STUDIES IN BRITISH ART

Seventeenth-Century Interior Decoration in England, France and Holland

Peter Thornton

Published for the Paul Mellon Centre
for Studies in British Art
by
Yale University Press
New Haven and London
1978

Library of Congress catalog card number: 77-91067
International standard book number: 0-300-021933

Designed by John Nicoll and set in Monophoto Bembo.
Printed in Great Britain by BAS Printers Limited, Over Wallop, Hampshire.
Colour illustrations printed in Great Britain by Jolly and Barber Limited, Rugby, Warwickshire.

Published in Great Britain, Europe, Africa, and Asia (except Japan) by Yale University Press, Limited, London. Distributed in Australia and New Zealand by Book & Film Services, Artarmon, N.S.W., Australia; and in Japan by Harper & Row, Publishers, Tokyo Office.

TO ANN, MY WIFE

IL SAVIO SA TROVAR TUTTO NEL POCO

To the wise man a trifle may reveal all

Inscription painted in the seventeenth century on the corridor-wall at Skokloster in Sweden

FOREWORD

UNDERLYING the survey of seventeenth-century interior decoration encompassed in these pages is a special way of looking at historic houses. It is an approach that my colleagues and I in the Department of Furniture and Woodwork in the Victoria and Albert Museum have as a group adopted and which is finding increasing favour with a number of other people who work in this general field. For my own part, my inclination towards treating the subject in this way springs from contacts with Scandinavian museum curators in the late 1940s, most notably with Dr Tove Clemmensen of the National Museum in Copenhagen who each summer used to take a small team of collaborators out to some country house where they spent several weeks studying, recording and photographing the rooms and their contents in great detail. The result was that they saw a great deal of antique furniture of all kinds in its intended context, and came to understand much about its purpose and the settings against which it was supposed to be seen. In the Scandinavian approach, much stress was laid on the study of contemporary illustrations and old photographs that provided information about the conventions governing decoration and the arrangement of furniture in the past.

The difficulty of applying this method to houses in England was largely one of scale (although money also came into it); there are so many more houses, they are larger and their contents are more numerous. Nevertheless, due largely to the enthusiastic and determined activities of John Hardy and Clive Wainwright, a remarkable survey has been made over the past decade or so. It is less thorough and consistent than the Danish version but is far more extensive and no less informative. It has been an essential factor in our growing understanding of the arrangement of rooms in the past and of the décor against which these arrangements were contrived.

A feature that became increasingly obvious (it is one of which most people are still only dimly aware) was how the rooms in ancient houses had not always been furnished with a random scattering of antique items, as they so often are today. There had been conventions, there had been a plan, there had been a host of special requirements that governed these matters—and these ground rules were quite different from those which have prevailed in recent times. None of this was explained as one went round English country houses, and there was no readily accessible literature to guide one. Although the architectural shell differed in each case and one might distinguish a specific piece of furniture here or a painting there, room after room had come to look very much alike. There seemed to be endless strings of drawing-rooms and very few interiors had any distinct character of their own. Certainly there were none which conveyed any genuine impression as a whole of an eighteenth-century room let alone one from the seventeenth century. All were presented according to aesthetic principles that have been paramount since about 1910. There was nothing inherently wrong with this; most people liked it that way. But it was rather monotonous and it did little to help the visitors to understand how these buildings came into being, what purposes they had served at various stages, what were the aspirations of those who built them.

The number of questions on these matters that reached us at the Victoria and Albert Museum began to increase. We also wanted to know for our own purposes. Here was a field that seemed in need of more purposeful tilling. Considerable impetus was given to our own craving for information in this area by our having in our care Ham House, a delightful seventeenth-century villa on the Thames about an hour's hard row upstream from Westminster, and Osterley Park, a magnificent Adam house near London Airport. Both had remained largely untouched, respectively since the 1670s and 1770s. Both contained the actual furniture provided for them at these stages. Moreover, in both cases inventories of the periods existed that help us the better to envisage how the respective rooms must originally have looked. And, finally, very little furniture from later periods remained in the two houses, so there was no reason why we should not strive to present them as nearly as possible in their original guises. At any rate, we needed to know more about furnishing in those two periods and the reader will very quickly become aware that the experience of myself and my colleagues with Ham House has been of immense importance to our appreciation of the background to, as well as many details of, seventeenth-century interior decoration. In my work as Keeper in charge of Ham House, I have been most ably supported by Maurice Tomlin. We have learned an enormous amount about the house while working together and many observations originally made by him are recorded in this volume. Indeed, I cannot adequately express my gratitude to the colleagues in my Department for the help they have given me over the years because, among other things, it takes the form of a protracted conversation in which these questions are discussed first from one angle and then from another. Theories are put forward, adjusted, refined. Fresh information comes pouring in daily. New opinions are voiced, criticisms are levelled against the wilder assumptions. The results are evident to ourselves and those who know us well, and we believe these results to be in every way worthwhile. But it is often impossible to recall who first came up with an idea, who first drew attention to some important point. All I can now do is thank them as a group of which I am proud to be a member, and list them in order of seniority—Simon Jervis, John Hardy, Maurice Tomlin, Clive Wainwright, Julia Raynsford, Gillian Walkling, Lisa Clinton, Frances Cooper and Griselda Chubb.

We have of course not been alone in thinking that the workings of historic houses needed more serious investigation. A scholar who is bringing about a fundamental change in our attitude to the country house is Dr Mark Girouard, an architectural historian whose stimulating talks on the radio and whose essays about the workings of the great Elizabethan houses and on the Victorian country house have already borne impressive fruit, and whose Slade lectures, delivered at Oxford University in 1976, are shortly to be published by the Yale University Press when they will undoubtedly have a very considerable impact. Another scholar who has thought a great deal about these matters and who has always been exceedingly generous in sharing his knowledge with those who are interested is John Nevinson. His many admirers eagerly await the publication of his study of the astonishing collection of Elizabethan textiles at Hardwick Hall. Equally stimulating and enjoyable have been the discussions I have had over the last few years with Gervase Jackson-Stops of the National Trust. Once again it is fervently hoped that the publication of his study of Daniel Marot and his contemporaries will not be too long delayed as it will clearly be of the greatest importance to our understanding of late seventeenth-century decoration.

From what has been said it will be seen that very little of a general nature has so far been published on the subject of historic interior decoration in this country, and one has had to turn to foreign authorities for serious information in this field. No one can afford to ignore, for example Henry Havard's *Dictionnaire de l'ameublement* which appeared in Paris between 1887 and 1890. It is a rich source from which not a few of my quotations have been culled. William Karlson's *Stât och Vardag i Stormaktidens herremanshem* (Lund, 1948) is a thorough survey of the contents of Swedish seventeenth-century country houses which is unfortunately only accessible to the relatively few people who can read Swedish. It was only brought to my attention fairly recently, but I was much relieved to discover that we had reached identical conclusions on many points, and that there were happily very few details over which we disagree. Another useful work is Walter Stengel's *Alte Wohnkultur* which appeared in 1958 in the depressing atmosphere of post-war Berlin, the result of a life-long study of life and domestic arrangements in and around that city in former times. Dreary in appearance and limited in its scope, this work was nonetheless a potent source of inspiration during the early stages of my own work.

However, a change is taking place in this country and as evidence one may cite John Fowler and John Cornforth's *English Decoration in the 18th Century* which appeared in 1974. It is a pioneering work that has laid a respectable foundation for further studies and we are naturally gratified that it incorporates, as the authors generously acknowledge, a number of ideas originally conceived in my Department as well as several discoveries made by myself and my colleagues. Their book and mine complement each other in considerable measure, especially as the authors have touched upon a certain number of seventeenth-century matters by way of introduction to their main theme.

Enough has been said to make it clear that a fresh way of studying historic houses has developed in this country in the past decade or so, and that the Fowler-Cornforth book and the present volume are early manifestations of this approach. Because the machinery for carrying out studies in this direction did not exist, my colleagues and I were forced to devise systems of self-help within the Department and I want to record with gratitude the imaginative assistance that has been given to us over the years by the Marc Fitch Fund, which has in all kinds of ways enabled us to achieve much that would otherwise have had to be left undone. We are especially grateful to Francis Steer, the former Secretary to the fund, whose work on the interpreting of inventories has incidentally been so useful to us all, and whose constant interest and encouragement have been so valuable to us.

While the present book was actually being written, it became clear to me that I needed to make a further visit to Holland. It was due to the assistance generously given me by the British Academy that I was enabled to accomplish this at the right moment and with special success. I would like to record my thanks to the Research Fund Committee for giving me this support.

Which brings me to the publication of this book. This would not have been possible without the assistance of the Paul Mellon Centre for Studies in British Art and I am very conscious of the debt of gratitude I owe the Centre and its Director, Christopher White, for the vote of confidence they have given me and my work by stepping in and sponsoring publication at the crucial moment. I should also like to thank my Director, Dr Roy Strong for the encouragement he has given me. The imaginative approach he has adopted in conservation matters had done a great deal to draw attention to problems that urgently need attention all over Britain, and this has in turn enabled me and my Department to give greater help to others in this direction, and has been a deep source of encouragement to us in the task that we find so fascinating. Friends and colleagues all over the world have given me much help over the years during which this book was in preparation. I hope I have recorded my appreciation in the appropriate places and hope to be forgiven for any omissions in this respect. I am also sincerely grateful to the owners of the objects illustrated in this work who have given me permission to publish them here. Acknowledgement is given at the end of the book, in the appropriate note to the illustration concerned.

Lastly, I want to mention Louisa Warburton-Lee, my assistant. Not only did she turn my manuscript from a nightmare scribble into a neat body of typing that in other circumstances, could perfectly well have been printed as it stood; she also saved me from a great deal of trouble and from making numerous mistakes. She achieved this, moreoever, not merely with hard work, but with patience and good humour. My debt to her is immense.

Victoria & Albert Museum,   Peter Thornton
London
July 1977

CONTENTS

Introduction

THE seventeenth century saw England and Northwestern Europe discarding the last
vestiges of a mediaeval way of life and adopting in its stead one that has formed the
basis of the western tradition ever since. An educated man of the seventeenth century
would be surprised by many aspects of our life today but we would be able to discuss
with him most of our daily problems and could expect to find his manner of
thinking very similar to our own. This would not be the case if one of our mediaeval
ancestors were to reappear amongst us.

Science, by the middle of the seventeenth century, had moved from the hesitant,
secretive, tradition-bound gropings of the age of Copernicus to a level-headed
inquisitiveness that sought to systematise knowledge, to discover order and
regularity in every facet of the universe. Symbolic of this new attitude was the
widespread adoption in the last years of the century of the pendulum clock—a piece
of mechanism that not only intrigued our ancestors on account of the regularity
which the pendulum imparted to the timepiece but was to set in motion what a
modern historian has described as 'the remorseless subjection of humanity to the
Clock'.[1] Although the working day of the labourer was still regulated by the hours
of daylight, the day was no longer divided by the liturgical hours and governed by
the ringing of a church bell. Regularity, precision and order came, indeed, to fire the
imagination of those with an intellectual cast of mind, to such a degree that the
world itself seemed, in Boyle's phrase, like 'a great piece of clockwork'.

Horrifying outrages were still perpetrated during the seventeenth century in the
name of religion but, as the fearful stresses set up by the Reformation and the
reaction against it were gradually resolved, men for the most part decided that it was
better to be tolerant than to kill one another or to destroy each other's means of
survival. This not only affected their attitude to spiritual matters but brought a
hitherto unknown measure of peace, safety and profit into their everyday activities.
In the Protestant countries particularly, this more liberal approach soon led to the
questioning of entrenched beliefs in every field, to the rooting out of old-established
practices that could be shown to have become outworn, to the revision of ancient
organisations, and the introduction of new methods and techniques.

In this new atmosphere commerce thrived. Energetic, enterprising and
determined men had better opportunities for growing rich than ever before—and
often did so. On the other hand the cost of living had risen enormously in the
sixteenth century and, although wages had been increased, the labouring classes
found their living standards had declined by the beginning of the seventeenth
century. Sporadic famines and furious epidemics, together with the appalling
upheavals brought about by the wars of religion and the revolutions of the middle of
the century brought widespread distress to the working population. The social
division between them and the ruling classes now became marked, and the latter
came to fear trouble less from other members of their class than from the many
distressed elements of the workforce. Indeed, the seventeenth century saw the ruling

classes coming increasingly to hang together in support of each other. A great lord was no longer simply the head of a family, governor of a large household with which he maintained personal contact, owner of estates, head of an extensive business enterprise, and surrounded with people who supported him and might even, if need be, fight for him. He was now a member of a class.

The great landed families were in fact able to entrench themselves ever more securely and they profited from the rise in prices to reinforce their position on the land. In a period of inflation the value of land is usually maintained and often increased. The merchant or banker who had made good in the seventeenth century was no less conscious of this than is his successor today, and many invested their freshly-won capital in country estates. Owning land became an important avenue to a rise in social rank and, in time and with luck, to political office. Socially this development was of course reactionary and did nothing to resolve the pressures that were building up in the labouring section of the population; but it established the landed aristocracy the more firmly and backed up this aristocracy with a substantial landed gentry, all of whom shared roughly identical interests.

If ownership of land was a source of power, an unmistakable symbol of that power was to have standing on one's own land a magnificent building, richly furnished, with the family's coat of arms much in evidence, and portraits of members of the royal and other great families prominently displayed as a reminder of one's connections. As Dr Mark Girouard has explained, by keeping up a handsome and impressive establishment, you could hope to make people feel it was 'a good thing to come in on your side'.[2] As he has also pointed out such advertising of your resources and of the potential support you could muster meant that the government tended to give you jobs and perquisites; so your income increased yet again while other members of the ruling class sought alliances with your family through marriage and you thus acquired even greater leverage for getting better jobs and perquisites—in fact, more influence and more power.

However, great families almost invariably also had an imposing house in the capital city. These houses were rarely as large as their country residences because the price of land in the cities was high and, as we shall see, they did not need to be so large. But these establishments were often even more grandly appointed than the country houses. What is more, some families found the journeys to their often distant country places so arduous that they could not visit them all that often, so they built themselves small *pieds-à-terre* in the countryside a few hours' ride from the capital. In seventeenth-century England, for instance, such sub-urban 'villas' sprang up along the banks of the Thames where they were equally convenient for getting into London or paying a visit to the Court when it was at Windsor or Hampton Court. Certain French noble families created similar small residences on the outskirts of Paris.

Yet, however powerful the aristocracy may have been on their estates, however imposing their country houses, however luxurious their sub-urban residences, it was at Court that offices and favours were acquired. And in France and England it was from the monarch that aspirants obtained positions of power—be it a political, clerical or military post. For, in order to protect the wider national interest in the face of growing hardship and unrest, the state had increasingly, during the sixteenth century, felt compelled to intervene in domestic affairs. This had led to tighter centralised control from the capital or seat of government—of which the monarch was head. This, and the fact that the nobility had rather too often proved unreliable in serving the interests of the state, encouraged monarchs to turn absolutist and speak more openly of the Divine Right of Kings,[3] setting up at the same time a middle-class administration steered by men who owed their position entirely to the monarch and whose allegiance was therefore hopefully beyond doubt. These men might belong to the gentry but were rarely of exalted birth. As they incidentally often came to wield great power, they were frequently able to amass great wealth, and could in consequence set themselves up in great luxury.

The monarchy in its turn found it essential to surround itself with a splendour that was even greater than that of its most wealthy subjects, so that everyone might be reminded of its close personal association with the divine power on high—or, failing that, of the yet more substantial wealth and power it could command through the state machinery.[4] In this respect it was the French monarchy that set the pattern that other kings strove to emulate. In England, although royal power was totally in eclipse during the period of the Commonwealth and was somewhat circumscribed after the Restoration, the later Stuart monarchs established themselves in considerable splendour in their royal palaces—St James's, Windsor, Holyrood, Hampton Court and Kensington—but the arrangements they made were for the most part based on French precepts.

Arrangements in the houses of the great noble families were closely modelled on those adopted by the respective royal households, the aim always being first and foremost to advance the power and status of their owners. As one moved down the social scale, so the splendour decreased but the standards of behaviour and taste set by the ruling families were recognised by all, and people adopted them as best they could, according to their means.

Great houses were built not merely for show, not merely as evidence of one's power or good taste. They were also intended as settings in which one could entertain one's equals or, if one were fortunate, one's superiors.[5] In town houses this did not require more space than the company would fill for the occasion. But, in a country house, suitable accommodation was needed for the visitors who might often stay quite a while (the journey there was rarely easy) and who were not infrequently accompanied by a substantial retinue. Important apartments had to be available for grand guests while lodgings of less splendour had to be provided for the supporting cast, each according to his degree. What is more, the owner's staff might itself be of considerable size and had likewise to be accommodated within the building—there being a permanent staff that always remained in residence as well as the retinue that habitually accompanied him from the capital or one of his other estates. The country residences of the principal noble families therefore tended to be extensive buildings, with a series of apartments, guest-rooms and accommodation for staff, as well as rooms for entertainment and ceremonial occasions.

The mediaeval lord had ruled by personal contact with those who supported him.[6] If necessary he was prepared to make his point with physical force, and evidence of valour in the field was at a premium. Holding estates that were often widely separated from one another meant that he had to visit each in order to supervise their management and, incidentally, to assert his authority by his presence and obvious signs of power. In many cases the lord was anyway forced to move on

3

because the quantity of provisions he and his accompanying retinue required was very substantial indeed and no neighbourhood could sustain so many people indefinitely. Thus the lord and his supporters tended to move from one great house to the next, travelling on when the provisions ran out, making his presence felt at each place ('showing the flag' as Girouard has called it) as well as seeing to his affairs.

This unsettled way of life among the seigneurial class dictated the form of furnishings that a great lord would take with him as he moved from one castle to the next, or from house to house. Some rugged pieces of furniture of no great value will have remained at each place, ready for use, but the more important furnishings had to be mobile,[7] they had to be capable of being packed onto a cart in the baggage-train, and set forth again at the next place of sojourn. Tapestries, that could be rolled up, and folding chairs met this requirement admirably; so did trestle-tables, folding beds and cushions. Hangings that could be used to transform a bare hall into an impressive setting for ceremony, a cosy bower or a charming bedchamber were likewise particularly in demand.

By the seventeenth century all this had changed. Grand people still travelled but they mostly travelled with only a few companions. They did not normally carry all their most treasured possessions with them. Their houses remained furnished all the time (even if the richest beds and wall-hangings were removed to the wardrobe-room and the rest was under cover when the family was not in residence).[8] Most of the old forms of furniture thus became obsolete. Tapestries and folding chairs happened to retain their importance as status symbols but no longer had any practical value; as for the rest, they were supplanted by new forms of furniture which were evolved to suit the new, static circumstances—the massive bed, the elaborate buffet, the writing-cabinet on a stand and the draw-table, for example. That these lost their massive character and became more delicate and graceful during the seventeenth century had to do with aesthetics and notions of comfort, and hardly at all with practical considerations.

Once the use of gunpowder had become widespread and artillery had become really effective, a lord could no longer hope to defend his castle against large-scale assault, and far less elaborate defences were adequate to cope with the sort of trouble that dissatisfied farm-labourers or resentful tenants might offer. The requirements of defence therefore gradually ceased to dictate the appearance and lay-out of seigneurial residences, and new types of buildings came to be devised—buildings with windows of more generous proportions that let in more light, for instance, and buildings arranged to accommodate rather more adequately the increasingly refined domestic arrangements that were gradually being adopted. Moreover, since there were severe practical limits to how far one could adapt an ancient castle to suit the new mode of life, it was quickly found to be easier to start afresh with an entirely new building.

For all the reasons given above, and no doubt for many others, there was incentive enough to build and the spate of significant building activity which started in France and England during the sixteenth century continued with only occasional losses of momentum right through the seventeenth century.[9] But we are beginning to trespass too deeply into the field of the architectural historian and the reader is referred to the works of such highly competent authorities as Sir Anthony Blunt and Sir John Summerson for surveys of this aspect of the matter.[10]

To whom could a nobleman or successful merchant turn when seeking to erect a new mansion in the seventeenth century? Sixteenth-century contracts to build were usually between the client and a contractor—a mason or a carpenter. There would not be any stipulation that the work had to satisfy a third party—an architect. Indeed, in 1600 there were still very few architects in France and hardly any in England, so that only extremely important buildings were erected with the aid of such a professional, a man versed in the mysteries of design and familiar with all aspects of building, who could co-ordinate the whole enterprise and ensure that each of its components met proper standards.[11] But as the principles of Italian Renaissance architecture came to be more widely assimilated in northern Europe, as a sense of order, regularity and discipline came to be an admired feature in a house, so any ambitious building enterprise came to require a governing mind to which the various craftsmen had to subordinate themselves. Even then an architect would mostly expect the individual contractors to submit designs for those features they were to construct; the notion that the architect should provide designs for all the required features was still not generally accepted even by the mid-seventeenth century, and most houses, even quite impressive ones, continued to be erected by craftsmen working on their own or in association, right through the century. The client therefore often had to steer the enterprise himself—or had to see that his agent did—and it is remarkable how many of them had an excellent grasp of the subject and were able to guide those working for them into creating harmonious and accommodating buildings.

Members of the nobility had of course often travelled abroad; some had even been to Italy and seen for themselves examples of the new style of building, and a few had sufficient understanding of these matters to enable them to recreate in their own country very creditable imitations, either for themselves or by way of providing guidance for other members of their class who were about to build. Sir Roger Pratt, who was himself one of the most influential of English architects in the middle of the century, advised those wishing to build at least to 'get some ingenious gentleman who has seen much of that kind abroad and been somewhat versed in the best authors of Architecture . . . to do it for you, and to give you a design of it in paper'.[12] The result will certainly be better than any builder can provide, he insists. His mention of 'the best authors of Architecture' reminds us that the sixteenth century had seen the publication in Italy of the first manuals of architecture and books of designs—just another aspect of the Renaissance demand for order, for codifying information. Such works appeared in increasing numbers during the seventeenth century,[13] and architects, both professional and amateur, who could procure these guides were greatly helped in their endeavours to bring order and discipline into their creations. But most patrons told their builders to copy an existing building or features from various buildings they admired. Certain buildings which were regarded as particularly successful therefore came to exert enormous influence on the history of architecture.[14]

What has all this to do with interior decoration, the reader may ask. One must not think that architects and gentlemen amateurs merely concerned themselves with questions of proportion, of how to draw correctly the different Classical orders of columns and other strictly architectural details. They were also interested in planning buildings so they would be more convenient for the sort of life that now had to be lived in them, and so as to provide greater comfort. Sir Henry Wotton, who was an ardent devotee of the new Italian taste in architecture, had this in mind when he explained in 1624 that 'Well building hath three Conditions— Commoditie, Firmness and Delight.' He places commodity, or convenience, first. However, it was the French who were to humanise the formalism of Italian house-planning and it is the French contribution in this field which remains paramount in countries north of the Alps throughout the seventeenth century.

The vital French contribution to the history of interior decoration during this period is the subject of the next chapter and is, indeed, the *leitmotif* in this book. Suffice it here to say that it was French architects who first insisted on controlling every aspect of creating an interior, who first thought it perfectly proper to provide designs for all the components, and who could then ensure that the various elements came together into a unified whole—the ultimate application of Renaissance principles to the creation of a building as an entity. Yet even in France it was only a handful of royal architects who took up such a dictatorial stance while, in England and Holland, it was only Daniel Marot who came to play such a role before the end of the century. Otherwise, it was not until the eighteenth century that leading architects, faced with an important commission, felt it necessary or desirable to attend to every detail of a scheme of interior decoration.

An important seventeenth-century house, then, might be the creation of an architect who would provide the ground-plan and elevations of the façades. When it came to the interior he might ask the various contractors for suitable designs for the features they were to provide—for example the plasterer who was to do the ceiling, the mason who was to create the chimneypiece, and the paviour or joiner who had to lay the floor. And he had to regulate the work of all these tradesmen as building proceeded. But the final appearance of any important seventeenth-century room depended largely on the contribution made by the upholsterer, who provided all the hangings (for walls, beds, windows, etc.) as well as coverings for seat-furniture, tables, floors, etc., and knew where to obtain furnishings of all kinds to complete the effect. Given the architectural shell, a great upholsterer could unaided provide a complete scheme of interior decoration and, although a handful of architects might presume to direct his contribution, the task was in most cases left to him. To a very large extent it was therefore still the upholsterer who governed fashion in this field and this is why he and his creations loom so large in the chapters that follow.

CHAPTER I
France and Aristocratic Fashion

MANUALS of deportment and polite behaviour had been published in the sixteenth century but European manners, even among the ruling classes, were still very rough when the new century opened in 1600. In France responsibility for bringing about the change to a less rude way of life has often been laid at the door of the Marquise de Rambouillet (1588–1665). It would of course be ludicrous to give her sole credit for this, but she clearly gave considerable impetus to this development and her rôle in it was no doubt exceedingly important. The famous *salon* she established at her house in Paris, the Hôtel de Rambouillet, became extremely influential and, while the subjects discussed were mainly literary, a pattern of well-mannered behaviour was forged there which spread right through the beau-monde and finally set the pattern for civilised behaviour throughout France and, ultimately, the whole of Europe. As Sir Harold Nicolson has said, 'In the history of French civility she remains a pioneer of wise and serious originality.'[1]

Her mother was a member of one of the oldest noble families in Rome (she was born a Princess Savelli) where her father was for a while French Ambassador. She herself was born in Rome and spent much of her childhood there. As a result she was atuned to Italian thinking and Italian behaviour before she came to live in Paris, and she must also have been familiar with some of the more advanced Italian ideas on questions of taste and manners at the turn of the century. Many aspects of life in Paris must have struck her as crude or provincial, but her husband's position as *Grand Maître de la Garde-Robe du Roi*, and her own very considerable fortune, enabled her to take up a central position in Parisian cultural life in the second decade of the century from which she was able to exert great influence on her entourage and material surroundings.

In 1619 she set about remodelling her father's old house which now came to be known as the Hôtel de Rambouillet. She took a lively personal interest in the enterprise and is said herself to have supplied such drawings and designs for it as were required.[2] We have noted that it was still in those days exceptional for someone setting out to build a house to engage an architect, and that a client who was well-informed in these matters might steer the undertaking himself, sketching ground-plans and details if he could, pointing to designs in pattern-books that appealed to him, and vetting sketches submitted to him by the mason or the carpenter. But that a woman should do so probably struck people as unusual and that the result turned out such a success was certainly thought remarkable at the time.[3] Moreover, because she came to have such enormous influence during the 1620s and 1630s, the arrangements this highly intelligent woman made in her house came to occupy an important position in the history of taste and interior decoration. For the presence of these features in her house[4] was a more certain advertisement for them than their presence in less celebrated buildings could ever have been.

In what directions did the advances made actually lie? Probably towards convenience and comfort on one hand, and harmony on the other.

Apart from its magnificence, what particularly struck the Parisians about her house was its 'regularité'. They also spoke of 'des agrémens, des commodités, des perfections',[5] and observed how the rooms were 'proportionnés & ordonnés avec tant d'art, qu'ils imposent à la vue, & paroissent beaucoup plus grand qu'ils ne sont en effet' [proportioned and ordered with such art, that they impress the onlooker, and seem much larger than they actually are].[6] This sense of spaciousness, these delightful aspects, seem to have been contrived by applying to the interior of this house the standard precepts of Italian Renaissance architecture—order, regularity and proportion—and these were matters the Marquise was well qualified to understand, intellectually and through her upbringing.

She may also have been more consistent than her predecessors in creating a unified effect in important rooms and this in turn added to the sense of order and harmony. We know that the famous *Chambre Bleue* where she regularly held her literary soirées was painted blue,[7] that the walls were covered with a blue material, and that the chair-covers and other textile components were also blue.[8] Occasionally bedchambers in the Middle Ages had been provided with wall-hangings and floor-coverings that were en suite with the bed-hangings, thus producing a totally uniform dressing for the room,[9] but it remained exceptional until early in the seventeenth century to have uniformity in the décor of a room as a whole, and it seems to be only from about 1625 onwards that this becomes a dominant feature of fashionable French interior decoration (Plates 1 and 2). It could well be that Madame de Rambouillet played a significant part in bringing this about.

But she may perhaps have made an even more personal contribution to what the French call *commodité*—to questions of convenience, ease and comfort. For she seems to have been prepared to scrap conventions in order to achieve this quality. This is reflected in the way she converted an old dressing-room into a small and private bedchamber (she suffered greatly from the cold and this little room could easily be kept warm).[10] She then turned her main bedchamber—the celebrated *Chambre Bleue*—into what we would call a drawing room. It is only when one comes to understand how rigid were the conventions that governed house-planning and room sequence at this period (see Chapter III) that one can appreciate what independence of mind such a move betrays.

Whatever the innovations to be seen at the Hôtel de Rambouillet may have been, we learn from contemporaries that features of the décor and arrangement soon came to be imitated 'dans tous les logis propres & superbes' [in all well-ordered and splendid houses].[11] Even the Queen Mother, Marie de Medici, is said to have 'ordered the architects to go and look at the Hôtel de Rambouillet' when she was building the Palais de Luxembourg and, while we do not know which particular aspects they went to see, we are told that 'ce soin ne leur fut pas inutile' [this precaution was not without benefit].[12] The architectural shell of the Luxembourg already existed by the time Madame de Rambouillet was starting to rebuild her house on the other side of the river Seine,[13] so it must have been in matters of detail that the Queen's designers were interested. Whatever the case, the Luxembourg was itself to exert a powerful influence on French architecture, particularly on account of its rich interior decoration.

Madame de Rambouillet brought to French manners a feminine pattern of elegance and it was principally through the women in her circle that she exerted her

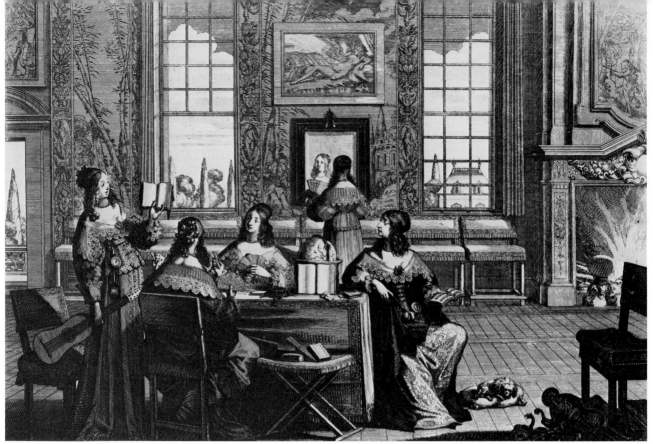

1. Upper-class Parisian girls in a fashionable interior of about 1640. The covers of the chairs are en suite with the fitted table-carpet. The single curtains to each window are pulled respectively to the left and right for the sake of symmetry.

2. Parisian interior of the 1630s. The covers of the chair and its cushion on the left are en suite with the bed-hangings.

influence. If, as seems likely, the innovations she made in the field of interior planning and decoration were chiefly of a practical nature leading to ease and greater comfort, it will have been to women that they first and foremost appealed. At any rate it was to a large extent women who created the distinctive character of French interior arrangements and decoration in the seventeenth century (Plates 3 and 4). As Christopher Wren noted when he was in Paris in 1665, 'the Women, as they make here the Language and Fashions, and meddle in Politicks and Philosophy, so they sway also in Architecture'.[14] Italian sixteenth-century architects had demonstrated, both in their buildings and in their published designs, how to produce order and clarity in an interior, but convenience and comfort were concepts that hardly came into their calculations at all. The French genius lay in adapting the formal schemes of Italian architectural theory in order to create interiors that were practical and comfortable as well as harmonious and imposing; indeed, this was to be the chief French contribution to European architecture during the seventeenth century and the influence of women on this development can scarcely be overrated. In the more public domain this is reflected in the enormous amount of attention given by the French to questions of planning in architecture—in working out how most conveniently to bring visitors up to the reception rooms, how to route them through the rooms so they saw the decoration to best advantage, how to lay out rooms so as to provide maximum comfort, how to ensure that servants could come and go with minimum disturbance, how to secure privacy for the family and how to contrive a means of retreat if one wanted to get away from unwelcome visitors. In the more personal field the feminine contribution lay in their insisting on having a high degree of comfort in their private rooms, particularly in their closets (*cabinets*). Closets had existed before but the elegant small rooms of retreat which became such a notable feature of well-appointed French houses at this period were a new development (see Chapter XII). They were the forerunners of the *petits appartements* so dear to the eighteenth century, ranges of private rooms set behind the more formal rooms of reception. Moreover, the luxurious comfort first contrived for private rooms gradually came to pervade and soften the formality of the grander, more public rooms—the *antichambres*, the *salons*, and so on. True comfort, as we understand it, was invented by the French in the seventeenth century.

However, the luxurious form of comfort evolved in Paris towards the end of the seventeenth century did not come to be widely adopted in Europe until well into the next century. What at the time principally struck foreigners about important French buildings was their magnificence. And it was particularly the details of their sumptuous interior decoration which impressed them. Writing to a correspondent in Paris to obtain information on 'what is to be found in the most distinguished town houses and more particularly in the State Apartment at Versailles', the Swedish architect Nicodemus Tessin remarked that in 'tout ce que concerne le dedans des appartements . . . on raffine en France de jour en jour et [c'est en quoy] où l'on reuscit avec beaucoup de succés' [all that concerns the interior of apartments . . . is improved upon daily in France and it is there they achieve such great success].[15]

After the building and decorating of the Luxembourg, the next important landmark in Parisian interior decoration was the embellishment of the mansion built for himself by the powerful minister, Cardinal Mazarin, right in the centre of Paris. At the Palais Cardinal, as it was called, richness and magnificence of quite a new

3. Feminine comforts in Paris, about 1640. In the corner is a daybed.

4. A Parisian woman receiving female friends in her bedchamber in the 1630s.

order were to be seen and it came to be regarded as one of the principal wonders of the city in its day. It was decorated between 1645 and 1647. One of the most impressive rooms was the *Galerie Mazarine*, the ceiling of which was painted by the great Roman artist G. F. Romanelli; this was to have a profound influence on Le Brun when he came to decorate the *Galerie d'Apollon* at the Louvre (commissioned in 1663). The chief decorative enterprises in the French capital until the 1660s were still for the most part entrusted to foreign artists. This had been so at the Luxembourg, and Mazarin is said likewise to have 'constraint presque toutes les Nations de la Terre à contribuer à l'ornement' [constrained most of the Nations of the Earth to contribute to the decoration] of the Galerie Mazarine which 'l'Art et la Nature semblent avoir pris plaisir à enrichir' [Art and Nature seem to have taken pleasure in adorning].[16]

But a truly national style of aristocratic interior decoration—based on Italian formulae, it is true, but with a quite distinctive flavour of its own—was being evolved in France and was embodied on a grand scale for the first time in the Château of Vaux-le-Vicomte which was built with unusual rapidity and decorated in a most sumptuous manner between 1652 and 1661 for the wealthy *Surintendant des Finances*, Nicolas Fouquet, to the designs of the famous architect, Louis Le Vau. It has been said of Fouquet that he was 'the actual founder of a school of French decorative art in the building and furnishing of his château of Vaux',[17] but the architecture itself was not all that remarkable; what was important about the house, what gave the château its special character, was its interior decoration which was conceived as a magnificent whole by Charles Le Brun and executed by a team of artists and craftsmen working under his personal and enormously talented direction (Plate 5). Here at last was a totally French achievement, conjured up by a French architect-decorator and carried out entirely by Frenchmen.

Unfortunately for Fouquet this spectacular building was altogether too blatant evidence of his growing power and the wealth he had somewhat dubiously amassed. Jealous and uneasy, Louis XIV therefore in 1661 had Fouquet arrested and charged with embezzlement. Shortly afterwards Le Brun and his team were engaged in the royal service. In 1664 Le Brun was created *Premier peintre du Roi* as well as *Directeur de la Manufacture Royale des Meubles de la Couronne*, the establishment at the Gobelins which produced not only superb tapestries woven to his designs but furnishings of all kinds created under his personal supervision. When he had in addition been made director of the *Académie Royale de Peinture et Sculpture*, it was fair to say, as the *Mercure Galant* did at the time, that 'all the Arts are carried on under him' and that 'there is no aspect that he is not concerned with' (Plates 6–10).[18]

Le Brun's first major work of interior decoration for the King was the *Galerie d'Apollon* at the Louvre, begun in 1663, but his great achievement was the internal decoration of the Château de Versailles which Le Vau had started to extend for his royal master in 1669. It was Le Brun, more than anyone else, who helped Louis create the grandeur and magnificence with which the King there surrounded himself—the glorious setting against which were enacted the dazzling ceremonies and entertainments that advertised unmistakably the King's absolute power (Plates 11 and 12). Uncomfortable, impractical and not especially distinguished as architecture, this vast palace overawed all who saw it. It served not only as an indication of French might, however; it also furnished a pattern for palace

5. Design by Charles Le Brun for a candlestand, probably intended for Vaux-le-Vicomte although not necessarily executed. About 1660.

6. Furnishings designed by Le Brun about 1670. Scene woven in tapestry 1671–6 at the Gobelins after a composition by Le Brun, depicting an audience given by Louis XIV in 1664. The candlestand on the right is similar to that shown in Plate 8.

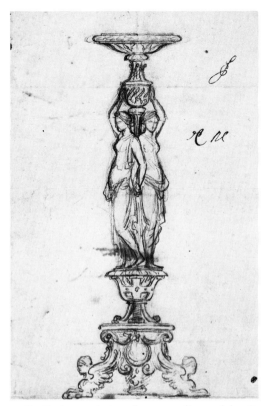

7. Preliminary design for a candlestand by Le Brun. About 1670?

8. Drawing, probably by a Parisian silversmith, of a candlestand based on the design by Le Brun reproduced in Plate 7 with alternative feet.

architecture, and more particularly for palatial interior decoration, that has been followed in its essentials all over Europe ever since.[19]

The ceremonial that Louis XIV introduced at Versailles was actually retrogressive. He re-imposed and formalised ancient customs that had almost fallen out of use, and enforced this elaborate and inflexible structure on court life. But this oppressive ceremonial had its reverse side which took two forms—diversion in the form of entertainments on the one hand, and the development of elegant, luxurious and comfortable retreats on the other. These two developments at the French Court in the seventeenth century pointed the way towards the graceful informality of the Rococo period and were therefore of more profound significance than the pomp and circumstance for which Versailles is mostly renowned.

In the park at Versailles were erected various pavilions or *maisons de plaisance* to which one could make excursions or which might form the focal point of some entertainment for the courtiers and the many visitors from abroad—ballets, collations, firework-displays and diversions of all kinds (Plate 13). In these places a playfulness and informality could be allowed to reign, both in the manners allowed there and in the décor. It was on a drawing with proposed ornaments for the little pleasure-house at the *Ménagerie* that Louis commented to his architect in 1699 that he felt something more youthful would be appropriate.[20] But something of the same spirit existed long before that. The arrangements at the *Trianon de Porcelaine*, for example, must have come as a delightful surprise to those who were invited there.

14

9. Preliminary
design for a
console-table by
Le Brun. 1670s?

10. Two designs
for console-tables,
probably executed
by a Parisian
silversmith, and
perhaps intended
for the *Grands
Appartements* at
Versailles. The
left-hand section of
the top proposal is
presumably based
on Le Brun's
sketch reproduced
as Plate 9.

11. (right) Contemporary view of one end of the *Grande Galerie* (the *Galerie des Glaces*) at Versailles showing Le Brun's ceiling and the array of silver furniture including vases with orange trees.

12. (below) The setting for this masquerade is probably based on a knowledge of similar scenes at the French court. Note the display of massive silver vessels at the sideboard, the orange trees in silver urns, and the crystal chandeliers.

13. (far right) Display of precious vessels on a *buffet*, perhaps set up in some *bosquet* near one of the royal *maisons de plaisance*. Some of the silver can apparently be identified with items in the French royal inventories and A. F. Desportes, who painted this scene in about 1700, is known to have assisted with the decoration at several of the French royal châteaux including Marly.

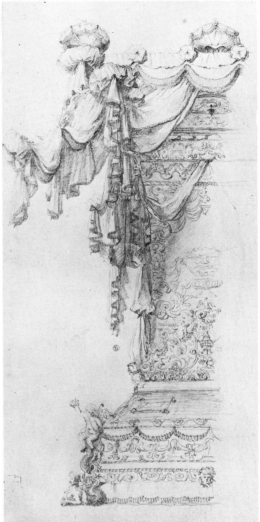

14. The bed set up in 1672 in the *Chambre des Amours* at the *Trianon de Porcelaine*. The French royal inventory described it as 'un lit extraordinaire'. This astonishing blue and white confection was no state bed but was the central feature of a royal love-nest where fantasy could be allowed free reign.

15. Presumably the second bed at the *Trianon de Porcelaine* (see Plate 14).

Begun already in 1670, this charming building consisted of little more than two bedchambers in which stood two fantastic beds (Plates 14–16), while the rest of the décor was exotic and whimsical in character. It was an attempt to conjure up a sort of fairyland and, although it was swept away not many years later, this little building was the ancestress of all those chinoiserie pavilions that were to be so fashionable in the eighteenth century.[21] Different styles of fantasy and informality prevailed at the other small pleasure-palaces in the grounds—the *Orangerie*, the *Ménagerie*, and (later) the *Trianon de Marbre* (Plate 17) which we know as the *Grand Trianon*—but all were created to counterbalance the overpowering character of the public rooms in the main Château which was being done over in the 1660s and was then greatly extended to its present guise in the 1670s.[22] The same purpose, incidentally, lay

16. A French engraving showing a fashionable lady resting on a small bed (possibly a daybed) similar in conformation to the bed shown in Plate 15.

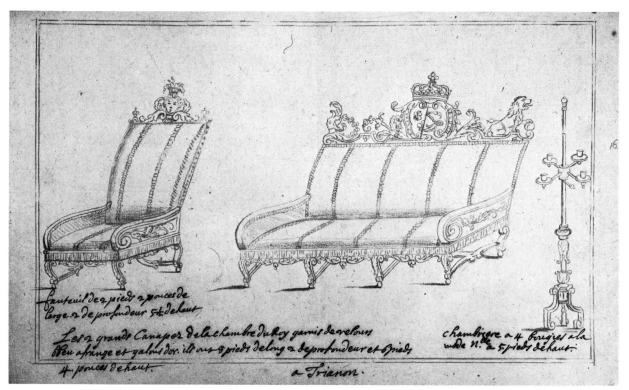

fauteuil de 2 pieds 2 pouces de
large 2 de profondeur 5 de haut

Les 2 grands Canapes de la chambre du Roy garnis de velours
bleu a frange et galons dor. ils ont 5 pieds de long 2 de profondeur et 5 pieds
4 pouces de haut.
a Trianon.

chambriere a 4 bougies a la
mode N.ce a 5 pieds de haut.

17. Furniture in the *Chambre du Roi* at the *Trianon de Marbre* (the Grand Trianon) probably drawn early in the 1690s.

18. Furniture in the most private rooms at the Château de Marly probably dating from the early 1680s.

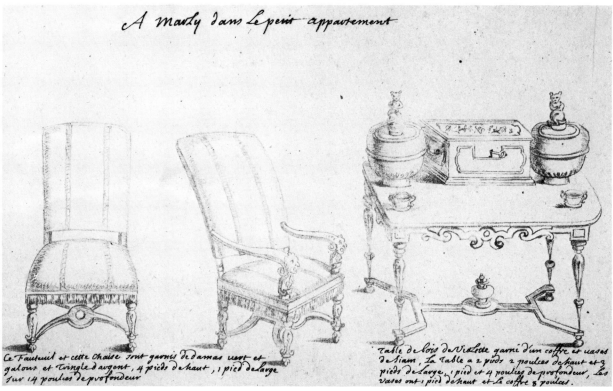

A Marly dans le petit appartement

Ce Fauteuil et cette Chaise sont garnis de damas vert et
galons et tringle d'argent, 4 pieds de haut, 1 pied de large
sur 14 pouces de profondeur

Table de bois de Violette garni d'un coffre et vases
de Siam, La Table a 2 pieds 2 pouces de haut et 3
pieds de large, 1 pied et 4 pouces de profondeur, Les
vases ont 1 pied de haut et Le coffre 8 pouces.

19. One of the eight fixed *buffets* installed at Marly in 1699–1700 when the château was radically altered.

behind the creation of the little Château de Marly which was built some miles from Versailles.[23] To be among those invited by the King to spend a few days there was regarded as an immense privilege, and considerable lack of formality characterised the stay.[24] Eventually the King spent too much on Marly; it became almost as sumptuous as Versailles itself and the early carefree atmosphere seems to have evaporated (Plates 18 and 19).[25]

However, it is often forgotten that in the main building at Versailles there were numerous private rooms in which the King or other members of the royal family could relax. He had his own private apartment behind the official rooms of reception—the *Grand Appartement*—to which he could retire and this included a private bedchamber where he frequently slept. The Dauphin likewise had a luxurious apartment on the ground floor where the décor was of an advanced character and considerable informality reigned. Moreover, each of the King's successive *maitresses en titre* was provided with a private suite of rooms close to the *Petit Appartement* of the King. The arrangement and decoration of Madame de Maintenon's apartment are well known to us through Saint-Simon's descriptions and it is clear that, for all her high-minded and austere way of life, a very considerable measure of comfort and ease was to be found there, so it is not surprising that the King during her 'reign', spent much of his time in this relaxed atmosphere, while she hardly left the rooms at all for weeks on end. Of her predecessor, Madame de Montespan's private apartment we know less but, judging from such evidence as is provided by her small château at Clagny, a stone's throw from Versailles, her surroundings were characterised by great charm and some novelty (Plate 20).[26] Moreover, immediately below the *Grand Appartement*, the

21

principal state rooms of the Palace, there was a luxury flat known as the *Appartement des Bains* which comprised not merely a sumptuous bathing room (Plate 21) but a whole suite of rooms that are said to have been of great beauty and must indeed have been delightful, for the King and Madame de Montespan spent many a long and happy hour in the relaxed atmosphere of this secluded retreat during the years when their liaison was at its height.[27]

At any rate, it needs to be borne in mind that an informal atmosphere, and a light-hearted and sometimes playful décor to go with it, existed side by side with the overpowering grandeur and formality of official French court life at this period. Madame de Rambouillet and her circle had shown the way to ease and comfort in the first quarter of the century. The last quarter of the century saw her ideas carried to a high degree of perfection within the orbit of the King himself (Plate 22 and 23).

20. (left) Probably the most luxuriously appointed house in its day, the 1670s, with furnishings in the most advanced taste— Madame de Montespan's Château de Clagny, just outside the park at Versailles. She reclines *en negligée* on an extremely elaborate canopied daybed. In the Gallery stand Oriental lacquer cabinets with porcelain massed on top.

21. Sketch for the scheme finally accepted for the *Cabinet des Bains* at Versailles; 1672. The walls were completely faced with marble of several sorts—apparently an early exercise in such treatment.

22. Seat-furniture in the *Antichambre* of the Dauphin's Apartment at Versailles in the 1690s. It was furnishings such as these that made the Dauphin's rooms one of the special marvels of the Palace. The colour-scheme was blue and gold, the loosely-hanging material on the walls, with its capping, presumably being en suite with the blue damask and 'brocard d'or piqué et d'or' on the *canapé* and *chaise*(s).

23. The Dauphin in his Closet at Meudon; about 1699. Decorated to the designs of Jean Bérain, the prince's personal and greatly appreciated interior architect. Several bronze-founders collaborated over the intricate mounts, including the *ébéniste et fondeur*, André-Charles Boulle, who presumably also provided the desk and glazed bookcases. Indeed, this is the kind of setting against which boullework is meant to be seen.

CHAPTER II
The Spread of the French Ideal

BY 1660 there was no longer any doubt that it was the French who set the pattern of civilised life indoors. The lay-out and arrangement of their buildings was widely studied, the details of their interior decoration was imitated, and the pattern of life led in such surroundings was copied. As has already noted, we have the word of the great Swedish architect, Nicodemus Tessin, for the fact that, as far as the interior of grand houses was concerned, here was a field in which the French were continually making admirable refinements (see p. 10). This was in 1694, but Christopher Wren implied much the same thing when he wrote from Paris in 1665 that the Palais du Louvre had so much to offer that it was 'for a while my daily Object' because not only was there much to be learned about the vast undertakings then in progress at the palace 'where no less than a thousand Hands are constantly employ'd in the Works' but he could also watch the artists and craftsmen engaged 'in Carving, Inlaying of Marbles, Plaistering, Painting, Gilding &c. Which altogether make a School of Architecture, the best probably, at this Day in Europe'.[1] He must be referring to the great programme of interior decoration then being carried out under Le Brun's direction including the decking out of the *Galerie d'Apollon*. At any rate there is evidence aplenty that what was being done in France in this field was being noted in many parts of Europe—not least in England and Holland, which are the countries that concern us here.

One must of course not think that French influence was in any way co-ordinated or was applied systematically. The impulses arrived haphazardly and in many various ways. Travellers to France took note of what they saw and the better-informed were often able to convey and interpret new French ideas to their own countrymen. Those architects who went abroad (and they now more frequently went to Paris as well as Rome, indeed, Wren never went to Italy at all) usually came back with notebooks full of observations and sketches that helped them introduce innovations to their homeland and it was increasingly often French ideas that caught their imagination. Engraved plans and proposals for ornament were published in Paris in ever growing quantity and, as they became more readily available abroad, so they came to constitute a powerful source of inspiration (e.g. Plates 27 and 28). The services of French artists and craftsmen likewise came into great demand; the emigration of large numbers of, for the most part, exceptionally capable Huguenot craftsmen and designers gave enormous impetus to the spread of French taste and techniques towards the end of the century (Plates 50 and 144), while francophile monarchs and aristocrats occasionally invited French artists to their countries to carry out specially important tasks.

Wren himself tells us that he had bought numerous engravings of the buildings he had seen in and around Paris 'that I might not lose the Impression of them'.[2] In fact he told his correspondent that he would 'bring you all France in Paper' and this gives one a measure of how great was the variety of engravings available in Paris already in the 1660s. He actually explains that those he was bringing home would 'give our

24. French art propaganda of the 1670s. Engravings by Jean Le Pautre (d. 1682) from a series showing candlestands but, in this instance, also providing information about fashionable Parisian frames, mural decoration and the draping of curtains. The style here depicted is that of Le Brun and his team of decorators. This stand, with its pair and the accompanying table, formed an important feature in the decoration of Versailles.

25. Drawing of a candlestand (*guéridon*) by Claude Ballin, the most renowned of Louis XIV's silversmiths, which was procured and sent in some triumph to Stockholm in 1693 at the request of the Swedish royal architect, Nicodemus Tessin. A drawing of the table which was flanked by two such stands was dispatched with it. The set must have constituted a spectacular feature of one of the principal state rooms at Versailles in the 1670s— which is presumably why Le Pautre chose to illustrate it (Plate 24).

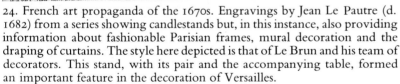

26. (right) Engraving of about 1665 providing information about modern Parisian bedchambers with one of the newly fashionable alcoves that has a raised *parquet* and is fronted by a balustrade.

Country-men Examples of Ornament and Grotesks, in which the Italians themselves confess the French to excel'.

Already in the sixteenth century the French were publishing engravings of ornament suited to interior decoration. The most famous work that included proposals in this line was Jacques Androuet Du Cerceau's *Les plus excellents bastiments de France* of 1576 and 1579 (it was in two volumes). The other French books on architecture which came to be widely known in the seventeenth century—the works of de l'Orme, Le Muet, Fréart, Jean Marot—concentrated on purely architectural matters, on façades, the Classical orders, pediments, etc.,[3] but of course the ground plans given in these books were a great help to those who were about to build and provided tips not merely on orderly planning but also on practical questions of access and so forth. This was particularly the case with Le Muet's treatise, which was found so useful in England that it was translated into English.[4] Incidentally, a book the importance of which may have been underrated by historians (perhaps because it is not illustrated) is Louis Savot's little handbook entitled *L'Architecture Françoise des bastimens particuliers* which first appears in 1624 but which Blondel re-issued in 1673 with comments. It is full of useful hints on the planning and arrangement of rooms—on which way particular rooms should face, on where to set the fireplace—as well as on such questions as rigging up a bathroom or building an ice-house. It also gives advice on how to order slates, quarry-tiles and window-glass, and makes observations on the merits of the respective architectural treatises then available.

27 & 28. Engravings by Jean Le Pautre from about 1660 showing bed-alcoves in which stand fashionable beds of the period.

Those decorating houses, on the other hand, could obtain inspiration from the astonishing number of engravings for ornament of various kinds that began to appear in Paris from the 1630s onwards. These usually took the form of sets of engravings devoted to a particular class of ornament or feature—panelling, doors, chimneypieces, ceilings, candlestands, tables, bed-alcoves, frames, vases, and every other sort of ornamental detail (Plates 24, 26 and 27). They were sold in sets or singly; sometimes various sets were combined and sold in a single volume. These prints, moreover, would often convey far more information about prevailing French tastes than the title of each set would imply. For example, the designs for a chimneypiece might show the latest form of fire-dog as well; there might also be a *garniture* of vases or a clock on the mantel-shelf, and the opening of the fireplace might be fitted with a decorated chimney-board (Plate 252). An illustration of a candlestand would be surrounded by a handsomely moulded frame, and the representation of one of the new bed-alcoves would indicate how to drape a curtain and would tell an intelligent observer much about balustrades and new forms of panelling (Plate 26 and 28). As a famous eighteenth-century printseller commented on the engravings of Jean Le Pautre, that most prolific artist whose delightful compositions (e.g. Plate 36) made the style of Charles Le Brun known to the world in the 1660s and 1670s, 'ce qu'il mettoit au jour étoit moins receu comme des modèles que comme des idées propres à échauffer le génie' [the things that he published were taken up less as [direct] models than as ideas guaged to fire the imagination].[5] One might say the same of many other Parisian designers of ornament. Jean Barbet's proposals for chimneypieces (Plates 65 and 66), for instance, were adapted by Inigo Jones in England and by the craftsmen working at Skokloster some forty miles north of Stockholm.[6] Indeed, they were found so useful that they were redrawn and slightly altered and then issued in Amsterdam not long after they had first appeared in Paris (Plate 67).[7] In the same way, Le Pautre's proposals for bed-alcoves (Plate 28) were copied (rather tamely) and published in London by Robert Pricke in 1674, about a decade after their publication in Paris.[8] In any case, this enormous output of engraved ornament in Paris, and the fact that others bothered to issue re-engraved copies, betokens a great need for information in this field. By feeding this need, the French generated yet more demands for what they had to offer.

French taste in these matters was also transmitted by means of genre scenes. The charming views of interiors by Abraham Bosse (1602–76) showing members of the Parisian *haute bourgeoisie* going about their daily lives in fashionable settings did much to convey an impression of how the various elements went together (Plates 1–4 and 84). They showed not only the new forms of bed or chair, but indicated how they should stand in the room. The way a harmonious atmosphere could be imparted by a unified décor also became clear from such illustrations. Indeed, the pattern of interior living evolved by Madame de Rambouillet and her friends is surely reflected in these scenes, even if the settings depicted by Bosse are perhaps rather less magnificent.

They must have done a great deal to help spread the civilised, graceful and comfortable way of life for which Paris was becoming renowned when these prints were new—in the 1630s and early 1640s. Later in the century many more prints were published showing fashionable people in various situations—a lady taking

29. (above) A Parisian fashion-plate of the 1690s giving details of contemporary interior decoration.

30. (upper right) A Parisian fashion-plate showing one of the new *cabarets* for serving chocolate.

31. (right) Fashion-plate showing a lady affixing a patch on her cheek, standing at her dressing-table which is *en forme de bureau* and would normally have been flanked by a pair of candlestands. The illustration also shows a sash-window.

32. Fan-leaf with a scene of the marriage of Louis XIV to Maria Theresa of Spain in 1660. Even such small ephemeral objects carried a message about fashionable French décor—the way the curtains of the canopy could be tied back with cats-whisker bows, the fancy dressing of a *lit à la Romaine*, the court ladies seated on *pliants*, etc.

33. The scene of an important royal event carrying information about fashionable French interior decoration in the 1640s. Note the magnificent rock-crystal chandeliers, the marquetry floor, the form of the state bed.

34. (left) Even the almanack for the year 1682 brings information about fashions at the French court; note the mirror-backed sconces, the *garniture de cheminée*, the chandeliers (probably of glass), and the upholstered *tabouret*.

35 & 36. (above) Two designs of the 1660s for bed-alcoves masquerading as scenes from Classical history (here respectively of Cleopatra and Alexander the Great). A bed of the sort shown in Plate 35 might perhaps not be suitable for a state bedchamber, but might very well be seen in the bedchamber of a royal mistress (see Plate 20).

chocolate, a couple playing cards, a girl washing her feet, a woman at her dressing-table—but all also serving as an excuse for illustrating current fashions in interior decoration, or aspects of it (Plates 30, 289 and 304). Thus one learns about the latest form of day-bed, the new *cabarets* used when serving chocolate, how to arrange flowers in vases or great 'cisterns'. Some of these scenes may be regarded as early fashion-plates, for often they concentrated particularly on the details of dress and *coiffure*. Related in this respect to genre scenes and fashion-plates are the scenes of some historical event in Classical history—the death of Cleopatra, the Rape of the Sabines–which offered a splendid excuse for illustrating an especially flamboyant setting. Such a design would probably not be considered at all suitable for a grand room but might provide ideas for settings where fantasy could be allowed free rein—in the rooms of a courtesan, for instance, or in some *maison de plaisance* (Plate 35).

French engravings were obtainable through printsellers in Amsterdam and London but a far wider selection, including the latest sets, was of course available in Paris and it was those who visited the French capital who got a more balanced idea of what French taste in the field really comprised. Indeed, Sir Roger Pratt remarked in 1660 that the man who 'deserves the name of an Architect' must have seen the old buildings of Rome 'as likewise the more modern of Italy and France' because it can never 'be supposed that anything should be in the Intellect, which was never in the senses'. The aspirant can study designs but, however good these may be, 'never having seen anything in its full proportions it is not to be thought that he can conceive of them as he ought'.[9] Go and see for yourself and then do as Wren was to do, bring back some engravings so as not to 'lose the Impression of them'. And many did go.

However, a visit of a few weeks was not really sufficient. Those who stayed longer had the advantage. Among those whose sojourn tended to last several years and whose duties brought them into contact with the grandest and most fashionable aspects of French life were the foreign ambassadors. Having once acquired a taste for

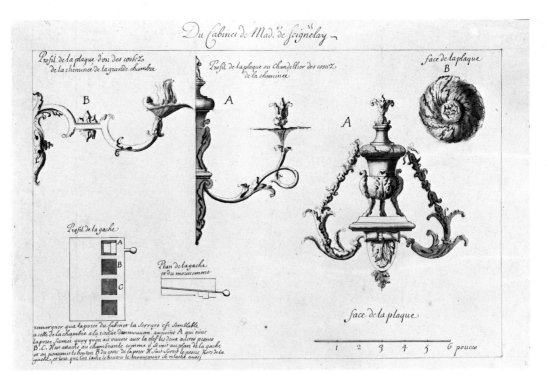

37. Evidence of the widespread interest shown in fashionable French décor is this drawing of cut steel ornaments in the newly-decorated closets of Mme. de Seignelay which were specially drawn in 1693 and sent to the architect to the Swedish Crown in Stockholm, Nicodemus Tessin, whose agent in Paris kept him informed of all the latest innovations in the French capital.

the new aristocratic pattern of life in Paris and at the French court, they were apt to try and introduce it to their homeland after their return, remodelling or rebuilding their residences along French lines, decorating them in the French style, bringing over French furniture with which to deck them out (Plates 38 and 39). Sometimes they even brought French artists and craftsmen over in order to carry out their schemes.[10] Moreover, they were often the recipients of handsome diplomatic gifts and these might also help spread notions of French magnificence and of French artistic and technical mastery. Louis XIV, for example, sometimes presented ambassadors with a splendid state bed and its associated kit of chairs and stools (Plate 41).[11] Gifts direct to foreign monarchs were also intended to convey the same message—we, the French, know how to do these things better than anyone else—and the message was widely believed.

I have discussed some of the ways in which knowledge of fresh developments in the field of interior decoration might be spread abroad from the French capital. I shall now briefly consider how this knowledge came to be assimilated in Holland and in England.

In the field of interior decoration, Dutch (also Flemish and North–German) taste during the first quarter of the seventeenth century was still entirely dominated by the kind of Mannerism embodied in the widely famed works of Hans Vredeman de Vries (1527–1604), notably in his *Variae Architecturae Formae* which was published at Antwerp in 1560. It was a style that borrowed elements from the works of the Italian authorities on Classical architecture but which relied greatly on the use of applied ornament that was often grotesque in character (Plates 42 and 43). It was a restless style, open to abuse and not readily lending itself to the creation of harmonious

38. (above left) Old photograph (1904) of one of a set of Parisian chairs brought back from Paris by an ambassador in 1682, showing their original upholstery.

39. (above centre) Chair from another set acquired in Paris by the same ambassador as that shown in Plate 38.

40. (above right) One of a set of chairs of markedly French conformation at Ham House which may have been procured from Paris in the 1670s when the building was being modernised in an advanced taste. It is even possible that they were a gift to the powerful Duke of Lauderdale from Louis XIV although no evidence for this suggestion has come to light. They still sport their original silk covers.

41. (left) State bed given to an ambassador by Louis XIV in about 1682. Such specimens of high-quality Parisian craftsmanship gave powerful impetus to the spread of French fashions and techniques.

effects.[12] A provincial and for the most part rather clumsy version of this Netherlandish Mannerist style reigned in England at the same time. In neither Holland nor England was there any real understanding of the basic principles of Classical architecture—exterior or interior. It was not appreciated that well-proportioned space and a well-developed sense of order were the key-notes of the style, and that no amount of plastering surfaces with Classical pediments, pilasters and friezes would produce the right effect.

At the beginning of the century, anyone in England wanting guidance on how to build had to read such architectural treatises as existed in their original language.[13] If one could not read Italian or French one was lost. Admittedly a Dutch version of Serlio was published in Antwerp in 1553 and new versions came out in Amsterdam in 1606 and 1616. The work was moreover re-translated into English in 1611 as *The First Book of Architecture made by Sebastian Serly*. For the rest one was obliged to fall back on the works of Hans Vredeman de Vries which purported to give information about Classical ornaments but left the builder to 'arrange them to his contentment according to the opportunity of his work', as the author himself disarmingly explained.[14]

The buildings which Inigo Jones erected in England between about 1620 and 1640 or so must therefore have seemed absolutely astonishing to contemporaries, for here suddenly was an architect who had absorbed the Italian Renaissance ideal and could create buildings in the Classical idiom that would have appealed even to his great Italian contemporaries. However, the Italian treatises of Scamozzi and Palladio that he so greatly admired cannot have been of much help when it came to decorating the interior of his buildings. He could produce Classical mural decoration, perhaps, and an Italian structure to the ceiling; but, as far as the details were concerned, he must have had to rely mostly on artists and craftsmen trained in the Netherlandish tradition.[15] What a help it must have been when engravings of French ornamental details began to appear on the market. He found particularly useful the designs for chimneypieces by Jean Barbet, published in 1632, which he copied freely as we have already noted. He also seems to have derived inspiration from the ceiling designs of Jean Cotelle (Plate 44 and Colour Plate V),[16] and there is a strong French flavour about much of his interior detailing. What is more, since some of the enterprises for which he was responsible were for Queen Henrietta Maria, the sister of Louis XIII of France and daughter of Marie de Medici, it is likely that the rooms concerned were furnished in something very like the current French manner (Plates 1–4), perhaps even with a certain amount of actual French furniture.

A central figure in cultural developments in England and Holland in the 1620s was Sir Henry Wotton (1568–1639). Much travelled, of an intellectual cast of mind, friend of Francis Bacon, Donne and Isaak Walton, this intelligent man was appointed Ambassador to the Venetian Republic in 1604 and was engaged in diplomatic duties in Venice with occasional breaks until 1624. He played an important part in bringing Francis Cleyn to England, having made Cleyn's acquaintance in Venice. Although Cleyn was a painter (he was thought by some to be 'il famosissimo pittore, miracolo del secolo') and is now mainly known as the chief designer at Charles I's tapestry manufactory at Mortlake, he was also able to turn his hand to interior decoration although his rôle in this field has not yet been properly evaluated.[17] It may well have been quite important. Wotton also wrote a

36

42. A Netherlandish interior decorated in the Mannerist style; about 1620. Although much of the ornament is Classical in derivation, the effect is made restless by the intrusive grotesque features (in this case, notably on the interior porch and buffet). The scale is misrepresented in this scene; the figures in front are too small, as the position of the door-handle shows.

43. A Dutch interior of about 1621 in the same style as that shown in Plate 42 but rather less grand.

44. A ceiling design drawn by Jean Cotelle (1607–76) in an album that may have been in Inigo Jones'
drawing-office. Perhaps a proposal for the Hôtel de Rohan in Paris, drawn in the 1630s.

guide to builders entitled *the Elements of Architecture* which was published in 1624 but
was reprinted many times and clearly met a need in its day. Not surprisingly
Wotton's book was a plea for the Italian form of architecture but he lists as the
qualities of a good building that it should possess 'Commoditie, Firmness, and
Delight'. He is here using commodity in the French sense meaning convenience, and
it was this same word that was used to describe the arrangements at Madame de
Rambouillet's house in Paris.[18] Clearly this need for practical yet well-ordered
architecture was becoming widely felt in the 1620s. In fact, he has sensible things to
say about planning.

Wotton's handbook was translated into Dutch, perhaps at the instigation of the
brilliant Constantijn Huygens (1596–1687) and certainly with his encouragement.[19]
During his boyhood at The Hague, Wotton had for a while been a neighbour and
had taught him to play the lute. Huygens visited England in 1618 and again for
seventeen months in 1621–3. He moved in court circles and can hardly have avoided
meeting Inigo Jones. He was certainly present when Jones' Banqueting House was
first used and records having seen several important works by Jones in London
including the famous galleries at Lord Arundel's house.[20] At any rate Huygens
seems to have sought to introduce 'ceste egalité regulière de part de l'autre . . . que

45. Design by John Webb, former pupil and assistant of Inigo Jones, for 'the Alcove in his Mats. Bedchamber, Greenwich 1665' which is clearly based on French proposals like those reproduced in Plates 27 and 28.

vous sçavez avoir tant pleu aux Anciens, et que les bons Italiens d'aujourd'huij recherchent encor aveq tant de soin' [that regular equivalance between one part and the other . . . which as you know formerly so appealed to the Ancients [i.e. in Classical Rome] and which the good Italians today so painstakingly seek to revive][21] into his own house which he built in the 1630s and of which he later sent an engraving that he hoped would convince Inigo Jones that 'le Bon Vitruve n'est pas du tout exclu d'Hollande' [the good Vitruvius is not totally excluded from Holland].[22]

Classical forms were being used with understanding in certain quarters in Holland by the 1630s (Plate 46) although it would seem that nothing so thoroughly Italian in conception as the buildings of Inigo Jones in England was produced there. On the other hand, certain French elements were apparently being introduced into Dutch architecture at this time, largely due to the personal intervention of the Stadholder, Frederik Hendrik, Prince of Orange (succeeded 1625, died 1647), to whom Constantijn Huygens was secretary. The Prince had strong leanings towards France. His mother was French and they had stayed a year in Paris together in 1598 at the court of Henri IV who was his godfather. He was extremely interested in architecture and later visited Paris again to study the latest developments. By 1630

46. This princess of the House of Orange-Nassau is portrayed in a Classical interior; she is Maria Stuart, daughter of Charles I and married to Willem II. Painted in the 1640s. Note the silver throne under a richly trimmed velvet canopy, and the splendid Persian carpet. The throne is of silver.

47. (far right) A portrait by the same artist as Plate 46 depicting a Dutch girl of a well-to-do family. This could well give an impression of a House of Orange interior in the 1640s.

the Stadholder's position was very strong and he set about re-planning the centre of The Hague along French lines.[23] Huygens' house and the well-known Mauritshuis, which is strongly French in character, formed part of this scheme. An English visitor to The Hague at this period (1634) noted 'The ladies and gentlemen here all Frenchified in French fashion.'[24] One may assume that the furnishing of these houses within the Stadholder's orbit was likewise based on French models, information about which was beginning to become more freely available at this stage, as we have already noted (Plate 47). A further instance of French influence on taste at the Stadholder's court is provided by the little Palace of Honselaarsdijk which the Prince started to build in 1621. Although much smaller, it had several features in common with the Palais de Luxembourg, Marie de Medici's residence that had been started only six years before—a building that has already been mentioned (see p. 8)—and it may well be that the plans for Honselaarsdijk were obtained from Paris. What is more, in 1634, the Prince secured the services of Jacques de la Vallée as his personal architect and the latter was the son of Marie de Medici's master of works at the Luxembourg.[25]

The court at The Hague of the Princes of Orange-Nassau, who became hereditary Stadholders of the United Provinces of the Free Netherlands, was the main avenue along which French influence was brought to bear on Dutch culture from about 1625 until the end of the century. Princely, almost royal at times, it remained none the less modest by comparison with the great royal courts of France, Vienna, Madrid and London. Indeed, the whole tenor of Dutch life in the seventeenth century

48. The pride and self-assurance of the Dutch middle-classes is admirably conveyed by paintings such as this. There is no ostentation; their dress and furnishings are costly but sober. The bed is tucked away into a corner; it does not dominate the centre of the room in the 'aristocratic' manner. About 1665. See also Colour Plate XIII.

remained anti-aristocratic. For the power lay with the Protestant élite in the cities, successful traders who came to form a self-perpetuating ruling caste—an upper middle class social and political dictatorship that was strongly opposed to the regal pretension of the House of Orange with which it waged an often bitter and sometimes bloody feud throughout the century. The regent or magistrate class in the chief cities at first led an austere life, without ostentation or pomp although they were imbued with a strong measure of self-assurance and civic pride that is embodied very clearly in the reticent but unmistakable magnificence of the Town Hall in Amsterdam (begun in 1648). Writing of Holland in the 1660s, Sir William Temple stated that

of the two chief officers in my time, Vice-Admiral de Ruyter and Pensioner de Witt . . . I never saw the first in clothes better than the commonest sea-captain . . . and in his own house neither was size, building, furniture or entertainment at all exceeding the use of every common merchant or tradesman . . . Nor was this manner of life used only by these particular men, but was the general fashion or mode among all the magistrates of the State.[26]

Such men viewed Frenchified ways with suspicion but, as commerce prospered and riches were amassed, a fresh generation grew up which drew its income from investments, land and houses; and this *rentier* class gradually came to demand the luxuries that French culture was known to be so skilful in devising. 'The old severe and frugal way of living is now almost out of date in Holland,' wrote Sir William Temple in 1673,[27] and greater opulence does indeed begin to pervade the scenes of interiors painted by the more fashionable Dutch artists at this time (Colour Plate I).

In 1672 France invaded Holland. After violent upheavals at home, the Dutch nation fell in behind the Stadholder, William III, Prince of Orange, who defended Holland with determination and skill. But although he had been the national leader in the war against France, he was a child of his time; for him Paris was still the centre of civilised life and the House of Orange remained the chief transmitter of French culture to the Dutch. A new phase in this movement began when thousands of Huguenot refugees arrived from France as a result of the fresh bout of persecutions that received official sanction in 1685 when the Edict of Nantes, which had granted French Protestants a measure of religious freedom, was revoked by Louis XIV.

Among the refugees were many who were prominent members of their trades and the effect their arrival had on the commercial and artistic life of the countries in which they settled was profound. As far as artistic developments in Holland are

49. Design for a study or small library by a Dutchman showing strong French influence (even the title is in French) and probably daring from the 1680s. The style is that of Jean Le Pautre and seems to owe nothing to Daniel Marot; it may have been composed before the latter arrived in Holland in 1684.

50. A complete, co-ordinated scheme of decoration designed by Daniel Marot, about 1695. The furbelows of the bed's tester are echoed in the pelmet-like cappings of the wall-hangings, while the festoons on the headcloth are repeated as 'pilasters' that divide the wall-hangings into panels. Waved falls edge both the bed-curtains and the hangings.

51. (right) Drawing by Daniel Marot for a pier-glass, table and pair of candlestands (only one is shown) for Het Loo, the House of Orange residence near Apeldoorn. Dated 1700.

concerned, the assimilation of the latest French style was given immense encouragement by the appearance on the scene of the Parisian designer Daniel Marot (1661–1752). Son of the architect Jean Marot, he had fled his native land already in 1684 and soon entered the service of the Stadholder. He was an exceptionally capable designer and could turn his hand to all branches of the decorative arts. He not only designed complete houses but could provide drawings for the decorations and all the furnishings (Plate 51). The small palace at Het Loo (begun in 1692) was perhaps his greatest triumph but his *oeuvre* was enormous and his influence extensive (Plates 141–4). The style he brought with him was that of Paris of 1680 although, once separated from the stimulating atmosphere of his native city which he must have understood so well, and forced to rely largely on his own inspiration or what he could glean from the latest French prints, his style evolved in a personal manner different from the main line in France. But he was a designer of international stature. What is more he was backed by a whole range of excellent craftsmen who were quick to pick up his style. As is well known, the master he served became King William III of England and Marot also provided designs for a

44

Le panneaux est fait à la hauteur marqué par la Lettre A-A, et je pourray
faire plus haut, pour ajuster la proportion de cette grandeur glace, à la
Lettre B.B.

La Largeur 48 pouces

le miroir ne doit avoir que 96 pouces de hauteur ce qui est 8 pieds

panneaux

moulure de la Croisée

La dessus de la Table de marbre blanc

Lambris 32 pouces
2 pi 7 4

2 pieds 7 pouces

13 pied
12
11
10
9
8
7
6
5
4
3
2
1 pied

Croi

D Marot fecit
à la Haye ce 20 de
Mes on est ée   17
achevée et passe den
la mois d'oust 1701
a los

good deal of work in this country in the 1690s, notably at Kensington Palace and at Hampton Court. At this point the artistic development of Holland and England ran parallel. But we must return to the England of Charles I to see how the British had accepted French influence in the meantime.

The purposeful francophile sentiments of Frederik Hendrik, Prince of Orange, were not strongly echoed at the English court. Charles I does not seem to have displayed any exceptional interest in French taste and it is difficult to judge how much the taste of his queen, the French princess Henriette Marie (1609–69), influenced artistic developments in this country. She was only sixteen when she arrived in England in 1625 and it is well known that Charles, a year later, dismissed her retinue of French personal attendants. However, she may have been rather more interested in art and decoration than is generally supposed. She would certainly have known something of her mother's great building enterprise, the Palais de Luxembourg. It may have been through her personal intervention that Inigo Jones was provided through the French Ambassador with a French design for a chimneypiece that he was to imitate for a fireplace in the Queen's apartment at Somerset House in the 1630s (see also Plate 64).[28] Furthermore, a French gardener, André Mollet, laid out her gardens at Wimbledon Palace and was retained out of her privy purse. It is not unreasonable to suppose that she had French furniture brought over for her rooms, and, if she had a French gardener, she may well somehow have secured the services of a French upholsterer to help do up her apartments. Her mother came over in 1638, admittedly as a refugee banished by her son Louis XIII but presumably still able to give impetus to any latent inclinations her daughter may have had towards introducing French ways at the English court.

By and large, however, the Queen must have been too pre-occupied with the acute political troubles that centred on her husband to give much thought to matters of decoration before the outbreak of the Civil War. She was in fact forced to leave the country in 1644, when she was still only thirty-five. She was provided with an apartment, first at Saint-Germain and then at the Louvre. While in France she naturally picked up fresh notions on fashionable French tastes and, on her return to England in 1660, she initiated changes in her apartment at Somerset House where, among other things, she had some parquetry floors laid which must have been inspired by floors in certain important rooms that she will have known in Paris (Plate 87).[29] It is unlikely that any English joiners would have been capable of executing such work in the 1660s and it may have been for this reason that some French joiners were working at the time at Somerset House.[30] We can see a new French fashion actually spreading in this case, for John Evelyn writes in his *Account of Architects and Architecture* that 'not to be forgotten are the Floorings of Wood which Her Majesty the Queen Mother has just brought into use in England at her Palace of Somerset-House, the like whereof I directed to be made in a Bed-chamber at Berkeley House; the French call it Parquetage'.

A childhood friend of Charles I was William Murray (1561–1654/5) who was appointed Gentleman of the Bedchamber in 1626 and had been among that band of constant companions of the future king who had formed the so-called 'Whitehall Group' of connoisseurs and art-collectors that included the Duke of Buckingham and Sir Balthazar Gerbier who will be mentioned again shortly. Murray redecorated Ham House, his villa on the Thames, in the late 1630s. As it probably remained virtually untouched right through the period of the Civil War the inventory of about 1654, which has recently come to light, is likely to give some indication of what the house was like once Murray's new schemes were completed.[31] It would seem that the house was most fashionably appointed and that the chief rooms were decorated in a unified manner, with complete matching suites of upholstery (the full *ammeublement*) in the principal rooms.[32] If the décor at Ham in some measure reflects tastes at the English court in the 1630s, as seems probable, this indicates that the basic principles of the new French thinking on interior decoration were by that date well understood in fashionable English circles (Colour Plate II).

A curious figure now appears on the stage who in a way symbolises the complexity of the network of influences being brought to bear on English taste at this time. Sir Balthazar Gerbier (1591?–1667) was born in Holland of French emigré parents—connoisseur, painter, diplomat, adventurer, pamphleteer and architect. He was familiar with everything and everyone in France, Holland and England, and was for a while the English ambassador in Brussels, so also knew the Spanish Netherlands. He came to England with the Dutch ambassador in 1616 and entered the service of the Duke of Buckingham whom he assisted in the acquisition of pictures for his famous collection. He was thus a key figure of the 'Whitehall Group' of connoisseurs, and accompanied the Duke and the future king Charles I on their famous visit to Spain in 1622. He was with the Duke in Paris in 1625 and shortly afterwards designed the Thames-side water-gate for York House, the Duke's chief residence, which he modelled on the Medici Fountain in the Gardens at the Palais de Luxembourg—a building whose seminal importance has already been mentioned. As Gerbier is said to have helped 'in contriving' some of the Duke's houses, he is very likely to have had a say in the decoration of their interiors, in which case he could have fallen back on his knowledge of Dutch and French practice and fashions. After a rather distressing interlude as ambassador in Brussels he was created Master of Ceremonies at court, in which capacity he may to some extent have been able to influence decorative arrangements in the royal residences. Certainly, after the restoration of the monarchy, he designed the triumphal arches that were needed for Charles II's coronation. In the 1660s, as an old man, he worked for the Earl of Craven, who had spent much time in Holland, and built for him a large country house (Hamstead Marshall, long ago demolished) and perhaps also the charming hunting-lodge at Ashdown—both of which echo the Franco-Dutch style of the 1640s. And, finally, Gerbier published in 1662 his *Brief Discourse concerning the Three principles of Magnificent Building*, a rambling and not particularly helpful little essay, and a year later his *Counsel and Advise to All Builders* which is, on the other hand, full of useful information. It seems to have been inspired by Louis Savot's work of 1624 with which it has many features in common. It may possibly be of some significance that Gerbier dedicated his work to (among others) Henrietta Maria, who was by then the Queen Mother.

Gerbier knew something of the latest fashions in building and decoration in Paris between 1625 and the outbreak of the English Civil War but his sympathies really lay with the Netherlandish tradition which was itself being shaped by French influence by that time. This was essentially the position right through the middle decades of the seventeenth century in England. The Mannerist tradition still had much impetus over here[33] and Dutch Classicism, evolved under Italian and French influence, then gradually came to affect English tastes. Direct inspiration from France was not apparent to any really noticeable extent outside a narrow court circle until after 1675 or so.

The fact that many upper-class Englishmen and women found it convenient to absent themselves from their country during the Commonwealth period on account of their royalist sympathies, or simply because life in England seemed uncongenial to them,[34] was of course to have great significance after the Restoration, for these people had learned about fashions on the Continent and could not fail to bring back with them many fresh ideas. It was not merely that the future Charles II and his court were exiled in Holland (Plate 257) and in France and had been able to study the Frenchified manners adopted by the House of Orange, as well as the genuine article at the Louvre and Saint-Germain; quite a few people who were not members of the court were also abroad. Sir Ralph Verney was an example and it is of interest to recall that he brought back with him in 1653 some Venetian mirrors and some ebony and tortoiseshell cabinets which he had purchased in Holland.[35] He proceeded to do over his family house shortly after his return. John Evelyn and Robert Boyle went abroad at this time; so did Sir Roger Pratt who took the opportunity to study architecture in France, Italy and the Low Countries on an extended tour lasting from 1642 to 1649. As a result he acquired an excellent understanding of these matters and put this to good use on his return. He was one of the three Commissioners appointed to supervise the rebuilding of the City of London after the Great Fire in 1666 and designed two highly influential houses, Coleshill in Berkshire and Clarendon House in Piccadilly (see p. 337). He favoured the French style and paid attention to details of interior furnishing—the most convenient height for bookshelves, how to contrive locks for windows so that 'women and short folk' might reach them.[36] One of the surveyors appointed to carry out the rebuilding of London after the Fire was Robert Hooke (1635–1703), the scientist and, like Pratt, an 'amateur' architect. Hooke records in his diary that he habitually purchased books on architecture and prints from France and Holland and some of his buildings betray marked French influence. Evelyn noted, for instance, that Montagu House (1675–9), which Hooke had designed, was 'built after the French pavilion-way'.[37]

But if Pratt and Hooke inclined to the French taste, Hugh May and William Winde preferred the Dutch style.[38] Hugh May (1622–84) has been described by H. M. Colvin as 'one of the two or three men who determined the character of English domestic architecture after the Restoration'. He accompanied Lely (who was of course Dutch) to Holland in 1653 and spent the years of the Commonwealth there. Later he was to give the brilliant Dutch carver, Grinling Gibbons, his first important commissions in this country. On the other hand, he was assisted at Windsor Castle by the decorative painter Antonio Verrio who worked in the French Baroque style of Le Brun which he had picked up while in France during the early 1670s.[39] Moreover, he collaborated with Evelyn on the translation of Fréart's *Parallèle de l'architecture antique et de la moderne* in 1664. William Winde (c. 1642–1722), for his part, was actually born in Holland while his royalist parents (his father had been Gentleman of the Privy Chamber to Charles I) were in exile there. Although a rather dashing cavalry officer, he could turn his hand to military architecture and Sir Balthazar Gerbier addressed to him one of the dedications of his *Counsel and Advise to*

All Builders of 1663. He had for a while served Elizabeth of Bohemia, daughter of James I and a friend of the Earl of Craven for whom Winde completed Hamstead Marshall after Gerbier's death and rebuilt Combe Abbey. But as Colvin remarked 'Winde's indebtedness to the Netherlands for his architectural ideas has sometimes been exaggerated.'

The other important figure on the architectural scene during the second half of the seventeenth century in this country was of course Sir Christopher Wren, but he towers so high above the others and the main lines of his career are so well known that I need not go into the matter here. However, it is worth recalling how impressed he had been with French interior decoration during his visit to Paris in 1665 and that he had on that occasion acquired a lot of engravings of French buildings and ornament. He will certainly have studied with interest any French engravings of this class of which he could subsequently gain a view and, as these were fairly readily available in London after about 1670, he will have been au fait with the main developments in his field during the last decades of the century.

Mention should also be made of Sir William Bruce, one of the most sensitive architects of the period, who built a number of charming houses in Scotland during the last part of the century (Plate 317) and carried out a major extension to the palace of Holyrood for Charles II. He had been in Holland in 1658 but the style he adopted with such success strongly reflects French mid-century taste with which he became familiar during a visit to France in 1663. Bruce was well-connected and influential; for example, he was a cousin of William Murray's daughter, Elizabeth Dysart, who was to marry the Duke of Lauderdale in 1672. It was from the Duke, whom Charles II had created Secretary for Scotland after the Restoration, that he received the commission for the work at Holyrood, which in turn led to his appointment as Surveyor-General of the King's Works in Scotland. He was friendly with Lauderdale, advising him on architectural matters of all kinds in connection with the Duke's several houses in Scotland and also with Ham House, on the Thames, which the Lauderdales were doing over in the latest fashion between 1672 and 1680 or so. As Elizabeth Dysart also went to France in 1670 it is hardly surprising that there are many French features among the decorations at Ham from that period (Plate 77).

While English architects at this stage concerned themselves with planning and the fixed elements of the interior, there is no evidence that they exerted any influence on the loose furnishings even of important rooms. They may sometimes have given a tip here, from their experience, or a sketch there. For the rest, this was something they were content to leave to the upholsterer. I shall discuss his rôle more fully in Chapter IV, but he provided many of the most prominent features of a room—the wall-hangings, the window-curtains, the seat-furniture which stood in serried ranks along the walls, the towering bed (if it was a bedchamber), and much else—and his part in creating the final appearance of such a room was all but paramount. It is therefore important to note that many of the chief upholsterers of the Stuart period bore French names and were presumably Frenchmen. John Casbert, John Poitevin (Paudevine), 'Monsieur La Grange', Francis La Pierre and Philip Guibert are names that appear prominently in the English royal accounts during the last three decades of the century, for instance (Colour Plate XII).[40] Some actual specimens of Parisian upholstery were to be seen in England and these of course demonstrated unmistakably the great superiority of the French in this field at the time. Particularly spectacular was the Parisian bed of Queen Catherine of Braganza at Hampton Court which, as Evelyn tells us in his diary, had cost £8,000, 'being a present made by the States of Holland when his Majesty returned' (presumably in 1660, that is).[41] Far less spectacular but none the less providing excellent examples of the new French line in comfort will have been chairs like those which Lord Montagu brought back from Paris in the 1670s.[42]

Carvers, who did so much to deck out a richly decorated room during the Restoration period, tended to work in the Dutch style and the best craftsmen in this field were at first Dutch. Grinling Gibbons is the best-known example but there was Anthony Verhuyck who also worked for the royal household. At the end of the century, however, the most prominent carvers were Frenchmen—Jean Pelletier and Robert Derignée, for instance, who were particularly well able to interpret the new style currently being introduced at some of the royal residences by Daniel Marot (Plate 51). Carvers produced not only ornamental cornices, door-frames and chimneypieces; they also made candlestands, tables, and supports for cabinets, and worked up elaborate chair-frames. Actual carved furniture found its way to England from Holland and France, and no doubt provided fresh inspiration. For example, it would seem that a carved table and accompanying candlestands at Ham House were acquired from Holland by the Duke of Lauderdale in 1672,[43] and some similar furniture at Hampton Court and elsewhere are also likely to be Dutch imports. The exceptionally handsome carved and gilt tables and stands at Knole, which were probably a gift from Louis XIV, cannot but have made a deep impression on anyone who saw them when they were newly arrived in 1671.[44]

The most exquisite cabinet making during this period, on the other hand, was produced in Paris and there is one of the most superb examples at Drumlanrig, Dumfriesshire, in the form of a marquetry cabinet which is believed to have been given by Louis XIV to Charles II.[45] However, it was Dutch cabinetmaking that had the most fundamental influence on English practice and, once again, some of the foremost practitioners in this country seem to have been Dutch or Flemish. Thomas Mallin, for instance who worked for Charles II in the 1660s may well have been a Fleming. Later in the century there were Cornelius Gole and Gerreit Jensen, both Dutch but working by that time in the French style. Indeed the intricacies of the network of influences being brought to bear on Holland and England at this stage are admirably brought out by these very men. Cornelis Golle, to give him his correct Dutch name, was the son of the celebrated cabinetmaker, Pierre Golle (d. 1684), whose name occurs prominently in the French royal accounts during the Louis XIV period. Cornelis presumably learned his trade in Paris and came over to England in the 1680s to serve Charles II. His brother Adriaan was cabinetmaker to the Princess of Orange (later Queen Mary of England); he had come from Paris to work in Amsterdam. To cap it all, their sister Catherine married Daniel Marot. But the links are even more remarkable for we find Pierre Golle in Paris owing money on his death to Gerreit Jensen in London for sending him a consignment of English glue, which was apparently especially efficacious.[46]

As far as we know, the Frenchman Daniel Marot was the first architect in Holland who attempted to co-ordinate all the decorative elements of a room (Plate 50) in the way Le Brun had done at Vaux-le-Vicomte and at the French royal palaces under Louis XIV. He apparently effected a similar form of co-ordination over certain schemes of decoration at Kensington Palace and Hampton Court but it was to be some while before any native English architect exerted a similar all-embracing influence on the décor of important rooms. However, that is an eighteenth century story and does not concern us here.

CHAPTER III
The Architectural Framework

IN ERECTING a building, the architect or whoever was responsible for the enterprise, created a shell the inside of which then had to be decorated and furnished. Although the rôle of the architect was still being defined during the seventeenth century, most really important buildings were being designed by such a professional, and he sought to co-ordinate the activities of the various contractors who were master-craftsmen of their respective trades. Designing a building at first consisted mainly in working out a suitable ground-plan and contriving tasteful elevations. When it came to the detailed features, these were discussed with the individual contractors concerned; they might provide a sketch of what they proposed to do and the architect could then either approve it or suggest something different. But, as a greater measure of unity was sought in the decoration of important rooms, it became necessary for the architects themselves to provide designs for the fixed decorative features and this was an aspect of their work which increasingly came to occupy their attention during the century. What is more, in the cases where an architect was trying to achieve a truly integrated scheme of interior decoration in a room, he tended also to concern himself with the design of the movable furniture, or at least the more eye-catching items. There was no consistent movement in this direction but once Le Brun had demonstrated at the French royal palaces and in certain Parisian *hôtels* how much more satisfactory a unified concept could be, ambitious architects began to try to exert an influence along the same lines. As far as we know, Daniel Marot was the first architect to apply this unifying principle to interior decoration in England and Holland, but the generation before—men like Sir William Bruce and Hugh May, for instance—seem to have taken a lively interest in interior embellishment and, even if they had to work through others (e.g. May supervised Verrio, and his team of decorators that included Grinling Gibbons, on the embellishment of important schemes at Windsor Castle), they may well have influenced the final appearance more than we can appreciate at present. One suspects that Inigo Jones, back in the 1620s and 1630s, cannot have been content to have his neatly ordered schemes ruined by the introduction of the ordinary run of clumsy Jacobean furniture. Something more elegant and in keeping must surely have been devised. The stools to be seen in the well-known view of the Earl of Arundel's famous sculpture gallery are Italian in form and may have been imported from Italy but Jones would have been perfectly capable of designing furniture of that kind, just as he could devise theatrical settings or costumes for masques. And there is evidence that suggests he may have relied quite considerably on men like Francis Cleyn to

I. (above right) The Dutch *haute bourgeoisie* adopted increasingly Frenchified ways in the third quarter of the century. There is a strong measure of French elegance in this scene of about 1670 showing the interior of a Dutch house in the country.

II. (right) Views of English seventeenth-century interiors are extremely rare but this charming picture of about 1638 is one of the earliest representations in colour of a suite of furniture (bed and seat-furniture) decorated in a unified manner.

contrive detailed decoration and even furniture that was suitable for the novel kind of interior architecture he was introducing (Plate 52).[1]

This is a big question that needs a great deal more investigation by architectural historians, but especially by those who can think of how buildings looked when they were completely finished, with all their furnishings in place. It is not sufficient for this purpose to view buildings merely as compilations of building materials rigged up according to certain rules into façades and spatial units. Architecture is far more than that and the seventeenth century architect was aware of it. Studying Vitruvius was all very well but people had to live in the buildings architects contrived. As Sir Francis Bacon so sensibly observed, 'Houses are built to Live in, and not to Looke on: Therefore let Use bee preferred before Uniformitie; Except where both may be had.'[2]

Even when it comes to the planning of houses, architectural historians have tended to think primarily in spatial terms and all too rarely help us understand how the great houses they study were actually supposed to be used. The rooms have different names but what purpose did each type of room serve? Were visitors to the house meant to see them in any particular order and, if so, why? These and related questions are only beginning to be answered. A seminal essay was H. Murray Baillie's on 'Etiquette and the Planning of the State Apartments in Baroque Palaces'.[3] This explains why the sequence of rooms in seventeenth-century royal palaces in England, France and Germany followed certain patterns and how these patterns varied in points of detail in the three countries as a result of variations in ceremonial at the respective courts. The subject has been greatly extended by

52. A chair from Holland House, said by Horace Walpole 'undoubtedly' to have been designed by Francis Cleyn. Such Italianate furniture would have suited the kind of Classical interior being devised for the English court and its immediate circle during the second quarter of the century by Inigo Jones and those, like Cleyn, who were associated with him.

III. (left) The State Bedchamber at Ham House as it must have looked in 1680. A small-scale reconstruction based on a careful study of the contemporary inventories, supported by the kind of evidence that is presented in this book. As the state bed, the balustrade, the tapestries and the chairs no longer survive, it is not possible to restore the room itself to its original guise.

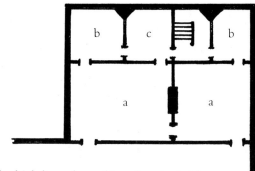

53. The basic formula for an apartment, with bedchamber (a) behind which lie a closet (b) and *garderobe*(c).

54. Approach to a state bedchamber through a sequence of rooms with doors *en enfilade*. Note how the chimneypieces face one as one progresses. The bed was considered so important that its position is commonly shown on plans of the period, as here. *Salle* (a), antechamber (b), bedchamber (c), closet (d), *garderobe*. There is a smaller apartment on the other side of the staircase with only a bedchamber (f) and closet (g). In the symmetrical wing beyond the Gallery (h) lies a chapel (j).

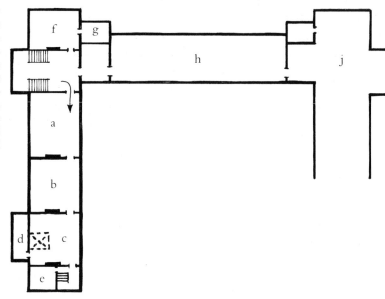

55. Twin principal apartments as shown in a French book of architecture in 1647. Vestibule (a), antechambers (b), bedchambers (c), closets (d), *garderobe* (e) which has a bed in it, presumably for a lady-in-waiting. A subsidiary apartment has an antechamber serving as *salle à manger* (g) with bedchamber (h) which has an alcove and *garderobe* (j) beyond. The gallery (f) occupies the opposite wing.

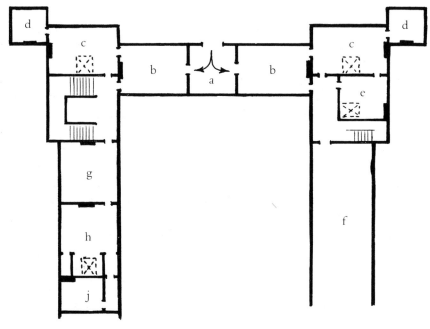

Girouard who, in his entertaining and informative book on great country houses,[4] has surveyed the whole organisation of these buildings and how this affected their planning from mediaeval times down to the present day. A chapter has also been devoted to the matter in Fowler and Cornforth's *English Decoration in the 18th Century*.[5] The reader is referred to these works for information on this fascinating and still not at all well understood subject. Here I shall only discuss it in so far as it affects interior decoration.

The arrangements made at court set the pattern for the great aristocratic families, and their arrangements were in turn imitated by those beneath them in rank—each according to his means. In royal palaces, the king had an apartment, a suite of rooms in which he resided. The principal room was the bedchamber which visitors approached through other rooms to which they were admitted according to their status and where the ceremonial of court life was performed (Plate 60). Behind the bedchamber were private rooms to which the monarch could retire. The high estate of the monarch was symbolised by the State Bed that formed the focal point of the State Bedchamber, and also by a throne and canopy (sometimes called 'an Estate' or 'Cloth of State') in the Presence Chamber. In the houses of the great nobility, where one might expect to have the king or queen coming to stay, a State Apartment had to be provided and it was arranged along similar lines, with a great symbolic bed at the culminating point of its sequence of rooms (Plates 54 and 59). Unless the monarch or an ambassador, or someone else of exceptionally high rank, were staying in the house, the State Bed was apparently not slept in, although the State Apartment was used for ceremonial occasions by the owner of the house—he 'held state' there.[6]

'You cannot have a Perfect Pallace,' wrote Francis Bacon, 'except you have two sevrall Sides; a Side for the Banquet ... And a Side for the household; the One for Feasts and Triumphs and the Other for Dwelling.'[7] Bacon is here saying that one side of a house should contain the State Apartment while the other should house the family. One should separate the ceremonial section in a grand house from the domestic part. The former was decked out in as impressive a manner as possible while the domestic quarters were rather less splendid but, depending on the inclinations and circumstances of the owner, might still be furnished with considerable opulence. These two distinct sets of rooms were actually more often to be found on different floors rather than in separate wings. In the sixteenth century and seventeenth century the State Apartments were normally on the first or even on the second floor, the domestic and family rooms being below. In the eighteenth century, this order was usually reversed so that the state rooms came to be on the raised *piano nobile*, with a view over the grounds, and the family then actually lived upstairs or sometimes in a wing. There were several permutations but all that needs concern us here is that there was this differentiation between the state and domestic apartments, and this difference in the status of the rooms came to be reflected in their décor.

In a royal palace an apartment was also set aside for the queen (Plate 61) and, because she usually symbolised an alliance with another country, she had to be treated with great respect and accorded much dignity. Her apartment was therefore usually almost as large and as grand as that of her husband. In some very large country houses, where they expected to have to entertain both the king and the

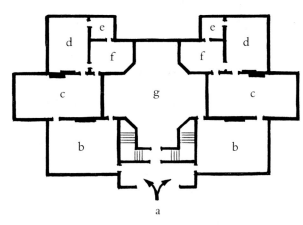

56. French principles of planning applied to a Dutch *maison de plaisance* (the Huis ten Bosch) built by Frederik Hendrik, Prince of Orange, and his consort, Amalia van Solms, in the second quarter of the century. Entrance hall (a), antechambers (b), bedchambers (c), great closets (d), little closets (e), *garderobes* (f) and saloon (g) (the *Oranjezaal* decorated with allegorical paintings honouring the House of Orange).

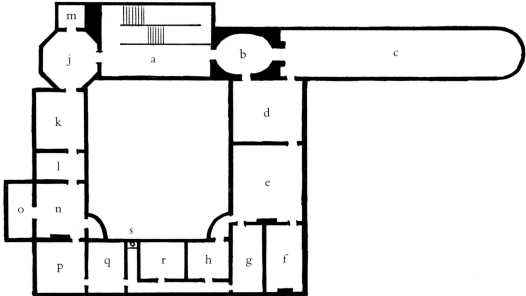

57. At the Hôtel Lambert in Paris, begun about 1640, ingenious planning enabled magnificence to be combined with great convenience. In spite of its complexity, the conventional sequence is maintained for the two principal apartments. Staircase (a), vestibule (b), gallery (c) decorated by Le Brun, antechamber (d), bedchamber (e), closet—the famous *Cabinet des Muses* decorated by Le Sueur (f), closet (g) and *garderobe* (h). Also antechamber (j), bedchamber (k), closet (l), *garderobe* (m). A subsidiary apartment (n–q) lies behind, as does a 'chambre pour les domestiques malades' (r) and a close-stool room (s).

queen, two equal State Apartments were provided[8] but most large houses were content to have just the single 'Great Apartment', as it was sometimes called (Plate 54). However, the owner and his wife also had an apartment each,[9] in the family section of the house. These consisted of the same general sequence of rooms leading to a grand bedchamber but they were naturally rather less formal than the rooms of the State Apartments. Faced with the need to incorporate such twin apartments in the ground-plan of a great house, the architects who were seeking to bring Classical order to their buildings seized upon the genial idea of making them into two equal apartments disposed symmetrically about a large central room lying on the central axis of the house (Plate 55). This plan was even adopted in quite small houses like

Ham House (as altered in the 1670s) where the Duke and Duchess had similar suites to either side of a central room, in this case a dining room, on the ground floor.

As well as the State Apartment and the suites of the owner and his wife, there would often be several other less important apartments[10] in a grand house—which could be used, for instance, by the eldest son, or the widowed mother, or an unmarried sister. The younger sons and the officers of the household—the steward, comptroller, tutor, gentleman usher, gentlewoman of the bedchamber, gentleman of the horse, etc.—had rooms that were a good deal less splendid but might still have closets attached so that they were essentially small private suites. The status of any room could readily be estimated by the richness of its appointment. The value of the textiles used for the upholstery in each case was usually the best indication but the rest of the furnishings tended to be commensurate. At Ham House, which still furnishes us with such excellent examples of seventeenth-century practice to this day, we find the most important rooms are those for which silver-handled fire-irons were provided; less important rooms have fire-irons with brass handles, or simply of iron.

Ordinary servants slept all over the place, often close to their place of work. The porter, whose job it was to guard the main door, slept alongside it. At Ham he had a bed in a chest that he could open out at night. In the early part of the century, personal servants frequently slept on a pallet bed[11] at the doors that gave access to their master's or mistress's bedchambers, thus forming a veritable bodyguard. Other servants slept in all kinds of small cubbyholes that we would today not think fit for human habitation—mere broom-cuboards! The seamstresses, the laundrymaids and other female members of the staff tended to sleep herded together in dormitories in the attic. The furnishing of the rooms occupied by the lower servants was sparse and inexpensive. Few had curtains to their beds, for instance.

Servants were much in evidence during the early part of the century but gradually they were swept away behind the scenes. The higher servants were no longer culled from the gentry and minor nobility; they rose from the ranks. The differentiation between the family and the servants became increasingly apparent and they now began to live apart. But, in order that servants should be able to attend to the wants of the family, a whole system of access-passages had then to be provided.

Let us return to the main rooms and see how they were organised. Girouard has described how the principal rooms in the great mediaeval house had been the hall, where the household dined, and a bedchamber beyond, where the master slept. Gradually this pattern changed so that, by the end of the sixteenth century, there was the hall at the entrance where the servants ate, supervised by the steward who was the chief officer of the household. Behind the hall was a parlour where the lord and his family dined but, on ceremonial occasions or if the lord considered himself especially grand, they would dine in the 'Great Chamber' which was now a large room upstairs. It had long ago lost its bed but the symbolism of high estate might still be embodied by a canopy suspended (in lieu of the bed, as it were) over the lord's 'high chair' or chair of state (Plates 166 and 46). Behind the Great Chamber there was a 'Withdrawing Chamber' to which the fine company could withdraw after a banquet. Here one could relax to some extent, perhaps waiting while the Great Chamber was cleared for dancing or some other form of entertainment. Behind the Withdrawing Chamber lay the State Bedchamber which contained the symbolic

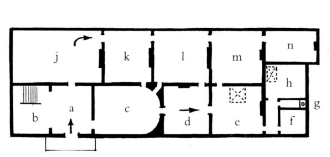

58. A late seventeenth-century project for a Parisian hôtel incorporating a *grand cabinet* (l) among the reception rooms. The direction of progress is indicated by the facing chimneypieces (j–n). Vestibule (a), staircase (b), *salle à manger* (c), antechamber (d), bedchamber (e), *petit garderobe* (f), *le lieu* (so named) for the close-stool (g), *garderobe* (h). Alongside run the receptions rooms: the *Grande salle* (j), antechamber (k), *grand cabinet* (l), *cabinet* (m), and *arrière cabinet* (n).

59. Diagram of the state-room sequence at Ham House. The sequence of the 1630s comprised the staircase (a), great dining room (b), with-drawing room (c), and gallery (d). To this was added in the 1670s a modern sequence with an antechamber (e), state bedchamber (f), called 'The Queens Bedchamber', and closet (g) with an alcove for the sleeping chairs, see Colour Plate XVI, opposite p. 290.

State Bed (Plate 54). And behind that were more private rooms called closets. The family used these grand rooms on formal occasions (the main meal of the day was often a formal occasion surrounded with much ceremony)[12] but had their own lodgings downstairs, while lesser lodgings for people of varying rank were tucked into the remaining spaces.

This was the picture around 1600: between the Great Chamber and the State Bedchamber there was already one room, a withdrawing chamber. The tendency thereafter was to increase the number of reception rooms between the Great Chamber, which now came to be renamed 'The Saloon', and the bedchamber. In a royal palace such rooms might be called 'presence chambers' and 'audience chambers' and might have thrones with canopies set up in them (Plate 60), but in the great aristocratic houses they were called antechambers (Plates 54–59). An important house from the 1670s onwards, therefore, would be entered via a hall, which was no longer used for dining (even by the lower servants who had by this time been moved out of sight to a 'servants' hall'), up a grand staircase on which architects now began to bestow much ingenuity, through a saloon, a withdrawing room, an antechamber (so called because it came *before* the bedchamber), to the bedchamber with its great bed and its small private rooms beyond—closets, *garde-robes* and dressing-rooms. Naturally there were variations on this pattern at different houses, and architects were kept busy thinking out clever ways of arranging the different rooms to best advantage (Plates 57 and 58).

Each room in this sequence was more elegantly appointed than that which lay before it, so anyone progressing through the sequence found the décor increasingly magnificent until the culmination was reached in the splendour of the bedchamber.[13] The impact of this sequence of splendour could be enhanced by

60

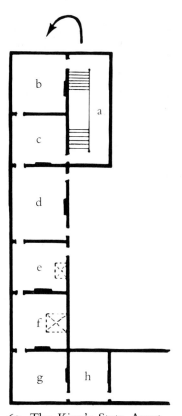

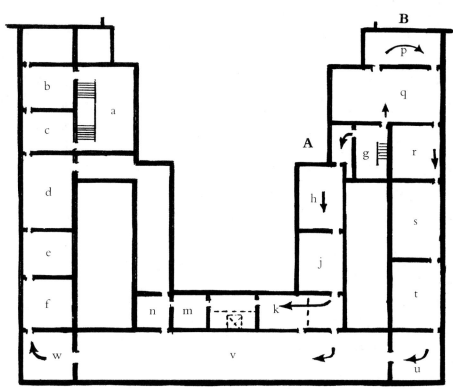

60. The King's State Apartment (*Les Grands Appartements*) at Versailles as built in the 1670s. The room-sequence advanced to the State Bedchamber (f), and a canopy or cloth of estate (see p. 57) was set up in the Antechamber (e). Louis XIV at this stage actually slept in a small bedchamber behind this sequence (h). Main staircase, *Escalier des Ambassadeurs* (a); reception room, *Salon de Vénus*) (b); reception room, *Salon de Diane* (c), guardchamber, *Salon de Mars* (d); Antechamber or Throne Room, *Salon de Mercure* (e); State Bedchamber, *Salon d'Apollon* (f); great closet, *grand Cabinet*, served as Privy Council Chamber (g); King's Private bedchamber (h) with minor closets attached.

61. The King's and the Queen's Apartments (**A** & **B**) at Versailles at the end of the century. The approach was now from the 'Queen's Staircase' (g) whence one could enter the King's Apartment (A: h–n) or the Queen's (B: p–t). Added was the *Grand Galerie* (v) with *salons* at each end, linking both apartments with the old sequence of *Grands Appartements* (a–f; see Plate 60) through which one now progressed in reverse, the ceremonial roles of (e) and (f) then being exchanged. The King now actually slept in his state bedchamber (l) which lay at the axial centre of the palace.

The King's Apartment (**A**): King's Guardchamber (h); *Antichambre du grand couvert* (j) where the King dined in public; *Antichambre de l'Oeil de Boeuf* (k) until 1701 comprising the King's Bedchamber and a smaller antechamber; the King's Bedchamber from 1701 (l) formerly the *Salon du Roi*; the Great Closet or Privy Council Chamber, *Cabinet de Conseil* (m); the King's gemstone collection, *Cabinet des Thermes* (n).

The Queen's Apartment (**B**); the Queen's Guard chamber, at this stage divided up as an apartment for Mme de Maintenon (p); the Great Guard Chamber (q); Antechamber (r); Great Closet (s) (with a canopy); curiously this closet came *before* the Queen's Bedchamber (t).

62. Design for a chimney piece by Pierre Collot, probably from his *Pieces d'architecture où sont comprises plusiers sortes de cheminées . . .* published in Paris in 1633. Such French suites of engraved proposals for architectural details were immensely influential.

63. French design for a chimneypiece by Jean Cotelle, which is included in a book of designs that probably belonged to Inigo Jones (see Plate 44). Coloured red and blue with touches of gold, this design is a reminder of how colourful French, and no doubt most, interiors were around 1630.

64. French drawing, possibly by Pierre Collot, copied directly by Inigo Jones in 1637 when designing a chimneypiece for the 'Cabinet room above behind ye round stair' in the Queen's House at Greenwich—a room intended for Henrietta Maria.

arranging the rooms in a line so that the connecting doorways were *en enfilade* and one could look right down the whole row of rooms (Colour Plate IV, Plate 54).[14] This was the commonest arrangement from about 1630 onwards. The doorways were placed close to the windows so that the main part of the room lay to one side as one proceeded along the line. There could be no doubt about the direction in which such a sequence was to be viewed because the chimneypieces were always set on the wall facing one—if they were not on the wall opposite the windows (e.g. Plates 54 and 60).[15] At any rate they were never to be found on the 'back' wall that one left behind as one proceeded, except when the architect had had to adapt an existing building. For it is no simple matter to move a fireplace: the flue is built into the masonry of the wall and there is often a massive, protruding chimney-breast as well. One can shift a chimneypiece a few feet to one side or the other, perhaps; but one cannot easily move it to the opposite side of the room. When Louis XIV reversed the direction of approach to the *Grand Appartement* at Versailles, the chimneypieces in three of the principal rooms (including the State Bedchamber and Throne Room) could not be seen by a visitor advancing through the sequence unless he turned and looked behind him (cf. Plates 60 and 61).

Having worked out a satisfactory ground plan, the architect could then proceed to think of the interior architecture. If he was good at his job he would consider the proportions of each important room as a spatial unit and he would try and dispose the fireplace, doors, windows and other essential fixed features in harmonious arrangements. Architectural historians deal with these matters in their works and what follows in this chapter is intended mainly to supplement their findings. It is not meant to be a consistent survey of the fixed elements of interior architecture and their decoration.

Since the chimneypiece was the principal feature of the room—the seat of warmth, light and therefore, by implication, of life itself—it is hardly surprising that architects took a lot of trouble to make it as striking as possible (Colour Plate V). In consequence this was a field in which demand for fresh inspiration was particularly strong. De l'Orme had included some designs for chimneypieces in his great architectural treatise of 1567[16] but separate sets of designs for these features began to become available in Paris in the 1630s. The most famous was that of Jean Barbet (Plates 65 and 66, see also Plate 1) but other selections were published from that point onwards.[17] So popular, indeed, was Barbet's *Livre d'architecture,* which first came out in Paris in 1632, that it was re-issued already in 1641 in both Paris and Amsterdam[18] while a set of simplified proposals based on his designs appeared under the title *Poorten en Shoorsteen-mantels en Autare* [Doorways, Chimney-mantels and Altars] at about the same time (Plate 67).[19] It must not, incidentally, be thought that every room had a fireplace in the seventeenth century. The Princess Palatine complained that, at the Château de Saint-Cloud, 'many of the rooms my people are lodged in have no fireplaces, which makes them unbearable in winter'.[20]

Sixteenth-century chimneypieces were massive structures, composed of architectural elements, with a large opening which was apt to be draughty. The seventeenth century saw the evolution in France of a form that was light and elegant, and totally lacked the overpowering character of its antecedents. This was brought about by a general refinement of the individual elements making up the whole. First, the great weight of sculptural ornament on the chimneybreast was tidied up. There

65 & 66. (above) Two designs for chimneypieces from Jean Barbet's *Livre d'architecture*, first published in 1632 and so popular that a second edition (from which the present reproductions are taken) was brought out in Paris and Amsterdam in 1641. Barbet's book was dedicated to Cardinal Richelieu and claimed to show 'ce qu'il a de beau dans Paris'. Inigo Jones used this work as a source of inspiration. See also Plate 1.

67. A simplified version of a Parisian design published in Amsterdam, presumably early in the 1640s. See Plate 160 where a chimneypiece in this style is depicted.

68. (above left) an example of the less over-powering form of chimneypiece that was beginning to be installed in fashionable Parisian houses in the 1650s. Engraving from Jean Le Pautre's *Cheminées à la moderne*, 1661.

69. (above right) The massive form of chimneypiece, albeit now more compact, continued in favour well into the third quarter of the century, as this title-page of a suite of designs for *Cheminées à l'Italienne* dated 1665 shows.

70. A chimneypiece of the compact model evolved towards the end of the century, with a panel of glass in the chimney-breast. Designs like this not only helped to spread the new fashion but gave information about fire-dogs, fire-backs and *garnitures de cheminées*.

71. Daniel Marot helping to spread the French fashion. The title-page of his *Nouvelle cheminées à panneaux de glace à la manière de France . . .*, published in Amsterdam about 1695.

72. Daniel Marot modernising the Dutch over-hanging form of chimneypiece late in the century. From his *Nouveaux lievre de cheminées à la Hollandoise.*

is still a certain lack of cohesion in Jean Barbet's designs of 1632 which are based on what was then recently completed work in Paris (Plates 65 and 66).[21] By 1665, however, the process had reached a point where Jean Le Pautre could publish a set of 'cheminées à l'italienne' which are proposals for compact chimneypieces of the sculptural type, usually with a central frame (oval, rectangular or fancily shaped) flanked by two figures (Plate 69). This form, also known as *à la Romaine*, was by now distinguishable from the new French form, *à la Moderne*, for which Le Pautre had brought out some designs in 1661 (Plate 68).[22] These reflect the new tendency towards lower openings for the fireplace, and often generally smaller openings, as well as a great simplification of the ornament of the chimneybreast, which ultimately came to be decorated with a simple panel en suite with those of the walls alongside, while the fireplace surround became a simple if bold moulding. As Blondel remarked in 1683 'l'on faisoit cy-devant beaucoup de dépense pour la structure & les ornmens des cheminées que l'on chargeoit excessivement: Mais presentement on les veue beaucoup plus legères, & L'on trouve plus belle dans leur simplicité' [formerly one spent much on the building and decoration of chimneypieces which were excessively loaded with ornament; but today they are far less massive and, with their simple lines, seem much more graceful].[23]

The great breakthrough in lightening the chimneypiece, however, was brought about by means of mirror-glass. A Venetian looking-glass had apparently been set into the panelling above a fireplace at Fontainebleau as early as 1601 but this seems to have been an isolated phenomenon. Glasses were not otherwise embedded in the chimney-breast until very late in the seventeenth century. Fiske Kimball suggested that the earliest executed scheme incorporating such a feature was the new *Chambre du Roi* at Versailles that was carried out in 1684 (Plate 82).[24] Once glass was being

66

73. One of Marot's *Nouvelle cheminées faittes en plusiers en droits de la Hollande et autres provinces.* The design on the title-page has a fire-back displaying the royal arms of England and Marot describes himself as 'Architecte des appartements de sa Majesté Britannique'.

74. Inscribed in the corner 'cheminée à l'angloise' and perhaps showing a chimneypiece for one of the English palaces for which Marot devised schemes of decoration. Note the royal crown.

used to face walls in fashionable rooms (Plate 80), it quickly crept out onto the chimney-breast, but such a feature is not shown in published engravings earlier than the 1690s, notably in Pierre Le Pautre's *Cheminées et Lambris à la mode* (Plate 70) which the title explains have been 'executez dans les nouveaux bâtiments de Paris' [erected in the most recent buildings in Paris]. In 1697 the Swedish architect Nicodemus Tessin, was advising Countess Piper on how to do up her house in Stockholm in the latest French taste and recommended 'pour les chiminées je les ferrois de glaces . . . du haut en bas; c'est le goust qui regne et qui est d'autant mieux fondé qu'avec 2 ou 4 bougies un appartement par la reverbération se trouve plus éclairé et plus guay qu'on autre avec 12' [for the chimneypieces I would make them with mirrors . . . from top to bottom; that is the taste that prevails here and which is all the more justified since with two or four candles a room, on account of the reflection, is lighter and more cheerful than another with twelve].[25] The magical effect of candles reflected in numerous panels of glass was still something of a novelty at this time, since relatively large plates of glass could not be produced at all easily.

At the end of the century, Daniel Marot, the Parisian emigré architect working in Holland for William of Orange, published a set of engravings in his personal variant of current French taste which he entitled *Nouvelle cheminées à panneaux de glace à la manière de France*, and there are chimneypieces in this style to be seen at Hampton Court and Kensington Palace, as well as in Holland (Plate 71). He also published a *Nouveaux lievre de cheminées à la Hollondoise* at about the same time; this will have been to satisfy conservative tastes in Holland, for they are all of the traditional Dutch type with a boldly protruding chimney-breast (with a mantelshelf) forming a large hood above the fireplace which is open on three sides (Plate 72). The French form was only open to the front.

75. French design for a ceiling signed by Jean Cotelle and dated 1647 (see also Colour Plate VI). It is signed by two master craftsmen at least one of whom was employed on Crown buildings in France. The crown above the cipher seems to be a royal one. This is from the album of drawings which was probably once in Inigo Jones' drawing office. Many of the other Cotelle ceiling-designs in the album are those actually published in his *Livre des divers ornemens pour Plafonds* . . .

The large Dutch openings lent themselves well to facing with tiles which were both decorative and easy to clean. There are numerous illustrations of such fireplaces in Dutch paintings (Plate 198) and they need no description here, but the practice of using tiles in this way spread into northern France and to England. Pepys had several fireplaces 'done with Dutch tiles' in the 1660s[26] and there are fireplaces faced with Dutch delftware tiles still to be seen at Ham House, dating from the 1670s. It is notworthy that some of the Ham fireplaces have undecorated white tiles (i.e. without the blue patterns that one so readily associates with this kind of tile) which, however, are haphazardly tinted and range from the normal creamy white of the tin-oxide glaze to pale mauve, pink and grey—very different from the harsh, even whiteness of modern bathroom tiles. These 'white' tiles are by no means set up in the least important rooms; for instance the Duchess of Lauderdale had them in her own bedchamber and Sir Roger Pratt ordered 'white tyles' for his withdrawing room in the 1660s.[27] But English interest in using Dutch tiles for lining fireplaces started well before the Civil War, for we find Sir William Brereton took a good deal of trouble, during his stay in Amsterdam in 1634–5, to acquire a set of such tiles which were decorated with soldiers of various kind, and then made careful note of how they were to be assembled back in England. 'Yesterday', he wrote, 'we bought four-score painted stones for one chimney; these postures of foot-men for the back of the chimney: care to be taken these to be placed half on one side of the hob[hearth], half on the other; half faces one way on one side, and so on the other side; drummers and officers to be placed in the most eminent places.' With the infantry thus marshalled facing each other, he could lay the 'Horsemen's postures for an hearth; fifty to be placed with as much care and in same manner as the other.' Brereton also bought a set of fifty flowered tiles and another of fifty birds for two more fireplaces. 'The horsemen and footmen cost nine gilders an hundred; the birds and flowers cost four gilders an hundred.'[28]

68

After the chimneypiece, the most noticeable feature of a room was usually the ceiling, and architects certainly gave much thought to the devising of striking ceilings in the seventeenth century. I will not say much about them because this is an aspect of interior decoration that has received much attention from art historians already.[29] However, let it just be said that here too the French published sets of designs to assist architects. The compositions of Jean Cotelle, for instance, seem to have inspired Inigo Jones and his followers (Colour Plate VI and Plates 44 and 75),[30] and Jean Le Pautre's ceiling designs were likewise influential.

While we know a good deal about the form modelled plasterwork ceilings could take in the seventeenth century we are still far from certain how they were decorated. Today we almost invariably see them painted white but were they originally so? In humbler houses, where the modelling was fairly simple, they no doubt were just white—but the white was far from pure and would almost certainly be regarded as a very light grey today. Grander ceilings sometimes had gilded elements—crowns and coronets, ciphers, ribbons binding festoons and wreaths, and similar features. And then there were even more elaborate schemes with

76. An architect's suggestion for the decoration of a ceiling. Inscribed 'for ye vault of ye Ceelings of ye Roomes East and West end' at Wilton, 1649, in the handwriting of John Webb, Inigo Jones' pupil and successor. Such a drawing would be used as a basis for large-scale drawings from which the actual painting was to be executed—in this case by Matthew Gooderick or Emmanuel de Critz.

77. The early Le Brun style of ceiling-painting translated to England. The ceiling of the Duchess of Lauderdale's magnificent 'White Closet' at Ham House dating from the latter 1670s, painted by Antonio Verrio who had worked in Paris for a while around 1671. The marbled surround is red and white, precisely echoing the actual marble on the fireplace and window-sill in this charming little room.

polychrome effects, fruit and foliage being coloured naturalistically. This is a big subject that needs a great deal of careful study but useful indications of contemporary practice may be found from studying the *trompe l'oeil* imitations of plasterwork ceilings that are painted on flat ceilings faced with canvas or boards, many of which survive in Sweden although examples may also be seen in Holland and no doubt elsewhere. The white of the Swedish ceilings of this class, at any rate, is invariably grey.

When it comes to mural decoration, one can once again say that a good deal has been written about panelling and about the better sorts of decorative painting, but

70

something more should be said about the finishing treatment given to panelling, even though a great deal more work needs to be done on this aspect of the matter.

The two principal timbers used for panelling in the seventeenth century were pine and oak. Deal was almost invariably painted[31] but oak was more often left uncovered except sometimes for a sealing coat of varnish.[32] In England and Holland, the grain and colour of oak was generally admired and it was mostly left to speak for itself although, during the first half of the century the bare wood often served as a background for painted or gilded ornament (arabesques, strapwork, coats of arms), while during the second half particularly rich panelling might have gilded details on carved mouldings and enrichments. If Evelyn can be trusted there ought to be less bold veining in oak panelling of the later part of the century, for he tells us that 'curiously veined' oak panels were 'of much esteem in former times, till the finer grain'd Spanish and Norway timber came among us'.[33] In France in the seventeenth century, on the other hand, oak panelling was usually painted (i.e. it was treated in the same way as deal, without ceremony) although in a few fashionable houses at the end of the century one might find rooms *boisé à la capucine*, which was the term used to describe varnished oak panelling because it seemed as stark as the walls of the cell of a Capucin monk.[34] Possibly this is an example of English influence on France.

A number of rooms in Elizabethan England were faced with unpainted oak panelling that was inlaid with patterns of contrasting woods. The fashion for decorating wood panels with such *intarsia* work originated in Italy in the late fifteenth century and was subsequently adopted in Germany and the Low Countries. German panelling of this class could be immensely elaborate but English examples were mostly rather simple. An exception seems to have been the panelling in the High Great Chamber in the old house at Chatsworth which was 'set forth with planets' executed 'in coulored woods markentrie'—the planets rendered in marquetry (or *intarsia*) of coloured woods.[35] Another room was 'very fayre waynscotted with coulored woods set out with portals [i.e. arcading or arched patterns] and some albaster and other stone'. Some detached panels of *intarsia* representing formalised architecture now preserved at Hardwick Hall may be from this room. Like most work of this sort, dirt and fading has effaced the contrast between the woods so it is difficult to visualise the original effect.[36] Such work went out of fashion in the seventeenth century but a certain amount of simply inlay (e.g. star-shaped patterns) was used in panelling late in the century. Panelling of oak with decoration carved in relief in the centre of each field was admired in France in the sixteenth century. It may well be that the 'French pannell' mentioned in the inventories of Chatsworth and Cockesden of, respectively, 1601 and 1610 was of this type.[37] During the seventeenth century the carving on panelling in France was for the most part confined to the surrounding mouldings while the fields remained plain and therefore lent themselves especially well to painted decoration—landscapes, portraits, etc.

Apart from oak and pine, other timbers were occasionally used for wall-panelling in the seventeenth century. The hall at Chippenham was 'wanscoated with wallnut tree, the pannells and rims round with mulberry tree that is a lemon coullour, and the mouldings beyond it round are of a sweete outlandish wood not much differing from cedar but of finer graine'.[38] The Great Chamber in the Mauritshuis at The Hague, built in about 1633, was panelled in 'a most rare Indian wood' that probably

71

78. Design for mural decoration, perhaps of a closet since the scale seems to be small. The lozenge-shaped mascle was the device of the Princesse de Rohan who was carrying out important schemes of interior decoration in Paris in the 1630s. The blank panels were probably to be filled with inset paintings. This is one of the designs that are likely to have been known to Inigo Jones, indeed, there is no reason why he should not actually have been responsible for procuring them from France.

79. (right) Proposal for mural decoration, perhaps by Jean Cotelle; 1630s? Once again this is from the collection that was probably in Inigo Jones' drawing-office. It seems to be for a closet, the owner of which sported a coronet and had the initials R.M.

came from Brazil.[39] However most of the exotic timber effects were obtained by means of graining (i.e. painted imitation of a timber) executed on deal panelling which was in itself relatively inexpensive. Thus one finds imitations of olive-wood and cedar at Ham House (Plate 314), a parlour at Broadlands was 'wanscoated and painted a cedar coullour',[40] while Sir Roger Pratt mentions also the imitation of 'prince's wood' which was a form of rosewood.[41] However, more commonly the imitations were of oak and walnut rather than of the fancy woods just mentioned.

The only type of wood Sir Balthazar Gerbier mentions in his list of prices for particular forms of paintwork is walnut; the other woods are merely 'timber colour'.[42]

Closely related to graining, of course, is marbling and this was equally popular in the seventeenth century. Indeed, these deceits might be practised in very grand settings. For instance, the Queen's attiring chamber at Denmark House had a chimney-piece painted in 1610–11 'with divers culloured stones as rance [i.e. red-and-white marble], white and black marble, serpentine and purfire'.[43] At Newby, Celia Fiennes noted that 'the best roome was painted just like marble, few roomes were hung' (i.e. with textiles), while at Barmiston there was a parlour 'with plaine wanscoate painted in veines like marble with white streaks'.[44] Remarkable examples of seventeenth-century marbling may still be seen at Dyrham, Ham House (Colour Plate V and Plate 77) and Belton.

A lot of work is currently being done on ancient paintwork and we shall soon be a great deal better informed about the composition of seventeenth-century paints and the techniques used in their application.[45] Nothing really useful can be said about colours in the space available here beyond propounding the general rule that colours were at first bold, and often in the primary range, becoming less strident towards the end of the century. Tessin was informed in 1693 that in Paris 'On ne peint les chambres boisées, les portes, les volets, les jassis [chassis], les plafonds, les portes, etc que de blanc avec le filet d'or ou sans or' [One no longer paints panelled rooms, doors, shutters, window-frames, ceilings, doors, etc. anything but white with or without narrow gilded mouldings],[46] but this fashion did not reach other countries until into the next century.

Before moving on from the subject of panelling, it should be noted that certain important rooms at Hardwick which were hung with textile materials had the sections of wall beneath the windows faced with panelling, presumably because any hangings put there might easily be damaged by rain or condensation. In the same way, Sir Roger Pratt stipulated that there should be 'wainscote under ye window' in his own and his wife's bedchamber when he was building Ryston Hall.[47]

Localised protection of walls could also be obtained by means of tiles. The Dutch frequently fitted a line of delftware tiles along the bottom of a plastered wall so as to form a shallow skirting that could not be marked by boots and chair-legs. Sometimes a similar line of tiles was set vertically on each side of a door-case to ward against finger-marks. Occasionally larger areas were faced with tiles. We have already spoken of tiled fireplaces and one sometimes sees in Dutch paintings a section of wall panelled with tiles.[48] Queen Mary II of England had a complete room faced with tiles, a dairy at Hampton Court which was built shortly before her death in 1694 and had large blue and white Delft tiles handsomely decorated with ornament designed by Daniel Marot.[49] The Trianon de Porcelaine, incidentally, which was built in the park at Versailles in 1670–71, was faced outside with tiles of delftware (i.e. faience, not porcelain) but the interior was of plasterwork painted in imitation of Chinese blue and white porcelain and tiles were, it seems, used only rather sparingly inside.[50]

We have already considered the use of mirror-glass in connection with the evolution of the chimneypiece in the late seventeenth century. Now something must be said about its use as a facing for walls in general.

Catherine de Medici (1519–89) had a *Cabinet de Miroirs* faced with 109 'miroirs plains de Venise . . . enchassez dans le lambris' [plain Venetian mirrors . . . set into the panelling].[51] The plates must have been quite small and the woodwork of the panelling into which they were set probably still remained the predominant feature. This little room seems to have been unique and, although we noted that Marie de Medici had a Venetian looking-glass[52] set into the chimney-breast of a fireplace at Fontainebleau in 1601, it seems that, for a while, those who wanted to achieve a striking effect with mirrors did so with looking-glasses suspended in front of the panelling or textile hangings. Francis Bacon spoke in 1624 of 'Rich Cabinets, Daintily Paved, Richly Hanged, Glased with Crystalline Glasse . . .',[53] indicating that the walls were clad with striking textiles and suggesting that the glass element was therefore subsidiary—just possibly inset but more probably loose in front. A ball was given at the Hôtel de Chevreuse in 1633 in a room that was 'tous revêtus de grands miroirs d'argent, de tapisseries exquises et garnis d'autres meubles dont la richesse ne trouve point ailleurs de comparaison' [completely dressed with large silver-framed looking-glasses and exquisite tapestries, and adorned with other furniture the richness of which has no comparison anywhere].[54] The looking-glasses with silver frames in this sumptuous interior must also have been hanging on the walls along with the tapestries (probably in front of them), but the effect was none the less impressive. The delightful effect such mirrors produced is indeed conveyed in a verse about a party given by the Archbishop of Sens in 1651.

> Cinquante miroirs de Venise,
> Des plus riches et des plus beaux
> Servoient d'agréables tableaux
> Pour representer les figures,
> Les grimaces, les grâces, les apas,
> Les ris, les mains et les bras
> De toute la belle cabale,
> Qu'on festoyoit dans cette sale.[55]

[Fifty of the richest and most beautiful Venetian mirrors serve as delightful pictures displaying the faces, the expressions and poses, the smiles, the graces, the charms, the bosom, the hands and arms of all the fine company that is entertained in this room.]

When 'La Grande Mademoiselle' (Anne, Duchess of Orléans, niece of Louis XIII) was sent into exile at Saint-Fargeau in 1653 she had her closet decorated 'avec quantité de tableaux et miroirs et je croyais avoir fait le plus beau chef d'oeuvre du monde' [with a quantity of pictures and mirrors and I believe it has made the finest masterpiece in the world].[56] She was no doubt putting a brave face on her situation and was trying to imitate effects with which she had been familiar in Paris (Plate 80).

By 1670 or so, however, one could see several rooms in France and England with large areas of wall entirely panelled with mirror-glass. Probably the earliest surviving example is a closet at the Château de Maisons of about 1660 (Plate 81). When, in 1668, Louis XIV did up a luxurious apartment for his new mistress, Madame de la Vallière, he had her *Grand Cabinet* faced with mirror-glass and we can be sure that this represented the most advanced taste of the day.[57] The Duchess of Portsmouth (Louise de Querouaille) and Nell Gwynne, the mistresses of Charles II, both had closets decorated in this new way, but already in 1667 Sir Samuel Morland

80. The closet attached to the principal bedchamber at the Hôtel Lauzun, Paris; about 1660. Instead of paintings inset in the middle band of decoration, panes of mirror-glass are here inserted—still in rather a primitive manner.

81. (right) The *Cabinet aux Miroirs* at the Château de Maisons. François Mansart's architectonic use of mirror-glass in this elegant little room, must have given rise to delighted astonishment when it was new, around 1660. Sir Thomas Browne saw it in 1664 and noted that 'whatsoever way you turn yourself you see an army of your owne selfe' reflected in the 'looking glasses quite round'. Note the elaborate marquetry floor which is apparently contemporary.

had had a room at his house at Vauxhall faced in the same manner.[58] Since it was not yet possible to produce plates of any great size, large areas were faced with abutted plates held in place by studs with large heads overlapping the corners. As was later explained to Tessin, one could fill panels 'de quarrés de glaces de telle grandeur que la depense que vous y voudriez faire permettroit, toutes les dites glaces sans bizeaux proprement jointes et ne composant pour aincy dire qu'une grande glace' [with panes of glass of such a size as the expenditure you have in mind will permit, all the panes being without bevelled edges, neatly juxtaposed so as to make as it were a single large glass].[59] Celia Fiennes saw something like this at Chippenham at the end of the century, describing it as '4 pannells of glass in length and 3 in breadth set together in the wanscoate' while the dining room 'had this looking-glass [i.e. with

76

panels set together] on the two piers between the three windows; it was from top to bottom 2 pannells in breadth and 7 in length' which means that each pier was faced with fourteen abutting panels forming one large pier-glass.[60]

What struck Celia Fiennes as so amazing about these composite mirrors at Chippenham, however, was that 'it shows one from top to toe'. It seemed incredible to people in the seventeenth century that one should be able to see the whole of oneself in a mirror. This is why rooms like the *Galerie des Glaces* at Versailles were considered so astonishing, for there one could see not only oneself, but the whole splendid company and the superb adornments reflected in the mirror-glass facing of this enormous room (Plate 11).

In 1684 Louis XIV planned a *Petite Galerie* at Versailles which was to be extensively faced with mirror-glass and was to have small brackets fixed to the glazed walls on which his fabulous collection of gemstone vessels could be displayed (Plate 236). The panels were rigged up at the Gobelins but were never erected at Versailles. Is it possible that the young Daniel Marot saw these panels before he was forced to go into exile in Holland? At any rate he created in Holland and England a number of rooms for the display of Mary II's large collection of Oriental porcelain. The engravings published in a suite entitled *Nouvelle cheminées faittes en plusier en droits de la Hollande et autres Provinces, du dessein de D. Marot, Architecte des appartements de sa Majesté Britannique* may perhaps show chimneypieces in rooms at the palaces favoured by the House of Orange in this country and in Holland (Plate 73; see also Plate 238). One engraving has a fire-back with the English royal arms while another is in addition described as 'à l'angloise' (Plate 74). They all have panels of mirror-glass in the French manner, and porcelain on small brackets is much in evidence. When Tessin visited the little palace of Honselaarsdijk, outside The Hague, in 1687, he saw one of the closets of the Princess of Orange (later Queen Mary II of England) which had probably been created the year before by Daniel Marot; it had a ceiling of mirror-glass and the walls were of Oriental lacquer.[61]

Large plates of glass were extremely difficult to make and were therefore very expensive. A plate had only to be a few inches larger to double in cost, so great were the hazards of trying to increase the size.[62] Until the 1660s almost all plate glass came from Venice[63] and when one is told that only something like two hundred cases of this costly material were imported into France each year, one can begin to appreciate why the first glazed closets caused such a sensation. By 1665 the demand for mirror-glass had so increased in France that a *Manufacture des Glaces de Venise* was established in Paris. The factory soon changed its title to *Manufacture Royale des Glaces de Miroirs*, reflecting the royal patronage it enjoyed.[64] It was able to fulfil official orders for mirror-glass by 1670 but the glass, as with all other plate-glass at this time, was produced by the blown method which placed a severe limitation on the size of plate that could be produced. To make larger plates, a new technique had to be invented.

Experiments in the casting of glass plate were carried out in the 1680s and a factory was set up in Paris in 1688 to make glass by this method which seemed to hold much promise. However, it was not until 1691 that four unblemished mirrors of this sort could be presented to Louis XIV. The casting process was laborious and attended by great risk of breakage; the polishing operation was unpleasant and noisy; and the silvering was difficult. By 1700 the French claimed to be able to make a plate 100 × 60 *pouces* in size (a *pouce* was about an inch), but between 1688 and 1699

82. Design for the chimney wall of the *Chambre du Roi* at Versailles; 1684. The large panels of mirror-glass set into the chimney-breast make this one of the earliest examples of what was to become the characteristic French chimneypiece in which the use of glass imparts lightness and grace. In order to obtain a sufficiently large area of glass, several plates had to be juxtaposed.

only eleven mirrors of 80 × 45 *pouces* had been produced and the breakage-rate during manufacture was enormous. Yet, by 1697, the Venetians had recognised that the French were the masters in this field and decided henceforth to confine their production to plates of 20 × 45 *pouces* and below.[65] By contrast, the French plate-glass manufactory was only permitted, by its letters patent of 1688, to produce glass of 60 × 40 *pouces* or more. At first it was allowed to sell broken pieces to foreigners but this was soon seen to be bad for business. In 1691 the firm moved to St. Gobain in Picardy and was shortly after amalgamated with the royal manufactory. Most of the large plates of glass produced right through the next century came from this single factory in Picardy. To the high cost of the product itself, had to be added the cost of transporting it from the point of manufacture to where it was to be set up.

It is hardly surprising that other nations tried to emulate the French but it was a long while before rivals captured any appreciable slice of the market. England, for instance, had sought to prohibit the importation of Venetian glass in 1620 in order to support home production[66] but this was clearly not successful as the prohibition had to be re-introduced in 1664 when the Worshipful Company of Looking-glass makers was incorporated. The Duke of Buckingham's 'glass-house' at Vauxhall enjoyed a certain amount of success. Evelyn claimed that they produced 'looking-glasses far larger and better than any that came from Venice' but they were still using the blown method so only small sizes of plate were obtainable. Robert Hooke, the scientist and architect is said to have taken out a patent for casting glass in 1691 but there is no evidence that any glass was ever produced by his method.[67]

Glass plates might be decorated in several ways. Slips of glass with bevelled edges,

83. Multiple interior shutters in a Parisian house early in the century, with leaded lights.

sometimes cut into fancy shapes, might be applied to the face of the mirror with screws or rivets. These slips were in some cases coloured.[68] One might engrave patterns at the edges that reflected the light in an interesting way.[69] And one could paint compositions on the glass. Catherine de Medici's *Cabinet de Miroirs* had a portrait of her husband painted on the glass that was set over the fireplace.[70] The glass walls of the *Apartement des Attiques*, built at Versailles in 1676, were painted with scenes by Bon Boulogne,[71] and at the end of the century we find Claude Audran painting with arabesques the borders of the mirror-glass panels of the Duchesse de Bouillon's closet.[72] The fashion also spread to England. Jean-Baptiste Monnoyer, who had been brought to England by Lord Montagu but who eventually came to work for Queen Mary, painted a glass at Kensington Palace that was 'tastefully decorated with festoons of flowers'.[73]

I have been discussing glazed wall-panels as part of a survey of fixed mural ornament contributing to the shell of interior architecture. Windows affect mural concepts as well but architectural historians mostly think of windows in terms of façades and their 'fenestration'. They rarely say much about the effect of windows on the interior. Yet again one has to admit that this is a large subject and that one can only touch upon certain aspects here. Madame de Rambouillet has been credited with introducing the tall 'French window' which reached right down to the floor. These 'fenêtres sans appui, qui regnent de haut en bas, depuis son plat-fond jusqu'à son parterre' make a room 'très gaie' and permit 'jouir sans obstacle de l'air, de la

80

vue & du plaisir du jardin' [These windows without sills, which extend from top to bottom, from ceiling to the ground, make a room extremely cheerful and permit one to enjoy without hindrance the air, the view, and the pleasures of the garden].[74] However, this form of window must have been invented some while after the Marquise rebuilt her family house (started 1619).[75]

The question of how light fell in a room was of course of paramount importance and there is good evidence that architects gave much thought to it. Savot explains why libraries, for instance, should face south while Wotton insisted that 'All the principal Chambers of Delight, All Studies and Libraries, be towards the East, for the Morning is a friend to the Muses.' Galleries and 'Repositories for works of rarity in Pictures or other Arts,' on the other hand, should face north as they 'require a steady light'.[76] Dutch painters were obviously interested in the play of light through windows and have recorded the many delightful effects that could be achieved by various combinations of shutters, open or closed, or with curtains drawn across one section (e.g. Plates 110 and 267). For windows during the first half of the century might have tiers of interior shutters (anything up to four tiers, one above the other (Plate 42) although one only fitted shutters up to a height that one could reach—any tier above that would have to have a curtain, if one wanted to exclude light or retain warmth). Indeed, interior shutters served both as insulation and as sun-blinds. Multiple interior shutters remained popular in Holland until the middle of the century but went out of fashion in France rather earlier (Plate 83). Windows with two tiers may be seen in engravings of Parisian interiors by Abraham Bosse, dating from the 1630s (Plate 84).

The earliest shutters consisted of a single leaf swinging on hinges at one side (Plate 133). This simple form had the great disadvantage that it projected into the room and clearly constituted quite a hazard. One could halve this projection by having pairs of shutters swinging from each side so as to meet in the middle of the window when closed, and this form could be made even more compact by arranging that each leaf could be folded back upon itself before it was folded away into a recess in the thickness of the window reveal. Bosse shows this stage evolving with a two-tiered system (Plate 84), but soon shutters of this type running the full height of the window were introduced. These were so much part of the architecture that they no longer appear in inventories. The earlier forms do, on the other hand, sometimes get listed—as 'window shutes', 'shute windows' and 'window leaves'.[77] The 'drawinge windowes' at Hatfield Priory in 1629 were probably also interior shutters and it would seem that they could be lifted off their hinges and stored in summer, for several were stacked in the 'wash-house', others were to be found in the apple loft and more were in the 'Folding Chamber'.[78]

Against the heat of the day one might fit blinds of various kinds, and these are dealt with in Chapter VI, but an effective measure adopted in parts of France was to fit abat-jours—slatted external shutters which excluded sun yet let through a current of air. On bright, sunny days they make a pleasant light indoors. A French edict of 1693 governed the amount abat-jours might project into the street so as not to inconvenience passers-by.[79] To exclude cold, on the other hand, one could fit curtains or mats inside a window, but in the present chapter we need only consider double windows which were certainly known in the late seventeenth century. The Duchess of Lauderdale had them in her closet which is in a rather exposed, eastern

Jey viennent à la haste,
Les Enfans de Mardy gras
Mettre la main à la paste,
S'escrimant à tour de bras.

La Cuisine les attire,
Soit par coustume, ou par jeu,
Et les bignets les font rire,
Tandis qu'ils sont pres du feu.

L'HYVER

Monsieur, dict vne Maistresse
Si vous touchez mon tein,
Ie repandray de la graisse
Sur vostre habit de satin.

Mais cette picotterie
Se termine incontinent,
Et toute leur raillerie
Est de Caresme-prenant.

84. Two-tiered, folding interior shutters in a Parisian house of the 1630s. The quarries of leaded glass are arranged in fancy patterns. Strengthening bars are fitted across the width.

corner at Ham House[80] and there were such windows at the *Orangerie* at Versailles in 1687, while Celia Fiennes saw some at Ashstead at the end of the century. She called them 'double sashes' and explains that they were 'to make the house warmer for it stands pretty bleake'.[81]

All houses of any pretensions had glazed windows by 1600,[82] but glass was still quite expensive and could only be obtained in relatively small pieces. The lattice-window, which only required small 'quarries' of glass, set in lead 'cames', therefore remained popular until larger panes of glass became more freely available (Plates 83 and 286). In 1613 it was still worth bringing out a pattern-book for the use of glaziers faced with the problem of devising varied patterns of lattices.[83] Occasionally a quarry was omitted and the space filled by an openwork panel of lead which served to ventilate the room[84] and many city-dwellers had small devices (usually their coats of arms) executed in stained glass set into their leaded windows. This was particularly popular in Holland during the first half of the century (Plate 232).

The opening of windows with leaded lights always posed problems. One could only have small opening sections as this delicate type of window was easily damaged

82

Baffe inu. et fe.   le Bleud grand auec Priuilege

L'Esprit en la Virilité   En cet âge là l'homme aspire   Alors sans creinte des dangers,   Que s'il voit que dans son mesnage
  Met les plus hautes entreprises   Aux principaux degrez d'honneur;   Au mestier de Mars il s'exerce,   Il gaigne des biens à foison;
 Dans vne juste eagalité,   Soit que le merité l'attire,   Et dans les païs estrangers,   N'aymant ny guerre ny voyage,
  Par les connoissances acquises.   Ou plustost son propre bon-heur.   Il se plaist à faire commerce.   Il vit paisible en sa maison.

85. A sash window in a Parisian house of about 1640? Abraham Bosse, who drew and engraved this scene, is usually so accurate on points of detail that this apparent representation of a sash window was unlikely to be mere artistic license.

by the buffeting of winds. A window that banged was apt to lose some of its quarries. It helped to have the section opening inwards, with the attendant inconvenience that also attached to the early single-leafed interior shutters. When the wooden framed window came into general use, with its larger, rectangular 'panes', it became possible to have windows opening outwards with reasonable safety. This form is so well known that nothing more need be said about it here, but on the other hand it is necessary to say something about the so-called 'sash window' which should strictly speaking be called the 'double sliding-sash window'.

The French term for any frame, and particularly any window-frame, is *chassis*—from which word comes our 'sash'. The word ought not to bear any implication that the frame can slide. Indeed, the French term for a 'sash window' is *fenêtre à chassis à coulisse* but luckily they have never been all that popular in France so they have not had to use this mouthful very often. Babelon claims that sash windows were used on staircases and other not easily accessible positions quite early in the century[85] and some of Bosse's scenes of Parisian interiors of the late 1630s and early 1640s seem to show this kind of window used in quite grand rooms (Plates 85 and 131). One is

83

certainly illustrated in a fashion-plate of the 1690s which indicates that the form was by then *à la mode* even if it did not sweep other types of window from the scene (Plate 31). In 1692 a tariff of dues payable on windows with fixed and sliding *chassis* was published in France and the latter were then described as being with a 'chassis à carreaux de verre à coulisse' [Window-frame with panes of glass that slides].[86]

Daniel Cronström wrote to Tessin in Stockholm in 1693 that 'Je vous envoiroy aussi, Monsieur [a drawing of] un invention de contre pieds [sic] nouveau pour les jassis de fenestre qui fait que les jassis demeure à la hauteur ou on le lève sans l'accrocher. Rien n'est plus commode et plus simple' [I will send you, Sir, a drawing of an invention of counter-weights for window-frames which make the frame stay at the height to which it is raised without fastening it. Nothing is more convenient or simpler].[87] But Tessin replied that 'J'ay vû une invention des contrepieds pour des jassis à [the Dutch palace of Het] Loo. Je seroy ravy de voir . . . si c'est la mesme ou non' [I have seen an invention of counter-weights for window frames at Loo. I shall be delighted to see . . . if it is the same or not]. When Tessin visited Het Loo in 1687 he did in fact record having seen the sliding sash windows.

> The upper section of the window which is of 5 large panes in height and the same in breadth is fixed. The lower section, which is just as large, goes all the time up and down with cords to which weights are hanging that run up over small pulleys and are fixed to small slots on each side of the window halfway up its height, so that the cords do not rub and yet cannot be seen. The two weights are proportioned to the weight of the window and are of lead, flat and rather like a small hand in size. They have holes at the top through which the cord is tied. It is to be noticed that all the window surrounds have two flat pieces of wood screwed into place forming a channel on one side of the window; this can be unscrewed so that one can get out an entire window and clean it. Large French window panes are fitted into the oak *chassis* and are fixed not with lead but with a certain compound.[88]

At the very same period, a sash-window with a counter-balancing system was being installed at Windsor Castle, but this was the period when Daniel Marot was architect to William III so any novelty of this kind in a Dutch or English palace would have been known within a short while in both countries.[89] Hitherto, one had had to lock the sash in position by means of small swivelling quadrants that engaged in a notched bead at the side of the window.[90] The occasional references to sashes with 'lines and pullies' prior to the 1680s may concern cords that facilitated the pulling up of the sliding sash (it was probably only the lower section that moved in the earliest forms of this type of window) as no mention is made of weights. This may have been the purpose of the '4 pairs of clock strings' that the Duke of Lauderdale bought in London in 1674 'to make strings for sash windows', and even the 'very strong shasses with their frames and brass pullies and very good lines to them' provided by a joiner for Whitehall Palace in November 1685 may have been of this early sort.[91] The Duke of Hamilton had sash windows fitted at Hamilton Palace in 1690 but his wright was sent to London three years later to inspect the new form of sash window—presumably because the Duke knew there was something better than the type with catches available by then.[92] The Maréchal de Lorge showed Dr Lister 'his great sash windows' in 1699 and demonstrated proudly 'how easily they might be lifted up and down and stood at any height; which contrivance he said he had out of

84

England by a small model brought on purpose thence, there being nothing of this poise in windows in France before'.[93]

In the 1570s, Harison explained that 'only the clearest glass is the most esteemed' and went on to say that 'we have divers sorts, some brought out of Burgundy, some out of Normandy, much out of Flanders, besides which it is made in England'.[94] This suggests that English glass was still of no consequence in his time. When Sir Roger Pratt was writing, almost a century later, the best glass from Newcastle was costing sevenpence per square foot while glass from Normandy cost seventeen pence and was considered much superior.[95] Indeed, during the seventeenth century Dutch and English privateers found it well worth trying to capture the shipments of Normandy glass that were regularly being sent from the factory at Tourlaville, via Cherbourg and up the Seine to Paris. So troublesome were their activities that the French had to send an armed escort to convoy the glass-boats.

Floors are of course also an important feature of the architectural shell which affect the appearance of an interior. We need not concern ourselves with how floors were supported and the other more purely structural aspects of the matter, but something needs to be said of the surfacing of floors in the present context.

86. Examples of paviour-work in various types of marble.

'Roomes on moist grounds do well to be paved with marble because the boarding otherwise is subject to rot,' wrote Sir Balthazar Gerbier in 1664[96] but not a few important rooms were paved with marble for the grand effect this produced. Much consideration was given by paviours (and perhaps also by the architects who were guiding their activities) to the patterns one could produce by combining stone 'quarries' of two or more colours (Plate 86). Several illustrations here show how intricate a pattern could be produced by using black and white quarries alone; it was particularly the Dutch who favoured floors of this kind, and Dutch marble was apparently exported in some quantity for this purpose (Colour Plate XIII and Plate 108).

The Dutch also exported thick tiles for flooring which were faced with a coloured lead glaze.[97] These were no longer a particularly fashionable type of flooring but tiles of some sort were laid as late as 1660 under the lantern in the Long Gallery at Knole (presumably because it leaked) and it was considered acceptable merely to renew old tile-work at Versailles in 1677 when the Château was being extended.[98] These are likely to have been of the more decorative kind—tiles of delftware (or maiolica) which have patterns executed in a limited range of colours on a white, tin-oxide ground. Italians had made much use of maiolica tiles in the sixteenth century and, when the potters of the Low Countries began to imitate Italian maiolica, tiles of this material were among their products. Indeed, Netherlandish maiolica tiles were exported all over northern Europe.[99] Moreover, Flemish potters versed in the techniques of producing this attractive ware emigrated and established themselves in many parts of Europe. Some settled in Norwich and, in 1567, proposed to make 'gally paving tiles and vessels for apothecaries and others'.[100] Strangely enough this was not to be a common form of flooring in the seventeenth century, however. The thin, and therefore rather delicate, delftware tiles by then being manufactured in Holland (at Rotterdam and elsewhere, apart from at Delft itself) were not really suitable for large floor areas although they lent themselves well to purposes like skirtings, fire-surrounds and even hearths.

In the three countries that primarily concern us here, wooden floors were primarily made of oak and it was considered noteworthy when Sir Bulstrode Whitelocke, who had been the English ambassador to Sweden in 1653, introduced the Scandinavian practice of having floors of deal when he had some boards of this timber imported and laid as a floor at Fawley Court.[101] The Scandinavians kept floors of this wood smooth and white, one method of doing this being to rub the floor with cold water and slaked lime, using a pad of straw knotted in a figure of eight.[102] The English method involved the use of wet sand, sometimes mixed with Fuller's earth. Floors were 'dry sanded' between-times and, in some parts of nineteenth-century America, a thin layer of sand was left on the floor and swept into decorative patterns—a practice which very probably reflects a much more ancient one stemming from northern Europe.[103]

IV. (right) Enfilade on the principal floor of the Hôtel Lauzun, Paris. View from the *Premier Salon*, through the *Salon de Musique* (antechamber) and *Chambre à alcove* to the *Cabinet* (see Plate 80). Built about 1656–7, probably by Louis Le Vau, for a financier, this gives a good idea of the kind of decoration to be seen in the most fashionable Parisian *hôtels* at about the time of Cardinal Mazarin's death.

Oak floors, on the other hand, were waxed. Cronström had to explain to Tessin in Stockholm how the floor of the *Grand Galerie* (the *Galerie des Glaces*) at Versailles was treated. They should be rubbed, he said with 'un peu de cire jaune . . . de sorte que les bois de chesne a sa couleur naturelle, à cela près que la cire le rend un peu plus jaune'[a little yellow wax . . . so that the oak wood keeps its natural colour, or perhaps the wax will make it a little yellower].[104] The almost black parquet one sees today in many old French houses is of course saturated with dirt that has become embedded in the wax over the centuries. Tessin was told that the floor needed to be polished with 'une brosse à frotter le parquet' [a brush for polishing the parquet] and a specimen of this implement was dispatched to him three months later.

In 1693 Tessin was also informed that, at Versailles 'il y a une frize ou bande de marbre noir de 8 pouces environ . . . qui regne tout au tour des lambris en bas' [there is a frieze or band of black marble about 8 inches wide . . . which runs right round the bottom of the panelling] while, at the Trianon, 'où il n'y a point de lambris de marbre, les parquets touchent aux lambris. Il n'y a qu'une seule piece à Versailles dont le parquet soit par quarrés . . . tout le reste est en lozanges à la nouvelle manière' [where the walls do not have panels of marble, the parquet floors reach the panelling. There is only one room at Versailles where the parquet is laid in squares . . . all the others are [laid] in lozenges in the new manner] (Plate 94).[105] Parquet laid diagonally *en lozanges* is still called *parquet de Versailles* in the trade.

Technically similar but far more elaborate were the floors which stemmed from the famous parquetry floors laid for Marie de Medici at the Luxembourg in 1620s, a type of floor-decoration that originated in Italy, as a contemporary noted.[106] Richard Symonds, who was in Paris in 1649, described the floor of the Queen's closet as being 'wrought in little workes all Sevvall forms pitcht in with Silver.'.[107] Such work would only be entrusted to joiners of the utmost capability; the Luxembourg floors were apparently laid by a man named Du Hancy and his skill was such that Martin Lister could still remark on their astonishing 'firmness, duration and intirenes' when he saw them in 1699, three quarters of a century later.[108] The floors of the next Queen of France, Anne d'Autriche, at the Palais Royal were furnished by the highly competent Jean Macé who would now qualify for the title of cabinet maker (Plates 33 and 81).[109] And her successor had floors laid by Pierre Golle who was nothing less than *ébéniste du roi*—cabinetmaker to His Majesty. A drawing of a floor laid by him in one of the Dauphin's closets shows how intricate such floors could be (Plate 90). In the record of payment to Golle it is justly called a 'parquet marqueté'. The famous cabinetmaker, André-Charles Boulle created another floor of this kind for the Dauphin in 1682–3.[110] No illustration of it survives but it is known to have been of extreme delicacy.

Around 1650 the Princess of Orange fitted out a closet at the Huis ten Bosch near The Hague where she had Oriental lacquerwork set into the panelling and the floor was of palisander wood with a large star in the middle, executed in woods of several colours; the whole was noted as being 'very curious'.[111] By French standards this floor was probably relatively simple, as was the roughly contemporary floor at Sir

V. (left) An imposing French chimneypiece bearing the arms of France and Navarre and intertwined L's for Louis XIII, who assumed power from his regent mother, Marie de Medici, in 1617 and died in 1643.

87. The patterns of parquetry floors laid in the apartment of Henrietta Maria, the Queen Mother, at Somerset House in 1661.

88 & 89. (far right) Patterns of parquetry. Presumably designs to be seen in the 1690s in important French buildings including the royal palaces (note the *fleur de lys*). One design has roundels with marquetry scenes.

John Danvers' house in Chelsea which John Aubrey described as being 'chequered like a cheese board of box and ewgh[yew] panels of about six inches square'.[112] Plate 87 shows the patterns of floors laid very early in the 1660s in the apartment of Queen Henrietta Maria at Somerset House, which work was said to have been 'a curiosity never practised before in England'. The Queen returned to England from exile in France in 1660 and will have seen, not only her mother's floors at the Luxembourg, but also some of the more recent manifestations of this form of decoration (e.g. Plate 33.).

A floor with an intricate strapwork pattern and with the crowned ciphers of the Duke and Duchess of Lauderdale may still be seen in the State Bedchamber and its attendant Closet at Ham House, which dates from 1673 (Colour Plate XV).[113] Probably of about the same date are the remains of an elaborate marquetry floor now mounted on a late seventeenth-century table at Boughton; it may have come from a closet at Montagu House which was built in the 1670s and damaged by fire in 1680. That it was thus re-used suggests it was prized in its day.[114] At Belton there is a closet with a floor painted black, red and brown in imitation of a floor of this kind; it may well give a truer indication of the original striking appearance of such floors than the mellow-toned survivals of the genuine article.[115]

The French term *parquet* comes from the small, fenced-in 'park' from which kings or other exalted persons had formerly administered justice. The floor of these small areas, which was usually raised, was often treated in some special manner in order to stress their separate character, and floors of *parquet* were presumably first used in such a context. Certainly, the very elaborate 'marquetry' floors were only laid in small

90. The 'parquet marqueté' of the Dauphin's *Cabinet Doré* at Versailles executed by the famous *ébéniste*, Pierre Golle, who was paid 7,500 *livres* for the work in 1682. The floor was taken up in 1688. The Dauphin's *Grand Cabinet* next door had a floor executed by the no less famous André-Charles Boulle, but floors of such complexity were exceptional.

rooms like closets, or in special areas like the raised step of the alcove in some grand bedchamber.[116] On the other hand, parquet, in the sense that we understand the term, had been widely adopted for all the principal rooms in important new French buildings by the end of the century, and this fashion was spreading to England and Holland by 1700.

Once the architectural shell existed, it had to be furnished. Just as one could rely on the plasterer to provide a suitable ceiling, and the marble contractor might supply a handsome chimneypiece in the prevailing style, so one could expect a fashionable upholsterer to provide hangings, beds and seat-furniture that would blend satisfactorily with the surroundings. But an ambitious architect, striving to create a special effect for some important commission, might guide the upholsterer by providing him with sketches of what he wanted. And he might do the same with the cabinetmaker, the joiner, the metalworkers and the other contractors engaged on the project. This is a matter that needs more investigation but a few comments are appropriate here.

Architects of the seventeenth century certainly did not concern themselves with the ordinary run of furniture; they will only have taken an interest in pieces which formed a salient feature in an important scheme of decoration on which they were engaged. Leading Italian architects were apparently already designing specially important pieces of furniture in the sixteenth century—a fancily inlaid marble table and its supporting frame, a cabinet to stand in some particularly eye-catching position, a candlestand, a state bed—and this tendency became more marked in the seventeenth century (Plates 7 and 51).[117] If Francis Cleyn really did design the shell-backed *sgabelli*-type chairs for Holland House (Plate 52) and for Ham House, it may well be that he was inspired to do so because he was following a practice that he had come across in Italy when he had stayed there early in the century.[118] Cleyn seems anyway to have worked within the circle where Inigo Jones was the presiding genius, and the latter is very likely to have wanted furniture in a style that needed to be specially created for the interiors he was devising for Charles I and his court in the 1620s and 1630s. Like Cleyn, he will also have known about current Italian practice and could well have provided sketches for furniture himself. Whether he actually did so is another matter. What we do know, however, is that his pupil and protégé, John Webb, did design an alcove with a state bed standing in it, for Charles II's apartment at Greenwich Palace (Plate 45). The drawing is dated 1665. The bed itself is a fairly straightforward structure of the type fashionable at the time, but Webb seems to have added an extra finial (cup with plumes of ostrich feathers) that distinguishes it from the more sketchy beds one sees in Jean Le Pautre's otherwise rather similar representations of alcoves (Plates 27 and 28), on which Webb's composition was no doubt based. Le Pautre's engravings, for their part, probably show the co-ordinated effects executed in Paris around 1660 by an important French architect.

We get on to rather firmer ground when Charles Le Brun appears on the scene. We have already discussed the superbly integrated schemes for which he was responsible, first at Vaux-le-Vicomte and then at the French royal palaces. Already at Vaux (i.e. around 1660) he was providing designs in sketch form for individual pieces of furniture (Plate 5) that the various craftsmen could develop into working drawings, and he continued this practice when he became director of the Gobelins, that incredible group of workshops, staffed by the best craftsmen of the day, which provided sumptuous furnishings of all kinds for the French royal household. For instance, a sketch from le Brun's own hand survives for what is believed to be one of the imposing silver tables that stood in the state rooms at Versailles (Plate 9), and a more finished drawing of the same table also exists, probably representing the silversmith's final conception deriving from Le Brun's inspirational sketch (Plate 10). The table itself, along with many other pieces of silver furniture, was constructed in the 1670s but all the silver furniture at Versailles was melted down in 1689 to help bolster up the then ailing French exchequer.[119]

The table in question was a console-table that was intended to stand against a window-pier, presumably with a mirror above and flanked by a pair of candlestands—an ensemble that became highly fashionable during the last two decades of the century (Plate 218).[120] The candlestands were later dispensed with (they got in the way of curtains and must always have been getting knocked over) but the mirror and its accompanying table were already then an essential part of the

8

91 & 92. Examples of designs for furniture published by architects to meet the need for unity of style in an interior. The joiners who bought this book, Paul Vredeman's *Verscheyden Schrynwerck* or *Plusiers Menuiseries*, could be sure that the 'doorcases, clothes-presses, buffets, beds, tables, chests, chairs, benches, stools, roller-towel holders, mirror-frames and works of many other kinds' would be in a fashionable style consonant with the interior architecture of the rooms in which they were to be set up.

architecture, so it is not surprising that architects paid special attention to this feature. A design by Daniel Marot for such a 'triad' (the term is modern) that was to be set up at Het Loo exists and shows the care he bestowed on its proportions (Plate 51). For, of course, an ensemble of this sort was designed to stand in a particular position in a special room; such furniture was not interchangeable, although it might still look very impressive even if moved from its intended surroundings. For the most part, however, such triads were produced by cabinetmakers or carvers to their own designs in a fashionable style that would blend perfectly adequately with the general décor of any newly decorated room. Such furniture was in these instances bought for a specific position but it was not actually designed for it.

In designing such important pieces (or groups) of furniture, master-craftsmen could turn to publish designs for inspiration. These were often composed by men who called themselves architects even though some of them seem to have concentrated on design as such rather than on erecting actual buildings. Nevertheless they will all have recognised that practising architects needed to have furniture

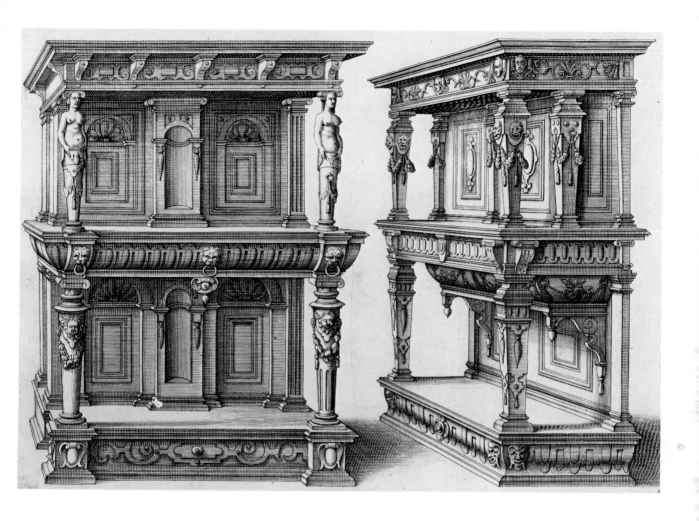

that was consonant in style with the architecture they were creating (Plates 91 and 92). The furniture that is illustrated in the published works of architects (e.g. Du Cerceau, Hans Vredeman, Jean Marot and Daniel Marot) may therefore be called 'architectural furniture', for the designs were put forward with the needs of the architect in mind. State beds, which formed the focal point of an important bedchamber and embodied such potent symbolism, therefore received a good deal of attention in such works. So, in the sixteenth century and the first half of the seventeenth century, did the great buffets on which valuable plate could be displayed, although these subsequently went out of fashion. The handsome draw-leaf dining table, with its associated stools, also figured in works of the early seventeenth century but the only kind of table that interested late seventeenth-century architects was the console-table which we have already discussed. Candlestands, urns, perfume-burners, thrones, cabinets, day-beds, clocks—all were the subject of such published designs: all therefore have claims to being called 'architectural furniture'.

Daniel Marot is a case rather on his own, as he practised as an architect but was also capable of designing all the furnishings and interior decoration—and, indeed, published many designs in this field (Plates 95 and 143). He no doubt found it necessary to spread as quickly as possible the style he introduced to Holland from Paris when he emigrated in 1684, so that his clients became familiar with it and would soon demand work only in that taste, and so that a supporting cast of craftsmen would spring up that could provide furnishings in the new style with a minimum of additional guidance.

In Daniel Marot's oeuvre the distinction between 'architectural furniture' and furniture in general is obscured by his versatility, but the distinction was never all that clear-cut. There was never a class of furniture that was invariably architect-designed. There were, however, certain classes of furniture for which architects occasionally took it upon themselves to provide the designs.

CHAPTER IV
The Upholsterer's Task

THE seigneurial pattern of life on the Middle Ages had involved frequent moves from one residence to another, as we have already noted. One of the purposes of these moves was to demonstrate a lord's power and high status. This was achieved by a display of wealth and luxury which clearly set him apart from lesser beings. It was also achieved through the performance of complicated ceremonial and the lavish entertainment of large numbers of people against a magnificent background. Devising suitable settings for these various activities seems to have been the responsibility of the *fourrier* in those days.[1] He carried out his task primarily with the aid of furnishings made of textile materials—wall-hangings, cushions, carpets, bed-hangings, padded chairs and canopies—with which he could quickly transform a bare interior into one of accommodating comfort and visual delight, and could contrive settings appropriate to each occasion. As these largely textile furnishings were made of extremely valuable materials that were conspicuous evidence of the lord's wealth, they were carefully protected and were not normally left at a residence once the lord had moved on elsewhere; they were taken along on the journey in the baggage train. Textile furnishings were of course particularly well suited to this way of life because they could be folded into manageable form for packing or they could be rolled up for stowing in the carts.[2]

Using these materials, the *fourrier* with the help of his staff could, for instance, divide off part of the great hall to make a smaller, more intimate compartment, he could rig up a daïs and canopy where the lord could sit in state, he could dress the staging of the buffet with a cup-board cloth on which the lord's collection of rich plate (his 'cups') could be proudly displayed. He might dress up a charming bower for my lady, strewing the seats with rich cloths and cushions, and he could furnish equally suitable lodgings for the rest of the family and for grand visitors—each according to his status. He knew the form for weddings, for christenings, for mournings, and could dress the house and chapel to an appropriate degree for each occasion. He could fix up a setting for a tournament and would remember to hang rich carpets and table-covers from the balconies when there was a parade. As we have said, he did all this primarily with the aid of textile materials made up in various ways.

When aristocratic life became more static, after 1500 or so, rich textile furnishings remained the symbol of high estate and still constituted the most conspicuous element of the décor in any house of importance. It took a long while before wooden furniture came into any great evidence and, even when it did, it was often largely masked with textiles. It was the hangings that were the most prominent part of the great carved beds of the sixteenth century; tables were covered with handsome 'carpets', and the massive buffets were dressed with their 'cupboard cloths'.

By the sixteenth century, responsibility for disposing the furnishings in a suitable manner for each occasion in a large household lay with the Gentleman Usher

97

93. Hangings still being used in the mediaeval manner. The verdure tapestries are nailed to the walls along the top edge and clad the walls down to the floor. They are roughly pulled back to disclose the door when necessary.

(*huissier*).[3] He was a senior member of the household (as the name indicates, he was classed as a gentleman and normally came from the ranks of the lesser nobility or gentry) and he was supported in his task by two Yeoman Ushers, who were respectively responsible for the arrangements in the Great Chamber and in the Hall, and they were in turn assisted by a staff of Grooms.[4] The furnishings were cared for by the Yeoman of the Wardrobe[5] who gave instructions to a bevy of seamstresses, laundry maids, joiners and so forth.[6]

The hierarchy of gentleman and yeoman servants in a household withered away during the seventeenth century (except in royal households where these posts lingered on vestigially) and the ordinary usher gradually became a waiter or flunkey. They could still arrange the furniture in the ordinary way but anything special had to be carried out by a man called an upholder or upholsterer.[7] Such a person might be attached to a great household[8] but he was more often brought in to attend to the now for the most part fixed textile furnishings that still formed so important a part of the décor (Plate 94).

The upholsterers had come up in the world since the Middle Ages. It seems they had originally been dealers in second-hand household goods and clothing but their status gradually improved and, by the beginning of the seventeenth century, they were involved entirely with the provision of new furnishings for houses or for doing over existing furnishings, but they were particularly concerned with those which had components of textile materials—beds, seat-furniture, wall-hangings, carpets.[9] It was no doubt in recognition of the altered character of the trade that the upholsterers' Company of the City of London, which had been in being since 1459 at least, was granted a fresh charter in 1626 but, as the document was burned in the Great Fire of London, we do not know anything of its provisions. By 1747, the upholsterer was being described as 'a Connoisseur in every article that belongs to a House'—he was an interior decorator.

In furnishing houses, the upholsterer had of course to visit the site so as to receive his instructions and take measurements. He might also have to return for further consultations and to check progress. He came to know about life in high society, and

94. The importance of upholstery. The bed-hangings, chair-covers, *portière* and table-carpet are en suite in a red material (velvet?) with gold trimmings. The sun-curtains match. The tapestries are fitted to the walls. Note the ostrich-feather plumes and aigrettes forming finials above the tester of the bed.

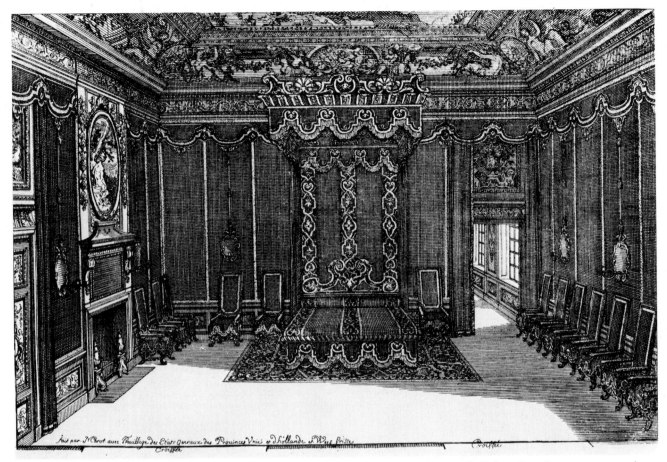

95. A scheme of decoration unified by upholstery. The flying-tester bed sets the key and all the other elements are en suite—the wall-hangings with their capping, the *portière*, and the chair-covers with their deep skirts (*pentes*). Design by Daniel Marot of about 1690.

to understand the aspirations and requirements of the rich. The top members of the trade saw for themselves what was fashionable and were able to help spread fashions; they gave advice to customers who found these matters bewildering or could not make up their minds. What is more they placed considerable orders with tradesmen of many different kinds for the wares they needed in order to make up their own goods, so they were to a large extent able to dictate what should be made by these craftsmen and how it should look. For instance, they patronised the silk mercer who dealt in silken goods and the finest of the woollen materials, and thus could have a say in what colours and patterns were produced. They could also guide the production of the *passementier*, the maker of trimmings who created the laces, fringes, tassels and galloons that played such an important part in the make-up of seventeenth-century upholstery (Plates 99 and 100). They likewise dealt with the embroiderer who could execute fancy needlework (Plates 98 and 106), the feather-dresser who not only provided stuffing for mattresses and pillows but also made the ostrich plumes that formed such spectacular finials on grand beds (Plate 94), the saddler who curled horsehair for stuffing chairs, the linen draper who dealt in linings and backing-materials, the blacksmith who made all the hooks and hinges that were

100

96. A late-seventeenth-century French design for a bed-head decorated with appliqué work. An upholsterer would have had such a drawing made to indicate what was desired from the embroiderers who would in turn have made full-scale drawings from which to work.

97. The upholsterer's art. The bed-head of the state bed of the first Earl of Melville; about 1695. Such an elaborate confection can only have been made by one of the leading London upholsterers, and very probably by one of French extraction like Guibert or Lapierre.

98. The counterpoint of the Melville Bed (see Plate 97).

99. Detail of the valance of a bed made in France for Queen Ulrika Eleonora of Sweden in 1680, showing the rich trimming incorporating the Queen's crowned monogram. The various kinds of gold thread would originally have been as bright as the detail in the bottom left-hand corner.

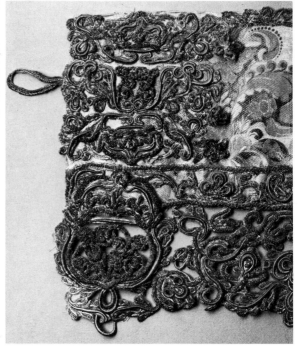

100. Tattered but still conveying an impression of richness, the valances and a finial (cup) of a 'French bed' of about 1665. Probably English.

101. Cups from a rich bed; probably French about 1660. Most of the bell-tassels have fallen away. The velvet is black, with a pale-blue ground. The undersides are of yellow silk as are the trimmings.

necessary as well as the curtain-rods and rings that were needed for bed-hangings, and they had to deal with the carver and gilder in connection with the more showy of the wooden components of beds and chairs. As the upholsterer gradually came to be entrusted with complete schemes of decoration, so he was forced to bring in other contractors—paviours for marble floors, cabinetmakers, painters, dealers in mirror-glass, joiners specialising in the laying of parquet, plasterers and so on (Plate 102). On all these people the upholsterer could bring his influence and tastes to bear. At a time when the architect still only occasionally took over total control of a building enterprise and only rarely attempted to dictate how the interior arrangements should look, the upholsterer still had matters very much his own way. It was therefore largely he who created the most eye-catching features of new schemes of interior decoration in the seventeenth century and it was invariably he who did so if it was merely a question of doing over existing rooms— which was something grand people were in the habit of having done frequently.

It is not surprising, therefore, that several seventeenth-century upholsterers became rich and some became famous. The name of Simon de Lobel, the principal *tapissier* to Louis XIV, was a household word around 1680, for instance. In the eighteenth century it was still a great deal more profitable to be an upholsterer than a mere cabinetmaker.[10]

Upholsterers (or their equivalent) brought a measure of unification to important rooms long before architects started to integrate the various elements into a cohesive scheme of decoration. Already in the Middle Ages, certain grand bedchambers were being completely hung with the same material as that which was used for the hangings of the bed. Such unity was not apparently common, however, until early in the seventeenth century. It became the convention when the concept of *regularité*,

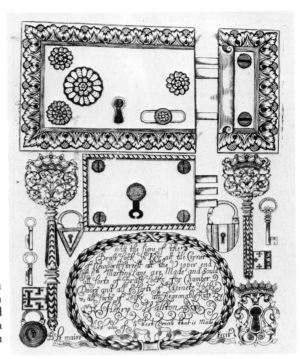

102. Among the many sub-contractors from whom an upholsterer might commission work was the locksmith. This bill-head of a London locksmith was drawn by a Frenchman, judging by his name which is inscribed in the bottom corner.

with which the name of Madame de Rambouillet is associated, came to be accepted as the basis for good taste in interior architecture. Sir Henry Unton, who had been ambassador to France and must have known what was fashionable in Paris in the late sixteenth century, does not seem to have had any properly unified suites of furnishings, *ammeublements* as the French called them, in his houses when inventories were taken in 1595, and this suggests that they were not yet common in France, even in smart circles. However, at Ingatestone five years later we find two chairs and a stool all covered 'sutable unto the bedd' or 'sutelike', although the rest of the furniture did not match.[11] The Earl of Northampton, in 1614, had most of the furnishings of his bedchamber 'all suteable to the bed' which had hangings of purple velvet trimmed with silver lace,[12] and in 1625 a French bedchamber is described as having a fine embroidered bed 'avec garniture de la chambre pareille' [with the furnishings of the room to match].[13] When Lady Leicester was in Paris in 1640 she notes that '6 chears of on sorte, 6 of on other, and 6 stooles . . . is just the number that is used hear to all good beds', which implies that this set of furniture was decorated en suite.[14] The Ham House inventory of about 1654, which probably reflects the state of the house prior to the outbreak of the Civil War, shows that several rooms there were unified in their *ammeublement*. For instance, one bed had two 'great chaires', eight stools, two table-covers and the window-curtains all en suite.[15] Indeed, by the 1640s, it must have been a commonplace in grand circles to have the textile furnishings of important rooms matching (Colour Plate II). Already in 1641, even a mere squire living in Devonshire might have the 'blew hangings' of his Little Parlour Chamber matching the bed which had 'curtaynes of the same'.[16] Nor was it solely the furnishings of bedchambers that could be en suite although it was at first primarily in this important room that such refinements were to be seen: at Easton Lodge in 1637 there were 'one high Chayer, one Low Chayer and three Low stooles all of Gillt Leather sutable to the hangings in the Clossett in the Chappell'.[17] Later inventories abound with descriptions of whole rooms decorated with textile furnishings decorated en suite.[18] When window-curtains became fashionable, and no longer simply served a utilitarian purpose, they were brought into the schemes and came to play an important rôle in the décor. Firescreens might also be en suite.

A careful reading of the three inventories of Ham House during the Lauderdale period (i.e. in the years around 1680)[19] shows how frequently changes were made to the furnishings of rooms at the time. In important rooms beds and their accompanying chairs were given new upholstery twice in five years, whole *ammeublements* were transferred to another room and adapted to the new surroundings.[20] Some sets were taken off to the wardrobe for storing and there was usually some spare material in store against the time when hangings needed repairing or altering. Presumably the new sets were provided by prominent London upholsterers but much of the work of adaptation and maintenance must have been done by the household staff. Upholsterers provided a cleaning service but the staff was supposed to see that the hangings were kept in proper order.

The cost of the materials of which upholstery was made was high. The raw materials (notably silk) had to be brought from distant parts of the world, and the process of weaving anything like a complicated pattern was laborious and slow.[21] The creating of intricate trimmings was also time-consuming. The making up by the upholsterer had then to be added to these prime costs. Once someone had paid for such expensive confections he took good care to protect them. All grand beds were provided with protective 'case curtains' (Plate 144); all expensive chair-covers had 'cases' to protect them or were themselves removeable.[22] Many of Cardinal Mazarin's most sumptuous wall-hangings had specially made bags in which they could be stored.[23] Indeed, valuable upholstery was often removed to the wardrobe-room and laid flat on shelves, at rest as it were, and seems only to have been put up when the family was in residence or on gala occasions.[24] For much of the year, the interiors of all grand houses must have been swathed in dust-covers.[25] It is only our own antique-besotted generation that expects what remains of these precious objects to be constantly on show—prey to the merciless ravages of light, to repeated fingering, to battering by assiduous cleaning staff, to corrosive dust, to rotting damp, and to the strains of hanging in one position, day after day, as they slowly tear themselves apart with their own weight. People in the past took enormous care although some of the instructions given to household staff do not always indicate this. Mazarin's servants, for instance, were expected to attend each day to the wall-hangings—'les bien ballayer et vergetter tous les jours pour en oster la poudre et empescher que les araignées ne s'y mettent et prendre garde que les souris ne gastent les tapisseries' [to brush them well and beat them every day so as to remove the dust, and to take care that the mice do not gnaw the tapestries].[26] That rats and mice might indeed attack the hangings is borne out by a Swedish inventory of 1672 where it is noted that the fringes of some fine hangings were 'något sönder skurit af rotter'—somewhat gnawed by rats.[27]

Hangings of tapestry or velvet and other thick materials are warm in character and are particularly suitable for clothing a room in wintertime. But in the summer heat they can seem hot and dusty. For this reason, particularly grand rooms were sometimes hung differently in summer and in winter. The State Bedchamber at

Ham House, a room decorated in the late 1670s, was provided with a set of tapestry hangings for the walls in winter while the bed was hung with a blue and gold velvet and the chairs were covered to match.[28] The 'Summer Furniture' (i.e. the complete *ammeublement*) for the room was of plain silk and must have seemed a lot cooler. There can be little doubt that this feature at Ham, which was merely the Lauderdales' suburban villa, reflected the practice in Paris. Indeed, the future Duchess (she was married to the Duke in 1672) may have seen something similar on her visit to the French capital in 1670 and there is a hint in a parody of 1674 of the opera *Alceste* suggesting that Parisian audiences were entirely familiar with such changes, for a character is mocked because 'vos rideaux sont d'esté et vos pentes d'hyver' [your bed-curtains are from the summer set, the valances from the winter set].[29] What may have been sets of winter and summer furniture were the alternative suites of hangings provided for the High Great Chamber at Hardwick, presumably in the 1590s. These consisted respectively of a set of tapestries (these are now on the walls the whole year through) and 'an other sute of of hangings for the same chamber being eight pieces of woollen cloth stayned with frett and storie and silk flowers', which have long ago disappeared.[30] These painted hangings seem to have had a fretted strapwork border, scenes from some story, and silk flowers that were probably embroidered. It was perhaps even more sensible to provide beds with two sets of hangings. Gabrielle d'Estrées, the mistress of Henri IV, had summer hangings on her bed of *taffetas de Chine* which must have seemed highly exotic in the Paris of 1599.[31] The parody on *Alceste* of 1674 shows that beds might then have alternative summer and winter sets of hangings sufficiently often to extract a laugh of recognition from a Parisian audience. Whether the two sets of hangings for the bed in the Duke's Chamber at Cockesden in 1626 served the same seasonal purpose, one cannot say, but there was certainly a second set for the 'great bed' in the cypress chest that stood in the room.[32]

With textiles playing so vital a rôle in seventeenth-century interior decoration, the task of the upholsterer was unending. That he drifted into providing services of many other kinds such as undertaking and furniture hire is hardly surprising. Moreover that his influence on taste and on the appearance of the seventeenth-century interior could be immense seems to be beyond doubt. We must now consider more specifically some of the things he provided and the materials he used.

CHAPTER V
The Upholsterer's Materials

UPHOLSTERERS used a very wide range of materials to make up the goods they created. In this chapter I shall review the different classes of materials available to them in the seventeenth century; in subsequent chapters, we shall see how they were used.

As far as the textile materials are concerned, scholars have no difficulty in defining the main classes but it is far from easy for them to agree about the identity of individual materials mentioned in contemporary documents. For example, there is as yet no general agreement as to what 'dornix' and 'mohair' were like although both terms occur frequently in seventeenth-century inventories. Dornix was clearly very different in character in the seventeenth century from what it became in the nineteenth. Mohair was the name of a woollen material with a distinctive finish in earlier times but by the late seventeenth century the name was undoubtedly used in reference to a silk material to which the same finish had been applied. As for the simpler forms of woollen materials, what was technically the same material could have several different names according to its weight, its quality, or the scale of its pattern, or due to some additional finish. Unfortunately no glossary of seventeenth-century textile terms exists as yet[1] and what follows must not be taken as anything more than a general guide, designed to help the reader understand the later chapters of this book. It should however be borne in mind when dealing with the names given to textile materials in household inventories that these names reflect differences that were easily recognised by normally intelligent people at the time. Although the differences might in the first place depend on some technical feature, these will not have been distinctions that only a textile historian can now detect; they will have been clearly visible to any casual observer.

TAPESTRIES, TAPISSERIES DE BERGAME AND DORNIX

Weaving tapestry is laborious and therefore expensive.[2] Like all weaving the technique requires a loom and, for the weaving of large tapestry hangings, the loom has to be correspondingly large. However the technique can be used for small, delicate wares, in which case the resulting material can have a superficial resemblance to some sorts of needlework with which tapestry-weaving otherwise has absolutely no connection.

There was no particular point in making firescreens and other small panels in this technique although it became fashionable to do so late in the seventeenth century (Colour Plate XIV). On the other hand, the comparatively robust and flexible character of larger tapestry-woven panels had made them particularly suitable for the mediaeval way of life in aristocratic circles. They could withstand the constant taking down from the walls, the bundling into carts and the fixing up again in some new setting that went with this mobile manner of living among the upper classes. Indeed, it can only have been because tapestry was so firmly associated in everyone's consciousness with aristocratic settings that it remained in fashion long after its practical advantages as a material had ceased to be of any real significance. For, in the largely static interior arrangements pertaining from the sixteenth century onwards, tapestry hangings tended to be fixed to the walls as permanent decoration and, if one simply wanted a picture on the wall, one executed in paint would have been far more satisfactory than one composed in this cumbersome technique. But an astute man like Colbert would never have established the extensive tapestry-weaving *ateliers* at the Gobelins in the mid-1660s if tapestries had not still been highly fashionable and had looked as if they would long remain so; nor would numerous high-class *ateliers* have been kept going in Brussels right through the sixteenth and seventeenth century. Incidentally, tapestry was often still called 'arras' in the early seventeenth century although particularly fine tapestries were no longer being woven at Arras.

Tapestries could be woven in huge panels; they did not have to be made up from several widths of material, as would have been the case if a panel of the same large size was to be made out of some other class of textile. Tapestries were normally made of wool but the highlights in a pictorial composition might be executed in silk in hangings of fine quality, and certain passages might be woven in gold thread in the most expensive quality of all. Because of the freedom this technique allowed the designer, it was well suited to large pictorial compositions, but formal and even repetitive patterns might also be produced by it although there was no practical advantage in doing so.

What might be called 'poor man's tapestry' was a class of rather coarse materials of wool which had large patterns that made them suitable for wall-hangings and other large-scale upholstery work. They were known as *Tapisseries de Bergame*.[3] The patterns were sometimes elaborate and were always repetitive rather than pictorial (Colour Plate VII). These materials were woven in a relatively straightforward manner on a wide loom, and large panels were made up by stitching widths together. The warps, which ran vertically, were usually of hemp which made these cloths very robust. The grandest sort might have passages rendered in metal thread or in silk but these materials were mainly intended for secondary rooms and offices in important buildings, and for a middle-class clientèle that could not afford real tapestries.[4] Their patterns included formal 'pomegranate' designs, flame-like *point d'Hongrie* and a related fish-scale form called *écaille*, and also crowned 'Ls' alternating with *fleurs-de-lis* which were presumably popular with those wishing to be known as supporters of the House of Bourbon and therefore perhaps date from after the Fronde.[5] Narrower border-widths of these weaves were available; with these one could frame widths of the main material and so make up hangings of any size.

Tapisseries de Bergame were made at Rouen and Elbeuf, and were sometimes called *tapisseries de Rouen*.[6] They were no doubt made elsewhere—at some of the other places noted for the production of woollen upholstery materials like Lille, Roubaix, Amiens and Tournai, for instance.[7] Moreover, it seems that these hangings were widely exported from France and Flanders,[8] and there is no reason to doubt that they were also brought into England.[9] Chambers' *Dictionary* of 1786 lists 'Bergamot' as a 'coarse tapestry' but the term does not seem to occur in seventeenth-century inventories.

It may well be that the 'dornix' which is so frequently mentioned in seventeenth-century inventories was identical with *tapisserie de Bergame* although, since we know that dornix came in several classes,[10] the term probably embraced a whole range of rather coarse, comparatively large-patterned upholstery materials that were readily distinguishable even if their patterns varied considerably.[11] Collections of ancient textiles usually contain examples of such materials; they have not so far attracted much attention from textile historians but it seems likely that at least some of them would have been recognised as dornix by a clerk compiling an inventory in the seventeenth century (Colour Plate VII b and c). Dornix, at any rate, derived its name from Tournai (Doornik) in the Low Countries which was a centre of tapestry-weaving and of the manufacture of woollen upholstery materials. It would be very natural if its products included the sort of material under discussion. As with *tapisserie de Bergame*, dornix was found in secondary rooms.[12]

Another rather coarse woollen material that was readily identifiable was 'Kidderminster stuff'. It is mentioned in inventories from about 1630 onwards, and remained in favour in the eighteenth century.[13] It was boldly patterned in a simple way. The same may be said of 'Scotch pladd' which was being used for the complete *ammeublements* of several rooms at Tart Hall in 1641 and at Dyrham at the end of the century.[14]

TURKEYWORK AND ORIENTAL CARPETS

When we speak of a carpet, we are usually thinking of a sturdy class of woven cloth with a thick pile surface that is easily recognisable, but the word 'carpet' simply meant a cover that lay flat, in the seventeenth century.[15] On the other hand, we tend to call all small carpets rugs but a 'rugg' was a coarse and often shaggy form of coverlet to our seventeenth-century ancestors, and they referred to all Oriental carpets or rugs as 'carpets'.

Oriental carpets have a pile that is produced by tying knots in rows as the fabric is being woven.[16] Most of the knotted-pile rugs brought to Europe in the seventeenth century came from Anatolia, the modern Turkey; these were usually boldly patterned in a few strong colours (Colour Plates XI and XIII). That they are frequently to be seen in early seventeenth-century portraits must, however, not be taken to mean that there were numerous rugs of this sort in every house at that date; the 'sitter' (who is usually standing in such portraits) was very likely painted with the rug because it was a prized possession.[17] Some of these small carpets were prayer-rugs, with a prayer-niche forming the chief feature of their design, and it would seem that these were sometimes called *mosquets* in French inventories and 'Musketta carpetts' in England.[18] Anatolian rugs were manufactured for the European market in considerable quantities and a lively trade in these exotic coverings grew up during the seventeenth century. Dutch paintings of the middle of the century show that they were relatively common, at least in Holland, by that stage.

Finer in quality, more subtle in design, and usually much larger, were Persian carpets (Plate 108). The finest of these, notably those made with a silk pile and with passages brocaded with gold thread, were often courtly presents from the Shah to people of influence,[19] and Persian carpets were not at all common in the seventeenth century.[20] Such weaves came from important centres; the ordinary rugs woven in the villages of Persia and by nomadic tribesmen—the equivalent of the Anatolian rugs—probably reached Europe only very rarely. On the other hand, the large Turkish court carpets woven at Ushak and the distinguished carpets from Cairo seem to have reached Europe in some quantity.[21] Large carpets of a Persian character were also commissioned in India for European consumption by the East India Company.[22] Suffice it to say that large Eastern carpets were expensive and still comparatively rare in Western Europe during the seventeenth century.

So greatly were Near Eastern carpets admired, however, that attempts to imitate them were made in several parts of Europe. Carpet-weaving had been introduced into Spain by the Moors in the Middle Ages and Spanish carpets had been widely famed right down to the sixteenth century but the industry had withered away by the seventeenth century. However, rugs with Anatolian patterns and using the Turkish technique were woven at Cuenca, although there is no indication that they were much exported and they hardly concern us here.[23] Carpets very similar in character, imitating Turkish patterns and constructed by Turkish methods, were being woven in England by the time of Elizabeth, as is proved by some famous specimens at Boughton, dated 1584 and 1585 and bearing the Montagu arms inwoven. There is also a panel with the royal arms of England and the date 1600 in the Victoria and Albert Museum.[24] Early in the seventeenth century carpets 'façon de Turquie' were also being made in Paris, and an *atelier* was established under the *Grand Galerie* of the Louvre in 1618 'travaillant pour le Roy en ouvrage de Turquie' [producing work in the Turkish manner for the King] (see Plate 6).[25] A decade later the famous workshops at Chaillot, set up in an old soap-factory (*savonnerie*), were established and the two factories were later amalgamated out there. The fact that they produced carpets 'façon de Perse' need not necessarily be taken to imply that the patterns of these weaves were Oriental in character, for some of the thirteen 'grand tapis ... façon de Levant, faits à la Savonnerie pour servir à la Gallerie d'Apollon du Louvre' [large carpets woven in the Levantine manner, made at the *Savonnerie* for the *Galerie d'Apollon* at the Louvre] still exist and are decorated with designs that are entirely in the European tradition.[26] Indeed, during the middle decades of the seventeenth century, the Savonnerie designers evolved a characteristic form of carpet-design, composed of naturalistic flowers in a formal framework based on the repertoire of Classical ornament, that has remained in favour for European carpets ever since.[27] However, as few Savonnerie carpets were exported, and then only as presents, and no other country was able to emulate the French example until well into the next century, this French development remained an isolated one in the seventeenth century.

In England, the local imitations of Turkish rugs went by the name of 'turkeywork'[28] but one cannot always be sure that what is described as a 'Turkie carpett' was not in fact a rug woven in England. For example, the Earl of Northampton had in 1614 'a large Turkie carpett of Englishe worke with the Earle of Northampton his armes, being 5 yeardes and 3 quarters large',[29] and Lady Dorchester spoke of 'my fower white turkey carpetts, and the long one that John Frithe wrought' in 1638.[30] At Ingatestone in 1600 there was an 'old Turkey foote carpett' that was probably woven in England because the pattern is indicated by the phrase 'the worke roses', which suggests a European style.[31]

Just as in France the Savonnerie weavers developed designs that owed nothing to Eastern traditions, so the English weavers of turkeywork gradually abandoned

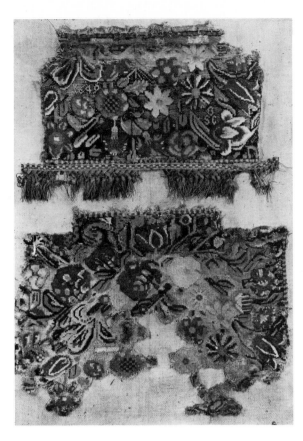

103. Fragments of English turkeywork panels made for covering chairs, one dated 1649 and trimmed with a worsted fringe. The panels have a 'barber's pole' border woven in the pile technique also used for the main pattern, showing that the panels were specially made for mounting on chairs of a standard size and no doubt of the 'farthingale' type.

Anatolian patterns and turned instead to the repertoire of the needleworker. Few traces of Eastern influence remained after 1625 or so; the patterns were now scaled-up and simplified versions of current fashions in embroidery (Plate 103).[32] Turkeywork was made on a large scale at Norwich and the industry was already well established there by the end of the sixteenth century.[33] Some turkeywork kneelers bearing the city arms were made for Norwich Cathedral in 1651 and provide well-documented specimens of what the local weavers could produce.[34] They also made carpets (Colour Plate II) but their main production consisted of panels suitable for upholstering the seats and backs of chairs. It is not always realised that English turkeywork (probably from Norwich) was exported to the Continent and colonies in substantial quantity. A French tariff of import-duties issued in 1664 makes it clear that a duty of a hundred *sols* was payable on each piece of 'tapis de Turquie, d'Angleterre ou d'ailleurs' while thirty *sols* was payable on 'tapis dudit pays d'Angleterre, pour faire chaises et emmeublement' [pile carpet from England, used for chairs and for upholstery].[35] Turkeywork appears to have been woven in Ireland as well, for 'an Irish turkey work carpott' is listed in an inventory of 1684 and there was an Irish carpet four yards long and two and three-quarter yards wide at Kilkenny Castle in the same year.[36]

Woollen Velvets

The pile of a velvet is produced mechanically by the weaving process and is not knotted into the weave, as in a carpet.[37] We are here concerned with moquette and other velvets with a woollen pile. Silk-pile velvets are dealt with under silks; velvets with a cotton pile did not come into widespread use until the mid-eighteenth century.

Woollen velvets are robust materials yet they are soft and yielding. They were popular in the nineteenth century—for instance, for the seats in railway-carriages. By that time the material was often called 'plush'. Woollen velvets were also much used in the seventeenth century, but the material is very vulnerable to attack by moths; it then quickly becomes unsightly and tends to be discarded. As a result, comparatively little ancient material of this class survives (Colour Plate VIII a). Moquette was also known in France as *moucade* (hence the English 'mockado').[38] It was made principally at Lille, Tournai, Abbeville and Rouen but weavers of this material established themselves in various other parts of Europe during the sixteenth and seventeenth centuries. It came with fancy patterns making it suitable for carpeting (in the tougher range) or the covering of seat-furniture; it could also be plain, and the plain material could have a pattern stamped onto it with heated metal plates (*gauffré*). In Holland and France both the plain and the patterned varieties went by the name of *trippe* or *trijp*.[39] A version was called *peluche* (hence 'plush') which may have had an especially long pile; and plain woollen velvets also seem to have been known as *pannes*.[40]

In England this class of material was not only called 'mockado' but we find 'vallure' (velure) and 'caffoy' or 'capha'.[41] The latter has a Dutch derivation: *Caffa werkers* were apparently weavers of this material. The Dutch made especially good materials of this class.[42] This may be why the misleading term 'Utrecht velvet' or *velours d'Utrecht* has come to be attached to it, but it seems these fabrics were never made at Utrecht; the term may derive from the fact that the figured versions were woven on a draw-loom and were thus a *velours de trek* (i.e. *à la tire*, drawn). The terminology within this whole class of materials is immensely confusing and deserves serious investigation. One might then be able to identify the different varieties, including 'tuft moccado' which was on some stools in 1585.[43]

RUGGS, BLANKETS AND FLEDGES

Ruggs, Blankets and Fledges were woollen materials, made up in recognisable forms, that one could place on a bed for warmth, although ruggs and fledges might sometimes also be used on the floor.

A rugg was a cloth of coarsely-woven material (*rug* means rough in Scandinavian) that served as a form of coverlet.[44] 'Irish ruggs' seem to have had a shaggy pile and may have resembled the *ryer* of Swedish and Finnish peasant-culture which were bed-hangings with a long pile, boldly patterned. In Ireland these ruggs were also used as cloaks[45] and one sees people wearing this shaggy garment in contemporary illustrations. Irish ruggs are sometimes described as being 'chequered', which presumably means they had a tartan effect in their weave.[46] They were apparently identical with the 'caddows' which Cotgrave explains was a type of 'couverture velouté' [coverlet with a pile] that we know could be checked.[47] In 1610 it was noted that Ireland produced 'course wool caddowes . . . or coverlets'.[48]

Irish ruggs were often to be seen on beds in grand English houses in England in the sixteenth and early seventeenth century[49] but the fact that someone could speak of 'outlandish caddows' in 1681 suggests that they had by then long disappeared from the fashionable scene.[50] Ruggs, on the other hand, continue to be mentioned among lists of bedclothes and the word had presumably come simply to mean a coarse woollen coverlet, as it does today. They tended to be colourful.

Exactly how a rugg differed from a blanket is not clear but most of the time there may have been no more difference than there is today. Superior to ordinary blankets were 'Spanish blankets'[51] which in France were often known as *catalonnes* or *castelognes* because they came from Catalonia.[52] However, these highly regarded bed-coverings were also referred to as ruggs—an inventory of 1603, for instance, included 'a large tawny Spanish rugge'.[53] By the middle of the century, fine blankets were being made in England. Cardinal Mazarin, who was highly discriminating in all such matters, had several sets of 'couvertures de laine trés fine d'Angleterre, ayant quatre couronnes bleues au quatre coins' [fine woollen coverlets [or blankets] from England, with four blue crowns in the four corners].[54] Blankets were apparently also woven on large estates for local use; the inventory of Ingatestone Hall of 1600 includes some 'home-made' blankets, one pair of which had black selvedges ('broad black lists').[55]

Blankets were normally of wool but the term comes from the mediaeval French word *blanchet* (pronounced *blanquet* in the west of France) which was a form of bed-clothing made of white linen,[56] and some seventeenth century blankets were in fact not of wool but of silk. The Duchess of Lauderdale, for example, had a silk blanket on her bed at Ham House,[57] while two that were 'quilted both sides' were bought in 1699 for a royal bed at Hampton Court[58]. William III's 'low bed' (i.e. his personal bed rather than his bed of state) had a pair of 'India sattan blankets'.[59] These were exceptional, however. Commonly referred to in lists of bedclothes are 'fustian blankets' or often simply 'fusteans'. Fustian in the seventeenth century seems to have been a material of cotton and linen but some fustians were classed with woollen materials.[60] It clearly had a fuzzy, napped surface which was distinctive. Some pillows at Ingatestone had 'the napp syde of the fustian outwarde'.[61]

In 1554 a fustian blanket was valued at 5s. 10d., a woollen blanket at 1s. 8d., and a 'fledge blanket' at only 12d.[62] Fledge was a material of which 'fledges' were made.[63] They are mentioned in the inventories of Hardwick and Chatsworth of 1601 when they were to be found on beds or on the floor round the bed. It has been suggested that fledges were eiderdowns or quilts filled with feathers (*flèches*) but it seems more likely that the material of which they were made, and from which they derived their name, had a distinctive feather-like pattern—a herringbone effect in the weave.[64] They do not appear in inventories much after the beginning of the seventeenth century.

WORSTED DAMASK AND PRINTED PARAGON

Damask is woven on a draw-loom with a pattern contrived by means of two contrasting weaves that catch the light in different ways. A damask can be of silk, of linen (see below), or of wool—or rather of worsted, which is spun from an especially long and well-combed woollen fibre so as to produce a particularly tough, smooth and shiny yarn. Damasks of worsted woven with large patterns suitable for hangings came into fashion in the late seventeenth century. Celia Fiennes saw a bed and wall-hangings at Ashstead Park 'of a fine damaske made of worsted. It looks pretty and with a gloss like camlett.'[65] 'Camlet', with its tougher relation, 'paragon' (*baracan* in French), was a ribbed worsted cloth but they could both be 'watered' (i.e. crushed so that the ribbed weave reflected light unevenly and so produced the characteristic wavy pattern of watering or *moirage*, as the French call it, giving a *moiré* or watered effect), or they could be printed with hot plates against a wooden block carved in intaglio with a pattern. The resulting 'printed paragon' was much used for hangings in the seventeenth century. A closet still hung with what is presumably this material is to be seen at Knole. The pattern is very similar to that which one might have found on a contemporary damask of worsted or silk. All are materials of a single colour with a pattern produced by the play of light on contrasting surfaces.

WOOLLEN STUFFS WITH LITTLE OR NO PATTERN

There was a very wide range of woollen stuffs with little or no pattern available in the seventeenth century. They came in many qualities, some of them far better than anything normally available today. There were numerous different types of weave and each had a different name. Some were given yet another name merely on account of a variation in quality or scale of pattern, while additional effects like 'watering' could also lead to their acquiring a fresh name. Moreover, the textile industry itself sometimes invented new names in order to promote sales. The main sorts were, however, fairly easy to recognise and their names occur in the inventories where they were presumably used properly. All the same, there was plenty of room for confusion at the time and the compilers of many inventories avoided the difficulty simply by calling all such materials 'stuffs' or 'cloth' (*drap* in French), and occasionally we find 'worsted stuff'.

Nevertheless, we must try and distinguish the chief sorts—not in a way that will satisfy the textile historian but sufficiently to give a general sense of the varieties that were available.

A material very commonly used in upholstery was 'serge' which has a pronounced twill (i.e. is woven in such a way as to produce a diagonal ribbed effect). London serges were admired but the principal centre of production, as with most woollen or worsted materials, was North-eastern France (Châlons, Rheims, Amiens). They also came from Chartres and from as far afield as Florence, Athens and Smyrna. 'Say(e)' was a light-weight form of serge;[66] in France it was known as *sayette* and it came chiefly from Amiens, but it was also woven at Norwich and at Sudbury in Suffolk. 'Shalloon' (named after Châlons) was also a form of serge. A tougher form of twilled worsted was 'perpetuana', known in French as *sempiterne*; some samples in a Swedish collection have a marked basket-like effect in the weave that is superimposed, as it were, on the twill ground.[67]

A common material at the time was 'kersey', which was flannel-like, but it was not much used in upholstery. The same applies to 'linsey woolsey', a coarse and often homespun cloth. Very similar to modern baize were the 'bays' of the seventeenth century although some had a longer nap. They came in many qualities but the finest bays were made at Colchester and bays from there and other towns in Essex were exported in large quantities. They were chiefly used for linings but were also suitable for making protective covers for furniture. 'Frieze' was a material that is usually associated with heavy outer clothing but some hangings of this heavily-napped stuff were to be seen in rather grand rooms at the Earl of Arundel's Tart Hall in 1641.[68] 'Homespun' was presumably woven locally and appears among the contents of unimportant rooms as 'wadmole' or 'woodmeale'.[69]

'Tammy' was a rather ordinary sort of worsted material in the eighteenth century, with a plain weave and a rather springy texture. It was originally called 'stamin' or 'stammel'; this was a corruption of the French term for the material, *estamine*. This in turn derives from the Italian for a strainer, *stamigna*, which indicates that it had an open weave[70]. Lady Leicester's 'best bed' had hangings of this material in 1634, it was obviously a very respectable material in her day.[71]

'Camlet' was a very important upholstery material. It had a ribbed effect and was raspy to the touch. It was very robust. Camlet could be 'watered', 'waved' or 'figured'.[72] A tougher form of camlet was 'paragon' which came in the same three forms, the 'figured' type being called 'printed paragon', as has already been noted.

SILKS, BROCATELLE AND HALF-SILKS

The most sumptuous and the most costly class of silk material was silk velvet[73] which could be plain (Plate 41) or figured. The type known as 'Genoa velvet', which had bold patterns rendered in one or more colours in silk pile against a plain or satin ground, was the most expensive of all in the seventeenth century (Colour Plate XI). Genoa was famous for its silk furnishing materials, of which the large-patterned velvets were the most spectacular, but 'Genoa velvet' was also woven elsewhere, notably at Lyons, from the middle of the century onwards. No other centre ever quite succeeded in improving on the Genoese product, however. Silk damask[74] came next in precedence but was probably the most popular of the luxury materials used for upholstery purposes. Once again, silk damasks with bold patterns suitable for this purpose were woven in great quantity at Genoa but were imitated in other centres of silk-weaving (Plate 38). Damasks were normally of a single colour but could be executed in two or more colours on occasion. If there were passages of gold in the pattern (or small areas of any second colour, for that matter) these would be 'brocaded' so as to save material. Brocading consisted of expressly inserting these passages with a separate bobbin of the required thread; this section of pattern did not appear automatically through the main weaving process.[75]

Silks of any sort could be brocaded. A handsome brocaded satin[76] dating from the 1670s is to be seen on the walls of the Queen's Closet at Ham House and on the two armchairs that belong there (Colour Plate XVI). A 'brocade' was strictly speaking any silk material incorporating brocading but in the seventeenth century it was more loosely used in reference to any silk material in which passages brocaded with gold or silver thread played a notable part.[77] 'Cloth of gold' was a term loosely used to describe any silk material where gold was much in evidence, either from heavy brocading with gilt thread of one or more kinds (Plate 140),[78] or because it was woven into the ground as part of the main weaving process. 'Cloth of silver' was similar but a material called 'tissue' seems to have been one with much silver woven into the ground.[79] Likewise 'tinsell' may have been the silk material, of which many specimens survive, which has strips of gold thread woven into the ground that made it sparkle (*étinceler*).[80]

Far more common, naturally, were the plain silken materials. I have mentioned plain velvet. Satin was also usually plain. Silk woven in plain weave was called 'taffeta' and a thin version of this, suitable for linings and sun-curtains, was known as 'sarcenet'.[81] A ribbed plain silk like *gros de Tours* was 'tabby' (*tabis* in French). It came plain or watered, but could also have a small pattern (probably self-coloured) when it came to be known as *tabis à fleurs*.[82] The 'spotted sad colour tabby' of the summer hangings in the Queen's Bedchamber at Ham House may have been of this last type.[83] Closely related to tabby was 'mohair' which some modern authorities insist was a woollen material, but the contexts in which mohair occurs in seventeenth-century inventories make this inconceivable, and it is actually called 'mohair silke' in some documents.[84] Taffetas might be 'changeable' which merely meant that they were what would now be called 'shot silks', with warps and wefts of two different colours which produces changing effects according to how the light falls on folds in the material. Satins (and taffetas later) might also be 'clouded' which is today called *chiné*; it is not easy to explain this process which involves dying the pattern onto the warps before they are woven. This produces a hazy pattern which can be very attractive.

Brocatelle (sometimes given as 'brocadillo') was specially designed for use as rich wall-hangings. It appears on the face to be all of silk and has large patterns similar to those on furnishing damasks and velvets. But the warps are of linen which make it robust and helped to take the weight of long 'drops' of the material when hung on a wall. Since it does not drape well, it was rarely used for other purposes. 'Brocatelle de Venise' was a very fashionable material in the late seventeenth century.

There were other half-silk materials available in the seventeenth century, and some had large patterns that made them suitable for upholstery. One finds specimens in large collections of historic textiles but, as with 'dornix' with which some of these materials have affinities, little serious study has so far been devoted to them. Common in the sixteenth and early seventeenth century was 'Bruges Satin' (rendered as 'Brydges satten' in some documents) which seems to have had a silk warp and linen weft (the latter probably only appeared on the face when there was a pattern).

COTTON AND LINEN MATERIALS, CANVAS AND TICKING

European cotton materials were not much used for upholstery in the seventeenth century.[85] On the other hand the delightful Indian painted cottons known as 'pintadoes' or 'chintes' were to be seen in some of the most fashionable settings during the second half of the century (Plate 115 and colour Plate XIII). These exotic materials were beginning to reach Europe in the late sixteenth century.[86] By 1609 the English East India Company was engaged in a lively trade in them[87] and, by 1620, was placing orders in India for specific types.[88] The Countess of Arundel so admired these materials that she had three whole rooms (including her own bedchamber) hung with them.[89] All the same, Pepys had to explain what 'a chinke' was when he bought some to hang his wife's study in 1663.[90] By the 1680s, however, plenty of these colourful materials were to be seen in every grand house in England, Holland and France. The 'Calleco Chamber' at Cowdray in 1682 was in no way exceptional. Not only the wall-hangings of this room were of 'painted caleco', but also the window-curtains, the table-covers and the hangings of the bed.[91]

Attempts were made in Europe to imitate these attractive Indian products. Patterns of an exotic character were printed (not painted) with wood blocks on cotton and on linen—but chiefly on the latter—in the seventeenth century; European printed cottons (*indiennes*) only really came into their own after about 1730.

Linen played little part in the more showy aspects of upholstery. Bed-hangings were very occasionally made of linen[92] but otherwise linen tended to be hidden away in the form of backings, inner coverings of chairs over which a finer material was fitted, and protective loose covers. Window-curtains were occasionally made of linen materials like 'buckram' and 'soultwich' (often rendered as 'southege') which must have been translucent so they acted as sun-blinds (Colour Plate I).[93] In the form of bed-linen and table-linen however the material truly came to the fore.

Sheets in the seventeenth century came in several qualities ranging from 'coarse' or 'towen' through 'flaxen' and 'dowlas' to 'Holland'.[94] Holland sheets were the finest—and whitest. In Elizabethan times, distinction was still being made between sheets of Holland and of Cambrick,[95] but Cambrai fell behind in the competition.

Table-linen also came in various qualities, with flaxen and towen at the coarse end and the linen damasks at the other. Some of the coarse grades were off-white and even brown (i.e. unbleached). Next came 'diaper' which had a regular all-over pattern,[96] with 'hucaback' which was even finer. There was 'French diaper' and 'Holland diaper', which was superior. Likewise there was 'course' and 'fine' damask, the latter almost certainly coming from Haarlem where the best linen-damasks were woven, although the weavers of Courtrai were scarcely less skilful.[97]

Mattresses, pillows and bolsters were usually composed of a bag made of canvas 'ticking' or 'tick' (*coutil* in French). Ticking was normally striped (Plate 116) and this was probably why it was possible to distinguish 'Bruxhill [Brussels] ticke' from 'Britanie ticke', or 'Flanders tick' from 'Dutch tike of small stripe';[98] for until quite recently, there were national preferences in the colour of ticking-stripes, the French preferring brown and white while the English liked black and white. However, 'tick' came also to mean the bag itself. There was at Ingatestone, for example, a 'fustian tick' filled with down whereas the other down mattresses were covered with 'ticke fyne . . . with blew stripes'.[99]

The padding of chairs was built up on an even coarser material—sackcloth. In the seat it would be supported on 'girthweb'—the webbing bands of which saddle-girths are made.[100] These materials were also commonly striped brown and white.

MATTING AND MATS

During the second half of the sixteenth century and the first three decades of the seventeenth century it was normal to have the floors of the grandest rooms fitted with an all-over covering of matting. This was made of rushes braided in strips, herringbone fashion, and could be stitched together to form what was presumably the earliest form of fitted carpet (Colour Plate X). Such floor-coverings may be seen in several Elizabethan portraits. The matting at Ingatestone came from Cornwall.[101] Cornish mats were famous in the eighteenth century and Dr Johnson stated that 'the women and children of Cornwall make mats of small bents there growing which serve to cover floors and walls.'[102] The 'natte anglaise tres fine' which was used in 1771 to protect a staircase in Paris was perhaps a Cornish product.[103] But matting had gone out of fashion for covering floors in important rooms by the mid-seventeenth century and one thereafter finds it in less noticeable places—'a flore matt & piece of corse cloth to cover ye stairs' and '2 church flore matts' being typical examples.[104]

This matting was plain, but mats could also have a coloured pattern. There were some 'fayre matts black and white' at Hardwick in 1601, and at the Nassau residence in Brussels in 1618 there were in store some 'marchepieds de joncqz d'Espagne grandz, de couleur noire et jaulne' [large [long?] runners of Spanish rushes, black and yellow coloured], and Cardinal Mazarin had 'un tapis de natte de Hollande, façonné de diverse couleurs' [a Dutch patterned mat of various colours].[105] A black and white mat is also visible in the portrait of a Spanish princess at Knole (Plate 117), and what could well be a Dutch mat is to be seen on the floor in a well known painting by Jan Steen (Plate 116). Such mats were clearly acceptable in fashionable settings. Some of them could well have been made in North Africa whence thin and colourful mats are still imported. Pepys saw 'a very fine African mat' in London in 1666 and maintained that it was entirely suitable 'to lay upon the ground under a bed of state'.[106] Under the bed of the Duchess of Ormonde at Kilkenny Castle in 1684 there was a 'Tangier mat' which could well have been similar to what Pepys saw.[107] In the Drawing Room at Kilkenny, moreover, there were some 'Portugal mats'. These must have been distinctive for they are mentioned in quite a few late seventeenth-century inventories of important houses. They were usually in the bedchamber and it would seem that it became the fashion to have grand beds standing on them (Plate 95).[108] Already in 1641 we find the Countess of Arundel's bed at Tart Hall standing on an 'Indian matt' and there was a roll of this material, comprising fourteen pieces, in the North Gallery which also sported many Turkish and Persian carpets.[109] Presumably we here have a transitional stage, with the Elizabethan tradition of a matted floor on which Oriental rugs could be placed, now carried out with exotic matting while an individual exotic mat is being placed in a strategic spot, as was to become the fashion later in the century. Matting and mats were, at any rate, to be seen in the grandest houses throughout the century.

The mattresses of beds were also frequently laid on mats supported on a network of ropes. Thick rush mats could also serve as insulation for windows in winter.

LEATHER

'Gilt leather' was extensively used for wall-hangings during the seventeenth century (Colour Plate XII and Plates 47, 104 and 227). It was also used for covering chairs during the second half of the century. 'Gilt leather' was not in fact gilt at all; it was made with 'skins' (of calves) that were faced with tin-foil. During the second half of the century these prepared skins might be embossed by pressing into a wooden mould carved in intaglio with a pattern. In all cases, however, the ground was then punched with small sub-patterns that would reflect the light, and the main pattern was then painted in one or more colours. Those parts of the tin-foil ground that had not been painted were then glazed with a markedly yellow varnish which imparted a golden look to the tin-foil.[110]

The skins could be made up into hangings of any required size. Border-patterns

104. Gilt leather providing a striking form of wall-decoration in a Dutch house; about 1640. Whole skins bearing a formal Renaissance pattern alternate in bands with a narrow border-pattern. A similar bordering is used at top and bottom.

were available and narrow strips of the material could be provided for disguising the nails that held the hangings in place on the walls.[111]

'Gilt leather' was first produced by the Islamic peoples, and Moorish Spain developed the technique. Indeed, this material has become so closely identified with Spain that some authorities still call it 'Spanish leather',[112] although the term is not commonly used to describe this material in seventeenth-century inventories. By this time the centre of production had anyway passed to the Low Countries—Malines (Mechlin) and Amsterdam being particularly famed for their gilt leathers. However, the material was also produced in France, and to a lesser extent in England, Brandenburg, Italy and Portugal. In the mid-seventeenth century some large pictorial hangings imitating tapestries were made in this technique (Plate 105) but, in most cases, each individual skin bore a complete repeat of the pattern concerned or was one of a set of four which made up a full repeat.

Chairs were sometimes covered with gilt leather (although not to the extent that some antique dealers and collectors would have us believe), but plain leather was much more commonly used (Plates 149 and 164). 'Russia leather' is mentioned frequently in this connection and 'Turkey leather' also appears; 'Morocco leather' only seems to make an appearance late in the century.[113] In Italy and Spain chairs

119

105. Gilt leather hangings with large-scale pictorial decoration, framed with widths of a border-pattern. Flemish; 1660s.

with leather backs that were heavily tooled and gilt, in the manner of rich book-bindings, were greatly in favour but this fashion was not widely accepted in the north. The 'couche of crimson leather printed border wise' mentioned in an inventory of 1614 probably had a tooled leather cover like this.[114] At Hardwick in 1601 there was 'a chare of black leather guilded'[115] which might also have been tooled and gilded, although the gilding could have been applied on some form of priming. In certain Dutch paintings, notably some by Vermeer, one sees chairs with what look like black leather backs that have gilded diamond-shaped patterns (Plate 227).

VI. (right) Design for a ceiling by Jean Cotelle; French, 1640s. This drawing may well have been procured from Paris for Inigo Jones and is likely to concern an important commission, perhaps in a French royal palace.

'Scorched leather' was a reddish-brown leather onto which a pattern was scorched with the aid of a hot plate applied to the face, and a mould applied under pressure to the back. The effect somewhat resembled that of damask (Plate 299) and there can be little doubt that the 'leather damask' of the inventories was in fact leather of this type, especially as 'to damask' also meant to stamp patterns on a material (see p. 124). It was much used for making protective covers—'cases' and 'carpets'—for furniture.

Printed, Painted and Flocked Hangings

We have already mentioned several printed, painted and flocked materials. We discussed printed linens and cottons, the imprinting of patterns on woollen velvets, on paragon and camlet, on ribbed silks, and on scorched leather. We also discussed Indian painted cottons (chintzes), and painted gilt-leather panels.

Large hangings that were painted with scenes similar to those woven into tapestries were not all that rare in the sixteenth and seventeenth centuries but not many specimens survive (Colour Plate VIII). They varied enormously in quality—from the 'paynted clothes about ye chamber' valued at 6s. 8d. to be seen in an Oxfordshire farmhouse in 1579,[116] which were substitutes for genuine tapestry, to the sumptuous and delicately executed hangings that were provided for the *Grande Galerie* at Versailles (presumably soon after 1680) which were described as 'une tenture de tapisserie peinte sur un fonds de toile d'argent trait, représentant partie de l'Histoire du Roy, dessein de Mr. Le Brun' [a tapestry [like] hanging, painted on a ground of drawn silver thread with a representation of part of the History of the King, designed by Mr. Le Brun].[117] At Hardwick the famous High Great Chamber was not only furnished with a set of tapestry hangings depicting the Story of Ulysses but had also 'another sute of hangings', no doubt for use in summer, which were of 'woollen cloth stayned [i.e. painted] with frett [strapwork patterns?] and storie and silk flowers.'[118] The Hardwick hangings very probably came from Flanders for the English industry was in decline in Elizabethan times.[119] At the end of the century there were painted satin hangings in a room at Dyrham[120] but these are likely to have been Chinese, since Chinese painted silk hangings were by then just coming into fashion.

In 1634, one Jerome Lanyer sought letters patent for 'by affixinge Wooll, Silke and other Material of divers Cullors, upon Lynnen, Cloath, Silke, Cotton, Leather, and other substances with Oyle, Size, and other Ciments, to make useful and serviceable Hangings'.[121] He was referring to hangings which had their patterns executed in flock of various kinds, but usually of wool flock (*tontisse*, in French). Flock applied in this way produced a tolerably good imitation of velvet and, since real velvet was both desirable and expensive, this cheap substitute was eagerly sought.

Flock hangings of some sort were already available in the sixteenth century and the Painter-Stainers Company of London claimed in 1626 that 'flock work' was one

VII. (left) *Tapisserie de Bergame*; probably woven in Northern France in the middle of the seventeenth century. Although rather coarse, such colourful, large-patterned materials were suitable for wall-hangings in all but the grandest settings. As this panel shows, separate borderings were available so that panels of any size could be made up.

of their monopolies.[122] How Lanyer's patent of a few years later differed is not clear now. A Scotsman visiting Amsterdam in 1693 reported that 'there is a . . . velvett and guilded leather [here] that is exported from this [country] to England',[123] and there is a late seventeenth-century model chair in the Saffron Walden Museum which is covered in a flocked gilt leather which might be a specimen of this Dutch product.[124] The famous Parisian decorative painter, Claude Audran III, organised 'une manufacture de tapisseries composées de laine hachée ou pilée, sur toile ciré' [a manufactory of hangings [with patterns] composed of chopped or crushed wool on [a ground of] oiled cloth] at the end of the century.[125] Audran's hangings are said to have become popular in Paris, probably because of the charm of Audran's designs rather than the technique in which they were rendered. Sadly, none seems to survive.

The Painter-Stainers' monopoly may primarily have concerned flocked *paper* hangings. Their monopoly only extended to England, of course, but they probably did not at this stage feel that the factory at Rouen producing *papier velouté* offered any serious competition.[126] Nevertheless, the industry was to wax, and flock wallpaper ('caffoy paper') was to become an English speciality in the eighteenth century.

Not all wallpaper was flocked, but wallpapers were not otherwise much used in the seventeenth century. It was still necessary for a writer in 1699 to explain that 'they are managed like wollen hangings' and are called 'paper tapestry'.[127] However, shops dealing in wallpaper existed in London from the time of Charles II onwards[128] and it had become worth levying a tax on wallpaper by 1712.

Pepys's wife had hangings of 'counterfeit damask' on the walls of her closet.[129] As it was an imitation of damask rather than velvet, it will not have been flocked. But the process involved printing for the word 'damask' also meant 'to stamp rude draughts on waste paper, etc.'[130] When books were censored, it was not unusual for the offending pages to be used as a ground for printing such patterns. In 1673 the Bishop of London, for instance, ordered the master and Wardens of the Stationers' Company 'to damask or obliterate whatever sheets you have seized of a book called *Leviathan*'.[131] Luckily some copies of Hobbes' book escaped the net and 'the greatest, perhaps the sole, masterpiece of political philosophy in the English language' is therefore still known to us.

NEEDLEWORK

Wall-hangings, chair-covers, table-carpets and most of the other confections that the upholsterer handled had to be assembled with the aid of a needle. Materials were made up into the desired form, trimming was applied, and the requisite hooks, rings and tapes were stitched in place. Upholstery has in this respect not changed in its essentials since the seventeenth century and there is no need to elaborate on this aspect here. What was created as a result of such labours can, however, best be studied from looking at contemporary illustrations including those in this book.

Needlework was also involved at a more artistic level in creating appliqué work which consists of taking ornamental shapes cut out (*découpé*) of one material and applying them to a ground material (Plates 96 and 107). One of the most striking examples of *appliqué* work in England is the 'Spangled Bed' at Knole which is traditionally associated with James I.[132] This has hangings of red satin to which a pattern of strapwork ornament cut from white silk has been applied. The edges of the *découpé* ornament are trimmed with silk cord that is 'couched', or stitched onto the surface. The spangles which have earned the bed its name are sequins stitched along the centre-line of the strapwork. Bold effects can readily be achieved by means of *appliqué* work, and there is a certain three-dimensional quality to materials assembled in this way. What may be regarded as an extension of *appliqué* work was the stitching to the face of a textile hanging or a chair-cover, of a braid or 'galloon' so as to form an inner border (Plate 162). This type of decoration could be quite elaborate, incorporating intricate scrollwork, and might be worked with two different widths of braid so that a counterpoint effect was achieved.

Actual embroidery, that is to say patterns worked with the needle on a textile ground (e.g. Plates 106 and 203),[133] came in many forms during the seventeenth century and the reader is referred to some of the numerous books on the subject which survey the technical and artistic aspects of this craft.[134] It was a highly versatile medium in which a needlewoman living, for instance, deep in the country could create decorative panels suitable for many purposes—cushion-covers, firescreen panels, coverlets, chair-covers, etc. She might copy a motif from one of the many pattern-books available, or she might get someone skilled with a pencil to draw a design for her to work—she might even do this herself if she felt she had the talent. Alternatively, she might imitate in needlework the pattern on a woven textile that was available to copy. At any rate, the panels created domestically in this way were rarely very big; the production of large hangings, table-carpets, and coverlets was on the whole left to the professional 'broderers', working in *ateliers* in the cities. They usually had access to skilful designers who could compose patterns suitable for any given purpose. The capabilities of individual professional embroiderers of course varied immensely, but the most skilful were able to produce work of the very greatest delicacy and beauty. The designs worked in the principal ateliers tended to be international in character, based on engraved compositions by Italian, Flemish, German or Parisian artists.

106. An embroidered bed-valance of about 1600. Executed in coloured silks and gold thread on cream-coloured silk and trimmed with two sorts of gold lace bordering. Although probably made in Germany, the pattern is in a style that was fashionable all over Europe at the time.

While the patterns executed with a needle might be described by someone making an inventory, they never specify what stitch was employed although the various kinds of stitches all had individual names that were known to embroiderers. It is therefore puzzling that inventories often mention 'Irish stitch',[135] until one realises that this was a pattern rather than a stitch. It was in fact the same as *point d'Hongrie,* the flame-like zig-zag pattern that was also executed as a woven pattern in materials like *tapisserie de Bergame.* It was a favourite pattern in the seventeenth century and has no other name in English inventories. Some hangings of this pattern survive at Chastleton that can with a fair degree of certainty be equated with the 'hangings of Irish stitch' mentioned in the inventory of 1633.[136]

Large hangings executed entirely in embroidery were anyway quite exceptional. Large pieces were more frequently decorated with bands of embroidery, with applied ornaments of embroidery, or with open patterns in which much ground was allowed to show between the elements. In fact, for large-scale work, embroidery was a form of embellishment and rarely served as a means of overall decoration.

The finest sorts of professional embroidery, executed perhaps in several kinds of gold thread with details worked with coloured silks, could be a most impressive form of decoration. Such work was also very expensive. Domestic work, on the other hand, was mostly worked or 'wrought' by the lady of the house or by the women of her entourage whose labour was free, so the only expense involved would lie in the purchasing of the materials.[137]

TRIMMINGS

Trimming serves two purposes. It can be used to finish off edges of upholstery work and to disguise seams, or it may serve merely as embellishment. In the seventeenth century it often did both at the same time.

To achieve a rich effect two or more materials could be assembled in a variety of ways, material could be decorated with *appliqué* work or with embroidery, or it could be loaded with trimmings of various kinds. Indeed, this last was the principal means by which the seventeenth-century upholsterer achieved his effects (Plate 95) and 193). By and large, seventeenth-century upholstery was not very well executed but failings could be disguised by these eye-catching ornaments. Trimmings were piled onto the richer kinds of seventeenth-century upholstery in great profusion, as contemporary descriptions sometimes prove and many illustrations show (Plate 140 and Colour Plate XXII). Surviving specimens of seventeenth century upholstery, on the other hand, have so often lost their complement of trimming that they no longer give anything like a true impression of how such confections looked when new. The contribution of the *passementier,* as the French called the maker of trimmings, to the final appearance of seventeenth-century upholstery must not be underestimated.

Randle Holme, writing in the middle of the century, explained that hangings might have 'inch fringe, caul fring, tufted fring, snailing fring, gimp fring with tufts and buttons, vellem fring, etc.',[138] but there were many sorts and some were of

107. (left) French appliqué work of about 1680. The headcloth of the Bielke Bed (see Plate 41). Strapwork of white silk, with foliate ornament in blue silk, all edged with couched silk cord, applied to crimson velvet. The tendrils are also rendered in the couched technique.

immense complexity. His list in fact seems to be arranged in increasing order of richness, the 'inch fringe' being a simple, straightforward fringe (Plate 40) while examples of what must be vellum fringe (because narrow strips of vellum are used to help produce loops and thus a three-dimensional build-up) show it to have been of extreme richness (Plate 100).[139] 'Snailing' was produced with a spiralling core; the fringe was usually uncut, and thus had loops rather than whiskers, as it were. 'Caul' means net, and fringes with a wide band of netting at the top were popular during the first half of the century (Colour Plate II and Plate 136). The strands were gathered into tassel-like bunches along the lower edge. 'Tufted fringe' had small bell-like tufts which led the French to call them *campanes* (Plate 38). In English this became 'campaign fringe'.[140] The terms used for fringes in France are most confusing. 'Lorsque la frange est tout-à-fait basse on l'apelle mollet; quand les fils en font plus longe que l'ordinaire & que la tête est large & ouvragée à jour, on lui donne le nom crépine' [When the fringe is quite short it is called *mollet*; when the threads are much longer than usual and the heading is wide and of open-work, it is known as *crépine*.] says Savary at the beginning of the eighteenth century.[141] But he is speaking of the well-established practice of the period of having long fringes, *crépines*, only in positions where they could hang straight down (i.e. along lower edges, or along top edges if affixed to hang downwards instead of upwards), while one had short fringes of the same pattern along the vertical edges and along the top, if the fringe at the top was not reversed.[142] On the other hand, as he also implies, *crépine* was the name given to any openwork fringe. It need not even display what we would understand by fringing; it could be an intricate network of metal thread (Plate 99) but used where *crépine* (or long fringe) would have been used.[143]

Rich fringes might be of gold thread, less commonly of silver, but were not infrequently of silver and gold together. Fringes were even more often made of silk, sometimes of two colours alternating along their length (Plate 40). Fringes on woollen or worsted hangings were often none the less of silk, but worsted (called 'crewel') fringe was also available (Plate 103). The heading of fringes could be plain or embellished in fancy ways, if a richer effect was required.

Another form of trimming was lace, which could be of silk, or of silver or gold thread.[144] It was applied in bands as inset bordering or so as to break up large areas of material into panels (Plate 2).[145] In inventories this is sometimes described as being 'striped with lace'.[146] Braids and galloons could be applied in the same way, as has already been noted.

The *passementier* also made up tassels, rosettes, cords and ribbons with which upholstery work could be completed.

Fillings and Stuffing

The upholsterer required soft materials with which to fill mattresses, bolsters and pillows, and to pad chairs and other forms of seat-furniture. I shall consider the various types of mattress in use in the seventeenth century when I come to discuss beds, but the fillings of mattresses ranged from swansdown and eiderdown, through ordinary feathers, wool clippings or flock, to straw and chaff.

Less common were cotton wool, beech leaves, and goose feathers. During the second half of the century, horsehair began to be used for mattresses.

Horsehair was not much used for padding seat-furniture before the 1660s (Plate 180).[147] The padding was otherwise achieved with the aid of down or of straw.

Securing stuffing so that it did not collect at one end of a mattress, or did not slide away from the pressure-points of a chair presented problems for the upholsterer. For coverlets and then mattresses, quilting provided the answer. This involved stitching right through the sandwich—cover, filling, cover—so that the stuffing was locked in position. Quilting is of course a form of needlework and the stitching could be organised into decorative patterns. It was not practical for thicker forms of mattress or squabs, however. For this purpose, what we would now call 'buttoning' was devised. Here the materials were secured by means of strong thread passed through at isolated spots with a long needle. The threads placed a considerable strain on the surface-material so the thread was looped over a tuft of linen which helped to spread the load (Plate 304). The tufts served the same purpose as buttons which were, however, not introduced until the late eighteenth century. Compared with the deep buttoning of the nineteenth century, incidentally, seventeenth and eighteenth century tufting or buttoning was quite shallow. The padding of chairs was also at first held in place by quilting (Plate 172) but, in the late seventeenth century, a few important pieces of French seat-furniture had their stuffing secured in position by tufting (Plate 170).

CHAPTER VI
The Upholsterer's Furnishings

HAVING surveyed the materials with which furnishings were made in the seventeenth century, we can now consider how the upholsterer made them up into 'furniture'—a term that embraced all the loose furnishings of a room, and not merely the wooden items, as it does today. In this chapter, I shall deal in turn with wall-hangings, portières, window-curtains and floor-coverings. Beds and seat-furniture constitute such important classes that separate chapters are devoted to them.

WALL-HANGINGS

Generally speaking, tapestries were the most valuable form of wall-covering in the seventeenth century and people tended to hang them in the most important rooms—in the Great Chamber, the Salon or Withdrawing Room, or the main bedchambers. There were two principal types of tapestry available. On the one hand were the pictorial kind with a three-dimensional scene. These are variously described as 'histories', 'of imagery' or 'with personages' (Plate 2 and 12).[1] Related to them were 'landskips (Plates 1, 93 and 94). On the other hand there were the essentially two-dimensional hangings with ornamental motifs like 'grotesques' and those displaying armorial bearings. One should perhaps class with these the so-called 'verdure tapestries' which show massed foliage and undergrowth (Plate 108). They often appear two-dimensional although they are in fact a variant of the landscape type. They were usually described as being of 'fforrest worke' and the 'buskedge' hangings, occasionally met with in English inventories are also likely to have been of this type.[2]

On rare occasions a set of tapestries would be designed with a special room in mind and then of course they would exactly fit the particular walls concerned.[3] Rather more commonly, a rich man might order a set of tapestries from a well-known series[4] and have them made so that they fitted a specific room. More modest people would buy a set of tapestries ready-made and adapt them to the walls of the room where they were to hang. A certain amount of adjustment could be obtained by playing around with the borders, which were usually separate weaves sewn on around the central panel (Plate 108). Part of the main scene could be folded under at one end and the border could be re-attached to make up the hanging tidily. Sometimes the piece that was not required was actually cut off. On other occasions a piece from a different scene was added to one side of the main panel to extend it. If such measures seemed too drastic, hangings could simply be taken past a corner of a room and round onto a bit of the next wall. As long as the walls were totally clad with the material, it did not matter too much that each panel did not precisely fit an individual wall (Plate 33). If a hanging obscured a doorway, it could be looped up out of the way at that place, with the aid of cords or hooks (Plate 93). It was preferable to arrange the hangings so that two abutted in line with the handle side of

108. Window with a single curtain pulled to one side and held up with a cord or ribbon. Note the rings attached with tapes. Dutch; 1660s.

the door (Plate 48); but, if necessary, a slit could even be cut in the hangings. If there was a narrow gap between the top of the hanging and the cornice, a narrow band of a neutral colour could be specially woven and stitched onto the top edge. The permutations were numerous; all that needs to be stressed is that, for all its associations with an aristocratic way of life, and in spite of its high cost, tapestry was not treated with all that much respect in the seventeenth century. No one thought twice about hanging pictures or a mirror in front of tapestries (Plates 1 and 311). A large nail was quite often driven straight through the hanging into the wall and that was that.

It was very much easier to adjust 'grotesques' and verdure tapestries. One could subtract a piece of the latter without spoiling the effect at all, while the open,

131

symmetrical patterns of grotesque compositions could quite easily be trimmed or extended by adjusting both sides equally.

Most other materials were rather more easy to adjust to a particular wall because they came in narrower widths and therefore had anyway to be made up into panels of the requisite size.

Coarse hangings like *tapisseries de Bergame* could be three or four feet wide but still needed to be joined to form a hanging of any great size. One could obtain lengths of bordering which could be sewn, not only round the edges of the whole hanging in the ordinary way (Colour Plate VII), but might be interposed between each width of the main material so as to make up a hanging with several rectangular panels. This was a very common formula for wall-hangings in the seventeenth century because it allowed almost infinite flexibility. Special borders were also available for gilt-leather hangings (Plate 104) and for brocatelle.[5] Few other materials had special bordering but one could make up borders with a different material and this was the commonest method used at the time (Colour Plate XVI). It would be pointless to try to list the many combinations that occur in seventeenth-century inventories but it was common in grand rooms to have two or three widths of a rich silk material—say, damask—framed into panels or 'panes'[6] with, for instance, a striped silk, or with a plain silk with an embroidered pattern, or with damask of another colour. Worsted materials might be treated in the same way. For a while in the middle of the century it seems to have been fashionable to have a worsted panel framed with gilt leather.[7]

Hangings could of course be made up simply with one material, and often were; but a paned effect could then be achieved by couching onto the surface lines of lace (of metal or coloured silks) which broke up the surface in much the same way. For the purposes of making an inventory, it was not usually necessary to describe every detail, so a bald statement that some hangings were of, say, blue damask often gives no indication that they in fact had various embellishments which one did not need to mention in order simply to identify the hangings.

With particularly ambitious sets of hangings, the sections of bordering interposed between the panels might be fashioned like columns or pilasters. Cardinal Mazarin had some especially rich hangings of 'brocart d'argent avec figures de chasseurs, d'animaux, oiseaux, fontaines, de soies de divers couleurs' [silver brocade with figures of hunters, animals, birds, fountains, executed in silks of various colours] and these had 'colonnes de brocart d'or' [columns of gold brocade] to go between them.[8] At the end of the century it became highly fashionable in Paris to have hangings decorated with applied *colonnes torses* [spiral columns].[9] With *découpage* one could, moreover, easily have panels of fancy shape, as some splendid *appliqué* hangings at Penshurst show (Colour Plate X).

Round most hangings one could expect to see a trimming of fringe.[10] These ranged from the straight fringe, the simple form that we understand by the term today, to extremely complicated confections like the *campane* or 'campaign fringe' which had a mass of small bell-like tassels. A hanging would normally be trimmed with two different lengths of the fringe concerned—a long version for the horizontal edges where the fringe could hang straight down, and a shorter version for the vertical edges where a long fringe would otherwise droop in an unfortunate way. Along the top edge of a hanging, one could either have a short fringe facing upwards, as it were; or one could have a long fringe reversed to hang downwards from the edge. Intricate edgings could also be made up with the aid of a needle. At Ham House, for instance, there is a fragment of a rich border trimmed with small gathered puffs of pink silk, all edged with a very narrow fringe. Even now, the effect is charming.

Some particularly splendid hangings had what amounted to a pelmet running along the top. At Tart Hall, for instance, there was 'a long valence for a roome' in store in 1641.[11] Daniel Marot included such a feature in several of his proposals for rooms at the end of the century and the Dauphin had a straight valance round the top of the red camlet hangings in one of his rooms at Versailles (Plates 22 and 95). An example survives at Rosenborg Castle, in Copenhagen, dating from the early years of the eighteenth century.[12]

All these applied details helped to give rich seventeenth-century hangings that lively, frothy appearance which was so greatly admired at the time. Straightforward hangings, of a single material, without any trimming at all, can only have been seen in the very humblest of homes. For the rest, it must have been the wall-hangings more than anything which gave each room in a seventeenth-century house its individual character. It is difficult for us today to envisage how enormous was the variety of effects that could be achieved by clever combinations of materials and by the subtle application of trimmings.

Reading through inventories gives one a general impression of the materials that were commonly used for wall-hangings and those which were more rarely so used. Tapestries were to be found in most important houses, usually in the principal rooms, but other kinds of expensive material might equally well be found in the same locations. Silk damask, for instance, was favoured for grand settings right through the century, crimson damask being particularly popular at the end of the period. Plain silk velvet was relatively common and was usually to be found in combination with another material, but it would seem that the large-patterned and very expensive Genoa velvets were by no means prevalent.[13] Mohair (which I have argued was a silk material; see p. 115) was to be found in many fashionable rooms during the last two decades of the century.

Gilt leather hangings were greatly in favour during the seventeenth century and provided a truly striking effect (Plate 227) but they were going out of fashion in Paris by the end of the century.[14] Coming into favour at that time were worsted damask and camlet. Chintz, which had been seen in a few rooms before the middle of the century, became popular after that in rooms of a not too formal character.

Down the scale somewhat came the *tapisseries de Bergame* and other coarse woollen upholstery materials, for instance dornix, which were to be found in rooms of secondary importance during most of the century (Colour Plates VII and VIII). The same may be said of 'Irish stitch'.

Worsted materials of various kinds were to be seen on the walls in rather humbler rooms. Perpetuana, camlet and paragon might be found in quite grand surroundings, Kidderminster stuffs in rather less so, and the many types of relatively inexpensive materials, often just called 'woollen stuff', were used in rooms of lower status.

Exceptional but rather grand must have been rooms hung with turkeywork and moquette.[15] The rooms at Tart Hall hung with frieze trimmed with gold lace seem to have been unique and it is difficult to imagine what they were like although it is clear that they were very splendid.[16] Rooms hung with Scots 'pladd' were not common but must have been striking; presumably they had a checked, tartan effect.[17] And then there was wallpaper, which was still rare at the end of the century although flock papers imitating velvet seem to have found a ready market.

The *Dictionnaire de Trévoux* of 1704 tells us that 'Il n'y a pas longtemps que toutes les murailles des maisons etoient tapissées de nattes' [It is not long since all the walls of houses were hung with mats] and it seems that it was the practice in the Middle Ages to use matting as insulation in winter, fitting *paillasons* against windows and doors.[18] At Saint-Germain-en-Laye in 1548 there were still 'nattes faictes de neuf contre les murs . . . tant contre des deux pans de murs au deux costez de la dicte Gallerye, que aux deux boutz d'icelle' [mats newly fitted to the walls . . . on the two sections of walls at the sides of the said Gallery, as well as at the two ends of it].[19] Galleries were always difficult rooms to keep warm; they by no means always had a fireplace. As late as 1669 mats were being fitted 'devant les croisées du grand salon des Thuilleries' [in front of the windows of the great *salon* at the Tuileries].[20] They had inner facings of *toile* which were no doubt neat and colourful. The practice of insulating with mats must have been known in England. Evelyn, anyway, advised gardeners in 1664 to 'keep the doors and windows of your conservatories well matted'.[21] In order to prevent children of high rank from hurting themselves, the walls and floors of their nurseries had in former times also been padded with matting. This practice was maintained in France in the seventeenth century, the apartments of royal children up to the age of twelve being padded with thick Savonnerie carpeting or with Gobelins tapestry 'qu'en jouent ils ne puissent se blesser'.[22]

Important hangings seem usually to have been kept in the Wardrobe and were only put up when the family was in residence. If there were summer and winter hangings for a room, at least one of the sets would have to be stored away at any given time. Delicate hangings also needed frequent attention—fringes repairing, wrinkles adjusting, etc. So hangings of any degree of richness must have been readily detachable from the walls. Some velvet and silk damask hangings at Ham House which are still on the walls for which they were created in the 1670s (and are not now taken down very often) have an arrangement of hooks and eyes. Very heavy hangings must have been nailed to battens fixed to the walls. Sometimes hangings were fixed to frames like picture-stretchers.[23] Wallpaper was usually pasted directly onto the wall but might first be pasted onto canvas.[24] Sometimes it was nailed with the pieces overlapping to hide the nails.

PORTIÈRES

It was common in especially grand rooms during the second half of the century to have hangings in front of the doors (Plate 94) These were usually en suite with the wall-hangings although they might be decorated with even greater elaboration. Such *portières* contributed to the unified appearance of the room. They are mentioned in the French royal inventories and in those of Cardinal Mazarin's collection,[25] for instance, and one can see them in some of the illustrations of rooms by Daniel Marot. Occasionally a *portière* might form a contrast to the wall-hangings, on the other hand. Such would seem to have been Mazarin's two pieces of 'tapisserie de Portugal servans de dessus de porte' [Portuguese tapestry for use over the door]; it seems unlikely that they were simply panels to be fitted as over-doors (i.e. above the door-case).

Although *portières* might form an important feature of the decoration, their original purpose was functional—they served to exclude draughts—and most *portières* were erected primarily with this in mind. The 'piece of old tapestry over the door' in Lady Teynham's Old Chamber at Cowdray must have been there as a draught-excluder and the Countess of Shrewsbury had a coverlet hung in front of one door in her bedchamber at Hardwick and 'a counterpoynt of tapestrie before another dore'.[26]

Portières tended to get dirty rather quickly as they had to be pushed aside each time someone passed through the doorway. The richest *portières*, like some of those in Mazarin's collection, therefore had to have their own protective curtains. Hitching up a *portière* always posed a problem. In one Elizabethan house there was a curtain of green kersey 'wth. a curtyn rod of iron wh. is to hand afore the dore, wth. a greate hooke to putt it up when it is not drawn.'[27] This hook must have been a primitive 'hold-back'. The same result could be achieved with a smaller hook and a cord. In many cases the wall-hangings themselves were carried in front of a door and matters would then be so arranged that the junction between two abutting hangings lined up with the handle side of the door. To prevent an awkward hitching-up of the hanging over the door when it was opened, one could extend the door with battens right up to the cornice so that the whole section of hanging above the doorway also would swing out from the wall. Such an arrangement may still be seen at Ham House.

What must have served as a double door was the frame covered in tapestry ['un chassis à tapisserie servant sur les portes'] which was in Mazarin's house.[28] Celia Fiennes certainly saw some double doors at Chippenham Park at the end of the century but they were lined, and served 'to prevent noise'.[29] At Dyrham, incidentally, there was 'an engine for closing the door' in one room.[30]

WINDOW-CURTAINS AND BLINDS

Window-curtains were by no means fitted to every window in the seventeenth century but they were not uncommon in rooms of any importance, particularly in rooms set aside for dining, as well as in bedchambers and in closets—in all of which a higher degree of comfort was required than in other types of room. Curtains were primarily fitted to exclude draughts or sunlight. Privacy was hardly a consideration at all because most important rooms were up on the first and second floor. Only in towns might it present a problem. It may well be that shutters were more common in city houses than in the country; if so, this might be due primarily to the wish to have a measure of privacy rather than from any desire for security or insulation.

A clear distinction was almost invariably made in seventeenth-century inventories between the curtains listed among the hangings of a bed and those provided for a window which are almost always specified as such.[31]

Mats were sometimes fitted into window-embrasures in winter as protection against the cold. One could presumably also hang a cloth to serve the same purpose, and the references to 'window pieces' and 'window cloths' which occur from the

109. Screening curtain in a doctor's surgery with taped rings, and cords for drawing backwards and forwards. A screen of wicker (with a handle) is inserted in the lower half of the window as an additional aid to privacy.

110. (right) Symmetry achieved at windows with single fitted curtains, by pulling them to opposite sides. The lower sections of the windows are dark because the outside shutters have been closed.

111. (far right) At present this appears to be the earliest known representation of divided window-curtains. The office of the Steward at the Danish royal castle, Rosenborg, in 1653.

Middle Ages down into the early seventeenth century seem to concern something of the kind.[32] Perhaps they were hooked in place at night or when it was particularly cold. Curtains that could be drawn (i.e. that had a rod and rings, or the equivalent) had occasionally been fitted to windows already in the Middle Ages.[33] They remained utilitarian until well into the seventeenth century. Curtains might be made of a pretty material but the rods and rings were not disguised and only a single curtain would be fitted to each window.[34] At that stage few people were worried about symmetry and a curtain that was simply pulled to one side did not offend the eye at all (Plate 1 and 108). Nor was it common to have the window-curtains matching the hangings until towards the middle of the century,[35] or so it would seem, although the wealthier citizens of Antwerp are said to have already had matching curtains by the middle of the sixteenth century.[36]

When the demand for greater order in interior architecture began to manifest itself, it was recognised that the single window-curtain could spoil the symmetry of a scheme of mural decoration. If there were two windows, one could pull the single curtains to opposite sides of the windows (Plate 110), and this would of course work with any even number of windows. But many rooms had an odd number so the solution was not fully satisfactory (Plate 219). Then the idea of dividing the single curtain down the middle was developed, so that the halves could be drawn to opposite sides of the window-opening during daytime. There were divided window-curtains at Ham House by the middle of the seventeenth century [37] and there is a picture of the steward at Rosenborg Castle, in Copenhagen, doing his accounts in 1653, in which one may discern a set of divided curtains suspended by rings from a rod (Plate 111). In 1673 the *Mercure Galant*, which kept Parisians informed of the latest gossip and fashions, told its readers of what it claimed was a new invention. 'Il n'y a pas jusques au rideaux qu'on met devant des fenestres, qui ne

soient aussi sujets aux caprices de la mode. Ils sont presentement fendus par le milieu, et au lieu qu'on ne les tiroit que d'une coste, on les tire maintenant des deux costez: et l'on a introduit cette mode parce qu'ils incommoderoirent moins, et que les fenestres en recevoient plus d'ornement.' [Even the curtains which are put in front of the windows are also subject to the caprices of fashion. They are now divided down the middle, and instead of pulling them to one side only they are now pulled to each side; and this fashion has been introduced because they are less inconvenient, and because the windows become more decorative.][38] Can it really be that divided curtains were unknown in France before that date? One suspects that, if they were to be seen at Ham in the 1640s, one could also by then have seen the device in certain places in France. But the French were placing much more emphasis on curtains and other hangings by the 1670s and it may well be that the *Mercure Galant* was merely pointing out that the old type of single curtain could no longer be tolerated in a fashionable interior. At any rate, thereafter the device was quickly adopted in fashionable circles. Dublin Castle, which was so elegantly appointed in the time of the Duke of Ormonde, certainly had divided curtains by 1679[39] and the curtains in the principal rooms at Ham House, fitted during the redecoration of the 1670s, were all of the divided type (Plate 112).

At about this time a new form of curtain was invented in France. This was the 'pull-up' curtain which, as its name implies, could be pulled up to the window-head by means of cords, and was so organised as to hang in festoons (Plate 238).[40] This form of curtain may have been developed from the 'tie-up' curtains used on beds of the *lit à housse* type (see p. 165), with which upholsterers would have been generally familiar by the middle of the century (Plate 132). Such curtains looked particularly good from inside the room and looked best if not pulled up too tightly against the top of the window. The fact that Louis XIV on one occasion gave explicit instructions as to how the holes for the pulleys at the top of the window-embrasure should be pierced is an indication of how important a contribution this type of curtain was thought to make to the decoration.[41] The new form was eagerly espoused by Daniel Marot in Holland and England, as several of his engravings show; he had no doubt seen early examples in Paris before he emigrated in 1684 (Plate 303). Pull-up curtains were anyway being installed in the English royal palaces at the end of the century, as an estimate for upholstery work at Hampton Court makes clear.[42]

It seems that pull-up curtains at first were fitted so as to pull up against the under-surface of the top of the window-embrasure. Later, a projecting board, pierced for the pulleys, came to be fitted at the window-head and the curtain was nailed to the front edge of this pulley-board, simply with a ruffled heading rising an inch or two above the board. The next development was to mask the pulley-board with a box-like window-cornice which might be of quite a fancy shape. This wooden box was often faced with the same material as that of the curtain below it.[43] Ordinary 'hanging' curtains were also thought to require a more decorative finish at the top and pelmets (called 'valances') were therefore added. An early reference to such a feature is one made in 1673 to curtains 'avec les petites pentes du haut' [with little valances at the top] while another in 1680 concerned 'deux rideaux et deux pentes de sarge violette pour les fenestres ...' [two curtains and two valances of violet coloured serge for the windows].[44] Some of the curtains illustrated by Daniel Marot

112. Divided window-curtains in a Dutch house in 1674. The red curtains are probably of thin silk (sarsnet). The lower half of the window is fitted with painted double-fold interior shutters.

have complicated pelmets with gathered pleats falling into festoons and tails. Celia Fiennes saw some white silk damask curtains at Lady Donegal's at the end of the century which had 'furbellows of callicoe printed [with] flowers'.[45]

Against the cold one chose a woollen material for one's window-curtains. Particularly popular in even the grandest settings during the first half of the century was dornix, which was warm and colourful.[46] Window-curtains of saye and other serges are mentioned frequently. Paragon was often used later in the century. Rather less common were Kidderminster stuff, shalloon, linsey-wolsey, pladd, and wadmole. The last was sufficiently thick to be 'unlyned'.[47] Tapestry was never used for curtains as it was too thick to draw backwards and forwards conveniently but it was still being used for window-cloths during the first decades of the century.[48]

An important bedchamber at Hardwick in 1601 had 'curtins of darnix for the windowes' against the cold, but also had 'curtins of damask and sarcenet for the windowes'.[49] The second set must have been there to reduce the amount of light coming into the room. The 'two great southege curtyons for ye great windowe' in the Great Chamber at Hengrave Hall must have served the same purpose; the cold was excluded by a 'window-cloth' of 'arras'.[50] Likewise there was a large curtain and rod in a window at Hatfield Priory a quarter of a century later but the additional 'rodds within the window' had three buckram curtains.[51] Southege and buckram, like the silk damask and sarcenet, would have been translucent, as must have been the curtains of 'greene cotten' at Cockesden in 1610 and the 'ffour ffrench green cotton window curtaines' at Edington in 1665.[52]

Window-curtains of silk are rarely mentioned in English inventories before the middle of the century. There were some at Hardwick at the beginning of the century, as we noted, but they were apparently exceptional. Very striking must have been the 'streamed tafata curtaines . . . without any lyning' which were hanging in the nine windows of the South Gallery at Tart Hall, one of the Arundels' magnificent residences, shortly before the outbreak of the Civil War.[53] After 1650, silk curtains are mentioned in the inventories of most grand houses.[54] They were effective as blinds against the sun and they were decorative. If they were to serve as blinds they were mostly of white silk[55] but, as window-curtains came increasingly to be embraced in the decoration of the room, the tendency was to have them matching the rest of the upholstery—the rest of the *ammeublement*.

At Cowdray there were some window-curtains of Indian painted callico—of chintz. They were en suite with the rest of the textile furnishings of the room which was appropriately named 'The Calleco Chamber'.[56] The effect of the light coming through the chintz must have been charming. A somewhat similar effect will have been seen in the room at Dyrham which had curtains of painted satin—presumably painted in China with exotic birds and foliage—at the end of the century.[57]

The *Mercure Galant* once again acquired a niche in the history of window-curtains when, in 1686, it brought news of some white damask curtains destined for the Château de Versailles which were brocaded in gold thread (which is heavy) with monograms and lyres, 'mais seulement d'éspace en éspace, parce ce qu'on ne doit pas trop charger d'or un rideau qui doit estre aisé à manier' [monograms and lyres of gold, but only here and there, because one must not overload a curtain which must be easy to manage].[58] However, if curtains were particularly delicate or very heavy, or were somehow awkward to manoeuvre, one might fix cords to the top and draw them backwards and forwards by pulling on these instead of tugging at the bottom of the hanging. Cardinal Mazarin, for instance, had some white taffeta curtains with 'cordons de soie blanche' attached, 'servans à couller les rideaux' [cords of white . . . used for drawing the curtains].[59] At Kilkenny Castle in 1684 some white shalloon curtains (which were hanging on a rod so were not of the pull-up kind) also had 'strings to draw'[60] and one occasionally sees curtains fitted with draw-strings in contemporary illustrations (Plates 94 and 109). Curtain-rings, incidentally, were usually of iron but could be of horn. Brass rings were not introduced until the eighteenth century.[61] The rings were sometimes sewn directly to the top edge, or to the back with a gathered heading. Not infrequently they were also attached with loops of tape which made the top of the curtain hang well below the rod (Plates 108 and 109). This presumably helped to prevent the ring binding on the rod. Rods were of iron and were sometimes gilded. They seem usually to have had loops at each end which fitted down onto hooks driven into the wall. Alternatively a rod might have a loop at one end only while the other end was fed through a ring like a modern screw-eye set in the wall at that end. During the second half of the century, curtains in luxurious settings were often trimmed with fringe (Plates 16 and 31).

Against the heat of the sun one might have blinds of straw or matting on rollers which could be pulled up by means of cords.[62] From this it was a simple step to adapt the roller to take a textile material and so produce a roller-blind. Such devices were being fitted to windows at Stockholm Palace in 1713[63] and it is reasonable to suppose that similar features could be seen in other parts of Europe. There were makers of 'window blinds' in London, at any rate by 1726 when a certain John Brown advertised that he could supply blinds of various materials 'the best painted of any in London'.[64] When Tessin was at Versailles in 1687 he noted that the pictures in the Dauphin's Closet were protected by blinds of a painted satin on rollers, fitted with a spring that held the blind down in front of the picture.[65] If one wanted to look at the picture, one raised the blind by means of a cord. The modern roller-blind with a spring, which seems to have been evolved in the eighteenth century, of course works the other way round. Slatted blinds (Venetian blinds or *jalousies à la persienne*) also seem to have been introduced in the eighteenth century but we have seen that *abat-jours* (outside slatted shutters) were much in evidence in parts of France in the late seventeenth century and Havard cites a reference of 1659 to what could possibly be an early form of *persienne*.[66] In Sweden, incidentally, it was customary to whitewash the inside of glass windows to protect the curtains from the sun in summer. Dexterous housemaids were able to produce decorative scrolls with the whiting-brush. This custom may have been widespread. It is not long since the glass of greenhouses was regularly whitewashed to reduce the heat in summer.

In his book on *The Art of Painting in Oyl*, published in 1687, John Smith devotes a whole chapter to 'The manner of painting cloth or sarsnet shash-windows'. I discussed windows with sliding sashes in Chapter III and noted that the word 'sash' derives from the French word for a frame—*chassis*. The sashes or frames to which Smith was referring were not fitted with panes of glass but were stretchers for paper, silk or linen which could be varnished and thus made transparent.[67] They were fitted inside glazed windows and acted as sun-blinds. Smith explains how one could mix verdegris with the varnish to make a green light that is 'very comfortable to the sight'. On the paper or silk one might 'paint upon them what fancy you please, but a landskip is most common and natural'.[68] Such 'transparencies' could be very decorative; one does occasionally see windows fitted with such 'sashes' in contemporary illustrations (Plates 113 and 114). The *chambre du Roi* at Fontainebleau was fitted with a 'grand chassis à verre et à pappier' in about 1640. This would seem to have been a 'double-window' with glass in the outer frame and a transparent paper sash inside.[69] Sashes were fitted inside windows at Skokloster, Count Wrangel's great country house north of Stockholm; in 1669 and in 1678 a Stockholm bookbinder charged a member of the Stenbock family for making up

De quel que façon que ie pense
A ce qui flatte nos defirs,
Ie ne treuue point de plaifirs
Plus charmans que ceux de l'Enfance.

Ces paffetemps fans artifice
Diuertiffent innocemment;
Et font exempts effgallement
De paffion et de malice.

Les IIII. AAGES DE l'Homme
faites par Maffe
Et ce Vend Anis Chez Ie Blond
Auec Priuilege du Roy. 1696.

Selon que l'humeur les conuie,
Les enfans fuiuent diuers ieux,
Et nous-mefme auons fait cóme eux
Aux premiers ans de noftre vie.

Pour moy, connoiffant leur aage
Bannit le chagrin et le dueil,
Ie voudrois iufques au cercueil
Pouuoir iouer leur perfonnage.

113. Painted sashes fitted
into windows in a
loggia. Scenes from
Genesis painted probably
on oiled silk stretched on
frames that formed
transparencies for the
light from the windows
to shine through.

114. What appear to be
hinged painted sashes
fitted inside windows at
a House of Orange
residence close to The
Hague, depicted in 1697.

two 'paper windows' and oiling them.[70] References to sashes are not all that common in English inventories or accounts but the fact that Smith thought it worth informing his readers how to make them suggests there was a steady demand for these fittings. Anthony Wood did, however, note that 'in most of the lower windows' of Oxford colleges numerous candles were placed on festive occasions and that, in one instance, there were 'severall emblems painted in colours on paper pasted on frames with mottoes under or neare describing them'.[71] Steele writing in 1712, told how his eye had been caught 'by the face of a very fair girl . . . fixed at the chin to a painted sash made part of the landscape'.[72] He must have seen the girl looking out of a window over the top of a transparency painted with a landscape in the manner described by John Smith.

FLOOR-COVERINGS

In the Middle Ages it had been the practice to strew loose rushes and straw on the floor. This seems to have been done in the grandest of houses and the French might still say of a very rich man in the seventeenth century that he was 'dans la paille jusques au ventre' [waist-deep in straw].[73] Nevertheless, rushes and straw were probably only used in this way on stone floors, which means that the family's more luxurious and private rooms, which were usually upstairs, would not have had such floor-coverings. It is even less probable that the floors of splendid rooms were strewn with rushes or straw in the late sixteenth century and early seventeenth century—in Elizabethan times—as it often claimed. This misconception probably springs from the apparent mis-translation of a statement made by Paul Hentzner who came to England in 1598. Hentzner was Swiss and he wrote his travel-account in Latin. His comments were translated and published nearly two centuries later by Horace Walpole, who makes him say of the royal palace of Greenwich that he found 'the floor, after the English fashion, strewed with hay'.[74] Walpole was translating the word 'faeno' but adds the comment that 'He probably means rushes,' and it was in fact a practice greatly favoured in this country to strew such greenery on the floor. Levinus Lemnius, writing in 1560, states that

> the better to qualifie and mitigate the heate, it shall be very good to sprinckle on the pavements and cool the floors of our houses or chambers with the springing water, and then strew them over with sedge, and to trimme up our parlours with green boughs, freshe herbes and vine leaves; which thing, although in the Low Country it be frequented, yet no nation more decently, more trimmely, nor more sightly than they doe in Englande.[75]

It will be noted that Lemnius was writing about a method of keeping a room fresh and cool in hot weather—with succulent, green foliage and not with dry straw—and it was probably to this practice, which the English had somehow perfected, that Hentzner was referring; hence his remark about it being 'after the English fashion'.[76]

Had Hentzner said that the floors were laid with straw mats, no one would subsequently have been misled. For it was a common practice in his day to lay rush matting on the floor. There is plenty of evidence that this was also the case in France in the sixteenth century and early seventeenth century.[77] A popular mid-sixteenth-century French poem refers to a 'chambre natée en toute place' (the French for a mat

115. Fitted rush matting in 1635. The plaited strips are sewn together; the stitching is clear. Even in this tragic scene recording the death of a wife in childbirth (note the wicker cradle draped with black and the black bed-hangings), some treasured possessions have been included—the valuable lute, the colourful globe and the exotic chintz on the table.

116. (right) A rush mat beside a Dutch bed in 1663. Thin mats of this kind are still imported from the East and, while this may possibly be a Dutch product, it is more likely to be an example of the class known as 'Tangier mats' imported from North Africa and perhaps related to the more elaborate 'Portugal mats' of the late seventeenth century. Note the Turkish carpet on the table.

being *natte*). This implies that the matting was fitted to the shape of the room which was made readily possible because it was plaited in strips about six inches wide. Fitted matting seems to have been quite common in England as well (Plate 115). The 'Best Chamber' at Walton, for instance, was 'matted under foote' when an inventory was taken in 1624 and the Gallery had three pieces of 'new matt'. At Chatsworth there was likewise a 'Matted Gallerie'.[78] Just fifteen years after Hentzner's visit to Greenwich Palace, the Duke of Saxe-Weimar visited Hampton Court and remarked on the fact that the floors of all the lodgings and galleries were fitted with plaited matting.[79] Maybe matting was used less frequently in Germany but it is more likely that he was impressed by the large number of rooms in the

144

English royal palace that were thus furnished. There is anyway no doubt that aristocratic Elizabethans and Jacobeans were very happy to be portrayed standing in a room laid with matting, even if they sometimes gilded the lily by laying a Turkish carpet on top of the matting (colour Plate XI).

Rush matting went out of fashion in the middle of the century. There was still matting in a bedchamber at Cowdray in 1682 but the house was by then appointed in an old-fashioned manner.[80] The Long Gallery at Ham House was still being called 'The Matted Gallery' in the inventory of 1677 although no mats are listed and it is very unlikely they were still present at that date. Thereafter, rush matting was mainly used in inconspicuous places—on landings, in the chapel, etc.[81] Mats were sometimes coloured (Plate 117) but those which were are likely to have been imported. Pepys' remark about an African mat being suitable to go under a bed of state suggests they were a very respectable form of floor-covering.[82]

'Portugal mats' and their relations were actual mats and probably had at least a border if not an overall pattern (Plate 95).[83] Rush matting, on the other hand, came in plaited strips and so could be made up into any size and fitted to the room, as already explained. It must have been the earliest form of fitted carpeting. Actual fitted carpet, that is to say, widths of pile carpeting sewn together into the shape of the room, does not seem to have been evolved until sometime in the second half of the eighteenth century but widths of moquette (see p. 112) were being joined and made up into carpets which were so large that they must have been for laying on the floor.[84] In the Chapel at Versailles, moreover, there was a large carpet of crimson velvet.[85] In this connection one should also mention 'fledges' which were made up of a material called 'fledge' (see p. 113). The Countess of Shrewsbury had fledges on the floor round her bed at Hardwick so it is clearly a fairly robust material although she also had some on the bed.[86] As for the 'peece of woolin hangeinge with birds and beasts under the beddes feett' at Cockesden in 1626,[87] this may well have been a hanging of dornix. Single widths of material of various kinds were also used on the floor as runners. There was 'a piece of corse cloath to cover ye stairs' at Dyrham, and borders of Savonnerie carpet were set aside 'pour servir aux marchepieds qui sont autour du sallon du billard de Trianon' [to serve as runners round the billiard room at the Trianon].[88]

The word 'carpet' had the same meaning in the seventeenth century as it has today but it was also used in reference to other large covers that lay flat—either on tables, as decoration, or as protective covers for delicate table-tops, marquetry floors, and so on. Table-carpets are discussed in Chapter IX but I shall here consider carpets of various kinds that were laid on the floor. In fact, a distinction was usually made between table-carpets and floor-carpets (or 'foot carpets'). The French likewise tended to speak of a *tapis à pied* or *tapis de pied*.[89]

I have already surveyed the various kinds of Oriental carpet that were available in Europe in the seventeenth century and we have discussed the European imitation of such pile-surfaced materials—principally turkeywork and Savonnerie carpets. Carpets were expensive and were therefore treated with respect. The Elector of Brandenburg was so proud of his Turkish carpets that, in 1617, he was still keeping them in his Cabinet of Curiosities—his *Wunderkammer* (see p. 302).[90] One gets the impression that carpets were commonly kept in store and only brought out on important occasions or when the family was in residence.[91] Large carpets had to be placed on the floor but small ones made a good show lying on a table, so there was a tendency first of all to place them there.[92] Only when carpets became fairly common, after the middle of the century, did it become rare in England and France to have pile carpets on tables, but the Dutch so liked the effect that they maintained the practice right through the century (Plate 108 and Colour Plate XIII).

Oriental carpets came in something like standard sizes. Occasionally commissions were placed through agents in the East for a carpet with some special feature—with the owner's coat-of-arms woven into the pattern, or of an unusual shape. However, it was easier to get special orders carried out in Europe. Turkeywork carpets might be made to fit a special position—usually a table-top but also, say, a space by a bed or in an alcove. They also not uncommonly had the owner's arms inwoven.[93] As for the carpets produced at the Savonnerie works, they were invariably ordered with a special position in mind[94] but, because they were all produced for royal consumption in France and nothing comparable was being made elsewhere in the seventeenth century, they constitute an exceptional form of floor-covering which hardly affects the general picture at all.

Tapestries were rarely laid on the floor[95] but carpets produced in the tapestry-weaving technique existed in the seventeenth century, although probably not in

117. Black and white rush matting illustrated in a Spanish painting of about 1620. Probably an African mat, an elaborate version of that to be seen in Plate 116.

large quantities. Cardinal Mazarin had a *tapis* of Brussels *haute-lisse* (which meant tapestry to the layman at the time)[96] and Savary des Bruslons tells us that, anyway by 1723, tapestry carpets were being woven at Rouen, Arras and Felletin.[97] The Aubusson factory, which has since given its name to tapestry-woven carpets as a class, was not started until 1743.

Blankets and 'ruggs' of various kinds might also be used on the floor in bedrooms, placed round the bed. Such materials came ready-made to size, although 'fledge blankets' were apparently made up from widths of a material known as 'fledge'.

Judging by inventories, embroidered floor-carpets were not at all common in the seventeenth century. On the floor round a bed at Hengrave Hall in Elizabethan times were three embroidered carpets 'of Englishe worke', and Lady Dorchester owned 'a black footcloth of cloth imbroydered round in borders with silk fringe' valued at £8.[98] Louis XIV had 'un petit tapis de toile de cotton blanche brodé . . . en or et argent' [a small carpet of white cotton . . . embroidered with gold and silver] and another quilted in small squares, but it is not certain that they were meant to go on the floor.[99]

When leather carpets are mentioned in seventeenth-century inventories, the reference is usually to a protective cover of some sort. These might lie on the floor, like the 'two leather Covers for the Stepp' which protected the elaborate marquetry of the daïs in the Queen's Bedchamber at Ham House,[100] in which case they were probably of scorched leather. But there do seem to have been actual carpets of leather which could be left in position even on grand occasions. For example, one closet at Tart Hall was 'covered with a carpett of yellow leather' while another had one of white leather.[101] One might perhaps think they there served as protection for elaborate floors (although no marquetry floors had apparently been made in England by that date) but the Earl of Arundel's bed also stood on a yellow leather floor-cover and this can only have been removable in exceptional circumstances. Cardinal Mazarin also owned 'un tapis de cuir rouge imprimé' which could have been 'printed' like a tooled book-binding.[102] It is listed among the other splendid *tapis* in his collection and certainly does not seem to have been merely a protective cover. Furs had been used on the floor in the Middle Ages but were rarely to be seen there in fashionable circles during the seventeenth century. William III had 'one baires skeen with the haire on' on the floor of his Great Closet at Kensington Palace and there was another bearskin on the floor of the Chapel,[103] but these seem to have been rarities.

CHAPTER VII
Beds, Cloths of Estate and Couches

ALL but the humblest beds in the seventeenth century had hangings. Being therefore large pieces of furniture, they automatically came to occupy a prominent position in the room where they stood. But the beds in important bedchambers also embodied a high degree of symbolism, coming thus to constitute the focal point of the bedchamber they occupied. For these reasons, a great deal of attention was paid to the design and decoration of beds in the seventeenth century and no further excuse need be made for devoting a separate chapter to them. Moreover, since canopies, or 'cloths of estate', were related to hung beds, both symbolically and structurally, it seems sensible to discuss them together. However, we must first survey the various types of bed; then we can consider bed-hangings and bed-clothes.

THE VARIOUS TYPES OF BED

The terms used for the various components of a seventeenth-century bed are set out in the key to the accompanying diagram of an imaginary bed (Plate 118). Only the word 'tester' needs special explanation. This was the word used throughout the century for the flat, roof-like component supported above the bed by the posts, although the mediaeval word 'ceilour' was still very occasionally used in reference to this component in early seventeenth-century inventories.[1] Most beds, incidentally, stood with their heads to the wall so that three sides were exposed. I shall discuss the exceptions to this rule later.

The simplest form of bed consists of a frame with four short posts at the corners forming legs. Greater rigidity can be obtained by carrying up the posts some inches above the frame and by fitting a cross-piece or board across at the head—the 'headboard'. Such beds existed in earliest times. In the seventeenth century, they were known in French as *couches* or *couchettes*, according to their size.[2] While a *couche* could be a simple structure, used by people of humble station, it could also be a very grand piece of furniture, perhaps with an elaborate headboard or with its posts extended to form notable features. The 'couch beddstead, the head posts, post[s], and feete thereof richly guilt' that belonged to Charles I (or perhaps to Henrietta Maria) was of this type, as must have been the 'couche de bois de chesne à pilliers tournez' [bed with an oak bedstock, with turned posts] mentioned in a French inventory of 1556.[3] Molière's 'couche à pieds d'aiglon, peints de bronze vert, avec un dossier peint et doré, sculpture et dorure' [*couche* with eagle's feet, painted a green bronze colour [i.e. bronzed], with painted and gilt headboard, carved and gilded] may also have been of this sort although it may equally well have been the sort of couch that we would now call a 'day-bed'.[4] Couches and day-beds are discussed below (see p. 172).

This basic form of bed could have hangings suspended round it; indeed, this was how bed-hangings first evolved in the early Middle Ages. The hangings had at first been held up on rods stretching across the room or by means of cords attached to hooks in the ceiling. At the Château de Turenne in 1615 there was what must have

149

118. Diagram showing the parts of a seventeenth-century bed with the main bed-curtains omitted for the sake of clarity.

   a. Tester.
   b. Cup with plumes (ostrich feather *panaches*, and *aigrettes*).
   c. Buttons and loops (originally linked the valances but became decorative, as here).
   d. Outer valance (*pente*).
   e. Inner valance (*pente*).
   f. Headcloth (*dossier*).
   g. Headboard.
   h. Counterpoint.
   j. Base valance (*pente* or *soubassement*).
   k. Cantoon (*cantonnière*).
   l. Bonegrace (*bonnegrâce*).
   m. Post with its case.
   n. Feet, the lowest part of the bedstock.

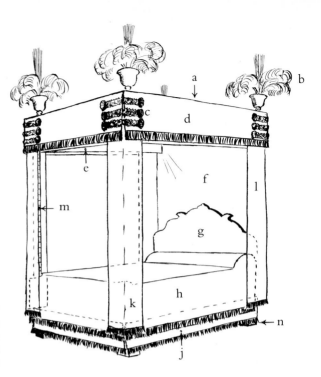

119. An elaborate version of the *couche* or *couchette* with a separate canopy suspended over it. This is probably the daybed of a fashionable French lady (compare with Madame de Montespan's couch shown in Plate 20).

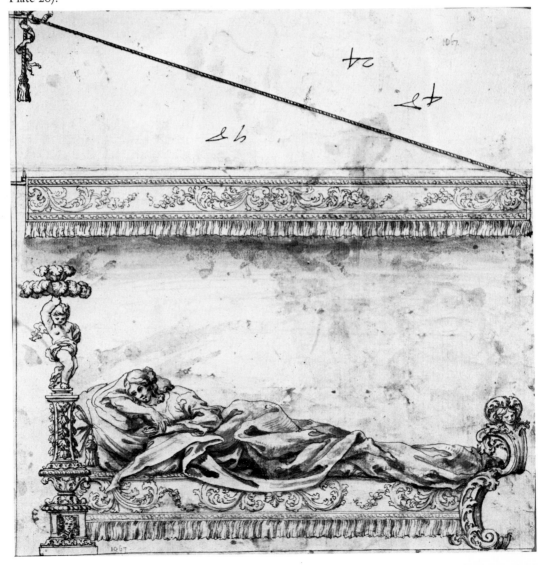

been a folding bed, intended for travelling, which is described as a 'couchette de bois de noyer . . . montant à vis' which was 'faictes à pavillon' [a *couchette* of walnut wood . . . that screws together . . . with a canopy].⁵ The travelling-bed of Henri IV's mistress, Gabrielle d'Estrées, which will have had hangings of great refinement, was likewise called a *couchette*⁶ and the bed shown in Plate 14, which stood in the *Trianon de Porcelaine* at Versailles, and has hangings of the greatest complexity, is described in the royal inventory as 'un lit extraordinaire dont le bois est une couchette' [an extraordinary bed of which the bedstock is a *couchette*]. The form of bed known as a *lit à la romaine* should presumably also be classed with the *couches* and *couchettes*: they too could have separate hangings (Plate 121).

At the other end of the social scale was the 'trundle-bedstead', or 'truckle bed', which was also a simple bedstead. It was mounted on wheels and could be stowed under the main bed in the room.⁷ An inventory of 1513 mentions a *couchette* that was 'soud ledict grant lit' [beneath the aforesaid large bed] while one of 1572 refers to a bed 'au-dessous duquel y a une couchette' [under which is a *couchette*].⁸ Personal

120. Seen from the foot-end, this magnificent bed must have been similar to that shown in Plate 119 but has a much more complicated canopy with a scene of Venus discovering Cupid painted or embroidered on the headcloth. Thought to date from 1669 and to be by Le Brun.

121. Two proposals for *lits à la Romaine* by Jean Le Pautre, probably published about 1670. Such *couches* were meant to have separate canopies as Plate 119 shows.

122. A very elaborate late sixteenth-century travelling bed (field bed), now lacking its bed-curtains and valances. The bedstock is held together with bolts (the heads of two may be seen at the foot end) while the head- and foot-boards are secured with hooks. The crestings are hinged and the posts can be dismantled.

123 & 124. (below) A seventeenth-century field bed that folds into itself and forms a travelling-box. The top section of the posts at the head are missing. Webbing straps ran lengthwise and were secured by a cord at the headboard.

servants could then sleep close to their masters.[9] A variant was the *couchette* on trestles (*sur pliant*) which was to be seen in a French country-house in 1688.[10] It had a *pavillon*—a suspended canopy—of serge.

The mediaeval form of bed-hangings, which were suspended with cords from the ceiling, somewhat resembled a hovering sparrowhawk and was therefore called an *épervier*. This was rendered as 'sparver' in English. A few beds of this kind seem to have lingered on into the seventeenth century. There was 'a fayre lardge sparver and beds' head with double vallance of cloth of golde' at Hardwick early in the century, while the 'furniture for a sparver bed' (consisting of a tester, headcloth, valances and five curtains) was in store at Knole in 1645.[11] But occasionally an additional canopy was suspended over a bed that already had its own tester (Plate 136). For example, in 1641 we find the Earl of Arundel had 'a great sparver about over the bed of the like stuff [as the bed], tyed up with yellow silk strings.'[12] Cardinal Mazarin had something similar—a bed complete with posts supporting the tester and valances, and with an additional *daïs* suspended above by means of silk cords.[13] As we shall see, the word *daïs* in French means a canopy.

Beds with posts supporting the tester (and therefore the curtains, valances and headcloth) had been evolved by the fifteenth century. The earliest form of bed with posts is likely to have been the so-called 'field bed' (*lit de camp*) which could be folded and was used, not only by military gentlemen in the field, but by all people of rank when travelling.[14] When travelling, one could not expect always to find convenient places in the ceiling from which to suspend the bed-hangings in the usual way, so it was necessary to provide posts with the bed to hold them up instead (Plate 122).

Field beds were first and foremost practical pieces of furniture. When dismantled they were stowed in a bag or a box (Plates 123 and 124).[15] They slotted together and the components were held in place by hooks or screws. They tended to be simple in outline but luxurious versions were made for rich people, with expensive hangings and decorated headboards.[16] Their testers did not have cornices, which could get damaged, but might have valances of intricate shape hanging from them.[17] Field beds might be rectangular, brick-shaped structures but some had hipped, pyramid-shaped testers.[18] Many seem to have had one end sloping (Plate 125) and some even

125. A Parisian field bed of the 1690s. It folds into a small bundle of wooden members and hangings which no doubt fitted into a bag. Such a bed might have been called a 'slope bedstead' in England.

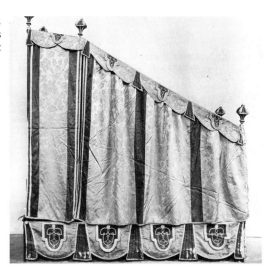

had both ends sloping.[19] The term 'slope bedstead' which occurs in several seventeenth-century inventories, must refer to beds of this form.[20] Randle Holme explains that a 'cant bed' can fit under a sloping roof, and many beds of this shape may merely have been simple beds used by relatively humble members of a household, living in rooms high under the roof.[21] Apart from the fact that such beds could not readily be dismantled, there would be little difference between them and the field bed version. Grand field beds must have been prized possessions and they were often set up in quite important rooms in the owner's house, particularly in the early part of the century.[22] Later, they become rarer. There was a 'camp bed' at Dyrham at the end of the century and Dr Martin Lister tells of a certain retired French field-marshal who in 1699 'very obligingly showed us his own apartment . . . and in his chamber his little red damask field bed, which he lay in now, and which had also served him when he commanded on the Rhine'.[23]

As aristocratic life became more static during the sixteenth century, the principal beds in a house could be allowed to remain where they were placed, year in, year out. There was no longer any need for them to be easily dismantled, and important beds could therefore be constructed in a far more substantial manner. The massive bed, with strikingly decorated wooden components, thus came to be developed, reaching the high point of its evolution shortly before 1600 (Plate 126). It is a form which is familiar to everyone, since, being robust, so many specimens have survived. It will, however, become clear that it was not the only form of bed that was in fashion at the time.

Such an obtrusive piece of furniture, standing in a prominent position in an important room, quickly gained the attention of the architect and those decorating interiors, and a number of designs for such beds were published in engraved form in the sixteenth century (Plate 91).[24] These proposals chiefly concerned the wooden components of the bed, incidentally; the design of the hangings was still in most cases left to the upholsterer. Nevertheless, these beds became architectural in character and, generally speaking, their ornament was made consonant with that of the rooms in which they were to stand.

Writers of inventories sometimes noted that a bed was of oak or of walnut, and we can usually then safely assume that the bed was of the massive sort, with the wooden members showing prominently. Otherwise beds in the seventeenth century were normally identified by the nature of their hangings (e.g. 'the green velvet bed'), so it would normally only be where the woodwork was especially prominent that it would be mentioned. The fact that the tester of such a bed was of wood (usually panelled) was also noteworthy.[25] On the other hand, the elaborate headboards, with their panelled and carved ornament, do not seem to have attracted much attention. Inlay, carving, painting and gilding are mentioned, however.[26] Far more care was taken in describing the hangings and we need to be reminded that, for all the ebullience of their wooden parts, the most conspicuous parts of these beds

VIII. (right) Seventeenth-century woollen (worsted) upholstery materials of the more elaborate sort.
    a. Two small pieces of woollen velvet made up as a panel about 32 cms high.
    b. Part of a woollen hanging (here shown partly reversed) which may be of 'dornix'. The yellow sprigs are about 7 cms high.
    c. Three specimens of wool and linen material which may also loosely have been classed as 'dornix' at the time.

a

b

c

remained their textile components, for the headboard would largely have been in shadow and the posts were masked by the curtains.

The term 'standing bed' occurs frequently in inventories from the first decades of the seventeenth century. It may refer to a specific type of bed[27] but it seems more probable that it was used in reference to any substantial and essentially immovable bed—including the massive type I have been discussing.[28] But clearly the standing bed with 'a tester of redde velvet and gold' at Sir Henry Unton's house in 1595[29] cannot have been of the type with a wooden tester. Moreover, one of the two standing beds in the nursery at Marton Hall is described as being 'with poulles' (i.e. poles or columns, rather than 'with posts' which implies carving) while the other was 'without poules'.[30] The latter would seem to have been a *couche* with only low posts at the corners. Whatever the case, it was presumably not intended that any of these beds were to be moved in the ordinary course of events.

IX. (left) A rare survival: a fine example of a painted hanging. Part of a set of canvas wall-hangings with scenes from the life of Alexander the Great signed by Jan and Daniel Smit of Amsterdam. Separate borderings were obtainable with which to trim a panel to any size required. This hanging is of unusually fine quality.

126. A bed of the massive kind, showing how the hangings masked much of the woodwork. A bed of the same general class as the Great Bed of Ware but with a hipped roof and finials. From a Danish engraving of 1645.

The massive type of bed, with its architectural form, had a bold cornice round the edges of the tester below which a valance of a textile material was invariably attached (Plate 126). Without this feature, the proportions of the whole structure are altered. As surviving beds of this class are today mostly shown without hangings, the impression now given is somewhat misleading, for not only does the tester look wrong without its valances but the carved posts were not meant to be so obtrusive; they were meant to peep out from a rich tumble of hangings and bedclothes.

This type of bed also seems normally to have had a flat top in France and England, but in Holland, Germany and Scandinavia domed or hipped testers were favoured (Plate 126). Beds with domed testers are also occasionally mentioned later in the century. The Duchess of Ormonde had one at Kilkenny in the 1680s. At the same time her husband had a 'pillar bedstead with a rising tester' which was presumably hipped.[31]

In the Netherlands a box-like form of bed was popular. It was enclosed with panelling on all sides but one, where there was a curtain over the opening (Plates 127 and 198)).[32] This form usually stood against the wall and in, some cases such beds were actually built into the wall or were incorporated into the scheme of panelling. Beds tended anyway to be placed in the corners of the room in the Low Countries, the 'aristocratic' position with the bed standing out from the central point of a wall being only gradually adopted, as far as one can judge—presumably as Frenchified ways came to be accepted.

Scholars have often been misled by the term 'canopy bed' which occurs frequently in inventories from the first half of the century. The 'canopy' was suspended over the head of the bed (which was of *couche* form) by means of a cord attached to the ceiling (Plates 36, 113 and 128). It usually consisted of a cone-shaped or domed 'bowl'[33] with a valance all round, and with two or three large curtains that were often called 'trains' because they had to drag (*trainer* in French) on the ground, in order to be long enough to reach out and also encompass the foot-end of the bed (Plate 129).[34] The French called such canopies *pavillons*.[35] The coat of arms of the Upholsterers' Company of London bears '3 pavilions ermine, lined azure, garnished or . . .' and, apart from the central tent-poles, these pavilions resemble the

127. (upper left) A Dutch box-bed with panelled wooden ends and base; 1624. Only one side was open and fitted with curtains. Note the warming-pan hanging at the foot end, and the striped bed-clothes. On the floor lies a farthingale, the padded waist-ring that was at this time fast going out of fashion.

128. (lower left) A 'canopy bed' showing the bowl suspended by a cord from the ceiling. Dutch; 1660s.

129. (right) Diagram of a canopy bed with its 'trains' tied back. The smaller sketch shows how the trains reached out to cover the foot end. The detail shows a 'soft' bowl depicted in several paintings by Terborch.

130. (far right) One of the three pavilions represented in the coat of arms of the Upholders' Company of London. When originally granted in 1465 the device was described as a 'sparver'.

131. What may be a 'lit à housse'. It has pairs of cords (the outer cords are clearly shown) by means of which the curtains can be tied up out of the way (see Plate 132). Note the *cantonnières* at the corners.

pavillons or canopies of 'canopy beds', with a fancy conical bowl topped by a finial, and depending curtains (Plate 130).[36] The top of such a canopy might of course be square instead of round, in which case it could be classed as a 'sparver' (see p. 153). The Upholsterers' bearings were actually called sparvers in the original grant of arms in 1465.[37] Jean Le Pautre was clearly fascinated by this type of bed and published a number of engravings depicting elaborate structures of this class in the middle of the century (Plate 36).

The type of bed which became far more popular than any other in the seventeenth century was that known all over Europe as a 'French bed' although its popularity between about 1620 and 1680 was such that most references to beds of an unspecified nature probably concern this type (Plate 136). They are to be seen in numerous illustrations of the period but hardly any specimens have survived because the wooden components were of such simple character that they were not considered worth preserving once the hangings had become soiled and tattered, and the bed was out of date.

The simple wooden framework of this type of bed supported the hangings so as to form a plain, rectangular box. There was no cornice running round the top; the

132. Tying up the curtains of a bed of a similar type to that shown in Plate 131. This bed does not have *cantonnières*. Note how the post is encased with a textile sheath trimmed en suite with the curtains.

curtains hung straight down from the top rails. In the simplest form of such beds, there were three curtains, one to each of the exposed sides, nailed to the top rails. These curtains could be tied up out of the way by means of pairs of cords hanging down from the same top rails, rather like the tapes used for tying up the door of a tent (Plates 2 and 131). An engraving by Bosse shows a servant in the act of tying up a curtain on such a bed, and the cords may be seen in several other contemporary illustrations (Plate 132). A bed in Charles I's possession must have been of this type as it had eighteen 'tassells with stringes', six to each side, so the curtains will have hung in four festoons on each side, when tied up[38].

The more complicated and common form of such beds had curtains that moved horizontally on rods in the usual way. In this case the rods and rings were masked by valances but there was still no cornice and the outline was still essentially brick-shaped (Plates 133–6). Both the pull-up and the sliding forms, however, had their outlines enlivened by four prominent finials on the flat top. The status of the bed was otherwise entirely demonstrated by the cost of the hangings and the degree of richness of the trimmings. No wooden components were visible; even the posts were encased in material.

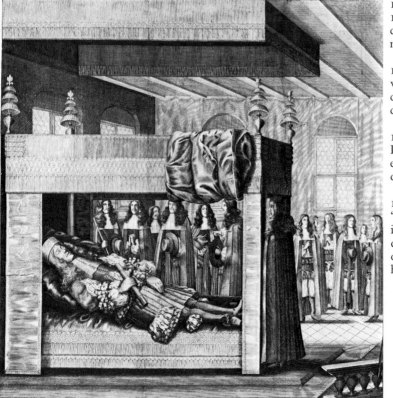

133. (upper far left) A Parisian engraving of about 1614 showing a fully-developed 'French bed'. It does not appear to have *cantonnières* but details are not drawn with much care in this picture.

134. (lower far left) A Dutch bedchamber in 1624 with a 'French bed' installed. On the quilted counter-point lie piled cushions and some bridal crowns.

135. (above) Two 'French beds' set up in a Danish bedchamber in 1645. Instead of draught-excluding *cantonnières*, these beds have their curtains joined with ribbons at the corners.

136. (left) A German prince lying in state on a 'French bed' above which an additional canopy is suspended. The *cantonnières* and *bonnegrâces* are clearly shown. The curtains have been slung up out of the way onto the top of the tester. The hangings appear to be of watered silk.

138. Even in the State Bedchamber of Louis XIV himself the bed would be simple in outline, as this proposal for the *Chambre du Roi* at Versailles of 1679 shows. In France, magnificence in state beds was achieved by means of sumptuous materials, rich trimmings and splendid *panaches*. Only in informal settings was the fancy given a free rein (see Plate 14). Note the alcove protected by its balustrade.

139. Sketch of Louis XIV's State Bed at Versailles in the early 1680s (based on contemporary illustrations) showing the rectilinear shape favoured for formal beds in France. Only a small cornice breaks the severe lines; richness is effected by the elaborate valances.

137. (left) A Parisian bed of 1680, still simple in outline but richly trimmed with gold lace. It has a slight doming in the tester which can hardly be seen from the front. The bed appears to have been cut down somewhat; the *pentes* of the counterpoint would normally have been deeper and the curtains longer to correspond.

These two related forms of bed were probably evolved from the field bed which also had a simple wooden structure and an uncomplicated outline. The shape must have struck someone as resembling a fine bed with its protective cover of an inexpensive material draped over it. At any rate, it seems at first to have been called a *lit à housse*, (the French for a loose-cover being *une housse*).[39] The link with the field bed is indicated by the 'lict de campagne à housse' which belonged to Gabrielle d'Estrées at the end of the sixteenth century.[40] This may have had curtains of the pull-up type. The 'lit carré' [rectangular bed] she also owned may have been of the more usual type of 'French bed' with sliding curtains.[41] But, once this sort of bed had become the most common form, there would no longer have been any reason to be specific and one could simply call it *un lit*—a bed.

Beds of this kind (both variants) were from an early date provided with *cantonnières* and *bonnegrâces* ('cantoons' and 'bonegraces', in English) which were narrow curtains at the corners that closed the gaps between the main curtains (Plate 118). If these features were at first peculiar to 'French beds', as seems possible, then it is perhaps worth noting that the earliest recorded reference to a bed with *bonnegrâces* seems to be in a French royal inventory of 1589, while *cantonnières* are at any rate mentioned early in the seventeenth century.[42] They must at first only have been fitted to beds of great luxury. There should, technically speaking, only be a pair of each on a bed but the terms were sometimes confused; the early reference of 1589, for instance, is to four *bonnegrâces*, two of which would normally have been called *cantonnières*, while a bed at Ham House was described in 1679 as having four

165

'cantoons'.[43] It would anyway seem that the 'French bed' was being evolved during the last decades of the sixteenth century. Three 'French beds' are listed in the inventory of Sir Henry Unton in 1596; although he had been ambassador to France in 1591–2, it is evident from the context that the references are to a class of bed. An early illustration of such a bed is to be seen in Salomon de Caus' *Perspective*, published in 1612, although it appears to lack *bonnegrâces* (perhaps because it seems to be a fairly humble bed) and its base is boxed in. An engraving published in Paris some two years later shows this kind of bed in its fully developed form (Plate 133).

Beds grew taller during the second half of the century (Plates 137 and 140). The French continued to favour the rectilinear form, even for the grandest settings,[44] the only concession to a lively outline being in the fancy contours given to the valances which, however, remained essentially two-dimensional (Plates 139 and 140). Moreover, the richness of the trimming continued to increase (Plate 137). The English and the Dutch, on the other hand, preferred a more elaborate form of tester with a cornice. These flaring cornices were often pierced and were generally covered with the same materials as the bed-hangings (Plate 142). Daniel Marot published many designs for beds of this sort, the complicated lineaments of which were in great contrast to the contemporary French form (Plate 50). However, the latter was current at the same time in England (and no doubt in Holland as well),[45] whereas the Marot type of bed does not seem to have found favour in France at all, at any rate, not for beds of a formal nature. But Marot may have been familiar with certain fantastic beds that had been created for light-hearted settings, such as the beds at the *Trianon de Porcelaine* (Plates 14 and 15), before he left his native country in 1684 to go into exile in Holland and England. These wild exercises were *tours de force* of the upholsterer's art and may have made a strong impression on the young artist who then subsequently applied similar features to state beds—a notion that would surely have struck stay-at-home Frenchmen as highly inappropriate!

Right from the beginning of the century there had been half-tester beds which were often called 'half-headed' (Plate 145).[46] Since the tester only covered the head-half of the bed, it would seem that many 'canopy-beds' were also described as 'half-headed', as a canopy (i.e. *pavillon*) is mentioned immediately afterwards.[47] Such beds were used by persons of secondary status—children of the family, tutors, ladies in waiting, etc. Towards the middle of the century a new form of grand bed became fashionable. This was the *lit d'ange* which had a flying tester suspended over the whole sleeping surface of the bed (Plate 141). Because the tester was suspended (with cords or chains) it in some respects resembled a canopy bed with its bowl hanging from a cord. The Dutch compiler of an inventory of the Palace at the Noordeinde at The Hague in 1633 recognised this when he explained that the Princess's bed had summer hangings 'op de maniere van een pavillioen, anders genaent een lict à l'ange' [in the manner of a *pavillon*, otherwise known as a *lit d'ange*].[48] Tessin saw the State

---

140. (right) State bed probably made for James II about 1685. This shows a late stage in the development of the grandest type of 'French bed', with valances of fancy outline, and with the increased height favoured late in the century. The form is still essentially rectilinear, however. Conflicting evidence makes it difficult to decide whether this actual bed was made in Paris or by a French upholsterer working for the Crown in London. This is the most splendid of the few surviving seventeenth-century beds. It is accompanied by a set of armchairs and squab-frames (in this view only the chair behind the bed is en suite; see Plate 152).

Bed of Louis XIV at Versailles in 1687 and described it minutely[49] 'Le lict est en forme de lict d'ange et admirablement beau', he wrote, 'le pavillon est suspendu au toict avec des cordons et houppes d'or, qui les soustiennent par les petits enroullements dorés au coins du pavillon.' [The bed is in the form of a *lit d'ange* and is astonishingly beautiful . . . the tester is suspended from the ceiling by means or cords and tassels of gold which are held by little gilt scrolls at the corners of the tester.][49] Five years later it was said that the ability to judge 'le grand art de retrousser les rideaux d'une lit d'ange' [the great art of tying up the curtains of a *lit d'ange*] was the sign of a true courtier,[50] and the tying back of the curtains did indeed offer the Parisian upholsterers of the day plenty of scope to display their skills. The tester of the *lit d'ange* at Versailles was called an *impériale* by Tessin although the whole ensemble he calls a *pavillon*. Indeed, such beds might be called 'lits à impériale'.[51] The bed Celia Fiennes saw in the Duke of Norfolk's apartment at Windsor Castle at the end of the century was presumably a *lit d'ange* and is likely to have been in the style Daniel Marot was then publicising in England and Holland (Plates 141–4). She called it 'a half bedstead as the new mode'.[52]

In inventories from the early part of the century, reference is often made to 'livery bedsteads'. They must have been fairly simple as they were to be found in relatively humble rooms in large houses. Sometimes they had their own separate canopy (Plate 146).[53] Maybe this was just a form of *couchette* that could be set up (*livré*) where required, for servants or guests. I have already discussed the *couchette* and its wheeled

141. (far left) Design for a state bed with a flying tester by Daniel Marot. Anglo-Dutch; about 1690. The iron rod running rather incongruously outside the tester is for the protective curtain (see Plate 144). The *portière* is en suite. This form of bed owes much to the Parisian *lits à la Romaine* or *couchettes* with canopies from the middle of the century (see Plates 14, 15, 119, 120 and 121).

142. (centre left) An English state bed of the 1690s. Note the pierced and flaring cornice so characteristic of English beds at this period. See Plates 97 and 98 for details from this bed which was made for the first Earl of Melville.

143. (left) Proposals by Marot for beds with flying testers; about 1700.

version, the trundle bed (p. 151). Beds for servants were tucked away into odd corners and various devices were adopted to hide away the bedding during the daytime. Squares of ticking or canvas, filled with straw, and called pallets could be laid directly on the floor or set out on some sort of board. Personal servants often slept by the doors to their master's or mistress's apartment and acted as a kind of bodyguard. On the landing outside the main entrance to the Countess of Shrewsbury's rooms at Hardwick stood 'a bedsted to turne up like a chest' while there were pallets by many of the other doors.[54] There was a 'trunke bedstead' at the Countess of Leicester's house and a 'settle bedstead' at Tart Hall.[55] Dean Goodwin had a 'press bedstead' which must have been similar to the 'banc à coucher en forme d'armoire' [sleeping-bench in the form of a cupboard] mentioned in a French inventory.[56] The porter at Ham House slept by the front door that he controlled; his bed was described as 'one presse bed of walnutree' and its bedding.[57]

When the famous hospital, the Hôtel de Dieu, was established in 1623, it was equipped with bedsteads of iron so they would be easier to keep clean and free of vermin. But the box-like hangings were of course still of a textile material so the gain can only have been partial.[58] Since wicker chairs were quite common in England in the seventeenth century one would expect to find beds of this material over here, too, but this is not the case. There was a basketwork bed (*Korbbette*) at Copenhagen Castle in 1638, however.[59] Hammocks were not unknown, on the other hand. There was a 'cotton hamocke' at Knole in 1645 and Prince Maurice of

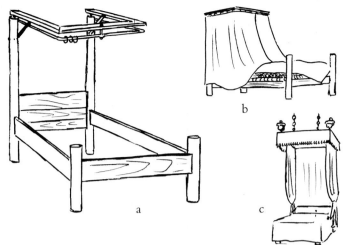

145.
  a. Sketch of a simple bed with a half-headed tester at Hardwick Hall dating from the seventeenth century.
  b. How the bed presumably looked when furnished with hangings.
  c. Sketch of a grander type of half-tester with the chains suspending the tester from the ceiling indicated.

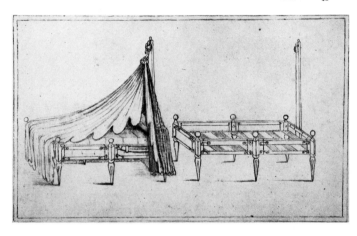

146. Sketch of a French folding bed, perhaps for servants or guards, or possibly for travelling.

147. Eighteenth century drawing of a ceremonial couch of state at Hardwick. The wooden structure of the couch itself survives (Plate 148), but this drawing indicates how it was originally dressed, under its canopy and flanked by a pair of stools. The arrangement is the same as that adopted for a more common form of chair of state like those shown in Plates 168 and 169.

144. (far left) Drawing by Marot of a bed with informative notes in his handwriting. For example, the iron rod (*verger d'assier*) encircling the tester is for a curtain that is a 'surtout, pour conserver le lict contre la poussier' which may be pulled 'jusque au millieu' (i.e. to meet in the middle at the foot end). The main bed-curtains run between 'les 2 campanes du lict marqué A'. The bed is of crimson velvet lined with an 'Estof d'or ou d'argent'.

Nassau (1604–79) once presented the King of France with 'un lit à la chinoise, fait de rezeaux de corde de fil vert pour estre suspendu' [a bed in the Chinese manner, made from a network of green fibre cords, which can be suspended].[60]

The 'clothes of estate' or canopies that were suspended over the principal seat of honour in a room set out for ceremonial use were formed like a tester of the period, with valances, curtains and a back-cloth (Plates 147 and 166). We have already noted that they might be suspended above the tester of an important bed (Plate 136). More often a canopy was hung over a chair of state or throne. Occasionally, they were hung above the portrait or the sculptured bust of some absent person who was being honoured (Plate 12). In England, it seems that anyone over the rank of earl rated a canopy when he or she was seated in state, and there might be more than one canopy set up in an important house.[61] The practice varied from country to country, however.[62] The chair of state, which was usually covered en suite with the canopy and might not only have a footstool but also one or more pairs of stools to flank it,[63] was normally placed on a raised platform or daïs. It should, incidentally, be noted that this word was used by the French to denote the cloth of estate, or the whole ensemble but not simply the raised platform.[64]

Chairs of state are discussed more fully in the next chapter but something should here be said about couches, a variant of which might serve as a ceremonial seat of estate.

We have seen that a *couche* or *couchette* was a simple form of bed, and it of course lent itself not only to sleeping on at night but could also be used as a day-bed. Day-beds seem already to have existed in the late Middle Ages and were certainly to be found in fashionable houses in France and England by 1600 (Plate 205). The couch must have acquired a high degree of symbolism because it was evidence of conspicuous luxury and therefore of presumed wealth and power, for only the very grand could spend time during the day lolling about. At any rate, a version of the couch was adopted to serve as a seat of state under a canopy, and we find several references to couches with canopies in inventories of the second quarter of the seventeenth century.[65] Judging from the surviving ceremonial couch at Hardwick, which is illustrated still standing under its square canopy in an eighteenth-century drawing, these formal pieces of seat-furniture stood with one side against the wall so that the ends of the *couche* now formed arms (Plate 147). The ends were made to slope outwards so as to accommodate large cushions against which one could lean.[66] The *couche* serving as a day-bed (a *lit de repos*), on the other hand, seems normally to have had a single end or head-board (Plate 208),[67] but such couches might also be furnished with a canopy, probably a *pavillon* rather than a square canopy of state.[68] No doubt the essentially informal day-bed ensemble was smaller in scale than the ceremonial variant but we now have only the context to guide us in deciding whether a reference to a couch and canopy concerns the one form or the other. The distinction was probably quite clear at the time, as an exchange in John Fletcher's play *Rule a Wife and Have a Wife* of 1624 suggests:

MARGARITA: Is the great couche up, the Duke of Medina sent?
ALTEA: 'Tis up and ready.
MARGARITA: And day-beds in all chambers?
ALTEA: In all, lady.

148. The remains of the ceremonial couch illustrated in Plate 147. Painted red. Only the top inner faces of the sloping ends are decorated since these areas were not masked by the upholstery. The scrolling floral ornament no doubt imitates that which was on the covers of the cushions, squab and valances, decorated with a scroll pattern executed in embroidery. On the ends are also painted the arms of the second Earl of Devonshire and his wife who inherited Hardwick in 1625–6 and probably first set up this couch of state, soon afterwards.

149. Couch with hinged arm-rests, that may be adjusted by means of iron rods. Covered with gilt leather. English; 1640s. Presumably this was a ceremonial seat that stood under a canopy like that shown in Plate 147.

150. Sumptuously upholstered couch with hinged arm-rests that are adjusted by irons at the back. This famous piece of furniture at Knole is often called a sofa although it would probably have been known as a 'couch chair' when new, in the second quarter of the seventeenth century.

The great couch was 'up', presumably because it had a canopy that had been set up.

Some double-ended couches had hinged ends so that these arm-supports could better accommodate the large cushions one leant against. There was a leather-covered couch with hinged ends secured by ratchets at Forde Abbey earlier in this century (Plate 149).[69] The *reposoir* in a French mansion in 1621, described as being 'à vice dorées' (with gilt screws) probably had some form of adjusting mechanism like this.[70] Single-ended day-beds might also be fitted with such an adjustment (Plate 207). Day-beds, which relate also very closely to sofas, are discussed in the next chapter.

BED-HANGINGS

There might be anything from two to six main curtains on a bed but four was the commonest number. Only half-headed and canopy beds had two curtains or 'trains'. It was chiefly beds with curtains of the pull-up variety that had three, while only exceptionally splendid beds had six curtains. Curtains other than those of the pull-up sort hung from rings running on iron rods exactly like those used for window-curtains. The rings might be of iron, or horn or copper.

174

151. The fleur-de-lis on the crestings of this magnificent piece of late-seventeenth-century seat-furniture suggests it was designed to stand in some royal setting in France. With its double ends this recalls the ceremonial couches of earlier in the century (Plate 147). Can this form have been a 'lit de repos en canapée'?

A fine bed might have paired valances (inner and outer) which could be of equal depth or might have the inner set shallower than the outer. The outer valances were often more richly decorated than the curtains hanging below. Early in the century the valances, tester and head-cloth of a grand bed might even be of a different material from the curtains.[71] The base valances ('bases' or *soubassements*), which hung down between the legs, were usually fairly plain.

The massive wooden beds of the early part of the century had intricate headboards but other sorts of bed, notably the 'French beds' that became so fashionable after 1620 or so, had headcloths which might constitute a fairly simple hanging, perhaps with the owner's arms embroidered on it. From the middle of the century a low headboard of fancy outline and covered with material was customarily fitted in front of the headcloth. In beds of the Marot type the headboard could be a very complicated piece of ornament with pierced scrollwork and rich trimming, the material of the hangings being pasted to the carved wooden backing.

Together with the tester, it was the 'counterpoint' (counterpane) that was most elaborately decorated, usually with needlework or patterns contrived with applied trimming.[72] Its pattern was often reflected more simply on the underside of the tester. The counterpoint was often shaped so as to fit round the posts at the foot end

175

and so as to encompass the bolster at the head. It also had *pentes*, the three panels falling down the sides of the bed.[73] The counterpoint was meant to lie flat and be squared at the edges. In order to make sure this happened, Cardinal Mazarin had a set of 'trois tringles couvertes de lames d'argent avec broquettes d'argent, servans à mettre sous la courte pointe pour la rendre quarrée et unie' [three rods covered with silver plate with silver fastenings, used to put under the counterpoint so as to make it square and flat].[74] The servant making the bed might use a *baton de lit* to aid the process of flattening or tucking the counterpoint in under the bolster (if the counterpoint did not have a built-in bag).

Bed-hangings were mostly lined, usually with a light-weight material that contrasted in colour with that of the main material. If decorated, it was in a comparatively restful manner. The counterpoint and headcloth were frequently faced with the lining material.

To cap off the whole edifice, finials were usually fitted above the tester, over the posts. As they were to be viewed from the front only, the two rearmost finials on late seventeenth century beds were sometimes halved, as if split down the middle so that the resulting flat face was nearest the wall at the back. Finials might be simple turned knobs, perhaps gilded, but often they were faceted and vase-shaped, in which case the material of the hanging was usually pasted to the wooden core and the edges were trimmed with braid.[75] Such 'cupps' might have 'spriggs' or *aigrettes* of egret feathers rising stiffly from a socket at the top. More showy were the *bouquets de plume* which consisted of a bunch of ostrich plumes (*panaches*), sometimes centred on an *aigrette*, which were fixed in a vase-like finial.[76] Plumes were usually white but could be coloured.[77] Sometimes the *bouquets* were made to resemble actual flowers, either in the form of silk or metal artificial flowers, or carved as a compact composition and gilded.[78] 'French beds' of the third quarter of the century seem often to have had tiered finials like those shown in Plate 136.[79]

Most of the materials that were used for wall-hangings or window-curtains could also be used for the hanging of beds (see Chapter V and p. 139). Tapestry, however, was far too heavy to be used at all commonly[80] although coverlets of 'arras' are sometimes mentioned.[81] Brocatelle, which did not drape well on account of its structure (see p. 116), was also rarely used on beds[82] and the same applies to turkey-work and gilt leather (pp. 109 and 118). Embroidered hangings, on the other hand, were common on beds (they were usually called 'wrought' or 'worked' beds) and it is noteworthy that they mostly belonged to ladies.[83] Although the quality of the needlework on such ladies' beds may often have been high, it was probably 'domestic' in character—that is to say, it was mostly executed by the women of the household and as a result lacked some of the finesse to be seen in the best professional work.[84] The patterns, moreover, will mostly have been charming rather than elegant. Professional embroidery, on the other hand, tended to be worked to patterns from the main line of current ornamental motifs, often with the lavish use of gold or silver thread of various kinds. The distinction was of course not always as clear cut as is here implied but when men had beds with embroidered hangings, it will probably have been of the professional kind, and this effectively means that only men of considerable wealth had needlework beds because professional embroidery was very expensive. It is incidentally widely supposed that a common type of embroidered bed-hanging in the second half of the seventeenth century was the so-called 'crewel work hanging' which has large-leafed patterns executed usually in dark green and blue crewels (worsted thread) on a cream-coloured cotton and linen ground. Because the material is robust, many specimens survive but references to what could be hangings of this class are not all that common in seventeenth-century inventories.[85] What is more, they were probably not to be found in the grandest surroundings, where something more splendid would have been used.

As for trimmings, the same varieties were used on bed-hangings as on other forms of upholstery (see p. 127), and they were made up in ways similar to those employed for wall-hangings. Peculiar to bed-hangings, however, were the 'buttons and loops' which were applied straps of braid that linked the valances together at the corners. Originally there really was a loop at one end of each strap that was hitched over the corresponding 'button' or toggle, but soon the junction was made with disguised hooks and eyes, and the feature became purely decorative. It was standard on 'French beds' of the grander sort but was no doubt used on other types of bed as well.

I have already mentioned the fact that very important beds might have two sets of hangings, one for summer and one for winter (p. 106), and that bed-hangings might be stored in the Wardrobe Room except when the family was in residence. Indeed, since people had spent so much money on a rich bed, every precaution was naturally taken to protect the fragile and valuable textiles and their delicate trimmings. I have already given some examples of beds being covered with sheets or with loose-covers but, towards the end of the seventeenth century when the upholstery of a great bed might be of immense complexity, special 'case-curtains' were provided as a permanent feature. Daniel Marot shows such curtains on several of his engravings of beds and on a drawing (Plate 144) actually states that the curtain was fitted 'pour conserver le lit contre la poussière' [to protect the bed from dust]. The curtain ran on an iron rod fixed to the top of the tester and running round some six or eight inches out from the cornice. It does not seem to have worried anyone that the iron bar was rather obtrusive, judging from the illustrations, but maybe a certain satisfaction was derived from demonstrating in this way that the hangings of one's bed required such special protection. A protective cover round a bed was in French called a *tour de lit* (*un tour*, a circuit). A bed at Ham House in 1683 had a 'tower de leet' which must have been a feature of this nature.[86]

BEDCLOTHES

Seventeenth-century bedclothes were not really all that different from those we use today, except that they did not have sprung or foam mattresses, and a decent bed therefore had several soft mattresses.[87] However, I shall deal with each layer separately, starting with the lowest.

The mattresses might lie on boards ('lath bottoms') or on cords stretched across the frame of the bedstock,[88] or could be supported by a 'sack-cloth bottom'. If cords were used, a 'bed matt' was placed over them to provide a bearing surface.[89]

The 'featherbed' so often met with in seventeenth-century inventories was of course a mattress, a bag of canvas ticking or *coutil* filled with feathers. In France this was known as a *couette* or *coite*. It was normally of ordinary feathers(*de plume*) but the finest featherbeds were filled with swansdown.[90] 'Eiderdowns' (bags filled with the feathers of the Eider duck which was fairly common round the Baltic) existed in

Germany and Scandinavia but were used as an overlay, not as a mattress, and did not come into common use in France and England until the eighteenth century.[91]

The *matelas* was a mattress filled with wool. The best were filled with *bourrelanisse* or *laveton* which were the cheap clippings of wool or flock.[92] In England we find the same distinction being made between the 'feather bed' and the 'flock bed' (sometimes called 'wool bed'). The 'dust bedds' mentioned as being on some beds in Devonshire farmhouses in the middle of the century were probably cheap flock beds, and such mattresses were no doubt very dusty at the best of times.[93] It is possible that some mattresses were filled with cotton wool.[94]

The commonest (in both senses) form of mattress was straw-filled. The 'straw bed' or *paillasse* (which in English became 'paliasse') was of course the oldest form of underbedding of all. The Vikings, for example, spoke disparagingly of a 'straw death' when a warrior had had the misfortune to die in bed; a true hero expired on the battlefield and was then carried off by the Valkyries to Valhalla. On the other hand, the Swiss Guard at Versailles slept on straw mattresses called *baudets* which must have been similar to the 'pallets' used by servants in England (see p. 169). People of high standing did not normally sleep directly on straw-filled mattresses in France and England in the seventeenth century[95] although a straw bed might constitute the lowest of a set of mattresses forming the underlay of a grand bed.

Mattresses filled with horsehair seem to have come into use in France during the middle of the seventeenth century. Molière had two mattresses on his bed; one of flock and one 'rempli de crin' [filled with horsehair].[96] Horsehair, although rather hard, was thought to be hygienic.

All but the very humblest beds seem to have had sheets of some kind in the seventeenth century. We have already discussed the various qualities of linen sheeting and the coarse sheets made of canvas. The finest linen sheets came from Holland and most of the best bed-linen probably had decorated edges. Certainly the top sheet, which had to be turned down, often had a wide band of decoration along the top edge. For example, some sheets 'de toille d'Ollande' at the Château de Turenne, early in the century, were enriched with 'gaze blanche' (white gauze, which could be of linen or silk) embroidered with black silk and silver roses,[97] while the top sheet on the bed occupied on his wedding night by the Duc de Bourgogne was trimmed with *point de Venise* lace a yard deep.[98] Louis XIV had some strange sheets which were 'peints tout autour d'une frize et cinq fleurons au milieu et dans les quatre coins' [painted all round with a border and with five flowers at the centre and in the four corners].[99] On the Continent bed-linen was quite often striped and might sometimes be checked,[100] but in the higher strata of society people wanted their sheets to be as white as possible. An exception was the great prince mentioned by Brantôme in his *Dames Galantes* who made his mistresses sleep between sheets of black taffeta 'afin que leur blancheur et delicatesse de chair parust bien mieux parmy ce noir, et donnant plus d'esbat' [so that their whiteness and delicacy of skin appeared even better against the black, and providing more entertainment].

On top of the sheets one might lay one or more blankets or a 'rugge'. Blankets were normally of wool but fustian blankets (often listed as 'fusteans') were presumably of cotton with a heavy nap, while a few exceptional 'blankets' were of silk. Ruggs were rough so Lady Beauchamp had 'one rugge with a false cotton cover' (i.e. a loose cover of cotton).

Uppermost lay one or more quilts. There were serviceable quilts, provided for warmth, and there was the decorative counterpoint, or counterpane, which lay on top and often formed part of the suit of bed-hangings. The word 'counterpoint' comes from *contre point* (often rendered as *courte-pointe*) because the quilting was executed by 'piquure faite pointe contre pointe'.[101] It would seem that the counterpoint was often left on the bed while the occupant was in it although Lord Montague instructed the Yeoman of his Wardrobe in 1595 to remove the quilts from the beds in the guest-rooms at night and replace them with Irish ruggs. Whether this was a general practice throughout the house or whether it only applied to guest-rooms is not clear.

Quilts that were decorative presumably lay on top of the more utilitarian quilted 'coverlets'—those of linen or of cotton.[102] The Dutch exported fine quilts of cotton in large quantity and they are mentioned in many inventories.[103] Marseilles quilts seem to have been distinctive; many are listed in the French royal inventories and Lady Dorchester's 'French quilt' may have been of this class.[104]

Pillows and bolsters were usually filled with feathers.[105] In England, few beds had more than two pillows[106] but on the Continent it was a sign of rank to have a large number. The Comtesse de Soissons is said to have had 'des oreillers dans son lit, de toutes les grandeurs imaginables; il y en en avait même pour son pouce' [pillows in her bed, of every imaginable size; there was even one for her thumb].[107] The bolster stretched right across the full width of the bed and the pillow rested against it. Husband and wife normally had separate beds (indeed, they usually had separate apartments, see p. 58) but one does occasionally see contemporary illustrations of beds prepared for two people, with a pair of pillows lying against the bolster (Plate 2).

Randle Holme mentions 'bed-staves' as being necessary to a bed and illustrates one (Plate 319 [81]), describing it as 'a Bed staffe, of some termed a Burthen staffe'.[108] They are occasionally mentioned in inventories; they seem to have come in sets of six and were sometimes kept in a case. They could be coloured.[109] Samuel Johnson in fact furnishes us with an explanation of how bed-staves were used, for in his *Dictionary* of 1755 he states that a bedstaff was 'a Wooden pin stuck anciently on the sides of a bedstead to hold the cloathes from slipping either side'. Presumably they were stuck vertically down the sides of the bed, two to each exposed flank, between the mattresses and the wooden rails of the bedstock. Swedish peasants had a similar device which they called a *Sänghäst* (a bed horse); it was comb-like but served the same purpose, for there was nothing else to prevent the multiple quilts from sliding off the bed.

CHAPTER VIII
Upholstered Seat-furniture

Cushions and Squabs

Cushions, like tapestries, can be easily moved about. For this reason they were much prized in the Middle Ages among the seigneurial classes. A window-seat of stone or a bench made of a plank fixed to the wall in a castle could be transformed into a comfortable seat in a trice by draping a cloth over it and placing a cushion upon it. With a cushion, the top of a chest could be made accommodating, and the hard seats of wooden stools and chairs made soft. Cushions were a symbol of luxury and ease and soon therefore became associated also with high status and dignity. In Dutch, the phrase 'op het kussen zitten' still means to hold high office. Since they were so important, much attention was paid to the decoration of cushions and this tradition lasted deep into the seventeenth century. The long and loving descriptions of the numerous cushions at Hardwick are eloquent evidence of this.[1] In Elizabethan portraits, moreover, great pains were taken by the artist to depict accurately the long cushions that lie across the arms of the chairs of state that are so often shown in the background.

In the sixteenth century a cushion-cover consisted of two rectangles of material, more or less richly decorated, laced together round the edges to produce an envelope for the stuffed inner bag (sometimes called 'the pillow'). The lace might be highly decorative and its zig-zag course through the eyelets, with the material of the bag inside peeping through, was itself an attractive feature. The lacing might be replaced by rows of buttons and loops. However, the modern envelope-like cushion, with an opening only at one end, existed by 1600. After about 1630 less trouble was taken to embroider cushions richly and more attention was paid to their trimming with fringes and galloon. Moreover, most fine cushions were furnished with four large tassels at the corners—prominent and expensive features. Cushions were not normally tightly stuffed and remained out of shape when squashed. The corners of a fat cushion might sometimes be pulled in so that the tassels nestled in the resulting indentations. At any rate, seventeenth century cushions did not as a rule have aggressively pointed corners. Cane-seated and 'rush-bottomed' chairs and couches were often provided with cushions or 'squabs' (Plate 320).[2] The latter were less yielding and might be constructed like a mattress, with vertical sides and even with 'tufting', i.e. primitive buttoning (see p. 128).[3] Cushions and squabs might have 'ribbons to tie at the corners', as did some at Kilkenny,[4] and French and Dutch caned chairs with caned backs sometimes had quilted padding tied to the inside back for additional comfort. Squabs were called *carreaux* in French, because they were often square although they could also be oblong.[5] The squared cushion that fitted into the bucket-seat of a late seventeenth century easy chair might also be called a *carreau* and this was the term used for the squabs normally provided for cane chairs.[6]

A large cushion might be provided for a chair of state instead of a footstool (Plate 166), but there was otherwise no tradition of using cushions on the floor in northern

Europe at the beginning of the seventeenth century. In Spain, on the other hand, the Moorish tradition had lingered on, and this ancient Eastern custom was adopted in fashionable circles in France during the sixteenth century. Since these floor-cushions were squab-like, they were called *carreaux* but the compiler of an inventory in Marseilles in 1583 felt it necessary to explain that the 'trois carreaux' he was listing were 'aureliers de tapisserie, doublés de cuir rouge, pour s'assessoir dessus' [pillows of tapestry, lined with red leather, for sitting upon]. The 'leather lining' was probably his way of describing the leather facing of the underside, provided to better withstand abrasion from the floor.[7] Catherine de Medici had many *carreaux* but the fashion does not seemed to have gained ground all that quickly, for Anne d'Autriche was still described in her time as being seated on 'des carreaux à la mode d'Espagne, au milieu de ses dames' [*carreaux* in the Spanish fashion, surrounded by her ladies].[8] On the other hand this may be a reference to a modification of the *carreau* which involved supporting it on a low stool—a *porte-carreaux* (Plate 152), for the *carreau* tended to be too low (Plate 153). They could be made more comfortable by using two, one piled on top of the other, but it was even better if they could be lifted off the ground by something more solid. One can see pairs of *carreaux* on such supporting stools in Plate 289. All this trouble to make this rather awkward form of seating comfortable can only have been taken because it was fashionable and, indeed, there are many references to *carreaux* in the literature describing life in high society at the time. Moreover, grand beds were often provided with a couple of *carreaux* as part of their complement of accompanying seat-furniture. The great cloth-of-gold state bed at Knole for instance has a pair, each with two squabs (Plate 152). There is a walnut squab-frame with a caned top at Knole which has for years masqueraded as a footstool[9] but has now regained one of its *carreaux* from which it had become

152. (below) A squab-frame (*porte-carreaux*) supporting one of its two squabs (compare with Plate 289). The top of the frame is caned. Originally gilded; now black. The apron-piece has largely broken away. One of a pair *en suite* with the state bed shown in Plate 140.

153. (right) Lady seated on a large *carreau*. Sitting upright on such a squab, with one's legs out to the side and with the then fashionable sharp-pointed corset digging into one's abdomen cannot have been all that comfortable. Small wonder that ladies tried to avoid sitting on *carreaux* except in informal circumstances where a decorous posture was not expected.

separated. In the same way, 'two small squob frames carv'd & guilt' at Ham House, which had long been upholstered as footstools, have now been recognised for what they are.[10] They originally had two cushions each. Sometimes on each *porte-carreau* one cushion was covered with the main material of the bed-hangings and the other cushion was covered with the lining, thus maintaining unity even here.

The most rudimentary type of form was constructed on the principle of the milking-stool, with a thick wooden seat drilled with large holes into which the legs were jammed. A six-legged form in the Pantry at Ingatestone in 1600, described as being 'with iiiiii stake feete', must have been of this class, as may have been the 'ploncke fformes' in the Hall at Hatfield Priory in 1629 which were distinguished from some 'Joyned fformes' that must have been of the more elaborate type, produced by the joiner using mortice and tenon joints to make a form of what one might call the 'school-room' variety.[11]

FORMS, BENCHES AND STOOLS

Forms were used with the long tables that had stood in the halls of great houses in earlier times but, with the advent of the draw-table (see p. 226), the form came to be dropped from politer settings and its place was taken by a multitude of stools. For, although the leaves of the draw-table could be pushed shut so that the table was half its normal length, a form could not. Stools allowed greater flexibility and forms were thenceforth only to be seen in old-fashioned halls, churches, school-rooms, alongside billiard-tables, and so forth. Occasionally a form was padded (Plate 155) like the four in Cardinal Mazarin's possession which were 'enbourrées de crin couvertes de moquette' [stuffed with horsehair and covered with plush].[12]

Randle Holme illustrates a plain form and describes it as 'a joynt forme or bench'[13] but normally a bench was a form which had a back-support. Indeed, the back-support could itself be called 'a bench'.[14] There was, anyway, no doubt in the minds of the members of the London Company of Joyners as to the distinction when they ordered one of their number to provide 'two forms at 2s. per foot and some benches at 22d. per foot', while the Ipswich carpenter who had to make 'a joyned forme of 4 foot long and a binch behind the table' presumably knew what was expected of him.[15]

A bench might have a panelled back[16] and might also have the space between the legs enclosed so it became what we would call a settle.[17] There were two 'close benches' at Ingatestone, and the *archebanc* met with in French inventories no doubt belonged to the same class.[18] Sometimes these disguised a bed.[19]

Garden-benches existed in the seventeenth century; a very handsome pair of carved oak may still be seen at Ham House. They date from the 1670s.

Randle Holme illustrates the varieties of stool to be found in England in the second quarter of the seventeenth century (Plate 319[71–76]). The 'staked stool', or 'countrey stoole' as he calls it, was only to be found in humble settings by his time. The 'turned stool', with its triangular boarded seat (Plate 197), remained popular in the Netherlands but was not any longer to be seen in fashionable surroundings (Plate 154). The type of stool with trestle ends had gone out of use by the early seventeenth century and was replaced by the 'joined stool' or 'joynt stoole', which had turned legs in the form of columns of balusters and, later, might have spiral twists. Any

154. Turned stools with T-shaped backs. A common form in Holland early in the seventeenth century, evolved from the common three-legged turned stool with a triangular wooden seat (see Plate 197). By this time such stools were normally supplied with a cushion, as here in a scene of fine company at an inn.

stool might be furnished with cushions but the 'joint stools' that were so commonly to be seen in the rooms of great houses around 1600 were mostly upholstered (Plates 84 and 133). The French called this form a *tabouret*. As Nicot, in his *Thresor de la langue française*, wrote in 1606, 'Tabouret signifie ce petit siège bas, embourré, couvert de tapisserie de point ou autre estoffe ou les femmes s'asséent tenans leurs cacquetoire ou faisant leur ouvrage.': it was stuffed, covered with needlework or some other material, and was sat on by women when chatting or doing their embroidery. Randle Holme states that in Cheshire a 'joynt stoole' was called a 'buffit stoole' (Plate 319[72]) but buffet stools are met with in inventories from all over the country.[20] Presumably they were primarily associated with the dining table, near which there would usually be a buffet (see p. 238).

Stools were often made en suite with a set of chairs for use round a dining-table. It is curious that many sets of stools comprised some that were 'high' while others are called 'low', yet the implication is that they went round the same table. Presumably the difference in height was minimal but still reflected the relative status of the sitters. Apparently the low version of the *tabouret* might in France be called a *respect* for this reason.[21] The upholstered *tabouret* continued in fashionable favour right through the century (Plates 133 and 199).

Randle Holme illustrates a nursing stool, for use when tending a baby (Plate 319[76]), and it is worth noting that grand people usually had a stool placed in the bath-tub so that they could sit on it while carrying out their ablutions (see p. 319).

La mine de cette accouchee
me semble si fort si bon poinct
que volontiers pour mon pourpoinct
je vaudrou sauoir empeschte.

A cette gentille Nourrice
coiffee de son baudet
quand on voudroit troubler son laict
seroit bon luy rendre service:

Et pour cette jeune seruente
qui chauffe la couche & l'enfant
qui luy voudroit en faire autant
ie croy quelle seroit contente

lentew à faire le mesnage
et sur tout a dresser vn lieF.
nulle pour, à prestre son deduict
ne faict mieux encor cet outrage.

Tauernier excudit

155. Assorted Parisian seat-
furniture of the 1630s. In the
background, an upholstered
bench, a 'farthingale chair' and a
'*pliant*'. The mother on the right
sits on a low nursing chair while
the fostermother swaddling the
baby may possibly be sitting on a
seat similar to those shown in
Plates 197 and 198.

156. A *perroquet* and a rush-
bottomed chair—a 'Dutch chair'.
The latter is here shown apparently
with a boarded seat but the illustration occurs in a treatise on
perspective where such details were
immaterial. On the right is a bedstock with a hipped tester. The
placing of a chamber-pot on a chair
alongside a bed seems to have been
normal practice (see Plate 127).

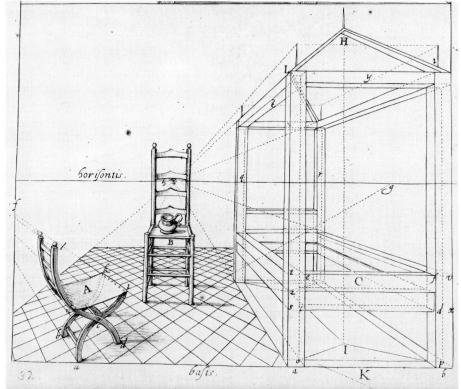

The French were fond of the folding stool with an X-frame which they called a *pliant* (Plates 1 and 155). Although seemingly a humble piece of furniture, it was to be seen in the grandest settings right through the century. It does not seem to have been very popular in England but a pair of mutilated specimens can still be seen at Knole.[22] The seat was formed by girth-webbing and was then covered with material, often richly. Sometimes the wooden members were painted; in other instances they were closely encased in the same material as that of the seat (the Knole specimen is thus decorated). The French royal inventories list several X-frame stools with silver mounts ('garnis d'argent cizelée') and a bed is mentioned which was accompanied by 'six sièges plians d'argent massif, cizelez et tres delicatement travaillez' [six folding seats of solid silver, chased and delicately worked].[23] The fact that such stools took up very little room may partly account for their popularity in France, but it may also have to do with the notion that such seats were associated by tradition with the mobile aristocratic life of former times. We still call them camp stools.

Chairs

A version of the folding stool, the *pliant* just discussed, was known as a *perroquet*.[24] It had a back, and the finials, which were often hooked forward, made it resemble a parakeet. The X-frame was hinged transversely so that the chair folded fore-and-aft (Plates 156), unlike the standard *pliant* where the sides came together. The *perroquet* came into fashion in France during the first half of the seventeenth century and was principally used at the dining table. Cardinal Richelieu had a set round his circular dining table with which, like King Arthur, he sought to overcome the problems of precedence.[25] They do not seem to have found favour in England, but why this should be so is difficult to explain.

Another form of chair which was essentially a stool with a back was Italian in origin and would today be called a *sgabello* although the term was in fact applied to stools of many kinds and not just to those with a back. This was a form of trestle-stool with a richly carved board of fancy shape forming the front 'legs' while the inside face of the back is equally richly worked. The seat was of wood and had a circular depression on top. The form may have been known in France but what is curious is that a pair can be seen in the background to the portrait of the Countess of Arundel, painted around 1616 or so, while chairs of this sort with shell-shaped backs were to be seen at Holland House and at Ham House, at both of which houses Francis Cleyn worked as a decorator (Plate 52). So this Italian form seems to have enjoyed a measure of favour within circles close to the court of Charles I and his architect, Inigo Jones (see pp. 53 and 93).

Also in a sense related to the stool, because it was essentially a *tabouret* with a back added, was the so-called 'back stool'. This was a simple form of upholstered chair but it was by far the commonest type of relatively comfortable chair in use between about 1615 and the 1660s, and it remained popular long after that. Randle Holme illustrates a 'back stool' and describes it as such (he shows one with finials which was seemingly an unusual feature on this class of chair), and they are to be seen in numerous illustrations of the period.[26] The back consisted of a rectangular pad attached to upright extensions of the back legs (Plate 158). These chairs tended to be

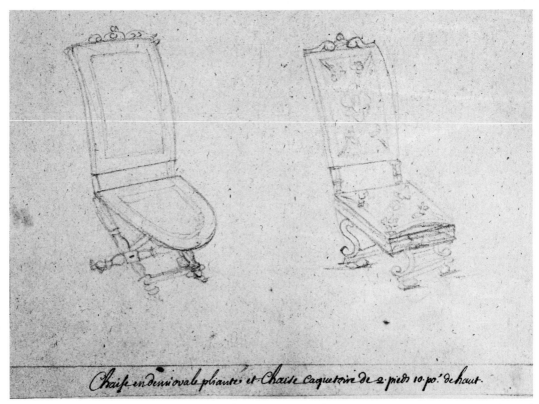

Chaise en demi ovale pliante et Chaise caquetoire de 2. pieds 10. po.' de haut.

157. Sketches from the 1690s presumably showing chairs to be seen in French court circles at the end of the seventeenth century. The 'chaise en demi ovale' appears to be a folding occasional seat evolved from the *perroquet*. The 'chaise caquetoire' may not have been very different from the chair shown in Plate 162 although it had a cresting and strange legs.

lower than other forms of seat-furniture[27] and were often used by women—for which reason they were sometimes called *chaises à demoiselles*.[28] As they had no arms and there was a gap between the lower edge of the back-pad and the seat, they were easy for women to sit in while wearing a farthingale—that large padded ring which women in about 1600 wore round their hips in order to hold out their voluminous skirts, like a barrel (Plate 127). Back-stools are often called 'farthingale chairs' by dealers and collectors but the term does not seem to occur in contemporary English inventories. On the other hand, *chaises à vertugadin* are quite often mentioned in French inventories of the period, and the meaning was the same, for a farthingale was called a *vertugadin* in French.[29] The term *chaise caquetoire* is also met with in French inventories at the time and probably refers to chairs of the 'farthingale' type rather than to an all-wooden form of armchair, as is often supposed; for references to *chaises caquetoires* (literally 'prattling chairs' or 'nattering chairs') usually mention upholstery and it is clear that they were low.[30]

When chair-backs became higher, at the end of the century, the form retained its name although the back was no longer low. The chair shown in Plate 157, drawn at the end of the century, is entitled 'un caquetoire' and Furetière, writing at this time, explains that a *caquetoire* is a 'chaise basse qui à le dos fort haut et qui n'a point de bras, où l'on babille à l'aise auprès du feu' [low chair with a very high back which has no arms, on which one chats at ease by the fireside].[31] The *chaises du four* [fireside chairs]

158. The so-called 'farthingale chair', the commonest form of chair in the seventeenth century, used all over Europe. Numerous variants of this basic form were produced. This example is shown in a Dutch drawing of 1672. In England they were commonly called 'back stools'. Note the domed padding on the seat of this simple specimen.

one also finds in French inventories were probably of this class as well.[32] Every now and then one comes across references in English inventories to 'back *chairs*' and one is probably once again dealing with chairs of this sort.[33] Maybe some people felt that they were so obviously chairs and not stools that it was misleading to call them 'back *stools*'. Nevertheless this was their common name throughout the period of their popularity. From about 1670 onwards, however, it seems that any chair without arms could be called a 'back stool'.[34] For this reason it is convenient to retain the term 'farthingale chair' for this once ubiquitous form of chair that I have been discussing (Plates 159, 162 and 164). Incidentally, the legs and stretchers of such chairs were left exposed and might simply have their wooden surfaces polished or varnished. Grand versions, however, had these parts painted or gilded. The two short sections of upright between the seat and the back-rest, on the other hand, were usually encased in the same material as these components.[35]

Although the farthingale chair was much used for relaxing in comfortable circumstances, it was the standard chair of its time and was also used for dining—in which case it was often covered in leather or in turkeywork (Plates 164 and 165). En suite with a set of farthingale dining-chairs there would often be a 'great chaire' which was a scaled-up version with arms. This was in turn the standard form of armchair during the middle of the century. The arms were usually covered with material, as were the short lengths of upright at the back (Plates 183). In the classical

X. (far right) Daybed and chairs upholstered en suite with appliqué wall-hangings, in a style fashionable in Paris late in the seventeenth century. The furniture, however, is English. The magnificent chandeliers are of about the same date.

159. (right) A middling grand farthingale chair of about 1630, with the remains of its original upholstery—a blue woollen cloth decorated with applied ornament executed in coloured silks. The remains of a red and blue fringe may be seen running round the lower edge of the seat-rails. Note the sheathed uprights to the back. The upholsterer attempted to square the padding of the seat. The lower ends of the legs have been cut off, no doubt because they were damaged.

160. The outside back of most seventeenth-century chairs was left uncovered (see also Plate 93). Only very grand seat-furniture had this part covered. The uprights to the back were covered, however.

161. (upper left) A grand version of the farthingale chair in 1663. Note the nail-patterning, the inset braid, the short fringe round the top and sides of the back, the braided sheath of the upright, and the long netted fringe along the lower edge of the back-rest and seat.

162. (above) Late-seventeenth-century chair evolved from the 'far-thingale' form, with the high back then fashionable. Note the rounded padding of seat and back. Trimmed with broad galloon round the outer edge. In England such a chair would doubtless still have been called a 'back stool'.

163. (left) A Dutch 'farthingale' chair of the late 1660s. Note the domed padding of the seat. The larger armed version of this type of chair is to be seen in the pendant portrait repro-duced in Plate 186.

XI. (far left) An English portrait of 1616 showing a Turkish carpet laid on a floor covered with rush matting that is fitted to the room (or it may be a tent, the armour perhaps indicating that the portrait was painted in the field). The red velvet table-carpet is richly embroidered with gold thread. However, it is still the clothes which are the most splendid items at this stage.

version, the arms consisted of two plain bars meeting at right-angles, but earlier versions had more substantial arm-rests sweeping downwards and showing that this form of chair supplanted the old form of all-wooden 'great chair' or 'high chair', which was itself probably not to be seen in fashionable surroundings after 1610 or so. The fact that so many all-wood Jacobean and Carolean 'great chairs' survive is due to their being robust and obviously showy pieces that seem valuable. Chairs of the scaled-up farthingale type (Plate 183) rarely seemed worth keeping once the upholstery had become worn and unsightly. The all-wooden 'great chair' of the seventeenth century belonged in the smaller country-house and the large farmhouses of the squirarchy.

The 'great chair' (of whatever type) was a seat of honour but was not in itself a symbol of rank. It reflected precedence in the context concerned. So, while a monarch might sit enthroned on a chair of state as his subjects stood around him, a mere squire would occupy the 'great chair' in his own house, honour being due to him as master of the household. However, if someone of superior rank paid the squire a visit, the latter would normally be bound to defer to the visitor and yield the seat of honour to him.[36] Questions of precedence bedevilled life at court in the seventeenth century but do not really concern us here. Honour was signified by raising the person to be honoured above the rest of the company. The 'high table' stood on a daïs at one end of the hall; a chair of state or throne likewise stood on a daïs. The seat of honour would also usually be of imposing proportions (hence 'great chair') and was often accompanied by a footstool—not merely to support the feet because the seat was higher than normal, but because the raising of the feet off the

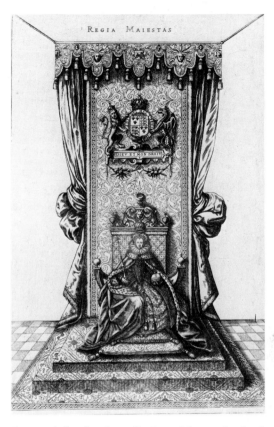

REGIA MAIESTAS

164 (far left) Two disparate 'back stools' covered with gilt leather. English, mid-seventeenth-century. The legs of the right-hand chair have been shortened.

165. (left) The back-stool remained in favour right to the end of the century. The backs grew taller late in the century as this chair, acquired for Christ Church, Oxford, in 1692, shows. Made locally, a set of twelve cost £6. It is covered in 'Russia leather'. The leather extends in one piece down the front edge of the uprights.

166. (right) Queen Elizabeth enthroned: an engraving of 1608 showing (seemingly none too accurately) an X-frame chair of state. However, the canopy (cloth of estate) is clearly depicted, as are the cushions that serve as a foot-rest. The canopy is suspended 'sparver fashion' by means of cords attached to hooks in the ceiling.

ground was in itself a symbol of authority. One might further distinguish a principal seat of honour by raising a canopy over it.

The 'chair of state' in the seventeenth century might be of conventional armchair form but the ancient folding-chair (Plate 168), which people still associated with the aristocratic way of life in former times, remained in favour as a seat of authority in England, right through to the middle of the century[37] and several seem still to have been used at the French court later in the century (Plate 170). Crude versions are, moreover, to be seen in many Dutch pictures of the seventeenth century, so the form must have remained popular even in relatively humble houses in Holland well into the century (Plate 268). But it was probably always a seat of honour. With its folding X-frame, it had been a practical piece of furniture, well suited to the mobile life of the aristocracy in mediaeval times but sixteenth and seventeenth-century examples were massive and could only fold slightly, if at all.[38] In the Middle Ages, this kind of chair was called a *fauldesteuil* in French (from the Latin *faldestolium*). Nicot (1606) explains that a *fauldesteuil* was 'une espèce de chaire à dossier et à accouldoirs, ayant le siège de sangles entrelacées, laquelle se plie pour plus commodément la porter d'un lieu a l'autre; et est un chaire de parade, laquelle on tenoit anciennement auprès d'un lict de parade' [a kind of chair with a back and arm-rests, having a seat formed with interlaced webbing, which folds so it may the more easily be carried from one place to the other; it is a chair of state which in ancient times stood close to a state bed].[39] The word *chaire* implies that it was a kind of 'great chair' or chair of state. Mary, Queen of Scots' 'twa auld faulding stuillis of cramosis velvot'[40] must have been of this type, and the Germans called them *faltstühle*. The French, on the other hand,

193

167. (left) To underline the fact that the lady here portrayed was of high rank (she was Countess of Denbigh) she is shown standing by a chair of state, a symbol of exalted status. This X-frame chair was entirely covered with red velvet. Note the long cushion lying across the armrests.

168. (above left) An X-frame chair of state from Hampton Court. It has an X-frame foot-stool en suite. Probably about 1620. Although fixed cross-members in the back and seat have always made this chair rigid, the crossing of the legs has still been made in the traditional manner to articulate scissor-wise. The woodwork is entirely masked with upholstery—red woollen cloth covered with a red and silver silk (probably 'silver tissue'), trimmed with silver braid and netted fringe.

169. (above right) The exposed woodwork of this X-frame chair of state gives a clue to its original appearance. Painted red with diagonal lines of simulated silver lace, inspection behind the present rather plausible and itself ancient covering revealed the former covering—red velvet laid vertically with silver lace, the impression of which is still to be seen in the pile. Finials are lacking and the original loose cushion has been built in when the present cover was put on.

shortened the word to *fauteuil*[41] which came to be the term used in reference to any important-looking armchair and then eventually to all fully upholstered armchairs.

It is difficult to trace how this transfer of meaning took place, but the two chairs with curtained cubicles shown in Plates 170 and 171 may throw light on the problem. Both chairs were probably to be seen somewhere in French court circles in the 1690s but neither need have been new at the time (see Plate 17). The Dauphin gave Madame de Maintenon a specially comfortable chair for use when she came to stay at his residence at Meudon. It was described as being 'un fauteuil à commodité apellé confessional' [an easy chair called 'a confessional'].[42] Could this chair have looked like one of those in the illustrations? Their curtained cubicles might indeed be likened to confessionals. At any rate, the term *fauteuil de commodité* had come by the 1680s to be applied to truly easy chairs, often with some contrivance for making them especially comfortable.[43] For example, the French royal inventory of 1687 lists

170. Sketches of important and probably royal French seat-furniture in the 1690s. On the right an X-frame chair with attached canopy. Was it a throne or a *fauteuil de commodité*? On the left, a rush-seated chair—probably one of the many 'petites chaises de paille' often mentioned in the French royal inventories in the time of Louis XIV. The other chair has 'tufted' upholstery.

thirty 'grands fauteuils de commodité à cremillière' [i.e. with *cremaillières* or ratchets] which suggests that they had adjustable backs like the so-called 'sleeping chairs' at Ham House which date from about 1678 (Plate 181).[44] Important bedchambers and closets were often furnished with an easy chair in which the occupant of the apartment could relax, perhaps in front of the fire; indeed, one such chair, or even a pair, became a standard part of the complement of seat-furniture that accompanied an important bed from about 1695 onwards. For example, 'six grands fauteuils de commodité' were supplied 'pour servir dans les chambres des seigneurs' [for use in the rooms of noblemen] in the French palaces at about this time.[45] Around 1700, the phrase à *commodité* was dropped and the accommodating armchair came simply to be called *un fauteuil*.

The earliest forms of adjustable chair seem to have been those devised for some illustrious invalid (Plate 172 and 175). They might have hinged backs, leg-supports, built-in reading desks, and even casters. 'Sleeping chairs' were evolved from such furniture. Evelyn saw something of the sort in Rome in 1644 which he described as a 'conceited chayre to sleepe in with legs stretch'd out with hooks & pieces of wood to draw out longer & shorter'.[46] Charles I had a 'sleepeinge chayre' covered in red velvet but it was valued at only £1 so cannot have been very elaborate.[47] The chair with ratchet-adjustments shown in Plate 178 would seem to date from the 1660s or early 1670s and may resemble the 'sleeping chair' provided by Richard Price for Windsor Castle in 1675 that was designed 'to fall in the back of iron worke'.[48] Two years later John Paudevine (Poitevin) supplied for 'Her Mats. Bed Chamber' at one of the royal palaces 'a sleeping chaire neatly carved and with the irons all gilt with gold' at a cost of £6. It may have been he that supplied the pair of 'sleeping chayres' for Ham House a year or so later. They have gilded iron quadrants drilled with a series of holes through which gilt pegs are pushed to lock the back at the desired

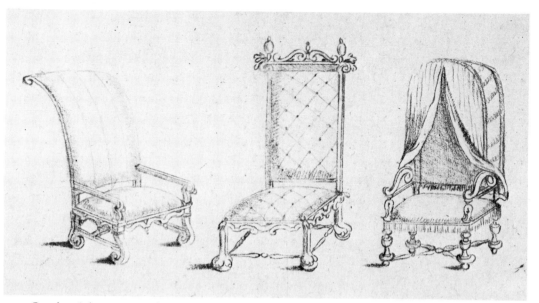

171. On the right, an easy chair with a canopy-like enclosure, perhaps a *'fauteuil en confessional'*, drawn at about the same time as Plate 170. Left, an arm-chair with a curved back; and, centre, 'tufted' upholstery on a strange chair with paw-and-ball feet.

172 & 173. The invalid chair of Philip II of Spain who died in 1658. Note the quilted upholstery, padded arms, hinged back and footrest, and spherical casters. The padding is stated to be of horsehair.

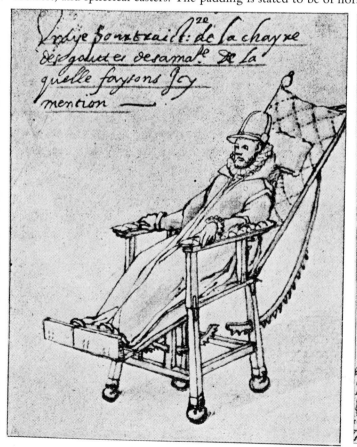

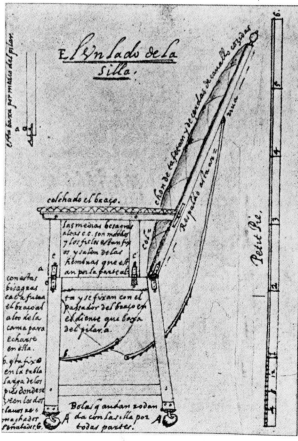

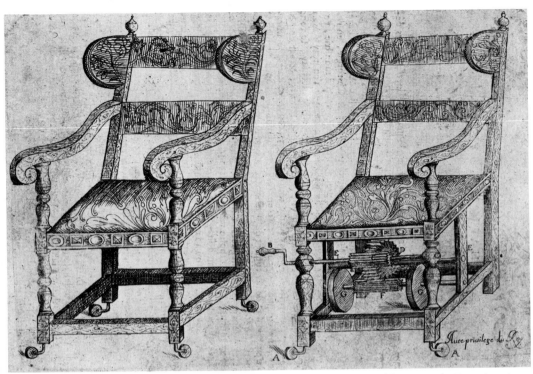

174. Easy chairs with casters, and a self-propelling mechanism operated by a crank. French, 1620s.

angle (Plate 182). A third 'sleeping chair' seems formerly to have been in the Duke's Closet at Ham; it has a different form of adjustment, one that is built into the arm-rests, and is in addition fitted with casters (Plate 179). It had a canopy[49] but this may not have been a ceremonial structure associated with the fact that its occupant was a Duke (for this chair stood in a closet, which was an informal location) but may rather have served the same purpose as the cubicles rising from *fauteuils de commodité*, like those shown in Plate 171. However, we know that the Duke's canopy was a separate item; it was not attached to the chair.

If the easy chair, with its wings and accommodating form (Colour Plate X), was developed from primitive invalid chairs, the more common type of upholstered armchair was evolved from the scaled-up, armed version of the 'farthingale' form that we have already discussed (p. 187 and Plate 183). It is reasonable to suppose that the 'French chairs' which are mentioned in English chairmakers' accounts from the 1660s and through the 1670s were representatives of this phase, because the French were at this stage leading the development towards greater comfort in this field.[50] The term 'French chair' first occurs in the royal accounts in the early 1660s and clearly meant something specific (Plate 186). In 1660–1 the London upholsterer, John Casbert, provided for royal use a 'crimson velvet french chair covered all over with gold and silver fringe and [with] a bagg [i.e. a cushion or squab] filled with downe'.[51] There can be no doubt the chair was intended to be comfortable, with its expensive cushioning of down. In 1674 Casbert supplied a 'French chaire hollow in ye back and quilted . . . of crimson damask . . .'. Chairs were occasionally given a concave (trough-like) curve to the back at this period the better to accommodate the sitter (Plate 177).[52] Backs also were made to slope backwards more pronouncedly to

198

175 & 176. The invalid chair of Charles X of Sweden who died in 1660. The hinged back and footrest are linked by straps running through the armrests and therefore move together. Note the crook in the back, probably a novel feature at this time. The seat lifts to reveal a compartment containing a close-stool pan that can be removed by a trap-door on one side. There is a further compartment on the other side. In the armrests are extension rods that can support an adjustable reading-desk. Originally all covered in velvet. The conformation of the spiral-turned legs suggests a Dutch provenance.

177. An English invalid chair with features similar to that shown in Plates 175 and 176. From the 1670s.

178. An English sleeping chair of 1665–75 with a hinged back adjusted by means of iron ratchets. Note the rods for supporting a reading-desk. The leather cover of the back, at least, seems to be original.

179 & 180. An English sleeping chair, perhaps that which stood in the Duke of Lauderdale's closet at Ham House, under a canopy. Mentioned in an inventory of 1679. The hinged back is adjusted by fore and aft movement of the armrest which can be held in the desired position by pegs passing through holes into the upright supports. Note the near spherical casters of *lignum vitae*, and the horsehair padding.

181. One of the pair of splendid sleeping chairs in the Queen's Closet at Ham House which were acquired between 1677 and 1679. Here shown with its back swung backwards to the full extent of the quadrant (see Plate 182), in which position the chair is liable to fall over.

182. (lower left) Adjustment of the Ham House sleeping chairs is made by pegs inserted through a quadrant in the direction of the black arrow.

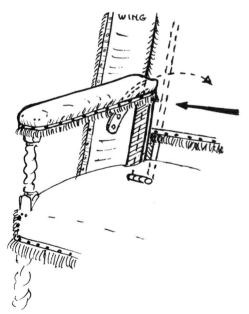

183. (right) Remains of an important 'great chaire'. Essentially a scaled-up version of a 'farthingale chair' (with a set of which it was no doubt en suite). The exposed parts of the wooden structure are gilded and painted with flowers. The chair will originally have had finials at the top of the uprights to the back. The dark line across the original red velvet of the back shows where a line of silver-gilt fringe once ran. More fringe will have trimmed the lower edges of the back-rest and the seat.

184. (right) Chair shown in a portrait of Sir Arthur Onslow (1622–88). The whole chair above the seat-rail is covered in velvet trimmed with a looped fringe (long, plain fringe along lower edges). Note the oval-headed nails on the seat-rail.

185. (far right) From an engraved portrait of Catherine of Braganza from the 1660s. The padding of the seat is highly domed. Note how some pendant fringe also trims the top edge of the back-support.

increase the comfort. In 1674 Richard Price, another royal upholsterer, provided a 'large chaire of Estate with a very crooked back'.[53] And once the back was thus tilted, most English chairmakers decided it was advisable either to rake the back legs backwards or to shape them so that they were crooked to make heels—'compass heeles', as they were called.[54] The French, on the other hand, did not rake their chair-legs backwards, relying on the weight to provide stability (cf. Plates 181 and 188). As for the arms, while these had consisted merely of a horizontal bar, there had been an incentive to cover them with material (Plate 186) but, once the arms began to be shaped (sweeping downwards in a comfortable curve and providing scope for decorative carving), they ceased to be covered. It was only the true 'easy chairs' that normally had padded arms.

Chairs with caned seats became popular in England after the Restoration (Plate 177). The Cane-Chair Makers Company, probably around 1680 or so, claimed that 'about the year 1664, cane-chairs came into use'. They were liked 'for their Durable, Lightness, and Cleanness from Dust, Worms and Moths which inseparably attend Turkey-work, Serge and other stuff chairs and couches, to the spoiling of them and all furniture near them'.[55] They were trying to counter the claim of the woollen manufacturers, made in a petition to Parliament, that the woollen industry would suffer greivously if cane chairs became popular. The cane-chair makers insisted that the number of people involved was not really so great and that, anyway, cane seats needed cushions (or 'quilts', as they are also called in this statement), the making of which provided much work for the woollen industry. Certainly cushions are often mentioned in connection with cane chairs in contemporary inventories, and it may be that, where no mention is made, the fact was merely overlooked because the fitting seemed an integral part of the chair. The cane chair makers also claimed that a great many cane chairs were exported 'into almost all parts of the world where heat renders turkey-work . . . useless'. Presumably, in hot countries, such chairs had to be used without squabs or this particular advantage would have been lost. Cane-seated chairs were popular in Holland but did not gain much favour in France before 1720 or so.[56] However, the sofa and chair shown in Plate 195, which have caned seats, show that such furniture was known (and presumably made) in France in the late seventeenth century although these actual pieces are described as being 'à l'Anglaise'.

Simple chairs with seats made of rushes were being produced in most parts of Europe during the eighteenth and nineteenth centuries, and are still being made in

186. (above left) The upholstered armchair becomes more refined in the 1660s. This pattern became international (here shown in a Dutch portrait). References to 'French chairs' in English documents at this period probably concern chairs of this type.

187. (above right) A French armchair of the 1670s with carved and gilt uprights to the armrests which appear to be padded. The velvet covering is of the slip-over variety, secured with hooks and eyes at the base of the back-rest, and at the four corners of the seat.

188. (right) Although curved the back legs of this grand French armchair of about 1675 are essentially upright and have forward-pointing feet in the characteristic French manner. Note the two lengths of fringe. The covers are of the slip-over kind.

189. A Dutch armchair of the 1680s showing the un-covered outside back and the domed seat covered with needlework. The covers are nailed in place through the bell-fringe, which is double banked. Very similar chairs were being made in England at the same time.

190. (right) Parisian armchair of the 1680s. The cover is of the slip-over variety. The armrests are not padded.

191. (far right) A fashionable Parisian arm-chair of 1687. An early example of the back with rounded corners. A broad galloon runs round the edge of the cover. It seems to be trimmed with a metal edging.

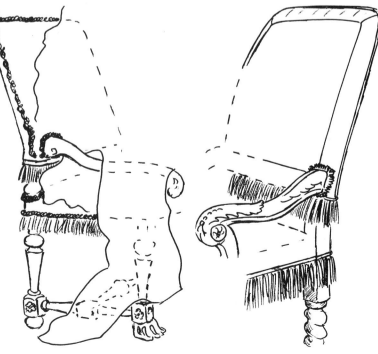

192. (above left) English armchair of the 1680s with slip-over covers of needlework in the French taste. The lower edge of the seat-cover was almost certainly trimmed with a heavy fringe hanging down to mask the square block of the front leg. A similar fringe will have run along the lower edge of the back.

193. (above right) Old photograph of an English armchair of about 1695 showing the original upholstery prior to restoration. The slip-over covers of red and silver silk are trimmed with an elaborate fringe—a long version along the scalloped lower edges, a short version round arms and uprights, and in a wavy line around the inside back. Knotted tassels are attached at strategic points like the indentations of the scalloping.

194. (left) A late-seventeenth-century Parisian armchair with arms padded—not seemingly a common feature at this date.

some rural areas today. The products of each area have their individual characteristics but the general conformation is the same. The uprights are usually turned on a lathe, and it was members of the guilds of Turners who mostly produced this sort of chair. Such chairs were certainly being made in Italy in the sixteenth century and it seems that there was a considerable export of them from Pisa. The inventory of a house at Marseilles taken in 1578, for example, refers to 'huit cheres de paille servant à femmes, à la fasson de Pise' [eight straw chairs for use by women, of Pisan type].[57] These chairs were clearly distinctive; the turned uprights of the back may have had quite fancy profiles and there may have been multiple spindles in the back. The woodwork may even have been stained. The implication of 'servant à femmes' is that they were low in the seat like the *chaises à vertugadin*.

The rush-seated chair was being made in Flanders by the beginning of the seventeenth century[58] and came to be produced in great quantities in Holland during the century. At first these may have had multiple spindles in the back but the Dutch seem to have developed the ladder-back form which has several shaped slats fitted across the back, like a ladder (Plates 127, 156 and 196). Such chairs are often to be seen in Dutch illustrations from the 1620s onwards and also appear in French and English scenes later in the century. No doubt they were made in France as well but many were apparently exported from Holland. Frequent reference is made in English inventories to 'Dutch chairs' or 'Holland chairs'; occasionally the fact that they had rush-seats is noted and we find also 'Dutch matted chairs' and 'Dutch flagg-chaires'.[59] A chair of this sort at Cowdray was described as being green, and Lady Rivers actually mentions a 'Greene Dutch chayre' in her will of 1644, which suggests she placed a certain value on it.[60] But most chairs of this sort were left with the wood in its natural state, which explains why fashionable people in France sometimes called them 'chaises à la capucine', as if they were only fit for the monastic life. This did not prevent them introducing such chairs to quite grand surroundings. Many 'petites chaises de paille' are, for instance, mentioned in the French royal

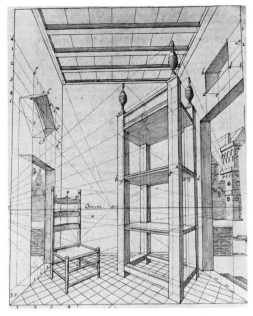

195. (far left) Caned furniture in fashionable French circles late in the seventeenth century. The large seat is described as a 'Sopha d'anglaise en caquetoire', the seat being 'de jonque'. The smaller chair is a 'Banquette d'anglaise'.

196. (left) A Dutch turned chair with a ladder-back shown in a work on perspective published in 1625. The seat will have been 'rush bottomed'.

inventories from the time of Louis XIV.[61] Some had arms and some were japanned ('façon de verny de la chine').[62] Plate 170 probably shows such a chair that was to be seen in one of the French palaces in the 1690s. Many had squabs and loose quilted padding tied to their backs.[63] A chair with such a padded overlay may be seen in the painting of a Dutch doll's house, reproduced in Plate 320.

There seems to be no evidence that rush-bottomed chairs were made in England before 1700 but, as so many were made here in the eighteenth century, it is probable that the industry was established in this country before the end of the seventeenth century. The English, on the other hand, developed the 'milking stool' formula of legs ('stakes') jammed into holes bored through a thick wooden seat and evolved what came to be known as the 'Windsor chair'. As there were 'staked stools' and forms with 'stake feete' in English houses in Elizabethan times, it is reasonable to suppose that backed versions (i.e. chairs) were being evolved during that century to become the ancestors of the ubiquitous 'Windsor chair' of the mid–eighteenth century. Mr Agius noted references to 'rodden' or 'rodd' chairs in Oxford inventories of the seventeenth century.[64] In one case, such a chair is mentioned directly after one made of wicker, which indicates that there was a distinction between the two.

Chairs of wicker were, anyway, common all over Europe in the seventeenth century, not least in England, and they were to be found in quite smart surroundings. Lady Rivers, for example, mentions in her will the 'great wicker chare with the cushion usually lying in it in my chamber'.[65] Wicker chairs had arms (not only for comfort but because they made the structure more rigid) and many had a hood rising up over the sitter like the later porter's chairs.[66] Randle Holme explains that 'chairs called Twiggen chaires . . . are made of owsiers and withen twigs; having round covers over the heads of them like a canopy. These are principally used by sick and infirm people and such women as have bine lately brought to bed.'[67] The extremely comfortable wicker armchair, with its 'winged'

197. A Dutch wickerwork swaddling seat, known as a *bakermat*. The Frenchwoman swaddling a baby in Plate 155 may be seated in a similar piece of furniture or she may simply be sitting on the floor. The *bakermat* must have been a practical aid to nursery routine. Note the three-legged, turned stool.

hood, not only made an excellent invalid chair but must have been the model for the great 'easy chairs' of the later decades of the seventeenth century and it was when the latter became common in grand circles that the wicker chair was relegated to humbler surroundings. A tray-like wicker seat with a low back was used in Holland for nursing and swaddling babies (Plates 197 and 198). The sitter's back was supported while her legs were stretched straight out to form a trough in which the baby lay safely as the swaddling proceeded. In Dutch they were called *bakermats*.[68] It may be that the 'one nurse twige chayre' in an English inventory of 1673 was of this class.[69]. There was a 'strowe chair' in the Master's Bedchamber at Gilling Castle in 1624[70] and it is possible that this was made of coils of plaited straw, as certain 'pouffes' still are today, but it is more likely to have been a wicker chair or a chair with a rush seat.

At Knole there was a 'Spanish chair wth. elbowes' in 1645 which was in some way distinctive; the term is frequently found in Dutch inventories of the early part of the century.[70] The twelve 'great Italian chairs with guilt frames covered with crimson velvet, with 12 stooles suteable, with brass tops' in Lady Dorchester's possession must have made an impressive show; they seem to have been of a well-known type,

198. A *bakermat* with a rather higher back than that shown in Plate 197 and with a handle. One is shown hanging on the wall by its handle in Plate 320 (top left-hand room). About 1670?

solid, fully upholstered and with small brass finials on the crest-rail.[72] At Tart Hall in 1641 there was an exotic group comprising an 'Indian chayre & 3 other India chayres' which were clearly Oriental in origin.[73] And what were 'Flanders chairs'? They are mentioned in many sixteenth and early seventeenth-century inventories both in England and France; some were covered with leather, others had rush seats.[74] They must have been distinctive, perhaps with turned members, but cannot yet be positively identified. And then there were 'scrowle chairs' which was probably the name for a small, upholstered chair of the early seventeenth century which had a back with a marked backwards scroll that is to be seen in several Netherlandish and German pictures.[75]

There were all kinds of scaled-down chairs for children, as well as a pulpit-like seat in which an infant could be placed before it could walk properly (Plate 231). In the Victoria and Albert museum there is a cage composed of turned members on swivelling casters into which a child could be locked until it learned to walk properly.

SOFAS AND DAYBEDS

I have already discussed how the simple form of bed, the *couche* or *couchette*, evolved in two ways—into the single-ended day-bed and into the double-ended ceremonial couch—and that the word 'couch' in English could be used for either type (see Plates 147 and 207, and p. 172). As the double-ended couch seems to have stood against the wall, usually under a canopy, it came to be a sort of backless sofa. The ends sloped outwards and were softened by two large cushions against which one could lean. The ends of later models were sometimes hinged so they could either be vertical, or inclined outwards for greater comfort. It was no doubt because one sat

199. Seat-furniture, probably in a French royal palace in the 1690s. The sofa is described as a 'Grand Canapé' and is six *pieds* in length. The chair is stated to be 'à la mode' and the stool is a 'banquette à la romaine'.

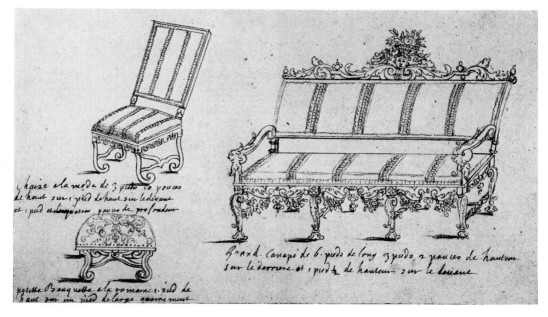

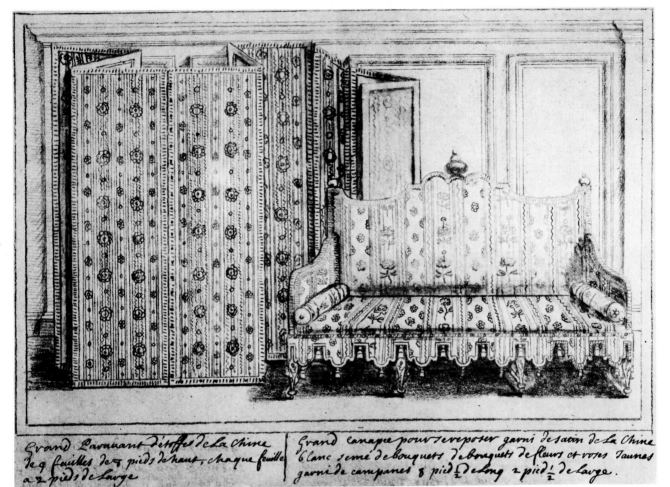

Grand Paravant d'étoffes de La Chine
de 9 feuilles de 7 pieds de haut, chaque feuille
a 2 pieds de large

Grand canapee pour se reposer garni de satin de La Chine
blanc seme de bouquets de bouquets de fleurs et roses Jaunes
garni de campanes 8 pied ½ de long 2 pied ½ de large.

200. This French sofa of the 1690s is described as a 'Grand canapée pour se reposer' which may imply that the piece could open forward to form a bed. Note the galloon round the edge and forming bands, the cylindrical bolsters, and the lappets here called 'campanes'. The covering is of Chinese white brocaded satin. The screen is of nine leaves, seven feet high, and is covered with a Chinese silk.

rather than lay on such couches that they were sometimes called 'couch chayres' (see p. 174). Once this stage had been reached (perhaps about 1630) it was a logical step to provide this form of seat with a back, and it then became a sofa in everything but name. A famous backed couch with hinged 'ends' or arm-rests is to be seen at Knole and represents this phase (Plate 150).[76]

The French seem to have called both types of couch (i.e. single- and double-ended) *lits de repos* or *reposoirs*. A 'reposoir à vice dorées' [couch with gilt screws] in a house in 1621 is likely to have been a double-ended couch with hinged arm-rests since the plural of the adjective suggests it had more than one screw-adjustment,[77] but normally there is no indication that a *lit de repos* in a French inventory was not of the single-ended variety like that shown in Plate 205, which were day-beds on which one could recline, informally and at ease.

In her bedchamber in 1684, Madame de Maintenon had a 'lit de repos en canapée'.[78] It had two bolsters and three valances so was evidently double-ended and stood with one long side to the wall. Perhaps this term was confined to the double-ended couch (Plate 151) and may reflect the fact that the ceremonial form had in earlier times had a canopy?[79] Insufficient evidence is at present to hand and all we

211

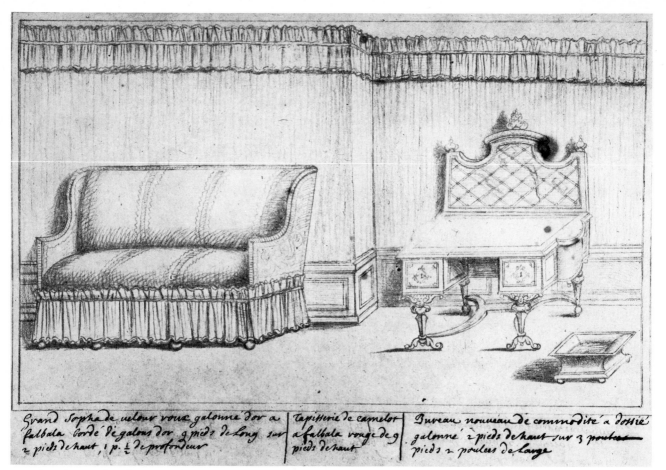

Grand Sopha de velour vous galonné d'or a
falbala bordé de galons d'or 9 pieds de long sur
2 pieds de haut, 1 p. ½ de profondeur

Tapisserie de camelot
a falbala rouge de 9
pieds de haut

Bureau nouveau de commodité a dossié
galonné 2 pieds de haut sur 3 pieds
pieds 2 poulces de large

201. A truly comfortable 'Grand Sopha' covered with a russet velvet trimmed with galloon and with a skirt 'à falbala[s]'
(with furbellows, which are echoed in the wall-hangings of red camlet). It may be that the filled-in arms and cheeks make
this a 'sofa' rather than a 'canapée'. The *bureau* is described as being 'nouveau' and 'de commodité'.

can now say is that another *canapée* (so described) was provided for royal use in the
mid-1680s,[80] while the term was being used in the 1690s to describe what we would
call a sofa, as the inscriptions under the drawings reproduced in Plates 17 and 199
show (they refer to 'grands canapés'). But two of the pieces are called *sophas* (Plate
201) although there does not seem to be any obvious difference between them and
those labelled as *canapés*. The fact that in 1692 someone explained that 'Un sofa [est]
une éspèce de lit de repos à la manière des Turcs' does not help to clarify the
problem[81] as far as the two sofas in question are concerned, although one could
understand it if the exotic double-seated affair shown in Plate 287 were called a *sopha
à la turque* (note the turban on a stand alongside). Unfortunately the inscription
below this drawing is indecipherable. But, even at the time, there seems to have been
some confusion. For example, Cronström, writing back to Stockholm from Paris in
1695, spoke of 'les sophas ou canappés', of which he said 'Il n'y a maintenant point de
chambre où il n'y en ait icy.' [There is now no room here where there is not one.][82]
What he says can, incidentally, only have been true of rooms (he cannot have meant
only *bed*-chambers) in houses of the most fashionable sort, and it may well be that
canapés and sofas were still at that period in some degree symbolic of high status and
may even occasionally have stood under canopies.[83]

212

Couches that can only have been day-beds (i.e. single-ended) had been furnished with canopies earlier in the century, presumably for the sake of comfort. The Duke of Lauderdale had a canopy over the sleeping-chair in his closet at Ham House around 1680 (Plate 180), as we have already noted, and we have illustrations of what must be French sleeping-chairs with attached canopies dating from the end of the century (Plate 171). Moreover, the *canapé* shown in Plate 200 is described as a 'grand canapé pour se reposer' (large *canapé* to sleep on) which may indicate that its base could pull out (and perhaps swing up and over) to form a bed-frame. If this is so, then it must be the direct ancestor of the sort of sofa-couches converting into beds that are illustrated in the works of Chippendale and of Ince and Mayhew in the middle of the next century.[84] These could have canopies, as the splendid Genoa velvet specimen at Holkham, installed in 1758, so magnificently shows.[85]

Sofas were by no means common in England before 1700 but some 'sophas in the Long Gallery' at Hampton Court were repaired in that year and were at the time described as being old.[86] The close resemblance between the opulent sofa made for the Duke of Leeds, now at Temple Newsam House near Leeds and some of those shown in the French drawings of furniture from the 1690s is not surprising if one realises that the leading upholsterers in London at that time were French or of French extraction.[87] The name of the maker of the Leeds sofa recently came to light and the same man, Philip Guibert, made what sounds like a very similar piece for William III in 1697 which was described in the bill as 'a fine black soffa of a new fashion, filled up with downe, the frieze and cheeks all molded and fringed'.[88] The Leeds sofa is accompanied by a no less magnificent day-bed upholstered en suite (Colour Plate

202. A strange sofa with rounded back in a closet panelled with mirror-glass (a 'Grand Cabinet de Glace' which is 'vue du grand Chambre'). French; 1690s.

CONTENTEMENT D'VNE DAME NOBLE.

SONNET EMBLEMATIQVE.

C'Eſt vn contentement & vne douce vie
  De voir la Damoiſelle ainſi dans ſa maiſon,
Prendre ſon Luth en main, eſtudier ſa leçon,
Et marier ſa voix auec ſon harmonie.

Elle banniſt de ſoy toute melancolie,
  Elle trouue repos en toute la ſaiſon;
  Elle chaſſe de ſoy de l'amour le tiſon,
  Et ne ſçait ce que c'eſt de l'infernale enuie.

Si quelqu'vn la vient voir dans le deuoir d'honneur,
  On voit rougir ſon front teſmoin de ſa pudeur,
  Et à peine peut-on entendre ſa parole:

Mais celle-là qui va, & qui court çà & là,
  Qui à baſtons rompus parle par cy par là,
  Monſtre des actions d'vne perſonne fole.

3

203. (upper far left) An English sofa of the 1690s formed like two adjacent easy chairs—a conformation frequently adopted in England. It may be that such sofas served a more formal, even ceremonial, purpose than we at present suppose. The red woollen material is superbly embroidered in coloured silks—no doubt professional work executed in London. The legs were originally gilded.

204. (lower far left) An English sofa of the late seventeenth century with integrated back and wings (note the line of the trimming on the armrests). Such imposing pieces of furniture are likely to have carried the implication that their owners held high rank. Made for the first Earl of Conyngsby about 1695.

205. (left) An early illustration of a daybed in a Parisian publication of about 1614. It has a drop-in squab and a large, shaped bolster.

206. A Dutch daybed; 1636. There must be some sort of upright head supporting the pillow. It has a loose coverlet.

207. Daybed with an adjustable head-rest organised in a similar manner to the double-ended couch shown in Plate 149. there is no indication that this piece ever had a hinged rest at the opposite end, so it must always have been a daybed, but a double-ended couch is en suite with it.

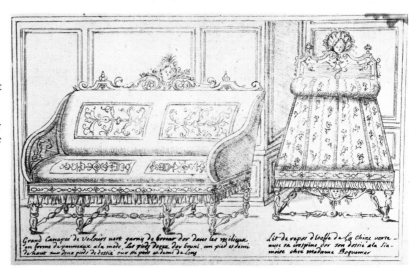

208. A French sofa and daybed in the 1690s. The daybed is described as a 'Lit de repos' with a headboard or backrest 'à la siamoise' (it is in fact decorated with appliqué work similar to that shown in Plate 96). The sofa is called a 'Grand Canapée', the paned covers (panels of gold brocade on green velvet) are stated to be 'à la mode'.

XII). Indeed, sofas and day beds were the two kinds of furniture on which the leading upholsterers of the day could display all their talents.

UPHOLSTERY

Before 1600, comfortable seating was generally achieved with the aid of cushions, and chairs with fixed upholstery were still something of a rarity. Moreover, such upholstery as was to be seen on seat-furniture at that period was of a most rudimentary kind. The devising of truly comfortable seat-furniture by means of cunningly placed padding and covering was left to the upholsterers of the seventeenth century and the technical advances made, particularly between 1660 and 1700, were immense. Nevertheless, it needs to be said that seventeenth century upholstery on seat-furniture was very poor when compared with that of the nineteenth century; it lacked firmness, it was often irregular and the workmanship can rarely have stood up to close inspection. One might say that it did the job, but the high traditions that one sees embodied in the best nineteenth-century upholstery had still to be evolved. The seventeenth century upholsterer achieved his effects with rich materials and by loading the confection with trimmings.

It is a comparatively simple matter to place a pile of padding (straw, hair, feathers, etc.) on a seat and to hold it down by nailing a cover over it. The result is a domed seat, and many seventeenth century upholstered chair-seats were of this simple shape (Plates 158, 163 and 186). To achieve anything more subtle required more elaborate techniques: the padding had to be stitched down and located in the desired position.

The earliest attempts to secure padding probably relied on attached quilted overlays to chair-backs and seats. Cane-seated and backed chairs were still being fitted with such overlays at the end of the seventeenth century and later. They were tied on with ribbons but the next step was to fix such padding to the framing with nails. Chairs with fixed quilting were apparently being made in both Spain and Italy before 1600; the invalid-chair of Philip II of Spain (d. 1598) seems to have this kind of padding (Plate 172). The stitching formed a lozenge pattern in this case but more decorative designs, such as scale-patterns, could be executed in this technique. It may be no accident that many of these early essays in fixing the padding of chairs were executed in leather, for it was probably the saddlers who first showed the way in this field.[89] They had perforce to make sure the padding of saddles stayed in place under the most rigorous conditions and, once evolved, such techniques could of course easily be applied to chairs. Maybe these techniques were first tried out on the seats of carriages and sedan chairs, for the saddlers and the carriage-makers naturally worked in close association.

Vermeer often painted a chair (it was presumably in his studio) which had padding stitched in such a way as to form long ridges round the edge and a cross in the middle (Plate 210). The technique seems primitive and probably reflects a Netherlandish practice from the early part of the century. Such padding could, however, never be very thick and it had to wait until buttoning (or tufting, see p. 128) had been evolved before anything more substantial could be fitted (Plates 170 and 171). This did probably not happen much before 1660.

Attempts were made from about 1630 onwards to produce squared edges to seats and backs but, as the distorted seat of the farthingale chair illustrated in Plate 159

217

shows, the techniques for securing such shapes rigidly had not been evolved and were not mastered until well into the eighteenth century. A certain squaring could be indicated by means of piped or corded edges but the essentially domed forms could not all that easily be disguised.

The padded back-rests of ordinary chairs remained rectangular until the end of the century and there was therefore always a gap between the lower edge of the rest and the top of the seat which no amount of fringing quite masked. Invalid chairs and easy chairs, on the other hand, often had no gap at the back.[90] On chairs of the farthingale type and the scaled-up armchair version made between about 1620 and 1670 the short sections of upright between the seat and the back-rest were often encased in material (Plates 160 and 184), as were the arms of the armchairs. There was a measure of padding on the top surfaces of the arm-rests in later models but the uprights and arm-rests of armchairs made after about 1670 tended to be left uncovered (Plate 191), it being left to the easy chair to take on the full padding of all surfaces.

Some X-frame chairs of state and some *pliants* had had their wooden members totally encased in material early in the century (Plate 168) but legs were mostly left natural, or were painted or gilded. When painted, the appearance of the textile covering material was often imitated. There is, for instance, an X-frame chair at Knole which has its legs painted red with a lace-pattern in white over it (Plate 169). Close inspection shows that the chair was originally covered in red velvet to which a silver lace was applied, so the paintwork on the legs would simply have carried on the decoration in a different medium.[91] Some farthingale chairs at Knole, dating from the 1620s and covered with red velvet trimmed with fringe, have their legs painted with translucent red varnish over a gold ground.[92] The red covering is reserved so as to leave the gold showing in a pattern of moresques but it also shows through the varnish to give the whole a brilliant effect. The same technique is used on 'Queen Elizabeth's Virginals', a Venetian spinet of about 1570 in the Victoria and Albert Museum. By and large, the colour of the painted woodwork formed an extension of the upholstered decoration but occasionally contrasting effects were sought—like the marbled stools in Cardinal Mazarin's collection.[93] Black, however, was much in favour for the wooden members of chairs right through the century. Many chairs with black leather covers to be seen in illustrations from the first third of the century seem to have their wooden members stained black; numerous cane chairs from the last third of the century had black frames as did some rush-seated chairs; and it was apparently fashionable for chairs in the 1680s and 90s to have black frames with gilt details (Colour Plate XII)[94] In fact, references to totally gilt seat-furniture are rare in the seventeenth century while references to silvered furniture occur rather more frequently than might be supposed from reading the average book on antique furniture.[95] Of course a gilded look could be achieved by applying a yellow varnish to a silvered finish—as was sometimes done on the stands of cabinets and to other carved work of the Restoration period.

But let us return to the actual upholstery. The padding of the seat was laid on a lattice of girth-webbing nailed across the seat-frame—just as it still is on many chairs today. Karin Walton has drawn attention to the fact that the French practice was to lace broad webs so closely as to form an unbroken surface, whereas the English preferred to use a narrow web spaced to form an open network.[96] This was certainly

209. (far left) Sketch of early stitched padding forming four mounds on a chair-seat, based on a painting of about 1625. The moulded seat-rails are faced with velvet as well. The chair is otherwise of a standard Netherlandish type.

210. (left) Stitching forming ridges in padding on a Dutch mid-seventeenth-century chair in Vermeer's studio.

true of chairs in the eighteenth century but these divergent practices may have become established well before 1700. The padding of the back was attached to a canvas or linen backing nailed to the front face of the back (the inside back as upholsterers call it). The covering material is then taken round the sides of the back-frame and nailed in position. A modern upholsterer will invariably cover the outside back with material so as to hide the wooden framing and the canvas or linen backing, but most seventeenth century chairs were left with these structural features exposed (Plates 160 and 189). After all, chairs were designed normally to stand with their backs to the wall, so there seemed little point in wasting money on decorating what was not often seen.[97] Only exceptionally grand chairs had coverings on the outside back as well. In some cases, late in the century, material was fitted closely to the wooden members at the back and then across the back of the canvas backing—that is to say, there was a rectangular recess covered in the fine material at the back.

The outer covering had to be fixed with nails and a virtue was often made out of this necessity by having the nails play a decorative part, in which case nails with gilded heads were used. 'Close-nailing' (i.e. with the nails close-set) was not used in the seventeenth century; they preferred a more open spacing with the nails hammered through a braid or the heading of a fringe. Sometimes nails with heads of fancy shapes were used, and it was not uncommon to have nails of two quite different sizes used in combination to form patterns (Plate 168). On the other hand, the material might be held with iron tacks that were not meant to be seen; in such cases, fringes of various kinds (notably the spiralling *mollet*, see p. 128) would be used to mask them.

Great freedom was allowed the upholsterer in the application of trimming (Plate 204), although there were in practice several conventions that most of them observed. These can best be understood by studying contemporary illustrations. The fact that silk materials of the period tended to be about twenty inches wide posed problems for the upholsterer when chair-backs and seats (not to speak of sofas) became wider and the material had to be seamed. Placing a decorative stripe at the join was one way of disguising it. Another was to have a rectangle of galloon applied to the back and to the seat.

When not in use, expensively covered chairs would invariably be protected against dust, light and fingering, and most will have been provided with loose covers of a less expensive material, often of serge or bays, or even taffeta. They often had vents at the sides of the back, or in the middle of the outside back, so that they were not too tight to put on, and they were then tied tight and secured with tapes or laces.[98] Later, hooks and eyes were used.[99]

The process might also be reversed so that it was the slip-over covering that was of the expensive material while a cheaper material remained fixed to the chair. Such 'slip-over' covers could be removed to the wardrobe room except when the family was in residence. Something of the kind may have been used quite early in the century[100] but the practice was well established by the 1670s, the 'dolphin chairs' at Ham House still providing excellent examples with their slip-over covers of 'rich brocard' (Plate 40).[101] These *housses* might have deep skirts. Cardinal Mazarin had eight armchairs 'en housse' in the 1650s which had 'pantes' (i.e. *pentes* or valances)[102] but it was left to the upholsterers of the 1690s to develop the heavy-skirted look, as several of Daniel Marot's engravings show (Plate 143).

Casters that swivelled had been evolved before 1600 and seem at first to have been applied to invalid chairs (Plate 173). They were later put on some easy chairs, for example that which stood in the Duke of Lauderdale's closet at Ham House in the 1670s (Plate 180), and the Duke of Ormonde had a 'crimson velvet easy chair on wheels' at Kilkenny Castle in 1684.[103] Such fittings were certainly not common, however. The wheels tended to be globular at this early stage. The Lauderdale chair has casters with sockets fitting over the ends of the legs.

As for the materials used for the covering of chairs, one might use almost any material as long as it was sufficiently strong. But, in practice, the commonest covering materials were plain silk velvet and silk damask at the upper end of the scale, and woollen cloths like serge at the lower end. Leather, which came in many forms, plain or decorated, was widely used—being strong, pliant and easy to clean, it was much in favour for dining chairs. Turkeywork and the various forms of woollen velvet were also very popular because they combined a yielding pile surface with bright colours. But let us consider these materials and their application to chairs in a little more detail.

Chair-covers of tapestry were uncommon in the seventeenth century although cushion-covers specially woven for the purpose were produced in great quantities, notably in Holland.[104] An armchair in the royal castle at Copenhagen in 1638 was covered in 'Flemish' ('mit flamsch überzogen') which indicates that it had a tapestry-woven material on it, tapestry being known as 'flamsk vaevning', Flemish weaving, in Scandinavia.[105] However, this material does not seem to have been used at all frequently for the covering of seat-furniture. The only English examples that can at present be cited are the tapestry-woven loose-covers for the large japanned squab-frames that already stood in the Gallery at Ham House in 1679 and are still there today.[106] In 1695 Daniel Cronström wrote from Paris advising Countess Piper in Stockholm that, if she wanted to do up her house in the latest Parisian fashion, she should have the chairs in her bedchamber covered with damask or *hautelisse* (by which he meant tapestry), or in Venetian brocatelle.[107] But he was no doubt recording the fashions current in a very thin stratum of Parisian society and there is no other indication that chairs covered with tapestry were to be seen at all frequently even there. Nor, for that matter, was it common to use brocatelle which was a rather stiff half-silk (see p. 116).

Dornix, which was so much used for hangings, was presumably too loosely woven to be suitable for chair-covering.[108] Another distinctive woollen material must have been 'Scotch pladd' which presumably had tartan checks. There was a room completely hung with this material at Tart Hall in 1641 and the couch, with its cushions and canopy, were of the same material, as were two small chairs and a table-carpet that completed the suite.[109] Right at the end of the century, there was a 'Plod' chamber at Dyrham which had hangings of 'Scots Plod' and seat-furniture covered en suite.[110] But this material does not seem to have been at all common, either. The woollen (or worsted) materials that were used for chair-covers in really substantial quantity were 'Cloth, Serge, Perpetuanoes, Chamlets, Bays, Kersies, Norwich Cheniis & Kidderminster Prints' with which, it was claimed (admittedly by members of the woollen industries) 240,000 new chairs were covered each year around 1685 or so.[111] Serge and dyed linen were, incidentally, often used for the fixed coverings of expensive chairs that had slip-over covers of a richer material.

Little need be said about silken materials, as far as their application to chair-covers is concerned, but it is interesting to note that grand people in the seventeenth century were not averse to having on chairs silken materials that were brocaded with gold or silver thread (Plates 168 and 181). In the eighteenth century, it was quite exceptional to use such materials, their scratchiness presumably being considered unacceptable for the purpose. The large-patterned 'Genoa velvets' do not seem to have been much used for chair-covering until the very end of the century (Colour Plate XII), when they began to enjoy a period of high favour that lasted into the middle of the next century. Sarsnet, that thin taffeta so suitable for sun-curtains, was only applied to chair-covers in the form of loose covers of the more expensive sort.

The various kinds of woollen velvet (see p. 111) were greatly favoured right through the seventeenth century for the covering of seat-furniture. For example, a 'chaize de bois à dam[ois]elle' [a woman's chair of wood] and twenty-one armchairs in a room at a house in Rheims in 1621 were covered in 'moquette de diverse couleurs' which was fixed with gilt nails, while a house at Marseilles in 1636 had 'trois tamboretz [tabourets] garnis de tripe de velours' [three stools covered with woollen velvet].[112] In a room at the Noordeinde residence at The Hague in 1632 were two old armchairs covered in *caffa*, and seat-furniture covered with this material and the related 'flowered trippe' are frequently mentioned in House of Orange inventories towards the end of the century.[113] In 1678 the *Académie Française* was provided with a set of walnut chairs covered with *moquade*.[114] There were numerous chairs and stools at Marly and Meudon covered with *tripe* and the 'six grand fauteuils de commodité' mentioned on p. 196 were covered splendidly in 'panne d'Hollande couleur de feu'.[115] At about the same time some chairs at Dyrham were being covered in 'stript plush' while at Tredegar House in South Wales a couch and some cane chairs were acquired which had cushions of 'flowered plush'.[116]

While technically different from the woollen velvets, turkeywork also had a woollen pile and was therefore popular for the same reason, namely that it had a comfortable resilient surface. The pile was usually rather coarser but it was also more robust. In the 'Little Dyning Chamber' at Hardwick in 1601 there was 'a chare of Turkie worke' with a stool covered en suite.[117] The other seat-furniture in the room consisted of 'joint stools'. It is not clear whether this room was used by the Countess of Shrewsbury as a private dining-room, or whether it was used by her steward or senior staff, but one can say that the seat of turkeywork was a fairly grand piece of furniture, inferior only to the opulent pieces in the state rooms. Many stools were covered in turkeywork during the early part of the century but the material really came into its own as covering for farthingale chairs which were produced in large quantities from about 1630 onwards.[118] Panels specially woven to go on such chairs were being made by the middle of the century (Plate 103). The royal household continued to order this simple but comfortable type of chair for use in offices and the like right into the eighteenth century.[119]

Technically related to turkeywork was Savonnerie carpeting and, likewise, it made excellent chair-covers. However, it was extremely expensive and its production was anyway under the king's control, so it was only to be found on seat-furniture in rather exceptional circumstances. Cardinal Mazarin had a whole set of furniture covered in this material—twelve armchairs, twelve ordinary chairs, a couch and two carpets—but then he always surrounded himself with objects of the most conspicuous luxury.[120] The Dauphin had some forms at Meudon in 1702 which were covered in yellow Savonnerie carpeting and a set of stools with Savonnerie covers that must have been specially designed as seat-covers because they each had inwoven a rose at the centre and a dolphin (*dauphin*) at each corner.[121]

Leather had been used for chair-seats and chair-backs since time immemorial; its properties make it particularly suitable for the purpose. Folding chairs and stools could have leather seats (and backs) which needed no further strengthening or padding, although they could of course have both. Moreover, leather can be decorated in various ways, and it is easy to keep clean—for which reason it was popular for dining-chairs. Most seventeenth century leather chair-seats were plain, made of 'Russia leather' which was relatively coarse, or of 'Turkey leather' which seems to have been finer. Towards the end of the century, 'Morocco leather' came into use for the purpose. Black leather with a certain amount of gilt tooling was popular in the Netherlands during the first half of the century,[122] but tooled and gilded leather was not unknown in England at the time, as several documents prove.[123] No doubt leather chair-backs and seats were sometimes painted, like so much other leatherwork of the period, such as the fire-buckets at Ham House, dating from the 1670s, which are painted with the Lauderdale's coat of arms. So-called 'gilt leather' was used to some small extent for chairs (Plate 164). There were eighteen chairs so covered in the 'Guilt Leather Room' at Cowdray in 1682, several sets at Ham House in the middle of the century had seats and backs covered with cloth bordered with gilt leather, while at the princely court at Groeningen in 1633 there were eight 'men's chairs' of gilt leather and a 'large English gilt leather chair'.[124] The material seems, however, to have gone out of fashion in England for the covering of chairs (it was never apparently favoured in France for this purpose and was not much used in Holland either) but it was put to this use in Germany and Scandinavia until well into the eighteenth century.

Embroidery, as has already been explained, could be executed in so many

XII. (right) Although made in London, this sumptuous daybed and its accompanying sofa exemplify better than any other surviving pieces the French style in luxurious seat-furniture at the end of the century. Richly carved, painted black and partly gilded, covered with polychrome Genoa velvet, and trimmed with bell-fringe, this furniture was made for the Duke of Leeds about 1700.

different ways and was so infinitely flexible as a medium for producing decorated textile covers for seat-furniture (Plates 189 and 204) that nothing can be gained by making generalisations here. However, one form of embroidery needs to be mentioned, because it was much used for the coverings of seat-furniture in the seventeenth century, and that is *point d'Hongrie* or 'Irish stitch' (see p. 125). I have also discussed the distinction between domestic and professional embroidery, explaining however that the distinction was by no means always clearly defined. But rich chair-covers worked by professional embroiderers could be very expensive, as Cronström pointed out when comparing them with covers of tapestry. 'Les chaises de haute lisse couteront mesme ou un peu moins que celles à l'aiguille' [Chairs with *hautelisse* cost the same or rather more than those with needlework], he wrote in 1695. He explained that the high cost of needlework was due to the fact that 'Il n'y a qu'une personne qui puisse travailler à chaque morceau' at a time and that therefore 'cela vas plus lentement.' [Only one person can work at each piece, which goes much more slowly.] What is more, he added, 'ces animaux de tapissiers' [those beasts of upholsterers] were always terribly slow and would invent reasons for late delivery. In Paris a finely embroidered chair-cover might then have cost 22 *écus*.[125]

Between June 1660 and Michaelmas of the following year, John Casbert supplied Charles II with a considerable amount of seat-furniture. Although based in London and working for the Royal Wardrobe, Casbert was probably a French upholsterer and his productions are likely to have been in the latest French taste. Indeed, he described several pieces in his account as 'french Chaires'.[126] He lists the various materials that he used for making up this furniture—sackcloth, girthweb, black tacks (i.e. of iron, as opposed to gilded nails), lining for the backs, crimson serge to cover the chairs, 'milland [Milan] fustion for baggs' (i.e. cushions), down to fill them with, 'curled haire to fill the chaire backs', 'gilt nailes for garnishing', and gold and silver fringe. He then charged for 'making and covering the chairs with crimson serge' and 'fitting false cases of crimson damaske'—these were detachable slip-over covers of the rich material. This is one of the earliest references to the use of horsehair (*crin*) in upholstery. Horsehair seems to have been used for padding the back of Philip II's gout-chair (Plate 173) in the late sixteenth century and Cardinal Mazarin had some forms stuffed with hair in the 1650s.[127] It will be noted that Casbert used horsehair only in the backs; presumably it was especially practical for this task as it was easier to keep in place than other forms of padding. Later it was used all over chairs where firm, springy padding was needed (Plate 179). For real softness, seventeenth-century upholstery relied on down and the accommodating *fauteuils de commodité* and *canapés* of the 1690s acquired their luxurious character through the lavish use of down in conjunction with forms carefully designed to support the human frame in maximum comfort. So great was the use of down for upholstery at the end of the century that an increase in the number of sufferers from piles in Paris was actually attributed to the too liberal use of down 'dans les chaise, les carrosses et autres sièges qui servoient à la commodité, au lieu de crin, dont on se servoit autrefois' [in sedan chairs and other seats which provided comfort, in place of horsehair, which was used formerly].[128]

XIII. (left) A looking-glass canted forward; the common method of hanging large framed items in the seventeenth century. The painting behind has a green protective curtain. Note also the vase of flowers. Dutch, 1678.

CHAPTER IX
Tables and Cup-boards

TABLES that could be dismantled or folded up had suited the mobile life of the ruling classes during the Middle Ages. As a more static life came to be adopted, a parallel development to that which we noted with beds took place—massive, heavy tables were evolved that were virtually impossible to move and therefore remained constantly in one position. But the mobile forms of table continued in favour for occasional use. The servants might bring one in so that dinner could be taken in warmth and comfort by the fire in winter, or they might set one up in the garden so that a meal could be eaten al fresco. Occasional tables were needed for all kinds of purposes—serving food, shaving, washing, accommodating extra people at meals, and so forth. Military gentlemen still needed such equipment on campaigns (Plate 211), moreover, and the rich might still have a folding table to go with the field-bed and the folding chairs when they travelled.

A simple and well-known form of portable table had two or more loose trestles each of which were hinged at the top and opened out into inverted V-shaped stands.[1] A development of this had trestle-like legs fixed with hinges to the underside of the table; the legs were locked in the open position with long iron hooks (Plate 213). This form seems to have been evolved in Spain and at any rate remained popular in that country for a long while.[2] It was known as a 'Spanish table' in the seventeenth century.[3] They are frequently mentioned in English inventories but were inexpensive and uninteresting pieces of furniture, so hardly any specimens have survived (Plate 212).[4] There were doubtless several other types of readily portable table; some were merely small, others had folding tops (Plates 214 and 215), while yet others must have stood on X-frame stands.[5]

Although the artistocracy in the mediaeval period carried their folding tables and trestle-tables with them, they often also had non-portable tables set up in their castles and residence. The long and heavy tables with their massive trestles that usually stood in the hall of great houses were fixtures of this kind[6] but by 1600 it was only the lower servants who would dine at such tables.[7] They would usually be presided over by the steward who would often sit at a draw-table—a table which had draw-leaves at each end by means of which the table area could be doubled at will.[8] The draw-table was itself somewhat massive and so tended to be kept in one place.

The draw-table was also the form commonly used by the owner and his family in their dining parlours or in other rooms where they frequently took meals (Plates 232 and 242).[9] It remained in favour until the middle of the century when the round or oval table with hinged flaps and a swinging gate-leg made its appearance.[10] These rounded shapes were convenient in the smaller and more intimate dining-rooms that were coming into fashion. They enabled the servants to circulate more easily, and questions of precedence were rarely much of a problem in such relatively informal surroundings. The gate-leg form could fold into a narrow compass and could then be placed out of the way against the wall (together with the dining chairs) or in an adjacent passageway.

211. A trestle table with folding, inverted 'V' trestles set up in a military tent. Note the velvet table-carpet. A folding X-frame chair may be seen in the background; at this date it would not only have been a practical piece of furniture to take on campaign but would in addition have underlined the owner's high estate.

212. A folding table of oak. This is likely to be an example of the 'Spanish tables' so often listed in English seventeenth-century inventories. The iron struts brace the folding legs when the table is in use.

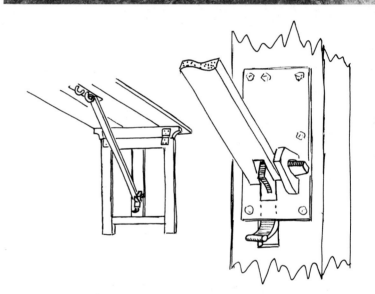

213. The locking action of the table shown in Plate 212. Pulling the spring-loaded catch downwards enables the strut to be un-hooked sideways from the protruding lug.

214 A late-seventeenth-century pinewood occasional table that can be folded. Provided for the use of a Queen of Sweden. The top folds upwards longitudinally; the gate-legs swing round outwards upon the other half-trestles which in turn fold up against the leaf (the trestle at one end is hinged from a deep block to allow the opposite trestle to fold under first).

215. An occasional table of pinewood dated 1696. Such simple furniture has very rarely survived. When in use it would normally have been covered with a cloth.

216. A tea-table of Javanese lacquer raised to a height suitable for Europeans by a Carolean joiner. About 1680.

217. Tea-table with markedly Dutch characteristics provided for royal use in a Danish palace, probably in 1696.

In the 'Great Dining Room' at Ham House in the 1670s there were eight folding tables of cedarwood.[11] They were no doubt humble structures that were usually hidden by the four Oriental screens that were also in the room. It is probable that they were rectangular and could be set out next to each other so as to make up a single table as large as circumstances at each mean required.[12] Extension-pieces were also known in the seventeenth century.[13]

There were of course many specialised forms of table. One type that must have been distinctive was an 'oyster table' at which one did in fact eat oysters, then a relatively inexpensive food. They were apparently circular, with a hole in the centre under which stood a basket for the empty shells.[14] They could be folded away[15] but a certain Mr Hastings, a squire living in Dorset who died in 1650, had in his parlour an 'oyster table at the lower end' which was 'of constant use twice a day all the year round'.[16] They were relatively common in the first half of the century but there was still 'a little oyster table' standing in the hall at Ham House in 1679.[17]

Tables specially designed for the taking of tea only made their appearance late in the century. A specimen at Rosenborg Castle in Copenhagen has a tray-like top with splayed sides, all covered with floral marquetry. It stands on four spiral-turned legs. It may have been made in Copenhagen by a Dutch cabinetmaker or it may have been imported from Holland (Plate 217). Also with a tray-like top is the East Indian lacquerwork tea-table at Ham House which is presumably to be equated with the 'Tea-Table carved and guilt' that stood in the Duchess of Lauderdale's private closet in 1683 (Plate 216).[18] There are similar tables at Dyrham and Lyme Park, and several more are to be seen at Schloss Charlottenburg, Berlin.[19] Since the latter was at that period the residence of a Dutch princess, it may well be that all these East Indian tables were acquired from a dealer in Amsterdam. The Lauderdales certainly bought furniture in Amsterdam although there is no evidence that this particular table came from Holland. By the turn of the century, the familiar form of tea-table with a tip-up top with a pillar and a tripod stand had been devised, probably in Holland.[20] One may be discerned standing in the corner of a room in the painting of a doll's house of about 1700 (Plate 320). Its painted top faces out into the room. The early models had a raised, moulded rim but it was soon found easier to have no rim so that a tea-tray could, so to speak, be slid onto the top.

The French, who were supreme masters in the creation of comfort in the seventeenth century, even devised small tables for taking meals in bed. At the end of the century there were six tables 'pour servir à manger sur le lit' at the Château de Marly, a royal residence where informality and relaxation were *de rigueur*.[21] But almost a century before there had been a 'table à metre devant madame lors qu'elle mange dans le lict' [table for placing before my lady when she takes a meal in bed] at the Château de Turenne.[22] No doubt other examples from the intervening decades could be found from a careful search in inventories.

In contemporary illustrations from about 1630 onwards, one often sees ladies at their *toilette* but no examples of dressing-tables from before about 1675 seem to survive, nor are references at all common in the documents. There were 'sixteene little dressinge Tables of severall sizes' at Easton Lodge in 1637 and there was one at Ham House in the middle of the century.[23] In many of the principal bedchambers at Ham in the 1670s there were small cedarwood tables which may well also have served this purpose, and one has to remember that the fashionable furniture ensemble of the 1670s and 1680s, comprising a side-table, looking-glass and pair of candlestands, might be used as a grand dressing-suite (see Plate 94), although such a triad was normally set up in a room just for show. Indeed, it was the principal fashionable furnishing unit of the period (Plate 218)[24] The group was commonly set against a pier between windows (Plate 273) and thus became the ancestor of the eighteenth century pier-glass and console-table (Plate 219). In that position it of course served well as a dressing-table for the light from the windows fell on the face of the lady in the daytime, while at night the light from the candles on the stands did the same. The looking-glass had to be canted forward so that the sitter could see her reflection. The tables initially associated with such groups tended to be rather insubstantial and therefore unsteady but in the 1680s the French introduced a more sturdy form of table with shorter legs and a knee-hole (Plate 31). This form is today often called a *bureau Mazarin* but, while some may actually have served as writing-desks, many were certainly dressing-tables.[25]

Elaborately decorated tables of various kinds were made right through the seventeenth century for purely decorative purposes—prized possessions of their owners. They were very naturally placed in prominent positions but, since each was unique and since they constituted such exceptional items there is no need to discuss them in the present context.[26]

One must not be misled by the term 'a pair of tables' which occurs in many early seventeenth-century inventories. This meant a games board which, at the time, usually took the form of a box with two tray-like halves hinged so as to open out to form a backgammon (*tric-trac*) board. On the outside faces were the boards for two other games—chess or draughts, and Nine-Men's Morris (Plate 160)[27] When closed, the box held the requisite 'men'. But, while chess-boards were not actual tables, there were several forms of table used for specific games—tables for billiards and *Trou-Madame*, and shovelboards. A mid-seventeenth century billiard-table is still to be seen at Knole and is probably the one mentioned in the inventory of 1645.[28] The drawing of a later example that stood at Chantilly is reproduced in Plate 225. It was faced with green cloth, just as it would be today, but there was a pillar with small bells at the top (*le but*) standing up in the centre. Shovelboards, being very long, are mostly to be found among the furnishings of galleries.[29] *Trou-Madame* was roughly like the modern bagatelle (Plate 83).[30] Some card-tables made for the Dauphin and the Prince de Condé are illustrated in Plates 223 and 224.

A form of table that remains a mystery was something called a 'brushing board' although it was easily recognisable for what it was in the early seventeenth century. In a room where some of the maids slept at Ingatestone, there was a 'brushing bourde of two breadthes lying upon a frame', while at Chatsworth there was 'a playne borde to brush on' in one small room.[31] The purpose of such tables is clear but their nature is not.

Finally, we must discuss cup-boards, a term that embraces a variety of forms, the common purpose of which was to provide a stage (or board) on which precious vessels ('cups') could be displayed.[32] Such furniture was usually to be found in rooms where grand company dined, but cup-boards might also sometimes be placed in bedchambers. Cup-boards had originally taken the form of a simple table but gradually acquired extra shelves or staging on which larger quantities of plate could be shown.[33] Eventually, the lower sections came to be enclosed, with a door in

Jean le Pautre Inv. et fecit

218 (left) The fashionable ensemble of the second half of the seventeenth century shown in a Parisian engraving of about 1670. From a suite entitled *Livre de Miroirs, Tables et Guéridons*. For convenience such a group is here called a 'triad'.

219. (above) A Dutch engraving of 1697 shows the eighteenth-century console-table and pier-glass evolving from the late-seventeenth-century 'triad'. The unstable candlestands have already been dispensed with.

front, and thus the term 'cupboard', as we understand it, gained its modern meaning.[34] Cup-boards in the form of *étagères* with enclosed cupboard-sections (i.e. with doors) were not uncommon in the sixteenth century (Plate 92). Being useful for other purposes as well as mere display, now that they could house objects and provide a measure of security, the cupboard came to be used in other rooms—notably in the bedchamber where it served also as a place in or on which to place the 'livery' of food or drink that was issued to important members of the household and guests for the night,[35] although this practice was fast going out of fashion by 1600.[36] The 'livery cupboard' seems finally to have acquired a generally recognisable form and, when it was placed in other rooms (for example, the dining parlour), it was still given this name even though it was presumably never expected to house liveries there. The cup-board with multiple stages (sometimes now with a small cupboard forming a centre section) evolved in England and came to be known as a 'court cupboard', presumably because it was a form that had in the first place been used at court.[37] At any rate, livery cupboards and court cupboards are frequently mentioned in English inventories of the first half of the seventeenth century. As both could have cupboard-sections and neither was invariably confined respectively to the bedchamber and the dining parlour, there was room for confusion at the time and it is no longer possible always to be sure which type of furniture was being described in a particular case.

220. (above) One of the massive silver tables at Versailles. Made by Claude Ballin (1615–78) in the 1670s. This actual table seems to be in the foreground of the view of the *Grand Galerie*, to which room it must have been moved early in the 1680s. Although the piece is there shown used as a pier-table, it appears to be a centre-table (i.e. with four decorated faces).

221. (right) The only surviving piece of silver furniture which faithfully conveys to us how the massive pieces at Versailles must have looked is this font, made by a French silversmith specially brought to Stockholm to execute important commissions for the Swedish Crown.

223. (far right) The Dauphin's card-table at Versailles late in the seventeenth century. The armchair was occupied by the Dauphin (note the dolphin armrests) while the rest of the company will have sat on circular *tabourets* like that illustrated.

222. Tables at Versailles late in the seventeenth century. From a suite of engravings entitled *Livre de tables qui sont dans les apartemens du Roy sur lesquelles sont posées les bijoux des Cabinet des Medailles.* This may be understood to mean that the tables stood in the *Cabinet de Medailles* (completed 1685) which certainly housed part of Louis XIV's collection of gemstone vessels. But the closet could hardly have contained so many tables (ten are illustrated) and we are probably meant to understand that the tables stood in the *Grands Apartments* but that the vessels are here merely shown standing on them. If so, the tables will be those of gilded wood that replaced the massive silver furniture that was melted down in 1689.

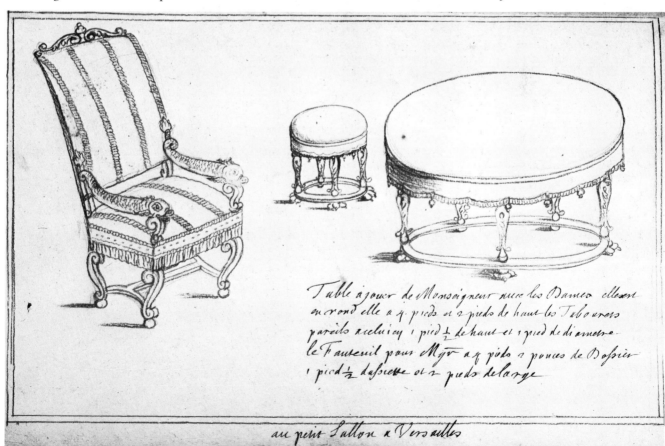

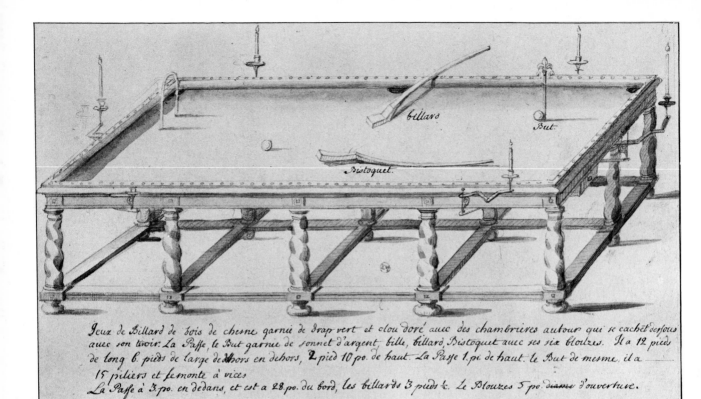

Jeux de Billard de bois de chesne garnie de drap vert et clou doré auec des chambrieres autour qui se cachet dessous
auec son tiroir. La Passe, le But garnie de sonnet d'argent, bille, billard, Bistoquet auec ses six bloutzes. Il a 12 pieds
de long 6. pieds de large dedhors en dehors, 2 pied 10 po. de haut. La Passe 1. pi. de haut. le But de mesme, il a
15 piliers et se monte à vices
La Passe à 3. po. en dedans, et est à 28. po. du bord, les billards 3 pieds ½. Le Blouzes 5 po. diam d'ouverture.

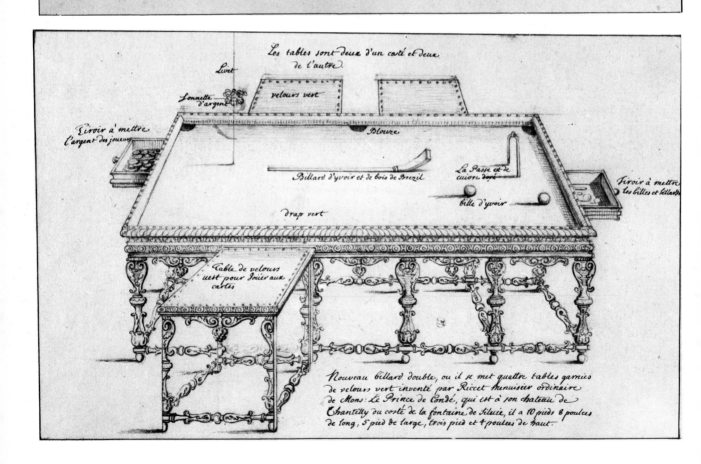

Nouveau billard double, ou il se met quattre tables garnies
de velours vert inventé par Ricet menuisier ordinaire
de Mons: Le Prince de Condé, qui est à son chateau de
Chantilly du coste de la fontaine de Silvie, il a 10 pieds 8 poulces
de long, 5 pied de large, trois pied et 4 poulces de haut.

224 & 225. (left) Two late-seventeenth-century French billiard-tables. The goal (*but*) is fitted with bells that will have rung when the post was struck. There is also a hoop (*passe*). The first table is covered with green cloth, the second, which stood at Chantilly, with green velvet. The latter is stated to be a new model by the Prince de Condé's joiner, Riccet (Ricetti?). A card-table is shown in front.

226. (above) The plain tables set against the window wall in this scene of an English royal banquet given in 1672 are described as 'court cupboards' in the contemporary key to the engraving.

227. An undressed *buffet* with superimposed staging for display of plate. The lower section must comprise two cupboard sections. Opposite stands a draw-table. The presence of these two pieces of furniture indicates that the room commonly served as a dining room.

The *étagère* type of court cupboard went out of fashion in the middle of the century but the term 'court cupboard' was still apparently used after that to describe a straightforward table used as a sideboard (Plate 226).[38] As Randle Holme stated, 'side-tables or court cubberts' were essential in a dining room.[39] The term 'sideboard' occurs in the inventory of Hatfield Priory already in 1629, while a 'side-board table' is mentioned in the mid-century inventory of Ham House.[40] The buffet with stages, conceived as a single piece of furniture, went out of fashion in the middle of the century, and was replaced by the sideboard. On very special occasions, when it was still desired to have a rich display of plate, a special side-table with staging entirely masked with a cloth was easily contrived (Plate 229).

The French called the cup-board with staging a *dressoir* (hence our 'dresser') in the Middle Ages, presumably because one dressed it with plate.[41] Later the common term for such a piece of furniture was *un buffet*, because from it one often dispensed drink (Plates 92 and 227).[42] Occasionally, it was also known as a *dessert*, perhaps because the dessert stood on it prior to being brought to the table.[43]

Continental buffets were altogether more elaborate than their English counterparts; they often had highly decorated back-boards, and many comprised cupboards in the lower stage. However, the more skeletal form (which the English called a 'court cupboard') was also known, at least in France, judging by two shown in an illustration in De Breuil's treatise on perspective of 1642–9.[44]

The various forms of buffet so far mentioned were movable (even if they were

228. A *buffet* or cup-board covered with a cupboard cloth and dressed with plate. Dutch; 1602. The master of the house has a 'great chair' with arms; his wife and children have less impressive forms of seating.

rarely moved because they were very heavy) but built-in buffets came into fashion late in the century. Plate 19 shows one of eight counter-like buffets of this sort that were provided for the central, octagonal Salon at the Château de Marly in 1699–1700. In the latter year, Jean Bérain, designer to the *Ménus Plaisirs*, the organisation that provided ephemeral equipment and decoration for the numerous elaborate festivities and ceremonies at the French Court, invented a special buffet which was 'fort propre pour les festes' [very suitable for banquets]. It was set in a niche and had sliding doors assisted by counterweights. It was decorated with 'figures à la Chine'.[45] In Holland, and also to some extent in England, buffets might be contrived in arched niches at one end of a dining-room.[46] Such buffet-niches were to become a common feature of Dutch interiors in the eighteenth century.

The seventeenth-century tables that one sees in museums and country houses today are almost all left bare—uncovered. This gives a false impression of their original appearance, for at that period they were, almost without exception, covered with a cloth of some kind (Plate 231). Draw-tables and other forms of table that stood in prominent places invariably had special 'table carpets' that were more or less splendid according to the depth of the owner's purse (Plate 232). Dining-tables were, moreover, covered with linen tablecloths at mealtimes.[47] When cup-boards or buffets were dressed with plate, a 'cup-board cloth' covered at least the uppermost stage and often the whole structure (Plate 228). Even the very splendid tables, decorated elaborately with inlay or marquetry and designed specially for show,

Plan, Elevation et Profil d'vn Buffet de Marbre et de Bronze, au milieu du quel est vn Tableau et aux côtez deux
Niches, dans lesquelles il y a des Cascades. Ce Buffet est executé chez Monsieur Thevenin a Paris.

I. Mariette excudit.

3.

74

299. (upper left) Proposal for dressing a *buffet* by Jean Bérain (1640–1711), showing an impressive array of plate including two perfume-burners (*casolettes*) with their pierced lids. The legs of this piece of furniture are not shown.

230. (lower left) End wall of a Parisian dining room late in the seventeenth century with a fixed *buffet* of marble flanked by niches containing fountains.

231. (above) The table-carpet constituted a prominent element in the décor of a room. Here is a relatively plain example, of woollen or silken velvet trimmed with fringe, on a table in Gerard Terborch's house in 1665.

would normally have been covered with a protective cover, only to be revealed in their full glory on festive occasions. However, such protective covers could be quite decorative in their own right as they had to be seen for much of the time.[48] Others, it must be admitted, were more purely utilitarian.[49]

In the seventeenth century, a 'table cloth' was a cover (usually of linen) that was placed over a table for dining. A 'table carpet', on the other hand, was a much more substantial covering. The equivalent in France was a *tapis de table*. The finest table-carpets were prized possessions that were treated with great care and perhaps were only displayed on special occasions. As tables with intricate marquetry decoration on their top surfaces became commoner, in the second half of the century, so the great age of the table-carpet receded into history. After that, the only form of table which was still in most cases covered with a 'carpet' was the dressing-table.

Table-carpets mostly consisted of a plain material (woollen cloth, or silk or woollen velvet) trimmed all round with a fringe.[50] Materials with a pile that was soft to the touch were of course in great favour for this purpose (Plate 211). During the first half of the century Turkish rugs, which were expensive and valued possessions were far more often to be seen on tables than on the floor, and this fashion

241

232. A draw-table with a table-carpet that fits it precisely. Maybe both were of standard sizes, or perhaps one was made to fit the other. This table-carpet is a characteristic product of Dutch tapestry-weaving *ateliers* of the second quarter of the seventeenth century. The cushions, pelmet round the chimneypiece, and bed-hangings are all en suite with the carpet.

continued in Holland right through the century (Colour Plate XIII and Plate 242).[51] Table-carpets of turkeywork were used in the same way as Oriental rugs.[52] Moquette, with or without pseudo-Oriental patterns,[53] was much used for table-covers, or so it seems. In Holland table-carpets were produced specially for the purpose in the tapestry-weaving technique; one may be seen in Plate 232 where it forms part of a complete suite comprising cushion-covers, bed-hangings and a pelmet round the over-hanging chimneypiece.[54] The class of material known as dornix was also used for covering tables on occasion.[55] I have considered covers for tables made of protective leather but table-carpets were also occasionally made of this material for show.[56] Gilt-leather, which is not pliant, could only be used for this purpose if the table-carpet was specially shaped (i.e. had four flaps or *pentes* that hung down the sides of the table from the rectangular top),[57] or if the central panel was of some less rigid material and only the borders were of gilt leather.[58] Occasionally one comes across references to unusual table-carpets, like the 'cubberd cloth of Indyan stuff' which was on a 'fayer court cubbard' at Cockesden in 1610, and the 'Indian twilt' (quilt?) on a small table at Tart Hall.[59] There is a chintz on the table to be seen in Plate 115.

Many table-carpets were embroidered and, as has been explained, needlework could be as varied in its delicacy and elaboration as the skills of each individual embroiderer permitted. Thus many quite plain cloths might have a simple border embroidered on them by one of the ladies of the household. At the other end of the scale were the sumptuous table-carpets worked by the professional 'broderers' working in some metropolitan *atelier* with all the facilities for obtaining expensive materials (silks of all kinds and a variety of gold and silver threads) and designs of advanced taste at their doorstep (Colour Plate X).[60]

On cup-boards and sideboards, it was usual to place a cupboard-cloth of linen when it was to be dressed with plate (Plate 228). Such cloths are usually listed with the household linen.[61] They tended to have lace edges which hung down over the sides of the shelf. As for the carpets on dining-tables, these were sometimes left in place under the linen tablecloth, when the table was being laid for a meal, but the practice seems to have varied from one country to another.[62]

Until the last years of the century, all dressing-tables were simple structures which required no decoration as they were entirely hidden by a 'carpet'. The carpet was at first protected from damage by powder and other cosmetics by a small linen cloth— a *toilette*—but this gradually became a more important feature until the *toilette* evolved as a richly trimmed cloth in its own right and might be of velvet or silk (Plates 29, 131 and 289).[63] Eventually, the word came to embrace the complete dressing-set which could comprise not just the cloth but comb-cases, brushes, mirrors, patch-boxes, flasks, trays and much else, as well as a container for it all, a dressing-gown and a pair of slippers. Such ensembles were given as expensive presents at the end of the century,[64] especially in connection with important weddings. About 1700 it became fashionable in Paris to have gauze or muslin covers, gathered in furbellows, laid over a silk *toilette*.[65] If there was a dressing-glass on the table, this would sometimes be provided with a 'scarf' of the same flimsy material which was fixed at the top of the frame and fell down the sides over the edge of the table.

CHAPTER X
Other Furniture and Decorative Features

ORNAMENTAL CABINETS

THE ornamental cabinet played a prominent part in the decoration of grand rooms during the seventeenth century (Plate 241). As the massive buffets and other varieties of cup-board went out of fashion, their place was taken on the one hand by straightforward tables that could assume the buffet's practical rôle by serving as sideboards, and on the other hand by the decorative cabinet which became *par excellence* the fashionable class of carcass-furniture of the period 1625–85. Its place was ultimately taken by the chest of drawers, the bureau-bookcase and the other highly decorative forms that were to dominate in the eighteenth century.

In the sixteenth century, cabinets had been sufficiently small to be portable and could therefore be placed on a table or some other piece of furniture at the owner's convenience.[1] They came in several qualities but the craftsmanship displayed in these small confections was generally of a much higher order than that bestowed on most other classes of furniture.[2] The exquisite workmanship of the best cabinets was a source of wonder and delight, and the proud owner tended to keep such valuable objects in the *Wunderkammer* or in his private study. But as the prestige and popularity of the cabinet grew, the tendency was to place it in more prominent positions: in the main bedchamber, in the withdrawing room or the gallery. In such positions, it was the decorative qualities of cabinets that came to the fore. In order to present a larger surface for ornament, the cabinet grew in size and eventually required a stand of its own (Plate 234). Soon the ornamental potential of this unit became widely apparent and considerable care was taken over the design of important specimens which came to be the subject of special commissions. Among the drawings at the Ashmolean Museum are several for imposing cabinets, one of which bears the cipher of Marie de Medici, and cannot therefore date from later than 1630 when she was deprived of her power (Plate 233).

The delicate work of the skilled cabinetmakers of Augsburg and Paris was beyond the means of all but the wealthiest clientèle; nevertheless there were many people who well appreciated the prestige that owning a handsome cabinet could bestow on its owner. As a result a lively industry sprang up in the Netherlands (notably at Antwerp but also at Amsterdam) which did a brisk business in what may be described as the second-class cabinet field (Plate 241).[3] The products of this trade are still to be found, now often sadly battered, in country houses all over Europe. They are showy objects on which the maximum decorative effect is achieved at relatively small expense;[4] they are typical confections of the Baroque age and must have given great pleasure when they were new.

Cabinets of an exotic character were greatly prized and were conspicuous evidence of wealth (Plate 20). In the principal bedchamber at Ham House stood a large ivory cabinet that still survives at the house. It is entirely faced with short lengths of ivory decorated with wave-moulding. To us it may seem rather a dull

233. An imposing French ornamental cabinet apparently intended for Queen Marie de Medici who was deprived of her power in 1630. A double M cipher under a royal crown occurs several times in this composition. The cabinet was probably to be faced entirely with ebony and set with gilt mounts, like the very similar cabinet recently acquired by the Victoria and Albert Museum. The drawing is here attributed to the architect Pierre Collot.

234. A published French design for an ornamental cabinet; about 1660. Such a piece was entirely for show.

235. Curiosities in a cabinet. Although the painting is German, this gives a vivid impression of the variety of goods one might expect to find in such a piece of furniture. Apart from the works of art, they include a baby's skull, sea shells and a document. Note the cup-hooks from which several items hang.

object but, if one considers how many elephants had to be sacrificed in order to clad this piece of furniture with ivory, one may start to appreciate why it was so highly rated and was placed in the most important room in the house.[5] There are at Ham also several Oriental cabinets faced with black lacquer which have carved and gilded stands that were specially made for them in Europe. They also stood in prominent positions in the main rooms.[6] Already in 1614 the Earl of Northampton had owned a 'china guilt cabonette upon a frame', but this must have been one of the earliest specimens to have made its appearance in England.[7] Cardinal Mazarin, who owned many cabinets, only seems to have had one Oriental piece although this was most certainly a curiosity, for it took the form of a pagoda.[8] With their more firmly established links with the Far East, the Dutch seem to have been able to procure Oriental lacquer cabinets slightly more easily than their neighbours. At the Prince of Orange's residence at The Hague there were several pieces by 1632[9] and, by the middle of the century, there were sufficient for it to be possible to cut them up and panel an entire closet with lacquer in the Huis ten Bosch. It should be added that not all Eastern cabinets were faced with lacquer; one cabinet in the Princess of Orange's closet was covered with Persian silk with a gold ground brocaded with flowers and had a gilt stand resembling a stool.[10] Towards the end of the century exotic cabinets became quite familiar in well-appointed houses. By 1688 the first handbook on how to paint imitation lacquer-work had made its appearance in London and 'Japanners'

246

were at work in most important cities, turning out fairly plausible renderings of these Oriental wares to satisfy the demand from those who could not afford the real thing—or who could not tell the difference.[11]

Since cabinets made such handsome and telling features in a room, and as they were increasingly displayed in the main (and therefore larger) rooms, they were sometimes made in pairs so as to contribute even more effectively to a symmetrical scheme of decoration (Plate 20).[12] In some cases cabinets came with a table decorated en suite: a cabinet veneered with red tortoiseshell in the Victoria and Albert Museum is still accompanied by its associated table, and there is a similar group decorated with floral marquetry at Ham House.[13] Cabinets seem also occasionally to have been accompanied by a pair of candlestands.[14] Flickering candlelight shining on the often gilded embellishments of a richly decorated cabinet would have produced a supremely decorative effect and, even if the cabinet did not have candlestands en suite, it is probable that candles were often placed flanking cabinets when a truly stunning effect was required after dark.

Cabinets mostly had flat tops that provided a convenient surface on which other decorative objects could be placed—clocks, small works of sculpture, caskets and boxes of all kinds, and vessels of precious metal or porcelain (Plates 291 to 293). Indeed, when the craze (no other word will do) for massed displays of Chinese porcelain gripped fashionable society in Europe, not only were porcelain vessels crammed onto the tops of cabinets but more vessels of this exotic ware were ranged between the legs of their stands. It was of course particularly cabinets of Oriental lacquer that were involved in these presentations of 'China ware'.

While cabinets could serve 'simplement d'ornement dans les chambres, galleries, ou autres appartements' [simply as ornaments in bedchambers, galleries or other rooms], as Savary des Bruslons pointed out early in the eighteenth century, he reminds us that they might also be receptacles in which 'les choses les plus precieuses' [objects of the most precious kind] could be kept (Plate 235).[15] Viscountess Dorchester had two cabinets 'in the roome, next my ladies Chamber' in which she kept, for example, some items of silver, six pairs of embroidered gloves and twelve plain pairs, some cups and dishes of amber, a looking-glass with a gold frame, a prayer-book with an embroidered cover, eleven purses and some caps.[16] Another detailed list of the contents of a cabinet is included in a French inventory of 1693. In it the owner kept not only several important documents but also various trinkets, some small boxes, reliquaries, watches, some precious balsam and some artificial flowers.[17] A similar miscellaneous collection of valued objects was to be found in a cabinet in Breda Castle in 1619—a cross and some bowls of rock crystal, some jewellery, a casket of mother-of-pearl, a little basket of silver filigree, two flasks and some medals.[18]

MASSED PORCELAIN AND SIMILAR FORMAL DISPLAYS

By the late sixteenth century Italian architects were organising collections of precious vessels and the like in formal arrangements on the wall, each piece standing on a separate bracket.[19] Such schemes conformed to the Renaissance sense of order that was already so strikingly embodied in the current Italian architecture and, as the Italian formula for orderly interior arrangements spread northwards across the Alps,

236. Precious vessels set on brackets arranged in formal patterns on the walls. Proposal for the mural decoration of the *Petite Galerie* at Versailles drawn by Lassurance in 1684. The room was to house Louis XIV's magnificent collection of gemstone vessels.

237. A collection of sculpture arranged formally. A display of François Girardon's works (and that of certain other sculptors, note the Chinese Dog of Fo under the table) in the gallery of his house in Paris at the end of the seventeenth century. Girardon (1628–1715) was the chief sculptor engaged at the Château de Versailles in the time of Louis XIV.

it is hardly surprising that formal displays of this kind gradually came to be adopted in the more northerly countries of Europe. However, it is not easy to plot the spread of this fashion.

The inventory of the Stadtholder's residence at The Hague, taken in 1632, provides us with our earliest impression of a carefully organised scheme of this sort.[20] There pottery of various apparently valuable kinds was displayed on shelves in massed arrangements round the room.[21] There were a few intrusive items (a cup of rhinoceros horn, two Oriental trays, some Eastern basketwork boxes and two vases of alabaster) but otherwise the assemblages were of a consistent nature and must have been striking.

There may have been other rooms in Holland decorated in this manner at the time, for the Earl and Countess of Arundel had what they called their 'Dutch Pranketing Room' rigged up in a similar manner at this period and this suggests that it was recognised as a characteristically Dutch form of decoration. The Arundels'

248

Banqueting Room was apparently a separate building standing in the garden at Tart Hall (rebuilt 1638–40) and a separate inventory of it survives which describes the various groups of rarities that were assembled in seemingly formal arrangements there—groups of glassware, basketwork and brassware as well as porcelain vessels and figures.[22] The groups comprising large numbers of objects were displayed between the windows, on a dresser, in the corners of the room, on the jambs of the chimneypiece, above the door, and on structures with up to seven shelves which, in the inventory, are called 'classes'. One such structure was 'a narrow classe in manner of a columne'.

The list of porcelain in the possession of Amalia van Solms, widow of Frederik Hendrik, Prince of Orange, in the middle of the century is very long and its relative importance may be judged from the fact that it follows immediately after that of her gold and silver plate, and before the objects of rock crystal, amber and semi-precious stones.[23] Amalia van Solms had caused a number of valuable Oriental lacquer cabinets to be dismembered and the resulting panels used to face the walls of a closet at her small villa, the Huis 'ten Bosch, outside The Hague. Some valuable Oriental lacquer screens suffered a similar fate when another closet was fitted out in the little palace of Honselaarsdijk in 1686, probably to the designs of Daniel Marot. Marot may have been inspired by what he had seen of a rich closet that was being created at Versailles for the Dauphin at the very time that the young designer was forced to emigrate in 1684.[24] The Swedish architect, Nicodemus Tessin saw the room at Honselaarsdijk the year after it was completed and carefully described its walls of Chinese lacquerwork, its ceiling of mirror-glass, and the massed porcelain on the chimney-piece.[25] We do not know much about the appearance of the Dauphin's closet but we have an inventory of his palace at Meudon, made in 1702, which informs us that in the Gallery, for instance, there were 'sur le cheminée & sous les cabinets, quatre porcelaines, six autres de Siam, neuf bronzes donnez par le Roy, [et] deux autre bronzes' [on the chimneypiece and beneath the cabinets, four porcelain vessels, six others from Siam, nine bronzes presented by the King and two other bronzes]. In the closet set aside for the use of Louis XIV when he paid a visit to his son, there were 'dessus et dessous des bureaux, quatre porcelaines de siam' [on and under the desks, four pieces of Siamese porcelain].[26] In another room porcelain stood both on and under a table, and so on.

Curiously enough, while his son derived much pleasure from porcelain, Louis XIV did not seem to care for it all that much, but he liked to have his treasures marshalled in an orderly manner that contributed to the mural schemes and the décor of his rooms as a whole. The Cabinet of Curiosities he built in 1684 to house his fabulous collection of hardstone vessels had these treasures set on brackets in a formal arrangement up the walls,[27] and Plate 236 shows a proposal of the same year for the Petite Galerie at Versailles that was to be dressed with valuable items of a similar nature, perched on brackets set in regular formation against panels of mirror-glass.

The porcelain cabinets that Daniel Marot began to create for Mary, Princess of Orange and soon to be Queen of England, shortly after his arrival in Holland combined Parisian stylishness in the most up-to-date fashion with the Dutch love of massed porcelain (Plates 72, 73 and 238). She brought the style to England, her appartment at Kensington Palace being decked out with very large numbers of

238. Massed arrays of porcelain integrated with the architecture. View of a 'China Closet' by Daniel Marot; about 1690. The triad against the window-pier closely resembles Marot's design of 1700, reproduced in Plate 51, which was to form part of the decoration at the Dutch palace of Het Loo; but, by the end of the century, rooms like this were to be seen in most of the House of Orange residences—Hampton Court, The Hague, Oranienburg, Leeuwarden, Kensington, etc.

porcelain vessels while several rooms at Hampton Court were dressed in a similar manner.[28]

All over northern Europe during the last half of the seventeenth century it was members of the House of Orange-Nassau who formed nucleii from which the china mania spread. Amalia van Solms' daughter, Luise Henriette, married the Elector of Brandenburg and seems to have introduced the fashion to that north-German state. At any rate, when her son Frederick I of Prussia rebuilt her small palace (appropriately named Schloss Oranienburg) between 1688 and 1695, he created a china closet dressed entirely with porcelain, using an architect (I. B. Broebes) who had been a pupil of Jean Marot (the father of Daniel) who was one of the principal designers in Paris during the third quarter of the century.[29] And when Albertina Agnes of Orange-Nassau had built Schloss Oranienstein (note the allusive name once more) on the Lahn near Koblenz, a task completed in about 1683, she began to collect porcelain on a large scale and soon amassed huge quantities which she too arranged in the new fashion.[30]

In the various House of Orange porcelain rooms at the end of the century there was the now obligatory stacking of vessels on top of cabinets, on chimneypieces, over doors and under tables. At Oranienstein more porcelain was set on *tablets* which

239. The hanging bookshelf, suspended merely on ribbons, was a common seventeenth century feature—apparently called a 'tablette' in France. This mid-seventeenth-century French still-life shows treasured objects including Chinese porcelain, a silver-gilt ewer and basin (for hand-washing) and a Japanese lacquer casket.

were pairs of hanging shelves separated by balusters. Some of the shelves were gilded (Plate 239). At Oranienburg there were some gilded *étagères* backed with mirror-glass that still survive although the room itself has long since gone. At Kensington there were special pedestals on which stood 'one fine Jar & cover [and] two fine large beakers' and there were 'two round black shelves to putt china on, ye under side covered with looking glass' which again were stacked with porcelain. Vessels were, moreover, combined in fanciful compositions. There were in a closet two 'fine basons of a sorte, one upon ye other, one fine little dish upon the bason; all this in one stand,' while nearby were 'two stands, each stand maide up with three jarrs & one china platt on the top'.[31] Marot's engraving of a china closet (Plate 238) gives a good impression of how such rooms looked. It will be seen how the porcelain is set so as to accentuate architectural features—up pilasters, in pyramid forms over the fireplace, along cornices, and so forth.

Defoe recorded how fashionable people in England fell over themselves trying to imitate the form of decoration Queen Mary had made so very much her own, 'till it became a grievance in the expence of it'.[32] It would be unfair to blame the Queen entirely for the porcelain mania, however, as such schemes were certainly known in these islands before she returned to England as William III's consort.[33] Her arrangements differed from earlier essays in this field of decoration chiefly in scale and probably also in the elegance of the presentation, for which Daniel Marot was largely responsible.

THE HANGING OF PICTURES AND LOOKING-GLASSES

As with precious vessels, paintings were sometimes already being hung in regular formations on walls in Italy in the sixteenth century.[34] In this way, the group of pictures formed part of the mural decoration, part of the architecture, and it was the rhythmic arrangement of rectangular, but sometimes round or oval, frames that formed the essential decorative element; the contents of the frame were in this respect of secondary importance. In important rooms of a formal nature paintings continued to be disposed on the walls in such regular arrangements, right through the seventeenth century (Plate 241). This fashion came to full fruition in the neo-classical period of the eighteenth century.

Most people in the seventeenth century did not however hang their pictures in such rigid patterns. In illustrations of Dutch interiors, which mostly show middle-class surroundings, paintings are hung in every conceivable position—high up under the cornice, in several tiers, haphazardly, tightly packed—no rules seem at first to have existed. Yet certain conventions must have governed these matters although it is difficult to get a clear impression of what they were.

Large paintings and looking-glasses, for instance, were rarely hung flat against the wall; they were mostly canted forward so that the top of the frame stood out several inches from the wall (Colour Plate XIII and Plate 94). If there were several rows of pictures, one above the other, the top row might be canted forward more than the lower rows but, once again, this does not invariably seem to have been the case. Experiments carried out at Ham House with the single row of portraits in the Gallery indicate that they were probably hung at a lower level than one might expect today. There was very little furniture in galleries in those days and pictures did not therefore have to be raised above cabinets and so forth; they could be set quite low.

Large pictures and looking-glasses were normally suspended from two rings or hooks at the back of the frame, from which one could either have two cords rising to be attached to two hooks under the frieze, or one could have a single cord running up to and over a single hook or nail in what is still the common fashion today (Plate 240). Inspection of the backs of seventeenth-century frames will show where the rings or hooks were originally fixed. In the case of frames that were meant to be canted forward, the hitching-point was quite far down from the top. This automatically threw the frame forward when it was hung from these points. Small frames would normally have a central ring at the top which fitted over a hook driven straight into the wall—if necessary, right through the wall-hangings (Plate 311). Hooks in the wall and rings on frames were often disguised by bows of silk ribbon (Plate 246),[35] and the cords might be masked with lengths of ribbon although cords might be made so decorative that they formed an embellishment in their own right. Sometimes the cords were organised in a decorative manner so that a tail ending in a tassel could hang down on each side of the frame (Plate 241). The permutations were numerous, it will be seen.

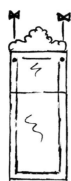

240. Diagram of the four principal ways of hanging framed objects in the seventeenth century. Here demonstrated with looking-glasses. Top left: canted forwards by having the hitching-points set low. Top right: with two cords, hanging flat. Lower left: small glass hanging on a single hook. Lower right: with a length of cord from a single hook. Bows were commonly used to disguise hooks and rings.

241. Various forms of picture hanging. Above the cornice are paintings set into frames in the wall. Against the chimneybreast is a large painting canted forward. Flanking the cabinet are two paintings hanging from hooks disguised by bows (the rings seem to be ornamental). The looking-glass probably rests on top of the cabinet and its angle of canting is adjusted by the cord attached to a single hook; the flanking cords and tassels are purely decorative. The ornamental cabinet, made in Antwerp, is decorated with paintings inside the doors. Flemish picture; 1660s.

An artist's handbook of 1675 explained which subjects were most suitable for the different classes of room.

> Let the *Hall* be adorned with Shepherds, Peasants, Milk-maids, Flocks of sheep and the like . . . Let the *Staircase* be set off with some admirable monument or building, either new or ruinous, to be seen and observed at a view passing up . . . Let landskips, Hunting, fishing, fowling, histories and antiquities be put up in the *Great Chamber* . . . In the Inward or *Withdrawing* Chambers put . . . draughts of the life, of Persons of Honor, intimate or special friends and acquaintance . . . in *Banqueting-rooms* put cheerful and merry paintings of Bacchus, Centaurs, satyrs, syrens and the like, but forbearing all obscene pictures. Histories, grave stories, and the best works become *Galleries*; where one may walk and exercise their senses in viewing, examining, delighting, judging and censuring . . . in the *Bedchamber* put your own, your wives and childrens pictures; as only becoming the most private room, and your modesty; lest (if your wife be a beauty) some wanton and libidinous guest should gaze too long on them and commend the work for her sake.[36]

The mention of a 'Great Chamber' suggests these rules were formulated earlier in the century. Certainly the Duke and Duchess of Lauderdale did not adhere to them when Ham House was done over the 1670s. Nevertheless there will have been conventions that led people to feel that one sort of picture was more appropriate than another in a given position. The inventory of pictures at Ham indicates in which room each item used to hang and, since most of the pictures concerned are still in the house, is a most revealing document.[37] Large portraits of high-ranking friends and relations were hung in the Long Gallery but there were many other portraits scattered throughout the house. In the Duke's Bedchamber the pictures embedded in the panelling were masculine in character (seascapes with men-o'-war and other shipping) while his wife had 'feminine' paintings (of birds) in hers.[38] In the closets, which were small rooms of an intimate and personal character, the pictures were correspondingly small ('cabinet pictures') and were often of high quality since they could be studied close to, an important consideration as many hours were spent in these places. In many of the rooms the over-door paintings are still in position and Ham therefore provides us with an especially good opportunity of studying 'furnishing pictures' that were designed for the actual spaces concerned. Some of them are good pictures but many are not.

A few people collected paintings for their own sake in the seventeenth century but most owners of houses bought pictures in the same way as they might acquire a fine cup of rock crystal, a splendidly inlaid cabinet, or a Persian carpet. These were valuable objects that projected the right image; they were acquired with an eye on the effect they would make. People might therefore often be content with a copy of a famous painting, and the quality of a picture tended to matter less than the subject it portrayed. Today, with the vast apparatus of scholarship in this field at our command, with comparative photographs to guide us, and the acute necessity of being able to differentiate forced upon us by overpowering commercial pressures, it is difficult to envisage how a seventeenth-century owner, living deep in the country, could be quite content with what would today be regarded as a mediocre assemblage. These things had significance for him; to understand this we need to consider the original context very carefully.[39]

Paintings that were particularly valued were sometimes provided with protective curtains of thin silk which hung from a rod fixed along the top of the frame (Colour Plate XIII). The Dauphin had roller-blinds on some of his pictures but this was certainly unusual (see p. 141). Since pictures were in many cases hung so as to contribute to the décor, their frames assumed great importance. An excellent frame might well be put round a painting that would today be rated as being of no great consequence.

SCREENS

The English word 'screen' should normally be rendered as *paravent* in French, while the French term *écran* is principally used in reference to firescreens. The *paravent* is usually a large structure which serves to keep off draughts, as the name indicates. When no specific indication is given in seventeenth-century inventories, one can assume that the term screen is being applied to a *paravent* but one cannot be altogether certain.[40]

There was a 'great foulding skreene of seaven foulds' in the Great Chamber at Hengrave Hall in 1603 but most seventeenth-century screens (*paravents*) had an even number of sections [41]. One of nine is, however, shown in Plate 200.

Early folding screens may have had detachable 'screen-cloths'[42] but most covers were nailed to the framing, the nails being driven through a tape running round the edge that prevented fraying (Plate 242). It would seem that these screens were usually covered on one side only.[43]

One could use almost any material for covering a screen. Worsted cloth of some

242. A simple folding screen (*paravent*) consisting of a wooden frame to which green cloth is nailed through a red tape.

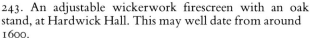

243. An adjustable wickerwork firescreen with an oak stand, at Hardwick Hall. This may well date from around 1600.

244. Stand for a screen-cloth to hang over, at Hardwick Hall. In 1601 such a screen was in the Best Bedchamber sporting a cloth of carnation-coloured velvet embroidered with gold thread and trimmed with gold fringe.

kind was the most usual[44] but silk was also used to some extent, especially towards the end of the century when the decorative potential of the screen began to be appreciated more widely.[45] There was a 'skrine [i.e. the wooden frame] & cloth of fine tapestrie' at Ham House in a room hung with tapestry during the middle of the century, but this was not a material commonly used for the purpose until the eighteenth century.[46] Gilt leather screens became popular at the end of the century and were extremely decorative.[47] European embroidery was not much to be seen on screens but there was a screen of embroidered Indian sarsnet at Ham in the 1670s.[48] A few particularly expensive folding screens were covered in Savonnerie carpetting, a material that would not seem especially well suited for the purpose but promised to be durable.[49]

Oriental screens were prized to quite a different degree and were indeed highly decorative. Already in 1614 a ship had arrived in the Port of London carrying 'Japanese Wares, as ritch scritores, trunckes, beoubes ... of a most excellent varnish.'[50] The merchandise was put up for sale and one of the lots consisted of 'a biobee or skreen Guilded and paynted with resemblances of warfare'. Such Oriental lacquer screens, however, remained a rarity in this country until well into the second

XIV (right) Tapestry-woven panel of a firescreen designed by Jean Bérain and woven at Beauvais late in the seventeenth century.

256

half of the century. There were several such 'Indian screens' at Ham House in the 1670s, for instance, and a number were cut up to panel rooms in Dutch palaces.[51] At Ham in 1679 there was an 'Indian paper screen' and in the inventory of 1683 mention was made of 'a litle Indian screen'; perhaps these entries concern a Chinese painted silk screen of four folds that still survives.[52] It is about thirty inches high.

From mediaeval times until the mid-seventeenth century the standard firescreen was of basketwork and seems usually to have been circular.[53] They came in different sizes and grades.[54] Several specimens may be seen at Hardwick, at least one of which may well date from around 1600 (Plate 243). The circular wicker firescreen was originally an adaptation of the hand-held bat-like implement which was often used for fanning the fire—and still is in many countries (Plate 84).[55] Randle Holme illustrates the pattern of 'hand-screen' current in his day in England; it was circular but of pleated paper. He explains that it 'is a thing made of crisped paper and set in an handle to hold before a ladies face when she sits neere the fire in winter tyme'.[56] The wicker firescreen went out of fashion in the second half of the century.[57]

When Horace Walpole visited Hardwick in 1760 he noticed some 'screens like stands to brush cloaths, with long pieces of carnation velvet hanging over them, fringed with gold; the velvet now turned yellow'.[58] There did in fact stand in the best bedchamber at Hardwick in Elizabethan times 'a skreyne with a cover for it of carnation velvet imbrodered with golde and a golde frenge' and there was a similar item in the Gallery.[59] Some T-shaped stands with tripod bases are still in the house and may be the supports for the screens in question (Plate 244). Maybe many of the references to 'screen cloths' in seventeenth-century inventories concern screens of this form.[60]

Although some 'screen cloths' were embroidered, little attention was paid to the decoration of firescreens until the second half of the century. Even the inventories of Ham House, taken between 1677 and 1683, say nothing about the leaves of the firescreens there listed although they linger lovingly over their descriptions of the stands, which were quite elaborate.[61] Tapestry-woven firescreen-leaves were being produced by 1700 at Beauvais and perhaps elsewhere (Colour Plate XIV), and it was only at this time that firescreens seem to have become an acceptable vehicle for domestic embroidery.[62]

A new form of firescreen was introduced towards the end of the century. This was a version of what would today be called a 'cheval' firescreen and had a sliding leaf which could be set at different heights. In France this was known as an *escran à coulisse* (Plate 245). Five were provided for the principal rooms at Marly in 1698.[63] Several examples from the time of William and Mary survive in the English Royal Collection.[64]

Chimney-boards (see p. 264) were sometimes fitted with small feet so that they could stand out on the floor and serve as cheval firescreens (Plate 251). Several examples of this form survive in Sweden but the modification seems such an obvious one to make that it would be surprising if this variant had not been known elsewhere in Europe.

XV. (left) Several ways of arranging flowers—in a vase, in a basket, in shallow *tazze*, as a nosegay, wrapped in a handkerchief, and as a garland.

245. An *écran à coulisse* (cheval fire-screen with a sliding leaf) in a smart Parisian bedchamber in 1688. Note the firedogs, the fire-irons set upright and embraced by hooks, and the *garniture de cheminée*.

CHIMNEY-FURNITURE

The fireplace was the dominant feature of a room and the care therefore bestowed on chimneypieces is a theme explored in the chapter devoted to the rôle of the architect. In the present section I shall consider the various fittings, implements and decorative objects that might be associated with the fireplace.

In the centre of the back wall of a fireplace it was usual to have a cast iron fire-back decorated with some motif in relief (Plate 73). The subjects were sometimes topical but most consisted of coats of arms or cyphers, or of mythological figures.[65] When coal came to be more widely used and the fire was confined to quite a narrow area, fire-backs became correspondingly narrow but were usually taller in proportion because the coals were burned in a grate that was raised above the hearth.

No grate was needed until coal was introduced. The logs of a wood fire rested on fire-dogs or andirons (from the French *l'andier* or *landier*) which raised them off the hearth. During the late sixteenth and early seventeenth century andirons became larger and more decorative (Plates 43 and 227), and the task of supporting the logs was sometimes actually performed by a smaller pair of fire-dogs set between the main andirons and known as 'creepers'.[66] An andiron consisted of a massive front pillar, usually standing straddled on two feet, with an iron bearing-bar ('billet-bar') stretching backwards and ending in a third support. When the smaller fire-place openings came into fashion (see p. 66) there was no longer room for the large form of andiron (and certainly not for creepers as well) so a combined form evolved which had an additional billet-bar reaching inwards at right-angles (Plate 70). Just as andirons might in England be called 'fire-dogs', because they could have some resemblance to dogs, so the French called them *chenets* (from *chienette*), this being the usual term during the second half of the century.

The ornamental pillars of fire-dogs were mostly made of brass ('latten' as it was often called in the inventories) and the huge andirons, with their grotesque figures or handsome great ball-finials, must have produced a striking effect in the large fireplace openings of the first half of the century (Plate 246).[67] Brass fire-dogs came principally from Flanders[68] although indigenous brass foundries in France and England must also have turned them out in great quantities. A peculiarly English variant had crude but effective decoration of cloisonné enamel.[69] Cast or wrought iron fire-dogs were the commonest form but the 'paire of Andirons of Noremburg worke' in the Long Gallery at the Earl of Northampton's house in 1614 may have been of wrought steel like an impressive pair at Knole dating from the 1530s.[70] A rarity must have been the marble andirons at Kilkenny Castle but they clearly served no practical purpose as they flanked 'an iron stove in the chimney with a grate'.[71] Grandest of all were fire-dogs with silver pillars: Cardinal Mazarin had numerous

246. Fire-dogs (andirons) often formed striking ornaments. The magnificent brass specimens to be seen in this Dutch picture of the 1660s may have been cast at Dinant, the principal centre of production of brassware. Note the bow at the top of the frame of the looking-glass.

247. Proposals by Jean Cotelle for fire-dogs (*chenets*). Parisian; about 1640.

248. Design by Charles Le Brun for a fire-dog for use in a royal setting; 1660s.

pairs and they became fashionable in France, or in circles where French fashions were imitated, during the second half of the century.[72]

'None but people of the first quality burn wood in London,' noted a French visitor in the 1690s; others burned coal, or 'sea-coal' as it was called because it came to London by sea, and in order to distinguish it from 'coals' which meant charcoal.[73] In the 1570s it had been stated that 'sea-coal beginneth to grow from the forge into the kitchen and hall of most towns' near the coast but, by the turn of the century, the practice had spread deep inland—there was for instance 'an iron for seacole' at Hardwick in 1601.[74] Eventually it was only in the principal staterooms that wood was still burned in England.[75] In other European countries, where coal was hard to come by, wood remained the principal fuel.

When grates were a novelty, those compiling inventories were not always sure how to describe them. At Chatsworth in 1601 one was listed as 'a landyron for seacole'; at Tart Hall in 1641 there was 'in the chimney a great bowing iron to keep up the coales'.[76] When fireplaces became smaller, towards the end of the century, and the hearth-stone decreased correspondingly in area, there was a greater danger that burning coals would fall from the grate and out onto the floor. At Ham in the 1670s metal 'hearth-rods' were sunk into the hearth-stone but must have offered only a token protection against this danger. Fenders, which were taller and more effective, were evolved for positions where it really mattered. Once again, an early specimen (of pierced brass) is to be seen at Ham.

Charcoal was burned in 'fyre pannes' of which there was an example at Henham

262

Hall at the beginning of the century, and of which several specimens (one with silver mounts) still survive at Ham.[77] Braziers of all kinds, often on stands and with pierced lids, were available and could be brought in to warm a room in much the same way as we can plug in an electric fire. Related to these braziers were the small chafing-dishes on which food could be kept warm at the table. And then there was the foot-warmer consisting of a small box-like wooden housing with one side left open, into which one inserted an earthenware container, with tiny peg-feet and a loop handle, that could hold the burning coals. These were especially favoured in Holland but must have been known all over Europe (Plates 93 and 283).

With wood fires one needed a 'fire fork' and a 'billet hook' with which to manipulate the logs. For coal one required a fire-shovel and a poker.[78] Tongs were needed for both.[79] Optional seems to have been 'one stiffe brush', or 'a haire broome' as it was called at Ham.[80] Bellows were fairly common in the seventeenth century but were not obligatory. They were often decorative and sometimes seem to have been carefully cherished.[81] Fire-irons generally tended to be largely ornamental and were stood or hung upright at the side of the fireplace (Plate 245). They often came in matching sets. Most had decorative handles of brass, because this metal reflected the heat, but the cheaper sort could be of iron, and especially grand ones had mounts of silver.[82] There were no coal-scuttles; fuel was kept in baskets (Plate 319[83]) in an adjacent locker awaiting the time when the fire needed topping up.[83]

Fireplaces should be 'garnished with green bowes or flowers' in summer, maintained the author of *The Rules of Civility* which appeared in 1671.[84] These *feuillards*, as the French called them, could be quite elaborate screens of verdure which, in the large fireplaces of the sixteenth and first half of the seventeenth century, incidentally provided effective hiding places, as several stories of the time make clear.[85] Right through the century, and irrespective of the size of the opening, large vases of flowers were often stood in the fireplace in summer (Plate 43).

249 & 250. Two French designs for fire-dogs; late-seventeenth-century.

251. Painted chimneyboard from a country house in Sweden. The two brass knobs are for lifting it into position in the fireplace opening and for removing it later. The small cross-pieces form feet that enable this screen to double as a firescreen. The decoration may well be based on a French design for such screens. The room whence this board came was decorated in a similar style. About 1690.

252. The title-sheet of a French suite of engravings of chimneypieces set in a cartouche which could be used as a model by an artist faced with the task of decorating a chimney-board.

Sometimes even a *jardinière* with a flowering bush might be placed there (Plate 253). If flowers were not available, handsome porcelain or delftware jars distracted the eye from the empty hearth quite effectively (Plate 238).

An even more effective way of filling the fireplace opening was to fit it with a chimney-board, which could either be a board made up with planks set side by side or it might be composed of a canvas nailed to a stretcher in exactly the same manner as a picture-canvas (Plates 251–3). The large flat surfaces of both the boarded and the canvas forms lent themselves well to decoration, which was usually painted but could consist of applied carving. Most of the paintings were of fairly simple motifs rendered with strict symmetry; sometimes they amounted to a true easel-painting, like the 'grand tableau peint sur toile representant un paysage et eaux jaillisantes, servant de devant de cheminée' [a large painting on canvas representing a landscape with fountains, serving to set before the fireplace] which was at the Château d'Humières in 1694.[86] From the closet fireplace in some House of Orange dwelling must come the two canvasses each painted with representations of an orange tree in a *jardinière* standing on a simulated hearth, one of which is in a Dutch collection (Plate 253), and one in an English collection. They probably date from the 1690s and may conceivably have been designed to go in some interior by Daniel Marot. Because chimney-boards were sometimes designed to go with the décor of a particular room, surviving examples can occasionally still provide information about the decoration of the room concerned. This is especially the case in the eighteenth century but it can anyway be well worth while searching the attics of ancient houses for what may look like paintings of no especial distinction but may

264

turn out to be chimney-boards. Instead of canvas, chimney-boards could also be faced with tapestry, embroidery, gilt leather, or paper.

Dutch chimney-pieces of the seventeenth century consisted of a hood-like over-mantel protruding from the wall over the actual fireplace which was mostly recessed into the wall. Smoke from the fire had to rise to about the height of a man before it was trapped by the hood of the chimney but, to assist in the trapping, a narrow textile hanging was often fixed like a pelmet all round the lower edge of the hood (Plate 241). Such features seem also to have been known in northern France where they were called *tours de cheminées*. They could be highly decorative, one mentioned in an inventory of 1628 being of 'tapisserie de Rouen'.[87] Close inspection of contemporary illustrations suggests that a detachable lining was often fitted behind these pelmets to ward off smoke and dirt. It seems possible that these small hangings were also known in England, for we find 'a chimneycase of ye same worke' as the 'Arras round ye chamber', but here the reference may simply be to a facing for the chimney-breast that was en suite with the other wall-hangings.[88] The same could be the case with the 'little peece on the chimney' that was in the principal bedchamber at St Giles House in 1639, and with the 'fowr chymey peeces valued att £13' which belonged to Charles I, but it would not be surprising if the *tour de cheminée*, which was so practical and decorative for large fireplaces, was also used in this country as well.[89]

Some chimney-pieces had a shelf or 'mantel-tree' in their composition. This was to become a notable feature of the *cheminées à la royale* of the last decades of the century (see p. 66, f.n. 24). For such shelves, special ornaments were devised. When they comprised a set of vases or jars, groups of such ornaments were called *garnitures de cheminée* (Plates 70 and 245). They usually consisted of five pieces and the potters at Delft produced sets specially designed for this purpose, or for standing in a row on the tops of cupboards. Small pieces of sculpture and busts were also sometimes stood on mantle-shelves (Plate 241). In a closet at Tart Hall, for instance, there stood 'eight brasse pieces' which are likely to have been small bronzes. Perhaps Lord Arundel had acquired them in Italy.[90] At Ham House, there were 'brasse figures' on the shelf over the withdrawing room fireplace, along with two brass candlesticks and two 'Indian boxes'.[91] The use of massed porcelain and delftware as decoration for chimneypieces was discussed in an earlier section of this chapter.

FLOWERS AND PLANTS INDOORS

People in the seventeenth century used flowers indoors in much the same way as we do today but they seem to have been more casual about it; they did not go in for 'flower arrangement' when it came to placing vases of flowers about the house. They mixed blooms of different kinds and no special care seems to have been given to achieving a balanced effect.[92] When one occasionally sees a vase of flowers standing on a piece of furniture in a contemporary illustration, it is there as a charming addition to the decoration and not as a significant feature (Colour Plate XIII). Only when the vase (then usually a large one) is standing in the hearth does it form a complement to a dominant feature of the room, but even then the flowers do not seem to have been arranged in any formal manner (Plate 43). Flowers seem only to have been used formally as components of garlands and similar motifs contrived for

253. Chimneyboard from one of the residences of William III, Prince of Orange, decorated with a *trompe l'oeil* representation of an orange-tree in a vase.

the bedecking of buffets, banqueting halls and settings for weddings (Plate 229).

Shrubs, on the other hand, might be dragooned most rigorously, and were thus often placed in precise rows so as to form part of the interior architecture—in a gallery, for instance, in covered 'walkes' and orangeries. Such regular arrangements of carefully trimmed shrubs standing in tubs or urns were an extension indoors of the formal garden which surrounded the house. This is not the place to discuss the formal garden, with its *parterres*, its carefully manicured hedges, its rows of urns and statues, and its strategically placed fountains: suffice it here to remind the reader that these regimented schemes were seen as an extension of the interior organisation of the house, the central axis of the gardens commonly passing through the principal or focal room in the house, so that it was not only the interior that was planned round this room but the exterior was focussed on it as well. Particularly favoured for putting indoors in tubs were small orange-trees, myrtle, jasmine, yew and certain conifers.

In the seventeenth century a 'flower pott' could be a large urn with two handles or it could be a vase (Plates 253 and 254).[93] In French a distinction was sometimes made between a *pot à bouquets* or a *vase à fleurs* on the one hand and a *pot à fleurs* which was usually an altogether more substantial vessel,[94] but the distinction is often blurred.

At Ham House in 1679 there were some 'boxes carved & guilt for tuby roses' and these small marbled and gilded *jardinières* are still in the Long Gallery although it is not today possible to keep them filled with sweet-smelling tuberoses.[95] There was incidentally a 'guardiniare' in the Earl of Kildare's house in Dublin in 1655.

At the end of the century Celia Fiennes reported that a pair of tables in the Gallery at Hampton Court was flanked by 'two great jarrs on each side of each table . . . to putt potts of orange and mirtle trees in', while at Chippenham 'there was a great flower pott gilt each side of the chimney in the dining roome for to sett trees in.'[96] In both instances, these were containers or *jardinières* in which one placed small trees or shrubs growing in flower pots. But what can have been the nature of the 'iron for a flower pott to stand in' which was at Tart Hall before the Civil War?[97]

According to Havard artificial flowers were much used during the seventeenth century.[98] Savary des Bruslons informs us that one made artificial flowers of paper, of feathers and of the cut open cocoons of silkworms.[99] He says nothing of those made of wax, glass, straw, or silk although they certainly existed.[100] A small silk rose may still be seen between the fingers of the wax effigy of Frances Stuart at Westminster Abbey. 'La Belle Stuart' died in 1702.

254. Proposal for a vase or urn suitable for shrubs, drawn by Charles Le Brun; about 1670 (?).

CHAPTER XI
Lighting

IT IS difficult for us to conceive how little light there normally was in a seventeenth-century house after dark (Plates 255 and 256). Good wax candles were expensive and other forms of lighting—tallow candles and rush lights—were either smelly, quickly consumed, or both.[1] The mathematician William Oughtred had a wife who was 'a penurious woman and would not allow him to burne candle after supper, by which means many a good [mathematical] notion is lost' wrote Aubrey.[2] Mrs Oughtred was no doubt excessively mean but extravagance in this direction was confined to a relatively small circle. When a large number of candles was lit for some special occasion, it was invariably remarked upon with wonder and delight.[3] For the rest of the time, lights were conserved[4] and life was lived as far as possible in the daylight hours.

In fact, the strongest light in a room after dark would mostly come from the fire. It was an exceptional occasion when the candles were so numerous that they equalled the fire in brightness. With the firelight playing so important a part, the surroundings of the fireplace became a focal point of the décor of the room in the evening. Masks and figures on the chimneypiece and firedogs came alive, marble glowed and brass andirons seemed liquid in the flickering firelight.

Candles did not burn steadily either; they moved and pulsed, and what they illuminated seemed to come alive in a manner quite unknown to generations familiar only with the unwinking stare of the electric-light bulb. When the level of light in a room is low, moreover, reflecting surfaces seem relatively bright. Gilding, particularly, stands out in the surrounding half-light; gilt picture frames sparkle (if they are not dulled with age), gilded mouldings on panelling shimmer, a glow emanates from the gilt leather, mounts and handles play counterpoint. Because they had to be lit and snuffed out, candles were normally set at a convenient height, usually between table height and shoulder level, and light from such a source was reflected more directly into the eye and thus revealed the fronts of objects (cabinets, vases, tables) rather than their top surfaces as is so often the case with modern gallery-type lighting which is usually set high up under the ceiling. When the light-source is low and not too powerful, the whole appearance of a room is altered.

There are three principal types of candle-holder. The candlestick which may be placed on a flat surface, the sconce which hangs on the wall, and the chandelier which is suspended from the ceiling. The French word *chandelier* originally meant a holder for *chandelles*, the name for tallow candles, wax candles being called *bougies*. However, by the seventeenth century *chandelier* had become the name for a holder of wax candles, but a holder of no specific kind and certainly not necessarily of the suspended type. Chandeliers with rock crystal or glass components came to be called *lustres* in France[5] and this subsequently became the generic term for all chandeliers. An arm with a nozzle at one end was called a 'branch' in English and a *bras* in French, but branch could be the generic term for all suspended candle-holders, whether of sconce or chandelier form. A candlestick with several branches might be known in

255 & 256. Writing by candlelight, one candle being in a lantern. It is worth remembering how very dark it was indoors in most houses except on special occasions. In such circumstances any reflecting surface would catch the light and stand out brilliantly in the surrounding darkness.

France as a *candelabre*, literally, a tree of candles—in England this became 'candelabrum'— although it came to be called a *girandole*, (from the Italian *girare*, to turn, and *girandola*, a pyrotechnic device that revolved like a horizontal Catherine wheel). There were usually six arms radiating from a central pillar (Plate 269), but half this amount (i.e. a *demi-girandole*) could be set on the wall against a back-plate of mirror-glass so that the candles were reflected to appear like a whole *girandole* (Plates 34 and 202).[6] Such multi-arm sconces were mostly called *bras* but, in the eighteenth century, the English adopted the form (enlarging the glass plate in the process) and then called it a 'gerandole' even though it was strictly speaking only half of one. A tall candlestick for a thick candle (*torche* because it had originally been composed of

257. Numerous candles used on a festive occasion. 'In the midst were four lustres, or christal candlesticks', the describer of this scene at The Hague in 1660 says of the four rock-crystal chandeliers, and adds that 'many other candlesticks, arms of silver, and a great number of torches, enlightened all corners much better than the Sun could have done at Midday. They gave, particularly, a most marvellous lustre to the bottoms of the chimney . . .' which must have been of polished marble. The 'arms of silver' are shaped like fore-arms protruding from mask-like bosses; they may be seen flanking the windows but are shown without candles. Some similar sconces are at Hardwick (see Plate 262).

several rods of wax twisted together—*torse*) was called a *torchier* or *torchère*. Particularly tall candlestands also came to be known as *torchères*, and some *torchères* actually sprouted candle-branches of their own.[7]

This is not the place to discuss the various forms of candlestick. Suffice it to say that, in house of any standing, they were mostly of brass or pewter but wooden candlesticks were still to be found in the kitchens and working quarters of great houses, early in the century.[8] During the second half of the century, it became fashionable to have candlesticks of silver and occasionally they were made of rare materials that were hard to work—amber, lignum vitae and rock crystal, for instance. There were many variants of the standard form, including the chamber candlestick which stood in a large drip-pan with a handle, and the miniature taper-stick. Cardinal Mazarin had some 'chandeliers à la financière' which were presumably specially suited for office-work and he owned a candlestick which was fitted with 'une feuille d'argent servant entre le feu de la lampe et la veue' [a leaf of silver to set between the flame of the candle and the eyes],[9] in fact a shade. Shades that clipped onto the light-holder were not all that uncommon, it would seem; one is to be seen in Plate 111 and there was 'a shadowe of mettle gelt' in the study at Marton Hall in Yorkshire, early in the century.[10] At the end of the previous century, Gabrielle d'Estrées had owned some 'chandeliers à tapisseries' which Havard suggests could be hung inside the bed-curtains.[11] One does sometimes see what looks like a lamp (perhaps an oil lamp in a glass container) suspended under the tester of a large bed—quite a sensible idea if one considers how difficult it would have been to obtain a light at night and that some people may have preferred to 'sleep with the light on'. In fact, it was common to place a candlestick in the hearth at night (Plate 258) and of course the fire, if it was lit, provided light after dark. A stubby form of night-light known as a 'morter' was provided at night for grand bedchambers.[12] These could have special holders to ensure they could not be knocked over, and to screen the light from the bed. The pierced metal holder shown in Plate 259 is probably for such a night-light. Among the Dauphin's silver plate at the end of the century were some silver-gilt *mortiers* which must have been particularly splendid versions of such functional light-fittings.[13]

The standard form of sconce at the beginning of the century had one or more branches springing from the lowest point of a reflecting back-plate which often took the form of a *repoussé* brass or copper dish that was suspended on the wall by a ring at the back (Plate 260). The 'fyftene plate candlesticks of copper to hang on the wales' of the Hall at Hardwick in 1601 will have been of this type; there were more in the Hall at Hengrave and at Marton there were some 'plate candlesticks of latten' (i.e. of brass).[14] In the Elizabethan period 'Candle plates of latten' of all sorts carried an

258. (below left) A candlestick on the hearth-stone serving as a night-light.

259. (below right) Holder for a night-light (morter). Of uncertain date but probably seventeenth century. Sheet iron, painted green. There is a ring fixed to the base-plate that locates the morter which must have been a stubby-shaped candle.

260. A 'plate candlestick'. A brass sconce with dish-shaped reflector. It bears the profile portrait of Queen Marie Thérèse of France and the date 1660 (the year in which she married Louis XIV). Presumably French and of that date.

261. Candlesticks on a dressing-table and an elaborate sconce on the wall. Paris; 1630s. This gives a good idea of normal lighting in a fairly luxurious house at the time.

import duty of three shillings a dozen when brought into England (presumably from Flanders), according to a tariff of duty-rates. Only items that were being imported in considerable quantities will have been included on such a list.

The 'plate candlestick' went out of fashion soon after the middle of the century (a late specimen is shown in Plate 260) and various forms of sconce became popular. Back-plates (*plaques*) of elaborate shape were evolved (Plate 189).[16] Sometimes they were fitted with reflectors of mirror-glass (Plates 34 and 202). The single 'hanging brass sconce' in the Earl of Arundel's own room at Tart Hall in 1641 is likely to have been something rather special.[17] Cardinal Mazarin owned in 1653 some sconces of polished tin-plate—'plaques de fer blanc avec leurs chandeliers' [back plates of tin-plate, with their branches]—and a decade later we find 'cinq petitz mirouers garnis de leur plaques et chandeliers' [five small mirrors with their back-plates and branches] in Fouquet's possession in 1661, which were presumably early versions of the 'six pettites plaques à miroir à huit angles' [six small octagonal back-plates of mirror] with copper-gilt frames surmounted by the royal cipher listed in the French royal inventories for 1673, each of which had two branches of copper-gilt (Plate 202).[18] But increasing use was now made of wood, painted or gilt, for sconces. At first they appear in halls and passageways like the 'foure wooden guilt candlesticks

262. A sconce or candle-branch in the form of a fore-arm protruding from a grotesque mask. Similar sconces are to be seen in Plates 257 and 33. Apparently of gilt *carton pierre*.

263. (right) Design for one of the 'beaux lustres d'argent' which Nicodemus Tessin saw in each of the state rooms (the *Grands Appartements*) when he visited Versailles in 1687. The preliminary sketch was no doubt made by Le Brun but this drawing is probably by Claude Ballin (compare with Plates 9 and 10, and 25).

fa[s]tned on the sides of the ffoure walles' in the Footmen's Hall at Tart Hall and those 'upon ye staires' at the Duke of Lauderdale's house in Westminster.[19] But then they begin to vie with metal sconces for grander positions; one 'large guilded skonce of wood' was to be seen in a bedchamber at Cowdray in 1682, for instance.[20] Carved and gilt wood was a substitute for gilt bronze, copper or silver, and a material known as *carton pierre* was a substitute for them all. This material was composed of moulded paper in layers and was the precursor of papier mâché (Plate 262). It already makes its appearance in the second quarter of the century at Fontainebleau where there were thirty-six 'bras de moullures de carton, dorez d'or brun, chacun de deux piedz de longueur ou environ pour . . . servir de chandelliers à porter des flambeaux' [branches moulded in *carton pierre*, gilded with dark gold, each two feet long or thereabouts . . . serving to carry candleholders for candles] and Mazarin had some 'bras de carton dorez avec leurs bobeches de fer blanc' (branches of *carton pierre* with nozzles of tinplate).[21] At Ham House there were 'four sconces of brasse hung with gould and silke strings with tassels',[22] which must have been early examples of the sconce suspended by a tasselled cord or a gathered ribbon with bows— a practice taken up enthusiastically by Daniel Marot and depicted in many of his engravings at the end of the century in which he shows sconces introduced for their decorative effect, hanging against the wall-hangings at regular intervals (Plates 95 and 141).

Chandeliers are not mentioned at all frequently in English inventories of the seventeenth century and it is probable that they were indeed by no means common over here. The same probably applies to France. In the Low Countries, on the other hand, brass chandeliers were popular (Plates 43 and 267) and one has of course to remember that the principal centres of the production of brassware lay in that part of the world. They came in many varieties and in several qualities; their radiating branches sprang from a central body of baluster or globular form. The brass type was exported all over northern Europe and was subsequently imitated in the other countries. The 'too great copper candlesticks' hanging in the Hall at Hardwick and the single 'great brannche of copper which hangs in the midst of the hall for lights' at Hengrave were all probably chandeliers of 'latten' imported from Flanders.[23]

Chandeliers, whether lit or not, could constitute an important decorative feature in a room, so considerable attention was paid to their embellishment. In order to obtain as much sparkle as possible, reflecting surfaces were increasingly introduced. The great polished globes and balusters of the brazen type glowed handsomely but the effect was sometimes enhanced by small plates set so as to catch the light. The most striking seventeenth-century innovation in this direction sprang from the use of rock crystal which was found to reflect light in a delightful manner. Beads of this material (globular or faceted) were threaded onto wire armatures to form arms, or were linked together to form chains (Plates 257 and 266). Plates of the material, with bevelled edges, were later suspended from the arms to increase the reflections. Rock crystal was principally worked at Milan but it seems to have been the French who developed the chandelier of rock crystal to its fullest splendour.[24] Four impressive specimens may be seen in the view of the King's Bedchamber at Fontainebleau in 1645 reproduced in Plate 33, and Madame de Rambouillet had a 'chandelier cuivre doré et cristal' [chandelier of gilt copper and crystal] in her famous *Chambre Bleue* in the 1660s;[25] it had fifteen branches. Rock crystal chandeliers were greatly admired and a few examples were brought over to England: the 'two crissal branches' listed

264. Chandelier of rock crystal which is said to have been presented by Louis XIV to the Danish Crown Prince Frederik (later King Frederik IV) when he visited France in 1693 although the tradition cannot be substantiated. It is nevertheless likely to date from the late seventeenth century and may well be French.

265. A Venetian twelve-branch chandelier with glass drops, some of them coloured. Perhaps among the glass objects given by the Venetian Senate to Frederik IV of Denmark when he visited Venice in 1709, although the style would appear to be that of the last decades of the seventeenth century.

266. A glass chandelier of an early form, now thought to have been made at a glassworks in northern Bohemia in the late 1680s but clearly inspired by the first glass chandeliers made in France, which in turn resembled those of rock crystal (see Plates 20 and 41). The conformation of the central pillar is reminiscent of that of brass chandeliers; it is however composed of large blue spheres alternating with small red ones.

in the inventories of goods that had belonged to Charles I are likely to have been French and may have been acquired through Henrietta Maria.[26] Charles II owned one for which his upholsterer provided a protective 'case of taffeter wth. ribbons' at a cost of two shillings in 1667.[27] The Duke of Ormonde also possessed a 'crystal chandelier' with ten branches which hung in his Drawing Room at Kilkenny Castle.[28] The 'guilt branche with crystall' in the grandly appointed Antechamber to the Queen's Bedchamber at Ham House in the late 1670s was perhaps also a chandelier although it could equally well have been a *girandole* (a candelabrum) since both forms of light-holder could have rock crystal components.[29] It is possible that this object was acquired when the future Duchess of Lauderdale was in Paris in 1670, for she can hardly have avoided being struck by the charming effect such lights were making in the most luxurious Parisian houses of the day, and she may well have decided that such an ornament would do much to lend a highly fashionable air to her own rooms back in England.

Rock crystal was expensive and hard to work but around 1670 chandeliers began to be produced in France which had components made of glass.[30] The general effect was the same and the conformation of the first glass chandeliers followed that of the rock crystal versions. The matter is further confused because clear glass went by the name of *cristal* in France.[31] The chandeliers to be seen in the engraving of 1682 reproduced as Plate 34 are likely to be early specimens of French glassware applied to this field. Some authorities believe that a handsome chandelier at Schloss Favorite, near Rastatt, may also be an example of French work in glass of about 1670 but others feel it is a more provincial expression of around 1690 (Plate 266).[32] In 1682 an Englishman could speak of a person 'living with lamps . . . intermixed with lustres or balls of glass', which indicates that the new type was then already familiar in England.[33] By the end of the century glass had almost totally supplanted rock crystal as the material from which such pleasing confections were made.

267. Candles were normally only fitted into the nozzles of chandeliers when they were about to be lit. Both the brass chandeliers in this charming picture are hanging empty. Dutch; 1670s.

268. Occasionally ones sees a single candle left in a chandelier, probably to serve in an emergency. A candle stub is to be seen in this brass chandelier hanging in a dentist's house. Note the adjustable double-branch candlestick on the table which only has a single candle. Dutch interior of the 1660s.

269. A *girandole* with a pyramid of glass drops and more drops below the branches. Probably French; 1680s.

270. A Venetian glass *girandole* or candelabrum, with six branches and a pyramid of glass reflectors of various kinds, some of them coloured. Probably part of the same gift from the Venetian Senate as Plate 265.

As has been pointed out, the French *girandole* of about 1670, with its short branches (usually six) radiating from a baluster stem, often had components of rock crystal. These were usually set in a pyramid round the central baluster so that they caught the light to advantage.[34] The glass models followed suit (Plate 269).

Such candelabra and ordinary candlesticks could be placed on any flat surface but these were not always in the right position or at the correct height. For this reason candlestands were devised. At first these were very simple structures. There are two early specimens (not a pair) at Knole, both crude constructions of wood, stained red (Plate 272). Red stands seem to have been popular at first; the Earl of Arundel had a pair in his room at Tart Hall in 1641, there was another pair at Edington in 1665 and at the Noordeinde residence at The Hague in 1632 there were two with gilding on a red ground.[35] Lady Arundel, on the other hand, owned 'a standard of greene for a candlestick to rest on'. The fact that it was still necessary to explain the purpose of her 'standards' suggests that they were still uncommon in England before the Civil War. Later, they were simply called 'stands'. What may be a pair of stands dating from the 1640s is to be seen at Ham House. They are of gilded wood, carved with floral trails on spiral columns with tripod stands in the form of masks. However, their dish-like tops appear to be of rather later date and it is not at present clear what form their

277

271. Candelabrum for a chimney-shelf. The four branches subtend 180°; there are none at the back so it can stand close to the chimneybreast. Brass with glass drops. Although made in Sweden in the 1680s this was no doubt a form used in all countries under strong French influence.

272. A simple candlestand of wood painted red. English; perhaps from the second quarter of the seventeenth century.

original tops can have taken. If they do date from just before the Civil War, they represent an altogether grander class than the simple painted stands just described. It gradually became common to make candlestands very elaborate; this was especially the case when they came to form part of a triad comprising a side-table, looking-glass and pair of stands, which was to become a favourite decorative ensemble from about 1670 right through into the eighteenth century (see p. 218). A splendid pair of stands and associated table believed to have been made in Paris in 1670, may be seen at Knole. In this case no mirror originally accompanied the set which comprised a second table, eight *carreaux*, and a second pair of stands.[36]

The fashion for elaborately decorated candlestands originated in Italy where a long tradition of carving tall candlesticks and candlestands existed. By the early seventeenth century Italian carvers were producing splendid candlestands with stems in the form of exotic or grotesque figures.[37] A pair of painted and carved stands in the shape of blackamoors, which are believed to be Venetian and to date from the 1670s, are still to be seen at Ham House and there is an almost identical pair at Knole.[38] Clearly such figures were popular at the time and the French evolved the form in many imaginative ways from the 1660s onwards (Plate 24). Because so many of the French stands also took the form of negroes, the name of a negro mentioned in a popular vaudeville song of the period[39] was adopted as the generic term for this class of furniture. Anne d'Autriche (d. 1666) owned a pair of *guéridons*, the negro figures of which were lacquered black over silver (or silvered wood); they supported her coat of arms.[40] Actual silver *guéridons* were made in some quantity for the French royal palaces from about 1670 until the vogue for silver furniture was stifled in the tide of economic difficulties that beset France at the end of the century. The famous royal goldsmith, Claude Ballin, made some of solid silver 'habillez à la turque, posez sur les piedestaux en triangle' [dressed in the Turkish manner, standing on tripod pedestals] and Nicodemus Tessin, visiting Versailles in 1687, was extremely impressed (as was the intention) by the 'tables et guéridons d'argent avec leurs flambeaux dessus' [tables and candlestands of silver with their candlesticks on top] and the other silver items in the Salon de Mars which, he said, were 'd'argent d'une pesanteur et grandeur prodigieuse' [of silver of a prodigious weight and size].[41] He went on to describe minutely the furnishings of the Chambre du Roi, taking care to note that 'sur les grands guéridons', which were of silver, 'il y avoient des girandoles d'argent fort jolyment imaginées avec une hydre dont les sept testes soustenoit . . . les chandelles, l'une au milieu et les autres six à l'entour' [on large candlestands . . . there were candelabra of silver very charmingly contrived, with a hydra the seven heads of which each held aloft the candles . . . one in the centre and

273. The fashionable triad comprising a table, looking-glass and pair of candlestands set against a window-pier, which seems to have been the most usual position for such groups in the second half of the seventeenth century.

274. A French hall lantern of the late seventeenth century. Presumably of sheet metal and glass.

the other six surrounding it]. *Guéridons* sometimes came in sets on their own but mostly they were associated with a table (often but not always accompanied by a looking glass) with which they were therefore made en suite (Plate 218). Many were in consequence decorated with marquetry or japanning; the fashion for carved and gilded *guéridons* or candlestands received much fresh impetus at the end of the century when actual silver furniture was scarcely being made any longer (see p. 23).

Guéridons were primarily candlestands but they could also be used to support vases or dishes of food.[42] They came in several heights: there were tall stands (*torchères*) for use in large and formal rooms, there was a standard form about three feet high, and a small type that was used with card-tables.[43] Care was taken to design candlestands so that they were difficult to knock over but this hazard could also be minimized by placing them close to the wall and especially in the corners of the room.[44] This position also ensured that light (and a striking, side-light at that) fell on the mural decorations—the chimneypiece, overmantel furniture, pictures and carved decoration. A variant of the standard forms was the *guéridon* in Cardinal Mazarin's possession which had 'bras qui s'allongent et accoursissent' (arms which lengthen and shorten).[45] The stand with branches that could be raised or lowered shown in Plate 17, is also noteworthy; it is there called a *chambrière*.

Chandeliers, incidentally, were probably not suspended as high up as they normally are today; it would have been difficult to light and snuff the candles if they had been hanging too high. La Bruyère tells the story of a man who 'passe sous un lustre où sa perruque s'accroche et demeure suspendu' [walks under a chandelier where his wig is caught up and held hanging], which could only have been possible if the chandelier was hanging fairly low down.[46] Chandeliers were usually suspended from a hook by means of a stout cord which could be decorative.[47] There is no indication that chains were used so the need to disguise them with an elaborate sleeve of silk had not yet occurred, but the brass chandelier shown in Plate 267 seems to be suspended with wire and this may well have been a common practice. Bows of silk were sometimes used to disguise the hooks and the rings at the top of the chandelier, as with picture frames.[48]

Lanterns were suspended in important passages. They were mostly made with small panes of glass (triangular or quadrangular) set in lead 'cames' or in a structure made of tinplate (Plate 274). At Hengrave Hall, however, the 'great lanterne of glasse' had a frame of 'Joyners worke, paynted', and was clearly a handsome affair.[49] On stairwells a modified form of lantern could be fixed to the wall; this form was essentially a glass housing for a candlestick. There are still some on a private staircase at Knole.

CHAPTER XII
Specific Rooms and their Decoration

ROOMS used for a specific activity tend naturally to assume a special character; they also require specialised equipment. In this last chapter I shall consider certain aspects of these matters and will thereby pick up various subjects that have not yet been touched upon.

Little would be gained from our here making general observations about the décor of the various types of reception room—the principal rooms in the house— because there was too much variety for such generalisations now to have much validity. However, the reader who has followed this survey through the last half dozen chapters will have formed some impression of how these matters were arranged and can supplement this impression by careful study of contemporary illustrations. It may, on the other hand, be rewarding to study in rather more detail the décor and furnishing of rooms like closets and libraries, and those set aside for dining, dressing, bathing, and so forth. Something further also needs to be said about bedchambers, for, while we have considered the bed itself and know something about the seat-furniture, the wall-hangings and floor-coverings that one could expect to find there, other specialised forms of furniture (here, used in its widest sense) associated with bedchambers deserve brief mention.

DINING-ROOMS

The unqualified term 'dining-room', used to signify a room where the family habitually dined, did not acquire its modern meaning until some time in the second half of the seventeenth century and this meaning was not generally accepted until well into the next century. Meals on ceremonial occasions had formerly either been taken in the hall or in the Great Chamber upstairs, while the family dined at less formal times in a parlour which was sometimes called the 'Dining Parlour' or 'Dining Chamber'.[1] We are often told, moreover, that the French term *salle à manger* was not coined until late in the eighteenth century but a room thus labelled is to be seen in a ground-plan published by Le Muet in 1647 (Plate 55) and the term occurs in an advertisement of a Parisian house that was for sale a decade before that.[2] But Frenchmen tended to dine ceremonially in the *salle* and less formally in a *salette* which was presumably the equivalent of a dining parlour.[3] As extra rooms, notably the *antichambre*, became interposed between the *salle* and the *chambre* (i.e. the chief reception room, and the bedchamber), it was often in one of these new rooms that the family dined, in the grander establishments. The 'Première Antichambre du Roi' at Versailles was also known as the 'Salle où le Roy mange' or the 'Salle du grand-couvert'.[4]

The important fact to remember is that one or more rooms in a seventeenth-century house would normally be equipped for dining; it was there that meals were normally taken, whatever the room's title may have been. One could not easily move the massive oak buffets and the heavy draw-tables of the early part of the seventeenth century; where they stood one dined. This was even more true of rooms, later in the century, which had built-in buffets. On the other hand, the owner or members of his family might decide to take a meal in some other room (a practice which seems to have been more common in France than in England), in which case light-weight tables (*tables volants*) were carried in and the chairs in the room were brought forward to it, in so far as was required.[5] It was anyway not apparently the practice, in the dining-rooms of the second half of the century, to leave the (usually oval) table standing out in the centre of the room. As it folded, it could either be removed entirely[6] or it could be stowed away against the wall along with the chairs. The floor was thus cleared and the room could serve other purposes. At Ham House the 'Marble Dining Room', the family's eating place, served as the central vestibule or salon of the domestic floor of the house, with the Duke and Duchess's respective apartments disposed symmetrically on either side. By the eighteenth century it had become the convention to hang family portraits in the dining-room (Long Galleries having gone out of fashion), and the late seventeenth-century dining-room was an obvious place to hang pictures so that, most of the day, they could be seen to advantage, without hindrance.

275. Different degrees of ceremony in dining are reflected in the names of the rooms given in a plan of Hamstead Marshall, built in the 1660s. To the left of the hall (a) lay a 'Little Parlour or Ordinary Roome to Eat In' (b) where the family presumably dined. Behind that was a 'Withdrawing Roome or Roome for the Lord to Eat In' (c), where the master of the household will have eaten when he wanted a higher degree of privacy. The 'Great Parlour' (d) was for grander occasions and had a 'Withdrawing Roome' beyond it (e). Quite separate, on the opposite side of the hall, were the dining quarters for two levels of servants—the 'Roome for the Gentlemen to eat in' and the 'Roome for Servants to eat in' ('f' and 'g'). If there was a suite of state rooms upstairs, there will have been a Great Dining Room among them.

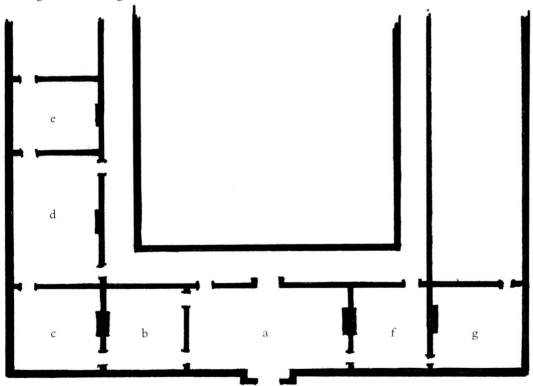

What primarily distinguished a dining-room, then, was the presence of a buffet (alias a cup-board, see p. 238) or sideboards at which drink could be dispensed or which would be of assistance to the servants in performing their duties during the meal. In Elizabethan times Lord Montagu ordered the Yeoman of his Cellar to 'stande att the . . . cupboorde and fill wyne wth. discretion to such as shall call for ytt' and, a little later, Fynes Moryson explained that one did not 'set drink on the table, for which no room is left, but the cups and glasses are served in upon a side-table, drink being offered to none till they call for it'.[7] By the cup-board or *buffet* there would in consequence stand 'a cistern of brass, pewter or lead to set flagons of beer or bottles of win in', as Randle Holme explained.[8] Today we call these cisterns wine-coolers and the French term for them was indeed *rafraichissoir*.[9] Such containers were mostly just filled with cold water but ice might be added if it could be obtained.[10] Adding camphor or saltpetre to the water also assisted refrigeration.[11] The contents of the flagons or bottles that stood in the coolant were then decanted into wine-jugs from which glasses were filled (Plate 160) and then taken on a salver to the individual diner who had asked for drink. Some of the large bottles to be seen standing in the cisterns shown in contemporary illustrations probably contained water, for watering one's wine was of course a widespread custom at the time. 'The Frenchman's glass is wrenched as often as he drinks,' Sir Balthazar Gerbier informs us;[12] if so, the French must also have had suitable containers for water in which to rinse the glasses. This practice may also have served to cool the glasses. It was anyway with this end in mind that the so-called 'Monteith' was evolved, a bowl with a notched rim that enabled glasses to be suspended bowl downwards in cold water.[13]

People in the seventeenth century might take supper seated at a small, often round, table that had been carried into a bedchamber or some other room but, for formal occasions, they at first dined at oblong tables (usually draw-tables, see p. 226) and this remained the fashion until well into the second half of the century. The table was usually placed across one end of the room and the diners sat at one of the long sides and perhaps also at the two ends, but the fourth side (that facing out into the room) was frequently left free so that the servants could wait on the table from the front. The principal diners sat at the centre of the long side, not at the ends. They might have armed chairs to set them apart from the diners of lower rank who sat on ordinary chairs or on stools.[14] Seniority was indicated by the relative heights of the actual seat. The position of the principal diners might in addition be marked out by a canopy hanging over the centre of the table (see p. 172 and Plate 257). At banquets, where large numbers of diners had to be accommodated, trestle- or folding-tables were commonly set together to form a 'U' or a 'T' (Plate 276).

During the second half of the century, when it became fashionable for the family and close friends to dine more informally in relatively small dining-rooms, oval and circular tables became common.[15] With them one no longer invariably needed special seating for the principal diners because one was eating with one's friends who all knew precisely what were the respective ranks of those present and there was therefore no need to stress precedence.[16]

The farthingale chair or back stool was the commonest form of chair from early in the seventeenth century until well into the last quarter, when it was supplanted by the cane-seated chair in England and by a variety of forms in France.[17] Chairs used for dining need to have backs that are almost upright and the back-stool was ideal for

A Paris Chez Melchior Tauernier Graueur et Imprimeur du Roy pour les Tailles Doulces demeurant en lisle du Pallais sur le Quay qui regarde la Megiserie.

Disposition du Festin fait par sa Majesté a M.rs les Cheualliers apres leurs Creations faitte a Fontaine blau le 14.me May 1633. Auec Priuilege du Roy.

276. A banquet at Fontainebleau in 1633. Louis XIII dines alone at a table on a dais under a canopy. A servant with a covered cup on a salver stands by with drink for the monarch. The rest of the company sit along the outside of two long trestle tables covered with carefully creased linen cloths. A fresh course is being carried in by a file of servants led by the Gentleman Usher. In the foreground wine is being carried to one of the diners; no glasses are on the table.

the purpose. When used in dining-rooms it was commonly covered in leather or with turkeywork.[18] The latter was perhaps not especially practical for the purpose but it was comfortable to sit on, and one has to remember that meals often lasted a long time in those days.

Great Chambers, which were formal rooms where ceremonial banqueting took place, were often hung with tapestries.[19] They were decorative, the scenes depicted in them gave one food for thought, and they were impressive evidence of wealth. Unfortunately they tended to retain the smell of food. For this reason Robert Adam in the next century advised against tapestries in dining-rooms[20] and this is no doubt why the smaller dining parlours of the seventeenth century were usually panelled or hung with gilt leather.[21] As Cronström observed, with panelling 'l'odeur des viandes ne se sentiroit point' [the odour of food will not be smelt at all];[22] with textile hangings it did. The laying of the table, as well as the serving of the food and drink, was attended by much ceremony in big houses.[23] Something has already

285

been said about tablecloths. Those made of linen damask were usually provided with napkins en suite and sometimes a set might still include a 'handcloth'—a long cloth which was laid across the diners' knees and was shared by all.[24] Napkins were likewise normally placed across the knees but the young Henri III and his friends, who were notorious for their outrageous behaviour, used to tie their napkins around their necks so as to protect their monstrous ruffs—and, in consequence, looked 'as if they were being shaved'(Plate 290). Napkins usually measured 70 by 100 cm. during most of the seventeenth century but increased in size up to about 90 by 115 cm. towards the end of the century.[25] Some napkins were trimmed with lace.[26] A large seventeenth-century house would usually be stocked with prodigious quantities of linen,[27] all of which was meticulously listed and stored separately, like the household plate.[28] Both tablecloths and napkins were supposed to be pressed with sharp folds[29] and, to this end, the laundrymaids' workroom was often provided with large tables where the cloths could be folded and presumably also pressed with irons, while napkins might likewise be ironed, although a truly sharp crease could more readily be obtained by means of a napkin-press (Plate 320).[30] Not all tablecloths were of linen, incidentally; at a banquet given for the young Duchesse de Bourgogne in 1700, the cloths were 'des riches indiennes'—of Indian chintz.[31]

The French seem to have excelled at folding napkins into fancy shapes and a manual of the period provides instructions for twenty-seven ways of doing so.[32] Mention is fairly often made in contemporary literature of napkins shaped like birds or animals or fruit; Tallement tells of a deaf-mute he had often seen 'pliant le linge admirablement bien en toutes sortes d'animaux' [folding linen astonishingly well into all sorts of animals].[33] Giles Rose, who was master cook to Charles II, explained to his own countrymen how napkins could be fancily folded in his book *The Perfect School of Instruction for Officers of the Mouth*, which was published in 1682.

Figures of various kinds, used as table decoration, were known already in the sixteenth century. Potters like Bernard Palissy and certain French silversmiths were already producing such *marmousets* well before 1600. The Italians were masters at such table ornaments which they called *trionfi* (Plates 277–80). When Marie de Medici was married at Florence in 1600, 'la table de la reine fut couverte d'un chasse de tous animaux avec grand arbres, partie faits de sucre et partie de linge ploie' [the queen's table was covered with a hunt of all kinds of animals with big trees, some made of sugar and some of folded linen].[34] No doubt Italians versed in these skills were brought into France to teach French pastry-cooks how to create such confectionary. At any rate, what would seem to have been Italian techniques were used to produce an astonishing table decoration for one of the *fêtes champêtres* held in the park at Versailles in 1668 which consisted of 'la face d'un palais basti de massepain et pastes sucrées' [the facade of a palace built with marzipan and sugar-paste].[35] Such *Schauessen*, as the Germans called them, often comprised mountains, trees and architectural features amid which the figures were placed, so that the table came to look like a park or landscape.[36] The earliest figures of porcelain, produced in Germany during the first decades of the eighteenth century, were generally made as table ornaments and were the direct descendants of the sugar-paste and wax *Schauessen* (Plates 279 and 280). Apart from figures made purely for show, there was of course a whole other form of *Schauessen* which was intended to be eaten after first having delighted the eye—the boar's head, the peacock with all its feathers put back,

277 & 278. Table decorations in 1667. The figures are of sugar-paste. The banquet in question took place in Rome where sculpture of an especially high order was executed in this medium at that period.

an ox head cooked and then entirely gilded, a seahorse of almond paste, a unicorn of butter.

Trionfi, marmousets and *Schauessen* are also closely related to centrepieces which were by no means a new invention in 1600. They had at first been associated with wine-fountains or containers of perfumed water; many groups of *Schauessen* and some of the early Meissen porcelain figures were likewise grouped round such fountains and all were prominent features of Baroque table-decoration on gala occasions.[37] The piling of dishes of food in decorative conformations was another popular form of table ornament that could also be indulged in at the sideboard (Plate 13). Randle Holme illustrates 'a stand for a dish' resembling a Victorian cake-stand, and comments that 'this is to set on a table full of dishes, to sett an other dish upon; which make the feast looke full and noble.'[38] Anthony Wood, describing a dinner given for Charles II at Oxford in 1687, records that the dishes were 'piled high, like so many ricks of high [hay]'. There were '24 little flat plates, like trencher plates, not piled: placed among the greater dishes scatteringly in vacant places to fill up the vacancies.'[39] Apparently also intended to raise dishes off the table were metal rings which are today sometimes known as 'potato rings' although they do not originally seem to have had anything to do with potatoes.[40]

A rather special form of seventeenth-century table decoration, reserved for royalty, was the *cadenas*, or 'caddinet' as it was called in English. This was a small platform of silver on which the royal person's cutlery was placed before the meal (Plate 281).[41] The *cadenas* had its origin in the custom of protecting the monarch from poisoning but became merely a symbol of rank. It had long been the practice to cover the monarch's bread and salt with a cloth.[42]

Many other items were used in the dining-room—cutlery, plates, salt cellars, chafing dishes and much else—but I should be drifting too far from the main theme if I pursued these subjects here. The same applies to the special equipment required

288

279 & 280. (far left) *Trionfi* executed in sugar-paste which formed part of the table decoration at a banquet held in honour of the English ambassador in Rome in 1688.

281. (left) A caddinet (*cadenas*) bearing the arms of King William III and Queen Mary engraved on the platform where the napkin would be laid. The receptacles are respectively for salt and for the royal cutlery. Bearing London hall-marks for 1683/4.

282. (below) Probably showing the gold *cadenas* provided in 1698 for the personal use of Louis XIV. Drawn by A. N. Cousinet in 1702.

283. A member of the supporting cast. A corner of the kitchen in a middle-class Dutch house in the 1660s. This servant is ironing linen coifs. An earthenware brazier standing on the table is probably being used for heating the iron. When the task was finished it was probably placed inside the foot warmer on which the girl has placed a foot (cf. Plate 93). Behind her stands the kitchen water-but. There is a pewter chamber-pot on the floor by the chicken coop.

XVI. (right) The Queen's Closet at Ham House was no doubt decorated in the most advanced taste when it was created late in the 1670s. The intricate marquetry floor must have been astonishing when it was new and the *scagliola* surround of the fireplace was presumably also a novel feature. The paintings set into the chimneybreast were provided specially for the purpose. The original wall-hangings may clearly be seen in this view; they are of brocaded satin bordered with a striped silk. The 'sleeping chayres' provided for the room about 1678, one of which is to be seen standing in the alcove, are covered en suite.

for serving tea, coffee and chocolate, although something has already been said about tea-tables (p. 230) and mention should perhaps just be made of *cabarets* which were small trays on which these exotic beverages could be served (Plate 30). They were often decorated in a correspondingly exotic manner, the most prized *cabarets* (comprising tray and cups) being of lacquerware and imported from the Far East.[43]

ACCESSORIES IN THE BEDCHAMBER[44]

People often received in their bedchambers (Plates 2 and 4) and the bedchamber was regarded as the innermost of the rooms of reception.[45] Bedchambers might be decorated in as many different ways as other reception rooms. As was pointed out at the beginning of this chapter, little would be gained from trying to analyse specifically the décor of seventeenth-century bedchambers, for they varied so widely, although it is true to say that principal bedchambers tended to be decorated in a rather formal manner and that the decoration of the room as a whole was usually governed by that of the bed itself (see Chapter VII).

XVII. (left) English fashionable decoration of about 1620 is reflected in this small library at Langley Marish, Bucks., which has miraculously been preserved largely untouched. The overmantel is delicately painted with grotesques on a gilt ground, there are Renaissance cartouches on the panels, and there is a frieze of small landscapes. The books are kept in cupboards, the inside of which are painted with open books *en trompe l'oeil*. In the now empty fireplace has been placed a board giving a catalogue of the contents of the shelves.

284. A French design for a bed-alcove with a balustrade across its mouth. Probably about 1640. Alternative treatments are offered. The balustrade has a hinged opening in the centre.

285. An engraved design for a bed-alcove published in Paris about 1660.

286. (right) Bed-steps with a pewter chamber-pot standing on them. Painted in 1671, the scene shows a Flemish bedchamber that seems rather old-fashioned.

In a royal bedchamber, or a State Bedchamber which was suitable for royalty to occupy if paying a visit to a house, there would often be a balustrade out in front of the bed to separate the area round the bed from the rest of the room and keep all but the most favoured at a distance.[46] The balustrade might run right across the room, cutting off the end where the bed stood (Plate 6). It could also run across the mouth of an alcove (Plate 284). In either case, the area enclosed was known in France as the *ruelle*[47] while the floor, which was often raised to form a daïs for the bed, was called the *parquet*. This term was subsequently used to describe the kind of ornamental woodwork that was commonly used to decorate this important floor area. (See also Colour Plate III.)

In most important seventeenth-century bedchambers there would usually be some form of storage furniture, not for clothes (which were rarely kept in an important bedchamber at night) but for the personal belongings of the owner of the room. During the first part of the century a buffet[48] with a cupboard-section below was often to be found in bedchambers; it was known as a 'livery cupboard' in England even though liveries were not regularly issued to a household much after 1600 (see p. 233). But there were no taps from which one could fetch water at night if one were thirsty, so it was common to have drink of some sort available and this could still stand on or in the livery cupboard, although it could of course equally well stand on a table. The livery cupboard was superseded by the ornamental cabinet which might also serve as a receptacle for valuables and personal possessions. In the sixteenth century chests had been common in bedchambers but they were fast going out of fashion by 1600 whereafter they were mostly to be found in farm-houses and the like (Plate 127).[49] Although one could use the chest as a seat (especially with a cushion) it was otherwise a rather impractical piece of furniture because one could not reach things stored at the bottom without first removing all the items lying above it; the difficulty could be mitigated by fitting drawers at the bottom and soon further tiers of drawers were fitted so that the chest eventually became a chest of drawers. This last class of furniture only came into its own at the end of the century but was then to be found in some important bedchambers. What were probably chests or coffers (the latter had rounded lids) of small size were the 'casette' of walnut

perched on a 'soubassement à colonnes torses' [stand with spiral columns] which was to be found in the bedchamber of a Breton country house in 1688 and the 'coffre de chambre' covered in black leather in the neighbouring bedroom.[50] Havard quotes a reference to a 'coffre de nuit de velours cramoisy rouge' [a night-box covered in crimson velvet] which contained a comb-case and 'un bonnet de nuit aussi de velours' [a nightcap also of velvet].[51] Lady Beauchamp had a 'velvett nighte-box and the cushionett of the same' in her bedchamber at Edington.[52] Maybe the 'cushionet' was a case for nightgown and nightcap, like the 'cover for nightgeere wth. checqr'd worke of several sorts in silver and gold' that belonged to Charles I.[53] Perhaps a night-box contained things that one might need at night. If so, it may have been placed alongside the bed, perhaps on a chair, so that one could reach it. There were no bedside tables in the seventeenth century.[54]

Other items commonly seen in bedchambers would have been portable candlesticks of various kinds—the morters, which were night-lights that could be left to burn right through the night, and chamber-candlesticks which had a dish-like base and handle (see pp. 270–271). But portable candlesticks are not listed in inventories of bedchambers because they were kept in a pantry or buttery during the day and only brought into the rooms where they were needed at nightfall. The same applies to chamber-pots. Warming-pans, those long-handled containers for hot coals, on the other hand, were sometimes kept in bedchambers (Plate 127). For this reason, they were often decorated. Some bed steps are shown in Plate 286; they do not seem to have been at all common.

CLOSETS

Any small room might be called a closet (*un cabinet* in French) but what concerns us here is the class of small room that was associated with a bedchamber.[55] The closet was a room to which the occupant of the bedchamber could retire and where he or she could normally expect to enjoy complete privacy to rest, read, study, write letters, or entertain intimate friends. When one recalls how very public a bedchamber could be in the seventeenth century, it is hardly surprising that there was a corresponding demand for a room of one's own.

When planning the principal apartments of a grand house, the closets were usually placed beyond the bedchamber with which they were associated (Plates 53–9), so that they formed the innermost and therefore most secluded room of the apartment concerned.[56] For although attached to the apartment, closets by their very nature were separate and were therefore freed from the conventions that governed the principal rooms. One could not only behave in them in a more relaxed manner, one could have them decorated and furnished in quite a different way. All formality was thrown to the winds and one could rig up these small rooms as one pleased, indeed, in as fanciful a manner as one liked (Plate 287). Thus it was often in closets that forms of decoration and furniture were first tried out that were subsequently to become widely fashionable—the setting of mirror-glass into pannelling, for instance, the display of precious vessels set on brackets in formal arrangements on the walls, and the facing of walls with panels of Oriental lacquer. The same applies to seat-furniture with truly accommodating upholstery which came into fashion in the last decades of the century, and probably also to tea-tables and other equipment necessary for the taking of the new exotic beverages.

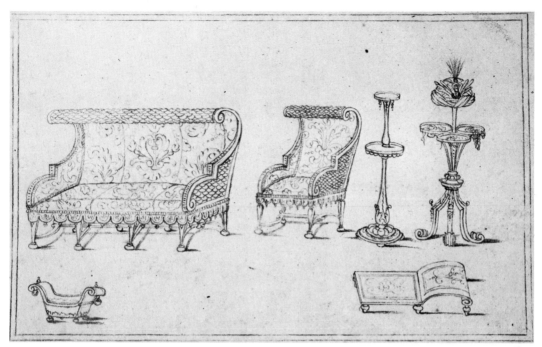

287. Fanciful furniture that may have stood in a French closet at the end of the century—perhaps in a *Cabinet turque* or one decorated in a *style indien* (note the turban on the stand). Certainly such crazy pieces would not have been suitable for any conventional room at the time. They include a footrest and a *jardinière*.

In closets one could display one's taste to advantage and, if one favoured exotic or advanced tastes, there was no better place in which to do so. We have many descriptions of particularly striking closets. The Dauphin's, which was designed by Jean Bérain and was executed by Boulle, had a floor worked in the most elaborate marquetry that seemed sensational to those who saw it. [57] By way of contrast the prince had another closet 'boisé à la capucine', faced with panels of untreated oak that were intended to conjure up a monastic atmosphere (see p. 71).[58] The Duchesse de Valentinois had what she called a 'cabinet de rocaille' that must have had rockwork and grotto-like elements in its décor. It was comfortably and charmingly furnished with 'piles de carreaux de drap d'or et de vases de porcelaine remplis de fleurs' [piles of squab-like cushions of cloth of gold and vases of porcelain filled with flowers]; (see p. 180).[59] And there was the *cabinet* of Madame de Rohan in the middle of the century which was unusual because its walls were clad with moquette (see p. 112). The favoured *habitués* of this apparently so delightful retreat were known collectively as 'La Moquette'. It would be interesting to know more about some of these charming little rooms which often had such a potent influence on the subsequent history of taste in Europe. It would also be pleasant to know what was so special about the panels 'which are to be seen at Paris in the Cabinets of the Palace called Orleans' that Sir Balthazar Gerbier, writing in 1664, clearly felt were remarkable.[60]

A gentleman's closet could be quite small: 'Nine feet upon three and a half deep . . . is the least you can allow to the Closet' maintained Sir Roger Pratt, writing in 1660.[61] Up to the end of the sixteenth century very little attention seems to have

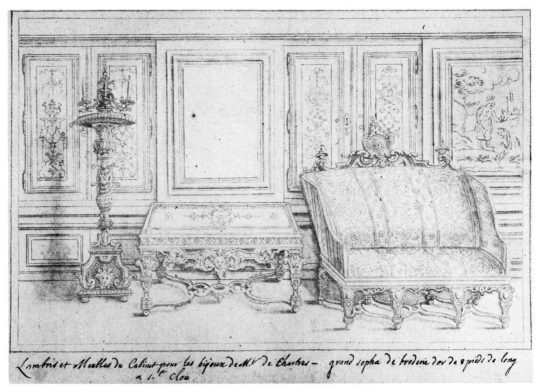

Lambris et Meubles du Cabinet pour les bijoux de M.r de Chartres — grand sopha de broderie d'or de 8 pieds de long a s.t Clou

288. Details of the furnishings in one of the Duc de Chartres' closets at the Château de Saint-Cloud in the late seventeenth century. This shows his *Cabinet des Bijoux*, the collection of jewellery and other treasures no doubt being housed in the cupboards that may be seen in the *lambris* (panelling). Chartres became Duc d'Orléans in 1701 (and was later Regent). On the right Titian's *Noli me tangere* is set into the panelling. It remained in the Orléans collection until 1792 and is now in the National Gallery in London.

been paid to the decoration of closets; for the most part they were rather utilitarian rooms of no particular distinction.[62] But quite a different spirit is to be sensed in the descriptions of certain *cabinets* after the turn of the century. We then find Francis Bacon speaking of 'rich cabinets, daintily paved, richly hanged, glazed with crystaline glass, and a rich cupola in the midst', all of which betokens a certain opulence.[63] Somewhat later (1626–7) we hear of John de Critz painting the panelling in Henrietta Maria's closet at Denmark House (later Somerset House) with simulated graining in 'wall nuttree couloure', and decorating the panels with 'antique worke . . . with badges in the midst of them, they being guilded with fyne gold and shadowed'.[64] The Green Closet at Ham House, which was decorated in the 1630s, still gives us some idea of what a rich closet of the earlier part of the century might look like.

The select gatherings in Madame de Rohan's *cabinet* must have required a room of some size and it was indeed from about the middle of the century that the French evolved the concept of the *Grand Cabinet* which was no longer quite so private and served as a reception room for select company. One can follow the development by noting the seating arrangements in the *cabinets* of Louis XIV's mistresses. Louis de la Vallière could seat eighteen people in her *Grand Cabinet* which was furnished with no less than six armchairs, the rest of the seats comprising six ordinary chairs and six folding stools (*pliants*); Madame de Maintenon at the end of the century had seating for up to twenty-nine people in hers.[65] As for the King's *Grand Cabinet*, this served as *Cabinet de Conseil* where his Privy Council (or Cabinet) met to discuss affairs of state. The fashion for having larger closets that served as small reception rooms was translated to England after the Restoration. There is a description of Catherine of Braganza's closet at Whitehall in 1669 which gives a vivid idea of how such a room was used 'as a place of amusement for their majesties and therefore they go into it every evening (unless particularly prevented) from the other apartments. The Queen sits in front of the door, and enters into conversation with the ladies who happen to be there, who form a circle round her Majesty'. A number of gentlemen were also present including most of the ambassadors and any distinguished foreigners visiting the English court. 'The King himself and the Duke [of York] are frequently seen there seeking relief from more mighty cares, and divesting themselves awhile of the restraint of royalty.' The King always stood or walked about, refusing to discuss affairs of state in these surroundings, 'those topics being always reserved for a proper and reasonable time'.[66]

Madame de la Vallière had to have a second and much smaller closet as well as the *Grand Cabinet* just mentioned, so that she still had somewhere truly private to which she could retire. Important apartments in the second half of the century anyway tended to be provided with two closets. For instance, the Duchess of Lauderdale had two closets lying next to each other at Ham House after she and her husband had extended the building in the 1670s. The 'White Closet' was a luxuriously appointed *cabinet* that was intended to impress visitors (there were six chairs in the room but only four people could ever have been in the room comfortably at a time) while her 'Private Closet' was in the nature of a study or office, although she also kept the equipment needed for drinking tea in this little room. These two small rooms survive and still convey much of the effect originally intended. The Duchess of Ormonde likewise had two closets at Dublin Castle at the same period, and 'My Lady's New Chamber' at Cowdray had one closet 'by My Lady's Chamber door' and another 'within My Lady's Chamber' (i.e. reached through the bedchamber).[67] Celia Fiennes noted that at Burfield there was 'within the dressingroome . . . a closset on one hand, the other side is a closet that leads to a little seate of easement'.[68] A description of Cardinal Mazarin's magnificent residence in Paris shows how, already before the middle of the century, the four principal apartments in this house, which had so many advanced features, were provided with 'des cabinets, des garde-robes, & des chambres de degagement' (Plate 58).[69]

A *garde-robe* was at first a place in which clothes were stored and the English word 'wardrobe' still carries the same meaning.[70] Both words can, by extension, also be used to designate a piece of furniture in which clothes are kept,[71] and this is indeed the common meaning in English today. In the seventeenth century, however, the *garde-robe* was not only a closet where clothes might be stored but was often also the place where the close-stool stood.[72] For this last reason *garde-robe* is in France today the term for what we equally euphemistically call a lavatory. The word 'wardrobe' also meant a room in which household effects, notably upholstery (in its widest sense), were stored and repaired.[73] At Chatsworth, in Elizabethan times, there were three wardrobes, one for her Ladyship's clothes, a 'Middle Wardrop' in which some dismantled beds and their bedding were stored along with a pair of virginals, some

Femme de qualitez a sa Toillette.

A Paris chez Jean Vander Bruggen rue S.t Jacque au grand Magasin d'Images. C.P.R.

289. *Femme de qualitez à sa Toilette* in the late 1680s, showing her luxuriously appointed dressing-room. Her dressing-table is covered with a *toilette* (apparently of silk) trimmed with a wide lace border. On the table is her dressing-set including a looking-glass, trays for bottles and boxes, and a folding comb-case. The man seated on a comfortable chair of ultra-modern form appears to be reading a book of music and singing.

chairs, some coffers and some presses, and there was a 'Lowe Wardrop' for such things as chamber-pots and candlesticks.[74] When beds were not in use they were often dismantled and the grandest beds sometimes had sets of both summer and winter hangings, so a considerable amount of storage space was needed for these prominent items of furniture in the seventeenth century; indeed, at Lady Leicester's house there was a special 'Bed Wardrobe'.[75] The French, more logically, called such a room a *garde-meuble*—a room where furniture was stored.

Garde-robe might also be the name for a dressing-room which would usually be a fairly small room, a closet, leading off a bedchamber (Plates 54, 55, 57 and 58). Evelyn saw the Duchess of Portsmouth 'in her dressing-roome within her bedchamber, where she was in her morning loose garments, her maids combing her, newly out of bed, his Majesty and the gallants about her'.[76] This room must have been of some size to have held so many people; no doubt it was really a *cabinet* of the large type then fashionable in France. The morning toilet of such a lady could be a

300

social occasion of some importance; news and gossip was exchanged, new ideas were discussed, and new fashions tried out. It was, for instance, at 'la grande toilette chez M. la duchesse de Bourgogne' on Friday, 25 September 1699, that the new lower hair-style which was to reign through the first half of the eighteenth century was first seen.[77]

The term 'dressing room' does not occur before the middle of the century, an early mention being that which occurs in an inventory of the Earl of Kildare's house in Dublin in 1656.[78] Anne of Denmark, however, had an '[At]Tiring Chamber' already in 1610.[79]

We have already in this chapter touched upon some of the more extraordinary forms of mural decoration to be seen in fashionable seventeenth-century closets, but most closets, even of the most luxurious class, had textile hangings on the walls that in no way differed from those on the walls in other fashionable rooms of the time, except perhaps in their scale. Catherine of Braganza's large closet mentioned above had hangings of 'sky blue damask . . . with divisions of gold lace'. A closet at Ham House furnished to receive the same queen still has on the walls its hangings of red satin brocaded with gold, empaned with a striped silk (Colour Plate XVI). Madame de la Vallière's two *cabinets* were respectively hung with 'broderie fond d'or, manière de velours à arabesques, rouge cramoisy' [crimson arabesques rendered in needlework on a gold ground, also embroidered] and 'velours rouge et brocat lamé d'or'[red velvet and brocade with gold thread]. At about the same period the 'inward chamber to Lady Isabella's Bedchamber' at Edington was hung with green

290. The man about town also needed a dressing-table. The table-carpet is protected by a *toilette* while his moustache is being curled. A small brazier or chafing-dish is being used to heat up curling tongs. On the floor stand a ewer, a barber's bowl and a sponge.

dornix while the 'Petit Garderobbe atenant ladite chambre' at a house at Rheims in 1621 was hung with *tapisserie de Bergame*.[80] In store at Lady Dorchester's was '1 sute gilt leather and green cloth hangings for my Ladies Closett'.[81] In 1695, David Cronström wrote from Paris to advise Countess Piper in Stockholm to hang her closet in accordance with the latest French fashion which was with green Genoa damask divided into panels by simulated pilasters cut out (*découpé*) of some rich material.[82] With the letter he sent some proposals for the scheme drawn by Jean Bérain himself, together with some sketches by an upholsterer of a similar scheme which had actually been carried out already in Paris.

Since ease, comfort and relaxation were sought in closets, it was also there that was first to be seen the truly comfortable seat-furniture that was so striking a product of the late seventeenth-century upholsterer's skills (see Plate 202). The two 'sleeping chayres' with adjustable backs in the Queen's Closet at Ham House are famous and early examples of this phenomenon, as is that with castors which formerly stood in the Duke's Closet and is now in a private collection. Such *fauteuils de commodité* and the related easy chairs, as well as well cushioned couches and sofas, formed focal points in these delightful rooms (Plate 22).

According to Cotgrave (*Dictionnarie of the French and English Tongues*, 1632) the French word *cabinet* could mean 'a closet, little chamber, or wardrobe wherein one keeps his best, or most esteemed, substance', so one could expect to find there precious belongings of all kinds. I have already discussed 'Porcelain Cabinets' and closets where other kinds of precious vessels were displayed. At Burghley, Celia Fiennes saw a closet where there was 'a great deale of worke under glasses and a glass-case full of all sorts of curyosityes of amber stone, curall and a world of fine things'.[83] Such 'Cabinets of Curiosities' or *Wunderkammern* were the ancestors of the modern museum (Plates 291–3); they were sometimes to be found attached to libraries, housing treasures other than the books which lived in the presses of the library itself. 'One's most esteemed substance' could also include important documents, jewellery, special articles of clothing, and mementoes of all kind—all suitable items for storage in the ornamental cabinets and writing-desks that are often listed in inventories as being in closets.

If, on the other hand, the closet was being used essentially as a dressing-room, a table of some kind that could serve as a dressing-table was of course needed, and an important feature of any luxuriously appointed *cabinet* being used in this way would have been the table-carpet laid over the dressing-table (Plate 309). Because this rich cloth needed protecting from spilt cosmetics, stray hairs and the like, it was usual to place over the carpet a *toilette* (see p. 243 and Plates 29, 131 and 309). Eventually complete sets, called *toilettes* collectively and comprising both the table-carpet and the toilette itself, as well as the full dressing set, all en suite, were produced for particularly splendid dressing-rooms. The dressing-table itself could be of any shape and, since it was covered with a cloth, did not need to be in any way elaborate.[84] Nevertheless, from about 1665 onwards, fancily-decorated dressing-tables were introduced.[85] The tables comprised in the ensemble of table, looking-glass and pair of candlestands, that I have called a triad might serve as dressing-tables in grand rooms, although it was probably only the plainer sets that were used, covered with a *toilette*, in this way. As these triads mostly stood against a pier between windows, daylight fell well on the sitter's face and the light from the flanking candlestands served the same purpose at night (Plate 94). The mirror had to be canted forward so the sitter could see herself in it. Later, a more solid form of bureau-like dressing table was evolved, as has already been noted (p. 231). Being steady, it was well suited for setting out the expensive dressing-sets that were fashionable at the end of the century,[86] and the dressing-mirror would henceforth invariably stand on the table and could be quite small (Plate 289). The large dressing-mirror hanging on the wall then went out of fashion. Once there, on the table, the small form of glass could be draped with a decorative cloth that fell down at the back and sides, integrating the glass with the table; this was the fashion in France at the end of the century.

The closet, then, was a highly personal room. Its decoration and furnishing varied widely according to the taste (one might even in some cases say whims) of the owner. The character of such rooms is well summed up by the list of the contents in the closet of the Princess Eleonore de Bourbon at Breda Castle taken after her death in 1619.[87] It lay next to her bedchamber and was hung with 'East Indian cloth of gold'. There was a large assortment of 'Indian' boxes and coffers of all shapes and sizes, some of them being of lacquer. An expensive piece of furniture was an ebony cabinet with silver-gilt figures and mounts, which probably came from Augsburg, as probably did her silver-mounted writing-desk. There was a plainer ebony cabinet and a coffer covered with velvet with a small looking-glass (in it?). Another cabinet, which was clearly quite large, contained numerous trinkets and treasured objects— some silk flowers, a turned ivory cup, a mother-of-pearl casket, some silver bottles, a silver-gilt bowl and cover set with pearls, and much else. On the walls were many small pictures, mostly of a religious nature, including a 'Last Supper' executed in silver relief. The list of '*porcheleyn*' is also long but one must not assume it all came from the Far East. It must have stood about on the various cabinets; no shelves are mentioned, and there were only two tables, one being a 'Spanish table' and therefore presumably folded. The table-carpets lying on them were of Oriental silk. There were two 'Spanish women's armchairs' (*twee vrouwe Spaens leynstoelen*) covered with green and white damask as well as six stools 'called tabourets' (*genoemt tamborees*). No floor-covers or window-curtains are listed. The room must have been crammed with small objects.

STUDIES AND LIBRARIES

'We doe call the most secret place in the house appropriate to our own studies . . . a closet,' explained a writer in 1586,[88] but he might have added that one could also call it 'a study'.[89] The 'Studdy Roome' at Cockesden in 1610 contained 'a fayer desk with his key' and 'a litle table, where uppon the desk doth stand'. On another table lay a second 'deske wereuppon the *Book of Martyrs* now standes'. There were also several maps, two 'fayre tronckes' with locks (which were probably for books and papers), a large chest, a standish for ink, etc., a chair with an embroidered seat and back, a looking-glass, a portrait of the owner's mother, twenty-four books, some almanacks and 'an ostrich egg hangs in the corner of the room'. With all this evidence of learning (the ostrich egg and the looking-glass would have been somewhat awe-inspiring items at the time) it comes as something of a surprise to find that there was also 'a black pyk for hay . . . behind the Study roome dore'. The

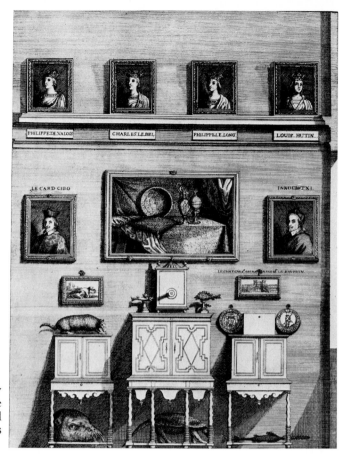

291–3. The Cabinet of Curiosities at one end of the Library at the Monastery of Sainte-Geneviève in Paris; 1688. Note how this wide variety of objects is organised in formal patterns against the three walls. The open display-cabinet is particularly noteworthy.

294. (below) The end wall of the Library outside the closet depicted in Plates 291–293. The room consisted of a long gallery flanked on both sides with bookcases separated by windows. The bookcases have doors with wire mesh and the shelves have dust-pelmets.

étude of the Archbishop of Bordeaux in 1680 was no doubt likewise a setting for intellectual pursuits but it seems to have had all the character of a large and luxurious French *cabinet*, with its hangings, chair-covers and table-carpet of red half-silk damask, its fifty pictures, its window-curtains of red serge, and its show of vessels of mother-of-pearl and porcelain.[90] The cabinet of purple wood, the red coffer containing cash, and the *prie-dieu* with a gilt crucifix hardly indicate that this was a room where studious activities were undertaken.

Studies were not only places in which to read and write, they were often also depositories for rarities of all kinds (e.g. the ostrich egg and mother-of-pearl vessels just mentioned). Books had of course also been rarities until the beginning of the seventeenth century[91] but when books became commoner, there was a tendency to separate them and house them in a library while the other rarities were kept in an adjacent small room (Plates 291–294).

When books had been very rare and costly, they were naturally stored with great care. It had been a common mediaeval practice to store one's books in a chest and this continued well into the seventeenth century. The Countess of Leicester was still keeping her books in a trunk by her bedside in 1634.[92] A gentleman living in Suffolk in 1648 owned 'a great chest of elming [elm] borde standing in the lower gallerie, for to put therein the bookes', while over in Ireland the Earl of Kildare still had 'a standard [massive chest] for bookes' as late as 1656.[93] These chests and trunks are all likely to have had locks.

As libraries grew, this form of storage became unpractical and proper book-cases began to be provided. The shelves behind lockable cupboard-doors that line the walls of the charming little Kederminster Library of 1623 at Langley Church in Buckinghamshire represent an early stage in this development (Colour Plate XVII Plate 301). Then, as book-bindings became increasingly attractive, it was desirable that at least the spines could be seen while the books rested on the shelves,[94] so bookcases fronted with wire mesh[95] or panes of glass came into being (Plates 294 and 295). The two original book-cases from Samuel Pepys' own house, which are now in the Pepysian Library at Magdalene College at Cambridge, are very early examples of such specialised cupboards with glazed doors.[96] They are markedly Dutch in character and are likely to have had Continental antecedents. These pieces of furniture were supplied in 1666 and Pepys had ten more made on the same model (with only minor differences) between that date and 1703 when he died.[97] Even the last in the series were still very early manifestations of the wish to have elegant and protective housing for a substantial number of books (Plate 303); the clerk drawing up a list of items destroyed when fire damaged Boulle's workshop in Paris in 1720 still felt obliged to explain that the three 'armoires en bibliothèques avec des glaces devant les portes' were 'servant à mettre des livres' [library cupboards with glass before the doors . . . used to put books in].[98] However, many libraries simply had shelves ranged against the walls, as is the case with the Library at Ham House that was fitted up in the 1670s (Plate 299). If one wanted to protect the books on such

295 & 296. (right) Samuel Pepys' library in London, about 1693. The first pair of bookcases was made in 1666 and those added subsequently vary only in points of detail. On the library-table (here shown entirely covered with a protective 'case') lies a reading desk. In the passage is a gate-leg table which might also serve as a desk. Note the fine looking-glass hanging against the window-pier, the portrait set into the chimneybreast, the other pictures canted forward, and the map of Paris.

297. The University Library at Leiden in 1610. The books are still chained to the presses which have reading desks below. There is a rail for the reader to rest a foot upon when standing at the desks. Note the globes with their protective covers, and the cupboard that presumably housed scrolls and other documents.

298. The 'Arts End' at the Bodleian Library, Oxford in 1675. Built in 1612 with an eye to the convenience and comfort of scholars. Note the seats where one may browse close to the shelves. The uprights of the benches are extended to form supports for a gallery. Beyond are book-presses and two library tables with a pair of globes presented by Sir Thomas Bodley who died in 1613.

299. (right) The library at Ham House, created in the 1670s. The book-shelves are simple structures and are not adjustable. The built-in writing cabinet of cedarwood is a delightful piece of furniture which has additional drawers superimposed. Originally there stood in the centre of the room a chest of drawers (no doubt a press for maps and the like) and a table. The globes, which still have their protective covers, formerly stood in the Gallery nearby.

shelves, one could fit a curtain in front (Plate 300).[99] With open shelves or bookcases with wire-mesh in their doors, a perennial problem was dust settling on the tops of the upright volumes—a problem that is still with us today. The eighteenth century often fitted a fringe or small pelmet below the front edge of the shelves to flick the dust off the volumes whenever they were withdrawn, but such a device seems to have been familiar in learned circles by the 1640s, as John Evelyn saw something of the sort in the Duke of Orléans' library in Paris in 1644.[100] The feature is to be seen in Plates 294 and 302 showing important French libraries at the end of the century. With such an arrangement it helps if all the volumes on a shelf are of the same height but a regular presentation of books in a library was anyway admired in learned circles towards the end of the century; Pepys actually had small pieces of wood, shaped and decorated to fit under his smaller volumes individually, so that they were raised and all the books on a shelf might seem to be of the same height.

'I can reach up to a shelfe 7 ft. high, from ye grounde,' wrote Sir Roger Pratt in a 'Mem[orandum] concerning shelves for my bookes of 20th August, 1671.'[101] 'From a chaire 18 ins. high consequently, $1\frac{1}{2}$ ft. higher, so yt. ye whole case may bee 9 ft. high an easy Joyners ladder may bee made about $4\frac{1}{2}$ ft. which be soe made as to thrust in at ye bottom of my table as part of it.' The table measured 5 ft 6 in. × 3 ft. and must have had solid stretchers near floor-level against which the foot of the ladder could be wedged. At Ham House there was 'one foulding ladder of cedar' in the Library but this was replaced by the massive eighteenth-century steps that are now there.[102] A late seventeenth-century pair of library steps is illustrated in Plate 302. An Oxford inventory of 1674 includes a reference to a 'boarded settle to reach down books' but exactly what this was like it would be difficult to say.

It was normal in libraries to have one or more sturdy tables on which large volumes could be opened or at which one could work. They were mostly simple structures without drawers, and were usually covered with a cloth.[103] As library bookcases became more architectural in character, so library tables also became more massive, the columnar legs being replaced by plinth-like pedestal supports which provided additional storage space inside. Pepys had a table of this type made for his library, probably not long before 1693, and several Continental libraries have substantial tables or presses of this kind dating from the late seventeenth century.

On the library table one could place the small portable desks (Plates 163 and 303) that remained common long after more substantial writing-cabinets of various kinds had become fashionable. Desks not only provided a conveniently sloping surface on which to write with a quill, they also served to prop up books—reading-desks. We have already noted a desk on which lay *The Book of Martyrs*; at Ingatestone the Bible in the chapel was provided with a similar 'deske for it to ly upon'.[104] These small desks could be richly decorated, like those Paul Hentzner saw at Whitehall Palace in 1598 in Queen Elizabeth's apartment and described as 'two little silver cabinets, of exquisite work . . . in which the Queen keeps her paper[s], and which she uses for writing boxes', or the 'little deske to write on guilded' at Marton Hall a few years later, and the 'escritoire de la Chine . . . vernie de couleur d'or' [writing-desk from China lacquered a gold colour] which belonged to Cardinal Mazarin.[105] Some desks at Hardwick were encased in leather but there was also 'a little deske of mother of pearle' in the best bedchamber.[106] Desks described as being covered with needlework are also likely to have belonged to this class of small

300. Books protected by a curtain. On the library table lies a large volume supported by a reading desk that cannot be seen. Alongside is a massive *torchère*.

furniture. In the inventories of Charles I's property appears the item 'A faire deske richly embroydered with silver and silk wherein is a silver inke pott and sand box' while the French royal inventory of 1673 notes 'une escritoire de petit point d'or et d'argent, enrichie de broderie d'or et d'argent' [a writing-desk of gold and silver tent-stitch embroidery, ornamented with embroidery in gold and silver] which had silver-gilt fittings.[107]

301. The Library at the Hôtel de Lauzun in Paris; about 1660. The books are housed in cupboards, the doors of which form an integral part of the richly decorated panelling.

At the end of the century, in England, these small desks were being placed on stands to serve as ladies' writing-desks and, when fitted with an adjustable looking-glass above, as dressing-tables.[108] Scaled up and furnished with more substantial stands, such desks finally evolved as the fall-front bureau so typical of the Georgian period. This is not the place to discuss in any detail the development of the writing-desk[109] but it needs to be said that the commonest form during the seventeenth century was that first evolved in Spain and called an *escritorio* (hence the French *escritoire* and English 'scriptor'). This was a box-like nest of drawers enclosed in the front by a flap that dropped down to form a writing-surface. Stands were often provided but small versions could stand on a table. There are four specimens at Ham House: two luxurious models with silver mounts which may be Dutch, a large utilitarian version which the Duchess used in her study ('Private Closet'), and the very handsome built-in cedarwood desk in the library which has sets of drawers above and below (Plate 299). During the second half of the century the French evolved quite a different form of desk (*bureau*) which was essentially a table with several stacks of drawers underneath, arranged so as to provide a 'knee-hole'. This is commonly called a 'bureau *Mazarin*' today;[110] it served equally well as a dressing-table (Plates 31 and 195). A few desks of this type were made in England at the end of the century[111] and the form was subsequently developed into the 'knee-hole desk' with the flanking stacks of drawers forming pedestals. In France, on the other hand, the fully developed knee-hole form was not favoured. Instead of multiple drawers (which could be housed just as conveniently in a separate piece of furniture as a filing cabinet—a *cartonnier*) three wide drawers sufficed and the characteristic French writing-desk became little more than an extensive working-surface on four sturdy legs—the *bureau plât*.

Pauline Agius noted a 'turning desk' in an Oxford inventory of 1659. Maybe this was a reading-desk on a turntable base but it could also have been of the sturdy mediaeval type with a tall upright that stood on the floor supporting a swinging arm at the end of which was the reading-desk.[112] There was at Knole in 1645 'a deske upon a skreene' which would seem to have been a firescreen with a reading-stand attached.[113] In the Elizabethan period, use was still being made of 'book pillows' which were often elaborately decorated with needlework.[114] A favourite or special book might lie on such a pillow which had the advantage that it was more kind to delicate bindings than the hard surface of a desk.

Some portable desks were fitted with an ink-well and a pounce-box for sand, but it was more common to have these accessories assembled in a separate unit known as

302. 'La Petite Bibliothèque . . . au Palais royale' at the end of the seventeenth century showing built-in book-cupboards, the shelves of which are fitted with dust-pelmets. Curious is the fact that the inside of the doors are undecorated. The battens on the wall to the left are also difficult to explain; it is as if the room were not completed when the sketch was made. Note the decidedly functional library-steps.

La petite Bibliotheque de Mr le Duc d'Orleans au Palais Royal proche son Cabinet

303. A library designed by Daniel Marot at the end of the century. The book-cases now form a prominent and fixed part of a unified scheme of decoration. Note the busts and globes used ornamentally, the barometer, the sturdy library table and comfortable chair with wings.

a 'standish' (Plates 109 and 163). Randle Holme, writing in the middle of the century, explained that ink-horns (hollowed horn-tips with a cap over the opening in which ink could be kept) were going out of use and being replaced by ink-wells of pewter or tin, and that a standish should 'have both inke place, sand box, candlestick and a long box to lay [sealing] wax' in.[115] A standish could either take the form of a small tray on which the various items stood, or could be a box with double lids swinging on a common hinge, covering two compartments, one of which could house the pens. Most pens were made from a quill but at Marton Hall there was apparently one made of brass.[116] This was listed among the writing materials in a Study which included another curious item, namely 'one bone to stirr incke'. A standish could be highly decorative: in his rooms at Oxford Lord Teviot had one of walnut and another that was inlaid; there was an 'Indian standishe' at Tart Hall which was probably lacquered, and at Kilkenny in the 1680s the Duchess of Ormonde had a 'standishe garnished with brass' which may very well have been French and perhaps of boulle-work.[117] They might also be made of silver. Another piece of equipment one might still find in a study early in the century was 'a little halff ynch board to cut parchement uppon'.[118] Parchment had of course long ago yielded to paper as the principal vehicle for writing but was still used for formal documents until well into the eighteenth century. As it was also quite expensive, one could cut slips of the size required from a skin.

314

Maps were popular in the seventeenth century, not merely for the information they gave but for their decorative effect. They are often to be seen in contemporary Dutch pictures of interiors and, because most maps were printed in Amsterdam, they may have been rather commoner in Holland than in other countries (Plate 231). But they are often mentioned in English inventories and were to be found in rooms of all kinds (Plate 296). Globes (normally in pairs, one terrestrial and one celestial) were also greatly in favour with those who could afford them. Once again, they had a fascination for the seventeenth-century mind as a revelation of Man's discovery of the physical world, but globes were also extremely pretty and it is quite obvious that they were treated equally as pleasing articles of decoration. The pair of large globes which are still at Ham House were not housed in the Library in the seventeenth century but were placed in the Gallery. They still have their original scorched leather protective covers (Plate 299).

Special lighting is required in places where people want to read after dark. This question is touched upon in Chapter XI. As I noted, some standishes were fitted with candle-holders, which would have provided a certain amount of light but would also have been useful for melting sealing-wax.

BATHS AND CLEANLINESS

How clean were our seventeenth-century ancestors? The evidence is scanty and one should not make sweeping statements on the matter. However, it is probable that many people were a good deal less dirty than is now generally supposed. It is not necessary to have a wash-basin in every bedroom and a bathroom next door in order to keep clean; it merely makes it easier.

On the days when he did not take a bath, Louis XIV wiped himself with a cloth moistened in spirits—probably a preparation akin to eau-de-Cologne or after-shave lotion. After meals he wiped both face and hands in a hot, damp napkin. Louis is not known to have been particularly fastidious in these matters and it is probable that many of his contemporaries took far greater pains to be clean than he. A seventeenth-century book on etiquette advises the gentry that 'tous les jours l'on prendra la peine de se laver avec le pain d'amande. Il faut aussi se faire laver le visage aussi souvent.' [every day one should take the trouble to wash with *pain d'amande*. It is also necessary to wash one's face almost as often.][119] The ewer and basin necessary for this last operation are to be seen in many contemporary illustrations, often standing on the dressing-table (Plates 29 and 309). The same equipment was brought in at meal-times so that the diners could rinse their fingers.[120] The staff were also expected to wash before the meal.[121]

Moreover, one must not think that, just because few houses had bathrooms in the seventeenth century, baths were not taken. All one needed was a tub—specially made for the purpose or cut from one end of a large barrel—and it was normally kept in the scullery or wash-house (Plates 305 and 319[58].[122] This was carried into the room where the bath was to be taken and removed again afterwards. Most baths were of wood but they might also be of copper.[123] A few were of silver but then are likely to have been comparatively small—footbaths, perhaps, like that illustrated in Plate 304.[124]

Queen Elizabeth is said to have taken a bath once a month 'whether she need it or

Femme de qualité déshabillée pour le bain.

304. A lady washing her feet in a vessel that might equally well serve as a wine-cooler or *jardinière*. This scene is a reminder that one could keep clean without the full paraphernalia of the modern bathroom. This *Femme de qualité* sits in her shift on a highly fashionable day-bed (the engraving is dated 1685) which seems to be set up in her dressing-room. A perfume-burner (*casolette*) stands in the foreground.

305. Taking a bath. Note that the bath is no more than a large laundry-tub and is probably lined with a cloth. Over it is suspended a *pavillon* embroidered with *fleurs-de-lis*. The lady must be seated on a stool. As she is wearing a bodice or shift it can only be the lower half of her body that is intended to benefit in this case. She may be enjoying a kind of localised steam bath.

no'.[125] The young Louis XIII apparently took frequent baths, according to his personal physician, Héroard, who records how on one occasion in 1611 the king rose at 7 a.m. to watch his bath being filled when red rose-petals were scattered on the water. The next day he again took a bath and this time we learn the tub was placed in his bedchamber. He called for his model boats on this occasion, filled them with rose-petals and pretended that the vessels were returning 'from the Indies or from Goa'.[126] If one did not have facilities at home for taking a bath one could hire a bath-tub for no great sum[127] or one could go to a public bath-house. The book on etiquette mentioned above actually recommended its readers that 'l'on peut aller quelque fois chez les beigneurs pour avoir le corps net' [one can occasionally go to the bath-house to keep the body clean] in addition to the daily ablutions already noted (Plate 308).

There is no denying, however, that actual bathrooms remained few and far between right through till the end of the century. What is more, it must be admitted that some of the more splendid bathrooms were installed principally to impress visitors rather than through any strong desire for hygiene. Celia Fiennes records in some detail the splendid 'batheing roome' at Chatsworth which she was shown on her tour of the house.[128] It had walls

> all with blew and white marble the pavement mix'd one stone white another black another red rance [i.e. varigated]; the bath is one entire marble all finely white veined with blew and is made smooth . . . it was as deep as one's middle on the outside and you went down steps into the bath big enough for two people; at the upper end are two cocks to lett in one hott the other cold water to attempt it as persons please; the windows are all private [obscured] glass.

The Chatsworth bathroom must have been modelled on that in the *Appartement des Bains* at Versailles which, as I have noted, was a luxury flat fitted out for Madame de Montespan. Because this was the preserve of the King's mistress, it was probably more private than the Chatsworth bathroom that was shown to tourists, but it was appointed with the utmost luxury. The baths were hewn from single pieces of marble, the largest being ten *pieds* wide and three deep. The walls were faced with marble marquetry decorated with bronze reliefs (Plate 21).[129] There were less grand bathrooms in some of the other principal apartments at Versailles and similar rooms were installed at a number of noble houses in Paris towards the end of the century.

The *Appartement des Bains* was being installed in the second half of the 1670s and it cannot therefore have influenced the Duchess of Lauderdale or her architect when they were building the bathroom at Ham House in the very same years. However, as we have noted, the Duchess was in Paris in 1670, so she may have seen other bathrooms over there. But what is perhaps more remarkable about her bathroom is that it was intended for actually taking baths and was not for show. This is obvious from the fact that it is approached from her bedchamber by only a very narrow spiralling staircase down which it would never have been possible to take visitors. So the Duchess of Lauderdale clearly wanted to take baths and, if she did so, how many of her contemporaries were likewise inclined? The bathroom at Eriksberg in Sweden is roughly contemporary and is sumptuously decorated (Plates 306 and 307). It probably reflects the sort of bathroom to be seen elsewhere in Europe during the third quarter of the century. It has twin copper bath-tubs set in niches, and a fountain in the centre of the room. There are ducts in the balustrades for hot air

306 & 307. A bathroom of about 1670. Two copper baths stand in niches; they have festoons on a black ground. The baths are filled from taps. Hot air could be introduced from the boiler-room below by means of ducts in the balustrade and under the benches.

generated from the boiler-room below. In a small cupboard is a control panel where servants can adjust separately the flow of air and water.

Taking a bath in the seventeenth century may well have been a lengthy process, perhaps more akin to the sauna than to modern bathroom practice. The French ambassador to Sweden in 1634 noted that every house of any consequence in that country had its own bathroom, by which he meant a steam-bath, and Savot explained that next to a bathroom should lie what he calls an *étuve*, with a copper set over a fire, which must have served a similar purpose.[130] It may well be that such an amenity was not all that uncommon in England at the time, for Robert Herrick referred to 'a sweating closset' in a manner that suggests that everyone would have known what he meant (Plate 308).[131] Francis Bacon seems to have been advocating a sweat-bath when he wrote that one should 'first, before bathing, rub and anoint the body with oyle and salves, that the bath's moistening heate and virtue may penetrate into the body, and not the liquor's watery part: then sit two hours in the bath'.[132] The Duchess of Lauderdale had her 'bathing tubb & little stoole within it' which suggests she followed the practice outlined by Bacon, and we know that Louis XIV sat on a stool in his bath. Plate 305 shows a woman taking

319

308. Taking a bath in an elongated vessel lined with a cloth. The man lying on the covered staging behind is enjoying a steam-bath. Although this shows a Swedish sauna in 1674, 'sweating closets' were certainly known in other countries at the time.

309. A pewter chamber-pot stands in the foreground. Behind the bed is a cubicle set into the wall with a screening door housing a fixed close-stool. The circular dressing-table has a velvet table carpet protected by a white linen *toilette*. A wash basin and ewer stand behind the dressing set.

a bath in this way but she only seems to be interested in bathing the lower half of her body as she has a cloth across the mouth of the tub with a hole in the centre through which her upper torso protrudes. She anyway sits under a tent and it was apparently a common practice to envelop the bather in this way. For example, at Marly there were 'deux pavillons pour les deux baignoires' in 1684.[133] Such tents or *pavillons* would have kept the bather warm during a prolonged period of bath-taking and would have served to contain steam if the bath being enjoyed was of the sauna kind (Plate 305). At Ham House there is a rod fixed below the ceiling above the place where the bath-tub must have stood; this could well be to hold up a tent over the tub. There is also a large hook from which, presumably, a container of hot water could be suspended so that the bath could be topped up when it had cooled off. In the tub it was usual to place a cloth which reduced the cold touch of marble or metal, or the clammy feel of a wooden bath-tub.

Three steps down through a handsome pair of doors leading out of the Ham bathroom is a second room which housed an 'Indian painted bedstead' with painted satin hangings.[134] In this room one presumably relaxed after the bath, for, as Bacon recommended, one should 'after bathing wrap the body in seare-cloth made of mastiche, myrrh, pomander and saffron, for staying the perspiration or breathing of the pores, until the softening of the body, having layne thus in seare-cloth 24 hours [sic], bee growne solid and hard'. To complete the treatment one had to anoint oneself with more ointment. At Hamstead Marshall, built in the 1660s, there was not only a 'Roome to Bathe' but next to it lay a 'Roome for to Repose after Bathing' which is probably what the room at Ham might also have been called.

Randle Holme illustrates a small circular table with a tripod stand which he explains 'is used to stand a bason on whilest washing, or a candle to read by, with many other uses for the chamber' (Plate 319[91]). Basins for washing and the en suite ewers for water are rarely listed as being in bedchambers, however,[135] probably because they were kept with other plate or household vessels in the serving quarters and brought in when needed.[136] Some of the small tables that are often found listed in the contents of a bedchamber may also have served as wash-stands.[137] On the Continent, hand-washing was often performed under a small cistern of water mounted on the wall with a basin below (Plate 128). In a house at Rheims in 1621 there was a 'pied de bois servant à laver les mains' which must have been a stand supporting a wash-basin rather like that to be seen in the illustration.[138]

In the best circles soap was used, Venetian soap being particularly good 'pour les mains' [for the hands]. 'Boites de savon de Milan'[boxes of soap from Milan] were considered a very acceptable present for a lady in the sixteenth century and in 1630 the Elector of Brandenburg was given eight pieces of Turkish soap. But most soap was made locally. In any event soap came either in slab form or in balls. Spherical containers were made for these 'wash balls'.[139]

Also normally only brought into the room when needed were chamber-pots, which were otherwise kept with the candlesticks in the pantry. Chamber-pots might sometimes be called *Nebstschale* in German, a term which carries the implication that they were placed next to the bed rather than under it. In fact, the chamber-pot was sometimes placed on an adjacent chair (Plate 127) and a special low table covered with gilt leather, 'en kleyn taflken . . . met goude leer overtrocken', was provided in a Dutch palace in the 1630s 'diende om den pispot op to setten'

310. A *chaise percée* insultingly included in an anti-spanish political tract of 1624.

311. A *chaise percée* being carried into a bedchamber in exceptional circumstances (the doctor is about to administer an enema). The padded ring and pewter pan are clearly shown.

312. Two mid-seventeenth-century close-stools of the box type.

313. (below left) A close-stool 'trunke fashion' covered with red velvet perhaps made for Charles I.

314. (below right) A japanned close-stool which was provided for the cubicle (stool room) set into the wall of the antechamber to the state bedchamber at Ham House late in the 1670s.

[serving as a stand for the chamber-pot].[140] Chamber-pots in the grander sort of house were commonly made of pewter in the seventeenth century; occasionally they were made of faience and perhaps also of porcelain, and more rarely of silver.[141] Pots of common earthenware were also used but the material was apt to be rather too brittle for the purpose.[142] Randle Holme illustrates a vessel of inverted conical form with a wide foot and turned over brim, which he calls a 'squatter' and explains was 'used by sick and infirm persons to ease nature in the bedchamber when they are not able to stire out'.[143] Bidets, incidentally, were unknown in the seventeenth century; Savary des Bruslons explains that a *bidet* was a small kind of horse and gives no other meaning.[144] The 'ewerinall' listed as being in the window-bay of a closet at Marton Hall will have been one of those long-necked flasks often illustrated in Dutch paintings being held up to the light by a physician who is usually shown in attendance on a sick woman (Plate 109).[145]

Altogether more substantial than the humble chamber-pot was the close-stool which took two distinct forms. What was presumably the earliest type consisted of an armchair with a padded ring-like seat (Plate 310). The term *chaise percée* accurately describes this form although it came to be used for both types of close-stool, under which the pewter pan fitted. The other type consisted of a box with a lid that closed over the ring-seat.[146] A few examples of the latter form survive (Plates 312–14).

Most close-stools were no doubt simple affairs but they could be quite elaborately decorated—like that at Hardwick which was inlaid, and the one at Ingatestone which was 'covered with black leather guilded in spotts'.[147] A handsome specimen covered in red velvet is at Hampton Court while one japanned black with chinoiseries

315. (below left) A 'lodging' or apartment in the late sixteenth century showing how the close-stool stood in a separate small closet or *garderobe* (c) behind the bedchamber (b). On the original plan the first room (a) is described as an 'Antecamera', using the Italian term. Room (c) is stated to be for 'Wood[,] cole and privy'. See also Plate 57 where a separate room for the close-stool is indicated.

316. (below centre) A privy in the thickness of the wall, approached from the alcove of a bedchamber. The Hôtel de Jars in Paris, designed by François Mansart about 1648.

317 (below right) The principal bedchamber at Kinross House with a 'stool room' in the thickness of the wall. Although Sir William Brice, who designed the house for himself in the 1680s, admired French practice in the planning of buildings, there was nothing strange in thus placing the 'house of office' discreetly out of the way. It was the normal thing to do, not only in Scotland but all over the civilised world.

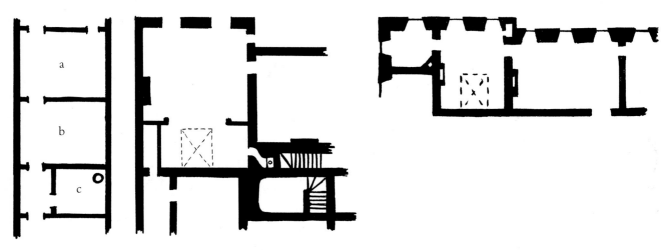

is to be seen at Ham House (Plate 314). Some close-stools were fitted with slip-over covers like that belonging to Cardinal Mazarin which had pendant flaps (*à pentes*) while another was covered with black leather and had an outer cover of red silk damask trimmed with silk fringe.[148] At Breda Castle in 1619 one close-stool had a red and yellow damask cover ['Eenen camerstoel met een behangsel van root en geel damast'] and the 'chaises d'affaires' at Marly were furnished with 'layettes de velour rouge' [loose covers of red velvet].[149] The inventories are rarely explicit about the actual seats but they must have been padded with straw or horsehair and covered with some material. At Ingatestone one had its 'seate lyned wth. yellow cotton' while one at Copenhagen Castle had red cloth on its seat-ring.[150] The pans or 'basons' fitted inside a close-stool were usually of pewter, but Mazarin had one of faience. Sometimes a stool was provided with two pans so that one served as a replacement while the other was being emptied.[152]

The close-stool is commonly listed in inventories among the contents of a bedchamber, but often it was in fact placed in a cubby-hole masked by a jib-door or disguised in some other way (Plate 309). The English version of Le Muet's work, published in 1670, tells us that 'the Privy shall be taken within the thickness of the wall' and such an arrangement can be seen in the plans reproduced in Plates 316 and 317. One sometimes also gets a hint that this was the practice from the inventories themselves. For example, the close-stool listed as being in Her Grace's Bedchamber at Kilkenny Castle in 1684 actually stood in such a cubicle, for we learn that there was 'a picture with flowers over the stool door'.[153] At Ingatestone right back in 1600 two bedchambers each had 'a little house of office within'.[154] The close-stool might also stand in a separate small room. At Ingatestone there was 'a little Stool house' containing a close-stool; at Petworth in 1670 there were 'two Close Stoole Roomes on the Middle Staires', at Tart Hall in 1641 a close-stool was located 'in ye lobby at ye back stayres', and Dr Thomas Lockey had his close-stool 'in a little place by . . . the parlour', while the close-stool at the Lauderdales' London house stood in a place known as 'The Hole'.[155] At Ham House one may still see two cubicles where close-stools once stood set in the walls behind the hangings in two antechambers, as the inventory proves: one of these rooms was called 'the Withdrawing Roome' and at Petworth there was likewise 'a Stoole Roome w'th[in] the Withdrawing Roome'. In his rooms at Oxford, Lord Teviot kept his close-stool 'in the Passage next the Dining Room'.[156]

Exactly the same may be seen on the Continent. The *camerstoel* in one of the principal apartments at the Noordeinde residence of the Prince of Orange stood in a special small closet [Het kleyn secreet camerken].[157] In a house at Rheims two close-stools were placed in a room called the *Garde-robe* and Louis XIV had his standing in a *garde-robe* off the closet known as the *Cabinet des Perruques*.[158] It was 'placée dans une niche garnie de gros de Tours rouge avec galon d'or' [placed in a niche faced with red *gros de Tours* taffeta trimmed with red galloon]. Although Louis XIV, who was old-fashioned in matters of court ceremony, revived the old tradition of receiving honoured callers while seated on his *chaise d'affaires*, it was no doubt all managed very discreetly,[159] the Noordeinde close-stool stood in a *secreet camerken*; in Germany such closets were also known as the *secret* or *das heimliches Gemach* [the secret room], in Sweden as the *privet* and in England as a 'privy'. The evidence all points to the conclusion that our seventeenth-century ancestors were a good deal

318. A French perfume-burner or *casolette* on a stand. Apparently dating from the last quarter of the seventeenth century this design was probably for an important object, perhaps to be made of silver. It may well have been quite large—up to 100 cm high.

more discreet about these matters than one is often led to suppose. Only in rather special circumstances (as that depicted in Plate 311 where an enema is about to be administered by the doctor) were close-stools brought right into an important bedchamber. At Burfield Lodge at the end of the century Celia Fiennes saw a closet that 'leads to a little place with a seate of easement of marble with sluices of water to wash it all down'.[160] She was clearly impressed by the arrangement which was no doubt a very early example of the water-closet. By the eighteenth century such an amenity was known in France as 'un lieux à l'anglaise' [an English place] which suggests that it was an English invention, although this may be just a further example of that long-standing and childish Anglo-French animosity which has, for instance, led one nation to speak of 'taking French leave' while this in French is called to 'filer à l'anglaise'. Incidentally, a common French name for the close-stool house or *lieu d'aisance* was simply *le lieu*—from which derives our own corruption, 'the loo'.

All this said, one could still cite many tales of dirty habits but the very fact that they were remarked upon suggests that the writer expected the reader to disapprove and at least indicates that a certain fastidiousness prevailed in some quarters.[161] It may well be that people in the seventeenth century were in general not so very different from what we would be if we did not have running hot and cold water freely available.

There was, whatever the case, incentive enough to surround oneself with fragrant

326

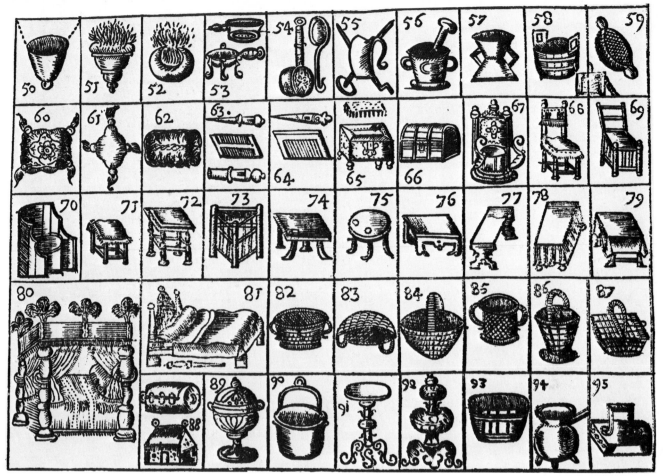

319. Mid-seventeenth-century English household furniture and utensils.

50–52   lamps

53   colander and chafing-dish. The purpose of the latter was 'to hold hot coales of fire in, and to set dish-meates thereon, to keepe them warme till the tyme of serving them up to the table . . .'.

54   warming pan and frying pan. The former was for airing beds.

55   a 'steel to strike fire', used in association with a tinder-box, and two spits for roasting.

56 & 57   mortars, one with its pestel

58   'A tub or turnell with handles' of the sort used by laundry-maids. It could also be used as a bath.

59   'a twiggen basket'

60 & 61   cushions

62   bolster, laced lengthways 'for the greater adornment and beauty of it'

63   two-sided head-comb and a bodkin, the latter to hold up long hair

64   single-sided comb and a bodkin

65   'a Bristle brush' and a 'kind of cabinett . . . such as ladyes keep their . . . jewells in; it stands constantly on the . . . dressing table . . .'.

66   coffer (with a curved lid). 'If it have a flat cover, it is called a Chest'.

67   throne 'or a cathedre'

68   'a stoole-chair, or back stoole'. If all made of joiner's work, then called 'a Joynt chaire, or a Buffet chaire'.

69   a 'turned chaire'

70   ancient form of chair, sometimes called a 'settle chair'. A variant made of osiers was a 'twiggen chaire'.

71   stool

72   'Joynt stoole', has wooden seat. In Cheshire called a 'buffit stool'.

73   'turned stoole'

74   'country stoole', also called a 'plancke or blocke stoole'

75   round 'country stoole'

76   nursing stool

77   'Joint forme, or bench'

78   long table

79   square table covered with a carpet

80   'a bed royall'

81   bed without a tester. Below is a 'bed staffe'.

82   'voyder basket' for carrying delicate clothes

83   'cloathes basket'; rough versions were for coal.

84   'hand basket'; might be coloured

85   fruit basket

86   'twiggen basket' for collecting eggs

87   egg or butter basket; has two lids and a partition

88   'port manteau' of tanned leather and an ark 'of wood and covered with haire cloth', which could be suspended from ceiling to 'secure all things . . . from the cruelty of devouring rates, mice, weesels and such like vermine'. Instead of horse-hair, panels of pierced tin might be used.

89   covered cup

90   hanging kettle or cauldron

91   'little round table . . . for to set a Bason on whilest washing, or a candle to read by, with many other uses for a chamber. Some call it a dressing table.'

92   andiron, 'for ornament more than profitt'.

93   tub

94   'posnett', used for boiling liquids

95   smoothing iron.

smells. Fragrant herbs were cultivated assiduously. The proper drying of such plants and the making of *pot-pourri* were subjects a young lady was expected to master. 'Swetebages' (sweet smelling bags or sachets) filled with lavender and other pleasant-smelling products of the garden[162] were laid among the clean sheets and clothes in their presses (see p. 299). Scented leather gloves and fans from Spain and Italy were much in demand, as were exotic confections like pomanders. Ladies sucked aniseed pastilles to sweeten the breath and covered themselves in scents imported from far afield. It is when one remembers how essential it was to kill the numerous malodours of daily life that one comes to realise why cargoes of spices and perfumes were so valuable and why so much money could be made when an East Indiaman loaded with such goods had braved the many hazards of the long journey from the Orient and succeeded in reaching port.

One of the principal ways of perfuming the air in a room was to install a perfume-burner. These took many forms and could be decorative (Plate 318). The huge specimens of silver that stood in the *Grand Galerie* at Versailles were especially striking. In French inventories the larger versions are called *casolettes*. They were more commonly of brass or faience. Such 'perfuming pannes' or 'perfuming dishes'[163] had a shallow upper container in which the scented pastille was placed under a pierced lid which let out the scent. In the lower container hot coals could be placed to make the pastille give off its scent (Plate 304). Candlesticks could be adapted to function in a similar manner.[164]

If all these devices had still not killed an evil smell, the final weapon in the perfumer's armoury, at Versailles at any rate, was the scent-spray. Louis had one described as 'une seringue, avec son manche d'ebenne garny d'argent' [a spray, with its ebony handle and silver mounts]. This must have resembled a modern bicycle-pump and was clearly a new invention, for it was necessary to explain that it was 'pour jetter des eaues de senteurs' [to spray scented waters].[165]

320. A Dutch dolls' house, about 1700. As this is a contemporary painting it records the actual state of the dolls' house at the time; a real dolls' house can lose its furnishings, they can be arranged quite incorrectly, and can be added to.

Top left:	Linen Room. A laundry-maid irons linen at a table. Opposite is a napkin-press and a *bakermat* hangs on the wall (see Plate 197).
Top centre:	Landing. A spinning-wheel and sconce for lighting the stairs.
Top right:	Nursery. The nurse has a canopy bed. Wicker cradle. Painted sashes in windows. Rush-bottomed chairs.
Centre left:	Parlour. Verdure tapestries. Sconce above the table. Painted tea-table withdrawn to side of the room with top tipped forward.
Centre:	Hall with view of garden. Hall bench and candlestands.
Centre right:	Bedchamber with box bed. Dressing table forming part of a triad. Sconces. Rush-bottomed chair with cushion. Six-leaf screen.
Lower left:	Dining Parlour? One wall fitted with a glass-fronted cupboard for chinaware; some of it is ranged on top. Brass birdcage. Painted sashes. Nursemaid making pillow-lace.
Lower centre:	Kitchen area. *Couvre feu* in corner fireplace. Cupboard. Waiter's table?
Lower right:	Closet or Library? Gilt leather hangings. Japanned cabinet with porcelain on top. The turned and black-stained chairs have slip-over covers with lappeted edges. An open door seems to reveal bookshelves.

The whole is housed in a fashionable cabinet with glazed doors that is furnished with a fitted protective cover. With its finials and valance, the whole piece would have looked very much like a contemporary bed when the curtains were drawn round it.

Abbreviations

In the notes references to works frequently cited are given in the following abbreviated forms. Occasionally, a slight but unmistakable variant has been used where the context so demands.

Agius	Pauline Agius, 'Late 16th and 17th century Furniture in Oxford', *Furniture History*, Vol. VII, 1971.
Bishop of Winchester's Invt.	Evelyn Philip Shirley, 'The Will, Inventories and Funeral Expenses of James Montague, Bishop of Winchester, anno 1618', *Archeologia,* Vol. XLIV, Pt. II, 1873
Books of Rates, 1582	T. S. Willan, *A Tudor Book of Rates (1582)*, London, 1962.
Celia Fiennes	*The Journeys of Celia Fiennes*, ed. Christopher Morris, London, 1947.
Charles I Invts., 1649–51	'The Inventory and Valuation of The King's Goods, 1649–1651,' ed. Oliver Millar; *Walpole Society Journal*, Vol. XLIII, 1973.
Chatsworth Invt., 1601	Transcript deposited in the Department of Textiles, Victoria and Albert Museum, London; from the archives of the Dukes of Devonshire.
Chenies Invt., 1585	'Inventory of Household Goods, etc. at Chenies, Com. Bucks., on the Death of Francis, 2nd Earl of Bedford, 1585.' From a typescript deposited with the Department of Furniture and Woodwork in the Victoria and Albert Museum by Miss Scott Thomson with the knowledge of the 11th Duke of Bedford.
Clonmell Invt., 1684	National Library of Ireland, MS. 2522. Kindly communicated to me by Desmond Fitz-Gerald, Knight of Glin. Clonmell belonged to the Duke of Ormonde.
Cockesden Invt., 1610	Inventory of a house at Cockesden, 1610; James O. Halliwell, *Ancient Inventories of Furniture, Pictures, Tapestries, Plate etc. illustrative of the domestic manner of the English in the 16th and 17th century*, 1854. The property concerned was probably one belonging to the Earls of Leicester.
Cockesden Invt., 1626	From the same source as the previous item and concerning the same house.
Countess of Leicester's Invt., 1634	Inventory of the effects of Lettice, Countess of Leicester, 1634; J. O. Halliwell, *op. cit.*, under

	'Cockesden Invt., 1610' above.
Cowdray Invt., 1682	Francis W. Steer, 'A Cowdray Inventory of 1682', *Sussex Archeological Society*, Vol. CV, 1927, pp. 84–102. Taken on the death of Francis, 3rd Viscount Montagu.
D.E.F.	Ralph Edwards, *The Dictionary of English Furniture*, 2nd edition, London, 1954.
Du Boisgelin Invt., 1688	Inventory of Monsieur Gilles Dubois Geslin, Seigneur de la Sourdière in Brittany; manuscript in the possession of Mr Cyril Staal who has generously allowed me to quote from it.
Devon Invts.	'Devon Inventories of the 16th and 17th Centuries,' *Devon and Cornwall Record Society*, New Series, Vol. II, Torquay, 1966.
Dublin Castle Invt., 1679	'Inventory of Dublin Castle, seat of the Duke of Ormonde, Lord Lieutenant of Ireland, 1679,' *Historical Manuscripts Commission*, New Series VII, 1912.
Duke of Norfolk Invt., 1684	'Inventory of the goods and Chattels of His Grace Henry Duke of Norfolk deceased taken at the house at Wabridg ... 1684.' Arundel Castle Archives (MS.IN53). Quotations published by kind permission of His Grace the Duke of Norfolk. I am much indebted to Mr Francis Steer for drawing my attention to this inventory.
Dyrham Invt., 1703	An Inventory of all the Goods and Furniture in Dirham House, 1703. Gloucestershire Record Office. Copy in the Victoria and Albert Museum.
Easton Lodge Invt., 1637	Francis W. Steer, 'The Easton Lodge Inventory, 1637', *The Essex Review*, Vol. LXI, January, 1952.
Ebba Brahe's Invt., 1665	William Karlson, *Ebba Brahe's Hem. Ett herremans inventarium från 1600-talet*, Lund, 1943. (Inventory of this powerful lady's house in Stockholm, made in 1665).
Edington Invt., 1665	Anne, Lady Beauchamp's Inventory at Edington, Wiltshire, 1665; *Wiltshire Archeological and Natural History Magazine*, LVIII, No. 211, 1963, pp. 383–93.
Evelyn's Diary	*The Diary of John Evelyn*, ed. by E. S. de Beer, Oxford, 1955.
Faringdon Invt., 1620	*An Inventairie of all such Implements and Household goods as allso Jewells, Plate and other Ornaments of the right honble the Ladie Dorothy Shirley ... att Farringdon, in the countie of Barkes ..., 1620.* See *The Unton Inventories ... 1596 and 1620, with a Memoir by John Gough Nichols*, printed for the Berkshire Ashmolean Society, London, 1841.
Gilling Castle Invt., 1594	'Inventories made for Sir William and Sir Thomas Fairfax, Knights of Walton, and of Gilling Castle',

	Yorkshire, *Archeologia*, Vol. XLVIII, 1884.
Gosfield Invt., 1638	F. W. Steer, 'Inventory of Anne, Viscountess Dorchester', *Notes & Queries*, March, April, September, October, November and December 1953 and January 1954 (the last being a transcription of her will). Gosfield Hall was in Essex.
Guiffrey, Inventaire	Jules Guiffrey, *Inventaire Général du mobilier de la couronne sous Louis XIV*, Paris, 1885.
Ham Invt., c. 1654	Unpublished inventory of the contents of Ham House, probably taken in 1654. The Victoria and Albert Museum intends to publish this in due course.
Ham Invt., 1677	Unpublished inventory of the house taken when much of the extension and re-decoration carried out by the Duke and Duchess of Lauderdale was largely completed. To be published (see previous note). It differs in several respects from that of 1679 (see below).
Ham Invt., 1679	The unpublished but well-known inventory of the house then recently enlarged by the Duke and Duchess of Lauderdale. To be published (see previous note).
Ham Invt., 1683	The inventory taken after the Duke's death. See previous note.
Hampton Court Estimates, 1699	'Estimates for Furniture, Upholstery, etc. for Hampton Court Palace, 1699, signed by the Earl of Montague, Master of the Great Wardrobe.' Photographic copy in the Victoria and Albert Museum Library.
Hardwick Invt., 1601	Lindsay Boynton (commentary by Peter Thornton), 'The Hardwick Inventory of 1601', *Furniture History*, Vol. VII, 1971
Hatfield Priory Invt., 1629	'Inventory of the Household Goods of Sir Thomas Barrington, Bart., at Hatfield Priory, 1629' [not 1626 as stated in title], *Transactions of the Essex Archeological Society*, III, New Series, 1889.
Havard	Henry Havard, *Dictionnaire de l'ameublement . . .*, Paris, 1887–90, in four volumes.
Hengrave Invt., 1603	John Gage, *The History and Antiquities of Hengrave in Suffolk*, London, 1822; p. 21 *et seq.*; inventory of Hengrave Hall, 1603
Henham Invt., 1602	A. Suckling, *The History and Antiquities of the County of Suffolk*, London, 1848; inventory of Henham Hall, 1602.
Ingatestone Invt., 1600	'Inventory of the furniture etc. at Ingatestone Hall, Essex,' typescript in the Victoria and Albert Museum Library; see also *Ingatestone Hall in 1600: an Inventory*, Essex Education Committee, 1954.

Karlson	William Karlson, *Stât och Vardag i Stormakstidens herremanshem*, Lund, 1945. A major survey of seventeenth-century furnishings in Sweden.
Kensington Palace Invt., 1697	T. Lunsingh Scheurleer, 'Documents on the Furnishings of Kensington House,' *Walpole Society*, Vol. XXXVIII, 1960–62.
Kensington Palace Invt., 1699	As for the previous entry.
Kildare Invt., 1656	'An Inventory of the Earl of Kildare's goods which is left in his house at Dublin, 1656.' Communicated to me by Desmond Fitz-Gerald, Knight of Glin. By kind permission of the Marquess of Kildare.
Kilkenny Invt., 1684	'Inventory of Kilkenny Castle, 1684', *Historical Manuscripts Commission*, New Series VII, 1912. The seat of the Duke of Ormonde, Lord Lieutenant of Ireland.
Knole Invt., 1645	Chas. J. Phillips, *History of the Sackville Family*, London, *c.* 1928, p. 353 'An Inventory of Goods at Knole, 1645.'
Lauderdale London Invt., 1679	Inventory of the house in Whitehall, London, of the Duke and Duchess of Lauderdale, 1679; included with the *Ham Invt., 1679*, see above.
Lockey Invt., 1679	'Inventory of Dr Thomas Lockey, 1679'; *Bodleian Library Record*, 1954–6, p. 82. Lockey was Bodley's Librarian 1660–5 and then Canon of Christ Church until his death.
Marton Invt., 1605	'An inventory of the goodes moveable and imoveable within the house at Marton, 1605.'
Mazarin Invt., 1653	Henri d'Orléans, *Inventaire de tous les meubles du Cardinal Mazarin*, London, 1861; the inventory was made in 1653.
Montague Household Book, 1595	Sir William St John Pope, *Cowdray and Easebourne Priory*, London, 1919. Appendix II.
Noordeinde Invt., 1633	'Inventaris van de Meublen van het Stadhouderlijk met het Speelhuis en van Huis in het Noodeinde te s'Gravenhage, 1633,' C. Hofstede de Groot and C. H. de Jonge (eds.), *Oud Holland*, 1930. Inventory of the Stadholder's Residence in the Noordeinde at The Hague. Possibly made in 1632. See also the *Orange Invts.* below.
Northampton Invt., 1614	'Inventory of the . . . Earl of Northampton . . . 1614,' *Archeologia*, Vol. XLII, Pt. II, 1862.
Northumberland House Invt., 1670	'Inventory of Northumberland House, 1670,' Jocelin, Earl of Northumberland's estate (see *Petworth Invt., 1670*, below).
Orange Invts.	*Inventarissen van de Inboedels in de verblijven van de Oranjes . . . 1567–1795*, ed. S. W. A. Drossaers and

	Th. H. Lunsingh Scheurleer (Rijks Geschiedkundige Publication), in three vols., The Hague, 1974–6. Inventories of members of the House of Orange.
Pepys' Diary	*The Diary of Samuel Pepys.* For the years 1660–1669, Robert Latham and William Matthews' edition was consulted; for subsequent dates, that of H. B. Wheatley of 1904.
Petworth Invt., 1670	'Inventory of the Rt Hon. Jocelin, Earl of Northumberland's Personal Estate at Petworth, 1670'; Manuscript shown to me by the Lady Victoria Percy, the quotations from it being published here by kind permission of His Grace, the Duke of Northumberland.
Princess Palatine's Letters	*Letters from Liselotte (Elizabeth Charlotte, Princess Palatine and Duchesse d'Orléans)*, ed. Maria Kroll, London, 1970.
Provost of King's Invt., 1660	J. W. Clark, 'On the Old Provost Lodge of King's College, with special reference to the furniture,' *Cambridge Antiquarian Society*, Communications, IV, 1876–80, 1881.
Randle Holme	Randle Holme, *The Academy of Armory or a Storehouse of Armory and Blazon*, 1688, The Roxburghe Club, London, 1905. Holme was writing in the middle of the century (see the note to Plate 319); he was a 'Deputy for the Kings of Arms' and well versed in heraldry.
Rambouillet Invt., 1652	*Deux inventaires de l'Hôtel de Rambouillet, 1652 & 1665; Bulletin Archéologique du Comité des Travaux Historiques et Scientifiques*, Paris, 1892.
Rambouillet Invt., 1665	See previous item.
Savary des Bruslons	Jacques Savary des Bruslons, *Dictionnaire universal de commerce*, Paris, 1723.
Standon Lordship invt., 1623	Sir Ambrose Heal, 'A Great Country House in 1623. The Inventory of Standon Lordship, near Ware, Herts.,' *Burlington Magazine*, May 1843.
Stengel	Walter Stengel, *Alte Wohnkultur in Berlin und der Mark*, Berlin, 1958.
Syon Invt., 1670	'Inventory of Syon House, 1670', Jocelin, Earl of Northumberland's estate (see *Petworth Invt., 1670*, above).
Tart Hall Invt., 1641	'A Memoriall of all the Roomes the Household Stuffe at Tart-Hall: and an Inventory of all the goods there belonging to The Rt. Hon. The Countess of Arundel ... 1641'. Lionel Cust, 'Notes on the Collections formed by Thomas Howard, Earl of Arundel and Surrey, K. G.,' *Burlington Magazine*, 1911, Pt. II, pp. 97–100; pp. 233–6; Pt. IV, p. 341–3.

Tessin-Cronström   *Les Relations artistiques entre France et Suède,*
Correspondence   *1693–1718. Extraits d'une correspondance entre*
                          l'architecte Nicodème Tessin le Jeune et Daniel Cronström.
                          Ed. R. A. Weigert and C. Hernmarck, Stockholm,
                          1964.

Tessin's Visit, 1687   Ragnar Josephson and Pierre Francastel eds., 'Nic-
                          odème Tessin le Jeune. Relation de sa visite à Marly,
                          Versailles, Clagny, Rueil et Saint-Cloud en 1687.'
                          Revue de l'histoire de Versailles et Seine et Oise, 28
                          Année, 1926, pp. 149–67.

Thiret Invt., 1621   'Inventaire des Meubles de l'Hotel de Mr. Claude
                          Thiret . . . Rheims . . . 1621.' *Travaux de l'Académie,*
                          Nationale de Reims, LXXV (1883–84), Nos. 1–2,
                          Rheims, 1885.

Tredegar Invt., 1688   Inventory of Tredegar House, 1688; manuscript in
                          the National Museum of Wales (Tredegar Papers;
                          MSS. 315).

Tredegar Invt., 1698   As previous item.

Turenne Invt., 1615   J. Deville, *Dictionnaire du tapissier, critique et historique*
                          de l'ammeublement Français, Paris, 1878–80; Inventaire
                          des meubles du Chàteau de Turenne, 1615.

Walton Invt., 1624   Household stuff at Walton, 1624; see *Gilling Castle*
                          Invt., 1594, above.

Notes to the Text

NOTES TO THE INTRODUCTION

1. Henry Kamen, *The Iron Century. Social Change in Europe, 1550–1660*, London, 1971, p. 1.
2. In his Slade Lectures held at Oxford in January and February 1976 under the title 'The Power Houses', published as *Life in the English Country House: A Social and Architectural History*, New Haven and London, 1978.
3. 'All authority . . . belongs to us. We hold it of God alone, and no person, of whatever quality he may be, can pretend to any part of it.' (Royal Declaration of Louis XIV, 31 July 1652). 'When Kings come to the crown, they swear on the Holy Gospels that they will maintain the Church of God to their best ability; that they will observe the fundamental laws of the State, and they will protect their subjects according to God and reason, as good Kings should do; in consideration of this oath, the people are obliged to obey them as Gods on earth . . .' (*Lettre d'avis à messieurs du Parlement de Paris*, 1649, see P. R. Doolin, *The Fronde*, Cambridge, Mass., 1935, pp. 79 and 135.)
4. In his *Instructions destinées au Dauphin*, Louis XIV explained how the endless round of parties, balls, *carrousels* and spectacles would serve this end, for one should always seek to entertain and please one's people so that by 'ces divertissements . . . nous tenons leurs esprits et leurs cœurs quelquefois plus fortement peut-être que par la recompense et les bienfaits' [these entertainments . . . we sometimes hold their imagination and their hearts more strongly perhaps than by rewards and favours]. With regard to foreign visitors, 'ce que se consume en ces depenses, qui peuvent passer pour superflues, fait sur eux une impression très advantageuse de magnificence, de puissance, de richesse et de grandeur' [what is spent on these occasions, which might be thought to be extravagant, makes on them a very favourable impression of magnificence, power and greatness]. (R. A. Weigert, Introduction to the catalogue to the exhibition *Louis XIV: faste et décors*, Musée des Arts Décoratifs, Paris, 1960, p. xv.)
5. Sir William Cavendish, for example, extended Bolsover in order to entertain Charles I and his Queen in the hope of being granted the guardianship of the young Prince of Wales, and wrote to a friend in 1634 that 'I have bent my estate with the hope of it.' (O. Hill and J. Cornforth, *English Country Houses, Caroline 1625–85*, London 1966, p. 9.)
6. See Girouard (note 2, above) and Penelope Eames, 'Furniture in England, France and the Netherlands from the twelfth to the fifteenth century', *Furniture History*, XIII, 1977.
7. One is reminded of the mobile character of ancient furniture by the Italian word for furniture, both in the modern narrow sense and in that embracing all furniture that is movable, which is *i mobile*. The French, German, Dutch and Scandinavian words for furniture (*les meubles, die Möbel, meubelen, møbler*) carry the same reminder.
8. A Swedish historian has concluded, however, that it was probably still uncommon in Sweden as late as 1640 for a noble family to keep all its houses fully furnished. (*Ebba Brahe's Invt., 1665*, p. 27.)
9. 'What has been created in the past is small in comparison with our own time, since we see the quality of buildings and the number of those who build them far exceed any yet known particularly among the nobility, who devote themselves to it more for glory than out of necessity', wrote La Noue in 1587. Francis Bacon could likewise say in 1592 that 'there was never the like number of fair and stately houses as have been built and set up from the ground' since the beginning of Queen Elizabeth's reign. A generation later another writer claimed that 'No kingdom in the world spent so much on building as we did in [King James'] time' although the phenomenon was not in fact confined to England (Kamen, *op. cit.*, pp. 144–5). So much building was being carried out in Paris early in the century as the result of new prosperity that Malherbe claimed that someone returning after a two-year absence would find the city unrecognisable (*Oeuvres*, letter of 3 October, 1608).
10. A. Blunt, *Art and Architecture in France, 1500–1700*, London, 2nd edition, 1970; J. Summerson, *Architecture in Britain 1530–1830*, London, 5th edition, 1969; O. Hill and J.

Cornforth, *op. cit.*; J. P. Babelon, *Demeures parisiennes sous Henri IV et Louis XIII*, Paris, 1965; L. Hautecoeur, *Histoire de l'architecture classique en France*, Paris, n.d.; and J. Rosenberg, S. Slive and E. H. Ter Kuile, *Dutch Art and Architecture, 1600–1800*, London, 1966.

11. There was of course still no special course of training for an architect in 1600 in France or England. The first architectural academy of all was that of San Luca, established in Rome in 1577. Before that, as Vasari pointed out in 1550, 'Architecture is to be adequately pursued only by such men as possess an excellent judgment, a good knowledge of design, or extensive practice in some such occupation as painting, sculpture, or woodwork, and have been thereby led to the habit of measuring figures, edifices and bodies of similar character in their several members . . .' Among the leading architects active in England during the seventeenth century we find a former painter (Inigo Jones), an astronomer (Wren), a military engineer (Winde) and a diplomatist-courtier with an interest in buildings (Gerbier). Only Webb had been brought up to practice in the profession, according to H. M. Colvin (*A Biographical Dictionary of English Architects*, London, 1954). The *Académie Royale d'Architecture* that was to offer French architects a formal training and provide a sound basis for future practice was established in 1671 but English architects had to rely on picking up what they could at schools of drawing or from older, practising architects until late in the next century. However, the Office of Works acted as a sort of academy for those whom the Surveyor of the King's Works selected to join his staff and, as those attached to the organisation had time to undertake private work as well as their official duties, the influence of this institution was considerable. As we shall see, the French equivalent of the Office of Works, the *Surintendance des Bâtiments Royales*, also became a cradle of influential and advanced ideas. This and related questions are also surveyed by Frank Jenkins in *Architect and Patron. A Survey of Professional Relations and Practice in England from the Sixteenth Century to the Present Day*, London, 1961 and in Malcolm Airs, *The Making of the English Country House, 1500–1640*, London, 1975.

12. R. Gunter, *The Architecture of Sir Roger Pratt*, Oxford, 1928, p. 60.

13. A list of the principal architectural books published before 1685 and probably known in England is given by Hill and Cornforth, *op. cit.*, pp. 250–1.

14. Clarendon House, for example, provided an especially favoured model that was imitated all over England. Erected between 1664 and 1667 in Piccadilly, admired by Pepys as 'the finest pile I ever did see in my life' and by Evelyn as 'the best contriv'd, the most usefull, graceful and magnificent house in England', and demolished already in 1683, its influence lived on and can still be traced in a great many country houses.

NOTES TO CHAPTER I

1. Harold Nicolson, *Good Behaviour, being a Study of Certain Types of Civility*, London, 1955, p. 164. Sauval, writing in the mid-seventeenth century, claimed that the Hôtel de Rambouillet was 'the most celebrated in the kingdom' and that 'every day there gathered a group of eminent people . . . only those of exquisite and refined taste met there'. (Henri Sauval, *Histoire et recherches des antiquités de la ville de Paris*, Livre III, Vol. II, pp. 200–1.) This work was first published in 1724 but Sauval died only four years after the Marquise and seems to have known her.

2. 'Nous ont appris qu'elle en a fait & donné le dessein, qu'elle seule l'a entrepris, conduit & achevé.' [We have been told that she actually made and provided the design, that she alone undertook, directed and brought about its execution.] (Sauval, *loc. cit.*)

3. Of the house Sauval (*loc. cit.*) said that 'one will not find many in Paris which equal it or surpass it'.

4. She placed the staircase to one side so that visitors, as they approached, might see the whole suite of state rooms through the *portes en enfilade*. Neither the siting of the staircase, however, nor the arrangement of doors in enfilade were entirely novel features. As Sir Anthony Blunt has pointed out, doors thus arranged had been known in the sixteenth century ('The Précieux and French Art', in *Fritz Saxl . . . A Volume of Memorial Essays*, London, 1957, pp. 326–38). See also J. P. Babelon, *Demeures parisiennes sous Henri IV et Louis XIII*, Paris, 1965, pp. 189–95.

5. Sauval, *loc. cit.*

6. *Ibid.*

7. G. Tallement des Réaux, *Historiettes* (c. 1657–9), II, p. 216.

8. Sauval (*loc. cit.*) speaks of the room being

'parée de son tems d'un emmeublement de velours bleu, rehaussé d'or & d'argent' [dressed at the time in an *ammeublement* of blue velvet, enriched with gold and silver]. The term *ammeublement* was normally applied to the complete textile furnishings of a room (i.e. wall-hangings, chair-covers, table-carpets, window-curtains if any, and bed-hangings if it was a bedchamber). But Babelon (*op. cit.*, p. 211) claims to have found the bill of 1620 for the wall-hangings which, he says, were of brocatelle with white and gold scrollwork on a blue ground. But he suggests this was for the summer hangings. Maybe in winter the wall-hangings were of the blue velvet while the chair-covers and other items remained unchanged all the year round.

9. Penelope Eames, 'Furniture in England, France and the Netherlands from the twelfth to the fifteenth century', *Furniture History*, XIII, 1977.

10. Babelon, *loc. cit.* He provides a reconstructed plan of the house, showing the layout of the main floor.

11. Sauval, *loc. cit.*

12. Tallement des Réaux, *loc. cit.* Rosalys Coope, in her excellent monograph on the architect of the Luxembourg, Salomon de Brosse (London, 1972, p. 131), discounts this story, however, but it must surely have some foundation.

13. Work on the Luxembourg started in 1615 and the main building seems to have been roofed in 1616 but the Queen could still apparently not stay in the building by 1623. The rebuilding of the Hôtel de Rambouillet was started in 1619 and it was again altered in 1627.

14. *Parentalia; or Memoirs of the Family of Wrens . . . but chiefly of Sir Christopher Wren . . . compiled by his son Christopher. Now published by his grandson, Stephen Wren, Esq.*, London, 1750, p. 261, quoting a letter of 1665 from Paris.

15. *Tessin-Cronström Correspondence*, letter of 3 Jan., 1694.

16. Le Comte Laborde, *Le Palais Mazarin . . .*, Paris, 1846, pp. 166–8. He quotes a pamphlet of 1649 entitled *Inventaire des merveilles du monde recontrées dans le palais de Cardinal Mazarin* which describes the superb tortoiseshell cabinets, the tables of Italian work in *pietre dure*, the statues, the silk damask on the walls, an ivory couch and a particularly noteworthy painting of the Virgin Mary which were among the wondrous objects to be seen in the *Galerie*. Next door was a second gallery, the *Galerie des Antiques*, where were displayed the Cardinal's rich collection of Classical sculptures. See in addition the *Mazarin Invt., 1653*, for a detailed description of the furnishing of this sumptuous building.

17. R. A. Weigert, Introduction to the Catalogue of the exhibition *Louis XIV: faste et décors*, Musée des Arts Décoratifs, Paris, 1960, p. xv.

18. *Ibid.*, p. xviii.

19. No other building can have been studied so much or written about so often as the Palace of Versailles. The history of its building in the seventeenth century is summarised by Sir Anthony Blunt, *op. cit.*, Chapter 7. A masterly and entertaining survey is Pierre Verlet's *Versailles*, Paris, 1961. But anyone seriously interested in the history of this important building in the seventeenth century should read Alfred Marie's *Naissance de Versailles*, Paris, 1968, and *Mansart à Versailles*, Paris, 1972.

20. 'Je me paroit qu'il y a quelque chose à changer, que les sujets sont trop sérieux, qu'il faut qu'il y ait de la jeunesse mêlée dans ce que l'on ferat . . . Il faut de l'enfance répandue partout.' F. J. B. Watson, *Wallace Collection Catalogue: Furniture*, London, 1956, p. xxvi.

21. The building of the *Trianon de Porcelaine*, which was seemingly created to please Madame de Montespan, began in 1670. Félibien spoke of it as 'un enchantement' because it sprang up so quickly. He mentioned the blue and white walls of the *salon* 'travaillé à la manière des ouvrages qui viennent de la Chine', i.e. in the Chinese manner. (See Alfred Marie, *Naissance de Versailles*, Vol. II, Paris, 1968, Chap. XI.)

22. The *Pavillon de la Ménagerie* was built in 1663–4 and had various novel features including several chimneypieces of rather low proportions (Marie, *op. cit.*, Vol. I, Chap. III). Le Vau created an Orangerie in the 1660s: this was replaced by the present building in the mid-1680s (see Alfred and Jeanne Marie, *Mansart à Versailles*, Paris, 1972, pp. 279–300). The *Trianon de Marbre* was begun in 1687.

23. Saint-Simon's account of how the King sought out the site for Marly is amusing. It was written in 1715, long after the event. 'The King, tired of elegance and of the crowd, became convinced that he needed a small place and privacy on some occasions. He searched around Versailles for something to satisfy this new fancy. He visited several places . . . He found . . . a narrow, deep valley, with steep sides, in-accessible on account of the boggy ground,

without any view, closed in by hills on all sides.' (Saint-Simon, *Mémoires*, ed. Pléiade, Vol. IV, p. 1008.) See also Jeanne and Alfred Marie, *Marly*, Paris, n.d.

24. 'The King never allowed ceremony at all at Marly. No ambassadors or envoys were permitted to come there; there was no etiquette and everything was higgledy-piggledy—in the *salon* everyone, right down to the captain and sub-lieutenants of the guard, was allowed to sit down', wrote the King's sister-in-law (see *Princess Palatine's Letters*, 11 August, 1716).

25. 'There is to be a further expenditure of a hundred thousand *livres*; Marly will soon be a second Versailles,' wrote Madame de Maintenon in 1698. France was at the time in a desperate financial state and the Marquise tried to remonstrate with the King at this enormous fresh outlay on such a frivolous exercise but 'I have not pleased [the King] in my conversation about the buildings and my sorrow is that I have offended without profit . . . One can only pray and grieve . . . But the People, what will become of them?' (A. Genevay, *Le Style Louis XIV: Charles Le Brun, décorateur*, Paris, 1886, p. 104.)

26. The Château de Clagny was built between 1674 and 1678. On a contemporary engraving it is described as 'Clagny, maison des délices'. Madame de Sévigné reported in 1675 that the Queen had visited Madame de Montespan at Clagny where 'elle trouvèrent la belle si occupée des ouvrages et des enchantements que l'on fait pour elle . . .'. There was a special room set aside for dining and actually called the *salle à manger* and some of the chimneypieces were of the new low proportions. (See Alfred and Jeanne Marie, *Mansart à Versailles*, Vol. I, Paris, 1972, Chap. I.)

27. The *Appartements des Bains* was created in the early 1670s. (See Alfred Marie, *Naissance de Versailles*, Vol. II, Paris, 1968, Chap. XIII.)

NOTES TO CHAPTER II

1. *Parentalia: or Memoirs of the Family of Wrens*, London, 1750, p. 261.

2. *Ibid.*, p. 262.

3. Philibert de l'Orme, *Le Premier tome de architecture*, 1567; Pierre Le Muet, *Manière de bien bâtir pour touttes sortes de personnes*, 1623, enlarged with *Augmentations de nouveaux bastimens* in 1647; Roland Fréart, *Parallèle de l'architecture antique et de la moderne*, 1650; Jean Marot, *L'Architecture François ou recueil des plans . . . batis dans Paris et ses environs*, c. 1670.

To be fair, however, it must be said that Jean Marot was also the publisher of suites of engravings of ornamental features and it is interesting to note that de l'Orme was tempted to give information about the interior decoration of palaces but felt his book was not the right place to do so. 'Ce lieu n'est à propos pour parler des mesures des chambres & dedans des logis, ny moins des meubles & ornemens des salles & chambres des Roys & Grands Seigneurs, veu [sic] que telle matiere est assez suffisante pour en faire un livre à part . . . peu personnes . . . sçachent bien orner & decorer les logis des Roys & Princes' [This is not the place to discuss the size of rooms and the interiors of apartments, nor even the furniture and decoration of the great chambers and bedchambers of kings and great noblemen, since the subject is so great that it would fill a separate volume . . . few people really understand how properly to decorate and furnish the apartments of kings and princes] (*Libre IX*). It would seem that already by the middle of the sixteenth century the French were more interested in such matters than other people.

4. Published in 1670 under the title *The Art of Fair Building*. Incidentally, John Evelyn translated Fréart's work in 1664.

5. See R. A. Weigert's introduction to the Catalogue of the exhibition entitled *Louis XIV: faste et décors* held at the Musée des Arts Décoratifs in Paris in 1960. This gives an excellent survey of the output of ornamental engravings in Paris during the period. It would be impossible to list here the huge number of sets of engravings available at the time.

6. John Harris, 'Inigo Jones and His French Sources', *Bulletin of the Metropolitan Museum*, New York, May 1961, discusses the use made by Jones and his pupil, John Webb, of Barbet's *Livre d'architecture, d'autels, et de cheminées* of 1632 in devising chimneypieces for Greenwich House and at Wilton in the late 1630s and 1640s. Several chimneypieces of the 1660s and early 1670s at Skokloster are modelled on plates in Barbet's work (see Erik Andrén, *Skokloster*, Stockholm, 1948, pp. 254, 267, 281, 287, 298 and 302). Some ceilings at Skokloster, incidentally, are based on engravings by Le Pautre.

7. Published by Cornelius Danckerts (c. 1603–56).

8. Robert Pricke, *The Architect's Store-house*, 1674. Pricke published and sold translations of many of the principal works on architecture and ornament including those of Vitruvius, Le Muet, Barbet and Francini. He advertised the 'choice of Mapps, Copy Books, chimney peeces and ceiling peeces' available at his shop near Cripplegate where he was established shortly after the Great Fire had destroyed much of the City of London and guidance was being eagerly sought by architects and decorators busy making good the devastation. In 1675 he advertised the wide selection of 'Italian, French & Dutch Prints, Books of Geometry, Perspective and Architecture' he had for sale (see L. Rostenberg, *English Publishing in the Graphic Arts 1599–1700*, New York, 1963, pp. 55–60).

9. Sir Roger Pratt, *Certain Short Notes Concerning Architecture*, 1660 (see R. T. Gunther, *The Architecture of Sir Roger Pratt*, London, 1928, p. 23).

10. The most obvious example is Ralph, Duke of Montagu (1638?–1709) who was Ambassador to the French court between 1669 and 1672, and again between 1676 and 1678.

11. See P. Thornton, 'The Parisian Fauteuil of 1680', *Apollo*, February 1975, and G. Jackson-Stops, 'The 6th Earl of Dorset's Furniture at Knole', *Country Life*, 2 and 9 June 1977, for further information on acquisitions by ambassadors to the French Court.

12. Karel van Mander, describing the way Michelangelo had freed Classical architecture from its bonds and of the 'free rein' and 'licence to invent' that architects had as a result been given, lashed out at his own countrymen in sharply critical terms, saying that now 'this rein is so free, and this licence so misused by our Netherlanders, that in the course of time in Building a Great Heresy has arisen among them, with a heap of craziness of decorations and breaking of pilasters in the middle, and adding, on pedestals, their usual coarse points of diamonds and such lameness, very disgusting to see' (*Schilderboeck*, fol. 168v).

13. Early in the seventeenth century the 9th Earl of Northumberland had in his library the works of Vitruvius, Alberti, Serlio, Vignola, Du Cerceau, de l'Orme, and Dietterlin. They must all have been in the original. (Frank Jenkins, *Architect and Patron*, London, 1961, p. 49).

14. Hans Vredeman de Vries, *Architectura, de oorden Thuschana . . .*, Antwerp, 1578.

15. For example, the cove in the Single Cube Room at Wilton and that in the Queen's Bedchamber at Greenwich are painted with grotesques in the Netherlandish Mannerist style (by Matthew Gooderick or John de Critz?). Those at Greenwich are rather more Italian in conception than those at Wilton which have pinnacles and all the 'craziness of decoration' about which van Mander was so scathing (see note 12).

16. Jean Cotelle, *Livre des Ornemens pour Plafonds . . .*, Paris, about 1640. A number of the original drawings for these ceiling designs are incorporated in a volume of mostly coloured drawings of interior architecture by various hands now in the Ashmolean Museum (see K. T. Parker, *Catalogue of the Collection of Drawings in the Ashmolean Museum*, Oxford, 1938, No. 395). Apart from a few interpolations they all seem to be Parisian and to date from the second quarter of the century. Several are for royal buildings, others bear ciphers with coronets indicating that they too are for decorative schemes of importance. It has very plausibly been suggested that the drawings come from the drawing-office of Inigo Jones or his pupil and successor John Webb (see John Harris, 'Inigo Jones and His French Sources', *Bulletin of the Metropolitan Museum*, New York, May 1961). What is more likely than that Jones and/or Webb made considerable efforts to acquire drawings of this sort which provided such helpful and vivid information about the newest schemes of interior decoration in important buildings in the French capital?

17. Frantz Cleyn was a German who was taken into the service of Christian IV of Denmark whose sister Anne was married to James I of England. James persuaded his brother-in-law to release Cleyn who finally came to England late in 1625, the year Charles I had come to the throne. In Denmark he had been a decorative painter (e.g. at Rosenborg Castle) and had apparently provided patterns for some rich cupboard carpets (see p. 241) that were made—woven or embroidered, it is not clear which—in Copenhagen in 1622. (I am indebted to Mrs Vibeke Woldbye for this information.) It is probable that James had intended that Cleyn should decorate rooms for Anne of Denmark but she died in 1619. Instead he executed work for Queen Henrietta Maria who arrived in England at about the same time as he did. He was apparently responsible for designing the tri-

umphal arches erected for her entry into the City, under the general supervision of Inigo Jones, and carried out decoration in her apartment at Somerset House. He also worked at Holland House, Carew House, Bolsover Castle and Ham House. Although he was primarily a painter, he was obviously capable of designing ornament and may even have devised quite extensive schemes of decoration. The chimneypiece in the North Drawing Room at Ham is plausibly attributed to him and he may well have designed the rich panelling still in that room, as well as the fireplace in the Hall which is in the current 'court style' of Inigo Jones—with which he must have been entirely familiar by the 1630s when Ham was being done over by William Murray. Some shell-back *sgabello*-type chairs to be seen in a view of the garden at Ham in the 1670s probably date from Cleyn's period and resemble closely a set which stood in the Gilt Room at Holland House that he is known to have decorated (Plate 52). This suggests that Cleyn could design Italianate furniture suitable for Classical interiors. If so, his services could well have been much in demand by Inigo Jones and his clients.

18. James Howell, in his *Instructions for Furreine Travel* of 1642, likewise claimed that 'commodity, firmness and beauty' were 'the three maine principles of Architecture'. These qualities were embodied, he claimed, in the buildings erected for the Earl of Arundel (1586–1646) who 'observing the uniforme and regular way of stone structure up and down Italy, hath introduced that forme of building to London and Westminster, and elsewhere'. He was presumably referring to buildings designed by Inigo Jones who had accompanied the Earl to Italy and certainly worked at Arundel House.

19. Katharine Fremantle, *The Baroque Town Hall of Amsterdam*, Utrecht, 1959, p. 99.

20. *Ibid.*, p. 101.

21. Letter of 2 July, 1639. (*Ibid.*, p. 98.)

22. Letter of 11–21 November, 1637. (*Ibid.*, p.102.)

23. D. F. Slothouwer, *De Paleizen van Frederik Hendrik*, Leiden, 1945, is the principal source of information on this matter. See also Fremantle, *op. cit.*, pp. 102–8.

24. Sir William Brereton, *Travels in Holland...*, Chetham Society, London, 1844, p. 33.

25. Fremantle, op. cit., p. 107.

26. Sir William Temple, *Observations on the United Provinces*, 1673.

27. *Ibid.*

28. John Harris, 'Inigo Jones and His French Sources', *Bulletin of the Metropolitan Museum*, New York, May 1961 (see notes 6 and 16).

29. At the Palais de Luxembourg her mother had several rooms with floors of marquetry of oak laid so as to form interlacing patterns which were 'merveilleuse & admirée de tous les gens du metier' [marvellous and admired by all those in the profession], that is, by other joiners and people who knew the trade and could appreciate how skilfully the joints were disguised (Sauval, *Antiquités de Paris, Livre XIV*, 1724, p. 8). An English visitor noted in particular the Queen's Closet which was 'floored with Wood wrought in little workes all Severall forms pitcht in with Silver' (O. Millar, 'The notebooks of Richard Symonds', *Studies in Renaissance and Baroque Art*, London, 1967). Dr Martin Lister commented in his *Journey to Paris* of 1699 that 'inward knots were inlaid with threads of silver' although it is likely that the metal was in fact pewter. He remarked on the astonishing 'firmness ... after so long laying' of these floors. At the Palais Royale, Anne d'Autriche in the 1640s had some parquet floors laid by the exceptionally skilful joiner, Jean Macé (see D. Alcouffe, 'Les Macés, ébénistes et peintres', *Bulletin de la Société de l'Histoire d'Art Français*, Paris, 1972). Henrietta Maria's floors were considered so remarkable in their time that engravings of them were available for sale shortly after their completion. In the English translation of Palladio's *First Book of Architecture* (published in 1663) designs of these floors were included and it is stated that the floors had been 'lately made in the Palace of the Queen Mother at Somerset-House. A curiosity never practised before in England' (see L. Rostenberg, *English Publishing in the Graphic Arts 1599–1700*, New York, 1963, p. 54); the designs are composed entirely of straight lines.

30. Information kindly provided by H. M. Colvin.

31. The inventory was drawn up by Murray's daughter, the future Duchess of Lauderdale, probably in 1654. See *Ham Invt.*, c. 1654.

32. In the parlour, for instance, the gilt leather hangings were red and gold, the covers of the couch and the eighteen chairs were of scarlet cloth bordered with the same gilt leather, while the window-curtains and table-covers were made up in the same fashion. It will be remembered that Francis Cleyn was responsible

for some of the decoration at Ham at this stage (see note 17, above).

33. It is noteworthy that Paul Vredeman de Vries' influential *Verscheyden Schryn werck* was only published in 1630. The style embodied in the many designs it offers its readers is only a slight modification of that brought forward in the *Variae Architecturae Formae* that his father, Hans, had published in 1560.

34. Sir Roger Pratt went abroad, as he said, 'to give myself some convenient education'.

35. *Memoirs of the Verney Family*.

36. Sir Roger Pratt, *Certain Short notes concerning Architecture*, 1660 (see R. T. Gunther, *The Architecture of Sir Roger Pratt*, London, 1928).

37. However, Montagu himself was a confirmed francophile. When his house was gutted in the 1680s he had a French architect reconstruct it. He is identified as Pierre Boujet by G. Jackson-Stops in 'The Building of Petworth', *Apollo*, May 1977. He is said to have been assisted by the French painter James Rousseau who was responsible for much of the interior decoration.

38. The facts supporting the assertions made in these passages may be found in the appropriate entries in H. M. Colvin's *Biographical Dictionary of English Architects, 1660–1840*, London, 1954.

39. Verrio had arrived in Paris by 1671 where he became a friend of Molière. He was invited to England by Lord Montagu. His main occupation between 1675 and 1684 was executing decorative work at Windsor Castle under Hugh May and, in 1684, he was created 'first & chief Painter to his *Matie*'. He worked with a troupe of foreign craftsmen including Grinling Gibbons (who was supported by two other Dutchmen), Jean-Baptiste Monnoyer (the flower-painter), René Cousin (gilder) and John Vanderstaine (stone carver). Clearly this band was able to create complete schemes of fixed decoration. Verrio's group, plus or minus a few members, also worked at Burghley and Chatsworth, and apparently also at Ham House (E. Croft-Murray, *Decorative Painting in England*, Vol. I, London, 1962).

40. John Casbert is mentioned in the royal accounts between 1667 and 1673, John Poitevin in the 1670s, 'Monsieur La Grange' in 1674, and Francis La Pierre and Philip Guibert in the 1690s. La Pierre worked also for the Duke of Devonshire and Guibert for the Duke of Leeds. Some of the chairs Casbert supplied were described as 'French' but this clearly refers to

their style (see the *Dictionary of English Furniture*; R. W. Symonds, 'Charles II: Couches, Chairs and Stools', *The Connoisseur*, January and February, 1934; and notes in the Department of Furniture and Woodwork, Victoria and Albert Museum). Incidentally, the principal upholsterer in The Hague serving William III was named Pierre Courtonne and died in 1714 (see *Orange Invts.*, I, p. 554).

41. *Evelyn's Diary*, 9 June, 1662. He tells us that the bed had been bought originally for the king's sister, the Princess of Orange (i.e. Maria Stuart, sister of Charles I, who died in 1660) but that the Estates General had then bought it back and presented it to the King. He must then in turn have given it to his bride on their marriage in 1662. Its high cost lay chiefly in the rich embroidery on a crimson velvet ground but the bed undoubtedly was accompanied by a set of seat-furniture and possibly also by a set of wall-hangings—all en suite.

42. See P. Thornton, 'The Parisian Fauteuil of 1680', *Apollo*, February 1975.

43. An account of money 'payed out for the Lady Dutchess of Lauderdale in Holland by Mistress v. der Huva' includes as its first item 'for a cabinet of black ebonie with a table and two Gadons [*guéridons*] cost ... 440 Guilders'. The French term for a candlestand at this date was *guéridon* (Scottish Record Office, Lauderdale Papers, 6/11).

44. See G. Jackson-Stops, 'The 6th Earl of Dorset's Furniture at Knole', *loc. cit.*

45. There is a splendid illustration of this cabinet in colour in Nancy Mitford's *The Sun King*, London, 1966, facing p. 192. The almost identical pair to this cabinet, which must also have belonged to Louis XIV will come to form one of the glories of the J. Paul Getty Museum in California not long after this book is published.

46. I am grateful to Professor Lunsingh Scheurleer for providing me with additional information about the Golle family.

NOTES TO CHAPTER III

1. See Chapter II, note 17.

2. Francis Bacon, *Essayes*, 1625, XLV, 'Of Building', 1625.

3. Published in *Archeologia*, Vol. CI, 1967.

4. M. Girouard, 'The Power Houses', Slade Lectures, Oxford 1976. Published as *Life in the*

English Country House: A Social and Architectural History, New Haven and London, 1978.

5. J. Fowler and J. Cornforth, *English Decoration in the 18th Century*, London, 1974, Chap. 3.

6. A writer in 1700 described the apartments at Dyrham as being 'more for State than use except upon Extraordinary occasion' (see Fowler and Cornforth, *op. cit.*, p. 60) and the Guide to Dyrham.

7. Bacon, *op. cit.*

8. Girouard (see note 4) has drawn attention to the two royal apartments created at Hatfield House early in the century.

9. Among the upper classes married couples did not share a bedchamber. Marriages were mostly arranged for dynastic reasons and while they might sometimes grow into love-matches, this was the exception.

10. In former times such sets of rooms had been called lodgings. The term apartment, and more especially the French *appartement*, has more stylish connotations but was essentially a lodging in a new guise.

11. A pallet was a small straw mattress. A pallet-bed usually consisted of three such pallets. Sometimes there may have been a very simple wooden framework underneath, to raise the mattresses off the ground.

12. The household regulations of the period give a good idea of the involved ceremonies that were associated with the laying of the table, the decking out of the cup-boards with splendid plate, the taking of seats, the testing of the food and drink and the serving of it, the bringing on of the various courses and their subsequent removal. See, e.g., Viscount Montagu's Household Book of 1595 (Sir William H. St. John Hope, *Cowdray and Easebourne Priory*, London, 1919, pp. 119–34) and also 'A Breviate touching the Order and Governmente of a Nobleman's house ... 1605' communicated by Sir Joseph Banks, *Archeologia*, XIII, 1800, pp. 315–89. Miss Rachel Cooper has informed me, it should be noted, that no date 1605 is actually given at the head of the manuscript and how Banks arrived at this date is at present a mystery. Other details have not been accurately transcribed either but there is no reason to doubt that the date is about right.

13. How far a person penetrated along the sequence of rooms leading to the bedchamber in a grand house was an indication of his standing with the owner. The greater the honour one wished to bestow on the visitor to the apartment, the further he was allowed to come. Especial honour was signified when the owner advanced to meet the visitor at the entrance and escorted him deep into the apartment. Intimate friends of the owner might be allowed to join him (or her) in the privacy of the closet that lay beyond the bedchamber. These are complicated questions and the etiquette varied somewhat from country to country. The reader is referred to the works of Murray Baillie and Girouard already mentioned.

14. Sir Henry Wotton was however not impressed with this arrangement which he will have seen in Italy. In his *Elements of Architecture* of 1624 he wrote that 'They do cast their partitions as when all doors are open, a man may see through the whole house, which doth necessarily put an intolerable servitude upon all the chambers save the innermost, where one can arrive but through the rest . . . I cannot commend the direct opposition of such overtures, being merely grounded upon the fond ambition of displaying to a stranger all our furniture at one sight.'

15. Sheraton, writing at the beginning of the nineteenth century, summed up the practice which was still current in his day. 'The chimney should always be situated so as to be immediately seen by those who enter the room. The middle of the partition-wall is the most proper place in halls, saloons, and other rooms of passage; but in drawing-rooms, dressing-rooms, and the like, the middle of the back wall is the best situation. In bed-rooms, the chimney is always in the middle of one of the partition-walls; and in closets and other very small places, to save room, it is put in a corner.' (T. Sheraton, *The Cabinet Maker, Upholsterer and General Artists Encyclopaedia*, London, 1804, 'Architecture'.) These rules were being formulated in the seventeenth century. Le Muet was more specific about the siting of the fireplace in a bedchamber which 'ought not be situate in the midst but distant therefrom about two feet, whereby place be allowed for the bed', unless the room was very large. The bed being about six feet square and standing with its head against the inner wall, it was naturally desirable to have the chimneypiece well to the window-side of the foot of the bed, allowing plenty of space round the fireplace (P. Le Muet, *The Art of Fair Building*, 1670, p. 2; translated from the original French version of 1623). Savot also discusses the best position for chimneypieces (L. Savot, *L'Architecture Francoise*

des Bastimens Particuliers, Paris, 1624). Evelyn remarked of Charles II's house at Newmarket that 'many of the rooms had chimnies plac'd in the angles and corners, a mode now introduced by His Majesty which I do at no hand approve of ... It does only well in very small and trifling rooms, but takes from the state of Greater' (*Evelyn's Diary*, 22 July 1670). However, some chimneypieces were set in strange places. Celia Fiennes saw one 'just under a window' at Wilton at the end of the century, arranged so that 'the tunnells [flues] runnes upon each side'. In another room she saw one alongside a window (*Celia Fiennes*, p. 9).

16. P. de l'Orme, *Le Premier Tome de l'Architecture*, 1567.

17. Apart from Barbet's work, there were those of Pierre Collot, Jean Le Pautre, L. Francart, Jean Marot, Antoine Perretz, Jean Bérain, Pierre Cottart and Pierre Le Pautre, together with quite a few anonymous sets brought out by the print-seller, Langlois.

18. Barbet's book actually contains more than just designs for chimneypieces but it was for these that it became famous. The engravings were by Abraham Bosse whose genre-scenes of Parisian interiors are famous. The 1641 edition was published by Frederik de Wit, a prominent print-seller of Amsterdam, with fresh engravings based on Bosse's by Cornelis Danckerts. 'Mr de Witt, ein alter mann, hat die besten zeichnungen undt kupffer stijckke zu verkauffen, wohnet neben den Statthaus ...' [Mr de Witt, an old man, has the best drawings and engravings for sale and lives next to the Town Hall] wrote Tessin in 1687 (Gustav Upmark, 'Ein Besuch in Holland 1687', *Oud Holland*, Vol. XVIII, 1900, p. 127).

19. Published by F. de Wit (see previous note) and presumably drawn by C. Danckerts. These simpler designs would have been better suited to a middle-class purse than Barbet's original proposals.

20. *Princess Palatine's Letters* 27 November 1717. One must remember, however, that a charcoal-burning brazier gave off much heat and these could easily be brought into a room when needed.

21. In his foreword, Barbet states that his designs are based on 'ce qu'il y a de beau dans Paris'. The book, incidentally, is dedicated to Cardinal Richelieu.

22. François Blondel, in his *Cours d'Architecture* of 1683, claims that *cheminées à la Romaine* were 'prises entierement dans l'épaiseur du mur' [entirely built into the thickness of the wall] while those *à la Lombarde* were partly so. Those called *à la Française*, however, stood out from the wall. None the less those called by Jean Le Pautre 'à l'Italienne' certainly protruded from the wall and were characterised by their wealth of ornament.

23. Blondel, *op. cit.*

24. See Fiske Kimball, *The Creation of the Rococo*, Philadelphia, 1943. See also his 'The Development of the "Cheminée à la Royale"', *Metropolitan Museum Studies*, Vol. V, 1934, where this phase is surveyed. A piece of bevelled mirror-glass is set into the chimney-breast (beneath a painting) in the Duchess's Private Closet at Ham House, a room created in the 1670s. If it is original, which seems possible, the fashion may have begun earlier than Kimball supposed.

25. *Tessin-Cronström Correspondence*, letter of 2 March 1697. On 11 October Cronström sent from Paris to Tessin in Stockholm 'quelques nouveaux desseins de cheminées' which may very well have been the set of which one is illustrated here (Plate 70).

26. *Pepys' Diary*, 19 January 1666.

27. R. T. Gunther, *The Architecture of Sir Roger Pratt*, Oxford, 1928, p. 192. Incidentally, Pratt gave instructions that the fireplace in his Great Parlour was 'for whiting' (i.e. to be white-washed) and this was probably the normal treatment for fireplaces in his day.

28. *Chetham Society Journal*, 1844. 'Travels in Holland ... of Sir William Brereton, Bt.' Brereton explains how to mend any tiles that get chipped. 'if any part of the corners break out, there is plaister of Paris powder, which is to be made as it were pap, and instantly with the point of a knife laid on; let it dry, and when it is dry, form it and scrape it even with a chisel or sharp knife. To cleanse it and even it, use a dog-fish's skin, or for want thereof, hair-cloth [i.e. horse-hair cloth].'

29. Geoffrey Beard, *Decorative Plasterwork in Great Britain*, London, 1975; G. Bankart, *The Art of the Plasterer*, London, 1909; Mr Jourdain, *English Decoration and Furniture ... 1500–1650*, London, 1924; A. Blunt, *Art and Architecture in France, 1500–1700*, 2nd edition, 1970; J. Rosenberg, S. Slive, E. H. Ter Kuile, *Dutch Art and Architecture, 1600–1800*, 1966; J. Summerson, *Architecture in Britain, 1530–1830*, 5th ed., 1969.

30. *Livre de divers ornemens . . . de l'invention de Jean Cotelle, peintre ordinaire du Roy,* was published about 1640 but a group of his actual drawings for ceilings (some of them subsequently engraved for the book) may have been in the possession of Inigo Jones or John Webb (see Chapter II, note 16).

31. It is possible that the Parlour at the old house at Chatsworth which was 'fayre waynscotted with whitewood' (*Chatsworth Invt., 1601*) may have had untreated white pine panelling. What is more, the room from Haynes Grange, which probably dates from about 1620 and may have been designed by Inigo Jones, is entirely faced with red pine that seems never to have been painted. If so, it must be exceptional. Could Inigo Jones, if it was he, have been thinking of rooms he had seen in Italy panelled with cypress wood? (The room is now in the Victoria and Albert Museum; see H. Clifford Smith, *The Haynes Grange Room*, London, 1935.)

32. When varnished, oak retains its light honey-colour and does not turn grey, as happens if it is left to itself, or go dark brown like molasses, which is the result of dirt becoming embedded in layers of polishing wax. Celia Fiennes saw panelling at Broadlands that was 'wanscoated and varnished' while the drawing room at Lady Donegal's house was likewise finished. (*Celia Fiennes*, pp. 85 and 90). Some panelling at Wimbledon Hall in 1649 was varnished green and decorated with golden stars and crosses. Was the varnish tinted or was there a green ground under a clear varnish? (See M. Jourdain, *English Decoration and Furniture of the Early Renaissance*, London, 1924, p. 96.)

33. John Evelyn, *Sylva*, London, 1664.

34. The Grand Dauphin had a closet made for his personal use at Meudon which was panelled in this manner in the 1690s (Comte Paul Biver, *Histoire du Château de Meudon*, Paris, 1923, Chap. XI).

35. *Chatsworth Invt., 1601.*

36. One of the most ambitious surviving schemes in this technique is the Inlaid Room from Sizergh Castle which dates from prior to 1582. When a panel was cleaned in 1968, the original contrast between the woods forming the white tendrils and black leaves, all set in the honey-coloured grounds, appeared decidedly bold. (See the Victoria and Albert Museum monograph, *The Inlaid Room from Sizergh Castle*, London, 1928.)

37. *Chatsworth Invt., 1601* and *Cockesden Invt., 1610.* It has been suggested (*Country Life*, 8 December, 1928, p. 813) that 'French panell' had mitred joints instead of the older mortised joints but compilers of inventories normally pick on some obvious feature to help identify an object. This tends to mean that they pick on a decorative characteristic rather than a technical feature.

38. *Celia Fiennes*, p. 153.

39. William Lower, *A Relation . . . of the Voiage and Residence which . . . Charles II . . . hath made in Holland . . . 1660,* The Hague, 1660. The Mauritshuis, built for Johan Maurits who was known as 'the Brazilian' on account of his exploits in that part of the world, was gutted by fire in the eighteenth century. I am grateful to Professor Lunsingh Scheurleer for throwing light on this matter.

40. *Celia Fiennes*, p. 56.

41. R. T. Gunther, *The Architecture of Sir Roger Pratt*, Oxford, 1928.

42. Sir Balthazar Gerbier, *Counsel and Advise to All builders*, 1663.

43. E. Croft-Murray, *Decorative Painting in England*, Vol. I, London, 1962, p. 199.

44. *Celia Fiennes*, pp. 85 and 90.

45. An important survey is being carried out by Mr Ian Bristow at the Institute of Advanced Architectural Studies at York University under the enlightened patronage of Messrs. Berger Paints, Ltd. Interesting work is also being done at the National Museum in Copenhagen and at several centres in the United States. A helpful but still very tentative essay appeared in J. Fowler and J. Cornforth, *English Decoration in the 18th Century*, London, 1974, Chap. 5, but great advances in this field can be expected soon.

46. *Tessin-Cronström Correspondence*, letter of 19 April 1693.

47. *Hardwick Invt., 1601* and Gunther, *op. cit.*, p. 189.

48. See Anne Berendsen and others, *Fliesen*, Munich, 1964, which has a chapter on wall-tiles and many excellent illustrations. See also Arthur Lane, *A Guide to the Collection of Tiles* (Victoria and Albert Museum) London, 1960; Dingeman Korf, *Dutch Tiles*, London, 1963; and C. H. de Jonge, *Oud-Nederlandsche Majolica en Delftsch Aardewerk*, Amsterdam, 1947.

49. See Arthur Lane, 'Daniel Marot: Designer of Delft Vases . . . at Hampton Court,' *The Connoisseur*, March 1949.

50. For information about the *Trianon de*

Porcelaine, see Alfred Marie, *La Naissance de Versailles*, II, Paris, 1968, pp. 197–225; see also note 19 to chapter 1.

51. *Havard, 'Miroir'.*

52. S. Roche, *Miroirs*, Paris, 1956, p. 22. The mirror was presented to the Queen (herself an Italian princess, of course) by the Republic of Venice in celebration of the birth of her son, the future Louis XIII.

53. Francis Bacon, *Essayes*, 1625, XLV, 'Of Building'.

54. *Havard,* 'Miroir'.

55. Elphège Frémy, *Histoire de la manufacture royale des glaces au 17e et 18e siècle*, Paris, 1909, p. 16.

56. *Ibid.*, p. 17.

57. *Havard,* 'Glace'.

58. Geoffrey Wills, *English Looking-glasses*, London, 1965, p. 16.

59. *Tessin-Cronström Correspondence,* letter of 22 March 1697.

60. *Celia Fiennes,* p. 153.

61. G. Upmark, 'Ein Besuch in Holland 1687 . . .,' *Oud Holland*, 18, 1900.

62. The tariff in 1682 in France was:

    10 × 10 *pouces* . . .   9 *livres*
    20 × 20 *pouces* . . .   24 *livres*
    30 × 30 *pouces* . . .   70 *livres*

In 1699 it was as follows:

    15 × 12 *pouces* . . .   7 *livres*
    40 × 30 *pouces* . . .   150 *livres*
    70 × 45 *pouces* . . .   750 *livres*
    90 × 55 *pouces* . . . 3,000 *livres*

A *pouce* was approximately equal to an inch. When one considers that the services of a good cook could be had for 300 *livres* per annum while a serving girl would work for 30 *livres*, and a shop with a room over is known to have cost 348 *livres*, one can more easily appreciate how the Comtesse de Fièsque came to sell an unfruitful estate in order to buy a mirror and why Louis XIV, who spent no less than 56,653 *livres* on mirror-glass in the year 1671 alone, arranged to pay for it at a 30 per cent discount. At least one lady sought the King's permission to buy her mirrors at the royal rate.

63. J. Barralet, *La Verrerie en France*, Paris, 1953, p. 83.

64. For information on this whole matter, see the works of Frémy and Barralet mentioned above.

65. Frémy, *op. cit.*, p. 197.

66. The Venetian Ambassador to England at the time commented that 'by this order they also mean to prohibit looking-glasses, of which they make a quantity here' (Wills, *op. cit.*, p. 42).

67. Wills, *op. cit.*, pp. 43–6.

68. The French royal manufactury was permitted to make 'ornements composés de glaces plates'. The flat pieces of glass could be 'coupées par bandes et par morceaux, figurez et taillez à facettes ou à bizeaux avec baguettes mince ou tortillés, colonnes torses, frontons et couronnements de toutes sortes de figures sur fonds colorez ou autrement' [cut into strips and small pieces, shaped and facetted or bevelled, with narrow or twisted beading, spiral columns, pediments and crestings of all kinds of figures on coloured or other grounds]. (Frémy, *op. cit.*, p. 78.) There are inset mirrors with such slips still to be seen at Hampton Court, some being of blue glass.

69. Cronström reported to Stockholm that in Paris there was a craftsman who knew the secret of how to 'creuser dans la glace: cela fait un assez joly effet' [engrave the glass: this produces a very pretty effect] and was known as 'ouvrage à la Mayenne' (*Tessin-Cronström Correspondence*, letter of 19 April 1693). Gerreit Jensen supplied 'a Peer Glass for ye Great Closett [at Hampton Court] with wrought work and Ingraved . . . £55' (R. W. Symonds, 'English Looking-glasses', *The Connoisseur*, May 1950).

70. *Havard,* 'Miroir'.

71. *Havard,* 'Glace'.

72. *Havard,* 'Miroir'.

73. R. Edwards, 'A Mirror with Painted Decoration', *Country Life*, 26 October 1935, quoting Faulkener's *History and Antiquities of Kensington*, 1820. Vertue also mentions 'the most curious of all is the Looking-Glass at Kensington House, which he [Monnoyer] painted for the late Queen Mary, of Glorious Memory, her Majesty sitting by him all the While'. A panel of what could be an example of Monnoyer's work is in the Victoria and Albert Museum; there are other sections in a closet off the Gallery at Syon House, and at Melbourne House.

74. H. Sauval, *Histoire et recherches des antiquités de la ville de Paris*, 1724 (but written before 1670), Livre VII, Vol. II, pp. 200–1.

75. See J. P. Babelon, *Demeures Parisiennes sous Henri IV et Louis XIII*, Paris, 1965, p. 190. Le Muet illustrates such a window, and explains how to calculate its proportions, in his *Divers Traictes* of 1646.

76. L. Savot, *L'Architecture Francoise des bastimens*

particuliers, Paris, 1624, Chapter VII, entitled 'De la position des membres du bastiments'; and Sir Henry Wotton, *Elements of Architecture*, 1624.

77. 'Three window shutes' (*Walton Invt., 1624*), '2 shuting windowes' (*Marton Invt., 1605*), 'wainscott shutts to both ye windowes' at King's College, Cambridge (*Provost of King's Invt., 1660*). '2 wyndow leaves and there wooden barres' are mentioned in the *Cockesden Invt. of 1610*, one only needs a locking bar for an interior shutter. In the same inventory mention is made of the 'double leaves to the wyndowe' in the Hall, which seems to indicate a paired arrangement rather than two tiers, while there was only 'one leafe to the other wyndowe'. 'Wyndowe levys of tymbre be made of bourdis joyned together with keys of tree let into them,' tells W. Horman, *Vulgaria*, 1619.

78. *Hatfield Priory Invt., 1629*. Also 'The wyndow wainescotted wth. two drawing wyndowes' (*Ingatestone Invt., 1600*); 'a draw window' (*Provost of King's Invt., 1660*; bill of 1616–17); 'drawers for the windowe (*Standen Lordship Invt., 1623*). The analogy is presumably with 'drawing the curtains' but it may be that the term was used in reference to some form of sliding shutter. Horman (*op. cit.*) says he had 'many pretty windowes shette with levys going up and downe . . .'.

79. *Havard*, 'Abat-jours'.

80. That certain windows at Ham House were double-glazed can be deduced from the accounts for 1674, the number of glass panes supplied being far greater for the rooms where the windows were thus furnished.

81. *Tessin's Visit, 1687* and *Celia Fiennes*, p. 339. The earliest mention of double glazing in Stockholm dates from 1729 (see G. Hazelius Berg, *Gardiner och Gardinuppsättningar*, Nordiska Museet, Stockholm, 1962, p. 12). An *Ode à l'Hiver*, written by Chapelle in 1520, tells how:

> On garnit les appartments
> De doubles chassis et de nattes,
> Et les grands foyers s'allumants.

[Apartments are furnished with double window-frames and mats, fires in the great hearths are kindled.] Although these 'double window-frames' may *both* have contained panes of glass, it is more likely that the inner frame had matting stretched over it.

82. In 1579 there was a legal wrangel as to whether glass windows were fixtures or movable chattels, and it was then claimed that 'without glass is no house perfect' (Nathaniel Lloyd, *History of the English House*, London, 1931, p. 71). However, stables, out-houses and many places in the country no doubt still had less expensive forms of 'glazing'. The stables at Versailles had panes of oiled cloth. Animal membrane (the diaphragms of cattle were best), oiled cloth and oiled paper (strengthened by two wires fixed diagonally from opposite corners of the frame) were all used for this purpose. 'Horne in windows is now quite laid downe in every place, so our Lattices [of thinly riven oak woven chequerwise, or of wicker] are also growne into lesse use because Glass is become so plentiful . . .' wrote William Harison in his *Description of England* in 1577, and by the beginning of the seventeenth century such wooden lattice-work can only have been used in humble dwellings. Nevertheless, it needs to be noted that the inventory of a house in Oxfordshire, drawn up in 1583, still drew attention to the fact that there was glass in three of the windows—implying that this was rather special. The fact that the glass windows at Alnwick Castle and at the Earl of Northumberland's other northern houses were 'taken doune and lade up in safety' when his lordship was not in residence has, incidentally, been taken to show that glass was rare even in grand establishments in sixteenth-century England but the actual passage from the survey of Alnwick in 1567 explains that it was because of the 'extreme winds' of Northumberland which caused the glazed windows to 'decay and waste'. It was cheaper to 'set uppe of newe with smale charges to his Lp. [Lordship] wher[eas] now the decaye thereof shall be verie costlie and chargeable to be repayred'. (*The Regulations and Establishment of the Household of Henry Algenon Percy, the Fifth Earl of Northumberland . . .*, London, 1827.)

83. Walter Gedde, *A Book of Sundry Draughts principally serving for Glaziers*, 1613. Many large houses at this period (see e.g. *Chatsworth Invt., 1601*) had a 'plumerie' and it is noteworthy that the task of a plumber in those days was as much concerned with repairing leaded windows as with the roofs and drainpipes.

84. M. Jourdain, *English Decoration and Furniture of the Early Renaissance*, London, 1924, p. 127. Some specimens may be seen in the Victoria and Albert Museum.

85. J. P. Babelon, *Demeures Parisiennes sous Henri IV et Louis XIII*, Paris, 1965, p. 78.
86. *Havard*, 'Chassis'.
87. *Tessin-Cronström Correspondence*, letter of 19 April 1693.
88. The author's translation from the original German which is given by Gustav Upmark, 'Ein Besuch in Holland, 1687', *Oud Holland*, Vol. XVIII, 1900, pp. 123–4.
89. Ada Polak, *Glass, its Makers and its Public*, London, 1975, Chap. 13: 'a Sash Window and Frame with Weights lynes and Pullies' (Windsor Castle Accounts, 1686–88).
90. According to Nathaniel Lloyd, *History of the English House*, London, 1931, p. 118. It will have been noticed that Cronström explained how the counter-balanced form could be fixed 'sans l'accrocher'.
91. R. K. Marshall, *Life in the Household of the Duchess Anne* [of Hamilton], London, 1973, p. 174; and Lloyd, *loc. cit.* Sash-windows with 'brass pulleys' were fitted at Ham House in 1673, incidentally, but no mention is made of weights there either.
92. R. K. Marshall, *loc. cit.*
93. Martin Lister, *A Journey to Paris*, London, 1691, p. 191. Publication of the researches of Mr H. J. Louw, a Dutch architectural historian, into the early history of the sash-window is eagerly awaited as this work goes to press. He is convinced that references to strings and pulleys do concern counter-balanced sashes in spite of the fact that weights are not mentioned, and he may well be right. He believes counter-balanced sashes were invented about 1670.
94. William Harison, *op. cit.*
95. R. T. Gunther, *The Architecture of Sir Roger Pratt*, Oxford, 1928, p. 72. Sir Roger Pratt was writing in 1660. In 1664 the rate was much the same, according to Sir Balthazar Gerbier, *op. cit.*, p. 83: The best French glasse . . . sixteen pence a foot
The best Englishe glasse . . . seven pence a foot
Ordinary glass for quarries . . . five pence half penny a foot.
Savot, in *L'Architecture Francoise des bastimens particuliers*, Paris, 1624, has a section on glass made in Normandy and in Lorraine. The former was of better quality and was sold in baskets each containing twenty-four circular pieces of blown glass about 70 centimetres in diameter.
96. Sir Balthazar Gerbier, *Counsel and Advise to All Builders*, 1663, p. 22. He lists the prices per

square foot of various types of stone paving then commonly used in England:
Portland stone . . . 8d.
Black and White marble, laid in London . . . 2s. 6d.
Black and White marble, laid in the provinces . . . 3s. 6d.
Namur stone, grey and white . . . as above
Rans[rance] . . . 5s. mixed with white
Rans and Purple . . .
White marble pavement . . . 3s.
Black marble pavement . . . 1s. 6d.
Black and White polished . . . 5s.
Red and White polished . . . 5s.
Black glazed Holland pan-tiles . . . £6 per 100.
97. 'Hollandische Floorsteenen' and 'neiderländische Flores' are terms occuring in late sixteenth and seventeenth-century German documents. Perhaps the 'steentjes' of Dutch sources were identical. Gerbier (see previous note) spoke of 'black glazed Holland pan-tiles'.
98. Chas. Phillips, *History of the Sackville Family*, London, *c.* 1928, p. 391; and *Havard* 'Carreau'. The tiles at Knole cost 6s. 8d. each so were probably rather handsomely decorated.
99. See C. H. de Jonge, *Oud-Nederlandsche Majolica en Delftsch Aardewerk*, Amsterdam, 1947; M. Boyken, *fliesen . . . de 17de und 18de Jahrhundert*, Darmstadt, 1954; and Anne Berendsen, *Fliesen*, Munich, 1964. The last has excellent illustrations in colour of tiled floors.
100. F. H. Garner, *English Delftware*, London, 1948, p. 2.
101. M. Jourdain, *English Decoration and Furniture of the Early Renaissance*, London, 1924.
102. This recipe was given me by Mrs Ellen Sørensen who had treated floors in this manner as a girl in provincial Denmark.
103. 'Fuller's earth and fine sand preserves the original colour and does not leave a white appearance as soap does,' advised Susanna Whatman in her *Housekeeping Book (1776–1800)*, edited by Thomas Balston, London, 1956. All her rooms were to be dry-scrubbed with white sand regularly. An American, writing of the town of Boscawen in 1800, states that no carpets were used there but the floors were 'strewn with clean white sand . . . and swept into curved lines, scrolls, and whorls, by a broom'. Another American, writing in the 1880s, tells how 'many years ago the kitchens and perhaps the sitting rooms were sanded over after

being scoured with sand and water. The sand, when the floor was dry, was scattered all over the floor and the next day was carefully and lightly swept in herringbone shape—this looking quite pretty' (see Nina Fletcher Little, *Floor Coverings in New England before 1850*, Old Sturbridge Village, Massachusetts, 1967).

104. *Tessin-Cronström Correspondence*, letter of 10 July 1693.

105. *Tessin-Cronström Correspondence*, letter of 22 May 1693.

106. 'Cette manière de placage est venue d'Italie' [This form of veneering comes from Italy] (Sauval, *Antiquités de Paris*, [written 1669–70], Paris, 1924, XIV, p. 17). A new monograph on decorated floors, H. Kier, *Schmuckfussböden in Renaissance und Barock*, Munich, 1976, does not seem to contradict what has been said in the present section but complements it substantially.

107. O. Millar, 'The Notebooks of Richard Symonds', *Studies in Renaissance and Baroque Art*, London, 1967. The floor is also described by Martin Lister (see note 108).

108. Dr Martin Lister, *A Journey to Paris*, London, 1699, p. 41. He adds that parquet floors 'in London and elsewhere in Paris . . . prove so noisy to tread on and faulty that they are in a few years intolerable'.

109. P. Verlet, *Versailles*, Paris, 1961, p. 33. See also D. Alcouffe, 'Les Macés, ébénistes et peintres', *Bulletin de la Société de l'Histoire de l'Art Français*, Paris, 1972, in which he assembles much information about the marquetry floors of Macé and others. Noteworthy are the careful instructions given for the laying of the intricate marquetry floor in the *Petite Galerie* at Versailles in 1685 (p. 63, f.n. 6); the marquetry of some dozen sorts of wood was to be laid over a complete new sub-floor of ancient oak boards and no singeing or dying was to be used.

110. See Gillian Wilson, 'Boulle', *Furniture History*, Vol. VIII, 1972. He also made floors for the Queen and the Dauphin.

111. *Orange Invts.*, I, p. 267).

112. John Aubrey, 'The Natural History of Wiltshire', Bodleian Library MSS. Aubrey 1 & 2.

113. The bill for laying this floor survives. The floor of the raised bed-alcove was provided with 'two leather covers for the step' by way of protection for this expensive feature when the room was not in use. The Closet also had a 'leather cover for the flore'. (*Evelyn's Diary*, 23 August 1678) noted that some floors at the Duke of Norfolk's new house at Weybridge were 'parqueted with cedar, yew and cypress' but, since he does not bother to describe them more fully, it seems probable that they were not as elaborate as those at Ham.

114. *D.E.F.*, Illus. 8, 'Tables, Side-, Console-, and Pier-.'

115. See Fowler and Cornforth, *English Decoration in the 18th Century*, London, 1974, Plate 193.

116. The December issue of the *Mercure Galant* for 1673 told its readers that 'les gens de qualité ne veulent plus de tapis de pied dans leurs alcoves à cause de la poudre qu'ils conservent. C'est pourquoy ils les font parqueter de bois de diverses couleurs et de pieces de rapport' [people of quality no longer want foot carpets in the alcoves on account of the way they harbour dust. That is why they have them parquetted with wood of different colours and with marquetry].

117. In the introduction to G. Lizzani's *Il Mobile Romano*, Milan, 1970, A. Gonzalez Palacios discusses certain furniture designed by Roman architects and illustrates a design for candlestands by Algardi (Plate XIV).

118. See p. 37 and note 17 to Chapter II and also p. 185.

119. When Nicodemus Tessin visited Versailles in 1687 he was much impressed by the silver furniture—as was the intention. The *Grande Galerie (des Glaces)* contained no less than seventy-six pieces comprising massive tables, candlestands, great urns and basins, stools and benches. Some were up to nine feet high. Tessin lists 167 items of silver furniture as being in the State Apartments (*Tessin's Visit, 1687*, p. 29). However, it must not be thought that it was only the King who had silver furniture in France. La Grande Madamoiselle had several imposing pieces in her apartment at the Palais Royal in 1679 and Monsieur, the King's brother, had more at Saint-Cloud; Madame du Lude is reported to have owned silver furniture which had cost her no less than 27,000 écus and Monsieur de Lavardin, according to Madame de Sevigné, had tables, candlestands, chandeliers and fire-dogs of this precious metal (*Havard*, 'Argent'). Earlier in the century, Sully saw some silver furniture at the house of the Comptroller-General of Castile and Cardinal Mazarin also owned several pieces. The fashion had spread to

NOTES TO PAGES 93–8

England. Charles I owned a folding table 'covered all over with silver plate ingraved' (C. C. Oman, *English Domestic Silver*, London, 1965, p. 183) and this is a reminder that most silver furniture consisted of thin sheets of the metal riveted to a wooden structure. A table, looking-glass and pair of candlestands given to Charles II by the City of London and now at Windsor Castle belongs to this category (Oman, *op. cit.*, pp. 183–4; see also his 'An XVIIIth Century Record of Silver Furniture at Windsor Castle', *Country Life*, 6 December 1930). What was remarkable about the Versailles furniture, on the other hand, was that it was apparently all of solid or 'massy' silver. Celia Fiennes visited the 'Silver Roome' at Lord Chesterfield's house at Bretby in 1696 and noted that the 'stands, table and fire utensils were all of massy silver' (*Celia Fiennes*, p, 171) and a table and looking-glass presented to William III by the City of London is of the same solid class. But a tax was introduced in Great Britain in 1697 which made it prohibitively expensive to have large objects of silver. As Celia Fiennes said of the Bretby items 'when plate was in nomination to pay tax, the Earle of Chester-field sold it all' (see J. F. Hayward, 'Silver Furniture', *Apollo*, LXVII, pp. 71, 124, 153 and 220). In France in 1690 it was even forbidden by law to cause large items of silver to be made. The result of these measures was two-fold: it gave an immense impetus to the faïence industry that now found great incentive to produce large, showy dishes, ewers and basins which could stand on buffets, replacing the silver pieces that had been melted down. And it greatly en-couraged the production of carved furniture with silvering or gilding that looked tolerably like real metal furniture but was more sym-pathetic to the touch and tended to be more graceful. For information on Dutch silver furniture, incidentally, see the article by Th. H. Lunsingh Scheurleer in *Opusculum in Honorem Carl Hernmarck*, Stockholm, 1966, pp. 141–158.
120. 'Devant les deux pilliers entre les croisées' of the Salon de Mars at Versailles, for instance, 'il y a de grands miroires, tables et guéridons d'argent avec leurs flambeaux dessus . . .' [In front of the two piers between the windows . . . there are large looking-glasses, tables and candlestands of silver with their candelabra on top . . .], wrote *Tessin* on his *Visit in 1687* (p. 25). These great mirrors, then, were pier-glasses with console-tables below; they were flanked by candlestands

with candlesticks standing on them; and it was all of silver. In addition '. . . la salle est toutte entourée des grands pièces, comme vases, cuves, cassettes et chesnests d'argent d'une pesanteur et grandeur prodigieuse . . .' [the room is furnished all round with large pieces, including urns, cisterns, chests and fire-dogs of silver of pro-digious weight and size . . .].

NOTES TO CHAPTER IV

1. Penelope Eames, 'Furniture in England, France and the Netherlands from the Twelfth to the Fifteenth Century', *Furniture History*, XIII, 1977.
2. The contents of each of the twenty-four 'cariages' in the Earl of Northumberland's baggage-train are listed in *The Regulations . . . of the Household of . . . Earl of Northumberland begun in Anno Domini M.D.XII* (1512), London, 1827, pp. 386–91. After 'my Lordes Chariot', the first three carts carried respectively the 'Stuf of the Dynyng Chambre and Gret Chambre,' that of 'my Ladies Chambre' and that of 'the Chambre wher my Lord makes him[self] redy' together with the Gentlewomen's belongings, and 'such Stuf remaynynge in the Wardrobe'. Each class of officer was allocated a cart onto which the appurtenances of their office or the tools of their trade, their beds and bedding, and their personal belongings were packed.
3. One Gentleman Usher was instructed to 'oversee the continewall furnisheinge and clea-nely keepinge of all lodgeinges, galleryes, greatchambers, dyneinge rooms, parlours, &c.', although the lord's own lodging was the particular responsibility of the Gentleman of the Chamber. (Viscount Montague's Household Book, 1595, see Sir William H. St. John Hope, *Cowdray and Easebourne Priory*, London, 1919, Appendix II.)
4. The Yeoman Usher of the Great Chamber (the site for ceremonial dining and banqueting) was expected to see that the room was 'orderly prepared . . . wth. tables, stooles, and chayres necessarye for the companye and after dynner, and supper to see them bestowed agayne decentlye into their several rooms [i.e. replaced where they belong]'. (Viscount Montague's Household Book, 1595, *op. cit.*).
5. The Yoeman of the Wardrobe was responsible for the 'furniture of all the chambers in the house, as they be furnishede, and what soever ells

350

is in the wardrobe [i.e. in store, not in use], and all these things to keepe well, and see there bee noe defectes in any of them, but to be presentlie amendede' ('A Breviate Touching the Order of a Nobleman's House . . . 1605', *Archeologia*, XIII, 1800, pp. 315–89).

6. The Yeoman of the Wardrobe who received the instructions in the previous note was expected to mend all the furnishings 'unlesse it bee joyners woorke as tables, stooles, bedsteedes, etc. which hee is to cause a joyner to mende'.

7. A law was enacted in 1750 granting certain privileges to the 'Art, Trade or Mystery of an Upholder otherwise called Upholsterers within the said City' of London. (See Karin Walton, 'The Worshipful Company of Upholders of the City of London', *Furniture History*, IX, 1973.)

8. 'This man Francis Oddy was servant to my father many years & hath since served me . . . He serves me in the way of upholsterer when there is a need to furnish the Lodging rooms and dress them up . . .' (written in 1638, *The Diary of Sir Henry Slingsby of Scriven . . .*, ed. Daniel Parsons, London, 1836, p. 5).

9. In 1613, for example, a payment is recorded to 'the uphoulster for sylck ffringe and making up chaires and stooles and window cusshen of damask', while Lord Cork paid 'Mr Argyll the uphoster' for wall-hangings, bedding and cushions in 1628. (*D.E.F.*, 'Upholder').

10. We do not yet know sufficient about the careers of any seventeenth-century upholsterers to give concrete examples but we know, for example, that Chippendale started off as a cabinetmaker but, in his will, he called himself 'upholsterer'. The latter was generally a far more lucrative trade.

11. *Ingatestone Invt., 1600.*

12. *Northampton Invt., 1614.*

13. Havard, 'Broderie'.

14. *Historical manuscripts Commission*, Vol. VI, p. 275, De L'Isle and Dudley 1955; letter from the Countess of Leicester to W. Hawkins, Paris, 1640. She was describing the kind of *ammeublement* to be seen in fashionable interiors like those illustrated by Bosse, comprising a bed, armchairs, 'backstools' and stools.

15. *Ham Invt., c. 1654.*

16. *Devon Invts.*

17. *Easton Lodge Invt., 1637.*

18. For example, Madame de Maintenon's bedchamber at St Cloud, furnished at the end of the century, had a bed hung with a green and gold damask lined with red damask, and these two materials were used for all the other furnishings in various ways. The counterpoint had a green and gold panel with red pendant edges (*pentes*) falling down the sides. The wall-hangings were of the two materials made up in alternating bands. The day-bed was dressed *en suite* and stood in a niche hung like the walls. The seat-furniture (three armchairs, twelve folding stools and four benches) were covered with the red damask framed (impaned) with a border of the green and gold. The window-curtains, portières and a five-leaf screen were likewise made up with the two materials, as was the small coverlet she used for covering her legs, as it was seemly for a woman to do when reclining on a day-bed. The only items that broke the sequence were the red cloth put on the table when the King had a Cabinet meeting, and the red velvet covering of the close-stool. The rest of the furniture comprised two small walnut desks inlaid with pewter, the writing-table of *bois de violette* (kingwood?) and two looking-glasses hanging on the wall (see *Havard*, 'Chambre'). So greatly did Madame de Maintenon love this room that the Duc d'Antin had an exact replica of it made in order that she would feel quite at home when she visited his château in 1707. He even had the markings in her favourite books copied.

19. The *Ham Invts.* of 1677, 1679 and 1683 are to be published by the Victoria and Albert Museum.

20. For example, the Duchess had a red and yellow damask *ammeublement* in her Bedchamber in 1677 and 1679. By 1683 the whole set had been exchanged for a set that was red and black, fringed blue and black. The hangings from the first set were used in the Duke's Dressing Room next door while the rest of the set was sent up to the Lauderdales' house in Whitehall. The Lauderdales were in the height of fashion; the Provosts of King's College, Cambridge, were probably not. At any rate the bed-hangings in the Provost's Lodge that had been acquired in 1609–10 were not replaced until 1631. *Provost of Kings Invt., 1660.*

21. For example, a silk damask might cost between 20 and 25 *livres* an ell (say 1.20 metres) in Paris (G. Mongrédien, *La Vie quotidienne sous Louis XIV*, Paris, 1948) while crimson damask suitable for use in the royal apartments at Hampton Court cost 22 shillings in 1699 and

green taffeta, a plain material, cost 16 shillings a yard (*Hampton Court Estimates, 1699*). A very richly brocaded silk, with much gold thread, might cost anything up to 100 shillings a yard. It is recorded that a certain French silk-weaver completed four pieces of silk totalling 393 *aunes* (one *aune* or ell equalled about 46 inches) in nine months—say 11 els per week or 84 inches a day. This was good going for a figured material; a plain material could be woven much more speedily but a complicated one with much brocading might proceed at the rate of only a few inches a day. The weaver concerned was working in the eighteenth century but there is no reason to suppose a seventeenth century weaver could work any faster. (See L. Bosseboeuf, 'La fabrique de soieries de Tours au XVIII et XIXe siècles', *Mémoires de la Société Archeologique de Touraine*, XLI, 1900, p. 349).

22. At Hardwick an embroidered bed had 'a curtain of darnix and a peece of buckerom about the bed to cover yt'. (*Hardwick Invt. 1601*). Daniel Marot shows an iron curtain rod protruding conspicuously round the tester of some of his beds from which the 'case-curtains' could be hung, 'pour conserver le lit contre la poussière' [in order to protect the bed from dust] as it says on the drawing reproduced in Plate 144.

23. The French called such cases *housses* and this term occurs in the *Cowdray Inventory of 1682* as 'a housse of printed paragon'.

24. At Chatsworth, *Celia Fiennes* (p. 100) saw that 'there were no beds up'. Presumably this means that their hangings had been removed and only the wooden structures remained in place.

25. The *Cockesden Inventory of 1610* records that one bed had its 'testerne and valence covered with a sheet', while *Celia Fiennes* (p. 100) saw 'clean sheets pinn'd about the beds and hangings' when she visited Ashstead Park at the end of the century.

26. Le Comte de laborde, *Le Palais Mazarin*, Paris, 1846, p. 299.

27. William Karlson, *Ebba Brahe's Hem . . .*, Lund, 1943.

28. *Ham Invts. 1677, 1679 & 1683.*

29. Laborde, *op. cit.*, p. 301.

30. *Hardwick Invt., 1601.*

31. *Havard, 'Lit'.*

32. *Cockesden Invt., 1626.*

NOTES TO CHAPTER V

1. Mrs Florence Montgomery, formerly curator of textiles at the Henry F. du Pont Museum at Winterthur, Delaware, and now textile consultant at the Metropolitan Museum, New York, has in manuscript form a glossary of historic textile terms which it is to be hoped will soon be published. The Department of Textiles at the Victoria and Albert Museum have a working index of such terms. Mrs Montogomery made numerous helpful comments on this chapter before it went to print, for which I am exceedingly grateful. The responsibility for all the statements made here nevertheless rests entirely with me.

2. This technique is described in most books on historic textiles. For this and related technical questions, see *Notes on Carpet-Knotting and Weaving* (which includes tapestry-woven carpets), Victoria and Albert Museum Handbook, London, 1969. See also François Tabard, 'The Weaver's Art' in *The Art of the Tapestry*, (ed. J. Jobé), London, 1965.

3. See P. Thornton, 'Tapisseries de Bergame', *Pantheon*, VI, XVIII Jahrgang, March, 1960. 'Une pièce de tapisserie de Bergame' is listed in a storeroom at the House of Nassau's residence in Brussels in 1618 (*Orange Invts.*, I, p. 118).

4. The French royal inventories list 160 pieces of hangings of this material 'dont la plus grande partie a esté employée à Versailles et pour les ballets' [of which the majority have been used at Versailles and for ballets] but they were probably not in any of the principal rooms (*Guiffrey, Inventaire*, II, p. 277). *Savary des Bruslons* claims that all artisans or 'gens de basse condition' had this material in their chambers—presumably only in Paris.

5. The crowned 'L' form is illustrated by Thornton, *loc. cit.*. Savary des Bruslons (1723) states that *tapisseries de Bergame* also came 'à grandes barres chargées de fleurs & oiseaux, ou d'autres animaux; d'autres à grandes & petites barres unies, sans aucune façon . . .' [with wide stripes on which are flowers and birds; others with plain wide and narrow stripes, without any decorative motives].

6. Hangings thus described were in the room of Monsieur Mancini, in Cardinal Mazarin's apartment at the Louvre (*Mazarin Invt., 1653*).

7. *Savary des Bruslons* says they were also made at Toulouse.

8. The 'Roanischen Tapeten' on the walls of the Palace of Potsdam in the late seventeenth century (*Stengel*, p. 36) were presumably 'hangings from Rouen'. Other German inventories refer to 'geflammte Teppiche' (flamed hangings) which presumably means they had a *point d'Hongrie* pattern that we know was much woven as *tapisserie de Bergame*. At Oranienstein, near Koblenz, there was in 1696 a 'kamer behangsel [set of wall-hangings] Rouans gevlamd tapeet' which must have been of the same class (*Orange Invts.*, II, p. 226). At Copenhagen Castle in 1688 there was likewise some 'fransk kammer haengsel' (French chamber hanging; G. Boesen, 'Kongelige Slotsinteriører omkring 1700', *Til Knud Fabricius*, Copenhagen, 1945) while Swedish inventories of the period make occasional reference to 'franska tapeter' (French hangings), some being specified as having violet stripes or bands while others are described as 'stora, nya grofva franska tapeter' (large, new, coarse French hangings; *Karlson*, p. 41). Some are listed as having silk details (medh silke in Wäfvet) and others had silver and gold flowers (med sölver och guld blommerat). These French hangings were evidently quite elaborate. There is also reference to 'flamska rums tapeter' (Flemish room hangings) which may concern actual Flemish tapestries but could just as well have to do with coarse woven materials of this kind, especially as some are described as being 'hem-väfna' (home woven) which suggests these materials were of a relatively simple character.

9. Many hangings listed among the belongings of Charles I are called 'course Elizens' and a reading of the original manuscript shows that this spelling is correct. Could they, all the same, be a mis-transcription of Elbeuf, for no other reference to 'coarse Elizens' seems to have been noted (*Charles I Invts., 1649–51*)? Maybe the 'Dover stuff' also mentioned in these royal inventories in the same way came from Douai rather than from Dover Castle, as has been suggested. This is pure conjecture but the terms have never been satisfactorily explained.

10. The *Book of Rates of 1582* lists the duties payable on three types of dornix:

Dornix called French dornix . . . 15d/ell.

Dornix with caddas [caddis = linen thread] . . . 10/- the piece of 15 yds.

Dornix with silk . . . 13/- the piece of 15 yds. The material 'called French Dornix' may have been of a distinctive type, perhaps with large patterns, and may not necessarily have been French in origin. It cost more than the other two classes (20 ells equalled about 15 yards). An Act of 1678 regulating the London cloth markets listed 'Dornix' with 'Birdsey[e] Carpeting, Bristol Carpeting and all sorts of Carpeting' on the one hand and as 'Darnix, narrow, for Garments' on the other—indicating a wide range of qualities (I am grateful to Miss Wendy Hefford for drawing my attention to this reference in W. Maitland, *The History of London*, 1761, Vol. I, p. 465).

11. Hangings of 'stript darnax' are mentioned in the *Cockesden Inventory of 1626*, as well as a dornix table-carpet 'of blue and white birdwork' and a coverlet of 'birdwork'. A room at Clonmell in 1684 was hung with yellow dornix 'with white flowers'. As shown in note 5 above, *tapisserie de Bergame* could be striped, or decorated with birds or flowers. (*Clonmell Invt., 1684*, National Library of Ireland, MS 2522, kindly communicated by Desmond Fitz-Gerald, Knight of Glin).

12. For example, the *Countess of Leicester's Invt., of 1634* shows that her ladyship had true tapestry in her own chamber but her daughter had hangings of dornix.

13. See the *Countess of Leicester's Invt., 1634*. The material is also mentioned in the *Charles I Invts., 1649–51*. Samples of eighteenth-century Kidderminster stuffs are to be seen in the Berch Collection in the Nordiska Museum, Stockholm; some are strongly banded by coloured wefts and have a warp pattern.

14. *Tart Hall Invt., 1641* and *Dyrham Invt., 1703*.

15. A 'table-carpet' might be an Oriental knotted-pile rug but it might equally well be an embroidered cloth or of a rich velvet trimmed with fringe. There was a 'carpet of black velvet for the little bord' in the 'Chiefe Chamber' at *Hengrave Hall (Invt., of 1603)*, for instance.

16. See note 2 above.

17. It is recorded that the Elector of Brandenburg still kept his Turkish rugs in his *Wunderkammer*—in his Cabinet of Curiosities—in 1617 (*Stengel*, p. 50).

18. In an inventory of a house at Marseilles in 1587, mention is made of 'trois masquetz neufs' (*Havard*, 'Moquette'). *Savary des Bruslons*, under the heading 'Tapis', lists *mosquets* as one of the three types of Oriental carpet available in Paris in his day (1723), the others being 'tapis de pic' and 'Cadene', but he fails to explain what they were

like. Several 'Musketta carpets' are listed in the *Gosfield Inventory of 1638*; some had 'redd grounds'. They seem to have been small; one lay on a table and two together were valued at only £1.

19. There is a famous example at Hardwick (see M. H. Beattie, 'Antique Rugs at Hardwick Hall', *Oriental Art*, Vol. V, No. 2, 1959). In the *Charles I Invts., 1649–51* we find 'two verie rich carpetts of Persian makeing, the ground of them gould & silver, wrought in workes of silver and silkes of sundry collors'. Some of Louis XIV's 'tapis de Perse' were also described as being 'estoffe razé, le milieu fonds d'or, avec quatre tigres qui devorent quatre cerfs' [a flat material [i.e. with only a shallow pile], the centre with a gold ground, with [representations of] four tigers devouring stags] (*Guiffrey, Inventaire*, I, p. 381). Fouquet likewise had a 'tapy de Perse de soye' (*Havard*, 'Perse') which he very sensibly had lined with black cloth (doublé de thoille noire).

20. Lady Dorchester, for instance, owned several Eastern carpets but only one 'long Pertian carpett of 6 yards long and two and a half broad'. It was valued at £38, which was a lot of money. (*Gosfield Invt., 1638*.)

21. Sir Philip Sidney wrote to a friend in 1602 that he had 'brought a Turkey carpet for my Lord Bergavenny, seven Dutch ells [about sixteen feet] long; it cost £27 sterling but is esteemed very fine and well worth the money' (S. W. Beck, *The Draper's Dictionary*, 1884, 'Carpet'). If it really was Turkish and not Persian, this might well have been an Ushak carpet. Lady Dorchester owned '2 Egiptian carpetts' valued at £10.10s. od. (see the previous note); Louis XIV owned a 'tapis du Kaire' (*Guiffrey, Inventaire*, I, p. 378) and *Charles I (Invt., 1659–51)* had 'one ould Carew Carpett' in his collection, valued at only £4. Carpets described as *Cairine, Kerrein*, and *Querin* occur in English and French inventories every now and then. For surveys of the use of Near Eastern carpets in Europe during the Middle Ages and later, see K. Erdmann, *Europe und der Orientteppich*, Mainz, 1962 and P. M. Campana, *Il Tappeto Orientale*, Milan, 1945.

22. They were made principally at Lahore (see J. Irwin, 'The Indian Textile Trade in the Seventeenth Century', *The Journal of Indian Textile History*, Vol. I, 1958).

23. See E. Kuehnel, *Catalogue of Spanish Rugs*, The Textile Museum, Washington, 1953.

24. See C. E. C. Tattersall, *A History of British Carpets*, revised by S. Reed, Leigh-on-Sea, 1966, pls. 2, 3 and 5.

25. *Havard*, 'Tapis'.

26. *Guiffrey, Inventaire*, I, p. 387. The bill for the *Galerie d'Apollon* carpets was paid in 1666. One is illustrated by M. Jarry, *The Carpets of Manufactory de la Savonnerie*, Leigh-on-Sea, 1966, fig. 11. Some of the carpets 'façon de Perse' woven at the Louvre (before the two factories were merged) were, however, of silk with gold brocading—like actual Persian court carpets.

27. Jarry, *op. cit.*, figs. 13–17.

28. A document of the 1680s refers to chairs of 'setwork (commonly called Turkey-work chairs)', see R. W. Symonds, 'English Cane Chairs', *The Connoisseur*, March and May 1951.

29. *Northampton Invt., 1614*. In the same room was 'a foot carpett of Turky Worke, the ground redd and yelowe' which may, on the other hand, actually have been Anatolian, as it is not specified as being 'of Englishe worke' like the large carpet, and red and yellow are colours characteristic of a well-known class of Anatolian rug.

30. *Gosfield Invt., 1638*. Frith's long carpet must have been English but the other four may well have been Oriental. Lady Dorchester also had '1 small Turkie carpett of English worke', valued at £1. 10s. od.

31. *Ingatestone Invt., 1600*.

32. Tattersall, *op. cit.*, figs. 14 and 15.

33. A Durham merchant owned 'ij carpetes noryshe wourke' in 1596 (*Surtees Society*, XII, 1906 'Durham Wills and Inventories', p. 260), while an inventory of 1584 includes a reference to a 'Turquey carpett of Norwiche work (J. O. Halliwell, *Ancient Inventories . . .*, London, 1854).

34. Tattersall, *op. cit.*, fig. 15.

35. *Havard*, 'Tapis'. This authority, however, suggested that 'tapis d'Angleterre' was a kind of moquette (see p. 112) although moquette was woven in France in great quantity so there would have been no need to import it to the extent that the introduction of an import-duty would imply. Turkeywork was certainly used both for chairs and floor-covering. Seventeenth-century chairs covered with what looks like English turkeywork are to be seen in several Scandinavian collections.

36. *Kilkenny and Clonmell Invts., 1684*.

37. See note 2, above.

38. *Savary des Bruslons*, (1723) had a heading 'Moquette, Mocade, Moucade'. 'Mockado of

Flaunders making' is listed in the *Book of Rates, 1582*.

39. In the Bibliothèque Forney, Paris, is an Italian sample-book of *c.* 1760 with specimens of 'Mocchetta unita denominata trippa' which are woollen-pile velvets. In 1601, 10,805 pieces of *trippe de velours* were woven at Lille. So excellent were the Lille products that the Procureur Générale of Tournai obtained from Lille in 1590–91 'une demi pieche de tripe de haultliche fin ouvrage' which he hoped would inspire the local weavers to do better (E. Houdoy, *Tapisseries de haute-lisse, . . . la fabrication Lilloise*, Lille, 1871, p. 70; note that at Lille and Tournai the *hautelisseurs* were not weavers of tapestries but made large-scale upholstery materials on a wide loom. This is made clear by E. Soil, *Tapisserie de Tournai, les tapissiers et hautelisseurs de cette ville*, tournai, 1891, who quotes many sixteenth-century references to *trippe* including one to 'pieces de haultliche . . . appelées trippes'). In the inventory of the Princess Albertina Agnes' possessions (1696) note is made of some flowered Tournai *trippe* (*Doornicks gebloemd trip; Orange Invts.*, II, p. 226).

40. In 1606 Claude Dangon, an inventive weaver of Lyons, devised a method of making a velvet with a shaggy reverse of 'panne ou pelluche' (Le Comte d'Hennezel, *Claude Dangon*, Lyons, 1926) but this was probably of silk, and there were certainly also 'pluches de soye' (silk plushes) available in the eighteenth century. Under 'Manufactures de Paris', *Savary des Bruslons* (1723) lists together 'velours, trippes de velours, pannes, pluches'. Savary, under 'Panne', also explains that 'pannes de laine' (woollen plushes) are usually known as *tripes* or *moquette*. At Marly some stools were covered 'de tripe ou peluche cramoisie' (D. Pitoin, *Marly-le-Roi*, Paris, 1904, p. 174). There was a room completely dressed with 'stript plush' at Dyrham at the end of the seventeenth century (*Dyrham Invt., 1703*) and at *Tredegar (Invt., of 1692)* some cane chairs had cushions of 'flowered plush'.

41. There are some seventeenth-century arm-chairs at Boughton still covered in a plain red woollen velvet that are described in an inventory of 1718 as being 'cover'd in vallure'. Whether this material was on the chairs when they were new (*c.* 1670?) has not yet been established but it is certainly possible. Some chairs of *c.* 1720 at Erthig have 'caffoy' covers (see J. Fowler and J. Cornforth, English Decoration in the 18th Century, London, 1974, fig. 90); the material originally had a bright yellow satin ground and a pattern rendered in red pile. 'Caffa' is mentioned in sixteenth-century records. In the eighteenth century, 'Caffoy paper' was a flocked wallpaper.

42. The *'Cafawerkers'* combined to form a guild with the *'Tripmakers'* at Hamburg in 1609 (K. Germann, *Die Deutsche Möbelplüsche*, Leipzig, 1913, p. 18). These names reflect the fact that the trades were run by immigrant Netherlandish craftsmen; there were *caffawerkers* at Tournai in 1532, for instance. There is a Swedish reference to a room being hung with red 'Harlemer trip' in 1706 and 'Harlemer plyss' occurs in another Swedish document of 1677 (*Karlson*, p. 276). In the *Orange Inventories* one finds 'Haarlems fluweel' (Haarlem velvet; I, p. 276) and 'Haarlems caffa' with black flowers on an orange ground (II, p. 226). Some accommodating chairs were provided at Versailles 'pour servire dans les chambres des seigneurs' [for use in the bedchambers of [set aside for] noblemen] and these were covered in 'panne d'Hollande couleur de feu' while some others had striped material of the same kind (*Guiffrey, Inventaire*, p. 414 and 433).

43. *Agius*, p. 76.

44. There is reference to 'a rugg coverlet' in the *Henham Inventory of 1602*.

45. A duty of no less than five shillings each was payable on the importation of 'Mantles, called Irish mantles' in 1582 (*Book of Rates, 1582*). An even higher duty (10/- to 13/4d) was paid on 'blankets called Paris mantles' which came white or coloured (often red, which is specifically mentioned).

46. In 1585 there was a 'checkey' Irish rugg at Chenies. 'Chicker' and 'chequered' ruggs are mentioned in the inventories of *Gilling Castle, 1594* and of *Marton, 1605*.

47. *O.E.D.*, 'Cadow'.

48. *Ibid.* Mr John Nevinson has kindly informed me that in an inventory of Worksop Hall of 1591 in the Sheffield Public Library there is a reference to 'Waterford ruggs'. Presumably these materials were exported from that port on the southeast coast of Ireland.

49. The Yeoman of the Wardrobe in Lord Montague's household had to see that 'the lodgeinges reserved for strangers' staying in the house were in proper order, making sure to remove the quilts at night and to have 'yrishe rugges lay'd in their places' (*Montague Household Book, 1595*).

50. *O.E.D.*, 'Cadow'. 'Outlandish' meant foreign but the implication is that the cadow was by this time strange and unfamiliar.

51. For instance, Spanish blankets are listed after ordinary blankets in the *Ham Inventory of 1679* but before silk blankets.

52. *Havard* and *Savary des Bruslons*, both under 'Castelogne'. Savary says they were woven in many parts of France in his day (1723).

53. *Hengrave Invt., 1603.*

54. *Mazarin Invt., 1653.*

55. *Ingatestone Invt., 1600.*

56. *Havard*, 'Blanchet'.

57. *Ham Invt., 1679.*

58. *Hampton Court Estimates, 1699.*

59. *Kensington Palace Invt., 1699.*

60. *Savary des Bruslons* says fustian was of cotton, sometimes with a linen warp, and a writer of a pamphlet on *Treasure and Traffic* of 1641 explained how Manchester bought in London 'cotton wool' from Cyprus and Smyrna 'and perfects it into fustians, vermillions, dimities and other such stuffs'; but in 1604 it was stated in an Act of Parliament that 'in Norwich, time out of mind, there had been a certain craft called Shearman, for sheering as well worsteds, stamins and fustians, as also all other woollen cloths' ('The House and Farm Accounts of the Shuttleworths of Gawthorpe Hall . . ., Pt. III, Notes, 'Fustian'' *Chetham Society*, 1857). 'Jeans fustian' (i.e. from Genoa) is often mentioned in seventeenth century inventories; 'jeans' is and was a cotton material. Fustian also came from Milan, Naples, Ulm (called Holmes) and from Holland.

61. *Ingatestone Invt., 1600.* A blanket at *Hatfield Priory (Invt., 1629)*, perhaps one of fustian, was 'napte on both sides'. A charter of 1641 mentions 'Naples Fustian Tripp, or Velvet' which must have been a cotton velvet (Beck, *Draper's Dictionary*). This material became popular in the late eighteenth century as 'Manchester velvet', now called velure and a ribbed version of which we still have as corduroy.

62. *Chetham Society*, 1861, 'Lancashire and Cheshire Wills and Inventories'.

63. 'whole clothes of fledge to make fledges of' occurs in an inventory of Sheffield Castle, taken in 1582, Mr John Nevinson has very kindly told me.

64. I am indebted to Professor Garnet Rees for suggesting this interpretation which I feel sure is correct.

65. *Celia Fiennes*, p. 339.

66. A seventeenth-century tariff of import duties lists together 'Sayes, Double Serges, or Flanders Serges, Double Saye or Serge . . .'.

67. Berch Collection, Nordiska Museet, Stockholm. W. Karlson (*Ebba Brahe's Hem . . .*, Lund, 1943) explains that perpetuana was a broad serge.

68. *Tart Hall Invt., 1641.*

69. From the Danish *'vadmel'*, homespun. See *Ingatestone Invt., 1600* and *Knole Invt., 1645.*

70. A document of 1732 in the Bibliothèque Centrale, Lyons, refers to 'crêpes appellé estamines' (*Inventaire Chappe*, Vol. VII, p. 591). Other authorities speak of it being 'slight' and suggest it had rather an open texture.

71. *Countess of Leicester's Invt., 1634.*

72. Evelyn 'went to see . . . the pressing and watering . . . [of] chamblettes' in 1644 (*O.E.D.*). *Savary des Bruslons* (1723) differentiates between *'camelots à eau'* which were pressed with a hot plate to impart a glaze, *'ondez'* which had waves imparted by pressing to give a 'watered' or 'moiré' effect, and *'gauffrez'* which had a figure imprinted on the surface by pressing it with a hot plate against a wood block carved with a pattern in intaglio. It should be noted that the watered or *moiré* effect was called 'waved' in England, whereas the plain, glazed sort of camlet was apparently called 'water camlet' because the process involved the application of water.

73. Velvets made of wool have been discussed above (p. 111). Velvet can also be made of cotton, as were 'Manchester velvets' in the eighteenth century (see note 61).

74. We have already considered the technique of weaving damask in connection with damasks made of worsted (see p. 113).

75. Brocading, as well as other weaving processes, is explained in many readily obtainable books. One of the most recent is Verla Birrell, *The Textile Arts*, New York, 1973.

76. Satin is a weave that gives the resulting material one shiny face. Although one can make satin of cotton, it is a weave that is particularly well suited to silk since it allows the shiny quality of the thread to come to the fore. See note 75.

77. 'Formerly the term restrained to cloths woven either wholey of gold . . . or of silver . . .' (*Chambers' Dictionary*, 1786).

78. Gold thread was in fact a narrow strip of silver-gilt metal wound on a silken core. It came in several sorts—straight (*filé*) or spiralling (*frisé*). It could also take the form of flat strips which could be woven into the ground.

79. A rich bed at *Ingatestone* (*Invt., 1600*) had its tester and valances of 'tysshew layde with crimson silke and goulde lace'. These were the richer components; the curtains were of taffeta (i.e. plain silk). Presumably the silver cloth was embroidered with red silk and trimmed with gold lace.

80. Lady Dorchester had a bed with a set of summer hangings of 'white tinsell wrought with flowers of several colours of silke', i.e. the white, shimmering material was embroidered with coloured silks (*Gosfield Invt., 1638*).

81. It is occasionally called 'taffeta sarsnett' (*Ingatestone Invt., 1600*) or 'taffety sercenet' (*Cockesden Invt., 1626*).

82. *Tabis à fleurs* was a major product of the Tours silk-weaving establishments in the later decades of the seventeenth century. The imparting of the 'tabby' (*tabisé*) effect is described in a document of 1638 (L. A. Bossebeuf, *La fabrique de soieries de Tours*, Tours, 1900, p. 257).

83. *Ham Invt., 1679.*

84. Given thus in the *Tredegar Invt., 1688* and the *Dyrham Invt., 1703*, and as 'Blak silk moyhair' in the accounts of John Clerk for the year 1649 (Register House, Edinburgh), a reference to which my attention was kindly drawn by Griselda Chubb. *Savary des Bruslons* (1723), under the heading 'Mohère, mouaire ou moire', explains that this is 'une étoffe ordinairement tout de soye . . . un espèce de gros de Tours mais plus faible'. When given a *moiré* or watered effect by being crushed in a calendering machine, it came to be known as *mohère tabisée*. In German and Scandinavian, watered silk is called '*Mohr*' in seventeenth-century inventories; some hangings of this material thus described are still to be seen on the walls of a room at Rosenborg Castle, Copenhagen, for instance. William III's bed at Honselaarsdijk at the end of the century was hung with blue English mohair (*blau Engels moor*; *Orange Invts.*, I, p. 462). The Countess of Manchester in 1675 had a room 'hung with six pieces of haire, called silk watered moehaire' (J. Fowler and J. Cornforth, *op. cit.*, p. 132): The Duchess of Lauderdale had the hangings of her bed and of her closet made of 'morello mohair' (*Ham Invt., 1679*). One might think that morello was the colour but the hangings are respectively described as being red and black, and white. Could 'morello' be a corruption of the Italian for watering 'marrezzo'? In 1646 Tours produced 'moires de soye' but also 'moires' of wool, cotton

and camel hair (Bossebeuf, *op. cit.*). Article LXXVIII of the *Regulations* of the Lyons silk-weavers, issued in 1737, concerned 'les moires de soye'. Beck's *Draper's Dictionary* (1884) explains that 'mohair' was in his day a cloth of mohair yarn but reminds his readers that Chambers' *Cyclopoedia* of 1741 describes it as 'A kind of stuff, ordinarily of silk . . . There are two kinds, the one smooth and plain, the other watered like tabbys'. Today the term is often used to describe a woollen velvet and is no longer associated with a silk material.

85. Apparently quite exceptional was the bed at Knole which had hangings of 'yellowe cotten trymde with blew and yellow silke fringe and lace sutable [i.e. matching blue and yellow lace]' (see Charles J. Phillips, *History of the Sackville Family*, London, *c.* 1928, p. 317; 'Household stuff sent . . . to Knole in 1624').

86. Chintzes began to come through the port of Marseilles in the 1570s and 1580s (see J. Irwin and K. Brett, *Origins of Chintz*, London, 1970, p. 4). They were subsequently imported through Lisbon and Antwerp—and then London. The name 'pintado' comes from the Portuguese likening these colourful materials to the speckled plumage of a peahen (*pintade* in French).

87. In 1609 a factor of the East India Company in Surat was writing about 'pintadoes of all sorts, especially the finest . . . I mean such as are for quilts and for fine hangings', (Irwin and Brett, *op. cit.*, p. 4).

88. One of the Company's factors actually stated that the *chintes* he was having made in 1619 were 'for hangings in England'. In 1630 a set of 'pintado hangings . . . for fitting a gallery or room' cost £30 (Irwin and Brett, *op. cit.*, p. 3).

89. *Tart Hall Invt., 1641.*

90. *Pepys's Diary*, 5 September 1663.

91. *Cowdray Invt., 1688.*

92. A bed at *Syon* House (*Invt., of 1670*) had hangings of 'white tufted Holland' and there was a bed with white linen hangings in a Prussian castle in 1695 but such examples are difficult to find. *Randle Holme* (Bk. III, Chap. XIV, p. 16) speaks of inner valances on beds being 'generally white silk or linen' but this is not borne out by contemporary inventories. The bed of John Evelyn and his wife had hangings lined with printed linen at the very end of the century (Inventory of Wotton House taken in 1702; deposited in the Library at Christ Church, Oxford).

93. e.g. 'two great southege curtyones for ye great windowe' (*Hengrave Invt., 1603*). Soultwich is listed among linen materials in seventeenth-century Books of Rates; so is buckram. There was a buckram curtain 'within the window' at *Hatfield Priory (Invt., 1629)*.

94. See F. W. Steer, *Farm and Cottage Inventories of Mid-Essex, 1635–1749*, Colchester, 1950. 'Dowles & Centin [Kenting]' sheets are listed separately from those of Holland in the *Tredegar Invt., 1688*.

95. e.g. *Hardwick Invt., 1601*.

96. At *Ham House (Invt., 1679)* the diaper cloths have patterns described as 'paviour work' (presumably chequered like marble paving), 'little rose', 'double rose' and 'holly'.

97. At Ham (see previous note) there were diaper table-cloths decorated with the Imperial crown, with 'flower and festoon border', with 'vine and grape', with 'fruit work', with 'forest worke' and with 'flowerpots'. The cloths with the Imperial crown were probably from Courtrai which lay in the Hapsburg territories; the same applies to the cloths 'wrought with a Spread Eagle' which are listed in the *Gilling Castle Inventory of 1594*, where there were also cloths with 'ye marigold and rose', and others 'with pictures'. At the same house in *1624* were some cloths 'wrought with mulberyes'.

98. *Chenies Invt., 1585, Dublin Castle invt., 1679,* and *Gosfield invt., 1638*.

99. *Ingatestone Invt., 1600*.

100. For instance, girthweb and sackcloth are among the materials listed in the bill John Casbert rendered after delivering a fine couch for use at Whitehall Palace in 1660–61 (R. W. Symonds, 'Charles II Couches, Chairs and Stools, Pt. I', *The Connoisseur*, February 1934).

101. *Ingatestone Invt., 1600*. 'The chamber [is] matted wth. cornishe matt somewhat worne.' Several other rooms in the house were fitted with Cornish matting.

102. *Johnson's Dictionary*, 1765, 'Mat'.

103. *Havard*, 'Natte'.

104. *Dyrham Invt., 1710*.

105. *Orange Invts.*, I, p. 114, and *Mazarin Invt., 1653*. The Dutch mat was large; it measured $5\frac{1}{2} \times 2\frac{3}{4}$ ells.

106. *Pepys' Diary*, 15 June, 1666. Miss Juliet Allen informs me that a bill for furnishing His Majesty's Bedchamber at Hampton Court in 1715 includes reference to a 'large Barbary mat' on which the bed stood.

107. *Kilkenny Castle Invt., 1684*. Kilkenny was rather grandly appointed at this time.

108. There were many Portugal mats at Kensington Palace (*Invt., 1699*) including one in the 'King's Low Bed Chamber'. In 1699 '4 larg Portugall Matts' were ordered for the Presence Chamber at Hampton Court for the throne to stand on (*Hampton Court Estimate, 1699*). Under William's bed in the Binnenhof at The Hague in 1700 was another (*Een Portugalise mat onder t' bedde*; *Orange Invts.*, I. p. 428). It is curious that nothing seems to be known of a great trade in mats in the seventeenth century although mats of *jonco* are still laid in Portuguese houses in summer. Perhaps 'Portugal mats' came from Africa, via Lisbon. *Savary des Bruslons* ('Jonc') says that 'nattes de jonc' were imported in his time from the Levant but makes no mention of Portugal.

109. *Tart Hall Invt., 1641*. The Arundel's matting was rolled up as it was not in use but Fouquet, not long after, had 'un roullean de bande de jong [jonc] servant à faire des tapis de pied' [a roll of rush runner for use as a foot carpet] (*Havard*, 'Natte').

110. At *Hardwick (Invt., 1601)* there were in store fifty pieces of 'wrought' gilt leather which presumably had a pattern and were finished, while there were thirty-four more pieces that were 'silverd but not fynished', which suggests they were blanks that could be used to repair existing hangings and merely had to be painted with a design to match.

111. Such trimming-strips may be seen on the gilt leather hangings in the Marble Dining Room at Ham House which were hung in the 1670s.

112. J. W. Waterer's excellent *Spanish Leather* (London, 1971) surveys the history of this material and explains the technique in greater detail. At Breda Castle in 1618 there were in store twenty-four skins of 'tapisserie de cuir d'Espagne' while the Audience Chamber had hangings of this material with a blue ground (*Orange Invts.*, I, p. 118).

113. In the splendidly furnished Gallery at Tart Hall (*Invt., 1641*) there were twelve black wooden chairs which had backs and seats covered in 'Rushia leather'. On the other hand an Oxford inventory of 1664 shows that eight chairs covered with 'Russia leather' cost only £1. 6s. 8d. (*Agius*, p. 78) while chairs thus covered were to be found in the 'Gentlewoman's

Eating Room' at Chapelizod (*Invt., 1679*). 'Turkey' leather was on some chairs at Oxford in 1669 (*Agius*, p. 78) and there were a dozen at Cowdray (*Invt., 1682*). A mattress (squab) of 'maroquin' is mentioned in the French royal accounts in 1681 (*Havard*, 'Maroquin').

114. *Northampton Invt., 1614*. The leather is stated to have been 'lined with silver and golde'; this can hardly be a reference to a lining and must mean it had lines on it of silver and gold—which suggests the 'printing' was in the same finish.

115. *Hardwick Invt., 1601*.

116. M. A. Havinden, *Household and Farm Inventories in Oxfordshire, 1550–90*, London, 1965, p. 113.

117. *Guiffrey, Inventaire*, p. 425. The silk was woven with flat silver strip in the ground.

118. *Hardwick Invt., 1601*.

119. 'Painting on Cloth is decayed,' wrote an observer in 1601, 'and not one hundred yards of new painted cloth made here in a year, by reason of so much Flanders pieces brought from thence.' (E. Croft-Murray, *Decorative Painting in England*, London, 1962, p. 30).

120. *Dyrham Invt., 1703*.

121. Waterer, *op. cit.*, p. 63.

122. *Ibid.*, p. 63.

123. *Ibid.*, p. 57.

124. *Ibid.*, fig. 47.

125. C. A. Weigert, *La tapisserie française*, Paris, 1956; also the Catalogue of an exhibition of French drawings from the Bibliothèque Nationale held in 1950 at the National Museum, Stockholm. *Savary des Bruslons*, under 'Tontisse', says Audran's establishment was at the Luxembourg.

126. *Havard*, 'Papier Peint'. See also C. C. Oman, *Catalogue of Wall-papers*, Victoria and Albert Museum, London, 1929, pp. 10–11.

127. E. A. Entwisle, *The Book of Wallpaper*, Bath, 1970, p. 22.

128. There was, for example, The Blew Paper Warehouse at Aldermanbury, in the City of London, at the end of the century which claimed that it 'sold the true sorts of figured paper hangings in pieces of twelve yards long, and others of the manner of real tapestry, and in imitation of Irish stitch [see p. 125] and flowered damask and also of marble & other coloured wainscot . . .' (Oman, *op. cit.*, pp. 2–4). Flemish and English harpsichord-makers frequently used papers for dressing the insides of the cases of their instruments in the seventeenth century. The

formal pattern of confronted dolphins printed in black on white paper which was used by the Antwerp firm of Ruckers on the keyboard-surrounds of their harpsichords and spinets is well known, but papers grained like wood and strips of gilt embossed paper resembling gilt gesso ornament that may be seen on such instruments also help to give us some idea of what seventeenth century wallpapers looked like.

129. *Pepys' Diary*, 8 January, 1665–6.

130. Edward Phillips, *New World of Words, or, Universal English Dictionary*, 1706.

131. C. R. Rivington, *The Stationers' Company*, London, 1883.

132. See *D.E.F.*, 'Beds' fig. 25, and J. Fowler and J. Cornforth, *op. cit.*, Pl. IX.

133. Very many of the textile materials we have been discussing could be embroidered. However, embroidery is usually most effective on a plain ground, rather than one with a pattern.

134. e.g. A. F. Kendrick, *English Needlework*, London, 1933; J. L. Nevinson, *Catalogue of English Domestic Embroidery of the 16th and 17th Centuries*, Victoria and Albert Museum, London 1938; P. Wardle, *Guide to English Embroidery*, Victoria and Albert Museum, London, 1970; G. F. Wingfield-Digby, *Elizabethan Embroidery*, London, 1963; L. de Farcy, *La Broderie du XIe siècle jusqu'au nos jours*, Paris, 1890.

135. Viscountess Dorchester bequeathed to her daughter 'my Irishe stitched furniture for a bedd' (*Gosfield Invt., 1638*).

136. Inventory of Chastleton House, Gloucestershire, 1633, kindly shown me by Mrs Alan Clutton-Brock. We have also the evidence of the Blew Paper Warehouse (see note 128), the trade-plate of which mentions 'Irish Stitch' as being one of the wallpaper patterns they sold while a roll of zig-zag patterned paper is displayed prominently on the counter.

137. Professional embroidery was not in those days anything like the female preserve that it was to become.

138. *Randle Holme*, Bk. III, Chap. XIV, p. 16.

139. Some fringe at Ham House, which is almost certainly the 'gould embroidered fringe' from the Queen's State Bed, has rosettes and bows of white vellum strip amid the rich spirals and loops of metal thread and the tufts of salmon-pink and cream-coloured silk.

140. e.g. The Duchess of Lauderdale's bed at *Ham House* (*Invt., 1679*) had 'campaign fringe'.

However, *campanes* could also mean the baggily gathered pleat hanging down between swags of material on valances or pelmets (see Plate. 144).

141. *Savary des Bruslons*, 'Frange'. See also *Havard*, 'Crépine' and 'Mollet'.

142. Thus a French inventory lists some red cloth bed-hangings that were trimmed with 'grand et petit frange' (*Du Boisgelin Invt., 1688*).

143. A Parisian bed in Sweden has rich silver lace trimming along the lower edges of its valances and these are described in a Swedish inventory of the period as '*krepiner*' (Åke Setterwall, 'Ulrika Eleonora d.ä's. paradsäng', *Gripsholm och des Konstskatter*, Stockholm, 1956).

144. Gabrielle d'Estrées had a splendid bed that was 'tout passementé de clinquant d'argent'. *Clinquant* was flat metal strip and the *passementerie* on her bed was therefore presumably of lace made up with such strip (*Havard*, 'Clinquant').

145. Some black and white damask hangings on a bed at *Hardwick* (*Invt., 1601*) were 'layde about with golde lace and golde frenge, and golde lace down the middest', while the 'Best Bed' was likewise 'layde with golde lace about the edges', while it had 'twist downe the seames' which probably means 'snailing fringe'.

146. The Countess of Shrewsbury's bed at *Hardwick* (*Invt., 1601*) had hangings 'stript' with lace; the bed-hangings in the Duke's Chamber at *Cockesden* (*Invt., 1626*) were 'stript with yealloew and redd lace'. At the end of the century, *Celia Fiennes* (p. 256) saw the State Bed at Windsor and described its green velvet hangings as 'strip'd down very thick with gold . . . lace of a hands breadth'.

147. The invalid chair specially created for Philip II of Spain (d. 1598) was padded with horsehair and quilted. John Casbert was supplying Charles II with chairs which had 'curled haire to fill the chaire backs' in 1660–61 (R. W. Symonds, 'Charles II Couches, Chairs and Stools', *The Connoisseur*, January and February, 1934) and Parisian upholsterers were certainly using *crin* for stuffing chairs by the 1670s (*Havard*, 'Crin'). The best horsehair apparently came from Ireland or from Holland; the Muscovite produce was thought to be less good. The curling of horsehair was most successfully carried out in Paris and at Rouen although the French conceded that the Dubliners were also good at it. (*Savary des Bruslons*, 'Crin' and 'Crespir de Crin').

NOTES TO CHAPTER VI

1. e.g. 'History of Vulcan' (*Ham Invt., 1679*); five pieces of 'new Flanders hangings with a storye' (*Ingatestone Invt., 1600*); 'tapestries of imagery' (*Lauderdale London Invt., 1679*); 'with personages' (*Hardwick Invt., 1601*).

2. 'foure pieces of fforrest worke hangings' were in Colonel Tollemache's room at Ham House (*Invt., 1679*) which was not one of the principal bedchambers. The Earl of Northampton (*Invt., 1614*) had some hangings of 'buskedge with redd and white and yelowe roses and bunches of grapes in the borders' as well as some 'busted hangings of a larger sort' and others 'of hunting worke'. It is possible that these were in fact of the dornix or *tapisserie de Bergame* class but they could also have been tapestries decorated with *boscage*(or *bocage*, as it is rendered in modern French). Some 'buscage tapestry' is listed with other tapestries in the *Syon Inventory of 1670*, although the collection also included some 'greenworke hangings' and some 'greenleafe hangings'. *Bossages* or *boschagies* are often mentioned in Dutch inventories of the late seventeenth century in a context where 'verdure tapestries' would seem an appropriate translation.

3. Painted hangings might also fall into the same category. The rooms of the Grand Apartement at Versailles, and the Grande Galerie, all apparently had alternative sets of tapestry hangings and painted hangings. They were designed specially to fit the rooms concerned. In the cases where large scenes painted on gilt leather were special commissions, they too fall into this small category (see note 14, below).

4. Pictorial tapestries were usually designed in a series with different scenes. Numerous weavings could be executed from these designs, or 'cartoons' as they were called, and a series might remain popular for many decades. A set of tapestries woven after the designs might not necessarily comprise all the scenes of the original series.

5. Cronström informs us that one could obtain half-width borders of *brocatelle de Venise* (*Tessin-Cronström Correspondence*, letter from Paris, 7 January, 1695).

6. The 'pane' or rectangle of the field of such hangings was 'impaned' with the secondary material but it is by no means always clear which of the two materials mentioned in an entry

concerning this kind of hanging is the main one. Did the room 'hanged with payned red and yellow damaske hangings' (*Tart Hall Invt., 1641*) have a panel of red damask framed by yellow or the reverse? Or was the damask red and yellow, with a framing of some quite other and unspecified material? At Ham House the 'Yellow Bedchamber' had hangings of yellow damask, fringed '& paind with blew mohair', i.e. empaned with blue silk (*Ham Invt., 1679*). Some of the Ham hangings are described as being 'paned and bordered' which suggests that 'paned' essentially meant that the rectangular panels were produced by alternate bands of material. But even so they are likely to have had a border at the bottom and probably at the top as well.

7. The hangings at Ham (*Invt.*, c. *1654*) were of 'blew perpetuanae' and gilt leather. At Gosfield (*Invt., 1638*) there was 'a sute gilt leather and greene cloth hangings for my Ladies closett', and the Banqueting House in the garden at Cowdray (*Invt., 1682*) had similar hangings made up with green printed paragon.

8. Le Comte de Cosnac, *Les riches du Palais Mazarin*, Paris, 1884, p. 787. Mazarin had several such sets with columns. They were so valuable that they were provided with loose covers of 'toille rouge' (a red material of linen or cotton rather than wool) and with a set of Beauvais serge covers in which they could lie when folded away in store.

9. Daniel Cronström, advising Count and Countess Piper in Stockholm in 1695, told them that 'l'on pourroit prendre un camelot couleur de feu et y faire des pilastres, ou montans, de brocatelle vert et aurore, ou violet et aurore, ou bleu et aurore, ou blanc au lieu d'aurore. L'on pourroit aussi prendre des satins de Turin et y faire des colonnes torses et des bordures ou frises, découppées suivant le dessein de M. Bérain. Tout cela seroit propre, nouveau et d'un goût nouveau' [one might take a flame-coloured camlet and on it make pilasters of green or pink brocatelle, or of blue and pink, or white instead of pink. One might also take a Turin satin and on it set spiralling columns or friezes cut out after designs by Mr Bérain. All this would be appropriate, new and in the latest taste] (*Tessin-Cronström Correspondence*, Letter of 7 January 1695).

10. Exceptions would be tapestry, *tapisserie de Bergame*, gilt leather and chintz.

11. *Tart Hall Invt., 1641*. It was of 'red & red and yellow damaske with a deep Fringe at the bottome & a narrow one at ye top'.

12. It is scalloped and has a border of braid accentuating the lobed edges, while a gathered band is stitched across the face of each lappet to form a simple pattern. Cronström (see note 9, above) advised that 'Si les déoupures ou gallons vous paroissent trop riches nous ne ferons qu'une campane,' which was a gathered valance 'qui regnera sous la corniche en haut, tout au tour de la chambre, galonné d'un petit bordé et d'un petit gallon d'argent, et qui sera couppée en festoon ou portique ... Les campanes faites et gallonnées sont maintenant si fort à la mode qu'on voit quasy que cela.' [If the cut-out ornaments or galloons seem too overloaded, we will merely make a *campane*... which runs round the cornice at the top, right round the room. It is trimmed with a narrow edging and a narrow silver galloon, and will be cut out like a festoon or arcading ... Made up valances with galloon are nowadays very much in fashion so that one hardly sees anything else.]

13. Cronström (see note 9, above) maintains that 'le velours n'est pas de toute saison' although perhaps in Stockholm 'nostre climat froid pourroit vous permettre l'usage du velours en hyver comme en esté'.

14. Cronström (see note 9, above) wrote that 'Mon avis n'est point de meubler la salle de cuir doré ... Parce que cela n'est point de toute saison, du moins selon la mode d'icy.' [My advice is not to hang the main room with gilt leather ... Because it is not at all suited for all seasons, at least, not according to the fashion here.] He advises the Pipers to use instead brocatelle or tapestry, or the camlet hangings with *découpage* mentioned in note 9. Mention should here be made of the large hangings, made up of many skins of gilt leather, on which large scenes similar to those on pictorial tapestries were painted. There is a famous set at Dunster Castle which includes a scene related to one designed for a Brussels tapestry by Julius van Egmont in 1661 but one does not get the impression such hangings were at all common in Britain. A Flemish artist arrive in Scotland in 1638 claiming that he had been trained in Rome in a new method of 'making great designs and representing histories upon leather hangings in chiaro scuro' but whether he produced anything of the sort in this country is not known (R. K.

Marshall, *Life in the Household of the Duchess of Hamilton*, 1636–1716, London, 1973, p. 41). In the Swedish Royal collection there is a superb set of gilt leather hangings with scenes depicting the Siege of Vienna by the Turks in 1688. One of the Dunster hangings is illustrated in Plate 105.

15. At Cowdray, which was appointed in an old-fashioned manner when the *Inventory* was taken *in 1682*, there were turkeywork hangings in four important rooms including the Great Dining Room, the Great Withdrawing Room and her ladyship's chamber. Tallement de Réaux (*Historiettes*, written 1657–59, Paris, 1834–40, III, p. 69) tells of Madame de Rohan's closet which was 'tout tapissé par haut et par bas de moquette'. For a while, he tells us, 'c'etoit là que la société faisoit ses conversations . . . et on appeloit cette cabale La Moquette'. There was a room at Dyrham (*Invt., 1703*) which was hung with 'striped plush'; and a Swedish account of 1706 refers to hangings for a room of red Haarlem *trippe* (see p. 112) but this was not a common material for wall-hangings.

16. *Tart Hall Invt., 1641*. The Great Chamber, for instance, had 'freeze hangings . . . laced with two gold galowne [galloon] laces in each space' which suggests they were plain with a panelled effect created with the gold braid. The frieze hangings in the Withdrawing Room were 'laced with parchment lace of gold' while those in 'My Lady's Chamber' had 'little silver laces in each seame and round the top.'

17. There was one in the old building at Tart Hall (*Invt., 1641*) and another at Dyrham (*Invt., 1703*).

18. *Havard*, 'Paillassons'.

19. *Havard*, 'Natte'.

20. *Ibid.*

21. J. Evelyn, *Kalendarium Hortense*.

22. *Havard* 'Matlassé', quoting Dufort de Cheverny.

23. Some gilt leather hangings from the 1670s and still on the walls at Ham House are fixed in this manner. The silk hangings painted by Bailly with 'toutes les victoires du Roy tres bien representé' which were provided from some of the principal rooms at Versailles had frames made for them by the joiner Prou (*Havard*, 'Peintre sur toile'). Some gilt leather hangings were put up at Dyrham in 1703 after instructions had been given that 'the opportunity of wett weather be taken'. In early August it must have been raining for we learn from a letter of 8 August that 'this is very good weather to putt up gilt leather'. (J. W. Waterer, *Spanish Leather*, London, 1971, p. 65.)

24. Mrs Delany tells us in 1750 that 'when you put up paper the best way is to have it pasted to the bare walls; when lined with canvas it always shrinks from the edges (*The Autobiography and Correspondence of Mary Granville, Mrs Delany*, ed. Lady Llanover, London 1861–62, p. 562). See also E. A. Entwisle, *The Book of Wallpaper*, London, 1954, p. 83. A writer in 1699 explained that, by his time, some wallpapers came in rolls and were therefore 'managed like wollen hangings' which means pasted to canvas and nailed to stretchers (Entwisle, p. 22).

25. See *Havard*, 'Dessus de Porte.'

26. *Cowdray Invt., 1682* and *Hardwick Invt., 1601*.

27. In the Gage inventory of 1556 (*Sussex Archaeological Collections*, XLV, 1892).

28. *Mazarin Invt., 1653*.

29. *Celia Fiennes*, p. 153.

30. *Dyrham Invt., 1710*.

31. In the early part of the century, when window curtains were still comparatively rare, there was a tendency to spell it out—two dornix curtains 'for the windows' were in 'The Nobleman's Chamber' at Chatsworth (*Invt., 1601*), and a Cockesden (*Invt., 1610*) there were 'for the wyndoes, 2 curteans of greene cotton'. Later the entries are made quite simply as 'window curtaines'.

32. 'Windowe peeces' are listed with window-curtains in the inventory of Kenilworth of 1584 (J. O. Halliwell, *Ancient Inventories . . .*, London, 1854). A distinction is made between the 'window-cloths' of 'arras' in the Great Chamber at Hengrave (*Invt., 1603*) and the 'two great southege [a linen material] curtyons for ye great window' in the same room. The 'sarges de Reins pour fenestres' (Rheims serge) mentioned in a French document of 1316 as well as the 'toile pour les fenestres de la chambre du Roy' required in 1359–60 for King Jean of France when he was held captive in England could both have been for window-pieces rather than curtains as we would understand them (*Havard*, 'Rideau' and 'Courtine'). Note is made in the English royal accounts in about 1470 of a payment to 'Rauf Underwood, wyre drawer, for iij and a quart'on of wyre for to hang verdours against the grete bay windowe in the Quenes old chamber' (S. W. Beck, *The Draper's Dictionary*, London, 1884, 'Verdure'). These

verdure tapestries could hardly have been made to draw on rings so were presumably hooked in place. The 'window cloth' of arras at Hengrave was probably fixed in a similar manner. The same applies to the 'two wyndow clothes of tapistry worke' at Henham (*Invt., 1602*), and to the 'rideau de tapisserie unie, servant au devant d'une croizée' [a curtain of plain tapestry for use in front of a window] mentioned in a French inventory of 1628 (see *Havard, 'Rideau'*).

33. The earliest certain reference so far published seems to be in a French inventory of 1380 where a 'courtine bleue de toille, qui se tire devant le fenestre' [blue curtain of linen [?] which may be drawn in front of the window] is mentioned (*Havard, 'Courtine'*). The word 'rideaux' came into general use in France early in the seventeenth century.

34. For example, at Ingatestone (*Invt., 1600*) there were 'three curtaines of grene saye to the wyndowes' in the Garden Chamber with 'three curtaine rodds to them'. Likewise at Walton (*Invt., 1624*) there was 'a dornix window curtaine & an iron rod for it'.

35. The *Inventory of Ham House*, drawn up about *1654* when the house was probably very much in the state it had been in before the Civil War, shows that several rooms there had window-curtains *en suite* with the wall-hangings. The fact that unity was stressed at Ham at that stage may reflect a connection with the thinking of Inigo Jones, working through Francis Cleyn (see p. *54*). When the house was re-decorated in the 1670s, the curtains were not made to match the hangings (see *Ham Invt., 1679*).

36. See *CIBA Review*, No. 126.

37. *Ham Invt., c. 1654* (see note 35 concerning its date). In the Parlour, which was one of the principal rooms, there was a pair of window-curtains of red cloth bordered with gilt leather 'and the curtaine rod'. The Countess of Dysart, later to become the Duchess of Lauderdale, likewise had a pair of divided curtains (with only one rod) in her bedchamber. There was apparently a set of divided curtains at Ingatestone already in 1600 (*Invt.*), which are described as old and with 'a curtaine rodd the length of the wyndow', but this is likely to have taken this form for purely practical reasons.

38. *Le Mercure Galant*, 1673, III, p. 203.

39. *Dublin Castle Invt., 1679*, and *Ham Invts., 1677, 1679* and *1683*.

40. A series of cords attached to the lower edge of

the curtains passed loosely through guide-rings at the back of the curtain and up over pulleys at the top of the window embrasure, or through a pulley-board, and then down to a cleat or pair of 'cloak pins' to which the cords could be tied so as to adjust the curtains at the right height when pulled up.

41. P. Verlet, *Versailles*, Paris, 1961, p. 258.

42. *Hampton Court Estimates, 1699*. One item concerns some white silk damask for window-curtains that were being ordered for His Majesty's Closet. In addition ninety-seven yards of 'white small silk stringe to drawe them up' were required together with two large white tassels which must have gone on the ends of the draw-strings.

43. The estimate mentioned in the previous note also referred to 'covering cornices'. Thirty yards of edging were required for this in addition to the silk damask that would have been needed.

44. *Havard, 'Rideaux'*. In a Swedish inventory of 1689 a window-curtain is described as being 'with a pelmet to it' (*Medh en kappa der til; Karlson*, pp. 49–50). There were matching 'window-curtains & Valens' at Dyrham in 1703 (*Invt.*).

45. *Celia Fiennes*, p. 345.

46. Dornix window-curtains are mentioned, for instance, in the *Hardwick, Chatsworth, Cockesden* and *Walton Inventories of 1600, 1601, 1610* and *1624* respectively.

47. *Ingatestone Invt., 1600*.

48. See note 32, above.

49. *Hardwick Invt., 1601*. This double set of curtains was in The Shipp Chamber, a relatively splendid room.

50. *Hengrave Invt., 1603*; see note 32, above.

51. *Hatfield Priory Invt., 1629*. The large curtain and rod may have been across the mouth of a window bay. Clive Wainwright has drawn my attention to a note by John Evelyn concerning the 'great bay windows jetting out within' gentlemen's houses in former times which had 'commonly a curtaine to draw before them for privacy'. Apparently people laid large cushions on the window-seats and used to retire there and 'discourse in private of business' (J. Aubrey, 'Monumenta Brittanica, MS Top Gen C.25, f.164 verso; Bodleian Library, Oxford).

52. *Cockesden Invt., 1610* and *Edington Invt., 1665*. The 'ffrench . . . curtaines' must have been in some way distinctive: could they possibly have been early specimens of the pull-up variety?

53. *Tart Hall Invt., 1641.*

54. Silk curtains were most frequently made of taffeta, especially the thin version known as sarcenet. Particularly grand rooms might have curtains of silk damask or, more rarely, of satin.

55. White sunlight-excluding curtains were not always plain white. A set at Ham House (*Invt., 1679*) was of grey and white striped taffeta and the stripes were no doubt intricately patterned; another was of white and purple chequered Indian sarcenet.

56. *Cowdray Invt., 1682.* The bed-hangings, wall-hangings, chair-covers and carpet, as well as the window-curtains, were all of the same material.

57. *Dyrham Invt., 1703.*

58. *Havard,* 'Damas'.

59. *Mazarin Invt., 1653.*

60. *Kilkenny Invt., 1684.*

61. In 1642 one could apparently order sets of rings by post—according to G. Hazelius Berg whose *Gardiner och Gardinuppsättningar*, Nordiska Museet, Stockholm, 1962, is still by far the best survey of the history of window-curtains. Being in Swedish and with only a very short English summary the information in it is unfortunately not readily accessible to most people.

62. At Copenhagen Castle in 1669, the windows of the Queen's Bedchamber were fitted with eight rollers 'on which are to roll the Dutch mats that shield the Queen's Chamber against the sun' (Hazelius Berg, *op. cit.*, p. 87).

63. *Ibid.* The blinds seem to have been of blue linen and had two cords.

64. Ambrose Heal, *The London Furniture Makers . . .*, London, 1952, p. 15 (illus.). John Brown's painted blinds must have been the successors of the 'painted sashes' that are discussed in the next paragraph, and the ancestors of the roller blinds printed with scenes that were so popular in the nineteenth century.

65. *Tessin's Visit, 1687*, p. 35. His description reads 'couverts d'satin sur lequel l'on a peint des branchissages et que se ferme à ressort, et que l'on tire en haute par moyen d'une corde à costé' [covered with satin on which scrollwork is painted and which are closed with a spring [catch?] and which may be pulled up by means of a cord at the side].

66. *Havard,* 'Jalousie'.

67. Smith states that the materials were wetted and then strained onto the frame, after which they were varnished 'so that they may appear all over clear and transparent'. Krünitz, in his *Oeconomiske Encyclopaedie* of 1777, explains how linen was treated with a mixture of Venetian turpentine, wax and tallow. Sashes covered with white silk were still being provided for windows at Osterley in the middle of the eighteenth century.

68. John Garret published in about 1670 *A Book of Six Large Land-skips* said to be 'fitting for sashes of windows' (see Leona Rostenberg, *English Publishers in the Graphic Arts, 1599–1700*, New York, 1963, p. 45). One could imitate stained glass windows, even down to the 'cames' of lead framing each quarry.

69. *Havard,* 'Chassis'. He also notes that, when the City of Lyons wished to honour a citizen in 1643, they undertook to do up his house in the smartest manner 'comme encores que les chassis tant de bois, pappier que vittres' [with, in addition, frames of wood fitted with paper and glass].

70. Hazelius Berg, *op. cit.*, p. 6. Dr Lars Sjöberg kindly informed me about the entry in the Stenbock accounts.

71. Andrew Clark, *The Life and Times of Anthony Wood, Antiquary, of Oxford, 1654–1695, described by himself*, Oxford, 1891, III, p. 271 and index, V, p. 208.

72. *The Spectator*, No. 510.

73. *Havard,* Paille'.

74. W. B. Rye, *England as seen by Foreigners*, London, 1865, p. 104.

75. Rye, *op. cit.*, p. 80.

76. Rushes are still strewn on the floor of the Council Chamber on important occasions at Trinity House, Hull, as they have been since time immemorial. The rushes were originally cut from reed-beds on the Humber but now have to come from further afield.

77. See *Havard,* 'Natte'. Matting was also much used in Sweden at the time (see *Karlson*, pp. 52–3) and one may presume that the fashion was widespread on the Continent.

78. *Walton Invt., 1624* and *Chatsworth Invt., 1601*. We are told that at Ingatestone (*Invt., 1600*) 'the chamber [is] matted wth. Cornishe matt somewhat worn'.

79. Rye, *op. cit.*, p. 204. The Duke's actual words were 'alle Gemächer und Galerien waren mit geflochtenen Decken aus Wintzen belegt'.

80. *Cowdray Invt., 1682.*

81. Listed together with a coarse cloth covering

the stairs at Dyrham (*Invt., 1710*) was 'a flore matt' which was clearly an insignificant object. There were also '2 church flore matts' in the Chapel.

82. *Pepys' Diary*, 15 June 1666.

83. For example, the Duke and Duchess of Ormonde had two 'Portugal mats' in the Drawing Room at Kilkenny Castle (*Invt., 1684*) and William III had one in his 'Low Bed Chamber' (i.e. his private bedroom) at Kensington Palace (*Invt., 1699*). '4 larg Portugall Matts' were laid on the daïs in the Presence Chamber at Hampton Court in 1699 (*Estimates*) and nailed to the flooring round the edge through a galloon.

84. There was, for instance a 'tapis de moquette de trois lais de large et trois aulnes et demye de long, fon[d]s jaune' at the Château de Turenne (*Havard*, 'Moquette'). The three widths were stitched together (making a total of about a yard and a half) while the carpet was three and a half ells wide. Cardinal Mazarin (*Invt., 1653*) had 'un grand tapis de moquette de quatre aunes trois quart de long, large de trois laiz, faisant une aune et demie'.

85. *Guiffrey, Inventaire*, II, p. 304.

86. *Hardwick Invt., 1601*

87. *Cockesden Invt., 1626.*

88. *Dyrham Invt., 1610* and *Guiffrey, Inventaire*, I, p. 414.

89. The equivalent German word is *Teppich*. When Constantijn Huygens visited Postdam in 1686, he saw there a workshop producing 'Tisch und Fussteppichen' (Table and Foot Carpets); they were presumably of moquette (*Stengel*, p. 52).

90. *Stengel*, p. 50.

91. The four Oriental carpets (two Turkish, one Persian and a silk carpet that must have been Persian, see p. 109 at Ham House were all in the Wardrobe Room when the Inventory was taken in 1679 although one was for a while noted as being in the drawing room.

92. In 1578 the King of Navarre had 'neuf tapis velus [i.e. pile carpets], desquels les deux sont grand pour servir soubs les pieds, et les aultres sept estoient pour servire à la table et buffet' [nine pile carpets of which two are large for laying on the floor, the other seven being for laying on tables and buffets] (F. Michel, *Recherches sur le commerce, la fabrication, et l'usage des etoffes de soie, d'or et d'argent . . . pendant le moyen age*, Paris, 1852–4, p. 165). The Duke of Pomerania asked

the art-dealer and agent, Philip Hainhofer, to secure for him some Turkish carpets of such a size that two or three would cover the entire floor of a room ('in der grösse dass zwei oder drei ein Ganzes Zimmer an der Erde bedeckten'; see *Stengel*, p. 50).

93. See pp. 110–111.

94. e.g. the thirteen 'grand tapis . . . facon de Levant, faits à la Savonnerie pour servir à la Gallerie d'Apollon du Louvre' (*Guiffrey, Inventaire*, p. 387).

95. In 1633 the King of Denmark ordered ten large chairs to be brought from Holland for some special festivity and apparently had each chair placed on its own individual carpet of tapestry (G. Garde, *Danske Silkebroderede Laeredsduge fra 16 og 17 arhundrede*, Copenhagen, 1961, p. 186).

96. *Mazarin Invt., 1653.* See p. 355 for a note on 'hautelisse'.

97. *Savary des Bruslons*, 'Tapis'.

98. *Hengrave Invt., 1603* and *Gosfield Invt., 1638.*

99. *Guiffrey, Inventaire*, II, p. 304.

100. *Ham Invt., 1679.* This was rendered as 'Two leathers to cover ye inlaid floore' in 1677.

101. *Tart Hall Invt., 1641.*

102. *Mazarin Invt., 1653.* It is unlikely the carpet was of scorched leather (see p. 120).

103. *Kensington Palace Invt., 1697.*

NOTES TO CHAPTER VII

1. Penelope Eames ('Documentary Evidence Concerning the Character and Use of Domestic Furnishings in England in the Fourteenth and Fifteenth Century', *Furniture History*, Vol. VII, note 10) has explained that, during the late mediaeval period, the 'tester' was the upright piece at the head (*tête* or *teste* in French) of the bed while the roof-like component above the bed was called the 'ceilour'. The French still called the latter the '*ciel*' in the seventeenth century. By this period, the English word 'ceilour' had largely fallen out of use and what had formerly been the 'tester' then became the 'head-cloth' or 'head-board'. That there was room for confusion even at the time is shown by the note concerning a set of bed-hangings that were sent down to Knole in 1624 which comprised five curtains, the valances and the 'test and tester' (see Charles J. Phillips, *History of the Sackville Family*, London, 1928, p. 317). Nevertheless there is absolutely no doubt that the word 'tester' almost invariably

meant the roof-like component in the seventeenth-century parlance. A 'half-tester' bed was one in which the tester only projected so far from the wall as to cover half the length of the sleeping-surface.

2. 'Quant les lits ne portoient que six pieds de long, sur autant de large, on leur donnoit le nom couchettes; mais lorsqu'ils étoient de huit pied et demi sur sept et demi, ou be onze sur dix ou de douze sur onze en ce cas là on les appeloit des couches' [When beds were only six feet long, by as much wide, they were simply given the name *couchettes*; but when they were eight and a half feet by seven and a half or eleven by ten or twelve by eleven, in that case they called them *couches*] (Sauval, *Antiquités de Paris*, written before 1669–70, Paris, 1724, II, p. 230).

3. *Charles I Invts., 1649–51* and *Havard*, 'Couches'.

4. *Havard*, 'Couche'.

5. *Turenne Invt., 1615*.

6. It was 'façon de camp', i.e. a field bed (see below) which 'se ploye et ferme' [which folds and shuts up] and was 'femant à quatre vis' [closed [locked in position?] with four screws] (*Havard*, 'Couche'). At the Brussels residence of the Prince of Orange in 1568 two ladies attending the Princess had 'Deux litz de camp en fachon de couches, avecq leurs fers de gordines, de bois' [two campbeds of wood in the form of *couches* with their iron curtain-rods] (*Orange Invts.*, I, p. 33).

7. The Germans called it a *Schaub-bette*, a 'shove-bed'. A French mediaeval inventory of 1471 refers to 'une petite couchete rouleresse' and another to 'une petite couchete roulante' (*Havard*, 'Couche'). The inventory of the Prince of Orange, mentioned in the previous note, refers to 'une couche rollé', 'une petite rolette' (pp. 29 and 32). The inventory of Breda Castle of 1597–1603 notes a gilt bed 'met rollebedt', with its rolling-bed (p. 76).

8. *Havard*, 'Couche'.

9. In the best bed the squire must lie,
   And John in truckle-bed hard by
a contemporary poet tells us, while another speaks of a servant who 'lay at his master's feet in a truckel bed' (*O.E.D.*, 'Truckle bed').

10. Du *Boisgeslin Invt., 1668*. Cardinal Mazarin's guards also had beds consisting of a plank laid on trestles (*Mazarin Invt., 1653*).

11. *Hardwick Invt., 1601* and *Knole Invt., 1645*.

12. *Tart Hall Invt., 1641*.

13. *Mazarin Invt., 1653*. Was the 'sempter [sumpter] hanging upp by the bedd' listed with the 'standing bedsted ... wth. a waneskote tester' at Marton Hall (*Invt., 1605*) a similar embellishment? And what about the 'French bedd, the tester and vallance of fugured [figured] sattin ... with a French canopie suteable to it'? Was this also such a double-tiered affair (*Gosfield Invt., 1638*)?

14. Gabrielle d'Estrées' bed 'façon de camp' has already been mentioned. Cardinal Mazarin also owned a very splendid 'lict de campagne' of red damask (*Mazarin Invt., 1653*). Henri IV, was forced to sleep on a plain straw-filled palliasse on one occasion in 1615 when he had arrived at some place in the evening and 'son lit n'etoit pas venu'. In 1608 he is recorded as having helped his servants to 'plier son lit' before moving off to Saint-Cloud (*Havard*, 'Lit', quoting from Héroard's life of Henri IV).

15. Mazarin's bed (see previous note) had its own leather-bound travelling coffer. At Copenhagen Castle (F. R. Friis, *Kjøbenhavn's Slots Inventarium, 1638*, Samlinger til Dansk Bygnings- og Kunsthistorie, Copenhagen, 1872–8) there was an old box (ein alter Kasten) with 'darin ein Reise bette'—in it a travelling bed. *Karlson* (p. 135) mentions several such containers including one of sealskin.

16. For example, the Earl of Northampton (*Invt., 1614*) had a 'field bedstead of China worke blacke and silver with the arms of the Earle of Northampton upon the head-piece, the toppe and valance of purple velvett striped downe wth. silver laces and knottes of silver'.

17. e.g. 'the vallans wth. bells' on a field bed at Marton Hall (*Invt., 1605*).

18. A splendid field bed with black velvet and silver-lace hangings at Hardwick (*Invt., 1601*) had five 'guilt knops to stand on top of the bed'. It is difficult to imagine five finials being disposed otherwise than on a tester of hipped conformation like that shown in Plate 122.

19. The Earl of Northampton's field bed (see note 16 above) had eight cups with plumes as finials. Had it been a bed with a single slope, it would only have needed six finials.

20. e.g. the inventories of *Hatfield Priory (1629)*, the *Countess of Leicester (1634)* and *Knole (1645)*.

21. *Randle Holme*, Bk. III, Chap. XIV, p. 16.

22. e.g. at Hardwick, Henham, Marton, Cockesden (*Invts. of 1601, 1602, 1605* and *1610*).

23. *Dyrham Invt., 1703*, and Martin Lister, *A Journey to Paris*, London, 1699, p. 191.

24. The chief groups of designs were those published by Jacques Androuet Ducerceau and by Hans Vredeman de Vries (see S. Jervis, *Printed Furniture Designs before 1650*, Furniture History Society, 1974, pp. 25 and 29).

25. e.g. the 'standing bedstead ... wth. a waneskot tester' at *Marton (Invt. 1605)*.

26. The Duke's bed at Cockesden (*Invt. 1626*) was inlaid, for example. There were several carved and gilt bedsteads in important rooms at Hardwick (*Invt., 1601*), while at Chatsworth (*Invt., 1601*) a splendid bed is described as being 'with sondrie coulers and golde'.

27. Karlson, p. 149, believed that the *Ståndsäng* of contemporary Swedish inventories was a bed without a superstructure but this hardly squares with the evidence.

28. The bed mentioned in note 25, above, seems to confirm this.

29. *Unton Invt., 1595*.

30. *Marton Invt., 1605*.

31. *Kilkenny Invt., 1684*. There was a *lit en dome* in the French royal collection in 1675 (*Guiffrey, Inventaire*, p. 263).

32. Could the 'Dutch bed' mentioned in the will of Mary, Countess Rivers (1644) have been of this sort? (J. Watney *Sole Account of St Osyth's Priory, Essex*, London, 1871.)

33. An upholsterer working for the royal household in 1595 was engaged on 'new guilding the bolle of a canopie' (information kindly given me by Mr John Nevinson) while there was 'a great guilt demi ball for a canopy' at Tart Hall (*Invt., 1641*), and 'one round canopy head' at Knole (*Invt., 1645*).

34. 'One Crimson velvett Canapie ... wth. two rich Tafata changeable Trayned Curtaynes to it' (*Easton Invt., 1637*), and '2 longe traynes of greene taffety sarcenet ... belongeinge to the canopy' (*Cockesden, Invt., 1626*). The same term occurs in the *Gilling Invts., 1594*.

35. In the *Turenne Inventory of 1615* the beds are listed in groups, one of them being headed 'Pavillons'. One, of red damask trimmed with silver, had 'le chapiteau de velours Cramoisy' [the cap of crimson velvet] and a deep fringe 'en rond' [all round] as well as a 'pomme paincte de rouge ... avec son cordon de soie' [finial painted red ... with its red silk cord]. Another French inventory refers to 'ung pavillons' which had a 'pomme dorée au dessus'—a gilt knob on top

(*Thiret Invt., 1621*).

36. A. C. Fox-Davies, *The Book of Public Arms*, London, 1894, p. 816.

37. See Penelope Eames, *Mediaeval Furniture*, London, 1977, p. 83; also published as Vol. XIII of *Furniture History*, where this question is also discussed.

38. *Charles I Invts., 1649–51*. One could of course fit pull-up curtains to beds of a more elaborate nature. The Duchess of Ormonde's domed bed at Kilkenny (*Invt., 1684*) had 'nine pairs of strings and tassels to tie the curtains'.

39. The beds in the *Turenne Invt., of 1615* are grouped under 'Litz Completz', 'Litz à housse', 'Pavillons' and 'couchettes'. The first group presumably concerned beds of the massive kind; *pavillons* and *couchettes* have already been discussed.

40. *Havard*, 'Couchette'.

41. *Havard*, see under 'Linomple', because the bed had hangings of linen.

42. *Havard*, 'Bonnegraces' and 'Cantonnières'. A 'French bed' with 'cantoons' is listed in the *Charles I Inventories of 1649–51*. A royal bed in Sweden, that was apparently imported in 1620, was noted as having 'corner-pieces' (*hörn-styckar*) in 1655 (Åke Setterwall, 'Gustaf II och Maria Eleonoras Bilägersäng', in *Uppländsk Bygd*, Stockholm, *1940*).

43. *Ham Invt., 1679*.

44. William III's ambassador in Paris in 1698 reported home to his royal master that 'les lits ... que l'on fait ici ... sont tous carré par dehors, jusques au haut' [the beds ... that are made here ... are all square outside right to the top] and went on to stress that 'en haut ... ils ne sont pas plus large qu'au bas' [at the top ... they are no wider than at the base], unlike the fashionable form of bed in England which had a spreading cornice as well as furbellows and excrescences of all kinds (G. Jackson-Stops, 'William III and French Furniture', *Furniture History*, VII, 1971).

45. The famous cloth-of-gold bed at Knole which probably belonged to James II is of the French type, with no cornice but with valances that are fanciful in outline. Whether it was made in Paris or London is a question that has not yet been settled. See G. Jackson-Stops, 'The 6th Earl of Dorset's Furniture at Knole, II', *Country Life*, 9 June 1977. See also Plate 140 here.

46. '2 halfe headed bedsteads' are listed as being in the 'Gentlemen's Chamber' (i.e. the gentle-

men servants) in the Earl of Northampton's *Inventory of 1614*, and there was such a bed in a 'Servant's Chamber' at Knole (*Invt., 1645*).

47. e.g. 'a halfe headed bedstead with a canopie' (*Northampton Invt., 1614*); 'A half headed bedstead . . .,' 'A featherbed' etc., 'A watchett [light blue] perpetuana cannopie[,] Curtaynes of the same . . .' (*St Giles Invt., 1639*); at Gosfield (*Invt., 1638*) a bed of this sort had a 'round canopie' which was presumably of the normal conical form.

48. *Noordeinde Invt., 1633.*

49. *Tessin's Visit, 1687.*

50. *Havard, 'Lit'.*

51. There was a bed of this sort in Mazarin's collection (*Invt., 1653*). The tester was held up by means of 'quatre cordons servans à attacher le dict lict' [four cords serving to suspend the said gauze bed]. It had six curtains. A bed at Meudon was described as 'un lit a l'Impérial et à la duchesse' but it is not easy to say precisely what the last term meant (*Havard*, 'Imperiale' and 'Duchesse').

52. *Celia Fiennes*, p. 277.

53. Dean Goodwin provided a livery bedstead for his maid; it had a separate canopy. 'Inventory of W. Goodwin, Dean of Christ Church, Oxon., 1621' (Manuscript in the Bodleian Library; by kind permission of the Keeper of the Archives, Oxford University). The same combination was to be seen at Henham (*Invt., 1602*). The Bishop of Winchester (*Invt., 1618*) had a livery bed among his household goods valued at 3s. 4d. while his half-headed beds cost between 2s. and 3s.

54. *Hardwick Invt., 1601.* A pallet normally lay on the floor, perhaps on a mat, but the Hardwick pallets seem to have had some sort of framework because the bedclothes are listed as being 'in ye pallet[s]'.

55. *Countess of Leicester's Invt., 1634* and *Tart Hall Invt., 1641*. At the Prince of Orange's residence at The Hague in 1632 there was a servant's 'sleeping bench' or couch (*Een Slaepbanck voor Dunois, camerdiener; Orange Invts.*, I, p. 235).

56. *Dean Goodwin's Invt., 1618 loc. cit.* and *Havard*, 'Banc'.

57. *Ham Invt., 1683.*

58. *Stengel*, p. 138. There is an engraving by Abraham Bosse showing the beds (of the 'French bed' type) standing in rows in one of the wards. Incidentally, Hans Fugger's sons each had an 'eysernes Pettstatt' (an iron bedstead) when they

attended the University of Padua in the fifteenth century.

59. *Copenhagen Castle Invt., 1638.*

60. *Knole Invt., 1645* and *Guiffrey, Inventaire*, p. 122.

61. At Knole (*Invt., 1645*) there were three, for instance.

62. An Italian visitor to Sweden in 1674 noted that even quite humble citizens might sport a canopy; it was not a sign of rank (L. Magalotti, *Sverige under år 1674*, ed. Carl Magnus Stenbock, Stockholm, 1912).

63. A rich canopy bearing the arms of Anne of Denmark, the consort of James I who died in 1619, had as its complement a chair and long cushion with a footstool, two other ceremonial chairs and their footstools, six back chairs and twenty-two high stools—all with painted and gilded frames (*Charles I Invts., 1649–51*).

64. Cotgrave in fact explains that the French word 'daïs' meant a 'cloth of estate, canopie or heaven, that stands over the head of Princes' thrones' but could also mean 'the whole state or seat of estate'. He does not mention platforms at all.

65. In her will, Lady Dorchester mentioned her 'canopie couche . . . which did stand on my Gallerie att Westminster' (*Gosfield Invt., 1638*); there was a 'coutch . . . wth. 2 taffeta curtaines & a canopie to it' in the Lower Gallery at Hatfield Priory (*Invt., 1629*) and, at Tart Hall (*Invt., 1641*), a couch with canopy stood in the North Gallery. At Knole (*Invt., 1645*) one of the couches was described as having not only a tester and a head-cloth (but no curtains?) but had a separate and additional canopy with a pair of curtains and double valances over it. An inventory of the possessions of Amalia van Sohms, Princess of Orange, of about 1654–58, refers to a canopy belonging to a couch of red velvet which had two ball-finials above (*Een canaby offte rustbedde van root flueweel . . . twee gardijnen . . . twee bollen bovenop't caneby; Orange Invts.*, I, p. 275).

66. Charles I had 'one seate couch fashion' with a canopy (*Charles I Invts., 1649–51*). At Cockesden (*Invt., 1626*) the 'fayre couch chaire of black feegurd sattin' was furnished with a single footstool (as well as two small stools, presumably to flank the couch) which suggests that one sat centrally and with a support for the feet. The 'couch of crimson leather printed borderwise' in the *Northampton Inventory of 1614* had a long

cushion (the mattress or squab) and two short cushions which were probably disposed, one at each end, as in the Hardwick drawing. At Tart Hall (*Invt., 1641*) the 'couch of painted wood on some partes thereof' (i.e. partly painted, like the Hardwick couch) likewise had 'thereon a couch bed [mattress or squab] & two long cushions'.

67. Some couches that started life as double-ended ceremonial couches have had one end sawn off so as to turn them into day-beds, when the ceremonial form went out of fashion. This has happened to a couch in the Victoria and Albert Museum, for instance (W. 57–1953).

68. Molière, for instance, had a *lit de repos* with a *pavillon* of Indian chintz (*Havard*, 'Pavillon').

69. See P. Thornton, 'Couches, Canopies and Chairs of State', *Apollo*, October 1974, pp. 292–9.

70. *Thiret Invt., 1621.*

71. e.g. The 'Pearl Bed' at Hardwick (*Invt., 1601*) had 'tester, bed's head and double vallens of black velvet imbroidered with silver, golde and pearle' but the five curtains were of a black and white damask. Lady Dorchester (*Gosfield Invt., 1638*) bequeathed to her daughter 'my white taffeta satten flowered piece of stuffe and cloake of the same for a valance and cantoones for a bedd, and thirtie pounds in money to buy her damaske' which must have been to make up the remaining hangings. Incidentally, *Randle Holme* states that the inner valances of beds in his day were 'generally white silk or linen' although this is not confirmed by the evidence of inventories. (Bk. III, Chap., XIV, p. 16).

72. Examples from the end of the seventeenth century survive (Plate 98) but inventories confirm that the counterpoint was habitually richly ornamented. At Gilling Castle (*Invt., 1594*) his Lordship slept in a bed with 'a fayre counter pointe shadowed with silke' while the 'Best Bed' at Hardwick (*Invt., 1601*) had a counterpoint 'payned with cloth of gold and silver, and a brode golde lace and golde fringe about it, lyned with crimson sarcenet.'

73. The *Thiret Inventory of 1621* refers to a brown serge coverlet on a bed 'pendante jusques en bas avec les courtines' (i.e. hanging down to the same level as the lower edge of the curtains) but such an arrangement would of course disguise the base valances. Normally their lower edges lined up with those of the curtains while the counterpoint reached down only over the top of the base valances. Elaborate beds of the Marot

type sometimes had the edges of the bed-stock accentuated by a textile-covered board of fancy shape. In such cases the counterpoint was tucked in under the mattresses and did not hang down.

74. *Mazarin Invt., 1653.*

75. *Randle Holme* (Bk. III, Chap. XIV, p. 16) explained that the tester of a bed might have 'bobbs of wood gilt, or covered sutable to the curtaines'. Charles I ordered that 'five gilt cupps for a feild bedd' be sent for melting down in 1626 (C. C. Oman, *English Domestic Silver*, London, 1963, p. 183).

76. Mazarin had a bed of embroidered velvet topped with four *panaches* each consisting of fifty large, twenty-two medium, and twenty-three small ostrich plumes 'blanches fines' as well as four *aigrettes* (*Havard*, 'Aigrette').

77. A bed at Versailles in 1682 had plumes that were white and *couleur de feu* while the Maréchale de Humières had green, yellow and white feathers on her bed (*Havard*, 'Bouquet de Plume').

78. Madame de Maintenon's bed at Saint-Cloud was surmounted by four carved vases of flowers which were gilded and 'glacé de rouge'— probably lacquered with a red-stained varnish (*Havard*, 'Chambre'). In the Thiret mansion (*Invt., 1621*) there was in store a special case containing 'quatre boucquets en feuilliage servans à mectre sur le lict' [four bouquets with foliage for putting on the bed] which must have been of artificial flowers. *Havard* ('Bouquet de Plume') mentions a bed of 1694 with metal flowers: they were presumably painted.

79. Apart from the one illustrated, which is at Cotehele in Cornwall, a pair from a bed that no longer survives is at Skokloster in Sweden, and the form may be seen in several contemporary illustrations.

80. A rare instance was the bed with 'three peeces of Arras hangings' at Edington (*Invt., 1665*).

81. Several 'Arras Coverletts' were on beds in the house of a West Country squire in 1641 (*Devon Invts.*). It is possible that they were specially woven as coverlets but the 'large counter pointe of verders' on a bed at Gilling Castle (*Invt., 1594*) must have simply been a verdure tapestry laid over the bedclothes.

82. There were 'green and white Broccadella' hangings on a bed at Petworth (*Invt., 1670*), however.

83. e.g. Lady Dorchester had a fine bed of 'purple

cloth embroydred in spaces' line with yellow taffeta that was valued at £150 (*Gosfield Invt., 1638*) and in 'My Lady's Old Chamber' at Cowdray (*Invt., 1682*) the bed was 'hung with embroidered cloth lined with clouded sattin'.

84. Lady Dorchester bequeathed to her daughter, among other items that she seems to have treasured, 'my tawny imbroidered cloth bedd which was wrought in my house' (*Gosfield Invt., 1638*). Celia Fiennes (p. 68) noted that Lady Burghley 'used to lye in winter' in a green velvet bed embroidered by her mother, the Countess of Devonshire.

85. The bed-hangings of 'wrought greene usted [worsted]' in the 'Greene Wrought Chamber' at Tredegar (*Invt., 1688*) and those of 'white dimity wrought wth. green worsted' in 'Young Master's' room ten years later (*Invt., 1698*) may have been of this distinctive class, as may have been another set of 'dymathy' hangings at Syon House (*Invt., 1670*) that were 'wrought with redd worsted'.

86. *Ham Invt., 1683*. The bed was the eldest son's; it had six main curtains along with the other bed-hangings of blue velvet and a 'tower de leet' of blue taffeta. A bed at Dieren in 1683 had silk hangings and a 'tour de lit' as well (*Orange Invts.*, I, p. 388).

87. Hans Andersen's fairy-tale about the princess who could feel a pea through twenty-four matresses was only a slight exaggeration. Many fine beds had four but lowly people had to make do with one filled with rough materials.

88. The Great of Bed of Ware, in the Victoria and Albert Museum, has holes bored into the side rails of the bedstock, through which the cords were threaded. Many early seventeenth-century beds have this feature.

89. *Randle Holme* (Bk. III, Chap. XIV, p. 16) lists the parts of a bed and mentions 'Mat or sack-cloth bottom.' There was a 'London mat' on a bed at Marton Hall (*Invt., 1605*) and a Cornish one on a bed at Ingatestone (*Invt., 1600*).

90. When a German prince slept in what must have been the 'Great Bed' at Ware in 1612, he told how 'je fus couché dans un lict de plume de cigne qui avoit huict pieds de largeur' [he slept in a bed of Swansdown which was eight feet wide] (W. B. Rye, *England as seen by Foreigners*, London, 1865, p. 62). See also *Havard*, 'Coite'.

91. King Christian IV, the brother of Anne of Denmark (the wife of James I of England) had an eiderdown on his camp-bed during his cam-

paigns in Germany during the Thirty Years' War (E. Fischer, *Linväverämbetet i Malmö*, Lund, 1959), and Pepys (*Diary, 9 September, 1605*) records how he 'lay the softest I ever did in my life, with a down bed after the Danish manner *upon* me' (my italics).

92. *Havard*, 'Matelas' and 'Bourralisse'. He cites a reference of 1697 to 'un matelas de bourralisse couverte de toile rayé' [a mattress of flock covered with striped linen]. In the *Du Boisgeslin Inventory of 1688* a bed is described as having both a wool and a 'boure' mattress.

93. *Devon Invts.*

94. The island of Chios apparently produced 'cotton wool etc., and also coarse wool, to make beds' (Gasper Campion, *Discourse of the Trade of Chio*, 1569).

95. It was remarked upon at the time when Henri IV had had to sleep on a straw-filled mattress on one occasion in 1598, and French courtiers considered it almost insufferable that one should have to sleep on such mattresses when staying at Saint-Germain in the middle of the century. By the end of the century such a thing would have been inconceivable (*Havard*, 'Paille').

96. *Havard*, 'Matelas'.

97. *Turenne Invt., 1615*.

98. *Princess Palatine's Letters*, letter of 8 December 1697.

99. *Havard*, 'Draps de Lit'.

100. One sees striped sheets in Dutch paintings of the period. *Stengel* (p. 171) states that blue and white striped sheets remained common in Berlin, even in quite grand houses, even in the eighteenth century, and quotes several references to checked bed linen.

101. *Savary des Bruslons*, 'Courtepointe'. He was probably describing quilting executed with a double running stitch where two threads appear alternately on the two faces to form a continuous line. Quilting is of course reversable.

102. There was a coverlet at Ingatestone (*Invt., 1600*) of 'taffeta sercenett . . . ymbrodered all over with yellow twyst, and lyned with fyne crimson wollen' while a handsome quilt at Hardwick (*Invt., 1601*) must have been that of 'India stuff imbroidered with beasts with frenge and tassells of white silk'. Counterpanes of 'painted quilted caleco' were on three beds at Cowdray (*Invt., 1682*).

103. Listed among Cardinal Mazarin's linen (*Invt., 1653*) are some 'couvertures de drap de toille d'Hollande fines'. There was a 'Hollon

quilt' at Edington (*Invt., 1665*) and a 'Holland quilt' at Chenies (*Invt., 1585*).

104. *Guiffrey, Inventaire*, III, p. 110; and *Gosfield Invt., 1638*.

105. Molière had a 'sommier de crin' which seems to have been a form of bolster filled with horse-hair and may have been wedge-shaped so as to tilt upward the top half of the body. Such 'triangular bolsters' were still to be found on many German beds until recently and the 'Kopfmatratze' (head-mattress) on the Queen of Prussia's bed in 1705 is likely to have been of a similar nature. English farmers occasionally had straw-filled bolsters but these were always used in conjunction with a feather bolster (*Havard*, 'Couche'; *Stengel*, pp. 146–8; *Devon Invts.*).

106. Lady Maynard, for instance, had two pillows while her lady-in-waiting had only one (*Ham Invt., 1679*).

107. La Comte de Laborde, *Le Palais Mazarin*, Paris, 1846, p. 301.

108. *Randle Holme*, Bk. III, Chap. XIV, p. 16.

109. e.g. 'Sixe colored turned bedstaves in a case of wood' (*Ingatestone Invt., 1600*).

NOTES TO CHAPTER VIII

1. *Hardwick Invt., 1601*. Note particularly the detailed description of the nineteen 'long cushions' that were in the Gallery. See also G. F. Wingfield-Digby, *Elizabethan Embroidery*, London, 1963. In the *Easton Lodge Inventory of 1637*, the cushions are listed separately as well; most of them were richly decorated and all must have been showy.

2. Lord Teviot (*Invt., 1694*) had two caned couches in his rooms at Oxford furnished with 'Irish Sticht squabs & six cushons of ye same' while a pair of 'Dutch chaires' (which had rush seats; see p. 206) had 'two Irish stitcht cushions'.

3. The mattress of Russia leather 'garni de petites touffes or et argent et d'un galon tout autour' mentioned in the French royal inventories of 1681 (*Havard*, 'Matelas') would seem to have been a squab with tufting (see p. 128).

4. *Kilkenny Invt., 1684*.

5. *Havard*, ('Carreau') quotes a reference of 1471 to 'carreaulx longs'.

6. A royal easy chair in 1693 was described as a 'grand fauteuil de commodité ... avec son carreau separé' (*Guiffrey, Inventaire*, II, p. 416);

Havard, ('Fauteuil') refers to several 'fauteuils de paille' [rush-seated chairs] with 'leurs carreaux'. Easy chairs are discussed on p. 195.

7. *Havard*, 'Carreau'. Mazarin (*Invt., 1653*) owned a *carreau* which had 'cuir rouge par dessous'.

8. *Ibid.*

9. It is illustrated in the *D.E.F.* under 'Stool', Plate 22.

10. *Ham Invt., 1683*.

11. *Ingatestone Invt., 1600*; *Hatfield Priory Invt., 1629*.

12. *Mazarin Invt., 1653*.

13. *Randle Holme*, Chap. XIV.

14. 'One forme with a back benshe of waynskot' and 'one forme with a bench bord' are quotations from inventories of 1619 cited by S. Wolsey and R. W. P. Luff, *Furniture in England, The Age of the Joiner*, London, 1968, p. 72.

15. Records of the Court of the Joyners' Company, Guildhall, London, Mx. 8046/2, 27 November 1694; and Ipswich Court Record, 26 March 1661 (both kindly communicated to me by Mr Benno Forman).

16. 'One forme with a joyned back' (*Agius*; given in the original typescript but deleted from the published version).

17. The 'settee' at Hatfield Priory (*Invt., 1629*) was probably of this class.

18. *Havard*, 'Archebanc'. An *arche* was a box-like container like our 'ark'. The 'banc de noyer à deux couverceaux et fermatures fermans à clef' [walnut bench with two lids with locks closed with a key] will have been an *archebanc* (*Thiret Invt., 1621*). The scene of the Assumption was painted on it, presumably on its panelled back.

19. 'Ung grand banc à coucher, en forme d'archebanc, bois noguier garny de couitte, cuissin, rempli de plume, couverte blanc' [A large sleeping bench in the form of a *archebanc*, of walnut, furnished with a mattress, cushion, filled with feathers with a white cover] (*Havard*, 'Archebanc'; inventory of 1635).

20. *Randle Holme*, Bk. III, Chap. XIV. 'Six joyned buffett stooles' were in the Parlour at Bramfield which was in Suffolk, for instance (Inventory of Arthur Coke of Bramfield, 1629, ed. F. W. Steer, *Proceedings of the Suffolk Institute of Archaeology*, XXV., p. 13, 1951); there were others at Tart Hall (*Invt., 1641*) which was in London.

21. *Havard*, 'respect'.

22. *D.E.F.*, 'Stool', fig. 5. See also G. Jackson-Stops, 'The 6th Duke of Dorset's Furniture at

Knole II', *Country Life*, 9 June 1977, fig. 3, where they are dated to the 1620s—in which case they may have been part of Queen Henrietta Maria's furniture; she arrived in this country from Paris in 1625. Some folding stools are mentioned in the *Petworth Inventory of 1670*.

23. *Havard*, 'Pliant'.

24. Furetière, in his *Dictionnaire* of 1690, states that *perroquets* were 'des sièges pliants' which 'ont un dossier'.

25. Furetière, *op. cit.*, also says that 'ils servent à s'asseoir à table' [they serve as seats at the table]. See *Havard*, 'Perroquet'.

26. What follows in this paragraph is a summary of an article on the identity of the 'back stool' (see P. Thornton, 'Back-stools and Chaises à Demoiselles', *The Connoisseur*, February 1974).

27. 'Low-back chairs' are mentioned in several inventories including that of Tart Hall of 1641. 'Half back chairs' (*Cockesden Invt., 1626*) and the 'two lowe chaires with lowe open backs' at Ingatestone (*Invt., 1600*) are likely to have been of the same class, the word 'open' presumably referring to the gap between the seat and the back-rest.

28. Contrasted with some 'chaize à bras' [armchairs] covered with embroidery in a room in a house at Rheims in 1621 were 'six chaises basses à dam[ois]elle' covered *en suite* (*Thiret Invt., 1621*). In another room were twenty-one 'chaizes a bras' of walnut covered with moquette and 'une autre chaize de bois a dam*elle*', covered in the same material. Women were being provided with low chairs well back in the sixteenth century; an inventory of 1568 refers to 'Une chayere basse pour dames à doz garny de volours rouge, viel' (*Orange Invts.*, I, p. 27).

29. Gabrielle d'Estrées had some gilt walnut chairs, four of which had arms while the rest were 'à vertugadin' (*Havard*, 'Chaise'). The farthingale itself had gone out of fashion by 1620 yet the hey-day of this type of chair was only reached about 1635; so, strictly speaking, it is only early versions which have a right to the name 'farthingale chair'.

30. An inventory of 1611 refers to some 'petites chaizes caquetoires en tapisserie' (E. Bonnaffé, *Le Meuble en France au XVIe siecle*, Paris, 1887, pp. 216–19). In 1580 the new regulations of the Parisian Guild of Huchiers-Menuisiers [Joiners] stipulated that those seeking to become masters of the Company had to make and submit for examination a 'chaise basse appellée caquetouère'

[low chairs called *caquetoires*]. It may well be that, at this early date, such chairs did not have padded backs but the sort of chair today mis-named 'a *caquetoire*' can certainly not be called low. This question is discussed by Thornton, *loc. cit.*

31. Bonnaffée, *loc. cit.*

32. e.g. in the *Du Boisgeslin Invts., 1688*.

33. In the Great Chamber at Faringdon (*Invt., 1620*), for instance, there was a 'greate chaier', a red velvet chair and a 'red velvett back chaier imbroydred' and seven more 'back chaiers'. There can be little doubt that, in such a setting, the fashionable chair of the day—the 'farthingale chair'— would have been present in some numbers. 'A little back chaire embrodred' was bought for the Provost's lodge at King's College Cambridge in 1609–10. (*Provost of Kings Invt., 1660*).

34. e.g. the famous set of 'dolphin chairs' at Ham House (see Plate 40, here) comprise armed and armless versions; the latter are called 'back stools' in the *Inventory of 1678* although they have little resemblance to the sort of chair we have been discussing. The term seems to have become synonymous with 'a chair without arms' during the last three decades of the century.

35. The type of 'farthingale chair' covered with turkeywork was probably always an exception to this general rule, for the uprights could not be conveniently covered in this thick material. In fact, rectangular panels of turkeywork with borders were made specially to go on the seats and backs of such chairs, the woollen manufacturers claiming towards the end of the century that '5,000 dozen' turkeywork chairs were produced in England each year. This is no doubt an exaggeration but it indicates that a lively industry existed and that the output was considerable (See R. W. Symonds, 'Turkey Work, Beech and Japanned Chaires', *The Connoisseur*, April, 1934). See Plate 103, here.

36. Mrs Eames has done much to clarify this subject, explaining how precedence rather than rank governed the use of chairs in mediaeval society (see P. Eames, 'Furniture in England, France and the Netherlands from the Twelfth to the Fifteenth Century', *Furniture History*, XIII, 1977).

37. In the Victoria and Albert Museum is a X-frame chair of state in which, tradition has it, Charles I sat during his trial in 1648 (see *D.E.F.*, 'Chairs', Plate 38).

38. It is curious that the chair-makers still bothered to make them foldable until well into the seventeenth century and still incorporated the scissor-action in the X-frame even after having made all movement impossible by introducing front and back seat-rails, and rails at the top and bottom of the back-support, thus effectively locking the frame in the open position. The late specimens of X-frame chairs of state at Knole exemplify this phase in the chair's development.

39. Jean Nicot, *Thresor de la langue francaise . . .*, 1606.

40. See 'Inventaires de la Royne Descosse Douairière de France, Catalogues of the . . . Furniture . . . of Mary Queen of Scots, 1556–1569', *The Bannantyne Club*, Edinburgh, 1863, Inventory of 1561.

41. The word appears in a French inventory of 1626. In one room were 'six chaires à vertugadin . . ., quatre chaires de bois de noier à dossier, façon de fauteuil, couverte de velours vert à ramages, trois chaires à bras et dossier de bois de noier . . .', i.e. six 'farthingale chairs' four walnut X-frame chairs covered with green velvet, and three walnut armchairs (*Havard*, 'Fauteuil').

42. P. Biver, *Histoire de Château de Meudon*, Paris, 1923, p. 141.

43. Some authorities have maintained that a *fauteuil à commodité* was a form of close stool (e.g. *Karlson*) but this was not the case. Eight chairs thus designated in the French royal inventories (*Guiffrey, Inventaire*, p. 433) had a leaf for writing at the end of one arm. It is unlikely that a close stool would have been fitted with such an accessory. What is more, no reference is ever made to pewter pans and the like in connection with such chairs.

44. *Guiffrey, Inventaire*, p. 368. A few years later (p. 433) were listed 'huit grands fauteuils de commodité à cremillières et joues', i.e. they had 'cheeks' or 'wings' against which one could rest the head—these were undoubtedly 'sleeping chairs'. The 'sleeping chayres' at Ham occur in the inventory of 1679 but not in that of 1677.

45. *Ibid.*, p. 414. The state bed at Clandon, dating from about 1700, is accompanied by a pair of easy chairs *en suite* (see J. Fowler and J. Cornforth, *English Decoration in the 18th century*, London, 1974, Plate 142). *Havard* ('Commodité' quotes a late seventeenth-century complaint about the fashionable young gentlemen at the French court who, 's'il y a des grandes chaises de commodité, ils s'en saisissent d'abord et ils auront l'incivilité de ne les pas offrir à une dame : ils s'y étendent, ils s'y renversent à demy couchez, ils s'y bercent, ils mettent leur jambes sur d'autre sièges ou sur l'un des bras de fauteuil où ils sont assis, ils les croisent et se mettent quelque fois en des postures encore plus indécentes croyant que cela a l'air de qualité d'en user ainsi' [if there are large easy chairs, they commandeer them straightaway and are so uncivil as not to offer them to a lady [first]; they stretch themselves upon them, they throw themselves back half lying down, they cradle themselves, they put their legs up on other seats or over one of the arms of the chair, they cross them and sometimes adopt postures that are even more indecent, believing that it lends an air of quality to use the chairs in this way].

46. *Evelyn's Diary*, 10 November, 1644.

47. *Charles I Invts., 1649–51.*

48. R. W. Symonds, 'Charles II couches, Chairs and Stools', *The Connoisseur*, January and February, 1934.

49. *Ham Invt., 1679 and 1683.*

50. Some indication of how great had been the advances made by the Parisian chairmakers in the 1670s is provided by the fact that both the English and the Swedish ambassadors to the French court took the trouble to take home sets of French chairs for the furnishing of their own homes (see P. Thornton, 'The Parisian Fauteuil of 1680', *Apollo*, February 1975).

51. Symonds, *loc. cit.*

52. *Ibid.* Casbert also supplied a chair for use at Whitehall which was 'round in the back and quilted' while at about the same time Richard Price, another craftsman working for the royal household, supplied some 'elbow chaires with compass backs'; these were probably both descriptions of the same 'hollow back' form.

53. *Ibid.*

54. *Ibid.* Richard Price provided some chairs in 1677 which had 'compass heeles and crooked backs'. These chairs had to be particularly stable as they were for the royal yacht.

55. R. W. Symonds, 'English Cane Chairs', *The Connoisseur*, March and May, 1951.

56. Under the heading 'Rotin', *Savary des Bruslons* (1723) tells us that this is a form of cane 'dont on fait en la fendant par morceaux, ces meubles de canne dont on fait un si grand usage et un si grand commerce en Angleterre et en Hollande, et qui commence a passer en France'

[of which have been made, by splitting it into pieces, the cane furnishings for which there is so much use and such a large trade in England and Holland, and which are beginning to enter France]. The Cane-chair Makers claimed that they exported some 2,000 dozen such chairs. So popular were they in Germany and Scandinavia that the indigenous makers of such furniture called themselves 'Englische Stuhlmacher' (or 'Engleske Stolemagere' in Danish).

57. *Havard*, 'Paille'.

58. An inventory of 1627 refers to 'une chayre de Flandre viele, garnye de paille' [an old Flanders chair, garnished with straw [i.e. rushes]] (*Ibid.*).

59. *Agius*, p. 78. There were three 'flagg bottomed chaires' in the housekeeper's room at Cowdray (*Invt.*, *1682*) which may have been Dutch, as may have been the four 'wooden chayres with bulrush bottoms' under the stairs at Tart Hall in 1641 (*Invt.*).

60. *Cowdray Invt.*, *1682* and J. Watney, *Sole Account of St Osyth's Priory, Essex*, London, 1871 (Will of Lady Rivers, 1644).

61. e.g. *Guiffrey, Inventaire*, II, pp. 241 and 243.

62. There are some black-japanned chairs of this sort at Boughton which may possibly have been imported from France along with some of the other furniture that the Duke of Montagu brought back from his embassies to that country between 1669 and 1672, and between 1676 and 1678 (see note 50). They were furnished with cushions of red damask. At Skokloster in Sweden there are some similar chairs.

63. 'garnis de carreaux et dossiers picquez' (Guiffrey, *loc. cit.*). An inventory of 1677 lists 'cinq petites chaises de bois tourne e garni de paille, et chacune de leur oreiller [here meaning a cushion rather than a pillow] et dossier rempli de plume et crain [crin, meaning horsehair, an early reference], couverte de brocatelle' (*Havard*, 'Chaise'; see also 'Fauteuil' for further examples).

64. *Agius* (p. 78) mentions one in a document of 1639. Steer (*Devon Invts.*) found another in an inventory of 1675. As Mrs Agius also found references to 'wicker rodds', she cautiously avoids drawing any firm conclusion about the nature of 'rodden chairs', but that primitive 'staked' chairs were being made at the time seems probable.

65. Lady Rivers' Will, 1644 (see note 60, above); see also *Ingatestone Invt.*, *1600* and *Edington Invt.*, *1665*.

66. e.g. a 'wicker chaire wth. a cover over the head' (*Hatfield Priory Invt.*, *1629*).

67. *Randle Holme*, Bk. III, Chap. XIV, p. 14.

68. I am indebted to Mrs Patricia Griffiths for this information.

69. *Agius*, loc. cit.

70. *Gilling Castle Invt.*, *1624*.

71. *Knole Invt.*, *1645*. Many of those mentioned in the *Orange Inventories* (e.g. p. 120, *passim*) had black leather covers; others were covered in cloth of gold or with silk damask. Some were specially for women (*2 Spaensches vrouwestolen*; p. 148) and some were for men (p. 153). They came with and without arms. In the Gage Inventory of 1556 (*Sussex Archeological Collections*, XLV, 1892) two chairs 'of Spanyshe making' are noted; one was 'garniyshed with collored woode' the other with coloured bone. There is no reason why all chairs from Spain should have been of the same class, but there was probably a distinctive form known as a 'Spanish chair'.

72. *Gosfield Invt.*, *1638*

73. *Tart Hall Invt.*, *1641*. Oriental furniture was still very rare in Europe at this date.

74. At the Vyne in 1541 there were some 'Flanders chairs covered with leather' (M. Jourdain, *English Decoration and Furniture of the early Renaissance* 1500–1650, London, 1924, p. 244), while some early seventeenth century French inventories have 'chaises de Flandres' that were 'basse, couverte de cyre' and others that were 'garnye de paille' (*Havard*, 'Chaise').

75. They occur, for instance at Hengrave (*Invt.*, *1603*) and in the Earl of Northampton's inventory of 1614. In Charles I's inventories (1649–51) mention is made of 'two scrowle or backed chaires'. Was the 'lowe role back chaire without armes' at Ingatestone (*Invt.*, *1600*) similar?

76. See also *D.E.F.*, 'Couch', Pl. V.

77. *Thiret Invt.*, *1621*.

78. *Guiffrey, Inventaire*, II, p. 346.

79. An item referred to as a *canapée* in a Dutch inventory of 1657 had mattresses and pillows, and seems to have had a canopy over it (*een geborduerd canopé met gehemelt*, a bordered canapée with a heaven; *Orange Invts.*; II, p. 77). presumably this was a couch and canopy (see p. 172) but it is here called a *canapée*. It may be worth recording that the earliest reference to a *Kanapee* in Germany so far noted occurs in a document of 1663 (P. W. Meister and H.

Jedding, *Das Schöne Möbel im Lauf der Jahrhunderts*, Munich, 1966, p. 21).

80. *Ibid.* p. 356.

81. *Havard*, 'Sopha'. Maybe the writer was thinking more of a kind of 'ottoman', for Saint-Simon some years later described something very like this piece of furniture that one tends to associate with the early nineteenth century. 'La sofa est une manière d'estrade,' he says, 'couverte de tapis, au fond de la chambre d'audience du grand vizier sur la quelle il est assis sur des carreaux' [The sofa is a kind of platform, covered with carpet, at the end of the audience chamber of the [Turkish] grand vizier, on which he is seated on squabs.]

82. *Tessin-Cronström Correspondence*, letter of 7 January, 1695.

83. See P. Thornton, 'Couches, Canopies and Chairs of State', *Apollo*, October 1974, where this question is discussed at greater length.

84. *Ibid.*, Plate 12. Some sofa-like settees standing under canopies, are illustrated in the article; they are presumably French and date from the 1690s.

85. *D.E.F.*, 'Settees and Sofas', Plate 51. This piece so closely resembles a sofa that its true nature is usually forgotten.

86. *D.E.F.*, 'Settees and Sofas'.

87. Among the upholsterers working for the royal household in the time of Charles II and William III, occur French-sounding names like Casbert, Paudevine, Guibert and 'Monsr. Le Grange'.

88. Having drawn his attention to this reference, it was gratifying that Mr Christopher Gilbert subsequently found the name 'Gilbert' (for Guibert) in the Duke of Leeds' accounts.

89. The future king Charles X of Sweden, who came to the throne in 1654, was provided with some stuffed chairs by the Court Saddler, it may be relevant to note in this connection. He stuffed the chairs in question with reindeer hair (see *Karlson*, p. 281).

90. Here again is an indication that the easy chair was evolved from the invalid chair rather than from standard forms of armchair, all of which had the gap at the back.

91. See R. W. Symonds, 'The Royal X Chair', *Apollo*, May 1937, Plate VII. It is at present covered in a green velvet which is itself fairly venerable but the red velvet, bearing the imprint of the applied lace, can be seen underneath. The double-ended couch at Hardwick (Plate 147) is painted with imitation embroidery which gives a very clear indication of what the textile covering of the mattress, valances, and two large cushions was like.

92. See Thornton, 'Backstools . . .', *loc. cit.*, Plate 6.

93. The folding stools were 'marbrez de diverses couleurs' (*Mazarin Invt., 1653*). The marbling of carcase furniture was common in the seventeenth century but it seems rather perverse to marble the slender wooden members of folding stools.

94. An important set of English armchairs at Ham House make a case in point. They were supplied about 1680 and the black areas were painted green (bronzed) in the Regency period, but the black paint may still be seen in places (P. Thornton, 'Some neo-Carolean Chairs at Ham House', *Furniture History*, Vol. X, 1974). The French armchairs at Salsta, in Sweden, also have black and gold frames (see P. Thornton, 'The Parisian *fauteuil* of 1680', *Apollo*, February 1975), and there were two black and gilt carved armchairs (*swarte vergulde gesneden armstoelen*) in William III's closet at Honselaarsdijk around 1695 (*Orange Invts.*, I, p. 470). See Plate 39, here.

95. At Hardwick (*Invt., 1601*) only one chair was gilt. Of the various chairs in the Leicester Gallery at Knole (*Invt., 1645*), several were painted but only one, with its accompanying pair of stools, was gilded and even that was only 'painted gold'. Daniel Cronström, advising Countess Piper on how to do up her house in Stockholm in close imitation of the latest Parisian fashion, suggested that 'les chaises du Cabinet de Madame seront à bois doré' [the chairs for My Lady's closet should be of gilded wood] but none of the other chairs in the house, which was to be very richly appointed, were to be gilded (*Tessin-Cronström Correspondence*, letter of 7 January 1695). As for silvering, no doubt considerable impetus was given to the fashion when Louis XIV in 1673 acquired 'un grand fauteuil de bois taille de plusieurs ornemens et argenté, pour servir de trosne au roi lorsqu'il donne ses audiences aux ambassadeurs' [a large armchair of wood carved with many ornaments and silvered, to serve as a throne for the King when he gives audience to ambassadors] (*Havard*, 'Argenture'). The Duke of Lauderdale had silvered chairs in his closet at Ham House in the late 1670s.

96. See Catalogue of the Exhibition, The Golden Age of English Furniture Upholstery, 1660–1840,

Temple Newsam, Leeds, 1973, Plates 31 and 32.

97. If the reader doubts this assertion, he or she should think of the many seventeenth-century cane chairs that survive; they all have backs that are rough and unfinished, while their fronts are handsomely carved.

98. The royal accounts for 1617–18 include an item for providing some armchairs, footstools and stools covered with crimson velvet and 'for making . . . cases of bayes for the same . . . and for the stringes & other necessaries to them (R. W. Symonds, 'The Craft of the Coffer and Trunk Maker . . .', *The Connoisseur*, March 1942).

99. The taffeta 'cases' of some chairs supplied for Hampton Court (*Estimates, 1699*) were closed in this way.

100. At Walton (*Invt., 1624*) there were six high stools with leather seats which in addition had 'covers of green cloth & fringe on them, which may be taken of at pleasure'. Was the 'mante verte' [green mantle] on a chair mentioned in a French inventory of 1621 (*Thiret*) also some form of slip-over cover?

101. *Ham Invt., 1679*. See P. Thornton, 'The Parisian fauteuil . . .', *loc. cit.*, where it is suggested that these chairs may be French.

102. *Mazarin Invt., 1653.*

103. *Kilkenny invt., 1684.* In the *garderobe* next to the Princess of Orange's Closet in the Noordeinde residence at The Hague, there stood an armchair on wheels (*Een armstoel staaende op rollen*; *Orange Invts.*, I, p. 206).

104. There were some tapestry-woven cushion covers at Cockesden in 1610 (*Invt.*).

105. F. R. Friis, *Kjøbenhavn's Slots Inventarium, 1638*, Samlinger til Dansk Bygnings- og Kunsthistorie, Copenhagen, 1872–8.

106. 'Four squobbs wth. covers of tapistry . . .' (*Ham Invts. 1679* and *1683*). The two surviving covers are, however, now too delicate to be shown on the squabs which are today covered in a checked cotton reflecting the fact that in 1679 the covers were protected by cases of purple and white chequered Indian sarsnet. The squabs *may* already have been present in the Gallery in the 1640s if they are identical with the 'three couches and their silk furniture on them' and a fourth in the adjacent closet which are listed in the Ham inventory of about 1654.

107. *Tessin-Cronström Correspondence*, letter of 7 January 1695.

108. There were '3 small stools covered with

dorney' at Cockesden (*Invt., 1610*) but no other reference has been noted.

109. *Tart Hall Invt., 1641.*

110. *Dyrham Invt., 1703.*

111. This statement was made in a petition laid before Parliament by members of the woollen industry who were seeking to curb the manufacture of cane-chairs. The cane-chair makers naturally disputed the matter and pointed out that the chairs concerned were anyway pretty humble confections (see note 56). The actual figure is given as '2000 dozen'.

112. *Thiret Invts., 1621* and *Havard*, 'Moquette'.

113. 'Twee oude spaensche stoelen van coleur kaffa . . .' (*Orange Invts.*, I, p. 198). In the Dieren inventory of 1683, for instance, mention is made of twelve 'gebloemde trijpe stoelen' in the dining-room (*Orange Invts.*, I, p. 389).

114. *Havard*, 'Chaise'.

115. See C. Pitoin, *Marly-le-Roi*, Paris, 1904, p. 174, and *Havard* 'Tabouret'. Of the 1,323 *tabourets* listed in the French royal inventoires under Louis XIV, 514 were covered in *moquette*, 24 with *panne* and 246 with 'peluche ou tripe'.

116. *Dyrham Invt.*, and *Tredegar Invt., 1692.*

117. *Hardwick Invt., 1601.*

118. The woollen industry (see note 111) claimed that 'there were yearly Vended in this Kingdom about five thousand dozen of Setwork (commonly called Turkey-work chairs though made in England)'.

119. The Crown acquired two dozen turkeywork chairs for Hampton Court in 1699, for instance, at a cost of £14. 8s. od. Similar orders were being placed for Holyrood Palace in Edinburgh right through the last decades of the century (see M. Swain, 'The furnishing of Holyrood House in 1668', *The Connoisseur*, February 1977).

120. *Mazarin Invt., 1653.* The frames of these pieces were 'façon d'ebeine à colonnes torses', i.e. of imitation ebony (probably black-stained pearwood) with spiral turning.

121. Le Comte de Biver, *Histoire du Château de Meudon*, Paris, 1923, p. 1495 *et seq.*

122. *Havard* ('Chaise') quotes an early seventeenth century reference to some 'chaises de Flandres . . . basse, couverte de cuyr' (see also p. 210).

123. The accounts of the Provost of King's College, Cambridge, for the year 1609–10 include a reference to 'le great red-leather chaire printed with gould, et 2 low-stooles eiusdem

'operis' which cost 16 shillings (*Provost of King's Invt., 1660*). The Earl of Northampton's couch with its 'crimson leather printed border wise . . . lined with silver and gold' was probably likewise tooled and gilded (*Northampton Invt., 1614*; see p. 119).

124. *Cowdray Invt., 1682, Ham Invt.,* c. *1651,* and *Orange Invts.,* II, p. 70 (*Acht goldenleeren manstoelen ende een groot Engels goldenleeren stoell*).

125. *Tessin-Cronström Correspondence,* letters of 4 May and 29 July, 1965. Clearly the *tapissiers* (upholsterers) had these particular embroiderers working for them. Charles II acquired '2 large elbow chairs of needlework richly wrought, one of blue and gold, the other of silver and pincke' in 1672 at a cost of £60 which was also a considerable sum (R. W. Symonds, 'Charles II Couches, Chairs and Stooles', *The Connoisseur,* January and February, 1934).

126. Symonds; *loc. cit.*

127. *Mazarin Invt., 1653.*

128. The Marquis de Sourches, *Memoires,* Vol. I, p. 82. He tells us that others blamed the malady on excessive consumption of *ragouts,* while some even suggested it could have been due to 'des debauches ultra montaines' [outlandish debauches]. The Marquis, however, felt that 'ce dernier avis n'etoit pas si bien fondé que les deux autres'.

Notes to Chapter IX

1. Presumably the tables 'appliquées sur des tréteaux qui se brisent' [laid on trestles which fold] which were in Catherine de Medici's possession in 1589 were of this kind (E. Bonnaffé, *Le Meuble en France au XVIe siècle,* Paris, 1887, p. 185).

2. A seventeenth-century Spanish specimen is represented in *St Bonaventura* by Zurbaran, painted in 1623 and now in the Gemäldegalerie Berlin-Dahlem. It is likely that the 'petite table à la mode d'Espaigne, qui s'ouvre et clot' [small table in the Spanish style, which opens and closes], listed in the inventory of Marguerite d'Autriche of 1523, was of this type (Bonnaffé, *loc. cit.*).

3. Mr Francis Steer, in his excellent introduction to the *Cowdray Inventory of 1682,* suggested that the 'Spanish tables' there mentioned might have been made of mahogany (the early shipments of which came from Spanish Honduras) but the inventory of Tart Hall (*1641*) included references to 'Spanish tables' of walnut and of oak. The term 'Spaens tafelken' [small Spanish table] occurs several times in the inventory of Breda Castle of 1619 (*Orange Invts.,* I, p. 150); this and the French reference of 1523 mentioned in the previous note, suggest that this type of table was in widespread use. They do not seem to have been regarded as of any importance. They came both with oval and with rectangular tops. The 'litle fir table with feet to fould up', mentioned in the *Walton Inventory of 1624* was very likely of the same class, as may have been the 'large table behind the hangings' at Marton Hall (*Invt., 1605*) which was fitted 'with iron hooks'.

4. Several oak tables of this type survive at Cotehele in Cornwall. Only one retains its original iron bracing-hooks which are secured by ingenious catches (Plate 213).

5. At Ingatestone (*Invt., 1600*) there was a little table which had 'two falling leaves', while the Countess of Shrewsbury had a 'little folding table' in her bedchamber at Hardwick (*Invt., 1601*). A 'foulding field table' is listed in the *Charles I Inventories* (1649–51); this echoes the description of a table that belonged to Catherine de Medici (1589; see Bonnaffé, *op. cit.,* p. 184) which is listed as 'une table de camp brisé'. She also had a 'table de camp pozée sur un pied brisé' which may have consisted of a top resting on an X-frame stand.

6. e.g. 'two longe Tables in the hall fastened to Tressells set in the ground' (*Easton Lodge Invt., 1637*).

7. In former times, when grand people still dined in the hall, the large trestle-tables had often been capable of being taken to pieces. In the late fifteenth century *Bokes of Keruyne and Curtasye,* the servants are instructed to 'lay some of the tables [tops] on the floor, and remove the trestles'. There is a seventeenth-century description of James I standing on a dismantled table-top and rinsing his hands after a meal. The long tables in early seventeenth century halls were no longer of the kind that could be dismantled. While it would appear that a static table might be called a 'table dormant' in the Middle Ages (see *D.E.F.,* 'Dining Table'), it is clear that trestles might be called 'dormants' or 'dormers' in the seventeenth century (e.g. 'one planke table wth. the Dorments' and 'a long thick elme planke for a table lyinge upon iiii dormers'—respectively from F. W. Steer, *Farm and Cottage Inventories of Mid-Essex, 1635–1749,*

Colchester, 1950, p. 12, and *Ingatestone Invt.,*
1600.

8. When Jacques Wecker, native of Colmar,
published his *De Secretis* at Basle in 1582, he
included a drawing of the construction of such a
table 'qui se redoublent' [which doubles itself], as
he put it. He stated that the invention had been
made in Flanders and that he had seen many such
tables at Ghent. The implication would seem to
be that they were still not all that common by the
1580s. However, Jacques Androuet Du Cerceau
published several designs for such tables in about
1560, so they must have been familiar in French
court circles by then. Bonnaffé (*op. cit.*, p. 186)
cities early French references to tables 'qui se tire'
[which draw out] or 'tirant par les deux bouts'
[drawing out at the ends] in 1566 and 1577. The
standard description was to become 'une table à
ralonge' [a table that extends] (e.g. in the 'Sale où
mange Son Ex[cellen]ce' the Prince of Orange in
his residence at Brussels in 1618: see *Orange Invts.*
I, p. 121). Many designs for this kind of table
appeared in Holland, principally in the works of
Hans Vredeman de Vries (*c.* 1586), of Paul, his
son (1630), and of Crispin van de Passe (1621 and
1642) (see S. Jervis, *Printed Furniture Designs*
before 1650, London, 1974). In the dining parlour
('Op de eetsael') in the Stadholder's residence at
The Hague there was a large oak table of this
type ('een groote wagenschotten uyttreckende
tafel') but the form went out of fashion in about
the 1640s (see *Orange Invts.*, I, p. 189).

9. It is an indication of the prominent position in
important rooms which such tables often occupied that designers of the calibre of Du
Cerceau and the de Vries, father and son, should
have published proposals for them (see the
previous note). Clearly they realised it was
desirable that such a feature should be decorated
as far as possible in a manner consonant with the
décor of the room concerned.

10. *Randle Holme* (Bk. III, Chap. XIV), listing the
'things necessary for and belonging to a dineing
roome' maintains that there should be a 'large
table in the middle, either square to draw out in
leaves, or long, or round or oval with falling
leaves'. He was writing just at the time when the
change-over was becoming apparent.

11. *Ham Invt., 1679.* 'A Lauderdale Table-Board
. . . 4 feet long, 3 feet Broad with twist-leggs all
of Walnut-tree wood' and costing twelve
shillings was in the 'little Parlour' of Dr Morris
of Wells in 1686 (G. Olive, 'Furniture in a West

Country Parish, 1576–1769', *Furniture History*,
Vol. XII, 1976); could this have been some form
of gate-leg dining-table, perhaps oval rather than
square?

12. At Dublin Castle (*Invt., 1679*) there was in a
closet 'another table to lengthen the other in the
dining-room'.

13. There was 'une ralongement de table' [table
extension] of oak in the Thiret mansion at
Rheims (*Invt., 1621*) which was 'garni d'un
pied'. Likewise, in the Gilt Parlour of Breda
Castle around 1600, two long tables were
described as being 'met een reloenje' [with an
extension-piece] (*Orange Invts.*, I, p. 75).

14. We learn that oyster tables had a 'hole in the
middle' and were circular from a reference in a
Restoration comedy. (A. Scouten and R. Hume,
'A lost Restoration comedy, *The Country*
Gentleman (1669)', *Times Literary Supplement*, 23
September 1973). In the *Easton Lodge Inventory of*
1637 there is mention of a basket 'to stand under
the oyster table'.

15. There were two oyster tables 'on folding
frames' at Ingatestone (*Invt., 1600*), while 'one
litle joyned bord, wth. feete to terne in, for
oysters' was to be found in the Winter Parlour at
Hengrave Hall (*Invt., 1603*). The latter may have
had an action like a 'Spanish table'.

16. M. Jourdain, *English Decoration and Furniture*
of the Early Renaissance, London, 1927, p. 5.

17. *Ham Invt., 1679.*

18. *Ham Invt., 1683*. It may also be identical with
the 'One table painted black and gould' that was
in the room in *1679*. In the adjacent closet (an
altogether grander room) there was 'One Indian
furnace for tea garnished with silver' which may
have been a kind of *samovar*. The tea-table stands
on six red and gold legs carved in the East Indian
taste; it was obviously found to be too low for
use with European chairs so an under-frame with
spiral-turned legs was added.

19. The Dyrham table was to be flanked by a
paid of stands in the form of kneeling blackamoors for, as the owner's clerk told him in a
letter of 1700, 'the two black boys have a proper
place on each side of the Indian tambour in one
of the best rooms' (*National Trust Guide to*
Dyrham). In the inventory of Dyrham made in
1703 the ensemble is described as 'a large tea table
and 2 blacks'. It stands on taller legs than did the
Ham table in its original guise. The Charlottenburg tables also stand somewhat taller. Some
of them are octagonal and drum-like (see

Catalogue of the Exhibition '*China und Europa*', Schloss Charlottenburg, Berlin, 1973, p. 53). There was also, incidentally, an East Indian tea-table at the Binnenhof at The Hague in 1700 (*Orange Invts.*, I, p. 434). It may also be relevant to note that a red and gold '*teetrommel*' (lit. tea-drum) was at the palace of Soestdijk in 1699–1712 (*ibid.*, II, p. 623). Th. Lunsingh Scheurleer discusses other examples in 'The Dutch at the Tea-Table', *The Connoisseur*, October 1976.

20. Scheurleer, *loc. cit.*, illustrates an early specimen in a painting of 1689, with a circular tray-like top.

21. C. Pitoin, *Marly-le-Roi*, Paris, 1904, pl 174.

22. *Turenne Invt.*, 1615.

23. *Easton Lodge Invt., 1637*. Had there been only two, one might have suspected that these tables were for dressing food in the dining parlour—that they were '*dressoirs*' or dressers. But the fact that there were no less than sixteen indicates that they were indeed what they seem. The *Ham Inventory of* c. *1654* probably reflects the state of the house before the Civil War broke out. A dressing-table is also mentioned in the *Edington Inventory of 1665*.

24. Of the several triads at Ham House in the 1670s, no complete set survives. There is a delightful black lacquered ensemble painted with flowers at Hopetoun House, near Edinburgh, and there is a famous silver set at Knole, Sevenoaks. William III acquired for one of his Dutch residences two complete silver ensembles (i.e. two looking-glasses, two tables and four candlestands) from Paris in 1697 (*Orange Invts.*, I, p. 421). It should in parentheses be added that the triad seems to have evolved from a group comprising a table and pair of candlestands only. For instance Amalia van Solms, the widow of Frederik Hendrick, Prince of Orange, owned a pair of candlestands and small table that was new in the period 1654–1668 (*Orange Invts.*, I, p. 279), and the well-known black table and stands at Ham House, with their strange caned tops, which were probably bought in Holland, do not seem from the outset to have had a looking-glass *en suite* although one was always hung above them.

25. The French royal inventories of 1686 note 'une table en forme de bureau ... avec un petit bord d'or pour y mettre une toilette de vermeil doré ...' [a table of desk shape ... with a small gallery of gold on which to stand a toilet set of silver gilt] (*Guiffrey, Inventaire*, II, p. 165). The red tortoiseshell 'bureau Mazarin' at Erthig in Denbighshire is listed as being in the state bedchamber in 1726 and is described as a dressing-table (see J. Hardy, Sheila Landi and Charles D. Wright, *A State Bed at Erthig*, Victoria and Albert Museum, 1972).

26. A few random examples can be given, however. There was the red coral table decorated with Latin sayings that a Danish visitor saw at Windsor Castle in 1613 (W. B. Rye, *England as Seen by Foreigners*, London, 1965, p. 164; see also p. 45 for a note on elaborate tables at Theobalds in 1592). At Tart Hall (*Invt., 1641*) there was an ebony table 'inlayde with torteaux shells' in the Drawing Chamber. In the Long Gallery at Northumberland House (*Invt., 1670*) stood a table of 'agott' as well as three tables of marble, all of which were presumably acquired in Italy. At Ham House (*Invt., 1679*) there stood in the Long Gallery a table and pair of candlestands of 'counterfeit marble' (i.e. of *scagliola*), of which the tops of the stands survive. And in the Hall at Dyrham (*Invt., 1703*) there was a table with a hone-stone top which is likely to have come from Solnhofen in Germany. Specimens survive in several German collections; they have ornament carved in shallow relief (see H. Kreissel, *Die Kunst des Deutschen Möbels*, I, Munich, 1968, Plates 71 and 271).

27. *The Walton Inventory of 1624* contains a reference to 'a paire of white & black checkered tables'. For further information on this matter see Julia Raynsford's forthcoming book on Gamesboards to be published shortly by George Bell & Sons.

28. *Knole Invt., 1645*. An early reference to a billiard-table is to be found in the *Hengrave Inventory of 1603*. It had 'two staves of bone, and two of wood, and four balls'. There was a billiard-table in the hall at *Ham House* in the 1670s (*Invt., 1679*).

29. See D.E.F., 'Tables, Shovel-board'.

30. There was a table for this game at Hatfield Priory in 1629 (*Invt.*) and 'one table to play Trolle Madame at' is listed in the Charles I inventories (*1649–51*).

31. *Ingatestone Invt., 1600* and *Chatsworth Invt., 1601*.

32. 'Her mistress ... set all her plate on the cubboorde for shewe' (1592; *O.E.D.*, 'Cupboard'). Lord Montague instructed the Yeoman of his Cellar to 'carrye uppe his plate ... and

place ytt uppon the cupborde' before dinner (*Montague's Household Book, 1595*). William Harrison, in his *Description of England* of 1577, speaks of the recent great increase in wealth and how the nobility now owned such great quantities of 'silver vessels, and so much other plate, as may furnish sundrie cupboards, to the summe oftentimes of a thousand or two thousand pounds at least'. The *Walton Inventory of 1624* includes a 'Note of Plate which stood upon the cupboard in your own Chamber' (i.e. the owner's bedchamber).

33. See Penelope Eames, *Mediaeval Furniture*, London, 1977, where the cup-board as a symbol of status in mediaeval times is discussed. The number of stages signified the owner's rank and was governed by an elaborate code of practice.

34. Cupboards created solely for storage (e.g. wardrobes and similar mostly rather large pieces of furniture) were generally known as 'presses' in the seventeenth century. The French term was 'armoire'.

35. The Earl of Northumberland set out in very specific detail 'the Order of all such Lyveryes of Breid Bere Wyne White-lights and Wax as shall be allow'd Dayly' in his houses (*The Regulations . . . of the Household of . . . The Fifth Earl of Northumberland . . ., begun in 1512*; London, 1827).

36. Lord Montague, in his *Household book of 1595*, instructed the Yeoman of his Wardrobe to see that the rooms in which visitors were staying were kept in proper order and to 'give his attendance to the servinge of lyveryes (if any be to be served)'. His Gentleman Usher was likewise to 'after supper . . . cause all lyveryes to be served' to the household, adding 'if any ought to be'. A year later Edmund Spenser seemed to find it surprising that in great Irish houses 'the lyverye is sayd to be served up for all night, that is theyr nyghtes allowance of drinke' (*View of the State of Ireland*, 1596).

37. I once put forward a rather different interpretation of the term (P. Thornton, 'Two Problems', *Furniture History*, Vol. VII, 1971) but now entirely accept that given here and proposed by Mrs Eames (*op. cit.*, p. 59, n. 154). In all other respects, I believe my suggestions in this direction remain acceptable.

38. See Elias Ashmole, *The Institution, Laws and Ceremonies of the Most Noble Order of the Garter*, London, 1672, p. 592, where is illustrated a banquet given by Charles II at which a series of plain tables standing against the window-piers are described as 'court cupboards'.

39. *Randle Holme, loc. cit.*

40. *Hatfield Priory Invt., 1629* and *Ham Invt., c. 1654*. The term 'cupboard table' occurs in a number of inventories from the 1620s until the middle of the century. At Cockesden (*Invt., 1626*) one was described as being 'with falling leaves' while at Tart Hall (*Invt., 1641*) there was one 'inlayde with bone and some slight stones' while another had a lock to a container (cupboard?) housing a box of oyster knives. Both were clearly distinguishable from ordinary tables, of which there were many in the house.

41. Nicot, in his dictionary of 1606, states that a 'Dressoir n'est jamais à armoire ne tiroir' (i.e. it had neither a cupboard or a drawer) and 'c'est le meuble qui est en chambre ou salle sur laquelle on estalle la vaisselle d'argent aux heures de disner ou de souper' [it is the piece of furniture that stands in the bedchamber or parlour on which one displays the silver vessels during dinner time or supper].

42. Furetière's dictionary of 1690 gives 'buffet' as 'une meuble qui sert pour mettre les pots et les verres, la vaiselle et autres choses nécessaires pour la service de table' [a piece of furniture on which are placed the jugs, glasses, plate and other things necessary for serving at table]. This piece of furniture often had 'numerous small columns' (Furetière died in 1688 so was probably writing this some years earlier). Cotgrave, in his French-English dictionary of 1632, gives 'buffet' as 'a court-cupboard, or high-standing cupboard'. It is interesting to note that, at Ingatestone in 1600 (*Invt.*), there were two 'courte buffett cupbourdes' as well as a 'high buffett lyerrie cupbourde' which indicates that both the 'court cupboard' and the 'livery cupboard' were variants of the buffet. When Marie de Medici was married in Florence in 1600, a Frenchman recorded that there was a 'credence ou buffect . . . qui montait jusqu'au plancher, garni tout de vases d'or et d'argent, de porcelaines, d'agathes, d'esmeraudes, rubis, saphirs et diamans par dedans, de la valeur de dix huit cent mil escus' [which reached up to the ceiling, decked all over with vases of gold and silver porcelain, agates, emeralds, rubies, sapphires and diamonds inside, to the value of eighteen hundred thousand *écus*] (A. Lebault, *La Table et le repas à Travers les siècles*, Paris, 1910, p. 462). The term 'credence' was not much used in France; it derived from the

Italian word 'credenza' which not only means a buffett but carries implications of the owner's high standing, the wealth of plate displayed on it being his 'credentials'.

43. In the *Thiret* mansion at Rheims (*Invt., 1621*) there stood 'ung grand dessert de bois de noyer à quatre grand colonnes et quatre petites' [a large buffet of walnut with four large columns and four small] which had a back-board painted with a scene of Susannah and the Elders. The dessert, a last course of sweetmeats, was brought on once the table had been cleared (thus from *de-servir*) after the main course.

44. See Jervis, *op. cit.*, Plate 438, where the type is described as a '*Buffet*'. One has a 'petit Cabinet, ou Armoire . . . au milieu' (i.e. a small enclosed section with a door between the top and middle shelves). The same illustration was published in 1672 by Robert Pricke in an English translation of de Breuil, where they are described as 'court cupboards'.

45. *Tessin-Cronström Correspondence*, letter of 1 October, 1700.

46. See *D.E.F.*, 'Buffet' (illus.).

47. An exception may have been the long tables still to be seen in many halls during the early part of the century. As we noted (p. 226), the lower servants dined at these tables which were probably just scrubbed. But it is possible that even these were usually covered with the cloths of coarse linen which are often listed in inventories.

48. The ebony table with silver mounts which is and was a notable feature of the decoration at Ham House (*Invt., 1679*) had a 'green sarsenet case for it fring'd'. Some of the magnificent tables that stood in Cardinal Mazarin's famous Gallery (*Invt., 1653*) had special covers of 'maroquain du Levant rouge cramoisy' that were trimmed with gold fringe.

49. At Kilkenny (*Invt., 1684*) there were some 'cases' of 'black leather to cover the table and [candle] stands' while other tables had 'printed leather carpets' which were perhaps tooled round the edges. A long table in the house had a cover of 'damask leather' (see p. 120). Several 'scorched leather' covers for tables were found at Ham House when the attics were cleared out around 1950. Some have now returned to the house, others are at Colonial Williamsburg.

50. For instance, a draw-table at Ingatestone (*Invt., 1600*) had two carpets of green cloth, one of which was for use when the table was 'at the

shortest' (i.e. closed). At Hengrave Hall (*Invt., 1603*) there was in the 'Chiefe Chamber' a 'carpet of black velvet for the little bord' which was 'laced and fringed with silver and gould, [and] lyned with taffita'. Table-carpets of velvet are frequently to be seen in contemporary illustrations; it is possible that not a few of these were of woollen rather than silk velvet.

51. In 1596 Richard Bellasio made a specific bequest of his 'best Turquey carpett for the long table, and other carpets for cobbarts'. The latter need not necessarily have been Oriental rugs at all (William Beck, *The Drapers' Dictionary*, 1884, 'Carpet'). In the 'Dyneing chamber' at Cockesden in 1610 (*Invt.*) there was a side-table with 'thereuppon a very good Turkey-carpett large'. The change from using Turkish rugs on tables to laying them on the floor in England is reflected in the list of carpets in the *Easton Lodge Inventory of 1637* where some 'little Turkey Carpitts' are described as being 'for foote Carpitts or side Tables' or 'for foote Carpitts or side Bordes'.

52. e.g. there was a turkeywork cup-board cloth at Hengrave Hall (*Invt., 1603*), while Lady Beauchamp owned a square table with 'one Turky worke carpet with a false [protective] bayes carpet' (*Edington Invt., 1665*). At Syon House (*Invt., 1670*) there was in the Wardrobe a 'Yorkshire carpett of Turkey-worke'. There were still some turkeywork table-covers at Woburn in 1703 (typescript in the Department of Textiles in the Victoria and Albert Museum) but these must by then have been old-fashioned.

53. In the Thiret mansion at Rheims in 1621 (*Invt.,*) there was a 'tapis de mocquette de couleur jaulne et rouge fasson de Turqy'.

54. In England such tapestry-woven carpets were called 'Arras Carpets' (see p. 108). The Provost of King's College, Cambridge, acquired '2 tapetis communiter vocat arrace carpetts' in 1610 (*Provost of King's Invt., 1660*).

55. In the French royal inventories of the Louis XIV period mentioned 'cinq tables de bois avec leurs tapis de Bergame' (*Guiffrey, Inventaire*, p. 240). There were cloths of 'Darnicks' and 'darnax', the latter being 'of bleu and white birds worke' at Marton (*Invt., 1605*) and Cockesden (*Invt., 1610*) respectively. In the inventory of Breda Castle, taken in 1619 (*Orange Invts.*, I, p. 131), one also finds mention of 'Dornicxse tafelkleedekens' (small Dornix table covers), while the inventory of the House of Nassau residence at Brussels of a year earlier (*ibid.*, p.

108) includes a note of some 'tapitz de table' of 'ouvrage de Tournay' (it will be remembered that Doornik was the Flemish name for Tournai). Some Tournai table-carpets, however, had a woollen pile and could thus be classed with moquettes. An inventory of 1654, for instance, notes a table covered with 'un tapis velu de Tournai, le fond bleu' (This reference and the whole question of Tournai table-covers is discussed by E. Soil, 'Tapisserie de Tournai', *Mémoires de la Société de l'Histoire de Tournai*, 1891, Vol. 22).

56. At Tart Hall (*Invt., 1641*) there was a closet where the floor was covered with white leather while a small table 'of firre' in the room was covered in the same material. On the table lay a cushion embroidered with the arms of Philip and Queen Mary—a treasured possession of fine workmanship, then already more than a century old, and deserving fine display.

57. The fitted table-carpet with four *pentes* was probably not uncommon (there is a dressing-table cover of the 1720s at Ham House with these features) and it was perhaps therefore not necessary to specify its character in inventories. A red damask cover which 'hangs down on four sides' (henger neder på fyrra sijdor) was in a house in Stockholm in 1665 (*Ebba Brahe's Hem*) and the 'three French gilt leather carpets fitted to the tables' in the Great Dining room at Kilkenny (*Invt., 1684*) were presumably of this form.

58. e.g. In the parlour at Ham House in the middle of the century (*Invt., c. 1654*) there were carpets on the two round tables and the sideboards made of green cloth bordered with gilt-leather. At Tart Hall (*Invt., 1641*) a large oval table with folding leaves standing in the hall had 'thereon a cover of red leather bordured with blew guilt leather'.

59. *Cockesden Invt., 1610* and *Tart Hall invt., 1641*. 'Six stayned Callico Carpitts' are listed in the *Easton Lodge Inventory of 1637*.

60. See G. F. Wingfield Digby, *Elizabethan Embroidery*, London, 1965. Of the forty-eight 'carpitts' at Easton Lodge in 1637 (*Invt.*), six were embroidered and it is clear that three of these were important items. The embroidered cloths are listed after the valuable Turkish and Persian rugs but before the plainer cloths.

61. At Gilling Castle (*Invt., 1594*) some 'newe cubberde clothes' were listed among the linen damask and there were several more of the rather coarse linen diaper. There were 'diaper sideboard clothes' at Dyrham a century later (*Invt., 1703*).

62. An Italian describing a French banquet in 1625 explains that 'sur la table était d'abord une nappe [linen tablecloth] ordinaire et sur cette dernière une seconde nappe damassée, très fine, pliée en deux et tombant jusqu'à terre formant ainsi nappe et tapis pour recouvrir la table' [on the table lies first an ordinary linen tablecloth and on this last lies a second damask cloth, very fine, folded in two and reaching to the ground thus forming cloth and carpet to cover the table] (*Havard*, 'Nappe'). This seems to imply that he would have expected a *tapis* to be left under the linen damask upper cloth. Lord Montague (*Household Book, 1595*) does not mention any table-carpet. On special occasions he wanted a second tablecloth which was revealed when the uppermost cloth was removed after the main courses had been cleared away. In Germany and other parts of Central Europe, however, it seems that it was normal to leave the carpet in place. Rumpolt, in his *Neu Kochbuch* of 1587 and 1666, (the second edition contained only minor changes), explains very carefully how two tablecloths should be laid over the table-carpet. The cloths should be so laid that a hand's breadth of the carpet shows all round, just above the floor. Comenius, writing in 1631, confirms what Rumpolt says (*Janua Linguarum Reserata*, 1631).

63. The French royal *toilettes* of 1673 were of brocade with a silver ground, trimmed with silver fringe and lace. They usually comprised three widths of material and were one ell long (about a yard). At each corner was an elaborate tassel or a bow.

64. Louis XIV gave Mary of Modena a rich *toilette* when she was living in exile at Saint-Germain. It was of green satin trimmed with lace, with borders of gold and silver galloon, and with a red taffeta lining.

65. *Havard* ('Toilette') cites a reference in an inventory of 1705 to 'une petit table de toilette de sapin, avec son Toilette, composée d'un dessous de toilette d'étoffe de soie, avec un dessus de toilette de mousseline à falbalas' [a small dressing-table of firwood with its *toilette* comprising an underlay of silk material with an overlay of muslin with furbelows].

NOTES TO CHAPTER X

1. A well-defined class of sixteenth-century

writing-cabinet that was popular in Spain (today often called a *vargueño*) had sometimes been furnished with a stand but these seem to have been exceptional in their day.

2. Such a high degree of craftsmanship was otherwise only bestowed on tables of special richness and on games-boards. The very fact that 'cabinet-maker' is the English term for a craftsman who creates fine furniture by means of skilfully applied woodworking techniques is evidence enough of the prestige cabinets enjoyed in former times.

3. See S. Jervis, 'A Tortoiseshell Cabinet and its precursors', *Victoria and Albert Museum Bulletin*, Vol. IV, No. 4, October 1968.

4. For example pearwood stained black was often used instead of the far more expensive ebony of the best cabinets; and rather than having the gilt mounts cast in bronze, they could more cheaply be stamped out of sheet copper and gilded, or they might be cast in brass and merely varnished.

5. In 1679 (*Ham Invt.*) it had stood in the North Drawing Room, one of the principal state rooms; it had been moved to the 'Queen's Bed Chamber' by 1683 (*Invt.*). It was furnished with a protective case of green paragon.

6. For instance there were 'Japan cabinets with frames' in the Green Closet and also in the Gallery and Antechamber, all of which formed part of the sequence of state rooms. At the time a stand for a cabinet was described as 'a frame'.

7. *Northampton Invt., 1614.* This cabinet was presumably of black lacquer with gilt decoration.

8. *Mazarin Invt., 1653.* The cabinet in question was 'en forme d'un temple d'ordre et structure du pays, vernis et peint de paysages, d'animaux et autres choses . . .' [in the form of a temple of the style and conformation of that country, lacquered and painted with landscapes, animals and other things]. To be fair, it must be added that Mazarin owned some lacquer boxes including a magnificent chest now in the Victoria and Albert Museum.

9. *Orange Invts.*, the residence at the Noordeinde, I, p. xxv; see also p. 193, a 'Jappaens cabinet met een tafelken daer't op staet . . .' [a Japan cabinet with a small table to stand it upon], p. 204, two 'cabinetten van Oostindien', one with a red and one with a black ground, and one Japan cabinet inlaid with mother-of-pearl.

10. *Orange Invts.*, I, p. 191. Noordeinde inventory, 1632; 'Een cabinet van buyten becleet

met Parsiansch stoff met een gouden gront ende versheyde blomkens, staende op een vergulde schabelle.'

11. John Stalker and George Parker's *Treatise of Japaning . . . Together with . . . Patterns of Japan-work . . . for . . . Cabinets, Boxes, etc.*, 1688. A Parisian harpsichord decorated with gilt *chinoiseries* on a black ground and dated 1681 (in the Victoria and Albert Museum) represents the parallel development in France, and Dutch equivalents could certainly be found.

12. This was especially so in royal circles in France as the *Comptes des Bâtiments* of the period show.

13. Jervis, *loc. cit.*, illustrates the tortoiseshell group.

14. In the French royal collection there were some 'guéridons de marqueterie' made to accompany a cabinet ('pour mettre au costé dudit cabinet' [placed on either side] *Guiffrey, Inventaire, II*, p. 144). *Havard* (Guéridon) cites a reference to a lacquer suite in Paris in 1694. A magnificent cabinet which is still associated with its pair of stands is at Knole (see G. Jackson-Stops, 'The 6th Earl of Dorset's Furniture at Knole', I, *Country Life*, 2 June 1977, Plate 1).

15. *Savary des Bruslons*, 'Cabinet'.

16. *Gosfield Invt., 1638.*

17. Inventory of Claudine Bouzonnet Stella, widow of Jacques Stella, *Nouvelle archives de l'art Français*, 1877.

18. *Orange Invts.*, I, p. 162.

19. See Fritz Heikamp, 'Zur Geschichte der Uffizien-Tribuna', *Zeitschrift für Kunstgeschichte*, 1963.

20. *Orange Invts.*, I, Inventory of the Oude Hof at the Noordeinde, 1632, pp. 204–206. The list is repeated in the *Nordeinde Invt., 1633.*

21. Some of the pottery is stated to have come from Fontainebleau and will therefore have been what is today called Palissy ware. The rest is described as 'porceleyne' although whether all of it came from the Far East is not clear. Since the quantity of 'porcelain' in the room was so large, it is likely that some of it was in fact European but this by no means certain. Some of the supports are described as 'richels' although precisely what these were like has not yet been discovered.

22. This 'Inventory of all the parcels of purselin, glasses & other goods now remayning in the Pranketing Roome at Tart Hall', taken on 8 November 1641, is unpublished (archives of

Arundel Castle, Ms.L.M.1). I am much indebted to Mr Francis Steer for drawing my attention to this important document and to His Grace the Duke of Norfolk for allowing me to quote from it here. Reference is made in the *Tart Hall Iventory of 1641* to the Banqueting Room, where it is specifically called 'Dutch', but the inventory concerned is a separate document. Among the porcelain items were '3 white little purselin figures, the first a man and a woeman; the second a dolphin' as well as 'a lyon on a pedestall of white purselin' which could be early specimens of Fukien *blanc-de-chine* ware.

23. *Orange Invts.*, I, pp. 250–2. See also pp. 310–11, for a later list.

24. See Th. H. Lunsingh Scheurleer, 'Stadhouderlijke Lakkabinetten', *Opstellen voor H. van der Waal*, Amsterdam/Leiden, 1970, p. 166. Marot may also have seen the drawing reproduced as Figure 236 here.

25. See G. Upmark, 'Ein Besuch in Holland, 1687; Aus der Reise schilderungen des schwedischen Architekten Nicodemus Tessin d.J.,' *Oud Holland*, 18, 1900.

26. Le Comte Biver, *Histoire du Château de Meudon*, Paris, 1923, p. 443 et seq. It may well be that the vessels of Siamese porcelain in the Dauphin's collection had been presented to him when the Siamese ambassadors were received at the Court of Versailles in 1686. Siamese porcelain was rather coarser than that of China but was technically similar. It is interesting that contemporary French connoisseurs could tell the difference. Clearly there were discriminating collectors at the time. Dr Martin Lister met one in Paris at the very end of the century and reported that this man owned 'the greatest variety, and best sorted China ware I ever saw, besides pagods and China pictures' (*A Journey to Paris*, London, 1699, p. 35).

27. See Fiske Kimball, *The Creation of the Rococo*, Philadelphia, 1942, Plate 22.

28. See Arthur Lane, 'Queen Mary II's Porcelain Collection At Hampton Court', *Transactions of the Oriental Ceramic Society*, 1945–50; also Joan Wilson, 'A Phenomenon of Taste; The Chinaware of Queen Mary II', *Apollo*, August 1973.

29. An illustration of the 'Porzellankammer' at Oranienburg was published in I. B. Broebes, *Prospect des Palläste . . .*, 1733. See also H. Kreisel, *Deutsche Spielgelkabinette*, Darmstadt, c. 1953.

30. See *Orange Invts.*, II, cf. 1684 inventory of Oranienstein with the 1695 inventory (pp. 121–33 and 159–203). The inventory of the Nassau-Dietz residence at Leeuwarden (pp. 147–52) also shows how extensive were these Dutch princely collections of porcelain.

31. *Kensington Palace Invts., 1697* and *1699*.

32. D. Defoe, *A Tour through England and Wales* (1724–27), Everyman edn., London, 1948, pp. 165–6. However, when the expense became prohibitive, painted wooden or plaster of Paris imitations of Chinese porcelain jars and vases could be used, at least in the less conspicuous corners. Such deceits 'mit blau und weissen Figuren auf Porcellanahrt' [with blue and white figures like those on porcelain] were noted in a Berlin inventory (*Stengel*, p. 73).

33. For example the Duchess of Ormonde had '4 pedestalls gilt for china' at Kilkenny Castle in 1684 (*Invt.*) which indicates that she had at least four groups of china ware forming conspicuous features in the décor of one room.

34. Heikamp, *op. cit.*

35. In the *Kilkenny Inventory of 1684* are listed many 'knots' of ribbon of various colours which must have been such bows. Fifteen were 'of several colours for the glass and sconces' in the Drawing Room. In Her Grace's Bedchamber there were 'three knots of ribbon to the looking glass'.

36. William Salmon, *Polygraphice, or the Arts of Drawing, Engraving, Etching, Limning, etc.*, London, 1675, III, Chap. XV. I am indebted to Mr Benno Forman for drawing my attention to this amusing passage.

37. 'An Inventory of the Pictures . . . Ham House . . . 1679'. This unpublished document was acquired by my colleague, Mr John Hardy, and presented to Ham House where it may now be seen.

38. When the Duke and Duchess subsequently exchanged bedrooms, it proved impossible to swap the fixed paintings over, so she ended up sleeping in a room with some 'masculine' pictures. The movable pictures of course presented no problem.

39. A thoughtful essay on this question by Sir Oliver Millar is to be found in *The Destruction of the Country House*, London, 1974, pp. 103–6, ed. Roy Strong, Marcus Binney and John Harris. See also J. Fowler and J. Cornforth, *English Decoration in the 18th century*, London, 1974, Chap. 8, 'Attitudes to pictures and picture hanging'.

40. Was the Earl of Northampton's 'skreene of

tabine fringed' which stood in a very grand bedchamber in 1614 (*Invt.*) an *écran* or a *paravent*? Tobine was a silk material.

41. *Hengrave Invt., 1603.* Six-leafed screens were commonest; many examples could be cited including the four at Marly which were fourteen feet high (Pitoin, *op. cit.*, p. 174). At Tart Hall (*Invt., 1641*) there was a screen of eight leaves in the Gallery.

42. The folding screen at Hengrave Hall (see previous note) had 'a skreene cloth upon it of green kersey'. In store at Easton Lodge (*Invt., 1637*) were some 'skreene Clothes for Foldinge skreines'.

43. Leather-covered screens survive in some quality and are invariably faced on one side only; the framing may be seen at the back. There is no reason to suppose other sorts of screen were normally treated differently although Cardinal *Mazarin* had 'une sorte de paravent à double face de serge cramoisy, garnie de petit passement d'argent[,] clouée' [a kind of screen with two faces of crimson serge, trimmed with a narrow silver galloon, nailed] (*Invt., 1653*).

44. The eight-leafed screen in the Gallery at Tart Hall (see note 40 above) was covered with blue baize.

45. Late seventeenth-century screens seem often to have been faced with silk damask. Those in the Council Chamber at Kensington Palace (*Invt., 1697*), for instance, were blue and one had a protective 'baize screen bagg'.

46. *Ham Invt., c. 1654.* This screen was in Elizabeth Dysart's own room so was presumably a valued object.

47. An early example would seem to be that at Tredegar in 1688 (*Invt.*); there was also one in the gilt leather Parlour at Dyrham in 1703 (*Invt.*) which may be that still in the house.

48. *Ham Invt., 1679*; it was in the Withdrawing Room and was probably quite a notable item in that reception room.

49. Nicodemus Tessin gave the Swedish Countess Piper a Savonnerie screen (*écran* or *paravent*?) in 1700; he felt that such 'ouvrages paroissent d'une grande durée' [such work seems to be exceptionally durable] (*Tessin-Cronström Correspondence*, letter of 31 January 1700).

50. See J. Irwin, 'A Jacobean Vogue for Oriental Lacquer-ware', *The Burlington Magazine*, December 1953, pp. 193–4. Scriptors were writing cabinets (*escritorios* in Spanish); *beobee* was the Japanese for a screen.

51. e.g. at Honselaarsdijk (see p. 78), and at Leeuwarden (*Orange Invts.*, pp. xxix and II, p. 147).

52. *Ham Invts. 1679 and 1683.*

53. One At Tart Hall is actually described as being circular (*Invt., 1641*). The lack of specific descriptions suggests that they were all the same shape and such evidence as we have all points to their having been circular.

54. At Hengrave Hall there was a 'little fine wicker skrene, sett in a frame of walnut tree' (*Invt., 1603*) and the Arundels had 'in the chimney, hanging on a rod with iron feete, a little wickar skreene' at Tart Hall (*Invt., 1641*). Was the 'wandel screen' at Gilling Castle in 1624 (*Invt.*) of a coarser sort, and how did the 'twiggen skreyne' at Hardwick (Old Hall) differ from the wicker ones also mentioned in the inventory of 1601?

55. There was a 'wicker fan for the fire' at Cockesden in 1610 (*Invt.*).

56. *Randle Holme*, Book III, Chap. 16, p. 83.

57. They may have lingered on in Ireland for, even at Kilkenny Castle (*Invt., 1684*) in the time of the great Duke of Ormonde, there was a wicker screen on 'a steel stem'.

58. *Walpole's Letters*, Walpole to Montague, 1 September, 1766.

59. *Hardwick Invt., 1601.*

60. For example, the several screen cloths listed in the *Charles I Inventories, 1649–51* were of two widths of material and were mostly $3\frac{1}{2}$ yards long although one was only $2\frac{1}{2}$ yards long. This last was embroidered with the arms of the Knights of the Garter within a circle. But we have shown that some screen cloths were for folding screens (see note 42).

61. 'One screen with a screen stick garnished with silver' is still in the house. It now has a tapestry-woven leaf which appears to date from the eighteenth century and may have replaced an original leaf of no great distinction.

62. Lady Johanna St John made a specific bequest of her 'crosstich screen' which stood in her dining room, when she wrote her will in 1705 (Somerset House, Gee 40; kindly communicated by Mr Frank Smallwood).

63. *Havard*, 'Ecran'.

64. *D.E.F.*, 'Screen', Plate 5. In the King's Library at Kensington Palace in 1697 (*Invt.*) there stood a 'sliding fire-screen, one side embroidered with silke'.

65. See *D.E.F.*, 'Chimney Furniture'.

66. A satirical pamphlet of 1642 likens bishops to 'andirons of state, standing in the chimney for show; but if a heavy block or red billets are brought to the fire there are four little creepers or cobirons underneath [i.e. the lesser clergy] who must bear all the weight' ('Threefold Discourse Between Three Neighbours'; quoted by F. Lenygon, *Decoration in England from 1640–1760*, London, 1927, p. 231). When creepers were present, a pair would normally have sufficed and it is not clear why the satirist speaks of four; maybe he wanted to exaggerate the difference.

67. So familiar were these objects that a writer in 1650 could make a comparison with 'brazen andirons in great men's chimnees' and expect to be understood (*O.E.D.*, 'Andiron'). References to andirons of brass or latten are so common that to cite any here is unnecessary but there was a splendid pair at Tart Hall (*Invt., 1641*) of which 'the upper part thereof [was] of cast brass pt. guilt'.

68. At Cockesden in 1610 (*Invt.*) there was a 'payre of Flaunders cobirones . . . and a payre of creepers'.

69. See *D.E.F.*, 'Chimney Furniture', Plate 7. At Cowdray (*Invt.*, 1682) there were some 'brass andirons enamelled' with a set of fire-irons *en suite*.

70. *Northampton Invt., 1614* and *D.E.F.* 'Chimney Furniture', Plate 2.

71. *Kilkenny Invt., 1684*. Stoves, incidentally, were not common in the British Isles but seem to have been familiar in Holland and to have gained some favour in France during the third quarter of the century (see *Havard*, 'Poêle').

72. *Mazarin Invt. 1653*. A particularly early example was the 'paire of andirons garnished with silver' that were listed in the *Charles I Inventories, 1649–51*.

73. *D.E.F.*, 'Chimney Furniture' (Misson's *Mémoires*, 1698). Already by 1606 one could speak of something being 'as common as coales from Newcastle' and the well-known proverb about people who 'carry coals to Newcastle' was certainly current by the middle of the century. (*O.E.D.*, 'Coal'; that 'coals' were charcoal is borne out by a reference of 1628 to the 'turning of trees to coals for fuel . . .').

74. William Harison, *Description of England*, 1577, and *Hardwick Invt., 1601*.

75. At Hengrave Hall (*Invt., 1603*) it is evident that coal was burned in the Hall but logs were burned in the Great Chamber.

76. *Chatsworth Invt., 1601* and *Tart Hall Invt., 1641*.

77. *Henham Invt., 1602* and *Ham Invt., 1679*.

78. At Hengrave Hall in 1603 (*Invt.*) there was a 'fier sholve made like a grate to seft the seacole with'.

79. *Randle Holme* (Bk. III, Chap. XIV, p. 7) claims that the more ornate forms of tongs were 'for ladys chambers and seldome used there, but hung by the fire-side more for shew and ornament then use'. He called the more serviceable sort 'useing tonges' or 'kitchen tongues'. There was a small-sized kind known as 'brand tongs' with which a live coal could be picked up for lighting a pipe although it is not certain this variant existed before 1700; perhaps it was identical with the '*tirebraize*' that was included in a set of fire-irons that belonged to Cardinal Mazarin (*Invt., 1653*).

80. *Edington Invt., 1665* and *Ham Invt., 1679*.

81. Nell Gwynn was given a pair of bellows decorated with marquetry which had silver mounts. A pair belonging to the Earl of Northampton (*Invt., 1614*) was inlaid with mother-of-pearl. A pair similarly decorated belonged to Lady Dorchester who kept hers with other valuable objects, including an ivory cup, some linen, 'certen beads' in a small box, some small cabinets and a 'tostinge forke', 'in the Deale chest' (*Gosfield Invt., 1638*). The silver-mounted pair at Ham is well known; at Hatfield Priory (*Invt., 1629*) there was a carved pair which is likely to have been Italian.

82. The status of the rooms at Ham House can be guaged by the richness of the fire-irons allocated to the respective fire-places, the grandest rooms have silver-mounted irons while those in less important rooms have mounts of brass.

83. At Ingatestone (*Invt., 1600*) in two instances the 'skepp baskett for cooles' was placed in the 'House of Office', the small closet where the close-stool lived. *Randle Holme* illustrates such a skep (Fig. 319[83]).

84. By Antoine de Courtin, originally published as the *Nouveau Traité de la Civilité*. The Yeoman Usher of the Great Chamber of an important household in 1605 was instructed to attend to the fire 'at the season of the yeare, or ells the chemney to bee garnished with greene bowes, or flowers' ('Breviate touching upon the Order and governement of a Noblemans House', *Archeologia*, XIII, 1800, p. 332).

85. Brantôme, for instance, tells of a certain

Admiral Bonnivet who one evening was surprised in the room of a lady of the court on whom King François I was also at the time wont to bestow his favours. The Admiral only just had time to scramble behind the foliage in the fireplace before the King came into the room and himself climbed into the bed alongside the lady. Later, the King felt a need to relieve himself and proceeded to do so in the fireplace. As Brantôme puts it, he 'la vint faire dans la cheminée, et arrousa le pauvre amoureux plus que si l'on luy eust jetté un seilleau d'eau' [came to do it in the fireplace, and soaked the poor lover more than if a bucket of water had been thrown on him].

86. *Havard*, 'Devant de Cheminée'; see also 'Papier de Cheminée'.

87. *Havard*, 'Tapis' and 'Cheminée'.

88. *Provost of King's Invt., 1660*.

89. 'Two 17th century Dorset inventories', ed. Lettice Ashley Cooper, *Dorset Record Society*, Publication No. 5, 1974 and *Charles I Invts., 1649–51*.

90. *Tart Hall Invt., 1641*.

91. *Ham Invt., 1679*. These may have been the bronzes after Giovanni Bologna and others which were still in the house at the beginning of the present century. Above the corner chimneypiece in the Duchess of Lauderdale's White Closet at Ham stood, and still stands, the gilded full-size bust of 'Her Grace's mother' now attributed to Dieussart.

92. Dutch flower-paintings may not always be strictly accurate (blooms that flower at different times of the year are sometimes depicted together) but probably convey the general spirit of seventeenth-century flower-arrangements. See R. Warner, *Dutch and Flemish Fruit and Flower Painters of the XVII and XVIII centuries*, London, 1928, and M. L. Hairs, *Les peintres flamands de fleurs au XVIIe siècle*, Paris and Brussels, 1955; also W. Blunt, *The Art of Botanical Illustration*, London, 1950.

93. The trade-plate of a Nottingham pottery dating from the late seventeenth century shows a massive bucket-shaped vessel with a pair of handles in which a shrub is growing (orange tree?); it is described as a 'flower pott' (see *World Ceramics*, ed. Robert Charleston, London, 1968, fig. 386). At Dyrham (*Invt., 1703*) there was in one room a 'Delf[t] flower pot in ye chimney'.

94. Cardinal Mazarin had 'quatre pots à bouquets d'argent blanc, façon de Paris' [four bouquet vases of silver in the Parisian taste] (*Invt., 1653*).

In the *Du Boisgeslin Inventory of 1688* mention is made 'vases à bouquets de terre blance' [vases for bouquets of white ware] which were painted and gilded; there were also some 'petites vases à fleurs en un grand de fayence' [small flower vases and a large one of fayence]. These all seem to have been for cut flowers. The 'pots à fleurs' in the French royal collection (*Guiffrey, Inventaire*, I, p. 44, 1673) which were one and a half *pieds* high may have been tall vases but could equally well have been containers for flower-pots. Some 'pots à fleurs' were of metal, in which case they must surely have been in the nature of *jardinières*, but the *pot à fleur* made of engraved rock crystal in the French royal collection (*Ibid*, p. 222) can only have been a vase for cut flowers.

95. *Ham Invt., 1679*.

96. *Celia Fiennes*, p. 154 and p. 355.

97. *Tart Hall Invt., 1641*. This does not seem to have been a *jardinière* for there were several 'flower potts' in the house, two of which were 'leaden . . . gilded' while others were of 'letany' (i.e. brass), and can only have been containers for actual pots with plants growing in them.

98. *Havard*, 'Fleur'.

99. *Savary des Bruslons*, 'Bouquets'. Artificial flowers were made in nunneries and sold by the *marchands merciers*.

100. The Swedish Countess Brahe owned a beadwork basket filled with wax fruit and silk flowers, as well as a glass vase in which stood some white lillies of silk. In a closet she had a glass vase with glass flowers, and a basket with straw flowers. When one of her sons got married she gave his wife some small silver vases filled with artificial flowers. At one of her country farms some delftware vases on the chimneypiece were filled with paper flowers (W. Karlson, *Ebba Brahe's Hem*, Lund, 1943, p. 47 and inventory of 1665).

NOTES TO CHAPTER XI

1. J. du Pradel, in his *Traité contre le luxe* of 1705, contrasts the simple tastes of yesteryear when people had been content to burn *chandelles* (tallow candles) at four *sous* per pound with the present extravagant age when one had to burn wax candles (*bougies*) costing twenty-two *sous* the pound. The cost of lights in England at the beginning of the seventeenth century is discussed in 'The House and Farm Accounts of the Shuttleworths of Gawthorpe Hall . . .' (ed. J.

Harland), *The Chetham Society*, 1857, Pt. III, Notes, 'Candles'). Rush lights were made of peeled meadow rushes (with a strip left to give strength) soaked in fat. A rush light fourteen inches long would burn in about half an hour. Tallow candles were made half of beef fat and half of mutton, refined; in Paris, at any rate, one was not permitted to add pork fat which was particularly smelly, but tallow candles were always smelly and gave an uneven light. 'Base and unlustrous as the smoky light that's fed with stinking tallow' is a passage that occurs in Shakespeare's *Cymbeline* (Act 1, Scene 7). Bees-wax candles were brighter and burned evenly; moreover they did not smell, and their wick required little snuffing as they did not 'gutter' or dribble down the sides. Samuel Pepys 'began to burn wax candles in my closet at the office [the Admiralty], to try the charge [expense], and to see whether the smoke offends like that of tallow candles' (*Pepys' Diary*, 15 December 1664). *Bougies* were normally tapered but 'bougies de table' were cylindrical. The whitest candles were called 'bougies de Venise' but some candles were 'citronnée' (see *Savary des Bruslons*, 'Bougies' and 'Chandelles'). At Somerset House in 1650 there was a 'chest of yellow wax lights' and another of white (*Charles I Invts., 1649–51*).

2. John Aubrey, *Brief Lives*, written between 1667 and 1680 (ed. O. L. Dick, Penguin Books, London, 1972). Madame de Maintenon's brother used only one pound of *chandelles* (tallow candles) a day—one in the *antichambre*, one in the kitchen and one in the stable (G. Mongrédien, *La vie quotidienne sous Louis XIV*, Paris, 1948).

3. For instance, at the banquet given for Charles II at the Mauritshuis at The Hague in 1660 (Fig. 257), there depended from the ceiling 'four lustres, or christal candlesticks [chandeliers]; which with many candlesticks, arms of silver, and a great number of torches, enlightened all the corners much better than the sun could have done at midday' (William Lower, *Voiage and Residence which ... Charles II ... hath made in Holland ... 1660*, The Hague, 1660). At a ball given in the Galerie des Glaces at Versailles there were 7,000 candles. With the lights multiplied over and over again by the mirror-glass panelling, the effect must have been breath-taking and extremely impressive—as was the intention (see *Tessin-Cronström Correspondence*, letter of 29 November 1695).

4. The same care was bestowed on candles as on the household linen. The Yeoman of the Ewery at Lord Montague's house (*Household Book, 1595*) was instructed to look after the linen, the candlesticks and the 'torches, lynkes and candles'. At Ingatestone (*Invt., 1600*) there was not only a 'plaine longe chest to laye linnen in' in the Buttery but 'a long shelfe to sett candlesticks upon', as well as a candlebox and a 'lock to the candle-house' door. Candle chests and candle boxes are listed quite frequently in seventeenth century inventories. Lady Rivers made a specific bequest of her 'cofer with partitions wherein my lights doe lye' J. Watney, *Some Account of St Osyth's Priory, Essex*, London, 1871. Incidentally, candles were never fitted in chandeliers except when actually needed, as numerous illustrations of the period show. A single candle at most was left in one of the branches to serve in an emergency.

5. Furetière (*Dictionnaire, 1690*) explains that a *lustre* could be a sconce with a mirror-glass back-plate and also a 'chandelier de cristal qu'on suspendu au plancher' [a candle-holder of crystal [glass] that one suspends from the ceiling].

6. At a ball given for the Duchesse de Bourgogne at Versailles in 1700 'il y avoit sur tous les pilastres des demi-girandoles à cinq branches d'argent. Ces girandoles ... ont été nouvellement inventées par M. Bérain' [there were on all the pilasters demi-girandoles with five branches of silver. These girandoles ... have been designed by Mr Bérain] (*Havard*, 'Girandole').

7. The Dictionary of the French Academy of 1696 explains that a *torchère* was 'une éspèce de guéridon fort eslevé, sur lequel on met un flambeau, une girandole ... dans les sales des ... grandes maisons' [a kind of very tall *guéridon* on which one places a candlestick or candelabrum ... in drawing rooms ... in great houses]. However, the royal silversmith, Claude Ballin, provided 'une grandissme torchère à cinq bobeshes [a very large torchère with five nozzles] for use in the French royal household in 1673.

8. Wooden candlesticks probably dropped from fashion because nozzles of wood have very little strength so, for a wooden candlestick, it was best to retain the old pricket form with an iron spike onto which the candle was fixed. Only thick candles could be used with a pricket. There were several wooden candlesticks in the kitchen at Ingatestone (*Invt., 1600*). The 'paynted candlesticks' in the High Great Chamber at Chatsworth (*Invt., 1601*) may also have been of wood and

will certainly have been very splendid (consonant with the richly inlaid panelling and the valuable contents of the room) but were probably old-fashioned and may anyway have been sconces rather than candlesticks as we understand them.

9. *Mazarin Invt., 1653*. *Havard* ('Chandelier') suggests that 'à la financière' implied adjustable in height.

10. *Marton Invt., 1605*

11. *Havard*, 'Chandelier'.

12. 'When your Soveraigne is in bed, draw the curtaines and see there be mortar of wax or perchours ready', advises J. Murrell in his *Cookery and Carving* of 1641. A 'percher' was a small candle that could be fixed to a stand called a perch.

13. Comte Paul Biver, *Histoire du Château de Meudon*, Paris, 1923, p. 395, inventory of 'Vaiselles de chambre de Monseigneur le Dauphin' taken in 1702.

14 *Hardwick Invt., 1601, Hengrave Invt., 1603*, and *Marton Invt., 1605*. The last were of 'latten' but although the others were both described as being of copper it is almost certain they too were of brass.

15. *Book of Rates, 1582*. Brassware was primarily made at Dinant and was particularly popular in the Low Countries. There were, for instance, no less than seventy copper (brass?) plate candlesticks (*pannecandelaers*) at Breda Castle in 1597–1603 (*Orange Invts.*, I, p. 75).

16. The back-plates might be decorated 'with Faces, others with Birds, Beasts, Fish, Trees and Flowers, some round or oval embossed works' (*Randle Holme*; see *D.E.F.*, 'Sconces' where this passage is quoted and some examples are illustrated).

17. *Tart Hall Invt., 1641*.

18. *Mazarin Invt., 1653*, and *Havard*, 'Plaques'.

19. *Tart Hall Invt., 1641*, and *Lauderdale London Invt., 1679*.

20. *Cowdray Invt., 1682*.

21. *Havard*, 'Carton Pierre', and *Mazarin Invt., 1653*.

22. *Ham Invt., 1679*.

23. *Hardwick Invt., 1601*, and *Hengrave Invt., 1603*. The Hardwick pair may be those now hanging in the bays of the Long Gallery.

24. The French royal inventories for 1685 include a specific reference to a 'chandelier . . . de cristal de Milan' (*Guiffrey, Inventaire*, II, No. 199). See J. Holey, 'Der Kristalkronleuchter;

seine Entstehung und Engwicklung', *Stifter Jahrbuch*, VIII, Locham bei München, 1964; he illustrates a splendid rock crystal chandelier of about 1690 in Genoa as well as two in Vienna which are likely to be Milanese. See also C. Waage Petersen, *Lysekroner*, Copenhagen, 1969, and the *D.E.F.* 'Chandelier'.

25. *Rambouillet Invt., 1665*. From about this time onwards, crystal chandeliers were commonly called *lustres*.

26. *D.E.F.*, 'Chandelier'.

27. *Ibid.* When the King gave Cosimo III a farewell banquet at the end of the Grand Duke's visit to this country in 1669 there was a 'chandelier of rock crystal with lighted tapers . . . suspended from the ceiling' (*The Travels of Cosmo the Third . . .*, London, 1821). It was very probably the identical piece.

28. *Kilkenny Invt., 1684*. The Ormondes owned several pieces of French furniture and this chandelier probably came from France as well.

29. *Ham Invt., 1679*.

30. See Holey, and Waage Petersen, *op. cit.*; also A. Polak, 'Om glas-lysekrone', Oslo Kunstindustrimuseum's *Yearbook*, 1943–9. There is a fine glass chandelier at Skokloster, Sweden, which was apparently in place by 1672 (E. Andrén, 'Melchior Jung's glasbruk i Stockholm . . .', *St Eriks Årsbok*, 1972).

31. e.g. the French royal inventory for 1684 includes the item 'une chandelier de cristal de Venise' which it is reasonable to suppose was composed of Venetian glass.

32. See Holey, *op. cit.*, and D. Rentsch, 'Bedeutung und Restaurierung des grossen Glaskronleuchters in Schloss Favorite', *Jahrbuch der Staatlichen Kunstsammlungen in Baden-Württemberg*, Bd, 12, 1975.

33. *O.E.D.*, 'Lustre'.

34. Perhaps Cardinal Mazarin's 'chandeliers à pyramides' were early versions of these.

35. *Tart Hall Invt., 1641, Edington Invt., 1665*, and *Orange Invts.*, I, p. 195 'twee flambeaupilaeren, vergult ende met rooden gront' [two candlestands, gilded and with a red ground].

36. See G. Jackson-Stops, 'The 6th Earl of Dorset's Furniture at Knole', I, *Country Life*, 2 June 1977, and illustrated in colour on the cover. What was apparently the payment for these items appears in the French royal treasurer's accounts for February 1671.

37. A drawing for four magnificent candlestands by Alessandro Algardi, the Roman sculptor, is

illustrated in G. Lizzani, *Il mobili Romano*, Milan, 1970, introduction by G. Gonzales-Palacios, Plate XIV.

38. 'Two Blackamore Stands' (*Ham Invt., 1679*).

39. The song had been current in the second half of the century. One heartless verse ran as follows:

> Guéridon est mort
> Depuis plus d'une heure,
> Sa femme la pleure,
> Hélas, Guéridon.
>
> [Guéridon has died
> more than an hour ago,
> his wife weeps,
> alas, Guéridon]

People at first gave the name to their negro servants and some wag then gave it to candlestands in the form of negroes. *Havard* ('Guéridon') noted an early use of the word in this sense in 1650.

40. *Ibid.*

41. *Ibid.*, and *Tessin's Visit, 1687*, p. 25.

42. The description of a party given by Madame de Chaulnes for Anne d'Autriche in 1651 makes this clear.

> A l'entour de la même sale,
> Et dans une distance égale,
> Des Mores noirs et non pas blonds,
> Fait en forme de guéridons,
> Chacun portant dessus sa teste,
> Un grand plat de viande preste,
> Et des autres entre leurs mains,
> Les uns remplis de massepains,
> Et les autres de marmelades
>
> [Around the same room,
> and at equal distances,
> black Moors and none fair,
> made in the shape of *guéridons*,
> each carrying on his head
> a large dish of prepared meat,
> and others in their hands,
> some filled with marchepain
> and others with marmalade.]

(*Havard*, 'Guéridon').

43. At Marly there were some 'paires de guéridons de 3 pieds de haut', which was an average height, and some smaller pairs 'pour tables de jeux' (C. Pitoin, *Marly-le-Roi*, Paris, 1904, p. 174). Three *pieds* would be roughly 91.5

cm. The heights of the *guéridons* shown at the Exhibition 'Louis XIV: Faste et Décors' (Musée des Arts-Décoratifs, Paris, 1960) ranged in height from 98 to 120 cm with three pairs being 175 cm and one 170 cm.

44. A drawing showing a room in a Roman *palazzo* with mural decoration couched in an ebullient Baroque style and attributed by Gonzales-Palacios (see Lizzani, *op. cit.*, Plate XXXVI) to G. P. Schor shows a candlestand placed in the corner of the room. Judging by the costume, this composition dates from about 1670. The Duc d'Orléans had some japanned (*vernis de Chine*) *guéridons* standing in the same position in his bedchamber at Versailles in 1708 (*Havard*, 'Chambre'), and there is a description of a masqued ball given in 1706 where 'the Duc de Bourgogne and three others—le Vidame, the Prince de Rohan and young Seignelay—were wittily dressed; they were in gold with golden masks and silver sashes like carved gilt guéridons. They wore candelabra on their heads and stationed themselves at the four corners of the room' (*Letters from Liselotte*, the letters of the Princess Palatine, ed. Maria Kroll, 1970; letter of 25 February 1706).

45. *Mazarin Invt., 1653.*

46. Jean de La Bruyère, *Charactères*, 1688.

47. The crystal chandelier at the Hôtel de Rambouillet (see note 25 above) was suspended with a 'cordon or et soie' [silk and gold cord], while *Mazarin* (*Invt., 1653*) owned several 'cordons d'argent et soie couleur de feu, garnis de boutons d'or et d'argent par les bouts, servant à suspendre les chandeliers' [cords of flame-coloured silk, furnished with gold and silver buttons [pom-poms?] at each end, used for hanging chandeliers].

48. At Kilkenny Castle (*Invt., 1684*) the crystal chandelier (see note 28 above) had 'a knot of ribbon on top'. The gold and silver 'boutons' mentioned in the previous note will also have served to disguise the hooks.

49. *Hengrave Invt., 1603.*

NOTES TO CHAPTER XII

1. Already in 1618 we find the Bishop of Winchester (*Invt.*) distinguishing between his Great Chamber and his Dining Parlour, calling them respectively the 'Great Dining Room' and the 'Little Dining Room'; but for a long time there was always a qualifying word. For in-

stance, the senior staff at the Countess of Leicester's (*Invt., 1634*) ate in 'The Mens Dyninge-roome' and those at Ham (*Invt., 1679*) in 'The Gentlemen's Dining Roome'. On the other hand, the 'Corner Dineing Room' at Cowdray in 1682 (*Invt.*) and the 'Marble Dining Room' at Ham (*Invt. 1679*) were both used solely by the family, the qualifying word having nothing to do with their size or purpose. A similar room at Petworth in 1670 (*Invt.*) was called the 'Supping Room', however, and the nomenclature was by no means firmly established by the end of the century when *Celia Fiennes* (p. 24) could still speak of 'The large dineinge roome or great parlour' at Coleshill.

2. J. P. Babelon, *Demeures Parisiennes sous Henri IV et Louis XIII*, Paris, 1965, p. 196. When the ambassadors from Siam visited Paris and Versailles in 1686 they were provided with an apartment that included a 'salle à manger' (Deville, *Dictionnaire de Tapissier*, Paris, 1878–80). There was also a room so entitled at the Mme. de Montespan's Château de Clagny (see A. and J. Marie, *Mansart à Versailles*, Paris, 1972, p. 31). *Havard* ('Salle à manger') noted what he called an early reference to the term in 1787 (*sic*) and even this was to 'une anti-chambre servant de salle à manger'.

3. In the Thiret mansion at Rheims in 1621 (*Invt.*), for example, 'La Grande Salle' was clearly intended for use as a dining-room—and was presumably the equivalent of a Great Chamber—while there was both a 'Salle Basse' and a 'Salette Basse' equipped for dining. The latter was next to the main bedchamber and seems to have been the family's private dining parlour, but maybe they normally dined in the 'Salle Basse', and only used the *salette* for informal *soupers*.

4. See P. Verlet, *Versailles*, Paris, 1961, p. 248, for further details. On less formal occasions the King dined in his closet 'à petit couvert'. Saint-Simon records having dined in the *anti-chambre* of the Cardinal de Rohan.

5. There are numberous references in the contemporary French literature to dining in bedchambers and closets. The poet Scarron wrote a charming verse inviting Pierre Mignard, the painter, to join him and dine 'dans ma chambre' (*Havard*, 'Salle à manger'). When Queen Christina of Sweden visited the French court it was noted that she 'ne dinoit pas souvent en public servie par ses officiers, mais presque toujours dans son petit cabinet servie par ses femmes' [did not often dine in public attended by her officers, but almost always in her private attended by her ladies] (*Ibid.*). Queen Elizabeth also preferred to dine in her 'inner and most private chamber', according to Paul Hentzner who visited England in 1598 (W. B. Rye, *England as Seen by Foreigners*, London, 1865, p. 100). Dr Martin Lister saw an Orangery in Paris which was 'the most beautiful room . . . I make no doubt it served to eat in in Summer when cleared of trees' (M. Lister, *A Journey to Paris*, London, 1699, p. 139).

6. Already in 1641 at Tart Hall (*Invt.*) there was an 'ovall Table of Wanscote wth. falling sides' in the Waiters' Room 'next the Little Parler' into which it could presumably be carried. In the Little Parlour itself stood a French draw-table and a small round table with 'falling leaves', so the oval table will have been for use when the company was large.

7. *Montague Household Book, 1595*, p. 129, and Fynes Moryson, *Itinerary*, 1617.

8. *Randle Holme*, Bk. III, Chap. XIV, p. 15. At Hengrave (*Invt., 1603*) there was 'a great coppr. sestourne to stand at the coobard'. At Ham (*Invt., 1679*) the wine-cooler of white marble is still in the house.

9. Near the 'grand dessert' or *buffet* in the Thiret mansion (*Invt. 1621*) stood 'ung rafrechissoir de cuivre avec le pied de bois' [a wine-cooler of copper with its stand].

10. So much ice was required in French fashionable circles that it was regarded as a valuable concession to be granted the monopoly of supplying ice to the whole of France, as happened to a certain Louis de Beaumont in 1700 (A. Lebault, *La Table et le repas à travers le siècle*, Paris, 1960, p. 136).

11. *Ibid.*

12. Balthazar Gerbier, *A Brief Discourse concerning the three Chief Principles of Magnificent Building*, 1662, p. 35.

13. 'This year [1683] came up a vessel or bason notched at the rim to let drinking glasses hang there by the foot, so that the body or drinking parte hang in the water to coole them' (Anthony à Wood, quoted by C. C. Oman, *English Domestic Silver*, 7th edn., London, 1968, p. 136).

14. 'Quand sa Mté. [i.e. Louis XIV] mange à Versailles en famille' he dined with considerable formality in the ancient tradition (*de l'ancienne institution*), we are told by Cronström. 'La table y

est d'un quarré long; le Roy et la Reine seuls ont des fauteuils . . .' [The table is oblong; only the King and Queen have armchairs] (*Tessin-Cronström Correspondence*, letter of 24 February 1702).

15. 'Quant le Roy mange à Marly, Trianon ou quelque autre maison de plaisance, alors le table est grande et ovalle . . . parce que les dames de la cour mangent avec le Roy' [When the King dines at Marly or some other *maison de plaisance*, then the table is large and oval . . . because the ladies of the Court dine with the King] (*Ibid.*). In fact the oval table measured 3 metres by 1.9 and sat eighteen, allowing 50 cm (19 pouces) per diner. This table seems to have been installed in 1699; previously there had been two circular tables each seating fourteen or fifteen people (see C. Pitoin, *Marly-le-Roi*, Paris, 1904, p. 157, with diagrams).

16. William III in 'The King's Pryvat Eating Room below stairs' at Kensington Palace also had 'a large oval table' accompanied by sixteen black leather chairs 'wth. ye large back' (i.e. with tall backs; see *Kensington Palace Invts. 1697* and *1699*). At Ham there were twelve chairs with cane seats in the family dining room; none of them had arms (*Ham Invt., 1679*). Likewise at Cowdray (*Invt., 1682*) the family dining-room contained twelve ordinary chairs, but there were 'two armeing chaires' along with twelve plain chairs in the 'Great Dineing Room'.

17. Louis XIV invariably dined seated in an armchair while those around him sat on stools (*tabourets*). This practice was maintained even at the Trianon where the atmosphere was supposed to be more relaxed ('un fauteuil pour Sa Majesté et vingt-quatre tabourets' [an armchair for His majesty and twenty-four stools] were provided for the Trianon in the 1680s; *Guiffrey, Inventaire*, II, p. 382).

18. *Randle Holme*, Bk. III, Chap. XIV, states that the chairs and stools in a dining-room should be 'of Turky work, Russia or calves leather, cloth or stuffe or needle work. Or els made all of Joynt work or cane chairs.'

19. e.g. The High Great Chamber at Hardwick (*Invt., 1601*), the 'Grande Salle' in the Thiret mansion at Rheims (*Invt., 1621*), the Great Dining Room at Ham (*Invt., 1651*) and the Great Dining Room at Edington (*Invt., 1665*). Large dining parlours like the Low Great Chamber at Hardwick and the Great Parlour at Edington might also be so hung.

20. Robert Adam, 'Instead of being hung with damask or tapestry etc.,' the walls of a dining-room should be of 'stucco, and adorned with statues and paintings, that they may not retain the smell of victuals.' (Robert and James Adam, *The Works in Architecture . . .*, Vol. I, 1773, p. 9.)

21. *Randle Holme* (Bk. III, Chap. XIV) stated that the walls of dining-rooms ought to be 'well wanscoted about, either with Mountan [muntin, the upright members between the panels] and panells, or carved as the fashion was; or else in large square panell'. The 'Little Dyning Chamber' at Hardwick (*Invt., 1601*) had 'waynscott rownde about the . . . roome'; the walls of the dining parlour at Ingatestone were likewise faced (*Invt., 1600*). As for gilt leather, we find it in the 'Salle basse' which served as dining-room in the Thiret mansion (*Invt., 1621*), in the family dining-room at Ham House (*Invt., 1679*) where it is still to be seen on the walls, and in the *Eetsael* at Dieren, the small residence in Holland that Queen Mary II liked so much (*Orange Invts.*, I, p. 289; inventory of 1683). There was also gilt leather on the walls of the 'Banqueting House in the garden' at Cowdray (*Invt., 1682*).

22. *Tessin-Cronström Correspondence*, letter of 24 February, 1702.

23. The 'household books' setting out instructions for the officers of important households mostly give information on these matters. Many survive but only a few have been published. Useful are 'Viscount Montague's Household Book, 1595', Appendix II to Sir William St John Hope, *Cowdray and Easebourne Priory*, London, 1919; and 'A Breviate touching the Order of Governmente of a Nobleman's House, etc.' c. 1605, *Archeologia*, XIII, 1800).

24. The whole company had used the handcloth for wiping their fingers during the meal in former times. After the introduction of napkins, the cloth was only used for drying the hands after the hand-rinsing that followed the meal. A set comprising two tablecloths, thirty-two napkins and a handcloth, all marked with the owner's initials and dated 1638 is cited by C. A. Burgers ('Tafelgoeds in vroeger tijd', *Voedings niews*, No. 60, 1969; 'Twee taffeltiens en 32 servetten int Jaer van 1638 getekent met EVK en d'handdoecken oock').

25. Burgers, *loc. cit.*

26. At Marton Hall (*Invt., 1605*) some napkins were 'wth. coventre thread wrought by the weaver at thende'. Coventry-thread was blue so

this set had an in-woven border of blue at each end.

27. At Breda Castle in 1618, for instance, there were no less than four hundred tablecloths, 3,600 napkins and forty-three handcloths (Burgers, *loc. cit.*).

28. The linen at Marton was wrapped in a worn linen diaper cloth and kept in an iron-bound chest (*Invt., 1605*) while Lady Dorchester kept her linen 'in the deale chest' at Gosfield in 1638 (*Invt.*). There is a famous painting by Pieter de Hoogh showing folded linen being carefully put into a large oak cupboard that stands in the main part of the house.

29. The creases usually formed squares (Plate 276) but fanciful patterns could also be produced like that 'ployée d'une certaine façon, que cela ressembloit fort à quelque rivière andoyante, qu'un petit vent fair doucement sous lever' [folded in a certain fashion so as to look very like some flowing river that a gentle breeze gently lifts] (*Description de l'Isle des Hermaphrodites nouvellement découverte*, 1605). According to G. P. Harsdörfer's *Vollständiges Trichir-Büchlein* of about 1650, linen with a fine damask figure ought not to be pressed with patterns as well.

30. In the Buttery at Hatfield Priory in 1629 (*Invt.*) there was a 'skrew presse for napkins'. The napkins were carefully folded, a small board was placed between each one, and the whole assemblage was compressed with the aid of the screw-thread.

31. *Havard*, 'Nappe'.

32. G. Mongrédien, *La vie quotidienne sous Louis XIV*, Paris, 1948, p. 95.

33. Gédéon Tallement des Réaux, *Historiettes*, (written 1657–9), Paris, 1834–40, VI, p. 96).

34. *Havard*, 'Nappe'. This presumably means that some of the figures were sculpted in sugar-paste, the rest were of folded linen.

35. P. Verlet, *Versailles*, Paris, 1961, p. 81.

36. An excellent survey of table ornament is provided by S. Bursche, *Tafelzier des Barock*, Munich, 1974. He quotes (p. 78) the description of a banquet held at Stuttgart in 1609 where the *Schauessen* were of wax and included scenes of Adam and Eve in the Garden of Eden, The Rape of the Sabines, Diana and Acteon, The Nine Muses with mount Helicon and a spring that ran with water for over an hour, and Jonah and the Whale where a splendid ship floated on a miniature pond with live fish, letting off squibs

that released perfume. Incidentally, when the pie was cut open, birds flew out.

37. *Ibid; passim.*

38. *Randle Holme*, Bk. III, Chap. XIV.

39. Andrew Clark, *The Life and Times of Anthony Wood . . .*; Oxford, 1891, Vol. III, p. 236.

40. At the King's table at Versailles, 'les plats sont servys sur des colliers, ou *ringar*' [the dishes were set forth on collars or rings] as the Swede, Daniel Cronström reported (*Tessin-Cronström Correspondence*; letter of 24 February 1702). At the Duke of Norfolk's house at Weybridge in 1684 (*Invt.*) there were in the Wardrobe Room '2 pewter rings to putt dishes upon'. There were two more at Dyrham in 1703 (*Invt.*). Modern caterers sometimes use tinned iron rings when they have to stack plates of food. Collectors of antique silver are familiar with rings, often of great elaboration, and always bearing Irish hall-marks—a fact that has led to the seemingly mistaken view that they have something to do with that Irish staple food, the potato.

41. See C. C. Oman, 'Caddinets . . .', *Burlington Magazine*, December 1958, 'Le Roy et la Reine seule ont des fauteuils et des cadenas' [The King and the Queen alone have armchairs and caddinets] said Cronström in the same letter from Paris as that quoted in the previous note. A *cadenas* of gold 'garny de sa cuillier, fourchette et cousteau' [furnished with its spoon, fork and knife] with the arms of Anne d'Autriche in enamel is listed in the French royal inventories of 1673 (*Guiffrey, Inventaire*, p. 10).

42. Charles I (*Invts. 1649–51*) owned a 'rich scarfe . . . to cover ye bread and salt'. At the Palace at Leeuwarden there was 'a silver-gilt caddinet on which to lay bread' ('een vergult candinae om broot op to legen'; *Orange Invts.*, list of silver made in 1681, p. 94).

43. *Savary des Bruslons*, 'Cabaret'.

44. See also Chapter VII on Beds, bed-hangings and bed-clothes, and sections relevant to the furnishing of bedchambers in Chapters VI, VIII and IX.

45. So common was the fashion of receiving in the bedchamber that Molière, in his *Les Précieuses Ridicules* (1659) makes a character say that 'ils me rendent tous visite' [they all pay me a visit] and that 'Je puis dire que je ne me lève jamais sans un demi-douzaine de beaux ésprits' [I may say that I never get up without half a dozen men of wit] being present in the bedroom. Saint-Simon (*Mémoires*, ed. La Pléiade, Vol. I, Chap. XV, p.

229) tells of a lady who on one occasion 'recut . . . sur son lit toute la France' [received . . . in her bed the whole of France]. Many other instances could be cited.

46. *Celia Fiennes* (p. 277), describing an unusual balustrade she had seen at Windsor Castle round the state bed there, said that 'this was insteade of the raile use to be quite round the king and queen's beds to keep off companyes coming near them'. At the French court, those permitted access beyond the balustrade were referred to as 'seigneurs à balustrade'.

47. 'Ruelle se dit . . . des alcoves et des lieux parés ou les dames reçoivent leurs visites, soit dans le lit, soit sur les siéges' [*Ruelle* means . . . the alcoves or separated areas where ladies receive their visits, either in bed, or on chairs] (Furetière, *Dictionnaire*, 1690). It was incidentally, 'une très grande indécence de s'asseoir sur le lit, et particulièrement si c'est d'une femme' [it is a great indelicacy to sit on the bed and particularly if it is that of a woman] (N. Courtin, *Traite de la civilité*, 1671).

48. For example at Breda Castle at the beginning of the seventeenth century the principal bedchamber contained a 'buffet van schreyn-werck' [a buffet of joiner's work] *Orange Invts.*, I, p. 75; many more references could be cited from this source alone).

49. We know that there was still a coffer in the bedchamber of the King of France in 1594 because the Maréchal de Biron is reported to have been so tactless as to fall asleep while sitting on it (*Havard*, 'Coffre'), but they were not to be seen in such places much after that.

50. *Du Boisgelin Invt., 1688*.

51. *Havard*, 'Toilette'. Amalia van Solms, Princess of Orange, owned a 'nacht-coffer' covered with a Persian silk material which stood in her closet at the Noordeinde residence at The Hague (*Orange Invts.*, I, p. 191).

52. *Edington Invt., 1665*.

53. *Charles I Invts., 1649–51*.

54. Rather exceptional may have been the Earl of Arundel's splendid bedchamber at Tart Hall (*Invt., 1641*) which had 'on the further side of the Bed a little square Table . . . on the other side of the Bed, a little Narrow table . . .'. The tables had carpets of Indian quilting *en suite* with the bed-hangings.

55. Sir Roger Pratt (1660) insisted that each bedchamber should have 'a closet, and a servant's lodging' (R. T. Gunther, *The Architecture of Sir*

Roger Pratt, Oxford, 1928, p. 27).

56. As one often reached the closet through the bedchamber, the former are commonly described in English seventeenth-century inventories as being 'within the bedchamber'. At Ham House, for instance, the future Duchess of Lauderdale, wrote of 'the Closet within my bedchamber' (*Invt., 1654*). The 'inward chamber to Lady Isabella's bedchamber' was likewise a closet, and the inventory (*Edington, 1665*) goes on to describe how 'the closet there [is] hanged with g[r]een dornex'. As both the chamber and the closet were particularly personal to the occupant of the apartment, the contents of the two rooms are not infrequently listed together.

57. Miss Gillian Wilson has assembled all the relevant material in her article on Boulle (*Furniture History*, Vol. VII, 1972). The room was decorated in 1683. The Dauphin's uncle also had a *cabinet* decorated in this manner while the Duc de Chartres had his decorated with 'menuiserie' which also suggests marquetry of some kind (*Havard*, 'Marqueterie').

58. *Havard*, 'Capucine'.

59. *Havard*, 'Porcelaine'.

60. Sir Balthazar Gerbier, *Council and Advise to all Builders*, 1664, p. 108.

61. R. T. Gunther, *The Architecture of Sir Roger Pratt*, Oxford, 1928.

62. For instance, the very splendid 'Shipp Bedchamber' at Hardwick (*Invt., 1601*) had a closet which only contained bedding and a stool, while that next to the 'Prodigall Chamber' housed only a close stool and a chamberpot. On the other hand, the closet next to 'The Noblemans Chamber' (i.e. the owner's room) at Chatsworth (*Invt., 1601*) was 'waynscotted and shelfed' which suggests a certain refinement.

63. Francis Bacon, essay 'On Building'. The last authorised edition of this essay was published in 1625, the year Bacon died. It presumably reflects fashionable taste of about 1610.

64. E. Croft-Murray, *Decorative Painting in England . . .*, Vol. I, London, 1962, pp. 198–9. The chimneypiece of the Kederminster Library at Langley, Buckinghamshire, probably gives a good impression of the style of the Somerset House decorations (Co. Pl. XVII); see also John Harris, 'A Rare and Precious Room', *Country Life*, 1 December 1977 with colour illustration.

65. *Havard*, 'Cabinet'.

66. *The Travels of Cosmo the Third, Grand Duke of*

Tuscany, through England during the reign of Charles II [1669], London, 1821, p. 177. Celia Fiennes (p. 345) noted seeing 'a large closet or musick room' at Lady Donegal's when she paid a visit at the end of the century.

67. Dublin Castle Invt., 1679 and Cowdray Invt., 1682.

68. Celia Fiennes, p. 358.

69. Sauval, Antiquités de Paris, Vol. VII, p. 173.

70. At Chatsworth (Invt., 1601) the room called 'My Lady's Wardrop' does not seem to have lain anywhere near 'My Lady's Chamber' but it was 'waynscotted with fayre presses rownde about' and these cupboards were presumably for her ladyship's clothes. At Ham there was a room called the 'Wardrobe' on the second storey containing 'two great presses for clothes', two 'standers' and some other large chests (Invt., c. 1654). In the French royal inventories of the time of Louis XIV mention is made of 'deux armoires de bois de noyer pour servir dans des garde-robbes' [two cupboards of walnut for use in garderobes] and of three other 'grands armoires qui sont posées dans les embrazures des croisées de la garde robbe du Roy' [large cupboards which were placed in the window embrasures of the King's garderobe] which were mounted on brass casters and were so formed that they blended with the panelling during the day (Guiffrey, Inventaire, p. 156 and p. 166).

71. 'Ung garde robe bois noyer à quatre portes et deux tiroirs' [A wardrobe of walnut with four drawers and two doors] is listed in a Lyons inventory of 1633 (Havard, 'Garde-robe'). Wardrobes were, however, normally called presses in the seventeenth century. In the 'Chamber under my mrs [mistress's]' at In-gatestone (Invt., 1600) there were, for instance 'two great open joyned presses with three rayles in them wth. turned pynns to hange gownes upon', while at Walton (Invt., 1624) there was 'a presse wherein hanges my lady's clothes' in the 'Middle Nursery'. Madame de Mercoeur, who formed part of Cardinal Mazarin's retinue (Invt., 1653) had 'deux grands amoires de bois de chesne à mettre des habits' [two large cupboards of oak in which to keep clothes] which were seven feet high and five wide.

72. e.g. The garderobe at the Thiret mansion at Rheims in 1621 (Invt.) contained two close-stools but apparently no storage for clothes. It did have two tables, however, and probably served mainly as a dressing-room (see below).

73. At Hengrave Hall in 1603 (Invt.), for instance, one notes that there were 'divers tents to serve for the embroyderers'. 'Tents' were frames on which work to be embroidered could be stretched (Fr. 'tendre', to stretch, hence 'tentures', wall-hangings).

74. Chatsworth Invt., 1601.

75. Countess of Leicester's Invt., 1634.

76 Evelyn's Diary, 4 october 1683. A garderobe with a table that probably served as a dressing-table is mentioned in note 72 above.

77. Havard, 'Toilette'.

78. Kildare Invt., 1656. The dressing-room also contained a still and one may be forgiven for at first suspecting that this was some ingenious Irish arrangement; but there was a 'clocke om water in te distilleren' [a vessel for distilling water] in a closet at Breda Castle in 1597/1603 (Orange Invts., I, p. 82). Perhaps distilling was associated with the preparation of certain cosmetics.

79. Croft-Murray, loc. cit.

80. Edington Invt., 1665.

81. Thiret Invt., 1621.

82. Tessin-Cronström Correspondence, letter of 23 August 1693.

83. Celia Fiennes, p. 69.

84. Some were portable and could fold (e.g. the 'huit tables brizées pour des toilettes' listed in the French royal inventory for 1685: Guiffrey, Inventaire, II, p. 165). The cedarwood tables noted in several rooms at Ham House probably also served as dressing-tables and/or wash-stands.

85. Plain dressing-tables still continued to be used nevertheless; e.g. Havard, 'Toilette', cites an inventory of 1705 which notes 'une petite table de toilette de sapin, avec son toilette, composée d'un dessous de toilette d'étoffe de soie, avec un dessus de toilette de mousseline à falbalas' [a small table of pinewood, with its toilette comprising an underlay of silk and an overlay of muslin with furbellows].

86. See C. C. Oman, English Domestic Silver, 7th edition, London, 1968, p. 190. John Evelyn's amusing verse, Mundus Muliebris, or the Ladies Dressing-room Unlock'd and her Toilette Spread (1690) describes the furnishings of a dressing-table in a most entertaining way. See also Havard, 'Toilette'.

87. Orange Invts., I, pp. 160–2. Although married to Philip Willem, Prince of Nassau-Orange, this French princess no doubt maintained strong links with her French background and the

arrangements in her rooms could well reflect contemporary Parisian taste.

88. *O.E.D.*, 'Closet'.

89. There was a room called 'The Studdy' at Marton Hall (*Invt., 1605*); James Montague, the Bishop of Winchester who died in 1618 (*Invt.*) had both a 'great' and a 'Little Study'. On the other hand the owner's own closet at Walton (*Invt., 1624*) in which it is recorded that he kept his 'own cabinet & bookes' was not graced with such a title.

90. *Havard*, 'Etude'.

91. The Countess of Shrewsbury kept her small personal library in her bedchamber at Hardwick (*Invt., 1601*). 'My Ladie's bookes' numbered only six titles and, while there may have been other books in the house, there was no separate library; since Hardwick seems to have represented the most advanced thinking on architecture and planning in this country when it was built in the 1590s, this dearth of books is revealing. At Gilling Castle in 1624 (*Invt.*) there were thirty-nine books in 'My Master's Closet', but George Marshall, the Warden of New College, Oxford, had a rather more substantial library when he died in 1659. It comprised sixty-five volumes in folio, 124 quarto, seven English Bibles, six translations of the Bible into different languages, some stitched books, nine other books, and a small group valued at 11s. 2d. The painter, Philippe de Champaigne, according to an inventory of 1674, owned sixty-five volumes in folio, 105 octavo and four in *douze*, 'le tout relié tant en veau qu'en parchemin' [all bound not only in calf, but in parchment]. Inventaire des biens de Philippe de Champaigne, *Nouvelle Archives de l'Art Français*, 3rd series, VIII, 1892. The books at Petworth (*Invt., 1670*) were valued at no less than £600, while the Canon of Christ Church who was also Bodley's Librarian between 1660 and 1665 owned books to the value of £200 (Invt. of Dr Thomas Lockey, 1679, *Bodleian Library Record* 1954–6, p. 82). No firm basis for comparison is provided by these figures but they reflect the fact that the size of private libraries increased strikingly during the seventeenth century.

92. The *Countess of Leicester's Invt., 1634*.

93. *Camden Society*, Wills and Inventories from the Registry of the Commissary of Bury St Edmunds, ed. Samuel Tymme, London, 1851, p. 209; and the *Kildare Invt., 1656*.

94. In earlier centuries particularly fine bindings had been displayed lying flat, on tables or sloping shelves and desks. Their spines were then of less consequence. When first set up on shelves they were placed with the spines inwards but the advantages of reversing them gradually became apparent, and the spine then became an important feature. When the effects of Henry Cooke, a painter who died in 1700, were put up for sale, it was pointed out that his books were in volumes 'most of them gilt on the back' (*The London Gazette*, 16/19th December 1700; Mr G. Jackson-Stops very kindly drew my attention to this reference).

95. The bookcases in the Ambrosian Library at Milan, built between 1603 and 1609, have wire mesh in their doors which is said to be original (J. W. Clarke, *The Care of Books*, London, 1901, pp. 260–5).

96. *D.E.F.*, 'Bookcase', Plate 5.

97. The bookcases were moved from Pepys' house in London to Magdalene early in the eighteenth century. My study of this furniture was greatly assisted by Mr Robert Latham, the well-known Pepys scholar to whom I am much indebted. Some very similar bookcases are at Dyrham (*A Short History of English Furniture*, Victoria & Albert Museum publication, London, 1966, Plate 221).

98. *Havard*, 'Bibliothèque'.

99. In the 'Boekcabinet' at the Binnenhof at The Hague in 1700, there were white damask curtains with pelmets in front of the books (*damast gardijnen met rabaten voor de boecken*; Orange *Invts.*, I, p. 434).

100. He describes 'The Valans of the shelves being greene Velvet, fring'd with gold' (see *Evelyn's Diary*, Vol. II, p. 128, 1 April 1644).

101. R. T. Gunther, *The Architecture of Sir Roger Pratt*, Oxford, 1928, p. 174.

102. *Ham Invt., 1679*.

103. The cloth made the table pleasanter to use and prevented the desk from sliding about. A rough woollen cloth named *bure* in France was often used for this purpose in earlier times and it was from this practice that the term *bureau* was coined for a writing-table or desk. According to *Havard* ('Bureau') the cloth had often been blue in former times but by the seventeenth century it had already been discovered that green was kinder to the eyes. At Marton (*Invt., 1605*) a table in the Study had a green cloth cover and the tables in Mazarin's library had covers 'de drap vert avec mollet de soye mesme couleur' [of

green cloth with a short silk fringe of the same colour] (*Invt., 1653*).

104. *Ingatestone Invt., 1600.*

105. W. B. Rye, *England as Seen by Foreigners*, London, 1865, p. 258; *Marton Invt., 1605*; and the *Mazarin Invt., 1653*. It is possible that the Queen's cabinets were of ebony with mounts of silver, of the kind produced by the silversmiths of Augsburg at that period.

106. *Hardwick Invt., 1600.*

107. *D.E.F.*, 'Desks'; and *Guiffrey, Inventaire*, II, p. 103.

108. What must have been quite a large desk on a stand was the 'deske and a frame' which was noted at Marton already in 1605 (*Invt.*) which contained many items in the 'rowmes' underneath it, but this seems to have been an exceptional object. The 'mettle writing box table' at Kensington Palace (*Invt., 1697*) was probably a sloping-topped desk on a gate-leg stand, faced with boullework marquetry of the sort produced in this country by Gerreit Jensen. Two less elaborate versions are illustrated in the *D.E.F.*, 'Bureau', Plates 3 and 4.

109. The article on Bureaux in the *D.E.F.* sums up the development in England admirably.

110. However, Mazarin (*Invt., 1653*) did own a strange desk described as being 'en forme de tombeau' (tomb-shaped). It was made of black touch-stone (*pierre de touche noire*), enriched with semi-precious stones, and was surmounted by the figure of a sphinx. It had feet in the form of four silver-gilt bats and the whole curious affair was housed in a case of red velvet. It may not have been very large and there is no cause to equate it with what is today called a *bureau Mazarin*, a form that can hardly have been evolved until well after the Cardinal's death.

111. *D.E.F.*, 'Bureau', Plate 2.

112. *Agius*, p. 81. The form was revived again in the second half of the eighteenth century and became popular in Regency England. No seventeenth-century specimens seem to survive but it would be surprising if this useful fitting had been totally abandoned by the studious during the intervening centuries.

113. *Knole Invt., 1645.*

114. See G. Wingfield Digby, *Elizabethan Embroidery*, London, 1963, pp. 107–8. At Tart Hall (*Invt., 1641*) there lay on a table in a closet a pillow embroidered with the arms of Philip I of Spain and Mary, by then a treasured antique, which is likely to have been a book-pillow.

115. *Randle Holme*, Bk. III, Chap. XIV.

116. *Marton Invt., 1605*. It is of course possible that a quill was fitted into this brass pen which should then have been described as a pen-holder.

117. 'Inventory of Robert, Viscount Teviot "lately deceased in his lodgings in Christ Church, Oxford" 1694', (Manuscript in the Bodleian Library, transcript shown me by Mrs Pauline Agius; by kind permission of the Keeper of the Archives, Oxford University); *Tart Hall Invt., 1641*; and *Kilkenny Invt., 1684*.

118. *Cockesden Invt., 1610.*

119. *Le Loi de la Galanterie Française*, 1640. See G. Mongrèdien, *op. cit.*, p. 71. 'Pain d'amande' was a paste. 'On sçait assez que les pâtes pour laver les mains, se font avec des amandes douces ou amerés, & quelques autres ingrédiens' [It is well known that the pastes used for hand-washing are made from sweet or bitter almonds, and various other ingredients] *Savary des Bruslons*, 'Amandes'.

120. 'The dynner beinge done . . . [the Gentleman Usher] shall come towards the table wth. a towell (gentlemen following wth. basons, and ewers) . . .' *Montague Household Book, 1595*. 'Quand les napes furent levées et que les mains furent lavées . . .' [when the tablecloths have been removed and the hands rinsed], wrote Loret in 1649 (*Havard*, 'Nappe').

121. 'When . . . I am redye for my dinner or supper, then my Gentleman Usher shall see the Carver and Sewer to washe att the ewerye table' where there were basins and ewers for the purpose (*Montague Household Book, 1595*).

122. In most cases there was probably no difference between a bath-tub and a wash-tub for laundry, so no distinction would have been made in an inventory.

123. *Savary des Bruslons*, 'Baignoires', confirms that these could be of copper or wood, the latter being made by members of the Coopers' Guild (*Tonneliers*).

124. Louis XIV had 'une grande cuvette d'argent qui seroit au roi à laver les pieds' [a large silver basin for the king to wash his feet in] (*Havard*, 'Cuvette'). The English royal accounts for 1623–4 refer to a payment for 'one large flatt coffer covered with leather lyned with bayes for the carriage of his higs. [His Highness, later Charles I] silver bathine sestorne [cistern]' (R. W. Symonds, 'The Craft of the Coffer-maker', *The Connoisseur*, March, 1942).

125. Lawrence Wright, *Clean and Decent*, London, 1960.

126. See P. Négrier, *Les Bains à travers les Ages*, Paris, 1925, quoting from Jean Héroard's journal of the life of the young Louis XIII.

127. Mongrédien, *loc. cit.*, states that a copper bath could be hired for 20 *sous* in Paris.

128. *Celia Fiennes*, p. 99.

129. *Havard*, 'Baignoire' and 'Salle des Bains'; and P. Verlet, *Versailles*, Paris, 1961, p. 102. One of the baths cost 15,000 *livres*. The ceiling of the Cabinet des Bains was painted and gilded, the cost of the gilding alone amounting to 24,000 *livres*. Along with two bronze figures by François Anguier, there was an imposing looking-glass. The bronze reliefs were by the famous *fondeur*, Domenico Cucci.

130. *Karlson*, pp. 620–2. This is confirmed by Lorenzo Magalotti who visited Sweden in 1674 and made a drawing of a sauna with tiered platforms on which the bathers reclined (C. M. Stenbock, *Sverige under År 1674*, Stockholm, 1912; see Plate 308, here). See also L. Savot, *L'Architecture Françoise des Bastimens Particuliers*, Paris, 1624, Chap. XVIII.

131. Robert Herrick, 'Panegerick to Sir Lewis Pemberton'. When Paul Hentzner visited Windsor Castle in Elizabeth's reign he remarked on the magnificent bedchambers, halls and 'hypocausts' (using the ancient Latin term for baths with ducted heating). Horace Walpole, editing his travelogue a century and a half later, translates this as 'bathing rooms' but adds that it might mean bedchambers equiped with stoves. It seems more likely Hentzner really meant that there were a number of steam-baths or 'sweating closets' at Windsor (P. Hentzner, *A Journey into England . . . in the year 1598*, translated by H. Walpole).

132. Francis Bacon, *The Historie of Life and Death*, London, 1638, pp. 249–250. Bacon died in 1626.

133. *Guiffrey, Inventaire*, II, p. 379. These tents were of a striped cotton material known as *bazin*.

134. *Ham Invts., 1677, 1679* and *1683*.

135. Lady Dorothy Shirley mentioned in her will 'my silver livery bason and ewer which are usually sett upon my cupboard in my chamber'. (Will proven in 1634; *Faringdon Invt., 1620*). The Bishop of Chester (Inventory of Hugh Bellot, Bishop of Chester, 1596, *Chetham Society*, Lancashire and Cheshire Wills and Inventories, Pt. III, ed. The Rev. G. J. Piccope, 1861) likewise had his pewter 'bason and laver' standing on a 'livery cupboard' which had a red cover.

136. At Henham (*Invt., 1602*) there were ten 'washing basons' in the Pantry and there were two pewter basins and ewers (with lids) in the Pantry at Ingatestone (*Invt., 1600*).

137. For example, the cedarwood tables that were in the Duke's dressing-room at Ham (*Invt., 1679*) and in that of Lady Maynard. Can the oak table 'covered with letaine' (laiton = brass) at Tart Hall (*Invt., 1641*) and the 'little table tinned-over' at Tredegar (*Invt., 1688*) also have been washstands?

138. *Thiret Invt., 1621*.

139. *Stengel*, p. 185. At Marton (*Invt., 1605*) there was a box with three 'washinge balls and one of them is a camphyre ball'.

140. *Noordeinde Invt., 1633*.

141. *Stengel*, p. 173, mentions a chamber-pot of 'porzellan' which may possibly have been of Oriental porcelain but was more likely of faience. Lady Joanna St John made a specific bequest of 'my oval silver chamber pott' in her will dated 17 February 1705 (Somerset House, Gee 40; kindly communicated by Mr F. T. Smallwood through my colleague Mr Simon Jervis). Mazarin (*Invt., 1653*) seems to have had a pot of glass ('un couverture de pot de chambre de verre de velours . . .').

142. The hazards of using an earthenware pot are vividly described by the Princess Palatine (*Lettres de Madame Palatine*, Le Club du Meilleur Livre, ed. H. Juin, Paris, 1961, p. 21; translated from the German). Finding that the close-stools in charge of the *garçon du château* at Saint-Germain were all too foul, she demanded a chamber-pot which turned out to be a humble vessel of earthenware. She placed it on a rush-seated chair but the pot unfortunately broke in two at the crucial moment. The Princess only saved herself from disaster by clutching at a nearby table. 'Je serais tombée, mollement si vous voulez, mais peu proprement' [I would have fallen gently, if you like, but hardly elegantly], she added.

143. *Randle Holme*, Bk. III, Chap. XIV; he spells 'squatter' with only one 't'.

144. *Savary des Bruslons*, 'Bidet'.

145. *Marton Invt., 1605*.

146. The form was probably new in the middle of the century when one in the royal palaces was described as a 'close stoole trunke fashion of redd velvet' (*Charles I Invts., 1649–51*).

147. *Ingatestone Invt., 1600*.

148. *Mazarin Invt., 1653*. At Ingatestone there

was a 'high close stoole with a lose cover all covered wth. black leather'.

149. *Orange Invts.*, I, p. 149 and C. Pitoin, *Marly-le-Roi*, Paris, 1904, p. 174.

150. *Ingatestone Invts.*, *1600* and F. R. Friis, *Kjøbenhavns Slots Inventarium*, *1638*, Samlinger til Dansk Bygnings- og Kunsthistorie, Copenhagen, 1872–8.

151 *Mazarin Invt.*, *1653*.

152. This was the case with the close-stool in the Countess of Shrewsbury's own apartment at Hardwick (*Invt.*, *1601*) and in the King's apartment at *Hampton Court* (Estimates, 1699), for instance. Incidentally, the Marquis of Hertford's accounts for 1641–42 include the item 'given to the woman who empties my Lordes close-stool . . . twentie shillings' (*Antiquaries Journal*, XXV, p. 23).

153. *Kilkenny Invt.*, *1684*. The close-stool in question was covered with Turkey leather.

154. *Ingatestone Invts.*, *1600*.

155. *Ingatestone Invts.*, *1600*; *Petworth Invt.*, *1670*; Invt. of Dr Thomas Lockey, *loc. cit.*, *Lauderdale London Invt.*, *1679*.

156. Teviot Invt., 1694, *loc. cit.*

157. *Noordeinde Invt.*, *1633*. A close-stool in the palace at Leeuwarden in 1633 is called a *secreetstoel* (*Orange Invts.*, II, p. 50).

158. Verlet, *op. cit.*, p. 264. Savot, *op. cit.*, p. 97, explains that 'L'arriere-garderobe n'est necessaire que pour y retirer un chaise percée' [the back *garderobe* is only necessary as a housing for the close-stool] and need only be four feet deep 'si ce n'est en celle des Princes, où il est besoin de plus de grande place' [unless it is in a princely house, in which case it needs to be larger].

159. The niche may well have had curtains behind which the King could retire. Lady Dorothy Shirley, whose husband had been our ambassador at the French court in the 1590s, had a curtain to hide the close-stool in her 'Close Rome' (*Faringdon Invt.*, *1620*).

160. *Celia Fiennes*, p. 358.

161. For example, the Princess Palatine writes that 'The Dutch understand cleanliness better than anyone in the world. Things are very different in France; there is one dirty thing at Court that I shall never get used to; the people stationed in front of our rooms piss in all the corners. It is impossible to leave one's apartments without seeing somebody pissing.' (*Letters from Liselotte*, ed. M. Kroll, London, 1970, letter of 23 July 1702).

162. G. Wingfield-Digby, in his *Elizabethan Embroidery*, (London, 1963, pp. 20–71) describes some richly decorated sweet-bags but suggests they were made to hold confectionery. Bulwer (*Artificial Changling*, 1653) refers to Montaigne's story of a man who was 'wont to find fault with Nature she had not made provision for a sweet-bag to hang under our noses . . . alleadging that his mustachoes served him to that purpose in retaining the sent of his perfumed gloves'. 'One sweett bage' is listed among the bedclothes in a chamber at Edington (*Invt.*, *1665*). Madame de Rambouillet (*Invt.*, *1665*) kept '2 petits sachets de parfums' trimmed with silver lace in a coffer in her bedroom. A recipe for 'a pouder for sweet baggs' dating from the late seventeenth century included 'orris' (ground up rhizomes of a type of iris), benhemen (a resinous gum), calamus (the rhizomes of sweet flag), lignum vitae sawdust, rosewood, musk, civet, ambergris, oil of orange-flowers, 'labdanum' (a sticky substance obtained from rock-roses) and 'chypre'. These were all 'separately beat by themselves and then mixed together, and to a pound of these pouders take a pound of roses dried' (see Beryl Platts, 'The Perfume and the Potters', *Country Life*, 2 June 1977).

163. 'A perfuming panne of brass with figures' (*Tart Hall Invt.*, *1641*).

164. *Walton Invt.*, *1624*.

165. *Guiffrey, Inventaire*, p. 63, 1673. The Dauphin had a 'seringue pour les eaux de senteurs' of silver-gilt in his bedchamber at Meudon (Le Comte de Biver, *Histoire du Château de Meudon*, Paris, 1923, p. 395).

Notes to the Plates

COLOUR PLATES

I (opposite p. 52) *The Music Party* by Pieter de Hoogh.
The Wellington Museum, Apsley House, Victoria and Albert Museum photograph.
II (opposite p. 52) Attributed to David des Granges (1611–*c*.75) who is said to have been a friend of Inigo Jones. Sir Richard Saltonstall (d. 1650) stands by the bed in which his wife has recently given birth to the baby held by the woman seated in the chair. What may be a turkeywork carpet lies on the floor.
The Tate Gallery, London, Victoria and Albert Museum photograph.
III (opposite p. 55) Model made in 1976–7 by Miss Lucy Henderson working under the guidance of the Department of Furniture and Woodwork in the Victoria and Albert Museum.
On show at Ham House, near Richmond.
Victoria and Albert Museum photograph.
IV (opposite p. 86) See Marcus Binney, 'The Hôtel Lauzun, Paris', *Country Life*, 11 May 1972. The parquet and chimneypiece in the second *salon* are of later date; the damask on the right is modern.
Country Life photograph.
V (opposite p. 89) From the volume of drawings, largely by French architects, which may have belonged to Inigo Jones (see note to Plate 44). Perhaps by Pierre Collot, about 1620.
The Ashmolean Museum, Oxford.
VI (opposite p. 120) From the album discussed in the note to Plate 44.
The Ashmolean Museum, Oxford.
VII (opposite p. 123) Victoria and Albert Museum, London.
VIII (opposite p. 154)
A, Red worsted cut pile on a linen ground.
B From Chastleton, Gloucestershire, where an inventory of 1633 mentions hangings of 'dornix' in one of the principal rooms, and hangings of this material are still on the walls of a landing to which position they may have been moved. It has thin linen warps; the yellow sprigs are brocaded. Some similar material, without the brocaded detail, is on a wall at Skokloster, Sweden.
C The patterns are produced by woollen wefts (in

two cases organised in bands) on the white linen ground. Such materials are usually called Italian and Mr Donald King informs me that the few specimens which have a firm provenance come from southern Europe.
Victoria and Albert Museum, London.
IX (opposite p. 157) From Hornsberg manorhouse in Kalmar County, Sweden. See also note to Plate 105.
Kulturhistoriska Museet, Lund, Sweden.
X (opposite p. 188) The Drawing Room at Penshurst, Kent. The *appliqué* work suite may have been made for Leicester House which was re-decorated between 1698 and 1700. An early photograph of the daybed shows that it originally had a row of heavy tassels beneath the seat-rail. A similar daybed was at Beningborough.
Country Life photograph.
XI (opposite p. 191) *Richard Sackville, Third Earl of Dorset*, Miniature by Isaac Oliver.
Victoria and Albert Museum, London.
XII (opposite p. 222) Perhaps made for Kiveton, the great house built by the Duke of Leeds (created 1694) between 1697 and 1702. Mr Christopher Gilbert informs me that a payment was made to 'Gilbert ye Joyner' in 1703 which is probably a reference to Philip Guibert who in 1697 had provided the Crown with a 'fine black soffa of a new fashion, filled with hair', its cushion 'filled up with downe, the frieze and cheeks all molded and fringed'.
Temple Newsam House, Leeds.
XIII (opposite p. 225) By Emanuel Witte.
Photograph by courtesy of the Terry-Engell Gallery, London.
XIV (opposite p. 256) Specially commissioned for Countess Piper who was re-decorating her town house in Stockholm in the fashionable Parisian manner, guided by the Swedish Court Architect, Nicodemus Tessin, and through the agency of Daniel Cronström in Paris (see *Tessin-Cronström Correspondence, passim*).
Now at Sövdeborg, Sweden (photograph by courtesy of Messrs Allhem, Malmö).
XV (opposite p. 259) By Frans Francken (1581–1642). Dutch; second quarter of the seventeenth century.

Photograph generously provided by Mr and Mrs Frank Woods (I am greatly indebted to Mr Brian Koetser for assisting me by tracing the painting which passed through his hands some years ago).

XVI (opposite p. 290) Ham House, Richmond. Victoria and Albert Museum photograph.

XVII (opposite p. 293) The Kederminster Library, Langley Marish, Buckinghamshire, about 1625(?); completed by 1631.

Photograph by permission of the Buckingham County Council.

BLACK AND WHITE PLATES

1. Engraving from the suite by Abraham Bosse (1602–76) entitled *Les Vierges folles*. While purporting to show frivolous girls, the artist in fact depicts with obvious delight an interior of considerable opulence. Note what appear to be sash-windows; also early parquet flooring and a chimney piece after a design by Barbet (1632).
By courtesy of the Trustees of the British Museum, London.

2. *Le Retour du baptême*, engraving by Bosse from a suite entitled *Mariage à la ville*. The bed has pillows for two; the counterpoint lies on the bed while occupied.
By courtesy of the Trustees of the British Museum, London.

3. Engraving from the same suite as Figure 1. A lighted sconce is masked by the chimneypiece but the principal light comes from the fire. Note how the fire-dogs catch the light. The decorative cup-board cloth forms a prominent feature.

4. *La Visite à l'accouchée*, engraving from the same suite as Figure 2. The cabinet with a 'carpet' may be a house-altar. The tapestry is pulled back so that the door can open.

5. See catalogue of the exhibition *Charles Le Brun* (Versailles, 1963, No. 96). The author is indebted to Mme. L. Buffet-Challie for information about this drawing.
National Museum, Stockholm (Cronstedt Collection).

Two extensive collections of drawings, now in the Print Room at the National Museum, were amassed by a succession of Swedish Court Architects, starting with Nicodemus Tessin the Younger (1654–1728) who formed the substantial nucleus of the first collection in the late seventeenth century. He was in France in 1687 (see *Tessin's Visit, 1687*) and made detailed notes

of what he saw. He no doubt also brought back drawings on that occasion but he remained avid for fresh information and obtained many further drawings from Paris later in the century (see the *Tessin-Cronström Correspondence*). The collection was subsequently much increased by his son, Carl Gustav Tessin (1695–1770), who was in Paris in 1728 and was ambassador there in 1735–36, and later became effectively *Surintendant des Bâtiments* in Sweden. Further additions were made by Carl Hårleman (1700–53) who visited Paris in the 1720s and succeeded C. G. Tessin as *Surintendant*. He was again in Paris in 1731–2 and 1744–5. The second collection was formed by C. J. Cronstedt who succeeded Hårleman as Court Architect and had himself been in Paris between 1732 and 1735. These men were all extremely well informed about artistic affairs in Paris between 1680 and 1770, and the drawings they assembled in Stockholm are all likely to have been of some special significance to the understanding of contemporary French taste and fashions. The author is much indebted to Dr Ulf Johnsson for his great help in selecting the drawings from these collections that are reproduced in the present work.

6. The audience given to Cardinal Chigi, the Papal Legate, on 29 July 1664 in the State Bedchamber at Fontainebleau. It is not known exactly when Le Brun drew the scene but it is likely that a designer of his standing would have shown furnishings in his latest style when composing such a scene. The tapestry was woven between 1671 and 1676. On the walls, three silver sconces may be seen. A carpet, which may have been woven at the Savonnerie factory or at Dupont's *atelier* at the Louvre, lies on the *parquet* behind the balustrade. Behind is a splendid cabinet. The richly-trimmed state bed is of simple outline.
Mobilier Nationale, Paris.

7. See catalogue of the exhibition *Charles Le Brun* (Versailles, 1963, No. 120).
Musée du Louvre, Paris.

8. Perhaps the design for the 'trois guéridons dont le corps est de trois figures de femmes qui portent le plâteau, posées sur un pied à trois consoles terminées en patte de lion pesans ensemble 1263 marcs, 5 onces, 0 g[ros]' [three candlestands of which the stem represents a female figure holding the plateau, standing on a tripod with lions-paws weighing . . .] listed in the French royal inventory in August 1685

(*Guiffrey, Inventaire*, pp. 347–8). The designer, working to Le Brun's preliminary sketch, has provided alternative proposals for the base.
National Museum, Stockholm (Cronstedt Collection; see note to Plate 5 above).

9. Musée du Louvre, Paris.

10. The central support under the top table suggests it was very heavy, as would have been the case if it was made of silver. These are likely to be some of the tables that were melted down in 1689.
National Museum, Stockholm (Cronstedt Collection; see note to Plate 5 above).

11. Engraving by Sébastian Le Clerc in Mlle de Scudéry's *Conversations nouvelles sur divers sujets, dédié au Roy*, Paris, 1684.
Bibliothèque Nationale, Paris.

12. Brussels tapestry, probably designed by Louis van Schoor; late seventeenth century.
By courtesy of Messrs. Sotheby, through the kindness of Mr Michael Webb; sale of 10 October 1969.

13. By A. F. Desportes (1661–1743). Note the pyramid of fruit.
The Metropolitan Museum, New York.

14. The complete *ammeublement* for the bedchamber, which is described in the French royal inventory (*Guiffrey, Inventaire*, II, p. 263), included four *carreaux* (see p. 181), four large *fauteuils de commodité* (see p. 195), four *portières* and a table with flanking candlestands (see p. 231). The 'enfans' supporting the looking-blass at the headboard were of *papier mâché* (*carton*). The Trianon de Porcelaine was destroyed in 1687.
National Museum, Stockholm (Tessin-Hårleman Collection; see note to Plate 5 (above).

15. National Museum, Stockholm (Tessin-Hårleman Collection: see note to Plate 5 above).

16. Engraving by J. D. de St Jean; 1680s. Perhaps based on knowledge of the *Chambre des Amours* at the Trianon de Porcelaine. Madame de Montespan, for whom this *maison de plaisance* was built in 1672, fell from royal favour in 1682 and the cipher over the bed is certainly not hers.
Bibliothèque Nationale, Paris.

17. Inscribed 'à Trianon' which must be in reference to the Trianon de Marbre (Grand Trianon) which was begun during the winter 1686–87, replacing the demolished Trianon de Porcelaine. The inscription concerning the sofa reads 'Les 2 grands canapez de la Chambre du Roy garnis de velours bleu à frange et galons

d'or' [The two large sofas in the King's Bedchamber covered with blue velvet with gold fringes and galloons] and gives their dimensions (eight feet long). It would seem that the crestings of the two sofas differed somewhat. The armchair is described as a *fauteuil* and the adjustable *torchère* is called a 'chambrière à 4 bougies à la mode' [a fashionable chamber light with four candles]. It was five feet high. The King's Apartment was completed in 1692.

This is one of a group of drawings in a volume belonging to the Bibliothèque de la Conservation of the Château de Versailles which Monsieur Gérald van der Kemp, Conservateur de Versailles, has most generously given me permission to publish here. A few have already been published by Monsieur Alfred Marie ('Louis XIV avait déja du mobilier Napoléon III', *Connaissances des arts*, February 1970; also in his *Mansart à Versailles*, Paris, 1972). Although the unidentified draughtsman seems to have been particularly interested in upholstery, he has drawn details of every kind (parquet patterns, iron grilles, topiary, etc.); he was clearly concerned to record items that struck him as strange or significant in the décor at the French royal palaces and other grand houses at the end of the seventeenth century. The drawings are not dated but are datable on internal evidence to somewhere between 1687 (or 1692) and 1701, the present drawing providing the evidence for the earliest date and Plate 288, which mentions the Duc de Chartres who became Duc d'Orléans in 1701, gives us the last possible date. Such sketches were probably drawn by architects and designers visiting Paris and Versailles, to record what they saw and in order to help them reproduce the latest French fashions in this field when they returned home. However, it may be that a Frenchman made these particular sketches for sale to such visitors; perhaps the fact that they are actually off-sets (produced by pressing down sheets of soft damp paper onto the original redchalk drawings, the impressions thus being in reverse) may be significant. Some of the images have subsequently been inked in and the inscriptions re-written. (I am much indebted to Mme Simone Hoog for the assistance she has given me in connection with my study of this material).

18. Inscribed 'A Marly dans le petit appartement'. The *Pavillon Royal* at Marly was largely completed by 1682–3 and the furniture illus-

trated in this drawing probably dates from that phase. The *fauteuil* and *chaise* were covered with green silk damask and stripes of galloon, trimmed with a silver rod (*tringle d'argent*). On the table of 'bois de violette' stand a 'coffre' and some Siamese vases. The latter may have been among the presents brought by the Siamese Ambassadors who visited Versailles in 1686.
Château de Versailles (see note to Plate 17).

19. Engraving by Pierre Le Pautre (1660–1744).
Victoria and Albert Museum, London.

20. Clagny was being built between 1674 and 1680 (Mme de Montespan fell from favour in 1684). The architecture visible in the background only agrees very approximately with the published plans and the scene is probably to a great extent imaginary (even a royal mistress would not set up her daybed at the top of stairs leading down to a large and no doubt draughty room, and even she cannot have persuaded cherubs to hold up its curtains). The furniture and costume otherwise seem totally plausible and are likely to be of the kind used to decorate this 'maison de délices' as it was called at the time. In the left foreground is a *carreau* on its stand, its second cushion supports her feet.
The Uffizi Gallery, Florence (Alinari photograph).

21. Probably by Antoine Desgodetz. An alternative proposal did not have the bath sunk so deeply into the floor (see Fiske Kimball, *The Creation of the Rococo*, Philadelphia, 1943, Plate 3; and A. Marie, *Naissance de Versailles*, Paris, 1968, Plates CXXIII and CXXIV).
Les Archives Nationales, Paris.

22. 'Chez Monseig[neu]r à Versailles' [In the Dauphin's apartment at Versailles]. The inscription under the *canapé* explains that it was covered with *damas bleu* and that 'le dossié' was of 'brocard d'or piqué et d'or[,] le falballa aussi bleu brodé de fleurs' [the back covered in gold brocade quilted with gold thread, the furbellow also being embroidered with flowers]. The dolphins forming armrests are an allusion to the prince's title. The rooms were being decorated in November 1684 and were so greatly occupying the time and energies of the best royal craftsmen that the exasperated King dropped a strong hint that his son should bring the work to a prompt conclusion (see A. and J. Marie, *Mansart à Versailles*, Paris, 1972, pp. 265–72 and 589–607).
Château de Versailles (see note to Plate 17).

23. Once again Mme Simone Hoog has greatly assisted me with information about this picture which belongs to the Musée du Château de Versailles. When acquired in 1898 it was thought to depict the *Cabinet du Regent* at Versailles, a room decorated by Boulle between 1682 and 1685, having originally been set up on the first floor and then moved downstairs. When the Dauphin died in 1711, the apartment was given to Philippe d'Orléans who became Regent in 1715. The boy standing on the left would then be the young Louis XV and the French authorities still adhere to this view. Fiske Kimball (*The Creation of the Rococo*, Philadelphia, 1943, pp. 64–5), on the other hand, advances cogent reasons for supposing that it shows the Dauphin's Closet at Meudon which was completed in 1699, with the Dauphin and his third son, the Duc de Berry who was born in 1686. If we accept this latter view, we here have a French royal prince in his ultra-fashionable room rather than one in a setting that was twenty years old. The fact that one can see a painting of *Mars and Venus* by Lanfranco, which is known to have been at Meudon, suggests that Kimball was correct. At any rate, the picture gives a convincing impression of a rich closet at the end of the seventeenth century.

24. From Jean Le Pautre's *Livre de miroirs*[,] *tables et guéridons*; about 1675?
Victoria and Albert Museum, London.

25. Daniel Cronström wrote to Tessin (*Tessin-Cronström Correspondence*, letter of 19 April, 1693) that he was sending him 'certains dessins de feu Baslin . . . ils sont veritablement de Baslin . . .' [certain drawings by the late Baslin . . . they really are by Baslin]. Tessin wrote back on 26 July concerning the 'table et guéridon avec des mors qui servent des soutiens' [the table and candlestand with blackamoors serving as supports]. No reference is made to the melting down of the silver furniture in 1689; can this set have been so important that it was allowed to survive a few years longer?
The National Museum, Stockholm (see note to Plate 5 above).

26. Note how the mouldings of the ceiling are shown in section.
Victoria and Albert Museum, London.

27 & 28. From a series of *Alcoves* which had immense influence all over Europe. For instance there is a painting of a Danish countess at Gisselfeld Kloster which is dated 1682 and shows a bed and alcove exactly like that illustrated in

Figure 27, while Robert Pricke in 1674 published a re-engraving of Figure 28 in *The Architects Store-house.*
Victoria and Albert Museum, London.

29. *Dame de qualité à sa toilette*, engraving by N. Bonnart (1636–1719); 1690s. Note the folding dressing-mirror, the *toilette* over the table-carpet.
The Pierpoint Morgan Library, New York.

30. *Un Cavalier, Et une Dame beuvant du Chocolat*, engraving *en suite* with Plate 29. The chocolate is being whipped in a special pot; glasses of cold water are brought by the negro servant (who might have been called *un guéridon* at the time). Note the fitted table-carpet.
The Pierpoint Morgan Library, New York.

31. Engraving by J. D. de St Jean; about 1690.
Bibliothèque Nationale, Paris.

32. By courtesy of the Trustees of the British Museum, London.

33. The signing of the contract of marriage between King Vladislas IV of Poland and Princess Louise Marie de Gonzaga on 25 September 1645, in the *Chambre du Roi* at Fontainebleau; engraving by Abraham Bosse. The young King Louis XIV, who had acceded to the throne only two years before, stands with his mother (Anne d'Autriche) and brother (Duc d'Anjou, later Duc de Chartres, then d'Orléans) 'enclos de la Balustrade'. A list of those who were not permitted beyond the balustrade is given in the inscription; they include Cardinal Mazarin, several dukes and ambassadors, and the 'dames de la Cour'.
Bibliothèque Nationale, Paris.

34. The engraving entitled *Bal à la Françoise* celebrates the return of Louis XIV and his Queen from Strasbourg in that year.
Bibliothèque Nationale, Paris.

35 & 36. From a series of engravings by Jean Le Pautre entitled *Differens desseins d'alcauve*, one edition of which was sold by Le Blond in 1667.
Victoria and Albert Museum, London.

37. 'Madame de Seignelay, dans le plus magnifiques et propres cabinets[,] faits apres la mort de son mary [d. 1670], et, qui sont des chefs d'oevres, n'a point voulu de serrurerie de cuivre doré n'y d'Angleterre; tout est de fer, mais d'un propreté qui passe tout ce qu'on a encore veu.' [Madame de Seignelay, in her most sumptuous and neatly-contrived closets, which she has created since her husband's death, and which are veritable masterpieces, did not want any locksmith's work of gilt copper or of the English

type; all is of iron [steel] but of a finish that surpasses anything one has ever seen before.] wrote Cronström (*Tessin-Cronström Correspondence*, letter of 11 September 1693). He added that he was sending a specimen of the work of the locksmith who had executed the Seignelay fittings; presumably this was in the form of the drawing here reproduced.
The National Museum, Stockholm (Tessin-Hårleman Collection).

38. Acquired by Count Niels Bielke, who was Ambassador to the French Court between 1679 and 1682, probably in 1680 according to surviving documents (see P. Thornton, 'The Parisian Fauteuil of 1680', *Apollo*, February, 1975).
Photograph from the Archives of the Nordiska Museum, Stockholm.

39. Acquired together with the preceding item. An old photograph shows that the modern re-upholstery of this chair has been carried out faithfully although the back is now perhaps a little too flat.
Photograph by courtesy of Bukowski Konsthandel, Stockholm.

40. The chairs were in the house by 1677 when they are listed in an inventory. The 1679 inventory describes the red and green material as a 'rich Brocard', using the French term for brocade; in 1727 it was described as being Venetian.
Photograph; Victoria and Albert Museum, London.

41. Given to Count Niels Bielke while Ambassador to the French Court between 1679 and 1682. Crimson velvet with *appliqué* ornament executed in white and light blue silk edged with silk cord.
The National Museum, Stockholm.

42. By Bartolomaeus van Bassen (1590–1652). This exercise in perspective is likely to be imaginary but is composed with elements in the fashionable style then current in the Netherlands. The architectural elements may in fact have been drawn by Paul Vredeman de Vries.
Hessisches Landesmuseum, Darmstadt.

43. By Nicholaes de Giselaer (1583–1654). Another exercise in perspective. As with the previous illustration, the architectural components may have been drawn by Paul Vredeman de Vries; these are anyway in the style he favoured.
The Fitzwilliam Museum, Cambridge.

44. The volume containing this drawing belonged to James Gibbs (1682–1754) but Mr John Harris has suggested that the volume had formerly belonged to John Webb and perhaps even to Inigo Jones—in fact that it belonged to the Office of Works. Some of the drawings are signed by Cotelle and a number (not the present subject) were published in his *Livre de divers ornemens pour plafonds* . . . in about 1640, a work that was dedicated to Anne de Rohan, Princesse de Guémené. The monogram on this ceiling occurs in conjunction with hers on another drawing in the volume.
The Ashmolean Museum, Oxford. (I am greatly indebted to Sir Anthony Blunt for drawing my attention to this extremely important album.)

45. This bedchamber lay in 'King Charles Block' (i.e. Charles II who was entirely familiar with French practice in this field) at Greenwich Hospital (then Palace). Engraved and mistakenly attributed to Webb's master, Inigo Jones, by John Vardy, *Some Designs of Mr. Inigo Jones and Mr. William Kent,* 1744.
The Devonshire Collection, Chatsworth. Reproduced by permission of the Trustees of the Chatsworth Settlement. (Courtauld Institute photograph.)

46. By Bartolomeus van der Helst (1613–70). Rijksmuseum, Amsterdam.

47. By courtesy of Messrs Thomas Agnew and Sons, Ltd., London.

48. By Pieter de Hoogh (1629–88). On top of the handsome oak cupboard (note its light colour) stand some Japanese lacquer coffers—expensive exotica.
The Cleveland Museum of Art, Cleveland, Ohio.

49. By J. van den Aveele, active in his native country from 1678 until he went to Sweden in 1698. The chairs have deeply skirted seat-covers.
Victoria and Albert Museum, London.

50. From the *Second livre d'appartemens inventé par Marot, architecte du Roy Guillaume III* (d. 1702). According to C. W. Royards (*Het Loo,* The Hague, 1972) this shows a bedchamber in that palace, which was begun in 1694.
Victoria and Albert Museum, London.

51. The architrave of the flanking window (*moulure de la Croisée*) is indicated. The sheet of glass is '96 pouces de hauteur—ce qui est 8 pieds' which does indeed make the plate a 'grande glace' as the inscription claims. Marot gives careful instructions concerning its proportions.
The Rijksmuseum, Amsterdam.

52. Victoria and Albert Museum, London.

53. Based on an original plan of Combe Abbey of about 1682 reproduced by Hill and Cornforth, *English Country Houses; Caroline,* Plate 243.

54. Based on a plan of the Château de Chavigny by Le Muet in his *Nouveaux bâtimens fait en France,* 1647.

55. Based on the plan of the Château de Pontz given by Le Muet (see previous note).

56. Based on a plan given by Th. H. Lunsingh Scheurleer, 'De Woonvertreken in Amalia's Huis ten Bosch', *Oud Holland,* LXXXIV, 1969.

57. Based on a plan reproduced by A. Blunt, *Art and Architecture in France, 1500–1700,* 1970 edn. The architect was Louis Le Vau.

58. Based on a plan reproduced by Blunt (see previous note). The design is by Jules Hardouin Mansart.

59. The Duchess of Lauderdale had been to Paris in 1670. Shortly afterwards, she began to modernise Ham House.

60. Based on Verlet, *Versailles,* Paris, 1961, and H. Murray Baillie, 'Etiquette and Planning of the State Apartments in Baroque Palaces', Society of Antiquaries of London, 1967.

61. Based on the same sources as Figure 60.

62. Collot's compositions often include rather graceful female figures in Classical dress.
Victoria and Albert Museum, London.

63. From the same album as Figure 44.
Ashmolean Museum, Oxford.

64. J. Harris, 'Inigo Jones and his French Sources', *Metropolitan Museum Bulletin,* May 1961, suggests the drawing is by François Derand the Elder, but makes no positive identification. The present attribution is the author's.
Royal Institute of British Architects, London.

65 & 66. Sold by C. Danckerts.
Victoria and Albert Museum, London.

67. From F. de Wit's *Poorten en schoorsteenmantels en Autare,* Amsterdam, 1640s. Based on a design in Barbet's *Livre d'architecture,* 1632.
Victoria and Albert Museum, London.

68. This seems to be fitted with a pair of doors across the opening, acting as a chimney-board.
Victoria and Albert Museum, London.

69. By Jean Le Pautre. The cartouche supported by putti was a motif no doubt intended to provide a source of inspiration for the decorators of chimney-boards (see Plate 252).
Victoria and Albert Museum, London.

70. The title-page of a suite of *Cheminées et lambris à la mode* by Pierre Le Pautre (1660–1744). Published in the 1690s and purporting to show chimneypieces that had been 'executez dans le nouveaux Batimens de Paris'.
Victoria and Albert Museum, London.

71. All but one design does indeed have a panel of mirror-glass inset.
Victoria and Albert Museum, London.

72. A perfume-burner (*casolette*) is represented in relief on the fire-back.
Victoria and Albert Museum, London.

73. Published in Holland, presumably in the 1690s (William III, to whom Marot was architect, died in 1702), this illustration is presumably based on schemes he had already devised in one of the Dutch residences of the House of Orange.
Victoria and Albert Museum, London.

74. From the same suite as Plate 73.
Victoria and Albert Museum, London.

75. In the same album as Plate 44.
The Ashmolean Museum, Oxford.

76. The attribution to Webb was made verbally to the author by Mr John Harris, the chief authority on the architectural drawings of Inigo Jones and his school. The style is Webb's and an earlier attribution to Inigo Jones can hardly be sustained on account of the late date (Jones died in 1652 and does not seem to have been an active architect during his last years). Inserted in the album discussed in the note to Plate 44.
The Ashmolean Museum, Oxford.

77. Ham House, Richmond (Victoria and Albert Museum, photograph).

78. From the same album as Plate 44.
The Ashmolean Museum, Oxford.

79. From the same album as Plate 44.
The Ashmolean Museum, Oxford.

80. See note to Colour Plate IV for information about the Hôtel Lauzun.
Country Life photograph.

81. The magnificent state rooms at the Château de Maisons bear eloquent witness to the sobriety and well-mannered reticence of the French Classical style as handled by its most talented advocate, François Mansart (d. 1666). This closet lies beyond the *Chambre du Roi*.
Country Life photograph.

82. At this stage the framing of the glass panel is still rectangular; soon, much attention was to be paid to framings of fanciful outline.
Archives National, Paris.

83. The group is playing *trou-madame*, a game somewhat like the modern *bagatelle*. Later, special tables were made for the game.
From Matthäus Merian, *Emblemata Amatoria*, Paris, about 1614. (See note to Plate 133.)
The National Museum, Stockholm.

84. *L'Hyver* from a suite of Seasons by Abraham Bosse. The company is making apple fritters at the fireplace (the apples await peeling on the stool; batter is in a bowl on the floor).
The Bibliothèque Nationale, Paris.

85. 'Maturity' from a series depicting *Les Quatres ages de l'homme*.
By courtesy of the Trustees of the British Museum, London.

86. From C. A. d'Avilers *Cours d'architecture . . .*, 1738 (first published in 1691).
The Victoria and Albert Museum, London.

87. Published in the English translation of Le Muet's *Palladio*, 1670, when the floors were described as having been 'lately made at Somerset House'.
The Avery Memorial Architectural Library, Columbia University, New York.

88 & 89. From the same collection as Plate 17.
Château de Versailles.

90. The *Cabinet Doré* was created to house the Dauphin's collection of bronzes and gemstone vessels which are said to have rivalled the King's and were likewise displayed on giltwood brackets on the white walls (see A. and J. Marie, *Mansart à Versailles*, Paris, 1972, p. 271).
Musée des Arts-Décoratifs, Paris.

91 & 92. Published at Amsterdam in 1630. Paul Vredeman de Vries was the son of Hans Vredeman, architect and designer. He collaborated with his father on the important *Architectura . . .*, published in 1607. See also Plates 42 and 43.
Victoria and Albert Museum, London.

93. *The Van Goyen Family* by Jan Steen (1626–79). Jan van Goyen was dead (1656) by the time his close friend Steen painted this picture but it no doubt gives a faithful impression of a well-to-do Dutch parlour of the 1660s.
The William Rockhill Nelson Gallery of Art, Kansas City, Missouri.

94. Probably French, about 1690; artist unknown. X-ray photographs show that the curtains have been repainted and formerly were shown pulled back to reveal a couple on the bed, having retired there after a scuffle at the dressing-table where they had been playing cards. Only

one candlestand is shown although there would normally have been a pair flanking the table.
Victoria and Albert Museum, London.

95. From a suite of engravings entitled *Nouveaux livre de paramens inventée et gravée par D. Marot, architecte de sa Majesté Britannique* (i.e. before 1702 when William III died). The word *croissée* at the front indicates the position of windows.
Victoria and Albert Museum photograph (from P. Jessen, *Daniel Marot*, Berlin, 1892).

96. The decoration resembles that on the Bielke Bed (see Plate 41) and the design may even be a proposal for it.
National Museum, Stockholm (see note to Plate 5 above).

97. The main hangings are of oyster-coloured Chinese silk damask. The bed-head is composed of a shaped three-dimensional wooden ground to which silk is pasted. The outlines are trimmed with red silk braid and 'campaign fringe'. It is possible that the bed was designed by Daniel Marot; it is anyway entirely in his style.
Victoria and Albert Museum, London.

98. Victoria and Albert Museum, London.

99. See Plate 137 where the complete bed is shown.
The Swedish Royal Collection (Gripsholm Castle).

100. The National Trust, Cotehele. (I am indebted to Mr Cyril Staal for answering technical enquiries about this important survival.)

101. A bed with cups of this sort may be seen in Figure 136.
Skokloster, Sweden.

102. On the sheet of paper with this heading is a memorandum dated 1694.
The National Trust, Dyrham (Victoria and Albert Museum photograph; I am indebted to Mr Anthony Mitchell for help in obtaining this photograph).

103. Mounted on a canvas backing awaiting restoration. The panel is now on a chair in the Victoria and Albert Museum.
Victoria and Albert Museum, Department of Furniture and Woodwork Archives.

104. By Gonzales Coques (1614–84). The wooden floor is bare (a common enough feature at the time). The painted harpsichord was an expensive item.
Staatliche Kunstsammlungen, Kassel.

105. *Anthony and Cleopatra*, one of a set at Dunster Castle. One of the scenes closely resembles that on a tapestry hanging designed by Julius van Egmont in Brussels in 1661; maybe the designers of tapestries were also prepared to provide the painters of this class of leather hanging with compositions to copy.
The National Trust, Dunster Castle (I am indebted to the late John Waterer for providing me with this photograph).

106. The bed was made for Queen Christina the Elder of Sweden (1573–1625). Daughter of the Duke of Holstein-Gottorp, she married Charles IX of Sweden in 1592.
The National Museum, Stockholm.

107. The National Museum, Stockholm.

108. By Pieter de Hoogh (1629–83).
Photograph from the Rijksbureau voor Kunsthistorische Documentatie, The Hague (by courtesy of the Frick Art Reference Library).

109. By Gothfried Schalcken, dated 1669.
Photograph by courtesy of Messrs. Christie, Manson and Wood (I am indebted to Mr Anthony Coleridge for his assistance in locating this picture which was in the sale of 1 May 1964).

110. By Pieter Janssens (1612–72), probably painted in the 1660s. The artist has had trouble with the scale; the catches of the windows are shown as being at eye level while the door seems too low. This may explain why the figure of the sweeping maid was painted out until recently again revealed.
The Städelsches Museum, Frankfurt-am-Main.

111. By Wolfgang Heimbach.
The Danish Royal Collection; Rosenborg Castle, Copenhagen.

112. By Jan Verkolje.
Photograph by courtesy of Messrs. Christie, Manson and Wood (sale of 28 November 1975).

113. From a suite of engravings of *Les quatres ages de l'homme* by Abraham Bosse; about 1640 (Plate 85 is from the same suite).
By courtesy of the Trustees of the British Museum, London.

114. This shows the closet at Ter Nieuburch at Rijswijk at the time of the signing of the Treaty of Ryswick in 1697 and furnished in a late seventeenth-century manner. However, the building was erected in the 1630s and 1640s to the designs of Jacques de la Vallée, architect to the House of Orange-Nassau. The drawing is faulty; the room is quite small. Engraved by J. van Vianen, published by Anna Beek.
The Rijksprentenkabinett, Amsterdam.

115. *Sir Thomas Aston at his Wife's Deathbed*, by

John Souch (1616–36). The picture is not painted from life, as the black hangings would not have been present at the event. The deceased wife is also depicted seated at the foot of the bed. The boy holds a fore-staff, an aid in surveying and navigation.

The City of Manchester Art Galleries.

116. By Jan Steen.

The Royal Collection; by Gracious permission of Her Majesty the Queen.

117. The Infanta Maria, sister of Philip IV of Spain and wife of Ferdinand III of Hungary (1606–45); painter unknown.

The National Trust, Knole, Sevenoaks. (I am indebted to Mr R. St John Gore for providing me with information about this picture.)

118. This sketch by the author is not to scale nor is it based on any particular contemporary illustration.

119. Probably from the 1660s; see the following note.

The National Museum, Stockholm (Tessin-Hårleman Collection; see note to Plate 5).

120. This may be the silver bed designed in 1669 by Charles Le Brun for the royal palace of Saint-Germain (see catalogue of the exhibition 'Versailles et les châteaux de France', held at Versailles in 1951, no. 125). This is no state bed; such a fanciful confection can presumably have been made only for a royal mistress. Louise de la Vallière became mistress to Louis XIV in 1668. Parts of this coloured design are rendered in silver which has since tarnished.

The National Museum, Stockholm (Tessin-Hårleman Collection; see note to Plate 5).

121. From a suite entitled *Livre de lit à la Romaine*.

Victoria and Albert Museum, London.

122. Made either at Augsburg or in Italy. Walnut inlaid with ivory. A very similar bed, still with its curtains, is at Gripsholm Castle in Sweden; it belonged to the father of Queen Eleonora of Sweden (born 1636) who was a Duke of Holstein-Gottorp.

Bayerisches Nationalmuseum, Munich.

123 & 124. Of oak with tinned iron mounts. Perhaps Swedish.

Eskilstuna Museum, Sweden (photograph by Lars Rannegårdh, kindly provided by Dr Carl Braunerhielm).

125. Originally the field bed of Count Carl Piper, the powerful minister of Charles XII of Sweden. He acquired it in Paris through the agency of Nicodemus Tessin. It was probably in

reference to this bed that, on 8 May 1695, the latter wrote to his agent in Paris that 'Mr. Piper vous fait faire ses compliments et protestation d'amitié plus que jamais, et il vous recommande fort son petit meuble du lict . . .' [Mr Piper sends you his compliments and expressions of friendship more than ever, and praises exceedingly his small bed]. *Tessin-Cronström Correspondence*.

The Royal Armoury, Stockholm.

126. From *Dend hyrdinde Astrea* by Søren Terkelsen, Copenhagen, 1645.

The Royal Library, Copenhagen.

127. From Johannes de Brune's *Emblemata of Zinnewerck*, 1624.

Victoria and Albert Museum, London.

128. From the family sketchbook of Gesina Terborch (1633–90).

The Rijksprentenkabinett, Amsterdam.

129. Sketches by the author.

130. Sketched from A. C. Fox-Davies, *The Book of Public Arms*, London, 1894, p. 816.

131. *La Veue* from a suite of engravings representing the Senses by Abraham Bosse. Paris; about 1635.

By courtesy of the Trustees of the British Museum, London.

132. *Le Touché* from the same suite as Plate 131.

Bibliothèque Nationale, Paris.

133. From an *Emblemata Amatoria* by Matthäus Merian (1595–1650) which appeared between 1612 and 1614 in Paris (see L. Wüthrich, *Das Druckgraphische Werk van Matthaeus Merian de. Ae.*, Basle, 1966).

The Bibliothèque Nationale, Paris.

134. From the same work as Plate 127.

135. From the same work as Plate 126.

136. The Lying-in-State of the Landgraf Wilhelm VI von Hessen-Kassel. Engraving by Elias von Lennep. 1663.

Staatliche Kunstsammlungen, Kassel.

137. A detail of the valance from this bed is shown in Plate 99. The property of the Danish princess Ulrika Eleonora who married Charles XI of Sweden in 1680. An inventory of that year describes 'the fine state and ordinary beds that have come out of France, with the great hangings belonging thereto, and their white plumes, the hangings of the former being trimmed with very rich gold and silver lace, both on the inside and outside and on the *cantonnières* and *bonnegrâces* . . .' (see Åke Setterwall, 'Ulrika Eleonora d. ä's. paradsäng' in *Gripsholm och des Konstskatter*, Stockholm, 1956; I am much

indebted to Dr Setterwall for providing information about this bed).

The Swedish Royal Collection, Gripsholm Castle.

138. From the French Royal Drawing-office, probably drawn by Antoine Desgodetz (see A. and J. Marie, *Mansart à Versailles*, Paris, 1972, pp. 340–6).

Archives Nationale, Paris.

139. Sketches by the author based on rather indistinct representations of the bed in paintings by F. Marot and A. Dieu (at Versailles) of scenes that took place respectively in August 1682 and May 1683.

140. Of cloth of gold (cream-coloured silk brocaded all over with two kinds of silver-gilt thread) lined with salmon-pink silk embroidered with couched decoration, trimmed with a rich 'campaign' fringe in places producing a three-dimensional effect. The sixth Earl of Dorset, who was Lord Chamberlain at the time, probably removed this suite from Whitehall Palace by way of a perquisite. An inventory of 1701 shows it formerly had a gilded rod running round the outside of the tester to support a dust-curtain like that shown in Plate 144. See G. Jackson-Stops, 'The 6th Earl of Dorset's Furniture at Knole', *Country Life*, 2 and 9 June 1977, I, Plates 2, 3 and 5; II, Plates 6 and 9.

The National Trust, Knole, Sevenoaks (*Country Life* photograph).

141. From the *Second livre d'appartements inventé par Marot, Architect du Roy Guillaume III* (i.e. published before 1702).

Victoria and Albert Museum photograph (from P. Jessen, *Daniel Marot*, Berlin, 1892).

142. Victoria and Albert Museum, London.

143. From the *Nouveau livre de licts de differentes penseez fait par Daniel Marot, Architecte du Roy Guillaume Troisième*.

Victoria and Albert Museum photograph (from Jessen, *op. cit.*).

144. The Biblioteca Communale, Siena (I am indebted to the late Professor Robert C. Smith for providing me with this photograph which he published in *Furniture History*, III, 1967).

145. Sketches by the author. The bed is one of several currently in store at Hardwick.

146. From the same collection as Plate 17.

147. Drawn by Samuel Hieronymus Grimm in 1775 in the Long Gallery at Hardwick.

By courtesy of the Trustees of the British Museum, London (Add. Mss. 15537).

148. Photograph from the Archives of the Department of Furniture and Woodwork, Victoria and Albert Museum, London.

149. Formerly at Forde Abbey; present whereabouts unknown.

150. The National Trust, Knole Park, Sevenoaks.

151. The Rijksmuseum, Amsterdam.

152. The National Trust, Knole.

153. *The Comtesse d'Olonne*, by A. Trouvain. French, 1694.

Victoria and Albert Museum, London.

154. By Dirck Hals, 1626.

National Gallery, London (by courtesy of the Trustees).

155. *La Visite à la nourrice* from the same suite of engravings as Plate 2. The servant in the background is using a stick to even out the bedclothes.

By courtesy of the Trustees of the British Museum, London.

156. From Hendrik Hondius, *Instruction en la science de perspective*, The Hague, 1623.

Victoria and Albert Museum, London.

157. From the series of drawings associated with Plate 17.

158. From the sketch book of Gesina Terborch. Note the pierced doors of the food cupboard. I am greatly indebted to Mr C. A. Burgers for drawing my attention to this important source of information about the Dutch interior around 1670.

The Rijksprentenkabinett, Amsterdam.

159. Much of the embroidery has disintegrated since this photograph was taken in 1912. Ancient upholstery has been treated with far too little respect in the intervening years.

Victoria and Albert Museum, London.

160. Parlour scene by Jan Steen; 1660s.

Museum Boymans van Beuningen, Rotterdam.

161. Portrait by Philippe de Champaigne of Jacques Tubeuf who was at this time *Surintendant des Finances* of Anne d'Autriche and Louis XIV as well as *Ordonateur* of the King's works.

Château de Versailles.

162. Sketch by the author after an engraving by J. D. de St Jean.

163. Portrait by Gerhard Terborch of Gosewijn Hogers who was elected to the city council of Deventer in 1668 and represented that city at the States General in 1672. It has been suggested that the furniture was painted in by Terborch later but the chairs would anyway have been up-to-

date in the late 1660s. See also Plate 186.
Private collection (photograph by courtesy of the National Gallery, London).

164. Powis Castle, Montgomeryshire (photograph kindly provided by the late J. W. Waterer).

165. By kind permission of the Governing Body of Christ Church, Oxford.

166. Engraving by Renold Elstrack (?) in Robert Glover's *Nobilitas Politica Civilis*.
Victoria and Albert Museum, London.

167. Susan Villiers, Countess of Denbigh, by Daniel Mytens, about 1625. (Mytens painted the lady's brother in 1626).
From the Collection at Parham Park, Sussex. (I am indebted to Miss R. Courcier for providing information about this portrait.)

168. The National Trust, Knole.

169. The National Trust, Knole.

170. From the same collection as Plate 17.

171. From the same collection as Plate 17.

172 & 173. Said to be in the Royal Library, Brussels, but not located there. Taken from *Havard*.

174. Illustrated in Mathurin Jousse, *La Fidelle ouverture de l'art de serrurerie*, La Flèche, 1627.
Victoria and Albert Museum, London.

175 & 176. Skokloster, Sweden.

177. Colonial Williamsburg Foundation, Virginia, U.S.A.

178. Victoria and Albert Museum. London.

179 & 180. Now in a private collection. Old photograph, taken before restoration, in the archives of the Department of Furniture and Woodwork, Victoria and Albert Museum.

181. Mentioned in the *Inventory of 1679* but not in that of *1677*. In that of *1683* they are called 'reposing chayres'. The royal accounts show that John Paudevine supplied Charles II with a sleeping chair 'neatly carved and the irons all gilt with gould' in 1677 at a cost of £6.
Victoria and Albert Museum photograph.

182. Sketch by the author.

183. Victoria and Albert Museum, London.

184. Sketch by the author from a painting at Clandon Park (The National Trust).

185. Sketch by the author from an engraving by Blooteling after a portrait by Lely (*The Connoisseur*, December 1944).

186. Gosewijn Hogers' wife; the pendant to the portrait shown in Plate 163.

187. Portrait of the brothers Henri and Charles Beaubrun by Martin Lambert, 1675.

Château de Versailles.

188. Portrait of Louis XIV based on an engraving by J. de St Jean (inscribed 'pinxit', suggesting he painted the original picture).
Esplunda, Närke, Sweden (photograph by courtesy of Messrs Allhem of Malmö).

189. *The Lying-in* by Mathys Naiveu (1647–1721). Although said to date from the early eighteenth century, the furnishings point to a rather earlier date.
Stedelijk Museum 'De Lakenhal', Leiden.

190. Based on Largillière's portrait of Charles Le Brun, painted in 1686 (see P. Thornton, 'The Parisian Fauteuil of 1680', *Apollo*, February 1975, where the portrait is illustrated).

191. Sketch by the author based on a portrait of Madame de Maintenon by Louis Elle, painted in 1687.

192. The woodwork is stained black. This chair is from a set en suite with a state bed at Drayton House, Northamptonshire.
Victoria and Albert Museum, London.

193. On loan from Lord Newton to The National Trust, Lyme Park (*Country life* photograph).

194. Sketch by the author based on a self-portrait of Pierre Mignard, the French court painter, executed in 1696.

195. From the same collection as Plate 17. The inscription under the 'Bureau' is unfortunately indecipherable.

196. From the same work as Plate 156.

197. From the same work as Plate 127.

198. *Nursing Twins* by Esias Boursse (1631–72). Photograph by courtesy of Messrs Appleby Bros Ltd, London.

199. From the same collection as Plate 17.

200. From the same collection as Plate 17.

201. It may be that the furniture shown here was made for the Dauphin; it is in a similar taste to that shown in Plate 22. From the same collection as Plate 17.

202. The identity of this room is unfortunately not indicated but it is likely to have been one of great importance, perhaps in the Dauphin's apartment.
From the same collection as Plate 17.

203. On loan from Lord Newton to The National Trust, Lyme Park (*Country Life* photograph).

204. Victoria and Albert Museum, London.

205. From the same source as Plate 133.

206. Engraving by Jacob van der Heyden.

Photograph by courtesy of Nordiska Museet, Stockholm.

207. Formerly at Nether Winchendon, Buckinghamshire.
(Photograph by kind permission of Mrs Spencer-Bernard).

208. From the same collection as Plate 17.
These pieces are stated to be 'chez Madame Boquemar', whose identity has not been established. Maybe whoever inked in the inscription misread the name Roquelaure.

209. Sketch by the author based on a painting in the London art-market in 1969.

210. Sketch by the author based on several Vermeer paintings, notably one in the Kunsthistorisches Museum, Vienna.

211. Miniature portrait of Sir Anthony Mildmay by Nicholas Hilliard (1547–1619), probably painted in 1596 when Mildmay was knighted. He died in 1617. The trunk covered with black leather and protected by tinned iron bands would have been for Mildmay's new suit of Greenwich armour, elements of which he is wearing (I am indebted to Mr John Hayward for making this observation).
The Cleveland Museum of Art, Ohio, (purchased from the J. H. Wade Fund).

212. The National Trust, Cotehele (I am greatly indebted to Mr Cyril Staal for helping me to obtain this photograph).

213. Sketch by the author.

214. From Gripsholm Castle, Sweden. Branded HERS GRIMSHOLM showing it was made for Queen Hedvig Eleonora who died in 1715.
Nordiska Museet, Stockholm.

215 Provided for the same Queen of Sweden as the table shown in Plate 214. Many tables of this highly serviceable type are still to be found in the Swedish palaces.
The Swedish Royal Collections, Gripsholm Castle (I am indebted to Dr Åke Setterwall for providing information about these tables).

216. Part of the furniture of the Duchess of Lauderdale's apartment at Ham House. Perhaps bought in Holland.
Victoria and Albert Museum, London.

217. It is certainly mentioned in an inventory of 1718. Veneered with ebony; decorated with floral marquetry and ivory stringing. Probably made in Copenhagen, perhaps by an immigrant Dutch craftsman.
The Danish Royal Collections, Rosenborg Castle.

218. By Jean Le Pautre (d. 1682). Perhaps inspired by a triad of silver in a French royal palace and certainly in the general style of Charles Le Brun.
Victoria and Albert Museum, London.

219. From the same work as Plate 114.

220. This is probably one of 'deux ou trois desseins de pièces d'orfèvrerie du Sr. Balin' that were sent to Stockholm on 10 July 1699 (see Plate 25 and Tessin-Cronström Correspondence; also C. Hernmarck, 'Claude Ballin . . .', Gazette des Beaux-Arts, 6e., XLI, 1953). The table is probably identical with item 926 in the French royal inventories (made between 1673 and 1681) which concerns 'une grande table d'argent, faite par Baslin . . . entourée d'une campanne, et portée par quatre cupidons assis sur des dauphins . . .' [a large table of silver, made by Baslin . . . with a lappeted apron all round, supported by four cupids seated on dolphins] (Guiffrey, Inventaire, p. 86). The Grande Galerie was not completed until 1684.
The National Museum, Stockholm (Tessin-Hårleman Collection; see Plate 5).

221. Made by Jean-François Cousinet between 1697 and 1707, under the guidance of Nicodemus Tessin, the Swedish Court Architect who had seen the silver furniture at Versailles in 1687.
The Swedish Royal Collection, Stockholm Palace.

222. Engraving by Pierre Le Pautre (1660–1744).
Victoria and Albert Museum, London.

223. The inscription states that this furniture was to be seen 'au petit Sallon'; this presumably means a room in the Dauphin's apartment, perhaps his Grand Cabinet or even the Cabinet doré next door (see Plate 90; also Marie op. cit., pp. 265–72 and 589–607).
From the same collection as Plate 17.

224 & 225. The National Museum, Stockholm (Tessin Collection; see Plate 5).

226. Banquet given by Charles II (seated under the canopy at a high table behind a barrier) for the Knights of the Garter. From Elias Ashmole, The Institutions, Laws and Ceremonies of the Most Noble Order of the Garter, London, 1672.
Victoria and Albert Museum, London.

227. A room in Rubens' house at Antwerp in the 1620s, painted by Frans Franken II (1581–1642). Strictly speaking this shows a Flemish interior but a grand Dutch room of the same date would have differed in no significant manner.

The National Museum, Stockholm.

228. Family portrait by Pieter Pieters. (1543–1603). Two children who died before this family portrait was painted are shown with palm fronds in the foreground.

American private collection (photograph by courtesy of the Isaac Delgado Museum of Arts, New Orleans).

229. Musée des Arts Décoratifs, Paris.

230. Engraving by M. Daigremont, about 1700. The inscription states that this had been executed 'chez Monsieur Thévenin à Paris'.

Victoria and Albert Museum, London.

231. From the album of watercolours by Gesina Terborch. See Plate 158.

232. By Gonzales Coques (1614–84). Musée d'art et d'Histoire, Geneva (Fondation Lucien Baszanges).

233. From the same collection as Plate 44.

234. By Jean Le Pautre (d. 1682). Victoria and Albert Museum, London.

235. By George Hainz of Altona; dated 1666. The kunsthalle, Hamburg (photograph by courtesy of the Museum für Kunst und Gewerbe).

236. Nicodemus Tessin saw the panels of this elaborate scheme of mural decoration set up at the Gobelins in 1687. In 1706 some panels were erected at the Tuileries when they were described as a 'tres riche lambris que l'on avoit destiné pour la petite galerie de Versailles, orné de glaces et de moulures de bronze doré, sur des fonds d'écaille de tortue et d'un lapis assez bien countrefait' [very rich panelling which had been intended for the small gallery at Versailles, decorated with mirrors and with gilt bronze mounts, on a background of tortoiseshell and of a lapis lazuli that is exceedingly well counterfeited] (see Marie, *op. cit.*, p. 291).

Les Archives Nationale, Paris.

237. It may well be that the arrangement is partly imaginary but the concept is characteristic of the period.

Metropolitan Museum, New York (Whittlesey Fund).

238. From Marot's *Nouveaux livre de paremens*, published before 1702. Victoria and Albert Museum, London (from P. Jessen, *Daniel Marot*, Berlin,

239. By Simon Renard de Saint-André (1613–77). If the inscription on the letter refers to the artist himself, he seemed to have served the Crown, as the words 'du Roy' are legible.

Staatsgemäldesammlung, Munich (displayed at Schloss Aschaffenburg).

240. Sketches by the author.

241. By Hieronymus Janssen. The Liechtenstein Collection, Schloss Vaduz, Duchy of Liechtenstein.

242. By Gerhard Terborch (1617–81). The Wallace Collection, London.

243. The National Trust, Hardwick Hall.

244. The National Trust, Hardwick Hall.

245. *Femme de qualité en deshabillé sortant du lit*; engraving by J. D. de St Jean. Victoria and Albert Museum, London.

246. Delft School; 1650–55. The National Gallery, London (by courtesy of the Trustees).

247. Engraving from a suite entitled *Livre de chenets*. Victoria and Albert Museum, London.

248. Musée du Louvre, Paris.

249 & 250. National Museum, Stockholm (Tessin-Hårleman Collection; see Plate 5).

251. Salsta, Uppland, Sweden (photograph by courtesy of Messrs. Allhem, Malmö).

252. From a suite of *Cheminées à l'italienne nouvellement inventées* by Jean le Pautre; about 1670 (?). Victoria and Albert Museum, London.

253. A similar chimneyboard, with an orange-tree growing in an urn in the style of Daniel Marot, is in a private collection in London. Stedelijk Museum, Amsterdam.

254. Musée du Louvre, Paris.

255 & 256. By Gerard Dou (copy by W. J. Laquy); 1660s. The Rijksmuseum, Amsterdam.

257. Banquet given at The Hague in honour of Charles II in 1660. The King is seated under a canopy, his two brothers, his aunt (Elizabeth of Bohemia), his sister, and the young Prince of Orange, later William III. From William Lower's *A Relation . . . of the Voiage and Residence which . . . Charles II . . . hath made in Holland . . .*, The Hague, 1660. Victoria and Albert Museum, London.

258. From the same work as Figure 127.

259. The National Trust, Knole (photograph from archives of the Department of Furniture and Woodwork, Victoria and Albert Museum).

260. Almnäs, Västergötland, Sweden (photograph by courtesy of Messrs Allhem, Malmö).

261. *La Rentrée des Mariées*, from the same suite as Plate 2.

Bibliothèque Nationale, Paris.

262. The National Trust, Hardwick Hall. (I am indebted to Air-Commodore C. C. M. Baker for his help in procuring this photograph.)

263. Probably identical with the 'deux très grands chandeliers d'argent, à six branches [only two are shown] en cornets, d'ou sortent six thermes de femmes qui portent chacun trois bobesches [nozzles]; les corps desdits chandeliers portez sur six consoles et couronnez d'une couronne royale soustenüe par trois Amours, [the drawing suggests there were to be six] lesdits chandeliers faits par Ballin, pesans ensembles 216 marcs, 5 onces, 4 g[ros]' which are listed in the French royal inventories as being in existence by February 1681 (*Guiffrey, Inventaire*, item 954–5). The figure of Fame seems to have been omitted. The National Museum, Stockholm (Cronstedt Collection; see Plate 5).

264. The Danish Royal Collections, Rosenborg Castle (I am greatly indebted to Dr Gudmund Boesen for providing information about this handsome object and that shown in Plate 265).

265. See G. Boesen, *Venezianske glas paa Rosenborg*, Copenhagen, 1960.
The Danish Royal Collections, Rosenborg Castle.

266. See D. Rentsche, 'Bedeutung und Restaurierung des grossen Glaskronleuchters in Schloss Favorite', *Jahrbuch der Staatlichen Kunstsammlungen in Baden-Württemberg*, Bd. 12, 1975.
Schloss Favorite (photograph by courtesy of the Badisches Landesmuseum, Karlsruhe. I am very grateful to Dr Rosemarie Stratmann for helping me to obtain this photograph on completion of the restoration).

267. By Emanuel de Witte (1617–92).
The Museum Boymans-van Beuningen, Rotterdam.

268. By Gerard Dou (associated with Plates 255 and 256).

269. The Royal Danish Collections, Rosenborg Castle.

270. From the same collection as Plate 265.

271. Made in Stockholm and paid for in December 1684 (see E. Andrén, 'Melchior Jung's glasbruk i Stockholm . . .', *St Erik's Årsbok*, 1972).
Skokloster, Sweden.

272. The National Trust, Knole (a second stand, not a pair, is at the house).

273. From the same work as Plate 114.

274. No information accompanies this drawing but it must have seemed significant to Nicodemus Tessin, probably as evidence of the modern taste in such fittings in Paris at the time. The National Museum, Stockholm (Tessin-Hårleman Collection; see Plate 5).

275. Based on a plan reproduced by Hill and Cornforth, *English Country Houses: Caroline*, Plate 227.

276. By courtesy of the Trustees of the British Museum, London.

277 & 278. Decorations at the banquet given by Pope Clement IX for Queen Christina of Sweden.
The National Museum, Stockholm (Tessin Collection; see Plate 5).

279 & 280. From Michael Wright, *An Account of His Excellence Roger Earl of Castlemaine's Embassy . . . to His Holiness Innocent XI*, London, 1688.
Victoria and Albert Museum, London.

281. The Earl of Lonsdale (Victoria and Albert Museum photograph).

282. Two other royal *cadenas* are illustrated in Marie, *op. cit.*, pp. 327–328.
The National Museum, Stockholm (Tessin-Hårleman Collection; see Plate 5: I am indebted to Dr Carl Hernmark for providing information about this drawing).

283. By Jacob Duck.
Central Museum, Utrecht.

284. Marked in *pieds*. Drawn in red chalk. From the collection that may have been in Inigo Jones' drawing-office (see Plate 44).
The Ashmolean Museum, Oxford.

285. From the same suite as Plates 27 and 28.

286. By Jan Siberechts, Antwerp.
The Royal Museum of Fine Arts, Copenhagen.

287. From the same collection as Plate 17.

288. From the same collection as Plate 17.

289. The Bibliothèque Nationale, Paris.

290. *Le Barbier* by Abraham Bosse; 1630s.
By courtesy of the Trustees of the British Museum, London.

291–4. From R. P. Claude du Molinet, *Le Cabinet de la bibliothèque de Saint-Geneviève*, Paris, 1692.
Victoria and Albert Museum, London.

295 & 296. Pen and ink drawings in Pepys' own manuscript catalogue to his Library, now set up at Magdalene College, Cambridge.
Reproduced by courtesy of the Master and Fellows of Magdalene College, Cambridge (I am greatly indebted to Mr Robert Latham for

providing me with much information about the Pepys Library and its furniture).

297. Leiden University.

298. Reproduced by the courtesy of the Curators of the Bodleian Library.

299. This library originally housed a valuable collection of books which was subsequently sold.

Ham House, Richmond (Victoria and Albert Museum photograph).

300. Painted by Jan van der Heyden when he was seventy-four (i.e. about 1711).

Reproduced by courtesy of Messrs Christie, Manson and Woods (I am indebted to Mr Anthony Coleridge for securing this photograph for me).

301. See Colour Plate IV.

Country Life photograph.

302. The harpsichord is shown in reverse because the illustration is an off-set image (see Plate 17 for an explanation concerning this and the related drawings). It is gilded and decorated with grotesques. The Duc d'Orléans died in 1701 and was succeeded by his son, the Duc de Chartres (see Plate 288).

303. From the *Nouveaux livre de paramens inventée & gravée par D. Marot, architecte de sa Majesté Britannique* (i.e. published before 1702). This no doubt reflects the general appearance of William III's library at Het Loo and perhaps also of libraries at Kensington Palace and Hampton Court.

Victoria and Albert Museum (from P. Jessen, *Daniel Marot*, Berlin, 1892).

304. Engraving by H. de St Jean. The *garniture* over the door-case is noteworthy, as are the bowls of flowers above the cornice.

The Bibliothèque Nationale, Paris.

305. A sixteenth century drawing said to represent a scene connected with the birth of François II in 1559.

Present location unknown (photograph from the archives of the Department of Furniture and Woodwork, Victoria and Albert Museum.

306 & 307. Eriksberg, Södermanland, Sweden (photographs by courtesy of Nordiska Museet, Stockholm).

308 From Lorenzo Magalotti's description of

Sweden published by C. M. Stenbock (*Severige Under År 1674*, Stockholm, 1912). Already in 1634 a French ambassador noted that the *sauna* attendants were women—a tradition that still pertains today.

Photograph by courtesy of Nordiska Museet, Stockholm.

309. By Jacob Ochtervelt (1634/5–1708/10). About 1670?

The Minneapolis Institute of Arts (The Putnam Dana McMillan Fund).

310. Title page by Crispin van de Passe in Part II of *Vox populi, or Gondomar appearing in his likeness of Mackiavell in a Spanish Parliament*, 1624.

By courtesy of the Trustees of the British Museum, London.

311. *Le Clystère* by Abraham Bosse; about 1635. The Bibliothèque Nationale, Paris.

312. Skokloster, Sweden.

313. Hampton Court Palace (reproduced by gracious permission of Her Majesty the Queen).

314. Ham House, Richmond (Victoria and Albert Museum, photograph).

315. Based on a plan reproduced in 'The Book of Architecture of John Thorpe in Sir John Soane's Museum', ed. by Sir John Summerson, *The Walpole Society*, 1966.

316. Based on a plan given by Blunt, *Art and Architecture in France 1500–1700*, 1970 edn.

317. Based on a plan in the care of the Royal Commission on the Ancient Monuments of Scotland.

318. The National Museum, Stockholm (Tessin Collection; see Plate 5).

319. From Randle Holme, *An Academie or Store of Armory & Blazon*, Book III, Chapter XIV, apparently published in 1688 although the title-page bears the date 1682 while the manuscript edition in the British Museum is dated 1649. Holme was born in Chester in 1622 and died in 1700. Some of the motifs would seem highly unsuitable for heraldry.

Victoria and Albert Museum, London.

320. The Rijksmuseum, Amsterdam.

Note. All Victoria and Albert Museum photographs are Crown copyright.

Index

415

furnishings, *also* Beds: *Lits à housse*

Howell, James (17 C. travel writer) 341n

Hucaback *see* Linen

Huis ten Bosch, near The Hague 89–90, 246, 249, Pl. 56

Huissier see Usher

Humbler furnishings 104

'Huva, Mistress van der' (Lauderdale's Dutch contact) 342n

Huygens, Constantijn (Secretary to Frederik Hendrik, Prince of Orange) 38–9, 40, 365n

Hygiene 169, 315–29

Ince & Mayhew (18 C. upholsterers and cabinet makers) 213

Informality 14–23, 296

Ingatestone Hall, Essex
    clothes storage 395n
    unified *ammeublement* 104
    Architectural features
        close-stool house 386n
        shutters 347n
        walls of dining room 392n
    Furniture
        brushing board 379n
        chairs 372n, 374n
        chest for linen and candles 388n
        close-stool 325, 398n
        cup-boards 380n
        desk 310
        forms 182
        tables 377n, 381n
    Upholstery
        bed-hangings 357n
        bedding 113, 117, 370n
        carpet 110
        hangings 360n
        matting 358n, 364n
        table-carpets 381n
        window-curtains 363n
    Miscellaneous
        basins and ewers 398n
        bed-staves 371n
        candlesticks 388n
        sarsnet 357n

Inkwells, inkhorns 311
    see also Standish

Intarsia 71, 345n

Irish
    horsehair 360n
    ruggs 112, 355n
    stitch (*point d'Hongrie*) 108, 125, 133, 225

James I, King of Scotland and England (1566–1625) 124, 340n, 377n

Jardinières 264

Jars, Hotel de, Paris Pl. 316

Jean, King of France (1296–1346) 362n

Jeans fustian (from Genoa) 356n

Jensen, Gerreit (17 C. cabinet maker) 50, 346n, 397n

Johnson, Dr Samuel (18 C. lexicographer) 117, 179

Joiners (Joyners), London Company of 182
    see also Guilds; Paris, *Huchiers-Menuisiers*

Jonc, Jonco (rushes; mats of) 358n

Jones, Inigo (17 C. architect)
    association with Cleyn 93, 340n, 363n, Pl. 52
    Arundel House 38, 341n
    Banqueting House 38
    copying French designs 29, 36, 46, 69, 340n, 345n, Pls 63, 64
    Court Circle 93
    furniture 185, Pl. 52
    meeting with Huygens 38–9
    unifying role 52–3
    see also Pls 44, 45, 75, 284

Jousse, Mathurin (17 C. locksmith) Pl. 174

Kederminster Library, Langley Marish, Buckinghamshire 306, 394n, Col. Pl. XVII

Kenilworth Castle, Warwickshire 362n

Kensington Palace, London 46, 51, 67, 80, 148, 250, 251, 346n, 358n, 385n, 392n, 397n
    see also William III

Kenting *see* Linen

Kersey (cloth) 114, 221

Kidderminster stuff 109, 133, 139, 221

Kildare, The Earl of (Inventory of 1656) 267, 301, 306, 395n

Kilkenny Castle, Ireland 111, 118, 140, 159, 180, 220, 261, 275, 314, 325, 365n, 376n, 381n, 384n, 385n, 389n, 390n

King's College, Cambridge 347n, 351n, 372n, 376n, 381n, 387n

Kinross House, Scotland Pl. 317

Kitchens Pl. 283

Kiveton Hall, Yorkshire Col. Pl. XII

Knole, Kent
    Furniture
        beds 181, 367n
        billiard table 231
        candlestands 277, Pl. 272
        chairs 208, 373n, 374n, 375n
        couches 368n, Pl. 150
        desk on screen 313
        hammock 169
        squabs 181
        stools 185
        triads 50, 278
    Upholstery:
        bed-hangings 124, 153, 357n
        canopy bowl 367n
        hangings 114
        matting 118
    Miscellaneous
        firedogs 261
        lantern 281
        nightlight holder Pl. 259
        tiles 86, 348n

Knops (bed finials) 366n, 369n

Krunitz, Johan Georg (18 C. encyclopaedist) 364n

Lace, openwork trimming of silk, silver or gold 148, 362n
    of linen 178

Lambert, Hotel de, Paris Pl. 57

Lamps 271, Pl. 319 (50–52)

Lanterns 281, Pls 256, 274

Langlois (17 C. print-seller; one of a dynasty) 344n

Lanyer, Jerome (flock hangings) 123

Lapierre, *see* Pierre, Francis La

Lath bottoms (under mattresses) 177

Lattice windows 82

Lauderdale, Elizabeth, Duchess of (17 C. aristocrat, daughter of William Murray) 49, 106, 275, 317, Pl. 59
    see also Ham House, Lauderdale (Duke of), and Murray
    furniture 342n, 385n, Pl. 216
    rooms and their features 59, 68, 81, 90, 230, 317, 319, 351n, 363n, Pls 77, 216
    upholstery 113

Lauderdale, John Maitland, Duke of (*see previous entry*) 49, 50, 84, 90, 274, 302, 325, 375n, Pls 40, 179–80

Lauderdale table 378n

Lauzun, Hotel de, Paris Pls 80, 301, Col. Pl. IV

Lavardin, Monsieur de, his silver furniture 349n

Laveton (flock) 178

Leather 118–23, 222
    carpets 148
    damask 120, 381n
    gloves 329
    on chairs 187, 217, 220, 222, 284, 392n
    see also gilt leather

Leeds, Thomas Osborne, Duke of, his seat furniture 213, 342n, Col. Pl. XII

Leeuwarden, The Residence at, 384n, 385n, 393n, 399n

Leicester, Lettice, Countess of (including Inventory of 1634) 104, 115, 169, 306, 353n, 356n, 366n, 368n, 391n

Leicester House, London Col. Pl. X

Leiden University, Library Pl. 297

Lely, Sir Peter (17 C. painter) 48

Lemnius, Levinus (16 C. humanist) 143

Libraries 302, 303–15, Pls 49, 291–303, Col. Pl. XVII

Library furniture
    ladders 310, Pl. 302
    steps 310
    table 310
    see also Bookcases and Desks

Lieu, le 326

Lighting 268–81
    candlelight Pls 3, 255–8, 261
    firelight 268, 261, Pls 65–74
    light on cabinets 247
    light reflected 67
    see also Liveries

Lille 108, 112, 355n

Linen 116–17, 178, 243, 286, 358n, 388n

Linsey woolsey (cloth) 114, 139

Liselotte, *see* Palatine, Princess

Lister, Dr Martin (17 C. traveller) 84, 89, 154, 341n, 348n, 349n, 384n, 391n

Lit de repos see Daybeds

Liveries 233, 294
    see also Beds, livery; *and* Cup-boards, livery

Lobel, Simon de (17 C. upholsterer) 103

Lockey, Dr Thomas (17 C. academic) 325, 396n, 399n

Lodgings 343n
    see also Apartment

Loo, Het, Palace of, Guelderland 44, 84, 94, Pls 51, 238, 303

Looking-glass Makers, Worshipful Company of 79

425

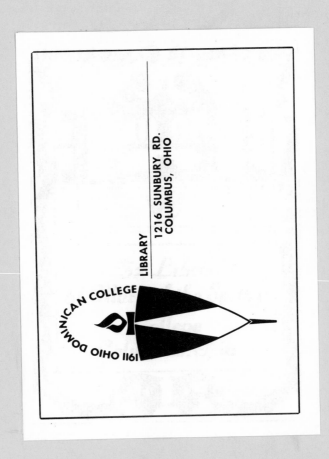

THE SECOND
ST. NICHOLAS ANTHOLOGY

S aid one bookworm to another, as they stopped one day to talk,
"I am getting so rheumatic, it is hard for me to walk;
But, in spite of close confinement, you are youthful, fresh, and gay.
Now what could cause the difference in our constitutions, pray?"
Answered then the youthful bookworm, "There's no need to feel
 so blue;
There was a period, long ago, when I was sickly too.
But for thirty years or more, since first it went to press,
My sole and daily diet has been St. Nicholas."

—By Miriam A. DeForde (Age 15)

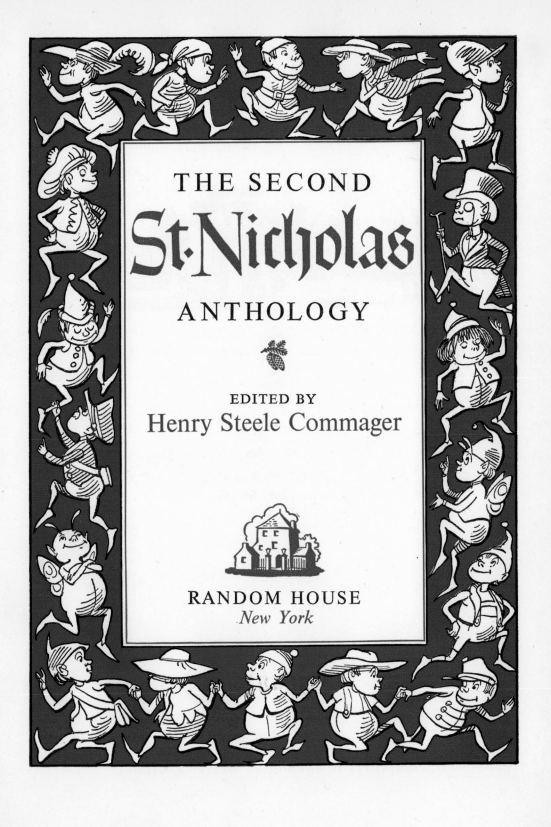

THE SECOND
St·Nicholas
ANTHOLOGY

EDITED BY
Henry Steele Commager

RANDOM HOUSE
New York

TO
LISA

TABLE OF CONTENTS

vii

THE ST. NICHOLAS LEAGUE

THE RIDDLE BOX

PREFACE

by Henry Steele Commager

THOSE of you who read the first *St. Nicholas Anthology* may recall—you won't, of course—a sentence from the preface. "Had we our own way," I wrote, "this anthology would probably have run to several volumes, and in our more ecstatic moments we talked of a second *St. Nicholas* anthology." Well, here it is, our wishes come true, just like in so many of the *St. Nicholas* stories—remember the street car that came in a stocking! The first *St. Nicholas Anthology* gave so much pleasure to so many people, including the editors, that it became more than just self-indulgence to prepare a second.

So here is another selection from the inexhaustible and enchanting volumes of *St. Nick*. Here are some of the old familiar names, and some newcomers. The list of contributors is, once more, a Hall of Fame, and not of juvenile literature alone. We have here old friends and favorites like Lucretia P. Hale of Peterkins fame, and Sophie Swett—we wanted to put in a half dozen of her wonderful stories—and Frank Stockton who wrote the best fairy tales (if you can call them that) of any one in our country, and Palmer Cox and his inimitable Brownies, and Ralph Henry Barbour of course—imagine *St. Nicholas* without Barbour! We have here the great names that turn out to be so simple and friendly, like Mark Twain and Louisa May Alcott

and Frances Hodgson Burnett and Joel Chandler Harris. And we have, too, those modern masters who are still, happily, with us, like Cornelia Meigs and Dorothy Canfield and Frank Dobie. The same illustrators, too, lend a hand: Reginald Birch, E. W. Kemble, Arthur Rackham, George Varian, Palmer Cox, and others.

In making this second anthology we have built, of course, upon our experience with its predecessor. We had a great mass of selections left over from that first one, but we weren't satisfied with that. Our judgment might have changed, or we might have missed something that was good. We had, too, a great many letters from *St. Nicholas* enthusiasts calling our attention to their particular favorites and invoking our interest in them. To all of these, and to the many, many others who wrote us, we are grateful. So we went back and started afresh, going through the volumes once again, making our choices all over again. We tried to keep pretty much the same recipe as before, too: mostly short stories, with a few long ones; a mixture of stories of family life, adventure, sailing, sports, history, and the like. We found room for a few—alas only a few—longer stories, like "Davy and the Goblins" and the "Two Biddicut Boys," everybody's first choice for the serial. We put in a few articles, interspersed the whole with poetry, spiced it with the League and the puzzles, and decorated it all with the best illustrations that any magazine ever had.

Like the original *St. Nicholas Anthology,* this one is a family enterprise; it wouldn't have been much fun any other way. Evan and I read everything, and agreed most of the time. Nell and Steele read everything, too, and their judgment was as sound as ever. But there is one important difference between this volume and its predecessor. When we compiled the first anthology Lisa was but an interested spectator. By the time we were ready to make this one she had graduated to a full partnership. No one read these stories more avidly than she and probably no one ever loved them better. It is only right that this *Second St. Nicholas Anthology* should be dedicated to her.

June, 1950

THE SECOND
ST. NICHOLAS ANTHOLOGY

THE PETERKINS' CHRISTMAS TREE

by Lucretia P. Hale

PRETTY early in the autumn the Peterkins began to prepare for their Christmas tree. Everything was done in great privacy, as it was to be a surprise to the neighbors, as well as to the rest of the family. Mr. Peterkin had been up to Mr. Bromwich's woodlot, and, with his consent, selected the tree. Agamemnon went to look at it occasionally after dark, and Solomon John made frequent visits to it, mornings, just after sunrise. Mr. Peterkin drove Elizabeth Eliza and her mother that way, and pointed furtively to it with his whip, but none of them ever spoke of it aloud to each other. It was suspected that the little boys had been to see it Wednesday and Saturday afternoons. But they came home with their pockets full of chestnuts, and said nothing about it.

At length Mr. Peterkin had it cut down, and brought secretly into the Larkins's barn. A week or two before Christmas, a measurement was made of it, with Elizabeth Eliza's yard measure. To Mr. Peterkin's great dismay, it was discovered that it was too high to stand in the back parlor. This fact was brought out at a secret council of Mr. and Mrs. Peterkin, Elizabeth Eliza, and Agamemnon.

Agamemnon suggested that it might be set up slanting, but Mrs. Peterkin was very sure it would make her dizzy, and the candles would drip.

But a brilliant idea came to Mr. Peterkin. He proposed that the ceiling of the parlor should be raised to make room for the top of the tree.

Elizabeth Eliza thought the space would need to be quite large. It must not be like a small box, or you could not see the tree.

"Yes," said Mr. Peterkin, "I should have the ceiling lifted all across the room; the effect would be finer."

Elizabeth Eliza objected to having the whole ceiling raised, because her room was over the back parlor, and she would have no floor while the alteration was going on, which would be very awkward. Besides, her room was not very high now, and if the floor were raised, perhaps she could not walk in it upright.

Mr. Peterkin explained that he didn't propose altering the whole ceiling, but to lift up a ridge across the room at the back part where the tree was to stand. This would make a hump, to be sure, in Elizabeth Eliza's room; but it would go across the whole room.

Elizabeth Eliza said she would not mind that. It would be like the cuddy thing that comes up on the deck of a ship, that you sit against, only here you would not have the seasickness. She thought she should like it for a rarity. She might use it for a divan.

Mrs. Peterkin thought it would come in the worn place of the carpet, and might be a convenience in making the carpet over.

Agamemnon was afraid there would be

3

trouble in keeping the matter secret, for it would be a long piece of work for a carpenter; but Mr. Peterkin proposed having the carpenter for a day or two, for a number of other jobs.

One of them was to make all the chairs in the house of the same height, for Mrs. Peterkin had nearly broken her spine, by sitting down in a chair that she had supposed was her own rocking-chair, and it had proved to be two inches lower. The little boys were now large enough to sit in any chair; so a medium was fixed upon to satisfy all the family, and the chairs were made uniformly of the same height.

On consulting the carpenter, however, he insisted that the tree could be cut off at the lower end to suit the height of the parlor, and demurred at so great a change as altering the ceiling. But Mr. Peterkin had set his mind upon the improvement, and Elizabeth Eliza had cut her carpet in preparation for it.

So the folding-doors into the back parlor were closed, and for nearly a fortnight before Christmas there was great litter of fallen plastering, and laths, and chips, and shavings; and Elizabeth Eliza's carpet was taken up, and the furniture had to be changed, and one night she had to sleep at the Bromwichs', for there was a long hole in her floor that might be dangerous.

All this delighted the little boys. They could not understand what was going on. Perhaps they suspected a Christmas tree, but they did not know why a Christmas tree should have so many chips, and were still more astonished at the hump that appeared in Elizabeth Eliza's room. It must be a Christmas present, or else the tree in a box.

Some aunts and uncles, too, arrived a day or two before Christmas, with some small cousins. These cousins occupied the attention of the little boys, and there was a great deal of whispering and mystery,

behind doors, and under the stairs, and in the corners of the entry.

Solomon John was busy, privately making some candles for the tree. He had been collecting some bayberries, as he understood they made very nice candles, so that it would not be necessary to buy any.

The elders of the family never all went into the back parlor together, and all tried not to see what was going on. Mrs. Peterkin would go in with Solomon John, or Mr. Peterkin with Elizabeth Eliza, or Elizabeth Eliza and Agamemnon and Solomon John. The little boys and the small cousins were never allowed even to look inside the room.

Elizabeth Eliza meanwhile went into town a number of times. She wanted to consult Amanda as to how much ice-cream they should need, and whether they could make it at home, as they had cream and ice. She was pretty busy in her own room; the furniture had to be changed, and the carpet altered. The "hump" was higher than she had expected. There was danger of bumping her own head whenever she crossed it. She had to nail some padding on the ceiling for fear of accidents.

The afternoon before Christmas, Elizabeth Eliza, Solomon John, and their father, collected in the back parlor for a council. The carpenters had done their work, and the tree stood at its full height at the back of the room, the top stretching up into the space arranged for it. All the chips and shavings were cleared away, and it stood on a neat box.

But what were they to put upon the tree?

Solomon John had brought in his supply of candles, but they proved to be very "stringy" and very few of them. It was strange how many bayberries it took to make a few candles! The little boys had helped him, and he had gathered as much as a bushel of bayberries. He had put them in water, and skimmed off the wax, according to the directions, but there was so little wax!

Solomon John had given the little boys some of the bits sawed off from the legs of the chairs. He had suggested they should cover them with gilt paper, to answer for gilt apples, without telling them what they were for.

These apples, a little blunt at the end, and the candles, were all they had for the tree.

After all her trips into town, Elizabeth Eliza had forgotten to bring anything for it.

"I thought of candies and sugar plums," she said, "but I concluded if we made caramels ourselves we should not need them. But, then, we have not made caramels. The fact is, that day my head was full of my carpet. I had bumped it pretty badly, too."

Mr. Peterkin wished he had taken, instead of a fir tree, an apple tree he had seen in October, full of red fruit.

"But the leaves would have fallen off by this time," said Elizabeth Eliza.

"And the apples too," said Solomon John.

"It is odd I should have forgotten, that day I went in on purpose to get the things," said Elizabeth Eliza, musingly. "But I went from shop to shop, and didn't know exactly what to get. I saw a great many gilt things for Christmas trees, but I knew the little boys were making the gilt apples; there were plenty of candles in the shops, but I knew Solomon John was making the candles."

Mr. Peterkin thought it was quite natural.

Solomon John wondered if it were too late for them to go into town now.

Elizabeth Eliza could not go in the next morning, for there was to be a grand Christmas dinner, and Mr. Peterkin could not be spared, and Solomon John was sure he and Agamemnon would not know what to buy. Besides, they would want to try the candles tonight.

Mr. Peterkin asked if the presents everybody had been preparing would not answer? But Elizabeth Eliza knew they would be too heavy.

A gloom came over the room. There was only a flickering gleam from one of Solomon John's candles that he had lighted by way of trial.

Solomon John again proposed going into town. He lighted a match to examine the newspaper about the trains. There were plenty of trains coming out at that hour, but none going in except a very late one. That would not leave time to do anything and come back.

"We could go in, Elizabeth Eliza and I," said Solomon John, "but we should not have time to buy anything."

Agamemnon was summoned in. Mrs. Peterkin was entertaining the uncles and aunts in the front parlor. Agamemnon wished there was time to study up something about electric lights. If they could only have a calcium light! Solomon John's candle sputtered and went out.

At this moment there was a loud knocking at the front door. The little boys, and the small cousins, and the uncles and aunts, and Mrs. Peterkin, hastened to see what was the matter.

The uncles and aunts thought somebody's house must be on fire. The door was opened, and there was a man, white with flakes, for it was beginning to snow, and he was pulling in a large box.

Mrs. Peterkin supposed it contained some of Elizabeth Eliza's purchases, so she ordered it to be pushed into the back parlor, and hastily called back her guests and the little boys into the other room. The little boys and the small cousins were sure they had seen Santa Claus himself.

Mr. Peterkin lighted the gas. The box was addressed to Elizabeth Eliza. It was from the lady from Philadelphia! She had gathered a hint from Elizabeth Eliza's letters that there was to be a Christmas-tree, and had filled this box with all that would be needed.

It was opened directly. There was every kind of gilt hanging thing, from gilt-pods to butterflies on springs. There were shining flags and lanterns, and bird-cages, and nests with birds sitting on them, baskets of fruit, gilt apples and bunches of grapes, and, at the bottom of the whole, a large box of candles and a box of Philadelphia bonbons!

Elizabeth Eliza and Solomon John could scarcely keep from screaming. The little boys and the small cousins knocked on the folding-doors to ask what was the matter.

Hastily Mr. Peterkin and the rest took out the things and hung them on the tree, and put on the candles.

When all was done, it looked so well that Mr. Peterkin exclaimed:

"Let us light the candles now, and send to invite all the neighbors to-night, and have the tree on Christmas Eve!"

And so it was that the Peterkins had their Christmas tree the day before, and on Christmas night could go and visit their neighbors.

GUESTS IN THE SMOKEHOUSE

by Cornelia Meigs

THE broad lake at the foot of Mt. Neshobe had been swept by the bitter wind until it was bare of snow, a smooth expanse of blue ice which reached away northward, winding and turning among the rocky spurs of the mountain. For more than an hour Richard Kent could see it spread out below as the sleigh, with its two fast, big, jingling horses, swung down the road cut from the steep hillside. The boy had the feeling, as he looked about him, that the

Vermont hills were familiar and friendly and yet totally strange, since, although he had seen them every summer for nearly ten years, he had never before looked at their ridges and sharp summits in the winter, when their abrupt slopes were

blanketed with hard-frozen snow instead of being shrouded in the abundant leafy green of the summer forests. The sky was gray behind the mountain tops, for it had snowed yesterday and would, in all probability, snow again before tomorrow. Richard burrowed a little deeper into the warm buffalo robes at the thought of it.

"We are lucky to find the way open," his Uncle Nathan observed, shifting his cold hands to get a new grip on the reins. "One more storm and the whole lake valley will be blocked."

Richard looked up at him, an erect, surprising figure with his tall, bell-crowned hat and close-fitting, caped greatcoat. He seemed curiously out of place, the boy thought vaguely, against that wild landscape of hill and snowdrift. Uncle Nathan Kent was always dressed just as a prosperous lawyer of the 1850's should be garbed, although just now he would have been more comfortable if he had buttoned himself into the old coat which Uncle Hiram Kent had sent along with the sleigh to meet the travelers, a coat which had belonged to a black bear before it had become Uncle Hiram's.

It was strange, also, Richard kept feeling, to be driving this last twenty miles of the accustomed journey without Uncle Hiram's cheerful presence, for it was his delighted face which they always saw first of all when they got down at the coaching station, stiff from the long ride up from Massachusetts. Travel was not easy in those days before the Civil War, but there was no difficulty too great to keep Richard from coming, summer after summer, to spend his vacation on the Vermont farm where his father and his two uncles had all grown up. Nathan and Thomas Kent, Richard's father, had long since made successful places for themselves in a Massachusetts manufacturing town and often wondered aloud how their elder brother could cling so stubbornly to those rocky acres above Neshobe Lake. Richard had wondered, too—until last summer. It was then that some inkling of an astonishing truth had suddenly burst upon him.

It had been a warm day, hot for Vermont, with brilliant sunshine everywhere, the most complete contrast to the present bleak afternoon. He and Selina had been picking summer apples, Selina being the lively granddaughter of that elderly cousin who kept house for Uncle Hiram. Selina lived the year round on the mountain farm; her cheerful company was always a taken-for-granted part of Richard's vacations. They were both tired on that afternoon, and a little dazzled by the bright sun. Richard, carrying the bushel basket of apples into the kitchen, was moved by a sudden fancy to seek the coolness of the dark cellar. He slipped down the stairs—groping, for he was quite blind in the dimness—and heard, all at once, under the vaulted arch of the farthest recess, the stirring of a big body, and a great voice sunk to a thick whisper saying:

"Is you coming to take me out of here, Mars'er Kent? Isn't you going to get me out of this pretty soon?"

He retreated abruptly, but stood for a long minute at the foot of the stairs, his heart hammering in his ears. Everything was still now, but Richard still thought that he could hear from that far, dusky corner a faint sound as of some great body trying to keep utterly silent, trying even to breathe as lightly as possible. Should he go forward boldly into the dark and demand who or what was there? Something kept him back, and it was not fear. This was Uncle Hiram's secret, and prying curiosity might bring disaster. He turned about and stumbled up the stairs. Out in the sunny orchard, Selina was still sitting, leaning against a twisted trunk with a yellow apple in her hand. Forbearance had its limits, nor could he have possibly helped putting that breathless question:

"Selina, what's—what's that in the cellar?"

Selina looked at him steadily. She was a year older than he; she had honest blue eyes which could, when she chose, be very determined in the guarding of secrets.

"I'm not to tell you," she answered. She set her lips resolutely, as though she were issuing the order to herself and not to him. "I—I only found out by accident, and Uncle Hiram knows I know, but we don't speak of it. My grandmother has never guessed, but I think Uncle Nathan has, and that he argues with Uncle Hiram about its being wrong."

This baffling statement was far from giving Richard satisfaction, but she told him no more, except to burst out a moment later, "Do you think, when your father and Uncle Nathan have done so much, away from here, that Uncle Hiram has stayed behind for nothing else than to grow hay and potatoes on this stony mountain? Did you ever think that he might be doing something special, too, that the others didn't even dare to think about?"

The time for Richard's departure came so soon after that day that he had little time to push the matter any further. He did slip into the cellar again, but realized from the very feel of the cool shadowy emptiness that there was now no presence there save his own. More than once he looked into Uncle Hiram's kind, sun-browned face and longed to frame a question, but went away without ever having found words for it.

During the next winter there was news that Uncle Hiram was less well than usual, crippled by rheumatism, an ancient and stoutly contested enemy. It was on an evening in early January that Uncle Nathan, immaculate in blue broadcloth and bright buttons, came to confer with Richard's father. Although it was still a number of years before the

Civil War, the shadow of that great upheaval was already on the horizon, and the question of slavery was drawing closer and closer to the hearts and souls of all citizens of the United States. It was not surprising, therefore, that the two Kent brothers plunged immediately into discussing the new laws which had to do with runaway slaves. What was odd was that Uncle Nathan should say suddenly in the midst of the heated talk, "I'm going up to see Hiram. I can get there, even through the snow. I worry about him more every day. I wrote him, and I am starting next week."

A few days later there came, rather surprisingly, a letter to Richard from Selina. She wrote very seldom and only when she had something particular to say. "When Uncle Nathan comes up," she directed now, "ask to come with him. I believe Uncle Hiram needs you." She had signed her name with proper messages and then added: "Do you remember that secret about the cellar? If ever Uncle Hiram told anyone about it of his own will, I do believe, Richard, that it would be you."

Richard had never been to the farm in winter, but there proved to be little difficulty in getting permission to go. Uncle Nathan was glad to have company on the stage journey, and it was holiday time from school. So here were uncle and nephew, driving down the freshly plowed road, with old Silas, who had brought the sleigh to meet them, tucked up in the back seat. Uncle Nathan, in spite of his elaborate clothes and manners, had not been brought up on a Vermont farm for nothing. He could not bear to drive behind a good pair of horses unless he held the reins himself. It was he who had taught Richard to drive, so that the boy now could appreciate the adroit skill with which his uncle eased the big grays down abrupt drops in the road and around the high-banked curves.

At a narrow place the sound of bells coming toward them made them pull up suddenly. A smaller sleigh drew out to make room for them to pass, and one of the two men in it first hailed Uncle Nathan, and then got down, knee deep in the drifts, to come over to speak to him. Richard had seen that rough-hewn face before, and knew that this was John Halloway, a neighbor of Uncle Hiram's and the sheriff of that county.

"Coming up to see Hiram Kent, be ye?" he asked. When Uncle Nathan answered yes, he went on in a lowered voice: "Just you tell Hiram, from me, that I've had orders to watch him." He jerked his head toward the other man in the smaller sleigh, a stranger with a narrow face sunk deep into the warmth of his big coat. "That fellow there is from down southward, a slave owners' agent, sent up to try to get back runaway property. You see it's my place to show him around, whether I like it or not. It's beyond my duty to say much, but you ask Hiram Kent just to read over the text of the Fugitive Slave Law. That's all."

He turned about hastily, climbed into his sleigh and slapped the reins over the horses' backs. Uncle Nathan drove on, looking straight ahead and making no comment upon the message. Richard, after glancing back to observe, as he had expected, that Silas was napping in the rear seat, asked abruptly, "Uncle Nathan, just what is the Fugitive Slave Law?"

"It's a regulation put through Congress by the men who support slavery," his uncle returned. "It says that any person who finds a runaway slave must return him to his master, or help to do so, otherwise he will be liable to arrest and fines. The owners of plantations in the South are complaining loudly over the number

of runaways who have been smuggled all the way north as far as Canada."

"Are they free when they get to Canada?" Richard asked.

"They are," answered his uncle, and concluded grimly, "The Canadian line, you may remember, is just forty miles from your Uncle Hiram's farm."

"Oh," was all that Richard could say, and was silent for a long time.

It had begun to snow when they drew up at the farm gate, but it was still light enough to see the row of buildings sheltered under the wall of the mountain— the big barns, the square brick smokehouse where the meat was cured for winter use, the long woodshed adjoining the broad, bright-windowed farmhouse itself. Selina was on the step to greet them and bring them in to the blazing fire.

"Uncle Hiram can't come down," she said, "and he wants you to have supper before you come up. You must be starving."

Selina and her grandmother had set forth a real banquet of country fare to which Richard did ample justice, but which seemed scarcely to tempt Uncle Nathan. He hurried through it and got up abruptly, just as Selina was bringing in the pumpkin pie. "I am going up to see my brother," he said. "You finish your supper, Richard, and come later when I call you."

THE bountiful meal had long been over and the dishes washed and put away before Richard heard Uncle Nathan's voice summoning him upstairs. Cousin Sarah, Selina's grandmother, had been in the room all the time, so that Selina had said nothing to him in private. But as he mounted the stair the words of her letter were burning within him—"Uncle Hiram needs you. If he ever tells anyone, of his own will, it would be you."

The eldest of the Kent brothers was sitting close to the narrow fireplace, which was all that gave warmth to the big, low-ceiled room. Hiram was taller than his brother Nathan, with a broader forehead and deeper, brighter eyes; with a general air of character and command which Nathan Kent, at that moment, seemed to lack. He stood behind his older brother and, in spite of his well-cut coat and his manner of ease and self-confidence, he was, very distinctly, less of a man than this crumpled giant who sat helpless in the great wooden chair. Hiram Kent sat looking at his nephew with twinkling gray eyes, but waited, obviously, for his brother to speak.

"You have surely guessed by now, Richard, what has brought me here—the fact that your Uncle Hiram has been smuggling slaves over the border into Canada, and the need of warning him that he is in danger. Such folly has to be stopped; he is under suspicion already. Even you can add a word. We can save him from his wrong-headed mistakes if we can make him listen to reason."

He walked toward the door, seeming to grow of more consequence the farther he got from that strangely powerful presence beside the fire. "I have used every argument I can to you," he concluded. "Any sane man can see the danger and what the end will be. I have nothing more to say."

He went out, and Richard came forward to sit on the stool beside the fire. For some minutes the burning wood snapped and crackled and neither of the two spoke.

"Selina sent for you?" Uncle Hiram began at last. "Selina is a wise girl. It is quite true that someone must save me tonight; must save me—and two others.

This rheumatism has caught me at a bad moment. I can't leave my chair—and it's forty miles to Canada."

Richard had been sitting with his hands clasped between his knees and his eyes on the floor. He looked up startled; Uncle Hiram gave him the quick flash of a smile and went on, "I can't ask you to involve yourself, Richard. Your Uncle Nathan is sensible and cautious; you will have to stand on his side or mine. You can try to save me from what he calls my folly, or you can save me where I have given my promise that another shall get away to safety. It is our fault, every living American's fault, that anything so hideous as slavery exists. It will continue to be our fault until we find some way to be rid of it. Mine is not a good way, Richard, I admit that; but it is, so far, the best way open. Now think a little, and choose. Don't decide too—"

They were interrupted by a sudden disturbance below by voices in the lower hall, and, a moment later, by Uncle Nathan's bursting into the room. "It's as I told you," he cried, his voice high with excitement. "John Holloway gave you one warning; what he could not tell you was that he was on his way to the village to take out a search warrant. He's here now with the slave owners' agent, a fellow named Atkins. They have authority to search the farm for runaway slaves and they're going to do it."

"Let them," returned Uncle Hiram easily and quite unmoved. "Give them the freedom of the place and tell them to look anywhere they want. But ask Sarah to give them some hot supper and have Selina light the fire in the front bedroom. They'll have to stay the night, with it snowing the way it is. A lot of guests we have this evening, for a quiet place like Neshobe Mountain Farm!" As Richard went downstairs to carry the message to the women he heard Hiram Kent chuckling.

As he came into the big kitchen, he saw that John Holloway was just taking a lamp from the table. "We can't waste any time," Holloway was saying in an undertone to his companion, Atkins, "especially after what we heard in the village of what had been seen up here." He led the way down a dark passage. Richard, unforbidden, came after the two, and Selina followed behind.

They went thoroughly up and down the whole of the rambling old house, poked their heads into closets, tapped on walls, flashed the light into dark places behind stairs. Richard stayed behind when they pushed into Uncle Hiram's room, but he heard cheerful voices and saw that both the men were laughing as they came out. He held his breath as they descended into the cellar. Here were a hundred shadows and hidden places, but search revealed them all as empty. For the first time he saw the big, arched niche from which he had heard that whispered voice the summer before. Nothing was there now save sacks of apples and a row of golden squashes. They all came tramping up the stairs again, with the long shadows trailing behind them.

The men armed themselves with lanterns before they sallied out to examine the barns, Richard and Selina still bringing up the rear. There was little wind, but the snow was coming down in a smooth white curtain, with the air feeling soft and moist. The slave agent shivered and drew his big coat closer about him. "Hideous weather you have in this wilderness," he observed, but he followed stoutly as John Holloway led the way.

It was a long journey all through the great barns, past the stalls where cows were munching comfortably in the dark or where a startled horse, now and again,

stamped and rolled a bright eye in the lantern light. In the farthest corner of the loft, where Richard and Selina had played when they were smaller, the expedition came to a brief halt. A ladder reached up to the rafters—a rather tall one which neither of the men seemed anxious to climb.

"Just get up there, Richard," directed Holloway, "and flash the light into that space between the beams."

As the boy hesitated, hoping to exchange glances with Selina and get a signal as to whether he would betray some desperate hiding place, the agent, Atkins, cut in roughly, "What are you waiting for when you have your orders? Don't you know what the law says, that any citizen, anywhere, can be summoned by an officer to help recover a runaway slave? Get up there of yourself or we'll make you."

Sudden, blind fury seized Richard. The man had thrust the lantern into his hand, but he threw it down as he cried hotly, "I won't go. You can't force me to go." He turned about and swung toward the stairs.

"Gently, there, gently, young man," came the sheriff's big voice as he caught up the lantern. "You don't want to burn down Hiram Kent's barn, no matter who is in it. Well, since no one else will, I'll just climb up myself." Glancing over his shoulder, Richard saw the tall man go clambering up the ladder, saw him lift the lantern high to illuminate the dark space and saw, with a gasp of relief, that it was unoccupied. He did not wait, but flung himself down the narrow stair and out of the big door. He breathed deeply of the cold wet air, so different from the warm, hay-perfumed atmosphere within.

There had been some doubt in his mind as he listened to Uncle Nathan and Uncle

Hiram—a wonder as to who was right; whether Uncle Hiram was wrong in running his whole household into danger by giving shelter to fugitive slaves. Uncle Nathan was very plausible, but his words no longer carried weight with Richard—not in the face of a law which not only dragged an escaped slave back into captivity, but even haled every free man into taking part in such cruelty. He stood a minute, seeing only faintly the bulk of the buildings about him, knowing that those great familiar mountains were all around—watching him, he almost felt, through the curtain of the dark; watching to see his mettle tried and his courage tested. He would not fail; his mind was made up now; he would help Uncle Hiram to the utmost that was in him.

He turned and saw the lights bobbing toward him from the barn. Selina, wrapped in an old shawl, came to stand beside him while the men strode past through the snow. "Here's one place we haven't looked," Richard heard Atkins say as they passed the brick smokehouse a few yards from the kitchen steps.

The sheriff fumbled at the low oak door, opened it and let out the dull glow of a smoldering fire and the sharp smell of smoke. "No one could abide in that stifling place," he said decisively. "We can be certain there's nothing here, at least."

They went up the steps, opened the kitchen door, showing a stream of ruddy light, and closed it. Even in the shrouding darkness Richard did not dare speak above a whisper, close to Selina. "Whatever has to be done, I am going to do it."

He could just see that she nodded. "You'll have to help. There are two here, and Uncle Hiram can't stir from his chair. I know how to tell you just what to do. But oh, Richard, are you sure?"

"Yes," he answered resolutely. "I'm sure

—now." Whatever his Uncle Hiram had dared and accomplished, Richard Kent would do also.

Selina turned about, lifted the latch of the smokehouse door and opened it. She bent her head to the choking smoke within, but pushed forward into the blackness, Richard behind her. An inner door swung open under her hand, through which they stepped and closed quickly behind them. Nobody ever could have guessed that the square smokehouse contained not one room, but a second also, reached through the forbidding interior of the first. There must have been hidden slits at the edge of the roof; for there were no windows in the blank, brick walls, yet it was a comfortable place, spotlessly clean, with its own fireplace and burning logs upon the small hearth.

Richard had not known what to expect, but he was completely unprepared for what he saw—a tall, grave-faced man who seemed of the same sort as Uncle Hiram himself, and a neat little lady garbed in gray, whose thin white hands were busy with knitting as she sat beside the fire. They were Quakers from Pennsylvania, they explained to him, friends of Hiram Kent for years, but through correspondence only; for they, at their end, shared in that slave-smuggling traffic which history has called the Underground Railroad. These two, so quiet in their manner, so bold and flagrant in their defiance of injustice, had finally been under such suspicion that they were forced to flee, also, to escape imprisonment and prosecution.

"Thee understands that there was nothing more that we could do for the poor blacks," the little lady said gently, "so it has seemed best for us to go away into Canada while we could. Some day we will come back and begin again in another place. Good friends have seen us thus far on our journey, and it is almost ended."

"Uncle Hiram only just finished building this room last autumn," Selina told them, "and you are the first to hide in it. He laid the first bricks the day the Fugitive Slave Law was brought up in Congress."

She had slipped out and returned, her arms laden with coats and blankets. She held out to Richard Uncle Hiram's bearskin coat and put his fur cap into her cousin's hands. While the other two were making ready, the boy and girl emerged again into the snow and took their way toward the barn. She was giving rapid and detailed directions as they went.

"You will have to drive on the ice; the road is blocked. Get well out into the middle and then face north. Uncle Hiram has sent you down his compass and says you are to put a lantern under the buffalo robe. That will keep your feet warm, at least."

They came within the cavernous door of the barn. Richard knew at once which sleigh to take and understood now why Uncle Hiram kept that team of swift black horses, too light for farm work. He backed one out of its stall and Selina the other, and the two harnessed quickly, as they so often had done in the summer. Selina was continuing those directions which it was not safe to seek at first hand from Hiram Kent. "It's twenty miles you have to go, to Seth Bronson's house, on the shore beyond Goose Neck Point. You remember that we sailed there last summer and the summer before. You must bear in toward shore as you pass the point, and when you get near enough you will see two lights shining from Seth's house for a signal. He will take Uncle Hiram's friends the rest of the way. This is the hardest and most dangerous part of the journey, for it is the one the gov-

ernment men are watching, since they suspect Uncle Hiram."

So many times had they harnessed together that both finished at exactly the same moment. The sleigh runners grated on the board floor, then glided out across the snow. In the recessed door of the smokehouse stood the Quaker pair, muffled to the eyes. The bright windows of the main house showed where the two officials were settling to an evening by the fire, with no intention of leaving shelter again that night.

The little lady murmured a word or two as she got in. "Tell thy uncle—just bless him, that is all."

Richard was in his place, with Selina looking up at him through the veil of white flakes. At the last moment misgivings seemed to have seized her. "Are you sure you can find the way?" she asked desperately.

"Yes," he nodded answer. "I will find it." He could see the two big pines which marked the track that led down to the shore. The little black Morgan mare pawed with anxiety to be off, partaking, as horses love to do, in the excitement of the errand. The sleigh slipped between the pines and the house with all its cheerful lights disappeared from view behind the swirling curtain of snow.

A FROZEN lake makes a magnificent highroad. The horses tugged at the bits as they swung into their course northward. Now and then the two in the rear seat stirred—from this time on, their liberty and even their lives depended on what Richard could do. The team was galloping wildly; now their pace increased and it was almost as though they were running away, only in this vast emptiness there was little sense of speed; no feeling of danger at all. He knew he must hold the horses; that otherwise they would exhaust themselves long before the journey's end. He braced his feet, took an iron grasp of the reins and drew them down to a more reasonable pace, although they still plunged forward the moment his hold relaxed.

They went on for hours; for untold time, it seemed to Richard. Once the snowfall lightened a little and he caught sight of a wooded island just where he had thought it ought to be. The white blanket came down again—still without wind, but with a steady, merciless increase of cold. His feet ached, his hands were numb, his arms up to his elbows were stiff as stone. The smaller of his two passengers had slipped down, completely hidden under the blankets. He heard a despairing voice behind him.

"Are we nearly there? I know thee is doing all thee can, but my poor wife—she can bear little more."

"It's not far now." His lips were so rigid that he could hardly make the words. He looked down at the compass; the needle was just visible. Then the lantern went out; the oil was spent. From that time on he drove blindly, so cold and exhausted that he did not know, and seemed scarcely to care, whether the way was right or not. A dark line of trees rose up before him. This was Goose Neck Point, or else he was hopelessly lost. He bore away to one side, but the line of trees seemed to have no end. He was lost—he wasn't—he was—. Suddenly beyond the last tall tree there was an opening. He rounded into it and saw a pair of twinkling lights, Seth Bronson's signal.

It was the horses, who had been on that errand before, who found their own path up to the house and stopped before a snowdrifted door. It was thrown open

as Richard got down, a wooden thing without feeling or joints. He indicated the heap of robes in the back of the sleigh. "Carry her in," he said hoarsely, not knowing his own voice. "I will get the horses into the barn."

They know in Vermont how to revive half-frozen travelers; they have so often had need to do so. Richard, warmed, fed, assured of the well-being of his fellow travelers, slept the day out until late afternoon. The storm had cleared when he came out again, the cold had softened, the black team, sobered to reason, trotted steadily with the sure pull of horses going home. The stars rode high, then began to sink, and the yellow winter dawn was showing behind Neshobe Mountain when he came in sight of Hiram Kent's farm.

The dark gables of the house and the tall bare elms showed plainly against the white hillside. There was a light in one window, growing fainter as the day brightened. Was it Selina's lamp, set there to guide him home? No, this was the upper chamber, where Uncle Hiram sat crippled in his great chair. Suddenly it came to Richard that his part in the work had been small and Hiram Kent's infinitely great. All the responsibility, many times the risk, had been Uncle Hiram's in planning this thing which must be done and done again and again—"until we find some way to be rid of slavery." Instead of excitement and striving and the thrill of triumph to repay him for the danger, he must simply sit and wait in pain and straining anxiety, while his own safety and Richard's and that of the two whom he had promised to save were all thrust into totally inexperienced hands.

It was certain that Uncle Hiram had sat there by the fire through both nights of waiting, watching the lamp, trying to pierce the darkness beyond the window.

Richard could see now, even at this distance, that the front door opened and a small figure which must be Selina's stood upon the step. It disappeared instantly and a moment later the light in the window went out. The gold of the sky behind the mountains was so bright now that it was no longer needed; the messenger had come safely home and the task was finished.

Selina came out to him as he was unharnessing the horses in the dusk of the barn. "Uncle Nathan stormed at first, when he found where you had gone," she told him, "but I think finally he was glad. He sat and talked with John Holloway and the other man, and never let them suspect."

The horses were fed and bedded, and the two came out together into the white dooryard. Richard knew within himself that he was going to help Hiram Kent not this once, but many times, as long as there was need, until a great evil was brought to its end. The mountains, clear and white against a brilliant sky, were witnesses of how unshakable was his determination to bear his part in all that remained to be done.

HOW THE SHOES FITTED THE BABY

by Sophie Swett

Such a pair of feet as the baby had!—plump and dimpled and satiny, and there was a bewitching little crease for an ankle, and the toe-nails were like bits of the inside of a sea-shell. I don't suppose there ever were such feet before, or, in fact, such a baby, altogether; at least, that was the opinion of the baby's little brothers and sisters, and, indeed, of the big brothers and sisters, and, now I think of it, the father and mother thought so, too. And there were, besides, some uncles and aunts and cousins (who had no babies of their own), and they were of the same opinion. And as for grandma, who had had a good many babies and grandbabies, she was sure of it. So it must have been so.

"Bless the darling! I wish she had some shoes," said grandma.

"She ought to have some shoes," said the baby's father.

"It's a *pity* she can't have some shoes," said the baby's mother.

"It's a *shame* that she's never had any shoes," said the older children—all except Jacob Abimelech.

"Can't she have some shoes?" said the younger children.

"She *shall have* some shoes!" said Jacob Abimelech.

Then they all knew that the baby would have some shoes. When Jacob Abimelech said a thing should be done, it was just as sure as roast turkey at Thanksgiving.

Jacob Abimelech was "smart." It was whispered in Brimfield that he could "spell down" the schoolmaster, and he had beaten the minister at checkers.

If Jacob Abimelech had said that a lovely little pair of shoes, with buttons on them, that exactly fitted the baby, would presently come skipping up the garden path to the front door, all by themselves, the children would have rushed to the window fully expecting to see them. They had such faith in Jacob Abimelech. But he did not say anything of that kind, and it wasn't probable that the shoes would come in any such fairy-book way as that, though it would be very convenient to have them; very convenient, indeed, for the Sparrows were poor—so poor that they had had to

Shoe the horse, and shoe the mare,
And let the little colt go bare.

To think of the baby having been in the world almost two years without having had a pair of shoes to shelter those pinky toes! I think nobody could blame the children for saying that it was a shame.

A squaw, who was wandering about, had once given the baby a pair of moccasins, gaily embroidered with beads, but they were too large,—almost large enough for Hannah,—and the baby would not keep them on.

Grandma knitted plenty of good, warm

17

little socks to keep Jack Frost from nipping her toes, but she knitted them of homespun yarn, and, though nobody wanted to hurt grandma's feelings by saying so, they were very clumsy, and not pretty at all, and, moreover, the baby could pull them off just when she liked.

Now, Jacob Abimelech had never said before that the baby *should have* some shoes. He had been the only one who had said nothing. Jacob Abimelech was one of those very uncommon people who, when they have nothing to say, say nothing. But his pumpkin had just taken the prize at the fair, and he had ten dollars of his own to do what he liked with. Although he was almost seventeen, I don't think he had ever before had ten dollars of his own in his life. They were so very poor! Mr. Sparrow had the rheumatism, and half of the time he could not work at all, and the farm was mortgaged, and seasons that were too wet, or too dry, or too cold, or too hot, came very often and spoiled the crops. And there were so many children to clothe and feed! But they found the world worth living in, after all; because there are so many beautiful things that money cannot buy.

It was such a delightful happening that Jacob Abimelech raised the prize pumpkin! And yet, like a great many good things that are called happenings, it had taken a good deal of patient care and labor to bring it about. And if it was like anybody in the world to raise a prize pumpkin, it was like Jacob Abimelech! He had chosen a place to plant the seeds where pumpkin seeds were never planted before; but it was on a sunny slope, and he made the earth rich, and that did its best to help; and the rain came along and helped at just the right time; and the sun—oh, how the sun did shine on that pumpkin-vine! and, by and by, it seemed to send its very first beam in the morning, and its very last beam at night, down on that particular pumpkin, so that it outstripped all the others, and grew and grew, until, one day, they stood the baby up beside it, and it reached to her shoulder, and a few weeks afterward they measured again, and it actually overtopped the baby's head!

You may believe that that *was* a pumpkin, and they were all very proud when Jacob Abimelech carried it to the fair, from Father Sparrow, who said he didn't know but Jacob Abimelech knew more about farming than he did, down to the baby, who understood more about it than they thought. And they were prouder still when he came home from the fair with the prize.

I have not space to tell you of the things that Jacob Abimelech had planned to buy with that ten dollars. He would have needed Aladdin's lamp, or Fortunatus's purse, to pay for them all, instead of only a ten-dollar bill. By retiring to the barn two or three times in a day, and making out a list of things he wanted most, and their probable prices, he had discovered how very few things he could have. He *did want* a gun. Jacob Abimelech was only a boy, if he was "smart." There was a fox that tried every night to get into the hen-coop; hawks and crows, too, that did great mischief. But then, there was the shawl that he wanted to get for his mother, the warm gloves for his father, and grandma's new spectacles—and the baby's shoes! He might waver a little about the shawl, and the gloves, and the spectacles,—that gun was such a temptation,—but the baby should have her shoes!

The next question was where they should be bought. There were no shoes worthy of such a baby as that in the one country store that Brimfield boasted, and at Mapleton, five miles away, where they did most of their shopping, there was a very small stock to choose from, and it was very doubtful whether there could be any found to fit her. Oh, if they could only get a pair from the city—the great city eighteen miles away, where there were shoes fit for a queen's baby—or for theirs!

"I'll tell you what!" said Jacob Abimelech, bring his hand down on his knee with great force, "Obadiah Cherrywinkle is going to the city to market to-morrow!"

"I wouldn't trust Obadiah to get them. He would never choose the right pair. They would be sure not to fit," said his mother.

"It's a pity we're so busy harvesting that one of us can't go," said Jacob Abimelech. "One of the children might go. There's James Albert; he isn't of much use at home, and he knows what's what, and is pretty sharp at a bargain."

"Oh, yes," cried all the children, in chorus. "Don't you remember the time when James Albert didn't let the tin-peddler cheat him?"

You could scarcely mention James Albert's name in that family without all the children shouting that out in chorus, it being considered one of the important events in the family history that James Albert, at the age of eight, had got the better of a tin-peddler, or, at least, had prevented the tin-peddler from getting the better of him.

"I don't know but James Albert might be trusted; he is such an old head," said his mother. "And we could measure the baby's foot exactly."

"I'll go right over and ask Obadiah if he'll take me," cried James Albert, seizing his hat.

He was back again in a very few minutes, and called out before he got the door open:

"He says *yes!* Obadiah says yes! And he says Hannah can go, too, as well as not!"

"Oh, James Albert, I'm awful sorry I told of you about the woodchuck, and you can have my bantam rooster to keep!" she exclaimed, in a gush of gratitude.

"Oh, pooh! who wants your old rooster? I just thought I'd take you for fear I'd be lonesome," replied James Albert, who did good by stealth and blushed to find it fame. "You'd better find out whether mother'll let you before you make such a fuss."

"It's a long ride. I'm afraid she'll be tired. And I suppose you'll have to be off by four o'clock in the morning. But if she wants to go, I don't know as it will do any harm," said their mother.

"It will do both the children good to see the world!" said grandma.

So it was settled, and Hannah dreamed, that night, that Jacob Abimelech's big pumpkin had turned into a coach, like Cinderella's fairy godmother's, and James Albert and she were going off to seek their fortunes in it. But they had hardly got started, it seemed to her, when James Albert was screaming "Spiders!" at her door. That was the only way they could wake Hannah, she was such a very sound sleeper. If she had not been terribly afraid of spiders I don't know what they would have done.

Jacob Abimelech had got up, and made a good hot fire in the kitchen stove, and put some potatoes in to bake, and they had a nice hot breakfast; and it seemed delightfully queer to be up eating breakfast in the night. Old Lion, who never approved of anything unusual, growled and barked; but Nebuchadnezzar got up and chased his tail as composedly as if he were in the habit of doing it at three o'clock in the morning.

There was scarcely a gleam of daylight when they heard Obadiah Cherrywinkle's heavy wagon creaking through the lane, and Obadiah's cheery voice called, "Halloo, youngsters!"

Obadiah was in a great hurry. "You have to get up early to get the start of them market fellers," he informed them. He hurried James Albert and Hannah into the wagon, cracked his whip over the horses' backs, and they were off.

James Albert had the money for the shoes, and a paper that was the exact measure of the baby's foot, carefully pinned into his jacket pocket, and Hannah had a bright new silver quarter, that Abimelech had given her, tied up in a corner of her pocket-handkerchief. And they would not have thought of changing places with the President or Queen Victoria!

They felt, too, a kind of proprietorship in the wagon that was very pleasant. The Cherrywinkles owned the largest farm in Brimfield, and the great wagon was filled with barrels of apples,—rosy-cheeked Hubbardstons, golden pippins, and little crimson-and-yellow snow apples, nicest of all, —barrels of golden squashes, and green and purple cabbages, a firkin of sweet, golden butter, and a big sage cheese; and hanging around the sides were rows of turkeys, poor things! that had strutted their last strut, and gobbled their last gobble in the pleasant Cherrywinkle farmyard. All these good things Obadiah was carrying to the unfortunate people who lived in the city, where nothing grew. James Albert and Hannah both felt that it would be the proudest day of their lives, even without that wonderful and delightful commission to buy the baby's shoes.

Obadiah fell fast asleep, and James Albert had the great privilege of driving the finest horses in Brimfield. It was a peculiarity of Obadiah's to fall asleep whenever he had to sit still; his father had tried to make a minister of him, and was forced to give it up because he could not keep awake. He did not wake until the wagon began to clatter over the pavements, and then he seized the reins from James Albert's hand, and said he was "beginnin' to feel kind of drowsy; guessed he should have come pooty nigh fallin' asleep if they hadn't got there pooty soon!" James Albert and Hannah thought it was not polite to say anything, but they had to make a great effort to smother their giggles.

But they were soon too much occupied with the delightful novelty of their surroundings to think of Obadiah. The streets were so queer, with houses "all hitched together in a row," as Hannah remarked, and so full of people that it seemed as if it must be the Fourth of July, or, at least, a circus day. When they reached the markets it looked as if all the farmers in the country had "got the start" of Obadiah. Vegetables, and fruit, and meat, and poultry seemed to have overflowed through all the doors and windows; the sidewalks were almost covered.

"Oh, Obadiah, we ought to have started the night before," cried Hannah, the tears coming into her eyes; she felt so sorry for Obadiah, who, she thought, might as well carry water to the well as to bring his wagon-load here.

But Obadiah only laughed. He was as wide awake now as a Yankee farmer ought to be. He jumped out of the wagon, and began to talk to men standing about on the sidewalk, and in a few minutes everything was sold, and they were driving gaily off, with an empty wagon, in search of the baby's shoes!

Hannah's heart beat fast when Obadiah lifted her down from the wagon in front of a large store whose plate-glass windows showed row after row of the most elegant boots and slippers imaginable. James Albert assumed a manly and assured bearing, but in truth he was almost as much frightened as Hannah. Inside they found the whole store, larger than the Brimfield meeting house, full of boots and shoes.

He walked up to a clerk as coolly as if it were an everyday occurrence for him to go shopping, and said:

"We want a pair of shoes for our baby."

The clerk did not seem to be struck with the importance of the occasion. He asked, carelessly, what kind and what size, and took a big box down from the shelf. Hannah was seized with violent admiration for a pair of dainty white kid slippers with white satin rosettes, but as they had been carefully enjoined to get shoes that would "wear well," she was forced to turn away from them. After many trials the clerk at last found a lovely little pair of black kid button boots that just fitted the measure, and James Albert put his hand into one of them as far as it would go, and decided that there was room enough,—the baby's feet were plump, if they were tiny,—and Hannah anxiously felt of the soles to be sure that they were not stiff enough to hurt the baby, and, after much deliberation and consultation, they decided to take them. The price was higher than they had expected to pay, but Jacob Abimelech had charged them to buy the best, and surely the best was not too good for such a baby as that!

They hurried out, impatient to show their purchase to Obadiah, but lo and behold! when they reached the sidewalk neither the wagon nor Obadiah was to be seen!

"We were so long he got tired, and went off and left us. Oh, James Albert, what shall we do?" exclaimed Hannah.

"I wouldn't have believed Obadiah would be so mean as that," said James Albert. And then he suddenly caught sight of a wagon that looked like Obadiah's going around a corner a few rods off, and started after it, Hannah following.

They followed it around three corners, and when at last they reached it, breathless, it was not Obadiah's at all, but an expressman's!

James Albert and Hannah looked at each other in dismay. Tears were running down Hannah's cheeks, and James Albert had a lump in his throat, but he suddenly remembered the tin-peddler, and the reputation for "smartness" which he had to maintain.

"We'll just go back to the shoe-store, and wait until Obadiah comes after us. He'll be sure to come. I suppose he just went off on an errand, and maybe he got lost. I don't think Obadiah is so very smart!"

It cheered Hannah very much to hear James Albert speak in this confident and easy manner, but, strange to say, when they reached the place where he thought the shoe-store ought to be, it wasn't there!

"Oh, James Albert, we're lost, we're lost!" cried Hannah.

"The shoe-store is lost, and Obadiah is lost, but we ain't, because here we are!" replied James Albert, stoutly.

This may have been very poor logic, but it made Hannah laugh.

"Let's go over there, and sit down, and get rested, and think it over," said James Albert, pointing to a large park with broad, shady walks, and a pond and a fountain shining through the trees.

Just inside the gate was a man with a Punch and Judy show, and they laughed at that until they almost forgot their trouble.

"Let's spend your quarter!" said James Albert, when they were tired of the show.

So they each had a glass of red lemonade which an old woman was dispensing from a large pail, and then James Albert advocated a "jawbreaker" apiece, because jawbreakers "lasted long." Hannah did not like them particularly, because they were flavored with cinnamon, but she deferred to James Albert's taste. Then both heartily agreed upon having a big paper bag full of peanuts, and with those and the "jawbreakers" they retired to a bench under a tree in a secluded corner.

The goodies were even more effective than the Punch and Judy show in helping them to forget Obadiah's mysterious disappearance, and they were laughing and making merry, just as if he might be

nah so much of grandma's drab parrot that it was quite startling; he had even the same way of holding his head on one side, and looking straight at one, with little sharp, beady eyes.

After he had looked at them long enough, he took off his hat, with a very polite bow, and remarked that it was a very fine day; to which remark the children responded, with their very best manners.

" 'I sell him to you sheap—so sheap as nozzing at all!'—said the ragman"

expected to drive up, all ready to carry them home, at any minute, when the queerest figure they had ever seen came hobbling along the walk, and stopped in front of them.

It was a little old man, with a huge bag of rags on his back, that bent him over nearly double. He had such a very long, large, hooked nose that his face looked all nose when you first saw him, and he had such a little bit of a chin that it was like having no chin at all. He reminded Han-

"You are all 'lone—all 'lone?" he inquired, looking cautiously around. "Zen I show you somezing bee-utiful! more bee-utiful as you evair have see!"

And setting his great bag of rags upon the ground, he drew from it a most beautiful doll. Hannah could hardly believe it was a doll. She had lovely blue eyes that opened and shut, golden hair that was "banged" in the most approved fashion, a pink silk dress trimmed with lace, and turquoise ear-rings in her ears. To be frank, her complexion was somewhat faded, and the tip of her nose was broken off, but those slight blemishes quite escaped Hannah's notice. Hannah, who had never in her life had any doll better than one made of a shawl, felt her heart yearn over this beautiful creature.

"I sell him to you sheap—so sheap as nozzing at all!" said the ragman.

There was only one cent left of Hannah's quarter. She held it out, saying mournfully, "That is all the money we have!"

"But vat is dis?" said the ragman, touching the package that was sticking out of James Albert's pocket.

"That is the baby's shoes," said James Albert, glad of an opportunity to display them.

The ragman looked at them, curling his lip and shaking his head contemptuously:

"No goot! no goot! Bad shoe! ver' bad shoe!" he said; and James Albert and Hannah felt their hearts sink within them, for of course he would not speak so confidently unless he were a judge of shoes!

"Poor shildern, I pity you! I mooch kind-heart man, and I pity you. I gif you ze doll, and I take ze shoe! No goot, but I take zem!"

And he stuffed the shoes hastily into his pocket, leaving the doll in Hannah's lap.

"Oh, we can't let you have the shoes; they're the baby's!" cried James Albert and Hannah, in chorus.

"You not gif doze bad shoe, good for nozzing at all, for dat bee-utiful doll wort' twenty dollar? You sell him for dozen pair shoe like dat, if you want!"

"It does seem a splendid bargain, James Albert!" said Hannah, hugging the doll.

It did seem so to James Albert, and he did want to have the credit of doing a fine stroke of business. If they *could* sell the doll for twenty dollars, he should distinguish himself even more than he had

done in that little affair with the tin-peddler.

While he was considering, with his forehead puckered into the deepest of frowns, the ragman was making off, with the baby's shoes.

Suddenly Hannah began to feel misgivings.

"Oh, James Albert, if we *couldn't* sell the doll, we should have to go home without the baby's shoes! And the tip of her nose is broken, and her dress isn't so very clean!"

"I'll run after him and get the shoes back. Give me the doll!" cried James Albert.

But not a trace of the ragman was to be seen. For an old man he must have walked very fast indeed after he turned the corner.

The children sat down again on the bench and looked at each other blankly, then they looked at the doll. It was astonishing to see how much worse her nose looked, and how much more soiled and disheveled she appeared, now that she belonged to them!

"We must go to a store and try to sell her right away," said James Albert. "But I am afraid nobody will buy her, she is so dirty!"

A young man was passing just then, and James Albert resolved to have the benefit of his opinion.

"Do you think this doll is worth twenty dollars, sir?" he asked.

"Twenty dollars! That old doll? Why, it isn't worth twenty cents," said the young man, with a laugh.

"And we have lost the baby's shoes! Oh, James Albert!" exclaimed Hannah, with a great sob.

"I just wish we had never seen the old doll! He was an awful bad man. He cheated us," said James Albert.

"He was worse than the tin-peddler, wasn't he? And you were not so smart as you were then, were you?"—which was somewhat aggravating to poor James Albert, although Hannah did not mean it to be so.

"It was awful wicked of us to do it, and I never should have thought of such a thing if it hadn't been for you. You wanted the horrid old doll so much!" he said, not very kindly.

Hannah's tears began to flow.

"It's no good to sit here and be a cry-baby!" said James Albert. "We'll go out into the street, and perhaps we shall come across Obadiah."

"I don't want to find Obadiah. I don't want to go home without the baby's shoes!" said Hannah. But as James Albert strode along crossly, with his hands in his pockets, she followed him, the tears rolling down her cheeks, and the doll tucked carelessly under her arm, a most melancholy picture.

As they were going through the park gates, one of a group of children playing near, under the care of what Hannah thought was a very queer-looking nurse, with a white cap on her head, came running up to Hannah, and seized the doll from under her arm, with a cry of delight.

"Oh, my own dear, sweet, darling Florabella!" she cried, hugging and kissing the doll. "I thought I never should see you again! Oh, dear, how she looks! The darling must have been through so much! But she would be my own darling Florabella if her nose were twice as bumped!"

And then the nurse came up, and asked Hannah, in a very severe manner, where she got the doll.

Before she had time to answer, James Albert constituted himself spokesman and told them all about it.

"Oh, what a wicked ragman!" cried the little girl, who was still hugging the doll. "Florabella fell out of the window onto the sidewalk; I ran down to pick her up, but when I got there she was gone. You come home with us, and tell mama about it, and she'll give you something to pay for Florabella—for of course you can't have her!" And she gave the doll an extra hug at the thought.

"We don't want her!" said James Albert and Hannah, in concert, and, indeed, the doll had caused them so much grief that she didn't look pretty, even to Hannah. "We only want the baby's shoes!"

"Well, perhaps mama can get them back for you; she can do almost anything," said the little girl, confidently.

So, feeling a little cheered, James Albert and Hannah went home with the children.

They lived in a house that made Hannah think of the palaces in her fairy-book, and their mother was as lovely and kind as one of the good fairies. Hannah would not have been very much surprised to see her whisk out a wand, and tap three times, and there would be the baby's shoes!

And she did do something that was almost as good as that.

After she had given them a nice luncheon, she said it would never do in the world for them to go home without the baby's shoes. So she ordered her carriage, and drove, with James Albert and Hannah, and all the children, to a shoe-store. But when they got there James Albert suddenly remembered that he had left the measure of the baby's foot in the store where they had bought the shoes; and where that was he could not tell.

Then what did the lady do but buy three pairs, graduated in size, like the porringers of the three bears, one "great big" pair (comparatively), and one "middle-sized" pair, and one "little wee" pair. And they were lovely shoes, even nicer than the pair that the children had lost.

Then each one of the children wanted to buy a present for the baby, and one bought a beautiful little white dress, and another a dainty little bonnet with white ribbons, and another a rubber doll, that the baby could not break; and then, after a great deal of whispered consultation, they bought a big doll like Florabella for Hannah, and a jackknife with four blades for James Albert.

It was no wonder that Hannah thought they had got into fairyland!

In the meantime the good fairy had sent a messenger to all the station-houses in the neighborhood, to give information of the children's whereabouts, because she thought Obadiah would know that those were the places to look for lost children; and when they drove back to her house, there was the wagon, with Obadiah calmly seated in it, standing before the door!

He told his adventures only after much urging and in a shamefaced way. Poor Obadiah! While the children were in the shoe-store he fell asleep, and the horses, thinking they had stood long enough, wandered along. A policeman caught sight of Obadiah and his horses,—that did not trouble themselves to turn out for anything—and thought Obadiah had been drinking, and took him, team and all, to the station-house!

Obadiah said, "It beat all natur' that he should 'a' done it, for he wa'n't generally one o' the sleepy kind!"

Hannah and James Albert were too happy to blame him, and they tried hard not to laugh.

They had a very exciting time telling their adventures when they got home that night. James Albert would have preferred not to tell about the ragman, but of course it had to be done, and I am afraid that now the tin-peddler will never be mentioned without the ragman being brought up to offset him!

As for the baby's shoes, the great big pair were entirely too large for her, but would do nicely for her by and by; the middle-sized pair gave so much room to her toes that they might have pushed ahead too fast; but the little wee pair fitted her as perfectly as if her feet had been melted and poured into them!

THE DOG THAT RETURNED TO MEXICO

by Ellis Parker Butler

SAMUEL DAZZARD was a great friend of mine and when I was working in the garden he often came and leaned over the fence and told me how the peons made gardens in Mexico.

Indeed, he told me many things about Mexico, for he had been there, and had walked all the way back to Iowa carrying a Mexican carved leather saddle and a braided-hair bridle, which were all he had to show for a herder's outfit that he assured me was the finest a man ever owned. He had a dog, a coal black one, that he had brought from Mexico, but it was a surprisingly mixed breed of dog, and not at all the kind that he could trade for a horse.

As a money-maker Sam Dazzard was a failure, but he was a powerfully lively thinker and he had a mechanical bent that would have made him rich if it had turned toward anything useful, but it didn't.

Sam—we all called him Sam—was a lank man, with innocent blue eyes and light hair. He had always a faraway expression, as if he was thinking of Mexico, and he was the most deadly serious man I ever knew.

I could hardly believe my ears when Sam came to me one day and offered to trade me the braided-hair bridle for the old buck-board that we were letting rot to pieces in the barnyard. One wheel of the buck-board was badly dished, and it had been a cheap vehicle when new.

"Have you got a horse, Sam?" I asked.

"No," he said. "No, I wouldn't have a horse in this country if you gave me one. A horse is all right in Mexico, but up here they eat their heads off. It doesn't pay to keep horses in Iowa."

"Then what do you want the buck-board for?" I ventured to ask.

Sam shook the bottom of the buck-board to see how sound it was.

"Well," he said, slowly, "I'll tell you. I am going to make an automobile. An automobile is the thing to have in this country. What a man wants up here is speed. Horses are all right in Mexico, where everybody takes plenty of time, but up here we have to move about fast. You mark my word; in ten years there won't be a horse left in Iowa."

He sat down and studied the buck-board for a while, and we waited.

"How are you going to run it?" I asked, after a while.

"Gasoline," he said, simply. "I prefer gasoline. You get more speed with gasoline, and that's what I'm after. I've got as fine a little gasoline engine as you ever saw—as soon as I get it in shape."

"Why, I thought that engine blew up and wrecked the launch!" I said, surprised.

"Well, it did blow up some," Sam admitted, reluctantly. "It blew up some! But I can put it in good shape again in no time, and it was a mighty fine engine when it was new. Two-horsepower en-

26

gine. Why!" he said, enthusiastically, "one horse could run away with this buck-board and not know it had anything behind it; and when I get *two*-horsepower in it, it will fly! That's what I want—speed."

He paused, thoughtfully.

"Oh, yes," he continued, "I've got some ideas that I'm going to use that will sur-

some ingenuity, he seemed to have more patience than anything else.

It was no trick at all for him to rig up a steering gear, but it troubled him to connect the engine with the rear wheels of the buck-board. He explained to us what he needed, and it seemed to be nearly everything he didn't have and couldn't get, and he admitted it frankly

"The hind wheels of that buck-board revolved so rapidly you couldn't see the spokes"

prise some people. I do wish that hind wheel was a little better, but I guess I can fix it up. It's got to stand a lot of speed. Maybe," he said, dreamily, "I'll buy a new wheel if it doesn't cost too much."

We boys spent a great deal of our spare time for the next month or two at Sam's cabin watching the progress of the automobile. It took no little ingenuity and a great amount of patience to patch up the gasoline engine, but, while Sam had

and said that if he just had a couple of good cog-wheels and a piece of endless chain he could do without the other things, but he didn't have the cog-wheels and chain either, and he finally rigged up a rope to drive the wheels.

He had the engine screwed to the floor slats of the buck-board and, for the test, he had the rear axle jacked up on a barrel so that the wheels were a foot or so above the ground, and there were almost tears in his eyes the first time he started the engine. The hind wheels of that buckboard revolved so rapidly you couldn't see the spokes. Sam said he figured they were going at the rate of at least one hundred miles an hour, but that he wouldn't drive the automobile that fast at first. He said it took some time to learn how to handle an automobile, and that until he learned he would not think of going over ten miles an hour, especially as he hadn't rigged up a brake yet. He explained that he could easily make a brake, if he had a few articles he didn't have, but there was no place to put it on the buck-board.

Sam's cabin was by the river bank, surrounded by brush and undergrowth, so we boys all lent a hand to carry the automobile to the road, which was not far. It was a good road for speeding an automobile, level as the top of a table—and we begged Sam to let the automobile go full speed, but he firmly refused. He said we might enjoy seeing him dashed to pieces, but that he was not going to trust himself at any hundred miles an hour until he learned to handle the machine properly.

He climbed in and braced himself firmly on the seat and turned on the power a little. The engine chugged and chugged away, as gasoline engines do, but nothing happened. Then Sam turned on more power, but the automobile sat still in the road and did not move. I could see that Sam was chagrined, but he said nothing. He turned the gasoline engine on at full power.

That engine certainly was a good one. It was full of life and vim, and it fairly jumped up and down on the buck-board, like a child romping on a spring bed, but the buck-board seemed frozen to the road. It did not move an inch.

Sam stopped the engine and got out and crawled under the buck-board, which was so much like what a man with a real automobile would have done that we all cheered. Then Sam got up and shook his head.

"It beats me!" he exclaimed, sadly. "I can't see what is wrong. I can't for a fact."

He leaned over the engine and turned on the power at the lowest notch and what do you think! The automobile moved! It did not run away; it did not dash off at a hundred miles an hour, but it moved. It went about as fast as a baby could creep.

Sam got in again and gave it the full power once more but the automobile would not budge. Then he got out and gave it half power and it started off so fast that he had to dog-trot to keep up with it, but the moment he got in, it stopped dead still. We found by experimenting that when Sam was in the automobile and the engine doing its best it was just an even balance. One of us boys could push the automobile along with one finger, but the moment we stopped pushing, the automobile stopped going. If the engine had been one fraction of a horse stronger the automobile would have run itself, or if Sam had been a couple of pounds lighter the engine would have been able to propel the automobile, but, as it was, it would not go alone. It would almost go, but not quite; but an automobile that will almost go is no better than one that will not go at all.

The first minute Muchito—that was the dog's name—heard the gasoline engine he crawled under Sam's cabin and refused to come out, and, when he found that Sam meant to keep the engine and make a sort of pet of it, Muchito took to going away during the day. He would come back to the cabin at night, with his coat full of burrs, but early the next morning he would run away again.

The next morning after that I was starting for a good day's fishing and had just got to the edge of the town when I heard a noise down the road like a steamboat trying to get off a sand-bar, and coming toward me I saw Sam in his automobile. He was holding to his steering bar with both hands and his hat pulled down over his ears to keep it from shaking off, and the engine was bouncing the bed of the buck-board so that Sam's teeth rattled like a stick drawn along a picket fence. Sam was jigging up and down on the seat like a man with the chills, and the whole outfit was palpitating as if it would be shaken to pieces the next minute. Everything was going at the rate of one hundred miles an hour except the wheels, and they were moving about as slowly as a tired turtle travels in the sun. I never saw so much noise and rattle and energy produce so little forward motion. I should say Sam was moving at the rate of about one mile an hour, but he was moving and his face showed his triumph.

I could walk so much faster than he could ride that I might say that I met him before he met me. He did not see me until I was right in front of him, for he was too busy being shaken, but the minute he saw me the automobile stopped.

Muchito saw me at the same moment, and jumped up on me, as a dog will. I never saw a dog so glad to see anyone as Muchito was to see me. We had always been good friends but not affectionate, but this time he wanted to love me to death. Sam had him fastened to the front axle of the automobile with a ten-foot rope.

"Hello, Sam," I said; "got the automobile so that it runs all right now, haven't you?"

"Yes! Oh, yes!" he said quickly. "She runs fine now. Not fast, but steady. That's what a man wants in an automobile—steadiness. This idea of speed is all wrong. You get too much speed and you run over people. It isn't safe. Steadiness is what a man wants in this country; a good, steady automobile that will go where he wants it to go. I was just going up to town," he added.

"You must have started pretty early," I ventured.

"Yes," he admitted, "pretty early. About four o'clock. I want to take my time. I want this machine to get down to good, steady work before I try any speed."

He looked anxiously over the front of the buck-board at Muchito, who was cowering close to my legs.

"Well," he said, "I guess I'll move on. I've got quite a way to go yet."

He turned on the power and the buck-board began to palpitate and bounce and jolt, but it did not move. Sam stood up and looked over at Muchito. Muchito was sitting on his tail looking sad and scared.

"Well, so long!" I shouted. "I want to get to the dam before the fish quit biting this morning."

I moved off down the road and Muchito followed me as far as the rope would allow. I looked back when I had gone a few yards and saw Sam get out of the automobile and take Muchito in his arms and carry him around to the front of the automobile and point him toward the city. Six times Sam carried Muchito to the front of the automobile and six times Muchito turned back and strained toward me at the end of the rope. Then Sam stood up and called to me.

"Hey!" he shouted. "Wait!"

I waited and saw Sam lift the rear wheels of the automobile around and straighten it out so that it was headed *away* from the city. Then he got in and turned on the power. Muchito was still straining toward me. The automobile moved toward me, slowly, but as Sam desired, steadily.

I understood Muchito was running away from the automobile, and if Muchito did not run neither did the automobile. His slight pull on the rope was all that was necessary to change the automobile from an inert but jolting buck-board into a slow but steady forward-moving vehicle.

"I guess I won't go to town today," chattered Sam, when he was near enough to make me hear; "I don't want to go to town much anyway. I enjoy riding one way as much as the other."

If he enjoyed being joggled I could admit it. I waited for him to come up with me, but as soon as Muchito reached me the dog sat down and the automobile stopped. Sam looked at me and at the dog.

"Suppose," he shouted, "suppose you walk on a little ahead. That dog—, I don't want to run over that dog. If you go on ahead he won't lag back. I wouldn't run over that dog for a good deal. That dog came from Mexico."

I started forward and whistled to Muchito. The dog jumped forward and the automobile moved, but the rope Sam had used was an old one and it snapped.

For one moment Muchito stood in surprise. The next moment Sam had jumped from his automobile and made a dash for Muchito, but the dog slipped quickly to one side, glanced once at the automobile which was moving rapidly into the fence at the side of the road, and then tucking his tail between his legs started down the road at a gallop. We saw him turn the bend in the road and we never saw him again. He was tired of being an assistant motor to an automobile and he was headed for Mexico, where there are peons and haciendas and rancheros, but no buck-board motor cars.

THE LAST MAN IN MARBLEHEAD

by Don C. Seitz

WE celebrate July 4, 1776, as the birthday of American Freedom because the Declaration of Independence was signed on that date; but its real anniversary is April 19, beginning with the year 1775, for then the battles of Concord and Lexington were fought, and armed conflicts continued thereafter between the forces of the colonies and those of the king.

Of course, there had long been friction and much hot oratory on this side of the ocean, but the War of the Revolution began with little real preparation on the part of the colonists. True, the direct clash arose because the British marched from Boston to seize munitions of the militia stored at Concord, but these supplies were scant; nor was there much to be found elsewhere; while upon the sea,

where a deal of the fighting was to be done, the "rebels" had no ships fitted for war.

Soon a slender squadron put to sea, but the bulk of the work had to be done by privateers, and here our story begins.

Until 1907, when, by international agreement, the practice of fitting out private armed vessels to prey upon enemy commerce was ruled off the ocean, it was legal for nations to issue "letters of marque and reprisal," under which individuals or companies could fit out ships to seize merchant vessels, wherever found, and do with them as they would.

Great Britain was rich upon the sea. She numbered war-ships by the hundred, and trading vessels by the thousand. These soon fell in fat harvests to the bold Yankee privateers, sailing from Charleston,

Baltimore, Philadelphia, New York, New Haven, New London, Providence, and, above all, Salem, Newburyport, Gloucester, and Marblehead. Nor did they limit their operations to home waters, but pushed into all of the seven seas, some even making haven at the Isle of France (Mauritius), in the far-off Indian Ocean, while swarms of them hovered off the English and Irish coasts, even venturing into the channel between them and that separating England from the European shore.

Now one of the boldest and most successful of these rovers was the *Lion* of Marblehead, that sturdy seaport of Cape Ann, where even to this day they breed the boldest of seamen, who sail in their slight vessels to the Grand Banks of Newfoundland, seeking cod, halibut, and like important members of the finny tribes. It is with the *Lion* and one of her crew that this tale is concerned. Great-grandfather Nathan Clapp used to tell it as he sat beside the glowing fireplace in his Cape Ann home, and a grandson told it to me long ago. It is such a valorous yarn as all youngsters of spirit like to hear.

In the year one thousand, seven hundred and eighty-one, when he was but eighteen, Nathan had sailed from Salem on the brig *Lark* for Oporto, in Spain, to come back with a rich cargo of Spanish wares—silks, drums of figs, cork, and wine.

They had easily evaded the British cruisers congregated off the Bay of Biscay and were returning full laden, when at the dawn of day they ran into a great convoy of more than three hundred sail.

This convoy, it must be explained, was a gathering of merchant ships proceeding, as nearly as they could, together for protection against raiding privateers. This great fleet of merchant craft was guarded by a dozen ships of war, the chief of

which was the *Royal George,* one of the biggest ships under the British flag and commanded by the master of the fleet, Admiral Sir Richard Kempenfelt. Several light cruisers were attached to the squadron, and two of these soon ran down the little *Lark.* Her captain, Josiah Lunt, surrendered at discretion, and because her barrels of port were taken to the flagship, the men went thither with them, while the *Lark,* under a prize crew, was sent into Portsmouth, so as not to encumber the convoy.

Some effort was made to make the Yankee seamen enlist in the English service, but none would join. They were well treated, however, and allowed to loiter about the ship while the convoy made its slow way toward Jamaica, whither it was bound, to scatter thence among the various islands of the West Indies belonging to the British.

The winds were baffling and the convoy made slow headway. It was difficult to keep them together, and the cruisers were always busy, like hens among their chicks, trying to herd their broods. One day a storm arose and the vessels were badly dispersed. The bulk of the convoy had to lie to, waiting for the others to come up. When nearly all were gathered, the Yankees on the *Royal George* were thrilled and startled to see a schooner heave in sight a league—three miles—away and pounce upon a luckless bark that was striving to beat up to the squadron. In almost a jiffy she was boarded and taken, the Stars and Stripes hoisted to her mizzen, and she was sailing away under guard of her captor.

Quite rudely, Nathan Clapp and his companions gave three cheers for the privateer, whoever she might be, for which they were clapped under hatches to cool off. The next day they were allowed up and saw the privateer repeat the performance. This time they were discreet enough to repress their joy.

But wasn't there a to-do on the king's ships! The admiral summoned all his captains and gave them a good dressing-down on the quarter-deck. Was the glory of England to be dimmed by a rascally Yankee but one degree removed from a pirate? He hinted grimly at courts-martial and losing numbers,—dreadful things to happen to naval gentlemen,—and the worthies departed to bestir themselves.

One of the smaller cruisers, the *Sprite,* captain the Honorable George Clowden, was hurriedly altered to look like a clumsy merchantman. With her ports painted out, her sails slack and gear loose, and straggling from the fleet, the *Sprite* became a well-baited trap. A few sailors in nondescript garb "worked" the ship. The others were kept below, lest some searching spy-glass might penetrate the disguise. On the morning of the third day that this trap was set, the sea became calm and a light mist obscured the view. Little puffs of wind rippled the water, and as it blew the mist away, a quarter of a mile to leeward lay the privateer. She spied the *Sprite,* and soon her long sweeps were out and brawny arms were propelling her toward the prospective prize. Clowden might have opened with a broadside, but he was not sure that he would not be outranged by the long pivot-gun of the privateer, which, in itself, carried heavier metal than any of his guns. He had set his heart on cutting her out by boarding and awaited events. In a quarter of an hour the *Lion* was alongside, bow to bow, the forward quarter almost touching, while the stern yawed off. The bulwarks of the privateer were lined with men ready to leap aboard the *Sprite,* on whose decks a dozen sailors in nondescript togs appeared to be listlessly resigned to their fate. A grappling-iron thrown from the

bow of the *Lion* lodged forward on the *Sprite* and bound them together, but the grapple cast from the stern failed to land, dropping into the water with a splash. This mishap saved the privateer.

As the bows touched, a score of the *Lion's* seamen leaped to the deck of the *Sprite,* and the first one to find footing was a boy—a brown-haired, blue-eyed, sunny-faced lad, quick of limb and eye. He had no more than touched the deck when he saw the glint of cutlasses, a hatch covering slide back, and men crowding each other to come up from below. The vessels had drifted a little apart, though the grappling-line held. Instantly the lad cast off the grapple and shouted:

"Look alive! Sheer off! She's a Britisher. Don't mind us!"

The privateer lost no time in heeding the warning cry. The helmsman put his wheel hard down and a handy puff moved her sixty feet away in almost as many seconds. On board the *Sprite* a volley of pistol shots came from the mizzen hatch, and uniformed seamen swarmed to the deck. They ranged themselves at once against the privateersmen. These now rallied to defend themselves. Two fell under the pistol-fire and there ended their cruising. The others, cutlass and pistol in hand, sustained the assault. They were soon overpowered; but in the confusion, Clowden failed to use his guns. The ports were tightly closed, and gummed with the paint that hid them. By the time a few were opened, the privateer was yards away. The pivot-gun on the forecastle sent a heavy shot into the *Sprite's* stern-post and the vessel ceased to mind the helm. Another shot from a long 18-pounder smashed the binnacle and struck down the man at the wheel. Then, opportunely, the wind rose and the *Lion* took to her heels. She was no match for broadsides and a crew double her own. Her speed was three knots better than that of her opponent, even had the latter not been disabled. It was not the policy of privateers to fight full-fledged warships, except in case of necessity, when they usually got the worst of it. The captain of the *Lion* was prudent in his getaway.

You may be sure that Captain Clowden was a very angry man at this outcome, and he vented his spite on the prisoners by putting them in irons and clapping them in the hold.

Repairs were made to the rudder, and in another day the *Sprite* found the convoy. Her captain had a very bad half-hour with the admiral, which ended in his being ordered to send the prisoners to the flagship. Their irons were knocked off and they were taken in the long-boat to the *Royal George.* The story of the boy's valor had become known, and every man on board wished to see the hero.

The prisoners of the *Lark* were not hindered from joining the eager crowd of sailors that manned the shrouds and bulwarks as the captives came over the side, and their hearts glowed at the sight of their countrymen. These bore themselves bravely. They were ranged abaft the mast for the inspection of the admiral. The great man regarded them curiously. They were nondescript to look at, coatless, hatless, bloody and scarred, but all were stalwart and young. One of them was very young. Indeed, he was nothing but a bit of a boy. He looked fourteen, and across his forehead was a bloody bandage that hid a cutlass scratch.

"What did he do?" asked the admiral of Captain Clowden.

"Fought like a lion's cub," replied the commander. "It took two men and a belaying-pin to subdue him."

The admiral looked at the boy kindly. "Come here, my lad," he said gently.

The youngster stepped out of the line of prisoners and stood before Kempenfelt.

"What is your name?" he asked.

"Nathaniel Libbey, sir."

"How old are you?"

"Fifteen, come next January." (It was then May.)

"Tell me," said the admiral, "how such a little fellow as you came to be in this mad adventure?"

"I was the last man in Marblehead," replied Nathaniel, proudly.

And indeed he was! The *Lion* had lacked one man to fill her hammocks, and the Widow Libbey gladly spared her only son to complete the company. There were no grown-ups left to go.

Well, the "last man in Marblehead" was soon a favorite aboard ship. The admiral even had him to dinner in the great cabin, and would much have liked to tempt him with a midshipman's cocked hat and dirk, but Nathaniel was too loyal to be led away from his flag.

When the fleet reached Jamaica they found there a cartel awaiting to exchange prisoners, and the admiral sent Nathaniel to his mother, with a couple of gold guineas jingling in his pockets so that he should not reach home poor. There was great rejoicing in Marblehead when he came back, and the owners of the *Lion* saw that he received more than a cub's share of prize-money.

Fate was unkind to the good admiral. Returning from his voyage, the *Royal George* was "careened" in Portsmouth Harbor that the dockmen might repair a leak below the water-line. It was a fair August day. Many visitors and nearly her entire crew of over seven hundred were on board. The admiral was writing in his cabin. A sudden squall struck the tilted ship and she careened still farther, until, the water entering her ports, she went down with nearly all on board, including her commander.

JIMMY'S MADE-TO-ORDER STORIES

by Dorothy Canfield

"WHAT I like best about your stories," said Jimmy, "is that there isn't any moral to them."

"Nor any sense," said a grown-up.

"Yes, that *is* another nice thing about them," said Jimmy, and continued:

"Seems as though we hadn't had any made-to-order stories for quite a while, and I'm sort of hungry for one."

"All right," said I. "Have you settled yet what you want to have in it this time?"

Jimmy fell into deep thought. You might, perhaps, imagine from the jumbled-up things he puts together for his stories that he grabs up any idea that comes into his head. But you'd be mistaken, for he often takes a long time to make his choice.

"As you haven't told me one for three whole days, the things I want have piled up and *piled* up!"

"Let's hear what they are."

"A little boy and a ship's anchor and a library full of old books and a woodchuck and a spider and a bed and a door-knob."

"Not on your life!" said I. "That's three days' worth, not one. There are too many."

"All right, I'll leave out the spider," said Jimmy. "I didn't want him in so very much, anyhow. It would probably turn out that he spun his web over the mouth of a cave and saved the life of somebody hiding inside. And I'd hate that."

As I have said, Jimmy's choice of what to put in a story is not wild and haphazard as it seems. He has one fixed aim, to avoid certain stale old combinations that make him groan in printed stories. For instance, he never has put into a story either a millionaire or an orphan child; but if he did, I know that nothing could make him put them into the same story. He would be afraid that the orphan couldn't help turning out to be the long-lost child of the millionaire. To prevent such a vexing thing, he would, I am sure, put the millionaire in with a cake of soap and have the orphan child in the story with a hippopotamus.

In this case, I asked him indignantly what made him think me capable of getting out that old cave-and-web combination; but he persisted, "Well, if he didn't do that, I bet he'd tell all about how many joints he has in his front legs and what spiders eat in winter; and I'd hate that worse. No, we'll leave the spider out."

ANCHOR HOUSE

"WELL, without the spider, it is, of course, the story about the little boy whose brothers and sisters got the measles, and the family weren't sure whether he'd been exposed, so they sent him off to Anchor House, which was the name of his old uncle's house down by the seashore."

"Was it in school-time?" asked Jimmy.

"Yes, right in the first part of May."

"Didn't he have the luck!" commented Jimmy.

"Oh, I don't know. Anchor House was 'way out on a sandy point, with no children in any of the farm-houses around. His uncle was a retired sea-captain, pretty deaf and awfully fat, who only wanted to read his newspaper all day and snore all night. And the old cook who did for them was as cross as two sticks and hated little boys in the kitchen. So he had to invent games to play all by himself. Mostly he played with the books in the library. They had belonged to his uncle's wife's father, who'd been a minister, and they were all full of theological facts that aren't so any more, so nobody thought of reading them. The little boy played blocks with them. They were big and thick and made splendid walls to forts. His uncle didn't mind, and the old cook didn't know anything about it, because she never went into the wing of the house where the library was. It was a good way from the kitchen, and she had rheumatism in her knee.

Well, one night the little boy woke up and remembered that he had carried a lot of books out on the porch of the wing to build a rampart there, and hadn't taken them back in. It was a nice clear night; but you never know for sure about the weather, so he thought he'd better go down and carry them back into the library, in case of rain.

It was lovely and warm, so he didn't need anything but his pajamas; and he'd been going barefoot daytimes, so he didn't stop for slippers. He trotted downstairs and along the hall that led to the wing, into the library and out on the porch that was back of the main part of the house. The books were a little damp, already, from the night air, so he was glad he had come down. He carried them into the library, armful after armful, dozens and dozens of armfuls, it seemed to him. It took him a long, long time, even though he didn't try to put them back on the shelves, but just piled them up anywhere. He was pretty tired when he finally got the last one in, and started back up the stairs.

He was yawning and stretching and thinking how nice it would be to get into bed and snuggle down and doze off, when he noticed that the door to his room stood open. This gave him rather a turn, for he was sure that he had shut it very carefully. But that was nothing compared to what he found when he stepped inside his room.

For his bed was gone!

Yes, just like that. The head-board was leaned up against the wall, and the footboard lay on the floor, and the bedclothes were tossed over the back of a chair; but the springs and mattress had disappeared! Not a sign nor a smitch of them was to be seen.

Of course, the little boy knew at once that this couldn't be so. Whatever else might get carried away out of a house at night, it wouldn't be a *bed*.

So he went out into the hall, shut his door behind him, waited a minute, and then opened it quick, expecting surely to see his bed all there, just as he'd left it.

But it wasn't, only just the head-board leaned up against the wall, and the foot-board lying on the floor.

You can't imagine how *queer* the little boy felt. Not scared, for there wasn't anything to be scared of; but so queer-feeling that he sat down quick in a chair.

"Let me think," he said to himself. "Let me *think*." But every thought he tried to think was perfectly impossible. How *could* his bed be gone, and he away for only a few minutes from his room, and not a soul awake in the house? And anyhow, why would anybody *want his bed*? Burglars didn't steal beds, any more than they stole kitchen stoves.

At this he gave a start. Maybe they *had* stolen the kitchen stove. He ran down the stairs and into the kitchen. But no, there it stood, in the dim starlight, nicely blacked, the way old Mary always left it, with no more notion of stirring than the big anchor half buried in the lawn, that his Uncle Peter had brought there from his last ship.

Well, if the stove was still there, maybe his bed was. He ran back upstairs and dashed open the door. No, it wasn't!

Good gracious! Now he was really a little scared. He decided he would go and tell Uncle Peter and find out— Oh mercy! suppose that Uncle Peter had disappeared, too, like the bed! This did scare him, really and truly, so that he could barely stagger across the hall to his uncle's door and turn the knob.

Uncle Peter always kept a little night-light burning, and by its light the little boy could see him plainly. He was oh so beautifully, comfortably asleep, as only deaf people can sleep, and snoring so loudly and so enjoyingly as only old sea-captains can snore. It made the little boy all right again, just in a minute, only to look at him. Nothing much could be the matter with Uncle Peter hitting the pillow like that.

He drew a long breath, stepped out again into the hall, and shut the door behind him. It would be a sin to wake up anybody who was having such a sleep as that. But all the same, it didn't get him back his bed.

Then he had another idea, that explained everything perfectly. This was all a dream, and he'd wake up in the morning just as usual. That was the way all the stories in books ended. The best thing for him to do was to turn over, curl up, drop off to sleep more soundly, and—

But how could he do all that without any bed to do it in?

Mercy! This was getting worse and worse. He put his hand up to his head to see if it were still on his neck and in the right place. It was. But that was all the good it did him.

Of course, he could have wrapped the bedclothes around him and lain down on the floor; but although he wasn't scared,— not *really* scared,—he wouldn't have lain down between that head-board and foot-board, not for a million dollars. Suppose whatever it was that had carried off the bed should carry him off to the same place. Not, of course, you know, that he really believed for a minute that his bed was gone. How could it be?

He began to feel a little chilly and went in to get his blanket. The phosphorescent hands of his alarm-clock showed him that it was nearly three o'clock. It would soon be day. He had an idea. He'd take his blanket and go out of doors for the rest of the night. He'd never seen dawn begin, and all the nature-books said that the animals got out and played more and moved around more just at dawn than at any other time. He wrapped the blanket around him and started out of the front door to go down to a big rock by the brook. There were woodchucks in the field beyond. Maybe he'd see them out feeding when it got light. He was sure of *one* thing! He wouldn't miss them from dropping off to sleep. He felt as though he never, never would sleep again—if, as a matter of fact, he wasn't sound asleep all this whole time!

As he stepped down the front path he saw something white lying there. And what do you suppose it was? The knob of his door. He recognized it because it was cracked in a funny way, with lines that made a triangle. He stooped over it to make sure, but you'd better believe he didn't pick it up or touch it. No, sir! All this was too queer for *him*. He stepped wide around it, left it lying there, and kept turning his head over his shoulder as he went on down the path. It wouldn't have surprised him to see it begin to roll along after him. But he was pretty sure that he could run faster than a door-knob —although, of course, he had never tried.

It seemed awfully good to get away from the house altogether and out on the rock, where he lay down with his blanket. The rock was hard and humpy, but he loved all the humps. They felt so natural and real. In a few minutes, as his eyes got used to the light, he saw that dawn was almost there. The sky was lighter in the east and the trees and bushes began to look gray. A big maple tree stood over the rock, and he heard a bird rustling around in the leaves and by and by it said *"Queet! queet!"* in a sleepy little voice.

And then, right under where the little boy lay, not two feet from his face, he saw something move and come slowly out of

a hole. It was a woodchuck's head. It looked around an instant and then dodged back so quickly that the little boy was afraid he had moved and frightened it, though he had hardly breathed for fear of making a noise. But in a minute, out it came again and looked all around, very cautiously. Then the whole woodchuck came out, and, behind it, four baby woodchucks, little soft, furry, gray things, all roly-poly and round. They toddled along after their mother for a few steps. Then, as she began to eat, they began to play— just like a family of puppies or kittens, rolling each other over and over, squealing and running around, or standing up on their hind legs to push each other. The little boy could hardly keep back his laughing, to see them, they were so jolly. After a while, their mother took them down to the brook for a drink, and he could hear them going on with their fun, pushing for the best place, falling into the water, squalling, and shaking themselves and starting another roughhouse the minute one was finished. They came racing back up the slope to the rock, bouncing along with their mother back of them. And now it was almost daylight, so the little boy could really see them. He had never seen wild animals close at hand before, when they were not frightened or angry, and he never forgot the gay look of fun on their bright little faces as they came scampering along toward him.

Something dreadful happened then. A shadow—or what the little boy had taken for a shadow—sprang up from beside the rock, pounced on the first of the baby woodchucks, and pinned it to the ground, with a horrid noise of snarling and craunching, like the noise a cat makes over a mouse. The mother woodchuck heard it too, and never hesitated an instant. The brave mother-thing made one

great jump and landed on top of the animal, whatever it was,—weasel perhaps,—
that had killed her baby. And then there
was a frightful fight, a snarling, snapping, growling ball rolling over and over,
with sharp yells when somebody got
bitten, and a gnashing click-click of angry
teeth snapping together that sounded to
the little boy ever so much fiercer than
the roaring of any lion at the zoo.

The little boy grabbed up a stick and
stood over them, trying to see where to hit,
for he didn't want to hurt the woodchuck.
For a minute they didn't notice him, they
were so set on tearing each other to pieces;
but all of a sudden they must have
caught a glimpse of him, for—whiz! flash!
In a jiff, they had both vanished, the
woodchuck back into the hole, and the
weasel off into the bushes. There was the
little boy, left alone, with the sun just
up over the horizon, and the poor little
woodchuck lying with its head bent
under it, all limp.

He picked it up to be sorry for it, and
thought he felt its heart still beating. Oh,
perhaps he could save its life and have it
for a pet! He left his blanket on the rock
and ran back into the house to the kitchen.
There was an old box there, with straw
in it and wire netting on two sides, that
somebody had brought a setting hen in,
the day before. He lifted the top, laid the
woodchuck in on the straw, and got a cup
of water to sprinkle on its face, in case it
had just fainted.

Old Mary came in as he was running
back to the box, and when he told her
about it, she advised him to try to see if
they couldn't get a little milk down the
poor thing's throat.

By the time they had some milk in a
saucer, with a bit of cloth to let it drip
from, the woodchuck had come to, had
got up on his feet, and backed off into a

corner. The little boy was so glad of this,
and knelt down in front of the box to put
his face close up to the netting to see how
the new pet looked. The woodchuck
sprang at him so savagely, clicking its
teeth so horridly, that he pulled away in a
hurry. It made him feel bad to have
the little creature hate him so; but, of
course, it didn't surprise him. Just caught
and imprisoned, it couldn't know who was
its friend. But he'd tame it; he'd be so
good to it, it would have to learn to love
him! That's what he told his uncle at the
breakfast table, where he set the box with
the little captive up beside him. His uncle
said that he didn't think anybody ever *had*
tamed a woodchuck; but the little boy was
sure *he* could.

Well, he certainly tried his best. For the
next two days he didn't think of another
thing. He sat right beside the cage by the
hour, so that the little wild thing would
get used to him. He tried everything he
could think of, to make it eat—from fresh
clover, to angleworms and sugar. But it
wouldn't even look at any of the foods, and
snarled and jumped wickedly at his hand
whenever he put something new into the
box. And when he sat still and looked in
lovingly at it, it would glare back at him,
hating him so that the little boy could
scarcely stand it.

Of course, not eating anything, it soon
grew weak, and could barely stand on its
feet. But even lying down and panting
for breath, it still had strength enough to
stare hatingly at the little boy if he came
near.

The second night after he'd caught it, he
couldn't sleep for thinking of it, and finally
got up to light a candle and go to look at
it again. It was crouched together in a
corner, its fur every which way, looking
miserably sick; but as the little boy came
up with his candle, it staggered to its feet

and made a feeble little spring toward him, gnashing its teeth and glaring its eyes. Then it fell over weakly on its side. But still it stretched its neck around to keep its hot eyes on the boy.

He remembered, then, how he had seen it playing and joking so happily with its brothers and sisters. He picked up the box in a great hurry and ran with all his might out to the big rock. There he opened the box, took the little woodchuck out, and laid it down on the ground in front of the hole. As soon as it felt the earth under it, it struggled up to its feet, and without once looking at the boy, it let itself slowly down into the hole. The last the little boy saw was a tiny black-striped hind leg, trembling with eagerness, as the little wild baby went home.

Jimmy drew a long breath. "I'm *glad* he let him go," he said softly, and fell into a dreaming silence.

I started to move away, but was recalled by an indignant yell from Jimmy, "But what about that *bed?*"

His eyes were fairly flashing fire.

"Oh," said I, "that turned out not to be interesting at all. One of the neighbors, going home late at night, had had an automobile accident around the turn of the road and his wife sprained her ankle. They came up to Uncle Peter's house to ask for a bedspring to carry her home on, and Uncle Peter stuck his head out of his door to say, sure, yes, they could have the one in the little bedroom on the right-hand side of the landing. They made a mistake and took the left-hand room. That was all.

"And as for the door-knob, that was loose and came off in the hand of one of the men, and he was so excited he didn't think about it till he got downstairs and out on the path."

DAVY AND THE GOBLIN

OR, WHAT FOLLOWED READING "ALICE'S ADVENTURES IN WONDERLAND"

by Charles Carryl

CHAPTER I

HOW THE GOBLIN CAME

IT happened one Christmas eve, when Davy was about eight years old, and this is the way it came about.

That particular Christmas eve was a snowy one and a blowy one, and one generally to be remembered. In the city, where Davy lived, the storm played all manner of pranks, swooping down upon unwary old gentlemen and turning their umbrellas wrong side out, and sometimes blowing their hats quite out of sight. And in the country, where Davy had come to pass Christmas with his dear old grandmother, things were not much better; but here people were very wise about the weather, and stayed indoors, huddled around great blazing wood fires; and the storm, finding no live game, buried up the roads and the fences, and such small-fry of houses as could readily be put out of sight, and howled and roared over the fields and through the trees in a fashion not to be forgotten.

Davy, being of the opinion that a snowstorm was a thing not to be wasted, had been out with his sled, trying to have a little fun with the weather; but presently, discovering that this particular storm was not friendly to little boys, he had retreated into the house, and having put his hat and his high shoes and his mittens by the kitchen fire to dry, he began to find his time hang heavily on his hands. He had wandered idly all over the house, and had tried how cold his nose could be made by holding it against the window-panes, and, I am sorry to say, had even been sliding down the balusters and teasing the cat; and at last, as evening was coming on, had curled himself up in the big easy-chair facing the fire, and had begun to read once more about the marvelous things that happened to little Alice in Wonderland. Then, as it grew darker, he laid aside the book and sat watching the blazing logs and listening to the solemn ticking of the high Dutch clock against the wall.

Then there stole in at the door a delicious odor of dinner cooking downstairs—an odor so suggestive of roast chickens and baked potatoes and gravy and pie as to make any little boy's mouth water; and presently Davy began softly telling himself what he would choose for his dinner. He had quite finished fancying the first part of his feast and was just coming, in his mind, to an extra-large slice of apple-pie well browned (staring meanwhile very hard at one of the brass knobs of the andirons to keep his thoughts from wandering), when he suddenly discovered a little man perched upon that identical knob and smiling at him with all his might.

This little man was a very curious-looking person indeed. He was only about a foot high, but his head was as big as a cocoanut, and he had great bulging eyes, like a frog, and a ridiculous turned-up nose. His legs were as slender as spindles, and he had long-pointed toes to his shoes, or rather to his stockings, or, for that matter, to his trousers,—for they were all of a piece—and bright scarlet in color, as were also his little coat and his high-pointed hat and a queer little cloak that hung over his shoulder. His mouth was so wide that when he smiled it seemed to go quite behind his ears, and there was no way of knowing where the smile ended, except by looking at it from behind—which Davy couldn't do without getting into the fire.

Now, there's no use in denying that Davy was frightened. The fact is, he was frightened almost out of his wits, particularly when he saw that the little man, still smiling furiously, was carefully picking the hottest and reddest embers out of the fire, and, after cracking them like nuts with his teeth, eating them with great relish. Davy watched this alarming meal, expecting every moment to see the little man burst into a blaze and disappear, but he finished his coals in safety, and then nodding cheerfully at Davy, said:

"I know you!"

"Do you?" said Davy faintly.

"Oh, yes!" said the little man. " I know you perfectly well. You are the little boy who doesn't believe in fairies, nor in giants, nor in goblins, nor in anything the story-books tell you."

Now, the truth was that Davy, having never met any giants when he was out walking, nor seen any fairies peeping out of the bushes, nor found any goblins about the house, had come to believe that all these kinds of people were purely imaginary beings, so that now he could do nothing but stare at the little man in a shamefaced sort of way and wonder what was coming next.

"Now all that," said the little man, shaking his finger at him in a reproving way, "all that is very foolish and very wrong. I'm a goblin myself,—a hob-goblin —and I've come to take you on a Believing Voyage."

"Oh, if you please, I can't go!" cried Davy, in great alarm at this proposal, "I can't, indeed. I haven't permission."

"Rubbish!" said the Goblin. "Ask the Colonel."

Now, the Colonel was nothing more nor less than a silly-looking little man made of lead that stood on the mantel shelf holding a clock in his arms. The clock never went, but, for that matter, the Colonel never went either, for he had been standing stock-still for years, and it seemed perfectly ridiculous to ask *him* anything about going anywhere, so Davy felt quite safe in looking up at him and asking permission to go on the Believing Voyage. To his dismay the Colonel nodded his head and cried out in a little cracked voice:

"Why, certainly!"

At this, the Goblin jumped down off the knob of the andiron, and skipping briskly across the room to the big Dutch clock, rapped sharply on the front of the case with his knuckles, when to Davy's amazement the great thing fell over on its face upon the floor as softly as if it had been a feather bed. Davy now saw that instead of being full of weights and brass wheels and curious works, as he had always supposed, the clock was really a sort of boat with a wide seat at each end; but before he had time to make any further discoveries, the Goblin, who had vanished for a moment, suddenly reappeared, carrying two large sponge-cakes in his arms. Now, Davy was perfectly sure that he had seen his grandmother putting those very sponge-cakes into the oven to bake, but before he could utter a word of remonstrance the Goblin clapped one into each seat, and scrambling into the clock sat down upon the smaller one, merely remarking:

"They make prime cushions, you know."

For a moment, Davy had a wild idea of rushing out of the room and calling for help; but the Goblin seemed so pleased with the arrangements he had made and, moreover, was smiling so good-naturedly that the little boy thought better of it, and after a moment's hesitation climbed into the clock and took his seat upon the other cake. It was as warm and springy and fragrant as a day in May. Then there was a whizzing sound, like a lot of wheels spinning around, and the clock rose from the floor and made a great swoop toward the window.

"I'll steer," shouted the Goblin, "and do you look out sharp for light-houses!"

Davy had just time to notice that the Colonel was hastily scrambling down from the mantel shelf with his beloved time-piece in his arms, when they, seated in the long Dutch clock, dashed through the window and out into the night.

CHAPTER II

THE BEGINNING OF THE BELIEVING VOYAGE

THE first thought that came into Davy's mind when he found himself out-of-doors was that he had started off on his journey without his hat, and he was therefore exceedingly pleased to find that it had stopped snowing and that the air was quite still and delightfully balmy and soft. The moon was shining brightly, and as he looked back at the house he was surprised to see that the window through which they had come, and which he was quite sure had always been a straight-up-and-down, old-fashioned window, was now a round affair with flaps running to a point in the center, like the holes the harlequin jumps through in the pantomime.

"How did that window ever get changed into a round hole?" he asked the Goblin, pointing to it in great astonishment.

"Oh," said the Goblin, carelessly, "that's one of the circular singumstances that happen on a Believing Voyage. It's nothing to what you'll see before we come back again. Ah!" he added, "there comes the Colonel!"

Sure enough, at this moment the Colonel's head appeared through the flaps. The clock was still in his arms, and he seemed to be having a great deal of trouble in getting it through, and his head kept coming into view and then disappearing again behind the flaps in so ridiculous a manner that Davy shouted with laughter, and the Goblin smiled harder than ever. Suddenly the poor little man made a desperate plunge and had almost made his way out when the flaps shut to with a loud snap and caught him about the waist. In his efforts to free himself, he dropped his clock to the ground outside, when it burst with a loud explosion and the house instantly disappeared.

This was so unexpected and seemed so serious a matter that Davy was much distressed, wondering what had become of his dear old grandmother and Mrs. Frump, the cook, and Mary Farina, the housemaid, and Solomon, the cat. However, before he had time to make any inquiries of the Goblin, his grandmother came dropping down through the air in her rocking-chair. She was quietly knitting, and her chair was gently rocking as she went by. Next came Mrs. Frump with her apron quite full of kettles and pots, and then Mary Farina, sitting on a step-ladder with the coal-scuttle in her lap. Solomon was nowhere to be seen. Davy, looking over the side of the clock, saw them disappear, one after the other, in a large tree on the lawn; and the Goblin informed him that they had fallen into the kitchen of a witch-hazel tree and would be well taken care of. Indeed, as the clock sailed over the tree, Davy saw that the trunk of it was hollow and that a bright light was shining far under-ground; and to make the matter quite sure, a smell of cooking was coming up through the hole. On one of the topmost boughs of the tree was a nest with two sparrows in it, and he was much astonished at discovering that they were lying side by side, fast asleep, with one of his mittens spread over them for a coverlet.

"I suppose my shoes are somewhere about," he said, sadly. "Perhaps the squirrels are filling them with nuts."

"You're quite right," replied the Goblin, cheerfully; "and there's a rabbit over by the hedge putting dried leaves into your hat; I rather fancy he's about moving into it for the winter."

Davy was about to complain against such liberties being taken with his property, when the clock began rolling over in the air, and he had just time to grasp the sides of it to keep himself from falling out.

"Don't be afraid!" cried the Goblin, "she's only rolling a little," and as he said this, the clock steadied itself and sailed serenely away past the spire of the village church and off over the fields.

Davy now noticed that the Goblin was glowing with a bright, rosy light, as

though a number of candles were burning in his stomach and shining out through his scarlet clothes.

"That's the coals he had for his supper," thought Davy; but as the Goblin continued to smile complacently and seemed to be feeling quite comfortable, he did not venture to ask any questions, and went on with his thoughts. "I suppose he'll soon have smoke coming out of his nose, as if he were a stove. If it were a cold night I'd

The rabbit takes liberties with Davy's property

ask him to come and sit in my lap. I think he must be as warm as a piece of toast!" And the little boy was laughing softly to himself over this conceit, when the Goblin, who had been staring intently at the sky, suddenly ducked his head and cried "Barkers!"—and the next instant a shower of little blue woolly balls came tumbling into the clock. To Davy's alarm they proved to be alive, and immediately began scrambling about in all directions, and yelping so ferociously that he climbed up on his cake in dismay, while the Goblin, hastily pulling a large magnifying glass out of his hat, began attentively examining these strange visitors.

"Bless me!" cried the Goblin, turning

very pale, "they're Skye-terriers. The dog-star must have turned upside down."

"What shall we do?" said Davy, feeling that this was a very bad state of affairs.

"The first thing to do," said the Goblin, "is to get away from these fellows before the solar sisters come after them. Here, jump into my hat!"

So many wonderful things had happened already that this seemed to Davy quite a natural and proper thing to do, and as the Goblin had already seated himself upon the brim, he took his place opposite to him without hesitation. As they sailed away from the clock, it quietly rolled over once, spilling out the sponge-cakes and all the little dogs, and was then wafted off, gently rocking from side to side as it went.

Davy was much surprised at finding that the hat was as large as a clothes-hamper, with plenty of room for him to swing his legs about in the crown. It proved, however, to be a very unpleasant thing to travel in. It spun around like a top as it sailed through the air, until Davy began to feel uncomfortably dizzy, and the Goblin himself seemed to be far from well. He had stopped smiling, and the rosy light had all faded away, as though the candles inside of him had gone out. His clothes, too, had changed from bright scarlet to a dull ashen color, and he sat stupidly upon the brim of the hat as if he were going to sleep.

"If he goes to sleep, he will certainly fall overboard," thought Davy; and with a view to rousing the Goblin, he ventured to remark, "I had no idea your hat was so big."

"I can make it any size I please, from a thimble to a sentry-box," said the Goblin. "And speaking of sentry-boxes—" here he stopped and looked more stupid than ever.

"I verily believe he's absent-minded," said Davy to himself.

"I'm worse than that," said the Goblin, as if Davy had spoken aloud. "I'm absent-bodied," and with these words he fell out of the hat and instantly disappeared. Davy peered anxiously over the edge of the brim, but the Goblin was nowhere to be seen, and the little boy found himself quite alone.

Strange-looking birds now began to swoop up and chuckle at him, and others flew around him, as the hat spun along through the air, gravely staring him in the face for a while, and then sailed away, sadly bleating like sheep. Then a great creature with rumpled feathers perched

"I'm a Cockalorum," he softly murmured

upon the brim of the hat where the Goblin had been sitting, and after solemnly gazing at him for a few moments, softly murmured, "I'm a Cockalorum," and flew heavily away. All this was very sad and distressing, and Davy was mournfully wondering what would happen to him next, when it suddenly struck him that his legs were feeling very cold, and looking down at them he discovered to his great alarm that the crown of the Goblin's hat had entirely disappeared, leaving nothing but the brim upon which he was sitting. He hurriedly examined this and found that the hat was really nothing but an enormous skein of wool, which was rapidly unwinding as it spun along. Indeed, the brim was disappearing at such a rate that he had hardly made this alarming discovery before the end of the skein was whisked away and he found himself falling through the air.

He was on the point of screaming out in his terror, when he discovered that he was falling very slowly and gently swaying from side to side, like a toy balloon. The next moment he struck something hard, which gave way with a sound like breaking glass and let him through, and he had just time to notice that the air had suddenly become deliciously scented with vanilla, when he fell crashing into the branches of a large tree.

CHAPTER III

IN THE SUGAR-PLUM GARDEN

THE bough upon which Davy had fallen bent far down with his weight, then sprang back, then bent again, and in this way fell into a sort of delightful up-and-down dipping motion, which he found very soothing and agreeable. Indeed, he was so pleased and comforted at finding himself near the ground once more that he lay back in a crotch between two branches, enjoying the rocking of the bough and lazily wondering what had become of the Goblin, and whether this was the end of the Believing Voyage, and a great many other things, until he chanced to wonder where he was. Then he sat up on the branch in great astonishment, for he saw that the tree was in full leaf and loaded with plums, and it flashed across his mind that the winter

had disappeared very suddenly, and that he had fallen into a place where it was broad daylight.

The plum-tree was the most beautiful and wonderful thing he had ever seen, for the leaves were perfectly white, and the plums, which looked extremely delicious, were of every imaginable color.

Now, it immediately occurred to Davy that he had never in his whole life had all the plums he wanted at any one time. Here was a rare chance for a feast, and he carefully selected the largest and most luscious-looking plum he could find, to begin with. To his disappointment it proved to be quite hard and as solid and heavy as a stone. He was looking at it in great perplexity, and punching it with his thumbs in the hope of finding a soft place in it, when he heard a rustling sound among the leaves, and looking up, he saw the Cockalorum perched upon the bough beside him. It was gazing sadly at the plum, and its feathers were more rumpled than ever. Presently it gave a long sigh and said, in its low, murmuring voice: "Perhaps it's a sugar-plum," and then flew clumsily away as before.

"Perhaps it is!" exclaimed Davy joyfully, taking a great bite of the plum. To his surprise and disgust, he found his mouth full of very bad-tasting soap, and at the same moment the white leaves of the plum-tree suddenly turned over and showed the words "APRIL FOOL" printed very distinctly on their under sides. To make the matter worse, the Cockalorum came back and flew slowly around the branches, laughing softly to itself with a sort of a chuckling sound, until Davy, almost crying with disappointment and mortification, scrambled down from the tree to the ground.

He found himself in a large garden planted with plum-trees, like the one he had fallen into, and with walks winding about among them in every direction. These walks were beautifully paved with sugar-almonds and bordered by long rows of many-colored motto-papers neatly planted in the ground. He was too much distressed, however, by what had happened in the plum-tree to be interested or pleased with this discovery, and was about walking away along one of the paths in the hope of finding his way out of the garden, when he suddenly caught sight of a small figure standing a little distance from him.

He was the strangest-looking creature Davy had ever seen, not even excepting the Goblin. In the first place, he was as flat as a pancake, and about as thick as one; and in the second place, he was so transparent that Davy could see through his head and his arms and his legs almost as clearly as though he had been made of glass. This was so surprising in itself that when Davy presently discovered that he was made of beautiful, clear lemon-candy, it seemed the most natural thing in the world, as explaining his transparency. He was neatly dressed in a sort of tunic of writing-paper, with a cocked hat of the same material, and he had under his arm a large book with the words "HOLE-KEEP-ER's VACUUM" printed on the cover. This curious-looking creature was standing before an extremely high wall with his back to Davy, intently watching a large hole in the wall about a foot from the ground. There was nothing extraordinary about the appearance of the hole (except that the lower edge of it was curiously tied in a large bow-knot like a cravat), but Davy watched it carefully for a few moments, thinking that perhaps something marvelous would come out of it. Nothing appeared, however, and Davy, walking up close behind the candy man, said very politely, "If you please, sir, I dropped in here——"

Before he could finish the sentence the Hole-keeper said snappishly, "Well, drop out again—quick!"

"But," pleaded Davy, "you can't drop out of a place, you know, unless the place should happen to turn upside down."

"I *don't* know anything about it," replied the Hole-keeper, without moving. "I never saw anything drop—except once. Then I saw a gumdrop. Are you a gum?" he added, suddenly turning around and staring at Davy.

"Of course I'm not," said Davy, indignantly. "If you'll only listen to me, you'll understand exactly how it happened."

"Well, go on," said the Hole-keeper, impatiently, "and don't be tiresome."

"I fell down ever so far," said Davy, beginning his story over again, "and at last I broke through something——"

"That was the sky-light!" shrieked the Hole-keeper, dashing his book upon the ground in a fury. "That was the barley-sugar sky-light, and I shall certainly be boiled!"

This was such a shocking idea that Davy stood speechless, staring at the Hole-keeper, who rushed to and fro in a convulsion of distress.

"Now, see here," said the Hole-keeper, at length, coming up to him and speaking in a low, trembling voice. "This must be a private secret between us. Do you solemsy promilse?"

"I prolemse," said Davy, earnestly. This wasn't at all what he meant to say, and it sounded very ridiculous; but somehow the words *wouldn't* come straight. The Hole-keeper, however, seemed perfectly satisfied, and picking up his book, said: "Well, just wait till I can't find your name," and began hurriedly turning over the leaves.

Davy saw, to his astonishment, that there was nothing whatever in the book, all the leaves being perfectly blank, and he couldn't help saying, rather contemptuously:

"How do you expect to find my name in *that* book? There's nothing in it."

"Ah! that's just it, you see," said the Hole-keeper, exultingly; "I look in it for the names that ought to be out of it. It's the completest system that ever was invented. Oh! here you aren't!" he added, staring with great satisfaction at one of the blank pages. "Your name is Rupsy Frimbles."

"It's nothing of the sort," said Davy, indignantly.

"Tut! Tut!" said the Hole-keeper. "Don't stop to contradict or you'll be too late"; and Davy felt himself gently lifted off his feet and pushed head-foremost into the hole. It was quite dark and rather sticky, and smelt strongly of burnt sugar, and Davy had a most unpleasant time of it crawling through on his hands and knees. To add to his distress, when he came out at the further end, instead of being, as he had hoped, in the open country, he found himself in a large room fairly swarming with creatures very like the Hole-keeper in appearance, but somewhat darker and denser in the way of complexion. The instant Davy came out of the hole, a harsh voice called out:

"Bring Frungles this way," and the crowd gathered around him and began to rudely hustle him across the room.

"That's not my name!" cried Davy, struggling desperately to free himself. "It isn't even the name I came in with!"

"Tut! Tut!" said a trembling voice near him, and Davy caught sight of the Hole-keeper, also struggling in the midst of the crowd with his great book hugged tightly to his breast. The next moment he found himself before a low platform on which a crowned figure was sitting in a gorgeous tin chair, holding in his hand a long white wand with red lines running screw-wise around it, like a barber's pole.

"Who broke the barley-sugar sky-light?" said the figure, in a terrible voice.

The Hole-keeper began fumbling at the leaves of his book in great agitation, when the king, pointing at him with his wand, roared furiously: "Boil *him,* at all events!"

"Tut! Tut! your majesty——" began the Hole-keeper confusedly, with his stiff little tunic fairly rustling with fright; but before he could utter another word he was dragged away, screaming with terror.

"Don't you go with them!" shouted Davy, made really desperate by the Hole-keeper's danger. "They're nothing but a lot of molasses candy!"

At this the king gave a frightful shriek, and aiming a furious blow at Davy with his wand, rolled off the platform into the midst of the struggling crowd. The wand broke into a hundred pieces, and the air was instantly filled with a choking odor of peppermint; then everything was wrapped in darkness, and Davy felt himself being whirled along, heels over head, through the air. Then there came a confused sound of bells and voices, and he found himself running rapidly down a long street with the Goblin at his side.

CHAPTER IV

THE BUTTERSCOTCHMEN

BELLS were pealing and tolling in all directions, and the air was filled with the sound of distant shouts and cries.

"What were they?" asked Davy, breathlessly.

"Butterscotchmen," said the Goblin.

"And what makes you that color?" said Davy, suddenly noticing that the Goblin had changed his color to a beautiful blue.

"Trouble and worry," said the Goblin. "I always get blue when the Butterscotchmen are after me."

"Are they coming after us now?" inquired Davy in great alarm.

"Of course they are," said the Goblin. "But the best of it is, they can't run till they get warm, and they can't get warm without running, you see. But the worst of it is that *we* can't stop without sticking fast," he added, anxiously. "We must keep it up until we get to the Amuserum."

"What's that?" said Davy.

"It's a place they have to amuse themselves with," said the Goblin,—"curiosities, and all that sort of thing, you know. By the way, how much money have you? We have to pay to get in."

Davy began to feel in his pocket (which is a very difficult thing to do when you're running fast) and found, to his astonishment, that they were completely filled with a most extraordinary lot of rubbish. First, he pulled out what seemed to be an iron ball, but it proved to be a hard-boiled egg, without the shell, stuck full of small tacks. Then came two slices of toast firmly tied together with a green cord. Then came a curious little glass jar filled with large flies. As Davy took this out of his pocket, the cork came out with a loud "pop!" and the flies flew away in all directions. Then came, one after another, a tart filled with gravel, two chicken bones, a bird's nest with some pieces of brown soap in it, some mustard in a pillbox and a cake of beeswax stuck full of caraway seeds. Davy remembered afterward that as he threw these things away they arranged themselves in a long row on the curb-stone of the street. The Goblin looked on with great interest as Davy fished them up out of his pockets, and finally said, enviously: "That's a splendid collection; where did they all come from?"

"I'm sure *I* don't know," said Davy, in great bewilderment.

"And I'm sure *I* don't know," repeated the Goblin. "What else is there?"

Davy felt about in his pockets again and found what seemed to be a piece of money. On taking it out, however, he was mortified to find that it was nothing but an old button; but the Goblin exclaimed in a tone of great satisfaction, "Ah! hold on to that!" and ran on faster than ever.

The sound of the distant voices had grown fainter and fainter still, and Davy was just hoping that their long run was almost over, when the street came abruptly to an end at a brick wall, over the top of which he could see the branches of trees. There was a small round hole in the wall with the words "PAY HERE" printed above it, and the Goblin whispered to Davy to hand in the button through this hole. Davy did so, feeling very much ashamed of himself, when to his surprise instead of receiving tickets in return, he heard a loud exclamation behind the wall, followed by a confused sound of scuffling, and the hole suddenly disappeared. The next moment, a little bell tinkled and the wall rose slowly before them like a curtain, carrying the trees with it, apparently, and he and the Goblin were left standing in a large open space paved with stone.

Davy was exceedingly alarmed at seeing a dense mass of Butterscotchmen in the center of the square, pushing and crowding one another in a very quarrelsome manner, and chattering like a flock of magpies, and he was just about to propose a hasty retreat, when a figure came hurrying through the square, carrying on a pole a large placard bearing the words:

"JUST RECEIVED!

THE GREAT FRUNGLES THING!

ON EXHIBITION IN THE PLUM-GARDEN!"

At the sight of these words, the mob set up a terrific shout, and began streaming out of the square after the pole-bearer, like a flock of sheep, jostling and shoving one another as they went, and leaving Davy and the Goblin quite alone.

"I verily believe they're gone to look at my button," cried Davy, beginning to laugh in spite of his fears. "They called *me* Frungles, you know."

"That's rather a nice name," said the Goblin, who had begun smiling again. "It's better than Snubgraddle, at all events. Let's have a look at the curiosities"; and here he walked boldly into the center of the square.

Davy followed close at his heels, and found to his astonishment and disappointment that the curiosities were simply the things that he had fished out of his pockets but a few minutes before, placed on little pedestals and carefully protected by transparent sugar shades. He was on the point of laughing outright at this ridiculous exhibition, when he saw that the Goblin had taken a large telescope out of his pocket and was examining the different objects with the closest attention, and muttering to himself, "Wonderful! wonderful!" as if he had never seen anything like them before.

"Pooh!" said Davy, contemptuously. "The only wonderful thing about them is how they ever came *here*."

At this remark the Goblin turned his telescope toward Davy and uttered a faint cry of surprise; and Davy, peering anxiously through the large end, saw him suddenly shrink to the size of a small

beetle and then disappear altogether. Davy hastily reached out with his hands to grasp the telescope; but it, too, disappeared.

The next moment he felt something spring upon his back. Before he could cry out in his terror, a head was thrust forward over his shoulder, and he found the Goblin, who was now of a bright purple color, staring him in the face and laughing with all his might.

CHAPTER V

THE GIANT BADORFUL

"GOBLIN," said Davy, very seriously, as the little man jumped down from off his back, "if you are going to play such tricks as *that* upon me, I should like to go home at once."

"Where's the harm?" said the Goblin, sitting down on the grass with his back against a wall and smiling contentedly.

"The harm is that I was frightened," said Davy, with great indignation. But as he spoke, a loud rumbling noise like distant thunder came from behind the wall against which the Goblin was leaning, followed by a tremendous sneeze that fairly shook the ground.

"What's that?" whispered Davy to the Goblin, in great alarm.

"It's only Badorful," said the Goblin, laughing. "He's always snoring and waking himself up, and I suppose it's sleeping on the ground that makes him sneeze. Let's have a look at him," and the Goblin led the way along the wall to a large grating.

Davy looked through the grating and was much alarmed at seeing a giant, at least twenty feet in height, sitting on the ground, with his legs crossed under him like a tailor. He was dressed in a shabby suit of red velveteen, with a great leathern belt about his waist and enormous boots, and Davy thought he looked terribly ferocious. On the grass beside him lay a huge club, thickly studded at one end with great iron knobs; but Davy noticed to his great relief that some little creeping vines were twining themselves among these knobs, and that moss was growing thickly upon one side of the club itself, as though it had been lying there untouched for a long time.

The giant was talking to himself in a low tone, and, after listening attentively at the grating for a moment, the Goblin shrieked:

"He's making poetry!" and throwing himself upon the ground kicked up his heels in a perfect ecstasy of delight.

"Oh, hush, hush!" cried Davy in terror. "Suppose he hears you!"

"Hears me!" said the Goblin, discontinuing his kicking and looking very much surprised. "What if he does?"

"Well, you know, he *might* not like being laughed at," said Davy, anxiously.

"There's something in that," said the Goblin, staring reflectively at the ground.

"And, you see," continued Davy, "a giant who doesn't like what's going on must be a dreadful creature."

"Oh! there's no fear of *him,*" said the Goblin, contemptuously, motioning with his head toward the giant. "He's too old. Why, I must have known him, off and on, for nearly two hundred years. Come in and see him."

"Will he do anything?" said Davy, anxiously.

"Bless you, no!" said the Goblin. "He's a perfect old kitten"; and with these words he pushed open the grating and passed through with Davy following tremblingly

at his heels. Badorful looked up with a feeble smile, and merely said, "Just listen to this:"

My age is three hundred and seventy-two,
    And I think, with the deepest regret,
How I used to pick up and voraciously
        chew
    The dear little boys whom I met.

I've eaten them raw in their holiday suits,
    I've eaten them curried with rice,
I've eaten them baked in their jackets and
        boots,
    And found them exceedingly nice.

But now that my jaws are too weak for
        such fare,
    I think it excessively rude
To do such a thing, when I'm quite well
        aware
    Little boys do not like to be chewed.

And so I contentedly live upon eels,
    And try to do nothing amiss,
And I pass all the time I can spare from
        my meals
    In innocent slumber—like this.

Here Badorful rolled over upon his side, and was instantly fast asleep.

"You see," said the Goblin, picking up a large stone and thumping with it upon the giant's head, "you see, he's quite weak *here.* Otherwise, considering his age, he's a very capable giant."

At this moment a farmer with bright red hair thrust his head in at the grating, and calling out, "Look out, there!" disappeared again. Davy and the Goblin rushed out and were just in time to see something go by like a flash with a crowd of people, armed with pitchforks, in hot pursuit. Davy and the Goblin were just setting off on a run to join in the chase, when a voice said, "Ahem!" and looking up, they saw Badorful staring at them over the top of the wall.

"How does this strike you?" he said, addressing himself to Davy:

Although I am a giant of the exhibition
*   size,*
I've been nicely educated, and I notice
*   with surprise,*
That the simplest rules of etiquette you
*   don't pretend to keep,*
For you skurry off to races while a gentle-
*   man's asleep.*

Don't reply that I was drowsy, for my nap
*   was but a kind*
Of dramatic illustration of a peaceful
*   frame of mind;*
And you really might have waited till I
*   woke again, instead*
Of indelicately pounding, with a stone,
*   upon my head.*

Very probably you'll argue that our views
*   do not agree,—*
I've often found that little boys have dis-
*   agreed with me;—*
But I'm properly entitled, on the com-
*   pensation plan,*
To three times as much politeness as an
*   ordinary man.*

Davy was greatly distressed at having these severe remarks addressed to him.

"If you please, sir," he said earnestly, "I didn't pound you."

At this the giant glared savagely at the Goblin and continued:

My remarks have been directed at the one
*   who, I supposed,*
Had been violently thumping on my per-
*   son while I dozed:*
By a simple calculation you will find that
*   there is due*
Just six times as much politeness from a
*   little chap like you.*

"Oh! you make me ill!" said the Goblin, flippantly. "Go to sleep."

Badorful stared at him for a moment, and then with a sickly smile, murmured: "Good afternoon," and disappeared behind the wall.

Davy and the Goblin now hurried off wildly to resume the chase, when the Goblin suddenly stopped, and by an ingenious twist of his body sat down on his long shoes or stockings, and began to rock to and fro like an animated little rocking-chair.

"Dear me!" exclaimed Davy, perfectly amazed, "I thought we were chasing something."

"Of course you did," said the Goblin, complacently; "but in this part of the world things very often turn out to be different from what they would have been if they hadn't been otherwise than as you expected they were going to be."

"But you thought so yourself——" began Davy, when to his distress the Goblin suddenly faded into a dull pinkish color, and then disappeared altogether. Davy looked about him and found that he was quite alone in a dense wood.

CHAPTER VI

THE MOVING FOREST

"OH, dear!" cried Davy, speaking aloud in his distress, "I do wish people and things wouldn't change about so! Just so soon as ever I get to a place, it goes away, and I'm somewhere else!" And the little boy's heart began to beat rapidly as he looked about him; for the wood was very dark and solemn and still.

Presently the trees and bushes directly before him moved silently apart and showed a broad path beautifully overgrown with soft turf; and as he stepped forward upon it, the trees and bushes beyond moved silently aside in their turn, and the path grew before him, as he walked along, like a green carpet slowly unrolling itself through the wood. It made him a little uneasy at first to find that the trees behind him came together again, quietly blotting out the path,—but then he thought:

"It really doesn't matter so long as I don't want to go back," and so he walked along very contentedly.

By and by, the path seemed to give itself a shake, and, turning abruptly around a large tree, brought Davy suddenly upon a little butcher's shop, snugly buried in the wood. There was a sign on the shop, reading, "ROBIN HOOD: VENISON," and Robin himself, wearing a clean white apron over his suit of Lincoln green, stood in the door-way, holding a knife and steel as though he were on the lookout for customers. As he caught sight of Davy, he said, "Steaks? Chops?" in an inquiring way, quite like an every-day butcher.

"Venison is deer, isn't it?" said Davy, looking up at the sign.

"Not at all," said Robin Hood, promptly. "It's the cheapest meat about here."

"Oh, I didn't mean that," replied Davy; "I meant that it comes off of a deer."

"Wrong again!" said Robin Hood, triumphantly. "It comes on a deer. I cut it off myself. Steaks? Chops?"

"No, I thank you," said Davy, giving up the argument. "I don't think I want anything to eat just now."

"Then what did you come here for?" said Robin Hood, peevishly. "What's the good, I'd like to know, of standing around and staring at an honest tradesman?"

"Well, you see," said Davy, beginning to feel frightened, "I didn't know you were this sort of person at all. I always thought you were an archer, like—like William Tell, you know."

"That's all a mistake about Tell," said Robin Hood, contemptuously. "He wasn't an archer. He was a crossbowman,—the crossest one that ever lived. By the way, you don't happen to want any steaks or chops today, do you?"

"No, not today, thank you," said Davy, very politely.

"Tomorrow?" inquired Robin Hood.

"No, I thank you," said Davy again.

"Will you want any yesterday?" inquired Robin Hood, rather doubtfully.

"I think not," said Davy, beginning to laugh.

Robin Hood stared at him for a moment with a puzzled expression, and then walked into his little shop and Davy turned away. As he did so, the path behind him began to unfold itself through the wood, and looking back over his shoulder, he saw the little shop swallowed up by the trees and bushes. Just as it disappeared from view, he caught a glimpse of a charming little girl peeping out of a latticed window beside the door. She wore a little red hood and looked wistfully after Davy as the shop went out of sight.

"I verily believe that was Little Red Riding Hood," said Davy to himself, "and I never knew before that Robin Hood was her father!" The thought of Red Riding Hood, however, brought the wolf to Davy's mind, and he began to anxiously watch the thickets on either side of the path, and even went so far as to whistle softly to himself, by way of showing that he wasn't in the least afraid. He went on and on, hoping the forest would soon come to an end, until the path shook itself, again disclosing to view a trim little brick shop in the densest part of the thicket. It had a neat little green door, with a bright brass knocker upon it, and a sign above it, bearing the words,

"SHAM-SHAM: BARGAINS IN WATCHES"

"Well!" exclaimed Davy in amazement. "Of all places to sell watches in, that's the preposterest!" But as he turned to walk away, he found the trees and bushes for the first time blocking his way, and refusing to move aside. This distressed him very much, until it suddenly occurred to him that this must mean that he was to go into the shop; and after a moment's hesitation he went up and knocked timidly at the door with the bright brass knocker. There was no response to the knock, and Davy cautiously pushed open the door and went in.

The place was so dark that at first he could see nothing, although he heard a rattling sound coming from the back part of the shop, but presently he discovered the figure of an old man, busily mixing something in a large iron pot. As Davy approached him, he saw that the pot was full of watches, which the old man was stirring about with a ladle. The old creature was very curiously dressed in a suit of rusty green velvet, with little silver buttons sewed over it, and he wore a pair of enormous yellow-leather boots; and Davy was quite alarmed at seeing that a broad leathern belt about his waist was stuck full of old-fashioned knives and pistols. Davy was about to retreat quickly from the shop, when the old man looked up and said, in a peevish voice:

"How many watches do you want?" and Davy saw that he was a very shocking-looking person, with wild, staring eyes, and with a skin as dark as mahogany, as if he had been soaked in something for ever so long.

"How many?" repeated the old man impatiently.

"If you please," said Davy, "I don't think I'll take any watches today. I'll call——"

"Drat 'em!" interrupted the old man, angrily beating the watches with his ladle, "I'll never get rid of 'em—never!"

"It seems to me—" began Davy, soothingly.

"Of course it does!" again interrupted the old man as crossly as before. "Of course it does! That's because you won't listen to the why of it."

"But I *will* listen," said Davy.

"Then sit down on the floor and hold up your ears," said the old man.

Davy did as he was told to do, so far as sitting down on the floor was concerned, and the old man pulled a paper out of one of his boots, and glaring at Davy over the top of it, said angrily:

"You're a pretty spectacle! I'm another. What does that make?"

"A pair of spectacles, I suppose," said Davy.

"Right!" said the old man. "Here they are." And pulling an enormous pair of spectacles out of the other boot he put them on, and began reading aloud from his paper:

> " 'My recollectest thoughts are those
> Which I remember yet;
> And bearing on, as you'd suppose,
> The things I don't forget.
>
> " 'But my resemblest thoughts are less
> Alike than they should be;
> A state of things, as you'll confess,
> You very seldom see.' "

"Clever, isn't it?" said the old man, peeping proudly over the top of the paper.

"Yes, I think it is," said Davy, rather doubtfully.

"Now comes the cream of the whole thing," said the old man. "Just listen to this:

*"'And yet the mostest thought I love
Is what no one believes—'"*

Here the old man hastily crammed the paper into his boot again, and stared solemnly at Davy.

"What is it?" said Davy, after waiting a moment for him to complete the verse. The old man glanced suspiciously about the shop, and then added, in a hoarse whisper:

*"'That I'm the sole survivor of
The famous Forty Thieves!'"*

"But I thought the Forty Thieves were all boiled to death," said Davy.

"All but me," said the old man, decidedly. "I was in the last jar, and when they came to me the oil was off the boil, or the boil was off the oil,—I forget which it was,—but it ruined my digestion and made me look like a ginger-bread man. What larks we used to have!" he continued, rocking himself back and forth and chuckling hoarsely. "Oh! we were a precious lot, we were! I'm Sham-Sham, you know. Then there was Anamanamona Mike—he was an Irishman from Hullaboo —and Barcelona Boner—he was a Spanish chap, and boned everything he could lay his hands on. Strike's real name was Gobang; but we called him Strike, because he was always asking for more pay. Hare Ware was a poacher, and used to catch Welsh rabbits in a trap; we called him 'Hardware' because he had so much *steal* about him. Good joke, wasn't it?"

"Oh, very!" said Davy, laughing.

"Frown Whack was a scowling fellow with a club," continued Sham-Sham. "My! how he could hit! And Harico and Barico were a couple of bad Society Islanders. Then there was Wee Wo; he was a little Chinese chap, and we used to send him down the chimneys to open front doors

for us. He used to say that sooted him to perfection. Wac——"

At this moment an extraordinary commotion began among the watches. There was no doubt about it, the pot was boiling. And Sham-Sham, angrily crying out "Don't tell *me* a watched pot never boils!" sprang to his feet, and pulling a pair of pistols from his belt, began firing at the watches, which were now bubbling over the side of the pot and rolling about the floor; while Davy, who had had quite enough of Sham-Sham by this time, ran out of the door.

To his great surprise, he found himself in a sort of underground passage lighted by grated openings overhead; but as he could still hear Sham-Sham, who now seemed to be firing all his pistols at once, he did not hesitate, but ran along the passage at the top of his speed.

Presently he came in sight of a figure hurrying toward him with a lighted candle, and as it approached he was perfectly astounded to see that it was Sham-Sham himself, dressed up in a neat calico frock and a dimity apron like a housekeeper, and with a bunch of keys hanging at his girdle. The old man seemed to be greatly agitated, and hurriedly whispering, "We thought you were *never* coming, sir!" led the way through the passage in great haste. Davy noticed that they were now in a sort of tunnel made of fine grass. The grass had a delightful fragrance, like new-mown hay, and was neatly wound around the tunnel like the inside of a bird's nest. The next moment they came out into an open space in the forest, where, to Davy's amazement, the Cockalorum was sitting bolt upright in an armchair, with its head wrapped up in flannel.

It seemed to be night, but the place was lighted up by a large chandelier that hung from the branches of a tree, and Davy saw that a number of odd-looking birds were roosting on the chandelier among the lights, gazing down upon the poor Cockalorum with a melancholy interest. As Sham-Sham made his appearance with Davy at his heels, there was a sudden commotion among the birds, and they all cried out together, "Here's the doctor!" Before Davy could reply, the Hole-keeper sud-

The Cockalorum is ill

denly made his appearance with his great book, and hurriedly turning over the leaves, said, pointing to Davy, *"He* isn't a doctor. His name is Gloopitch." At these words, there arose a long, wailing cry, the lights disappeared, and Davy found himself on a broad path in the forest with the Hole-keeper walking quietly beside him.

CHAPTER VII

SINDBAD THE SAILOR'S HOUSE

"You had no right to tell those birds my name was Gloopitch!" said Davy, angrily. "That's the second time you've got it wrong."

"Well, it's of no consequence," said the Hole-keeper, complacently. "I'll make it something else the next time. By the way, you're not the postman, are you?"

"Of course I'm not," said Davy.

"I'm glad of that," said the Hole-keeper; "postmen are always so dreadfully busy. Would you mind delivering a letter for me?" he added, lowering his voice confidentially.

"Oh, no," answered Davy, rather reluctantly; "not if it will be in my way."

"It's sure to be in your way because it's so big," said the Hole-keeper; and taking the letter out of his pocket, he handed it to Davy. It certainly was a very large letter, curiously folded like a dinner-napkin and sealed in a great many places with red and white peppermint drops; and Davy was much pleased to see that it was addressed:

> *Captain Robinson Crusoe,*
> *Jeran Feranderperandamam,*
> *B. G.*

"What does B. G. stand for?" said Davy.

"Baldergong's Geography, of course," said the Hole-keeper.

"But why do you put *that* on the letter?" inquired Davy.

"Because you can't find Jeran Feranderperandamam anywhere else, stupid," said the Hole-keeper, impatiently. "But I can't stop to argue about it now," and saying this, he turned into a side path, and disappeared in the wood.

As Davy walked mournfully along, turning the big letter over and over in his hands, and feeling very confused by the Hole-keeper's last remark, he presently saw, lying on the walk before him, a small book beautifully bound in crimson morocco, and picking it up, he saw that it was marked on the cover:

"Perhaps this will tell me where to go," he thought as he opened it; but it proved to be far more confusing than the Hole-keeper himself had been. The first page was headed "How to frill griddlepigs"; the second page, "Two ways of frumpling crumbles"; the third page, "The best snub for feastie spralls"; and so on, until Davy felt as if he were taking leave of his senses. He was just about to throw the book down in disgust, when it was suddenly snatched out of his hands; and turning hastily, he saw a savage glaring at him from the bushes.

Now Davy knew perfectly well, as all little boys should know, that when you meet a savage in the woods you must get behind a tree as quickly as possible; but he did this in such haste that he found to his dismay that he and the savage had chosen the same tree, and in the next instant the savage was after him. The tree was a very large one, and Davy in his fright went around it a number of times so rapidly that he presently caught sight of the back of the savage, and he was surprised to see that he was no bigger than a large monkey; and moreover, that he was gorgeously dressed in a beautiful blue coat, with brass buttons on the tail of it, and pink striped trousers. Davy had hardly made this discovery, when the savage suddenly disappeared through a door in a high paling of logs that began at the tree and extended in a straight line far out into the forest.

It was very puzzling to Davy when it occurred to him that, although he had been around the tree at least a dozen times, he had never seen this paling before. The door through which the savage had disappeared also bothered him; for, though it was quite an ordinary-looking door, it had

no knob nor latch, nor indeed any way of being opened that he could perceive. On one side of it, in the paling, was a row of bell-pulls, marked:

> *Family*
> *Butcher*
> *Baker*
> *Police*
> *Candlestickmaker*

and on the door itself was a large knocker, marked:

> *Postman*

After examining all these, Davy decided that, as he had a letter in charge, he was more of a postman than anything else, and he therefore raised the knocker and rapped loudly. Immediately all the bell-pulls began flying in and out of their own accord, with a deafening clangor of bells behind the paling; and then the door swung slowly back upon its hinges.

Davy walked through the doorway and found himself in the oddest-looking little country place that could possibly be imagined. There was a little lawn laid out on which a sort of soft fur was growing instead of grass, and here and there about the lawn, in the place of flower-beds, little footstools, neatly covered with carpet, were growing out of the fur. The trees were simply large feather-dusters; but they seemed, nevertheless, to be growing in a very thriving manner. And on a little mound at the back of the lawn, stood a small house built entirely of big conch-shells with their pink mouths turned outward. This gave the house a very cheerful appearance, as if it were constantly on a broad grin.

The savage was sitting in the shade of one of the dusters, complacently reading the little red book; and as Davy approached, he saw, to his astonishment, that he was the Goblin dressed up like an Ethiopian serenader.

"Oh! you dear, delicious old Goblin!" cried Davy, in an ecstasy of joy at again finding his traveling-companion. "And were you the savage that was chasing me just now?"

The Goblin nodded his head, and exclaiming, "My, how you did cut and run!" rolled over and over, kicking his heels about in a delirium of enjoyment.

"Goblin," said Davy, gravely, "I think we can have just as good a time without any such doings as that. And now tell me what place this is."

"Sindbad the Sailor's house," said the Goblin, sitting up again.

"Really and truly?" said the delighted Davy.

"Really and treally truly," said the Goblin. "And here he comes now!"

Davy looked around and saw an old man coming toward them across the lawn. He was dressed in a Turkish costume, and wore a large turban and red morocco slippers turned up at the toes like skates; and his white beard was so long that at every fourth step he trod upon it, and fell forward to the ground. He took no notice whatever of either Davy or the Goblin, and after falling down a number of times, took his seat upon one of the little carpet foot-stools. Taking off his turban, he began stirring about in it with a large wooden spoon. As he took off his turban, Davy saw that his head, which was perfectly bald, was neatly laid out in black and white squares like a chess-board.

"He's the most absent-minded story-teller that ever was born," said the Goblin, pointing with his thumb over his shoulder at Sindbad.

As Davy and the Goblin sat down beside him, Sindbad hastily put on his turban, and after scowling at Davy for a mo-

ment, said to the Goblin, "It's no use telling *him* anything; he's as deaf as a trunk."

"Then tell it to me," said the Goblin, with great presence of mind.

"All right," said Sindbad, "I'll give you a nautical one."

Here he rose for a moment, hitched up his big trousers like a sailor, cocked his turban on one side of his head, and sitting down again, began:

"A capital ship for an ocean trip,
  Was 'The Walloping Window Blind';
No gale that blew dismayed her crew
  Or troubled the captain's mind.
The man at the wheel was taught to feel
  Contempt for the wildest blow,
And it often appeared, when the weather
    had cleared,
  That he'd been in his bunk below.

"The boatswain's mate was very sedate,
  Yet fond of amusement, too;
And he played hop-scotch with the star-
    board watch,
  While the captain tickled the crew.
And the gunner we had was apparently
    mad,
  For he sat on the after-rail,
And fired salutes with the captain's boots,
  In the teeth of the booming gale.

"The captain sat in a commodore's hat
  And dined in a royal way
On toasted pigs and pickles and figs
  And gummery bread each day.
But the cook was Dutch and behaved as
    such;
  For the diet he gave the crew
Was a number of tons of hot-cross buns
  Prepared with sugar and glue.

"All nautical pride we laid aside,
  And we cast the vessel ashore
On the Gulliby Isles, where the Pooh-
    pooh smiles,

And the Rumbletumbunders roar.
And we sat on the edge of a sandy ledge
  And shot at the whistling bee;
And the cinnamon-bats wore water-proof
    hats
  As they danced in the sounding sea.

"On rubgub bark, from dawn to dark,
  We fed, till we all had grown
Uncommonly shrunk,—when a Chinese
    junk
  Came by from the torriby zone.
She was stubby and square, but we didn't
    much care,
  And we cheerily put to sea;
And we left the crew of the junk to chew
  The bark of the rubgub-tree."

Here Sindbad stopped, and gazed solemnly at Davy and the Goblin.

"If you please, sir," said Davy, respectfully, "what is gummery bread?"

"It's bread stuffed with molasses," said Sindbad; "but I never saw it anywhere, except aboard of 'The Prodigal Pig.'"

"But," said Davy, in great surprise, "you said the name of your ship was——"

"So I did, and so it was," interrupted Sindbad, testily. "The name of a ship sticks to it like wax to a wig. You *can't* change it."

"Who gave it that name?" said the Goblin.

"What name?" said Sindbad, looking very much astonished.

"Why, 'The Cantering Soup Tureen,'" said the Goblin, winking at Davy.

"Oh, *that* name!" said Sindbad; "that was given to her when—— But speaking of soup-tureens—let's go and have some pie;" and rising to his feet, he gave one hand to Davy and the other to the Goblin, and they all walked off in a row toward the little shell house. This, however, proved to be a very troublesome arrangement, for Sindbad was constantly stepping on his long beard and falling down; and as he kept a firm hold of his companions' hands, they all went down in a heap together a great many times. At last Sindbad's turban fell off, and as he sat up on the grass and began stirring in it again with his wooden spoon, Davy saw that it was full of broken chessmen.

"It's a great improvement, isn't it?" said Sindbad.

"What is?" said Davy, very much puzzled.

"Why, this way of playing the game," said Sindbad, looking up at him complacently. "You see, you make all the moves at once."

"It must be a very easy way," said Davy.

"It's nothing of the sort," said Sindbad, sharply. "There are more moves in one of my games than in twenty ordinary games;" and here he stirred up the chessmen furiously for a moment, and then, triumphantly calling out "Check!" clapped the turban on his head.

As they set out again for the little house, Davy saw that it was slowly moving around the edge of the lawn, as if it were on a circular railway, and Sindbad followed it around, dragging Davy and the Goblin with him, but never getting any nearer to the house.

"Don't you think," said Davy, after a while, "that it would be a good plan to stand still and wait until the house came around to us?"

"Here, drop that!" exclaimed Sindbad, excitedly, "that's my idea. I was just about proposing it myself."

"So was I," said the Goblin to Sindbad. "Just leave my ideas alone, will you?"

"*Your* ideas!" retorted Sindbad, scornfully. "I didn't know you'd brought any with you."

"I had to," replied the Goblin, with great contempt, "otherwise there wouldn't have been any on the premises."

"Oh! come, I say!" cried Sindbad, "that's my sneer, you know. Don't go to putting the point of it the wrong way."

"Take it back, if it's the only one you have," retorted the Goblin, with another wink at Davy.

"Thank you, I believe I will," replied Sindbad, meekly; and as the little house came along just then, they all stepped in at the door as it went by. As they did so, to Davy's amazement Sindbad and the Goblin quietly vanished, and Davy, instead of being inside the house, found himself standing in a dusty road, quite alone.

CHAPTER VIII

LAYOVERS FOR MEDDLERS

As Davy stood in the road, in doubt which way to go, a Roc came around the corner of the house. She was a large bird, nearly six feet tall, and was comfortably dressed in a bonnet and a plaid shawl, and wore overshoes. About her neck was hung a covered basket and a door key, and Davy at once concluded that she was Sindbad's housekeeper.

"I didn't mean to keep you waiting," said the Roc, leading the way along the road; "but I declare that, what with combing that lawn every morning with a fine-tooth comb, and brushing those shells every evening with a fine tooth-brush, I don't get time for anything else, let alone feeding the animals."

"What animals?" said Davy, beginning to be interested.

"Why, *his,* of course," said the Roc, rattling on in her harsh voice. "There's an Emphasis and two Periodicals and a Spotted Disaster, all crawlin' and creepin' and screechin'——"

Here Davy, unable to control himself, burst into a fit of laughter, in which the Roc joined heartily, rolling her head from side to side and repeating "All crawlin' and creepin' and screechin'" over and over again, as if that were the cream of the joke. Suddenly she stopped laughing and said in a low voice, "You don't happen to have a beefsteak about you, do you?"

Davy confessed that he had not, and the Roc continued, "Then I must go back. Just hold my basket, like a good child." Here there was a scuffling sound in the basket and the Roc rapped on the cover with her hard beak and cried, "Hush!"

"What's in it?" said Davy, cautiously taking the basket.

"Layovers for meddlers," said the Roc, and hurrying back along the road, was soon out of sight.

"I wonder what they're like," said Davy to himself, getting down upon his hands and knees and listening curiously with his ear against the cover of the basket. The scuffling sound continued, mingled with little sneezes and squeaking sobs as if some very small kittens had bad colds and were crying about it.

"I think I'll take a peep," said Davy, looking cautiously about him. There was no one in sight, and he carefully raised the cover a little way and tried to look in. The scuffling sound and the sobs ceased, and the next instant the cover flew off the basket and out poured a swarm of little brown creatures like snuff-boxes with legs. As they scampered off in all directions, Davy made a frantic grab at one of them, when it instantly turned over on its back and blew a puff of smoke into his face, and he rolled over in the road almost stifled. When he was able to sit up again and look about him, the empty basket was lying on its side near him, and not a layover was to be seen. At that moment, the Roc came in sight, hurrying along the road with her shawl and her bonnet-strings fluttering behind her; and Davy, clapping the cover on the basket, took to his heels and ran for dear life.

CHAPTER IX

RIBSY

The road was very dreary and dusty, and wound in and out in the most tiresome way until it seemed to have no end to it, and Davy ran on and on, half expecting at any moment to feel the Roc's great beak pecking at his back. Fortunately his legs carried him along so remarkably well that he felt he could run for a week; and indeed he might have done so if he had not, at a sharp turn in the road, come suddenly upon a horse and cab. The horse was fast asleep when Davy dashed against him, but he woke up with a start, and, after whistling like a locomotive once or twice in a very alarming manner, went to sleep again. He was a very frowsy-looking horse with great lumps at his knees and a long, crooked neck like a camel's; but what attracted Davy's attention particularly was the word "Ribsy" painted in whitewash on his side in large letters. He was looking at this and wondering if it were the horse's name, when the door of the cab flew open and a man fell out, and after rolling over in the dust, sat up in the middle of the road and began yawning. He was even a more ridiculous-looking object than the horse, being dressed in a clown's suit, with a morning gown over it by way of a topcoat, and a field marshal's cocked hat. In fact, if he had not had a whip in his hand no one would ever have taken him for a cabman. After yawning heartily, he looked up at Davy and said drowsily: "Where?"

"To B. G.," said Davy, hastily referring to the Hole-keeper's letter.

"All right," said the cabman, yawning again. "Climb in, and don't put your feet on the cushions."

Now, this was a ridiculous thing for him to say, for when Davy stepped inside he found the only seats were some three-legged stools huddled together in the back part of the cab, all the rest of the space being taken up by a large bathtub that ran across the front end of it. Davy turned on one of the faucets, but nothing came out except some dust and a few small bits of gravel, and he shut it off again, and sitting down on one of the little stools, waited patiently for the cab to start.

Just then the cabman put his head in at the window, and winking at him confidentially, said: "Can you tell me why this horse is like an umbrella?"

"No," said Davy.

"Because he's used *up*," said the cabman.

"I don't think that's a very good conundrum," said Davy.

"So do I," said the cabman. "But it's the best one I can make with this horse. Do you say N. B.?" he asked.

"No; I said B. G.," said Davy.

"All right," said the cabman again, and disappeared from the window. Presently there was a loud trampling overhead, and Davy, putting his head out at the window, saw that the cabman had climbed up on top of the cab and was throwing stones at the horse, which was still sleeping peacefully.

"Oh! don't do that," said Davy, anxiously. "I'd rather get out and walk."

"Well, I wish you would," said the cabman, in a tone of great relief. "This is a very valuable stand, and I don't care to lose my place on it;" and Davy accordingly jumped out of the cab and walked away.

Presently there was a clattering of hoofs behind him, and Ribsy came galloping along the road with nothing on him but his collar. He was holding his big head high in the air, like a giraffe, and gazing proudly about him as he ran. He stopped short when he saw the little boy, and giving a triumphant whistle, said cheerfully: "How are you again?"

It seemed rather strange to be spoken to by a cab-horse, but Davy answered that he was feeling quite well.

"So am I," said Ribsy. "The fact is, that when it comes to beating a horse about the head with a three-legged stool, if that horse is going to leave at all, it's time he was off."

"I should think it was," said Davy, earnestly.

"You'll observe, of course, that I've kept on my shoes and my collar," said Ribsy. "It isn't genteel to go barefoot, and nothing makes a fellow look so untidy as going about without a collar. The truth is"—he continued, sitting down in the road on his hind legs, "the truth is, I'm not an ordinary horse by any means. I have a history, and I've arranged it in a popular form in six canters—I mean cantos," he added, hastily correcting himself.

"I'd like to hear it, if you please," said Davy, politely.

"Well, I'm a little hoarse——" began Ribsy.

"I think you're a very big horse," said Davy, in great surprise.

"I'm referring to my voice," said Ribsy, haughtily. "Be good enough not to interrupt me again;" and giving two or three preliminary whistles to clear his throat, he began:

"It's very confining, this living in stables,
 And passing one's time among wagons
  and carts;

I much prefer dining at gentlemen's
  tables,
 And living on turkeys and cranberry
  tarts."

"That's rather a high-toned idea," said Ribsy, proudly.

"Oh! yes, indeed," said Davy, laughing; and Ribsy continued:

"As spry as a kid and as trim as a spider
  Was I in the days of the Turnip-top
   Hunt,
 When I used to get rid of the weight of
  my rider
  And canter contentedly in at the front."

"By the way, that trick led to my being sold to a circus," said Ribsy. "I suppose you've never been a circus-horse?"

"Never," said Davy.

"Then you don't know anything about it," said Ribsy. "Here we go again!"

"It made me a wreck, with no hope of im-
  provement,
 Too feeble to race with an invalid crab;
 I'm wry in the neck, with a rickety move-
  ment
  Peculiarly suited for drawing a cab."

"I may as well say *here*," broke in Ribsy again, "that the price old Patsey Bolivar, the cabman, paid for me was simply ridiculous."

"I find with surprise that I'm constantly
  sneezing;
 I'm stiff in the legs, and I'm often for
  sale;
 And the blue-bottle flies, with their tire-
  some teasing,
  Are quite out of reach of my weary old
   tail."

"I see them!" cried Davy eagerly.

"Thank you," said Ribsy, haughtily. "As the next verse is the last, you needn't

trouble yourself to make any further observations.

"*I think my remarks will determine the
    question
Of why I am bony and thin as a rail;
I'm off for some larks to improve my di-
    gestion,
And point the stern moral conveyed by
    my tail.*"

Here Ribsy got upon his legs again,
and after a refreshing fillip with his heels,
cantered off along the road, whistling as
he went. Two large blue-bottle flies were
on his back, and his tail was flying around
with an angry whisk like a pin-wheel; but
as he disappeared in the distance, the flies
were still sitting calmly on the ridge of
his spine, apparently enjoying the scenery.

Davy was about to start out again on
his journey, when he heard a voice shouting "Hi! Hi!" and looking back, he saw
the poor cabman coming along the road
on a brisk trot, dragging his cab after him.
He had on Ribsy's harness, and seemed to
be in a state of tremendous excitement.

As he came up with Davy, the door of
the cab flew open again, and the three-
legged stools came tumbling out, followed
by a dense cloud of dust.

"Get in! Get in!" shouted the cabman,
excitedly. "Never mind the dust; I've
turned it on to make believe we're going
tremendously fast."

Davy hastily scrambled in, and the cabman started off again. The dust was pouring out of both faucets, and a heavy
shower of gravel was rattling into the
bath-tub; and, to make matters worse, the
cabman was now going along at such an
astonishing speed that the cab rocked violently from side to side, like a boat in a
stormy sea. Davy made a frantic attempt
to shut off the dust, but it seemed to come
faster and faster, until he was almost
choked. At this moment the cab came
suddenly to a stop, and Davy, rushing to
the window, found himself staring into a
farm-yard, where a red cow stood gazing
up at him.

CHAPTER X

JACK AND THE BEANSTALK'S FARM

IT was quite an ordinary-looking farm-
yard and quite an ordinary-looking
cow, but she stared so earnestly up at
Davy that he felt positively certain she
had something to say to him. "Every creature I meet *does* have something to say,"
he thought, "and I should really like to
hear a cow—" and just at this moment the
cab door suddenly flew open and he
pitched headforemost out upon a pile of
hay in the farmyard and rolled from it
off upon the ground. As he sat up, feeling
exceedingly foolish, he looked anxiously
at the cow, expecting to see her laughing
at his misfortune, but she stood gazing
at him with a very serious expression of
countenance, solemnly chewing, and slowly
swishing her tail from side to side. As
Davy really didn't know how to begin a
conversation with a cow, he waited for her
to speak first, and there was consequently
a long pause. Presently the Cow said, in a
melancholy, lowing tone of voice:

"Are you a market-gardener?"

"No," said Davy. "Why?"

"Because," said the Cow, mournfully,
"there's a feather-bed growing in the
vegetable garden, and I thought you might
explain how it came there."

"That's very curious," said Davy.

"Curious, but comfortable for the pig," said the Cow. "He's taken to sleeping there, lately. He calls it his quill pen."

"That's a capital name for it," said Davy, laughing. "What else is there in the garden?"

"Nothing but the beanstalk," said the Cow. "You've heard of 'Jack and the Beanstalk,' haven't you?"

"Oh, yes, indeed!" said Davy, beginning to be very much interested. "I should like to see the beanstalk."

"You can't *see* the beans talk," said the Cow, gravely. "You might *hear* them talk —that is, if they had anything to say, and you listened long enough. By the way, that's the house that Jack built. Pretty, isn't it?"

Davy turned and looked up at the house. It certainly was a very pretty house, built of bright red brick with little gables, and dormer windows in the roof, and with a trim little porch quite overgrown with climbing roses. But it had a very comical appearance, for all that, as the cab-door was standing wide open in the walk just a little above the porch. Suddenly an idea struck him, and he exclaimed:

"Then you must be the cow with the crumpled horn!"

"It's not crumpled," said the Cow with great dignity. "There's a slight crimp in it, to be sure, but nothing that can properly be called a crump. Then the story was all wrong about my tossing the dog. It was the cat that ate the malt. He was a Maltese cat, and his name was Flipmegilder."

"Did you toss *him?*" inquired Davy.

"Certainly not," said the Cow, indignantly. "Who ever heard of a cow tossing a cat? The fact is, I've never had a fair chance to toss *anything*. As for the dog, Mother Hubbard never permitted any liberties to be taken with *him*."

"I'd dearly love to see Mother Hubbard," said Davy, eagerly.

"Well, you can," said the Cow, indifferently. "She isn't much to see. If you'll look in at the kitchen window, you'll probably find her performing on the piano and singing a song. She's always at it."

Dave stole softly to the kitchen window and peeped in, and, as the Cow had said,

Mother Hubbard sings a song

Mother Hubbard was there, sitting at the piano and evidently just preparing to sing. The piano was very remarkable, and Davy could not remember ever having seen one like it before. The top of it was arranged with shelves on which stood all the kitchen crockery, and in the under part of it, at one end, was an oven with glass doors, through which he could see several pies baking.

Mother Hubbard was dressed, just as he expected, in a very ornamental flowered gown with high-heeled shoes and buckles, and wore a tall pointed hat over her nightcap. She was so like the pictures Davy had seen of her that he thought he would have recognized her anywhere. She sang in a high key with a very quavering voice, and this was the song:

"I had an educated pug,
  His name was Tommy Jones;
He lived upon the parlor rug
  Exclusively on bones.

"I went to a secluded room
  To get one from a shelf;
It wasn't there, and I presume
  He'd gone and helped himself.

"He had an entertaining trick
  Of feigning he was dead;
Then, with a reassuring kick,
  Would stand upon his head.

"I could not take the proper change
  And go to buy him shoes,
But what he'd sit upon the range
  And read the latest news.

"And when I ventured out one day
  To order him a coat,
I found him, in his artless way,
  Careering on a goat.

"I could not go to look at hats
  But that, with childish glee,
He'd ask in all the neighbors' cats
  To join him at his tea!"

While Mother Hubbard was singing this song, little handfuls of gravel were constantly thrown at her through one of the kitchen windows, and by the time the song was finished, her lap was quite full of it.

"I'd just like to know who is throwing that gravel," said Davy, indignantly.

"It's Gobobbles," said the Cow, calmly. "You'll find him around at the front of the house. By the way, have you any chewing-gum about you?"

"No," said Davy, greatly surprised at the question.

"So I supposed," said the Cow. "It's precisely what I should expect of a person who would fall out of a cab."

"But I couldn't help *that*," said Davy.

"Of course you couldn't," said the Cow, yawning indolently. "It's precisely what I should expect of a person who hadn't any chewing gum." And with this the Cow walked gravely away, just as Mother Hubbard made her appearance at the window.

"Boy," said Mother Hubbard, beaming mildly upon Davy through her spectacles, "you shouldn't throw gravel."

"I haven't thrown any," said Davy.

"Fie!" said Mother Hubbard, shaking her head; "always speak the truth."

"I am speaking the truth," said Davy, indignantly. "It was Gobobbles."

"So I supposed," said Mother Hubbard, gently shaking her head again. "It would have been far better if he had been cooked last Christmas instead of being left over. Stuffing him and then letting him go has made a very proud creature of him. You should never be proud."

"I'm not proud," replied Davy, provoked at being mixed up with Gobobbles in this way.

"You may define the word *proud*, and give a few examples," continued Mother Hubbard, and Davy was just noticing with astonishment that she was beginning to look exactly like old Miss Peggs, his school-teacher, when a thumping sound was heard, and the next moment Gobobbles came tearing around the corner of the house, and Mother Hubbard threw up her hands with a little shriek and disappeared from the window.

Gobobbles proved to be a large and very bold-mannered turkey, with all his feathers taken off except a frowsy tuft about his neck. He was pounding his chest with his wings in a very disagreeable manner, and altogether his appearance was so formidable that Davy was half inclined to take to his heels at once, but Gobobbles stopped short upon seeing him, and discontinuing his pounding, stared at him suspiciously for a moment, and then said:

"I can't abide boys!"

"Why not?" said Davy.

"Oh, they're so hungry!" said Gobobbles, passionately. "They're so everlastingly hungry. Now, don't deny that you're fond of turkey."

"Well, I *do* like turkey," said Davy, seeing no way out of the difficulty.

"Of course you do!" said Gobobbles, tossing his head. "Now, you might as well know," he continued, resuming his thumping with increased energy, "that I'm as hollow as a drum and as tough as a hatbox. Just mention that fact to any one you meet, will you? I suppose Christmas is coming, of course."

"Of course it is!" replied Davy.

"It's *always* coming!" said Gobobbles, angrily; and with this he strutted away, pounding himself like a bass-drum.

CHAPTER XI

ROBINSON CRUSOE'S ISLAND

"THIS is a very sloppy road," said Davy to himself, as he walked along in the direction taken by the turkey; and it was, indeed, a *very* sloppy road. The dust had quite disappeared, and the sloppiness soon changed to such a degree of wetness that Davy presently found himself in water up to his ankles. He turned to go back, and saw, to his alarm, that the land in every direction seemed to be miles away, and the depth of the water increased so rapidly that, before he could make up his mind what to do, it had risen to his shoulders, and he was carried off his feet and found himself apparently drifting out to sea. The water, however, was warm and pleasant, and he discovered that instead of sinking he was floated gently along, slowly turning in the water like a float on a fishing-line. This was very agreeable, but he was, nevertheless, greatly relieved when a boat came in sight sailing toward him. As it came near, it proved to be the clock with a sail hoisted and the Goblin sitting complacently in the stern.

"How d'ye do, Gobsy?" said Davy.

"Prime!" said the Goblin, enthusiastically.

"Well, stop the clock," said Davy; "I want to get aboard."

"I haven't any board," said the Goblin, in great surprise.

"I mean I want to get into the clock," said Davy, laughing. "I don't think you're much of a sailor."

"I'm not," said the Goblin, as Davy climbed in. "I've been sailing one way for ever so long, because I don't know how to turn around. But there's a landing-place just ahead."

Davy looked over his shoulder and found that they were rapidly approaching a little wooden pier standing about a foot out of the water. Beyond it stretched a broad expanse of sandy beach.

"What place is it?" said Davy.

"It's called Hickory Dickory Dock," said the Goblin. "All the eight-day clocks stop here," and at this moment the clock struck against the timbers with a violent thump, and Davy was thrown out, heels over head, upon the dock. He scrambled upon his feet again as quickly as possible, and saw to his dismay that the clock had been turned completely around by the shock and was rapidly drifting out to sea again. The Goblin looked back despairingly, and Davy just caught the words, "I don't know how to turn around!" when the clock was carried out of hearing distance and soon disappeared on the horizon.

The beach was covered in every direction with little hills of sand, like haycocks, with scraggy bunches of sea-weed sticking out of the tops of them; and Davy was wondering how they came to be there, when he caught sight of a man walking along the edge of the water and now and then stopping and gazing earnestly out to sea. As the man drew nearer, Davy saw that he was dressed in a suit of brown leather and wore a high-peaked hat, and that a little procession, consisting of a dog, a cat, and a goat, was following patiently at his heels, while a parrot was perched upon his shoulder. They all wore large standing linen collars and black cravats, which gave them a very serious appearance.

Davy was morally certain that the man was Robinson Crusoe. He carried an enormous gun, which he loaded from time to time, and then, aiming carefully at the sea, fired. There was nothing very alarming about this, for the gun, when fired, only gave a faint squeak, and the bullet, which was about the size of a small orange, dropped out quietly upon the sand. Robinson, for it was really he, always seemed to be greatly astonished at this result, peering long and anxiously out to sea, after every shot. His animal companions, however, seemed to be greatly alarmed whenever he prepared to fire; and scampering off, hid behind the little hills of sand until the gun was discharged, when they would return, and after solemnly watching their master reload his piece, follow him along the beach as before. This was all so ridiculous that Davy had

great difficulty in keeping a serious expression on his face as he walked up to Robinson and handed him the Hole-keeper's letter. Robinson looked at him suspiciously as he took it, and the animals eyed him with evident distrust.

Robinson had some difficulty in opening the letter, which was sopping wet, and took a long time to read it, Davy meanwhile waiting patiently. Sometimes Robinson would scowl horribly as if puzzled, and then again he would chuckle to himself as if vastly amused with the contents; but as he turned the letter over in reading it, Davy could not help seeing that it was simply a blank sheet of paper with no writing whatever upon it except the address. This, however, was so like the Hole-keeper's way of doing things that Davy was not much surprised when Robinson remarked: "He has left out the greatest lot of comical things!" and stooping down, buried the letter in the sand. Then picking up his gun, he said: "You may walk about in the grove as long as you please, provided you don't pick anything."

"What grove?" said Davy, very much surprised.

"This one," said Robinson, proudly pointing out the tufts of sea-weed. "They're beach trees, you know; I planted 'em myself. I had to have some place to go shooting in, of course."

"Can you shoot with *that* gun?" said Davy.

"Shoot? Why, it's a splendid gun!" said Robinson, gazing at it proudly. "I made it myself—out of a spy-glass."

"It doesn't seem to go off," said Davy, doubtfully.

"That's the beauty of it!" exclaimed Robinson, with great enthusiasm. "Some guns go off, and you never see 'em again."

"But I mean that it doesn't make any noise," persisted Davy.

"Of course it doesn't," said Robinson.

"That's because I load it with tooth powder."

"But I don't see what you can shoot with it," said Davy, feeling that he was somehow getting the worst of the argument.

Robinson stood gazing thoughtfully at him for a moment, while the big bullet rolled out of the gun with a rumbling sound and fell into the sea. "I see what you want," he said, at length. "You're after my personal history. Just take a seat in the family circle and I'll give it to you."

Davy looked around and saw that the dog, the goat, and the cat were seated respectfully in a semicircle, with the parrot, which had dismounted, sitting beside the goat. He seated himself on the sand at the other end of the line, and Robinson began as follows:

"The night was thick and hazy
    When the 'Piccadilly Daisy'
Carried down the crew and captain in the
        sea;
    And I think the water drowned 'em,
    For they never, never found 'em,
And I know they didn't come ashore with
        me.

"Oh! 't was very sad and lonely
    When I found myself the only
Population on this cultivated shore;
    But I've made a little tavern
    In a rocky little cavern,
And I sit and watch for people at the door.

"I spent no time in looking
    For a girl to do my cooking,
As I'm quite a clever hand at making
        stews;
    But I had that fellow Friday,
    Just to keep the tavern tidy
And to put a Sunday polish on my shoes.

"I have a little garden
    That I'm cultivating lard in,

As the things I eat are rather tough and
        dry;
    For I live on toasted lizards,
    Prickly pears and parrot gizzards,
And I'm really very fond of beetle pie.

"The clothes I had were furry,
    And it made me fret and worry
When I found the moths were eating off
        the hair;
    And I had to scrape and sand 'em,
    And I boiled 'em and I tanned 'em,
'Till I got the fine morocco suit I wear.

"I sometimes seek diversion
    In a family excursion
With the few domestic animals you see;
    And we take along a carrot
    As refreshment for the parrot,
And a little can of jungleberry tea.

"Then we gather as we travel
    Bits of moss and dirty gravel,
And we chip off little specimens of stone;
    And we carry home as prizes
    Funny bugs of handy sizes,
Just to give the day a scientific tone.

"If the roads are wet and muddy,
    We remain at home and study,—
For the goat is very clever at a sum,—
    And the dog, instead of fighting,
    Studies ornamental writing,
While the cat is taking lessons on the
        drum.

"We retire at eleven,
    And we rise again at seven,
And I wish to call attention as I close
    To the fact that all the scholars
    Are correct about their collars
And particular in turning out their toes."

Here Robinson called out in a loud voice, "First class in arithmetic!" but the animals sat perfectly motionless, sedately staring at him.

"Oh! by the way," said Robinson, confidentially to Davy, "this *is* the first class in arithmetic. That's the reason they didn't move, you see. Now, then!" he continued sharply, addressing the class, "how many halves are there in a whole?"

There was a dead silence for a moment, and then the Cat said gravely, "What kind of a hole?"

"That has nothing to do with it," said Robinson, impatiently.

"Oh! hasn't it though!" exclaimed the Dog, scornfully. "I should think a big hole could have more halves in it than a little one."

"Well, *rather*," put in the Parrot, contemptuously.

Here the Goat, who apparently had been carefully thinking the matter over, said in a low, quavering voice: "Must all the halves be of the same size?"

"Certainly not," said Robinson, promptly; then nudging Davy with his elbow, he whispered, "He's bringing his mind to bear on it. He's prodigious when he gets started!"

"Who taught him arithmetic?" said Davy, who was beginning to think Robinson didn't know much about it himself.

"Well, the fact is," said Robinson, confidentially, "he picked it up from an old adder that he met in the woods."

Here the Goat, who evidently was not yet quite started, inquired, "Must all the halves be of the same shape?"

"Not at all," said Robinson, cheerfully. "Have 'em any shape you like."

"Then I give it up," said the Goat.

"Well!" exclaimed Davy, quite out of patience. "You are certainly the stupidest lot of creatures I ever saw."

At this, the animals stared mournfully at him for a moment, and then rose up and walked gravely away.

"Now you've spoiled the exercises," said Robinson, peevishly. "I'm sorry I gave 'em such a staggerer to begin with."

"Pooh!" said Davy, contemptuously. "If they couldn't do that sum, they couldn't do anything."

Robinson gazed at him admiringly for a moment, and then, looking cautiously about him to make sure that the procession was out of hearing, said coaxingly:

"What's the right answer? Tell us, like a good fellow."

"Two, of course," said Davy.

"Is that all?" exclaimed Robinson, in a tone of great astonishment.

"Certainly," said Davy, who began to feel very proud of his learning. "Don't you know that when they divide a whole into four parts they call them fourths, and when they divide it into two parts they call them halves?"

"Why don't they call them tooths?" said Robinson, obstinately. "The fact is, they ought to call 'em teeth. That's what puzzled the Goat. Next time I'll say, 'How many teeth in a whole?'"

"Then the Cat will ask if it's a rat-hole," said Davy, laughing at the idea.

"You positively convulse me, you're so very humorous," said Robinson, without a vestige of a smile. "You're almost as droll as Friday was. He used to call the Goat 'Pat'; because he said he was a little butter. I told him that was altogether too funny for a lonely place like this, and he went away and joined the minstrels."

Here Robinson suddenly turned pale, and hastily reaching out for his gun, sprang to his feet.

Davy looked out to sea and saw that the clock, with the Goblin standing in the stern, had come in sight again, and was heading directly for the shore with tremendous speed. The poor Goblin, who had turned sea-green in color, was frantically waving his hands to and fro, as if

motioning for the beach to get out of the
way; and Davy watched his approach
with the greatest anxiety. Meanwhile, the
animals had mounted on four sand-hills,
and were solemnly looking on, while Robinson, who seemed to have run out of
tooth-powder, was hurriedly loading his
gun with sand. The next moment the
clock struck the beach with great force,
and turning completely over on the sand,
buried the Goblin beneath it. Robinson
was just making a convulsive effort to fire
off his gun when the clock began striking loudly, and he and the animals fled in
all directions in the wildest dismay.

CHAPTER XII

A WHALE IN A WAISTCOAT

DAVY rushed up to the clock, and
pulling open the little door in the
front of it, looked inside. To his
great disappointment, the Goblin had
again disappeared, and there was a smooth
round hole running down into the sand,
as though he had gone directly through
the beach. He was listening at this hole in
the hope of hearing from the Goblin,
when a voice said, "I suppose that's what
they call going into the interior of the
country," and looking up, he saw the Hole-
keeper sitting on a little mound in the
sand, with his great book in his lap.

His complexion had quite lost its beautiful transparency, and his jaunty little
paper tunic was sadly rumpled, and, moreover, he had lost his cocked hat. All this,
however, had not at all disturbed his complacent conceit; he was, if anything, more
pompous than ever.

"How did *you* get here?" asked Davy
in astonishment.

"I'm banished," said the Hole-keeper
cheerfully. "That's better than being
boiled, any day. Did you give Robinson
my letter?"

"Yes, I did," said Davy, as they walked
along the beach together; "but I got it
very wet coming here."

"That was quite right," said the Hole-
keeper. "There's nothing so tiresome as a
dry letter. Well, I suppose Robinson is expecting me, by this time,—isn't he?"

"I don't know, I'm sure," said Davy.
"He didn't say that he was expecting you."

"He *must* be," said the Hole-keeper,
positively. "I never even mentioned it in
my letter—so, of course, he'll know I'm
coming. It strikes me the sun is very hot
here," he added faintly.

The sun certainly was very hot, and
Davy, looking at the Hole-keeper as he
said this, saw that his face was gradually
and very curiously losing its expression,
and that his nose had almost entirely disappeared.

"What's the matter?" inquired Davy,
anxiously.

"The matter is that I'm going back into
the raw material," said the Hole-keeper,
dropping his book and sitting down helplessly in the sand. "See here, Frinkles," he
continued, beginning to speak very
thickly. "Wrap me up in my shirt and
mark the packish distingly. Take off shir
quigly!" and Davy had just time to pull
the poor creature's shirt over his head and
spread it quickly on the beach, when the
Hole-keeper fell down, rolled over upon
the garment, and bubbling once or twice,
as if he were boiling, melted away into a
compact lump of brown sugar.

Davy was deeply affected by this sad incident, and though he had never really
liked the Hole-keeper, he could hardly

keep back his tears as he wrapped up the lump in the paper shirt and laid it carefully on the big book. In fact, he was so disturbed in his mind that he was on the point of going away without marking the package, when, looking over his shoulder, he suddenly caught sight of the Cockalorum standing close beside him, carefully holding an inkstand, with a pen in it, in one of his claws.

"Oh! thank you very much," said Davy, taking the pen and dipping it in the ink. "And will you please tell me his name?"

The Cockalorum, who still had his head done up in flannel and was looking rather ill, paused for a moment to reflect, and then murmured, "Mark him 'Confectionery.'"

This struck Davy as being a very happy idea, and he accordingly printed "CONFEXIONRY" on the package in his very best manner. The Cockalorum, with his head turned critically on one side, carefully inspected the marking, and then, after earnestly gazing for a moment at the inkstand, gravely drank the rest of the ink and offered the empty inkstand to Davy.

"I don't want it, thank you," said Davy, stepping back.

"No more do I," murmured the Cockalorum, and tossing the inkstand into the sea, flew away in his usual clumsy fashion.

Davy, after a last mournful look at the package of brown sugar, turned away, and was setting off along the beach again, when he heard a gurgling sound coming from behind a great hummock of sand, and peeping cautiously around one end of it, he was startled at seeing an enormous Whale on the beach lazily basking in the sun. The creature was dressed in a huge white garment buttoned up in front, with a bunch of live seals flopping at one of the button-holes and a great chain cable leading from them to a pocket at one side. Before Davy could retreat, the Whale caught sight of him and called out in a tremendous voice, "How d'ye do, Bub?"

"I'm pretty well, I thank you," said Davy, with his usual politeness to man and beast. "How are you, sir?"

"Hearty!" thundered the Whale; "never felt better in all my life. But it's rather warm lying here in the sun."

"Why don't you take off your——," here Davy stopped, not knowing exactly what it was the Whale had on.

"Waistcoat," said the Whale, condescendingly. "It's a canvas-back-duck waistcoat. The front of it is made of wild duck, you see, and the back of it out of the fore-top-sail of a brig."

"Is it nice, being a Whale?" inquired Davy curiously.

"Famous!" said the Whale, with an affable roar. "Great fun, I assure you! We have fish-balls every night, you know."

"Fish-balls at night!" exclaimed Davy. "Why, we always have ours for breakfast."

"Nonsense!" thundered the Whale, with a laugh that made the beach quake; "I don't mean anything to eat. I mean dancing parties."

"And do you dance?" said Davy, thinking that if he did, it must be a very extraordinary performance.

"Dance?" said the Whale with a reverberating chuckle. "Bless you! I'm as nimble as a six-pence. By the way, I'll show you the advantage of having a bit of whale-bone in one's composition," and with these words the Whale curled himself up, then flattened out suddenly with a tremendous flop, and shooting through the air like a flying elephant, disappeared with a great splash in the sea.

Davy stood anxiously watching the spot where he went down, in the hope that he would come up again; but instead of this, the waves began tossing angrily, and a roaring sound came from over the sea, as though a storm were coming up. Then a cloud of spray was dashed into his face, and presently the air was filled with lobsters, eels, and wriggling fishes that were being carried inshore by the gale. Suddenly, to Davy's astonishment, a dog came sailing along. He was being helplessly blown about among the lobsters, uneasily jerking his tail from side to side to keep it out of reach of their great claws, and giving short, nervous barks from time to time, as though he were firing signal-guns of distress. In fact, he seemed to be having such a hard time of it that Davy caught him by the ear as he was going by, and landed him in safety on the beach. He proved to be a very shaggy, battered-looking animal with a weather-beaten tarpaulin hat jammed on the side of his head, and a patch over one eye; and as he had on an old pilot coat, Davy thought he must be an old sea-dog, and so, indeed, he proved to be. He stared doubtfully at Davy for a moment, and then said in a husky voice:

"What's *your* name?" as if he had just mentioned his own.

"Davy,——" began the little boy, but before he could say another word, the old sea-dog growled:

"Right you are!" and handing him a folded paper, trotted gravely away, swaggering as he went, like a sea-faring man.

The paper was addressed to *"Davy Jones,"* and was headed inside *"Binnacle Bob: His Werses,"* and below these words Davy found the following story:

"To inactivity inclined
  Was Captain Parker Pitch's mind;
  In point of fact, 't was fitted for
  An easy-going life ashore.

"His disposition, so to speak,
  Was nautically soft and weak;
  He feared the rolling ocean, and
  He very much preferred the land.

"A stronger-minded man by far
  Was gallant Captain Thompson Tar;
  And (what was very wrong, I think,)
  He marked himself with India ink.

"He boldly sailed 'The Soaking Sue'
  When angry gales and tempests blew,
  And even from the nor-nor-east
  He didn't mind 'em in the least.

"Now Captain Parker Pitch's sloop
  Was called 'The Cozy Chickencoop'—
  A truly comfortable craft
  With ample state-rooms fore and aft.

"No foolish customs of the deep,
  Like 'watches,' robbed his crew of sleep;
  That estimable lot of men
  Were all in bed at half-past ten.

"At seven bells, one stormy day,
  Bold Captain Tar came by that way,
  And in a voice extremely coarse
  He roared 'Ahoy!' till he was hoarse.

"Next morning of his own accord
  This able seaman came aboard,
  And made the following remark
  Concerning Captain Pitch's bark:

"'Avast!' says he, 'Belay! What cheer!
  How comes this little wessel here?
  Come, tumble up your crew,' says he,
  'And navigate a bit with me!'

"Says Captain Pitch, 'I can't refuse
  To join you on a friendly cruise;
  But you'll oblige me, Captain Tar,
  By not a-taking of me far.'

"At this reply from Captain Pitch,
  Bold Thompson gave himself a hitch;
  It cut him to the heart to find
  A seaman in this frame of mind.

"'Avast!' says he; 'We'll bear away
For Madagascar and Bombay,
Then down the coast to Yucatan,
Kamchatka, Guinea, and Japan.

"'Stand off for Egypt, Turkey, Spain,
Australia, and the Spanish Main,
Then through the nor-west passage for
Van Diemen's Land and Labrador.'

"Says Captain Pitch: 'The ocean swell
Makes me exceedingly unwell,
And, Captain Tar, before we start,
Pray join me in a friendly tart.'

"And shall I go and take and hide
The sneaking trick that Parker tried?
Oh! no. I very much prefer
To state his actions as they were:

"With marmalade he first began
To tempt that bluff sea-faring man,
Then fed him all the afternoon
With custard in a table-spoon.

"No mariner, however tough,
Can thrive upon this kind of stuff;
And Thompson soon appeared to be
A feeble-minded child of three.

"He cried for cakes and lollipops—
He played with dolls and humming
tops—
He even ceased to roar 'I'm blowed!'
And shook a rattle, laughed, and
crowed.

"When Parker saw the seamen gaze
Upon the Captain's cunning ways,
Base envy thrilled him through and
through
And he became a child of two.

"Now, Thompson had in his employ
A mate, two seamen, and a boy;
The mate was fond as he could be
Of babies, and he says, says he,

"'Why, messmates, as we're all agreed
Sea-bathing is the thing they need;
Let's drop these hinfants off the quar-
ter!'
—(They did, in fourteen fathom water)."

Just as Davy finished these verses, he discovered to his alarm that he was sinking into the beach as though the sand were running down through an hourglass, and before he could make any effort to save himself, he had gone completely through and found himself lying flat on his back with tall grass waving about him.

CHAPTER XIII

THE END OF THE
BELIEVING VOYAGE

WHEN Davy sat up and looked around him, he found himself in a beautiful meadow with the sun shining brightly on the grass and the wild-flowers. The air was filled with dainty colored insects darting about in the warm sunshine, and chirping cheerily as they flew, and at a little distance the Goblin was sitting on the grass attentively examining a great, struggling creature that he was holding down by its wings.

"I suppose,"—said the Goblin, as if Davy's sudden appearance was the most ordinary thing in the world,—"I suppose that this is about the funniest bug that flies."

"What is it?" said Davy, cautiously edging away.

"It's a cricket-bat," said the Goblin, rapping familiarly with his knuckles on its hard shell. "His body is like a boot-jack, and his wings are like a pair of umbrellas."

"But, you know, a cricket-bat is something to play with!" said Davy, surprised at the Goblin's ignorance.

"Well, *you* may play with it if you like. *I* don't want to!" said the Goblin, carelessly tossing the great creature over to Davy, and walking away.

The cricket-bat made a swoop at Davy, knocking him over like a feather, and then with a loud snort flew away across the meadow. It dashed here and there at flying things of every kind, and turning on its side, knocked them, one after another, quite out of sight, and finally, to Davy's great relief, disappeared in a distant wood.

"Come on! come on!" cried a voice; and Davy, looking across the meadow, saw the Goblin beckoning vigorously to him, apparently in great excitement.

"What's the matter?" cried Davy, pushing his way through the thick grass.

"Oh, my! oh, my!" shrieked the Goblin, who was almost bursting with laughter. "Here's that literary hack again!"

Davy peered through a clump of bushes and discovered a large red animal with white spots on its sides, clumsily rummaging about in the tall grass and weeds. Its appearance was so formidable that he was just about whispering to the Goblin, "Let's run!" when the monster raised its head and, after gazing about for an instant, gave a loud, triumphant whistle.

"Why, it's Ribsy!" cried Davy, running forward. "It's Ribsy, only he's grown enormously fat."

It was Ribsy, indeed, eating with all his might. The name on his side was twisted about beyond all hope of making it out, and his collar had quite disappeared in a deep crease about his neck. In fact, his whole appearance was so alarming that Davy anxiously inquired of him what he had been eating.

"Everything!" said Ribsy enthusiastically. "Grass, nuts, bugs, birds, and ber-

ries! All of 'em taste good. I could eat both of you, easily," he added, glaring hungrily down upon Davy and the Goblin.

"Try that fellow first," said the Goblin, pointing to a large round insect that went flying by, humming like a top. Ribsy snapped at it and swallowed it, and the next instant disappeared with a tremendous explosion in a great cloud of smoke.

"What was that?" said Davy, in a terrified whisper.

"A Hum Bug," said the Goblin calmly. "When a cab-horse on a vacation talks about eating you, a Hum Bug is a pretty good thing to take the conceit out of him. They're loaded, you see, and they go booming along as innocently as you please, but if you touch 'em—why, 'there you aren't!' as the Hole-keeper says."

"The Hole-keeper isn't himself any more," said Davy mournfully.

"Not altogether himself, but somewhat," said a voice; and Davy, looking around, was astonished to find the Hole-keeper standing beside him. He was a most extraordinary-looking object, being nothing but Davy's parcel marked, "Confexionry," with arms and legs and a head to it. At the sight of him the Goblin fell flat on his back, and covered his face with his hands.

"I'm quite aware that my appearance is not prepossessing," said the Hole-keeper, with a scornful look at the Goblin. "In fact, I'm nothing but a quarter of a pound of *'plain,'* and the price isn't worth mentioning."

"But how did you ever come to be alive again, at all?" said Davy.

"Well," said the Hole-keeper, "the truth of the matter is that after you went away, the Cockalorum fell to reading the *Vacuum;* and if you'll believe it, there wasn't a word in it about my going back into the raw material."

"I *do* believe that," said Davy; but the Hole-keeper, without noticing the interruption, went on:

"*Then,* of course, I got up and came away. Meanwhile, the Cockalorum is filling himself with information."

"I don't think he'll find much in your book," said Davy, laughing.

"Ah! but just think of the lots and lots of things he *won't* find," exclaimed the Hole-keeper. "Everything he doesn't find in it is something worth knowing. By the way, your friend seems to be having some sort of a fit. Give him some dubbygrums," and with this, the Hole-keeper stalked pompously away.

"The smell of sugar always gives me the craw-craws," said the Goblin, in a stifled voice, rolling on the ground, and keeping his hands over his face. "Get me some water."

"I haven't anything to get it in," said Davy, helplessly.

"There's a buttercup behind you," groaned the Goblin, and Davy, turning, saw a buttercup growing on a stem almost as tall as he was himself. He picked it, and hurried away across the meadow to look for water, the buttercup, meanwhile, growing in his hand in a surprising manner, until it became a full-sized tea-cup, with a handle conveniently growing on one side. Davy, however, had become so accustomed to this sort of thing that he would not have been greatly surprised if a saucer had also made its appearance.

Presently he came upon a sparkling little spring, gently bubbling up in a marshy place with high sedgy grass growing about it, and being a very neat little boy, he took off his shoes and stockings and carefully picked his way over the oozy ground to the edge of the spring itself. He was just bending over to dip the cup into the spring, when the ground under his feet began trembling like jelly, and then, giving itself a convulsive shake, threw him head-foremost into the water.

For a moment Davy had a very curious sensation as though his head and his arms and his legs were all trying to get inside of his jacket, and then he came sputtering to the top of the water and scrambled ashore. To his astonishment he saw that the spring had spread itself out into a little lake, and that the sedge-grass had grown to an enormous height and was waving far above his head. Then he was startled by a tremendous roar of laughter, and looking around, he saw the Goblin, who was now apparently at least twenty feet high, standing beside the spring.

"Oh, my!" cried the Goblin, in an uncontrollable fit of merriment. "Another minute and you wouldn't have been bigger than a peanut!"

"What's the matter with me?" said Davy, not knowing what to make of it all.

"Matter?" cried the Goblin. "Why, you've been and gone and fallen into an Elastic Spring, that's all. If you'd got in at stretch tide, early in the morning, you'd have been a perfect giraffe, but you got in at shrink tide and—oh, my! oh, my!" and here he went off into another fit of laughter.

"I don't think it's anything to laugh at," cried Davy, with the tears starting to his eyes, "and I'm sure I don't know what I'm going to do."

"Oh! don't worry," said the Goblin, good-naturedly. "I'll take a dip myself, just to be companionable, and to-morrow morning we can get back to any size you like."

"I wish you'd take these in with you," said Davy, pointing to his shoes and stockings. "They're big enough now for Badorful."

"All right!" cried the Goblin. "Here we go;" and taking the shoes and stockings in his hand he plunged into the spring, and a moment afterward scrambled out exactly Davy's size.

"Now, that's what I call a nice, tidy size," said the Goblin complacently, while Davy was squeezing his feet into his wet shoes. "What do you say to a ride on a field-mouse?"

"That will be glorious!" said Davy.

"Well, there goes the sun," said the Goblin; "it will be moonlight presently," and as he spoke, the sun went down with a boom like a distant gun and left them in the dark. The next moment a beautiful moon rose above the trees and beamed down pleasantly upon them, and the Goblin, taking Davy by the hand, led him into the wood.

*   *   *   *   *

"Freckles," said the Goblin, "what time is it?"

They were now in the densest part of the wood, where the moon was shining brightly on a little pool with rushes growing about it, and the Goblin was speaking to a large toad.

"Forty croaks," said the Toad, in a husky whisper; and then, as a frog croaked in the pool, he added: "That makes it forty-one. The Snoopers have come in, and Thimbletoes is shaking in his boots." And with these words the Toad coughed, and then hopped heavily away.

"What does he mean?" whispered Davy.

"He means that the Fairies are here, and *that* means that we won't get our ride," said the Goblin, rather sulkily.

"And who is Thimbletoes?" said Davy.

"He's the Prime Minister," said the Goblin. "You see, if any one of the Snoopers finds out something the Queen didn't know before, out goes the Prime Minister, and the Snooper pops into his boots. Thimbletoes doesn't fancy that, you know, because the Prime Minister has all the honey he wants, by way of a salary. Now,

here's the mouse-stable, and don't you speak a word, mind!"

As the Goblin said this, they came upon a little thatched building, about the size of a baby-house, standing just beyond the pool; and the Goblin, cautiously pushing open the door, stole noiselessly in, with Davy following at his heels, trembling with excitement.

The little building was curiously lighted up by a vast number of fire-flies, hung from the ceiling by loops of cobweb; and Davy could see several spiders hurrying about among them and stirring them up when the light grew dim. The field-mice were stabled in little stalls on either side, each one with his tail neatly tied in a bow-knot to a ring at one side; and at the farther end of the stable was a buzzing throng of fairies, with their shining clothes and gauzy wings sparkling beautifully in the soft light. Just beyond them Davy saw the Queen sitting on a raised throne, with a little mullen-stalk for a scepter, and beside her was the Prime Minister, in a terrible state of agitation.

"Now, here's this Bandybug," the Prime Minister was saying. "What does *he* know about untying the knots in a cord of wood?"

"Nothing!" said the Queen, positively. "Absolutely nothing."

"And then," continued the Prime Minister, "the idea of his presuming to tell your Gossamer Majesty that he can hear the bark of the dogwood trees——"

"Bosh!" cried the Queen. "Paint him with raspberry jam and put him to bed in a bee-hive. That'll make him smart, at all events."

Here the Prime Minister began dancing about in an ecstasy, until the Queen knocked him over with the mullen-stalk, and shouted, "Silence! and plenty of it, too. Bring in Berrylegs."

Berrylegs, who proved to be a wiry little

fairy, with a silver coat and tight, cherry-colored trousers, was immediately brought in. His little wings fairly bristled with defiance, and his manner, as he stood before the Queen, was so impudent that Davy felt morally certain there was going to be a scene.

"May it please your Transparent Highness—" began Berrylegs.

"Skip all that!" interrupted the Queen, flourishing her mullen-stalk.

"Skip, yourself!" said Berrylegs, boldly, in reply. "Don't you suppose I know how to talk to a queen!"

The Queen turned very pale, and after a hurried consultation with the Prime Minister, said, faintly, "Have it your own way," and Berrylegs began again.

"May it please your Transparent Highness, I've found out how the needles get into the hay-stacks."

As Berrylegs said this, a terrible commotion arose at once among the Fairies. The Prime Minister cried out, "Oh, come, I say! That's not fair, you know," and the Queen became so agitated that she began taking great bites off the end of the mullen-stalk in a dazed sort of way; and Davy noticed that the Goblin, in his excitement, was trying to climb up on one of the mouse-stalls so as to get a better view of what was going on. At last the Queen, whose mouth was now quite filled with bits of the mullen-stalk, mumbled, "Get to the point."

"It ought to be a sharp one, being about needles," said the Prime Minister, attempting a joke with a feeble laugh, but no one paid the slightest attention to him; and Berrylegs, who was now positively swelling with importance, called out in a loud voice: "It comes from using sewing machines when they sow the hay-seed!"

The Prime Minister gave a shriek and fell flat on his face, and the Queen began jumping frantically up and down and beating about on all sides of her with the end of the mullen-stalk, when suddenly a large cat walked into the stable and the Fairies fled in all directions. There was no mistaking the cat, and Davy, forgetting entirely the Goblin's caution, exclaimed, "Why! it's Solomon!"

The next instant the lights disappeared, and Davy found himself in total darkness, with Solomon's eyes shining at him like two balls of fire. There was a confused sound of sobs and cries and the squeaking of mice, among which could be heard the Goblin's voice crying, "Davy! Davy!" in a reproachful way; then the eyes disappeared, and a moment afterward the stable was lifted off the ground and violently shaken.

"That's Solomon, trying to get at the mice," thought Davy. "I wish the old thing had stayed away!" he added aloud, and as he said this the little stable was broken all to bits, and he found himself sitting on the ground in the forest.

The moon had disappeared, and snow was falling rapidly, and the sound of distant chimes reminded Davy that it must be past midnight, and that Christmas-day had come. Solomon's eyes were shining in the darkness like a pair of coach-lamps, and as Davy sat looking at them, a ruddy light began to glow between them, and presently the figure of the Goblin appeared dressed in scarlet, as when he had first come. The reddish light was shining through his stomach again, as though the coals had been fanned into life once more, and as Davy gazed at him it grew brighter and stronger, and finally burst into a blaze. Then Solomon's eyes gradually took the form of great brass balls, and presently the figure of the long-lost Colonel came into view just above them, affectionately hugging his clock. He was gazing mournfully down upon the poor Goblin, who was now blazing like a dry chip, and as the light of the fire grew brighter and stronger, the trees about slowly took the shape of an old-fashioned fire-place with a high mantel-shelf above it, and then Davy found himself curled up in the big easy-chair, with his dear old grandmother bending over him, and saying, gently, "Davy! Davy! Come and have some dinner, my dear."

In fact, the Believing Voyage was ended.

THE OWL, THE PUSSY-CAT, AND THE LITTLE BOY

By J. G. Francis

THE Owl and the Pussy-Cat went to see
A Boy of diminutive size,
Who was full of contrition, remorse, and crust
From lemon and gooseberry pies.
They lifted him up, and they cast him down,
And rolled him over the floor,
And the Boy resolved, when they vanished away,
That he'd sleep after dinner no more.

UNDER COVER OF APOLOGIES

by Geoffrey Household

WHEN the draft of the naval pact was stolen from the archives of the Foreign Office in London, the American ambassador and the British officials despaired. They knew who had it—Cosmo Casals, the popular but unscrupulous first secretary of a foreign embassy—but they could not hope to get it back. Embassies may not be raided, and diplomats cannot be prosecuted.

In a Knightsbridge apartment two young men sat gloomily in front of an array of empty dishes, digesting their breakfast and reading their mail. They had every right to be gloomy, for the work of years had been undone by the daring coup of Mr. Casals. The owner of the apartment was Oscar Lund, an attaché of the American Embassy. All Lund's duties were obscure; nothing was expected of him except that he should have information on every subject when the ambassador wanted it. His guest was Lord Reginald Bathgate, a tall, hatchet-faced, monocled Englishman, who, so far as London society knew, did nothing at all for a living, and did it very gracefully. But on the continent of Europe various mysterious travelers knew him as Number 4X. He was one of the unsuspected chiefs of the British secret service.

"Casals is leaving for his own country today," said the American. "He'll carry a diplomatic mail bag, and the pact will be inside it. Can't you stage a hold-up, Bats?"

"I could, old chap," answered the Englishman, "but I daren't risk it. If Casals were a spy, I could do anything to him short of murder. If he were a criminal, I could set the police on him. But since he's a diplomat, his person is sacred."

"Oh, all right!" said Lund wearily, and went on reading his mail. He slit open a pale blue envelop and glanced through the enclosed letter.

"Just listen to this, Bats," he groaned, turning to his friend.

"Dear Mr. Lund: I *do* hate to trouble you again, but I know you will forgive me, as we are such *old* friends. My little Teddy is leaving London for his school in Switzerland, and I can't *bear* to think of him traveling alone. Would you send him in charge of one of your charming diplomatic friends, so that he doesn't get frightened and has no trouble with the customs? Please tell your friend to see that he has a glass of milk at eleven, and that he keeps his throat *well* covered up on the boat. . . ."

"And two pages more of the same," said Lund. "But that's nothing. I once had to forward her Pekingese to a dog show!"

"Who is this mother's darling?" asked Bats.

"Teddy van Ness. The first time he was over here he ran away and joined a Paris circus. Then his tutor lost him in Constantinople, and he turned up as the Wonder Boy Drummer in a German cabaret.

He knows Europe better than I do, and I'm supposed to nurse him."

"Send him with Casals!" snorted Lord Reginald.

"That's an idea!" the American exclaimed.

Bats screwed his monocle well home and stared at his friend.

"Are you serious?" he asked.

"Sure! Listen here! If young Teddy steals the bag, nobody can say he's one of your agents. He'll be taken for a spoiled, mischievous child playing at being a gangster. You people over here believe anything of our American boys."

"But can he keep his mouth shut?"

"Can he?" answered Lund. "That kid could keep his mouth shut if he had a hot potato in it. I'll call him over and you can judge for yourself."

Lund telephoned Teddy at his hotel, and the boy promised to be right over. Then the attaché telephoned Cosmo Casals.

"Mayfair 1756, please. Hello, is that you, Cosmo? Sorry to call you so early, old man. . . . I hear you're leaving us today. . . . Isn't that just too bad! What's a London season without our Cosmo? I wonder if you'll do me a favor? Will you take a fifteen-year-old pet of the embassy as far as Lausanne with you? . . . That's fine! He won't give you any trouble. Momma says keep his throat well covered—he's that kind of boy."

Bats, who was seldom deceived by appearances, liked Teddy at first sight. There was a suggestion of a thoroughbred greyhound about Theodore van Ness. When he was bored he looked a pampered pet; but when he was aroused his pale face became keen and remarkably intelligent, and the sleek young muscles tautened all over his lanky body. Deep down in his eyes was a wicked sense of humor—unless

Teddy was suspected of wrongdoing, when they were blue, innocent, and appealing.

"Teddy," said Lund, "we've a job for you. Promise me on your honor that you will keep to yourself what I'm to tell you."

"On my honor," replied Teddy.

"In the event of any nation declaring war on another," Lund explained, "the United States and Great Britain have agreed to pool their naval and air forces to prevent it. The pact hasn't been ratified by the Senate or by Parliament, but it will be if we can choose our moment to get it passed. Other countries are pretty sure that the unofficial agreement exists, but they daren't say so unless they have an authentic copy of it. Teddy, Cosmo Casals has such a copy. He will show it to his government and then to the newspapers; the whole world will ring with it prematurely, and it will never be signed.

"Now, then! Mr. Casals, at your mother's request, has consented to escort you as far as Lausanne, and to give you your glass of milk at eleven."

Teddy grinned broadly.

"Be the nastiest kind of spoiled child you can imagine. Watch him closely. Note who talks to him. And keep your eyes on his mail bag."

"Shall I grab it if I can?" asked Teddy.

"This is where I chip in," interrupted Lord Reginald. "Get the bag if you can, and bring it to Mr. Lund. But remember —there would be a first-class international row if it were known that we were behind you. So if you're caught, you must pretend you did it for a lark."

"And if I succeed?" asked Teddy. He had grown serious.

"If you succeed," answered Lund, "I shall have to disown you, and apologize for you, and probably the ambassador will send you home in disgrace."

"Gee!" Teddy gasped. "Then I get it in the neck both ways."

"You do," admitted Lord Reginald. "That's why there are very few men in the world brave enough to be secret agents."

"I don't know about brave," said Teddy, "but I do love excitement. When do I start?"

"This morning," answered Lund, putting his hands on Teddy's shoulders. "Our men will be near you, though they can't help you much. If anyone addresses you as Mr. Thwaite, show no particular interest, but listen to what he has to say."

Teddy spent a frantically busy hour at his hotel and then returned to Lund's apartment, where he was handed over to the care of Casals, an exquisite young diplomat, dark, slim, and beautifully dressed.

When the diplomat saw Teddy he wished to Heaven that he had not been so obliging. The boy looked sulky, he was bad-mannered, he had an indecent quantity of baggage. Although it was a warm spring day, the fur collar of his overcoat was turned up to his ears.

"Well, well, my little man! So you're going back to school!" remarked Casals, as soon as they were settled on the gorgeous cherry-colored cushions of the boat train, and roaring smoothly from London to Dover.

"Don't want to!" replied Teddy, and started to kick the mahogany paneling.

"I wouldn't do that, if I were you," said the diplomat firmly.

"Why wouldn't you?" asked Teddy, continuing to kick.

There was a strained silence for some minutes. Then Teddy, pointing rudely at the small white mail sack with the arms of Mr. Casals' country stamped on the outside, asked, "What's in that bag?"

"Just letters and reports," said Casals politely.

"Huh!" Teddy grunted. "If it's got money in it, you'd better be careful I don't steal it!"

Mr. Casals, sighing at this crude boast, called the attendant, and ordered lunch for them both.

"Soup, sir?" the attendant asked, turning to the sulky boy.

"No," said Teddy. "I want a big cream puff. Right away!"

"That isn't very good for you," suggested Mr. Casals. "Try a—"

"I want a cream puff!" Teddy repeated in a loud voice.

Mr. Casals glanced nervously at his grinning fellow passengers, and ordered one.

"Make it four," said Teddy to the attendant.

The attendant made it four. On top of them Teddy ate a whole lobster and a pound of strawberries. He then lay back in his corner, munching a candy bar. Casals lighted a dainty cigarette, and then looked at the boy with unconcealed disgust.

At Dover two blue-jerseyed porters seized their hand baggage and led them through the dungeon-like vestibules under the station and out upon the windy quay. While one of them escorted Casals to his stateroom, the other, who appeared to be nothing more than one of the regular porters, touched his cap to Teddy.

"Hope you have a smooth crossing, Mr. Thwaite," he said. "Stand in the corridor when your train leaves Calais."

The boat churned up the water, and stood out of the harbor for the distant gray hills of France. Teddy joined Casals in his stateroom. He made himself a nuisance by examining all the fittings of the tiny cabin, leaving the port open so that it banged, and losing the soap under Casals' chair.

"Will you please sit down!" ordered the diplomat, who by now was calculating how many more hours he would have to spend in the company of this beastly boy.

Teddy obediently sat down. The boat began to roll in the ceaseless swell of the Channel. The boy's face took on an injured expression. He was so quiet that Casals actually managed to read three pages of his book.

"Mr. Casals!" cried Teddy suddenly. "Oh, Mr. Casals!"

"What is it?"

"Mr. Casals, I think I'm going to be seasick!"

He clutched the unfortunate diplomat, and gave a heart-rending hiccup. Casals led him firmly to the side of the boat, but he was too late. Teddy had had the greatest difficulty in making himself seasick, and having succeeded, he wasn't going to waste his efforts.

Casals, cursing in four languages, mopped his exquisite trousers with an inadequate silk handkerchief and returned to his stateroom. Teddy chuckled to himself. Casals had actually left the bag unguarded while he rushed the boy to the open air. Teddy rightly guessed that by this time he had got so thoroughly on the diplomat's nerves that the man had forgotten everything except his hatred of him.

The desolate-looking town of Calais came racing up from the horizon, and soon the boat nosed alongside the jetty. Casals showed his diplomatic passport, and the two walked serenely through the customs, and on to the station platform. Gold-laced, bearded, and magnificent, the stationmaster led them to their reserved compartment on the Simplon-Orient Express. A narrow corridor ran along one side of the coach, and out of it opened luxurious little rooms. Casals dropped dejectedly into the corner nearest the corridor, with the precious bag on the seat beside him. Teddy sulked in the corner by the window. The famous express slid silently out of the station, and settled down to its seventy miles an hour.

Teddy pushed past Casals' legs and went out into the corridor. Two men, looking like solid English manufacturers, edged past him.

"I hear, Mr. Thwaite," said one, apparently speaking to the other, "that there's a slight obstacle on the line. The train will slow up in five minutes."

Teddy returned to the compartment. "Feeling better now!" he announced. "I guess I could eat another candy bar."

He pulled a half-melted bar from his pocket and started to eat it noisily. The trick worked. Casals got up and stood at the entrance to the compartment, his back to Teddy. The bag remained on the seat. Teddy banged the window down and thrust his head out. Casals glanced around, saw the boy's shoulders heaving, and looked away again, hoping fiercely that the revolting child would fall out. Anything to get rid of him!

As they passed outside the port of Boulogne, the brakes jarred on quietly. Teddy thrust his legs through the open window and balanced on the sill. The speed of the train dropped to ten miles an hour. He leaned back, grabbed the mail sack, and slid, feet foremost, to the track. The bag and his heavy coat broke the fall, and in an instant he was up and skidding down the embankment. At the bottom he shed his coat and sprinted across the open fields toward the gray cottages on the outskirts of Boulogne.

Teddy was no mean runner. He had done the 100 yards in 10 seconds, which was well for the two great countries whose plans depended on his legs. He took a low hedge in his stride, and dropped on one knee behind it to see what was happening. Casals was standing on the embankment, raving. Some of the train crew and passengers were pounding after the fugitive, strung out over the field like a pack of hounds.

"*Au voleur!*" they yelled. "Stop thief!"

Teddy sprang up and skimmed over the ground toward a narrow, cobbled street that seemed to promise dark corners and yards where he might hide. He was nearly in it when out shot a mob of honest citizens, headed by a blue-cloaked French policeman. Teddy swerved like a hare, but he was too late. The *flic* caught him by the collar.

"I arrest you in the name of the law!" he said.

He led Teddy down the street at a rapid walk, surrounded by the excited crowd.

Suddenly he stopped and looked the crowd over, twirling his glorious moustaches with his free hand.

"*Circulez!*" he ordered grandly. "*Circulez donc!*"

The crowd obediently dispersed, but followed at a distance. The policeman turned a corner, and with a catlike spring leaped into a tiny, dark cottage, dragging Teddy after him.

"That was a close shave, Mr. Thwaite!" he said in English.

"Gosh!" exclaimed Teddy. "Are you a Mr. Thwaite, too?"

"Exactly!" replied the policeman.

He hurled his cloak, uniform, and moustaches into a corner, and slipped on a loud tweed suit. In an instant he was transformed into a middle-class English tourist, spending a jolly week-end in Boulogne.

"If anyone catches us," he said, "say that you escaped from the police. I wish I could help you more, old boy. But

you've got to play a lone hand. They told you that, I suppose?"

"Sure!" answered Teddy, grinning. "I don't know there are such things as secret agents."

He dressed Teddy in the blue jersey and trousers of a French fishing boy, and tanned his face. The mail sack he dropped into a stout paper bag, and covered it with rolls of bread.

"Off No. 2 pier," he said, "is my motor launch, the *Baby Mine*. She's fast and seaworthy, in spite of her disgusting name. Steal her. Make Folkestone, not Dover, if you can. Your course is due west till the tide starts running down channel, then northwest. I'll have to make an awful row when I find she's gone, but I'll delay pursuit as long as I can."

The two shook hands with a single swift grip. Teddy left the cottage and strolled through the streets toward the port. He saw Casals standing outside the telegraph office, and shot hastily around a corner. Nobody took any interest in him. He might have been a boy from any of the brown-sailed fishing smacks that worked the coast from Ostend to Dieppe.

He got himself rowed out to the *Baby Mine* on the pretense of delivering stores. Standing with his back to the man in the dinghy, so that the movements of his hands were hidden, he started the motor. It roared into life, and before the boatman could recover from his surprise, Teddy had slipped the moorings and was tearing out to sea at a speed absolutely prohibited by the port of Boulogne.

He settled down at the wheel and relaxed. He had the gift of trusting to his luck when there was nothing else to trust to. The *Baby Mine* purred into the sunset at twenty knots an hour. The misty shores of England gradually took on definite shape, and a white cliff gave him a landmark. He found that he was drifting down channel, and altered his course to the northwest. The lights of Folkestone winked in the dusk and he aimed straight for the harbor.

" 'Eave to, and stop yer engines!" came a sharp command.

Teddy, gazing fixedly into the growing darkness, had not noticed the coast-guard cutter that foamed up on his port quarter. He disobeyed the order, trusting to his superior speed. Three times he was challenged; then a fountain of water deluged him as a one-pounder shot plumped into the sea a yard ahead of the *Baby Mine's* bows.

"The next un'll knock yer 'ead off," remarked a grieved voice through a megaphone. "I don't want ter 'ave ter do it."

Teddy promptly hove to, and the cutter came alongside.

"Aye!" said the captain. "This 'ere's the boat wot was pinched from Boulong 'arbor. Come aboard, young un!"

"But I'm Mr. Thwaite," protested Teddy firmly.

"I don't care if yer the bloomin' prince of Wales," replied the captain. "Come on quietly now!"

Teddy went aboard, and the cutter, taking the *Baby Mine* in tow, ran into Folkestone.

With a seaman on each side of him, he was marched along the jetty to the port offices, still clutching his paper bag, and deposited in a whitewashed and depressing cell. Teddy sat there dejectedly, hoping that his unknown friend in Boulogne had been able to wire Lord Reginald that he was on the way. It was maddening to think that all his work might be undone by the clumsy questioning of the police.

After a short wait he was escorted to the charge room, where a stern inspector looked him up and down disdainfully.

"Name?" asked the inspector.

"Theodore van Ness."

"Nationality?"

"United States citizen."

"Did you steal the launch *Baby Mine* from Boulogne Harbor?"

"I did," answered Teddy calmly.

The inspector snorted, and looked over a telegram lying on his desk. Then he pulled a bell at his side. A stout and helmeted police sergeant answered the ring.

"Sergeant Hawkins," ordered the inspector, "we have instructions from the Foreign Office to send this boy under arrest to No. 6 Clarendon Crescent, where an attaché of the American Embassy will hold him for inquiries. Take him there. Resist any attempt at rescue, and above all, see that his baggage is not disturbed. Where's your baggage?" he asked Teddy.

"Here," said Teddy, indicating the paper bag, and trying hard not to show his delight.

"Balmy!" exclaimed the inspector. "That's what they are, balmy! Still, it's no business of mine. Get a move on, Sergeant Hawkins! You'll just make the boat train if you run."

Sergeant Hawkins trotted leisurely to the station, with the dignified gait of an old cab-horse. He heaved his prisoner and himself into the baggage van just as the train was pulling out. Then he released Teddy, took off his helmet, and mopped his brow.

"Watcher been up to?" he asked sternly. "Been shootin' peas at Mussolini?"

"Yes, sergeant," replied Teddy with the utmost innocence.

The sergeant kept a disapproving silence for a while, but finally slapped his massive knee and winked at Teddy.

"You're a bit of orl right!" he said. "Ever play the game o' 'earts?"

Teddy had. The baggage master pulled out a pack of greasy cards, and the three sat down on the trunks to play.

" 'Alfpenny points?" asked Hawkins.

"Go on!" said the baggage master. "The kid's too young!"

"No, 'e ain't," answered the sergeant. "Not after bein' mixed up with all them dirty furriners, 'e ain't!"

Sergeant Hawkins was right. When the train rattled over the switches into Victoria Station, the pair of them had a profound respect for Teddy's game.

The sergeant led his prisoner to a taxi, and they drove out into the murky London night. A drizzling fog shrouded the great city. The street lamps were pale yellow globes dimly reflected in the soaking pavement. The taxi crawled toward Clarendon Crescent through a maze of wide, elegant squares and terraces, deserted at this hour.

A powerful Rolls Royce pulled up alongside them.

"Hand over your prisoner, sergeant," said a quiet voice with a slight foreign accent.

Sergeant Hawkins jumped. He was looking down the barrel of a revolver. A second was trained on Teddy, while a third man covered the taxi driver. The car stopped with a jerk.

"Nah then!" said Sergeant Hawkins calmly, reaching for his whistle. "Yer can't do this in London, yer know."

"No?" answered Casals' agent. "If you blow that whistle, sergeant, you're a dead man."

"Say, mister!" interrupted Teddy sulkily. "Here's your bag! I only took it for a joke."

He opened the door of the taxi, stepped onto the running board, and offered the bag to the man who had spoken. The secret agent grasped it eagerly. At the same instant Teddy jerked the bottom. The wet paper gave way, leaving the mail-sack in Teddy's hands. He hurled himself sideways under a shower of stale rolls, and ducked behind the back of the car. Two tongues of fire spat at him. A bullet ripped through his sleeve. Another cut a part through his hair. In a fraction of a second he was up and zigzagging through the fog—an impossible target. He heard Sergeant Hawkins blow his whistle, heard it answered at once from the next block. The Rolls Royce whizzed around a corner on two wheels and disappeared.

Teddy jumped the railings of one of the little gardens that line the residential terraces of London, and took cover in some shrubbery. His first impulse was to make a dash for Lund's apartment, but then decided that he should appear to be brought there against his will. The police were scattering through the adjoining street and gardens in search of him. He marked the burly figure of friendly Sergeant Hawkins, to whom he wished to give the honor of his recapture, dashed across the road in front of him, and tripped deliberately over the curb. The sergeant grabbed him in triumph.

"Well," he remarked, "that there was the queerest rescue I ever did see. 'Ang me if them furriners h'acted like yer friends!"

He waited for an explanation, but Teddy offered none, and allowed himself to be led in stony silence to No. 6 Clarendon Crescent, and handed over to Mr. Lund. The attaché looked so sternly at Teddy that Sergeant Hawkins felt positively sorry for the boy.

As soon as the sergeant had left, Lord Reginald, who had kept discreetly out of sight, appeared from the bedroom. Teddy was overwhelmed by his reception. The diplomats, apparently mad with joy, danced around him, cheering incoherently and slapping him on the back.

"Well done! Well done, my Thwaiteling!" yelled Bats. "Lord! I can't and I won't let this boy go without credit! You'll have to wait till the pact is signed, Teddy, but then I'm going to let this tale leak out —and leak where it will do you the most good!"

He ripped open the bag and removed a simple, typewritten document, each paragraph initialed in several hands.

"That's it!" he said, pocketing the document. "They'll miss it, but they can't say anything. Why, our efficient police even recovered the bag for them within eight hours!"

"And now your lordship had better shut up, and take itself down the backstairs," said Lund. "I'll call Casals' chief over, and deliver the bag with many apologies for our spoiled American children. Whatever made you do such a shocking thing, Van Ness?"

Teddy opened his big blue eyes and pretended to be on the verge of tears. "I guess I must have seen too many gangster films!" he whimpered.

Fritz the Master-Fiddler

by John Bennett

A LONG time ago, in fact several years before there was any such thing as time, there lived a sturdy miller and his wife in a cottage at the edge of a great black forest near the village of Weisnichtwo, in the southeast corner of the kingdom of Niemandweis, just this side of the other end of nowhere.

This worthy couple had one son, Fritz, a funny little tow-headed fellow with big blue eyes, rosy cheeks, and baggy little trousers that he could almost turn around in. He was a queer little chap, too; for when the other boys played along the dusty highway and narrow street with whoop and halloo, Fritz crept quietly away to the field or forest, where, among the kaiserblumen or the fern, he would sit alone for hours, singing baby-songs to the brook as it babbled out of the woods, and making quaint little tunes for the lambs to play to—tunes that sounded like the wind in the pines, the birds calling in the tree-tops, or the stream rippling down the rocks to the water-wheel at the mill.

"Father," said he one day, "when I grow up I will be a master-fiddler and make music on the fiddle."

"Stuff and nonsense!" said his father; but he bought him a little yellow fiddle at the next kermess, and let him play it all day long.

It was surprising how soon Fritz could draw melody out of that Swiss-pine box with his stubby bow! He made it fairly laugh and cry and sing and gurgle and whistle and hum, until the birds flew down from the tree-tops and hopped about him; and the lambs came and lay down at his feet; and mother-sheep rubbed their noses against his knees; and the marmots peeped from among the rocks; and the rabbits paused in the thick grass with listening ears; and the brown bees buzzed about his head. None of them were afraid, for Fritz seemed one of themselves.

But he grew up,—as healthy boys will do, who eat good meat, and sweet brown bread, and amber honey with creamy milk as rich as nectar,—and he fiddled better and better every day, until at last he said: "Father, I fiddle too well for Weisnichtwo. These dull villagers care only for the drone of the dudelsack and a bawling song with their muddy beer. I must go out into the world and seek my fortune."

"The little boys followed him down the street"

So he took his cap and his fiddle, was blessed by his father and kissed by his mother, waved a farewell to Weisnichtwo, and went out into the world.

At first he fiddled merrily as he went along, and thought to fiddle himself into a fortune soon. But no one stopped to listen; no one seemed to care whether he fiddled or not; and, no one offering to pay for his music, he might fairly have fiddled himself into the poorhouse if one angry goose-herd had not rated him soundly for scaring the geese with his "nonsensical noise." After that Fritz indignantly tucked his unappreciated fiddle under his arm and trudged on silent and discouraged.

"Oh, dear!" he sighed wearily, "if they won't let me fiddle, how can I ever find my fortune? I wonder where it can be."

So he began to ask the passers-by, "Good sir,"—or "madam," as the case might be,—"have you seen my fortune?"

Some laughed at him. Some told him to mind his business. Others were too busy hunting their own fortunes to pay him any attention whatever. And at last, in one rough village, they called him a silly dunder-head, and pelted him with mud and stones until he took to his heels and ran off. All out of breath as he turned into the cross-road, he tripped over a stone and fell flat upon his fiddle with a dreadful crunch. And when he picked it up out of the dust it was spoiled beyond all hope of repair, with one peg bent up, and one peg down, and one this way, and the other that, while the neck was twisted hopelessly awry.

"Oh, my fiddle, my little fiddle, my dear little fiddle, it is ruined!" he sobbed; and, clasping the spoiled instrument to his breast, he limped ruefully on, hardly caring where he went or what became of him, and only knowing that his beloved fiddle would never make sweet music again.

Just at nightfall he came to the city of the king, and wandered through the gloomy streets heedless of them all.

"Hullo, Master-Fiddler!" called some revelers beside a cozy inn. "Come fiddle for us, and we will pay you well!"

"I do not care to play—pay or no pay," said Fritz bitterly, as he clutched his ruined fiddle to his bosom and passed on.

"What?" cried the amazed revelers, "a fiddler who will not fiddle for pay!" And the little boys took up the shout, and followed him down the street, crying, "Look, here is a fiddler who will not fiddle for pay!" And all the people stopped to see; and many came out of their houses, hearing the cry; and soon the narrow way was so crowded that the king's carriage could not pass, and a footman came to learn the cause of the blockade.

"It is a fiddler who will not fiddle for pay!" yelled the gamins in the gutter.

"Indeed?" exclaimed the king. "Then he must surely be a great fiddler! Tell him he may come to my palace and play."

But Fritz thought only of his poor, twisted fiddle, and replied, "I do not care to play, king or no king!"

"Dear me!" cried his Majesty, surprised; "this must be a very fine fiddler, indeed, who does not fairly jump at the chance to play before a king. I surely must hear him!"

So he sent his coach and a regiment of grenadiers to bring Fritz to the palace, or to take him to prison if he would not play —for he gave him his choice, being a magnanimous king.

Then Fritz was at his wit's end. His clothes were torn, his fiddle was spoiled,— but there was no way to escape; so in sheer despair he faced the music like a man. "If the king *will* hear me play, he shall!" said he grimly, as he climbed into the coach and was whirled to the palace.

"So," said the king, "you are here, are you?"

"Yes," replied Fritz, as he looked about; "I believe I am."

"Then call the court," cried the king; "we will have some first-class A No. 1 music! But where are your notes?"

"This fiddle does not play by note," faltered Fritz; which was very true—it certainly did not!

"Ah," whispered the king to the vice-chancellor, "what did I tell you? This fellow is a genius—he does not fiddle by note."

"Yes," whispered the vice-chancellor, "he must indeed be a genius—just see how very shabby he is!"

But, "Oh, dear!" groaned Fritz to him-self, "it is all up with me!" And then, with his heart clear up in his throat, though outwardly smiling, he hastily filled his ears with cotton and began to play.

Such a shrieking, such a squeaking, such a wild, ear-piercing scream as came out of that crooked fiddle! Ugh-h-h-h!

Why, even the sparrows under the palace eaves jumped out of their nests, flew over the fence, and never came back again; the king's pet cat crawled under the cellar door and yowled with fear; while, for a moment, paralyzed with amazement, the courtiers sat motionless and dumb!

They had never heard any such music as that before. It set their teeth on edge, made their flesh creep, and raised goose-flesh in the very marrow of their shivering bones! But there stood Fritz, placidly playing away as if he were producing the sweetest sounds in the world. And had not the king himself said that this fiddler was a genius? Certainly he had! And since the king had said it, it must be so. Consequently, every man Jack of them was afraid to say he did not like it. And no one dared to admit that he saw nothing lovely in it, for fear he would appear more stupid than his neighbor. So they all clasped their hands, and, turning to each other, cried in one ecstatic voice, "Oh, this must be a new school of music—it must be a new school! Isn't it overpowering— isn't it forceful—isn't it thrilling—isn't **it** just too utterly *ne-plus-ultra* for any-thing!"

"Ah," said one, "it isn't everybody who can have taste for such music!"

"No, indeed," answered another; "one should know how to listen!"

And then they all listened with rapt at-tention and clasped hands, while they fairly squirmed, and longed for the roof to fly off, the walls to fall in, the floor to blow up, or something—or anything, oh, anything!—just to stop that horrible noise!

Now it happened that, seven years before, the Crown Princess Hilda's favorite wax doll had fallen head first into the royal soup-tureen one day at dinner; and the soup, being hot, had melted off her nose. Whereat, after one wild burst of childish grief, the princess had been seized with profound grief, and had gone into deep mourning for her disfigured darling, refusing to be comforted, and had never smiled again. The court physician had given her potions and powders until she was pale as a ghost. She had traveled to all of the fashionable watering-places for change of air until she was worn to a shadow. Fabulous rewards had been offered for anything to break her sorrow, but in vain. Her sorrow remained unbroken.

There, attended by a favorite maiden, and with a trusty grenadier within call, upon a raised dais at the end of the great hall, a fragile little waxen princess in gloomy black, brown-haired and hazel-eyed, she sat so deeply wrapped in melancholy that nothing seemed to move her.

But at the first shriek of Fritz's crooked fiddle she jumped with surprise and looked up with a sudden sparkle in her heavy eyes. And as she listened to the squeaking, screaming, shrieking squeal, a gleam lit up her face, she cast one quick look around the vast audience all in its rapt attention, and falling back into her chair broke into a peal of uncontrollable laughter.

"Oh, my!—oh, my!—oh, my!" she cried, holding her sides; "it sounds like—a little pig under—a—gate!" and she laughed until the tears ran down her face.

Oh, the scene of wild excitement that ensued! The king tossed his crown up to the ceiling, the lord high chamberlain fell over two small pages trying to dance a jig,

the whole court rolled off their chairs in delighted surprise, and the court physician had three conniption fits in rapid succession behind the Japanese screen—for the melancholy spell was broken, the princess was cured, and his high-salaried situation was at an end!

Then the king fell upon Fritz's neck and kissed him, to his great embarrassment; and the courtiers, delighted that the fiddling had stopped, cheered until they were hoarse, crying, "Long live Fritz, the Master-Fiddler!" And the populace outside, hearing the shout, took up the cry until they were twice as hoarse: "Long live Fritz, the Master-Fiddler!" although they had not the slightest idea what it was all about—which made no difference at all with the populace.

"And now, Sir Master-Fiddler," exclaimed the king, when the hullabaloo had stopped; "since you have cured the princess, of course you will marry her."

"Shall I?" stammered Fritz, blushing like a girl. "Why?"

"Because that is the way I am going to have this story end," said the king, firmly. "And I am not going to have it spoiled by any nonsense!"

"Well," said Fritz, thoughtfully, rubbing his chin; "if I must, I suppose I must —but," he continued uneasily, "I would like to ask the princess one thing before the wedding takes place."

"What is that?" asked the princess, smiling up into his face.

"Will—will—will," he stammered bashfully—"will you marry me?"

"Yes," replied she, shyly dropping her dark eyelashes, and laying her little hand confidingly upon his broad shoulder; "but—"

"But what?" cried Fritz anxiously.

"You must never—"

"What?" gasped Fritz, turning pale with apprehension.

"Play that horrible fiddle around the house!"

"Oh!" ejaculated Fritz, with a smile of relief that spoke volumes, as he removed the cotton from his ears; "I promise you I never will."

And he never did.

"And all went merry as a marriage-bell"

ONAWANDAH

FOURTH SPINNING WHEEL STORY

by Louisa M. Alcott

Long ago, when hostile Indians haunted the great forests, and every settlement had its fort for the protection of the inhabitants, in one of the towns on the Connecticut River lived Parson Bain and his little son and daughter. The wife and mother was dead; but an old servant took care of them, and did her best to make Reuben and Eunice good children. Her direst threat, when they were naughty, was, "The Indians will come and fetch you, if you don't behave." So they grew up in great fear of the red men. Even the friendly Indians, who sometimes came for food or powder, were regarded with suspicion by the people. No man went to work without his gun near by. On Sundays, when they trudged to the rude meeting house, all carried the trusty rifle on the shoulder, and while the pastor preached, a sentinel mounted guard at the door, to give warning if canoes came down the river or a dark face peered from the wood.

One autumn night, when the first heavy rains were falling and a cold wind whistled through the valley, a knock came at the minister's door and, opening it, he found an Indian boy, ragged, hungry, and footsore, who begged for food and shelter. In his broken way, he told how he had fallen ill and been left to die by enemies who had taken him from his own people, months before; how he had wandered for days

till almost sinking; and that he had come now to ask for help, led by the hospitable light in the parsonage window.

"Send him away, Master, or harm will come of it. He is a spy, and we shall all be scalped by the murdering Injuns who are waiting in the wood," said old Becky, harshly; while little Eunice hid in the old servant's ample skirts, and twelve-year-old Reuben laid his hand on his cross-bow, ready to defend his sister if need be.

But the good man drew the poor lad in, saying, with his friendly smile: "Shall not a Christian be as hospitable as a godless savage? Come in, child, and be fed; you sorely need rest and shelter."

Leaving his face to express the gratitude he had no words to tell, the boy sat by the comfortable fire and ate like a famished wolf, while Becky muttered her forebodings and the children eyed the dark youth at a safe distance. Something in his pinched face, wounded foot, and eyes full of dumb pain and patience, touched the little girl's tender heart, and, yielding to a pitiful impulse, she brought her own basin of new milk and, setting it beside the stranger, ran to hide behind her father, suddenly remembering that this was one of the dreaded Indians.

"That was well done, little daughter. Thou shalt love thine enemies, and share thy bread with the needy. See, he is smiling; that pleased him, and he wishes us to be his friends."

But Eunice ventured no more that night, and quaked in her little bed at the thought of the strange boy sleeping on a blanket before the fire below. Reuben hid his fears better, and resolved to watch while others slept; but was off as soon as his curly head touched the pillow, and dreamed of tomahawks and war-whoops till morning.

Next day, neighbors came to see the waif, and one and all advised sending him away as soon as possible, since he was doubtless a spy, as Becky said, and would bring trouble of some sort.

"When he is well, he may go whithersoever he will; but while he is too lame to walk, weak with hunger, and worn out with weariness, I will harbor him. He can not feign suffering and starvation like this. I shall do my duty, and leave the consequences to the Lord," answered the parson, with such pious firmness that the neighbors said no more.

But they kept a close watch upon Onawandah, when he went among them, silent and submissive, but with the proud air of a captive prince, and sometimes a fierce flash in his black eyes when the other lads taunted him with his red skin. He was very lame for weeks, and could only sit in the sun, weaving pretty baskets for Eunice, and shaping bows and arrows for Reuben. The children were soon his friends, for with them he was always gentle, trying in his soft language and expressive gestures to show his good will and gratitude; for they defended him against their ruder playmates, and, following their father's example, trusted and cherished the homeless youth.

When he was able to walk, he taught the boy to shoot and trap the wild creatures of the wood, to find fish where others failed, and to guide himself in the wilderness by star and sun, wind and

water. To Eunice he brought little offerings of bark and feathers; taught her to make moccasins of skin, belts of shells, or pouches gay with porcupine quills and colored grass. He would not work for old Becky—who plainly showed her distrust—saying: "A brave does not grind corn and bring wood; that is squaw's work. Onawandah will hunt and fish and fight for you, but no more." And even the request of the parson could not win obedience in this, though the boy would have died for the good man.

"We cannot tame an eagle as we can a barn-yard fowl. Let him remember only kindness of us, and so we turn a foe into a friend," said Parson Bain, stroking the sleek, dark head, that always bowed before him, with a docile reverence shown to no other living creature.

Winter came, and the settlers fared hardly through the long months, when the drifts rose to the eaves of their low cabins, and the stores, carefully harvested, failed to supply even their simple wants. But the minister's family never lacked wild meat, for Onawandah proved himself a better hunter than any man in the town, and the boy of sixteen led the way on his snow-shoes when they went to track a bear to its den, chase the deer for miles, or shoot the wolves that howled about their homes in the winter nights.

But he never joined in their games, and sat apart when the young folk made merry, as if he scorned such childish pastimes and longed to be a man in all things. Why he stayed when he was well again, no one could tell, unless he waited for spring to make his way to his own people. But Reuben and Eunice rejoiced to keep him; for while he taught them many things, he was their pupil also, learning English rapidly, and proving himself a very affectionate and devoted friend and servant, in his own quiet way.

"Be of good cheer, little daughter; I shall be gone but three days, and our brave Onawandah will guard you well," said the parson, one April morning, as he mounted his horse to visit a distant settlement, where the bitter winter had brought sickness and death to more than one household.

The boy showed his white teeth in a bright smile as he stood beside the children, while Becky croaked, with a shake of the head:

"I hope you mayn't find you've warmed a viper in your bosom, Master."

Two days later, it seemed as if Becky was a true prophet, and that the confiding minister *had* been terribly deceived; for Onawandah went away to hunt, and, that night, the awful war-whoop woke the sleeping villagers to find their houses burning, while the hidden Indians shot at them by the light of the fires kindled by dusky scouts. In terror and confusion the whites flew to the fort; and, while the men fought bravely, the women held blankets to catch arrows and bullets, or bound up the hurts of their defenders.

It was all over by daylight, and the red men sped away up the river, with several prisoners, and such booty as they could plunder from the deserted houses. Not till all fear of a return of their enemies was over, did the poor people venture to leave the fort and seek their ruined homes. Then it was discovered that Becky and the parson's children were gone, and great was the bewailing, for the good man was much beloved by all his flock.

Suddenly the smothered voice of Becky was heard by a party of visitors, calling dolefully:

"I am here, betwixt the beds. Pull me out, neighbors, for I am half dead with fright and smothering."

The old woman was quickly extricated from her hiding-place, and with much energy declared that she had seen Onawandah, disguised with war-paint, among the Indians, and that he had torn away the children from her arms before she could fly from the house.

"He chose his time well, when they were defenseless, dear lambs! Spite of all my warnings, Master trusted him, and this is the thanks we get. Oh, my poor Master! How can I tell him this heavy news?"

There was no need to tell it; for, as Becky sat moaning and beating her breast on the fireless hearth, and the sympathizing neighbors stood about her, the sound of a horse's hoofs was heard, and the parson came down the hilly road like one riding for his life. He had seen the smoke afar off, guessed the sad truth, and hurried on, to find his home in ruins and to learn by his first glance at the faces around him that his children were gone.

When he had heard all there was to tell, he sat down upon his door-stone with his head in his hands, praying for strength to bear a grief too deep for words. The wounded and weary men tried to comfort him with hope, and the women wept with him as they hugged their own babies closer to the hearts that ached for the lost children. Suddenly a stir went through the mournful group, as Onawandah came from the wood with a young deer upon his shoulders, and amazement in his face as he saw the desolation before him. Dropping his burden, he stood an instant looking with eyes that kindled fiercely; then he came bounding toward them, undaunted by the hatred, suspicion, and surprise plainly written on the countenances before him. He missed his playmates, and asked but one question:

"The boy? the little squaw?—where gone?"

His answer was a rough one, for the men seized him and poured forth the tale, heaping reproaches upon him for such treachery and ingratitude. He bore it all in proud silence till they pointed to the poor father whose dumb sorrow was more eloquent than all their wrath. Onawandah looked at him, and the fire died out of his eyes as if quenched by the tears he would not shed. Shaking off the hands that held him, he went to his good friend, saying with passionate earnestness:

"Onawandah is *not* traitor! Onawandah remembers. Onawandah grateful! You believe?"

The poor parson looked up at him, and could not doubt his truth; for genuine love and sorrow ennobled the dark face, and he had never known the boy to lie.

"I believe and trust you still, but others will not. Go, you are no longer safe here, and I have no home to offer you," said the parson, sadly, feeling that he cared for none, unless his children were restored to him.

"Onawandah has no fear. He goes; but he comes again to bring the boy, the little squaw."

Few words, but they were so solemnly spoken that the most unbelieving were impressed; for the youth laid one hand on the gray head bowed before him, and lifted the other toward heaven, as if calling the Great Spirit to hear his vow.

A relenting murmur went through the crowd, but the boy paid no heed, as he turned away, and with no arms but his hunting knife and bow, no food but such as he could find, no guide but the sun by day, the stars by night, plunged into the pathless forest and was gone.

Then the people drew a long breath, and muttered to one another:

"He will never do it, yet he is a brave lad for his years."

"Only a shift to get off with a whole skin, I warrant you. These varlets are as cunning as foxes," added Becky, sourly.

The parson alone believed and hoped, though weeks and months went by, and his children did not come.

Meantime, Reuben and Eunice were far away in an Indian camp, resting as best they could, after the long journey that followed that dreadful night. Their captors were not cruel to them, for Reuben was a stout fellow and, thanks, to Onawandah, could hold his own with the boys who would have tormented him if he had been feeble or cowardly. Eunice also was a hardy creature for her years, and when her first fright and fatigue were over, made herself useful in many ways among the squaws, who did not let the pretty child suffer greatly; though she was neglected, because they knew no better.

Life in a wigwam was not a life of ease, and fortunately the children were accustomed to simple habits and the hardships that all endured in those early times. But they mourned for home till their young faces were pathetic with the longing, and their pillows of dry leaves were often wet with tears in the night. Their clothes grew ragged, their hair unkempt, their faces tanned by sun and wind. Scanty food and exposure to all weathers tried the strength of their bodies, and uncertainty as to their fate saddened their spirits; yet they bore up bravely, and said their prayers faithfully, feeling sure that God would bring them home to father in His own good time.

One day, when Reuben was snaring birds in the wood,—for the Indians had no fear of such young children venturing to escape,—he heard the cry of a quail, and followed it deeper and deeper into the forest, till it ceased, and, with a sudden rustle, Onawandah rose up from the brakes, his finger on his lips to prevent any exclamation that might betray him to other ears and eyes.

"I come for you and little Laraka,"—
(the name he gave Eunice, meaning "Wild
Rose.") "I take you home. Not know me
yet. Go and wait."

He spoke low and fast; but the joy in his
face told how glad he was to find the boy
after his long search, and Reuben clung
to him, trying not to disgrace himself by
crying like a girl, in his surprise and delight.

Lying hidden in the tall brakes they
talked in whispers, while one told of the
capture, and the other of a plan of escape;
for, though a friendly tribe, these Indians
were not Onawandah's people, and they
must not suspect that he knew the children, else they might be separated at once.

"Little squaw betray me. You watch
her. Tell her not to cry out, not speak me
any time. When I say come, we go,—
fast,—in the night. Not ready yet."

These were the orders Reuben received,
and, when he could compose himself, he
went back to the wigwams, leaving his
friend in the wood, while he told the good
news to Eunice, and prepared her for the
part she must play.

Fear had taught her self-control, and
the poor child stood the test well, working off her relief and rapture by pounding corn in the stone mortar till her little
hands were blistered, and her arms ached
for hours afterward.

Not till the next day did Onawandah
make his appearance, and then he came
limping into the village, weary, lame, and
half starved after his long wandering in
the wilderness. He was kindly welcomed,
and his story believed, for he told only
the first part, and said nothing of his life
among the white men. He hardly glanced
at the children when they were pointed
out to him by their captors, and scowled
at poor Eunice, who forgot her part in
her joy, and smiled as she met the dark
eyes that till now had always looked

kindly at her. A touch from Reuben
warned her, and she was glad to hide her
confusion by shaking her long hair over
her face, as if afraid of the stranger.

Onawandah took no further notice of
them, but seemed to be very lame with
the old wound in his foot, which prevented his being obliged to hunt with the
men. He was resting and slowly gathering
strength for the hard task he had set himself, while he waited for a safe time to
save the children. They understood, but
the suspense proved too much for little
Eunice, and she pined with impatience
to be gone. She lost appetite and color,
and cast such appealing glances at Onawandah that he could not seem quite indifferent, and gave her a soft word now
and then, or did such acts of kindness as he
could perform unsuspected. When she lay
awake at night thinking of home, a cricket
would chirp outside the wigwam, and a
hand slip in a leaf full of berries, or a
bark-cup of fresh water for the feverish
little mouth. Sometimes it was only a
caress or a whisper of encouragement, that
reassured the childish heart, and sent her
to sleep with a comfortable sense of love
and protection, like a sheltering wing over
a motherless bird.

Reuben stood it better, and entered
heartily into the excitement of the plot,
for he had grown tall and strong in
these trying months, and felt that he must
prove himself a man to sustain and defend his sister. Quietly he put away each
day a bit of dried meat, a handful of
parched corn, or a well-sharpened arrow-
head, as provision for the journey; while
Onawandah seemed to be amusing himself with making moccasins and a little
vest of deerskin for an Indian child about
the age of Eunice.

At last, in the early autumn, all the
men went off on the war-path, leaving
only boys and women behind. Then Ona-

wandah's eyes began to kindle, and Reuben's heart to beat fast, for both felt that their time for escape had come.

All was ready, and one moonless night the signal was given. A cricket chirped shrilly outside the tent where the children slept with one old squaw. A strong hand cut the skin beside their bed of fir boughs, and two trembling creatures crept out to follow the tall shadow that flitted noiselessly before them into the darkness of the wood. Not a broken twig, a careless step, or a whispered word betrayed them, and they vanished as swiftly and silently as hunted deer flying for their lives.

Till dawn they hurried on, Onawandah carrying Eunice, whose strength soon failed, and Reuben manfully shouldering the hatchet and the pouch of food. At sunrise they hid in a thicket by a spring and rested, while waiting for the friendly night to come again. Then they pushed on, and fear gave wings to their feet, so that by another morning they were far enough away to venture to travel more slowly and sleep at night.

If the children had learned to love and trust the Indian boy in happier times, they adored him now, and came to regard him as an earthly Providence, so faithful, brave, and tender was he; so forgetful of himself, so bent on saving them. He never seemed to sleep, ate the poorest morsels, or went without any food when provisions failed; let no danger daunt him, no hardship wring complaint from him; but went on through the wild forest, led by guides invisible to them, till they began to hope that home was near.

Twice he saved their lives. Once, when he went in search of food, leaving Reuben to guard his sister, the children, being very hungry, ignorantly ate some poisonous berries which looked like wild cherries, and were deliciously sweet. The boy generously gave most of them to Eunice, and soon was terror-stricken to see her grow pale and cold and deathly ill. Not knowing what to do, he could only rub her hands and call wildly for Onawandah.

The name echoed through the silent wood, and, though far away, the keen ear of the Indian heard it, his fleet feet brought him back in time, and his knowledge of wild roots and herbs made it possible to save the child when no other help was at hand.

"Make fire. Keep warm. I soon come," he said, after hearing the story and examining Eunice, who could only lift her eyes to him, full of childish confidence and patience.

Then he was off again, scouring the woods like a hound on the scent, searching everywhere for the precious little herb that would counteract the poison. Anyone watching him would have thought him crazy as he rushed hither and thither, tearing up the leaves, creeping on his hands and knees that it might not escape him, and when he found it, springing up with a cry that startled the birds, and carried hope to poor Reuben, who was trying to forget his own pain in his anxiety for Eunice, whom he thought dying.

"Eat, eat, while I make drink. All safe now," cried Onawandah, as he came leaping toward them with his hands full of green leaves, and his dark face shining with joy.

The boy was soon relieved, but for hours they hung over the girl, who suffered sadly, till she grew unconscious and lay as if dead. Reuben's courage failed then, and he cried bitterly, thinking how hard it would be to leave the dear little creature under the pines and go home alone to father. Even Onawandah lost hope for a while, and sat like a bronze statue of despair, with his eyes fixed on his Wild Rose, who seemed fading away too soon.

Suddenly he rose, stretched his arms to the west, where the sun was setting splendidly, and in his own musical language prayed to the Great Spirit. The Christian boy fell upon his knees, feeling that the only help was in the Father Who saw and heard them even in the wilderness. Both were comforted, and when they turned to Eunice there was a faint tinge of color on the pale cheeks, as if the evening red kissed her, the look of pain was gone, and she slept quietly without the moans that had made their hearts ache before.

"He hears! He hears!" cried Onawandah, and for the first time Reuben saw tears in his keen eyes, as the Indian boy turned his face to the sky full of a gratitude that no words were sweet enough to tell.

All night, Eunice lay peacefully sleeping, and the moon lighted Onawandah's lonely watch, for the boy Reuben was worn out with suspense, and slept beside his sister.

In the morning she was safe, and great was the rejoicing; but for two days the little invalid was not allowed to continue the journey, much as they longed to hurry on. It was a pretty sight, the bed of hemlock boughs spread under a green tent of woven branches, and on the pillow of moss the pale child watching the flicker of sunshine through the leaves, listening to the babble of a brook close by or sleeping tranquilly, lulled by the murmur of the pines. Patient, loving, and grateful, it was a pleasure to serve her, and both the lads were faithful nurses. Onawandah cooked birds for her to eat, and made a pleasant drink of the wild raspberry leaves to quench her thirst. Reuben snared rabbits, that she might have nourishing food, and longed to shoot a deer for provision, that she might not suffer hunger again on their journey. This boyish desire led him deeper in the wood than it was wise for him to go

alone, for it was near night-fall, and wild creatures haunted the forest in those days. The fire, which Onawandah kept constantly burning, guarded their little camp where Eunice lay; but Reuben, with no weapon but his bow and hunting knife, was beyond this protection when he at last gave up his vain hunt and turned homeward. Suddenly, the sound of stealthy steps startled him, but he could see nothing through the dusk at first, and hurried on, fearing that some treacherous Indian was following him. Then he remembered his sister, and resolved not to betray her resting-place if he could help it, for he had learned courage of Onawandah, and longed to be as brave and generous as his dusky hero.

So he paused to watch and wait, and soon saw the gleam of two fiery eyes, not behind, but above him, in a tree. Then he knew that it was an "Indian devil," as they called a species of fierce wild-cat that lurked in the thickets and sprang on its prey like a small tiger.

"If I could only kill it alone, how proud Onawandah would be of me," thought Reuben, burning for the good opinion of his friend.

It would have been wiser to hurry on and give the beast no time to spring; but the boy was overbold, and, fitting an arrow to the string, aimed at the bright eye-ball and let fly. A sharp snarl showed that some harm was done, and, rather daunted by the savage sound, Reuben raced away, meaning to come back next day for the prize he hoped he had secured.

But soon he heard the creature bounding after him, and he uttered one ringing shout for help, feeling too late that he had been foolhardy. Fortunately he was nearer camp than he thought. Onawandah heard him and was there in time to receive the wild-cat, as, mad with the pain of the wound, it sprang at Reuben. There was no time for words, and the boy could only watch in breathless interest and anxiety the fight which went on between the brute and the Indian.

It was sharp but short, for Onawandah had his knife, and as soon as he could get the snarling, struggling beast down, he killed it with a skillful stroke. But not before it had torn and bitten him more dangerously than he knew; for the dusk hid the wounds, and excitement kept him from feeling them at first. Reuben thanked him heartily, and accepted his few words of warning with grateful docility; then both hurried back to Eunice, who till next day knew nothing of her brother's danger.

Onawandah made light of his scratches, as he called them, got their supper, and sent Reuben early to bed, for tomorrow they were to start again.

Excited by his adventure, the boy slept lightly, and waking in the night saw by the flicker of the fire Onawandah binding up a deep wound in his breast with wet moss and his own belt. A stifled groan betrayed how much he suffered; but when Reuben went to him, he would accept no help, said it was nothing, and sent him back to bed, preferring to endure the pain in stern silence, with true Indian pride and courage.

Next morning, they set out and pushed on as fast as Eunice's strength allowed. But it was evident that Onawandah suffered much, though he would not rest, forbade the children to speak of his wounds, and pressed on with feverish haste, as if he feared that his strength might not hold out. Reuben watched him anxiously, for there was a look in his face that troubled the boy and filled him with alarm, as well as with remorse and love. Eunice would not let him carry her as before, but trudged bravely behind him,

though her feet ached and her breath often failed as she tried to keep up; and both children did all they could to comfort and sustain their friend, who seemed glad to give his life for them.

In three days they reached the river, and, as if Heaven helped them in their greatest need, found a canoe, left by some hunter, near the shore. In they sprang, and let the swift current bear them along, Eunice kneeling in the bow like a little figure-head of Hope, Reuben steering with his paddle, and Onawandah sitting with arms tightly folded over his breast, as if to control the sharp anguish of the neglected wound. He knew that it was past help now, and only cared to see the children safe; then, worn out but happy, he was proud to die, having paid his debt to the good parson, and proved that he was not a liar nor a traitor.

Hour after hour they floated down the great river, looking eagerly for signs of home, and when at last they entered the familiar valley, while the little girl cried for joy, and the boy paddled as he had never done before, Onawandah sat erect with his haggard eyes fixed on the dim distance, and sang his death-song in a clear, strong voice—though every breath was pain,—bent on dying like a brave, without complaint or fear.

At last they saw the smoke from the cabins on the hill-side and, hastily mooring the canoe, all sprang out, eager to be at home after their long and perilous wandering. But as his foot touched the land, Onawandah felt that he could do no more, and stretching his arms toward the parsonage, the windows of which glimmered as hospitably as they had done when he first saw them, he said, with a pathetic sort of triumph in his broken voice: "Go. I cannot.—Tell the good father, Onawandah not lie, not forget. He keep his promise."

Then he dropped upon the grass and lay as if dead, while Reuben, bidding Eunice keep watch, ran as fast as his tired legs could carry him to tell the tale and bring help.

The little girl did her part tenderly, carrying water in her hands to wet the white lips, tearing up her ragged skirt to lay fresh bandages on the wound that had been bleeding the brave boy's life away, and, sitting by him, gathered his head into her arms, begging him to wait till father came.

But poor Onawandah had waited too long; now he could only look up into the dear, loving, little face bent over him, and whisper wistfully: "Wild Rose will remember Onawandah?" as the light went out of his eyes, and his last breath was a smile for her.

When the parson and his people came hurrying up full of wonder, joy, and good will, they found Eunice weeping bitterly, and the Indian boy lying like a young warrior smiling at death.

"Ah, my neighbors, the savage has taught us a lesson we never can forget. Let us imitate his virtues, and do honor to his memory," said the pastor, as he held his little daughter close and looked down at the pathetic figure at his feet, whose silence was more eloquent than any words.

All felt it, and even old Becky had a remorseful sigh for the boy who had kept his word so well and given back her darlings safe.

They buried him where he lay; and for years the lonely mound under the great oak was kept green by loving hands. Wild roses bloomed there, and the murmur of the Long River of Pines was a fit lullaby for faithful Onawandah.

THE FLOATING PRINCE

by Frank R. Stockton

THERE was once an orphan prince, named Nassime, who had been carefully educated to take his place upon the throne of his native country. Everything that a king ought to know had been taught him, and he was considered, by the best judges, to be in every way qualified to wear a crown and to wield a scepter.

But when he became of age, and was just about to take his place upon the throne, a relative, of great power and influence in the country, concluded that he would be king himself, and so the young prince was thrown out upon the world. The new king did not want him in his dominions, and it was therefore determined, by his teachers and guardians, that he would have to become a "floating prince." By this, they meant that he must travel about, from place to place, until he found some kingdom which needed a king, and which was willing to accept him to rule over it. If such a situation were vacant, he easily could obtain it.

He was therefore furnished with a new suit of clothes and a good sword; a small crown and a scepter were packed into his bag; and he was started out to seek his fortune, as best he could.

As the prince walked away from the walls of his native city, he felt quite downhearted, although he was by nature gay and hopeful. He did not believe that he could find any country which would want him for a ruler.

"That is all nonsense," he said to himself. "There are always plenty of heirs or usurpers to take a throne when it is empty. If I want a kingdom, I must build up one for myself, and that is just what I will do. I will gather together my subjects as I go along. The first person I meet shall be my chief councilor of state, the second shall be head of the army, the third shall be admiral of the navy, the next shall be chief treasurer, and then I will collect subjects of various classes."

Cheered by this plan, he stepped gayly on, and just as he was entering a wood, through which his pathway led him, he heard some one singing.

Looking about him, he saw a little lady, about five inches high, sitting upon a twig of a flowering bush near by, and singing to herself. Nassime instantly perceived that she was a fairy, and said to himself: "Oho! I did not expect a meeting of this sort." But as he was a bold and frank young fellow, he stepped up to her and said: "Good-morning, lady fairy. How would you like to be chief councilor to a king?"

"It would be splendid!" said the lively little fairy, her eyes sparkling with delight. "But where is the king?"

"I am the king," said Nassime, "or, rather, I am to be, as soon as I get my kingdom together."

And then he told her his story and his plans. The fairy was charmed. The plan suited her exactly.

"You might get a larger councilor than

I am," she said, "but I know a good deal about government. I have been governed ever so much, and I could not help learning how it is done. I'm glad enough to have a chance to help somebody govern other people. I'll be your chief councilor."

"All right," said the prince, who was much pleased with the merry little creature. "Now we'll go and hunt up the rest of the kingdom."

He took the little fairy in his hand and placed her in one of the folds of his silken girdle, where she could rest, as if in a tiny hammock, and then he asked her name.

"My name," she answered, "is Lorilla, chief councilor of the kingdom of—what are you going to call your kingdom?"

"Oh, I haven't thought of a name, yet."

"Let it be Nassimia, after yourself," said Lorilla.

"Very well," answered the prince, "we will call it Nassimia. That will save trouble and disputes, after the kingdom is established."

Nassime now stepped along quite briskly, talking to his little companion as he went, and explaining to her his various ideas regarding his future kingdom. Suddenly he stumbled over what he supposed was the trunk of a fallen tree, and then he was quickly raised into the air, astride of the supposed tree-trunk, which seemed to have a hinge in it.

"What now?" said a great voice, and the prince perceived that he was sitting on the knee of a giant, who had been lying on his back in the wood.

"Don't be afraid," said Lorilla, looking out of her little hammock. "He won't hurt you."

"Excuse me," said the prince, "I did not see you, or I should have been more careful. How would you like to be general of the army of the kingdom of Nassimia?"

"That sounds splendid!" cried little Lorilla.

The giant looked bewildered. He could not understand, at all, what the prince was talking about. But when Nassime explained it all to him, he said he would like very well to be head general of the army, and he accepted the position.

Rising to his feet, the giant offered to carry the prince on his arm, so that they could get along faster, and in this way they traveled, all discussing, with much zest, the scheme of the new kingdom.

About noon, they began to be hungry, and so they sat down in a shady place, the giant having said that he had something to eat in a bag which he carried at his side. He opened this bag, and spread out half a dozen enormous loaves of bread, two joints of roast meat, a boiled ham, and about a bushel of roasted potatoes.

"Is that the food for your whole army?" asked Lorilla.

"Oh, no," answered the giant, who was a young fellow with a good appetite. "I brought this for myself, but there will be enough for you two. I don't believe I should have eaten it quite all, anyway."

"I should hope not," said the prince. "Why, that would last me several weeks."

"And me a thousand years," said Lorilla.

"You will talk differently, if you ever grow to be as big as I am," said the giant, smiling, as he took a bite from a loaf of bread.

When the meal was over, they all felt refreshed, and quite eager to meet the next comer, who was to be the admiral, or commander of the navy, of the new kingdom. For some time, they went on without seeing any one, but, at last, they perceived, in a field at some distance, a man on stilts. He was tending sheep, and wore the stilts so that he could the better see his flock, as it wandered about.

"There's the admiral!" said the giant. "Let me put you down, and run over and catch him."

So saying, he set the prince on the ground, and ran toward the shepherd, who, seeing him coming, at once took to flight. His stilts were so long that he made enormous steps, and he got over the ground very fast. The giant had long legs, and he ran swiftly, but he had a great deal of trouble to get near the man on stilts, who dodged in every direction, and rushed about like an enormous crane. The poor frightened sheep scattered themselves over the fields, and hid in the bushes.

At last, the giant made a vigorous dash, and swooping his long arm around, he caught the shepherd by one stilt, and waving him around his head, shouted in triumph.

The prince and Lorilla, who had been watching this chase with great interest, cheered in return.

"Now we have an admiral," said the fairy, as the giant approached, proudly bearing the shepherd aloft. "Don't you think it would be well for you to get out your crown and scepter? He ought to understand, at once, that you are the king."

So Nassime took his crown and scepter from his bag, and putting the first on his head, held the other in his hand. He looked quite kingly when the giant came up, and set the shepherd down on his knees before him, with his stilts sticking out ever so far behind.

"I am glad to see you," said the prince, "and I herewith make you admiral of my royal navy."

"Admiral?" cried the poor frightened man. "I don't understand."

"Oh, it's all right," exclaimed the merry little Lorilla, as she slipped out of the prince's sash, and ran up to the shepherd. "We're going to have a splendid kingdom, and we're just getting together the head officers. I'm chief councilor, that giant is the general of the army, and we want you to command the navy. There'll be a salary,

after a while, and I know you'll like it."

When she went on to explain the whole matter to the shepherd, his fear left him, and he smiled. "I shall be very glad to be your admiral," he then said, to the prince, whereupon the giant lifted him up on his feet, or rather on to the stilts, which were strapped to his feet and ankles, and the affair was settled. The party now went on, the giant and man on stilts side by side, the prince on the giant's arm, and Lorilla in Nassime's sash.

"What other great officer must we have?" asked she of Nassime.

"The chief officer of the treasury, or chancellor of the exchequer. I see him now."

It was true. Along a road in a valley below them, a man was walking. Instantly all were excited. The giant and the man on stilts wished to run after the newcomer, but the prince forbade it, saying it would be better to approach him quietly.

The man, who halted when he saw them, proved to be a clam-digger, with his clam-rake over one shoulder, and a large basket in his hand. The prince did not waste many words with this person, who was a rather humble-minded man, but briefly explained the situation to him, and told him that he was now the chancellor of the exchequer, in charge of the treasury of the kingdom of Nassimia.

The man, remarking that he saw no objection to such a position, and that it might, in the end, be better than clam-digging, joined the prince's party, which again proceeded on its way.

That night, they all slept in a palm-grove, first making a supper of cocoa-nuts, which the giant and the admiral picked from the tops of the trees.

"Now, then," said Nassime, in the morning, "what we must have next is an aristocracy. Out of this upper class we can then fill the government offices."

"Very true," said the giant, "and we shall want an army. I do not feel altogether like a general, without some soldiers under me."

"And *I* must have a navy," said the admiral.

"And there must be common people," remarked the chancellor of the exchequer. "For we shall need some folks on whom I can levy taxes with which to carry on the government."

"You are all right," said Nassime, "and this is the way we will manage matters. All the people we meet to-day shall be the aristocrats of Nassimia; all we meet to-morrow shall form the army, and all we see the next day shall be taken to make up the navy. After that, we will collect common people, until we have enough."

"I can tell you now," said the admiral, "how to get a lot of aristocrats all together in a bunch. A mile ahead of where we now are is a school-house, and it is full of boys, with a gray-headed master. Those fellows ought to make excellent aristocrats."

"They will do very well," said Nassime, "and we will go quietly forward and capture them all."

When they reached the school-house, Nassime, with his crown on his head and his scepter in his hand, took his position at the front door, the giant crouched down by the back door, the chancellor stood by one window and the admiral tried to stand by the other, but his stilts were so long that he looked over the roof instead of into the window.

"Is not that a well near you?" said the little councilor Lorilla, who was perched on a vine, for safe-keeping. "Step into that, and you will, most likely, be just tall enough."

The admiral stepped into the well, which was close to the house, and found that he stood exactly high enough to command the window. When all were posted,

Nassime opened his door, and stepping a short distance into the room, declared his title and position, and called upon them all to consider themselves members of the aristocracy of his kingdom. The moment he said this, the astonished and frightened boys sprang to their feet and made a rush for the back door, but when they threw it open, there squatted the giant, with a broad grin on his face, and his hands spread out before the door-way. They then turned and ran, some for one window and some for the other, but at one stood the treasurer, brandishing his clam-rake, and at the other the admiral, shaking his fists. There was no escape,—one or two, who tried to pass by Nassime, having been stopped by a tap on the head from his scepter,—and so the boys crowded together in the middle of the room, while some of the smaller ones began to cry. The master was too much startled and astonished to say a word.

Then came running into the room little Lorilla, and mounting to the top of the school-master's table, she addressed the school, telling them all about the new kingdom, and explaining what a jolly time they would have. It would be like a long holiday, and although their master would go with them, to teach them what they would have to know in their new positions, it would not be a bit like going to school.

As soon as the boys heard that they would not have to go to school, they agreed to the plan on the spot. Some of them even went out to talk to the giant. As to the master, he said that if his school was to be taken into the new kingdom he would go, too, for he had promised the parents that he would take care of their boys.

So, when all was settled, the whole school, headed by the master, made ready to follow Nassime and his officers. The giant pulled the admiral out of the well, much to the delight of the boys, and all started off in high good humor.

The company went into camp on the edge of a wood, quite early in the evening, because Lorilla said that boys ought not to

The general and the admiral led the procession

be up late. If it had not been for the luncheons which the boys had in their baskets, and which they cheerfully shared with their older companions, many of the party would have gone to sleep hungry that night. As for the giant, it is probable that he did go to sleep hungry, for it would

have taken the contents of all the baskets to have entirely satisfied his appetite.

Early the next morning, he aroused the party.

"Here are a few bushels of coco-nuts," he cried, emptying a great bag on the ground. "I gathered them before any of you were awake. Eat them quickly, for we must be off. To-day is my army day, and I want to get as many soldiers as I can."

As every one was very willing to please the giant, an early start was made, and, before very long, the party reached the edge of a desert. They journeyed over the sand nearly all day, but not a living being did they see. Late in the afternoon, a black man, on an ostrich, was seen coming from behind a hillock of sand, and immediately, with a great shout, the whole party set out in chase.

It is probable that the man on the bird would have soon got away from his pursuers, had not the ostrich persisted in running around in a great circle, while, with whoops and shouts, the giant and the rest succeeded in heading off the ostrich, which tumbled over, throwing his rider on the sand. The bird then ran off as fast as he could go, while the negro was seized by every aristocrat who could get near enough to lay hold of him. The giant now came up, and lifted the man from the midst of his young captors. "You need not be frightened," said he. "You are to belong to my army. That is all. I will treat you well."

"And not kill me?" whimpered the black man.

"Certainly not," said the giant. "I need soldiers too much to want to kill the only one I've got. Fall into line, behind me, and we'll march on and see if we cannot find you some comrades."

But by night-fall the giant's army still consisted of one black man. The party encamped in an oasis, where grew a number of date-palms, the fruit of which afforded a plentiful supper for everybody. The giant had not much appetite, and he looked solemn while gazing at his army, as it sat cross-legged on the ground, eating dates.

The next morning, the admiral earnestly petitioned that they should try to get out of the desert as soon as possible. "For," said he, "I have a dreadful time in this sand with my stilts, and I really need more men in my navy than the giant has in his army. Besides, the best kind of sailors can never be found in a dry desert like this."

As no one could object to this reasoning, they set forth, turning to the east, and, before noon, they saw before them fields and vegetation, and shortly afterward they came to a broad river. Journeying down the bank of this for a mile or two, they perceived, lying at anchor in the stream, a good-sized vessel, with a tall mast, and a great sail hauled down on the deck.

"Hurrah!" shouted the admiral, the moment he set his eyes upon this prize, and away he went for it, as fast as his stilts would carry him. When he reached the water, he waded right in, and was soon standing looking over the vessel's side.

He did not get on board, but, after standing for some time talking to a person inside, he waded back to the shore, where his companions were anxiously waiting to hear what he had discovered.

"There are not many persons on board," he said, rather ruefully. "Only an old woman and a girl. One is the cook and the other washes bottles. There were a good many men on the ship, but the old woman says that they all went away yesterday, carrying with them a vast number of packages. She thinks they were a lot of thieves, and that they have gone off with their booty and have deserted the vessel. She and the girl were simply hired as servants, and knew nothing about the crew. It isn't exactly the kind of navy I wanted, but it

will do, and we may see some men before night."

It was unanimously agreed that the government of Nassimia should take possession of this deserted vessel, and the giant soon managed to pull her to shore, anchor and all. Everybody excepting the giant went on board, Nassime and Lorilla going first, then the government officers, the aristocracy, and the army. The admiral stood on his stilts, with his head up in the rigging, and the ship was formally placed under his command. When all was ready, the

The Kingdom of Nassimia afloat

giant ran the ship out into the stream, wading in up to his middle; and then he very carefully clambered on board. The vessel rocked a good deal as he got in, but it could carry him as long as he kept quiet.

"As my navy is not large enough, just now, to work the ship," said the admiral to Nassime, "and, also, as it doesn't know anything about such work, I shall have to have the help of the aristocracy, and also to ask the general to lend me his army."

"All right," said the giant, "you can have him."

A number of the larger boys, assisted by the negro, now went to work and hoisted the sail. Then the army was sent to the helm, the vessel was put before the wind, and the kingdom of Nassimia began to sail away.

There was a large quantity of provisions on board, enough to last many days, and everybody ate heartily. But not a person was seen that day on either bank of the river.

They anchored at night, and the next morning, setting sail again, they soon entered a broad sea or lake. They sailed on, with the wind behind them, and everybody enjoyed the trip. The admiral sat on the stern, with his stilts dangling behind in the water, as the ship sailed on, and was very happy.

"Now," said the chancellor of the exchequer, as the officers of the government were talking together on deck, "all we want is some common people, and then we can begin the kingdom in real earnest."

"We must have some houses and streets," said Nassime, "and a palace. All those will be necessary before we can settle down as a kingdom."

They sailed all night, and the next day they saw land before them. And, slowly moving near the shore, they perceived a long caravan.

"Hi!" shouted the chancellor of the exchequer, "there are the common people!"

Everybody was now very much excited, and everybody wanted to go ashore, but this Nassime would not permit. Capturing a caravan would be a very different thing from capturing a negro on an ostrich, and the matter must be undertaken with caution and prudence. So, ordering the ship brought near the shore, he made ready to land, accompanied only by the giant and Lorilla.

The giant had found a spare mast on the vessel, and he had trimmed and whittled it into a convenient club. This he took under one arm, and, with Nassime on the other, wearing his crown and carrying

Lorilla in his sash, the giant waded ashore, and stopped a short distance in front of the approaching caravan.

Nassime, having been set on the ground, advanced to the leader of the caravan, and, drawing his sword, called upon him to halt. Instantly the procession stopped, and the leader, dismounting from his horse, approached Nassime, and bowed low before him, offering to pay tribute if necessary.

"We will not speak of tribute," said Nassime, "at least, not now. What I wish, is to know who you all are, and where you are going."

"That is easily answered," said the other, giving a glance upward at the giant, who stood leaning on his club, behind Nassime; "we are a company of men of high degree; philosophers and rich merchants, who have joined together to visit foreign lands, to enjoy ourselves and improve our minds. We have brought with us our families, our slaves, and our flocks and other possessions. We wish to offend no one, and if you object to our passing through your dominions——"

"I do not object," said Nassime, "I am very glad you came this way. These are not my dominions. I am king of Nassimia."

"And where is that, your majesty?"

"It is not anywhere in particular, just now," said Nassime, "but we shall soon fix upon a spot where its boundaries will be established. It is a new kingdom, and only needed a body of com—"

"Say populace," whispered Lorilla, from his sash, "the other might offend him."

"And only needed a populace," continued Nassime, "to make it complete. I am the king—of royal blood and education. I have ministers of state and finance; an admiral and a navy; a general of the army, whom you see here," pointing to the giant, "and an aristocracy, which is at present on board of that ship. I have been looking for a populace, and am very glad to have met you. You and your companions are now my people."

"What, your majesty?" cried the astonished leader of the caravan. "I do not comprehend."

Nassime then explained the plan and purpose of his kingdom, and assured the other that he and his countrymen could nowhere be more happy than in the kingdom of Nassimia, where every opportunity of enjoyment and the improvement of the mind would be offered to the people.

The leader, on hearing this, begged permission to consult with his fellow-travelers. Some advised one thing and some another, but the sight of the giant, who every now and then playfully struck the earth with the end of his club in such a way as to make the ground tremble, hastened their decision.

"If we were poor men," said one of the philosophers, "and had no treasures with us, we might scatter in various directions, and many of us might escape. That giant could not kill us all. But we are too rich for that. We cannot run away from our great possessions. We must submit in peace."

So it was settled that they should submit to the king of Nassimia and become his people, and the leader carried the decision to Nassime.

The chancellor of the exchequer now became very anxious to go on shore. He had cast off his clam-digger's clothes, and wore a magnificent suit which he had found in the ship, and which had belonged to the robber captain. He stood on the deck and made signs for the giant to come for him. So the giant was sent for him, and soon returned, bringing also the army, which the chancellor had borrowed of him for a time. This officer, as soon as he had landed, approached Nassime and said:

"These, then, are the common people.

I suppose I might as well go to work and collect taxes."

"You need not hurry about that," said Nassime.

"They will never believe in your government until you do it," urged the chancellor, and so Nassime allowed him to do as he wished, only telling him not to levy his taxes too heavily.

Then the chancellor, with the negro behind him, carrying his old clam-basket, over which a cloth had been thrown, went through the caravan and collected taxes enough in gold and silver to fill his basket. He also collected a horse for himself and one for Nassime. "Now," said he, "we have the foundation of a treasury, and the thing begins to look like a kingdom."

Everything being now satisfactorily arranged, the company began to move on. The giant, with his army at his heels, and his club over his shoulder, marched first. Then rode Nassime with Lorilla, then the chancellor, with his basket of treasure before him on his horse, and after him the caravan. The ship sailed along a short distance from the shore.

In the evening, the land party encamped near the shore, and the vessel came to anchor, the giant shouting to the admiral Nassime's commands. The chancellor wished to make another collection of taxes after supper, but this Nassime forbade.

Lorilla then had a long talk with Nassime, apart from the company, assuring him that what was needed next was the royal city.

"Yes, indeed," said Nassime, "and we are not likely to meet with that as we have met with everything else. We must build a city, I suppose."

"No," said Lorilla, gayly. "We can do much better. Do you see that heavy forest on the hills back of us? Well, in that forest is the great capital city of my people, the fairies. We are scattered in colonies all over the country, but there is our court and our queen. And it is the fairies who can help you to get a royal city. This very evening I will go and see what can be done."

So, that evening, Nassime took Lorilla to the edge of the forest, and while she ran swiftly into its depths, he lay down and slept. Early the next morning, while the stars were still shining, she returned and awoke him, and while they were going to the camp she told him her news.

"Our queen," she said, "will have a city built for you, all complete, with everything that a city needs; but before she will have this done, she commands that someone in your party shall be changed into a fairy, to take my place! This must be a grown person who consents to the exchange, as I have agreed to be your chief councilor of state. And it must be someone whose mind has never been occupied with human affairs."

"I don't believe you will find any such person among us," said Nassime, ruefully.

But Lorilla clapped her hands and cried merrily:

"Ah, yes! The bottle-washer! I believe she is the very person."

Nassime was cheered by this idea, and as soon as they reached the shore, he asked the giant to carry him and Lorilla to the ship. Early as it was, they found the young girl sitting on the deck, quietly washing bottles. She had lost her parents when an infant, and had never had any one to care for. She had passed her life, since she was a very small child, in washing bottles, and as this employment does not require any mental labor, she had never concerned herself about anything.

"She will do," exclaimed Lorilla, when she had found out all this. "I don't believe her mind was ever occupied at all. It is perfectly fresh for her to begin as a fairy."

When the girl was asked if she would be a fairy, she readily consented, for it made no difference to her what she was, and

when the admiral was asked if he would give her up, he said: "Oh, yes! To be sure, it will reduce my navy to one person, but, even then, it will be as large as the army. You may take her, and welcome." The bottle-washer therefore was taken to the shore, and Nassime conducted her to the woods with Lorilla. There he left them, promising to return at sunset.

"You must be careful of one thing," said Lorilla to him, before he left, "and that is, not to let those aristocrats come on shore. If they once get among the populace, they will begin to lord it over them in a way that will raise a dreadful commotion."

Nassime promised to attend to this, and when he went back he sent orders to the admiral, on no account to allow any aristocrat to come on shore. This order caused great discontent on the vessel. The boys couldn't see why they alone should be shut up in the ship. They had expected to have lots of fun when the common people were found.

It was, therefore, with great difficulty that they were restrained from jumping overboard and swimming ashore in a body. The master had been made an ancient noble, but his authority was of little avail, and the poor admiral had his hands full. Indeed, he would have been in despair, had it not been for the gallant conduct of his navy. That brave woman seized a broom, and marching around the deck, kept watchful guard. Whenever she saw a boy attempting to climb over the side of the vessel, she brought down the broom with a whack upon him, and tumbled him back on the deck. In the afternoon, however, the giant came to the vessel with a double arm-load of rich fruit, cakes, pastry and confectionery, an offering from the common people, which so delighted the aristocrats that there was peace on board for the rest of the day.

At sunset, Nassime went to the woods and met Lorilla, who was waiting for him.

"It's all right!" she cried; "the bottle-washer is to be magically dwindled down to-night. And when everybody is asleep, the fairies will come here and will see how many people there are and what they are like, and they will build a city just to suit. It will be done to-morrow."

Nassime could scarcely believe all this, but there was nothing to be done but to wait and see. That night, everybody went to sleep quite early. And if the fairies came and measured them for a city, they did not know it.

In the morning, Nassime arose, and walked down toward the shore. As he did so, a lady came out of a tent and approached him. He thought he knew her features, but he could not remember who she was. But when she spoke, he started back and cried out: "Lorilla!"

"Yes," said the lady, laughing, "it is Lorilla. The king of Nassimia ought to have a chief councilor of state who is somewhat longer than his finger, and last night, as the girl who took my place dwindled down to the size of a fairy, I grew larger and larger, until I became as large as she used to be. Do you like the change?"

Lorilla was beautiful. She was richly dressed, and her lovely face was as merry and gay as ever.

Nassime approached her and took her hand.

"The chief councilor of my kingdom shall be its queen," he said, and calling a priest from the populace, the two were married on the spot.

Great were the rejoicings on land and water; but there was no delay in getting ready to march to the royal city, the domes and spires of which Lorilla pointed out to them behind some lovely groves.

Nassime was about to signal for the ship to come to shore, but Lorilla checked him.

"I'm really sorry for those poor aristo-crats, but it will never do to take them to the royal city. They are not needed, and they would make all sorts of trouble. There is nothing to be done but to let the admiral sail away with them, and keep on sailing until they are grown up. Then they will come back, fit to be members of the nobil-ity. They will have their master with them, and you can put three or four philosophers on board, and they can be as well educated, traveling about in this way, as if they were going to school."

Nassime felt sorry for the aristocrats, but he saw that this was good advice, and he took it. A quantity of provisions and four philosophers were sent on board the ship, and the admiral was ordered to sail away until the boys grew up. As he liked nothing better than sailing, this suited the admiral exactly; and after having a few sheep sent on board, with which to amuse himself during calms, he hoisted sail, and was soon far away.

The rest of the kingdom marched on, and in good time reached the royal city. There it stood, with its houses, streets, shops, and everything that a city should have. The royal palace glittered in the center, and upon a hill there stood a splendid castle for the giant!

Everybody hurried forward. The name of the owner was on every house, and every house was fully furnished, so in a few minutes the whole city was at home.

The king, leading his queen up the steps of his royal palace, paused at the door:

"All this," he said, "I owe to you. From the very beginning, you have given me nothing but good advice."

"But that is not the best of it," she said, laughing. "You always took it."

The vessel carrying the aristocrats sailed away and away, with the admiral sitting on the stern, his stilts dangling in the water behind, as the ship moved on.

HOW THE ARISTOCRATS SAILED AWAY

by Frank R. Stockton

For many and many a day, the ship of the admiral of the kingdom of Nassimia, containing the admiral himself, the company of school-boys who had been made aristocrats, the old school-master, the four philosophers, and the old woman, who was cook and navy all in one, sailed and sailed away.

The admiral sat on the stern, his long stilts dangling in the water behind, as the ship sailed on. He was happy, for this was just what he liked; and the four philosophers and the old master and the navy were happy; but the aristocrats gradually became very discontented. They did not want to sail so much; they wanted to go somewhere, and see something. The ship had stopped several times at towns on the coast, and the boys had gone on shore, but, in every case, the leading people of the town had come to the admiral, bearing rich presents, and begging him to sail away in the night. So it happened that the lively young aristocrats had been on land very little since they started on their travels.

Finding, at last, that the admiral had no intention of landing again, the aristocrats determined to rebel, and, under the leadership of the Tail-boy, who was the poorest scholar among them but first in all mischief, they formed a plan to take possession of the ship.

Accordingly, one fine afternoon, as the admiral, the master, and the four philosophers were sitting on the deck of the vessel, enjoying the breeze, six aristocrats, each carrying a bag, slipped quietly up behind them, and, in an instant, a bag was clapped over the head of each man. It was in vain to kick and struggle. The other aristocrats rushed up, the bags were tied securely around the necks of the victims, their hands and feet were bound, and they were seated in a row at the stern of the ship, the admiral's stilts lying along the deck. The Tail-boy then took a pair of scissors and cut a hole in each bag, opposite the mouth of its wearer, so that he could breathe. The six unfortunate men were now informed that if they behaved well they should be treated well, and that, on the next day, a hole should be cut in each of their bags, so that they could see with one eye; on the next day, a hole for one ear; on the next, a hole for the nose; and if they still behaved well, holes should be cut on the two succeeding days for the other ears and eyes. The smartest boy of the school had said, when this arrangement was proposed, that by the time they got this far they might as well take off the bags, but the rest of the aristocrats did not think so; a prisoner whose head was even partly bagged was more secure than one not bagged at all.

The admiral and his companions could think of nothing to do but to agree to these terms, and so they agreed, hoping that, by some happy chance, they would soon be released. It was suggested by a few

III

aristocrats that it would be well to bring up the navy and bag her head also, but the majority decided that she was needed to do the cooking, and so she was shut down below, and ordered to cook away as hard as she could.

The prisoners were plentifully fed, at meal-times, by their captors, who put the food through the mouth-holes of their bags. At first, the aristocrats found this to be such fun that the poor men could scarcely prevent themselves from being overfed. At night, cushions were brought for them to lie upon, and a rope was fastened to the ends of the admiral's stilts, which were hoisted up into the rigging, so as to be out of the way.

The aristocrats now did just as they pleased. They steered in the direction in which they supposed the coast should lie, and, as they were sailing on, they gave themselves up to all manner of amusements. Among other things, they found a number of pots of paints stowed away in the vessel's hold, and with these they set to work to decorate the vessel.

They painted the masts crimson, the sails in stripes of pink and blue, the deck light green, spotted with yellow stars; and nearly everything on board shone in some lively color. The admiral's sheep were adorned with bands of green, yellow, and crimson, and his stilts were painted bright blue, with a corkscrew red line running around them. Indeed, the smell of paint soon became so strong, that three of the philosophers requested that the nose-holes in their bags should be sewed up.

There is no knowing what other strange things these aristocrats would have done, had they not, on the fourth day of their rule on the vessel, perceived they were in sight of land, and of what seemed to be a large city on the coast. Instantly the vessel was steered straight for the city, which

they soon reached. The ship was made fast, and every aristocrat went on shore. The cook was locked below, and the admiral and his companions were told to sit still and be good until the boys should return.

Each of the prisoners now had holes in his bag for his mouth, his nose, one eye, and an ear, but as the eye-holes were all on the side toward the water, the poor men could not see much that was going on. They twisted themselves around, however, as well as they could, and so got an occasional glimpse of the shore.

The aristocrats swarmed up into the city, but although it was nearly midday, not a living soul did they meet. The buildings were large and handsome, and the streets were wide and well laid out; there were temples and palaces and splendid edifices of various kinds, but every door and shutter and gate of every house was closely shut, and not a person could be seen, nor a sound heard.

The silence and loneliness of the place quieted the spirits of the aristocrats, and they now walked slowly and kept together.

"What does it all mean?" said one. "Is the place bewitched, or has everybody gone out of town and taken along the dogs, and the birds, and the flies, and every living thing?"

"We might go back after one of the philosophers," said another. "He could tell us all about it."

"I don't believe he'd know any more than we do," said the Tail-boy, who had now forced his way to the front. "Let us go ahead, and find out for ourselves."

So they walked on until they came to a splendid edifice, which looked like a palace, and, much to their surprise, the great doors stood wide open. After a little hesitation, they went up the steps and peeped in. Seeing no one, they cautiously entered. Everything was grand and gorgeous within, and they gradually penetrated to a large hall, at one end of which they saw a wide stair-way, carpeted with the richest tapestry.

Reaching this, they concluded to go up and see what they could find upstairs. But as no one wished to be the first in such a bold proceeding, they went in a solid body. The stair-way was very wide, so that twelve boys could go up, abreast, and they thus filled three of the stairs, with several little boys on the next stair below.

On they went, up, up, and up, keeping step together. There was a landing above them, but it seemed to be farther up than they had supposed. Some of the little aristocrats complained of being tired; but as they did not wish to be left behind, they kept on.

"Look here," said one of the front row; "do you see that window up there? Well, we're not any nearer to it now than we were when we started."

"That's true," said another, and then the Smart-boy spoke up:

"I'll tell you what it is. We're not going up at all. These stairs are turning around and around, as we step on them. It's a kind of a tread-mill!"

"Let's stop!" cried some of the boys; but others exclaimed, "Oh, no! Don't do that, or we shall be ground up!"

"Oh, please don't stop!" cried the little fellows below, forgetting their tired legs, "or we shall be ground up first."

So on they kept, stepping up and up, but never advancing, while some of them tried to devise some plan by which they all could turn around and jump off at the same instant. But this would be difficult and dangerous, and those little fellows would certainly be crushed by the others if they were not ground up by the stairs.

Around and around went the stairs, each step disappearing under the floor beneath, and appearing again above them; while the boys stepped up and up, wondering if the thing would ever stop. They were silent now, and they could hear a steady click, click, click, as the great stair-way went slowly around.

"Oh, I'll tell you!" suddenly exclaimed the Smart-boy. "We're winding it up!"

"Winding up what?" cried several of the others.

"Everything!" said the Smart-boy; "we're winding up the city!"

This was true. Directly, sounds were heard outside; a dog barked; some cocks crew, and windows and doors were heard to open. The boys trembled, and forgot their weariness, as they stepped up and up. Some voices were heard below, and then, with a sudden jar, the stairs stopped.

"She's wound!" said the Smart-boy, under his breath, and every aristocrat turned around and hurried off the stairs.

What a change had taken place in everything! From without, came the noise and bustle of a great city, and, within, doors were opening, curtains were being pulled aside, and people were running here, there, and everywhere. The boys huddled together in a corner of the hall. Nobody seemed to notice them.

Suddenly, a great gilded door, directly opposite to them, was thrown wide open, and a king and queen came forth. The king glanced around, eagerly.

"Hello!" he cried, as his eyes fell upon the cluster of frightened aristocrats. "I believe it is those boys! Look here," said he, advancing, "did you boys wind us up?"

"Yes, sir," said the Head-boy, "I think we did. But we didn't mean to. If you'd let us off this time, we'd never——"

"Let you off!" cried the king. "Not until we've made you the happiest boys on earth! Do you suppose we're angry? Never such a mistake! What do you think of that?" he said, turning to the queen.

This royal lady, who was very fat, made no answer, but smiled, good-humoredly.

"You're our greatest benefactors," continued the king. "I don't know what we can do for you. You didn't imagine, perhaps, that you were winding us up. Few people, besides ourselves, know how things are with us. This city goes all right for ten years, and then it runs down, and has to be wound up. When we feel we have nearly run down, we go into our houses and apartments, and shut up everything tight and strong. Only this hall is left open, so that somebody can come in, and wind us up. It takes a good many people to do it, and I'm glad there were so many of you. Once we were wound up by a lot of bears, who wandered in and tried to go upstairs. But they didn't half do it, and we only ran four years. The city has been still —like a clock with its works stopped—for as long as a hundred years at once. I don't know how long it was this time. I'm going to get here?"

The boys then told how they had come in a ship, with the admiral, their master, and four philosophers.

"And the ship is here!" cried the king. "Run!" he shouted to his attendants, "and bring hither those worthy men, that they may share in the honor and rewards of their pupils."

While the attendants were gone, the aristocrats waited in the hall, and the king went away to attend to other matters. The queen sat down on a sofa near by.

"It tires me dreadfully to smile," she said, as she wiped her brow; "but I have to take some exercise."

"I hope they won't bring 'em here, bags and all," whispered the Tail-boy. "It would look funny, but I shouldn't like it."

In a short time the king came back in a hurry.

"How's this?" he cried. "My messengers tell me that there's no ship at our piers excepting our own vessels. Have you deceived me?"

The aristocrats gazed at each other in dismay. Had their ship sailed away and left them? If so, they had only been served aright. They looked so downcast and guilty that the king knew something was wrong.

"What have you done?" said he.

The Head-boy saw that there was no help for it, and he told all.

The king looked sad, but the queen smiled two or three times.

"And you put their heads in bags?" said the king.

"Yes, sir," replied the Head-boy.

"Well, well!" said the king; "I am sorry. After all you have done for us, too. I will send out a swift cruiser after that ship, which will be easy to find if it is painted as you say, and, until it is brought back to the city, I must keep you in custody. Look you," said he to his attendants; "take these young people to a luxurious apartment, and see that they are well fed and cared for, and also be very careful that none of them escape."

Thereupon the aristocrats were taken away to an inner chamber of the palace.

When the admiral and his companions had been left on board the vessel, they felt very uneasy, for they did not know what might happen to them next. In a short time, however, when the voices of the aristocrats had died away as they proceeded into the city, the admiral perceived the point of a gimlet coming up through the deck, close to him. Then the gimlet was withdrawn, and these words came up through the hole:

"Have no fear. Your navy will stand by you!"

"It will be all right," said the admiral to the others. "I can depend upon her."

And now was heard a noise of banging and chopping, and soon the cook cut her way from her imprisonment below, and made her appearance on deck. She went to work vigorously, and, taking the bags from the prisoners' heads, unbound them, and set them at liberty. Then she gave them a piece of advice.

"The thing for us to do," said she, "is to get away from here as fast as we can. If those young rascals come back, there's no knowin' what they'll do."

"Do you mean," said the master, "that we should sail away and desert my scholars? Who can tell what might happen to them, left here by themselves?"

"We should not consider what might happen to them if they were left," said one of the philosophers, "but what might happen to us if they were not left. We must away."

"Certainly!" cried the admiral. "While I have the soul of the commander of the navy of Nassimia left within me, I will not stay here to have my head put in a bag! Never! Set sail!"

It was not easy to set sail, for the cook and the philosophers were not very good at that sort of work; but they got the sail up at last, and cast loose from shore, first landing the old master, who positively refused to desert his scholars. The admiral took the helm, and, the wind being fair, the ship sailed away.

The swift cruiser, which was sent in the direction taken by the admiral's vessel, passed her in the night, and as she was a very fast cruiser, and it was therefore impossible for the admiral's ship to catch up with her, the two vessels never met.

"Now, then," said the admiral the next day, as he sat with the helm in his hand,

"we are free again to sail where we please. But I do not like to sail without an object. What shall be our object?"

The philosophers immediately declared that nothing could be more proper than that they should take a voyage to make some great scientific discovery.

"All right," said the admiral. "That suits me. What discovery shall we make?"

The philosophers were not prepared to answer this question at that moment, but they said they would try to think of some good discovery to make.

So the philosophers sat in a row behind the admiral, and thought and thought; and the admiral sat at the helm, with his blue-and-red stilts dangling in the water behind; and the cook prepared the meals, swept the deck, dusted the sail, and put things in order.

After several hours, the admiral turned around to ask the philosophers if they had thought of any discovery yet, when, to his amazement, he saw that each one of them had put his bag upon his head.

"What did you do that for?" cried the admiral, and each of the philosophers gave a little jump; and then they explained that it was much easier to think with one's head in a bag. The outer world was thus shut out, and trains of thought were not so likely to be broken up.

So, for day after day, the philosophers, with their heads in their bags, sat, and thought, and thought; and the admiral sat and steered, and the navy cooked and dusted and kept things clean. Sometimes, when she thought the sail did not catch the wind properly, she would move the admiral toward one side or the other, and thus change the course of the vessel.

"If I knew," said the admiral one day, "the exact age of the youngest of those aristocrats, I should know just how long we should have to sail, before they would all be grown up; when it would be time for us to go back after them, and take them to Nassimia."

The cook remembered that the smallest boy had told her he was ten years old.

"Then," said the admiral, "we must sail for eleven years."

And they sailed for eleven years; the philosophers, with their heads in their bags, trying their best to think of some good thing to discover.

The day after the aristocrats had been shut up in their luxurious apartment, the queen sent a messenger to them, to tell them that she thought the idea of putting people's heads in bags was one of the most amusing things she ever heard of, and that she would be much obliged if they would send her the pattern of the proper kind of bag, so that she could have some made for her slaves.

The messenger brought scissors, and papers, and pins, and the boys cut a pattern of a very comfortable bag, with holes for the eyes, nose, mouth, and ears, which they sent with their respects to the queen. This royal lady had two bags made, which she put upon two of her servants, and their appearance amused her so much that she smiled a great deal, and yet scarcely felt tired at all.

But, in the course of a day or two, the king happened to see these bag-headed slaves sitting in an ante-chamber. He was struck with consternation, and instantly called a council of his chief ministers.

"We are threatened with a terrible danger," he said to them, when all the doors were shut. "We have among us a body of Bagists! Little did we think, in our gratitude, that we were wound up merely that we might go through life with our heads bagged! Better far that we should stay stopped forever! How can we know but that the ship which brought them here may soon return, with a cargo of bag stuffs, needles, thread, and thimbles, and

that every head in our city may be bagged in a few days? Already, signs of this approaching evil have shown themselves. Notwithstanding the fact that these dangerous characters have been closely confined, no less than two of the inmates of my palace have already had their heads bagged!"

At these words, a thrill of horror pervaded the ministers, and they discussed the matter for a long time. It was finally decided that a lookout should be constantly kept on the top of a high tower, to give notice of the approach of the ship, should she return; additional guards were posted at the door of the aristocrats' apartment, and it was ordered that the city be searched every day, to see if any new cases of bagism could be discovered.

The aristocrats now began to be very discontented. Although they had everything they could possibly want to eat and drink, and were even furnished with toys and other sources of amusement, they did not like to be shut up.

"I'll tell you what it is," said the Tailboy. "I can't stand this any longer. Let's get away."

"But where shall we get away to?" asked several of the others.

"We'll see about that when we're outside," was the answer. "Anything's better than being shut up here."

After some talk, everybody agreed that they ought to try to escape, and they set about to devise some plan for doing so. The windows were not very high from the ground, but they were too high for a jump, and not a thing could be found in the room which was strong enough to make a rope. Every piece of silk or muslin in the curtains or bed-clothes was fine, and delicate, and flimsy. At last, the Smart-boy hit upon a plan. The apartment was a very long one, and was floored with narrow boards, of costly wood, which ran from one end to the other of it. He proposed that they should take up one of these boards, and, putting it out of the window, should rest one end on the ground, and the other on the window-sill. Then they could slide down.

Instantly, every aristocrat set to work, with knife, or piece of tin, or small coin, to take out the silver screws which held down one of the boards.

"It is very narrow," said the Head-boy. "I am afraid we shall slip off."

"Oh, there is no danger of that," replied the Smart-boy. "If we only go fast enough, we cannot slip off. We will grease the board, and then we shall go fast enough."

So the board was taken up, and, after having been well greased with oil from the lamps, was put out of the window.

Then the boys, one at a time, got on the board and slid, with the speed of lightning, to the ground. Most of them came down with such rapidity and force that they shot over the smooth grass to a considerable distance. As soon as they were all down, the Smart-boy took the end of the board, and moved it to one side, so that it rested on the edge of a deep tank.

"Now, then," said he, "if any of the guards slide down after us, they will go into the tank."

It was now nearly dark, and the boys set about finding some place where they could spend the night. They soon came to a large building, the doors of which were shut, but, as they were not locked, they had no trouble in entering. This building was a public library, which was closed very early every afternoon, and opened very late every morning. Here the aristocrats found very comfortable quarters, and having lighted a candle which one of them had in his pockets, they held a meeting, to determine what they should do next.

"Of course the ship will come back, some

day," said the Smart-boy, "for that admiral would be afraid to go home without us. The giant would smash him and his old ship if he did that. So we shall have to wait here until the ship comes."

"But how are we going to live?" asked several of his companions.

"We can sleep here," he answered. "It's a nice, big place, and nobody will ever disturb us, for a notice on the door says it's closed two hours before sunset. And as to victuals, we shall have to work at something."

This was thought good reasoning, and they now began to consider what they should work at. It was agreed that it would be wise for them all to select the same trade, because then they could stand by each other in case of any business disputes, and their trade was to be chosen in this way: Every boy was to write on a piece of paper the business he liked best, and whatever trade or profession was written on the most papers, was to be adopted by the whole company.

When the papers were read by the Head-boy, it was found that nearly every one had selected a different calling; but three of the smaller boys happened to want to be letter-carriers, and so, as there was no business which had so many votes as this, it was determined that they should all be letter-carriers.

The three little boys shouted for joy at this.

"But where shall we get letters to carry?" asked some of the older fellows.

"Oh, we'll see about that in the morning," said the Smart-boy. "There'll be plenty of time before the library opens."

They slept that night on piles of parchments, and in the morning the building was searched to see if any letters could be found for them to carry. In the cellar they discovered a great many huge boxes, filled with manuscripts which had been collecting ever since the city was first wound up and started. These, they concluded, would do just as well as letters, and each boy filled his satchel with them, and started off to deliver them.

Each carrier was assigned by the Head-boy to a different street, and all went to work with a will. The people were glad

"in trying to escape, have all slid into the tank. Let it be walled over, and that will be the end of it. We are fortunate to get rid of them so easily."

But the watch on the high tower was still kept up, for no one knew when the ship might come back with more Bagists.

One day, as the Head-boy was deliver-

The aristocrats winding up the city

to get the manuscripts, for many of them were very instructive and interesting, and they gave the boys a small piece of money for each one. This went on, day after day, and every morning each person in the whole city got a letter.

When the king was informed of the escape of his prisoners, he hurried, in great trouble, to see how they had got away. But when he saw the board which they had left resting on the edge of the tank, he was delighted.

"Those wretched Bagists," he exclaimed,

ing his letters, he met an old man, whom he instantly recognized as his master. At first, he felt like running away; but when the master told him that he was alone, and forgave everything, they embraced in tears. The old man had not been able to find his boys in the town, and had wandered into the surrounding country. In this way, he had never had a letter.

The Head-boy took him to the library that night, and he afterward spent most of his time reading the old manuscripts, and sorting them out for the carriers. Nobody ever came into the cellar to disturb him.

The people of the city were very much benefited by the instructive papers which were brought to them every day, and many of them became quite learned. The aristocrats also learned a great deal by reading the papers to those persons who could not read themselves, and, every evening, the master gave them lessons in the library. So they gradually became more and more educated.

They often looked up to the high tower, because they had heard that a flag was to be hoisted there whenever a ship with a pink and blue sail was seen approaching the city.

Ten years passed, and they saw no flag, but one day they saw, posted up all over the city, a notice from the king, stating that, on the next day, the city would run down, and ordering all the people to retire into their houses, and to shut up their doors and windows. This struck the aristocrats with dismay, for how were they to get a living if they could not deliver their letters?

So they all boldly marched to the palace, and, asking for the king, proposed to him that they should be allowed to wind up his city.

The king gazed upon them in amazement. "What!" he cried. "Do you letter-carriers venture to come to me with such a bold request? Do you think for a moment that you know anything about what you propose doing?"

"We can do it a great deal easier than we did it before," said one of the younger aristocrats, "for some of us were very small then, and didn't weigh much."

"Did it before?" exclaimed the bewildered king, staring at the sturdy group before him.

The Head-boy, who was by this time entirely grown up, now came forward, and,

acknowledging that he and his companions were the boys who had been shut up in the luxurious apartment, told their whole story since their escape.

"And you have lived among us all this time, and have not tried to bag our heads?" said the king.

"Not a bit of it," replied the other.

"I am very glad, indeed, to hear this," said the king, "and now, if you please, I would like you to try if you really can wind us up, for I feel that I am running down very fast."

At this, the whole body of aristocrats ran to the great stair-way, and began quickly to mount the steps. Around and around went the revolving stair-way, twice as fast as it had ever gone before. Click! click! click! went the machinery, and before anybody could really imagine that the thing was true, the stair-way stopped with a bump, and the city was wound up for another ten years!

It would be useless to try to describe the joy and gratitude of the king and the people. The aristocrats were loaded with honors and presents; they and their old master were sumptuously lodged in the palace, and, in their honor, the public library was ordered to be kept open every evening, in order that the people who were busy in the day-time might go there and read the papers, which were no longer carried to them.

At the end of a year, a flag was raised on the top of the high tower, and the admiral's ship came in. The philosophers took off their bags, which were now very old and thin, and the aristocrats, with their master, were warmly welcomed on board. Being all grown up, they were no longer feared. In a few days, the ship sailed for Nassimia, and, as the aristocrats were taking leave of the sorrowing citizens, the Smart-boy stepped up to the king, and said:

"I'll tell you what I should do, if I were you. About a week before the time you expect to run down again, I'd make a lot of men go to work and wind up the city. You can do it yourselves, just as well as to wait for other people to do it for you."

"That's exactly what I'll do!" cried the king. "I never thought of it before!"

He did it, and, so far as is known, the city is running yet.

When the aristocrats reached the city of Nassimia, everybody was glad to see them, for they had become a fine, well-behaved, and well-educated body of nobility, and the admiral, standing high upon his stilts, looked down upon them with honest pride, as he presented them to the king and queen.

Lorilla shook each one of them by the hand. They did not recognize the little fairy in this handsome woman, but when she explained how the change had taken place, they were delighted.

"To think of it!" cried one of the younger aristocrats. "We never missed that bottle-washer!"

"No," said Lorilla; "nobody ever missed her. That is one reason why she was such a good one to be made a fairy. And now you must tell us your whole story."

And so the king and the queen, the giant and his army, the chancellor of the exchequer, and as many of the populace as could get near enough, crowded around to hear the story of the adventures of the aristocrats, which the Head-boy told very well.

"I should like very much to go to that curious city," said Lorilla, "especially at a time when it had run down, and everything had stopped."

"Oh, I don't believe it will ever stop any more," cried the Tail-boy. "We told them how to keep themselves agoing all the time."

THE MAN WHO MADE INSECTS FAMOUS

by Louise Seymour Hasbrouck

Jean Henri Fabre

A LITTLE boy stood in the sunlight in front of a poor farmer's hut on a desolate, wolf-haunted moor in France. His soiled, coarse frock flapped about his bare ankles; his grimy handkerchief, all too frequently lost, had been tied to his waist by a string. One would never have taken him for a scientist. But he was! He was conducting an important experiment.

It had occurred to him to wonder whether he enjoyed the sunlight with his mouth or his eyes! He set about finding out. First, he shut his eyes and opened his

mouth. No sunlight! Then he shut his mouth and opened his eyes. The sunlight was there! He repeated each process, with the same result. He had proved, then, by deduction, in the scientific manner, that he saw the sunlight with his eyes. What a discovery! That evening at supper he told the family all about it. Strange to say, they laughed at the "little simpleton," all except the fond grandmother, who was sure her grandchild was a prodigy.

A few days, or perhaps a few months, later, the same little boy heard one evening a faint "jingling" sound from some bushes. What caused it? He must know. But the bushes were very awe-inspiring in the darkness. Wolves had been known to lurk in them before now. All the same, the boy stationed himself behind some tall grass and waited. The evening passed, with no result. The next evening he was there again, and this time he was more fortunate. *Whoosh!* The singer jumped out and was promptly caught in a chubby hand. It was a grasshopper. But this particular child was not nearly so much interested in the fact that the grasshopper was a wonderful jumper, as in the discovery that a grasshopper made that kind of a song. This time, though, he did not tell the family. He did not wish to be laughed at again.

The little boy's name was Jean Henri Fabre, and he was to become one of the greatest entomologists—perhaps *the* greatest—the world has ever known. Some one at this point may say, "Oh, if he was one of those people who collect butterflies and bugs and pin them to cardboard, with long Latin names underneath, I don't want to hear about him." But wait a moment. That is what an entomologist means to most people—but Fabre was one of a different kind. Fabre's entomology meant a study of the live insects; it meant finding out all about their births and deaths, their babies and ways of caring for them, their game-hunting, their building, and their wonderful instincts—those instincts which involve a knowledge, conscious or unconscious on the part of the insect, of laws of higher mathematics, chemistry, and physics which are beyond the comprehension of most humans. It meant finding out about all these things, and then writing about them in such an interesting, vivid, poetic way that even people who are not scientists get as much pleasure out of reading Fabre's works as they do out of reading the most absorbing fiction. If an American were to describe Fabre, he might say he was "the man who made the insect famous." A Frenchman—possibly Victor Hugo—long ago gave him the striking and well-deserved title of the "Homer of the insects."

This scientist, whose works have been widely known only during the last few years, spent all of his long life in poverty, and most of it in obscurity. He was born in 1823 of a poor peasant family. How did he, whose parents and grandparents in most cases could neither read nor write—how did he come by his scientific curiosity and the mind with which to gratify it? Nobody knew—least of all, himself. "Heredity—" he wrote, "the darkness that lies behind that word! There was nothing in heredity to explain my taste for observation."

When a small boy, Fabre attended the village school, a wretched hovel which was not only a school, but a kitchen, bedroom, dining-room, and, at times, chicken-house and piggery as well. The schoolmaster, Fabre's godfather, was also a barber, bell-ringer, farmer, and choir-singer. Naturally, he did not have much time to teach. The youngsters studied their A B C's out of little penny primers at their own sweet will. There were many diversions. Often they slyly opened the door into the barn-yard, so that the hens, with their "velvet-coated chicks," and the tiny piggies entered, the latter, in Fabre's words, "troting and grumbling, curling their little tails," poking "their cold pink snouts into our hands in search of a scrap." Little Jean Fabre was much more interested in these animals than in his lessons. He was induced to study his A B C's only by a woodcut of a pigeon that embellished one of the leaves of his primer, and a large print, afterward given him, containing an "animal alphabet."

One of the duties connected with the school was to remove snails from the master's box-hedge. Instead of killing his snails, Jean took them home in his pockets. "They are so pretty!" he wrote long after. "Just think! there are yellow ones and pink, white ones and brown, all with dark spiral streaks." Sometimes the scholars turned out to help the master make hay. Then Jean made the acquaintance of the frog, and the "Hoplia, the splendid scarab who pales the azure of the heavens," the locusts, "spreading their wings, some into a blue fan, others into red," and various other fascinating creatures.

His father, the first of the family to forsake the fields for the town, was a poor innkeeper, always failing in his business. At one of these crises Jean had to leave school and earn his living as best he could, one day selling lemons at a country fair, another working with a gang of laborers on the roads. Once he dined on a few grapes, after exchanging his last sous for a volume of poems. But he never forgot his little winged and creeping friends. In this period of misery, which he felt keenly, he had time to notice the pine-chafer, "that superb beetle whose black or chestnut coat is sprinkled with specks of white velvet; which squeaks when captured, emitting a slight complaining sound, like the vibration of a pane of glass rubbed with the tip of a finger."

After this period of wandering, he managed to attend a secondary and normal school. Natural history at that time was held in utter contempt in educational circles. No one taught it—no one wanted to learn it. The necessity of earning his living made Fabre give up his nature studies, bury his specimens and notes deep in the bottom of his trunk, where they would not tempt him, and apply himself to mathematics and the physical sciences. He made rapid progress, and at the age of nineteen was appointed to a place as primary teacher in the college of Carpentras. His salary here was about $140 a year! It was a melancholy place, looking like a penitentiary rather than a school. The only recreation place was "a yard between four high walls, a sort of bear-pit, where the scholars fought for room for their games." After a few years of discontent, he received a more congenial post at the college at Ajaccio, Corsica, at a salary of about $360 a year. The beauty and interest of the surrounding country was a more considerable gain than the gain in salary. During his scanty spare time, the young schoolteacher applied himself to mathematics, to chemistry, and to collecting geological specimens, shells, and ancient coins, in which the country was rich. He met in some of his walks two traveling scientists, one of whom gave him some sound advice:

"Leave your mathematics," said he. "No one will take the least interest in your formulæ. Get to the beast, the plant; and if, as I believe, the fever burns in your veins, you will find men to listen to you. You interest yourself in shells," he went on. "That is something; but it is not enough. You must look into the animal itself. I will show you how it's done." He took a pair of sharp scissors from a nearby work-basket (this happened at dinner, between the "fruit and the cheese") and then and there showed him the anatomy of the snail in a soup-plate filled with water. It was the first and the only natural-history lesson Fabre ever received. But it was the only one he needed.

From that time on, Fabre took pains to develop his peculiar genius. When he was thirty-two, he finished his first memoir on the insect, a wonderful study of a wasp and its manner of paralyzing its prey. Two years later he published another essay, equally illuminating, on a species of beetle. These papers attracted the attention of scientists and gained him a prize from the French Institute. But, owing to his many school duties and the outside tutoring necessary to support his family, he could devote very little time to his insects, and it was twenty-five long years before the first volume of his "Souvenirs Entomologiques" appeared, a series destined to comprise many volumes.

Printed unattractively and without illustrations, they were read at first by scientists only. Some of these worthy men were displeased because the books were too interesting! They feared, Fabre said, "lest a page that is read without fatigue should not always be the expression of the truth." Fabre defended himself from this extraordinary complaint in a characteristic way:

"Come here, one and all of you," he wrote, addressing his friends the insects, "you, the sting-bearer, and you, the wing-cased armor-clads—take up my defense and bear witness in my favor. Tell of the intimate terms on which I live with you, of the patience with which I observe you, of the care with which I record your actions. Your evidence is unanimous; yes, my pages, though they bristle not with hollow formulas nor learned smatterings, are the exact narrative of facts observed, neither more nor less; and whoso cares to question you in his turn will obtain the same replies.

"And then, my dear insects, if you cannot convince these good people because you do not carry the weight of tedium, I, in my turn, will say to them:

"'You rip up the animal, and I study it alive; you turn it into an object of horror and pity, whereas I cause it to be loved; you labor in a torture-chamber and dissecting-room, I make my observation under the blue sky to the song of the cicadas; you subject cell and protoplasm to chemical tests, I study instinct in its loftiest manifestations; you pry into death, I pry into life. . . . I write, above all, for the young. I want to make them love the natural history which you make them hate; and that is why, while keeping strictly in the domain of truth, I avoid your scientific prose, which, too often, alas, seems borrowed from some Iroquois idiom.'"

The twenty-five years just alluded to formed for Fabre a season of bitter struggle and disappointment. He had married young, his family was large, and though devoted to his wife and children, it was no easy matter to support them and still have time left to develop his specialty. He was a splendid teacher, but had no talent for pushing himself, and consequently did not advance beyond an assistant professorship at a tiny salary. He was not even free from persecution. The other professors at Avignon, where he taught for twenty years, were jealous of him because the free lectures he gave on natural history attracted much favorable attention. In ridicule of his pet study, they nicknamed him "The Fly."

Yet there were a few bright spots in this period. Through his writings and genius, Fabre had gained the friendship of several celebrated men. One of these was Darwin, then at the height of his fame, who called him "the incomparable observer." Another was John Stuart Mill, the celebrated English logician, who lent him three thousand francs without security at a time of special need. The minister of education in France invited him to Paris, had him made a Chevalier of the Legion of Honor, and presented him to the emperor, Napoleon III. This honor did not destroy in the least the poise and simplicity of the country professor. As he stood at court in his shabby-genteel frock-coat (a garb he hated, but was obliged to wear on account of his profession), he thought the emperor a "simple man," and compared the chamberlains in livery who waited on the monarch to "great beetles, clad with café-au-lait wing-cases, moving with a formal gait."

At last, after forty years of drudgery and severest privation, he secured the desire of his heart—a small independent income from his books, releasing him from teaching and enabling him to own his own small cottage and garden, and, more important than either, a piece of waste ground, dedicated to thistles and insects. How he exulted in it!

"This cursed ground," he wrote, "which no one would have had as a gift to sow with a pinch of turnip-seed, is an earthly paradise for bees and wasps. Its mighty growth of thistle and centauries draws them all to me from everywhere around. Never, in my insect-hunting memories, have I seen so large a population at a single spot; all the trades have made it their rallying point. Here are hunters of every kind of game, builders in clay, weavers of cotton goods, collectors of pieces cut from a leaf or the petals of a flower, architects in pasteboard, plasterers mixing mortar, carpenters boring wood, miners digging underground galleries, workers handling goldbeater's skin, and many more.

"It is a little late, O my pretty insects," he writes pathetically,—he was at this time nearly seventy years old,—"I greatly fear the peach is offered to me only when I am beginning to have no teeth wherewith to eat it." But his misgivings were not justified. In his home-made cottage laboratory, in this barren, sun-scorched bit of ground, he was to spend more than twenty happy, laborious years, the devoted wife and young children of his second marriage caring for him and helping him in his work.

Here he completed observations and experiments begun in his young manhood. As an example of his patience, it may be recorded that his observations on the sacred beetle, or "tumble-bug," as we call it, extended over a period of forty years. The remarkable things he found out about it—its bold highway robberies, its stupendous feasts, when it sits over twenty-four hours "at table," the exquisitely shaped little "pear" the mother beetle makes for a couch and for food for her babies—all these discoveries make us regard the tumble-bug with a new and respectful interest as we watch its antics in the fields. His study of the bees and wasps took nearly as long and resulted in even more surprising knowledge. What learned surgeon can surpass in skill the wasp, who, desiring live animal food for her children, who will arrive at the eating stage some months hence, paralyzes without killing a grub by inserting her sting at exactly the spot in the neck which connects with the nerve centers? No battle tale is more exciting and gruesome than the recital of the terrible encounters of the wasp and tarantula; and few stories from human life are more pathetic than that of the shabby Grandmother Bee, who, too old for the labors of the hive, makes herself into a portress to guard its door. But space here is too short to give you more than the barest glimpse of Fabre's true wonder stories—you must read them all for yourself some day. And when you do, you will wonder how one man, with no more elaborate apparatus than you yourself could construct, could discover so many new and wonderful secrets in a domain of science hitherto considered unimportant.

During the last few years of his life, Fabre's fame gradually spread. In 1910, in his eighty-eighth year, some of his devoted disciples arranged a jubilee celebration at his dwelling-place, Serignan. On that day many famous men visited the old man in his cottage; letters and telegrams of congratulation poured in from all parts of the world. There was a banquet, and the presentation of a gold plaque engraved with his portrait. The venerable poet-scientist, so long neglected, so poor, was almost overcome. Tears came into his eyes, and into the eyes of those who watched him. The recognition was indeed belated, but it came in time to brighten the last five years of his life. He died in the fall of 1915; and people in all countries stopped for a time their talk of war and battles to mourn for the man who, loving so much his "pretty insects," interpreted their little lives in a way to illumine the great mystery of the universe itself.

A Tender-hearted Monster

by Alice Calhoun Haines

"Now, see here," said the Dragon, "are you going to betray me?"

"I—I don't know," faltered Molly, clutching her dolly nervously. "I—I don't think mama'd like it if she knew you were here."

"That's just the point," the Dragon answered; "of course she wouldn't. No lady would; and yet, what harm have I done or what harm do I do? It's the only home I've got."

"But it's our garden," Molly said; "and we like to walk in it."

"Well," answered the Dragon, "I don't mind. You may walk in it all you please, and I'll never say a word. I've been here a month already, and nobody's ever guessed it. You wouldn't know it now, but that I told you; and I wouldn't have told you only that I hated to see you crying so hard about your doll when I could give it back to you just as easy as not."

"Yes," said Molly, "it was very good of you." She hugged Arabella, her favorite wax beauty, closer to her heart. "Oh,

Bella," she whispered, "what an adventure you've had! Tumbling into the dried-up well, and spending all this time with a dragon! Goodness, child, I don't see how you ever lived through it! But it *was* good of him to give you back."

"You know," the Dragon continued, "if the Prince should find out my hiding-place it would settle things pretty thoroughly for me. I've almost forgotten how to fight. Anyhow, dragons never *do* beat the princes; you must know that, if you know anything."

"But there isn't any prince," said Molly.

"You don't say!"—the Dragon raised himself high on his hind legs and peered out at her—"you don't say so!" His head was thrust far out of the well now, and Molly drew back in terror. He was a very dreadful-looking beast; but there was also something quite familiar about his appearance. For a moment this puzzled her; but then she saw it was his likeness to a picture in her new fairy-book that caused the feeling.

"Don't be afraid," he said, when he saw

her shrink away; "I won't hurt you. But do you really mean to tell me that there isn't any prince at all?"

"Why, yes," Molly answered faintly; "they all died long ago. At least, there aren't any in this country, I'm quite sure. I thought the dragons were all dead, too."

"I believe they are—all but me. And if it hadn't been for the old fairy Merenthusa I shouldn't be here either. It's a queer story—" he shook his head sadly.

"Oh, tell it," cried Molly—she was a little girl who dearly loved to listen to stories.

"Now, see here," said the Dragon, "I'll tell you the story, if you will promise not to tell your folks about my being here. Come, now—is it a bargain?"

Molly considered for a few moments.

"I'd love to hear the story," she said, "but just think how dreadful it would be if mama or papa were walking alone in the garden, and you should snap off one of their feet."

"I wouldn't;" the Dragon answered; "I never eat anybody but just princesses. I say, you aren't a princess, are you?"

"Oh, no!" cried Molly, hastily, "indeed, I'm not. I'm just a little girl—Molly Forster."

"I'm glad of that," he assured her; "I wouldn't like to eat you a bit, but it would be my duty, you know, if you were a princess."

"Would it? How dreadful!" Molly's little face grew quite white with horror.

"You needn't think I'd enjoy it," said the Dragon, "for I never did one bit. I want to whisper to you. It's a terrible thing I have to say, and I'd rather not speak it aloud."

"There's nobody near," Molly objected; "there isn't a soul in the garden but just you and me. I—I'd rather not put my ear down. Can't you say it without that?"

"Well, if I must, I must," grumbled the Dragon. "I did not think you were so suspicious; but nobody trusts me. I'm beginning to get used to it; and yet all the time, you know, *I've got a tender heart.*" He patted his chest with his paw as he spoke. "Yes; I've got a tender heart."

"I'm very glad to hear it," said Molly, cheerfully. "It's a nice thing to have."

"Not for a dragon, my dear," the monster answered; "you're all off there. On the contrary, it's a drawback, a most terrible drawback!"

"Why, I don't see that," Molly cried. "My mama says that there is nothing so bad as a hard heart. You can cure other things, you know, but you can't cure that. If you are really hard-hearted you have just got to stay so. Why, I believe it's the very worst fault there is."

"For a little girl, I'll admit, or for a princess; but not for us. It's what we all aspire after, and most of us have it. I never did." He sighed deeply. "That's one of the particular features of my story. Shall I tell it to you?"

"Yes, indeed," cried Molly.

"Well," said the Dragon, "there were seven of us, and we lived in a cave in the mountains. It was a big cave with lots of cracks and crevices and crannies to play hide-and-seek in, and my! but we had a good time! Our father died when we were babies, and our mother let us do just whatever we chose. She was the most indulgent parent that dragon ever had; and yet *she* didn't have a tender heart. She could eat a princess with all the gusto in the world; and that is the thing I never did manage. Oh! h-m-m! It has embittered my whole life; however, I'm not up to that yet.

"As I said, we had a glorious time up there in our old cave in the mountains. We never went away to school—our mother couldn't part with us—so we had a private tutor, and that was fun, too.

My!—we led him a life! The jokes we played on that poor old fellow would make you split your sides laughing; but I haven't time to tell about them now. I remember one morning in particular—but never mind; I guess I won't tell you that."

"Oh, please do," cried Molly; "I love to hear about naughtinesses."

"No," said the Dragon, "I don't think it would be strictly honorable. You see I'm here in your mother's garden, enjoying

"We had a private tutor, and that was fun, too"

her hospitality,—her guest you might almost say,—so I must be doubly careful, and tell you only those stories that she would care for you to hear—stories that have a moral."

"I don't like that kind," pouted Molly.

"Well, you ought to," said the Dragon; "that's all that concerns me. Shall I go on?"

Molly thought a moment. "What is the moral of this one?" she asked.

"Never be tender-hearted," the Dragon answered. "It's the best one I know."

"Oh," cried Molly, "why, that's not a moral at all!"

"You wait and see if it's not," said the Dragon, with much confidence. "I think I am the best judge of that."

"Go on," Molly whispered. She felt that

she was a very naughty little girl, but she had not time to grieve over the matter just then.

"Well," said the Dragon, "one by one my brothers left the old cave, till at last I alone was left. I had always been delicate, and then, too, I was the baby, so my mother naturally hated to part with me. But when I was about five years old I grew impatient of that quiet life, and determined that it was time for me also to go forth to seek my fortune.

"My mother felt very sad when I told her what was in my mind. 'My dear child,' she said, 'it is what I have been dreading for a long time, but if you feel that you cannot be happy here any longer, why, of course, I can't keep you. Nothing would induce me to make one of my children unhappy for a single moment.' Now wasn't she a good creature?"

"Indeed she was," said Molly.

"Next morning I started upon my travels. I shall never forget how strange everything seemed to me, secluded as I had always been in my happy home among the rocks. I remember well seeing my first man—my heart leaped within me, for I had never see anything like him before, and 'twas only by hearsay that I knew what he was. Of course, the correct thing was to chase him; all my brothers had told me that, so I began at once. I never thought that I should mind. My brothers all enjoyed it, and I expected to also; but when I saw the horror depicted upon the poor fellow's face and heard his breath coming in quick, panting gasps, it gave me such a queer, sick sort of feeling that I stopped running and the man got away.

"At first I could not imagine what was the cause of my weakness, but the meaning flashed upon me all of a sudden. I was tender-hearted! The conviction forced itself upon me and nearly drove me mad."

"Poor Dragon!" said Molly; and then she thought, "Oh, what a bad, bad little girl I am, to be sorry because he did not eat the man! I didn't think I could be so wicked!"

"Yes," said the dragon, "that was how I first knew it, and from that day to this I have never known a happy moment! It's been the same way with everything I've undertaken; I'd go out in the woods and see a lovely princess tied to a tree, a sight that would make most dragons leap for joy, and it would just make me cry! I could not help it, somehow, the tears would come.

"I'd say over and over to myself, 'You're a dragon. You're a dragon. It's your duty to eat her. She won't mind. Princesses never do. It's what they're made for.' But try as I would I could not bring myself to do it. I'd go away and hide in a cave till some one had untied her, and sometimes I'd overhear remarks like this: "They say there is a dragon around here, and, do you know, the Princess Rose, or Belinda, was tied to this tree for three whole days and he never came near her. I wouldn't give much for a beast like that!' Oh, it was most humiliating, and the older I grew the worse it was.

"At last one day things came to a crisis. I was walking in the forest when suddenly I came upon three beautiful maidens, all in a row, tied to sycamore trees. I just turned about and ran! I'm sorry to confess it, but it's true. I scuttled over the ground as fast as I could crawl, slipping under the brushwood and whisking around the tree-trunks, till suddenly I stopped spell-bound, for there—right in front of me—was another of them! I just stood still and looked at her, my eyes almost bulging out of my head!

" 'So this is the way you bear yourself, oh, valiant one!' she cried, her voice full of fury. 'This is the way you devour princesses, oh, ranger of the woods! Very pretty conduct; very pretty, indeed!'

" 'Good gracious!' I gasped, 'do you want me to eat you?' I had never expected this. 'Let others scoff as they will,' I always thought, 'at least I have the sympathy of the princesses.'

" 'Look at me,' she commanded; and then I understood. She was not a woman at all, but a fairy. I knew her at once by her eyes; they were pale green and twinkled like stars. Her name was Merenthusa, and she was both wicked and powerful.

" 'They were my step-daughters,' she said, 'and I tied them to the trees this morning. I knew that there was a dragon near and I wanted to get rid of them. Then I tied myself to this tree, intending to make myself invisible when you passed, and so escape unharmed. When my husband returned he would find me here weeping and wailing over the fate of his three lovely daughters. I would have told him that you were frightened away before you had eaten me. That would have been true, at all events.'

" 'No, it wouldn't,' I cried, and I jumped at her; and, do you know, I really believe I should have eaten her, but she raised her wand, and—that is all I can remember.

"I think she must have put me into a magic sleep, in which I lay for years and years, for about two months ago I woke and found myself in what used to be the forest—it is only a patch of woods now; a great thicket had grown up around me, and I suppose that is how I had escaped detection.

"When I scrambled from it everything seemed changed; nothing was as it used to be, and I felt lost and strange. I traveled a great many miles, always during the night, and hid in the daytime, and after a while I made my way into your garden, found this old well, and here I have been ever since. That's my story. Now remember, you promised not to tell."

"Molly! Molly! Molly!" It was her mother's voice calling.

The little girl started up from the ground, where she had been sitting, and ran toward the house. She felt queer and stiff.

"I don't suppose I can break my word," she whispered, "though mama would love to hear about him. Oh, I wish to-morrow would hurry up and come. I am going to get him to tell me a new story every day."

But, strange to say, next morning when Molly sought her friend the dragon in the garden he was nowhere to be found, and the little girl never saw nor heard of him again.

SOME MAN-EATERS

by Ernest Ingersoll

How the title "man-eaters" is to be understood depends a great deal upon what part of the world you happen to be in. To us North Americans, and to our English cousins, it has a very foreign sound, since there is no animal in our forests, nor hardly any along our coasts, to which the term is commonly applied or would properly belong. If you should say "man-eater" in South America, the native would at once think of the cayman and the jaguar, and similarly, in India, the crocodile would be suggested along the Ganges, and the royal tiger in Bengal. In Africa, it is the lion which would at once be brought to mind. To a West Indian, or to the pearl-fishers of any coast, the shark is the dreaded foe, while the Vancouver Indian looks upon the ugly cuttle-fish as the man-eater of his region, and the Eskimo fears the polar bear.

While all wild carnivorous beasts capable of coping with men may become man-eaters,—since human flesh is no doubt quite as palatable as the flesh of any of the other animals upon which they are accustomed to feed,—yet, properly speaking, only those are called "man-eaters" that, having once tasted human blood, are supposed always afterward to be hankering for it, and never to be quite satisfied with any less noble diet. They are thought to be forever on the watch for men, lying in ambush and seeking every means of destroying them, and never feeding on anything else, excepting to satisfy extreme hunger. Such beasts, being especially dreaded, are credited with extraordinary size, strength and ferocity.

In Africa, every district has a lion of this kind, which is feared by the whole region as much as all the rest of the lions there put together, and the case is equally true of central India. The lion truly deserves the royal name he bears. Although by no means of great size, the strength of his massive shoulders and forelegs, and of the thick muscles of his great neck and firm, square jaws, is so enormous that he can drag down the heaviest buffalo and overthrow the powerful giraffe, whose head towers above the trees, and whose skin is nearly an inch thick. There is no animal, even the elephant, which the lion hesitates to attack; yet notwithstanding the power of the machinery which has been given him for this purpose, it has been packed in such small compass in his lithe body that he can overtake and prey upon quadrupeds as fleet as zebras and antelopes.

Although he has great speed, the lion does not depend so much upon chase in the open field as upon strategy, in securing his prey. He follows about from pasture to pasture, and from spring to spring, the herds of deer and buffaloes as they change their feeding-places at different seasons. Remaining asleep, and concealed in the recesses of the forest or among secluded rocks, during the day, he sallies out at night in company with one or two friends, or perhaps with his mate and two half-grown cubs, or often alone, and repairs to the nearest water-hole. In Africa, water is very scarce. The springs are few and far between, and the animals of the whole region must resort to a particular fountain, sometime during the night, to quench the thirst which there alone can be allayed. The lion knows this, and goes to the vicinity of this spring, choosing the early part of the evening, if the moon is to rise early, or waiting until morning, after the moon has set, if it be on the wane, so as not to show himself. When some convenient prey approaches, he leaps upon it, bears it down with his weight, breaking its neck by the stroke of his heavy paw or the crushing strength of his jaws, and drags the body away into the jungle, to be feasted upon at leisure.

At such times, if you should happen to pass near him, you would hear a low, deep moaning as he eats, repeated five or six times, and ending in faintly audible sighs. At other times, he startles the forest with loud, deep-toned, solemn roars, uttered in quick succession. Often, a troop may be heard roaring in concert, making music inconceivably grand to the hunter's ear. The effect is greatly enhanced when the hearer chances to be all alone in the depths of the forest, at the dead hour of midnight, and within twenty yards of the fountain which the troop of lions is approaching.

In central Africa, many of the native tribes do not bury the bodies of their dead, but simply carry them forth and leave them lying anywhere on the plain. Lions are always prowling about, and, finding many of these corpses, do not hesitate to dine off them, for it is not true that the king of beasts will not eat what he himself has not killed. Afterward, that

lion, particularly if he is an old and cunning fellow, becomes a very dangerous neighbor. I do not believe that the lion has from the first a preference for the flesh of men over fresh venison or beef, but that it is an agreeable discovery to him that men are animals, and good to eat; and, furthermore, that he soon recognizes unarmed men as less able to resist or escape from him than are the four-footed beasts. He therefore keeps an eye out for human prey, since it costs him less trouble.

In the tropical wastes of India, the forest, or jungle, is grown up very densely with cane, stout, tangled grass, creepers, vines, and so on, until the only way to get through it is by following paths kept open by constant traveling. In traversing these dark and narrow passages, the traveler is peculiarly exposed to attack from the lions and tigers which make the jungle their home, and the native Hindoos are often stricken down. Then ensues a grand hunt from the nearest village, assisted by some English officer, who, with his cool courage and precise shooting, usually does more to kill the beast (if he is killed) than all the rest of the villagers combined.

Generally, the animal will try to get away and hide, when he hears the hunters approaching. But if he is a hardened old man-eater, it does not take long to bring him to bay, since he has grown courageous, or reckless, or both. Then those who are on foot look out for their safety as best they can, usually by climbing the nearest tree, and those who are on horseback dismount and get upon the back of an elephant, where, in a sort of basket strapped upon the great animal, two or three will stand together, ready to shoot the moment they get a chance, while the elephant slowly crushes his way toward that spot in the thick jungle where the tiger is heard growling. The books about life in

India, and the letters which sportsmen write home to the English newspapers, are full of accounts of such hunts; but none that I know of is more thrilling, or better shows the terrific danger sometimes encountered in such contests of men-eating lions and tigers with lion-killing men, than an incident related by Charles Waterton, in his charming "Essays on Natural History."

Three English officers and a lot of natives were hunting for two lions, which had made a raid upon a village the night before, and in the course of the day one of the pair was killed, but the other escaped to the jungle. When at last his hiding-place was discovered, the three officers got upon an elephant and proceeded toward the heart of the jungle, to rouse the royal fugitive a second time. They found him standing under a large bush, with his face directly toward them. He allowed them to approach within range of his spring, when he made a sudden leap, and clung upon the elephant's trunk. The men fired, but without avail, and the elephant managed to shake his troublesome visitor off, but was so frightened that he became uncontrollable, and when the lion made another spring at him, rushed in headlong fear out into the clearing. The officers, therefore, had to give up all idea of forcing the elephant to face the lion again, but one of them, Captain Woodhouse, took the desperate resolution to proceed on foot in quest of the game; and finally seeing him, fired though the bushes, the only effect of which was to make the lion retire still deeper into the brake.

Resolved not to let the game escape, his companions, the two lieutenants, now took the elephant, intending to proceed around the jungle, so as to discover the route the lion had taken on the other side. But Captain Woodhouse reloaded his rifle, and alone followed the tracks through the thicket. Finally, Lieutenant Delamain joined him.

Proceeding cautiously, after a few steps the lieutenant saw the lion, and instantly fired, which enraged the beast so that he rushed toward him at full speed. Captain Woodhouse saw the movement, and knew that if he tried to get into a better position for firing, he would put himself directly in the way of the charge, so decided to stand still, trusting that the lion would pass close by him, unaware, when he could perhaps shoot to advantage. But he was deceived. The furious animal saw him, and flew at him with a dreadful roar. In an instant the rifle was broken and thrown out of the captain's hand, his left arm at the same moment being seized by the claws, and his right by the teeth, of his antagonist. At this desperate juncture, Lieutenant Delamain ran up and discharged his piece full at the lion. This caused both beast and man to fall to the ground together, while the lieutenant hastened out of the thicket to reload his gun. The lion now began to crunch the captain's arm; but as the brave man, notwithstanding the pain which this horrid process caused, had the cool, determined resolution to lie still, the lordly savage let the arm drop out of his mouth, and quietly placed himself in a crouching posture, with both his paws upon the thigh of his fallen foe. While things were in this untoward position, the captain unthinkingly raised his hand to support his head, which had got placed ill at ease in his fall. Instantly the lion seized the lacerated arm a second time, and crunched it as before, breaking the bone higher up. This hint was not lost on Captain Woodhouse, who saw at once the imprudence of stirring, and to the motionless attitude which this lesson taught him to keep thereafter he undoubtedly owed his life.

But while death was close upon him, as he lay bleeding and broken in the power of the most mighty enemy which a man can meet in the forest, and was closing his eyes to a world on the point of vanishing forever, he heard the welcome sound of feet approaching. But the lieutenants were in the wrong direction. Aware that, if his friends fired, the balls would hit him after they had passed through the lion's body, Captain Woodhouse quietly spoke, in a low voice, "To the other side! To the other side!" Hearing the voice, they for the first time saw the horrible position of their commander, and having cautiously but quickly made the circuit, Lieutenant Delamain, whose coolness had been conspicuous in many an encounter with wild beasts, fired from a short distance at the lion, over the person of the prostrate warrior. The beast started up a little, quivered, the massive head sank down, and in an instant he lay dead, close beside his intended victim.

The lesson to be learned from this true story of nerve and heroism is that, when a person is in the power of a lion, tiger, leopard or panther, or any other of the great cats, he must feign death and lie absolutely still, if he hopes for life. Let him make a motion, and his foe will pounce upon him as the house-cat does on an escaping mouse; but so long as he keeps still, he has a chance. Yet not every one has the nerve to do so. With dogs, wolves and bears, on the other hand, the only way, when attacked, is to resist sturdily to the last limit of your strength, since, once having a victim in their power, they never cease worrying it until it is utterly dead. Sometimes, nevertheless, resolution and nerve are no protection, since there is no opportunity to exercise them. This was the case in a dreadful tragedy which happened in the lonely camp of that great Nimrod, Gordon Cumming,

during one of his hunting expeditions to the far interior of Africa. Lions had been roaring about all day, but at last their voices ceased, and apparently they all went off. After their supper, three of the men went off to a little fire they had built, near some bushes, at some distance from the main camp-fire, and lay down—two of them under the same blanket.

"Suddenly," says Mr. Cumming, "the appalling voice of an angry lion burst upon our ear, within a few yards of us, followed by the shrieking of the Hottentots. Again and again the deafening roar was repeated. We heard John and Ruyter shriek, 'The lion! the lion!'

"Still, for a few minutes, we thought the lion was no doubt only chasing one of the dogs around the kraal; but, all at once, John Stofolus rushed into the midst of us, almost speechless with fear and terror, his eyes bursting from their sockets, and shrieked out: 'The lion! the lion! the lion! He has got Hendric; he dragged him away from the fire beside me. I struck him with the burning brands upon his head, but he would not let go his hold. Hendric is dead! Oh! Hendric is dead! Let us take fire and seek him!' The rest of my people rushed about, shrieking and yelling as if they were mad. I was at once angry with them for their folly, and told them that if they did not stand still and keep quiet, the lion would have another of us; and that very likely there was a troop of them. I ordered the dogs, which were nearly all fast, to be let loose, and the fire to be increased as far as could be. I then shouted Hendric's name, but all was still. I told my men that Hendric was dead, and that a regiment of soldiers could not help him; and, hunting my dogs forward, I had everything brought within the cattle-kraal, when we lighted our fire, and closed the entrance as well as we could.

"It appeared that, when the unfortunate

Hendric rose to drive in the oxen, the lion had watched him to his fireside; and he had scarcely lain down when the brute sprang upon him and Ruyter (for both lay under one blanket), with his appalling, thunderous roar, and, roaring as he lay, grappled him with his fearful claws, and kept biting him on the breast and shoulder, all the while feeling for his neck, having got hold of which, he at once dragged him away backward around the bush into the dense shade."

The next day, toward evening, knowing the lion would return for a second victim that night, Mr. Cumming decided to seek him out and kill him. So, setting his dogs to work, and following the track along which the mangled body of poor Hendric had been dragged, the hunter soon came up with the savage beast, among some thornbrush. But let him tell it:

"As I approached, he stood, his horrid head right to me, with open jaws, growling fiercely, his tail waving from side to side. On beholding him, I dashed my steed forward within thirty yards of him, and shouted, 'Your time is up, old fellow!' I halted my horse, and, placing my rifle to my shoulder, waiting for a broadside. This the next moment he exposed, when I sent a bullet through his shoulder, and dropped him on the spot. . . . I ordered John to cut off his head and forepaws and bring them to the wagons, and, mounting my horse, galloped home, having been absent about fifteen minutes. When the Bakalahari women heard that the man-eater was dead, they all commenced dancing about with joy, calling me their father."

Perhaps the next most important class of animal-enemies of men is that of the sharks. Of sharks, there is a large number of species. They are of various sizes and inhabit all seas, from Arctic and Antarctic to tropical latitudes. They are most abundant, of greatest size and of most impor-

tance, in the tropics, however; and it is among the coral rings of the Pacific Islands, and along the shining sands of the Gold Coast, that the shark is the most dreaded.

In the South Sea Islands, everybody swims from infancy, like so many water-dogs. It is asserted that a Mexican is taught to ride before he learns to walk. It is just as near truth—and, indeed, very little removed—to say that a native of the Sandwich or Society Islands can swim before he can creep. Babies a few months old are tossed into the surf, and, before they have cut their teeth, they become as lively and safe in the water as ducks. We have accounts of these people swimming incredible distances. Ten or a dozen miles seem to offer no difficulty whatever to them; and when ships approach the shores of the less civilized islands, they are surrounded by men and women and children, who sport about the bows like dolphins, long before the sailors have thought of taking in sail or preparing to anchor.

But along a tropical coast, where hundreds of people are constantly at play in the surf, and often are far out from shore, it is to be expected that sharks will often get a good meal. Fortunately, all sharks, or nearly all, are surface-swimmers. They do not lurk at the bottom or float in the depths, like the true bony fishes; usually, therefore, their great triangular back-fins appear above the water and give the bathers warning. The sight always produces great consternation, and a rush for the shore takes place, though sometimes the crowd will unite, and, by shouting and splashing, frighten the great fish away. Yet, not infrequently he comes upon them unawares, and, dashing into their midst like a streak of white light, is scarcely observed before the death-scream of some wretched bather is drowned, almost before uttered, as he is dragged down, and the next wave rolls in red with blood, or casts high upon the gleaming beach some torn fragments of what was once their friend. Looking seaward, they see the shark cruising back and forth, eager for another victim, and perhaps they go out to attack him, in revenge. But the surf-riding is over for that day, for the shark will stay there many hours, in hope of more prey.

Perhaps the metropolis of shark life is off the western coast of Africa. They found there always plenty of food, furnished by the slave-ships which used to haunt those waters. There are few good harbors along the whole of that extensive sea-coast. The ships, therefore, were obliged to anchor some distance away, and send back and forth to the shore by the small boats. It was thus that the slaves were taken on board. But the passage through the surf was always dangerous, and often the yawls were capsized. On such occasions, few of the blacks were ever seen again. The sudden activity of the swarms of ever-present sharks, and the blood-stained water, told sufficiently well their fate. Troops of these same sharks would follow a slave-ship clear across the Atlantic, sure of their daily meal of dead and dying captives, which were thrown overboard from those floating dens of the most awful human misery the world has ever seen—misery that we cannot even think of without a sick and shuddering sense of horror.

Some of the Polynesian fishermen before alluded to, nevertheless, do not hesitate to attack and conquer the largest shark in his native element. The fish does not see very well, and is not very quick in any but a straight-ahead movement. The swimmer, armed with a long knife, watches the shark's onslaught coolly, and just as the great fish opens his horrid mouth to seize the brave man in his jaws, the fisherman dives out of reach, and plunges his knife deep into the shark's belly, as the disap-

pointed monster passes over his head. This feat is attempted only by the coolest and ablest divers, you may be sure, but it is done; and it is one of the most splendid examples I know of the success of human pluck against animal force greatly its superior. Should the swimmer fail in his plan by an instant of time, his life must pay the penalty. The pearl-divers in the Gulf of California are said to employ an equally audacious method of fighting the sharks which torment them when at work on the deep-sea beds of the pearl-oyster. They carry with them a stick of hard wood about a foot long, sharp-pointed at both ends. Finding that a shark is meditating an attack, they grasp this stick in the middle, and calmly await him. When he opens wide his mouth, they dexterously shove in the sharp stick, crosswise, and then get out of his way as fast as possible, while the too-eager shark shuts his jaws only to find that he has mortally wounded himself by punching holes in the roof and floor of his mouth. I cannot vouch for this story; the reader must take it for what it is worth.

Not long ago I read, in the New York *Herald,* a diver's narrative of how he escaped from a shark which seemed to have too great curiosity as to his edible qualities. This man was known as "On Deck," and he had an eventful life. A sailor in youth, a diver in manhood, and a "ne'er-do-weel" in old age, he saw more than falls to the lot of most men. In California, in 1851, a ship lost an anchor in the harbor of San Francisco, and "On Deck" was sent for to recover it. While so engaged, he noticed a shark hovering a few feet above him, evidently observing his movements. The fish was at least eighteen feet long, and was known as the "bottle-nose," one of the most voracious of the shark kind. This discovery naturally alarmed the diver. He had found the anchor, made a cable fast to it, and was about ascending, when the appearance of the shark made him pause. He had heard that sharks did not molest men in armor. He doubted this, and did not feel now like risking the experiment. He moved a few paces from the anchor— the shark moved, too. He returned to his former place—the shark followed. He was evidently, to use his own words, "spotted by the bottle-nose for a supper," and, unless signally favored, would fall a victim to its voracity. He hardly knew how to act, when he thought how the cuttle-fish often escapes its enemies by darkening the waters with an inky liquor ejected from its body. He accordingly stirred up the mud at the bottom till the water was darkened around him, cast off weights, and signaled the man to haul him up. The shark snapped at him as he ascended, and three of his toes were taken off. A little more and his foot would have gone, a stout boot only saving it. The happy idea of muddying the water was all that preserved his life.

The shark's mouth is one of the most formidable means of destruction I know of among animals anywhere. It is on the under side of the head, some distance back of the end of the snout, and crescent-shaped. The teeth are in three to seven close, crescentic, parallel rows, the largest and oldest in front, the smaller ones behind—that is, farthest inside the mouth. Some sharks have more than 200 of these teeth. They are three-cornered, exceedingly thin and sharp-pointed, and in some cases have saw-edges. When the mouth is wide open they stand erect, and almost protrude from the lips, but when it is closed they lie down flat, out of the way. When those in the front row wear out or break off, the next row behind is gradually pushed forward to take their places. The shark thus has reserves of teeth which, operated by the tough and exceedingly

muscular mechanism of the jaws, are able to bite through anything, especially since the bite is nearly always accompanied by a rolling or wrenching movement which causes the teeth to act like a saw, and thus cut through the quicker. For some of the larger sharks in the South Seas, it would be only a moderate mouthful to take half a man's body in, and clip him off at the waist. Nevertheless, I believe fewer persons have lost their lives by sharks than we generally suppose, though many narrow escapes are constantly happening.

There are some other fishes which would regard it as very good luck to find a human body in their power,—the old piratical threat, of making "food for the fishes" out of their captives, was not altogether an idle one,—but there are few, if any, besides the sword-fish, that could do a man much harm, or would be likely to. A friend at my elbow suggests the whale; but I object. The whale is not a fish!

There is a sea-beast, nevertheless, which makes a formidable antagonist to man, and does not hesitate to attack him, or anything else that comes in its way. This is the cuttle-fish, which is also known as the devil-fish, in allusion to its frightful appearance and evil disposition. It has a shapeless pouch of a body, spotted, rough and wrinkled, from all sides of which branch stout, elastic arms of a leathery character, some of which are stretched far away, winding in and out among the slimy rocks and stems of sea-weed, and others are shortened up close to the body, as the animal lies concealed in a dark and muddy crevice of a broken rock at the bottom of the sea, patiently waiting for its prey. Two enormous round, bulging eyes are ever staring about, and nothing escapes their attention. Let a living thing come within reach of those arms, and its fate is sealed. Quick as thought, the snaky member clutches the prey, and holds on by a host of little suckers and tiny hooks, in the grasp of which the strongest and slipperiest animal is fast. Other arms whip out to the help of the first, paralysis soon overpowers the unfortunate captive, and slowly the arms are contracted until the prey is brought within reach of the sharp, parrot-like jaws, when it is deliberately eaten up.

Some of these cuttle-fishes are of vast size. They are abundant in the Eastern Mediterranean, on the coast of British Columbia, on the Pacific coast of Asia, on the Banks of Newfoundland and else-where. They lurk near the shore, hiding very quietly among the rocks, where, as they are mud-color, they are not easily seen.

The Indians of Puget Sound eat these cuttle-fishes, baking the flesh in the ground. They go in canoes and hunt for them, spearing them with a long handled harpoon when discovered. It is exceed-ingly dangerous business, and many have lost their lives at it, besides those who now and then are dragged down when bathing over the spot where a cuttle-fish lies in wait.

This frightful tyrant over all the inhabit-ants of the ocean must be allowed a place among our man-eaters; and a great deal more might be said about his peculiar and interesting, though always deadly, habits, were there room.

Turning from salt to fresh waters, no more feared and hated animals stand in the way of human enjoyment than the crocodiles and alligators, which swarm in all tropical rivers from Borneo to Guate-mala. The most famous of these ugly rep-tiles are the long-snouted, hungry gavial of the Ganges, the crocodile of the Nile, the cayman of the Amazonian region, and the alligator of our own Southern States. Their jaws are of great extent and strength, and filled with strong, sharp teeth, while the broad tail is able to deliver so effective a blow as to stun almost any animal which it strikes, and even splinter a stout boat. Nothing can exceed the ugli-ness of their rough, knotted hide, so thick that a rifle bullet glances off without harm, or equal the stony glare of the cold, glassy eyes. The crocodiles haunt the shallows of streams, lurking among the rank vegeta-tion which grows along marshy shores, or lying asleep upon banks and half-sub-merged islands of mud. Sometimes per-sons, finding one thus, have mistaken it for an old water-soaked log of drift-wood, and stepped upon it. It was fortunate if they discovered their mistake in time to get out of the reach of the powerful tail. When swimming, crocodiles move about with only the tip of the snout, where the nostrils are, out of water; and, if they want to escape notice, they will sink altogether beneath the surface so quietly that not a ripple disturbs the water. Thus they stealthily approach any animal swimming in the stream, or drinking upon the mar-gin, and, making a sudden rush when close by, drag it down before it has time to make an effort to escape. The South American and West Indian species, known as caymans, are the most active and dan-gerous of all, and a great many negro slaves and Indians lose their lives through them every year. The same thing happens on the Nile, and, to a less extent, in the bayous of Louisiana and Florida. The peo-ple there get somewhat careless, and forget how quietly the alligator approaches, and how terrible is his attack when within reach. In the United States, however, not many of these disagreeable creatures reach a sufficient size to make them able to drag down and devour a full-grown man.

The history of the natives of India is full of dark and bloody rites, which shock all civilized hearts by their blind superstition and cruelty. Human life seems of very small account to those Eastern nations, and most of their deities are fearful tyrants, to be dreaded and appeased rather than loved and honored. It has always been a pagan idea that, when any misfortune came upon a family or a nation, it was an expression of anger on the part of a god, and that the only way to get rid of present distress, or avert a threatened disaster, was to sacrifice, on an altar consecrated to the particular deity from which the affliction was supposed to come, something of great value. Sometimes it was the first of a farmer's fruit or crops; sometimes the fattest ox or the whitest dove; sometimes quantities of gold and precious stones, which were given for the support of the temples of this god, or made into images of him; and along the Ganges, the Hindoo mothers bid their tender babes a heart-rending farewell, and set them afloat on the tide of that vast stream for the crocodiles to eat.

The subjection of India to England has put a stop to this terrible custom to a great extent, but it is still occasionally followed. The Hindoo mother is suffering under some real trouble, or the village in which she lives is visited by pestilence or some other calamity, or her priest tells her that a catastrophe will follow unless she sacrifices her child. Perhaps there are many mothers who hope similarly to avert the frown of their god and save their neighbors from calamity,—for I do not believe any woman would put her baby to death merely to save herself from suffering; and so these women make little boats of rushes, dress the laughing and crowing infants as though for a festival, heap the little boat up with flowers, and, with the semblance of joy but with hearts almost dead with grief, commit their darlings to the wide, rolling, merciless river, and watch the pigmy craft as the eddies toss it this way

and that, while the current bears it on to where the chubby little hands will be held up in vain, and the delicate voice be hushed forever.

Surely the crocodiles belong in the horrible society of man-eaters.

Returning to four-footed beasts, it is hard to find any, besides the lion and other large cats, that will attack man without any provocation. Some of the bears, when severely pressed by hunger, are very savage, and may perhaps prey upon man at such times, but instances of their doing so are, I think, very rare. The grizzly bear of our Rocky Mountains is the most ferocious of its race, and one authority says of it: "If it is not certain that he will voluntarily attack a human being, it is certain that, if attacked, he will pursue the assailant to the last, nor quit the conflict while life remains." The bears can hardly be classed among man-eaters, I think; yet they are very dangerous enemies of man, and certainly the grizzly and the polar bear should be numbered with the animals that *kill* man. And if such beasts may be mentioned here, we must not forget the "rogue" elephant, as certain old cross leaders of the herd are called, for he is a very dangerous fellow to be in the same grove with; and the black rhinoceros of South Africa, who, when on his native heath, does not wait to do the polite thing, but introduces himself by a fierce snort and a headlong charge as unexpected as it is impetuous. But, of course, the elephant and rhinoceros could not eat any portion of their victims,—their food is wholly vegetable; at the same time, I do not know of beasts more dangerous to meet.

There are no other animals that I know of which could properly be called man-eaters, excepting wolves, and they are timid about attacking, unless they are in packs and starving. So much has been written about them of late, that I refrain from saying a great deal. You cannot do better than to read Mr. Hamerton's talk on this subject in his "Chapters on Animals." It is very rare that a man's life is lost by the attack of wolves, though, like other beasts, they will fight when put in a corner. On our western plains, there is a tradition which seems to have a considerable foundation of truth concerning a mad wolf, which can properly be told here:

Half a century ago, bands of trappers used to wander through the northern Rocky Mountains, shooting and trapping bears, wolves, foxes, beavers, otters, and other animals, for the sake of their fur. When winter came on, it was their custom to settle in a fixed camp at some convenient spot, and make short excursions, while in summer they roamed about the cañons. One winter night, where several companies happened to be close together, the men were all asleep, when suddenly a cry of

"Mad wolf! Mad wolf!" rang through the silent camp, and frightened men leaped up from their blankets only in time to see a dark form vanishing swiftly into the darkness, and hear shrill howls die away in the distance. It was not long before the effects began to be seen. Dogs were seized with hydrophobia and shot, till nearly all were gone. Not one alone, but nearly all the camps had been visited, and, one by one, men in each of these little, far-isolated communities were seized with the dreadful disease, and were left to die. How many lives were thus lost I do not know, and no one ever can tell, but there were many; and all through the next summer the skeletons and bodies of wolves were found scattered over that region, and these evidently had been bitten by the rabid animal and died of hydrophobia. It is a horrible story to think of, and a fit conclusion to a talk about "Man-Eaters."

MIDSUMMER PIRATES

by Richard H. Davis

THE boys living at the Atlantic House, and the boys boarding at Chadwick's, held mutual sentiments of something not unlike enmity—feelings of hostility from which even the older boarders were not altogether free. Nor was this unnatural under the circumstances. When Judge Henry S. Carter and his friend Dr. Prescott first discovered Manasquan, such an institution as the Atlantic House seemed an impossibility, and land improvement companies, Queen Anne cottages, and hacks to and from the railroad station, were out of all calculation. At that time "Captain" Chadwick's farmhouse, though not rich in all the modern improvements of a seaside hotel, rejoiced in a table covered three times a day with the good things from the farm. The river, back of the house, was full of fish, and the pine-woods along its banks were intended by Nature expressly for the hanging of hammocks.

The chief amusements were picnics to the head of the river (or as near the head as the boats could get through the lily-pads), crabbing along the shore, and races on the river itself, which, if it was broad, was so absurdly shallow that an upset meant nothing more serious than a wetting and a temporary loss of reputation as a sailor.

But all this had been spoiled by the advance of civilization and the erection of the Atlantic House.

The railroad surveyors, with their high-top boots and transits, were the first signs of the approaching evils. After them came the Ozone Land Company, which bought up all the sand hills bordering on the ocean, and proceeded to stake out a flourishing "city by the sea" and to erect sign-posts in the marshes to show where they would lay out streets, named after the directors of the Ozone Land Company and the Presidents of the United States.

It was not unnatural, therefore, that the Carters, and the Prescotts, and all the Judge's clients, and the Doctor's patients, who had been coming to Manasquan for many years, and loved it for its simplicity and quiet, should feel aggrieved at these great changes. And though the young Carters and Prescotts endeavored to impede the march of civilization by pulling up the surveyor's stakes and tearing down the Land Company's sign-posts, the inevitable improvements marched steadily on.

I hope all this will show why it was that the boys who lived at the Atlantic House —and dressed as if they were still in the city, and had "hops" every evening—were not pleasing to the boys who boarded at Chadwick's, who never changed their flannel suits for anything more formal than their bathing-dresses, and spent the summer nights on the river.

This spirit of hostility and its past history were explained to the new arrival at Chadwick's by young Teddy Carter, as the two sat under the willow tree watching a game of tennis. The new arrival had just expressed his surprise at the earnest desire manifest on the part of the entire Chadwick establishment to defeat the Atlantic House people in the great race which was to occur on the day following.

"Well, you see, sir," said Teddy, "considerable depends on this race. As it is now, we stand about even. The Atlantic House beat us playing base-ball—though they had to get the waiters to help them —and we beat them at tennis. Our house is great on tennis. Then we had a boat-race, and our boat won. They claimed it wasn't a fair race, because their best boat was stuck on the sand-bar, and so we agreed to sail it over again. The second time the wind gave out, and all the boats had to be poled home. The Atlantic House boat was poled in first, and her crew claimed the race. Wasn't it silly of them? Why, Charley Prescott told them, if they'd only said it was to be a *poling* match, he'd have entered a mud-scow and left his sail-boat at the dock!"

"And so you are going to race again to-morrow?" asked the new arrival.

"Well, it isn't exactly a race," explained Teddy. "It's a game we boys have invented. We call it 'Pirates and Smugglers.' It's something like tag, only we play it on the water, in boats. We divide boats and boys up into two sides; half of them are pirates or smugglers, and half of them are revenue officers or man-o'-war's-men. The 'Pirate's Lair' is at the island, and our dock is 'Cuba.' That's where the smugglers run in for cargoes of cigars and brandy. Mr. Moore gives us his empty cigar boxes, and Miss Sherrill (the lady who's down here for her health) lets us have all the empty Apollinaris bottles. We fill the bottles with water colored with crushed blackberries, and that answers for brandy.

"The revenue officers are stationed at Annapolis (that's the Atlantic House dock), and when they see a pirate start from the island, or from our dock, they sail after him. If they can touch him with the bow of their boat, or if one of their men can board him, that counts one for the revenue officers; and they take down his sail and the pirate captain gives up his tiller as a sign of surrender.

"Then they tow him back to Annapolis, where they keep him a prisoner until he is exchanged. But if the pirate can dodge the Custom House boat, and get to the place he started for, without being caught, that counts one for him."

"Very interesting, indeed," said the new arrival; "but suppose the pirate won't be captured or give up his tiller, what then?"

"Oh, well, in that case," said Teddy, reflectively, "they'd cut his sheet-rope, or splash water on him, or hit him with an oar, or something. But he generally gives right up. Now, to-morrow the Atlantic House boys are to be the revenue officers and we are to be the pirates. They have been watching us as we played the game, all summer, and they think they understand it well enough to capture our boats without any trouble at all."

"And what do you think?" asked the new arrival.

"Well, I can't say, certainly. They have faster boats than ours, but they don't know how to sail them. If we had their boats, or if they knew as much about the river as we do, it would be easy enough to name the winners. But, as it is, it's about even."

Every one who owned a boat was on the river the following afternoon, and those who didn't own a boat hired or borrowed one—with or without the owner's permission.

The shore from Chadwick's to the Atlantic House dock was crowded with people. All Manasquan seemed to be ranged in line along the river's bank. Crab-men and clam-diggers mixed indiscriminately with the summer boarders; and the beach-wagons and stages from Chadwick's grazed the wheels of the dog-carts and drags from the Atlantic's livery-stables.

It does not take much to overthrow the pleasant routine of summer-resort life, and the state of temporary excitement existing at the two houses on the eve of the race was not limited to the youthful contestants.

The proprietor of the Atlantic House had already announced an elaborate supper in honor of the anticipated victory, and every father and mother whose son was to take part in the day's race felt the importance of the occasion even more keenly than the son himself.

"Of course," said Judge Carter, "it's only a game, and for my part, so long as no one is drowned, I don't really care who wins; *but,* if our boys" ("our boys" meaning all three crews) "allow those young whippersnappers from the Atlantic House to win the pennant, they deserve to have their boats taken from them and exchanged for hoops and marbles!"

Which goes to show how serious a matter was the success of the Chadwick crews.

At three o'clock the amateur pirates started from the dock to take up their positions at the island. Each of the three small cat-boats held two boys: one at the helm and one in charge of the center-board and sheet-rope. Each pirate wore a jersey striped with differing colors, and the head of each bore the sanguinary red, knitted cap in which all genuine pirates are wont to appear. From the peaks of the three boats floated black flags, bearing the emblematic skull and bones of Captain Kidd's followers.

As they left the dock the Chadwick's people cheered with delight at their appearance and shouted encouragement,

while the remaining youngsters fired salutes with a small cannon, which added to the uproar as well as increased the excitement of the moment by its likelihood to explode.

At the Atlantic House dock, also, the excitement was at fever heat.

Clad in white flannel suits and white duck yachting-caps with gilt buttons, the revenue officers strolled up and down the pier with an air of cool and determined purpose such as Decatur may have worn as he paced the deck of his man-of-war and scanned the horizon for Algerine pirates. The stars-and-stripes floated bravely from the peaks of the three cat-boats, soon to leap in pursuit of the pirate craft which were conspicuously making for the starting-point at the island.

At half-past three the judges' steam-launch, the "Gracie," made for the middle of the river, carrying two representatives from both houses and a dozen undergraduates from different colleges, who had chartered the boat for the purpose of following the race and seeing at close quarters all that was to be seen.

They enlivened the occasion by courteously and impartially giving the special yell of each college of which there was a representative present, whether they knew him or not, or whether he happened to be an undergraduate, a professor, or an alumnus. Lest someone might inadvertently be overlooked, they continued to yell throughout the course of the afternoon, giving, in time, the shibboleth of every known institution of learning.

"Which do I think is going to win?" said the veteran boat-builder of Manasquan to the inquiring group around his boat-house. "Well, I wouldn't like to say. You see, I built every one of those boats that sails to-day, and every time I make a boat I make it better than the last one. Now, the Chadwick boats I built near five years ago, and the Atlantic House boats I built last summer, and I've learned a good deal in five years."

"So you think our side will win?" eagerly interrupted an Atlantic House boarder.

"Well, I didn't say so, did I?" inquired

boats; and if the Chadwick boys win, they'll win because they're the better sailors."

In the fashion of all first-class aquatic contests, it was fully an hour after the time appointed for the race to begin before the first pirate boat left the island.

" 'Which do I think is going to win?' said the veteran boat-builder to the inquiring group around his boat-house"

the veteran, with crushing slowness of speech. "I didn't say so. For though these boats the Chadwick's boys have are five years old, they're good boats still; and those boys know every trick and turn of 'em—and they know every current and sand-bar just as though it was marked with a piece of chalk. So, if the Atlantic folks win, it'll be because they've got the best

The *Ripple,* with Judge Carter's two sons in command, was the leader; and when her sail filled and showed above the shore, a cheer from the Chadwick's dock was carried to the ears of the pirate crew who sat perched on the rail as she started on her first long tack.

In a moment, two of the Atlantic House heroes tumbled into the *Osprey,* a dozen over-hasty hands had cast off her painter, had shoved her head into the stream, and the great race was begun.

The wind was down the river, or toward the island, so that while the *Osprey* was sailing before the wind, the *Ripple* had her sail close-hauled and was tacking.

"They're after us!" said Charley Carter, excitedly. "It's the *Osprey,* but I can't make out who's handling her. From the way they are pointing, I think they expect to reach us on this tack as we go about."

The crew of the *Osprey* evidently thought so too, for her bow was pointed at a spot on the shore, near which the *Ripple* must turn if she continued much longer on the same tack.

"Do you see that?" gasped Charley, who was acting as lookout. "They're letting her drift in the wind so as not to get there before us. I tell you what it is, Gus, they know what they're doing, and I think we'd better go about now."

"Do you?" inquired the younger brother, who had a lofty contempt for the other's judgment as a sailor. "Well, I don't. My plan is simply this: I am going to run as near the shore as I can, then go about sharp, and let them drift by us by a boat's length. A boat's length is as good as a mile, and then, when we are both heading the same way, I would like to see them touch us!"

"What's the use of taking such risks?" demanded the elder brother. "I tell you we can't afford to let them get so near as that."

"At the same time," replied the man at the helm, "that is what we are going to do. I am commanding this boat, please to remember, and if I take the risks I am willing to take the blame."

"You'll be doing well if you get off with nothing but blame," growled the elder brother. "If you let those kids catch us, I'll throw you overboard!"

"I'll put you in irons for threatening a superior officer if you don't keep quiet," answered the younger Carter, with a grin, and the mutiny ended.

It certainly would have been great sport to have run almost into the arms of the revenue officers, and then to have turned and led them a race to the goal, but the humor of young Carter's plan was not so apparent to the anxious throng of sympathizers on Chadwick's dock.

"What's the matter with the boys! Why don't they go about?" asked Captain Chadwick, excitedly. "One would think they were trying to be caught."

As he spoke, the sail of the *Ripple* fluttered in the wind, her head went about sharply, and, as her crew scrambled up on the windward rail, she bent and bowed gracefully on the homeward tack.

But, before the boat was fully under way, the *Osprey* came down upon her with a rush. The Carters hauled in the sail until their sheet lay almost flat with the surface of the river, the water came pouring over the leeward rail, and the boys threw their bodies far over the other side, in an effort to right her. The next instant there was a crash, the despised boat of the Atlantic House struck her fairly in the side, and one of the Atlantic House crew had boarded the *Ripple* with a painter in one hand and his hat in the other.

Whether it was the shock of the collision, or disgust at having been captured, no one could tell; but when the *Osprey's* bow struck the *Ripple,* the younger Carter calmly let himself go over backward and remained in the mud with the water up to his chin and without making any effort to help himself, until the judges' boat picked him up and carried him, an ignominious prisoner-of-war, to the Atlantic House dock.

The disgust over the catastrophe to the pirate crew was manifested on the part of

the Chadwick sympathizers by gloomy silence or loudly expressed indignation. On
the whole, it was perhaps just as well that
the two Carters, as prisoners-of-war, were
forced to remain at the Atlantic House
dock, for their reception at home would
not have been a gracious one.

Their captors, on the other hand, were
received with all the honor due triumphant heroes, and were trotted off the pier
on the shoulders of their cheering admirers; while the girls in the carriages waved
their parasols and handkerchiefs and the
colored waiters on the banks danced up
and down and shouted like so many human calliopes.

The victories of John Paul Jones and the
rescue of Lieutenant Greely became
aquatic events of little importance in comparison. Everybody was so encouraged at
this first success, that Atlantic House stock
rose fifty points in as many seconds, and
the next crew to sally forth from that
favored party felt that the second and de-
cisive victory was already theirs.

Again the black flag appeared around
the bank of the island, and on the instant
a second picked crew of the Atlantic House
was in pursuit. But the boys who commanded the pirate craft had no intention
of taking or giving any chances. They
put their boat about long before the revenue officers expected them to do so, forcing their adversaries to go so directly
before the wind that their boat rocked
violently. It was not long before the boats
drew nearer and nearer together, again,
as if they must certainly meet at a point
not more than a hundred yards from the
Atlantic House pier, where the excitement had passed the noisy point and had
reached that of titillating silence.

"Go about sharp!" snapped out the captain of the pirate boat, pushing his tiller
from him and throwing his weight upon
it. His first officer pulled the sail close over

the deck, the wind caught it fairly, and,
almost before the spectators were aware of
it, the pirate boat had gone about and was
speeding away on another tack. The revenue officers were not prepared for this.
They naturally thought the pirates would
run as close to the shore as they possibly
could before they tacked, and were aiming
for the point at which they calculated their
opponents would go about, just as did the
officers in the first race.

Seeing this, and not wishing to sail too
close to them, the pirates had gone about
much farther from the shore than was
needful. In order to follow them the revenue officers were now forced to come
about and tack, which, going before the
wind as they were, they found less easy.
The sudden change in their opponents'
tactics puzzled them, and one of the two
boys bungled. On future occasions each
confidentially informed his friends that it
was the other who was responsible; but,
however that may have been, the boat
missed stays, her sail flapped weakly in
the breeze, and, while the crew were vigorously trying to set her in the wind by lashing the water with her rudder, the pirate
boat was off and away, one hundred yards
to the good, and the remainder of the race
was a procession of two boats with the
pirates easily in the lead.

And now came the final struggle. Now
came the momentous "rubber," which was
to plunge Chadwick's into gloom, or keep
them still the champions of the river. The
appetites of both were whetted for victory
by the single triumph each had already
won, and their representatives felt that,
for them, success or a watery grave were
the alternatives.

The Atlantic House boat, the *Wave,*
and the boat upon which the Chadwicks'
hopes were set, the *Rover,* were evenly
matched, their crews were composed of
equally good sailors, and each was deter-

mined to tow the other ignominiously into port.

The two Prescotts watched the *Wave* critically and admiringly, as she came toward them with her crew perched on her side and the water showing white under her bow.

"They're coming entirely too fast to suit *me*," said the elder Prescott. "I want more room and I have a plan to get it. Stand ready to go about." The younger brother stood ready to go about, keeping the *Rover* on her first tack until she was clear of the island's high banks and had the full sweep of the wind; then, to the surprise of her pursuers and the bewilderment of the spectators, she went smartly about, and, turning her bow directly away from the goal, started before the wind back past the island and toward the wide stretch of river on the upper side.

"What's your man doing that for?" excitedly asked one of the Atlantic House people, of the prisoners-of-war.

"I don't know, certainly," one of the Carters answered, "but I suppose he thinks his boat can go faster before the wind than the *Wave* can, and is counting on getting a long lead on her before he turns to come back. There is much more room up there, and the opportunities for dodging are about twice as good."

"Why didn't *we* think of that, Gus?" whispered the other Carter.

"We were too anxious to show what smart sailors we were, to think of anything!" answered his brother, ruefully.

Beyond the island the *Rover* gained rapidly; but, as soon as she turned and began beating homeward, the *Wave* showed that tacking was her strong point and began, in turn, to make up all the advantage the *Rover* had gained.

The *Rover's* pirate-king cast a troubled eye at the distant goal and at the slowly but steadily advancing *Wave*.

His younger brother noticed the look.

"If one could only *do* something," he exclaimed, impatiently. "That's the worst of sailing races. In a rowing race you can pull till you break your back, if you want to; but here you must just sit still and watch the other fellow creep up, inch by inch, without being able to do anything to help yourself. If I could only get out and push, or pole! It's this trying to keep still that drives me crazy."

"I think we'd better go about, now," said the commander quietly, "and instead of going about again when we are off the bar, I intend to try to cross it."

"What!" gasped the younger Prescott, "go across the bar at low water? You can't do it. You'll stick sure. Don't try it. Don't think of it!"

"It is rather a forlorn hope, I know," said his brother; "but you can see yourself they're bound to overhaul us if we keep on—we don't draw as much water as they do, and if they try to follow us we'll leave them high and dry on the bar."

The island stood in the center of the river, separated from the shore on one side by the channel, through which both boats had already passed, and on the other by a narrow stretch of water which barely covered the bar the *Rover* purposed to cross.

When she pointed for it, the *Wave* promptly gave up chasing her, and made for the channel with the intention of heading her off in the event of her crossing the bar.

"She's turned back!" exclaimed the captain of the *Rover*. "Now, if we only can clear it, we'll have a beautiful start on her. Sit perfectly still, and, if you hear her center-board scrape, pull it up, and balance so as to keep her keel level."

Slowly the *Rover* drifted toward the bar; once her center-board touched, and as the boat moved further into the shallow water the waves rose higher in proportion at the stern.

But her keel did not touch, and as soon as the dark water showed again, her crew gave an exultant shout and pointed her bow toward the Chadwick dock, whence a welcoming cheer came faintly over the mile of water.

"I'll bet they didn't cheer much when we were crossing the bar!" said the younger brother, with a grim chuckle. "I'll bet they thought we were mighty foolish."

"We couldn't have done anything else," returned the superior officer. "It was risky, though. If we'd moved an inch she would have grounded, sure."

"I was scared so stiff that I couldn't have moved if I'd tried to," testified the younger sailor with cheerful frankness.

Meanwhile the wind had freshened, and white-caps began to show over the roughened surface of the river, while sharp, ugly flaws struck the sails of the two contesting boats from all directions, making them bow before the sudden gusts of wind until the water poured over the sides.

But the sharpness of the wind made the racing only more exciting, and such a series of maneuvers as followed, and such a naval battle, was never before seen on the Manasquan River.

The boys handled their boats like veterans, and the boats answered every movement of the rudders and shortening of the sails as a thoroughbred horse obeys its bridle. They ducked and dodged, turned and followed in pursuit, now going free before the wind, now racing, close-hauled into the teeth of it. Several times a capture seemed inevitable, but a quick turn of the tiller would send the pirates out of danger. And as many times the pirate crew almost succeeded in crossing the line, but before they could reach it the revenue

cutter would sweep down upon them and frighten them away again.

"We can't keep this up much longer," said the elder Prescott. "There's more water in the boat now than is safe; and every time we go about we ship three or four bucketfuls more."

As he spoke, a heavy flaw keeled the boat over again, and, before her crew could right her, the water came pouring over the side with the steadiness of a small waterfall. "That settles it for us," exclaimed Prescott, grimly; "we *must* pass the line on this tack, or we sink."

"They're as badly off as we are," returned his brother. "See how she's wobbling—but she's gaining on us, just the same," he added.

"Keep her to it, then," said the man at the helm. "Hold on to that sheet, no matter how much water she ships."

"If I don't let it out a little, she'll sink!"

"Let her sink, then," growled the chief officer. "I'd rather upset than be caught."

The people on the shore and on the judges' boat appreciated the situation fully as well as the racers. They had seen, for some time, how slowly the boats responded to their rudders and how deeply they were sunk in the water.

All the maneuvering for the past ten minutes had been off the Chadwick dock, and the Atlantic House people, in order to get a better view of the finish, were racing along the bank on foot and in carriages, cheering their champions as they came.

The *Rover* was pointed to cross an imaginary line between the judges' steam-launch and Chadwick's dock. Behind her, not three boat-lengths in the rear, so close that her wash impeded their headway, came the revenue officers, their white caps off, their hair flying in the wind, and every muscle strained.

Both crews were hanging far over the sides of the boats, while each wave washed the water into the already half-filled cockpits.

"Look out!" shouted the younger Prescott, "here comes another flaw!"

"Don't let that sail out!" shouted back his brother, and as the full force of the flaw struck her, the boat's rail buried itself in the water and her sail swept along the surface of the river.

For an instant it looked as if the boat was swamped, but as the force of the flaw passed over her, she slowly righted again, and with her sail dripping and heavy, and rolling like a log, she plunged forward on her way to the goal.

When the flaw struck the *Wave,* her crew let their sheet go free, saving themselves the inundation of water which had almost swamped the *Rover,* but losing the headway which the *Rover* had kept.

Before the *Wave* regained it, the pirate craft had increased her lead, though it was only for a moment.

"We can't make it," shouted the younger Prescott, turning his face toward his brother so that the wind might not drown his voice. "They're after us again, and we're settling fast."

"So are they," shouted his brother. "We can't be far from the line now, and as soon as we cross that, it doesn't matter what happens to us!"

As he spoke another heavy gust of wind came sweeping toward them, turning the surface of the river dark blue as it passed over, and flattening out the waves.

"Look at that!" groaned the pirate-king, adding, with professional disregard for the Queen's English, "We're done for now, that's certain!" But before the flaw reached them, and almost before the prophetic words were uttered, the cannon on the judges' boat banged forth merrily, and the crowds on the Chadwick dock answered its signal with an unearthly yell of triumph.

"We're across, we're across!" shouted the younger Prescott, jumping up to his knees in the water in the bottom of the boat and letting the wet sheet-rope run freely through his stiff and blistered fingers.

But the movement was an unfortunate one.

The flaw struck the boat with her heavy sail dragging in the water, and with young Prescott's weight removed from the rail. She reeled under the gust as a tree bows in a storm, bent gracefully before it, and then turned over slowly on her side.

The next instant the *Wave* swept by her, and as the two Prescotts scrambled up on the gunwale of their boat the defeated crew saluted them with cheers, in response to which the victors bowed as gracefully as their uncertain position would permit.

The new arrival, who had come to Manasquan in the hope of finding something to shoot, stood among the people on the bank and discharged his gun until the barrels were so hot that he had to lay the gun down to cool. And every other man and boy who owned a gun or pistol of any sort, fired it off and yelled at the same time, as if the contents of the gun or pistol had entered his own body. Unfortunately, every boat possessed a tin horn with which the helmsman was wont to warn of his approach the keeper of the draw-bridge. One evil-minded captain blew a blast of triumph, and in a minute's time the air was rent with tootings little less vicious than those of the steam whistle of a locomotive.

The last had been so hard-fought a race, and both crews had acquitted themselves so well, that their respective followers joined in cheering them indiscriminately.

The *Wave* just succeeded in reaching the dock before she settled and sank. A dozen of Chadwick's boarders seized the crew by their coat-collars and arms as they leaped from the sinking boat to the pier and assisted them to their feet, forgetful in the excitement of the moment that the sailors were already as wet as sponges on their native rocks.

"I suppose I should have stuck to my ship as Prescott did," said the captain of the *Wave* with a smile, pointing to where the judges' boat was towing in the *Rover* with her crew still clinging to her side; "but I'd already thrown you my rope, you know, and there really isn't anything heroic in sticking to a sinking ship when she goes down in two feet of water."

As soon as the Prescotts reached the pier they pushed their way to their late rivals and shook them heartily by their hands. Then the Atlantic House people carried their crew around on their shoulders, and the two Chadwick's crews were honored in the same embarrassing manner. The proprietor of the Atlantic House invited the entire Chadwick establishment over to a dance and a late supper.

"I prepared it for the victors," he said, "and though these victors don't happen to be the ones I prepared it for, the victors must eat it."

The sun had gone down for over half an hour before the boats and carriages had left the Chadwick dock, and the Chadwick people had an opportunity to rush home to dress. They put on their very best clothes, "just to show the Atlantic people that they *had* something else besides flannels," and danced in the big hall of the Atlantic House until late in the evening.

When the supper was served, the victors were toasted and cheered and presented with a very handsome set of colors, and then Judge Carter made a stirring speech.

He went over the history of the rival houses in a way that pleased everybody, and made all the people at the table feel ashamed of themselves for ever having been rivals at all.

He pointed out in courtly phrases how excellent and varied were the modern features of the Atlantic House, and yet how healthful and satisfying was the old-fashioned simplicity of Chadwick's. He expressed the hope that the two houses would learn to appreciate each other's virtues, and hoped that in the future they would see more of each other.

To which sentiment everybody assented most noisily and enthusiastically, and the proprietor of the Atlantic House said that, in his opinion, Judge Carter's speech was one of the finest he had ever listened to, and he considered that part of it which touched on the excellent attractions of the Atlantic House as simply sublime, and that, with his Honor's permission, he intended to use it in his advertisements and circulars, with Judge Carter's name attached.

THE LATEST NEWS ABOUT THE THREE WISHES

by Rupert Hughes

As every one knows, young folks that never do what they should not do, and never leave undone what they ought to do, run a great risk of meeting some day a good fairy who will say, in a musical voice:

"Thomas" (or "Richard" or "Henry," as the case may be), "since you have been a good boy, the gracious King of the Fairies has decided to reward you bountifully. Any three wishes you may make will be granted, whatever they are. But be very careful what you choose!"

Now, there was once a lad named Albert Crane. He was related to the King of the Fairies by the marriage of a great-uncle, on his mother's side, to the second cousin of an intimate friend of a passing acquaintance of a young man who had once saved the life of a fairy who was caught in a rain-storm about midnight and could not fly home. If she had stayed out till sunrise she would have died, as you all know; and her wings were so wet that she was having a sorry time of it when this young man picked her gently up by the nape of the neck, and hid her under a candle-snuffer till the next night, thus saving her from the fatal glance of the sun. And this is a thing you must all do when you find a fairy in distress; for fairies are like the unfixed proofs of a photograph: they fade into nothing under the glare of the sun.

Well, then, since this young man had befriended the fairy, the fairy King was eager to show his gratitude in any way and every way possible, even to relatives as far removed as the eye could reach. He was very anxious, for this reason, to grant the three wishes to Albert Crane. But Albert was such a mischievous little fellow that it seemed he would never be able to express his gratitude in that direction. The lowest average of good behavior on which the diploma of the three wishes will be granted is three weeks. (No wonder so few young people ever get the wishes!) Albert Crane seemed the most hopeless of all. He was so far from being able to stay good three weeks in succession that nothing could trap him into being good even one day in succession. There is no need of telling you all the mischievous things he did, because, if you have not already done them all yourself before, you might learn something new.

But just as the fairy King was giving up in despair, Albert fell sick, and was kept in bed for a whole month. He was too weak to carry out any mischief, or even to plan it; and the fairy King jumped at the chance to relieve himself of the debt he thought he owed to Albert's mother's uncle's second cousin's intimate friend's passing acquaintance's young man.

So one day,—the first day Albert was strong enough to go out into the woods alone, and before he could rob any birds' nests or do anything else wrongful,—he was surprised beyond expression to see standing before him a beautiful girl with long brown hair and bright blue eyes, and a wand with a star on it. And on her shoulders grew beautiful butterfly wings that must have cost between $3.99 at Browny & Pixie's bargain-counter. Albert recognized her at once from her resemblance to the fairies in the picture-books; and for the first time he saw how true all such pictures are.

Before Albert could make up his mind

to do what he usually did when he met pretty girls,—pull their hair till the tears came,—the fairy spoke to him, and said the words quoted above, except that in the printed blank the King had given her was written the name Albert instead of Tom, Dick, or Harry.

When Albert heard the fairy's little speech, which she delivered like a Friday afternoon recitation,—only she forgot the curtsy at the end,—he was too much amazed for a moment to say a word. His memory ran back over all the similar experiences of youngsters who had been accosted by fairies for some good deed. He had never expected any such experience himself, and was not prepared with an immediate answer; but he remembered the fates of several of the children to whom the gift of three wishes had been given.

Some of the boys asked, first, for all the candy they could eat; second, for all the red circus-lemonade they could drink; and third, for all the baseball runs they could score. Albert never forgot the fate of these poor wretches—the terrible stomach-aches the candy gave them, how sick they grew of lemonade, and how their baseball games lasted so long they could never go home to dinner or to bed. Because, of course, the three wishes they wished were fulfilled to the last degree, and they had no extra wish to save them from the penalty of the first three. Albert had read of other boys, who, unlike him, had always enjoyed Sunday-school, and never stole a ride on a wagon or threw a rock through a street-lamp. They always wished, first, for virtue; second, for wisdom; and third, for a chance to do good in the world. But these things did not appeal to Albert at all, for he was a little imp. His father called him a limb, though he never specified whether he was a hickory limb or a limb of "slippery-ellum."

Albert was very much puzzled over his

wishes. He wanted so many things at once that his brain went into a whirl. He felt as if he had been tied in a merry-go-round for weeks. The whole world was one great merry-go-round to him.

The fairy stood and watched the boy till she remembered an appointment she had in China, a few minutes later, to carry the three wishes to a little pigtail, who would probably wish, first, for as much rice as he could eat; second, for as many fire-crackers as he could set off; and last (and least), for good luck with his lessons.

Then the fairy spoke as sharply as a street-car conductor saying "Step lively, there!" and brought Albert to his senses in a moment. Now, Albert was a lawyer's son, and a happy thought struck him. Instead of choosing any three wishes out of the thousands things a boy of his age could wish, he suddenly said, with a bluntness that took the fairy's breath away:

"If I choose one wish only, will you make me three times as sure of getting it?"

The fairy was too much startled to understand what this strange request might mean, and before she thought she accepted:

"Yes, if you wish."

"You promise?" persisted Albert.

"I promise," said the fairy.

"Well, then," said Albert, with the slowness of a judge, "I make this one wish: that every wish I make in all the rest of my life shall be granted."

This was something the fairy had not expected. She had never heard of such a thing, and it almost scared her to death to think what she had done. It would have scared her to death, if there were any death for fairies.

"I shall have to see the King," she cried; and before Albert could grab her by her back hair she had disappeared.

Then Albert stood nonplussed for a moment, and wished he had not been so greedy. It made him sicker than he had been all the month before, and he felt very much like lying down and crying his eyes out. In fact, he had just decided that would be a good thing to do, when there was a buzz and a whizz and a flash, and there stood the King of the Fairies himself.

Albert dropped down on his knees before the bright apparition, and heard the King saying:

"What trick is this you are trying to play on us? You are the worst boy that ever lived! I have been trying for half a year to keep you good long enough to grant you the three wishes, and now you try to play a trick upon me! As a punishment for your presumption, you shall have no wish at all."

But Albert, being a lawyer's son, was not to be put out of countenance, and he said, as if it were the Fourth of July and he were saying, "Give me liberty, or give me death":

"Your Majesty, whatever my past history may be, you have given your sacred promise, and you cannot break it."

The fairy King blustered and stormed and threatened and pleaded; but Albert was obstinate, and finally the King flew away in a great huff, snapping:

"Keep your old wish, then!"

So Albert went home very triumphant. Finding that he had walked a long way and was a little tired and weak from his illness, he wished for a beautiful Shetland pony; and before he knew how it came, there it was. So he got on its back, and just as he wished it would gallop away, even before he could say "Get up," it galloped. But Albert had never learned to ride before, and he was being jolted into a cream-cheese, when he wished that he might be an expert rider. So he was.

Remembering that his home was not a very beautiful one, for his father was a poor lawyer,—in both senses of the word,—he wished that he might find his mother and father and brothers and sisters in a beautiful mansion. So he did.

But when he went into this beautiful home he found that the butcher and the baker and the grocer had got tired of having their bills unpaid, and had refused to give his father any more credit; so, for all the beautiful house, there was nothing to eat; and much as the family was mystified at the change in their dwelling, they were not too much mystified to be hungry. So Albert simply wished all his father's bills receipted, and a beautiful dinner served in the magnificent dining-room. So everything was done as he wished.

It would take all the rest of your life to tell all the beautiful experiences he had, so if you have anything else to do this year, we'll skip most of it. He got his wisher so well trained that he could wish for so many things at one time that the whole fairy court had to quit all other work and attend to him. On beautiful moonlight nights they were too tired to dance in the woods. Besides, Albert was just as likely to wish in his sleep as when he was awake.

The fine thing about Albert's experience was that it was unlike that of the bad boys who had wished for candy and red lemonade. When they made themselves sick, there was nothing to do but suffer. When Albert overate, all he had to do was to wish himself cured. If there was an especially beautiful dinner before him, he wished himself an extra good appetite and digestion till he had finished all there was in sight and was tired of eating.

He wished to have Christmas every day until he got as tired of it as Mr. Howells' little girl grew. Then he wished for Fourth of July every day till that bored

him. Then he wished that he might know all his lessons without going to school, until he found that one of the chief pleasures of knowledge is the pleasure of getting it. He wished that all the trees with birds' nests in them would be easy to climb until he saw how much pain he was causing the mother birds, and how many songs he was hushing in the woods by robbing the nests of the eggs which would some day be songsters.

He wished his baseball nine to win all the games by tremendous scores, till he saw how uninteresting it was to be certain of everything.

In fact, in time he came to believe that, after all, life was very good and full of pleasures and opportunities just as it was, and without fairy power to change it. He saw the use of pain, and, understanding this, came to sympathize with the rest of the world, and to be very merciful and very charitable and very thoughtful.

But even this happiness palled on him. He was ashamed to be so different from the other boys, and he felt that he had no friends at all, because he was no fit companion for boys who had to work hard for all the fun they had, as well as all the serious things they accomplished. He saw that his life was merely one continued story of good luck—a mere fairy story; and he felt that he never deserved pleasures, because he had done nothing to earn them.

Besides, the other boys began to let him severely alone. They wouldn't play with him, they wouldn't go to school with him, and they wouldn't even fight with him. It would have been bad enough to becalled "teacher's pet"; he couldn't endure being called "fairy's pet."

One day, in his loneliness, he cried, "Plague take the wish! I wish I were without it!"

Suddenly he felt something rip, and in a

great fright he gasped, "No; I wish my wish to come back!" But when he wished for a glass of chocolate ice-cream soda to appear on a tree-stump near by, not a thing happened.

The fairy court stood on their heads with joy when Albert's wish came crashing through a window, and they knew their long service was over.

But Albert was happier still, for he was admitted to a ball game when he said he was no longer a professional wisher. And when he put up his hands to catch a "beauty" fly, he muffed it and got a bruised finger to boot. And when he went to bat he missed the ball three times. And he was so happy at being a human boy again that he hugged himself; and that evening he ran home crying: "Hooray! hooray! We lost the game!"

THE SWIFTWATER BUCK

by William Gerard Chapman

Across the sunlit swale came stalking cautiously a whitetail doe with her five-months' fawn stepping daintily at her side, the weanling showing a curious, long, whitish scar on its flank. Before emerging from the dark recesses of the wood, they had stood in the spruce tangle at the forest's edge for several minutes, the doe searching the open with eyes and nose and ears, her fawn as motionless as herself in obedience to an unspoken command.

The mother deer was in mighty fear of humankind, but it is doubtful if the fawn would have evidenced any great terror had one of the tribe appeared, for the same recent experience from which sprang the doe's overpowering dread of man had left the fawn with as great a curiosity concerning him. Early in the spring the doe, driven by wolves, had, in her extremity, leaped among the pasturing herd of a settler, and the cattle, alarmed by her abrupt advent and catching the fever of her fear, had raced to the barn-yard. The doe and her fawn, which had followed at her heels, tolled along by the rush, soon found themselves in a strange, fenced enclosure, and, falling exhausted from their terrific effort, had been captured and imprisoned within a calf-pen by the backwoods farmer. The man had acted on impulse, and, once the pair was safely railed in, wondered what he should do with them, his first thought naturally being of the venison they would provide for his table.

The next day, however, his young son, coming early to the pen to feed and make overtures to the captives, was overjoyed by the sight of the fawn, and thenceforth he devoted himself to cultivating the friendship of the agile and beautiful creature.

One morning, some days later, the boy, peering into the pen, was cut short in his salutations by the sight of a red gash in the flank of the baby deer. The fawn had torn his side deeply, but not dangerously, on a protruding splinter, and the crimson streak in his delicate coat smote the child's heart with horror and sympathy. He lifted the latch of the pen door, which could be fastened only on the outside, and ran to comfort his wounded protégé. The doe backed into the far corner, trembling with terror, then suddenly sprang for the opening, bowling the child over in her rush. At her bleat of command the fawn dashed after her, maternal authority overcoming whatever of reluctance he may have felt in deserting the kind little two-legged animal, and the boy, rising bewildered and with the hot tears springing to his eyes, emerged from the pen just in time to glimpse the two gracefully leaping forms disappearing over the crest of a rise in mid-pasture. With her white flag guiding the youngling, the freed mother deer streaked for the friendly cover that loomed invitingly before her eyes, and quickly doe and fawn were swallowed up in the cool, dim sanctuary of the forest.

SEVERAL years passed, and in the settlements a "scar-sided buck" began to achieve a reputation beyond that of any of his fellows. Known and recognized both by the livid mark on his right flank and the immense size to which he grew, he became famous throughout the Swiftwater country. He was credited either with possessing uncanny craft or the gift of uncommonly good luck, for no magnificently antlered head was more coveted, or more assiduously hunted, than the one that reared itself proudly on his broad, powerful shoulders. And frequently something more than desire to possess the finest head they had known inspired the efforts of the hunters of the region. His depredations on the fields and truck patches of the scattered farmsteads periodically sent irate backwoods farmers on his trail vowing to exterminate this despoiler of their crops. But these usually returned without having seen the big buck, or else, if they caught a glimpse of him, he got himself so swiftly out of sight that no chance offered for a successful shot.

That the buck knew the difference between a man unarmed and a man with a gun was an opinion shrewdly held by one young hunter, who kept this view to himself for reasons of his own. Probably some early experience in being creased by a bullet from one of those fire-spouting, loud-voiced sticks that men sometimes carried had brought an idea into the buck's head. Dogs did not seem to excite any great terror in him, and on numerous occasions he had turned on those that followed his trail and driven them off. But usually he accepted the challenge and gave them an exhilarating run, and, when the game palled, broke his trail craftily and left the dogs to plod back home foot-sore and chop-fallen.

The history of "Old Scarside," which was the name by which the great buck finally came to be known, was familiar to the settlement folk. Laban Knowles, the farmer who had imprisoned the doe and fawn, and his son Lonny held themselves his sponsors; indeed, Lonny maintained that the buck belonged to him, and always was driven to white anger by the often expressed designs on the deer's life.

Lonny desired above all things that his big buck, who only a few years before, as a captive fawn, had plainly shown his willingness to be friends with him, should live unharmed. Old Scarside, magnificent and storied buck whitetail of the Swiftwater country, had responded to his voice and nuzzled his hand when both were hardly more than babies! The intimate association, unfortunately, had been terminated after all too brief a life, else surely it would have progressed to a thorough understanding; but the friendship so begun still held with one of the parties to it, and the boy's assumption of proprietorship in the biggest deer of the region was known to all the inhabitants of the border country.

Lonny Knowles was by way of becoming a top-notch woodsman, and his skill as a marksman with his twenty-two rifle was a matter of note among his fellows. Whenever his farm duties permitted, he roamed the woods, shooting what small game was needed for the home table, but finding his greatest pleasure in studying the wild life of the great timbered stretches that enclosed the settlement. Of all the wild-wood folk, the scar-sided whitetail deer held first place in his interest. Noiselessly he ranged the feeding-grounds and runways that he had come to know were used by "his buck," and often his careful stalking was rewarded by a sight of the noble animal. His great wish was to overcome the buck's instinctive fear, in the boyish hope that eventually he would succeed in reëstablishing an understanding with his one-time friend. And very patiently and persistently he sought to accustom the buck to his presence. Whenever he came upon his track, easily distinguishable by its size, he trailed him with the silent efficiency of an Indian. When, finally, Old Scarside was sighted, Lonny drew as near to him as cover and wind permitted, and watched him long and admiringly. Then, leaving his rifle on the ground, he would silently rise and show himself, all his movements quiet and restrained and his manner casual. Up would come the buck's head with a snort of surprise at the sudden apparition. Usually he would bound away the instant Lonny showed himself. Sometimes, when Lonny stood forth while the buck's eyes were turned aside, Scarside would suddenly become aware of an alien figure standing astonishingly close where no figure had been an instant before, and, snorting and stamping petulantly, with eyes and nose would seek to penetrate the mystery. Then, suspicion overcoming curiosity, he would wheel and plunge swiftly from the spot.

But gradually, very gradually, the painstaking methods of the young woodsman began to have their effect on the buck. The casual approach, unthreatening manner, and eyes that never fixed themselves disquietingly upon his own, were strangely at variance with what his experience had taught him of the ways of the man tribe, though sometimes the evidence carried on a veering puff of wind would unmistakably proclaim the intruder a member of it. And as time went on, a growing familiarity with this seemingly harmless individual, smaller in stature than his other persecutors and never bearing that abhorrent instrument of noise and flame asso-

ciated with these enemies, slowly wore down the fine edge of his fear. Often he would stand and stamp and snort for minutes, merely backing off slowly as Lonny advanced upon him inch by inch. Then, as a quiver of muscles rippled the sheen of his coat and signaled a break for cover, Lonny would stay him with a bleated *"Mah!"* And for an instant longer the wondering buck would tarry, to puzzle out the meaning of this, before discretion sent him bounding away into the green forest depths. Later, when the buck's departure was still longer delayed, Lonny would utter soothing words to him.

"You ain't afeard o' me, are you, old feller? 'Member when you an' me was babies, you licked my hand. We're friends still, ain't we? Now, don't get skeery an' cut an' run—I ain't a-goin' to harm you!"

Awed and fascinated by the softly spoken words, Scarside would stand a-quiver, then run back a few steps and halt, half hidden, in a near-by thicket, pawing and whistling, his big liquid eyes never leaving this strangely ingratiating one of the enemy kind. In the dim recesses of his brain did some faint memory stir at the voice that, in the first days of his life, spoke to him in the universal language of infant brotherhood? Or perhaps some remnant of that early curiosity of his concerning man creatures remained to weaken the ancestral dread.

The buck's whistling Lonny chose to interpret as a reply to his own remarks.

"Remember, do you? Well, then don't be so bashful. I ain't never a-goin' to hurt you, Old Scarside—it's all along o' that scar that you got away from me when you were jest a little feller. You ain't forgotten, have you? Well, good-by then, if you're a-goin'."

When Lonny described his adventures in friendliness with the deer, Laban scoffed amusedly at his son's firm belief in Scarside's memory of the early incident.

"A deer hain't got no memory—don't you ever believe it. He's jest gittin' used to you an' your quiet ways, like any wild critter will ef you show yourself often enough an' don't pay special attention to 'em at first. He's jest curious about you, an' a deer's as curious a critter as any woman.

"But ef he's your deer, like you claim, you better learn him to keep out o' the clearin's," Laban continued, his whimsical tone changing to half-angry seriousness as he thought of the devastated field of rutabagas he had just visited. "The pesky critter's gittin' to be a blame nuisance, eatin' up half the crops. Last night he liked to spile the hull 'baga patch, tromplin' what he didn't eat. I ain't a-goin' to stand him much longer. Ef he don't quit ruinin' the fields, I'll put a bullet inter his big carcass!"

"Don't you never do it, Pa!" burst out Lonny. "He's only takin' what he thinks is rightly his'n, an' we oughter be able to spare a few 'bagas an' such like. He is my deer, and I won't stand to have him hurted!"

Laban grumbled in his throat and turned away. The generous-hearted farmer was troubled by the knowledge that Old Scarside's continued depredations had reached the unbearable stage. Fences were as nothing to him, and his despoiling of growing crops was now a matter of almost nightly occurrence. The countryside was becoming inflamed against the big buck, who left his sign manual in each invaded area in the form of tracks that in size resembled those of a calf.

Leaving the boy protesting against the threat, Laban strode off on his way to a neighbor's to assist in raising a new barnframe. A short cut could be made by paddling across the lake that lay between the farmsteads, the trail to this leading over a hard-wood ridge, beyond which stretched the broad sheet of water. On the shelving beach his birch-bark lay among the bushes, and, noting as he shoved it in that a stiff breeze was blowing in his face, he decided to weight the bow with a small rock. Otherwise, the light craft would expose so much free-board to the gale that he would have difficulty in keeping its prow in the wind's eye. Bending forward, he was about to deposit the rock carefully in the canoe, when his design was rudely frustrated. His next conscious thought was that the Wendigo—that demon of northern Indian legend which seizes men in its talons and bears them off on journeys through space—had savagely snatched at him and sent him whirling dizzily through the air.

Back in the timber of the ridge a big, nobly antlered buck, the pride—and bane—of the Swiftwater country, had watched the striding man with arrogant eyes, eyes that for the moment held no glint of fear. The fever of the sweethearting time was in his blood this crisp November morning, and dread of man was forgotten in the swift anger that blazed within him when his trysting was disturbed. Stiffly he stood for a moment in his screen of bushy hemlock, neck swollen with the madness in his veins, bloodshot eyes glaring upon the unsuspecting interloper. Then, intent upon vengeance, he followed after the figure noisily descending the slope. His progress was a series of prancing steps, though his feet fell cunningly without sound, and he shook his magnificent head threateningly.

He was only a few paces behind when the man, reaching the shore, suddenly swerved to look about; and the buck froze for a moment before the expected stare of those disconcerting eyes. But the man's gaze did not lift from the ground.

He picked up something and turned his back again and bent over at the water's edge.

The opportunity was too tempting. The buck plunged forward, his lowered head aimed at the crouching figure, and drove at it with all the power of his hard-muscled body. The impact was terrific and the result startling—no less to the object of his attack than to the deer. For the man, with a grunt of astonishment, shot from the shore, turning upside down as he went, and out of the splash that followed emerged not the man, but what appeared to be a smooth brown log, that trembled and rolled crazily among the wavelets and gave forth weird, muffled bellowings!

The backwoodsman, lifted into the air by the amazing assault from the rear, had let go the rock (which at the instant was poised above the canoe) as his hands instinctively reached for the gunwales. As he catapulted into the lake, his grasp on the birch-bark turned it over on him, and he found himself upright in the water, his face above the surface, but in darkness. For a moment utter bewilderment possessed him; then, realizing that he was standing in over five feet of freezing water, his head in the hollow of his capsized canoe, to which he still clung tenaciously, he burst into language and sought to extricate himself.

With a wrench of his arms, he threw the canoe over and turned a wrathful glare toward the bank. Hot indignation choked him momentarily as his eyes fell on the author of his plight pawing the gravel and shaking his antlers in invitation to combat. Then he found his voice.

"Ye confounded, tarnation critter!" sputtered Laban, at a loss for adequate words with which to express his feelings. "So 'twas you butted me into the lake! Ye'll pay fer this—with a bullet through yer hide afore ye're a day older, ye scar-

sided imp o' Satan!" He shook his fist at the animal and started to scramble up the steep bottom, continuing his abuse vigorously. But half-way up he came to a stop, perplexed. What should he do when he reached the bank? The buck plainly was in a fighting mood, and no unarmed man was a match for those driving, keen-rimmed hoofs and dagger-like antler-points. Scarside stood his ground, stamping and snorting and lowering his head in challenge.

Laban wondered angrily if he would have to stand there waist-deep in the icy lake until some one came to drive the buck away—and to witness his humiliation! The blood rushed to his bronzed and bearded cheeks at the thought, though he was now shivering to his marrow with the combined cold of water and wind.

In desperation, he suddenly made a great splashing and waved his arms wildly about his head, then gave a piercing yell.

This inexplicable behavior of his victim had its effect on the buck. Irresolutely he fell back a few steps, startled by the wild commotion; and at the terrifying sound that followed, his ardor for battle died. His madness cooling as suddenly as aroused, with a snort of dismay, Scarside whirled in his tracks and dashed off through the trees.

Grim of visage, but with chattering teeth, Laban climbed out of the water, beached his canoe, and hurried homeward, flailing his great arms against his body to restore the circulation of the sluggish blood. Half-way home, he met Lonny coming over the trail.

"Was that you that yelled, Pop? Sounded like some one was terribly hurted, or somethin'. What in time's the matter, anyway? Upset?" Lonny gazed wonderingly at the dripping, angry-faced figure of his father.

"Yes, somethin' happened; but you needn't blat it 'round 'mongst the neighbors. An' somethin' else's goin' to happen, too, mighty soon!"

As his father related his adventure with Old Scarside, Lonny had difficulty in repressing the chuckles that rose to his lips. He covered his mouth with his hand to hide the grin that would persist.

" 'Tain't no laughin' matter," protested Laban, noting the action. "Ef I don't catch pneumony from it, I'll be lucky. Jest as soon as I c'n get some dry duds on, I'm a-goin' to take the rifle an' trail that blame' critter till I git him. 'Tain't enough fer him to be destroyin' the crops; he's started to attack folks, an' he's too dangerous to let live."

He clamped his mouth on his resolution; and Lonny knew that the big buck of the Swiftwater country was doomed.

The scar-sided buck, resting on a mossy knoll in the depths of the spruce wood, raised his head to a suspicious odor that drifted down the wind. He rose to his feet and ran with the breeze for a short distance, then swung around and headed back, paralleling his trail. He halted in a clump of tangled low growth a few rods from it, and waited. Soon a man came swinging along, silent footed, carrying that dreaded black stick, his eyes bent on the ground, but now and again lifting to scan the surrounding bush. Manifestly, as the evidence of nose and eyes indicated, this was the same human so lately visited with his displeasure; and some elemental intuition that reprisal was to be expected warned him that he must be discreet.

When the man had passed, the buck quietly withdrew from his hiding-place and bounded off at right angles to the trail. A mixture of wariness and confidence guided his actions during the succeeding hours. He well knew the danger of giving the man a glimpse of himself in circumstances like these, but his great craft, so often successfully exercised, and his long immunity from harm had bred in him a confidence in his powers that stayed his flight to the barest necessity of keeping out of range. Doggedly the hunter followed, untangling the puzzles of the trail so cunningly woven, his skill the fruit of many a previous stalking of the wily old buck. But whereas on these other occasions he had been content to consider himself the victor in the contest of wits when he finally had come within easy shooting distance of his quarry, bravely withstanding the itch of his trigger-finger, this time there would be a different ending to the hunt.

As the pursuit lengthened, familiar landmarks apprized the backwoodsman that the buck was circling back toward the settlement. This was fortunate, for the afternoon was waning; and furthermore, it afforded him the opportunity of cutting across to the runways along the ridge where, logically, the buck would pass. And then, the finish!

Laban put his plan into operation. If he hurried, he could obtain a vantage-point on a rise of ground commanding the flank of the ridge, and here he would have an ideal chance for a shot as the buck swept across the burning that gashed its forested sides. He neared the spot somewhat winded from his exertions, and paused a moment to regain his breath before carefully threading the thicket of young alder and birch, beyond which the earth fell away into the little valley that lay between. Reaching the fringe of the growth, the opposite slope was revealed to his sight, and he exulted inwardly as he glimpsed the object of his chase just about to cross the burned area. The deer was going steadily, but at no great speed, and though the shot was a long one, he presented an easy chance for a marksman of Laban's skill.

Without hurry, he raised his rifle to his shoulder. At the same instant the buck swerved, stood tense for a second, and began to rear and whirl about in a most astonishing manner. Puzzled by this behavior, which made a killing shot uncertain, Laban lowered his rifle to study the meaning of it. He could discern nothing at first to account for the deer's actions, and when the buck momentarily presented a broadside target, he aimed quickly and pressed the trigger. As he did so, there came to him a flash of understanding— the scene suddenly cleared to his eyes, and his brain fought to restrain the pressure of his finger—but too late! The rifle cracked and the buck went down, and Laban rushed over to the hillside, a numbing fear rising in his heart.

THE scar-sided buck had begun to be annoyed at the pertinacity of the man who followed him. All the cunning that so often in the past had served him seemed of no avail against this creature, who solved each mystery of the trail with such seeming ease. But he was not yet fearful; his bag of tricks was still far from empty. Therefore, without panic, he broke through the trees that bordered the fire-devastated sweep of ground, heading diagonally for the summit, from whence, in the shielding second growth that clothed the spine of the ridge, a view of his adversary's progress might be had. Midway in his flight up the acclivity, a terrifying odor suddenly smote his nostrils. He pivoted sharply as the mingled scent of man and an even worse-hated enemy warned him of danger close by, and he sought warily to locate it.

As his head lifted, his gaze fell on a long, tawny, furtive beast, crawling serpent-wise through the low brush, its tail twitching at the tip, while, at a little distance in front, a small man creature lay twisted on the ground, wriggling frantically, but not moving from the spot. The stricken one's eyes bore on him at the same instant, and a cry came from his lips, cut short as he sagged into an inert heap.

Who shall say what promptings stirred within the whitetail buck, impelling him to leap furiously upon the most dreaded of his animal foes? Whether, at the cry, he recognized the young human who had grown so engagingly familiar to him and sensed the appeal in it, or whether it was that, in the season of his queer flashes of insane courage, his hatred for the slinking beast flamed into uncontrollable rage, no man may say; but the big cat, crouching for the spring and unaware, or unmindful, of the new-comer upon the scene, was assailed from behind by a fury of fierce-driven blows from feet that cut into his flesh like steel knives. His spine was crushed at the first onslaught, and, turning with an agonized snarl, he was flattened to the ground by an irresistible array of stabbing bayonet-points. So sudden and overwhelming was the attack that the panther had never a chance. Almost before he could realize his plight, the deep-cutting feet and battering antlers had reached his vitals, and the spark of his savage life flickered out. But as the victorious buck prodded at the now unresponsive form, a rifle shot shattered the silence, and at the report he gave a convulsive leap forward and fell asprawl, his nose lying against the same hand that he had nuzzled confidingly in a long-past day.

As Laban breathlessly drew near, the full meaning of the strange scene was made plain to him. A sharp pang of regret for the slaying of his son's deliverer came to the backwoodsman as he bent over the huddled, unconscious form, and saw that the child was not seriously hurt. A foot, tightly held in a clump of roots and twisted at the ankle, indicated the nature of Lonny's mishap. Thankful that it was no worse, Laban cut away the detaining tangle and gently chafed the boy back to life. In a few minutes Lonny was sitting up, nursing his sprained ankle, the pain of which was almost forgotten in his wonder at what he beheld.

"Old Scarside saved ye from the painter, Lonny, an' what he got fer it was a bullet! I'd give my rifle if I could have sensed what was up a second sooner. I saw somethin' of what was happenin' all in a flash, but 't was too late. I'm mortal sorry I killed the critter."

Lonny sorrowfully patted the sleek, tawny neck that lay stretched at his feet. Tears were not far from his eyes, but not for the pain of his wrenched foot. "The old feller knew it was me—I allus told you he knew me!—an' he wasn't goin' to let me be chawed up by no painter!" Never thereafter, in the many tellings of the story, was either father or son to permit this altruistic motive for the buck's action to be gainsaid.

"How 'd you git inter such a mess, I want t' know?" asked his father, as the boy thoughtlessly tried to rise to his feet for a closer view of the mangled body of the panther.

Lonny sank back, stifling a yelp of pain. "I come out here to see if I couldn't turn Old Scarside off the ridge, if he happened along with you after him," he admitted; "an' I ketched my foot in this here mess o' creepers an' like to broke my ankle when I fell. I couldn't move, hardly, an' then that ornery painter come lopin' along an' saw me an' started creepin' up——" He shivered at memory of the sinister, stealthy approach of the big cat, its brassy, malevolent eyes fastened with savage purpose on the shrinking lad whom, in its cowardly heart, it knew to be disabled. "I tried to crawl off, but my foot was held tight; an' I jest looked at the varmint an' tried to yell, but was too scairt. An' then I saw Old Scarside amblin' out o' the woods, like he was comin' to help me, an' I called to him—an' that's all I remember.

"You come, didn't you, old feller?" he said, addressing his fallen champion. "It's a blame' shame you got killed fer what you did fer me." The hot tears this time overflowed.

"Wonder where I hit him?" questioned Laban, awkwardly seeking to cover his own very real misery. "Don't see nary mark, an' there ain't no blood far as I kin tell. 'Spose I might as well bleed him," he added, practicalities not to be lost sight of even in the face of tragedy. He drew his knife from its sheath and bent over the body, one hand grasping the antlers.

The moment that followed was the most bewildering in the lives of father and son. For an instant they seemed to be inextricably entangled in a maze of wildly threshing limbs—their own and a deer's—as the "dead" buck rose in the air with a terrified snort, sending Laban spread-eagling over beyond Lonny, and, finding his feet after a few frantic seconds, sped off into the timber.

Astonishment held the two speechless for a space. Then Lonny, ignoring the pain of his foot, throbbing fiercely from the shaking up, gave voice to a yell of joy.

"Go it, Scarside, go it!" he shrieked jubilantly after the vanishing buck. "Couldn't kill you after all, you old rip-snorter, could they?" Full vent for his feelings at the deer's startling resurrection demanded nothing less than the throwing of several handsprings, but Lonny could only toss his hat in the air and wave his arms exultantly. He turned shining eyes on his father, over whose face a delighted grin was breaking as he rubbed his bruises.

"You must've just creased him, Pa, an' only knocked him out fer a spell. Gosh, but I'm glad!"

"You bet I'm glad, too," chuckled Laban, "even ef 't was the second time to-day the critter sent me sprawlin'! Reckon when I pulled the trigger an' then tried not to, all at once, I must've lost my bead an' shot high. Likely the ball nicked him at the base o' the antlers, an' the shock keeled him over, but didn't hurt him none. 'T was a rank miss that I'm proud of—an' 'twill be the last time any one from here-abouts takes a shot at the old buck, I promise ye that! Well, I reckon we better be gittin' home; I'll carry ye pickaback." He swung the lad up to his broad shoulders and started along the back trail for the clearing; and as he strode homeward through the lengthening woodland shadows, his chattering, light-hearted burden clinging to his neck, he marveled thankfully at the outcome of the day's adventures, and framed the edict he would send forth upon the morrow—to be violated only at peril of Laban Knowles's vengeance.

The scar-sided buck, plunging through the twilight aisles of the spruce wood, could not know that from this day he would have nothing to fear from his human neighbors of the wilderness border, nor that, before many hours, the story of his exploit would go ringing through the settlements, colored into a supreme act of devotion to his youthful patron and given an imperishable page in the annals of the Swiftwater country.

THE POOR UNFORTUNATE HOTTENTOT

(NONSENSE VERSE)

by Laura E. Richards

THIS poor unfortunate Hottentot,
    He was not content with his lotten-
        tot;
    Quoth he, "For my dinner,
    As I am a sinner,
There's nothing to put in the pottentot!"

This poor unfortunate Hottentot
Cried: "Yield to starvation I'll nottentot;
    I'll get me a cantaloup,
    Or else a young antelope,
One who'll enjoy being shottentot."

This poor unfortunate Hottentot,
His bow and his arrows he gottentot;
    And being stout-hearted,
    At once he departed,
And struck through the bush at a trotten-
        tot.

This poor unfortunate Hottentot,
When several miles from his cottentot,
    He chanced to set eyes on
    A snake that was p'ison,
A-tying itself in a knottentot.

Then this poor unfortunate Hottentot
Remarked: "This for me is no spottentot!
    I'd better be going;
    There's really no knowing
If he's trying to charm me, or whattentot!"

This poor unfortunate Hottentot
Was turning to flee to his grottentot,
　　　When a lioness met him,
　　　And suddenly "et" him,
As a penny's engulfed by the slottentot.

MORAL:

This poor unfortunate Hottentot
Had better have borne with his lottentot,
　　　And grown even thinner
　　　For lack of a dinner.
But *I* should have had, then, no plottentot!

UNDER THE HEADLIGHT

by Albert Bigelow Paine

ONE summer morning, nearly twenty years ago, I found myself in New Orleans, Louisiana, with very little money indeed. Being rich in youth and health, this fact did not trouble me. I was rather expert in certain branches of photography, and at once set about obtaining employment at what I was pleased to call my profession.

But it was a poor year and a dull season. I tramped day after day from gallery to gallery, getting always the same reply: "More help than we need now. No chance before cotton time," which was then about three months distant. Finally I went to the photographic supply depot and learned there that a customer at Winona, Mississippi, wanted at once an operator and retoucher, and would pay for his work a fair price, as wages went. I thanked my informant, and said that I would start immediately.

But alas! Winona was more than two hundred and seventy miles from New Orleans, and the fare something over eight dollars. A year or so later I should have stated my case frankly to the supply-dealer and arranged for my ticket. But I did not know of this custom then, and also, being very young, was too proud, or too timid, perhaps, to confess my predicament. Instead, I went back to my cheap room to devise ways and means.

There seemed very few of either. I had precisely twenty-five cents after paying my bill, and the sale of a half-worn heavy coat—not needed in this climate and season—brought me fifty cents more. The remainder of my wardrobe I put into a small valise, and presently set out on foot for the Illinois Central Railroad yards, where freight-trains for the North were made up. I had resolved to beat my way.

I was not altogether unfitted for the undertaking. In still earlier youth I had for one summer been station-agent's assistant, or "cub," at a small Western village, and had learned a good deal about cars, as well as to climb over them while in motion; also the lingo and manner of railroad men, and the kind of talk most likely to obtain a free ride. In fact, during the summer that followed, I had made an extensive trip, in company with a boyfriend, through the great wheat districts of the Central West, earning a good deal of money in the harvest-fields, and paying no railroad fare whatever, though often riding with the trainmen, and in such style as the caboose afforded. I felt confident, therefore, of my ability to get about handily on any part of a running train, and relied as well on a certain railroad freemasonry, though I am bound to say the latter did not count for much in this adventure.

It was a warm day. Even the small valise and my light attire became a burden. Arriving at the yards, the sun beat fiercely down on the cinders and shining steel rails.

Then, the constant switching was confusing, and there seemed to be no train making up that would be ready to start for some hours at least.

I resolved at length to walk to the first small station outside the city, and wait somewhere in the shade until a train came along. Remembering past experience, I counted on making an average of a hundred miles a day, at which rate it would take me about three days to reach Winona.

Beyond the outskirts of the city the road led through a semi-tropical Louisiana swamp, from which the sun drew steam and heavy odors. Here and there I passed gangs of negro railroad laborers, whose shiny blue-black bodies, bare above the waist, and gleaming like polished gun-metal, had a wild look of South African savagery. They chopped and dug at the rank tropical vegetation, and didn't seem to mind the heat, which to me was stifling.

My valise began to drag on me fearfully, and it would bother me still worse later; I resolved to express it, charges collect, from the little station at which, almost overcome by the heat, I at length arrived. Here also I bought a few cents' worth of crackers and, with cold water from a public well, was soon refreshed. Then I went over near the track, and sat down in a shady place to wait.

I had barely rested when a construction train ran in, pausing just long enough for telegraphic orders. When it pulled out, I mounted an empty flat-car at the rear end. By-and-by an employee came back to where I was sitting.

"Where you goin'?" he shouted, above the clatter of the wheels.

"Winona!" I shouted back.

"Can't ride here! Against the rules!"

"Sorry, but I *must go.*"

"Can't allow it. You must get off next stop."

"All right."

The train was for hauling gravel and was very long. I sat on the edge of the flat-car and let my feet swing over the side. The cool wind fanned by, and I enjoyed the scenery. We were making time, too, for a gravel-train, and I thought if I could just keep this up I could increase the daily average. After about a dozen miles, however, we stopped, and I jumped off, as I had agreed to do.

We were at another little village, and I walked for a short distance up a shady street. Then my train whistled to start, and as she got under good headway I resumed my old place on the rear flat-car. Presently my former acquaintance returned and shouted:

"Thought I told you you couldn't ride here!"

"Yes, I believe you did."

"Why didn't you get off back there, then?"

"I did."

He smiled then, too.

"Well," he said, "you can go as far as the lake. We stop there to work. But it's a bad place to lay up in. Mosquitoes will kill you."

"When does the next train come along?"

"About nine o'clock. Passenger-train. Stops at the tank there for water."

That suited me exactly. I could make a station, perhaps two, on the passenger, and some time during the night catch a freight, which, with good luck, I could "hold down" till morning, thus completing my first hundred miles or more.

By and by we came to Lake Pontchartrain bridge, and just beyond it my train ran into a switch and laid up. A gang of painters were employed on the bridge, and with these I soon struck up an acquaintance; for, among the many occupations of a restless youth, I had also painted. The foreman offered me a job, presently, at two dollars a day and board. I thought at first I would take it temporarily, but finally declined, fearing the delay would cause me to lose the other position.

The lake was picturesque. The tall moss-hung cypresses and the placid waters were just as I had seen them in the pictures. The bridge had a draw in the middle of it, and presently this was opened to let a lumber-schooner pass—the *Mary Polly* of New Orleans. As she passed through I looked down on her peaceful decks and wished she were going my way.

At the end of the bridge there was a little store where I ate a light lunch. I did find the mosquitoes rather fierce, but I had nothing to do except to defend myself, and night brought, at last, the rumble of my approaching train. I knew it only stopped here for water, and I could tell just about where the pilot, or cow-catcher, of the engine would be when it stopped. In a line with this and near the track I stood waiting behind some tall weeds and bushes, while the headlight streamed across the bridge, passed me, and the heavy train slowed down and stood panting at the tank. When the big water-pipe was hoisted back to its place and the locomotive began to move slowly, I stepped out and, putting my toe on the lower crosspiece of the cow-catcher, swung myself lightly into place, directly in front of the boiler and beneath the great glaring headlight.

It had grown quite dark by this time, and neither the engineer nor fireman was looking. I felt quite sure I had not been noticed.

Presently we began to go much faster, then still faster. Then we settled down into a steady thirty to thirty-five mile swing, and the rushing wind swept heat, mosquitoes, and weariness far behind.

Faster and still faster! The engine began to rock and hum, and a cloud of small sharp cinders swirled down from above.

They stung my face, but I did not mind them. I was cutting off good miles now. How long I would be allowed to do so, I had no idea; but every two minutes that it lasted meant a mile, at least, nearer my journey's end, and the sensation and excitement of it were glorious. The light from the great eye above me streamed far ahead up the track. On each side was a black wall of night, and between them I was plunging northward at a fearful speed.

On, and still on. Suddenly, with a wild scream from above, we swept through a town without stopping. Country stores were built along the track, after the usual fashion of Southern villages. I saw lights and people. Then woods and blackness again, with the great light streaming ahead.

A new joy now swept over me. My train was the express—the fast mail. It would stop only where railroads crossed, or at large towns, and for water. There are very few railroads or large towns in Mississippi,—fewer then than now,—and an express-locomotive does not take water often. I was good for thirty miles, perhaps, before the first stop. How much better it was than the plodding freights! I looked down the shining steel rails that drew together and vanished in the gloom far ahead, and was exultant, with the careless happiness of youth.

Another village fled by, and another. I was quite settled down to a sense of enjoyment and ownership by this time, and when at last we whistled "down brakes," and I felt our speed slacken for the first stop, it was with a sense of personal injury and ill usage. Perhaps this was to be the end of my glorious ride. It would be more difficult to escape notice in the town than it had been at the lonely water-tank. To add to my dismay, some boys saw me as we swept up to the platform, and ran along by the engine, pointing and calling to the engineer. It was all up, of course. I must get off, and stay off. They had fallen a little behind, however, by the time the engine stopped. I slid off directly in front of the pilot, and walked carelessly away as if I had reached my journey's end. Opposite the platform some ties were piled near the track, and there it was dark. I stepped between them and waited. The boys came up to the pilot, whooping eagerly, and found me gone. I heard them talking loudly and laughing; then their voices grew fainter. The bell clanged to go, and from my place in the shadow I saw the engine move. I stepped out quickly, though with no undue haste, and resumed my place on the pilot. I was, I believe, quite cool. I realized that a scramble might mean a misstep, and a misstep, death. The engineer or fireman may have seen me, but, if so, they gave no sign. The town became scattering houses, with only here and there a light; then came woods again, and the rushing black walls.

I rejoiced greatly that I was good for at least one more stage of my journey. I believed that I had already covered no less than thirty miles on the pilot, and that the next stop would mean as many more. Every village that we dashed through added to my satisfaction; and when the engine screamed, I shouted with it. Then I sang hymns and jubilee songs to the roar and rhythm and rock of the locomotive.

No boys troubled me at the next stop. Perhaps it was too late for them. Nevertheless, I got off instantly, on the side opposite the platform, and walked back to the mail-car. I knew that it had a step on the front, and that the door leading out to this step was rarely opened. It was dark there, and I sat on the end of a tie just below until the train moved; then I

climbed aboard, and away we went once more.

This was a harder place to ride, for the cinders and smoke were terrible; but I was determined to make at least one more run, and I felt that the engineer and fireman, who must have seen me, would be on the watch and prevent my boarding the pilot again.

Either the run was unusually long this time, or it seemed so because of the discomforts of my position. Then, too, for some reason, a postal employee came out there and found me. He shouted to me to get off, and stay off, at the next stop. I did not waste words with him. It was no place for argument. I had resolved to "get off and stay off" his old car, anyway. I did so, and went quietly forward to the friendly engine.

My engineer and fireman were off their guard now, it seemed, and I lay in the shadow of some freight-cars on the siding until the pilot moved. Then I mounted as before, and with renewed joy and confidence. This was something like. On the mail-car was no proper place for a gentleman to ride. Perhaps the wildness and excitement of it all had made me desperate by this time, for I was seized with a determination to ride till daybreak.

"I won't get off till morning!
I won't get off till morning!
I won't get off till morning,
Till daylight doth appear!"

I shouted.

But there are some things easier to sing than to do. I went along without difficulty and with increasing confidence for several stations. Then, all at once,—at Canton, I think,—we changed engines. There was broad light everywhere, and a number of employees were about the cab. The conductor, too, came up presently to chat with the engineer, and from my concealment in the shadow of a small tool-house I could hear what they said. I heard the conductor speak of the hot night and a black cloud, and say that it was going to rain. I wished that it would pour instantly, so that everybody would go away.

This it did not do, and the engineer oiled and wiped while the conductor and yard employees lingered and talked. There would be no chance whatever to get back on the pilot,—none, so far as I could see, to get anywhere,—unless these fellows went away. The employees did so presently, but the conductor lingered and talked on. Then, for some unknown reason, he turned and walked directly to where I was sitting. It would have been foolish to run. I closed my eyes and pretended to be asleep. He came up and held his lantern to my face. Then he called to the engineer: "Here's a fellow going to get wet, Bill!"

The engineer laughed, but did not seem interested enough to look. The conductor left me, and I heard him talking to the engineer again—something about tramps and getting killed. He talked on, and I concluded that he meant to stay there until the train started and get on the first coach as it passed. The situation was becoming desperate. After all, perhaps it would be as well to stop over one train at Canton.

But when the bell began to ring it brought me to my feet. The conductor had walked back a few yards to the end of the platform. If he got on the step of the mail-car there was no hope. The train was moving now, and gaining speed with every foot. He was a heavy man, and would hardly take chances on waiting for the coach. The baggage-car passed him, and the mail-car came on at good speed.

He looked at the step as it came abreast of him, made a slight movement with his body, and—let it pass.

I hesitated no longer. He would not look around again. I stepped quickly over to the track, and as the mail-car step swept by, almost on a level with my head, I caught the handles and made a quick, swinging leap. An instant later I was seated on the upper step, my heart thumping and my breath coming quick and hard. The step had been very high and was going very fast. It was the greatest feat of my life.

The postal employee did not come out this time, perhaps because it was sprinkling and very discouraging out there. At the next stop I went back to my old post on the pilot.

Now it began to rain in earnest—great splashing drops at first, with quick lightning and thunder. I was drenched through at once, of course. Then followed one of the fiercest thunder-storms of that semi-tropical country: a continuous blue flare, crashing thunder, a torrent of water that bore upon me as if from a broken dam. The conductor's prophecy had come true: I *was* wet. It was cool, though, and a relief after the mail-step. I bent my head to it, and laughed aloud at the wildness of the situation. I thought, if we should only strike a cow now, there would be nothing left to happen, and the fact that we were rushing on to the North through it all exhilarated me till I shouted and sang and laughed wth the rain beating and blinding me. The storm slackened at last, then ceased. The air was much cooler, and I began to feel chilly with the rushing wind in my wet clothes. But the boiler behind me was warm, and I pressed back against it. As my clothes dried I grew very sleepy.

For a time I could scarcely hold my

eyes open, and it was only the occasional stop, and the interest and exercise of regaining my position, that kept me awake.

And so on through the night. I do not know how many stops we made in all—how many times I concealed myself behind the ties, weeds, cars, sheds, or whatever came handiest; but it could not have been less than a dozen in all. Of these places I caught a few of the names as we passed the station placards. I remember dimly Crystal Spring, Jackson, the State capital, and, more clearly, Canton (I think), where we changed engines. I had counted on the night seeming very long, and I could scarcely believe that it was more than two o'clock when all at once I realized that daylight was coming. The sky was clear now, and the stars were fading back into the white light of morning. Bushes and trees on either side began to show in dim outline as we whirled past. At the next stop the fireman came around and met me as I left my seat. He carried a lantern and an oil-can, and did not seem surprised.

"Don't you ever get tired?" he asked.

I knew then that he must have been aware of me for some time. I said that I *was* rather tired—that travel was not all pleasure. He laughed, and throwing his light in my face, looked at me intently. Then he laughed again. I suppose the soot and cinders that had gathered on my features and mixed with the rain had something to do with his mirth. He was good-hearted, though, and went back to his cab with a pleasant word. If he sees this, and remembers, I want him to know that if I wasn't clean, I was grateful for his kindness.

The next stop was a water-tank in the woods. The sun was on the horizon, and the wet green trees were loud with birds. The conductor came forward and saw me.

"This is your place to get off," he said.

"Well," I replied, "I guess I *will* stop over here."

I sat down on a green bank, and the train went on. Then I went to a barrel of fresh rain-water that stood near the tank, and plunged in my arms and head. When I had finished I believed I had the soot and cinders pretty well off. I learned my mistake when, later, I came face to face with a mirror. But, at least, I was refreshed, and sat down to think and congratulate myself on the night's run. I believed that it was about four o'clock, and that I had been seven hours on the train. I could not have made less than two hundred miles, which, with the distance beyond Lake Pontchartrain, would make a total not far from two hundred and twenty-five, leaving perhaps fifty still to go. I could take a good rest, and, with any luck at all, still complete my journey a day sooner than I had calculated.

I realized suddenly that I was thinking all this aloud, and repeating some of it over and over. My head felt light, and I knew that I was slightly delirious from loss of sleep and excitement. I was tempted to lie down at once, but decided to walk on to the first village and get something to eat. There were open fields just ahead, where meadow-larks sang and the grass sparkled with dew. The morning air was fresh and sweet—much better, I thought, than the heavy Louisiana atmosphere. I felt perfectly well in body, but found it hard not to think aloud. The mind is very easily unsettled.

All at once I came to a little road that led across the track and connected two fields. A small negro boy was driving a cow across, and just beyond him was a white post with black figures on it. I looked closer and saw that they formed the number "271." I stared at them steadily

—272 would be my destination. I was not quite sure of my brain. Then I asked of the little darky:

"How far is it to the next town?"

He looked at me, grinning, before he spoke.

" 'Bout a mile," he said. "You can see it f'm right up yon'er a li'l' piece."

"What's the name of it?"

"Winona."

I made him repeat it to be sure.

"Yes, sah; Winona. Mighty nice town, sah."

I gave him five of the sixty cents still left in my pocket. Then I hurried on, and going to a cheap railroad restaurant, ate whatever I could get the most of for the least money. They had a wash-room there, and a mirror. In the latter I saw what I most needed, and took it, for towel and basin were there and soap that was strong and plentiful. After breakfast I went to a barber shop, and came out penniless but respectable. I reached my employer's gallery just as he was opening his morning mail. It contained a letter from New Orleans, stating that a man such as he needed would start at once. It referred to me, and had come on the same train. He was glad to see me, and I remained with him a year. We became the best of friends in time, and one day I told him about my trip.

"Well," he laughed, "you were here on time, anyway."

And so I was. But I would not willingly go through such a night again, and many a poor fellow since then has lost his life in just that sort of an undertaking.

THE BROWNIES MEND THE DAM

by Palmer Cox

As Brownies talked in spirits good,
   Beside a broken dam they stood,
   To watch the water as it flew
From many holes the timbers through.
Said one: "The noise that strikes the ear
Would tell that something's lacking here,

If one had not an eye to see
The water spouting out so free;
It surely finds no lack of room
To make escape without the flume,
Where it's supposed to lie and wait
With patience till they raise the gate."

Another said: "This dam supplied
The needs of all the country wide;
It drove the millstone round about,
And ground the grain that kept folk stout,
From grandsires, with their gruel bowl,
To babes just learning how to roll.
It made the saw play up and down,
And furnished lumber for the town
To build its homes so snug and warm,
And give protection from the storm."
A third exclaimed: "Now here's a task
That will have all that one could ask,
In way of struggle and of strain,
Who seeks distinction to attain!
And I, for one, don't want to miss
Or put aside a chance like this.

The work begun was work indeed,
Of all their strength they felt the need,
And skill to plan, and power to stick,
Or make a leap both sure and quick.
For water, if there be enough
And running fast, is dangerous stuff,
And those who went above the flow
Were not more safe than those below.

We all can see there's danger here,
Even for us, who never fear,
And, if a river talks at all,
Quite plainly says this waterfall,
'Begin, begin, to stop the leaks,
You'll need no other bath for weeks.'
But where the human kind would dread
To make a move, we push ahead,
And in this way the honor win
That only comes from wading in.
If men with chisel, saw, and bore,
Could patch this break, we can do more,
Because their skill is ours too,
Besides some gifts they never knew."
What need we with our knowledge great
Of Brownie band do more than state
The task, as you've already guessed,
Was soon commenced with all their zest?

'T was hard above to check the rush,
And hard below to meet the gush;
The logs, that down the stream they ran
To aid in working out their plan,
Were seldom checked at boom or bar,
And, to their sorrow, went too far,
While Brownies with the sticks were
    tossed,
And for a time were counted lost.
For logs rolled over as they ran,
And changed at once the Brownies' plan,
By keeping heads a foot below
Where it was thought the feet would go.
Some might have laughed who saw the
    sight,
But there's no fun in such a plight.
Some bravely faced the danger great,
While more went backward to their fate,
And on the timbers round or square

That they had shaped with art and care,
There was no moment, do their best,
When one could let his prudence rest.
'T would have been painful to behold
If one knew not traditions old,
That these wee people can win through
The trials that would us undo.

To carry out their plans entire,
That failure may not mock desire.
Like bees in hive, or ants in hill,
They show a common stir and will,
And though at times they crowded seem,
They're only working out their scheme,
Each calculation made aright

There is no mourning at the home
When they lose breath beneath the foam,
Or grieving at the fireplace,
If they are missing for a space.
They're up and active as a clock
Nor ever suffer from the shock,
Or they would not for years have run
From page to page as they have done.
A mortal scarce can comprehend
The energy they all expend

To reach success and honor bright.
If one would judge them ere they're
    through,
While all's confusion and to-do,
You'd think success would never crown
Such crazy acts, or bring renown.
At such a time advice is lost,
As all have plans and won't be bossed,
But carry out as firm as stone
The part each thinks to be his own.

Strange things were into service press'd
That in their hurry promised best,
And few the objects that escaped
Their eyes, if they were rightly shaped,
Or could with labor small be made
To stop a leak if rightly laid.
They used some gates that long had swung
A welcome wide to old and young,
But now were sagging in their place
With faithless hinge and broken brace.
The task was hard, and tried the best,
And all were anxious for a rest.

But that was not the place to stay
And face the coming glare of day.
So those who still had strength to spare
To weaker comrades gave their care,
For some were heated, some were chilled,
And some with aches and pains were filled,
While more had bruises, or were sore
With work they never tried before.
They hastened to a safe retreat
Where no surprises they would meet,
However bright the day might be,
Or mortals hope to find the key.

MORE · THAN · CONQVERORS

BY ARIADNE GILBERT

THE DEAF MUSICIAN

IT was over a hundred and thirty years ago. The opposite neighbor of the Beethovens, who was standing in front of his comfortable home, saw Ludwig, Carl, and Johann Beethoven turn in at their gate and bravely help their staggering father up the steps. He watched them solemnly. "Herr van Beethoven has been drinking again," he thought. Many times after that he saw the same sight—the three Beethoven boys almost lifting that sagging burden into the house.

But what wonderful music came through the open door of the house across the way! At his best, Herr van Beethoven sang beautifully. Ludwig, when he was only four, had sat in his father's lap at the harpsichord, rapt not in the fascination of flying fingers, but in satisfied love of the music. Then Herr van Beethoven had stopped, and, letting the baby hands take their turn on the cold, white keys, had felt with a thrilling, bounding confidence that no ordinary child touched the instrument. Out of it stole the same melody that he had played. And so, when Ludwig was only four or five, his father began his musical training; when he was nine years old,

a big man named Pfeiffer, who lived with the Beethovens, gave him regular lessons. As the oldest son and a possible genius, Ludwig was to have his chance. While the Beethoven boys were playing, Herr Pfeiffer would come to the door and thunder, *"Ludwig, komm' ins Haus";* and the child, sometimes crying, would stop his fun and stamp into the house to that dull practising. At times, they say, his teacher had to use something harsher than his big, harsh voice.

But once indoors, Ludwig was not miserable; he handled the keys with love. Sometimes Herr Pfeiffer would pick up a sweet-voiced flute, and, standing there beside the boy, he too would play. And the people going by would stand still to listen, and perhaps even Carl and Johann would stop their games to listen, too, for they were German boys, and music made them happy.

One day, the neighbors learned that the Beethovens had sold their linen and their silver service; another day, that much of the furniture and tableware had been sold. Frau van Beethoven grew paler and paler, and the father kept on drinking. Sometimes Ludwig would go away to play at public concerts. At that time, no one knew that Herr van Beethoven, in order to gain a large audience, reported the child a year younger than he really was. He was such a little fellow for his age that this was easily believed. When, "aged six," he was advertised to give a series of concerts in Cologne, he was really seven. But he was only ten when he made a concert tour through Holland with his mother, and he was only fourteen when he was appointed assistant to the court organist.

People used to love to have him "describe the character of some well-known person" on the piano. He could do with the piano what a painter does with his brush.

Before Beethoven was out of his teens, his brave, good mother died. "There was once some one to hear me when I said, 'Mutter,'" thought the lonely boy. Soon after, his father, who was less than a cipher, lost his position through drink, and so Ludwig was made head of the family, with the weight of his brothers' education and all his father's debts.

Hoping to have his genius recognized and perhaps to take a few lessons, he went from Bonn to Vienna to play before the great Mozart. But Mozart was absorbed in composing an opera; he did not want to be bothered. He looked at the short young man with the "snub nose," and thought little of him; heard him play, and still thought him commonplace. In fact, he believed that Beethoven had learned his pieces by heart just to show off. Then, on fire with disappointment, Beethoven asked Mozart to give him a subject, and, just as an author might make up a story on a given subject, he sat down and played a wonderful piece of music. The older genius was astounded. "This youth will some day make a noise in the world!" he exclaimed.

Before Beethoven was thirty, he began to grow deaf. Think of it! Think of a painter losing his sight; never again to see the changing beauty of cloud and river, the chasing light on a field of waving grain, or the sparkle in a baby's eyes. It was as heart-breaking for a musician to grow deaf as for a painter to be struck blind. "The noblest part of me, my sense of hearing, has become very weak," Beethoven wrote in sorrowing confidence. "Please keep as a great secret what I have told you about my hearing." Then followed years of torment mingled with terrible sensitiveness, even to the point of running away for fear people would learn that he was deaf, and show pity in their faces. It was not possible for him to say, "Speak louder, shout, for I am deaf." "A feeling of hot anxiety" overwhelmed him, and at the same time a pathetic wistfulness, when he thought that perhaps his companions could hear "a distant flute" or a "shepherd singing." When he went to concerts, he had to lean forward close to the orchestra to get the sound. This sealing of his dearest sense must have made him feel like "a house half ruined ere the lease be out."

With time, in spite of all his doctors, the humming in his ears grew worse. At last, deafness drove him to ear-trumpets and written conversations; saddest of all, he could no longer hear the sounds made by his own fingers on the piano.

It would be both impossible and misleading to systematize a life of Beethoven. Eccentric genius that he was, his life had next to no system. Though many of his days were much alike, domestic explosions of one kind or another broke into them and kept him harried and confused. We must think of him as seldom at peace. His youth was spent in the city of Bonn, his manhood in or near Vienna, with some of his summers at Baden. He never married, and he never had a home, in any real sense, though his great, affectionate heart would have dearly loved one.

Now fretted by small suspicions and petty wants, now upborne by the power of great emotion, he was a wonderful combination of pygmy and giant. Judged by his letters, the veriest trifles made up life; judged by his music, life was too vast for our poor human groping. And so one person called him "a growling old bear"; another, "the cloud-compeller of the world of music." Almost as helpless as a child, in some respects, he expected his friends to look after all sorts of things: wrote to Ries for half a dozen sewing-needles, and to the ever patient Zmeskall for quills for his pens, a watch, the cost of re-vamping his servant's boots, and, at last, "Please send me for a few hours the looking-glass which hangs next to your window; mine is broken"; and even, "Send me at once your servant."

If ever a man needed a guardian, it was Beethoven. Wholesome Frau Streicher, the wife of one of his friends, did all she could to help him in his many domestic difficulties. "Yes, indeed," he wrote her, "all this housekeeping is still without keeping, and much resembles an *allegro di confusione.*" To her the poor man turned for dusters, blankets, linen, scissors, knives, and servants; and to her he complained of having to "carry in his head so many pairs of trousers, stockings, shoes, etc."

"Man stands but little above other animals, if his chief enjoyments are limited to the table," Beethoven would often say. Under inspiration, for days together he "forgot all about time and rest and food." On the other hand, when he did eat, he was particular. He generally made his own coffee for breakfast, allowing sixty beans to a cup, and counting them as precisely as if coffee were all-important. Not only

was he as fond of soup as are most other Germans, but he thought himself the highest authority on that great subject, and would argue hotly on the best way to make it. "If Schindler had declared a bad soup good, after some time he would get a note to this effect: 'I do not value your judgment about the soup in the least, *it is bad,*'" or perhaps a savory sample to prove Beethoven's knowledge. Indeed, Germany's mighty composer made very superior soup!

"There is music in running water," says Van Dyke. To Beethoven there surely was; but his landladies must have regretted it. If, for any reason, Beethoven could not go out-of-doors, he had a way of creating inspiration in his room. He would go to the wash-bowl, "pour several jugs" of water over his wrists, and dabble there till his clothes were drenched. If this had been all, no one else would have cared; but often, in his absent-minded rapture, he poured out a great deal more water than the bowl would hold, and, before long, buxom old Frau von R——, who roomed below him, would find her ceiling dripping. To her there was no "music in running water," and she took pains to explain as much to the landlady. And then there would be one more change of lodging for Beethoven. Often, when he moved, he would leave part of his things behind, and sometimes he was paying for "two, three, and at one time four, dwelling-places at once."

One day, a ten-year-old boy was taken to see Beethoven, and this is his memory of the visit:

"We mounted five or six stories high ... and were announced by a rather dirty-looking servant. In a very desolate room, with papers and articles of dress strewn in all directions, bare walls, a few chests, hardly a chair except the rickety one standing by the piano, there was a party of six or eight people. Beethoven was dressed in a jacket and trousers of long, dark goat's-hair, which at once reminded me of 'Robinson Crusoe,' which I had just been reading. He had a shock of jet-black hair, standing straight upright."

When Frau Streicher was in Baden, Beethoven wrote to her: "If you wander through the mysterious fir-forests, think it was there Beethoven often poetized, or, as it is called, composed." "Strolling among the mountain clefts and valleys," with a sheet of music-paper in his hand, he would "scribble a lot for the sake of bread and money—daub work for the sake of money," so that he might "stand the strain of a great work."

Never understood, that great, mysterious soul with its tremendous inner struggles must have suffered incurable loneliness. Indeed, Beethoven was twice solitary—through deafness and through greatness. In all seasons and in all weathers, beneath the open heavens, he sought society in winds and lightning, as well as gurgling brooks and restful moonlight. Away into the woods he would go. The hurry of business, the clatter of wagons and of many feet—these things suffocated his inspiration. Solitude gave it life. Tempests filled him with power; clouds, with their far-away peace; but not even in his greatest music could he utter it all. And so he had the pain, not only of loneliness, but of being forever unsatisfied. After his deafness came on, he could not hear the wind in the pine-trees, or the singing-bird that soared up, up into the blue; but he could see the green boughs bend, and watch the joyous flight, and he could *remember*. In his little notebook he would feverishly jot down his ideas, waiting a while to let the melody and its variations settle. Then at dusk, half afraid that it might all slip

away, his hat gone and his bushy head bowed, he would stride home through the city streets, seeing and hearing no one, not even his best friends.

"Just Beethoven!" they would laugh, getting out of his mad way; "only his body is in the world!"—or some such thing. Though he had lost nothing in the woods but his hat, very likely strangers thought he had lost his wits. On the contrary, he had found a wonderful something that made his heart swell. In that heart a great symphony struggled for creation and release, and all the elements of earth and sky cried out to be immortalized in music.

God has a few of us whom He whispers
    in the ear;
The rest may reason and welcome; 't is
    we musicians know.

When Beethoven reached home, he dashed in, and, keeping his hat still on (if he *happened* not to have lost it) and throwing his coat anywhere, he rushed to the piano. There, leaning low over the keys, to catch all the beauty his deafness would allow, he played rapturously, not knowing who or where he was, not knowing, above all, that a crowd had gathered outside the forgotten open door to hear the great, free concert.

"He has three sets of apartments in which he alternately secretes himself," said a friend—"one in the country, one in the town, and a third on the ramparts." Just as his eccentricity scattered his servants and enraged his landladies, so it broke out to his friends, his orchestra, his pupils, in a hundred hot-headed actions.

His friends had to be very patient and believing. Von Breuning, Ries, and Schindler were repeatedly tested by his shifting trust and suspicion. There would be a terrible word-explosion or a letter of the never-speak-again kind, and then, "warm out of the heart," but in abominably illegible handwriting, would gush a little note begging for forgiveness and the same old place in their affections. It was a fragment of the child left in him. "I fly to you, . . . Your contrite, faithful, and loving friend, Beethoven." "I know I have rent thy heart." Then, after pages of penitent pleading, "Now perhaps thou wilt fly back into my arms." Notes of two successive days read: "Do not come any more to me. You are a false fellow," and "You are an honorable fellow . . . so come this afternoon to me." One day he calls Schindler "arch-scoundrel," later, "best of friends" or "trusty one, I kiss the hem of your coat." This is one unique invitation: "You can come to midday meal, bring your provisions with you—be ready—we are ready."

Once, in the middle of a public concert, when his orchestra had not pleased him, he stopped, quite as if he were giving a lesson, and shouted, "Begin again! From the beginning!" The orchestra obeyed. He never treated a lord with a whit more respect than a peasant. When Duke Raimer came late to his music-lesson, Beethoven revenged himself on the young man's fingers.

"Why are you so impatient?" asked the duke.

"You make me lose my time in the anteroom, and now I cannot get patient again," answered Beethoven. After that, Duke Raimer never kept him waiting. As we can imagine, the tediousness of counting his pupils' time wore terribly on the great composer. He did it for bread. But rather often he excused himself, on the ground of illness, from lessons to the Archduke Rudolph. "Your Imperial Highness," he called him, or oftener, "Y. I. H." The same old reason crept again and again into his profoundly respectful letters. We must re-

member, however, that Beethoven suffered for years from rheumatism, indigestion, and finally from dropsy. He seems never to have been really well.

Just as eccentric in public as in private, when he led an orchestra he would make himself smaller and smaller to compel softened sounds. Then, as he wanted the sounds louder, his head would "gradually rise up as if out of an abyss; and when the full force of the united instruments broke upon the ear, raising himself on tiptoe, he looked of gigantic stature, and, with both his arms floating about in undulating motion, seemed as if he would soar to the clouds. He was all motion, no part of him remained inactive."

Few things are more irritating to musical people than drifting attention. It is as if, sensitive to every thought and feeling, the power to play leaves the musician's hands if his listeners are not with him. A frivolous audience scattered the great Beethoven's inspiration like wind-blown leaves. And he could not recall it. As a rule, though, he did not care to; he gave way to justified impatience. One day, during a duet by Beethoven and Ries, some young people began to talk and laugh in the next room. Suddenly Beethoven stopped, grabbed Ries's hands from the piano, and sprang to his feet with an angry exclamation. And no one could persuade him to finish the piece.

"You prelude a great while; when are you going to begin?" was his tart comment when Himmer competed with him in improvising. It sounds bitter and conceited, but Beethoven was equally hearty in his appreciation, and in offers of assistance. "Truly in Schubert dwells a divine fire," he said. He admired the "scene-painting" of Rossini; but particularly the work of Mozart, Bach, and Handel. And he was unstinted in his praise of "The Messiah." "Handel is the greatest composer who ever lived," he sweepingly declared. One letter, practical, loving, tender, he wrote to help raise money for Bach's daughter, who was "aged and in want." He asked earnestly for help—"before this daughter of Bach dies, before this *brook* dies up, and we can no longer supply it with water." (Bach is German for brook.) Beethoven was apt to make puns in his letters, just as he was to begin them with a bar of music.

With his hands too full of his own work, he wrote, nobly and freely, "With pleasure, my dear Drieberg, will I look through your compositions, and if you think me able to say anything to you about them, I am heartily ready to do it." And he wrote to a little girl of eight or ten who "raved over him": "If, my dear Emilie, you at any time wish to know something, write without hesitation to me. The true artist is not proud; he unfortunately sees that art has no limits; he feels darkly how far he is from the goal. . . . I would, perhaps, rather come to you and your people than to many rich folks who display inward poverty."

Just such a democratic spirit as this ruled his life. Passion and pride moved him to all sorts of unexpected acts. He refused to take off his hat to royalty. When his brother Johann wrote him a letter signed "Landowner," Beethoven signed his answer "Brain-owner." When he was asked in court to prove his right to his title of nobility, he said, raising his rough head grandly and flashing his brilliant little eyes, "My nobility is here and here," and he pointed to his head and heart. In his warm hero-worship he had dreamed that Napoleon meant to make France a republic, and he intended to dedicate his "Heroic Symphony" to him. But, just as he was completing it, he heard that the emperor had been crowned. With mingled passion and disappointment, he tore off

the title page bearing the word "Bonaparte," and flung the whole thing to the floor. "After all, he's nothing but an ordinary mortal!" he exclaimed bitterly. And so, though the original manuscript still bears faint traces of the fallen hero's name, it was published merely: "To the Memory of a Great Man."

As Louis Nohl says, the march in this symphony gathers into one picture "the glad tramp of warlike hosts, the rhythm of trampling steeds, the waving of standards, and the sound of trumpets."

To Beethoven the greatest element in music was spiritual. Not only did he long to lift the audience heavenward, but every one of the orchestra. His own feeling was so immense that he judged the best musical performance as nothing if it had no soul. "Read Shakspere," he said to some one who wanted to play. Those who would interpret Beethoven must be full of poetry. For that reason, those who are mere piano gymnasts, no matter how good, had better try shallower compositions.

There is the music of imitation and the music of feeling. One of Beethoven's early teachers had complained, in despair, "He will never do anything according to rule; he has learned nothing." But even then the young genius was *feeling* something no follower of rules could teach. Before him lay a conquest of sound so glorious that strong men would bow their heads and sob aloud at its power.

Like a mighty heart the music seemed,
That yearns with melodies it cannot speak.

Sir George Grove said of Beethoven's "Funeral March," "If ever horns talked like flesh and blood, they do it here." That solemn march stirs us to the depths. But hard labor had gone hand in hand with feeling. Though Beethoven could neither play nor write formally, he often worked for years on a piece of music, changing, cutting, and improving. They say that of his opera "Fidelio" he made as many as eighteen different versions.

He had the power of imitation, too, though that was not his greatest strength. As we can see the sunlight flash on the leaping fish in Schubert's "Trout," so we can see a heavenly shimmer in Beethoven's "Moonlight Sonata." His "Pastoral Symphony" carries us from the scene by the brook, through the gathering of the peasants, a thunder-storm, a shepherd's song, and a final rejoicing. We hear the murmur of the brook and the mutter of thunder; the violins make flashes of lightning; the flute, oboe, and clarinet mimic the nightingale, quail, and cuckoo. One part of the symphony pictures "a rustic merry-making, the awkward, good-natured gambols of peasants," and one old fellow who sits on a barrel and is able to play only three tones.

The great, lonely composer gave and craved much love. But no friend, no *one* ever held a place in his heart equal to his nephew Carl's. At eight, the boy had been left by his father's will to his Uncle Ludwig, and immediately that uncle assumed all a father's responsibility and love. His one great thought, aside from music, was Carl. Much of his music, even, was written to get money for the boy's education. We follow the uncle through all his early hopes. Believing he saw scientific genius "in the dear pledge intrusted" to him, he sent the boy to a fine school and gave him, besides, lessons in drawing, French, and music. For years he chose him the best tutors, watched over him like a mother, and called him all kinds of pet names: "lovely lad," "my Carl," "dear little rascal," "best ragamuffin," "dear jewel," but, oftenest of all, "my son." How willingly he adjusted his own program to suit the boy's convenience! He believed he found

in the handsome little fellow all the things he longed for: honor, tenderness, affection; and he vowed to do his "best for him to the end of his life," and leave him everything after death.

To those who read Beethoven's letters, even the awful, increasing deafness seems less cruel than Carl's ingratitude. The empty-hearted fellow had no loyalty. As he grew older, he grew calculating and defiant. It is not too hard to say that he loved his uncle's money, not his uncle. At twenty, he was publicly expelled from the university, and later sent to prison, his uncle getting him out and securing him a commission in the army. With all this, the selfish nephew even begrudged Beethoven his society. The uncle, in his wistful loneliness, wrote him the most pathetic letters. "I should be so glad to have a human heart about me in my solitude," he said, touchingly.

How often the great composer must have looked from his sick-room window! The long days lagged by, and many suns set gloriously behind the trees; but Carl, beloved and longed for, did not come.

Meanwhile, "in his remote house on the hill," the "Solitary of the Mountain" fought out his final conquest. On his writing-table stood his framed motto: "I am all that is, all that was, and all that shall be; no mortal man hath my veil uplifted." "He had learned in suffering what he taught in song." His life had been one battle after another, all the way: the child Ludwig had begun by caring for a drunken father and shouldering big debts; the man had driven himself through humdrum lessons. Then came the approach of closing deafness, and, in the darkness of desperation, Beethoven had looked up and said, "Art, when persecuted, finds everywhere a place of refuge; Dædalus, though inclosed in the labyrinth, invented wings which carried him into the air; oh! I also will find those wings." Lonely for Carl and hungry for his own music, he said to himself, "Poor Beethoven, there is no external happiness for you! You must create your own happiness." "O God, grant me strength to conquer myself," he prayed. And so he determined to give to others what he, himself, could not get— a wonderful rapture of sound; he would not leave this earth till he had revealed what lay within him. For this, he had been sent of God.

His tempestuous fight ended March 26, 1827, after a long illness. He died in the midst of a great thunder-storm. None of his dearest friends were with him. Carl was not there; Schindler and von Breun-ing had gone out on errands. Beethoven's clock stopped, as it had often done when it lightened. But the warring elements had been the composer's lifelong friends, and often before had carried his soul above this little world. In the midst of the flashes and the rumbling, he thought, "I shall hear, in heaven."

He might have thought that he would be immortalized on earth. Twenty great composers bore Beethoven to his last sleeping-place, and twenty others carried torches in the grand, somber procession.

"No mourning wife, no son, no daughter wept at his grave; but a world wept at it."

TAKEN AT HIS WORD

by Elizabeth Stuart Phelps

HEROD'S STORY

"THERE, go!" said I; "and I don't care if I never see you again!"

I am almost an old man now, with gray hairs and rheumatism, and an objection to draughts; so old that I wear my rubbers in dry, cold weather, and don't take off a comforter before May, and don't go out after dewfall in the summer, and don't keep track of the last engagement, and don't think much about the church sociables and whom I shall take to a lecture.

You can think how old that must be! But old as I am, I remember just how I said those words; where the accent fell; how they sounded; how the wind caught them and blew them around the corners of the house; and how they seemed to come around and knock on the windows, to be let in again, after I had shut the door. Nothing has happened to me in all my life since they were spoken that has helped in the least to make me forget them.

It may be only an old man's notion, but sometimes I am forced to wonder if anything will happen in the next life that can make me forget them.

There is this about a next world's life, girls and boys: It is no fun, to my mind, to carry a thing on into it that you want to forget and *can't* forget. And we all know how dreary anything is when there's "no fun" in it.

There was fun enough in what I have to tell, at the first of it. At least Trollo thought so, I suppose. Trollo was my brother. He was a little chap, eight years old. I was fourteen. They all had gone off and left us alone in the house, and Trollo had plagued me half out of my senses. That's the way, you know, it seemed to *me*. It seemed to *him* quite different, I've no doubt.

This is how it happened.

My sister Mary lived in New Haven. That was fifteen miles away. Mary's husband had got into some trouble about money, and father thought he would go on and see about it; and Mary's baby was sick with something or other, and mother thought she would go on and see about that.

Mary's husband was always getting into trouble about money, and Mary's baby was always getting sick; but they didn't often come on poor Mary together. At any rate, father and mother thought they would go on; and as they would be gone only over the second night, and because I was fourteen years old, and because Trollo said he would be good, and because Keziah Phipps said she would come over and "do" for us, and stay nights, unless "the old man got his back up,"—and because, on the whole, we didn't very much care, but thought it would be rather nice, and that if Keziah Phipps' old man *should,* by any providential accident, "get his back up," we would make molasses corn-balls, with vanilla in them,—we were left alone.

It was dark and cloudy, the day they went away. Mother said she was afraid it was blowing up for a storm; but father said he thought not. And he told me to be sure and not let the fire go out, nor the pigs go hungry, nor the horse go un-blanketed; and mother kissed us both— but she kissed Trollo twice—and told me to take good care of Trollo, and let the cat sit by the fire; and then the stage rattled away with them, and Trollo and I stood looking after it.

"I wish they'd come back to-morrow; don't you, Herod?" said Trollo.

My name was Hurdley. But Trollo used to call me Herod, just to see what I would say; and when he found I didn't say any-thing, he called me so because he had got into the way of calling me so; and by the time he'd got into the way of calling me so, I didn't much mind, but rather liked it. Only when the boys laughed at it, or I felt cross, it used to seem an ugly name. But Trollo had a gentle, little, pleasant voice, and generally I liked the sound he gave it.

I said no, I didn't wish they were com-ing *right* back; for I was thinking about the vanilla corn-balls. And Trollo said he didn't know as he did either.

"But you're to be good, you know," said I.

I felt very old and superior to Trollo, and I rather liked it to feel that I could order him around for two days.

"I hadn't said I wasn't, had I?" said Trollo, firing up to begin with.

Then I fired up a little, and told him he was to behave himself, at all events; and that was the beginning of it. I thought

afterwards it would have been nicer in me not to have preached at him before he'd had a chance to behave one way or another. But I didn't think of it at the time. Boys don't, you know.

So we both sulked a little, and Trollo went to school; but when he came home to dinner we'd got over it, or very nearly. We only quarreled about his piece of pie. I said it was bigger than mother let him have. And we got the foot-rule and a tape-measure, and measured it off. Then he ate it down in three mouthfuls, to pay me for that.

I didn't go to school myself. I was to stay and watch the house, and look after the horse, and so forth; for it was only two days, and I could study at home, and such a thing might never happen again. And Keziah Phipps came over and got dinner and went away again, and came again to supper, and stayed all night. Keziah Phipps was our nearest neighbor; she lived a quarter of a mile away. Ours was rather a lonesome house, with pine trees in the front yard and a long stretch of fields behind, where the snow drifted; it always drifted in the road by our house, too. We lived on a very windy road.

It was a cold day, and the wind blew pretty high. Trollo came in from school the last time that afternoon with red cheeks, and as full of mischief as he could hold. He stamped off the snow in the entry and flung his mittens at me when I told him not to. One of them hit me in the eye.

Trollo was a good aim—a lithe, little quick-eyed chap, always up to something.

"Oh! I didn't mean to!" he said, when the mitten hit.

But I was mad. It didn't hurt me much; but I'd been having a cold time with the horse and had spilled the pigs' supper, and, I suppose, didn't feel like myself exactly, from not going to school as usual, but loafing around and sitting by the fire so much. At any rate, I was mad. So I shook him.

He didn't say much, and I don't think he cared much. He'd come home as wild as a witch, and there wasn't anything he wasn't ready to do to make mischief that night. And because I was mad, he wouldn't mind me.

He tied his rubber boots to the door-bell. He stuffed his wet mittens down my neck. He set the cat in the platter with the turkey bones, and then set platter, cat, bones and all upon the table, when Keziah Phipps had begun to eat. He ran out with a new squash pie to give to the horse, and dropped it and fell on it before he got there. He put salt in my tea, and sugar on my pickles, and green wood on the fire; and when I scolded him, he whistled.

Then, after tea, we sat down to study. Somehow, everything that Trollo did seemed to me to be wrong that night. He banged his boots against the table-leg. He wouldn't put on his slippers. His nails were dirty; he wouldn't clean them. He asked Keziah for another piece of cake, and, after all he had done, he got it. He sang "Hail, Columbia!" on a very flat squeak for twenty minutes. He sat down on the cat. He wouldn't brush his hair. He got Keziah to show him his sums. He flung sofa-pillows at the ceiling, and they came down on the custard batter. He seemed to me the most disagreeable boy I ever knew. When he went to bed, I told him so.

I remember just how he looked, standing—with our little brass bed-lamp in his hand—in the entry, to say good-night. It was one of those old-fashioned, one-wicked lamps, that gave almost no light. His face looked dim and odd behind it in the dark entry.

He started to say something, but gave

it up and didn't speak,—only laughed,—and trotted off up stairs, kicking his boots off and letting them drop down through the balusters. He was a merry, happy-go-lucky little chap. If he minded anything, he wouldn't say so. If you were cross to him, he might plague you; but he wouldn't scold a great deal himself.

The next morning it was much the same. It was a very dark morning, and snowing in a slow, hard way. We woke late, and I had to hurry Trollo up. I don't suppose I was very gentle. And he threw pillows at me, and when I ordered him down to see if Keziah had got breakfast, he hid my tooth-brush. I needn't have ordered him around so much, but I thought that was part of the fun of having father and mother gone. I rather liked it to be able to say "you must" and "you mustn't" to Trollo. It didn't occur to me to wonder how Trollo liked it.

Well, it was one thing and another between Trollo and me till school-time. Such little things they seem now! But they did not seem little to me then. I was cross and cold. And I was afraid Keziah Phipps' old man wouldn't get his back up, after all, and we shouldn't get our corn-balls. And everything hit me, somehow, just the crooked way. You know how it is on a cold morning. Not that I want to excuse myself. I wouldn't excuse myself for the wide, wide world, for what I said to Rollo at the last.

He'd plagued me about his luncheon,—for it was so snowy Keziah thought he'd better stay over till afternoon,—or I thought he plagued me. He nibbled at the pie, and took a squash cooky Keziah made for me. And when I told him how much trouble he was, he said:

"Hee-he-hee-e-e-ee!"

He had a funny way of laughing out, like a waterfall or a little bell, or a little shower. When I felt pleasant, I liked to hear him laugh. When I didn't, it didn't make me any pleasanter.

"It's nothing to laugh at," said I.

"Hee-hee-he-ee-ee!" said Trollo.

I didn't say anything to that, but hurried him along a little to the door. I didn't push him *exactly*.

"Come, Herod!" said Trollo; "le' me alone, and say good-by!"

"My name is *not* Herod!" said I, with an awful air.

"Oh, well," said Trollo, "don't let's be so cross. I wished you were coming, too. Just see it snow!"

He stood a minute on the steps, turning his face towards the road—the pretty, mischievous little round, red face! It looked graver, somehow, that minute, as he stood looking at the storm. And he spoke back in his gentlest, prettiest little way, as he went down the steps and waded into the snow that had already begun to drift in shallow, grayish piles against the fence.

"Good-by, Herod!" said Trollo.

But still I felt a little cross; and he called me Herod. And I didn't want to give in to him that way, I suppose. However it came about, I called after him down the walk:

"There, go! And I don't care if I never see you again!"

Trollo did not answer. The wind blew in between us. He trudged off stoutly into the storm, his little red tippet flying in the wind across his shoulder. The snow whirled up, and in a minute or less I lost sight of the little tippet, and came in and shut the door.

I shut the door, but I did not shut away the words I had spoken to Trollo. As I told you, they seemed to me to come back and knock on the window to be let in again. If I could, I would have unsaid them, I think, even then. I wished I had said something a little different, somehow.

I passed rather a lonesome morning. The storm grew worse. Keziah Phipps warmed over the hash and a piece of squash pie for me, and went home early. She said maybe she shouldn't come over again. "The old man was riley about it to-day, anyhow—his potatoes burned yesterday—and then it did set in and snow at such a rate!" But she'd come if she could, for she'd promised my ma, and I could heat up the coffee myself, for she'd cut the bread and butter.

So I said, "Very well," and I didn't urge her to come, for I was thinking about the corn-balls. I hoped Trollo would get home in good season, and we'd have some fun. I opened Keziah's old umbrella for her, and kicked her a little path to the gate, and then came back and stood in the door till she had got out of sight, and then I came into the house alone.

It did seem lonesome, do the best I would. My footsteps echoed up and down the stairs. The doors slammed after me and made me start. The fire winked at me, as if it were going to sleep. I built it up, and put things in order a little, picking up some slippers and an old mitten of Trollo's, that he had left kicking around. I wished that Trollo would come. It gave me an unhappy feeling to see the little slippers, as if I had been homesick.

I went to the barn for company before long, and fed the pigs and shook down hay for Hautboy—that was the horse—for the night, although it was early, and locked everything up, and came back again, wondering what I should do next. I wished that Trollo would come.

I had been in the barn some time, and when I crossed the little side-yard to come from the barn to the house, I was surprised to see how the storm had gained. It was blowing, by that time, a furious gale; the wind came up in long waves like an incoming tide. It took my breath as I stood in the barn door. The air was gray and dense with snow and sleet. There was a deep drift in the yard at the corner where I crossed. I waded through to get to the house. It came almost to my waist. I could hardly get the door together. I wished that Trollo were at home.

I wished so again when I had got into the house by the fire. It looked so deadly cold out of doors, I wondered how anyone could see his way to walk in that great whirl of snow and wind. And such a little fellow—only eight years old!

I looked at the clock. It was almost four. Just about that time he would be starting to come home. The school-house was a mile and a quarter away, beyond the church and beyond the town. Trollo had rather a lonely road to come, and a very windy one, as I said. There were two ways, where the road branched off. He might take one or he might take another; but both were bad enough.

I began to think that I should feel better to go and meet him. But I remembered that he would have started long before I could get there, and that I could not tell which way he would come. If he came alone, he would come by the church. When he came with Jenny Fairweather, he came the other way. Jenny Fairweather and Trollo were rivals in the spelling class, but the best of friends outside of it.

So I gave up the idea of going to meet him, for if I missed him, and he came home cold and found me gone, I should be sorry, I thought. I ran up into the attic once, to see if I could see anything of him. It had begun to grow a little dark. I thought I could see as far as the church clock, for I often got the time by the attic window. But I could not even see the church. I could not see the road. I could see nothing but wind and snow. It seemed to me as if I could *see* the wind. From the

attic window, the whole world seemed to have become a whirlpool of wind and snow. Oh, for a sight of the little red tippet! a glimpse of the round, red, mischievous little face!

It seemed to me still as if those ugly words were blowing about in the storm, and had come up to the attic window, and were knocking and knocking to be let in.

"I don't care if I never see you again!"

"I—don't—care if I—never—see you—again!" I actually tried to open the window and let them in,—I felt so uncomfortable in the attic. But the window was frozen and stuck.

I went downstairs and tried to amuse myself by putting the molasses candy on to boil. Keziah Phipps had not appeared, and I thought it as good as settled that the old man's back would be up to-night. She would not come. We would have the candy. Trollo would be so pleased! He would come in wet and cold. I would have a good, hot fire. I would get him some dry stockings. Perhaps we would roast some apples in the ashes. Trollo always liked to roast apples. We should have a nice time that night. He should see that I *was* glad to see him again, after all! He should know that I *didn't* think him the most disagreeable boy I ever knew. I shouldn't say much about it, for it was not our way. But he should know.

So I put the molasses on, and then I went to the window to look for Trollo. Then I got out the bread and butter and coffee, that they might be ready for his supper; and I went down into the cellar and picked out the biggest Baldwin I could find, to roast for him. Then I went to the window again. I was very restless. I could not keep away from the window. The storm was beating against the house in an awful way.

Half-past four. Trollo had not come. Five. No Trollo. Quarter past five. Where *was* Trollo?

It came upon me very suddenly that it was dark, and that Trollo ought to have been at home half an hour ago,—three-quarters, perhaps. It came *into* me, like the thrust of a sharp knife, that something had happened to keep the child away. Had he gone home with Jenny Fairweather? Had he not started at all? Had he got angry with me because of what I said, and gone on to Keziah's to frighten me? Or had he started, and *not* got anywhere? Where *could* he be?

I was too restless, wretched and anxious by that time to sit any longer, asking myself questions to which I got no answer. I determined to harness up the horse, and start out to find my brother.

It took me some time to do this, for Hautboy was of the opinion that the barn was the warmest place for a horse of any sense that night. He would not take the bits, and made me trouble. I had to hunt up a barrel and stand on it to reach his head—for I was not tall for my age. It was quite dark by the time I got harnessed and drove out into the yard.

I drove as fast as I could, but that was scarcely over a walk. The long, dim, bleak road stretched, a solid drift, before me. Hautboy broke it angrily, tossing the snow back into my face, and blinding me again and again. I took the road to Jenny Fairweather's, as nearly as I could make out where the road might be. I thought I would inquire there first.

"Surely Trollo must be there!" I said to myself, as I drove along. "Trollo will be there!"

I looked out into the drifts as I rode along. An awful fear had crept into my heart. I would not own it to myself. I said, "He will be at Jenny Fairweather's." But I looked at all the drifts. Sometimes I poked them with the butt end of my whip. Sometimes I called out. I did not call Trollo,—for, of course, Trollo *must* be at Jenny Fairweather's. But I thought I would shout a little,—it did no harm.

I knew the Fairweathers' by the light in the sitting-room behind the red curtains. I drove up close to the back door, and went in without knocking. I carried the reins in with me, so that Hautboy should not overturn the sleigh in the drifts, from being restless. I knocked with my whip on the sitting-room door.

Mrs. Fairweather came to the door. She held a light, and had her hand up before her eyes to shield them. I could see into the sitting-room. Jenny Fairweather sat there alone, studying her atlas at the table. My heart gave a sickening bound; but I spoke up—or I tried to—manfully:

"Is Trollo here, Mrs. Fairweather?"

"Trollo? No! Where is he?"

"That's what I don't know. He hasn't come home from school at all. I thought he must have come with Jenny. I thought you had kept him on account of the storm."

"Why, he started when I did!" said Jenny. She, too, came to the door and looked at me. "He started, but he went the other way. I came with Tommy Larkins. Trollo didn't come with us at all. He went the other way, alone."

"Where can he be?" exclaimed Mrs. Fairweather.

I did not answer. I could not speak. Mrs. Fairweather and Jenny followed me to the door. They said things that I did not hear. I only remember telling Mrs. Fairweather that he must have gone to some of the neighbors, and that I should drive up the other way; and I remember her saying that I must have help,—the child must be found! And that she wished she and Jenny were men, to go with me.

I got into the sleigh, and started out again into the storm.

I was now very cold; but I did not think much about it. I whipped and whipped poor Hautboy, and we blundered along,—freezing, frightened, stumbling,— into the other road. I could just see the church. I thought if I could get as far as the church, I would go to the first house I came to and get help. I shouted as I went along, and called out Trollo's name. But I could scarcely hear my own voice. I could not see. I could not breathe. My hands were stiff. I dropped the reins two or three times. The wind blew savagely up the other road. It blew in our faces. Hautboy did not like it. He puffed and backed and bothered me.

The first thing I knew, the horse stood still. I whipped him, but it did no good. I shouted, but he would not stir. I got out to see what was the matter. We had stuck in a mighty drift, which came to the creature's haunches.

So fast and so frightfully our old-fashioned Connecticut storms come down!

I turned around as well as I could, and Hautboy put for home. I sat still, in a stupid way, in the sleigh. I let the reins hang, for I could not hold them. I felt very numb and sleepy. I wondered if I were freezing to death. I thought how I should look, when Trollo found me in the morning; how Hautboy would get as far as the barn-door, and stick, with the sleigh; how I should be sitting up there, straight under the buffalo, half in, half out the door.

Then I thought that, perhaps, Trollo would never find me at all. Stupidly, I seemed to think that Trollo was frozen too. In a dreamy, meaningless way, I remembered telling Trollo that I hoped I should never see him again; and I won-

dered if, when *he* was freezing, *he* remembered it too.

All at once I felt myself aroused. Something had happened. Hautboy stood stock still beside a fence. He whinnied, and turned his neck to look at me.

"What is it, Hautboy?" said I, sleepily. I managed to get out. Had we got home? Had we gone on to Keziah's? What had happened?

We had got home—or nearly. We were just outside the gate, in an enormous drift. I could see the light in the kitchen and the cat sitting in the uncurtained window.

That brought me to my senses. Perhaps Trollo had got home. I called out as loud as I could: "Trollo! Trollo! Oh, *Trol*-lo!" Did something answer me? Did Hautboy whinny? Was it the cat mewing in the window? Or was it—? Oh, what was that?

Whoa, Hautboy! Whoa! Whoa, sir! Whoa! You'll tread on it! You'll crush him! Back, sir! Back!

Is it under your feet—across the drift! I have my hand beneath it! I can lift it up—the still, cold thing! The awful precious thing!

I have it in my arms. Oh, Hautboy, I'm so weak! Don't tread on me! We shall drop back beneath the drift! Back, sir! back! Good pony. Good old fellow. There!

Oh, Trollo, here we are! Here's the door-latch! We are getting up the steps. It's warm inside; and I set the candy on, and I went to meet you, Trollo. Oh, Trollo, can you hear?

Can he hear? Can he ever hear again? Does he know that I hold him; that I love him; that my heart is breaking, while we crouch by the stove that he may feel the red-hot glow? Does he stir? Do his eyelids move? Has Heaven taken me at my word?—that dreadful word! Shall I never see him move again?

Oh, what shall I do? What shall I do? All alone in the house this awful night with this awful little burden in my lap! If any grown-up soul were here, they would know how to save the child!

I do the best I can. I rub him and rub him with my numb, cold hands; I get hot water—for the fire has kept like a furnace, thank God! I fetch water and mother's blankets, and I get him upon the old lounge, and I rub and rub and wrap him and breathe on him. Now and then I speak to him, but I get no answer. Once or twice I think I will say my prayers, but I only say, "Our Father," for I can think of nothing else.

There! While I am rubbing and sobbing, curled on my knees in a little helpless heap beside the lounge,—oh, there! he *did* draw a little, little breath. He chokes and stirs; his eyelids flutter.

I remember then that there is brandy on the lower cupboard shelf. I spring to get it, calling, "Trollo! Trollo!" lest he drop away and lie still again before I can get back. I get it, somehow, down his throat. I keep on calling, "Trollo! Trollo! Trollo!" How long before it happens I cannot say; how it happens I do not know; but while I am kneeling and sobbing, calling and spilling brandy wildly down his neck, and doing everything wrong, and nothing right, except to love him and to hate myself, as if my heart would break with love and hate, a little feeble, pleasant voice speaks up:

"Her-od?"

"Oh, Trollo, I *did* want to see you all the afternoon! I did! I did!"

"Yes, Herod; I *hoped* you'd come to meet me, Herod."

"Oh, Trollo, just look here! You *know* you're not the most disagreeable boy I ever——"

"Oh, yes, I know. It isn't any matter, Herod. I'm warm as toast, I guess, only

a little queer, somehow. But the pains ain't *very* bad. Did Keziah's old man get his back up? Did you put the candy on?"

Our poor candy has bubbled and boiled away to a burn on the stove. But little want have we of candy this long, strange night. Trollo is very weak and suffers much. I cannot leave him to get help. I do the best I can. Towards morning he feels better, and I crawl out to look at Hautboy, who has broken his harness and got safely under cover. In the gray, cold dawn in the breaking storm I crawl into mother's bed beside my brother, and we drop asleep heavily, holding hands.

We sleep long and late,—I don't know how late it is. I am wakened by Keziah Phipps; she has fires going and hot coffee, and she throws up her hands and says: "Laws mercy on me! What is the matter? What has ever happened to you?"

And when she knew what it was that happened, she says we are to lie in bed till our ma comes home, and she makes beef-soup for Trollo, and cries into it, so that he makes faces when he drinks it.

Trollo is very weak, but pretty well. So when the broth is gone, we both lie still. By-and-by Jenny Fairweather comes over to see if Trollo has been found, but we feel too weak to see her. Then, by-and-by, we hear the whistle of the early train, —well-belated this morning,—by which father and mother will be hurrying home to see how we have stood the storm.

We do not talk much. We lie very still, holding each other's hands in bed.

Only once, I say, "Trollo?" and Trollo says, "Well, Herod?" and I say, "If I live to be an old, old man I shall never forget this night. Shall you?"

Trollo says, no, he doesn't think he ever shall. Then I say again, "Trollo?" But when he says, "What, Herod?" I only hold his hand a little closer, for I cannot speak.

AN ALPHABET FROM ENGLAND

by Christina G. Rossetti

A is the Alphabet, A at its head;
A is an Antelope, agile to run.

B is the Baker Boy bringing the bread,
Or black Bear and brown Bear, both
    begging for bun.

C is a Cornflower, come with the corn;
C is a Cat with a comical look.

D is a dinner which Dahlias adorn;
D is a Duchess who dines with a Duke.

The comical cat

E is an elegant, eloquent Earl;
E is an Egg whence an Eaglet emerges.

F is a Falcon, with feathers to furl;
F is a Fountain of full foaming surges.

The eloquent earl

G is the Gander, the Gosling, the Goose;
G is a Garnet in girdle of gold.

The gander, the gosling, the goose

H is a Heartsease, harmonious of hues;
H is a huge Hammer, heavy to hold.

I is an Idler who idles on ice;
I am I—who will say I am not **I**?

A hammer heavy to hold

J is a Jacinth, a jewel of price;
J is a Jay full of joy in July.

K is a King, or a Kaiser still higher;
K is a Kitten, or quaint Kangaroo.

L is a Lute or a lovely-toned Lyre;
L is a Lily all laden with dew.

A jay full of joy in July

M is a Meadow where Meadow-sweet
    blows;
M is a Mountain made dim by a mist.

N is a nut—in a nutshell it grows;
Or a Nest full of Nightingales singing—
    oh, list!

O is an Opal, with only one spark;
O is an Olive, with oil on its skin.

A pony, a pet in a park

P is a Pony, a pet in a park;
P is the Point of a Pen or a Pin.

Q is a Quail, quick chirping at morn;
Q is a Quince quite ripe and near drop-
    ping.

A red-breasted robin

R is a Rose, rosy red on a thorn;
R is a red-breasted Robin come hopping.

The umbrella

S is a Snowstorm that sweeps o'er the Sea;
S is the Song that the swift Swallows sing.

T is the Tea-table set out for tea;
T is a Tiger with terrible spring.

U, the Umbrella, went up in a shower;
Or Unit is useful with ten to unite.

Policeman X exercised

V is a Violet veined in the flower;
V is a Viper of venomous bite.

W stands for the water-bred Whale;
Stands for the wonderful Wax-work so
    gay.

X, or X X, or X X X is ale,
Or Policeman X, exercised day after day.

Y is a yellow Yacht, yellow its boat;
Y is the Yucca, the Yam, or the Yew.

Z is a Zebra, zigzagged his coat,
Or Zebu, or Zoöphyte, seen at the Zoo.

"Seen at the Zoo"

PARLOR MAGIC

by Leo H. Grindon

EXPERIMENTS REQUIRING CHEMICAL SOLUTIONS

To prepare these solutions, purchase of a druggist a small quantity of the solid crystals of the substance needed for the experiment you wish to try. Dissolve the crystals in clear pure water, and keep the solution in a little bottle, labeled with the name. It is seldom that the solutions need be strong. When the crystal is a colored one, enough should be used to give the water a light tint, blue, yellow, or what it may be. None of these solutions will do any harm to the hands, unless there is a cut or a wound of any kind upon the skin. It is well also, not to let a drop of any of them fall upon the clothes, or upon furniture, for some of them will stain. And none of them should ever be tasted, or touched by the lips or tongue, many of them being acrid and even poisonous.

With the acids still greater care is needed, the stronger acids being corrosive and poisonous. The greater portion of these substances must likewise not be smelled, as the fumes or vapors would affect the nostrils painfully.

For the proper performance of these experiments with solutions, etc.,—at all events for the neatest and most elegant performance of them,—there should be obtained from the chemist's shop about a dozen test-tubes. These are little glass vessels, manufactured on purpose, and very cheap. Do not take glasses that may afterward be used for drinking or household purposes. Be careful to have every one of your experiment glasses perfectly clean.

To Produce a Beautiful Violet-Purple Color

Take a nearly colorless solution of any salt of copper. The sulphate is the cheapest and handiest. Fill the test-tube or other experimenting-glass about two-thirds full. Then drop in, slowly, a little liquid ammonia. It will cause a beautiful blue to appear, and presently a most lovely violet-purple, which, by stirring with a glass rod, extends all through the fluid.

If now you drop into this a very little nitric acid, the fluid will again become as clear as pure water.

To Make a Splendid Scarlet

Again take some solution of sulphate of copper. Add to it a little solution of bichromate of potash. Then add a little solution of nitrate of silver, and there is produced a splendid scarlet color.

To Make a Deep Blue

Now, take a nearly colorless solution of sulphate of iron, and drop into it, slowly, a small quantity of solution of yellow prussiate of potash. This will induce a beautiful deep blue, quite different from the blues that are produced from copper salts.

To Make a Yellow Color

Take a solution of acetate of lead, and add a few drops of solution of iodide of potassium, and a most lovely canary-yellow color is produced.

Invisible Inks

Nearly all those experiments which result in the production of color may be performed in another way, and be then applied to the purposes of secret writing. Thus:

Write with dilute solution of sulphate of copper. The writing will be quite invisible, but become blue when held over the vapor of liquid ammonia.

Write with the same solution, and wash the paper with solution of yellow prussiate of potash, and the writing, previously invisible, will become brown. If you choose you may reverse this method, writing with solution of the prussiate of potash, and washing the paper with solution of the copper salt.

Write with solution of sulphate of iron, and the writing will again be invisible. Wash it over with tincture of galls, and it becomes black.

Write with sulphate of iron, and use a wash of yellow prussiate of potash, and the writing will come out blue. This experiment may likewise be reversed, and with similar result.

How to Copper a Knife-Blade

Make a rather strong solution of sulphate of copper. Let a clean and polished piece of steel or iron, such as the blade of a knife, stand in it for a few minutes, and the iron will become covered or encrusted with a deposit of pure copper.

To Make Beautiful Crystals

Dissolve, in different vessels, half an ounce each of the sulphates of iron, zinc, copper, soda, alumina, magnesia, and potash. The solutions can be made more rapidly by using warm water. When the salts are all completely dissolved, pour the whole seven solutions into a large dish, stir the mixture with a glass rod, then place it in a warm place, where it will not be disturbed. By degrees, the water will evaporate, and then the salts will recrystallize, each kind preserving its own proper form and color. Some occur in groups, some as single crystals. If carefully protected from dust, these form extremely pretty ornaments for the parlor.

Alum Baskets

These may be prepared by dissolving alum in water in such quantity that at last the water can take up no more, and the undissolved alum lies at the bottom of the vessel. The solution thus obtained is called a saturated one. Then procure a common ornamental wire basket, and suspend it in the solution, so as to be well covered in every part. There should be twice as much solution as will cover the basket. The wires of the basket should be wound with worsted, so that the surface may be rough. Leave it undisturbed in the solution, and gradually the crystals will form all over the surface. Before putting in the basket, it is best to further strengthen the solution by boiling it down to one half, after which it should be strained.

The Lead-Tree

Dissolve half an ounce of acetate of lead in six ounces of water. The solution will be turbid, so clarify it with a few drops of acetic acid. Now put the solution into a clean phial, nearly filling the phial. Suspend in the solution, by means of a thread attached to the cork, a piece of clean zinc wire. By degrees the wire will become covered with beautiful metallic spangles, like the foliage of a tree.

UN ALPHABET FRANÇAIS

par Laura Caxton

A—ANNETTE A UN TRÈS JOLI PETIT AGNEAU.

B—BAPTISTE A UNE PAIRE DE GRANDES BOTTES.

C—CÉCILE EST CHARMÉE DE FAIRE ROULER SON CERCEAU.

D—DENIS PLEURE PARCEQU'IL A MAL AUX DENTS.

E—ÉDOUARD VA GAIEMENT À L'ÉCOLE,
AVEC SES LIVRES.

F—FANCHON FAIT UNE CRAVATE POUR
SON FRÈRE.

G—GABRIELLE A ÉTÉ GRONDÉE PAR
SON GRAND-PÈRE.

H—HENRI VA PATINER SUR LA GLACE
PENDANT L'HIVER.

I—ISABELLE EST UNE PAUVRE PETITE
INVALIDE

J—JACQUES S'AMUSE TOUTE LA JOURNÉE
AVEC SES JOUJOUX.

K—K EST LA LETTRE QUE JEAN TIENT
SOUS LA MAIN.

L—LOUISE DONNE DES LÉGUMES À SES
PETITS LAPINS.

M—MARIE A DES MARGUERITES POUR
SA CHÈRE MAMAN.

N—NARCISSE A TROUVÉ DES OISEAUX
DANS UN NID.

O—OLIVIER, AVEC SON PARAPLUIE, N'A
PAS PEUR DE L'ORAGE.

P—PAULINE A BEAUCOUP DE PLAISIR
AVEC SA PETITE POUPÉE.

Q —QUENTIN AIME À JOUER AUX
QUILLES DE BOIS.

R —ROLAND REMPLIT UN POT POUR Y
PLANTER SON ROSIER.

S —SUSETTE A UN MORCEAU DE SUCRE
POUR SON SERIN.

T —THÉRÈSE EST TRISTE PARCEQUE SON
TABLIER EST SALE.

U—URBAIN A LE DRAPEAU DES ÉTATS-
UNIS.

V—VIRGINIE ARROSE SES VIOLETTES
CHAQUE MATIN ET CHAQUE SOIR.

W—WINIFRED EST AMÉRICAINE, ELLE
N'EST PAS UNE PETITE FRANÇAISE.

X—XÉNOPHON EST LE GÉNÉRAL RENOMMÉ
À QUI PAUL CROIT RESSEMBLER.

Y—Y A-T-IL UNE AUTRE PETITE FILLE
DE SI JOLIS YEUX?

Z—ZÉNOBIE SAIT COMPTER D'UN JUSQU'À
ZÉRO.

THE CREATURE WITH NO CLAWS

by Joel Chandler Harris

"W'EN you git a leetle bit older dan w'at you is, honey," said Uncle Remus to the little boy, "you'll know lots mo' dan you does now."

The old man had a pile of white oak splits by his side and these he was weaving into a chair-bottom. He was an expert in the art of "bottoming chairs," and he earned many a silver quarter in this way. The little boy seemed to be much interested in the process.

"Hit's des like I tell you," the old man went on; "I done had de speunce un it. I done got so now dat I don't b'lieve w'at I see, much less w'at I year. It got ter be whar I kin put my han' on it en fumble wid it. Folks kin fool deyse'f lots wuss dan yuther folks kin fool um, en ef you don't b'lieve w'at I'm a-tellin' un you, you kin des ax Brer Wolf de nex' time you meet 'im in de big road."

"What about Brother Wolf, Uncle Remus?" the little boy asked, as the old man paused to refill his pipe.

"Well, honey, 't ain't no great long riga-marole; hit's des one er deze yer tales w'at goes in a gallop twel it gits ter de jumpin'-off place.

"One time Brer Wolf wuz gwine 'long de big road feelin' mighty proud en high-strung. He wuz a mighty high-up man in dem days, Brer Wolf wuz, en 'mos' all de yuther creeturs wuz feard un 'im. Well, he wuz gwine 'long lickin' his chops en walkin' sorter stiff-kneed, w'en he happen ter look down 'pon de groun' en dar he seed a track in de san'. Brer Wolf stop, he did, en look at it, en den he 'low:

"'Heyo! w'at kind er creetur dish yer? Brer Dog ain't make dat track, en needer is Brer Fox. Hit's one er deze yer kind er creeturs w'at ain't got no claws. I'll des 'bout foller 'im up, en ef I ketch 'im he'll sholy be my meat.'

"Dat de way Brer Wolf talk. He followed 'long atter de track, he did, en he look at it close, but he ain't see no print er no claw. Bimeby de track tuck 'n tu'n out de road en go up a dreen whar de rain done wash out. De track wuz plain dar in de wet san', but Brer Wolf ain't see no sign er no claws.

"He foller en foller, Brer Wolf did, en de track git fresher en fresher, but still he ain't see no print er no claw. Bimeby he come in sight er de creetur, en Brer Wolf stop, he did, en look at 'im. He stop stock-still en look. De creetur wuz mighty quare-lookin', en he wuz cuttin' up some mighty quare capers. He had big head, sharp nose, en bob tail; en he wuz walkin' roun' en roun' a big dog-wood tree, rub-bin' his sides ag'in it. Brer Wolf watch 'im a right smart while, he acts so quare, en den he 'low:

"'Shoo! dat creetur done bin in a fight en los' de bes' part er he tail; en w'at make he scratch hisse'f dat away? I lay I'll let 'im know who he foolin' 'long wid.'

"Atter 'while, Brer Wolf went up a leetle nigher de creetur, en holler out:

"'Heyo, dar! w'at you doin' scratchin'

yo' scaly hide on my tree, en tryin' fer ter break hit down?'

"De creetur ain't make no answer. He des walk 'roun' en 'roun' de tree scratchin' he sides en back. Brer Wolf holler out:

"'I lay I'll make you year me ef I hatter come dar whar you is!'

"De creetur des walk 'roun' en 'roun' de tree, en ain't make no answer. Den Brer Wolf hail 'im ag'in, en talk like he mighty mad:

I fus' holler atter you, but I ain't gwine ter let you off now. I'm a-gwine ter l'arn you a lesson dat 'll stick by you.'

"Den de creetur sorter wrinkle up he face en mouf, en Brer Wolf 'low:

"'Oh, you nee'n'ter swell up en cry, you 'ceitful vilyun. I'm a-gwine ter gi' you a frailin' dat I boun' you won't forget.'

"Brer Wolf make like he gwine ter hit de creetur, en den——"

Here Uncle Remus paused and looked

"Well, suh, dat creetur des fotch one swipe dis away, en 'n'er swipe dat away"

"'Ain't you gwine ter min' me, you imperdent scoundul? Ain't you gwine ter mozey outer my woods en let my tree 'lone?'

"Wid dat, Brer Wolf march todes de creetur des like he gwine ter squ'sh 'im in de groun'. De creetur rub hisse'f ag'in de tree en look like he feel mighty good. Brer Wolf keep on gwine todes 'im, en bimeby w'en he git sorter close de creetur tuck'n sot up on his behime legs des like you see squir'ls do. Den Brer Wolf, he 'low, he did:

"'Ah-yi! you beggin', is you? But 'tain't gwine ter do you no good. I mout er let you off ef you'd a-minded me w'en

all around the room and up at the rafters. When he began again his voice was very solemn.

—"Well, suh, dat creetur des fotch one swipe dis away, en 'n'er swipe dat away, en mos' 'fo' you can wink yo' eye-balls, Brer Wolf hide wuz mighty nigh teetotally tor'd off 'n 'im. Atter dat de creetur s'antered off in de woods, en 'gun ter rub hisse'f on 'n'er tree."

"What kind of a creature was it, Uncle Remus?" asked the little boy.

"Well, honey," replied the old man in a confidential whisper, "hit want nobody on de top-side er de yeth but old Brer Wildcat."

EDITHA'S BURGLAR

by Frances Hodgson Burnett

I WILL begin by saying that Editha was always rather a queer little girl, and not much like other children. She was not a strong, healthy little girl, and had never been able to run about and play; and, as she had no sisters or brothers, or companions of her own size, she was rather old-fashioned, as her aunts used to call it. She had always been very fond of books, and had learned to read when she was such a tiny child, that I should almost be afraid to say how tiny she was when she read her first volume through. Her papa wrote books himself, and was also the editor of a newspaper; and, as he had a large library, Editha perhaps read more than was quite good for her. She lived in London; and, as her mamma was very young and pretty, and went out a great deal, and her papa was so busy, and her governess only came in the morning, she was left to herself a good many hours in the day, and when she was left to herself, she spent the greater part of her time in the library reading her papa's big books, and even his newspapers.

She was very fond of the newspapers, because she found so many curious things in them,—stories, for instance, of strange events which happened every day in the great city of London, and yet never seemed to happen anywhere near where she lived. Through the newspapers, she found that there were actually men who lived by breaking into people's houses and stealing all the nice things they could carry away, and she read that such men were called burglars. When she first began to read about burglars, she was very much troubled. In the first place, she felt rather timid about going to bed at night, and, in the second place, she felt rather sorry for the burglars.

"I suppose no one ever taught them any better," she thought.

In fact, she thought so much about the matter, that she could not help asking her papa some questions one morning when he was at breakfast. He was reading his paper and eating his chops both at once when she spoke to him.

"Papa," she said, in a solemn little voice, and looking at him in a very solemn manner, "papa dear, what do you think of burglars—as a class?" (She said "as a class," because she had heard one of her papa's friends say it, and as he was a gentleman she admired very much, she liked to talk as he did.) Her papa gave a little jump in his chair, as if she had startled him, and then he pushed his hair off his forehead and stared at her.

"Burglars! As a class!" he said, and then he stared at her a minute again in rather a puzzled way. "Bless my soul!" he said. "As a class, Nixie!" (that was his queer pet name for her.) "Nixie, where is your mother?"

"She is in bed, papa dear, and we mustn't disturb her," said Editha. "The party last night tired her out. I peeped into her room softly as I came down. She looks so pretty, when she is asleep. What *do* you think of burglars, papa?"

"I think they're a bad lot, Nixie," said her papa, "a bad lot."

"Are there no good burglars, papa?"

"Well, Nixie," answered papa, "I should say not. As a rule, you know,—" and here he began to smile, as people often smiled at Editha when she asked questions, —"as a rule, burglars are not distinguished for moral perspicuity and blameless character."

But Editha did not understand what moral perspicuity meant, and besides she was thinking again.

"Miss Lane was talking to me the other day, about some poor children who had never been taught anything; they had never had any French or music lessons, and scarcely knew how to read, and she said they had never had any advantages. Perhaps that is the way with the burglars, papa,—perhaps they have never had any advantages,—perhaps if they had had advantages they might n't have been burglars."

"Lessons in French and music are very elevating to the mind, my dear Nixie," papa began in his laughing way, which was always a trial to Editha, but suddenly he stopped, and looked at her rather sadly.

"How old are you, Nixie?" he asked.

"I am seven," answered Editha, "seven years, going on eight."

Papa sighed.

"Come here, little one," he said, holding out his strong white hand to her.

She left her chair and went to him, and he put his arms around her, and kissed her, and stroked her long brown hair.

"Don't puzzle your little brain too much," he said, "never mind about the burglars, Nixie."

"Well," said Editha, "I can't help think-ing about them a little, and it seems to me that there must be, perhaps, one good burglar among all the bad ones, and I can't help being rather sorry, even for the bad ones. You see, they must have to be up all night, and out in the rain some-times, and they can't help not having had advantages."

It was strange that the first thing she heard, when she went up to her mamma's room, was something about burglars.

She was very, very fond of her mamma, and very proud of her. She even tried to take care of her in her small way; she never disturbed her when she was asleep, and she always helped her to dress, bring-ing her things to her, buttoning her little shoes and gloves, putting the perfume on her handkerchiefs, and holding her wraps until she wanted them.

This morning, when she went into the dressing-room, she found the chamber-maid there before her, and her dear little mamma looking very pale.

"Ah, mem! if you please, mem!" the chamber-maid was saying, "what a bless-ing it was they didn't come here!"

"Who, Janet?" Editha asked.

"The burglars, Miss, that broke into Number Eighteen last night, and carried off all the silver, and the missus's jewelry."

"If burglars ever do break in here," said mamma, "I hope none of us will hear them, though it would almost break my heart to have my things taken. If I should waken in the night, and find a burglar in my room, I think it would kill me, and I know I should scream, and then there is no knowing what they might do. If ever you think there is a burglar in the house, Nixie, whatever you do, don't scream or make any noise. It would be better to have one's things stolen, than to be killed by burglars for screaming."

She was not a very wise little mamma, and often said rather thoughtless things;

but she was very gentle and loving, and Editha was so fond of her that she put her arms round her waist and said to her:

"Mamma, dearest, I will never let any burglars hurt you or frighten you if I can help it. I do believe I could persuade them not to. I should think even a burglar would listen to reason."

That made her mamma laugh, so that she forgot all about the burglars and began to get her color again, and it was not long before she was quite gay, and was singing a song she had heard at the opera, while Editha was helping her to dress.

But that very night Editha met a burglar.

Just before dinner, her papa came up from the city in a great hurry. He dashed up to the front door in a cab, and, jumping out, ran upstairs to mamma, who was sitting in the drawing-room, while Editha read aloud to her.

"Kitty, my dear," he said, "I am obliged to go to Glasgow by the 'five' train. I must throw a few things into a pormanteau and go at once."

"Oh, Francis!" said mamma. "And just after that burglary at the Norris's! I don't like to be left alone."

"The servants are here," said papa, "and Nixie will take care of you; won't you, Nixie? Nixie is interested in burglars."

"I am sure Nixie could do more than the servants," said mamma. "All three of them sleep in one room at the top of the house when you are away, and even if they awakened they would only scream."

"Nixie wouldn't scream," said papa, laughing; "Nixie would do something heroic. I will leave you in her hands."

He was only joking, but Editha did not think of what he said as a joke; she felt that her mamma was really left in her care, and that it was a very serious matter.

She thought about it so seriously that she hardly talked at all at dinner, and was so quiet afterward that her mamma said, "Dear me, Nixie, what *are* you thinking of? You look as solemn as a little owl."

"I am thinking of you, mamma," the child answered.

And then her mamma laughed and kissed her, and said: "Well, I must say I don't see why you should look so grave about me. I didn't think I was such a solemn subject."

At last bedtime came, and the little girl went to her mother's room, because she was to sleep there.

"I am glad I have you with me, Nixie," said mamma, with a rather nervous little laugh. "I am sure I shouldn't like to sleep in this big room alone."

But, after she was in bed, she soon fell asleep, and lay looking so happy and sweet and comfortable that Editha thought it was lovely to see her.

Editha did not go to sleep for a long time. She thought of her papa trying to sleep on the train, rushing through the dark night on its way to Scotland; she thought of a new book she had just begun to read; she thought of a child she had once heard singing in the street; and when her eyes closed at length, her mind had just gone back to the burglars at Number Eighteen. She slept until midnight, and then something wakened her. At first she did not know what it was, but in a few minutes she found that it was a queer little sound coming from down-stairs,—a sound like a stealthy filing of iron.

She understood in a moment then, because she had heard the chamber-maid say that the burglars broke into Number Eighteen by filing through the bars of the shutters.

"It is a burglar," she thought, "and he will awaken mamma."

If she had been older, and had known more of the habits of burglars, she might have been more frightened than she was. She did not think of herself at all, however, but of her mother.

She began to reason the matter over as quickly as possible, and she made up her mind that the burglar must not be allowed to make a noise.

"I'll go down and ask him to please be as quiet as he can," she said to herself, "and I'll tell him why."

Certainly, this was a queer thing to think of doing, but I told you when I began my story that she was a queer little girl.

She slipped out of bed so quietly that she scarcely stirred the clothes, and then slipped just as quietly out of the room and down the stairs.

The filing had ceased, but she heard a sound of stealthy feet in the kitchen; and, though it must be confessed her heart beat rather faster than usual, she made her way to the kitchen and opened the door.

Imagine the astonishment of that burglar when, on hearing the door open, he turned round and found himself looking at a slender little girl, in a white frilled night-gown, and with bare feet,—a little girl whose large brown eyes rested on him in a by no means unfriendly way.

"I'll be polite to him," Editha had said, as she was coming down-stairs. "I am sure he'll be more obliging if I am very polite. Miss Lane says politeness always wins its way."

So the first words she spoke were as polite as she could make them.

"Don't be frightened," she said, in a soft voice. "I don't want to hurt you; I came to ask a favor of you."

The burglar was so amazed that he actually forgot he was a burglar, and staggered back against the wall. I think he thought at first that Editha was a little ghost. "You see I couldn't hurt you if I wanted to," she went on, wishing to encourage him. "I'm too little. I'm only seven,—and a little over,—and I'm not going to scream, because that would waken mamma, and that's just what I don't want to do."

That did encourage the burglar, but still he was so astonished that he did not know what to do.

"Well, I'm blowed," he said in a whisper, "if this aint a rummy go!" which was extremely vulgar language; but, unfortunately, he was one of those burglars who, as Miss Lane said, "had not had any advantages," which is indeed the case with the majority of the burglars of my acquaintance.

Then he began to laugh,—in a whisper also, if one can be said to laugh in a whisper. He put his hand over his mouth, and made no noise, but he laughed so hard that he doubled up and rocked himself to and fro.

"The rummiest go!" he said, in his uneducated way. "An' she haint agoin' to 'urt me. Oh, my heye!"

He was evidently very badly educated, indeed, for he not only used singular words, but sounded his h's all in the wrong places. Editha noticed this, even in the midst of her surprise at his laughter. She could not understand what he was laughing at. Then it occurred to her that she might have made a mistake.

"If you please," she said, with great delicacy, "are you really a burglar?"

He stopped laughing just long enough to answer her.

"Lor' no, miss," he said, "by no manner o' means. I'm a dear friend o' yer Par's, come to make a evenin' call, an' not a wishin' to trouble the servants, I stepped in through the winder."

"Ah!" said Editha, looking very gravely at him; "I see you are joking with me, as papa does sometimes. But what I wanted to say to you was this: Papa has gone to

Scotland, and all our servants are women, and mamma would be so frightened if you were to waken her, that I am sure it would make her ill. And if you are going to burgle, would you please burgle as quietly as you can, so that you wont disturb her?"

The burglar stopped laughing, and, staring at her, once more uttered his vulgar exclamation:

"Well, I'll be blowed!"

"Why don't you say, 'I'll be blown?'" asked Editha. "I'm sure it isn't correct to say you'll be blowed."

She thought he was going off into one of his unaccountable fits of laughter again, but he did not; he seemed to check himself with an effort.

"There haint no time to waste," she heard him mutter.

"No, I suppose there isn't," she answered. "Mamma might wake and miss me. What are you going to burgle first?"

"You'd better go upstairs to yer mar," he said, rather sulkily.

Editha thought deeply for a few seconds.

"You oughtn't to burgle anything," she said. "Of course you know that, but if you have really made up your mind to do it, I would like to show you the things you'd better take."

"What, fer instance?" said the burglar, with interest.

"You mustn't take any of mamma's things," said Editha, "because they are all in her room, and you would waken her, and besides, she said it would break her heart; and don't take any of the things papa is fond of. I'll tell you what," turning rather pale, "you can take my things."

"What kind o' things?" asked the burglar.

"My locket, and the little watch papa gave me, and the necklace and bracelets my grandmamma left me,—they are worth a great deal of money, and they are very pretty, and I was to wear them when I grew to be a young lady, but—but you can take them. And—then—" very slowly, and with a deep sigh, "there are—my books. I'm very fond of them, but——"

"I don't want no books," said the burglar.

"Don't you?" exclaimed she. "Ah, thank you."

"Well," said the burglar, as if to himself, and staring hard at her brightening face, "I never see no sich a start afore."

"Shall I go upstairs and get the other things?" said Editha.

"No," he said. "You stay where you are —or stay, come along o' me inter the pantry, an' sit down while I'm occypied."

He led the way into the pantry, and pushed her down on a step, and then began to open the drawers where the silver was kept.

"It's curious that you should know just where to look for things, and that your key should fit, isn't it?" said Editha.

"Yes," he answered, "it's werry sing'lar, indeed. There's a good deal in bein' eddicated."

"Are you educated?" asked Editha, with a look of surprise.

"Did yer think I wasn't?" said the burglar.

"Well," said Editha, not wishing to offend him, "you see, you pronounce your words so very strangely."

"It's all a matter o' taste," interrupted the burglar. "Oxford an' Cambridge 'as different vocabillaries."

"Did you go to Oxford?" asked Editha, politely.

"No," said he, "nor yet to Cambridge."

Then he laughed again, and seemed to be quite enjoying himself as he made some forks and spoons up into a bundle. "I 'ope there haint no plated stuff 'ere," he said. "Plate's wulgar, an' I 'ope yer parents haint wulgar, cos that 'd be settin' yer a werry bad example an' sp'ilin' yer morals."

"I am sure papa and mamma are not vulgar," said Editha.

The burglar opened another drawer, and chuckled again, and this suggested to Editha's mind another question.

"Is your business a good one?" she suddenly inquired of him.

"'Taint as good as it ought to be, by no manner o' means," said the burglar. "Every one haint as hobligin' as you, my little dear."

"Oh!" said Editha. "You know you obliged me by not making a noise."

"Well," said the burglar, "as a rule, we don't make a practice o' makin' no more noise than we can help. It haint considered 'ealthy in the perfession."

"Would you mind leaving us a few forks and spoons to eat with, if you please? I beg pardon for interrupting you, but I'm afraid we shall not have any to use at breakfast."

"Haint yer got no steel uns?" inquired the burglar.

"Mamma wouldn't like to use steel ones, I'm sure," Editha answered. "I'll tell you what you can do: please leave out enough for mamma, and I can use steel. I don't care about myself, much."

The man seemed to think a moment, and then he was really so accommodating as to do as she asked, and even went to the length of leaving out her own little fork and knife and spoon.

"Oh! you are very kind," said Editha, when she saw him do this.

"That's a reward o' merit, cos yer didn't squeal," said the burglar.

He was so busy for the next few minutes that he did not speak, though now and then he broke into a low laugh, as if he was thinking of something very funny indeed. During the silence, Editha sat holding her little feet in her nightgown, and watching him very curiously. A great many new thoughts came into her active brain, and at last she could not help asking some more questions.

"Would you really rather be a burglar than anything else?" she inquired, respectfully.

"Well," said the man, "p'r'aps I'd prefer to be Lord Mayor, or a member o' the 'Ouse o' Lords, or heven the Prince o' Wales, honly for there bein' hobstacles in the way of it."

"Oh!" said Editha; "you couldn't be the Prince of Wales, you know. I meant wouldn't you rather be in some other profession? My papa is an editor," she added. "How would you like to be an editor?"

"Well," said the burglar, "hif yer par ud change with me, or hif he chanced to know hany heditor with a roarin' trade as ud be so hobligin' as to 'and it hover, hit's wot I've allers 'ad a leanin' to."

"I am sure papa would not like to be a burglar," said Editha, thoughtfully; "but perhaps he might speak to his friends about you, if you would give me your name and address, and if I were to tell him how obliging you were, and if I told him you really didn't like being a burglar."

The burglar put his hand to his pocket and gave a start of great surprise.

"To think o' me a forgettin' my card-case," he said, "an' a leavin' it on the pianner when I come hout. I'm sich a bloomin' forgetful cove. I might hev knowed I'd hev wanted it."

"It is a pity," said Editha; "but if you told me your name and your number, I think I could remember it."

"I'm afeared yer couldn't," said the burglar, regretfully, "but I'll try yer. Lord Halgernon Hedward Halbert de Pentonwille, Yde Park. Can you think o' that?"

"Are you a lord?" exclaimed Editha. "Dear me, how strange!"

"It is sing'lar," said the burglar, shaking his head. "I've hoften thought so myself. But not wishin' to detain a lady no longer than can be 'elped, s'pose we take a turn in the lib'ery among yer respected par's things."

"Don't make a noise," said Editha, as she led the way.

But when they reached the library her loving little heart failed her. All the things her father valued most were there, and he would be sure to be so sorry if one thing was missing when he returned. She stood on the threshold a moment and looked about her.

"Oh," she whispered, "please do me another favor, wont you? Please let me slip quietly upstairs and bring down my own things instead. They will be so easy to carry away, and they are very valuable, and—and I will make you a present of them if you will not touch anything that belongs to papa. He is so fond of his things and, besides that, he is so good."

The burglar gave a rather strange and disturbed look at her.

"Go an' get yer gimcracks," he said in a somewhat grumbling voice.

Her treasures were in her own room, and her bare feet made no sound as she crept slowly up the staircase and then down again. But when she handed the little box to the burglar her eyes were wet.

"Pape gave me the watch, and mamma gave me the locket," she whispered, tremulously; "and the pearls were grandmamma's and grandmamma is in heaven."

It would not be easy to know what the burglar thought; he looked queerer than ever. Perhaps he was not quite so bad as some burglars, and felt rather ashamed of taking her treasures from a little girl who loved other people so much better than she loved herself. But he did not touch any of papa's belongings, and, indeed, did not remain much longer. He grumbled a little when he looked into the drawing-room, saying something to himself about "folks never 'avin' no consideration for a cove, an' leavin' nothin' portable 'andy, a-expectin' of him to carry off seventy-five pound bronze clocks an' marble stattoos;" but though Editha was sorry to see that he appeared annoyed, she did not understand him.

After that, he returned to the pantry and helped himself to some cold game pie, and seemed to enjoy it, and then poured out a tumbler of wine, which Editha thought a great deal to drink at once.

"Yer 'e'lth, my dear," he said, "an' 'appy returns, an' many on 'em. May yer grow up a hornyment to yer sect, an' a comfort to yer respected mar an' par."

And he threw his head very far back, and drank the very last drop in the glass, which was vulgar, to say the least of it.

Then he took up his bundles of silver and the other articles he had appropriated, and seeing that he was going away, Editha rose from the pantry step.

"Are you going out through the window?" she asked.

"Yes, my dear," he answered, with a chuckle, "it's a little 'abit I've got into. I prefers 'em to doors."

"Well, good-bye," she said, holding out her hand politely. "And thank you, my lord."

She felt it only respectful to say that, even if he had fallen into bad habits and become a burglar.

He shook hands with her in quite a friendly manner, and even made a bow.

"Yer welcome, my dear," he said. "An' I must hadd that if I ever see a queerer or better behaved little kid, may I be blowed —or, as yer told me it would be more correcter to say, I'll be blown."

Editha did not know he was joking; she thought he was improving, and that if he had had advantages he might have been a very nice man.

It was astonishing how neatly he slipped through the window; he was gone in a second, and Editha found herself standing alone in the dark, as he had taken his lantern with him.

She groped her way out and up the stairs, and then, for the first time, she began to feel cold and rather weak and strange; it was more like being frightened than any feeling she had had while the burglar was in the house.

"Perhaps, if he had been a very bad burglar, he might have killed me," she said to herself, trembling a little. "I am very glad he did not kill me, for—for it would have hurt mamma so, and papa too, when he came back, and they told him."

Her mamma wakened in the morning with a bright smile.

"Nobody hurt us, Nixie," she said. "We are all right, aren't we?"

"Yes, mamma dear," said Editha.

She did not want to startle her just then, so she said nothing more, and she even said nothing all through the excitement that followed the discovery of the robbery, and indeed, said nothing until her papa came home, and then he wondered so at her pale face, and petted her so tenderly, and thought it so strange that nothing but her treasures had been taken from upstairs, that she could keep her secret no longer.

"Papa," she cried out all at once in a trembling voice, "I gave them to him myself."

"You, Nixie! You!" exclaimed her papa, looking alarmed. "Kitty, the fright has made the poor little thing ill."

"No, papa," said Editha, her hands shaking, and the tears rushing into her eyes, she did not know why. "I heard him, and —I knew mamma would be so frightened,—and it came into my mind to ask

him—not to waken her,—and I crept down-stairs—and asked him;—and he was not at all unkind though he laughed. And I stayed with him, and—and told him I would give him all my things if he would not touch yours nor mamma's. He—he wasn't such a bad burglar, papa,—and he told me he would rather be something more respectable."

And she hid her face on her papa's shoulder.

"Kitty!" papa cried out. "Oh, Kitty!"

Then her mamma flew to her and knelt down by her, kissing her, and crying aloud:

"Oh, Nixie! if he had hurt you,—if he had hurt you."

"He knew I was not going to scream, mamma," said Editha. "And he knew I was too little to hurt him. I told him so."

She scarcely understood why mamma cried so much more at this, and why even papa's eyes were wet as he held her close up to his breast.

"It is my fault, Francis," wept the poor little mamma. "I have left her too much to herself, and I have not been a wise mother. Oh, to think of her risking her dear little life just to save me from being frightened, and to think of her giving up the things she loves for our sakes. I will be a better mother to her, after this, and take care of her more."

But I am happy to say that the watch and locket and pearls were not altogether lost, and came back to their gentle little owner in time. About six months after, the burglar was caught, as burglars are apt to be, and, after being tried and sentenced to transportation to the penal settlements (which means that he was to be sent away to be a prisoner in a far country), a police officer came one day to see Editha's papa, and he actually came from that burglar, who was in jail and wanted to see Editha for a special reason. Editha's papa took her to see him, and the moment she entered his cell she knew him.

"How do you do, my lord?" she said, in a gentle tone.

"Not as lively as common, miss," he answered, "in consekence o' the confinement not bein' good fer my 'e'lth."

"None of your chaff," said the police officer. "Say what you have to say."

And then, strange to say, the burglar brought forth from under his mattress a box, which he handed to the little girl.

"One o' my wisitors brought 'em in to me this mornin'," he said. "I thought yer might as well hev 'em. I kep' 'em partly 'cos it was more convenienter, an' partly 'cos I took a fancy to yer. I've seed a many curi's things, sir," he said to Editha's papa, "but never nothin' as bloomin' queer as that little kid a-comin' in an' tellin' me she wont 'urt me, nor yet wont scream, and please wont I burgle quietly so as to not disturb her mar. It brought my 'art in my mouth when first I see her, an' then, Lor', how I larft. I almost made up my mind to give her things back to her afore I left, but I didn't quite do that—it was agin human natur'."

But they were in the box now, and Editha was so glad to see them that she could scarcely speak for a few seconds. Then she thanked the burglar politely.

"I am much obliged to you," she said, "and I'm really very sorry you are to be sent so far away. I am sure papa would have tried to help you if he could, though he says he is afraid you would not do for an editor."

The burglar closed one eye and made a very singular grimace at the police officer, who turned away suddenly and did not look round until Editha had bidden her acquaintance good-bye.

And even this was not quite all. A few weeks later, a box was left for Editha by a very shabby, queer-looking man, who quickly disappeared as soon as he had given it to the servant at the door; and in this box was a very large old-fashioned silver watch, almost as big as a turnip, and inside the lid were scratched these words:

To the little Kid,
From 'er fr'end and wel wisher,
Lord halgernon hedward halbert
de pentonwill, ide park.

MAULED BY AN ELEPHANT

by J. Alden Loring

"BUTIABA, Uganda, Africa; Jan. 5, 1910. On the shore of Albert Nyanza." So begins one of the entries in my journal during the Roosevelt African Expedition, of which I had the good fortune to be a member.

We were due at Butiaba the day before, but were detained a day by waiting at the last camp to secure the tusks and feet of an ugly old rogue elephant that the Colonel had killed at the earnest solicitation of the natives.

The great brute was a sort of outcast among his fellows, and for some time had been wandering about terrorizing the people by visiting the "shambas" (gardens) at night and feeding on the crops. He had wrecked several grass huts and killed one native; and, as our coming was heralded through the country several months in advance, the childish people, who were apparently at the brute's mercy, anxiously awaited our arrival.

We were not in camp fifteen minutes before the chief of the district appeared and asked the Colonel to relieve his people of their tormentor. For several days, the cunning old native had stationed men to watch the rogue, and he said that the two men who accompanied him were guides that had just left the brute taking his midday siesta under a tree less than a mile from camp.

The Colonel heard the story in silence, and then said: "But, Cuninghame, tell him that I have secured all the elephants I want, and that we lack the men to carry the skin and skeleton even though we *did* want it."

"Yes, Colonel, that's true," said Cuninghame; "but this animal is really a pest to the country, and, if he is not killed, his depredations may compel the people to desert their village and move from the locality. Such an occurrence is not unusual. Besides, it is one of the customs of the country, a thing that these natives expect of a white man—that he should deliver them from a rogue elephant—and if you do not acquiesce, they will look upon it as a lack of courtesy, so to speak."

"Oh, well, if that's the case, certainly I will try my best."

So saying, he called to Kermit, and in a few minutes the two, accompanied by their gun-bearers, left with the guides, after being warned by the chief that the rogue was dangerous, and would probably charge as soon as it saw or scented them.

As they disappeared, I thought how typical of the Colonel this dialogue was, for, during the eleven months that we were in Africa, he rarely shot an animal that was not used for a specimen or for food,—the only exception being crocodiles, which every year kill hundreds of women and children as they wade out to fill their water-jars.

Seizing a bag of traps, I called to my boys and started out to collect some small mammals. I had set only a few traps when I heard a shot, then another, and finally several in rapid succession. The roar of the heavy 405 Winchester and the double report of the Colonel's Holland rifle were unmistakable. A few minutes later I heard the exultant shouts of the gun-bearers and the guides, and I knew that the rogue elephant was an animal of the past.

The hunters had come upon the brute in the tall grass, and, true to the chief's warning, it charged the instant that it saw them, and before a shot had been fired.

After seeing the brute, I did not wonder that the natives hesitated about attacking it, for it measured ten feet nine inches from the soles of its front feet to the top of the back, and its tusks weighed one hundred and ten pounds.

As we marched into Butiaba, we were met by Captain Hutchison, then head of the Uganda Marine, which was at the time a fleet of several miniature naphtha launches. He congratulated the Colonel on his recent feat, adding that escape from a charging elephant of any kind, and particularly a "rogue," deserved congratulations, as he could testify from a certain "close call" he once had in elephant-hunting.

"Now, Captain," spoke up the Colonel, "I feel sure that you have an interesting story to relate, so please give it to us at once."

"Well, it was a bit awkward, I must admit," began the captain, "and so upset me that I have never 'taken on' an elephant since.

"It happened just north of the Lado country. I had been out ivory hunting for some time without having much luck, when one of my boys brought in word that he had struck a herd in which, judging from the enormous track, there was

an immense tusker. He guided me to the spot, and, sure enough, there was a huge track that was well worth following.

"The trail was made several hours before, and evidently there were about twenty elephants in the bunch. They were traveling at a good rate, and we knew that they probably would not stop before feeding time, late in the afternoon.

"Elephants may look slow and clumsy in captivity, but when they are walking at an ordinary gait, a person must step along at almost a dog-trot in order to overhaul them. It was about ten o'clock when we took the 'spoor' (a sign of any kind), and we knew that it meant a hard twenty-mile journey at least, before we should overtake them. Frequently ivory hunters will follow a herd of elephants for days before catching up with their game. The trail was not hard to keep, for a herd of twenty elephants, following single file through the ten-foot elephant-grass, makes more than a well-worn path.

"As they marched along, they had amused themselves by snatching a bunch of grass and tossing it aside; then, as they had passed through a grove of thorn-trees, they had broken off limbs and dragged them a hundred yards or more before dropping them. Several times one had halted long enough to dig a hole in the ground three or four feet in diameter with his tusks, and then we saw where he had galloped on to overtake his comrades. Once they gave us an advantage by stopping for some time to wallow in a water-hole, and, as they emerged, they rubbed their bodies against the first trees they passed, leaving the mud plastered ten feet high on the bark. These and other signs, growing fresher and fresher all the time, told us that we were slowly overtaking our game.

"About five o'clock, we surmised that, if the elephants were still traveling, we must be within five miles of them; but, as it was feeding time, I thought it practical to send my best tracker ahead to reconnoiter, while we followed more slowly. In an hour he returned, and reported that he had overhauled the herd feeding in a grove of thorn-trees, of which they are particularly fond.

"By the time we had arrived, they had passed out of the grove and were again in the elephant-grass, which, owing to its height and density, made it impossible for us to see them. Even when we mounted an ant-hill, the growth was so tall that we got only an occasional glimpse of a back or of a few snakelike trunks waving about in the air. The wind was scarcely in our favor, so we circled them to a large tree, and I sent one of the boys up to see if he could locate the big tusker.

"Our prize was on the far side of the herd, and in such a position that, should we attempt to stalk him, there would be risk of some of the elephants catching the scent and giving the alarm. Nothing could be done, therefore, but to keep watch until he had worked around to a more favorable position.

"At last, the long-looked-for time arrived, for the tusker was on the outskirts of the herd, and the wind was favorable. We circled to his side, and stealthily drew near—my gun-bearer, tracker, and myself—while the other boys remained in the rear.

"The tall grass prevented us from even catching a glimpse of the beasts, but it was easy to locate them by the noise they made while feeding.

"We held to the elephant trails, as no one could penetrate that jungle of grass and travel silently. Next to silence we had to watch the wind, for, once the animals caught our scent, they would either dash away or charge.

"So far, our plans had worked out admirably; the elephants, unconscious of our presence, were still tearing up the grass directly in our front, while my boys and myself proceeded inch by inch and strained our eyes to catch sight of the brutes. These boys had been my companions on many an elephant-hunt, and I had the utmost confidence in them, knowing well that, if it were necessary, they would not hesitate to give up their lives to save mine.

"I don't care how many elephants a man may have encountered, while he is sneaking up on his game, a feeling of uneasiness steals over him until the critical moment arrives; then things happen so quickly and his brain works so rapidly, that all sense of fear is for the moment lost.

"With both hammers of my rifle raised, I cautiously sneaked nearer and nearer, my faithful boys following at my very heels. At last, we were within fifty feet of the elephant, and, as he moved toward me, I could see the top of the grass swaying violently from side to side. Suddenly, fate turned against us, for a shifting current of air must have warned the brute of danger. I saw a huge trunk rise above the grass, heard a shrill, deafening trumpet, and knew that the fight was on. The grass parted as though a snow-plow were being driven through it, and the next instant there loomed up, not twenty feet away, a monster head with wing-like ears protruding on either side like the sails on a dhow. Two shiny tusks of ivory, fully six feet long, were pointed at my chest, and the towering trunk between them gave the head a fiendish look not often found outside of Hades. The other elephants took up the trumpeting, and the uproar was appalling.

"My rifle was at my shoulder from the second the brute began his charge, and the instant that he hove in sight, I fired both barrels point-blank into his face. Without a second's hesitation, I reached back to my gun-bearer for the '450,' and brought it to position. Immense though the brute was, he looked three times his normal size as I cast my eyes along the barrels leveled at his head not five feet away. I pressed one trigger, then the other, but there was no report, and, with a sickening feeling of horror, I realized that my gun-bearer, in the excitement of the moment, had failed to raise the hammers.

"Before I could lower the rifle from my shoulder, the brute was upon me! With a scream of rage he twined his trunk about my body, and, lifting me high above his head, brandished me about in the air as though I were a feather. Every instant I expected to be hurled fifty feet or more through space, which I welcomed as the only possible likelihood of escape. But no, at that moment I struck the ground with a thud. Three times I was lifted high and brought crashing through the grass to earth. The last time the elephant uncoiled his trunk and left me lying there, stunned and dazed, and staring blankly into his wicked little eyes, now hot with rage.

"Then dropping to his knees before me, he knelt there hesitating, as though to give me time to deliberate before the end should come. But he did not keep me waiting long, for slowly the two great tusks began descending. With all my waning strength I threw my body snug up against his bending knees, and the tusks passed harmlessly over me, just grazing my back, and tore great holes in the earth beyond. Again the ponderous head was raised, and again his tusks bore down upon me and probed deeply into the earth behind me.

"Evidently the animal had been somewhat blinded by my shots, for, assuming that he had done his work, he started to rise, and as he did so, the sudden thought came over me that he would probably attempt to trample me to death, the usual method that an elephant employs to obliterate an enemy. So, as he slowly rose, in some unaccountable manner I managed to scramble between his fore feet, and grabbed him by the leg, then loosed my grip, and, working back, seized hold of his hind foot.

"Once more I felt the snakelike trunk being wound around me, next I was being waved about over the grass-top—then the ground seemed suddenly to rise and meet me, and I lost consciousness. How many times I was hammered on the ground I do not know.

"Three hours later, I came to myself and found my boys dashing water into my face. When I opened my eyes, I saw the gun-bearer holding a smoking rifle in his hands. He had just returned from the scene of my mauling, and brought in my rifles, one of which he had attempted to unload, and, in some manner, had accidentally discharged. The explosion had no doubt assisted to revive me.

"My men told me that my life was saved by the quick action of my tracker, who appeared on the scene with a spear at about the time that I lost consciousness, and, rushing in, plunged the spear into the elephant's side. Leaving me, the animal took after its new tormentor, and the agile native, twisting and doubling in the thick grass, managed finally to escape. The elephant had devastated the grass, bushes, and small trees in his search for the man, and, fortunately, had not returned to me.

"While it is undoubtedly true that the native's action had much to do with saving me, one reason why I was not dashed to death lies in the fact that an elephant's trunk is the tenderest part of his body, and being twined about me, it received the brunt of the blow each time that I struck the ground, and evidently the pain kept the animal from using the force needed to kill me.

"As a result of this mauling, I was laid up for six weeks before I was well enough to hobble about again.

"That elephant may be alive at this present moment, for all I know. My native attendants were too terror-stricken over the outcome of the hunt to give the brute any further attention after I was mauled, so no one followed him up to discover what damage my shots had done. But, judging from the amount of vigor that was left in his great hulk at the time he put me to sleep, he could not have been seriously wounded.

"Well, as I have said, Colonel," concluded Captain Hutchison, "that hunt used up my stock of courage, and I doubt if I shall ever 'take on' another elephant, unless in self-defense."

The Gossips

Painted by Arthur Rackham

Marjorie and Margaret

Painted by Arthur Rackham

Mother Goose

Painted by Arthur Rackham

A BARREL OF TACKS

by Foster Rhea Dulles

JOHN COLLINGS gripped his oar and pulled as he never had before in his life. He dared not look around—that was the first rule of the whaleboat—but from the excited and frantic pleas of the first mate, clinging grimly to his long steering oar as they shot through the crested waves which broke in a fine spray over the boat's crew, he knew that they must be getting close to the whale. But that was not his business. He had only to row; and with the sweat pouring down his face and his heart thumping noisily, he put every ounce of energy into it. No one would be able to say that he was not worth his weight when it came to chasing whales.

They had lowered from the whaleship *Angus Parker* so quickly that the lookout's long-drawn-out call of "There she blows!" was still reverberating in their ears when they pushed off and headed toward that distant spot where the whale's filmy jet had broken the surface. It was the first whale they had sighted in three weeks. Captain Hooker had become so gloomy that not even the mates dared approach him, and the crew were so sick of loafing about the decks that they grumbled all day and half the night. If they didn't get this whale there was bound to be trouble. Nerves had been stretched to the breaking point.

But if this was the way the *Angus Parker's* crew in general felt about things,

the lowering was even more important to John Collings. It was his first chance in the boats. Ten months before, he had shipped as a cabin boy. Throughout the long voyage about Cape Horn, throughout those endless weeks of cruising in the South Pacific, he was always afraid that Captain Hooker would never give him his opportunity. He was afraid that he would be helping the cook and the steward, running errands, until the *Angus Parker* at last tied up again at her berth in New Bedford. And that was not what he had come to sea for. He had come to hunt whales. But now here he was in the first mate's boat, actually going after a whale. John pulled with all the strength of his eighteen years.

"Give it to her, boys," the mate was shouting. "Oh, he's a beaut, a beaut. Just a hundred yards ahead of us now. Pull, you scoundrels, pull! What are you loafing for? Do you think this is some blamed regatta? We're after whales and we're going to get this one. Come on now, all together. Pull, pull. What are you holding back for? Do you think we're out here for fun? It's oil we're after and this thumping crittur is just oozy with it. We can get him if you'll only wake up. Pull, will you, pull, pull!"

The boat was now shooting through the water, each man almost breaking his back as he dragged on his heavy oar. The waves cascaded over the bow and drenched

227

them to the skin. The water shot by. Any minute now should see them close enough for the harpooner to let his iron fly. He was ready there in the bow, the long weapon in his hands, his knee braced against the gunwale. The line still lay loose along the thwarts and there was not a hitch in the neat coils in the after tub, but it was not hard to imagine it running out when the harpoon had been hurled. Any minute now and they might be fast, off for a "Nantucket sleigh ride" as the whale made its dash for freedom.

John was so excited he could hardly breathe. His hands seemed stuck to the oar, his heart had stopped. He thought he could hear the whale wallowing in the deep swells; he thought he could smell it. The spray which broke over him seemed hot and scalding. He was sure it was from the whale's spout. He'd have given anything for a quick glance over his shoulder to see what was happening. But he clung to his oar and pulled as if his life depended on it.

Suddenly the mate whispered a command to the harpooner to stand ready. The time had come. John leaned forward for a final long stroke, caught his oar on the top of a wave, and was tumbled off the thwart as he swung back. The whaleboat seemed to hesitate a fraction of a second and just at that moment the harpooner let go his iron. But he was thrown off his balance and the harpoon fell short. Before a second could be hurled, the whale had sounded. As the whaleboat rocked in the rolling swells, a cloud of bubbles rose to the surface as sole evidence that there had ever been a whale.

No one in the boat said a word except the mate, who was cursing steadily under his breath. John struggled up and grabbed the oar which had been knocked out of his hand.

"I . . ." but he could get no further. Never did a boy wear a more rueful expression, a more beaten, hang-dog look. He had had his chance. He had failed. He would have given anything in the world to be back home on his father's farm. He couldn't face the men in the boat.

For a little while the whaleboat remained at the spot where the whale had sounded, its weary and discouraged crew resting on their oars. They kept their thoughts to themselves but John could feel the unspoken bitterness of their resentment. If the whale should break water again not too far off, the chase might be renewed, but as minute after minute passed without a sign of it, this hope slowly faded. Finally far in the distance a faint spout was sighted by the harpooner, but he merely pointed at it with a listless gesture. It was much too far away to make any renewal of the hunt at all practical. As the whale disappeared in the distance the whaleboat's bow was swung around toward the waiting *Angus Parker* and the boat crew started on the long row back to the ship.

As they drew near Captain Hooker could be seen on the quarterdeck and from his angry expression it was clear he had some idea of what had happened.

"Well, what do you think you were doing?" he shouted as soon as the boat was within hailing distance. "Did you trip over yourselves or did you get scared? Of all the stupid, clumsy, dodgasted ways of going on a whale . . ."

"What do you expect when you give us a farmer who still thinks he's handling a hoe instead of an oar?" shot back the mate angrily. "Your smart young cabin boy is about as much use in a boat as a blind organ grinder furling sails in a Cape Horn blow."

As John clambered up the ropes and

stood on deck he steeled himself for a terrible dressing-down. But Captain Hooker took one look at him and turned abruptly.

"Go back to the galley," he ordered in a gloomy tone, "and tell the cook you're to do whatever he wants from now on. If I ever let you in a boat again, may the barnacles on the ship's bottom turn into pansies!"

For five weeks after this incident John was kept hopping about by the cook and by anyone else who could think of a disagreeable task which would keep him busy. He could hardly face a potato, he had peeled so many of them; the sight of food made him ill, he had spent so many hours in the stifling galley. Never was a boy's life more completely miserable. If more whales had been sighted and there had been a chance to lower and make a kill, it would not have been so bad. But not once in those five weeks did the glad cry of "There she blows!" ring out. Even though John knew he would not be allowed in the boat, he would have given anything for a little excitement to break the deadly monotony of working in the galley.

For the officers and men it was almost as bad. Every day they became more morose and quarrelsome. They blamed John not only for missing that one whale, but for all their bad luck. No one would speak to him. He felt himself to be a Jonah and hardly dared to go down in the forecastle.

Finally, with supplies running low, the *Angus Parker* was headed toward the Pelew Islands, where Captain Hooker thought he could get some fresh vegetables and fruit by bartering with the natives. The ship's stores were broken out to see what they had for trade. Among the miscellaneous assortment of cloth goods, trinkets, iron nails, and other such stuff, was a barrel of tacks.

"By the flukes of the great white whale," Captain Hooker exploded, "what do they expect me to do with tacks? Do they think we came out here to lay a carpet or to catch whales?" Suddenly he had an idea. "Here you, Collings," he called. "No shore leave for you while we're layin' off the Pelews and here's something you can do. Count these tacks so I can make a report to the owners showing how careful I am of the ship's supplies. And count 'em right."

A few days later they anchored in a little harbor on a palm-fringed island with a long sandy beach. In spite of himself John could not help getting excited. What fun it would be to go ashore! What fun to swim off that beach! The other members of the crew gathered at the rail and began to talk of what they were going to do. Forgetting the captain's orders, John started to join them. At that moment the mate spied him.

"What about those tacks?" he shouted.

With a start John remembered, and sadly went over to where the barrel had been put in the ship's waist with another empty barrel beside it. One by one he began taking the tacks out of the first barrel and putting them into the second. "So this is what a whaling voyage is," he thought bitterly. "So this is why I've sailed around Cape Horn and across the Pacific. To be made sport of by Captain Hooker! To count a barrel of tacks!"

When a number of canoes put out from the shore filled with natives—fierce-looking beings with wild, unkempt hair and roving eyes—it was all he could do to keep from rushing over to the ship's side to get a better look at them. They were the first South Sea Islanders he had ever seen and it made him more than ever bitter to be kept at such a stupid task when he might be trying to barter with these fascinating natives for the yams, coconuts, oranges, and pineapples they were bringing out to the *Angus Parker*.

Among the other members of the crew little attention was paid to the natives. It was often necessary to be pretty much on guard when such savages came aboard ship. One could not tell what they might do if their cupidity was aroused by sight of a vessel's stores. But these islanders seemed peaceful enough, for all the savagery of their appearance, and they had no weapons of any kind with them. Captain Hooker carelessly motioned to them to stay forward and leisurely prepared to look over their fruits and vegetables before trying to barter with them. The crew were ordered not to trade until he had arranged for what the ship needed.

Suddenly there was a startling yell from one of the natives and at that abrupt signal the savages rushed amidships with hair-raising shouts. There on the racks the whalemen kept the weapons of their trade: long harpoons with their heads sharpened to a razor-like edge, keen-pointed lances, cutting-in spades and heavy axes. Before the startled crew of the *Angus Parker* realized what was happening the savages had seized these weapons, and, brandishing them aloft with bloodcurdling yells, started to advance upon the quarterdeck.

Captain Hooker and the mates had instinctively retreated to their own deck at the savage chief's first signal. Some of the crew were with them but most of the foremast hands had by now either dived down the open hatchways or sprung into the rigging. The natives appeared to have won control of the deck by their unexpected rush for the ship's whaling weapons, and the fate of the men on the quarterdeck

and eventually of every man on the ship hung in precarious balance.

It had all happened too quickly for the crew to take any effective measures to defend themselves and in their wild panic their only thought was of immediate escape. Even Captain Hooker was staggered by the sudden attack. Another minute and he knew the savages would be upon him, and against the harpoons, lances, and spades with which they had armed themselves, there was no protection.

At this moment, when every man's life was at stake, an idea flashed into the mind of John Collings. He had jumped up at the first bloodcurdling yell and sprung into the rigging. But now he dropped lightly to the deck and dashed back to where he had been counting the tacks. Plunging his hands into the open barrel he scooped out great handfuls of them and began to strew them over the deck. Again and again he plunged in his hands and, with the sweeping motion he had learned in planting seed, scattered the tacks full across the ship. The deck was soon covered with them.

The savages paid no attention to him. They had their eyes on the quarterdeck. They knew that if they could cut down the little group of officers and men still holding their ground, the ship was theirs. They could pick off the rest of the crew at will and plunder to their hearts' content. As their chief sprang forward they followed him in a rush aft. But their charge was halted as quickly as it had started. Some enchantment had converted the wooden deck into a torturous field of knives and spears which cut cruelly into their bare feet and burned like fire.

A chorus of frightful shrieks rose from the pain-maddened savages. They jumped and danced about the deck in agony and with every jump more tacks were embedded in their bare soles. The attack had become a rout. The natives howled and yelled. First one man and then another dove over the ship's side to escape this stabbing deck. Soon the whole savage band had dropped their weapons and plunged headlong into the sea. They did not stop to climb into their canoes; they swam for shore without a backward glance. The ship was enchanted!

John himself scarcely realized what had happened. He was wildly excited. The frantic din made by the pain-maddened savages still rang in his ears as he looked at his bleeding hands and at the half-emptied barrel of tacks.

Captain Hooker strode from the quarterdeck and looked at the boy a moment without saying anything. Then he stretched out his hand, caught sight of the boy's bleeding fingers, and withdrew it. He hesitated, cleared his throat gruffly.

"Well, John, never mind about counting the tacks. Get your hands in shape so you'll be able to pull the bow oar in my boat next time we lower."

OLD MORDECAI'S COCKEREL

by Sargent Flint

"GRAND old trees," said Mamma, "a fine view from the piazza, and pleasant inside."

"I see no fault," said Papa.

"Except that hideous little house at the foot of the garden," said Aunt Amy.

"And that horrible old man, sitting all day close up to our fence," said Bob.

"Both his legs is shorter than the other," said little Lucy.

"He sits on his own land," said Papa.

"And he minds his own business," said Mamma.

"Nevertheless, he is a very Mordecai at our back gate," said Aunt Amy.

But the summer went, and, despite the hideous little house at the foot of the garden, and the old man smoking his pipe so near the fence, everybody had seemed quite merry. The grand old trees were bare now, and a great, melancholy pile of leaves in the garden was all that was left of their glory. Aunt Amy wished the pile had been a little higher, that it might have hidden old Mordecai's house.

"I like Old Mortify," said Lucy; "he hands me my kitten when she runs away." She had grown used to seeing the old man walking from side to side, on his poor old rheumatic legs, and felt kindly toward him. She had smiled first at his little grand-daughter, and then asked her if she were Mortify's little girl.

"What you mean?" said the child.

"Are you his little girl?" asked Lucy. "He is my grandpa; I am Sadie."

Lucy handed some white roses through the fence, and Sadie handed back a plum. To be sure, the plum was very hard, and Lucy could not eat it; but she believed it was the best her little neighbor had, and always spoke to her afterward.

Now the weather had become so cold that Mordecai no longer sat by the fence, or walked in his little garden; and Lucy had not seen Sadie for a long time.

In a week it would be Thanksgiving. The sky was gray and cold, and the tall trees waved their bare branches to keep warm until the snow should come to cover them.

"Everything looks awfully homesick," said Bob, standing at the window. "This is the meanest place I ever saw."

At that moment a loud, defiant crow fell upon his ears.

"That's Old Mordecai's cockerel," he said angrily.

"Yes," said Lucy. "I can see him down at the pile of leaves."

"I told him never to crow on our side of the fence," said Bob.

Lucy laughed.

"You may laugh, but you just see if he crows on our side again, Lucy Jackson."

Once again the cockerel crowed, loudly and triumphantly. Once more Lucy laughed. Bob went out, and Lucy saw the cockerel scratching the leaves. Then she saw Bob creeping toward him with a bow and arrow. She laughed again, for she considered Bob a very poor shot. Aunt Amy had often said that, if no one but Bob cared for archery, a target would last forever.

Mordecai's cockerel seemed to be of the same opinion, for he stopped a moment to turn his eye toward the young archer, then began to scratch again more diligently than before.

Lucy did not see the arrow fly from the bow, but she saw Bob flying to the stable with the cockerel in his arms. She was so much excited that she ran out at once, bare-headed, to find Bob just drawing out the arrow from the poor fowl's breast.

"Oh, Bob!" she whispered, "that will hurt him dreadfully."

"Do you 'spose he likes it that way?" said Bob, sarcastically.

"Oh, Bob!" she continued, "I didn't believe you could ever hit anything."

"Nor I, either."

She turned away her head while he drew out the arrow. The cockerel flapped his wings a little, then closed his eyes and lay quite still.

"He's going to die," whispered Lucy.

"That's just like a girl! Why don't you help a fellow out?"

"I will do anything you want me to, Bob."

"A girl ought to know more about such things than a boy."

"I know it," sighed Lucy. "I'm trying to think, but all I can remember is arsenicum and Jamaica ginger. He hasn't sneezed, so I don't believe it's arsenicum he needs. Shall I go for some ginger?"

"Do you think it would do any good?"

"He opened one eye; maybe, if he had some ginger, he could open both."

"Well, go get it; we can try it." And Lucy went for the ginger.

"Hope you stayed long enough," said Bob, when she appeared at the stable-door with a cup in her hand.

"That mean cook wouldn't give me the sugar, and I hurried so I spilled the ginger in the closet. How is he?"

"He keeps on breathing, but he doesn't notice much."

Bob took the cup, and gave the cockerel a spoonful of the ginger. The bird staggered to his feet and flapped his wings. Lucy thought surely he meant to crow again on their side of the fence, but the next instant he lay motionless before them.

"He's gone!" said Bob, solemnly.

"I wish we had tried the arsenicum," said Lucy, sadly. "What will Old Mortify say?"

"I guess I shall be Old Mortify, if Papa finds it out. How strong this ginger smells! —how much did you put in?"

"Five spoonfuls. I thought he was so awful sick he ought to have a lot."

"Five spoonfuls! Then you killed him."

"Oh, Bob, don't say that!" she cried. "What would Sadie say to me?" and she lifted the bird's head tenderly, but it fell back again upon the stable-floor. Old Mordecai's cockerel would never crow again on either side of the fence. Little Lucy stood shivering, with tears in her eyes.

"Run in the house," said Bob.

"What shall you do?"

"I am going to hide him under the leaves. And mind you, it's my place to tell of it, and not yours."

"But you are going to tell, Bob?"

"You run in, and wait and see."

She went in and stood by the window, and saw him come carelessly out of the stable and walk about the garden, then return with the dead cock and cover him hastily with leaves.

When he came in, he said: "Don't stand

staring at that pile of leaves. It's done, and can't be helped. Nothing but an old rooster, anyway! No business crowing on our side of the fence. I gave him fair warning."

"But he didn't understand, Bob."

"Well, he does now," said Bob.

That night, after the children had gone to bed, the old man came up to inquire if any one had seen his cockerel.

Aunt Amy went up to ask Bob.

"Yes," said that young gentleman; "tell him I saw him on the wrong side of the fence about four o'clock."

As the days went by, little Lucy felt more and more uneasy, as she thought of what lay under the leaves. She had seen Sadie out, and had heard her call and call for the poor cockerel that never came. Still she had kept quiet, waiting for Bob to speak.

The day before Thanksgiving she sat alone in the library. Her mother and Aunt Amy had gone to the city to meet her grandmother, and Lucy felt a little lonely. Bob saw her as he passed the door, and stepped in, saying:

"What is the matter with you, Lucy? Why can't you brighten up? You've had the doleful dumps for a week."

"Oh, Bob!" she answered, "why don't you tell about that cockerel? It worries me awfully."

He glanced around at all the doors, then came savagely up to his sister and took her roughly by the arm. "I suppose," he whispered almost fiercely, "you mean that old rooster under the leaves. Now, never say another word to me about it. You have twitted me enough."

She looked very much astonished, as she had never referred to it in any way before. A mightier voice than little Lucy's had been calling to him ever since he hid the bird under the leaves.

She saw that his conscience troubled

him, and gained courage. "If you would only tell Mamma, she would tell you what to do. Oh, Bob! I can't walk on that side of the garden for fear I shall see Sadie. She came out yesterday, and looked over our fence, and I heard her call the cockerel several times."

Bob looked down into Lucy's face and wished he had not taken hold of her quite so roughly. He went back to the kitchen and got a large bunch of raisins and gave them to her, with a pat on the head, which she understood very well. "Too bad," he declared, "that you can't go out to-day."

After he had gone, she took up the raisins, when, happening to look out of the window, she saw Sadie looking over the fence. "I will give her my raisins," thought Lucy.

The cook rapped sharply as she passed the kitchen window, for she knew Lucy ought not to go out.

"Don't give me all," said Sadie, as Lucy passed the great bunch through the fence.

"Tomorrow we shall have a whole box-ful," said Lucy.

"We can't find our rooster," said Sadie. "Grandpa sold all but him; we kept him for Thanksgiving. I don't see how he got out of the coop. We can't have any Thanksgiving now."

"Too bad!" said little Lucy, very faintly.

"Grandpa's looked everywhere for him, till he tired himself out, and got rheumatism dreadfully. He thinks some of the neighbors have killed him."

Lucy turned a little pale, and said she had a very bad cold and must go in.

Sadie would have been surprised had she looked out a few minutes later, for she would have seen Lucy running toward the provision store.

"Anything wrong, Miss Lucy?" said the red-cheeked boy who drove the wagon.

She went in timidly, and when she stood

close by his side, she whispered, "How much do you ask for roosters?"

"A hen wouldn't do?" he asked, laughing.

"No," she said, with a sigh, as she compared in her mind the proud strut of Mordecai's cockerel with the walk of any hen she had ever met. "No, I want a rooster."

"What's it for?" he said, confidentially.

"For Thanksgiving."

"I just took two fine gobblers up."

"It's for—for somebody else's Thanksgiving."

"Oho! Why not get a small turkey? Just the thing."

Why had she not thought of it before! Perhaps that would help Mordecai to forgive them. (She had begun to blame herself with Bob, for had she not prepared the fatal ginger?)

The red-cheeked boy held up a plump little turkey.

"Is that a dollar?" she asked.

"That's heavier than I thought," he said, after he had thrown it into the scales. "That will cost, all told,—let me see,—one dollar thirty-eight."

She began feeling about her neck, as if she kept her money concealed somewhere about her jugular veins, and the tears came to her eyes.

The red-cheeked boy became again confidential. "Come, now," he said, in a low tone, "how much do we want to pay? What is just the little sum we were thinking of, when we came in?"

"I have only one dollar," answered Lucy, with her hand still guarding a jugular.

"A dollar is quite enough to pay for a small, nice, plump little turkey, if the right person comes for it."

Lucy hoped she was the right person. "If you please," she said, as he showed her another turkey, the smallest one she

had ever seen, "are you sure it's a turkey? I don't want a rooster, now."

"My word for it, Miss Lucy, yesterday afternoon that fowl said 'Gobble.' Shall I send it to your house?"

"If you would do him up so he would look like a dress, I would be very much obliged to you."

While he was gone, she again put her hand to her neck and took off a small gold chain; attached to this was a gold dollar. She had worn it since she was a baby; her fingers seemed unwilling to take it off. Her little head said, "Take it off!" and her little heart said, "Oh, no!"

When the boy came back with the turkey, looking as much like a dress as a provision man could make it, the small coin still remained firmly attached to the chain.

"If you please, will you undo this?" said Lucy.

He looked at it a moment, without taking it in his hands, and said, "Why don't you charge it, Miss Lucy?"

"Oh, no, no," she said, hastily; "Papa is not to pay for this. I must pay for it myself."

"I understand; you don't want your good works talked about either, Miss Lucy. But I don't want to take this."

"Come, come," said his employer from the other side of the store; "fly around there!"

The boy hurriedly unfastened the dollar, and said: "You may have it back any time, Miss Lucy."

She took the turkey in her arms and went out. When she had walked a few steps she stopped suddenly and turned and went back. The boy was just getting into the wagon. She pulled his coat, and, as he turned, said timidly: "You are so kind, will you tell me how to spell 'Mordecai?' Not Mortify, but Mordecai."

"It's a joke," he said, grinning.

"Oh, no!" groaned poor Lucy.

"Mordecai," he said, pausing, with one foot on the wheel: "M-o-r—Mor—d-y—Mordy—k-i—Mordyki."

She thanked him and hurried home.

When Bob came in, she pulled him into a corner and whispered: "I have bought a little turkey, the littlest one you ever saw, but a sure turkey, for Mordecai! Run out, before you take off your coat, for it's in the stable, in the oat-box; and will you take it to Mordecai's house? Go quick, before it gets dark."

He turned toward her with an angry gesture.

"Oh, Bob! Sadie can't have any Thanksgiving, because we killed the rooster, and I knew you would be so sorry."

He made no reply, but ran with great haste to the stable. He soon found the bundle and brought it to the little window, when he saw there was a little letter, pinned with several pins, on the outside. The afternoon light was fast fading, and it was with some difficulty he read the note, of which this is a copy:

> "DEAR MISTER MORDYKI BOB AND ME KILLED YOUR RUSTER PLEAS TAKE THIS
>
> LUCY"

"The good, generous little thing!" muttered Bob, gazing solemnly at the brown bundle, which was supposed to resemble dry goods. "I wonder where in time she got the money! And to say *she* killed it, or had anything to do with killing it! Oh, I hope she wont grow up and be one of those good kind of folks that never have any fun and give all their money away. Where in the world *did* she get the money?" He folded the note carefully and put it in his pocket. "I never felt meaner," he thought, as he seized the turkey, with no gentle hand, and ran to Mordecai's house.

The old man sat at the front window, and Bob thought he looked a little sour as the gate opened; but he came to the door as fast as he could hobble, for fear Mrs. Mordecai might get there first. Bob held out the turkey and said: "I shot your rooster, sir. My little sister thought you were saving him for Thanksgiving, and she sent you this turkey."

"So *you* killed my cockerel, did ye?" said the old man; "a mighty fine cockerel he was!" He punched with his thumb the turkey that he could not see, as if he wondered if it could possibly be as fine as the cockerel.

"I had no idea I should hit him," said Bob. "I am a most awful shot, sir. Would you rather have a live rooster?"

"N-no," said old Mordecai. "Though my wife misses his crowing in the morning—overslept every morning since he went."

"We should have killed him for Thanksgiving," said Mrs. Mordecai, a tired-looking little woman, who looked as if she could oversleep, in spite of all the warnings that might be sounded. "A turkey, Father, is better than a cockerel; and so we have lost nothing."

"You don't like to feel that yer neighbors is standin' round armed, ready to destroy yer property,—do you, eh?"

"No, but I like to know that, if they do happen to destroy it, they stand ready to pay more than it's worth."

"Yer allays did like young folks," said Mordecai, dryly, and hobbled back to the front window.

"You are a good boy," said his wife. "Don't mind him; he'll speak better of you behind your back."

"'T was Lucy sent it; I only killed the cockerel," said Bob, turning away.

"I have carried the turkey down," he said to Lucy on his return. "Now, tell me where you got the money."

"I had to take my gold dollar." Lucy

could not keep the tears from filling her eyes.

"Whew!" he said, "the one on your chain?"

She nodded.

"Born with it on, weren't you?"

"I don't 'member when I got it," said she, a little more cheerfully. "Don't go out again, Bob," as he started suddenly toward the door, and she saw him run across the garden with his skate-bag under his arm.

"Hang the old rooster!" he said, as he passed the little house and saw old Mordecai sitting at the window. "It's going to cost me a pretty sum. I won't do it!— It's good enough for her, to go spend that dollar—just like a girl—I hope he won't take them. Hang Mordecai!" Still he walked on rapidly until he came to Johnny Bang's house. "Hope he's gone away," he said, as he pulled the bell, which was answered by young John himself, whose eyes brightened as he saw the skate-bag; but he waited for Bob to speak.

"You said last night you would give me two and a half; say three and they're yours," said Bob.

"Do you suppose I made a half a dollar in my sleep?" said Johnny, with a grin.

"Can you give me three?"

"No, I can't."

"Jerry will; I came to you first, because you made the first offer. I must have three or nothing."

"You come in and sit down, and I'll see if I can work Mother up to it."

Johnny's mother proved a person easily "worked up," for in a few minutes he returned with three crisp bills in his hand.

"I told her they cost five dollars, and you had had them only two weeks; was that straight?"

"Yes," said Bob, "that's straight."

"She asked me if you had a right to sell them without asking your father, and I told her you bought them yourself with your own money that you had saved; was that straight?"

"Yes," said Bob, his mouth twitching a little, "that's straight."

He took the skates from the bag and handed them to his friend.

"Won't throw in the bag?" said Johnny.

"Oh, I'll throw in the whole family," said Bob, sarcastically, as he left the house.

The first call he made was on the red-cheeked boy at the provision store; then he went to the city.

After supper, when little Lucy was sitting with her father, talking about Thanksgiving, he came in, looking rather tired, and gave her a tiny box. She opened it and found first a note, which said to her:

"DEAR LUCY: You did the square thing by me and I won't forget it. Hang these on your chain in remembrance of Old Mordecai's rooster.　　　　"BOB."

And under some pink cotton lay her own little dollar, and beside it a small gold cockerel, as proud-looking as Old Mordecai's before Bob's unlucky shot.

A WONDERFUL PAIR OF SLIPPERS

*(WITH LETTERS CONCERNING THEM FROM
MARK TWAIN AND ELSIE LESLIE LYDE)*

MARK TWAIN'S LETTER

Hartford, Oct. 5, '89.

Dear Elsie: The way of it was this. Away last spring, Gillette and I pooled intellects on this proposition: to get up a pleasant surprise of some kind for you against your next visit—the surprise to take the form of a tasteful and beautiful testimonial of some sort or other, which should express somewhat of the love we felt for you. Together we hit upon just the right thing—a pair of slippers. Either one of us could have thought of a single slipper, but it took both of us to think of two slippers. In fact, one of us did think of one slipper, and then, quick as a flash, the other thought of the other one. It shows how wonderful the human mind is. It is really paleontological; you give one mind a bone, and the other one instantly divines the rest of the animal.

Gillette embroidered his slipper with astonishing facility and splendor, but I have been a long time pulling through with mine. You see, it was my very first attempt at art, and I couldn't rightly get the hang of it along at first. And then I was so busy that I couldn't get a chance to work at it at home, and they wouldn't let me embroider on the cars; they said it made the other passengers afraid. They didn't like the light that flared into my eye when I had an inspiration. And even the most fair-minded people doubted me when I explained what it was I was making—especially brakemen. Brakemen always swore at it, and carried on, the way ignorant people do, about art. They wouldn't take my word that it was a slipper; they said they believed it was a snow-shoe that had some kind of a disease.

But I have pulled through, and within twenty-four hours of the time I told you I would—day before yesterday. There ought to be a key to the designs, but I haven't had time to get one up. However, if you will lay the work before you with the forecastle pointing north, I will begin at that end and explain the whole thing, layer by layer, so that you can understand it.

I began with that first red bar, and without ulterior design, or plan of any sort—just as I would begin a Prince and Pauper, or any other tale. And mind you it is the easiest and surest way; because if you invent two or three people and turn them loose in your manuscript, something is bound to happen to them,—you can't help it; and then it will take you the rest of the book to get them out of the natural consequences of that occurrence, and so, first thing you know, there's your book all finished up and never cost you an idea. Well, the red stripe, with a bias stitch, naturally suggested a blue one with a perpendicular stitch, and I slammed it in, though when it came daylight I saw it was green—which didn't make any difference, because green and blue are much the same anyway, and in fact from a purely moral point of view are regarded by the best authorities as identical. Well, if you will notice, a blue perpendicular stitch always suggests a ropy red involved stitch, like a family of angle-worms trying to climb in under each other to keep warm—it would suggest that, every time, without the author of the slipper ever having to think about it at all.

Now at that point, young Dr. Root came in, and of course he was interested in the slipper right away, because he has always had a passion for art himself, but has never had a chance to try, because his folks are opposed to it and superstitious about it, and have done all they could to keep him back; and so he was eager to take a hand and see what he could do. And it was beautiful to see him sit there and tell Mrs. Clemens what had been happening while we were off on summer vacation, and hold the slipper up toward the end of his nose, and forget the sordid world, and imagine the canvas was a "subject" with a scalp wound, and nimbly whirl in that lovely surgical stitch which you see there—and never hesitating a moment in his talk except to say "Ouch" when he stuck himself, and then going right on again as smooth and easy as nothing. Yes, it was a charming spectacle. And it was real art, too,—realistic; just native untaught genius; you can see the very scalp itself, showing through between the stitches.

Well, next I threw in that sheaf of green rods which the lictors used to carry before the Roman Consuls to lick them with when they didn't behave, — they turned blue in the morning, but that is the way green always acts.

The next week, after a good rest, I snowed in that sea of frothy waves, and set that yellow thing afloat in it and those two things that are skewered through it. It isn't a home-plate, and it isn't a papal tiara with the keys of St. Peter; no, it is a heart—my heart—with two arrows stuck through it—arrows that go in blue and come out crimson—crimson with the best drops in that heart, and gladly shed for love of you, dear.

Now, then, as you strike to the south'ard and drift along down the starboard side, abaft the main-to'-gallant scuppers you come to that blue quarter-deck which runs the rest of the way aft to the jumping-off place. In the midst of that blue you will see some big red letters—M. T.; and west'ard, over on the port side, you will see some more red letters—to E. L. Aggregated, these several groups of letters signify, Mark Twain to Elsie Leslie. And you will notice that you have a gift for art yourself, for the southern half of the L, embroidered by yourself, is as good as anything I can do, after all my experience.

There, now you understand the whole work. From a professional point of view I consider the Heart and Arrows by all odds the greatest triumph of the whole thing; in fact, one of the ablest examples of civil engineering in a beginner I ever saw—for it was all inspiration, just the lightning-like inspiration of the moment. I couldn't do it again in a hundred years,—even if I recover this time and get just as well and strong as I was before. You notice what fire there is in it—what rapture, enthusiasm, frenzy—what blinding explosions of color. It is just a "Turner"—that is what it is. It is just like his "Slave Ship," that immortal work. What you see in the "Slave Ship" is a terrific explosion of radiating rags and fragments of flaming crimson flying from a common center of intense yellow which is in violent commotion—insomuch that a Boston reporter said it reminded him of a yellow cat dying in a platter of tomatoes.

Take the slippers and wear them next your heart, Elsie dear; for every stitch in them is a testimony of the affection which two of your loyalest friends bear you. Every single stitch cost us blood. I've got twice as many pores in me now as I used to have; and you would never believe how many places you can stick a needle into yourself until you go into the embroidery line and devote yourself to art.

Do not wear these slippers in public, dear; it would only excite envy; and, as like as not, somebody would try to shoot you.

Merely use them to assist you in remembering that among the many, many people who think all the world of you is your friend,

Mark Twain.

ELSIE'S REPLY

New York, October 9, 1889.

My dear Mr. Clemens: The slipper the long letter and all the rest came this afternoon, I think they are splendid and shall have them framed and keep them among my very most prechus things. I have had a great many nice things given to me and people often say very pleasant things but I am not quite shure they always mean it or that they are as trustable as you and "Leo," and I am very shure they would not spend their prechus time and shed their blood for me so you see that is one reason why I will think so much of it and then it was all so funny to think of two great big men like you and "little Willie" (that is what "Leo" calls himself to me) imbroidering a pair of slippers for a little girl like me of corse you have a great many large words in your letter that I do not quite understand. One word comencing with P. has fifteen letters in it and I do not know what you mean by pooled unless you mean you and Leo put your two minds together to make the slippers which was very nice of you both I think you are just right about the angle worms thay did look like that this summer when I used to dig them for bate to fish with please tell Dr. Root I will think of him when I look at the part he did the Surgicle Stich I mean I hope you will be quite well and strong by the time you get this letter as you were before you made my slipper it would make me very sad if you were to be ill. Give my love to Mrs. Clemens Susie Clara Gene I-know and you-know and Vix and all of my Hartford friends tell Gene I wish I was with her and we would have a nice jump in the hay loft. When you come to New York you must call and see me then we will see about those big words my address is up in the top left corner of this letter.

To my loyal friend
Mark Twain
From his little friend
Elsie Leslie Lyde.

THE FAIRPORT NINE

by Noah Brooks

CHARACTERS IN THE STORY

THE FAIRPORT NINE	THE WHITE BEARS
Pitcher—Ned Martin	*Pitcher*—Jake Coombs
Catcher—John Hale, otherwise "The Lob"	*Catcher*—Eph Weeks
1st Base—Jo Murch	*1st Base*—Joe Patchen
2d Base—Hi Hatch	*2d Base*—George Bridges
3d Base—James Pat Adams	*3d Base*—Sam Booden, Captain
Short Stop—Sam Perkins, Captain	*Short Stop*—Eph Mullett, otherwise "Nosey"
Left Field—Sam Black, otherwise "Blackie"	*Left Field*—Dan Morey
Center Field—Billy Hetherington	*Center Field*—Joe Fitts
Right Field—Bill Watson, otherwise "Chunky"	*Right Field*—Peletiah Snelgro

The whole assisted by a large number of young ladies and gentlemen, who do not belong to any base-ball nine, but who hope to, if they live long enough.

CHAPTER I

RINGING THE BELL

IN Fairport, every boy slept with some other boy on the night before the Fourth of July. If any boy did sleep in his own bed, it was because he had a playmate with him. But, for the most part, the boys of that period thought it poor fun to sleep at home on that eventful night. They all preferred to sleep in barns, hay-mows, or some other out-of-the-way and unusual place. It was a sign that a fellow was a milk-sop if he slept in a real bed on that night, except under such circumstances as have just been referred to. For there was a great deal to be done on the night before the Fourth. In the first place, there was a bonfire to be built on the common. There was a large, bare spot in the middle of the common where the grass refused to grow from one year's end to another, because the bonfire was built there on the night before the Fourth. And to feed that fire, it was necessary to gather

much fuel from various and distant places. Spare barrels, store-boxes, and occasionally a loose board from off some careless person's fence, were to be brought in. The boys did not take gates off their hinges to kindle the fire, as tradition said that their older brothers did, when they were boys. The time of which I write was a great improvement on that elder period. No boy fed the bonfire with anything more valuable than the few loose things that could be picked up without alarming the neighbors. The neighbors were easily alarmed, anyhow. There was a class of old ladies in Fairport who never remembered from one Fourth of July to another that, on the night before it, the boys, ever since there were any boys, built a bonfire on the common. So, when the bright flames began to rise up in the darkness, one or more of these timid women would be sure to come out on her door-step and cry: "Boys! Boys! What are you doing? You'll set the town a-fire, you pesky boys!"

Jo Murch (his whole name was Jotham Augustus Murch) used to be very much mortified when his mother came out like that, and he would say: "Now, Ma, don't be so foolish. There isn't any danger of our setting anything a-fire!" Once, one of the Selectmen of the town, a very dignified and truly awful person, came upon the common to see what the boys were at. It was nearly midnight, and it seemed as if something alarming was about to happen when the great man came out at that time of night. But he only looked the party of boys all over, as if to be sure that he would know them again, if anything happened, and then he went away, telling them to be careful of the sparks.

"My! Wasn't I afraid he would see old Snelgro's wheelbarrow!" said Ned Martin, when the Selectman was gone.

At midnight, as near as they could guess, it was necessary that the meeting-house bell should be rung. At least, every Fairport boy thought it was necessary; and it was rung. There was a bell on the school-house at the right of the common, only, as nobody but the nearest neighbors objected to the ringing of this bell, the boys did not much enjoy ringing it. They took a pull at it, once in a while, for fear that the folks around would not know that the glorious Fourth had arrived. The folks usually found it out before day-break. The town bell was on the Unitarian meeting-house, below the school-house, and facing the street which skirted the bottom of the common. To ring this bell was not only necessary, but it was also a great feat. The Selectmen had forbidden that the bell should be rung by anybody but the town sexton, except in case of fire. From time immemorial, Old Fitts had been the town sexton, and if any man really hated boys, Old Fitts did. Probably he never was a boy. It seemed absurd to think that he ever could have been a boy. Boys were his natural enemies. They used to shin up the lightning-rod of the church and catch the pigeons which he reared in the belfry; and they used to ring the bell on the night before the Fourth of July. Generation after generation of boys had done this; but, somehow, Old Fitts could never become reconciled to it. On the particular night about which I am going to write, Old Fitts had not only nailed up one of the two church doors and put an extra padlock on the other, but he had carried away the bell-rope. The Fairport boys were a curious set. They laughed among themselves when they saw him going home, after he had rung the nine o'clock bell, with the long bell-rope coiled up on his back. But when they flew to the doors, after he was well out of sight, and beheld the defenses which he had put on them, they began to think that, for the first time in the history of the world, the bell would not be rung on the night before the Fourth of July.

As the boys scattered to the barns and hay-mows where they had chosen to sleep, Ned Martin said to his crony, Sam Perkins:

"I'll ring that bell before daylight, you see."

"But how, Ned?"

Now, Sam was the leader of the boys in almost all of the mischief that was afoot, and he was, besides all that, the captain of the Fairport Nine. For Fairport had a baseball nine, and it was the terror of the surrounding villages. Of course, Sam did not want any other boy to lead off in a feat of this kind unless he had a hand in it himself. But Ned Martin knew a thing or two, and Sam was sure that he would ring the bell, if he said so. And when the boys, three of them, for Hi Hatch bunked in with them that night, were safely hidden in the hay, Ned unfolded to them his plan. It was a good scheme, and all agreed to it.

In all the world, probably, there is no stillness like that which comes between

THE FAIRPORT NINE 243

nine o'clock and the time when the Fairport boys get up to ring the bell and build their bonfire, on the night before the Fourth of July. At least, Hiram Hatch thought so that night, as he lay awake in the hay in his father's barn, listening to the heavy breathing of his mates. The spears of hay tickled his ear so that he could not get to sleep; and the stillness was awful. He almost wished that he was snug in his own bed, and he wondered why Ned and Sam should go to sleep so soon, and he should be so broad awake. There was a sound of something on the barn floor below. It was a tread! Then he heard a ghostly whisper, and he felt the hair rising on his head. Desperately poking Sam in the back he whispered:

"There is something climbing up the ladder!"

Sam bounced up and cried: "What's—what's that!"

There was a scrambling and a rush of feet below, and all was still again. But Hiram was too badly scared to go to sleep at once, and when, tired out by his long vigil, he did drop off into slumber, he slept so soundly that Sam had hard work to wake him, as he shook him and shouted in his ear:

"Remember you have got to play second base, to-day."

"What do you s'pose that was in the barn, just now?" shivered Hiram, for the midnights in Fairport are cool, seeing that the town is on Penobscot Bay, on the cold coast of Maine.

"Oh bother!" said Sam. "Let's get out of this as still as we can. If your father should hear us, as likely as not he'd fire that double-barreled shotgun at us."

Hiram held his peace, for the double-barreled shotgun was a sore subject with him, since he had promised to carry it off on the sly and have it for firing the usual midnight salute. He was comforted now by the reflection that he had not the responsibility of that gun on his mind; and Ned assured him that the noise in the night was probably only made by some of the other boys who had intended to steal a place to sleep, without waking up the rightful tenants.

Silently, and as if bent on some dreadful deed, dark forms now stole in from all around, and clustered in the middle of the common. A crockery crate, filled with straw, and stuck all around with pickets from some slothful man's dilapidated fence, was set on fire. The cheerful blaze, ascending, lighted up the fronts of the houses on the edge of the common, and shed a lurid glare on the tall elms which stood tremulously in the midnight air. The flames warmed the boys, and revived their spirits, somewhat damped by cold and lack of sleep.

"Hurrah for the Fourth of July!" shouted Bill Watson, a burly little chap, the right fielder, and better known as "Chunky." Then every other fellow cried "Hurrah for the Fourth of July!" And it was felt that the fun had begun.

Amidst great enthusiasm, Pat Adams now fired off his gun. It was only a single-barreled one, to be sure, but it spoke well for itself. Pat's name was James Patterson Adams, but he was known, for short, as Pat Adams, and, when the boys were not in much of a hurry, he was called Jim Pat Adams, to distinguish him from another Jim whose name was not Adams. When the bang of Pat's gun rent the air, there was a sound of opening windows, and the boys knew that angry looks were directed toward them from some of the houses roundabout. There was a wild hurrah when Sam Black, assisted by Billy Hetherington, staggered up to the fire with the better part of a tar-barrel, which they had hidden away some days before. There is no aristocracy among real boys, and it was an evidence of this truth that Sam Black, who was the only Negro boy in Fairport, was a crony of Billy Hetherington, whose father was the county judge, and had been to Congress. If any boy had a right to be "stuck up," it was Billy, whose family held themselves very high in Fairport. But Billy never once thought of such a thing. If he had, his mates would have cut him at once, and he would have found himself alone in the village of boys. It was curious that the only black boy in the town should be Black by name. So Sam, who was a great favorite with his comrades, was usually called "Blackie," a term which carried with it no idea of contempt. Blackie was the best fellow of the boys of that generation, and, moreover, he knew more of the habits of the birds, beasts, fish, and all manner of living wild things, than most of the naturalists who write thick books about the animal kingdom. The times and seasons when birds come and go, and when they mate, and where they build their nests, as well as the secret lairs of the small game of the woods and fields, were all as familiar to Blackie as if he had been born in the wilderness, and not in a house on stilts at the harbor's edge.

"Three cheers for the left fielder!" cried Jo Murch, as Blackie, his face shining with satisfaction and pride, helped Billy Hetherington heave the tar-barrel on the blazing pile. "And now, boys, for the bell," he added, for it was already past twelve, one of the boys having reconnoitered, through the kitchen window of a neighboring house, to ascertain the time of night.

Ned Martin looked around on the little group of lads in his superior way, and said:

"Which of you fellows is the best on shinning a lightning-rod?" There was a great laugh when John Hale stoutly answered: "I am!" for John was so big and lubberly that he was never called anything

but the "lob." In Fairport, the 'longshoremen call any craft which is clumsy and unwieldy "lob-sided," meaning, perhaps, that it is lop-sided, a phrase which may be found in the dictionaries. If one but stuck out a fist at Johnny Hale he fell over. And when the schoolmaster tried to get him up on the tall stool where it was the custom for boys to be hoisted for punishment, the master and Johnny invariably came down in a heap together on the floor, the "lob" was so very clumsy and so very heavy. Nevertheless, the "lob," for all his awkwardness, was the champion catcher in Fairport, and the envy of the White Bears, the rival club from the south end of town.

The "lob" was rejected as the champion climber, however, and little Sam Murch, Jo's brother, was selected for the feat of shinning up the lightning-rod of the church.

As an aid, in case of need, the volunteered services of Blackie were also promptly accepted, for the Fairport Nine never did anything that was not "shipshape and Bristol fashion," or, otherwise, according to rule and discipline.

Old Major Boffin's house stood so near the meeting-house that one could toss a biscuit from the roof of one to the other; and the Major's grandson, Ike, was a member of the party, though not of the famous "Nine." This was lucky; and it was also lucky that the roof of the Major's house was nearly flat, and that it had at each of the angles of said roof a big, square chimney, so big that two or three boys might hide behind one of them without fear of detection. And when it was remembered that the roof of the Major's house could be reached by a lightning-rod, much easier of ascent than that on the meeting-house, it was evident that fortune favored the brave when it was necessary for the brave to ring the bell on the night before the Fourth of July. The testy old Major, calmly sleeping in his bed, could not have dreamed how much his property was contributing to the celebration of the glorious Fourth, when, in addition to all this, Ned Martin, carefully stripping the sheets, shirts and pillow-cases from the clothes-line in the Major's garden, took the line and making one end fast to the ankle of little Murch, gave him a hoist, and told him to "go it" up the lightning-rod of the meeting-house.

The projection of the eaves of the building set the rod out from the side of it a great way, and, as the rod was jointed in two or three places, it swayed fearfully while Sam laboriously shinned up it. Now and again he would be flung round and round by the swinging rod, as he passed over the clanking joints, the clatter of which threatened to bring the choleric Major down upon them at any moment.

"Hold fast, little one," hoarsely whispered Captain Sam from below, for Sam, with his usual facility for taking command, had now assumed the direction of things. "Hold fast, or Blackie will be on your heels." And Blackie, dancing up and down with impatience, was ready to make a spring at the rod when little Murch should be out of his way.

"Bully for Sam," half shouted Ned Martin, for the little fellow had reached the edge of the far-projecting eaves, and was now struggling to get over the most difficult part. The boys below held their breath, for it was a perilous place. The lightning-rod, after turning up the edge of the shingles, was fastened to the roof by strong staples which held it firmly down and afforded almost no hold to which even a boy's small and hook-like fingers could cling. But little Sam was "clear grit," as his brother proudly remarked in a suppressed whisper, and while the silent spectators below all looked up, with their hearts in their mouths, he turned the edge

of the eaves and went picking his way up the roof, hand over hand. It was now Blackie's turn to go up, but Captain Sam interfered, and declared that if both of the best climbers went up into the meeting-house belfry, there would be nobody to shin up to the roof of the Major's house and carry the rope from the bell, when it was made fast. Half-a-dozen boys volunteered to go up the Major's lightning-rod, but Ike Boffin agreed to "hook in" by the back door, steal up the stairs to the roof, and take care of the rope when there.

"So, then, you are to have all the fun of ringing the bell, are you?" demanded Captain Sam, sarcastically.

"Well," said Ike, "you pick out four other fellows, and I will undertake to get them up on our roof, if they will promise to be mighty still about it."

Accordingly, Captain Sam, Ned Martin, Hi Hatch and Chunky were chosen to go up on the Major's roof, guided by Ike, who, with a quaking heart, opened the back door and let in these midnight conspirators. No cat could have climbed the stairs more softly than the five boys, Ike at the head. Barefoot and breathless, they stole by the door of the sacred chamber where the old Major, snoring manfully, was sleeping in happy unconsciousness of what was going on around him. Drawing a long breath, the five boys found themselves out on the roof at last. To their great delight and relief, they saw little Murch just shinning up the part of the rod which led from the roof to the belfry, not a very difficult job, in comparison with that which he had just finished. In a moment more he was in the belfry, and pausing on the balustrade which decorated the rim, he gave a noiseless cheer, dropped over to the inner side, and made fast to the clapper of the bell the end of the line which he had brought up with him. Ned Martin now dropped down from the roof of the Major's house one end of a mackerel line which he had with him. To this the boys below fastened the end of the line from the bell-clapper, and it was drawn up to Captain Sam, who took it up behind his chimney with great joy. The boys on the ground now scattered to all parts of the common, at a whispered command from Captain Sam, and then the big bell struck a peal of mighty strokes, pulled by the sinewy hand of Sam. The night air quivered with the blows on the bell. Old Fitts' pigeons, affrighted by the midnight booming of the bell, flew out in crowds, scaring Sam Murch as they dashed in his face. The brave little lad swung himself over the balustrade, and sliding down the roof in a hurry, was soon on the long and swaying rod below, and on firm ground once more, and then safe among his comrades.

"Those pesky boys," sighed Grandmother Boffin, as she turned uneasily in her sleep, but awake enough to know what was the cause of the horrible din which rent the air. The Major got out of bed, and, putting his head out of the window, addressed the darkness, commanding all in sound of his voice to disperse and go home, or take the consequences. But the old Major never forgot that he had been a boy once himself, although that was a great many years ago; and when he went back to bed, smiling grimly to himself as the bell answered his warning with a yet louder peal, he said: "Well, mother, boys will be boys, you know. There's no law ag'in ringing the meeting-house bell on the night before the Fourth." The Major, although a hot-tempered man, remembered that he had fought in "the last war" —that of 1812—and something was due, he thought, to the day we celebrate.

A sudden idea struck the good grandmother. She crept out of bed, stole to the bedroom of her grandson, passed her hand over the vacant bed, and then going back to her chamber-window, cried into the air, as the Major had done, "You, Ike, wherever you are, don't you dare to come into the house for your breakfast!" Ike, who was now taking his turn at the clothesline, laughed to himself. He remembered that he had a share in a boiled ham, a basket of apples and a paper of crackers, stowed away in Hatch's barn, under the hay.

Suddenly there was an alarm of "Fitts! Fitts!" from the boys stationed on the court-house steps, from which post they could see all the way down Howe's lane, up which the old sexton must come to the defense of his precious bell. Fortunately for the boys, Fitts never stirred out of doors, no matter how light the night, without his lantern. And the rays from that familiar lantern, "like a lightning-bug," as Billy Hetherington declared, now bobbed along the ground as Fitts climbed the hilly lane.

Warned in time, not a boy was in sight when the old sexton, grumbling to himself, reached the top of the hill and went across the bottom of the common toward the meeting-house. The bell continued to ring, much to the delight of the boys hidden behind the chimneys and stowed away in various nooks and corners below. With infinite trouble, Old Fitts got the door open, and with many a hard word for the boys, toiled up the long stairs which led to the belfry. "Now, then, Ned, give her a good one," whispered Captain Sam, as the old Sexton's lantern, shining through the belfry windows, showed that he was almost up to the bell, and, sure enough, as Fitts put his head out of the scuttle which opened to the deck of the belfry, a tremendous and audacious peal boomed directly over his head.

The old man walked all around the big bell. Not a boy was to be seen. The rope, he knew, was safe in his own house, and there was no sign of anything by which the bell could be rung. The light line leading to the roof of the Boffin house was too small to be noticed as it lay on the slanting deck of the belfry. The boys chuckled to themselves as they watched the puzzled old man walking around the bell, again and again peering over the balustrade, as if to see if some small boy were circling around in the air with the scared pigeons which silently flew about their master's head. It was very queer, so it was.

Just then, the "lob," who was never known to stand up when he could fall down, slipped on the roof behind the Boffin chimney that hid him. He might have slid off to the ground below if he had not put out his hand to save himself by grabbing at the boy next to him, which happened to be Sam, who tried to shake the "lob" from him. It was in vain, and the two boys came down in a heap behind the chimney, Sam pulling the rope with him. As he fell, the bell, of course, was given another peal, and the rope in the belfry flew up before the astonished eyes of the old sexton. Fitts stopped, cut the line, and, shaking his fist in the direction of the Major's house, cried, "I've stopped your fun this time, you young varmints;" and so he had. When he had carefully locked the scuttle of the belfry, descended the stairs and gone home, his light disappearing in the distance, the four boys on the roof, somewhat crestfallen, silently slid down the Major's lightning-rod, and made their way up to the bonfire. The "lob" was overwhelmed with ridicule for his share in the failure of the bell-ringing feat. "And he wanted to shin up the meeting-house lightning-rod!" said Captain Sam, derisively.

Blackie, however, soon found a way to remedy the mischief. He went up the lightning-rod again with the agility of a cat, spliced the line, then, disdaining to go up through the Major's house, he shinned up its lightning-rod and speedily had the bell a-ringing merrily. Meantime, the boys about the bonfire were doing their best to celebrate the night by firing the few pieces of small-arms which they had; and their fire-crackers were exploded—sparingly, however, as it was borne in mind that the Fourth was yet to come, and more noise would be needed for the day.

Hiram Hatch, returning from a visit to the back of Major Boffin's house to encourage Blackie, who was pulling away lustily at the bell-rope, cast his eyes on the fire, and, to his horror, spied the remains of the leaching-tub which he knew ought to be standing on his father's barn floor. "Where did that come from?" he demanded. Nobody knew, but Chunky guessed that Jo Murch and George Bridges had thrown it on the fire.

"That came out of my father's barn," said Hi, stoutly, "and the fellow that took it is a mean sneak, and I don't care who he is."

"I don't see that it is any meaner to take that leaching-tub out of Deacon Hatch's barn than it is to steal old Boffin's clothes-line, or Judge Nelson's chicken-coop, so there," said Jo Murch.

As the Judge's coop had been ravished by Hiram, he felt condemned; but he replied, hotly, that there was a big difference between taking an old chicken-coop, only fit for kindlings, anyhow, and stealing a leaching-tub out of a man's barn. Then, suddenly remembering the mysterious noises which he had heard while he was trying to go to sleep, he exclaimed, with his small fist before Jo Murch's nose, "And you came in there and stole that tub while we were in the hay-loft. I heard you."

"Yes, and mighty scared you were, too," Jo replied, with an unpleasant sneer.

There were symptoms of a fight, when one of the sentries on the court-house steps shouted "Fitts! Fitts!" Then all the boys, in their anxiety for the bell, scattered to points about the meeting-house from which they could see the fate of Blackie, who, perceiving the lantern of the old sexton coming, improved the time by giving the bell as many and as vigorous strokes as possible.

Grumbling and groaning to himself, the sexton slowly climbed the belfry stairs once more, and was soon on the upper deck. "Why, oh why, didn't I nail down that scuttle?" groaned little Blackie, as, from behind his chimney, he saw the old man emerge upon the belfry deck. Blackie consoled himself with the reflection that he would do this the next time the coast was clear. But he was doomed to disappointment. Fitts, as soon as he had cut the line, for the second time, gave it a strong pull, and a sudden pull, and poor Blackie, not for a moment dreaming what was going to happen, was jerked out from behind the chimney, and, still holding on, across the scuttle, which had been left open.

"Aha! It's you, is it? you, you black limb, is it?" cried Old Fitts, exultingly, as the boy came dimly into sight from behind the chimney. "Major Boffin! There's a burglar on your roof!" shouted the old man, as he tugged at the line which Blackie sturdily refused to let go.

"Shame! Shame! Old Fitts!" shrieked several of the boys below, in their concealment. "He's no burglar, and you know it."

In the midst of the racket, Major Boffin, with a grim smile on his face, put his head out of the window, and, after shouting

"Thieves! Thieves!" at the top of his voice, fired into the sky a horse-pistol which he kept loaded for the entertainment of the midnight cats that sometimes disturbed his slumbers. A profound silence followed this volley. Even Old Fitts was quiet in his belfry; and Blackie, taking advantage of the lull, dropped the line which he had held, and softly crept down the roof, clutched the lightning-rod, slid to the ground, and made off in the darkness.

"If I catch those pesky boys around here again to-night," said the angry sexton, "I'll put a load of buckshot into some of 'em."

"Never you fear," answered the Major, "you will never catch them. Sooner catch a lot of weasels." And the old man shut down his window with a bang.

Fitts descended into the little loft below the belfry, and, though the boys waited for his appearance beneath, his lantern did not shed its beams again on the outside of the meeting-house.

"He's camping in the steeple!" cried the boys, in alarm. And so he was. Determined to stop the ringing of the bell, and afraid to leave his post of duty, the old man lay down on the floor of the loft, secure in the knowledge that no enemy could scale the roof without awakening him. The boys gathered in a knot below, examined the ground and confessed that, for once, they were circumvented.

It was growing toward morning. The east was pale with the first streaks of dawn. It had been a tiresome night. The great baseball match was coming off on that day. The bell had been rung. The Nine went to bed, and Fairport was quiet at last.

HOW PINKEY DELIVERED AN ADDRESS

by Captain Harold Hammond, U.S.A.

CHILDREN'S DAY at the church was drawing near, and each day Pinkey Perkins was becoming more and more impressed with a sense of his personal importance. He had been selected to deliver the "Welcome Address to the Fathers and Mothers" on that occasion. When he had been informed of the fact in the beginning, he had not looked on it with favor. Heretofore his oratorical efforts had been confined to the school-room, and he lacked the necessary confidence to attempt such a courageous feat. But his mother had been assured by the lady who consulted her on the subject, that the committee had carefully considered all the boys available for the honor, and had decided that of all these Pinkey was the one to make the address.

When the task had been turned over to him and he had set about practising, it was with a pardonable air of superiority that Pinkey, on occasions, when invited to join in some after-school game of "scrub" or take part in an attack on some newly discovered bumble-bees' nest, would reply, with a sort of bored air: "I wish I could, but I've got to go and rehearse."

True, there were others who had "to go and rehearse," but not in the way that Pinkey did. While they devoted their time to singing and went to practise collectively, he went alone to Miss Lyon, his Sunday-school teacher. That lady, being a teacher of elocution, had taken the task of drilling Pinkey in the most effective delivery for his first public oration.

"Humph! You needn't feel so smart," retorted Bunny Morris one day when Pinkey had referred rather loftily to "my address"; "you're not the only one who has to practise."

It happened that Bunny was one of eight who were to sing in chorus on Children's Day, and, although he would not admit it, the fact that Pinkey had been selected to make the "Welcome Address" rankled in Bunny's bosom.

When Bunny had made this stinging remark, Pinkey merely replied in his condescending way: "I don't 'practise.' I rehearse."

Pinkey had really entered on his work with a will, and a week before the eventful Sunday he had committed the whole of his address to memory and could recite it perfectly.

This statement, however, must be slightly modified. Sometimes, in rehearsing, he would have difficulty with certain portions of it, and that difficulty came about in this way:

Once in two weeks Miss Vance, Pinkey's school-teacher, required one half of her pupils to "recite a piece," either prose or poetry. For Pinkey's part in one of these bi-weekly punishments, as they were looked upon by the pupils, she had assigned him "The Supposed Speech of John Adams." Pinkey had surprised her by acquitting himself with credit on the occasion, for he had spent hours and days of careful preparation on it—"just to make her think it was easy," as he expressed it.

For some time, Red Feather, as she was known among her pupils, had not made Pinkey's school-life a bed or roses. Since one memorable Monday morning, when she had found four able-bodied mice secreted in her desk, she had always felt certain that he was responsible for their presence. From that day, the examples hardest to work, the States hardest to bound, and the words hardest to parse, according to Pinkey's standard, had fallen to his lot. It was to this "partiality" that Pinkey attributed his assignment of the "Supposed Speech."

Now, the author of the "Welcome Address," when in search of suitable material for that literary effort, had evidently used as a reference work "Great Speeches of Great Men," wherein was printed "The Supposed Speech of John Adams." Owing to this fact, several portions of the "Supposed Speech," either word for word or slightly modified, had found their way into the "Address." Oratorical flights were scattered all through it, such as: "Let not those beneath these vaulted roofs, within these hallowed walls, upon this memorable occasion, forget the incontestable vital truth that it is the young blood, the young mind, that we look to for our support," and so forth—sentiments more appropriate to John Adams's speech than to a Children's Day address.

In rehearsing, Pinkey found it hard not to confuse the two orations. In fact, neither was to him much more than a series of high-sounding phrases, intended more to impress the ear than to enlighten the mind. This is why it is necessary to modify the statement that Pinkey knew his address perfectly a week before the date appointed for its delivery.

As a reward for his diligence, Pinkey's mother promised him what had long been his heart's desire—a pair of patent-leather shoes that laced up the front and had sharp-pointed toes incased in fancy-edged tips.

Besides, since his unfortunate experience on the way home from Red Feather's party, he felt that he had been continually losing ground with his Affinity, and he hoped that the possession of a pair of patent-leather shoes might turn her in his favor.

Eddie Lewis, his arch-rival for her affections, had been paying her marked attention of late, and to Pinkey it seemed that she regarded these attentions as more or less acceptable.

Pinkey felt that the important moment when his Affinity must choose once and for all between him and Eddie would be when he should appear on the rostrum and, by his manly bearing and glowing oratory, win everlasting approval or disapproval. Consequently, he set great store by the promised shoes, which he felt would be not a small factor in making his appearance all that could be desired and thereby serve as an aid in fanning back to life the waning affections of his Affinity.

Saturday evening came at last, and, to Pinkey's delight, he was allowed to go down-town with his father and try on the coveted shoes, and to carry them home. He insisted on putting them on again when he got home, just to show his mother how well they fitted him and how far superior they were to anything he or any of the boys had ever had before, and how high the heels were and how bright and shiny the toes. And Pinkey was doubly proud of them on account of the squeak that accompanied each step. Before he went to bed, he carefully wrapped them up again and replaced them in their box, in order that no speck of dust might get on them and mar the luster that he depended on to melt the heart of his Affinity.

As he lay in bed that night, reciting his address over and over, and making his gestures in the darkness, he pictured the envy of the others as they saw him in his new shoes mount the platform to declaim his welcome. He had said nothing to any-one about the shoes his mother had prom-ised him,—not even to Bunny,—and he looked forward to the envy they would arouse among his less fortunate compan-ions.

When Pinkey awoke next morning, it was raining; but no rain could dampen his

spirits on such an occasion as this. He wore his ordinary "Sunday shoes" to Sun-day-school that morning, desiring not to show his patent-leathers until the time came for his address.

On account of the rain and mud, Mrs. Perkins suggested that it might be better not to wear the new shoes to the exercises; but Pinkey could not think of such a blow to his plans, and his mother had not the heart to wound his pride by insisting on her suggestion, and, besides, she feared he might not do so well with his speech if he were plunged into disappointment after all his anticipations.

"Pinkey," said his mother, after putting

the last finishing touches to his toilet, "since you *must* wear your new shoes in all this rain and mud, I want you to put on these high overshoes of mine, to keep your shoes clean."

To this compromise Pinkey reluctantly assented, but later found his action to be a wise one, as he encountered the muddy crossings on the way to church, against which his own rubbers would have been but little protection.

Pinkey's heart swelled with pride as he strutted along between his father and mother on the way to the church. But as he saw the people entering the building, several of whom spoke encouraging words to him about his forthcoming address, he began to feel a little shaky and noticed his heart beating faster than he liked. He kept trying to swallow a lump of suppressed ex-citement that would go neither up nor down.

If Pinkey gave these symptoms more than a passing thought, he attributed them to his inward exultation and not to any manifestation of stage-fright—a malady of which, up to that time, he had never known the existence.

Pinkey left his parents at their pew and marched on up the carpeted aisle, looking neither to right nor left. He mounted the rostrum and took his seat on one of the uncomfortable, high-backed, hair-cloth chairs which, since time immemorial, had occupied space at either end of the equally uncomfortable, though not so high-backed, hair-cloth sofa on the platform. The top of the seat was rounded in form, and Pinkey found it hard to retain his position and his composure at the same time.

As the time drew near for the exercises to begin, Pinkey became more and more nervous. The church became full to over-flowing, despite the bad weather, and, look where he would, Pinkey found hundreds of eyes gazing at him. He envied those in the chorus, because they each had seven others to assist in the singing, but he must get up and do his part all alone.

Presently the minister appeared and attempted to put the children at their ease by shaking hands with each one and uttering a few words of encouragement.

The members of the chorus were seated on a long bench on one side of the rostrum, and were partly hidden by the banks of flowers, while Pinkey sat alone on the other side, out in full view of the congregation, where he could get only an occasional, uncertain view of the others. His Affinity was there, but he could not muster up the courage to look at her.

He tried to look unconcerned, but he knew the utter failure he was making. Once he saw Putty Black grin and whisper something behind his hand to the girl next to him, and then they both looked at Pinkey and tittered.

By and by the last bell stopped ringing and the exercises began. By the time the chorus had sung the "Welcome Carol," and the minister had made the opening prayer, Pinkey had partly regained his composure. But the minister's reference to the "bright young faces" around him, and the pleasure he felt and that he was sure every member of the congregation must feel "on such an occasion," made the pitapat of Pinkey's heart seem to him loud enough to drown all other sounds.

After a few other appropriate remarks, during which Pinkey's discomfort became more and more marked, the minister announced his "pleasure in presenting to the congregation the orator of the day," who would welcome the fathers and mothers on this joyous occasion—"Master Pinkerton Perkins."

Pinkey slid from his perch on the haircloth chair as the minister seated himself on the mate to it at the other end of the sofa.

With shaking knees, he walked to the front. When he stopped, his legs trembled so violently that he felt sure every one in the congregation must notice his quaking knees.

He could distinguish nothing. All before him was an indistinct blur. Beyond, at the rear of the auditorium, he could make out a hazy, arched opening. That, he knew, was the door. He looked for his mother, but his eyes would focus on nothing, and the intense stillness that pervaded the whole room only added to the suffering he was undergoing.

Then he began. Automatically the words came, but his voice sounded hollow and strange. His throat was parched, and it was with difficulty that he could get his breath. The roaring in his ears made his voice sound as though it came from far in the distance. The perspiration stood in beads on his forehead, and he felt hot and cold by turns. Still on he went, though it seemed that each word must be his last.

About midway of his speech, in order to allow the full import of his words to awe his hearers, Pinkey had been taught to strike an attitude and pause for effect. Reaching that point, he paused, right hand uplifted, left foot advanced. As he put his foot forward, a nauseating wave of sudden mortification swept over him. *Now* he knew why Putty Black had whispered to the girl next to him. *Now* he knew why they had both tittered as they looked at him. Gradually he bent his head and looked down until his gaze met his feet. The sight that greeted his eyes sickened him.

He had forgotten to take off his mother's overshoes!

The shock of this realization, combined with his stage-fright, rendered Pinkey utterly helpless. He stood as one petrified, speechless, before the assembled throng. He stared glassily at his overshoes; they seemed fascinating in their hideousness. A stir in the congregation awakened him to the fact that he had been standing mute, he knew not how long.

He tried to continue his address, but the words had taken wings. Miss Lyon attempted to prompt him, but all her efforts proved futile. He could not take up the broken thread.

Yet he dare not quit the platform with his speech unfinished and go down to ignominious failure before the eyes of the congregation, of his father, his mother, and, above all, his Affinity.

Then came a brilliant thought. "The Supposed Speech of John Adams"! Since the two speeches were so similar, why would not that do instead of the one he could not remember?

Without further delay, he began: "Sink or swim! live or die! survive or perish! I give *my* hand and *my* heart to this vote! It is true that, in the beginning, we aimed not at Independence; but there's a Divinity that shapes our ends—" and so on, without hesitation, clear to the end.

Delivering his school-room speech, he regained his school-room composure, and as he spoke he gathered courage. His voice became natural and his lost faculties, one by one, returned. His knees became firm again, and his heart became normal. What had been but a hazy blur became a sea of faces, and all within the church began to take definite form.

As Pinkey concluded, he made a sweeping bow, once more possessed of all his customary assurance.

Spontaneously the congregation burst into applause, such as the old walls had never heard on any occasion. Every one had seen his overshoes, and had been moved to sympathy when they saw his embarrassment on discovering them. That he had left out part of his address, which he had plainly forgotten, and delivered another entirely out of keeping with his subject and the occasion, only increased their admiration for his determination and grit.

With his head erect, Pinkey faced about and returned to his chair. As he did so he gave a look of triumph at his Affinity, and received in return a look that told him, plainer than words, that, overshoes or no overshoes, he had won her unqualified approval.

When he reached his place, he knelt down, calmly removed the overshoes, and, with his heart swelling with pride at the ringing applause, resumed his seat on the hair-cloth chair.

ANN MARY—HER TWO THANKSGIVINGS

by Mary E. Wilkins

"Grandma."

"What is it, child?"

"You goin' to put that cup cake into the pan to bake it now, Grandma?"

"Yes; I guess so. It's beat 'bout enough."

"You ain't put in a mite of nutmeg, Grandma."

The grandmother turned around to Ann Mary. "Don't you be quite so anxious," said she with sarcastic emphasis. "I allers put the nutmeg in cup-cake the very last thing. I ruther guess I shouldn't have put this cake into the oven without nutmeg!"

The old woman beat fiercely on the cake. She used her hand instead of a spoon, and she held the yellow mixing-bowl poised on her hip under her arm. She was stout and rosy-faced. She had crinkly white hair, and she always wore a string of gold beads around her creasy neck. She never took off the gold beads except to put them under her pillow at night, she was so afraid of their being stolen. Old Mrs. Little had always been nervous about thieves, although none had ever troubled her.

"You may go into the pantry, an' bring out the nutmeg now, Ann Mary," said she presently, with dignity.

Ann Mary soberly slipped down from her chair and went. She realized that she had made a mistake. It was quite an understood thing for Ann Mary to have an eye upon her grandmother while she was cooking, to be sure that she put in everything that she should, and nothing that she should not, for the old woman was absent-minded. But it had to be managed with great delicacy, and the corrections had to be quite irrefutable, or Ann Mary was reprimanded for her pains.

When Ann Mary had deposited the nutmeg-box and the grater at her grandmother's elbow, she took up her station again. She sat at a corner of the table in one of the high kitchen-chairs. Her feet could not touch the floor, and they dangled uneasily in their stout leather shoes, but she never rested them on the chair round, nor even swung them by way of solace. Ann Mary's grandmother did not like to have her chair rounds all marked up by shoes, and swinging feet disturbed her while she was cooking. Ann Mary sat up, grave and straight. She was a delicate, slender little girl, but she never stooped. She had an odd resemblance to her grandmother; a resemblance more of manner than of feature. She held back her narrow shoulders in the same determined way in which the old woman held her broad ones; she walked as she did, and spoke as she did.

Mrs. Little was very proud of Ann Mary Evans; Ann Mary was her only daughter's child, and had lived with her grandmother ever since she was a baby. The child could

254

not remember either her father or mother, she was so little when they died.

Ann Mary was delicate, so she did not go to the village to the public school. Miss Loretta Adams, a young lady who lived in the neighborhood, gave her lessons. Loretta had graduated in a beautiful white muslin dress at the high-school over in the village, and Ann Mary had a great respect and admiration for her. Loretta had a parlor-organ and could play on it, and she was going to give Ann Mary lessons after Thanksgiving. Just now there was a vacation. Loretta had gone to Boston to spend two weeks with her cousin.

Ann Mary was all in brown, a brown calico dress and a brown calico, long-sleeved apron; and her brown hair was braided in two tight little tails that were tied with some old brown bonnet-strings of Mrs. Little's, and flared out stiffly behind the ears. Once, when Ann Mary was at her house, Loretta Adams had taken it upon herself to comb out the tight braids and set the hair flowing in a fluffy mass over the shoulders; but when Ann Mary came home her grandmother was properly indignant. She seized her and re-braided the tails with stout and painful jerks. "I ain't goin' to have Loretty Adams meddlin' with your hair," said she, "an' she can jest understand it. If she wants to have her own hair all in a frowzle, an' look like a wild Injun, she can; you sha'n't!"

And Ann Mary, standing before her grandmother with head meekly bent and watery eyes, decided that she would have to tell Loretta that she mustn't touch the braids, if she proposed it again.

That morning, while Mrs. Little was making the pies and the cake and the pudding, Ann Mary was sitting idle, for her part of the Thanksgiving cooking was done. She had worked so fast, the day before and early that morning, that she had the raisins all picked over and seeded, and the apples pared and sliced; and that was about all that her grandmother thought she could do. Ann Mary herself was of a different opinion; she was twelve years old, if she *was* small for her age, and she considered herself quite capable of making pies and cup-cake.

However, it was something to sit there at the table and have that covert sense of superintending her grandmother; and to be reasonably sure that some of the food would have a strange flavor were it not for her vigilance.

Mrs. Little's mince-pies had all been baked the Saturday before; to-day, as she said, she was "making apple and squash." While the apple-pies were in progress, Ann Mary watched her narrowly. Her small folded hands twitched and her little neck seemed to elongate above her apron; but she waited until her grandmother took up an upper crust, and was just about to lay it over a pie. Then she spoke up suddenly. Her voice had a timid yet assertive chirp like a bird's.

"Grandma!"

"Well, what is it, child?"

"You goin' to put that crust on that pie now, Grandma?"

Mrs. Little stood uneasily reflective. She eyed the pie sharply. "Yes, I be. Why?" she returned in a doubtful yet defiant manner.

"You haven't put one bit of sugar in."

"For the land sakes!" Mrs. Little did not take correction of this kind happily, but when she was made to fairly acknowledge the need of it, she showed no resentment. She laid the upper crust back on the board and sweetened the pie. Ann Mary watched her gravely, but she was inwardly complacent. After she had rescued the pudding from being baked without the plums, and it was nearly dinner-time, her grandfather came home. He had been over to the village to buy the Thanksgiving turkey. Ann Mary looked out with delight when he drove past the windows on his way to the barn.

"Grandpa's got home," said she.

It was snowing quite hard, and she saw the old man and the steadily tramping white horse and the tilting wagon through a thick mist of falling snowflakes.

Before Mr. Little came into the kitchen, his wife warned him to be sure to wipe all the snow from his feet, and not to track in any, so he stamped vigorously out in the shed. Then he entered with an air of pride. "There!" said he, "what do ye think of that for a turkey?" Mr. Little was generally slow and gentle in his ways, but today he was quite excited over the turkey. He held it up with considerable difficulty. He was a small old man, and the cords on his lean hands knotted. "It weighs a good fifteen pound'," said he, "an' there wasn't a better one in the store. Adkins didn't have a very big lot on hand."

"I should think that was queer, the day before Thanksgivin'," said Mrs. Little. She was examining the turkey critically. "I guess it'll do," she declared finally. That was her highest expression of approbation. "Well, I rayther thought you'd think so," rejoined the old man, beaming. "I guess it's about as good a one as can be got,— they said 'twas, down there. Sam White he was in there, and he said 'twas; he said I was goin' to get it in pretty good season for Thanksgivin', he thought."

"I don't think it's such very extra season, the day before Thanksgivin'," said Mrs. Little.

"Well, I don't think 'twas, nuther. I didn't see jest what Sam meant by it."

Ann Mary was dumb with admiration. When the turkey was laid on the broad shelf in the pantry, she went and gazed upon it. In the afternoon there was great enjoyment seeing it stuffed and made ready for the oven. Indeed, this day was

throughout one of great enjoyment, being full of the very aroma of festivity and good cheer and gala times, and even sweeter than the occasion which it preceded. Ann Mary had only one damper all day, and that was the non-arrival of a letter. Mrs. Little had invited her son and his family to spend Thanksgiving, but now they probably were not coming, since not a word in reply had been received. When Mr. Little said there was no letter in the post-office, Ann Mary's face fell. "Oh, dear," said she, "don't you suppose Lucy will come, Grandma?"

"No," replied her grandmother, "I don't. Edward never did such a thing as not to send me word when he was comin', in his life, nor Maria neither. I ain't no idee they'll come."

"Oh, dear!" said Ann Mary again.

"Well, you'll have to make up your mind to it," returned her grandmother; she was sore over her own disappointment, and so was irascible toward Ann Mary's. "It's no worse for you than for the rest of us. I guess you can keep one Thanksgivin' without Lucy."

For a while it almost seemed to Ann Mary that she could not. Lucy was her only cousin. She loved Lucy dearly, and she was lonesome for another little girl; nobody knew how she had counted upon seeing her cousin. Ann Mary herself had a forlorn hope that Lucy still might come, even if Uncle Edward *was* always so particular about sending word and no word had been received. On Thanksgiving morning she kept running to the window, and looking down the road. But when the stage from the village came, it passed right by the house without slackening its speed.

Then there was no hope left at all.

"You might jest as well be easy," said her grandmother. "I guess you can have a good Thanksgivin' if Lucy *ain't* here. This evenin' you can ask Loretty to come over a little while, if you want to, an' you can make some nut-candy."

"Loretta ain't at home."

"She'll come home for Thanksgivin', I guess. It ain't very likely she's stayed away over that. When I get the dinner ready to take up, you can carry a plateful down to Sarah Bean's, an' that'll be somethin' for you to do, too. I guess you can manage."

Thanksgiving day was a very pleasant day, although there was considerable snow on the ground, for it had snowed all the day before. Mr. Little and Ann Mary did not go to church as usual, on that account.

The old man did not like to drive to the village before the roads were beaten out. Mrs. Little lamented not a little over it. It was the custom for her husband and granddaughter to attend church Thanksgiving morning, while she stayed at home and cooked the dinner. "It does seem dreadful heathenish for nobody to go to meetin' Thanksgivin' day," said she; "an' we ain't even heard the proclamation read, neither. It rained so hard last Sabbath that we couldn't go."

The season was unusually wintry and severe, and lately the family had been prevented from church-going. It was two Sundays since any of the family had gone. The village was three miles away, and the road was rough. Mr. Little was too old to drive over it in very bad weather.

When Ann Mary went to carry the plate of Thanksgiving dinner to Sarah Bean, she wore a pair of her grandfather's blue woolen socks drawn over her shoes to keep out the snow. The snow was rather deep for easy walking, but she did not mind that. She carried the dinner with great care; there was a large plate well filled, and a tin dish was turned over it to keep it warm. Sarah Bean was an old woman who lived alone. Her house was about a quarter of a mile from the Littles'.

When Ann Mary reached the house, she found the old woman making a cup of tea. There did not seem to be much of anything but tea and bread and butter for her dinner. She was very deaf and infirm, all her joints shook when she tried to use them, and her voice quavered when she talked. She took the plate, and her hands trembled so that the tin dish played on the plate like a clapper. "Why," said she, overjoyed, "this looks just like Thanksgiving day, tell your Grandma!"

"Why it *is* Thanksgiving day," declared Ann Mary, with some wonder.

"What?" asked Sarah Bean.

"It is Thanksgiving day, you know." But it was of no use, the old woman could not hear a word. Ann Mary's voice was too low.

Ann Mary could not walk very fast on account of the snow. She was absent some three-quarters of an hour; her grandmother had told her that dinner would be all on the table when she returned. She was enjoying the nice things in anticipation all the way; when she came near the house, she could smell roasted turkey, and there was also a sweet spicy odor in the air.

She noticed with surprise that a sleigh had been in the yard. "I wonder who's come," she said to herself. She thought of Lucy, and whether they *could* have driven over from the village. She ran in. "Why, who's come?" she cried out.

Her voice sounded like a shout in her own ears; it seemed to awaken echoes. She fairly startled herself, for there was no one in the room. There was absolute quiet through all the house. There was even no sizzling from the kettles on the stove, for everything had been dished up. The vegetables, all salted and peppered and buttered, were on the table—but the turkey was not there. In the great vacant place where the turkey should have been was a piece of white paper. Ann Mary spied it in a moment. She caught it up and looked at it. It was a note from her grandmother:

We have had word that Aunt Betsey has had a bad turn. Lizz wants us to come. The dinner is all ready for you. If we ain't home to-night, you can get Loretty to stay with you. Be a good girl.
GRANDMA

Derby, and Derby was fourteeen miles away. It seemed a long distance to Ann Mary, and she felt sure that her grandparents could not come home that night. She looked around the empty room, and sighed. After a while she sat down and pulled off the snowy socks; she thought she might as well eat her dinner, although she did not feel so hungry as she had expected. Everything was on the table but the turkey and plum-pudding. Ann Mary

"When Ann Mary reached the house, she found the old woman making a cup of tea"

Ann Mary read the note and stood reflecting, her mouth drooping at the corners. Aunt Betsey was Mrs. Little's sister; Lizz was her daughter who lived with her and took care of her. They lived in

supposed these were in the oven keeping warm; the door was ajar. But, when she looked, they were not there. She went into the pantry; they were not there either. It was very strange; there was the dripping-pan in which the turkey had been baked, on the back of the stove, with some gravy in it; and there was the empty pudding-dish on the hearth.

"What has Grandma done with the turkey and the plum-pudding?" said Ann Mary aloud.

She looked again in the pantry; then she went down cellar—there seemed to be so few places in the house in which it was reasonable to search for a turkey and a plum-pudding!

Finally she gave it up, and sat down to dinner. There was plenty of squash, and potatoes, and turnips, and onions, and beets, and cranberry-sauce, and pies; but it was no Thanksgiving dinner without turkey and plum-pudding. It was like a great flourish of accompaniment without any song.

Ann Mary did as well as she could; she put some turkey-gravy on her potato and filled up her plate with vegetables; but she did not enjoy the dinner. She felt more and more lonely, too. She resolved that after she had washed up the dinner dishes, and changed her dress, she would go over to Loretta Adams's. It was quite a piece of work, washing the dinner dishes, there were so many pans and kettles; it was the middle of the afternoon when she finished. Then Ann Mary put on her best plaid dress, and tied her best red ribbons on her braids, and it was four o'clock before she started for Loretta's.

Loretta lived in a white cottage about half a mile away toward the village. The front yard had many bushes in it, and the front path was bordered with box; the bushes were now mounds of snow, and the box was indicated by two snowy ridges.

The house had a shut-up look; the sitting-room curtains were down. Ann Mary went around to the side door; but it was locked. Then she went up the front walk between the snowy ridges of box, and tried the front door; that also was locked. The Adamses had gone away. Ann Mary did not know what to do. The tears stood in her eyes, and she choked a little. She went back and forth between the two doors, and shook and pounded; she peeked around the corner of the curtain into the sitting-room. She could see Loretta's organ, with the music book, and all the familiar furniture, but the room wore an utterly deserted air.

Finally, Ann Mary sat down on the front doorstep, after she had brushed off the snow a little. She had made up her mind to wait a little while, and see if the folks would not come home. She had on her red hood, and her grandmother's old plaid shawl. She pulled the shawl tightly around her, and muffled her face in it; it was extremely cold weather for sitting on a doorstep. Just across the road was a low clump of birches; through and above the birches the sky showed red and clear where the sun was setting. Everything looked cold and bare and desolate to the little girl who was trying to keep Thanksgiving. Suddenly she heard a little cry, and Loretta's white cat came around the corner of the house.

"Kitty, Kitty, Kitty," called Ann Mary. She was very fond of Loretta's cat; she had none of her own.

The cat came close and brushed around Ann Mary. So she took it up in her lap, and wrapped the shawl around it, and felt a little comforted.

She sat there on the doorstep and held the cat, until it was quite dusky, and she was very stiff with the cold. Then she put down the cat, and prepared to go home. But she had not gone far along the road when she found out that the cat was following her. The little white creature floundered through the snow at her heels, and mewed constantly. Sometimes it darted ahead and waited until she came up, but it did not seem willing to be carried in her arms.

When Ann Mary reached her own house the lonesome look of it sent a chill all over her; she was afraid to go in. She made up her mind to go down to Sarah Bean's and ask whether she could not stay all night there.

So she kept on, and Loretta's white cat still followed her. There was no light in Sarah Bean's house. Ann Mary knocked and pounded, but it was of no use; the old woman had gone to bed, and she could not make her hear.

Ann Mary turned about and went home; the tears were running down her cold red cheeks. The cat mewed louder than ever. When she got home she took the cat up and carried it into the house. She determined to keep it for company, anyway. She was sure, now, that she would have to stay alone all night; the Adamses and Sarah Bean were the only neighbors, and it was so late now that she had no hope of her grandparents' return. Ann Mary was timid and nervous, but she had a vein of philosophy, and she generally grasped the situation with all the strength she had, when she became convinced that she must. She had laid her plans while walking home through the keen winter air, even as the tears were streaming over her cheeks, and she proceeded to carry them into execution. She gave Loretta's cat its supper, and she ate a piece of mince-pie herself; then she fixed the kitchen and the sitting-room fires, and locked up the house very thoroughly. Next, she took the cat and the lamp and went into the dark-bedroom, and locked the door; then she and the cat were as safe as she knew how to make them. The dark-bedroom was in the very middle of the house, the center of a nest of rooms. It was small and square, had no windows, and only one

door. It was a sort of fastness. Ann Mary made up her mind that she would not undress herself, and that she would keep the lamp burning all night. She climbed into the big yellow-posted bedstead, and the cat cuddled up to her and purred.

Ann Mary lay in bed and stared at the white satin scrolls on the wall-paper, and listened for noises. She heard a great many, but they were all mysterious and indefinable, till about ten o'clock. Then she sat straight up in bed and her heart beat fast. She certainly heard sleigh-bells; the sound penetrated even to the dark-bedroom. Then came a jarring pounding on the side door. Ann Mary got up, unfastened the bedroom door, took the lamp, and stepped out into the sitting-room. The pounding came again. "Ann Mary, Ann Mary!" cried a voice. It was her grandmother's.

"I'm comin', I'm comin', Grandma!" shouted Ann Mary. She had never felt so happy in her life. She pushed back the bolt of the side door with trembling haste. There stood her grandmother all muffled up, with a shawl over her head; and out in the yard were her grandfather and another man, and a horse and sleigh. The men were turning the sleigh around.

"Put the lamp in the window, Ann Mary," called Mr. Little, and Ann Mary obeyed. Her grandmother sank into a chair. "I'm jest about tuckered out," she groaned. "If I don't ketch my death with this day's work, I'm lucky. There ain't any more feelin' in my feet than as if they was lumps of stone."

Ann Mary stood at her grandmother's elbow, and her face was all beaming. "I thought you weren't coming," said she.

"Well, I shouldn't have come a step to-night, if it hadn't been for you—and the cow," said her grandmother in an indignant voice. "I was kind of uneasy about you, an' we knew the cow wouldn't be milked unless you got Mr. Adams to come over."

"Was Aunt Betsey very sick?" inquired Ann Mary.

Her grandmother gave her head a toss. "Sick! No, there wa'n't a thing the matter with her, except she ate some sassage-meat, an' had a little faint turn. Lizz was scairt to death, the way she always is. She didn't act as if she knew whether her head was on, all the time we were there. She didn't act as if she knew 'twas Thanksgivin' day; an' she didn't have no turkey that I could see. Aunt Betsey bein' took sick seemed to put everythin' out of her head. I never saw such a nervous thing as she is. I was all out of patience when I got there. Betsey didn't seem to be very bad off, an' there we'd hurried enough to break our necks. We didn't dare to drive around to Sarah Bean's to let you know about it, for we was afraid we'd miss the train. We jest got in with the man that brought the word, an' he driv as fast as he could over to the village, an' then we lost the train, an' had to sit there in the depot two mortal hours. An' now we've come fourteen mile' in an open sleigh. The man that lives next door to Betsey said he'd bring us home, an' I thought we'd better come. He's goin' over to the village to-night; he's got folks there. I told him he'd a good deal better stay here, but he won't. He's as deaf as an adder, an' you can't make him hear anythin', anyway. We ain't spoke a word all the way home. Where's Loretty? She came over to stay with you, didn't she?"

Ann Mary explained that Loretta was not at home.

"That's queer, seems to me. Thanksgivin' day," said her grandmother. "Massy sakes, what cat's that? She came out of the settin'-room!"

Ann Mary explained about Loretta's

cat. Then she burst forth with the question that had been uppermost in her mind ever since her grandmother came in. "Grandma," said she, "what did you do with the turkey and the plum-pudding?"

"What?"

"What did you do with the turkey and the plum-pudding?"

"The turkey an' the plum-puddin'?"

"Yes; I couldn't find 'em anywhere."

Mrs. Little, who had removed her wraps, and was crouching over the kitchen-stove, with her feet in the oven, looked at Ann Mary with a dazed expression.

"I dunno what you mean, child," said she.

Mr. Little had helped the man with the sleigh to start, and had now come in. He was pulling off his boots.

"Don't you remember, Mother," said he, "how you run back in the house, an' said you was goin' to set that turkey an' plum-pudding away, for you was afraid to leave 'em settin' right out in plain sight on the table, for fear that somebody might come in?"

"Yes; I do remember," said Mrs. Little. "I thought they looked 'most too temptin'. I set 'em in the pantry. I thought Ann Mary could get 'em when she came in."

"They ain't in the pantry," said Ann Mary.

Her grandmother arose and went into the pantry with a masterful air. "Ain't in the pantry?" she repeated. "I don't s'pose you more 'n gave one look."

Ann Mary followed her grandmother. She fairly expected to see the turkey and the pudding before her eyes on the shelf and to admit that she had been mistaken. Mr. Little also followed, and they all stood in the pantry and looked about.

"I guess they ain't here, Mother," said Mr. Little. "Can't you think where you set 'em?"

The old woman took up the lamp and

stepped out of the pantry with dignity. "I've set 'em somewhere," said she in a curt voice, "an' I'll find 'em in the mornin'. You don't want any turkey or plum-puddin' to-night, neither of you!"

But Mrs. Little did not find the turkey and the plum-pudding in the morning. Some days went by, and their whereabouts as much a mystery as ever. Mrs. Little could not remember where she had put them; but it had been in some secure hiding-place, since her own wit which had placed them there could not find it out. She was so mortified and worried over it, that she was nearly ill. She tried to propound the theory, and believe in it herself, that she had really set the turkey and the pudding in the pantry, and that they had been stolen; but she was too honest. "I've heerd of folks puttin' things in such safe places that they couldn't find 'em, before now," said she; "but I never heerd of losin' a turkey an' a plum-puddin' that way. I dunno but I'm losin' what little wits I ever did have." She went about with a humble and resentful air. She promised Ann Mary that she would cook another turkey and pudding the first of the week, if the missing ones were not found.

Sunday came and they were not discovered. It was a pleasant day, and the Littles went to the village to church. Ann Mary looked over across the church after they were seated and saw Loretta, with the pretty brown frizzes over her forehead, sitting between her father and mother, and she wondered when Loretta had come home.

The choir sang and the minister prayed. Suddenly Ann Mary saw him, standing there in the pulpit, unfold a paper. Then *the minister began to read the Thanksgiving Proclamation.* Ann Mary cast one scared glance at her grandmother, who returned it with one of inexpressible dignity and severity.

As soon as meeting was done, her grandmother clutched her by the arm. "Don't you say a word about it to anybody," she whispered. "You mind!"

When they were in the sleigh going home, she charged her husband. "You mind, you keep still, Father," said she. "It'll be town-talk if you don't."

The old man chuckled. "Don't you know, I said once that I hed kind of an idee that Thanksgivin' weren't quite so early, and you shut me up, Mother," he remarked. He looked good-naturedly malicious.

"Well, I dunno as it's anything so very queer," said Mrs. Little. "It comes a whole week later than it did last year, and I s'posed we'd missed hearin' the proclamation."

The next day a letter arrived saying that Lucy and her father and mother were coming to spend Thanksgiving. "I feel jest about beat," Mrs. Little said when she read the letter.

Really, she did feel about at her wit's end. The turkey and pudding were not yet found, and she had made up her mind that she would not dare wait much longer before providing more. She knew that another turkey must be procured, at all events. However, she waited until the last minute Wednesday afternoon, then she went to work mixing a pudding. Mr. Little had gone to the store for the turkey. "Sam White was over there, an' he said he thought we was goin' right into turkeys this year," he reported when he got home.

That night the guests arrived. Thanksgiving morning, Lucy, and Ann Mary, and their grandfather, and Lucy's father and mother, were all going to meeting. Mrs. Little was to stay at home and cook the dinner.

Thanksgiving morning, Mr. Little made a fire in the best-parlor air-tight stove, and just before they started for meeting, Lucy and Ann Mary were in the room. Lucy, in the big rocking-chair that was opposite the sofa, was rocking to and fro and talking. Ann Mary sat near the window. Each of the little girls had on her coat and hat.

Suddenly Lucy stopped rocking and looked intently over toward the sofa.

"What you lookin' at, Lucy?" asked Ann Mary, curiously.

Lucy still looked. "Why—I was wondering what was under that sofa," said she slowly. Then she turned to Ann Mary, and her face was quite pale and startled— she had heard the turkey and pudding story. "Oh, Ann Mary, it does look like —oh——"

Both little girls rushed to the sofa, and threw themselves on the floor. "Oh, oh, oh!" they shrieked. "Grandma—Mother! Come quick, come quick!"

When the others came in, there sat Ann Mary and Lucy on the floor, and between them were the turkey and the plum-pud-ding, each carefully covered with a snow-white napkin.

Mrs. Little was quite pale and trembling. "I remember now," said she faintly, "I run in here with 'em."

She was so overcome that the others tried to take it quietly and not to laugh much. But every little while, after Lucy and Ann Mary were seated in church, they would look at each other and have to put their handkerchiefs to their faces. However, Ann Mary tried hard to listen to the sermon, and to behave well. In the depths of her childish heart she felt grateful and happy. There, by her side, sat her dear Lucy, whose sweet little face peeped out from a furry winter hat. Just across the aisle was Loretta, who was coming in the evening, and then they would pop corn and make nut-candy. At home there was the beautiful new turkey and unlimited pudding and good cheer, and all disappointment and mystery were done away with.

Ann Mary felt as if all her troubles would be followed by thanksgivings.

THE BILGED MIDSHIPMAN

by Thomas A. Janvier

I USED to know a Bilged Midshipman. He was rather a nice sort of fellow, and we got along together very well. But we should have liked him much better, at first, I think, if he had not been so dismal a character. I never did know any boy (except a boy whom we named the "Sea-Calf," because he was all the time blubbering) who seemed to be so thoroughly miserable. Why, I've known that Bilged Midshipman to refuse to join a swimming party of five as good fellows as ever walked—I was one of them, myself—and to spend all the afternoon of a half-holiday in moping.

None of us knew much about him except that he had been a midshipman and had been bilged. This much he said himself, when Clarence Detwiler, by virtue of seniority, asked him about himself on the first day that he came to the school. He didn't begin regularly, but in the middle of the term, and so he was something of a curiosity.

"Yes," he said sadly, "I was a midshipman at Annapolis, but I was bilged!" Then he turned away and looked as if he might take to crying—blinky about the eyes, you know.

Now, not one of us had the least idea of what "bilged" was, or how it felt to be in that condition. But as he seemed to take it hard we concluded that it must be an uncommonly bad thing to have, and we came to an understanding among ourselves not to bother him by talking about it. I think that he understood our good intentions and was grateful to us for trying to do the handsome thing by him. Anyhow, he certainly tried to make himself agreeable, in a cheerfully dismal sort of fashion; and sometimes he succeeded.

His first success was won by splicing the clothes-line. In the interest of Science, a lot of us had borrowed the clothes-line from the laundry and had begun a series of very interesting experiments on the Levitation of Solids. For want of better solids to work with, we were using ourselves—each one of us knew about how much he weighed—and we were levitating ourselves up into some remarkably fine chestnut-trees. In the midst of an interesting experiment—we had Pud Douglass up in the air—the clothes-line broke. It was a new line, but Pud was too much for it. Luckily, he was only about ten feet up, and the tumble didn't hurt him. But the clothes-line separated into two pieces; and what made it worse was that the break was just about in the middle.

We were in something of a dilemma. We knew that a knot in the middle of the new line would excite critical comment, and probably would lead to very unpleasant consequences. For, apart from the fact that we had obtained the line rather informally, the chestnut-trees were quite out-of-bounds. We felt low in our minds. Then we all went back to the school and

264

were as dismal as possible. However, we comforted ourselves a little by abusing Pud for being so inordinately fat.

Close by the wood-shed we fell in with the Bilged Midshipman. He was in his usual mournful mood; but we were mournful too, so we stopped to tell him of our tribulations.

"Pooh!" said the Bilged Midshipman, when we had told our tale of woe. "Is that all?"

We said that it was, and that we rather thought it was more than enough.

"Pooh!" said he again (he was a great fellow to say "Pooh!"). "Just you let me have the line and I'll splice it so its own mother won't know it's been broken!"

We were too much pleased to stop for argument with him over a clothes-line's having a mother, and we all sat down in a row behind the wood-shed, and little Billy Jenks pulled the line out from under his jacket. What Billy wished to do, was to go straight to the Doctor and tell him all about it and offer to pay for the clothes-line—but that always was Billy's way.

The Bilged Midshipman really seemed almost cheerful for once; and he went to work with a will. He made what he called a "long splice." It was a wonderful piece of work. He untwisted two strands of the rope for three or four feet, and then he "crutched them together," as he called it. Then he untwisted some more from one of the ends, and into the space where the strand had been he twisted a strand from the other. He did this both ways from the "crutch," and ended up by tucking all the ends snugly away. When he had cut the ends off smoothly and had rolled the rope under his foot, it would have taken a pretty good pair of eyes to see that it ever had been broken! It seemed almost a miracle to us, and only prudential reasons kept us from giving the Bilged Midshipman three cheers on the spot. But

we all shook hands with him and told him solemnly that we thought that he was "a brick." For a minute or two he seemed really pleased. Then he subsided suddenly and his countenance grew as dismal as Clarence Detwiler's on the day when he ate more green apples than were good for him.

"What's the use of it all?" he said, half to himself. "I'm bilged,—bilged!" Then he went sorrowfully away.

After that he often did bits of knotting and splicing for us, and seemed to find it rather comforting. But he always ended by going moping off, muttering to himself something about bilging. It was very mysterious.

We looked up "bilged" in the dictionary, and found that it was "nautical" and meant "having a fracture in the bilge." As applied to a midshipman, the "nautical" was good; but the rest wasn't. To cut things short, I may say that we all were completely puzzled. Finally, we concluded to have the matter settled definitely. It was growing too rasping to be borne. So we called a meeting of the school and elected Clarence Detwiler Chairman, and little Billy Jenks Secretary—not because there was anything in particular for a secretary to do, but because we wanted to make things pleasant for Billy. You see, Billy's father had just failed and he was naturally a little cut up about it.

When the meeting was fairly under way, the chairman appointed Pud Douglass and me a Committee of Two to bring in the Bilged Midshipman. As he was just around the corner of the wood-shed, waiting to be brought, this did not take long— and he could have been brought even sooner if "Clumsy" Skimples hadn't tumbled down from above among the rafters just as the procession was entering, and so spoiled the effect. But "Clumsy" was always tumbling down from somewhere or other,—he generally kept himself bumped black and blue,—so nobody minded it much.

Detwiler made a speech, in which he explained that we all were curious to know how a fellow who seemed to be all right could be bilged, if the dictionary gave the true meaning of the word; that we did not wish to press him too hard upon a delicate subject; but that, as we now cherished a very high esteem for him as a companion and as a—a boy, we should be very much obliged to him if he would explain this mysterious matter once and for all. Detwiler was a capital hand at speech-making, and this speech was even better than usual. When he concluded, we all clapped our hands, and then we looked at the Bilged Midshipman and waited for him to begin.

He blinked his eyes for a minute or two, in his queer, sorrowful way, and then he braced up and said he supposed he might as well tell about it, and have done with it;—we'd all been kind to him and we had a right to know.

"You see," said the Bilged Midshipman, "down at Annapolis 'bilged' is what they call it when a cadet fails to pass his examinations, or is sent adrift for misconduct. It's a sea term, and means that a barrel, or cask, is stove in and done for; a cadet is done for when the Academy throws him overboard, and so the sailors say that he is bilged. That's all;—I was bilged—terribly!" Then he hitched up his trousers in sailor fashion—he was as fond of this action as Dick Deadeye—and looked dismaler than ever.

"If you don't mind telling," said Clarence Detwiler, "the meeting would like very much to know what bilged you. Everybody in favor of his telling what bilged him, will please say 'aye.'" (Of course we all said "aye.") "The ayes have it, gentlemen."

"Well," said the Bilged Midshipman, in a most forlorn and solemn way, "it was a cat; a big, black tom-cat! Yes, I know it sounds queer, but it's true, all the same; that cat finished my naval career—bilged me! You see, it happened in this way: It was the beginning of my second year at the Academy, and my prospects were bright. I had passed the examinations and stood well up in my class, and the professors seemed to like me. But I couldn't get along comfortably with the Commandant of Cadets. He was a peppery sort of a man, a Commander in the service; and he had a way of snapping a fellow up short and setting him down hard, that made it uncomfortable to get along with him. And then he never would listen to what a fellow had to say. He was always talking about discipline. His pet speech was: 'The discipline of the service demands, my boy, that when I give an order you are to obey it, instantly and implicitly. Discipline and argument are utterly incompatible.' He'd say this over a dozen times a day: and so we always called him 'Old Discipline.'

"Well, I had a way of sliding into scrapes and Old Discipline had a way of catching me. At last things began to look squally. The Admiral—who was a trump—sent for me and gave me a good talking-to, just such a talking-to as my father gives me sometimes; and he made me see that it really wouldn't do for me to be careless, if I 'ever hoped to be an officer and a credit to the service,' as he put it. He was just as kind as he could be, but he wound up by telling me that I must steer a straight course or take the consequences; and, to give me a clear idea of what the consequences would be, he said that if I was reported to him again for misconduct during the term I certainly would be sent adrift from the Academy. I promised him with all my heart that I would turn over a new leaf then and there. And then the old gentleman, in his kind way, shook hands with me and said that he was sure I really meant to be steady, and would live to be as good an officer as ever trod a deck."

The Bilged Midshipman stopped for a minute or two and seemed very low in his mind. "It makes me feel dismal," he said presently, "when I think what the Admiral must think of me now. But it wasn't my fault that I was bilged—at least, not entirely.

"For a week or two after I was 'warned,' I was the best-behaved cadet in the Academy. 'Old Discipline' was on the lookout to catch me tripping, but I was on the lookout not to trip, and he couldn't. Two or three times he thought he had me, for the cadets were always playing tricks on him, but every time it turned out to be somebody else, and I was not in the wrong.

"But he did catch me at last, and that wretch of a black tom-cat was at the bottom of it. The cat was a good-for-nothing sort of a cat that used to drift about the Academy grounds by the kitchen. It was forever getting picked up by the cadets and put into places where a cat didn't belong—such as the professors' desks and the officers' hat-boxes.

"Well, one day it happened that the Commandant had to go down to the Norfolk Navy Yard for some stores, and a detail of cadets was told off to go with him. On the strength of my recent good conduct I was put in the detail; and I was glad enough to have the little cruise. Just as the tug was pushing off from the Academy wharf, 'Old Discipline' found that he had forgotten his valise—and as he was going to stay all night at Norfolk and go to a ball, and as the valise contained his dress-uniform, leaving it behind was not to be thought of. So he ordered the tug back to the wharf and, as I had the bad luck to be standing close by him, he directed me to jump ashore and run up to the Academy and get it. It was in his room, he said, all ready. Now this was orderly-service, and he had no business to send me on it. But I did not dare to hesitate; and I feared, too, that if I made the least objection, he would order me ashore and go off without me. I didn't like to give in when I knew I was right, but neither did I like to lose the cruise; so away I went as fast as my legs would carry me.

"I found the valise all right, seized it and bolted back to the tug—but I hadn't taken a dozen steps before I thought I felt something alive, squirming around inside the valise. Then it flashed upon me, all in a minute, that one of the fellows had stowed the old black Tom there, in a coil with the Commandant's dress-uniform. When I found that the Commandant, in his hurry, had left his keys hanging in the lock of the valise, the whole business was clear to me, and I just chuckled with delight. I put the keys into my pocket and hurried toward the wharf. But before I reached the tug I had stopped chuckling, and was thinking over the matter seriously. Of course I hadn't much sympathy with the Commandant, but I could not help worrying over my promise to the Admiral that I would keep out of scrapes. I stopped and attempted to open the valise; but either I mistook the key or failed to understand the lock, for I really could not open it. I tried faithfully until I dared delay no longer, and then feeling I had done my best, I ran for the tug. Still, I was very uneasy, and afraid of blame or something worse. To be sure, I hadn't put the cat in the valise, and I didn't even know, positively, that there was a cat in it at all. It wasn't my valise and it wasn't my cat; and, finally, the Commandant had no right to send me on orderly-duty. This was one side of the case. On the other was my promise to the Admiral that I would do my best to behave like an officer and a gentleman while I remained at the Academy—and I couldn't help admitting to myself that a cadet reasonably suspected of having anything to do with stowing a cat in the same valise with a dress-uniform might well be thought neither officer-like nor gentlemanly.

"Well, the long and short of it was that by the time I got down to the tug, I had made up my mind to tell the Commandant about the cat, and thus to clear my conscience of breaking my promise to the Admiral; and I must confess that I thought it would be rather good fun to see the Commandant open his valise and let black 'Tommy' come bouncing out of it on the deck, while all the sailors and cadets would be grinning at the jolly lark and at the way 'Old Discipline' would rage over it. But, as things turned out, I didn't have a chance to tell, after all,—more's the pity!" Here the Bilged Midshipman stopped for a minute or two to be miserable.

"When I got down to the tug," he went on, "the Commandant was hurried and flurried—for the Admiral had come down to the dock in the interval, and had asked why the tug had not started—and so, as I tumbled on board and handed him his keys, he blazed away:

"'Now, sir, I should like to know where you have been spending the morning. Are you so utterly incapable of all useful duty that you cannot run an errand without dawdling over it all day? Take the valise below, at once, and remain below until we reach Norfolk! Boatswain, see that the lines are cast off. Mr. Pivot, you will oblige me by getting under way immediately.'

"I was all in a rage at this unfair attack. It wasn't my fault that the Commandant

had come off without his valise, that he had ordered the tug to wait while he sent back for it, and that the Admiral had come down and caught him at the dock when he ought to have been well downstream; and I knew that I hadn't dawdled a bit. Then, to crown it all, he had ordered me below for the cruise, and so spoiled every bit of my fun. A big lump came up in my throat, and I felt rather wicked.

"But somehow, right in the thick of it I remembered my promise to the Admiral. So I gulped down the lump, by a great effort, and began:

"'If you please, sir, I——'

"'But I don't please,' he said angrily. 'Go below, sir!'

"'If you please,' I began again, for I was determined to do my duty, 'in the valise there's——'

"I don't think he heard what I was saying, he was in such a passion. He burst out: 'How *dare* you reply! The discipline of the service demands that when I give an order you are to obey it instantly and implicitly. Discipline and argument are utterly incompatible. Go below, this instant! You are under arrest. I shall report you to the Admiral for gross misconduct!'

"That settled the whole thing. There was nothing more to be said. I went down into the cabin and—I hope you fellows won't think it was mawkish—I just burst out crying. The whole business was so wretchedly full of injustice. Here I was trying my best to do my duty as an officer and a gentleman, and, for no fault of mine, I was under arrest and was to be reported for misconduct."

A sort of sympathetic thrill ran around the wood-shed. Clarence Detwiler formulated the sense of the meeting by observing that the Commandant was "a terror"; and little Billy Jenks crossed over from the secretary's seat—on the saw-horse—and put his arm over the Bilged Midshipman's shoulder. Billy always was a good-hearted little beggar.

After a while the Bilged Midshipman went on with his story: "After all," he said, "I don't believe that the Commandant would have reported me, when he came to think the matter over quietly, if it hadn't been for the cat—and he certainly had a right to raise a row over that part of the performance. You see, there was a stiff east-wind blowing that kicked up a heavy swell in the bay, and the tug rolled and tumbled about so that you fairly had to 'hang on with your teeth to keep your footing,' as one of the cadets said. Down in the cabin, things went bumping around in a very reckless sort of way, and I had to stow myself between a locker and the after-bulkhead to keep from bumping about, too. The valise was down in the cabin; and as it was not clewed fast it had the range of the whole place—sailing away first to starboard and next to port, and then taking a long roll up and down amidships, as the tug pitched in the short seas. Of course no cat was going to stand such nonsense as that without remonstrance; especially such a determined old scoundrel as Tommy. At first he sent up a lot of plantive 'me-ows!' but presently, when he found that 'me-owing' didn't do any good, he took to howling at the very top of his voice, and trying to scratch his way out. I could hear the sound of tearing cloth as he rattled his claws through and through the Commandant's dress-uniform, and—as I was in a rather wicked frame of mind by that time—I didn't object. If ever poetical justice got hold of a fellow it was then and there—and the fellow was 'Old Discipline' and the poetical justice was that ripping and raging cat who was tearing those ball-room clothes to scraps and tatters. I felt in my

bones that there was a tremendous storm ahead for me; but I was so angry that I hadn't much sympathy with the Commandant."

The wood-shed responded promptly to this sentiment, Clarence Detwiler leading a roar of laughter at the Commandant's expense. Only little Billy Jenks looked solemn. When we had got through laughing he said that he thought it was all right so far as the Commandant was concerned, but he couldn't help feeling that it was rather rough on the old cat. (You see, Billy was a very soft-hearted little chap about animals. Why, that little fellow once wanted to fight Clarence Detwiler, who was three years older and a whole head taller and who had taken boxing lessons, because Detwiler was going to drown a stray puppy so as to see whether or not he could bring it to life again by a plan that he had been reading about in some scientific paper. Detwiler was angry at first, but Billy was so much in earnest about it that he wound up by shaking hands with Billy and letting the puppy go—"sacrificing Science to Friendship," as he explained in his clever way. But that has nothing to do with the story.)

When we were all through laughing, the Bilged Midshipman continued:

"Well, the Commandant did not go to the ball! He came back to the Academy the next day, raging, and the storm which I knew to be brewing burst out at once. I have never heard what he said to the Admiral, but the case against me was black enough. The upshot of the matter was that I was dismissed from the Academy right out-of-hand—just 'bilged' without being summoned or having a chance to say a word in my own defense. This seemed to me the crowning injustice of all. I did not think that the Admiral would have treated me in that way, and I had expected to make it all right when I was summoned; for, you see, I really had tried to do my duty, and could have explained the whole matter so that the Admiral and all other officers would have seen that I was not to blame. But I had been in mischief several times since I entered the Academy and so everybody believed I had been larking again: and so I came to grief. Instead of believing me innocent until I was proved guilty, I was believed guilty from the start,—for there certainly seemed to be plenty of evidence against me,—and I wasn't given even an opportunity to prove my innocence.

"But I didn't see all this as plainly then as I do now, and I was angry at the clear injustice which had been done me, and concluded that the sooner I got away from the Academy the better. If the Admiral did not believe in me after my promise, it was he who was not behaving like an officer and a gentleman, this time. I hated him, and I hated everybody, myself included; and I was eager to get away, and so I didn't even try to explain matters and have my dismissal canceled. The Admiral had lost faith in me, and that settled the whole matter.

"And so, the short and long of it was, that I was 'bilged'—kicked out of the service in disgrace—all because some other fellow had put that miserable black cat in with 'Old Discipline's' dress-uniform! That's all there is to tell. And the reason I'm so miserable is that I can't help thinking all the time that if I'd kept reasonably steady from the start I should not have been dismissed at all. It was the cat that finished me, but the root of the whole wretched business was my bad name.

"I did love the service with all my heart, and I'd give almost anything to get back into it again; but I'm out of it forever—and I've nobody but myself to thank for my bad luck!"

The Bilged Midshipman sat down on the pile of kindling-wood just behind him and blinked his eyes quickly. I'm not sure that he wouldn't have broken down altogether, but just then Clumsy Skimples managed to tumble from the top of the wood-pile, bringing a whole load of wood down with him, and this raised a general laugh, and gave the Bilged Midshipman time to recover. When Clumsy had finished piling up the wood, and things were quiet again, Clarence Detwiler made a very handsome speech, in which he told the Bilged Midshipman how sorry we all felt for him and how badly we thought that he had been treated "while in the service of our common country" (Detwiler said that over twice, and we all applauded); and how, in short, we all hoped that it wouldn't happen again. Others of us made sympathetic speeches, and the meeting wound up by adopting a preamble and resolutions in which we just gave it to the United States Government in general and to the Commandant at the Naval Academy in particular.

But what seemed to please the Bilged Midshipman more than anything else, was the way in which little Billy Jenks got up from the saw-horse, walked across the wood-shed and said that he thought the Bilged Midshipman was a "gentleman, all the way through!" and he would like to have the honor of shaking hands with him. So Billy and the Bilged Midshipman solemnly shook hands, and then the small chap, in his dignified way, walked back across the wood-shed and sat down on the saw-horse again. Billy was such a queer little dick! He was always doing odd, old-fashioned things in the most natural sort of a way;—and yet, when you came to think about them, you always saw that they were just the right things to do, and you couldn't help respecting Billy for doing them. It is a solemn fact that there was more real, downright dignity about that little fellow than there was about Clarence Detwiler himself—though, of course, nobody at the school would have dared say so. And so the Bilged Midshipman seemed better pleased with Billy's shaking hands with him that way, than he was with our vote of censure upon the National Government.

Then the meeting broke up.

Now perhaps you think that this is the whole story of the Bilged Midshipman. But it isn't. At least, it has a very short sequel that is a great deal pleasanter than the story itself.

When the Bilged Midshipman was sent home, it seems, he told his father just how the whole thing happened, and his father, without saying anything to his son, wrote it all out and forwarded it to the Admiral. The Admiral immediately began an investigation of the case, and the result of it all was that the cadet who put the cat in the valise was found out, and was "bilged" in no time. Then the Admiral wrote back that he thought it would be a good plan to let our Bilged Midshipman stay at school quietly until the next term at the Academy began, without telling him that he was all right, so as to give him a good opportunity to think over what had happened and see what his failure to maintain a good record at the Academy had cost him,—it was to give him a sort of moral lesson, you see. And that was just what his father had concluded to do. Next year he was reinstated at the Academy, and two years later he was graduated, almost at the head of his class. He is an Ensign now, cruising around out on the East India Station. I had a letter from him the other day, telling how he had been in a rumpus with a Malay pirate, and had ridden on an elephant, and had eaten mangoes.

And so, the short and long of it was, you see, that the Bilged Midshipman was not really bilged, after all!

DEBORAH'S CHANGE OF HEART

by Helen Ward Banks

"OF course I can't have what the others have. I'm too homely," murmured Deborah. "But I hate her when she talks like that."

The corners of her mouth drooped, and her eyes filled with tears. There were so many things Deborah hated: the bare, angular house perched on the hillside, the plainness of her daily living, the vision she saw reflected in the mirror,—a small figure clothed in checked-brown gingham, and a pale face with drooping mouth and hair drawn tightly back into two braids. She could have seen eyes blue as gentians if she had looked long enough, but she always turned away after the first glance.

"I don't love a thing but my garden," thought Deborah. "It's the only beautiful thing I have. Maybe I love Aunty Jones a little scrap, and I used to love Josie, because she's so pretty. I hate ugly things. I'm going to hate people now, too. I hate Josie when she talks like that."

Pretty Josie Fenton walked on down the hill with Fred Dillon, unconscious that her words had been overheard. "It's too bad Debby is so homely," she had said carelessly.

Deborah watched them out of sight. She would have given all she owned to walk unconcernedly down the street with Fred. He was so merry and good-looking; any girl would be glad to have him for a friend. She picked up her trowel from the door-sill, and went slowly down the walk, her back to the ugly little house. She knelt among her flowers, and laid a caressing hand on the nearest. The garden was gay now with foxglove and sweet-William and columbine. Later it would run riot with tiger-lilies and larkspur and hollyhocks.

"I love you! I love you!" she whispered passionately. "You're the only thing I have to love. Why do I have to be so ugly when I hate ugly things with all my soul!"

She dug vigorously among her pansies for some time. Presently she left the trowel sticking in the earth, and settled back, her hands clasped around her brown gingham knees. She was too shy to have friends to talk to; she was used to thinking things out for herself.

"I am ugly," she thought, "and Aunty Jones is ugly, and the house is ugly. It must hurt everybody to look at us all, for ugliness is hateful. Why can't the world just be full of beauty?"

For a long time she sat thinking about it, and then she slowly went back to her pansies.

"I suppose really to make all the world beautiful, everyone ought to put a little beauty into it. All I have is my garden, but that's the prettiest in town, and I can make it prettier even than it is. It's the only point I have to start from, but I'll do it. I sha'n't pay any more attention to people, whether they're pretty or not. I'm going to hate people, and hate ugly things all my life, and just give myself up to putting beauty into the world."

She rose to her feet and surveyed her garden with a dreamy look. Her eyes showed the blue in this direct glance, and the corners of her mouth did not droop quite so pitifully. She had at least an object in life.

"Yes," she said. "The larkspur is in just the right place, and the hollyhocks will be lovely against the fence. The phlox needs thinning,—but it's time to go and help Aunty Jones get dinner now."

As she walked back toward the house, her eyes traveled farther up the hill. A new house was rising on the hilltop, and the newly graded earth made more raw ugliness in the landscape.

"It's a beautiful house," thought Deborah. "It makes ours worse than ever by contrast. But it will take forever to get the new look off the place. How lovely rock-pinks would be on that slope!"

A sudden thought struck her, so daring that it sent the unaccustomed color over her face. Was this a broader chance in her mission of bringing beauty into the world? Could she take it out of the confines of her own little garden and spread it abroad?

"Oh, I couldn't! I'd never dare!" she exclaimed. "I've plenty of pinks, and they spread like lightning, but I'd never dare offer Mr. Danvers any."

She could not get the thought out of her mind, however. Every morning for a week, with a quick-beating heart, she watched Mr. Danvers walk by on his visit of inspection to his new house. Then one day, before she knew she had done it, she had opened the gate and was speaking to him.

"Rock-pinks would be lovely on that slope," she gasped, her cheeks aflame. "I have lots of them. Could I plant some out there?"

Mr. Danvers looked at her quizzically.

"You're the girl with the pretty garden, aren't you?" he said, "and we are neighbors. I've tried to speak to you before, but you always looked the other way. And you want to share with me? That's very kind of you."

"Don't you mind?" stammered Deborah.

"I shall be very grateful. I'm not much at flowers, and Mrs. Danvers won't be coming till later, for I want things settled before she arrives."

"And could I put a little bunch of pink phlox by the barn?" asked Deborah, eagerly. "The color will be so pretty against the gray."

"It will be extremely pretty. Do whatever you want to. How do you like my house?"

"I love to look at it," said Deborah, fervently.

The glow stayed on Deborah's face all through dinner-time. She had never before spoken to a stranger of her own accord, and it was exciting. So was the permission to pour some of the beauty of her own little garden-plot into her neighbor's wide domain.

"I'm really doing it!" she thought. "I'm really putting beauty into the world out of my own garden!"

Then she stopped, struck by a sudden thought. Was she going to be able to carry out perfectly her plan of hating people as she spread beauty? How could she hate Mr. Danvers while she was giving him flowers out of her garden?

She did not have time to find an answer to her question just then, for transplanting kept her very busy. Josie Fenton's father was building the house, and he watched Deborah with interest as, day by day, she came over with a new perennial clump to tuck into its fitting nook. Deborah did not know he was watching her until he spoke to her.

"Are you sharing up that white piny? It's the handsomest one in town."

"Do you think so?" Deborah asked shyly. "I didn't know any one ever noticed it."

"When it's in bloom, I come down this way just to look at it," Mr. Fenton said.

"Oh, do you?" Deborah asked, with a little smile. She did not often smile. Then she added, shyly, "Would you like a root, too?"

"Indeed I would, if it won't be robbing you."

"I'd like to give it to you," Deborah answered, and went home wondering if she could leave out from her hating the people who loved flowers.

She dug so hard at her peony roots that before she knew it she had kneed a hole straight through her brown gingham frock. She showed it in dismay to Aunty Jones.

"Never mind," said the kind old lady. "It's an old one. You go up to the store this afternoon and get you some new gingham, and I'll make you some new dresses. I'm slack of work just now; and I don't read as easy as I did once."

To the second brown gingham, clean and starched, Deborah added a brown sailor hat over hair tied tightly with a brown ribbon, and went to the store. She had to wait a long time for attention, for an automobile stood outside, and the two ladies who owned it were inside buying many things. Deborah sat patiently on a high stool and waited. She looked a good deal at the young lady who was matching embroidery silk, for she was very pretty. Presently the young lady looked up and met the gaze. She smiled at Deborah,

and Deborah had shyly smiled back before she knew what she was doing.

"I'm afraid we're keeping you waiting," said the older girl.

"I don't mind," answered Deborah. "I only want some brown gingham, and I have lots of time."

"If you're going to buy yourself a dress," the automobile girl said impulsively, "don't buy another brown; buy blue, to match your eyes. See, there's a lovely piece up there."

"Why," faltered Deborah, "I've always had brown."

"But that's no reason you always should. The blue costs the same, and pretty things are much nicer to look at than ugly ones, aren't they?" said her new friend, with a smile.

"Oh, yes!" exclaimed Deborah.

The young lady had the blue-and-white check pulled down, and held it against Deborah's face. Her cheeks flushed, and her eyes were bright as she looked up.

"It's very becoming," said the older lady, with a satisfied nod. "I am going to make you a present of a blue hair-ribbon to match, so that when you look in the glass and find how nice you look, you will remember what I tell you. Outside beauty doesn't always strike in, but inside beauty always strikes out in time, though young folk aren't apt to think so. Will you remember that? Every girl wants to be pretty, and no girl can carry a brave, honest, merry heart without having it shine through, finally, to make people call her beautiful."

"My mother is preaching you quite a sermon," laughed the young lady. "Now remember, too, what I tell you. Just wear blue always, and never touch another inch of brown. Wait a minute! I have a hat out in the car that would just suit you, I know, and it isn't my style at all. Will you take it to remember *my* little sermon? My mother's ribbon will make you remember to be good, and my hat will make you remember to wear becoming clothes. They're both very important."

The young lady dashed out to find the hat, and dashed back to leave it on Deborah's lap. Then she smiled once more, and she and her mother buzzed off in the automobile, leaving Deborah's head buzzing as fast as the car. She went home, scarcely knowing who she was, the blue gingham and the blue hair-ribbon done up in one parcel, and the hat—such a pretty one!—in another.

"I'm getting all mixed up on my hating plan," she thought as she went. "I've given Mr. Danvers and Mr. Fenton flowers; that's all right. But I like them both. And I like the pretty young lady and the hair-ribbon lady, too."

Aunty Jones chuckled comfortably when she saw the gingham. "I declare, Debby! I don't know as my needle'll take to anything but brown. We might have thought of blue long ago, for it's a sight prettier. I'll enjoy sewing on it."

"I could read to you while you sew, if you like," ventured Deborah, quite thrilling with the soft, clear shade of her new dress. Aunty Jones's face brightened. "It would be a great treat. Maybe you'd read me my Bible piece first."

Deborah found the Bible marker at the account of Jehoshaphat going to meet the Moabites. She liked the swing of the old Jewish story. "He appointed singers unto the Lord and that they should praise the beauty of holiness," she read finally, and stopped to think what the words meant. The beauty of holiness was a thing she had not thought about, but in a flash she saw it was the only true beauty in the world; one must cultivate beautiful thoughts and deeds as well as beautiful

flowers. That was what her hair-ribbon lady had meant, and that was why she found it hard really to hate people. Hating must always be ugly. To bring beauty into the world, one must bring love into it. Oh, but it would be much harder than transplanting flowers and wearing blue ribbons!

She finished the story, and shyly kissed Aunty Jones when she went to bed. The old lady looked up lovingly.

"She isn't so awfully ugly," thought Deborah, wonderingly, as she went upstairs. "I guess she's beautiful inside, and it's shining through. I never noticed. I wonder if I couldn't make her something soft and white to wear at her neck. Then she would look like the hair-ribbon lady."

Even transplanting the beauty of love wasn't so hard when Deborah really tried it. Maybe the blue frock helped along, for it was much more friendly than the old brown ones. Deborah, before she knew it, was having long flower discussions with Mr. Fenton, and a good many of her roots made their way into his garden. She found, too, that Mr. Danvers's head painter was very fond of milk, and she carried him a pitcherful for his lunch every day. When she proposed white muslin curtains for the sitting-room, Aunty Jones was quite ready to agree, and she brought out bags of carpet-rag pieces to start a new rug. Deborah chose all the blue, and while the old lady peacefully cut and sewed and rolled, her niece read aloud all sorts of books that they both enjoyed. For the first time, the house had a gleam of home in it, because somebody had begun to love it.

All her spare time Deborah spent in Mr. Danvers's place. He had been away for a fortnight, and came back to find new little bunches of growing things in all sorts of odd places, and Deborah busy with her seedling zinnias.

"You're a born gardener," said Mr. Danvers, "but you need more material for this big place. Suppose you had everything you wanted, what would you put in over here?"

"Oh," said Deborah, "I've shut my eyes and seen that place over and over; it's full of dahlias—yellow ones!"

Mr. Danvers nodded approvingly. "Yes, that's good. I'll get some. Now how about over here?"

Before the morning was over, Deborah and Mr. Danvers had planned the entire garden. Deborah forgot to be dumb or bashful. She chattered and laughed and glowed like any other happy, human creature.

Presently Mr. Danvers looked at his watch. "My! how the time runs away. I don't know when I've enjoyed a morning more. I have a train to catch now, and I shan't be back till next month. Are you going to oversee all this planting for me? If you will, I'll give you a percentage for yourself out of the dahlias and all the other things. And now I tell you what I want to do, Miss Deborah. If you have to look up at my place, I have to look down at yours. You have beautified my slopes; now I want to add a little beauty to your house. I have lumber here I'm not going to use, and I want Fenton to put a porch along the south side of your house. Will you let him? It will take down the height and will make a pretty little house of it. I want to do it for my own sake, if you'll let me."

Then he ran for his train, and Deborah did not really know whether she had said "No, thank you," or "Yes, thank you." But it must have been yes, for the very next morning Mr. Fenton's men began to saw and fit and hammer by the little, dingy house.

Those were exciting days. Boxes of plants and seeds arrived, and there was an experienced gardener at Mr. Danvers's who lived for nothing but to plant beauty as Deborah ordered it. The porch took on its outline and filled out to completeness. One day the painter whom Deborah had fed with milk handed back the jug with a very grave face.

"That there milk seems to have some magic in it," he said solemnly. "I declare if it ain't turned into white paint; enough to cover your whole house. If you'll say the word, I'll smear it over odd times after hours; it'll be a good-looking little place when it gets whitened up."

"Haven't you got some green cheese around, too?" laughed Mr. Fenton. "I was just thinking I've got some blinds piled under a lot of rubbish over at the shop that would just fit these little windows. I took 'em off an old house ten years ago. I'll hang 'em if you'll daub 'em over with green cheese."

"Oh!" cried Deborah. "Everybody is so good. Could I really have blinds? Not having them has always made the house look like a person without any eyebrows."

"It's nothing to put those on," Mr. Fenton said; "and it's all the house needs to make it match the garden. My new flowers are doing finely. Why don't you come over and see 'em? Don't you ever come to see my girl?"

"She wouldn't want to me to," stammered Deborah. She could not forget how homely Josie thought her.

"Of course she'd want you," answered Mr. Fenton. "I'll send her down here to prove it."

"Oh, don't," Deborah wanted to protest, but she didn't. Would she even have to love Josie Fenton?

The paint and the blinds were on before Josie came. Debby tried to be cordial and entertaining, but it was Josie who did most of the talking. They discussed the weather and the garden, and all the time Josie was casting little flying glances at Deborah.

"Oh, Debby!" she exclaimed abruptly at last. "Will you be mad? I'm just crazy to fix your hair. I never noticed before how thick and soft it is. You could be stunning if you did it right. Come on upstairs and let me try."

Most unwillingly Deborah led the way to her room and sat down before her dressing-table.

"Why, it's gorgeous!" cried Josie, as Debby's loosened hair flowed over her shoulders. "But you mustn't drag it back tight as if you were stuffing a pincushion. It's got lots of wave in it. There, you must always roll it like that and keep it soft—so. Now where's your blue ribbon? Why, Debby, you're *lovely!* Just look!"

Confused, yet pleased, Deborah looked in the mirror which had so often reflected her plain face. But what did she see now? A warm flush in the pale cheeks; a happy smile on the discontented lips; a friendly look in the downcast eyes; softly waving hair instead of the scalp-tight locks—and all this set off by a blue ribbon and a blue dress that made her eyes look like forget-me-nots. It wasn't herself; it couldn't be! She was so ugly, and this girl was a joy to look at! It was too good to be true.

"Don't you ever dare do it any other way!" said Josie. "There's Father going home. I'll catch a ride. Come and see me, Debby."

Debby felt almost too conscious to go down to supper. She stole another glance at herself in the mirror, and smiled at what she saw. "I'm not ugly," she thought with a throb of joy. "People won't have to hate looking at me. Something has shined through, but I don't know what it is."

She went out to water her flowers after supper, with the smile still in the corners of her lips, the flush on her cheeks, and the brightness in her eyes. When Fred Dillon walked by, instead of turning her back, Deborah looked up and smiled. It was a friendly smile, born of her new sense of self-assurance.

"Hello, Debby!" the boy said. "If you'll invite me in, I'll carry that water-pot for you. My, what a dandy porch you've got! You'll have to have a house-warming for that, for sure!"

"So I can!" cried Deborah. "I'll do it just as soon as the moon is full."

"Then I'm invited, am I?"

"Yes," said Debby, "only I can't let you pass lemonade if you spill as much as you're spilling out of that watering-pot."

"They're wet enough anyhow," said the boy. "Let's go sit on the porch and look at how much good we've done them."

Debby led the way to the porch, her heart beating with a new glad glow of life. It was all so wonderful. Above her, Mr. Danvers's beautiful house stood against the evening sky, and his lawns sloped to her own pretty little home, painted and porched and shuttered, worthy of the garden in which it stood. Fred had come to see her, as he called to see other girls, and she was talking and laughing, and she wasn't homely. Life was full of joy, where a few months ago there had been only heaviness and hopeless loneliness. And she loved everything and everybody.

"Loving is the biggest beauty in the world," Deborah thought. "The really ugly things are just hating and hatefulness. I guess we can put beauty anywhere if we have loving enough."

WHEN I WAS A BOY ON THE RANCH

by J. Frank Dobie

THERE were six of us children and our ranch was down in the brush country of Texas between the Nueces River and the Rio Grande. The automobiles have outrun the horses since then; radios have drowned out many a cricket's voice and many a coyote's wailing cry; in many a ranch yard the lights of Delco plants have dimmed the glowing points of the fireflies—"lightning bugs," we called them. But the ranch of our childhood is still a ranch. And south of it clear to the Mexican border, and northwest of it into the Rocky Mountains and on up beyond the line where Montana joins Canada, there are millions and millions of acres of other ranches on which boys and girls live.

Despite automobiles these boys and girls still ride horses. Despite radios they still listen in the evening to crickets and frogs, and sometimes in the night to the wailing cries of coyotes. As for electric lights on the ranches, they light such small spaces that the fireflies in the grass and the stars in the sky never notice them. The country is still country. For all the changes brought by invention, ranches are still ranches.

So if I tell how we children lived on our ranch, I'll also be telling how children still live on other ranches scattered all over the western half of the United States.

We liked ranching so much that our best game used to be "playing ranch." There were fine live oak trees between the yard fence and the pens about the stables and barns, and it was in the shade of these trees, especially during the summer, that we built our "ranches."

To build a pasture we drove little stakes close together in the ground until a plot about as big as a kitchenette was inclosed; sometimes the pasture was made by setting up "posts" of stakes in the ground and then stretching cords, in imitation of barbed wire, from one corner of the "pasture" to the other. Each ranch had several pastures, and of course each ranch had headquarters, where houses and corrals were built. The houses were generally of boards; the corrals were of pickets laid between pairs of upright posts.

Fencing in the pastures was never so much fun as getting them stocked. It took work to fence in land and improve it with dirt tanks, which never would hold water very long. It took patience to construct corral gates that would open and shut and to make a house that would not fall down when a turkey stepped on it or a pup ran against it. But stocking this land with cattle and horses and goats was nothing but fun.

We had two kinds of cattle—high-grade cattle and common "stuff." The horn tips of real cattle—which were clipped off at branding time—became our pure-bred animals. Sometimes we had hundreds of them. Our "common Mexican cattle" were represented by oak balls.

But we prized our horses far more than

our cattle. Horses consisted of sewing-thread spools; most of our clothes were made on the ranch, and those clothes took an astonishing amount of thread. Moreover, when we went visiting we had our eyes open for discarded spools, but visits of any kind were rare and those that brought spools were rarer. A spool has a long "side" that can be branded and it has a long "back" that can be saddled. I can't think of any better kind of play-horse than a spool.

The ranches in our part of the country had herds of white Mexican goats. White-shelled snails were abundant in our neighborhood, and these shells became our goats. A live snail would not stay in a pasture, for he can climb straight up and carry his shell with him, so our goats were always empty shells. There were no sheep in the country; we had never heard anything particularly good connected with sheep men; and so we had no sheep—just cattle, horses, and goats.

Each of us had a brand. Mine was N̄v, which an uncle of mine ♋ named Neville used. Fannie's was Ⅺ, Elrich's was an *E;* Lee's brand was *L.* The two younger children were too small to build ranches and brand herds by themselves; consequently if Henry and Martha got into the game, they got in as "hired help." Our branding irons were short pieces of bailing wire, with a crook at one end. This kind of branding iron is called a "running iron." When we had occasion to brand, we built a fire close to ranch headquarters, heated the "running irons," and burned our brands on the spool-horses, the common oak-ball cattle, and the fine horn cattle.

Like real ranchmen, we bought and sold stock. When a trade was made, the cattle or horses—we seldom traded goats—had to be gathered up, driven to the shipping pens, loaded on the railroad cars, trans-

ported, and delivered. Then after they were delivered they had to be branded with the brand of the new owner. (A great many of the "common cattle" were decayed on the inside and when they were branded collapsed into nothing!) We had to sell cheap for the very simple reason that dollars were scarce and cattle were plentiful.

The dollars we had, however, were extraordinarily good dollars of sound coinage and pure metal. The ranch kitchen used a considerable amount of canned goods, particularly canned tomatoes, salmon, and sardines, along with some peaches and corn. We held the empty can in a fire with tongs until the solder started to run, and then caught the solder in an old spoon, pouring it into a round wooden box that had once held bluing. The diameter of this round bluing box was—and still is—about that of a silver dollar. The dollars we coined were sometimes thicker than a silver dollar and they were always heavier, but in buying cattle they were worth just as much.

We had another source of metal for our dollars. In the fall of the year hunters would be on the ranch, either camped out or staying with us at the house. They usually shot up a good many boxes of shells practicing on trees. After the shooting was over, we children gouged out the lead bullets lodged in the trees and melted them into dollars.

I spoke of shipping cattle. The train was a string of empty sardine cans coupled to each other with wire hooks. Motive power was the chief problem. We tried hitching horned frogs and green lizards to it, but neither pulled with any strength. A horned frog would sometimes pull an empty wagon made of a cardboard match box. Old Joe, the best dog we ever had, would pull the train pretty well if he went in a straight line, but when he didn't, he caused several bad wrecks that overturned cars and spilled cattle out. If a delivery of cattle had to be made promptly, the simplest and surest way to make the engine pull the train was to tie a string to it and pull it yourself.

Of course there were *real* horses and *real* cattle to interest us. Children brought up on a ranch usually learn to ride only a little later than they learn to walk. Old Stray, Dandy, and Baldy were the horses on our ranch that could be trusted with the youngest children. Old Stray was a common Mexican pony that some Mexican had ridden down and turned loose on our ranch. When we first saw him he was as thin as a stick-horse. Nobody claimed him, so after a while we used him. He seemed to appreciate having plenty of grass to eat but he had no intention of ever exerting himself again. In short, he was not only gentle but "pokey." If a child fell off him, he would stop and graze until the child got up again. Baldy was an enormous horse, and by the time a boy was big enough to scramble upon his back without help from a man or a friendly fence, that boy was nearly ready for "long pants."

Dandy was a black horse of thoroughbred trotting stock. He alone of all the horses was entitled to corn the year around. The other horses lived mostly on grass. We rode Dandy sometimes as well as drove him, but he had too much life in him for mere beginners. He was as kind and intelligent as he was lively. One time when my brother Elrich was very small he toddled into Dandy's stall while Dandy was eating. The flies were bothering Dandy and he was switching his tail and stamping his feet. He knew that the little boy was in danger. He put a hind foot against the child and shoved him out of the stall. He did not kick him—just shoved him.

By the time I was eight years old I had several horses to ride. There was Maudie, a little Spanish mare, that would kick up when I punched her in the shoulder with my finger or pointed my hand down toward her flank or tail. Later there was Buck, a horse raised on the ranch. He was a bay with a white face and stocking feet. I kept him as long as he lived and he died on the ranch where he was born. He could be turned loose in camp and would not stray off. Once when I was running to head some wild steers and Buck gave a quick dodge, the saddle, which was loosely girted, turned, throwing me to the ground and nearly breaking my hip. Buck could "turn on a dime" and stop as quickly as one can snap a finger. On this occasion he stopped so suddenly that he did not drag me a foot, though I was still in the saddle when my hip struck the ground. He was the best cowhorse I ever rode. Often when we were alone I talked to him. By the time I was twelve years old and a regular ranch hand, I was sometimes on him from daylight until long after dark. More than once I went to sleep riding him. I loved him and he loved me. I think of Buck oftener now than I think of many people who have been my friends.

As range cows do not give as much milk as dairy cows, we usually had a pen full of them to milk, especially in the summertime. Each cow had her calf, and the calves were allowed part of the milk. A Mexican man usually did the milking, but it was the privilege of us boys to bring in the calves from the calf pasture each evening and then to ride them.

Now, riding calves is about as much fun as a ranch boy can possibly have. The calf is roped around the neck, and a half hitch, called a "bosal," is put around its nose. Then, using the rope as a bridle, the boy mounts. Until the calf is gentled, it will "pitch like a bay steer." One calf that I remember particularly was a black heifer with a white face. She became very gentle and we named her Pet. I trained Pet so well that I could mount her and guide her all over the calf pasture. Usually, no matter how well "broke" to riding, a calf won't go where you want it to go. It won't go anywhere. Saddles don't fit calves, or grown cattle and, although it was sometimes fun to saddle yearlings, what actual riding we did was bareback. As we grew older we caught range cattle coming into the big pen to water and rode the calves and yearlings.

Each of us children had a few head of cattle to call our own. They were for the most part dogies or of dogie origin. A "dogie" is a motherless calf. When one was found on the range, it would be brought in and some cow with a calf of like age would be tied at night and morning and forced to let the motherless calf share her milk. We had one old muley cow that was so kind to dogies that the dogie always fared better than her own offspring. She would moo to it and lick its hair and otherwise mother it.

Pet was originally a dogie. When she grew up and had calves of her own, we milked her. If she was a good "saddle horse," a red-roan calf that she had was a better one. Pet had so many calves and those calves grew up and had so many calves of their own that the little stock of cattle coming from her helped materially to put me through college one year.

We went to a country school, which was on our own ranch, where the children of five or six other ranch families attended. Most of them rode to school horseback. One of our games was "cats and dogs." This we boys—for girls did not join in it— played at noon recess. The "cats" would set out in the brush afoot. About three minutes later the "dogs," mounted on horses and yelling like Apache Indians, would take after them. The brush had thorns and

the idea of the "cat" was to get into brush so thick that the "dog" could not follow him, or to crawl into a thicket where he could not be seen. Sometimes the chase would last until long after the bell had sounded. I remember one great chase that kept us out until three o'clock. An hour later eight or nine boys were alone with the teacher and a pile of *huajilla* switches.

Another game on horseback that the older boys played was "tournament." Three posts are erected in a line a hundred yards apart. Each post has an arm of wood about a yard long. Hanging from this arm is a metal ring about two inches in diameter. It is held by a spring clasp so that it can be easily disengaged. The runner takes a sharpened pole—the "tournament pole"—in his right hand and, holding it level, with the point out in front of him, runs lickety-split down the line of rings trying to spear them. The game requires skill. Buck was a wonderfully smooth-running horse, and he and I together hooked plenty of rings.

My sisters and girl cousins joined us in playing Indian and in making houses. Our ranch was built on a dry arroyo, or creek, named Long Hollow. Just below the house this creek had bluffs about forty feet high. For years we children worked periodically at digging caves back into the bluffs. Here we played Indian. If the soil had not been so gravelly and consequently inclined to cave in, we might have made dwelling places as ample as some of the ancient cliff dwellings. As it was, we got the caves big enough for us to hide in. When Long Hollow ran water after a rain, we made water wheels of sticks and cornstalks and watched them turn.

The house of our own construction that we enjoyed most was in a tree. It was a live oak called "the Coon Tree," from the fact that a coon hungry for chickens had once been found in it. Climbing up into this tree was an enormous mustang grape-vine. This grapevine afforded us a kind of ladder to the limbs of the Coon Tree. We took planks up to these limbs and nailed them so that we had a solid floor.

In our country we did not have many fruits, but around the ranch house were prolific pomegranate bushes. No matter how dry the season, these pomegranates always bore fruit. In the summertime we would pick pomegranates, borrow some sugar, spoons, and glasses from the kitchen, and, with a jug of water, gather on the platform in the Coon Tree for a picnic. We had a rope with which to pull up the jug and a bucket containing the other articles. The point of the picnic was to make "pomegranateade" out of sugar, the fruit seeds, and water.

Sometimes we took books and read in the Coon Tree. *Beautiful Joe* and *Black Beauty* were favorites. Our real house had matting on the floor, and when this mat-ting was discarded and we covered the platform in the Coon Tree with it, we felt that we had reached the height of luxury. I don't understand why none of us ever fell out of the Coon Tree.

I have spoken of our life with horses and calves. There were other animals to interest us, as there always are in the country. The trees about the ranch were inhabited each spring and summer by hun-dreds of jackdaws, a kind of blackbird. They built their nests in the trees so flimsily that disaster to the newly hatched birds was inevitable. Before they could fly or even walk, young birds would fall out of the trees and sprawl helpless on the ground, a ready prey for cats, turkeys, and other enemies. The distressed cries of the parent jackdaws were at times almost deafening, but these parents could do noth-ing toward getting their young back into the nests. We used to pick up the young birds and put them in straw-filled

wooden nail-kegs, which we placed on the roofs of a shed and smokehouse under the Coon Tree. I have seen three or four par-ent jackdaws feeding their young at the same time in one of these kegs. Some-times each keg held as many as eight young birds.

Scissortails built their hanging nests in the very tops of the higher trees, but their young never fell out. We never tired of watching the scissortails fly, especially if they were chasing a hawk, darting at his head and driving him away. The wrens nested in tool boxes in the stable, in coils of rope, even in the leather toe-fenders—called *tapaderos*—covering the stirrups of saddles. When we found these nests, we made it our duty to warn our father and the Mexican laborers not to disturb them. One time a saddle had to go unused for weeks until a wren that had built in the *tapadero* of one stirrup had brought off her brood.

Under Mother's direction we raised chickens, turkeys, and guineas. The guineas were good "watchdogs," alarm-ing, with their wild cries, everything and everybody within hearing distance when a hawk was approaching. Hawks, chicken snakes, and coyotes were constant enemies of the barnyard. We boys sometimes set traps for the coyotes. I remember seeing my mother, before I was old enough to handle a gun, shoot one with a rifle very near the house.

The evening call of the bob-white brought—as it yet brings—a wonderful peace. In the early mornings of certain times of the year we could hear wild tur-keys "yelping" out in the brush back of the field. Once a large flock of them grazed up to the schoolhouse, but the teacher would not let us out to chase them. Al-though deer were plentiful, and some other children in the country had a pet fawn, we never had one. Once while riding in the pasture I halted a long time to watch a doe kill a rattlesnake.

I can honestly say that we did not enjoy "tormenting" animals and that we did not rob birds' nests. But when we snared lizards with a horse hair looped on the end of a pole; when we poured buckets of water down the holes of ground squirrels to make them come out; and when we hitched horned toads to match boxes, we no doubt did torment those animals, though we seldom injured them. I have since killed noble buck deer, mountain lions, wild boars, and other game, but no memory of hunting is so pleasant as that of rescuing little jackdaws, of restoring a tiny dove fallen from its nest, and of watching, without molesting them, baby jack-rabbits in their cotton-lined nest against the cow pen fence—memories all of a ranch boy.

Ranch girls and boys always find so many ways to play and so many creatures of nature to interest them that the days are never long enough. And no life can be long enough for a ranch-bred boy or girl to forget the full times of childhood.

PERCY RAY'S TRICK BOAT

Nathan Haskell Dole

"FATHER, I'm going to build a boat."
"Build a boat! You couldn't build a boat!"

There was no conviction in the father's tone. Alexander Ray, who was satisfied with himself, with all his possessions, and, above all, with his only son, in his heart believed that his son could do anything, just as he believed that he himself could do anything. Percy looked like his father. He had the same bright blue eyes, the same aquiline nose, the same determined mouth. His hair stood up on his head with the same aggressive fierceness. They both had a quick, eager way of speaking.

"What is your plan?" asked Percy's father.

"Well, I'm going to build it in the barn. I'll get some wood over at the sawmill. I saw some over there which looked just right."

"What kind of a boat?"

"No flat-bottomed punt, I tell you! I want one that will sail. I'll build her with a keel and a rudder."

"Have you made a sketch of it?"

"No; only in my own mind."

"You want a carefully drawn sketch of it. I'll help you."

Mr. Ray got some large sheets of brown paper, and he and Percy were soon deeply engrossed in making measurements to scale. Both had considerable skill in drawing, and the boat as it took shape gave promise of being a joy forever. They reckoned about how much lumber would be necessary, and Percy borrowed a team of a neighbor and went to the mill to make his purchase.

The old harness-room in the barn had been converted into a carpenter's shop; it contained a solid bench, and a fairly complete assortment of tools. The main body of the barn afforded ample room for the boat-building. The big folding doors could be flung wide open, and the view, as one looked out, comprised a small grove of maple-trees with one big oak and one tall pine, and, far beyond, the main village and the slope of a high hill covered with old apple-trees. Out of sight lay the wide river into which the boat would be launched. The barn stood lower than the house, which was of brick, with huge chimneys. One could stand on the front door-step and fling a stone into the water.

Percy went to school in the morning; he had, therefore, only three or four afternoon hours and his Saturdays in which to work on the boat. If he had not been eager to have it finished by the beginning of the summer vacation, he would have been rather jealous, and have objected to his father's pushing it forward while he himself was engaged in reading how Cæsar constructed the bridge or Odysseus made his raft. Mr. Ray puttered more or less, but Percy did the larger part of the work. It was wonderful to see the boat grow. The keel was laid with great care, and the ribs, skilfully shaped, took their proper places. One thing Percy's father could do, and that was to make shavings. He handled the plane like a master, and he did yeoman's work in smoothing the boards. It was to be a lapstreak.

The pounding and general clatter could not fail to attract attention, and there was always a little crowd of critics who watched the operations with the keenest interest. When the work began, the ice was still in the river. It went out as usual on Sunday, and there was even a first-class freshet. Another barn, standing a little lower, was inundated, and Caleb Loring had to take a flat-bottomed punt and rescue the Widow Jones's cow. Percy was sorry that his craft was not in readiness to engage in such a deed of mercy.

At last, the school examinations were finished, and the boat was ready to be launched. All the boys of the village, and not a few men, gathered to watch and assist. In the olden days, before the bridge was built, long before the war, there had been a ferry, and the road leading diagonally down the rather steep bank still existed. Indeed, it was always used in winter when there was teaming on the ice. Percy arranged two pairs of wheels taken from a hay-cart, and, with the assistance of willing hands, got the boat safely and steadily established between solid crutches. Strong ropes were attached to the forward axle. Ropes were also fastened to the rear axle, so as to hold back when going down the incline. A team of shouting boys were waiting the word of command to march forward with the glittering equipage. Glittering? It was painted white, with two parallel green lines. The name, *Speranza,* was delicately lettered on the stern. Two parts of brass rowlocks were in place. Four small boys disputed the honor of carrying the four oars.

The procession started. An excited crowd was on hand to witness the launching. Percy had in some way procured a small yacht-cannon. It was all ready to fire a salute to the young queen of the river. Everything went like clockwork. The lads at the ropes walked in step. A couple of the taller ones moved at each side to give a steadying hand if it were necessary. Under the tall hackmatack trees that lined the street, the sunlight pouring down from a cloudless sky, went the boat. It soon reached the old ferry road. The team changed places, taking hold of the rear ropes. It was all admirably managed. Percy's heart swelled with pride. He realized that he occupied a commanding position among his fellows. Every one in town had been praising his enterprise and ingenuity. This was his day of triumph.

The river flowed by in a calm and sedate manner. There was not a breeze. Every bush and tree was reflected in its soft brown water. Occasionally, a little fountain of bubbles would mount to the surface— gas from some decaying log buried in the muddy bottom. Now and then a fish would leap and cause a spreading circle to mar the images depicted on the mirror. There was a beach of clean white sand; the bottom sloped gradually for perhaps ten feet, and then went down suddenly. It was an ideal place to launch the bonny craft. It did not take much imagination to see that the *Speranza* was quivering with anticipation. It seemed to be actually alive. Very carefully she was pushed out into the stream until she floated. Then Percy, taking the end of the painter, towed her round to his float. This was constructed of large logs fastened together with parallel planks and securely anchored. All the boys would have piled in at once, but he kept them off. "No," said he, "I'll try it myself first. You shall have your show afterward." He took one pair of the oars, and carefully, so as not to scratch the paint, stepped in. He was just inserting one oar into the rowlock, having drifted away a few feet from the float, when suddenly, without the least warning, the boat rolled over, tipping the proud owner into the river. A shout went up from the crowd on the bank; but they all knew Percy could swim like a duck. He came up sputtering, but a few strokes brought him and the boat to shallow water.

Here Mr. Ray asserted himself.

"You were careless," he said; "there's no sense in managing a boat like that! I thought you knew how to handle oars. Here, give it to me. I will show you how!"

It was hot in the sun, so there was no danger of Percy's getting cold, though the water was streaming from his clothes and from his thick hair.

Mr. Ray, assisted by several of the boys, brought the boat to the float again.

He took the oars, and crept cautiously over the bow and seated himself on the middle thwart. He then tried to insert both oars simultaneously, saying rather boastfully, "I was brought up in a boat. I know all about them—" The next instant he was floundering in the water. When the crowd saw the expression of his face, a mighty howl of unholy joy went up which might have been heard a mile. It was too bad, but Mr. Ray, in spite of many admirable qualities, enjoyed among his fellow-townsmen the reputation of being a little too boastful. He was so often justified in his pretensions that, to see him for once humiliated, relieved the disappointment which all felt at the failure of the *Speranza* as a passenger-carrying craft. Both oars and Mr. Ray's new hat went sailing down the current together. Percy had to swim after them and bring them back.

As poor Mr. Ray waded ruefully ashore, he was overwhelmed with suggestions as to what should be done. One thought that the keel should have a lead shoe; another proposed to get some bricks for ballast.

"She sets just like a swan," said Harry Manning. "She doesn't look as if she'd be so cranky. Here comes Caleb Loring; perhaps he'll try her."

Caleb Loring was a half-witted fellow who got his living from the river. He had a flat-bottomed punt which he navigated backward or forward with a paddle. With it he collected cords of driftwood; from it he fished near the sunken piers of the old bridge that had been carried away during a January thaw, many years before. Caleb Loring was always the first to cross the river on the ice after it had closed over.

"What's the trouble?" he asked as he came lumbering down over the bank. He wore a ragged straw hat, a blue flannel shirt, and trousers hitched to his shoulders by pieces of hemp rope. He was barefooted. "Oh, I see," he continued, "boat too high-studded. Wait, I'll get a stun'." He went a few rods up the bank, and soon returned, bringing a water-worn boulder which he had used for an anchor. "There!" he exclaimed, "this'll make her set deeper. Now she'll be all right."

"You try her, Caleb," shouted several.

"I'd ruther paddle her," said Caleb; "I'll use the oar f'r a paddle."

With perfect confidence he stepped into the *Speranza*, but he had not taken two strokes before the mischievous craft, with all the agility of a bucking bronco at a circus, flopped on her side, spilling Caleb Loring, just as she had spilled Percy and his father, into the smiling river.

Loring came up puffing like a grampus —a most ludicrous object. His straw hat and one oar went sailing down the current. The boat righted herself and floated gracefully, looking as innocent as she was beautiful.

"There's something wrong with her," said Mr. Ray, with the water still dripping from all his garments; "I can't imagine what it is. She was built on measurements. We've got to take her up to the barn again."

This time it was more like a funeral than like a wedding procession. The boys hauled her out of the stream and lifted her on the wheels. Then they all took hold and rushed her up the bank, and back to the place of her nativity. Nothing was talked about in the village during the next few days except Percy Ray's "bucking boat," and those who missed the great spectacle of Alexander Ray following Percy over her side, had no difficulty in imagining the scene, so vividly was it narrated by the various eye-witnesses.

Percy and his father were sitting, a few days later,—in dry clothes, of course, and with a somewhat chastened spirit—talking about the still unsolved problem of the bucking boat, as it was universally called. The door-bell rang. The visitor was the proprietor of a little hotel at "the Pond." This was a resort about six miles from the village. Picnic parties frequently went there for sailing, swimming, rowing, and fishing. Ebenezer Junkins had originally been a farmer, and his acres skirted the Pond. He had found it more profitable to rent his grove, to take boarders, and gradually to enlarge his fleet of boats, than to practise farming. He was a character. He had very blue eyes, sandy hair, and a straggly beard under his chin. His clothes consisted of a pair of very baggy pantaloons, a rusty black coat, and cowhide boots. He was regarded as extremely shrewd. He took a seat, and, twisting his broad-brimmed rusty black hat in his big, hairy hands, which carried around with them a goodly share of the rich soil of his farm, he hemmed and hawed for a while, and then burst out suddenly:

"I hearn tell about that there boat o' yourn. That was plum funny—the way she upsot ye. I'd 'a' giv' a dime to 'a' seen that circus-show. What I come f'r is to find out if ye'd sell her."

"I don't think it would be fair to palm her off on any one," said Mr. Ray; "do you, Percy?"

"Why, no; it wouldn't be safe for any one to try to go out in her," said the boy.

"Well, I'd take the resk o' that," eagerly urged Mr. Junkins. "I've got quite a stack o' boats, and I'm mighty keerful how I let 'em. What will ye take f'r her?"

"Let me see," mused Mr. Ray. "It cost us about twenty dollars, didn't it, Percy?"

"I kept the accounts very carefully," replied Percy. "Not reckoning our time, the bare materials stood us about twelve dollors. That doesn't include the oars. One of them went down the river."

"I'll give ye six dollars f'r her. She ain't no good to you nohow."

"I don't think I want to sell her," decided Percy. "I'm bound to discover what was the trouble with her, and if I can't make her carry me, I'll take the material and build another. What do you want of her, anyway?"

Ebenezer Junkins's desire to get the boat was so evident that the boy's bright mind was filled with all sorts of conjectures.

"Ef ye don't want to sell her, will ye rent her to me?"

"Tell us what you want to do with her," insisted Mr. Ray.

"If ye'll either sell her or rent her, I'll tell ye what my scheme is," replied Ebenezer, after a little consideration, during which he scratched his sandy hair vigorously.

"I'd just as lief rent it," said Percy. "Now tell us what you propose to do."

"Wall, I went to the circus onc't, and I see a bucking mule named Maud. Ther' was a standin' offer of five dollars to any one who'd stay three minutes on her back, an' I never see no one git it. When I heerd about your 'buckin' *boat,*' 't occurred to me that I might try the same scheme with *her.* I'll offer a dollar to the boy or man who will row or paddle her acrost fr'm the float over to the p'int 'thout gittin' tipped over—'t 's about as fur 's fr'm here up to the corner yonder. I'll charge ten cents a try at it. There's hundreds o' boys an' men come every season an' go in swimmin'. 'T'will be a grand card."

"What would you be willing to pay for it for the summer?"

At first he offered a lump sum, but, after some bargaining, it was decided that Percy should have twenty-five per cent. of all the profits.

"I come down in my hay-cart," said Ebenezer, "an' I s'pose I may 's well take her now 's any time. That's all right, ain't it?"

A little later, the village was astonished to see Ebenezer Junkins, whom every one knew, deliberately driving through the streets and across the bridge with the *Speranza,* apparently enjoying the sensation she was creating.

A week later, the Sunday-school which Percy was regularly attending held its annual picnic at the Pond. Every one was going. It was known that Percy's trick boat would be going through her paces. All the boys and a good many of the girls carried their bathing-suits, and an extra dime and the resolution to conquer the mischievous little craft. It was a perfect summer day, not even the prospect or threat of a shower to mar its festivity. There was the usual motley array of equipages—wagons which looked as if they had been made before the flood, old-fashioned chaises, barges, and carts piled high with sweet-scented new hay. Baskets filled with home-made goodies were not lacking, and the train started off promptly, with shouts and songs.

Percy, though he was going to play on the side of the Academy boys against the outsiders in a game of base-ball, managed, first of all, to steal away and get a look at his masterpiece—the bonny *Speranza.* Yes, there she floated, demure and graceful! He could not help feeling proud of her nice lines—a pride tempered, indeed, by the consciousness that she had played him false. Ebenezer saw him as he stood contemplating her.

"She's a swan!" exclaimed Percy, with a burst of enthusiasm he could not repress.

"I sh'd call her a duck!" chuckled Ebenezer. "Nobody ain't tamed her yit. More 'n forty's tried her so fur. That gives ye a dollar. Guess we'll make ye another to-day."

There was a hurry call for Percy, whose heart, it must be confessed, was not in the game. At least he did not play so well as usual. Nevertheless, the Academy boys came out ahead: the score stood five to four. When the nine innings were finished, there was a rush for the water. Three or four boys piled into each of the bath-houses, and, in an incredibly short time, the pond was alive with heads of every color—black, yellow, brown, red. Some dived from the float; others jumped; many raced in, leaving a foamy wake and making a prodigious splash. Several tried to see how far they could swim under water. But after the first general cooling off, there was a simultaneous convention gathered to tame Percy's trick boat. Ebenezer supervised the trials. A painted sign announced the terms: each competitor was to pay ten cents; any number might try at once. Whoever succeeded in propelling the *Speranza* from the float to the point without overturning should receive a dollar.

Percy himself was the first to try the game. He had an inward lurking hope that his first experience with his beautiful boat might have been only a dream—a dreadful nightmare. But the trick boat was true to her principles. She seemed to be actually alive. She took a mischievous delight in deceiving, for a moment, the careful venturer, and then, with a little shake, flinging him into the shining waters of the pond, the next moment riding calm and serene, as if no such impulse had ever entered her perverse feminine heart.

Half a dozen of the larger boys in succession tried to tame her; they all floundered, one after the other. Then companies of twos, threes, and fours, and, finally, half a dozen at once, experimented. The *Speranza* stood nobly to her reputation. She was no Atalanta: she would not be bribed by a golden apple; she was as tameless as Pegasus. She and her antics made the event of the picnic. Even the girls—a few of them, at least—with no little self-confidence, thought they might have better success; but the *Speranza* was proof against even this appeal to the sex pride— she refused to be wheedled.

Ebenezer pocketed the dimes.

It chanced that a sailor on shore leave arrived at the Pond. He heard of the unruly lady of the waters. He knew he could conquer her. He scorned to take off his watch. "I never saw a boat yet that I couldn't manage," he boasted. The *Speranza* heard him; she played with him after the manner of her kind. She let him row away ten or a dozen strokes from the dock. "This is an easy one!" he was saying to himself; but—the thought was finished in the cooling, gurgling waters. From the shore it could be seen how the tameless one exulted in her pride. The sailor knew not how to swim, but half a dozen of the boys bore down to his aid, and got him ashore, where he stood for a rueful moment, his wide trousers clinging limply to his legs, and streams of water like tears running

from his head; then he disappeared, all his boastfulness melted within him.

All that summer, Percy Ray's trick boat was the drawing attraction of Ebenezer Junkins's picnic grounds. Her fame traveled far and wide; men came from distant places to discover the cause of such a freak. As the *Speranza* sat on the water, she looked as innocent and harmless as a dove. Yet ever there lurked that tricksy spirit of mischief, ready to spill the would-be conqueror.

Percy's receipts for the season amounted to about fifty dollars. When the autumn came, it was the time for fairs; in such places as had streams or ponds easily accessible, there Ebenezer exhibited the *Speranza,* offering a prize of ten dollars for the successful mastery of the boat, and charging a quarter for the privilege. As the price went up, the boat's pride increased. She bridled with the witchery of her unconquerable nature. One would have thought that a more docile spirit might have come to her in time—that she would have tired of exhibiting what has been called "the total depravity of inanimate things." Inanimate? If ever a boat was animate, she was! She exerted an irresistible fascination. Men could not seem to help making the futile attempt to manage the fickle creature. But never once did the ten-dollar gold piece change hands.

When the weather became too cold, the *Speranza* was stored in a shed on Ebenezer Junkins's farm. One October morning, the shed was burned to the ground. It was supposed that some tramp who had slept in it had smoked his pipe and thrown a match into rubbish. The *Speranza* perished in the conflagration, with several more innocent boats. Ebenezer was inconsolable. She was the only boat of her class. Percy, with a part of the money which he received as his share of the sea-

son's proceeds, bought a second-hand mo-
tor-boat at a great bargain. It was an innovation on the river, and he soon covered the cost of it in taking excursion
parties to the Glen and the Old Indian
village, and other points of interest on
the river.

But he will wonder to his dying day
what caused the *Speranza* to deceive the
promise of its beautiful lines.

THE BOY WHO BORROWED TROUBLE

By FREDERICK B. OPPER

THOUGH extremely fond of coasting, this most peculiar lad,
　　While flying swiftly down the hill, would wear a look of pain;—
For already he was thinking—and it really made him sad—
　　That very soon he'd have to climb the whole way up again.

THE MAN WHO DID N'T BELIEVE IN CHRISTMAS

BY MARY AUSTIN

Albertine
Randall
Wheelan

PERSONS OF THE DRAMA

THE REAL PEOPLE
Alan, a lonely boy   Mr. Hardmann,
                 his father
Mammy Delia, the housekeeper

THE PASSERS-BY
Grocer's Boy   Shopping Girl
Old Woman   Newsboy

THE STORY PEOPLE
Red Riding Hood   The Three Bears
Captain Kidd   Fairy Princess
Toby, the Clown   The Wizard of Oz
Dare-Devil Dick, the Indian Fighter
Clarice, the World's Empress
Bareback Rider
TIME: The Present, Christmas Eve.

ACT FIRST

SCENE.—The living-room of a comfortably
furnished house in any American city. At
the back is a deep window-seat looking on
the street; at the left, a fireplace, with a
dull glow of coals; in front of it, a table
with a reading-lamp, unlighted; near that
a Morris chair. One or two other chairs
are arranged about the room, and over
the mantel is the portrait of a lady. A
strong light comes in from the window,
but the corners of the room are in darkness.

A boy of seven or eight is seated among
the cushions of the window-seat, turning
over a pile of books. From time to time
he glances out of the window.

A grocer's boy goes by with a basket from
which the top of a bunch of celery and a
chicken's legs may be seen sticking out.
The boy inside opens a small book and
begins to read. Little Red Riding Hood
comes out of the dusk on the right of the
room and goes briskly across with her
basket. As she disappears on the left you
can just see the Wolf, joining her. The
boy turns the pages, and from somewhere
in the dusk the Three Bears materialize,

each with his appropriate spoon. ("Who's been eating out of my spoon?") The boy keeps his eyes on the book and wriggles with appreciation.

A pretty girl, with her arms full of parcels, passes outside and calls, "Hello, Alan!" Turning to look at her and wave his hand, the boy lets his book fall, and the Three Bears disappear. He watches the girl out of sight. An old woman with wreaths of holly on her arm holds up one, inviting him to buy, but he shakes his head, and with a sigh turns to his books again. This time he selects a larger one; and as he reads, the Fairy Princess, who looks very like the young lady who just smiled at him, steps daintily across the room, and then other figures appear indistinctly. A newsboy outside, passing, cries, "Merry Christmas," and a man with a small fir-tree in his arms goes by. Alan answers, "Merry Christmas," but it ends in a sigh and a choke, and he turns to his books.

Now the shadowy figures grow plainer. Captain Kidd, with a cutlass in his mouth, buries a chest of Spanish Treasure behind the Morris chair, and Dare-Devil Dick, the Indian Fighter, comes scouting along the trail. Dick catches sight of the largest of the Three Bears, draws a bead on him, misses fire, and, drawing his bowie-knife as the bear rears on his hind legs, they clinch.

Just at the most dramatic moment the sound of a door opening causes them all to vanish; and Alan, who has been showing the most intense appreciation of what he reads, puts down his book to talk to the housekeeper, who enters from the right.

All this time the room has been growing dark, lit only by the glow of the street lamp outside. Now delicate flakes of snow begin to fall. Mammy Delia brings in a tray with Alan's supper, which she places on the table, turning on the reading-lamp, diffusing a warm glow over the room.

DELIA. Law sakes, honey, ef you ain't a-strainin' of you' eyes ag'in over them old story-bookses! Ef you' daddy was to catch you at it, you gonna hear somepin go smack, I reckon.

ALAN (*still absorbed in what he has been reading*). Mammy Delia, were you ever scalped? Or had to walk a plank?

DELIA. Who, me? (*Alan nods.*) Law bless you, chile, ain't no plank gonna hold me; I take the whole sidewalk.

ALAN. Oh, no, Delia, I mean as a pirate makes you. Captain Kidd, you know (*Pantomime*). But I guess they didn't do that to ladies. Pirates were always awfully kind to ladies; and the ladies sometimes got so fond of them that the pirates just couldn't drive them away.

DELIA (*moving about the room, drawing the curtains and setting the furniture to rights*). Oh, couldn't they!

ALAN. No. Don't you think that shows they have kind hearts, Delia?

DELIA (*placing a chair at the table*). Well, I reckon pirates is a whole lot like other people. They got as kind hearts as they can affo'd to have 'ithout spilin' their business.

ALAN. I'm glad you think so, because I really wouldn't *care* to be a pirate if they weren't kind. Sometimes I think I'd rather be an Indian fighter, because pirates have to fight perfectly good people sometimes; but Indian fighters only kill bears and red-skins and things of that kind. (*While Delia has her back turned he creeps upon her from behind with pantomime of scalping.*) Scalped! (*War-whoop*).

DELIA (*in mock terror*). Fo' de laws' sake, you ain't skelped me ag'in, is you? I reckon you' daddy'll do that, though, ef he comes home and catches you settin' up. (*She draws a chair invitingly.*) Come, now!

ALAN. It's very perplexing, don't you think, Delia, trying to decide what you'll be when you grow up?

DELIA (*tying his napkin*). Well, I guess havin' you' supper will help some with the growin'. (*Pushes him up.*)

ALAN (*catching sight of the bread and jam*). Oh—e! Strawberry jam! (*He reaches for it, but Delia catches his hand*).

DELIA. Porridge first! (*She brings a cushion to make him high enough, giving his napkin a final tuck*). Mind now, don't spot! You know you' daddy says you got to be a gen'man jes' the same when you's alone as when you got company.

ALAN. Uh—huh (*eating carefully*). Delia, why don't we have some Christmas in this house?

DELIA. Well, you know, you' pa, he don't believe in Chris'mus.

ALAN. Yes, but isn't it *there*? In the street and everywhere, just like Thanksgiving and—Sunday? I don't see how you can help believing in it if it is *there*.

DELIA. Well, leastways, he don't believe in makin' a fuss about it.

ALAN. Every window in this street has got some Christmas in it but ours.

DELIA (*with a quick glance up at the portrait on the wall*). You poor lamb!

ALAN (*following her glance*). If we had a mother in our house, *we'd* have a Christmas, too, wouldn't we, Delia?

DELIA. Yes, honey, you' mother, she was one for all kinds of doin's and fixin's. Seemed like we wasn't hardly done with Thanksgivin' till we was fixin' for Chris-mus. An' them ole story-books what you been readin', she was fond of 'em up to the last. 'Pears like this ole house ought to be plumb full of pirates an' b'ars an' fairy princesses an' sich, they was that alive to her.

ALAN (*kindling*). Oh, it is. Every time I open a book they just come right out. (*Mysteriously*) There's a chest of Spanish Treasure right over there behind that chair, Delia, and back there in that corner there's the most awful, horrible—grizzly bear!

DELIA. Awk! (*She gives a squeal of fright, and then recovers herself*). If you ain't the beatenest chile!

ALAN. I should think they wouldn't like it not to have any Christmas in the window.

DELIA (*to herself*). Poor lamb! (*Aloud*) But we don't have to have Chris'mus in the window, honey. We can have it right here in ou' hearts.

ALAN (*taking it seriously*). I don't know just what that means, Delia.

DELIA. Why, jus' lovin' and givin'. That's what Chris'mus is, honey lamb. We can love people in ou' hearts and give them things in ou' hearts. We can have that kind of Chris'mus.

ALAN (*soberly*). Can we? (*Absorbed in the subject, he absently lets the porridge fall from his spoon, and then puts the spoon in his mouth without noticing*).

DELIA. Mind you' napkin! You know what you' pa is always sayin'.

ALAN (*regarding the drip of his spoon thoughtfully, and then suddenly taken with an idea*). Why—of course we can have that kind of a Christmas. (*He finishes his porridge carefully, with great attention to keeping his napkin spotless, takes a careful drink of milk, and begins on his bread and jam.*)

DELIA. Besides, you jes' wait an' see what I got for dinner to-morrow.

ALAN (*interested*). Turkey?

DELIA. You jes' wait an' see!

ALAN. I know. Turkey and stuffing and celery—and mashed potato—and cranberry—and mince pie—ouch! (*In his excitement he has almost dripped the jam, but remedies that by licking the crust once around.*)

DELIA. (*Who has been piling up the books with her back to him.*) Ain't you 'most finished? You' pa is likely to be along home any minute now.

ALAN (*bolting the last mouthful*). Almost—Thank you. (*He licks his fingers, and, taking off his napkin, surveys its spotlessness with satisfaction.*) Not a one!

DELIA (*taking it from him*). Quite the little gen'man you're gettin' to be. Wait a minute! (*She attempts to wipe on the napkin the jam which he has not quite succeeded in removing from his countenance with his tongue*).

ALAN (*drawing back*). No, no. No, sir-ee! (*He takes out his handkerchief and polishes his cheeks with it.*) Now it's all right.

DELIA. And now you better run along to bed before you' pa—

ALAN. Please, Delia—I just have to stay up tonight until Daddy comes. There's something I have to ask him.

DELIA. You know what he said—

ALAN. He said I could stay up when it was necessary, and this is, Delia. It's *most* important.

DELIA (*reluctantly, as the boy strokes her cheek coaxingly*). Oh, well— But don't you try no 'maginary pufformances on you' pa, honey; he ain't built for 'em. (*Goes out with the tray.*)

(*Alan brings his book to the table, kneels in the chair to bring himself in the right relation to the lamp, and begins to turn the pages slowly. As he turns, Captain Kidd and Dare-Devil Dick come out of the shadow; they are joined by the Fairy Princess, and as the three talk the Three Bears lumber up and stand listening*).

CAPTAIN KIDD (*motioning to Dare-Devil Dick to draw near and regarding Alan with pride*). What a pirate he'd have made if they'd just let him have his chance in life!

DICK. Well, now, *I* think he rather favors trailin' an' scalpin'. But ain't it a plumb shame the poor kid don't have no Christmas? Ain't there nothing we can do about it?

CAPTAIN KIDD. Well, maybe if we made that father of his walk the plank—

PRINCESS. Oh, no, *she* wouldn't like that (*indicates picture*). You know, if it hadn't been for her, we wouldn't be here.

DICK. No, we can't go against the feelings of a lady.

PRINCESS. Don't you remember how all the time the boy was a tiny baby she kept calling us around her? She was afraid she would have to leave him, and she said if he could have *us* for friends—

CAPTAIN KIDD (*much moved*). Well, the *Jolly Roger* isn't exactly the school for Christmas angels, ma'am, but if you think of anything—

PRINCESS. We must *all* think—

DICK. The first thing is to lay for the father—

PRINCESS. Hush! I think he's coming! (*They slip back into the shadow and as the outer door is heard to close, Alan closes his book and they completely disappear. Mr. Hardmann is heard stamping in the entry, and immediately enters with his coat still on and hat in hand.*)

ALAN (*getting down from chair*). Hello, Daddy!

HARDMANN. Well, son! Been a good boy to-day?

ALAN. Yes, Daddy. (*They kiss formally.*)

HARDMANN. (*To Delia, who has en-*

tered and who takes his coat.) Just hang it where it will dry; there's quite a bit of snow falling. (*Exit Delia. Hardmann takes newspaper from pocket and draws up the Morris chair.*) A bit late, isn't it, for you, young man?

ALAN (*who stands touching him with timid affection.*) I wanted to ask you something.

HARDMANN. Well, out with it. (*He takes the boy's hand, not unkindly, but with stiffness.*)

ALAN. I wanted—to ask—if you would mind our having a little Christmas in the window to-morrow—

HARDMANN (*stiffening*). Who's been talking to you about Christmas? I thought I had made Delia understand—

ALAN (*alarmed*). No, Father, truly. I just thought of it by myself. You see, every house but ours—

HARDMANN. *Of* course! It's a conspiracy of tradespeople. The more fools they can get to buy their gimcracks—Christmas giving! Christmas getting would be more like it. I'll have nothing to do with it.

ALAN (*desperately*). I thought you wouldn't mind. I could take the money out of my bank—and we needn't put it up until after you had gone to the office— Daddy!

HARDMANN (*rising and taking an attitude before the fireplace*). Now, Alan, you have really hurt my feelings! You are talking as though I were a cruel and neglectful parent. I thought I had made you understand that, in doing my best to bring you up useful and successful, I had tried to avoid everything that is not eminently practical.

ALAN (*forlornly*). Yes, Daddy.

HARDMANN. Now what is there practical about Christmas? And Santa Claus? What's Santa Claus? Driving reindeer through the air! Sliding down chimneys! Stuff and nonsense! Do you understand?

ALAN (*choking back his disappointment and glancing back toward his storybook for support*). I—I think so, Daddy.

HARDMANN. Well, then, you mustn't disappoint me by indulging in such nonsense. It stimulates the imagination unduly. Your poor dear mother had too much imagination. It was her one failing, and I shouldn't be doing right by her son if I didn't try to correct it. Come now, kiss me good night, and let us hear no more of Christmas.

ALAN (*kissing him*). Good night, Daddy. (*He looks at his book and then back at his father, and, when he thinks the latter isn't looking, tries to slip the book away unobtrusively.*)

HARDMANN. Here, what's this? Reading in bed?

ALAN. I wasn't going to read. I was just —taking it. For company.

HARDMANN. Well, let me see what company you keep. I suppose it is time I began to supervise your reading. Come.

ALAN (*reluctantly yielding it*). It's a very nice book, Father. It—it isn't at all— imaginative.

HARDMANN (*reading the title*). Boy's Story-book. We'll see (*turning the pages*). Captain Kidd—h'm—Aladdin—Sindbad—

ALAN. Good night, Father.

HARDMANN (*abstracted*). Good night, son.

(*He adjusts the light and the Morris chair and begins to turn over the pages of the book, showing strong disapproval. He says "Pish!" and "Tut-tut!" and "This is worse than I thought!" But in spite of himself he grows interested, tries to pretend he is not, finally surrenders and settles down to enjoyment. As he reads, the story people gather in the dark corners of the room. They whisper and make signs to one another. Captain Kidd takes off his sash and offers it to Dare-Devil Dick, making signs what he shall do with it. Dick and Captain Kidd steal up on either side of Hardmann.*)

DICK. "Hands up!" (*They bind his hands behind him with the sash, and Dick takes off his own handkerchief to make a gag. Hardmann sputters.*)

CAPTAIN KIDD. There now, don't you make any more noise than you have to!

DICK (*with the gag*). He won't have any more chance to than the coon had with Davy Crockett. Now then! (*Slumping him back in the chair*). You look more the way a man ought to look who's been putting it all over a poor kid. Just because he's your'n! I've a notion to skelp you. Eh, Cap?

CAPTAIN KIDD. Walking the plank is too good for *him*. Shiver my timbers! Don't believe in Christmas!

RED RIDING HOOD. Why doesn't he?

ALL. *Yes, why don't you?* (*Hardmann makes inarticulate protest.*)

CAPTAIN KIDD. There wasn't a pirate ship on the Spanish Main that didn't have an extra grog and a plum pudding for Christmas.

RED RIDING HOOD. Why, you're worse than a pirate!

THE OTHERS. Yes, you are worse than a pirate!

PRINCESS. A great deal worse. You've had a chance to learn better.

RED RIDING HOOD. I think he ought to be magicked away to some place *where nothing ever happens.*

DICK. That's no good. That kind don't know when anything happens, anyway.

PRINCESS. Oh, I've thought of something! Listen! (*They all gather around her to whisper.*)

DICK. Hist! You, Pete! (*He motions to the Father Bear to take his place while he joins the others.*)

CAPTAIN KIDD. You, mate! (*He panto-*

mimes to the Mother Bear to take her place beside the prisoner*). Fo'castle council!

(*Hardmann, who has not seen the bears, as soon as the others turn their backs tries to get out of his chair on one side, and is terrified back by the open jaws of Father Bear; he tries to sneak out on the other side, and confronts Mother Bear. He sinks back in the chair, and Baby Bear comes sniffing about his toes. He begins to kick out frantically and makes sputtering noises. This attracts the others.*)

DICK. Hold on there, hold on! (*Separating him from Baby Bear.*) Ain't you got no feelings for the young? He was just having fun with you. Why, I knew a man had his whole arm et off and didn't make so much fuss about it. Take his gag off and let him talk some. It'll relieve his feelings.

(*While this is being done there is music and a whoop-halloo outside, and Toby the Clown comes tumbling into the room, holding a hoop through which the Bareback Empress suddenly bounces and pirouettes about the circle.*)

PRINCESS. Oh! I never saw you before. Did *you* come out of a book?

CLARICE. Out of a circus, and that's pretty near the same thing. I heard you were having a party, and this gentleman (*kissing her hand to Hardmann*) is a friend of mine.

HARDMANN. I—really, there's some mistake, I—really!

CLARICE. And what's more, he once admired me very much. (*Sensation.*)

HARDMANN. I?—preposterous!

CLARICE. You did. You were eleven and a half when your father took you to a circus, and you saw me there.

CLOWN. What's more, you admired *me*. You were going to be *me* when you grew up. You used to practise this out in the barn (*tumbles*).

CLARICE. Yes, and when your own boy wanted to go to the circus this summer you—said—it was—enervating!

THE OTHERS. Oh! You never! How could you!

HARDMANN. I didn't! That is—I mean I don't know this lady. I won't be responsible for what people like that say about me.

DICK. Why, it's the best thing I ever heard about you. If you was to *be* one of them things, you'd have to be doing something every minute.

CLOWN. You betcha! (*Business of clowning*) Like that!

CAPTAIN KIDD. That's why boys like to read us, real healthy boys. We're always doing something.

PRINCESS. It's very stimulating to the imagination.

THE OTHERS. Yes. Of course it is. Didn't you know *that?*

PRINCESS. And that's what gave me my idea.

CLARICE. What's that?

PRINCESS. Why, that he should have to be each one of us in turn until he finds out what we are for.

THE OTHERS. Yes! That's the idea. Make him find out!

CLARICE. Well, you're rather old to begin my business. They generally break a leg or an arm when they begin at your age. Still, that's nothing, and if you fall, the horses hardly ever step on you.

HARDMANN (*alarmed*). Really, I—

CAPTAIN KIDD. There's nothing like pirating to keep you limber. Why, I've seen the time when the scuppers were running full and the rigging half over, and the sea swarming with sharks—And there was Old Flint. Remember Flint? (*Sings*).

Fifteen men on the dead man's chest,

(*The others join*)

Yoho, and a bottle of rum!

HARDMANN. I'm a respectable citizen—

DICK. That won't do you no good when you get into the redskin's country. (*Fixes his gag again.*) Now, don't you try no funny business. We're going to learn you something. Let's begin. (*Hardmann shows extreme terror as Dick begins pantomime of Indian war-dance and scalping.*)

CLARICE. Well, I think we ought to do something for the poor kid first.

RED RIDING HOOD. He ought to have some kind of Christmas.

THE OTHERS. Yes, of course he ought. (*They consider.*)

PRINCESS. I know! Let's ask the Wizard of Oz.

CLARICE. Well, he doesn't seem to be among those present—

PRINCESS. Oh, *that's* easy. I only have to make a figure like this with my wand, and wave it like this—and this—and turn around three times—and stamp my foot—

(*There is a flash of light, a flash of darkness, then the lights are at normal again and the Wizard of Oz is seen.*)

And there he is!

WIZARD (*proceeding at once to do tricks of magic and legerdemain*). What can I do for you?

PRINCESS. We want you to make a Christmas.

RED RIDING HOOD. For a little boy who never had any.

CLARICE. Christmas-trees and toys and candy.

WIZARD. Produce your boy.

PRINCESS. Why, we can't, you know. He's upstairs, asleep.

WIZARD. I see. You want a dream Christmas. Nothing easier. Make the magic circle there.

(*They make a circle, pushing back the furniture, the Wizard producing whatever he needs by magic, describes circles in the air with his wand, and begins to pace a magic figure, chanting*)

Cabala, quabala,
Abracadabra,
Zamiel, Amiel, Abaron, Tymayel,
Shemeshiel, Malkahiel,
Tetragram, Pentagon,
Fee! Foo! Fum!

(*As he paces, the others circle in back, moving from right to left as he moves from left to right, each one using movements appropriate to his character.*)

STORY PEOPLE (*dancing and chanting*).
Intry, Mintry, Cutery corn,
Apple seed and briar thorn,
Onery, oery, ichory Ann,
Phillison, phollison,
Nicholas, John—

WIZARD OF OZ (*his voice rising above the others as smoke begins to arise within the circle and a strange light shines about him*).
Shemeshiel, Malkahiel,
Macaroni, piebald pony,
Samiel and Grimalkin,
Cabala, quabala,
Abracadabra,
Ding, Dong, Dell—

(*As the last word thunders out, the smoke clears and shows a small Christmas-tree in the middle of the circle.*)

ALL. Oh, lovely!

WIZARD. Now for the gifts. (*He goes about extracting small toys from each of them—a ball, a top, etc.*)

PRINCESS. But I want to give him something my own self. Christmas-trees have stars, don't they? (*She takes the star from her wand and fixes it to the top of the tree. The Wizard waves his wand, and suddenly the star glows, amid exclamations of delight.*)

CLARICE. I want to be in on this. (*She takes the spangles from her dress; the clown hangs up his whistle.*)

CAPTAIN KIDD (*lugging his treasure-chest*). Just let him get his hands into this! (*He opens it at the foot of the tree and holds up a handful of gold*). Spanish Treasure!

DICK (*showing a bowie-knife*). These long marks are for the Injuns I've killed, and these notches are for grizzly bears, and the crosses are for life-and-death struggles.

PRINCESS. Dear me, there seem to be a great many of them!

DICK. Yes, ma'am; and if he finds he needs any more, I can easy put 'em on for him. (*He hangs it on the tree and at the same time Red Riding Hood produces a cake from her basket and puts it on the treasure-chest.*)

WIZARD. Now, produce your boy! (*They all look blank.*)

PRINCESS. Well, of course, it's only a dream Christmas—(*she looks troubled*).

CLARENCE. Well, he could walk in his sleep, couldn't he?

PRINCESS. The very thing. I know a fairy spell! You must all help me. Somebody open the door.

(*Red Riding Hood sets the door open. The Princess begins to dance and to sing softly. A fairy light plays over the whole scene. The others stand back and accompany her dance with a low crooning*).

PRINCESS (*singing*)

All you sleeping in this house,
Man and child and creeping mouse,
Hearken to my fairy spell!

(*Chorus*)
Hearken to her fairy spell!

Hark, but do not wake to hear,
Be your slumber without fear,
While the dream is hovering near,
Slumber deep and well!
(*Chorus*)
Slumber deep and well!

You, dear child, for whom we wait,
Come you through the Dreamland Gate,
Listening to my fairy spell!
(*Chorus*)
Listening to her fairy spell!

Come you softly down the stair,
Of the darkness unaware,
Come to those who speak you fair
And who love you well!
(*Chorus*)
All who love you well!

(*She pauses to listen at the doorway, turns to the others and nods reassuringly, and sings softly*)

Now the dream is at its best,
Day is neither East nor West,
Come but do not break your rest,
Come, oh come!
(*Chorus*)
Come, dear dreamer, come!

(*The Princess backs away from the door, dancing still with beckoning movements as she draws Alan, who appears at the door in his night things, with his shoes and stockings in one hand and his little coat in the other.*)

ALAN (*vaguely*). I thought somebody called me. Oh—ee! (*catching sight of the tree*). Christmas-tree! (*He drops his clothes and advances, entranced, discovering the others*). Why, you are all here! (*Timid for a moment, he suddenly remembers*) Merry Christmas! Everybody!

ALL. Merry Christmas! Merry Christmas!

ALAN. Captain Kidd, and Dare-Devil Dick the Indian Fighter, and the Fairy Princess, and—and everybody. (*Wistfully*) Is that your tree?

PRINCESS. No, it's yours. See, this is what I gave you. (*Alan is overcome*).

DICK. And look-a-here, Pard. This is from me.

CAPTAIN KIDD (*thrusting his hands in the chest*). Pieces of Eight!

RED RIDING HOOD (*giving him cake*). Now sit right down and eat every bit. It's got pink icing.

ALAN (*sitting down, cake in hand, on the treasure-chest*). And who is this? I don't believe I know your story?

CLARICE. Oh, I'm Mademoiselle Clarice, the World's Bareback Empress!

ALAN (*looking at her back interestedly*). Oh! (*Wishing to be polite*) Don't you ever catch cold?

CLARICE. Well, what do you think of that? That's what comes of keepin' kids away from the circus.

ALAN. Oh—ee, circus! Oh, won't you please do a little of it now?

CLARICE. Why, sure. That's what I'm here for. Hoop-la, Toby!

(*The clown and Clarice begin their act, and one by one the others join in, doing things for Alan's entertainment, the Wizard pulling rabbits out of people's collars, etc., Captain Kidd dancing a hornpipe with Father Bear, until the boy is quite beside himself with laughter and sounds of delight. In the meantime Alan's father, who has been sitting in the background, gagged and tied, has worked the handkerchief from his mouth, and calls attention to himself with various spluttering noises. When the fun is at its height he breaks out.*)

HARDMANN. Stop, stop! I object. That's not the sort of thing I want my son to see. It's foolish, it's impractical—

ALAN. Father! (*Goes up to him.*) Why, your hands are tied!

HARDMANN. I tell you, I'll not sit here and have my son hear such things—

DICK. Easy, old scout.

ALAN. What are you doing to my father? Untie his hands!

PRINCESS. You see, my dear, we don't regard him as a suitable kind of father for a nice, imaginative boy like you—

ALAN (*almost crying*). What are you going to do with him?

CAPTAIN KIDD. Walking the plank's too good for—

DICK (*stopping him*). Why, you see, he was going to take your book away. And then where would you be without us?

RED RIDING HOOD. And he doesn't believe in Christmas!

PRINCESS. And the fairy folk don't care much about staying around a house where there isn't any Christmas, not a teenty little smidge of it.

ALAN (*laying his hand on his father's arm*). You—you mean that you won't stay if my father stays—

PRINCESS. You see, it isn't only the fairy folk who leave! There are lots of other nice things go out of a house where there isn't any Christmas—you'll find when you grow up—and lots of ugly things come in — You'll have to choose.

ALAN (*stoutly struggling with tears*). It isn't true that there isn't any Christmas in this house. There is some right here in my heart. Christmas is loving—Mammy Delia said it was. And—I love you, and I love my father—

PRINCESS. Christmas is giving, too, little boy.

ALAN (*dashing away the tears triumphantly*). Well, I was giving some-thing, too. I was giving my father a Christmas gift. I—I'm a nawful careless little boy—an' I spot my napkin and sometimes the tablecloth—and disappoint my father. And I didn't spot them to-night. And I wasn't going to, *ever*—and I was giving it to him for a Christmas gift. (*He bursts into tears and throws himself upon his father's breast*). And I don't want him to go away, I want him to sta—ay!

(*At the boy's first sob, the story people look at one another in consternation, and at the next, all the lights but the reading-lamp go out, and they all vanish. The lights go up a little and show Alan sobbing in his father's arms in the Morris chair.*)

HARDMANN. There, there, son (*petting him*).

ALAN. Father, Father! I don't want you to go away!

HARDMANN. Why, I'm not going. I'm here, son. You've been dreaming. Hush—hush.

DELIA (*entering, in dressing-gown*). 'Scuse me, Mr. Hardmann, I thought I heard Master Alan cryin'.

HARDMANN. He's been walking in his sleep, and he's had a dream or two.

ALAN (*now fully awake and puzzled*). I thought Daddy was going away.

HARDMANN. Why, I couldn't leave you, son. I—why, I would get to be quite an old fogy without my boy—I— Isn't that so, Delia?

DELIA. Well, you suttenly was aidgin' in that direction, Mr. Hardmann.

HARDMANN. Yes, I—(*embarrassed*)—I think you'd better take him right up to bed. There are—several things I want to do (*gives her the boy*). I—suppose you couldn't tell me if the shops on this street are open, Delia?

DELIA (*as she takes Alan, now drowsing*

off again). Yes, sir, they's right smart sto's, keeps open till midnight, along of to-morrow bein' Chris'mus.

ALAN (*rousing sleepily*). Merry Christmas, Daddy.

HARDMANN. Aw—er—Merry Christmas! (*Delia bursts into a laugh which she tries discreetly, but unsuccessfully, to check as she goes out with Alan in her arms or drowsily stumbling along beside her*).

(*Left alone, Hardmann goes to the window, drawing the curtain to look up and down the street. The old woman with holly wreaths holds up one. Hardmann makes signs that he wishes to buy, opens the sash, hands out the money, and is heard to say emphatically, "Two, please." Receives the two wreaths, hangs them up in the window and hurries to the door. He stumbles over Alan's shoes and stockings, picks them up, is struck with an idea, and, timidly looking up at his wife's picture for approval, hangs up one stocking at the mantelpiece, and then hurries out at the door like a man bent on a pleasant errand. Christmas chimes are heard.*

CURTAIN.

THE COOPER AND THE WOLVES

by Hjalmar H. Boyesen

TOLLEF KOLSTAD was a cooper, and a very skillful cooper he was said to be. He had a little son named Thor, who was as fond of his father as his father was of him. Whatever Tollef did or said, Thor was sure to imitate; if Tollef was angry and flung a piece of wood at the dog who used to come into the shop and bother him, Thor, thinking it was a manly thing to do, flung another piece at poor Hector, who ran out whimpering through the door.

Thor, of course, was not very old before he had a corner in his father's shop, where, with a small set of tools which had been especially made for him, he used to make little pails and buckets and barrels, which he sold for five or ten cents apiece, to the boys of the neighborhood. All the money earned in this way he put into a bank of tin, made like a drum, of which his mother kept the key. When he grew up, he thought, he would be a rich man.

The last weeks before Christmas are, in Norway, always the briskest season in all trades; then the farmer wants his horses shod, so that he may take his wife and children to church in his fine, swan-shaped sleigh; he wants bread and cakes made to last through the holidays, so that his servants may be able to amuse themselves and his guests may be well entertained when they call; and, above all, he wants large tubs and barrels, stoutly made of beech staves, for his beer and mead, with which he pledges every stranger who, during the festival, happens to pass his door. You may imagine, then, that at Christmas time coopers are much in demand, and that it is not to be wondered at if sometimes they are behindhand with their orders. This was unfortunately the case with Tollef Kolstad at the time when the strange thing happened which I am about to tell you. He had been at work since the early dawn, upon a huge tub or barrel, which had been ordered by Grim Berglund, the richest peasant in the parish. Grim was to give a large party on the following day (which was Christmas eve), and he had made Tollef promise to bring the barrel that same night, so that he might pour the beer into it, and have all in readiness for the holidays, when it would be wrong to do any work. It was about ten o'clock at night when Tollef made the last stroke with his hatchet on the large hollow thing, upon which every blow resounded as on a drum. He went to a neighbor and hired from him his horse and flat sleigh, and was about to start on his errand, when he heard a tiny voice calling behind him:

"Father, do take me along, too!"

"I can't, my boy. There may be wolves on the lake to-night, and they might like to eat up little boys who stay out of bed so late."

"But I am not afraid of them, Father. I have my whip and my hatchet, and I'll whip them and cut them."

Thor here made some threatening flourishes with his weapons in the air, indicating how he would give it to the wolves in case they should venture to approach him.

"Well, come along, you little rascal," said his father, laughing, and feeling rather proud of his boy's dauntless spirit. "You and I are not to be trifled with when we are angered, are we, Thor?"

"No, indeed, Father," said Thor, and clenched his little mittened fist.

Tollef then lifted him up, wrapped him warmly in his sheep-skin jacket, and put him between his knees, while he himself seized the reins and urged the horse on.

It was a glorious winter night. The snow sparkled and shone as if sprinkled with starry diamonds, the aurora borealis flashed in pale, shifting colors along the horizon, and the moon sailed calmly through a vast, dark-blue sea of air. Little Thor shouted with delight as he saw the broad expanse of glittering ice, which they were about to cross, stretching out before them like a polished shield of steel.

"Oh, Father, I wish we had taken our skates along, and pulled your barrel across on a sled," cried the boy, ecstatically.

"That I might have done, if I had had a sled large enough for the barrel," replied the father. "But then we should have been obliged to pull it up the hills on the other side."

The sleigh now struck the ice and shot forward, swinging from side to side, as the horse pulled a little unevenly. Whew! how the cold air cut in their faces. How it whizzed and howled in the tree-tops! Hark! What was that? Tollef instinctively pressed his boy more closely to him. Hush!—his heart stood still, while that

of the boy, who merely felt the reflex shock of his father's agitation, hammered away the more rapidly. A terrible, long-drawn howl, as from a chorus of wild, far-away voices, came floating away over the crowns of the pine-trees.

"What was that, Father?" asked Thor, a little tremulously.

"It was wolves, my child," said Tollef, calmly.

"Are you afraid, Father?" asked the boy again.

"No, child, I am not afraid of one wolf, nor of ten wolves; but if they are in a flock of twenty or thirty, they are dangerous. And if they scent our track, as probably they will, they will be on us in five minutes."

"How will they scent our track, Father?"

"They smell us in the wind; and the wind is from us and to them, and then they howl to notify their comrades, so that they may attack us in sufficient force."

"Why don't we return home, then?" inquired the boy, still with a tolerably steady voice, but with sinking courage.

"They are behind us. Our only chance is to reach the shore before they overtake us."

The horse, sniffing the presence of wild beasts, snorted wildly as it ran, but, electrified, as it were, with the sense of danger, strained every nerve in its efforts to reach the farther shore. The howls now came nearer and nearer, and they rose with a frightful distinctness in the clear, wintry air, and resounded again from the border of the forest.

"Why don't you throw away the barrel, Father?" said Thor, who, for his father's sake, strove hard to keep brave. "Then the sleigh will run so much the faster."

"If we are overtaken, our safety is in the barrel. Fortunately, it is large enough for two, and it has no ears and will fit close to the ice."

Tollef was still calm; but, with his one disengaged arm, hugged his little son convulsively.

"Now, keep brave, my boy," he whispered in his ear. "They will soon be upon us. Give me your whip."

It just occurred to Tollef that he had heard that wolves were very suspicious, and that men had often escaped them by dragging some small object on the ground behind them. He, therefore, broke a chip from one of the hoops of the barrel, and tied it to the lash of the whip; just then he heard a short, hungry bark behind him, and turning his head, saw a pack of wolves, numbering more than a dozen, the foremost of which was within a few yards of the sleigh. He saw the red, frothy tongue hanging out of its mouth, and he smelt that penetrating, wild smell with which every one is familiar who has met a wild beast in its native haunts. While encouraging the reeking, foam-flecked horse, Tollef, who had only half faith in the experiment with the whip, watched anxiously the leader of the wolves, and observed to his astonishment that it seemed to be getting no nearer. One moment it seemed to be gaining upon them, but invariably, as soon as it reached the little chip which was dragging along the ice, this suddenly arrested its attention and immediately its speed slackened. The cooper's hope began to revive, and he thought that perhaps there was yet a possibility that they might see the morrow's sun. But his courage again began to ebb when he discovered in the distance a second pack of wolves, larger than the first, and which, with terrific speed, came running, leaping, and whirling toward them from another direction. And while this terrible discovery was breaking through his almost callous sense, he forgot, for an in-

stant, the whip, the lash of which swung under the runners of the sleigh and snapped. The horse, too, was showing signs of exhaustion, and Tollef, seeing that only one chance was left, rose up with his boy in his arms, and upsetting the barrel on a great ledge of ice, concealed himself and the child under it. Hardly had he had time to brace himself against its sides, pressing his feet against one side and his back against the other, when he heard the horse giving a wild scream, while the short, whining bark of the wolves told him that the poor beast was selling its life dearly. Then there was a desperate scratching and scraping of horseshoes, and all of a sudden the sound of galloping hoof-beats on the ice, growing fainter and fainter. The horse had evidently succeeded in breaking away from the sleigh, and was testing his speed in a race for life. Some of the wolves were apparently pursuing him, while the greater number remained to investigate the contents of the barrel. The howling and barking of these furious creatures without was now incessant. Within the barrel was pitch darkness.

"Now, keep steady!" said Tollef, feeling a sudden shock, as if a wolf had leaped against their improvised house with a view to upsetting it. He felt himself and the boy gliding a foot or two over the smooth ice, but there was no further result from the attack. A minute passed; again there came a shock, and a stronger one than the first. A long, terrible howl followed this second failure. The little boy, clutching his small cooper's hatchet in one hand, sat pale but determined in the dark, while with the other he clung to his father's arm.

"Oh, Father!" he cried, in terror, "I feel something on my back."

The father quickly struck a light, for he fortunately had a supply of matches in his pocket, and saw a wolf's paw wedged in between the ice and the rim of the barrel; and in the same instant he tore the hatchet from his son's hand and buried its edge in the ice. Then he handed the amputated paw to Thor, and said:

"Put that into your wallet, and the sheriff will pay you a reward for it. For a wolf without paws couldn't do much harm."

While he was yet speaking, a third assault upon the barrel lifted one side of it from the ice, and almost upset it. Instead of pushing against the part nearest the ice, a wolf more cunning than the rest had leaped against the upturned bottom.

You can imagine what a terrible night father and son spent together in this constant struggle with the voracious beasts, that never grew weary of attacking their hiding-place. The father was less warmly clad than the son, and, moreover, was obliged to sit on the ice, while Thor could stand erect without knocking against the bottom of the barrel; and if it had not been for the excitement of the situation, which made Tollef's blood course with unwonted rapidity, it is more than probable that the intense cold would have made him drowsy, and thus lessened his power of resistance. The warmth of his body had made a slight cavity where he was sitting, and whenever he remained a moment still, his trousers froze fast to the ice. It was only the presence of his boy that inspired him with fresh courage whenever hope seemed about to desert him.

About an hour after the flight of the horse, when five or six wolves' paws had been cut off in the same manner as the first, there was a lull in the attack, but a sudden increase of the howling, whining, yelping, and barking noise without. Tollef concluded that the wolves, maddened by the smell of blood, were attacking their wounded fellows; and as their howls seemed to come from a short distance, he cautiously lifted one side of the barrel and peered forth; but in the same instant a snarling bark rang right in his ear, and two paws were thrust into the opening. Then came a howl of pain, and another paw was put into Thor's wallet.

But hark! What is that? It sounds like a song, or more like a hymn. The strain comes nearer and nearer, resounding from mountain to mountain, floating peacefully through the pure and still air:

"Who knows how near I am mine
    ending;
  So quickly time doth pass away."

Tollef, in whose breast hope again was reviving, put his ear to the ice, and heard distinctly the tread of a horse and of many human feet. He listened for a minute or more, but could not discover whether the sound was coming any nearer. It occurred to him that in all probability the people, being unarmed, would have no desire to cope with a large pack of wolves, especially as to them there could be no object in it. If they saw the barrel, how could they know that there was anybody under it? He comprehended instantly that his only chance of life was in joining those people, before they were too far away. And, quickly resolved, he lifted the boy on his left arm, and grasped the hatchet in his disengaged hand. Then, with a violent thrust, he flung the barrel from over him, and ran in the direction of the sound. The wolves, as he had inferred, were lacerating their bleeding comrades; but the moment they saw him, a pack of about a dozen immediately started in pursuit. They leaped up against him on all sides, while he struck furiously about him with his small weapon. Fortunately, he had sharp steel pegs on his boots, and kept his footing well; otherwise the combat would have been a short one.

His voice, too, was powerful, and his shouts rose high above the howling of the beasts. He soon perceived that he had been observed, and he saw in the bright moonlight six or eight men running toward him. Just then, as perhaps in his joy his vigilance was for a fraction of a second relaxed, he felt a pull in the fleshy part of his right arm. He was not conscious of any sharp pain, and was astonished to see the blood flowing from an ugly wound. But he only held his boy the more tightly, while he fought and ran with the strength of despair.

Now, the men were near. He could hear their voices. But his brain was dizzy, and he saw but dimly.

"Hello, friend; don't crack my skull for my pains!" some one was shouting close to his ear, and he let his hatchet fall, and fell himself, too, prostrate on the ice.

The wolves, at the sight of the men, had retired to a safe distance, from which they watched the proceedings, as if uncertain whether to return.

As soon as Tollef had recovered some- what from his exhaustion and his loss of blood, he and his boy were placed upon a sleigh, and his wound was carefully bandaged. He now learned that his rescuers were on their way to a funeral, which was to take place on the next day, but, on account of the distance to the church, they had been obliged to start during the night. Hence their solemn mood, and their singing of funeral hymns.

After an hour's ride they reached the cooper's cottage, and were invited to rest and to share such hospitality as the house could offer. But when they were gone, Tollef clasped his sleeping boy in his arms and said to his wife: "If it had not been for him, you would have had no husband to-day. It was his little whip and toy hatchet that saved our lives."

Eleven wolves'-paws were found in Thor's wallet, and, on Christmas eve, he went to the sheriff with them and received a reward which nearly burst his old savings-bank, and compelled his mother to buy a new one.

"CHRISTMAS GIF'"

by Ralph Henry Barbour

Jimmy stroud slammed the door behind him and joyfully assaulted his room-mate. "I got you in!" he announced triumphantly. "I worked it!"

"Hey, hold on!" protested Tom Wayne. "Got me in what?"

"Hal's Christmas party, of course. I told you about it yesterday, stupid!"

"Yes, but you didn't say anything about me!"

"Course not." Jimmy slid into a chair and beamed. "Wasn't certain I could swing it for you and didn't want you disappointed. But it's all right, old chap. Trust little James! Hal was about decided for Ted Winslow, but I fixed that. Why, shucks, Ted wouldn't fit in at all! Not in this bunch."

"Well, but—"

"Hal will be around to invite you pretty soon. Say, it's going to be some party, Tom! He was telling about this house where he lives, and I'll bet it's a corker. It's in the country, sort of, only you can get into New York in almost no time, he says. And it's got just about everything; billiard-room and skating-pond—"

"In the house?" ejaculated Tom.

"And cars and horses and—and—"

"But look here, Jimmy," the listener interrupted, "I didn't suppose you were going to—to get Hal to ask me! Do you think he really wants me?" Tom's incredulity was natural, for Hal Townsend was the acknowledged and admired leader of a considerable coterie at Embury School, of which Tom was at the best no more than a quasi-member—and that by virtue of his acquaintance with Jimmy. He couldn't help feeling flattered.

"Of course he wants you," answered Jimmy impatiently. "I had to talk you up a bit, but he came around. Besides, I showed him what a dim bulb Ted would be at a house-party. Why, gosh, I don't suppose he even owns a dress-suit!"

"I kind of wish you hadn't knocked him, though. Ted's an awfully decent sort."

"Sure, but listen, Tom. You don't get it. This is a bang-up affair. Dinners and dances and theaters. 'Evening clothes obligatory.' Where'd Ted be? He wouldn't enjoy it a bit!"

"Still," Tom murmured, "I don't see why Hal asks me."

"You don't, eh?" Jimmy chuckled. "Well, for one thing, you had a mighty good press-agent. Besides, Hal likes you anyhow. He says you know how to wear your clothes and aren't dumb. And you dance pretty well, too, and there'll be girls there. Say, what are you looking so sunk for? Gee, I thought you'd be tickled!"

"I am, Jimmy, and it was awfully decent of you to take so much trouble," answered Tom earnestly. There were occasions when he wasn't particularly enthusiastic about his room-mate, but present gratitude oblit-

307

erated the memory of them. "I'd like awfully to go, too, but—oh, gosh, Jimmy, I don't see how I can!"

"Why not, for Pete's sake?" asked the other amazedly.

"Well, I—I've always been home for Christmas. I don't believe Mother would like me to be away. You see, there's just the three of us, and—no, I guess it wouldn't do, Jimmy." Tom shook his head regretfully. "Maybe if I'd known sooner I could have kind of prepared them, but it's all settled now."

"Sooner! Why, gee, it's eleven days to Christmas, Tom! What's eating you? Write home and say you've had a bid to a corking house-party and that you simply can't afford to turn it down. And you really can't, Tom. It means a lot to a fellow to be invited home by Hal Townsend. In a way it's your duty to accept. Hal's a fine chap, but if he's down on you—and don't forget that you haven't got your place on the team cinched by any means, Tom. Of course Hal isn't one of the baseball crowd, but he's a senior and he can pull a lot of strings. I don't mean that he'd do anything nasty—"

"I wouldn't be afraid of what he'd do to me," replied Tom a trifle coldly. "I'd really like to go, of course. But if I can't—well, I just can't. If he asks me I'll simply tell him how it is, and—"

"No, wait! Don't be a goof, Tom! Tell him you'll go. Then if anything happens you can get out of it later. But I don't see why your mother shouldn't let you; honest, I don't!"

"Oh, I guess she'd *let* me," murmured Tom, "it isn't that."

"What is it, then?"

"I'm afraid they'd be awfully disappointed, Jimmy; Mother and Ellen. They sort of look forward to having me home at Christmas, and there's been no question of

my not going, and so—well, I sort of hate to—spoil it."

"Shucks, what's one Christmas in so many? Besides, Hal's only asking us from Wednesday to Monday. That'll give you a whole week at home. Be your age, Tom!"

"That's so," replied Tom, brightening a little. "Well, I—I guess it won't do any harm to write and see how Mother feels about it."

"Course it won't! And, listen, Tom, put it strong, eh?"

The invitation came a few hours later, and Tom, although forewarned, accepted it with such evidences of embarrassment and gratitude that Hal's vanity was pleased and he concluded that perhaps, after all, he hadn't erred in allowing Jimmy Stroud to persuade him against Ted Winslow. Tom tried hard to approach that difficult letter to his mother, but it wasn't until the following afternoon that he finally got it off. And all the rest of the day, after he had dropped it in the letter-box he wished it back again.

Jimmy professed to hold it certain that Tom was to be one of the fortunate five destined to enjoy the hospitality of the Townsends, and brought frequent tidings regarding the magnificence of the Townsend home, the number of servants employed there, the plans for entertainment, and so on. "Hal says there'll be something doing every night. His father has already bought theater tickets for two shows in New York, and we're to dine in town beforehand. Then there's a dinner-dance at the Country Club on Christmas Eve, and a luncheon somewhere on Christmas Day—"

"But don't we eat at home ever?" asked Tom perplexedly.

Jimmy shrugged. "Oh, I guess so, but Hal says they dine out a lot. More fun, I dare say."

"Y-yes, but what's the good of all those servants you told about? Gee, that's a funny way to live!"

The letter from his mother didn't come until Saturday, and when it did Tom hesitated for a long minute before he opened it. But having read it he sighed with vast relief. Everything was quite all right! "Of course, dear," Mrs. Wayne wrote, "we're a little disappointed, for Ellen and I have been looking forward to seeing you for so long, but I quite understand your wish to accept such a nice invitation, and since we're to have you from Tuesday on it won't seem quite so bad. I suspect that Ellen means to write, too, dear, but you mustn't mind what she says. She is young and thoughtless, and a little upset just now. When she is older she will learn that she can't always have things her own way. I do hope you'll have a splendid time in New York, but don't let your friends keep you too long. We shall be thinking of you often on Christmas Day, my dear boy."

There was much more: news of Aunt Emmie and Uncle Marsh; of the horses and dogs and cousins and neighbors; also the announcement that Tom's presents would be awaiting him at home. But this portion Tom only skimmed over on first reading, the fact that he was free to attend Hal's party overshadowing everything else. It was only when he reread the letter that doubts assailed him. Mother had made light of her disappointment, he mused, but she wasn't fooling him. For some moments he wavered. It still wasn't too late to change his mind. But in the end he placed the letter back in its envelope and frowningly locked it away.

His sister's letter arrived the next morning. It wasn't a pleasant letter, for Ellen called him a selfish pig and several other things no more flattering; said that Mother had cried when his news had arrived; declared that for her part she didn't care a picayune if he didn't come home at all, that she hoped he'd have a perfectly beastly time in New York and that she hated him. Tom scowled considerably during the perusal and then crumpled up the agitated epistle and hurled it in the wastebasket. "She's crazy," he muttered angrily. "Wish I hadn't sent her a thing!" But it was too late now, for he had despatched his mother's present and hers the day before. They weren't as nice as he had intended, for, although this visit to the Townsends was, theoretically at least, to entail no expenditure on his part, Jimmy had reminded him that it would cost a lot in tips. "It's a quarter every time you turn around in New York," he said complacently. "And then you're expected to tip the servants when you leave. Better take plenty, Tom."

Not so easy, though, for Tom had had to buy a pair of new patent leathers, not to mention four dress collars and a tie, and these expenditures left him woefully short; moreover, there was still the price of a ticket to Carver's Run, Virginia, to be reckoned with. However, financial worries were soon forgotten in the joys of anticipation as the term neared its end and Christmas holidays drew closer. The only incident to mar that period of pleasant suspense was a near quarrel with Jimmy. They were discussing the social merits of the other three fellows whom Hal had selected for his party, comparing them with several who had been considered and passed over, when Jimmy inadvertently revealed a secret.

"He asked Bruce Ellery first of all, but Ellery turned him down," said Jimmy thoughtlessly. And then, observing Tom's expression, he tried to cover up his indiscretion, but too late.

"Bruce Ellery!" exclaimed Tom. "Jimmy, he never! You mean he actually invited *him?*"

"Sure! Why not?"

"Why—why—but Bruce Ellery! I don't see how Hal had the nerve, Jimmy!"

Jimmy bristled. "Where's the nerve?" he demanded. "I guess Ellery would have been glad to go if—if he hadn't had another date or something. He said so!"

But Tom smiled gently and shook his head. "Hal ought to have known he couldn't get *him,* Jimmy."

"Oh, you make me tired! Listen, Bruce Ellery isn't any better than Hal Townsend, even if he is so high-and-mighty!"

"Bruce Ellery," said Tom firmly, "is about everything a fellow can get to be. He's President of the Student Government, Senior Class President, President of S. D. S., Chairman—"

"Well, what of it? That doesn't—"

"And he's the only fellow in the history of the school," continued Tom inspiredly, "who ever refused a football captaincy! He won the Norton game for us—"

"Aw, rats! Now listen here—"

"And he can have his pick of Graduation Day offices—"

"He's a swell-head, if you want my opinion!"

"And I don't believe there's another fellow in school cheeky enough to do what Hal did! It's a wonder to me he didn't ask Prexy to his party!"

"That's all right," declared Jimmy irately. "Ellery was asked, and he'd have accepted too, if he could have. You're perfectly daffy about him. He makes fellows think he's the grandest thing around, but he's no better than lots of others. Hal says his folks aren't even known in New York!"

"Never mind," answered Tom loyally. "He's known here!"

It continued for another ten minutes,

at the end of which period Jimmy went out and slammed the door very hard behind him. But the disagreement was forgotten by morning.

Christmas recess began on Wednesday, the twenty-second, to last twelve days. The exodus started almost the moment that breakfast was over, and in something less than two hours nearly three hundred joyous youths took their departure. Most of them left by train, but many sped away in motor-cars, and of the latter were Hal Townsend and his five guests. There was a big limousine for the boys and a smaller car for the baggage, and no automobile that rolled away from the school that morning was so well-appointed, so immaculately shining, so impressively chauffeured as those. Tom's vacation began on a high note of luxury and never faltered from it during his stay at Valley View.

The house was enormous, and even more wonderful than Jimmy had pictured it. There were acres of grounds surrounding it. There were servants galore, indoors and out, anticipating one's every intention. And there were Mr. and Mrs. Townsend. The former was stout, jovial of manner, rather loud of voice; a man of well on toward fifty trying to look thirty-five, and almost succeeding. Tom liked Mrs. Townsend better; a tall, pretty woman, much younger than her husband, who wore beautiful clothes and much jewelry and was never still. For that matter, remaining quiet for more than a half-hour was evidently an impossibility for any one at Valley View. The boys reached the house in time for a late luncheon and then were whisked off immediately to a round of neighboring houses. Tom recalled the afternoon as a confusion of things to eat and drink, of dozens of girls, youths, and older folks, of music and impromptu dances. He returned dazed, tumbled into a bath, dressed, and went down to dinner. It had been explained by Mrs. Townsend that this first evening was to be spent quietly at home, and so subsequent proceedings rather surprised him. Fourteen persons, many of whose names he never learned, sat down at table. Later as many more arrived, appearing and disappearing bewilderingly. The music-room rug was rolled away and dancing began. Tom liked to dance, but the steps indulged in by his partners were often most disconcerting. There was a light supper at midnight, and after experimenting with two kinds of salad and a lot of strange delicacies, he stole off to bed in the big yellow-toned room which he had all to himself. He didn't fall asleep readily, but the music and voices from downstairs were still in his ears when he did.

Thursday was a day of rain, but that made little difference to the restless spirits of the house-party. Their motto was, evidently, "Never a dull moment"! Breakfast almost merged into luncheon, luncheon into tea, and tea into dinner in town. Between times Tom was sped here and there, trotted after Hal and the others, tried his hand at billiards, danced a few times, changed his clothes twice, longed for a moment's respite and failed to find it save in the big amber-hued bathtub. The party, fifteen strong, dined at a hotel, hurried to a theater to occupy three boxes, took supper at a second hostelry and finally, long after midnight, sped back over wet, glistening roads to Chesterville. Tom enjoyed the play, although he thought some of it rather silly, ate his first broiled lobster, nodded most of the way back and had horrible dreams when he got to bed.

Perhaps the lobster was to blame, not only for his dreams, but for the state of mind in which he awoke. The rain had changed in the night to snow, and the view from his window was lovely, but somehow the Christmas landscape increased rather than dissipated his depression. He sat down on the edge of his bed and looked facts in the face.

He wasn't having a good time, after all. On the contrary, he was bored and tired and rebellious and—yes, he might as well say it—homesick. Hal, in his own home, was irritatingly bossy and patronizing. Two of the other fellows, distantly admired by Tom at school, were distinctly ill-mannered. Even Jimmy was changed. He dogged Hal about and truckled to him disgustingly. The place was oppressively comfortable. Everything was soft and pillowed, and Tom longed for a hard angle once more. Besides, although he had locked his mother's letter away from sight days ago, he couldn't get it out of his mind. Nor Ellen's, either, although he discounted that; Ellen was just a crazy kid. And to-morrow was Christmas Day and no one seemed to think a thing about it here. Why, they probably wouldn't even stay at home long enough to find out! This afternoon there was a shindig somewhere and to-night they were to dine at the Country Club; and if they made him sit next to that doll-faced girl they called Pam just once more he'd—he'd—

He got up and turned the water on in the tub, taking satisfaction in the thought that he had beaten the lantern-faced valet to it. He was Spartan this morning, only tempering the icy flood with a brief flow from the hot faucet. He plunged in, shivering, dried himself on a towel so large that he became all tangled up in it, and finally emerged from the bathroom with his mind made up. He was going home.

It required courage. He hid himself in the big drawing-room with a morning paper, deaf to the summons of Jimmy and the others, and awaited the appearance of his hostess, who was seldom visible until just before luncheon. Mrs. Townsend was very nice about it, although it was plain that she considered him slightly deficient. That any one could deliberately renounce the hospitality of Valley View was strong evidence of mental failing. But she helped him break the news to Hal after luncheon, and kindly invited him to come again. Hal, after the first shock of the announcement, was pitying and ironical. Oh, of course, if Tom was bored with them he was quite right to go. Probably they couldn't hope to provide the entertainment awaiting him in—what was the place? Oh, yes—Carver's Run! Tom felt so guilty that he fairly groveled in apologies, without, however, winning forgiveness from Hal. Jimmy was, in a way, even worse, for he charged Tom with a total lack of appreciation of his efforts in his behalf, accused him of being "small-town," and finally intimated that Tom had disappointed him most terribly. He ended his tirade on a note of warning. Tom was making an enemy of Hal, and that, he declared, was dangerous.

The others apparently cared little whether Tom went or stayed. Mr. Townsend was in the city, and the deserter was spared one leave-taking. At the last Jimmy relented somewhat and offered to accompany Tom to the station—the latter had declined Mrs. Townsend's offer to have him driven to New York—but Tom refused the sacrifice and departed alone, trying to look at ease but feeling exceedingly otherwise. To increase his discomfort, he remembered that he had come away without giving a single tip, and the two dollars he slipped into the willing palm of the chauffeur at the little station failed to restore his self-respect.

It was almost four o'clock when he finally reached the Pennsylvania Station, and he had most of an hour to wait. He bought his ticket and a parlor-car seat and

repaired to a bench. The station was crowded and grew more so from minute to minute. The snow had turned back to rain at noon, and the hurrying throng trailed moisture from coats and umbrellas, giving off odors of rubber and damp garments. Almost everyone was burdened with parcels, evidences of last-minute Christmas buying, and it seemed to Tom that a holiday spirit somewhat softened their irritable excitement. Suddenly he began to feel excited, too; excited and very happy. He could forget his social failure and realize that in the morning—Christmas morning—he would be at home with his mother and Ellen, good old Aunt Emmie and Uncle Marsh, and Stuart and Tug. The last two were just dogs, but they seemed most important factors of the reunion. Gee, it was great! Christmas at home!

Presently he had an idea, and, finding that the hands of his watch had hardly moved since his last inspection, surreptitiously counted his money. He mentally laid aside a dollar for his supper, twenty-five cents for the porter, a half-dollar for unforeseen incidentals, and found that he had nearly four dollars left. Afraid to leave his two bags behind, he tugged them to a distant counter and there bought two boxes of candy; very beautiful boxes bearing winter scenes and much red ribbon. It was while he was retracing his steps to his bench that the stupendous happened. Dodging through the stream of traffic he brought a suitcase into violent collision with a pair of long legs and a patiently remonstrant voice exclaimed: "Hey, feller! Look out where—" And then the tone changed and the assaulted pedestrian said, "Why, hello, Wayne!"

As Tom told himself later, you could have knocked him down with a baseball bat! For there was Bruce Ellery smiling down at him! Tom stared gasping out something made up of surprise, embarrassment and apology, and Bruce shoved him into a back-water of the stream. "Where are you off to?" he inquired. "Thought you were at Townsend's house-party."

"I am," answered Tom. "I mean I was! But—but I thought I'd go home."

"H'm, that sounds like a wise thought. When does your train go? Oh, well, you've gobs of time. Come over and sit down a minute." Tom followed, incredulous of his fortune. Why, at school if Bruce Ellery even recognized him with a smile and a nod he had been proud for hours! And here he was invited to sit and talk with him! Well, this was turning out to be a wonderful Christmas; Bruce had left his bag on a bench, something Tom wouldn't have dared, and when he had removed it there was room for them both. "So you decided to tear yourself away from the fleshpots, eh?" he asked, smiling encouragingly. "What was it like there?"

Tom started circumspectly, but was presently opening his heart. "I shouldn't have gone in the first place, you see," he ended.

"Oh, well, I can't say I blame you," replied Bruce, taking a quizzical look at the other. "Sounded pretty attractive, I guess. Where do you live, Wayne?"

Tom told him, and Bruce said, nodding, "Virginia, eh? I was in Richmond once with my father. I was only about seven or eight, I think, but I can remember it pretty clearly. It was in winter, late winter, I guess; but there was always sunlight, as I remember it. Do you suppose the sun will be shining when you get home?"

"Oh, yes," answered Tom confidently. "And not a bit like this. Maybe there'll be ice on the ponds—just a skin, you know; but it'll be right warm by ten or eleven. Gee, Virginia winters are great, Ellery!"

"Are, eh?" He looked at his watch. "Hello!" he muttered, made as though to seize his suitcase and then relaxed again. "My train's just about pulling out," he said.

"Oh, I'm sorry! Can't you make it?"

Bruce shrugged. "Shan't try. There'll be another one after a while. This is the second I've missed since I got here. Fact is, Wayne, I'm not awfully keen on my visit. You see, I haven't any folks now. Father was killed in France. My guardian's a foggy old chap and we don't enjoy each other much. I've just spent a couple of days with him and now I'm off to my aunt's, my mother's sister. She's an estimable lady, but I can't bear the kids. There are three of them, from nine to fourteen, and they make things."

"Make things?" repeated Tom vaguely.

Bruce nodded gloomily. "Yes. Last year it was model airplanes. The Christmas before it was ships. They all do it. There's a workshop off the living-room and the house smells of glue and paint and shavings. They never do anything else, it seems. Not when I'm there. Pestiferous kids, I call 'em. Christmas at Aunt Justine's is about as merry as the Burial of Sir John Moore!"

Tom tried to think who Sir John Moore was, but didn't, because words sprang to his lips and got past before he could stop them. "Gee, I wish you could come home with me!" he exclaimed. The enormity of his offense brought the blood to his cheeks, and Bruce's startled *"What?"* added to his discomfort. Embarrassment held him, and Bruce was making the situation more painful by staring hard. Then, while Tom still struggled for speech, Bruce spoke again.

"What did you say, Wayne?" he insisted.

"I said—" Tom gulped nervously, tried a placating smile that faded almost before it was under way, and tried again. "I didn't mean to be cheeky, Ellery! I didn't think when—"

"Cheeky be hanged!" replied the big

fellow surprisingly. "Do you mean you'd really like me to go with you?"

Tom nodded silently but vehemently.

"Well, but—but what would your folks say?" Bruce sounded and looked almost excited.

"They'd love it," said Tom earnestly. "I —they've heard about you. You don't mean that—that you could, Ellery!"

"No, I don't suppose I do." Bruce sighed and settled back. "Only, you oughtn't to tempt a fellow, Wayne. Virginia sounds —well, it sounds pretty wonderful to me. If you knew Hopewell-in-the-Hills and Aunt Justine—bless her heart—and those three plaguy kids as I do, you'd understand. And—" Bruce turned a threatening scowl on his companion—"it would serve you right if I held you to it. Only," he muttered, "I shan't."

Tom never knew afterwards how he got the courage for what he did next. He actually grabbed Bruce Ellery by the arm and cried, "Quick! Let's get your parlor-car seat before they're all gone! And you can send a wire to Aunt Whose-this. We've got thirteen minutes! Oh, do hurry, *please!*"

Wonderful, miraculous things still happen in this delightful world, and perhaps, if the facts could be known, most of them happen around Christmas-time. That, at least, was Tom's conclusion as he and Bruce sped through the rain-swept darkness toward Washington. Having crossed his Rubicon, Bruce was the most delightful of companions. He still pretended to view pessimistically the effect on Tom's mother of his appearance at "Far Fields," but that didn't keep him from being very care-free and jolly. Tom found himself wondering why he had held Bruce Ellery in such awe, because when you knew him he wasn't awe-inspiring at all. He was just —well, he was just corking!

They had supper in the dining-car and made it a very merry meal. At Washington they alighted, whiled away almost two hours, and then embarked on a leisurely train for Carver's Run. Fortunately they obtained berths, even if they were uppers, and long after midnight Tom, too blissfully excited to sleep, lay and tried to realize that farther along the swaying, darkened car was Bruce Ellery! He was still trying when slumber at last claimed him.

They were awakened at dawn, dressed, and presently stepped out into a frosty world. At the end of the tiny station a weather-beaten sign proclaimed "Carver's Run." They left their bags and started off along the red clay road that rose and fell before them between broad fields. There was a good two-mile walk ahead, but they swung out briskly and merrily, Bruce proclaiming to the wide and empty world in a fine tenor that
"The old team fights till it can't fight no
    more,
Pilin' up, pilin' up a great big score!"

The sun came up, the stubble of the fields turned to gold, birds twittered, and a covey of quail took flight across a rail fence. The frosty clay began to yield to the warmth, and their feet skidded at times and got themselves laughed at. The sound of distant bells reached them and Bruce stopped to listen and wonder. "Christmas chimes," laughed Tom. But it sounded like fairy music until at last the big wagon came into sight and Bruce saw that the bells were on the three great black horses that drew it. "That's one of Cousin Harrison's," explained Tom, and when the wagon drew abreast, the negro driver, astride a wheel-horse, stilled the jangling bells and he and Tom exchanged news while Bruce marveled at and admired the gay caparisons.

The bells took up their pleasant song again and the big, wide-tired wheels rolled on. Trees marched across a sunny field to meet the travelers, drenched them with cool shadow for a while, and retreated. A low white house appeared on a distant rise and a column of blue smoke arose straightly against the sky. A dog barked and another answered. Tom tried to keep his voice steady. "Yonder it is," he said. "That's 'Far Fields'."

"It's lovely," answered Bruce softly.

Tom only nodded, keeping his face averted. It was so silly to have your eyes get moist at the sight of sunlit fields, a kind of tumble-down old white house, a grove of leafless trees, and the barking of a dog! But it all spelled home, and, wonder of wonders, he was coming back to it! And—why, he had almost forgotten! This was Christmas Day! He turned suddenly to cry, "Christmas gif', Bruce!"

"Say, that's right! Same to you, old man. But what's 'Christmas gift' mean?"

"Means you must give me a present, of course," Tom explained, laughing. "I said it first, you see."

"Oh, that's it, eh? The idea being to pop out on folks and yell 'Christmas gift!' before they beat you to it?"

"Yes. 'Chrismas gif' the darkies say it. You'll hear it plenty of times to-day when they begin to come around."

They turned in at a gate and followed a lane. A red-and-white setter came bounding toward them, followed no less eagerly but, of necessity, less speedily, by a basset-hound. There were joyous barks and bays, whines and yelps, and Tom's voice trying to hush the clamor. It was still no more than breakfast-time, if so late, and he wanted to walk in unannounced. Bruce had suggested sending a warning telegram from Washington, but Tom had laughingly assured him that unless they delivered it themselves it probably wouldn't reach its destination before noon. After a prolonged frenzy of welcome the dogs con-

sented to "hush up," and Tom and Bruce went on silently to the house, Bruce lagging as they reached it.

Tom tried the front door, found it unlocked as usual, and entered stealthily. A wonderful aroma of coffee almost made him gasp! He tiptoed along the hall, tried to peek in the dining-room where, as he knew from the sounds, fat old Aunt Emmie was lumbering around the table, and would have done so undetected if Stuart, the setter, hadn't gone bounding past him. Aunt Emmie gave a shout and a dish clattered to the floor.

"Miss Lizzie! Miss Lizzie! He's done come home!"

There was a startled exclamation beyond the door and then Tom was holding his mother very tightly, and an amazed but happy voice was crying: "Why, Tom! Oh, I can't believe it! My dear, dear boy, is it really you?"

"Yes'm," said Tom sort of chokily. "You see, Mother, I—I changed my mind."

Then Ellen was there, trying to kiss him, too, and Uncle Marsh, attracted by the hubbub, was scraping and bobbing at the back door and grinning all over his old black face. And Stuart and Tug barked as loud as they could.

"Oh, gee!" gasped Tom. "Bruce! Bruce, where are you?"

"Here," answered a voice from the hall, and the momentarily forgotten guest appeared. If Mrs. Wayne was surprised she kept it quite to herself, and Bruce could have no doubt of his welcome.

"And this," went on Tom, with an almost approving glance at his pretty sister, "is Ellen, Bruce."

"How do you do, Miss Wayne?" said Bruce gravely as he shook hands. "Christmas gif'!"

"Of course," said Jimmy weightily a week later, "it was a pretty rotten thing to do, Tom, and Hal was mighty sore about it, but I guess he's most over it now. If I were you, though, I'd see him and sort of—well, you know; sort of smooth him down."

"What for?" asked Tom, looking up from the bag he was unpacking.

"What for?" gasped Jimmy. "Gee whiz, you aren't crazy, are you? Why, you can't afford to have as—as influential a fellow as Hal Townsend down on you! Not if you're going to get anywhere next spring! Don't be a goof, Tom. Just drop over there and tell him—"

He was interrupted by a knock on the door, and when it opened, there, to Jimmy's amazement, stood Bruce Ellery.

"Say, Tom," announced Bruce, "I called up Wiggins on the 'phone and he says he's got a couple of pretty decent saddle nags. I told him to feed 'em some oats and we'd try 'em about four o'clock. How's that? Suit you?"

"Sure, Bruce," replied Tom. "I'd like a ride mighty well."

"Good," said the visitor, and nodded. "Meet you downstairs at quarter to four."

The door closed. Tom stole a glance at Jimmy. Jimmy's mouth was wide open and his eyes looked glazed.

A STORY OF A VERY NAUGHTY GIRL; OR, MY VISIT TO MARY JANE

from the pen of 'Lizbeth Hall

WHEN Mary Jane Hunt left Tuckertown last summer, she invited me to come to the city and make her a visit.

"If I were sure Mrs. Hunt wanted you, 'Lizbeth, I would like to have you go," said Mother, "for it's good for young folks to widen their horizon now and then, and you would enjoy seeing the sights."

I didn't care anything about my horizon, but I did want most awfully to see the sights; but, although I teased and teased, Mother wouldn't let me go.

There was a great church bother in Tuckertown that year, but our folks weren't in it. The trouble began in the choir, who couldn't agree about the tunes. On some Sundays the organist wouldn't play, and on others the singers wouldn't sing. Once, they all stopped short in the middle of "Greenland's Icy Mountains," and it was real exciting at church, for you never knew what might happen before you came out; but folks said it was disgraceful, and I suppose it was. They complained of the minister because he didn't put a stop to it; so at last he took sides with the organist, and dismissed the choir, and declared we would have congregational singing in the future. 'Most everybody thought that would be the end of the trouble; but, mercy! it was hardly the beginning! Things grew worse and worse. To begin

with, the congregation wouldn't sing. You see, they had had a choir so long, people were sort of afraid to let out their voices; and besides, there was Elvira Tucker, who had studied music in Boston, just ready to make fun of them if they did. For she was one of the choir, and they were all as mad as hornets.

In fact, the whole Tucker family were offended. They said folks didn't appreciate Elvira, nor what she had done, since she returned from Boston, to raise the standard in Tuckertown. I don't know, I am sure, what they meant by that, for I never saw Elvira raise any standard; but I do know that they were real mad with the minister, and lots of people took their side and called 'emselves "Tuckerites."

You see, the Tuckers stand very high in Tuckertown, and other people try to be just as like them as they can. They were first settlers, for one thing, and have the most money, for another; and they lay down the law generally. The post-office and the station are at *their* end of the village. *They* decide when the sewing-societies shall meet, and the fairs take place, and the strawberry festivals come off. If there is to be a picnic, *they* decide when we shall go, and where we shall go, and just who shall sit in each wagon. If anybody is sick, Mrs. Tucker visits 'em just as regularly as the doctor, and she brings grapes and jelly, and is very kind, though she always scolds the sick person for not dieting, or for going without her rubbers, or something of that sort. If Mother had a hand in this story, not a word of all this would go down. She says they are very public-spirited people, and that they do a great deal for Tuckertown. I suppose they do; but I've heard other people say that they domineer much more than is agreeable.

The people on the minister's side were called "Anti-Tuckerites"; but, as I said, our folks weren't in the quarrel at all. The consequence of being on the fence was, that I could not join in the fun on either side, and I think it was real mean. Every now and then, the Tuckerites would plan some lovely picnic or party, just so as not to invite the Anti-Tuckerites. Then, in turn, *they* would get up an excursion, and not invite any of the Tuckerites. Of course, *I* wasn't invited to either, and it was just as provoking as it could be.

One day, when I went to school, I found that Elvira Tucker was going to train a choir of children to take the place of the old choir.

"I went over to call on Elvira last evening," I heard Miss Green tell our schoolteacher, "and I found her at the piano playing for little Nell to sing. It was just at dusk, and they did not see me; so I stood and listened, and wondered why we couldn't have a choir of children instead of the congregational singing. Elvira said she thought it would be lovely."

Now, I had been to singing-school for two winters, and the singing-master said I had a good voice; so I thought I ought to belong to the choir.

"You can't, 'cause only Tuckerites are going to belong," said 'Melia Stone. "And your folks are just on the fence. They aren't one thing or another."

I couldn't stand being left out of all the fun any longer, so I said: "I'm as much a Tuckerite as anybody, only our folks don't approve of making so much trouble about a small affair."

"I want to know!" said Abby Ann Curtiss. "Well, I'll ask Miss Elvira if you can belong there."

Mercy me! I had jumped from the fence and found myself a Tuckerite! I was sure Mother would be real mad if she knew what I had said, for I suspected in my heart of hearts that, if *she* had jumped from the fence, she would have landed on the minister's side. I made up my mind that I would not tell her what had passed, for maybe, after all, Miss Elvira would decide that I was no real Tuckerite. But the very next day she sent word to me by Abby Ann that she would like to have me join the choir.

I told Mother that I was wanted in the children's choir because I had a good voice, and I never said a word about being a Tuckerite.

"A children's choir," said she. "That's a real good idea—a beautiful idea."

She never suspected how I was deceiving her.

Well, we had real fun practicing. That week we learned a chant and two hymns.

One day Miss Green came in.

"How does *she* happen to be here?" I heard her ask Miss Elvira, with a significant look at me.

"Oh, she has a real good voice," answered Miss Elvira, laughing. "Most of the children who can sing are on the Tuckerite side. Besides, from something she said to Abby Ann, I think at heart the Halls sympathize with us."

What would my folks have said to that? I felt half sick of the whole affair, and went home and teased Mother to let me go to the city and visit Mary Jane.

I never shall forget the Sunday I sang in the choir. Miss Elvira played for us on the organ, for when the real organist heard that only the Tuckerite children were to belong to it she refused to play. Everybody seemed surprised to see me in it, and even Dr. Scott looked at me in a mournful sort of way, as if he thought the Halls had gone over to the enemy. What troubled me most, though, was the look Mother gave me when she first realized that the choir was formed only of the

But I never sang but just that once in the choir, for next Sunday I spent with Mary Jane, in Boston.

The way it happened was this. That night Mother sent me to bed right after supper, as a punishment for not telling her all about the choir before I joined it; and, as I undressed, she had a great deal to say about the defects in my character. She talked to me a long time about my faults,

"Mercy! how we did sing!"

Tuckerite children, and that she had not found it out before.

But, in spite of all this, I enjoyed the singing. We sat, a long row of us, in the singers' seats up in the gallery. After the hymn was given out and we stood up, Miss Elvira nodded to me and whispered: "Now, don't be afraid, girls. Sing as loud as you can."

Mercy! how we *did* sing! Twice as loud as the grown-up choir. Luella Howe said, afterward, that we looked as if we were trying to swallow the meeting-house.

and she went down-stairs without kissing me goodnight. I was thinking what a miserable sinner I must be, and was trying to cry about it, when I heard her go into the sitting-room and say to Father, who was reading his paper there:

"I just put 'Lizbeth to bed; but she isn't half so much to blame as some other folks. If grown people act in such a way, you can't expect much of the children. I declare, I wish I could send her away from Tuckertown till this choir-matter is settled."

"Well," says Father, "why don't you let her go and see Hunt's girl? You know she invited her, and 'Lizbeth wants to go."

"Oh, no," says Mother. "They have so much sickness there. I'm afraid she would be in the way," and she ended her sentence by shutting the door with a slam.

I got right up and sat on the stairs for a long time, to see if they would say anything more about my visiting Mary Jane, but they didn't. Father began to talk of the black heifer he had just bought, and then about the Presidential campaign, and several other unimportant things like that. Not a word about me.

But I began early the next morning and teased steadily to go and visit Mary Jane. Finally, Tuesday morning Mother said I might write Mary Jane that, if it were perfectly agreeable to her mother, I would now make them the promised visit, and, if I heard nothing to the contrary from them, would start on Friday in the early train for Boston.

Well, Tuesday passed and Wednesday came, and Thursday came, and at last—at last Friday came, and no letter from Mary Jane. My trunk was all packed. I took my best dress and my second-best dress, and most of the every-day ones, and Mother lent me her hair jewelry. I had my shade hat, and my common one, and my too-good hat. That last is one I've had for years—ever so many years,—fully two years, I guess,— and it's always too good to wear anywhere, and that's why it lasts so long. At the last, Mother declared she was sorry she had ever consented to let me go, for she was afraid Mrs. Hunt didn't like to write that my coming would be inconvenient. She declared that I ought to have written I would go if I heard that it would be agreeable.

I had fifty frights that morning before I was finally put in Deacon Hobart's care in the cars, for he, too, was going to Boston that day.

He promised my mother that, if no one was at the depot for me, he would put me in a carriage, so that I should get safely to Mrs. Hunt's house.

I was real mad to have him tag along— it would have been such fun to travel alone, and I did hope, when he stood so long on the platform talking to Father, the cars would go off without him; but he jumped on just as they were starting. However, when we finally got to Boston, and I found that nobody was waiting for me there, I was glad enough to have him with me.

I must say that, as I rode along in the carriage, I thought it was real queer and rude for no one to come to meet me; but the city was so interesting, I had forgotten about it by the time we had stopped at the Hunts' door. The house had a kind of shut-up look, and I felt queer for a moment, as I thought perhaps they were all away from home; but, just then, Mary Jane flew down the steps, and Dot came squealing behind her.

"Now, you just hush!" said Mary Jane to her, after she had kissed me. "You wake Lucy up, and see what you'll get." (She is always awful domineering to Dot, Mary Jane is.)

"Why, what's the matter with Lucy?" I asked. "Why is she asleep in the day-time?"

"Why, she is sick," said Mary Jane.

"Oh, awful sick!" cried Dot.

"'T isn't catching, though; so come right in, Beth," added Mary Jane, and in we went.

She had the hackman carry my trunk up into her room, and she went up behind him all the way, ordering him to be quiet, and slapping Dot and holding up her finger at me, and making more noise herself than all the rest of us put together.

"You see, I have to take care of everything," she said, when we were up at last. "Mother has to stay with Lucy all the time, and Dot is so thoughtless. But, what have you got in your trunk?"

"Yes, why don't you unpack?" asked Dot.

It took me some time to get to the bottom of my trunk, but I showed them everything that was in it. After that, Mary Jane said she must go and see about tea. When we got down-stairs we found the table set.

"Why! there's no preserves on it," said Mary Jane to Bridget, who tossed her head, and answered:

"Your ma didn't order any, and I won't open 'em without her telling me."

"Oh, my!" cried Mary Jane; "you are very particular just now, aren't you? You don't mind so much when your aunt's step-mother's cousin comes."

Bridget turned as red as a beet. "Now, just you take yourselves out of my kitchen!" she said, and, as true as you live, she shut the door right in my face!

"Hateful old thing!" cried Mary Jane. "Well, never mind, I'm going to the china-closet to get some. But, which do you like best, peach preserves or raspberry jam?"

"Peach preserves, o' course," answered Dot. "Everybody does."

I don't see why Dot had to say that. It was just enough, and I knew it would be, to make Mary Jane take the jam. When we went back to the dining-room, we found Susan (that's the nurse) had come in with the baby.

"Here, Mary Jane," said she, "your ma said you were to take care of Baby while I'm upstairs."

Mary Jane looked as cross as two sticks. "Oh, bother! I can't! I have Dot to take care of, and Beth and the house, and everything. Bridget ought to do that."

But just then Mr. Hunt came down. He looked real worried, but he spoke to me just as kind, and asked after the Tucker-town folks. I tried to tell him about the singing affair, but he didn't seem to take much interest, and soon went upstairs again.

"He hasn't eaten any of his supper," said Dot. "I'm going to give his jam to Baby."

The baby had been sitting in a high chair up to the table, and hadn't had a thing but a piece of graham cracker to eat. I thought he was real good.

"He can't have any jam. Here! give it to me," said Mary Jane. "I'll eat it."

Of course, at that he banged his cracker on the floor, and began to cry for the jam. But Mary Jane didn't take the slightest notice of him. She went on eating the jam as calmly as if he was asleep in his cradle. Dot had been sent out on an errand, so I tried to amuse him; but he was afraid of me, and screamed louder than before.

"Don't pay any attention to him," said Mary Jane. "I'm going to break him of screaming so much. I always longed to break him of it, and at last I've got a chance. When he finds no one takes any notice of him, he'll stop it, I guess."

While he was still screaming, Mrs. Hunt came down. She had on her wrapper, and her hair was just bobbed up, and she looked as if she hadn't slept for a month.

"Mary Jane, why don't you amuse him?" she said, after she had shaken hands with me, and had taken Baby in her arms. "You know that the noise disturbs Lucy, and yet you'll let him cry."

"It's too bad," said I. "I would amuse him, only he is afraid of me."

"Why, I'll amuse him, of course," said Mary Jane.

So her mother went upstairs again, and we had that child on our hands till seven o'clock, when Susan came and took him to bed.

The next morning I told Mary Jane that I thought I ought to go home.

"Oh no!" she begged. "You are here, and you might as well stay, and Lucy will be better soon."

"Oh," said Dot, "don't go! You can help us take care of Baby, you know."

"I don't see how I can be in your mother's way, when I hardly ever see her," said I. "Besides, it would be real mean to leave you while you are in trouble." So I decided to stay.

I should have had a splendid time of it, had it not been for the baby; but we never began any interesting play but Susan would come and leave him with us, and then he always had to be amused. I never saw such a child—never quiet a moment. They said it was because he was so bright. If I ever have a child, I hope it will be one of the stupid kind, that will sit on the floor and suck its thumb all day.

He was particularly in the way when we went to see the sights. We went to the State-house and the Art Museum, and one day Mary Jane showed me a place where they were having a baby show.

"Mercy!" said Mary Jane, "*who* would ever want to go to that?"

"Lots o' people are going in, anyhow," said Dot.

We had started on, but all at once Mary Jane stopped short. "Lizbeth," said she, "I'll tell you what. Let's take Baby to the baby show. I mean to exhibit him, and p'raps he'll take a prize, and we will have the money."

Wasn't it a splendid idea? The trouble was, we didn't know how to get in. At last, Mary Jane told the ticket-master what we wanted, and he sent for the manager.

"And so you want to put this little chap in the show," said he. "How old is he?"

Mary Jane told him.

"Well, he *is* a whopper," said the man.

"Is it too late for him to get the prize?" we asked.

"Oh, he won't stand so good a chance as if he had come at first. You see, the babies are all numbered, and each person, when he goes out of the show, gives the number of the baby he thinks is the finest, and the one that has the most votes, so to speak, gets the prize. Those folks that came yesterday, you see, haven't voted for *your* baby, but then you'll have part of to-day and to-morrow."

"Why, will we have to stay all the time?" asked Mary Jane.

"No, you can take him out when you choose; but the more he is here the more votes he'll get."

"Well, if there's a prize for the baby that can cry loudest, he'll get it," said Dot.

But they didn't give any prize for that.

We gave Baby's name and address to the manager, who then took us in to the show. His number was three hundred and twelve, and a paper telling his age, and number of teeth, and so on, was tacked over the little booth where we sat.

There were lots of people in the room, but when any one came near *our* baby he cried.

"I do believe he won't get a single vote," said Mary Jane, in despair. But somebody gave him some candy, and that pacified him for a while, and ever so many persons said he was the finest child in the show. We were so encouraged, we planned just how we would spend the money, and we stayed till dinner-time, when Mary Jane thought we ought to go home.

Mrs. Hunt was real pleased that we had kept him out so long. It was a pleasant day, she said, and the air would do him good.

"We will take him out again this afternoon," said Mary Jane.

When we went back, Baby was so tired he went to sleep in Dot's lap. They looked awful cunning, and everybody raved over them; but we had to promise Dot everything under the sun to keep her quiet.

Lucy was worse that night, and the next morning Mrs. Hunt sent us right out after breakfast. We stayed at the show all day, but the baby wasn't good a bit. He screamed and kicked, and looked, oh, so red and ugly! We had to send Dot for some candy for him, and we felt worried and uncomfortable.

The doctor's carriage was at the door when we went home at last, and Mr. Hunt was walking up and down in the parlor. He called Mary Jane and Dot in, and I went upstairs, for Susan said the postman had left a letter for me. I thought it was from Mother; but it was a printed thing from the Dead-letter Office, saying that a letter for me was detained there for want of postage. It had been sent to Tuckertown, and the postmaster had forwarded it to Boston. I had spent all my money, except just enough to buy my ticket home; but I thought I would take out enough for the stamps, and borrow six cents from Mrs. Hunt. I went out right off and mailed my letter with the stamps, so as to get the other letter that was in the Dead-letter Office. When I came back I found Mary Jane crying in the hall.

Lucy was worse and the doctor had given her up.

"And I have always been so cross to her," sobbed Mary Jane.

"Yes, so you have!" put in Susan, who was coming down stairs with a tray. "I hope you'll remember now to be kinder to Dot and the baby."

"But they are so healthy," she sniffed. but she seemed to feel real bad, and it's no wonder, for Lucy is a darling! I couldn't help crying myself.

That night, poor little Three Hundred and Twelve was taken sick. Mr. Hunt and the doctor came to our room to ask what we had given him to eat, and when we told them about the candy (we didn't dare say a word about the show) they were angry enough.

I sha'n't forget that night in a hurry. I didn't think it would ever come to an end, and we both lay and cried till the sun shone into our window in the morning, when Susan came to tell us that Lucy was sleeping beautifully, and was going to get well, after all. After breakfast, we went into Mrs. Hunt's room, which was next to the nursery, where Lucy lay, and she took us all in her arms—there was room for me too—and we just cried with joy together.

The baby had got all over his colic, and Mary Jane and I had just concluded we had better tell Mrs. Hunt where we had taken him, when a letter came for Mrs. Hunt.

It was a notice that number three hundred and twelve had taken the third prize at the baby show.

It could not have come at a better time for us, for how could she scold, with Lucy coming back to life, as it were, after those dreadful hours of suspense and suffering? But I know she did scold Mary Jane afterward, for it wasn't right to keep the baby in that stuffy place when she thought he was in the fresh air; but that was after I went home, which happened a few days later.

And what do you think!—Just as the carriage came to take me to the depot, the postman left a sealed envelope from the Dead-letter Office. I opened it as the cars started, and while I was traveling home, I read the very letter Mrs. Hunt had written in answer to the one I wrote her to tell her I was about to visit them in Boston. And in that letter she had asked me to postpone my visit till some later date, on account of the illness of little Lucy!

RALPH CHANTS A DITTY

by Franklin M. Reck

WHEN Ralph Pickens gets inspired, he's pretty sure to carry the day. I think he could argue a marble statue into doing setting-up exercises.

Anyhow, he got me to go to Prince Edward Island with him. Not only that, but he talked me into passing all my final exams two weeks ahead of time so that we could leave State College the last week in May. And that's talking.

"Prince Edward Island is a paradise," he told me up in my room, where I had become slightly unconscious from organic chemistry. "It's a sparkling emerald set in the Atlantic Ocean. It's a land of beautiful trout-streams, cultivated farms, pine forests, and red cliffs dipping down into the sea."

"Swell," I murmured. "What are we going to do in paradise?"

"Catch codfish."

I woke up in alarm. But Ralph was in earnest.

"You can catch a thousand pounds a day," he asserted. "You get a cent and a half a pound. We'll earn a lot of money, have a great vacation, and fill ourselves with sea-food."

I wasn't particularly interested in sea-food, but the thought of riding the gray Atlantic every day, seeing new sights, swimming in the surf, and making money attracted me aplenty. So the last week in May, with our exams safely behind us and a slim fund of cash in our pockets, we took the train to Chicago and got on a Grand Trunk for Montreal.

It wasn't until we arrived at Charlottetown, the capital of Prince Edward Island, that I began to suspect Ralph of having some other purpose besides codfishing in planning this far-off trip. Riding in a day-coach up the St. Lawrence through Quebec, down the wild and beautiful Matapoedia valley, and through New Brunswick to Cape Tormentine, we planned and chatted until in our minds we became codfish millionaires. But the minute the train-ferry had taken us across twelve miles of rough and rolling Atlantic to the island, Ralph grew abstracted.

And when we registered at the hotel in Charlottetown for the night, I detected an excited glow in his eyes. He was humming a tune in his snappiest tenor when we signed our names:

"Casey Jones, mounted to the cabin,
  Casey Jones, with his orders in his hand—"

He put down the pen and looked at the room-clerk affably. "My favorite tune," he grinned. "Ever hear it before?"

"Can't say I have," replied the clerk, and I'll be blamed if Ralph's face didn't fall noticeably!

The next morning, on the train for Couris, the fishing town at the eastern end of the island, Ralph was humming it again when the conductor came through for our tickets:

"—mounted to the cabin,
And he took his farewell trip to the Promised Land."

The conductor smiled at us.

"That song has about a thousand verses," Ralph said casually.

"I've heard at least nine hundred," ad-

Souris," I told the official. I was getting nervous over Ralph's behavior. "How are they running this year?"

"Dunno," he said. "The fishermen are just getting their lines out."

"Hm," Ralph murmured. "I thought they started earlier than that!"

"It's a late season. There's been ice on the shore up to last week."

"Holy Smoses!" breathed Ralph. "Holy Smoses!"

" 'Just what does "Casey Jones" have to do with codfishing?' I asked."

mitted the conductor, punching our tickets.

"Where?" Ralph asked eagerly.

"I used to work in the States."

"Oh," muttered Ralph, disappointed. "Thought maybe you'd heard it up here."

"We're going to do some codfishing at

Startled, I looked at Ralph and caught him gazing at the conductor with what seemed to be pleading hope in his eyes. But the conductor merely said:

"Codfishing's always good at Souris."

Again it seemed to me that Ralph's face fell, as though he had hoped for some kind of response to his fool expression. When the conductor had passed on, I turned to Ralph half-peeved.

"Just what does 'Casey Jones' have to do with codfishing?" I asked him. "Do you use him for bait? And is 'Holy Smoses' the patron saint of fishermen, or what?"

But Ralph didn't answer.

DURING our first two days at Souris, we were a pair of excited and busy land-lubbers. We got a room for next to nothing per week and arranged to use a small oil-burner so that we could cook our own meals. We figured it wouldn't cost us more than five dollars a week, apiece, to live, providing we ate lobster and fish most of the time.

Ralph had studied up on the art of catching cod, but we learned a lot from William Poole, who runs the general store. We learned that we'd have to set out about a mile of trawl-line, with at least 1,400 hooks on it. We learned that we'd need a buoy at each end of the line and one in the middle, and three anchors to hold the line in place. The best fishing-ground was about five miles out, where the water was twenty fathoms deep.

Mr. Poole solved the boat problem for us by renting us his for two dollars a trip. But we'd have to go out for our cod at eleven in the morning—not at six, as the rest of the fishermen did, because Mr. Poole used the boat himself at the earlier hour.

That afternoon, loaded with gear, we marched down the straggling street to the water's edge. We were in high spirits and chattering like parrots. Suddenly Ralph burst into song:

"Casey Jones, mounted to the cabin,
  Casey Jones, with his orders in his
    hand—"

Then he turned to Mr. Poole, who was going with us to show us the boat.

"Ever hear that song?" he asked.

"I don't recollect it."

Ralph seemed to bear up under the sad news better this time, and he was still talking gaily when we walked out on the long wharf.

"Here's the boat," Mr. Poole said, cutting in on Ralph's babbling. "Know how to start it?"

"Sure," Ralph replied. "I've run lots of engines."

So after a few final instructions, the storekeeper left us and we started loading things into the boat. It was a stout one, with a heavy-duty one-cylinder engine. As we worked, I began to get all excited over the prospect of chugging through those Atlantic rollers and wresting a living from the green depths.

"What you going to do with all that gear?" asked a voice.

I looked up and saw several men standing on the dock, gazing down at us. They were all dressed in oilskins, and their lined faces were the color of tanned leather. The speaker, a broad, stumpy guy with a square jaw, looked distinctly hostile.

"See if we can't catch a little cod this summer," I explained.

"Plannin' on living here?" he asked.

"Until fall," I replied. "We go back to school then."

"Going to catch all the fish you can and then leave?" he queried coldly.

"Any objections?" I asked, getting a little hot under the collar. I wondered why Ralph wasn't taking any part, and I looked around half expecting to see him preparing to jump out of the boat and swim to a more friendly spot. But instead he was gazing at the stumpy guy with a curious interest.

"The banks are crowded now," grunted the fisherman, walking away. He was followed by one of the others. The man who was left had a friendly wrinkle around his eyes. He was square-shouldered and well set up. I looked at him doubtfully.

"Don't mind Follabee," he said. "He's all right."

"Do the rest of 'em feel the way he does?" I asked, worried.

"I don't think so. Follabee's lived by himself too long. But at heart he's a good enough man."

"Has he always lived here?" asked Ralph in a tone of suppressed excitement, breaking into the conversation for the first time.

" 'Bout fifteen years, I think."

"Where'd he come from?" Ralph asked quickly.

"Don't think he's ever told anybody."

"I wonder—" Ralph began, but instead of finishing what he was wondering he started to stow buoys in the stern. I got busy myself, because we had a lot to do in the next few hours. In a couple of more minutes, after the fisherman had told us how to cut the herring into diagonal chunks for bait, we were plowing toward the end of the breakwater at a snappy five miles an hour. Beyond the breakwater, the gentle swells hit us, and before we knew it the shore began to look far away.

I acquired a funny feeling inside of me —not seasickness—but a sort of excitement like what you feel when you step to the platform for your first public speech.

I steered and Ralph stood in the front of the boat.

"I feel like a viking," he said happily. Then he swept his arm toward the horizon and I knew he was about to be seized with an attack of poetry. "Think of it! The boundless ocean, stretching out before our eyes! Away off there is England and Europe. What if we kept on going east— away from the setting sun?"

"We'd go about thirty miles and then run out of gas," I told him. "Let's catch cod instead."

All the while, I was looking back at shore. Mr. Poole had told me to set a course by two points on shore, and I had selected a little white farm-house overhanging the red cliffs and a clump of high trees on a hill, farther inland.

For about thirty minutes we steered straight out to sea on this course, and then we began to look for buoys. We passed one about fifty yards to port—a bobbing calked keg just like the ones we had in the boat. For about five minutes more we chugged along, and then we took soundings. The water was about a hundred feet deep and, after shaking hands solemnly, we let out our first anchor and moored our first buoy. Then we began paying out the long trawl, I steering my course and Ralph baiting each hook with a chunk of herring.

Before we were finished, I was feeling a lot funnier inside. I got so I couldn't bear to see Ralph bait a hook—it wasn't seasickness, but just an unwillingness to see even a dead herring cut up in that remorseless fashion. It pained me to think of his tail on one hook and his head on another, may be twenty feet away.

Ralph chattered unceasingly on the way back. He sat on the engine-housing, his eyes dancing and his round, firm body all tense. Ralph looks fat, but if you try to poke your finger in him any place, you're likely to break it. He's hard. Three years of high-school football did it.

"To-morrow at eleven," he chortled, "we go out and haul in our first cod. A thousand pounds! Enough for fifteen hundred meals of flaky, creamed—" He broke off and looked at me. "You look pale," he accused me. "You're seasick. Why don't you use a little will-power?"

I didn't bother to reply to his insult. I was steering straight for the edge of the breakwater, three miles away, and I was in one of those moods where you don't want to think about more than one thing at a time.

I felt more talkative after we'd been on shore a while, and that night, in our rooms, we visioned ourselves reaching the very pinnacle of the codfish aristocracy.

To learn, first-hand, the way to haul in a trawl, we went out at six in the morning with Mr. Poole. He's a big, knotty, large-boned man, just about as kindly as they make 'em, and he taught us a lot. The way you do is to haul up your line from the bottom and run it over the bow of the boat. The line is guided sternward by sticks set upright in the bow. Then you just haul, pulling the boat forward and unhooking each cod as you come to it. Some of 'em weigh more than eighty pounds!

Cod isn't all you get, either. Now and then you bring up a haddock, a less freckled fish than the cod, and flatfish— queer things about a foot from top to bottom and about an inch thick. On the menu they're called sole. Then again you get skates, scrapping fish shaped like a flatfish, but all gristle. Skates are a total loss, and so are starfish, with their six tentacles wrapped around the bait.

We felt like old-timers when we set out alone at eleven. I'd like to tell you how elated we were when we started hauling our own line—when the tug got heavy, and looking down into the green depths we caught the flash of a white belly! The first one must have weighed about thirty pounds, but it looked like a whale to us!

A cod is a submissive creature. He hardly struggles at all when you take him up, and when you toss him back into the boat he just heaves a big sigh, gazes at you reproachfully, and passes out without a wiggle. He seems to know, somehow, that he's destined to be creamed and eaten on potatoes.

At the dock, in the middle of the afternoon, our friendly fisherman—Mr. Poole had told us his name was John Roach— showed us how to clean the fish. Weighed in, our catch totaled 900 pounds. That was $13.50 and, deducting our costs, we figured we'd netted a profit of at least $8.00! We slept sweetly that night.

The next afternoon we came in with our boat loaded half-way to the gunwales, and when we started tossing them out on the dock, we caught the stumpy, hostile fisherman, Follabee, looking at us in a manner that made us feel uncomfortable. But the catch weighed in at 1200 pounds—$18.00—and we didn't care what Follabee thought.

The third day's catch was 1100, and we began to compare ourselves favorably with the wealthy oil and automobile magnates. Only one thing marred my joy in our good fortune. One night we called on Cliff Cox, the resort owner, and Ralph sang him about six verses of "Casey Jones."

"Aside from the fact that your voice is even less your fortune than your face," I told him later, in our room, "most people have heard 'Casey Jones' and they get practically no kick at all from hearing you repeat it. Why do you do it? You used to be a good guy."

But Ralph just rolled over and shut his eyes. I went on:

"You've sung it both to Mr. Poole and Mr. Cox. What have those two men done to you?"

No reply from Ralph, so I continued:

"Furthermore, you pretend to get excited about something, and then you bark 'Holy Smoses!' Explain yourself."

But Ralph was snoring. When a guy acts like that there's nothing much you can say, so I went to sleep myself.

THE next day we were due for a shock. Ralph steered the boat out to our line and I took a turn at hauling the trawl. Before we had pulled the boat a hundred yards I knew something was wrong. In that distance I took in only one twenty-pound cod. I pulled a couple of hundred yards more and got one skate and a haddock.

"What are you doing to 'em?" Ralph asked. "Throwin' 'em back into the water?"

"No, eating 'em," I grunted. "Didn't have enough breakfast."

It ceased to be funny before we got half through our line. In that time we had just four fish, and at the last buoy our catch wasn't more than two hundred pounds. We just sat there and looked at each other with a gone feeling in the pit of our stomachs.

"Did you bait the hooks yesterday?" I asked, knowing blamed well that he did.

I wondered if some fisherman—maybe Mr. Follabee—had taken our cod. But the more I thought about it, the more incredible it seemed that anybody would deliberately rob us.

"Probably just an off day," Ralph suggested, and I agreed with him because there was nothing else to do.

Just the same, when we chugged out past the breakwater the next day, I had a gnawing fear that our disappointment was going to be repeated. The waves were crested just a bit with white, this morning, and Ralph had a hard time steering.

I hauled the trawl again, and when we had gone a short distance, my worst fears were justified. Not a fish!

In desperation I pulled feverishly until my arms were sore, and the reward was one small cod. I quit and faced Ralph.

"Somebody's stealing our fish!" I announced emphatically. "And I'll bet it's old man Follabee. He doesn't like us and he doesn't care if we know it."

"Somebody's taking 'em, that's a cinch," Ralph agreed. "But I don't think it's Follabee."

"Why not?"

But Ralph just looked at me queerly. "I —" he started—and then shut his lips tightly.

Exasperated, I turned and started hauling. I kept it up for fifteen minutes and then stopped in disgust.

"There's no use in going on," I told Ralph, "because we won't find any fish. If we don't want our summer to be a total flop, we've got to find out who's robbing our line!"

Down in my heart, I felt sure that if anybody would do it, Follabee was our man. But how could we catch him at it? He was probably robbing us early in the morning, but we couldn't get a boat at that time because they were all in use. I suggested going to Mr. Poole, or the friendly Mr. Roach, but Ralph shook his head. I could see that he was doing some deep and painful thinking, so I waited quietly. Suddenly his face brightened.

"I know what we can do," he muttered. "Pull along until we come to the first good fish and then mark him! To-morrow, when the fishermen come in, we'll watch as they throw 'em out on the dock. See which one has the marked cod!"

"Good old Sherlock," I murmured delightedly. "That's brain-work."

I turned to and started hauling again.

The waves were choppy and the pulling was twice as hard as ordinarily, but I made the boat fairly sing through the crests. After about twenty empty hooks, I came to a good-sized fish—a forty-pounder.

"Cut a diagonal piece off his tail," Ralph suggested. "Not too big."

I did it without taking him off the hook.

THAT night we strolled over to Cox's hotel. A few tourists were beginning to arrive and we anticipated talking to somebody from the United States. About half-way there, we passed a small shack close to the road. The door was partly open and the sound of whistling floated out. Ralph stopped and grabbed my arm.

"Do you hear that?" he hissed.

"Sure," I said. "What of it?"

"He's whistling 'Casey Jones'!"

There it was again! Ralph getting mysterious about that old bromide! But before I could remonstrate, he had pushed through the little gate and entered the house. I followed.

Ralph stood near the door, facing Follabee, who was sitting in a rocker with a newspaper in his hand, looking blankly at the intruder.

"Where did you live before you came here?" Ralph asked, right out of a clear sky.

Follabee recovered from his surprise. "What business is it of yours?" he asked quietly.

But a knowing look stole into Ralph's eyes. "Did you ever sing 'Casey Jones' at a high-school concert?" he asked.

I don't know what kind of a response Ralph expected, but all he got was a blank look—just the kind of look such a question deserved. Ralph seemed to realize he was on the wrong track. For a moment he stood there, while a red flush crept up his neck, and then he stammered an awkward apology and backed out.

When we were on the street once more, I took him by the arm.

"We're not going to the hotel," I told him. "We're going back to the room and we're going to stay there until you tell me what all this tommyrot is about."

We didn't exchange a word as we walked back, and when I lit the lamp in our room I could see that Ralph looked weary.

"We're about as close to each other as two fellows can get," I told him. "Why did you come to Prince Edward Island?"

"To catch codfish," he said firmly.

"That doesn't go," I declared flatly, "and you know it. I don't like to be left out in the cold this way. Why did you come here?"

"Partly to catch cod," Ralph insisted defiantly, "and partly"—he hesitated—"to find my uncle."

"Your uncle!"

Ralph nodded. After a moment's silence he cleared his throat.

"My uncle disappeared twenty years ago."

The statement surprised me, but Ralph's queer conduct had led me to expect anything, and I waited quietly for him to go on.

"After Dad died, Uncle Walter took care of money matters for Mom. He was a bug for aviation—even in those days—and he urged Mom, against our lawyer's advice, to buy stock in an airplane company. She put nearly all her money into it."

"And the company went broke?" I asked, trying to be helpful.

"Went out of business," he said. "But that wasn't the worst of it. Our lawyer told Mom that the deal looked funny. A sort of a stock swindle, with Uncle Walter getting his share out of it.

"Mom didn't believe it, but she let the

lawyer call a little conference with just the three of them present. The old fellow sort of hemmed and hawed and talked a lot about family honor and all that. When Uncle finally got what the lawyer was driving at, he just looked at Mom, and back at the lawyer. Then, without a word, he got up and left the room. That's the last time she ever saw him. She can't forget how hurt he looked."

"But—" I started.

"During the war," Ralph went on, "the airplane company reorganized under a new name. And since then it's made a lot of money. But there wasn't anything in the papers about the reorganization and I don't suppose Uncle Walter knows anything about it. Mother's been hoping for years he'd come back."

"But why did you come *here* to look for him?" I began to feel like a detective grilling a victim, but I had to get the whole story.

"Once or twice a year we get an unsigned letter. It usually has two or three hundred-dollar bills in it—Canadian bills, wrapped in plain paper. And they're mailed from Nova Scotia."

"That's not Prince Edward Island."

"But it's not far away—just across the Northumberland Straits. Uncle Walt served two years on a coastwise boat and he used to talk about Prince Edward Island a lot—called it a paradise, a land of red cliffs dipping down into the sea, and all that."

"Same line you fed me," I murmured. "Then this vacation—"

"A shot in the dark."

"But why did you pick on Souris? Prince Edward Island is more than a hundred miles long and has a score of towns."

"Souris is on the eastern end of the island, and I had a notion Uncle Walt would pick some little town as far away as possible—where we wouldn't be likely to look for him. Mom says he was mighty sensitive, prob'ly wouldn't ever show up until he thought the account was squared."

"But where does 'Casey Jones' come in?"

"Well," Ralph cleared his throat and half grinned. "Mom told me the story. It seems that Uncle Walt was on the program to sing 'Casey Jones' at a country-school concert. You know how it goes: 'Casey Jones, mounted to the cabin, Casey Jones with his orders in his hand, Casey Jones, mounted to the cabin and took his farewell trip to the Promised Land—'"

"Never mind!" I groaned, "I've heard it before. Go on."

"Uncle Walt got up, sang the verse and chorus through once, and couldn't remember the second verse. But his accompanist started right out and began to get ahead of him, so he couldn't do anything but sing the first verse and chorus through again. Well, he sang it through four times before the audience broke down and drowned him out. Uncle Walt used to say that experience was the making of him. And ever since, whenever he had a big job to do, he used to sing the whole song through to prove he had his wits about him. He was always humming it, Mom says.

"I figured that wherever he went he probably took a new name, and I'd have to trace him down through his favorite song or his favorite expression—'Holy Smoses!' I didn't have anything else to go by."

"Don't you even have a picture of him?"

"The only picture we have shows him at sixteen."

"What made you think Follabee was your uncle?"

"Well, he lives by himself, he doesn't talk much to anybody, he's been here about the right number of years, and when I heard him whistling that tune I thought maybe he might be. Uncle was a square-set guy. Besides, Mr. Poole told me that Follabee goes to Nova Scotia pretty often."

I whistled. Talk about slim clues! Right then I decided that there wasn't one chance in a thousand of locating the lost uncle, and that the best thing to do was to get Ralph to forget it.

"Better get some sleep," I suggested. "Our job, now, is to catch the codfish thief. If we earn enough money at this business, I'll travel all over Canada with you, singing 'Casey Jones' and shouting 'Holy Smoses!'"

And we shook hands on it.

THE next morning, at nine thirty, we were down on the dock waiting for the first fisherman to return with his catch. Two fellows we didn't know came in at ten, and we eagerly watched them toss out their fish. But we didn't see the marked cod. Then Mr. Poole came in. We knew he didn't have it. A half-dozen more and no bob-tailed fish. We weren't discouraged, because we figured that the man who hauled two lines—his own and ours—would be late.

The last two were Roach and Follabee. With a significant glance at Ralph I went over and helped Follabee tie up his boat, while Ralph went to the friendly Mr. Roach. I kept my eyes glued on each fish as it skidded on the wet boards. Right down to the last fish—and no bob-tail.

Half disappointed, I strolled over to Ralph, sure that he had discovered nothing—sure that our luckless cod was still moored to a hook five miles off-shore. But the minute I looked at his face, I knew differently. His eyes, big as saucers, were fixed on a mess of fish. I followed his gaze. And there it was—a forty-pounder with a diagonal piece cut off his tail. No mistaking it.

He looked at each other blankly, dismayed. The friendly Mr. Roach who'd showed us how to clean fish! Slowly we walked off the dock—neither of us felt like accusing him.

"He's the one," Ralph muttered when we were on shore.

"What'll we do?" I asked.

Ralph's lips were set in a firm line and I could see he was getting red-headed.

"The old hypocrite," he grated. "He said hello to me like an old friend and tossed those fish of ours out on the dock without a quiver. Let's—let's get a boat and catch him at it to-morrow morning."

"All the boats are in use," I pointed out.

We were strolling along aimlessly and found ourselves opposite the Cox Hotel. An idea struck both of us at the same time.

"Maybe Mr. Cox has a boat," Ralph ventured, and I nodded.

Mr. Cox had one, a four-cylinder, fairly speedy launch, for the convenience of his guests. In jig time we arranged to use it the next morning.

"He can't get away from us—not with us in this baby," Ralph whispered to me.

We didn't go out for our cod that afternoon—we knew it'd be no use. Instead we took a long walk east of town, along the cliffs overhanging the sea. For a long time we watched the gulls swooping down to the water and mewing at each other. Neither of us had any taste for our job—to catch, red-handed, the man who had been so thoroughly friendly in two short contacts. But it was either that or leave Souris—and we intended to stay. We loved it. Ralph's Uncle Walt had named it correctly—Paradise.

The next morning at seven, gray-eyed from lack of sleep, we purred out into the harbor from Mr. Cox's wharf. There was no sun—the sky was overcast, and the crests of the waves beyond the break-water were curling. By this time, we figured, the fishermen would be at their buoys, commencing to haul.

The going was hard, farther out, and I found myself hanging to the gunwale. Ralph steered. As he set the course by our two points on shore, he slowed down the engine. Mr. Roach might haul his own line first. We didn't want to interrupt him until he started on ours.

The shore receded. After a while I made out, far to the east, a tiny spot. Away south, another. Neither of them near our line. Gradually, as we bucked the waves seaward, I saw another speck—squarely ahead of us. My heart began to pound furiously.

In another ten minutes, we felt certain that we had our man. A half-mile more and I knew that the boat contained Mr. Roach. Ralph's eyes were glowing with battle-light.

It seemed strange to me that as we drew close to Mr. Roach he made no move to escape, or showed any concern whatsoever.

"Hallo, boys!" he hailed. "You're out early."

There he was, calmly hauling *our* line —tossing *our* cod into his boat. Cast-iron nerve! I lost all patience with him, and so did Ralph. We drew alongside.

"What's the idea!" burst out Ralph, his voice trembling slightly.

"Which idea?" Mr. Roach asked pleasantly.

Ralph had let go the helm and the launch had turned broadside to the waves. The crest of a roller splashed against the side and drenched us both. But Ralph didn't notice it.

"The idea," sputtered Ralph, almost lurching out of the launch, "of standing there like an oily hypocrite, smiling at us, and swiping our fish—"

Mr. Roach quit hauling and watched in amazement while another wave drenched my indignant pal. Ralph was so hot I almost expected the water to sizzle when it hit him.

"You've been pulling this off for two days—coming out here and cleaning our line—and you're going to cut it out!"

I could see that Mr. Roach didn't know whether to laugh or reach over and gaff Ralph with that mean-looking hook he had in his hand. But if he did, he'd find Ralph harder to handle than a meek, fat cod. Ralph can scrap.

"You're just a common thief!" Ralph concluded.

And then Mr. Roach exploded.

"Are you trying to say that I'm taking your cod?" he boomed, and his eyes burned at Ralph so fiercely that I thought they'd singe the blond hair off his head. "Why, you fresh skate, you! Why—" For a moment he stopped, utterly dumfounded, and then he bellowed, "Why, HOLY SMOSES! You two youngsters—"

Ralph's jaw dropped. His eyes popped out. He sank back into the stern of the boat with one arm over the side. Awe crept into his eyes.

"Uncle—Uncle Walt," he said weakly. "Uncle Walt!"

At those words it was Mr. Roach's turn to stop and stare. The gaff he was holding dropped from his limp hand.

"Who—who are you?" he asked, huskily.

"Ralph Pickens," Ralph almost whispered.

"Nan Pickens's boy—my nephew?"

Mr. Roach's Adam's apple was doing its daily dozen and his hand was trembling slightly. I felt something choking my own throat, and just to be doing things I stumbled back to the helm and tried to turn the boat into the wind.

Of the two limp relatives, Mr. Roach came to life first. He quickly cast off the trawl-line, tied his boat to the stern of ours, and climbed over.

Things were explained in no time at all. Mr. Roach—Uncle Walt—hadn't been hauling our line at all. We'd been hauling his. On the two days when the catch had been so poor, Ralph had been steering the boat and he'd unerringly guided us to the wrong buoy. They all look alike. The ocean is a wide place, without traffic signs or route marks, and it's the easiest thing in the world to get a point or two off the course. Even the old-timers sometimes have trouble locating the right buoys. We had been the robbers—only we hadn't stolen much. Our own line—untouched for two days—was probably loaded with cod.

But that wasn't important anyhow. The important thing was that Ralph had found his uncle and was able to tell him that the investment he'd made for Ralph's mother had kept her in bread and butter for ten years. And all the money Uncle Walt had sent home was in a bank, waiting for him.

Gosh, it was one of the sweetest fairytales in which I ever acted. In fact we almost had a lovely ride home. Almost.

"We'll celebrate to-night," smiled Uncle Walt.

"You bet," Ralph said dreamily, sitting close to the big, stalwart fisherman.

The launch was diving up and down like an indignant bronco, only less jerky. A sudden rising—then a falling away that left your stomach suspended.

"Sure—sure will," Ralph repeated faintly.

"We'll start out with cod tongue. Did you ever eat it?" Uncle Walt said contentedly.

Ralph shook his head and looked a little pale.

"Then creamed haddock for entrée—" Ralph shut his eyes.

"Oysters, maybe. And lobsters—two or three fat ones—broiled—"

Ralph's nerveless hand fell to his lap.

"—a slice of bacon on top. And then pie. Your mother used to bake big, juicy mince-pies—"

The pies finished Ralph. Finished him with a completeness that left very little to the imagination. He felt much better when we reached shore. Good, solid ground. And eventually we had our feast. Mr. Follabee was invited because he was the man who'd mailed all those anonymous letters for Uncle Walt from Nova Scotia.

Boy, we had a wonderful summer! Uncle Walt staked us to another complete outfit and we hauled two trawls instead of one—doubled our income. We went home with $600 net profit apiece.

And before we got to Chicago, Uncle Walt had taught us thirty-nine verses of "Casey Jones."

THE INDIA-RUBBER TREE

bp William B. MacHarg

This yarn was told to a pea-jacket boy,
  On a wide breakwater walk,
By a short old salt with auburn hair,
And a most engaging, experienced air,
  And a tendency to talk:

———

Now, a-settin' right here on this empty
    cask,
  A-talkin' this way with you,
It'd sound kind o' queer, it seems to me,
If you was to say, "Your Majestee,"
  An' give me a bow or two.

Yet I oncet was a king (said the sailor-
    man);
  I don't look it now (said he);
But I oncet was king of a savage race
In a sort of exceedin' bewilderin' place
  In the middle of Afrikee.

I had hunderds of servants a-standin'
    around,
  Withouten a thing to do
But just keep fandin' of me with fands,
An' just continual obey the commands
  I continual told 'em to.

But I give 'em a too benif'cent rule,
  Peace bein' my only port,
An' a enemy come when the night was
    dark,
A-sailin' along in their boats of bark,
  An' a-cuttin' my kingdom short.

335

They walloped them peaceful soldiers of
    mine
  Like they didn't amount to a thing;
An' when there weren't any more to be
    found,
Why, then they started a-lookin' around,
  A-seekin' the peaceful king.

An' that peaceful king he was me, you
    know,
  An' as scared as scared could be;
An' a single soldier of dusky 'ue,
As painted his features white an' blue.
  Was all that was left with me.

An' together we flees through the forest
    thick,
  An' we flees 'crost the burnin' sand;
But a-gaining be'ind us all the w'ile,
An' a-comin' closer with every mile,
  Is a blood-stained African band.

I couldn't see no way out o' that mess,
  Not *one* way out could I see;
But that peaceful soldier of dusky 'ue,
Though there weren't much else he was
    fit to do,
  Knowed the country better 'n me,

An' after a time we come to a place
  Where trees was a-growin' round,
With their tops a-pointin' up to the sky
Maybe several feet, maybe not so high,
  An' their roots stuck into the ground.

An' in one of them trees is a little hole,
  It might be as big as a pea;
An' the soldier puts his finger inside,
An' he stretches it out till it's two foot
    wide—
  It's an injia-rubber tree!

An' in we climbs, an' the tree snaps shut,
  An' the heathens they rage an' shout;
But there we're as safe as a bug in a rug,
An' just as contented, an' just as snug,
  With a little hole to look out.

An' so I escapes them savage troops
  In a way as I'm proud to boast,
An' comes back home in the "Adam
    M'Cue";
But that peaceful soldier of dusky 'ue
  Keeps store on the Guinea Coast.

The Prince's Councilors

by Tudor Jenks

As the Prince and a Page were coming from a game of tennis, a newsboy ran along crying: "Extra—extra-a! Here y' are; extra-a! Ter'ble los' life!"

"Boy!" called the Prince.

"Extra?" asked the boy.

"Yes, please," answered the Prince, drawing a gold coin from his purse.

"I can't change that," said the boy.

"Never mind the change," said the Prince. The boy's eyes sparkled. He hastily handed over two papers, and ran off with the coin, shouting as before, while heads popped from windows and people tried to find out the news without paying for it.

Meanwhile the Prince and the Page read their papers.

EXTRA

THE PRINCESS PARAGON!
POSSIBLY PERISHING!!
ALONE AND ADRIFT!!
ROYALTY TO THE RESCUE!!!

By this time both had dropped the rackets and were reading rapidly down the big print so as to get at the facts. The finer print told the story in simple words.

The position of the Princess Paragon—at present entirely unknown—is for that very reason most alarming. With her Royal Father she this morning went sailing in their private yacht. In spite of His Majesty's well-known skill with tiller and tackle, he lost control for an instant of the stanch little vessel, and, fearing the worst, courageously jumped overboard and waded ashore, intending to bring assistance to her Royal Highness, the unfortunate Princess. Having lost one of his shoes in the wet sand, His Majesty was delayed by his efforts to find it that the yacht had drifted beyond reach of those on shore before the fishermen sent by the intrepid King could reach the beach.

Distracted by his loss, the King now most generously offers his daughter's hand and a princely dowry, also half his Kingdom (subject to a first and second mortgage), to the noble youth who shall restore to him his daughter and the valuable necklace of diamonds she wears.

We commend the quest to the young Prince and the brave youths of his court. Further particulars in the regular edition this afternoon. The boat, we learn, was fully insured.

"There!" said the page, throwing aside the paper. "That's just what I'm looking for!"

"What is that?" asked the Prince, as he folded his paper and put it in his pocket.

"An opportunity to distinguish myself—to become renowned!" said the Page, proudly.

"You shall have it," answered the Prince, graciously. "You have always served me well, and you play tennis nearly as well as I do." (The score that afternoon was six sets love in favor of the Page.)

"Then you are willing I should try this adventure?" asked the Page, in surprise.

"Certainly," replied the Prince. "I shall take you with me, of course."

"Oh!" said the Page, in quite a different tone. He had been surprised at the Prince's generosity, but now he understood it better. Then he turned to the Prince and said, "When shall you start?"

"In a few days, I think," said the Prince, as he stooped to pick up his racket. "It depends on how long it will take to decide upon the best plan, to get things ready, and to pack up my robes, and put my fleet in order."

"Indeed!" said the Page. Then he added, "As I'm quite willing to go alone, because I'm in a hurry, I think I won't wait. In fact, I'll start now."

Then, coolly turning on his heel, he walked off down the street, leaving his racket where it had fallen, and the Prince where he stood.

"His last week's wages aren't paid, either," said the Prince to himself; "and I don't believe he'll ever come back for that racket of his. Reckless boy!"

The Prince picked up the racket and went leisurely home to the palace, where he was received by two long lines of footmen, who bowed low as he entered.

There were quail on toast for supper, and the Prince was so fond of these little birds that he ate seven of them, and was so busied over it that he could not find time to say a word until he was quite done. The Queen was telling the King all about a new gown; and the King was thinking how he could persuade the treasurer that there was a little too much money instead of much too little; and the Jester was wondering what chance he might have to make a living as a farmer; and the nobles were trying to attract the King's attention; so there was hardly a word spoken at the table until the Prince was quite through with his seven small birds. Then said the Prince:

"Oh, by the way, Papa, I almost forgot to ask you something. Will you please tell the treasurer to give me three or four bags of gold to-morrow? I'm going to take a little journey."

But the King at first paid no attention.

"What did you say?" he asked, at length.

"You tell him," suggested the Prince to the Jester.

So the Jester gave the King a hasty outline of the news in the paper, and told him that the Prince thought of going in search of the Princess. The King took little interest in the story until there was mention of the three or four bags of gold. Then he awoke to animation.

"To be sure," he cried. "It is an excellent plan. I will give you an order on the treasurer for six bags of gold, and I will keep the rest so as to send out a search expedition for you when you get lost."

The King knew the treasurer would not dare refuse the money for so worthy an object as the rescue of a princess adrift. Even if the treasurer did not want to give up the money, the people would never support an economy that would keep the Prince from so worthy an expedition. Indeed, the King's order was at once obeyed, and the Prince began his preparations.

First the Prince called a council of the wisest of the court.

"I suppose you have all read the news about the Princess?" he asked, when his councilors had assembled.

"Yes," they answered.

"I am desirous of not making a blunder at the outset, and so have resolved to secure the assistance of the wisest men of the kingdom. What, then, would you advise?"

"It seems to me," said the Chief Secretary, who was so venerable that his hair and beard seemed turned to cotton-batting, "that we ought first to ascertain whether the report is confirmed."

A low murmur of assent arose from them all; and the Prince, accepting the suggestion, said: "Let us then appoint a committee of investigation. Who knows how to go about the appointing of a committee?"

After a brief pause for consideration, another old courtier arose and said that he had a neighbor who was skilled in such matters, and if they would take an adjournment for a day or two he would ascertain just how to go about it.

The Prince thought the request was very reasonable, and announced that the council would meet again in two days. So they separated, and the Prince betook himself to the tennis-courts again, this time, however, with another page. The Prince found during the games that the former page's racket was a very good one; and this reminded him that the owner of it had started to seek the lost Princess.

Suddenly stopping the game, he said to one of his attendants:

"On second thought, I think I ought not to have sent after the man who knows how to appoint a committee. Suppose you go after the man who went after him, and tell him to come back."

Away went the attendant, and the Prince returned to the palace, resolved to prosecute the search with vigor. The council was again called together, and the Prince told them that without waiting to verify the report of the loss of the Princess, he meant to seek her at once.

"But in which direction will you go?" asked the Court Geographer.

"Oh, in any direction!" said the Prince, indifferently. "There is no telling where a boat may drift to."

"In that case," said the Court Mathematician, smiling, "the chances are about one in three hundred and sixty that you will hit upon the right way. Let me show you."

So the Court Mathematician sent a page to the kitchen for some beans. Away ran the boy; only to return in a few moments with the report that the cook wished to know whether he wanted "a pint, or a quart, or how many?"

"I want three hundred and sixty white ones, and one black one," said the Mathematician.

This time the page was gone a long while. When he returned, he explained that it took the cook longer to count the beans than one would think. That they had disagreed, and had counted them twice, to make sure; and then

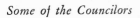

Some of the Councilors

had to send to the grocer's for a black bean, since there was none in the palace.

"There was no need of that," said the Mathematician, impatiently. "I can mark one of the white ones, and it will do quite as well."

So the page ran to overtake the messenger who had started for the grocer's, and meanwhile the Mathematician made an ink mark on one of the white beans, put them all into a hat, and shook them well. "Now, draw one," he said, offering the hat to the Prince.

The Prince drew one. It was the marked bean.

"Well," he said, "what does that prove?"

"It really doesn't prove anything," said the Mathematician, a little out of temper. "Try again." So the Prince returned the marked white bean to the hat, and after they were well shaken, drew again. This time he drew a plain bean.

"You see," said the Mathematician, triumphantly.

"What do I see?" asked the Prince.

"You didn't get the right one."

"But I did the first time," argued the Prince. "All your experiment proves is that I may hit it right the first time, and miss it the second, if I should try again. But if I hit it right the first time, I sha'n't have to try over again; so your rule doesn't apply. Isn't that so?"

"It does sound reasonable," answered the Mathematician, who was honest though clever.

"Perhaps you'd like to go home and try the experiment for yourself," said the Prince, kindly.

The Mathematician borrowed the beans, and went home, promising to send a written report of his trials after a few days.

"Now that we have settled the mathematical side of the question," said the Court Meteorologist, "we can go at the

problem scientifically. Here is the way it appears to me, your Royal Highness."

Then the Meteorologist unrolled a map and pinned it on the wall.

"The present position of the lost Princess," said he, "depends upon the joint action of the winds and tides. The Gulf Stream has little or nothing to do with the problem, as the boat was abandoned beyond the sphere of its influence. The trade-winds for a similar reason may perhaps be disregarded. There is no question here of simoon or sirocco, and—"

"Maybe it would be as well to leave out the things that have nothing to do with it," suggested the Prince, a little impatiently.

"But how shall we know what to leave out unless we go over them to see?" asked the lecturer.

"True," said the Prince; "but as that will take some time, you might run over the list at home and report to me, say, the day after to-morrow."

"I will do so," replied the Meteorologist, rolling up his map and departing with an air of great importance.

"I don't see," remarked the Prince, uneasily, "that we are making real progress."

"There has been nothing but nonsense, so far," said a bluff old Admiral. "What I say is to take a boat and go after the young lady in shipshape style!"

The Prince was so much encouraged by this direct way of putting the matter that he let the undignified mention of the Princess pass without reproof.

"And what would you advise?" he asked the Admiral.

"Take the fastest brigantine you can find —" begun the officer; but he was interrupted.

"In a case of less importance," broke in the voice of a portly Commodore, "I should not venture to interrupt my superior officer. But here the matter admits of no false hesitation because of etiquette."

"What suggestion have you to make?" inquired the Prince.

"A brigantine," the Commodore said impressively, "is an unreliable craft at best. I say, take a frigate, at once."

"Pshaw!" broke in the Admiral explosively.

"Gentlemen," said the perplexed Prince, "I cannot presume to decide between you. I am a novice in these matters. Suppose you discuss the question fully, and report in writing?"

When the naval officers had departed, there were left only a few small fry who asked that they might have a day or two to think the whole matter over before committing themselves to a decided opinion. Upon their withdrawal, the Prince found only the Jester.

"Perhaps," said the Prince, a little sarcastically, "you have some advice to give?"

"Perhaps," replied the Jester; "but first I have a plan to suggest."

"What is that?"

"You might take a small army and go after the page who started out to seek the Princess. By the time you have come up with him, he will perhaps have found her. Then you can sail in and take her away from him, and bring her home yourself. That's the way kings and princes often do."

"But that seems hardly fair," said the Prince, after a few moments' reflection.

"Of course it isn't fair," said the Jester; "but it's your only chance. I have no doubt he has found the Princess long ago."

"Do you think so?" asked the Prince.

"No doubt of it," said the Jester. "You see, he didn't wait for any advice, but started off at once."

"Isn't advice a good thing?"

"Yes," said the Jester, "for lawyers and councilors. They make their living by it. Advice is good, when it's good; but the best qualities are hard to find, and the time it takes to find them is sometimes worth more than the advice when found."

"Then you wouldn't advise me to take advice?" said the Prince, thoughtfully.

"My advice is," said the Jester, "don't take mine, or anybody's."

"Isn't that rather a difficult course to follow?" asked the Prince, after a momen's reflection.

"Very," the Jester agreed.

"I think," the Prince went on, "that I shall start now, and take my chances."

"I'll go with you," replied his companion.

So they started toward the palace gate; but just as they reached it and had called for the gate-keeper, there came a summons from without. When the gate was opened there was the Page. He seemed weary, and his shoes showed that he had traveled a long way on foot.

"Did you find the Princess?" asked the Prince, eagerly.

"Yes," said the Page, very calmly. "I found her."

"Fortunate boy!" said the Prince, a little enviously.

"I don't know about that," said the Page. "She was as cross as two sticks about having been left to go adrift. It rained, you know; and when I rowed out to the yacht, I found that everything on board was soaking wet, and she hadn't had anything to eat for two days, and—my goodness!—she was hopping mad!"

"What did she say?" asked the Jester.

"She said she'd like to box my ears," said the Page, earnestly. "Then I told her if she wasn't more polite I wouldn't rescue her. That quieted her, quick! So then she didn't say anything, but she looked about as pleasant as cold gravy. As soon as I towed the boat ashore, she gave me some money and told me to get along home. So I did, and I was glad to get away. I didn't tell her who I was, and I don't think she will ever find me. You won't tell, will you?" pleaded the Page, as he finished.

"No," said the Prince, laughing. "I won't tell. But perhaps you didn't treat the Princess with proper courtesy. No wonder she was out of humor, after being adrift so long."

"I'll tell you," said the Page, suddenly, "what we'll do. I found the Princess, and I suppose I'm entitled to the reward. Now, can't you arrange it that you'll marry the Princess? I think she'll just suit you. She is a fine-looking Princess, and I don't believe she meant to be cross. Do you think you can arrange it? It would be a splendid thing for the kingdom, you know. It would unite the two kingdoms, and there'd be all sorts of advantages. You can say that I went with your permission, you know, and that I'm engaged to be married, and wouldn't presume to aspire to a princess's hand."

"It's a good suggestion," said the Jester; "for otherwise there'll be war, of course. The other king will be bound to know why this young man won't accept his daughter's hand, and then there'll be a lot of diplomatic correspondence, ultimatums, protocols, and all sorts of goings-on. If you don't mind, I think you would do well to marry this Princess."

"I don't mind at all," answered the Prince; "and I think I'll write a letter to her this very day. But how," he went on, turning to the Page, "did you come to be engaged? I didn't know anything about it."

"The fact is," said the Page, "I'm not quite engaged; but there's one of the maids of honor who will have me, I'm sure. She told me the other day that she wished it was leap-year every day; and I think that's

a distinct encouragement, don't you?"

His friend agreed that it was a marked observation.

"You'll be safe for a day or two," remarked the Jester to the Page; "and meanwhile you can be getting your clothes brushed and your shoes mended. The Prince will write to-day."

Early on the following morning, as the Prince came down to breakfast, he was told that a deputation was awaiting him in the Council-Room. "Who are they?" he asked.

"The Councilors with their reports," answered the messenger.

"But," said the Prince, "they are—"

"Hush!" said the Jester; "let us not lose their words of wisdom."

"Very well," the Prince agreed, smiling.

So the Prince, the Jester, and the Page entered the room where the Council were assembled. All bowed profoundly.

"Your Royal Highness," began the Secretary, "in order to verify the report of the loss of the Princess, I sent an inquiry to a friend of mine who stands very high in favor at her father's court. It was thus worded: 'Is the Royal Princess absent from the Court?' And I have his sealed reply: 'She is not.' That I consider conclusive. Is it not?"

"Yes," said the Jester; "it is not."

"I have no doubt," said the Prince, "that your information is correct; and I thank you for your diligence."

The Secretary bowed and was seated.

"I," began the Meteorologist, "have prepared a list of the things that may be disregarded in the search. It contains 872 items, with two appendices and voluminous notes. I will read it."

"Never mind," said the Prince, very graciously. "I will order it filed in the Royal Archives. We will now listen to the Mathematician."

"I have tried the bean-experiment several hundreds of times," said the Mathemati-

cian, "and have not yet succeeded in drawing the marked bean. The formula of
chances I have worked out. I find that 'If

"I am not prepared to dispute you," said
the Prince, "and I will ask leave therefore
to express my indebtedness to you."

The Councilors return to the palace with their reports

Henry puts 360 white beans into a hat, and
John draws a good many times, no one can
tell whether he will draw the marked bean
the first time, or not at all.' I consider that
an exact statement of the matter."

"We," said the Admiral, speaking for
himself and the Commodore, "I regret to
say, have as yet arrived at nothing more
advanced than a compromise. We have
agreed to recommend a squadron com-

posed of equal numbers of brigantines and frigates. Thus you will secure the advantages of both forms of craft."

"A wise conclusion," said the Prince; "and I gladly offer to you both my fervent gratitude."

A few of the smaller fry of Councilors yet remained to be heard, but the Prince announced that he had bestowed upon each councilor The Order of the Brazen Owl. But, as he was about to leave the room, the Councilors, after a moment's consultation, begged permission to ask a question. It was granted.

"We should like to know what use Your Highness wished to make of the information we have furnished?"

"To find the Princess who was lost," answered the Prince.

"Oh, yes," said the Councilors' spokesman. "We had forgotten what it was all about. But it's of no consequence now."

"No," said the Prince; "she is rescued."

"Indeed?" said the Councilors, with polite interest. Then they put on their cloaks, and went their several ways, all reading their reports to one another, and none listening.

The Prince and Princess were married soon after, and the Page and the Maid of Honor were best man and bridesmaid.

The Prince pensioned the Councilors and sent them to America. They all sailed in one ship. The vessel is several days overdue, but undoubtedly will arrive in safety after the Admiral and the Commodore have settled a little difference of opinion as to where they had better land.

The Page and the Maid of Honor are married, and keep a candy-store where they sell a dollar's worth of candy for five cents. They sent me the address, but you'll be sorry to learn that I have mislaid it.

IN THE KNOB MOUNTAIN TOWER

by Merritt P. Allen

As far back as he could remember, Ray Rand had loved the woods; and about the time he was ten years old he had decided to spend his life in them. This determination did not waver as time advanced; but from his early dreams of being a hermit or a trapper, he turned to an earnest, whole-hearted desire to enter the forestry service, not as a second-rate man, but as a college graduate with an M.F. (Master of Forestry) after his name.

It takes money to go to college, especially to a high-class forestry college, and there was very, very little money in the Rand family. Ray was seventeen when he graduated from high school, a time when a boy's life must necessarily take a turn, for he either goes to college then or he never goes, as a rule. Sometimes circumstances force the decision, but more often it depends on the boy himself.

When Ray graduated he had less than ten dollars of his own, but he had an abundance of clean, solid grit. Searching the papers for a summer's job, he found an announcement by the chief forester of the Adirondack Mountain region that a man was wanted to watch for forest fires from the Knob Mountain lookout-station. The salary was one hundred dollars a month and camp. It sounded good, and eventually Ray appeared in the chief forester's office.

"What can I do for you?" the broad-shouldered, keen-eyed official asked.

"I am applying for the Knob Mountain job."

"Know what it is like?"

"No, sir; but I think I can watch for fires."

"It is a man-sized job, son. The work isn't much, but it is the solitude that gets you, unless you like it. I seldom get a man to stay the season through. It is seven miles straight back in the woods. There are no camps near, and you are not allowed to leave your post night or day. There is a telephone, but you don't use it for pleasure, since it only runs to this office. Twice a month we send a man up with supplies, and I drop in occasionally; you will probably see no other persons until you come out in the fall."

"I like the woods," Ray said. "I shouldn't be lonesome."

The chief looked doubtful. "Why not get a pal to go with you?" he suggested. "You could make a camping-trip out of it and have considerable fun, alternate the work and divide the wages."

Ray shook his head. "I need all the money," he said.

The chief's face became thoughtful, for he had once been a boy in need of money.

"What's the idea?" he asked kindly.

Ray told him.

The chief smiled. "Want to enter the service, eh? Well, that puts a different face on the matter. I guess, after all, there is no reason why you shouldn't have the job."

Within a week, Ray was established on Knob Mountain with two weeks' provisions, a few books, a clock, a camera, and a light rifle of his own, besides the professional equipment provided by the service. His camp was the watch-tower itself. It was of steel, round, and rose twenty feet above the rocks of the mountain peak. The ground floor was a tiny kitchen, the next a sleeping-room, and the third and top, the observation-post. Such a view! On clear days Ray could see through the binoculars hundreds and thousands of acres of land and water, deep forest for the most part, except for occasional small valley clearings and lakes, and on the east, the long, glistening expanse of Lake Champlain. When the sun was just right, the spires of Montreal glistened a hundred and more miles to the north; and at night, lights, none nearer than seven miles, twinkled here and there below.

Over this mighty tract it was Ray's duty to watch and, should smoke appear, to locate it as best he could on his maps and telephone the news to the chief's office. There was plenty of rain that season, and he had but two small fires to report.

The chief called up frequently, partly to keep in touch with the boy to whom he had taken a fancy, and partly in an attempt to catch him away from his post. But he never did; for though Ray longed to steal away for a ramble in the woods, he always kept within sound of the telephone-bell as he had promised to do. A man came up with fresh supplies once a fortnight, and the chief dropped in unannounced three or four times; but aside from them, Ray saw no one except at a distance through the glasses.

On a sleepy afternoon in August, the chief was on the wire. "I am going to be away for a few days," he said, among other things. "If anything happens, ask for Mr. Adams, who will be in charge here."

"Yes, sir," Ray answered. And after more talk, he asked as usual, "Any news?"

"No. Oh, yes! the Lake Placid bank was robbed last night of a hundred thousand in cash. The police think the thieves got away through Malone. That's all. Good-by."

Lake Placid, the famous summer resort, was not so very far away, about fifteen miles through the woods to the southwest, but hidden from the Knob tower by an interposing mountain. The robbery was of no consequence to Ray, but for some reason it was so much in his thoughts after that, that at first he believed it to be a dream when he was awakened in the night by a light and opened his eyes to see three men in his room, one with a drawn revolver.

"Get up," the man commanded, "and find us some grub."

"Who are you?" Ray asked, knowing it was no dream.

"Never mind that."

Ray looked about quickly.

"We've got your rifle," the man said. "No use making a fuss. Get up!"

Ray got up, dressed, and went downstairs between two of the men. Without a word, he set out some provisions, and the men ate hungrily, one of them standing guard at the door and all of them casting frequent glances at three canvas packs on the floor. When they finished, dawn was breaking, and he could see their faces better—cruel, hard faces.

"Climb!" the leader said suddenly, pointing up the stairs with his revolver. "Go clean to the top and stay there, or I'll shoot you down like a hedgehog." And there was no doubt but that he meant it.

Ray went up the stairs obediently, for there was nothing else to do; he stood no show against three armed men.

"He can't signal from there, can he?" one asked anxiously.

"No," another answered. "Nothing there but the 'phone. I know these places."

Ray went up through his bedroom to the observation-post, and, looking through the window, saw, as he expected to, the severed telephone-wires dangling from their rock-propped pole a hundred feet away. He went back to the head of the stairs. The two flights were in line, so that from where he stood, he could look directly down on the table on the ground floor. The men were dumping the three canvas packs upon the table—and those packs were full of money. Gold, silver, but mostly bank-notes, lay in a great pile. The leader glanced up suddenly, saw Ray, and, quick as lightning, snatched his gun and fired. The bullet missed the boy by a few inches, glanced from the steel roof over his head, and crashed through a window. Not a word was said, and none was necessary. Ray tumbled back out of range and sat down.

He had seen enough, though, to tell him that those men were the bank-robbers who, instead of going through Malone, had fled straight into the woods. While the police were searching every car on the highways and railways, the bandits were counting their loot on the mountain-top. Only one person besides themselves knew this, and that one was cooped up in the top of a steel tower, helpless.

There was no possible way of getting down, for the outside of the tower was smooth, and to jump the twenty feet to the rocks below would mean a broken leg if nothing more. There was nothing to do but wait; so he waited. If only some one would happen along! He took up his post by the window, and about noon could scarcely believe his eyes when up the trail came the man who brought his supplies.

Regardless of the circumstances, Ray leaned as far out as he dared and shouted wildly: "The men who robbed the Lake Placid bank are downstairs. They will shoot. Run!"

The man stopped in his tracks, then came on again; and out of the tower door calmly walked the leader to meet him. They were in league!

Ray sank back in dismay. His last hope was gone. There was not one chance in a thousand that another person would come that way. How long would the bandits stay in the tower? What would they do with him? They dare not let him go. Would they kill him? They looked capable of it. Whatever they did, it would not be pleasant.

Ray could hear them talking, and, dropping flat on the floor, put his ear as near the head of the stairs as he dared and listened. The supply man was relating how the search was progressing, which was the very reason for which he had been planted in the village below. The fact that they were supposed to have gone west or north pleased the men immensely, and in louder and more confident tones they began outlining their plans. At dark they would go down into separate valleys, and the next day, passing as trampers, would go to the nearest railroad points and get away by train. The supply man would go back as usual, but would soon receive a telegram saying that his brother was dead in New York, after which, of course, he might be expected to depart hurriedly. "And the boy?" some one asked. They would tie him up and leave him, they decided. It might mean his death by starvation, but they couldn't help it. Ray shivered.

After a while the supply man left the others and came up the two flights of stairs.

"Make out a list of the things you want brought up next time," he said. "I'm going down about three o'clock."

He made no attempt to explain his friendship with the bandits. Ray wondered if the man thought him fool enough to be unable to put two and two together. At any rate, he decided to be as taciturn as the next one and merely agreed to have the list ready.

The man went downstairs again, and shortly after, Ray heard the tower door shut and the key turn on the outside. Looking down from his window he saw the supply man and two others spreading blankets and coats on the rocks in the shade of the tower. They were tired after their night's work and lay down heavily. Evidently the leader preferred a softer couch, for Ray heard him coming up the first flight of stairs; then the cot in the tiny bedroom creaked, and soon all was still below.

The boy sat down to think, and decided that rather than be tied in the tower to die by inches, perhaps, he would jump to the rocks, when the time came, and take his chances, slim as they were. As he laid his plans the only sound was the ticking of his alarm-clock on a shelf beside him. It was a very small clock, which he had bought because it could be easily packed up the mountain, thicker, but not much more in diameter, than a watch. It had a modest tick, for a clock, but when it was aroused, it *would* ring!

Ray's thoughts turned idly to this clock; and of a sudden he had an idea. He pondered it for a full two minutes, then, looking down again and making sure that the men outside the tower were sound asleep, he stole to the stairs and peered into his bedroom. The bandit leader was sleeping furiously. The boy went back for the clock and holding it carefully in his hands, began descending the stairs very, very cautiously. His heart was in his throat, for he knew that if he awoke the man, he might be shot. He reached the floor, and, not daring to pause, so precious was every fraction of a second, crept past the cot on his tiptoes and so on down to the ground floor.

The three packs full of money were on the table and he had a great desire to open them, but he knew that time was more precious than money, and went about his work. Moving silently as a ghost, he took down a good-sized tin can partly full of dried hulled corn, emptied two thirds of the corn out on the table, leveled off the remainder inside the can, and on this corn placed an empty cocoa can. Taking a pencil and a leaf from his note-book, he wrote:

The three men who robbed the Lake Placid bank are in the Knob tower with the money. They will leave at dark, separately, for railroad stations. The man who brings me supplies is in with them and will get away to-night if you don't nab him. Telephone wires are cut and I am a prisoner in the tower.   RAY RAND.

This note he placed in the small can inside the larger one, then, taking up the little clock, he wound it and set the alarm at half-past five. Smiling a little, he placed the clock upon the note, put the cover on the cocoa can, then proceeded to bury it completely with the corn from the table. He felt the weight of the large can in his hands, held it close to his ear in an attempt to detect the clock's ticking, then set it back on the shelf, confident that no one could guess that it contained anything but the article advertised on its outside. Three minutes later he was safely back upstairs.

"Got that list ready?" the supply man called up from the kitchen an hour later.

Ray dropped it down to the man, who eyed it sharply to see that it contained no hidden message, then put it in his pocket.

"I wish that you would take back that package of hulled corn and tell the merchant you got it of that I ordered popcorn," Ray said to him.

"I ain't going to fuss with that," the man growled.

"Take it along," the leader commanded. "It will make things look more natural."

"Well, where is it?"

Ray directed him to the shelf and held his breath while he took down the can and thrust it into his pack-basket. But the man suspected nothing and soon started away.

It was already dark in the valleys when the bandit chief ordered Ray to come down. As the boy stepped into the kitchen he was seized, and in two minutes was bound hand and foot and laid on the floor.

"You're a gritty chap," the leader said, standing over him in the darkness. "I hate to leave you this way, but we must get away and don't want you telling what you know too soon. If things go right, I may be able to send you help in two or three days. I will leave a dish of water and some food on the floor and perhaps you can get enough of it to keep you going."

Two or three days or a week to remain bound, with only a little food and water picked off the floor, dog fashion! He might never be found until it was too late. He wished then that he had jumped to the rocks as he had planned.

"We'll be moving," the bandit said to the others. "You know where to go from here."

Silently they picked up their precious packs and stepped out into the darkness. Then came the sound of many feet, blows, a couple of shots, and presently a big voice boomed:

"Got 'em tied up, boys? Anybody hurt? Good! Now where's Rand?"

"Here!" Ray shouted, "inside!"

Two electric torches flashed through the doorway. A man wearing a sheriff's badge entered and cut Ray's bonds.

"There's your friends," he said, pointing outside, where the robbers were nicely handcuffed and guarded by a dozen men. "We got the other one down in the village. Found your note, you see. And say! that was a mighty bright idea fixing the alarm-clock as you did. I happened to be in the store when the fellow brought in that hulled corn. The clerk set it back on the shelf, and a few minutes later—*rippity bang!* We couldn't think what was up till we dug into the corn and found the little clock going like a cyclone. And there was the note under it! Best thing I ever heard of. Say, I guess you'll come in for a fat slice of the reward."

Ray did come in for his share of it, and later, after the chief had heard the story, he received a scholarship to a forestry school that is second to none. He is there now.

TOM SAWYER ABROAD

by Huck Finn. Edited by Mark Twain

CHAPTER X

Tom said it happened like this.

A dervish was stumping it along through the desert, on foot, one blazing hot day, and he had come a thousand miles and was pretty poor, and hungry, and ornery and tired, and along about where we are now, he run across a camel-driver with a hundred camels, and asked him for some alms. But the camel-driver he asked to be excused. The dervish says—

"Don't you own these camels?"

"Yes, they're mine."

"Are you in debt?"

"Who—me? No."

"Well, a man that owns a hundred camels and ain't in debt, is rich—and not only rich, but very rich. Ain't it so?"

The camel-driver owned up that it was so. Then the dervish says—

"Allah has made you rich, and He has made me poor. He has His reasons, and they are wise, blessed be His name. But He has willed that His rich shall help His poor, and you have turned away from me, your brother, in my need, and He will remember this, and you will lose by it."

That made the camel-driver feel shaky, but all the same he was born hungry after money and didn't like to let go a cent, so he begun to whine and explain, and said times was hard, and although he had took a full freight down to Balsora and got a fat rate for it, he couldn't git no return freight, and so he warn't making no great things out of his trip. So the dervish starts along again, and says—

"All right, if you want to take the risk, but I reckon you've made a mistake this time, and missed a chance."

Of course the camel-driver wanted to know what kind of a chance he had missed, because maybe there was money in it; so he run after the dervish and begged him so hard and earnest to take pity on him and tell him, that at last the dervish give in, and says—

"Do you see that hill yonder? Well, in that hill is all the treasures of the earth, and I was looking around for a man with a particular good kind heart and a noble generous disposition, because if I could find just that man, I've got a kind of salve I could put on his eyes and he could see the treasures and get them out."

So then the camel-driver was in a state; and he cried, and begged, and took on, and went down on his knees, and said he was just that kind of a man, and said he could fetch a thousand people that would say he wasn't ever described so exact before.

"Well, then," says the dervish, "all right. If we load the hundred camels, can I have half of them?"

The driver was so glad he couldn't hardly hold in, and says—

"Now you're shouting."

So they shook hands on the bargain, and the dervish got out his box and rubbed the salve on the driver's right eye, and the hill opened and he went in, and there, sure enough, was piles and piles of gold and jewels sparkling like all the stars in heaven had fell down.

So him and the dervish laid into it and they loaded every camel till he couldn't carry no more, then they said good-by, and each of them started off with his fifty. But pretty soon the camel-driver came a-running and overtook the dervish and says—

"You ain't in society, you know, and you don't really need all you've got. Won't you be good, and let me have ten of your camels?"

"Well," the dervish says, "I don't know but what you say is reasonable enough."

So he done it, and they separated and the dervish started off again with his forty. But pretty soon here comes the camel-driver bawling after him again, and whines and whimpers around and begs another ten off of him, saying thirty camel-loads of treasures was enough to see a dervish through, because they live very simple, you know, and don't keep house but board around and give their note.

But that warn't the end, yet. That camel-driver kept coming and coming till he had begged back all the camels and had the whole hundred. Then he was satisfied, and ever so grateful, and said he wouldn't ever forgit the dervish as long as he lived, and nobody hadn't ever been so good to him before, and liberal. So they shook hands good-by, and separated and started off again.

But do you know, it warn't ten minutes till the camel-driver was unsatisfied again —he was the lowdownest reptile in seven counties—and he come a-running again. And this time the thing he wanted was to get the dervish to rub some of the salve on his other eye.

"Why?" said the dervish.

"Oh, you know," says the driver.

"Know what?" says the dervish.

Says the driver—

"Well, you can't fool me. You're trying to keep back something from me, you know it mighty well. You know, I reckon, that if I had the salve on the other eye I could see a lot more things that's valuable. Come—please put it on."

The dervish says—

"I wasn't keeping anything back from you. I don't mind telling you what would happen if I put it on. You'd never see again. You'd be stone blind the rest of your days."

But do you know, that beat wouldn't believe him. No, he begged and begged, and whined and cried, till at last the dervish opened his box and told him to put it on, if he wanted to. So the man done it, and sure enough he was as blind as a bat, in a minute.

Then the dervish laughed at him and mocked at him and made fun of him; and says—

"Good-by—a man that's blind hain't got no use for jewelry."

And he cleared out with the hundred camels, and left that man to wander around poor and miserable and friendless the rest of his days in the desert.

Jim said he'd bet it was a lesson to him.

"Yes," Tom says, "and like a considerable many lessons a body gets. They ain't no account, because the thing don't ever happen the same way again—and can't. The time Hen Scovil fell down the chimbly and crippled his back for life, everybody said it would be a lesson to him. What kind of a lesson? How was he going to use it? He couldn't climb chimblies no more, and he hadn't no more backs to break."

"All de same, Mars Tom," Jim said, "dey *is* sich a thing as learnin' by expe'ence. De Good Book say de burnt chile shun de fire."

"Well, I ain't denying that a thing's a lesson if it's a thing that can happen twice just the same way. There's lots of such things, and *they* educate a person, that's what Uncle Abner always said; but there's forty *million* lots of the other kind—the kind that don't happen the same way twice —and they ain't no real use, they ain't no more instructive than the smallpox. When you've got it, it ain't no good to find out you ought to been vaccinated, and it ain't no good to get vaccinated afterwards, because the smallpox don't come but once. But on the other hand Uncle Abner said that a person that had took a bull by the tail once had learnt sixty or seventy times as much as a person that hadn't, and said a person that started in to carry a cat home by the tail was gitting knowledge that was always going to be useful to him, and warn't ever going to grow dim or doubtful. But I can just tell you, Jim, Uncle Abner was down on them people that's all the time trying to dig a lesson out of everything that happens, no matter whether—"

But Jim was asleep. Tom looked kind of ashamed, because you know a person always feels bad when he is talking uncommon fine and thinks the other person is admiring, and that other person goes to sleep that way. Of course he oughtn't to go to sleep, because it's shabby; but the finer a person talks the certainer it is to make you sleep, and so when you come to look at it it ain't nobody's fault in particlar, both of them's to blame.

Jim begun to snore—soft and easy-like, at first, then a long rasp, then a stronger one, then a half a dozen horrible ones like the last water sucking down the plug-hole of a bathtub, then the same with more power to it. And when the person has got to that point he is at his level best, and can wake up a man in the next block, but can't wake himself up although all that awful noise of his'n ain't but three inches from his own ears. And that is the curiosest thing in the world, seems to me. But you rake a match to light the candle, and that little bit of a noise will fetch him. I wish I knowed what was the reason of that, but there don't seem to be no way to find out. Now there was Jim alarming the whole Desert, and yanking the animals out for miles and miles around, to see what in the nation was going on up there; there warn't nobody nor nothing that was as close to the noise as *he* was, and yet he was the only cretur that wasn't anyways disturbed by it.

We yelled at him and whooped at him, it never done no good, but the first time there come a little wee noise that wasn't of a usual kind it woke him up. No, sir, I've thought it all over, and so has Tom, and there ain't no way to find out why a snorer can't hear himself snore.

Jim said he hadn't been asleep, he just shut his eyes so he could listen better.

Tom said nobody warn't accusing him.

That made him look like he wished he hadn't said anything. And he wanted to git away from the subject, I reckon, because he begun to abuse the camel-driver, just the way a person does when he has got catched in something and wants to take it out of somebody else. He lit into the camel-driver the hardest he knowed how, and I had to agree with him; and he praised up the dervish the highest he could, and I had to agree with him there, too. But Tom says—

"I ain't so sure. You call that dervish so dreadful liberal and good and unselfish, but I don't quite see it. He didn't hunt up another poor dervish, did he? No, he didn't. If he was so unselfish, why didn't he go in there himself and take a pocket-full of jewels and go along and be satisfied? No, sir, the person he was hunting for was a man with a hundred camels. He wanted to get away with all the treasure he could."

"Why, Mars Tom, the dervish was willin' to divide, fair and square; he only struck for fifty camels."

"Because he knowed how he was going to get all of them by and by."

"Mars Tom, he *tole* de man de truck would make him blind."

"Yes, because he knowed the man's character. It was just the kind of a man he was hunting for—a man that never believes in anybody's word or anybody's honorableness, because he ain't got none of his own. I reckon there's lots of people like that dervish. They swindle right and left, but they always make the other person *seem* to swindle himself. They keep inside of the letter of the law all the time, and there ain't no way to git hold of them. *They* don't put the salve on—oh, no, that would be sin; but they know how to fool *you* into putting it on, then it's you that blinds yourself. I reckon the dervish and the camel-driver was just a pair—a fine, smart, brainy rascal, and a dull, coarse, ignorant one, but both of them rascals, just the same."

"Mars Tom, does you reckon dey's any o' dat kind o' salve in de worl' now?"

"Yes, Uncle Abner says there is. He says they've got it in New York, and they put it on country people's eyes and show them all the railroads in the world, and they go in and get them, and then when they rub the salve on the other eye the other man bids them good-by and goes off with their railroads. Here's the treasure-hill, now. Lower away!"

We landed, but it warn't as interesting as I thought it was going to be, because we couldn't find the place where they went in to git the treasure. Still, it was plenty interesting enough, just to see the mere hill itself where such a wonderful thing happened. Jim said he wouldn't a-missed it for three dollars, and I felt the same way.

And to me and Jim, as wonderful a thing as any was the way Tom could come into a strange big country like this and go straight and find a little hump like that and tell it in a minute from a million other humps that was almost just like it, and nothing to help him but only his own learning and his own natural smartness. We talked and talked it over together, but couldn't make out how he done it. He had the best head on him I ever see; and all he lacked was age, to make a name for himself equal to Captain Kidd or George Washington. I bet you it would a-crowded either of *them* to find that hill, with all their gifts, but it warn't nothing to Tom Sawyer; he went clear across the Sahara and put his finger right on it.

We found a pond of salt water close by and scraped up a raft of salt around the edges and loaded up the lion's skin and the tiger's so as they would keep till Jim could tan them.

CHAPTER XI

WE went a-fooling along for a day or two, and then just as the full moon was touching the ground on the other side of the Desert, we see a string of little black figgers moving across its big silver face. You could see them as plain as if they was painted on the moon with ink. It was another caravan. We cooled down our speed and tagged along after it, just to have company, though it warn't going our way. It was a rattler, that caravan, and a mighty fine sight to look at, next morning when the sun come a-streaming across the Desert and flung the long shadders of the camels on the gold sand like a thousand grand-daddy-longlegses marching in procession. We never went very near it, because we knowed better, now, than to act like that and scare people's camels and break up their caravans. It was the gayest outfit you ever see, for rich clothes and nobby style. Some of the chiefs rode on dromedaries, the first we ever see, and very tall, and they go plunging along like they was on stilts, and they rock the man that is on them pretty violent and stir him up considerable, I bet you; but they make noble good time and a camel ain't nowheres with them for speed.

The caravan camped, during the middle part of the day, and then started again about the middle of the afternoon. Before long the sun begun to look very curious. First it kind of turned to brass, and then to copper, and after that it begun to look like a blood red ball, and the air got hot and close, and pretty soon all the sky in the west darkened up and looked thick and foggy, but fiery and dreadful like it looks through a piece of red glass, you know. We looked down and see a big confusion going on in the caravan and a rushing every which way like they was scared, and then they all flopped down flat in the sand and laid there perfectly still.

Pretty soon we see something coming that stood up like an amazing wide wall, and reached from the Desert up into the sky and hid the sun, and it was coming like the nation, too. Then a little faint breeze struck us, and then it come harder, and grains of sand begun to sift against our faces and sting like fire, and Tom sung out—

"It's a sand-storm—turn your backs to it!"

We done it, and in another minute it was blowing a gale and the sand beat against us by the shovel-full, and the air was so thick with it we couldn't see a thing. In five minutes the boat was level full and we was setting on the lockers, all

of us buried up to the chin in sand and only our heads out and we could hardly breathe.

Then the storm thinned, and we see that monstrous wall go a-sailing off across the Desert, awful to look at, I tell you. We dug ourselves out and looked down, and where the caravan was before, there wasn't anything but just the sand ocean, now, and all still and quiet. All them people and camels was smothered and dead and buried—buried under ten foot of sand, we reckoned, and Tom allowed it might be years before the wind uncovered them, and all that time their friends wouldn't ever know what become of that caravan.

Tom said—

"Now we know what it was that happened to the people we got the swords and pistols from."

Yes, sir, that was just it. It was as plain as day, now. They got buried in a sand-storm, and the wild animals couldn't get at them, and the wind never uncovered them again till they was dried to leather. It seemed to me we had felt as sorry for them poor people as a person could for anybody, and as mournful, too, but we was mistaken; this last caravan's death went harder with us, a good deal harder. You see, the others was total strangers, and we never got really acquainted with them at all. But it was different with this last caravan. We was huvvering around them a whole night and most a whole day, and had got to feeling real friendly with them, and acquainted. I have found out that there ain't no surer way to find out whether you like people or hate them, than to travel with them. Just so with these. We kind of liked them from the start, and traveling with them put on the finisher. The longer we traveled with them, and the more we got used to their ways, the better and better we liked them and the gladder and gladder we was that we run across them. We had come to know some of them so well that we called them by name when we was talking about them, and soon got so familiar and sociable that we even dropped the Miss and the Mister and just used their plain names without any handle, and it did not seem unpolite, but just the right thing. Of course it wasn't their own names, but names we give them. There was Mr. Elexander Robinson and Miss Adaline Robinson, and Colonel Jacob McDougal, and Miss Harryet McDougal, and Judge Jeremiah Butler, and young Bushrod Butler, and these was big chiefs, mostly, that wore splendid great turbans and simmeters, and dressed like the Grand Mogul, and their families. But as soon as we come to know them good, and like them very much, it warn't Mister, nor Judge, nor nothing, any more, but only Elleck, and Addy, and Jake, and Hattie, and Jerry, and Buck, and so on.

And you know, the more you join in with people in their joys and their sorrows, the more nearer and dearer they come to be to you. Now we warn't cold and indifferent, the way most travelers is, we was right down friendly and sociable, and took a chance in everything that was going, and the caravan could depend on us to be on hand every time, it didn't make no difference what it was.

When they camped, we camped right over them, ten or twelve hundred foot up in the air. When they et a meal, we et ourn, and it made it ever so much homeliker to have their company. When they had a wedding, that night, and Buck and Addy got married, we got ourselves up in the very starchiest of the Professor's duds for the blow-out, and when they danced we jined in and shook a foot up there.

But it is sorrow and trouble that brings you the nearest, and it was a funeral that done it with us. It was next morning, just in the still dawn. We didn't know the diseased, but that never made no difference, he belonged to the caravan, and that was enough.

Yes, parting with this caravan was much more bitterer than it was to part with them others, which was comparative strangers, and been dead so long, anyway. We had knowed these in their lives, and was fond of them, too, and now to have 'em snatched from right before our faces whilst we was looking, and leave us so lonesome and friendless in the middle of that big Desert, it did hurt us.

We couldn't keep from talking about them, and they was all the time coming up in our memory, and looking just the way they looked when we was all alive and happy together. We could see the line marching, and the shiny spear-heads a-winking in the sun, we could see the dromedaries lumbering along, we could see the wedding and the funeral, and more oftener than anything else we could see them praying, because they don't allow nothing to prevent that; whenever the call come, several times a day, they would stop right there, and stand up and face to the east, and lift back their heads, and spread out their arms and begin, and four or five times they would go down on their knees, and then fall forwards and touch their forehead to the ground.

Well, it warn't good to go on talking about them, because it didn't do no good, and made us too downhearted.

When we woke up next morning we was feeling a little cheerfuller, and had had a most powerful good sleep, because sand is the comfortablest bed there is, and I don't see why people that can afford it don't have it more. And it's terrible good ballast, too; I never see the balloon so steady before.

Tom allowed we had twenty tons of it, and wondered what we better do with it;

it was good sand, and it didn't seem good sense to throw it away. Jim says—

"Mars Tom, can't we tote it back home en sell it? How long'll it take?"

"Depends on the way we go."

"Well, sah, she's wuth a quarter of a dollar a load, at home, en I reckon we's got as much as twenty loads, hain't we? How much would dat be?"

"Five dollars."

"By jings, Mars Tom, le's shove for home right on de spot! Hit's more'n a dollar en a half apiece, hain't it?"

"Yes."

"Well, ef dat ain't makin' money de easiest ever I struck! She jes' rained in—never cos' us a lick o' work. Le's mosey right along, Mars Tom."

But Tom was thinking and ciphering away so busy and excited he never heard him. Pretty soon he says—

"Five dollars—sho! Look here, this sand's worth—worth—why, it's worth no end of money."

"How is dat, Mars Tom? Go on, honey, go on!"

"Well, the minute people knows its genuwyne sand from the genuwyne Desert of Sahara, they'll just be in a perfect state of mind to git hold of some of it to keep on the whatnot in a vial with a label on it for a curiosity. All we got to do is, to put it up in vials and float around all over the United States and peddle them out at ten cents apiece. We've got all of ten thousand dollars' worth of sand in this boat."

Me and Jim went all to pieces with joy, and began to shout whoopjamboreehoo, and Tom says—

"And we can keep on coming back and fetching sand, and coming back and fetching more sand, and just keep it agoing till we've carted this whole Desert over there and sold it out; and there ain't ever going to be any opposition, either, because we'll take out a patent."

"My goodness," I says, "we'll be as rich as Creosote, won't we, Tom?"

"Yes,—Creesus, you mean. Why, that dervish was hunting in that little hill for the treasures of the earth, and didn't know he was walking over the real ones for a thousand miles. He was blinder than he made the driver."

"Mars Tom, how much is we gwyne to be worth?"

"Well, I don't know, yet. It's got to be ciphered, and it ain't the easiest job to do, either, because it's over four million square miles of sand at ten cents a vial."

Jim was awful excited, but this faded it out considerable, and he shook his head and says—

"Mars Tom, we can't 'ford all dem vials—a king couldn't. We better not try to take de whole Desert, Mars Tom, de vials gwyne to bust us, sho'."

Tom's excitement died out, too, now, and I reckoned it was on account of the vials, but it wasn't. He set there thinking, and got bluer and bluer, and at last he says—

"Boys, it won't work; we got to give it up."

"Why, Tom?"

"On account of the duties."

I couldn't make nothing out of that, neither could Jim. I says—

"What is our duty, Tom? Because, if we can't git around it, why can't we just do it? People often has to."

But he says—

"Oh, it ain't that kind of duty. The kind I mean is a tax. Whenever you strike a frontier—that's the border of a country, you know—you find a custom-house there, and the gov'ment officers comes and rummages amongst your things and charges a big tax, which they call a duty because it's their duty to bust you if they can, and if you don't pay the duty they'll take your sand. They call it confiscating. Now if we try to carry this sand home the way we're pointed now, we got to climb fences till we git tired—just frontier after frontier—Egypt, Arabia, Hindostan, and so on, and they'll all whack on a duty, and so you see, easy enough, we *can't* go *that* road."

"Why, Tom," I says, "we can sail right over their old frontiers; how are *they* going to stop us?"

He looked sorrowful at me, and says, very grave—

"Huck Finn, do you think that would be honest?"

I hate them kind of interruptions. But I said nothin'. I didn't feel no more interest in such things, as long as we couldn't git our sand through, and it made me low-spirited, and Jim the same. Tom he tried to cheer us up by saying he would think up another speculation for us that would be just as good as this one and better, but it didn't do no good, we didn't believe there was any as big as this. It was mighty hard; such a little while ago we was so rich, and could 'a' bought a country and started a kingdom and been celebrated and happy, and now we was so poor and ornery again, and had our sand left on our hands. The sand was looking so lovely, before, just like gold and diamonds, and the feel of it was so soft and so silky and nice, but now I couldn't bear the sight of it, it made me sick to look at it, and I knowed I wouldn't ever feel comfortable again till we got shut of it, and I didn't have it there no more to remind us of what we had been and what we had got degraded down to. The others was feeling the same way about it that I was. I knowed it, because they cheered up so the minute I says, "Le's throw this truck overboard."

Well, it was going to be work, you know, and pretty solid work, too; so Tom he divided it up according to fairness and strength. He said me and him would clear out a fifth apiece, of the sand, and Jim three fifths. Jim he didn't quite like that arrangement. He says—

" 'Course I's de stronges', en I's willin' to do a share accordin', but by jings you's kinder pilin' it onto ole Jim this time, Mars Tom, hain't you?"

"Well, I didn't think so, Jim, but you try your hand at fixing it, and let's see."

So Jim he reckoned it wouldn't be no more than fair if me and Tom done a *tenth* apiece. Tom he turned his back to git room and be private, and then he smole a smile that spread around and covered the whole Sahara to the westward, back to the Atlantic edge of it where we come from. Then he turned around again and said it was a good enough arrangement, and we was satisfied if Jim was. Jim said he was.

So then Tom measured off our two tenths in the bow and left the rest for Jim, and it surprised Jim a good deal to see how much difference there was and what a raging lot of sand his share come to, an' he said he was powerful glad, now, that he had spoke up in time and got the first arrangement altered, for he said that even the way it was now, there was more sand than enjoyment in his end of the contract, he believed.

Then we laid into it. It was mighty hot work, and tough; so hot we had to move up into cooler weather or we couldn't 'a' stood it. Me and Tom took turn about, and one worked while t' other rested, but there warn't nobody to spell poor old Jim. We couldn't work good, we was so full of laugh, and Jim he kept fretting and fuming and wanting to know what tickled us so, and we had to keep making up things to account for it, and they was pretty poor inventions, but they done well enough, Jim didn't see through them. At last when we got done we was most dead, but not with work but with laughing. By and by Jim was most dead too, but it was with work; then we took turns and spelled him, and he was as thankful as he could be, and would set on the gunnel and heave and pant, and say how good we was to him, and he wouldn't ever forgit us. He was always the gratefulest feller I ever see, for any little thing you done for him. He was only black outside; inside he was as white as you be.

MARCH

By Lucy Larcom

March! March! March! They are coming
  In troops, to the tune of the wind
Red-headed woodpeckers drumming,
  Gold-crested thrushes behind;
Sparrows in brown jackets hopping
  Past every gateway and door;
Finches with crimson caps stopping
  Just where they stopped years before.

March! March! March! They are slipping
  Into their places at last,—
Little white lily-buds, dripping
  Under the showers that fall fast;

Buttercups, violets, roses;
  Snowdrop and bluebell and pink;
Throng upon throng of sweet posies,
  Bending the dewdrops to drink.

March! March! March! They will hurry
  Forth at the wild bugle-sound,
Blossoms and birds in a flurry,
  Fluttering all over the ground.
Hang out your flags, birch and willow!
  Shake out your red tassels, larch!
Grass-blades, up from your earth-pillow
  Hear who is calling you—March!

THE BLACK HERO OF THE RANGES

by Enoch J. Mills

THE pungent odor of the camp-fire drifted down the swale, and carried with it the savory smell of the cooking supper. All afternoon, the Diamond H riders had been arriving; word had been passed that a feast would be spread at sundown, in honor of the owner of the "Diamond H" ranch, who had arrived for his first visit to the ranch in three years.

The riders had all arrived but young "Hank"—he of the shiny spurs and new "chaps." No rider in the outfit possessed such complete trappings. Though Hank was not a regular "puncher," it pleased him mightily to be called one. He was a kind of messenger-boy for the outfit, and rode far and wide carrying orders from the foreman, or going down to the post for the mail. When in camp, he assisted the cook, a task he detested as being beneath his dignity. But Hank was proud of the Diamond H, and boasted that no ranch in Nevada had such riders and ropers.

The feast was nearing the end in the soft dusk of evening, when Hank charged down upon the scene at a reckless gallop, and stopped abruptly within the circle of the firelight.

The foreman straightened up with observing eye upon the foaming horse. "Didn't I tell you not to run Old Baldy any more?"

Every cow-puncher eyed Hank, and several tried to divert the foreman by witty remarks and laughter.

But Hank did not wither under the accusation.

"I had a try at the Black Stallion," he observed, as he fixed his eyes on the owner.

"Where?" came a half-dozen demands at once. "Where?" rapped out the owner. It was like an explosion in their midst. The feast was scattered, and instantly there was a stampede of talk. Each rider was possessed of the same thought—to capture that wonderful steed that had so long led his herd whither he would, defying capture, daring to go where no horse ever had gone before, and upon whose head was set a price.

"I thought you said the Black Stallion never came down from the rough country?" The owner waited eagerly for the foreman's answer.

"It's the first time he's shown up, down here, since we had the chase after him two years ago."

"Jess, I'd like to have that horse, and I'm willing to go to any amount of trouble to get him. But the question is, 'can we?'"

The foreman looked into the fire and ran his hands thoughtfully through his hair. At length he turned to the owner. "I believe we've got the best chance at him, now that he's left the rough country, that we've ever had. He's an old fox, though, and there's nothing he doesn't know about

359

being chased. It's about as easy to round
up a bird as to try to corner him. Still, the
water's all gone, higher up, and he's got
to range down here. If we only had more
men and a mustang outfit, I believe we
could—" The owner's heavy hand reached
the foreman's shoulder and stopped him
midway of the prediction.

"Get the men and the outfit. I'll foot
the bills. If you get him, I'll hand you a
year's salary. You can promise the men
whatever reward you like, but the thing
is, *get that horse!*"

Hank moved opposite the two men, and
leaned forward across the embers of the
fire.

"Where did you see him, Hank?"

"About three miles up the valley by the
spring. There were twenty in the herd
he was leading."

"All right, Hank; get a fresh horse and
ride down to the post and pick up every
rider you can. Find old Sam Higler, and
tell him he's to be here with his canvas
corral outfit by to-morrow night. Tell
every one you see that the black's come
down, and there's a reward of a thousand
dollars for the man who drops his rope
on him and brings him in." Hank vanished in the direction of the rope corral,
and five minutes later was riding rapidly
toward the post. After he had gone, the
owner turned to the foreman. "Jess," said
he, "did I ever tell you where the stallion
came from?" The foreman's interested
face invited him to proceed.

"It was five years ago that a Syrian ped-
dler was killed by a couple of half-breeds
because he had this wonderful black stallion. The Indians took the horse clear
across the desert to make their escape, but
just when they were about to sell him, the
stallion killed one, and lamed the other
with his heels, and got away. It was not
long before he appeared with a wild-horse
herd, and since then he's been the terror

of the range, and there's not a man in Nevada who can boast of ever getting near
enough to drop his rope on him. I doubt
if he's ever taken alive. Before I quit the
ranch three years ago, I'd ridden in a
couple of chases after him, and I tell you
he's got sense, and legs that can put him
over a hundred miles any day."

They sat in silence, each looking into
the embers of the fire.

TWENTY Diamond H riders surrounded
the valley early in the morning, and from
the passes looked down at the wild-horse
band led by the big black stallion. It was
a long, narrow valley, and the eastern
wall had but a single pass where anything
but winged creatures could escape. At the
upper end the valley narrowed, and leading down into it was an old, time-worn
pass; here were posted three men with as
many extra horses. West of the valley, the
ridge rose abruptly. In ten miles it had
only five breaks, where steep cañons penetrated its rocky top and broke the barrier.
At each break, two men posted themselves
and waited. They gained these passes by
circuitous routes. The lower end of the
valley was guarded by three men, who
lounged about, allowing their horses to
graze.

At noon, Hank arrived upon a jaded
horse, and singly, or by twos and threes,
the other "punchers" came in during the
afternoon, each mounted on his best
horse, and with carefully coiled ropes.
At dark, Sam Higler put in appearance
with his mustang trap, which was set up
over night across the lower end of the
valley. This trap consisted of a brown
canvas twelve feet high, which represented
an impassable wall. Near the center the
wall curved sharply, making a natural
corner with an inviting opening leading
into a canvas corral beyond. It was a cunning contrivance, and in it scores of wild

mustangs had been captured. It was here that they hoped to capture the famous stallion.

Extra men were sent to reinforce the guards at all the passes. Fifteen of the best ropers were kept at camp, and these were to take part at the finish of the chase.

From the main ranch there had been sent up a dozen thoroughbred, long-legged, racing horses, which were to be used in case the stallion broke through the barrier and escaped from the valley, or were to be held in reserve until the chase had tired out the crafty leader. Then they were to appear suddenly from behind the canvas wall, and go after the herd like the wind.

Orders were to shoot the stallion if he broke through the lines. The rest of the herd was worth four thousand dollars, and their addition to the ranch stock would be valuable.

The only ones at breakfast at the chuck wagon that morning were the owner, the foreman, and Hank. While the men settled the final details of the chase, Hank tidied up the camp things and saddled his horse.

"Hank, one of the boys rode back yesterday to report that there's still a little water at the muddy spring water-hole." Hank was silent; sudden fear had chilled him. The foreman continued: "If the foxy old stallion gets away from us in the valley, that's the only place in a hundred miles he can get water; and I guess after we've run him a hundred miles or so, he'll be wanting water, too. You'd better ride up to the muddy spring, Hank, and stick it out there until dark. There's no telling what may happen to-day, but whatever comes, the chase will end at dark."

Hank turned away, blinking fast and swallowing hard. His hopes of riding with the foreman and the owner were thus suddenly blasted, leaving behind a sense of revolt that fairly hurt. After discover-ing the horse, he would lose all the excitement of the chase.

Soon after daylight, the foreman and the owner rode into the valley above the canvas wall. They galloped easily toward the spring where Hank had seen the horses two days before. When they rounded a knoll a half-mile below the water-hole, they sighted the wonderful stallion on guard on a slight elevation, with the herd feeding quietly below. Instantly the band was off up the valley, and the foreman was riding rapidly in pursuit. The owner stopped at the spring, where he would wait until the time came for the concerted dash and capture of the big black. It was a waiting game, and patience was to play an important part.

Ten miles up the valley, straight for the steep trail at the upper end, swept the black leader at the head of his herd. But a quarter of a mile from the pass he stopped, wheeled, and doubled back. The foreman was riding near the western wall, and the band passed him on its return trip without being forced into too close quarters.

One of the men on guard at the pass dashed down with a fresh horse, and five minutes later the foreman was after the herd again with the second horse. He galloped along a half-mile behind the stallion, and not once did he press the chase or excite the band unduly.

At the sight of the brown canvas wall barring his way, the stallion spun around and fled wildly up the valley again. But three of the others went straight on through the narrow opening at the center, and were easy victims in the canvas corral. On another fresh horse, the foreman continued the chase. Not once did he come nearer than the half-mile, and never did he permit the band to stop for more than a minute or two at a time.

When within a quarter of a mile of

the pass, the stallion again scented danger, and again wheeled back down the valley. Once more a man dashed out from hiding with a fresh horse, and the chase continued. It was settling down now to one of dogged endurance, with the odds against the stallion. Fresh horses were in plenty for the foreman, but the wonderful black kept on, hour after hour, leading his dwindling band with what seemed tireless energy. Ceaselessly they kept him moving. Three round trips of the valley, sixty miles, and ten of his mates were out of the chase, and before the fourth round of the valley was finished, they were dropping out rapidly, being roped and dragged in submission to the canvas corral.

Frequently now the stallion would stop and watch until his relentless pursuer was within a hundred yards; then he would be off again. His black coat was covered with foam; he was becoming uncertain on his feet, and stumbled often. He approached the water-hole, but it was guarded. Wearily he turned back down the valley because it was easier going.

The foreman fired three quick signal shots, and from behind the brown canvas wall rode the best ropers of the region, mounted on the fleetest horses. The stallion sloped his flight and went on down the valley along the western side. The riders waited across the valley until he had passed, then they spread out across the level floor.

Ten abreast, and absolutely certain of success, they galloped easily along behind the stallion as he went on straight toward the canvas barrier. They did not hurry; there was no need; an easy gallop kept pace with the stallion's now unsteady gait.

A hundred yards from the barrier, he wheeled defiantly. Facing them, he waited. The foreman shouted an order, and they dashed wildly forward, each eager to be first to drop his rope over the wary head

and win eternal fame in the region as the subduer of the most wonderful horse in Nevada.

The stallion waited their coming with heaving sides and flaming eyes. When the nearest riders were fifty feet away, he charged directly toward them, getting into his full stride in spite of his weariness, and by the time he reached them, he was going at top speed. His unexpected charge threw the riders into confusion. Their racing horses were not trained to the roping game like their cow-horses; besides, each rider was racing wildly, and each had his full length of rope ready for a long cast in order to be first.

Straight between two riders went the stallion. The men were alert and active in spite of their mounts. They made casts at the same instant, and their ropes met in mid air above his head. One loop dropped short, and the other was so large that he leaped half through before the man could snake the slack with a quick backward jerk of his hand and tighten up. Even then, his horse was broadside when the plunging stallion reached the end of the rope with a tremendous charge that lifted the racer clear of his feet and flung him violently to the ground.

To save himself, the man instinctively let go the rope, which he had snubbed around the saddle horn, and at the stallion's first lunge it slipped from the saddle and went trailing off behind the black. Three leaps more, and it dropped harmlessly to the ground. The stallion was free again.

The very number of his pursuers was his advantage. A hundred feet away the side of the valley rose at half pitch, and rough rocks and dense scrub were scattered thickly up the slope. Up he went over ragged rock slabs, forcing his way through the scrub where no ridden horse could follow.

Straight up the mountain the great horse fought his way, though it was strewn with huge blocks of bare rock piled in a forbidding mass of debris. The route looked impossible to any animal except a man.

"Don't shoot! He's all in," ordered the foreman. From above came the shouts of the men guarding the pass: "Let him come! We'll get him."

Desperately the men below tried to follow, and impatiently the men at the top waited and watched his slow upward progress. They straightened their ropes, tightened their cinches, and made sure that every detail was ready. Behind them, back of the ridge top, lay a narrow plateau, and beyond rose a second ridge. Upon this level bench they would capture the famous stallion, and the reward.

A hundred feet from the top, the stallion doubled back, leaped boldly over a narrow chasm, and followed along a narrow ledge of bare rock that ran along the face of the cliff. It was barely wide enough for him to edge along, and there was every chance that it might pinch out.

But the ledge did not pinch out, and the stallion came to the end of it fifty yards farther, where a section of the barrier had gone out with the rock slide. Up over the rock slabs the horse fought his mad way, always toward the top. His progress was slow and painful. Often he was minutes gaining a few feet. Still, nothing daunted nor defeated him. The men watching from above laughed, exulted at the sight.

A narrow rock-filled gully ran back across the plateau toward the ridge beyond. Scrub growth filled in between the rocks. It was to the mouth of this gully that the horse finally forced his way.

The men were waiting for him on foot. Each dropped his rope over the coveted head with a yell of triumph.

No sooner did the ropes tighten upon the stallion's neck than he became an explosion of action. Up the slope toward the level ground he charged, and the men, confident of success, let him go.

Once in the open, they stopped him by throwing their weight against their ropes. With flaming eyes, mouth open, and ears laid flat, the stallion came down at them, a terrible monster of rage.

The horse was within ten feet of the men, when one of them let go his rope and dived aside as the black bulk lurched by. The other threw his weight against his rope, and the stallion turned upon him with bared teeth, and awful, flashing eyes. He saved himself only by leaping blindly into the scrub in the gully.

When the men recovered their feet, they rushed to their horses, and were after the runaway pell-mell. But the stallion continued along the broken top of the ridge, where it seemed as if he would surely tumble headlong back into the valley. He dared every obstacle for liberty, leaped treacherous gaps in the rock barrier where his enemies dared not follow, and made his way across fields of huge, broken rocks where no other horse had ever dared.

On the level, the fresh horses of the men could easily have overtaken him; but among the rocks and chasms of the ridge top, they had difficulty in keeping him in sight. Their horses were not fighting a life-and-death battle, and could not follow the way the stallion went. They had to make detours where the black forged straight up the slope.

Seeing that he was about to gain the second ridge top, the men opened on him with their six-shooters, but he plunged desperately into the growth of scrub just back of the second ridge top, and went crashing headlong out of sight, and safe from the spiteful guns.

Ten minutes after the stallion disappeared in the scrub, the men reached the top of the ridge and saw the plain trail where he had entered the thicket. They separated and started circling around the copse in opposite directions, chagrined at their failure to either capture or kill the wonderful black horse. They rode desperately to intercept him when he should emerge from the far side of the sheltering growth. But, as soon as they were out of hearing, the crafty animal came out at the spot where he had entered the thicket, and started westward along the rough ridge top. Sometimes he stopped for a moment to rest, and always he watched the back trail. When he went on again, he followed the roughest way he could find.

An hour later, the men from the valley came up and found his tracks, which told once more how the big black stallion had won his freedom. In the second valley, they found where he had joined another wild-horse band. But they knew he would soon leave the band and seek shelter; so they scattered and began careful search for tracks near every thicket. They hoped to find him before he had sufficiently rested to run away from them.

It was a game for life and freedom by the stallion, and he never gave up. Leaving the wild herd abruptly, he rested a few minutes, then pushed on to a hiding-place. But he allowed little time for rest; always he went on and on, putting as much distance between himself and his enemies as his strength would permit. Thus it was, he worked his way to the lonely water-hole.

Through all the long hours, Hank waited at the muddy spring beside it. While he kept lonely vigil, his heart welled up against the foreman and the others. He almost hoped that the stallion would get away. Surely the chase was over, long

since, for the sun was dropping low. However, his orders were to wait until dark, and he would stick it out. Not because he cared what any of them thought, or said, or did, but because he was a boy—and almost a man. They had not given him a fair chance, and he knew that they would give the stallion even less.

At four in the afternoon, Hank unsaddled Old Baldy, hobbled him, and allowed him to graze away from the spring. Behind a scrub where the sand had drifted, he scooped out a hole with his hands, and snuggled in the bottom with his six-shooter within touch. Long rides, loss of sleep, and constant vigil had wearied him more than he knew. In five minutes he was asleep. The sun touched the distant mountains and sank slowly behind them.

A wild snort awakened him, and he started up stupidly, half awake, gun in hand. He arose cautiously. Thirty feet away stood the stallion, legs braced wide apart to keep from falling, muscles all a-quiver. He was reeking with foam and dirt. But his eyes were blazing with that terrible fear and hate of man. The breeze carried the man-smell away from the stallion, and undersized Hank, standing knee-deep in the sand-pit, did not look formidable.

For a moment they faced each other across the water-hole, each immovable with surprise. Instinctively, Hank's gun hand crept out and rose slowly in front, sliding out toward the stallion. He covered a foam fleck between the blazing eyes, held the gun steady there for a second, then he lowered it. "He can't get away anyhow," he said aloud.

At the sound of his voice, the stallion pulled himself together with a jerk. Plainly though, he was at the end of his race. He must have water or perish. Slowly he advanced. A few steps from the spring he halted, his instinct warning him against nearer approach to his hated enemy. But he was too weak to run away, and, after hesitating, he staggered forward and dropped to his knees at the water-hole.

"All right, old fellow, you win!" and Hank replaced his gun in its holster and stood watching as the horse buried his nose in the muddy water and drank in great, sobbing gulps, until the water-hole was empty. Hank was glad he had dug it out in the morning. The little hole held perhaps two buckets of dark water, but it made only a taste for the stallion.

"Looks like they'd given you a run for your life, old fellow," and Hank moved forward slowly, continued talking, and edging nearer. Soothingly he talked his way forward while the horse held his hot muzzle pressed against the wet sand, eagerly sucking up the water as it flowed slowly forth. Its slowness made him impatient, and he began pawing wildly.

"Now don't do that!" Hank chided; "don't you see you've filled up the hole?"

Far back in his mind, the stallion must have remembered that men *had* been kind to him, for he was not afraid now of this first man-being who had been kind to him since he escaped the Indians. There was something in the gentle touch of the boy that thrilled him with vague memories. He waited patiently while with bare hands Hank scooped out the water-hole.

Tears were streaming down Hank's boyish face as he loosened the two ropes and tossed them aside. Patting the foam-flecked neck, he talked on and on. The horse waited impatiently for the water that came so maddeningly slow. After his second draft, he nosed Hank and whinnied eagerly.

Darkness settled unnoticed. Suddenly the stallion lifted his head alert and looked intently toward the east, ears pricked sharply forward, and alarm in his manner. Hank could see or hear nothing, but he watched the revived horse keenly. A moment later came distant hoof-beats, and the stallion galloped stiffly away into the darkness.

Soon the rough voice of a man greeted Hank as he stood motionless by the water-hole.

"Hello, fellows! Did you get him?" his question saved him from having to answer that question himself, and conveyed to the men exactly what he wished it to. He had scooped out a hole in the sand, tossed the ropes into it, and smoothed the sand over them.

Hank was silent on the homeward ride. His heart was filled with conflicting emotions, and he heard only part of the talk about the dare-devil horse that had climbed rock walls and fought for his freedom. It seemed to be the general opinion that the stallion had joined another band.

FIFTEEN miles across the rough country Hank rode every Saturday afternoon. He had asked, then demanded, of the foreman this half-holiday, and had at last secured it through strategy. In his pockets were lumps of sugar, offerings of salt, bread, and other treats for the stallion. Twice during the first month he had sighted the wonderful black, and had coaxed him to approach and accept the offerings he had brought to cement their friendship. If the stallion failed to keep the tryst, Hank would return to the ranch dejected and morose.

It was near round-up time, and some extra work had delayed Hank past his usual starting time. He did not take the precaution of starting off and circling back to throw the others off his trail, but took a short cut up the valley, climbed the steep trail at its upper end, and emerged through the pass that overlooked the muddy spring. He went down the opposite slope at a rapid pace. Baldy had once been a famous cow-horse, but had grown too old for active service. They were going down the smooth slope like the wind, when Baldy stepped into a hole and plunged downward, turning completely over in his fall. Hank was flung from the saddle, but one foot stuck in its stirrup. Then he lost consciousness.

Pain in his leg roused him after a few minutes, and he sat up, dazed.

Noticing that his right toe was twisted in, he tried to reach out to it, but his hand refused to obey the summons—his collarbone was injured, too. His head cleared, and he realized what had happened. Baldy lay with his head doubled under his body; his neck was broken.

Hank crawled painfully to his saddle and cut the thongs that bound his slicker. Out of it, with his left hand, he cut strips and slowly bound the throbbing ankle, and made a sling for his useless arm. When he had finished his bandaging, he started crawling slowly toward the spring. On one hand and both knees he dragged himself along, stopping often to rest.

The stallion snorted at the strange crawling object and circled until he got the wind; the smell convinced him, and he decided to venture nearer. Sitting quiet, Hank coaxed, gave sugar sparingly, and a little salt too. When the stallion was used to his new appearance, he pressed firmly with his left hand behind the horse's knees. "Lie down, lie down, lie down," he begged, but the black horse did not understand, and edged away.

Water at the hole revived Hank, but at times during the night he was half delirious, calling out for the stallion to come to him; and all night the stallion kept vigil about the spring. Frequently at the call, he would approach and nose the boy, whinny eagerly, and walk round and round him.

At daylight, the great black horse was still waiting beside the boy. Sometimes

Hank would rouse himself with an effort and try to get the horse to lie down. Toward noon, Hank's head cleared, and he crawled slowly to an upthrust of rock and coaxed the stallion to him. With a painful effort he dragged himself upon the mighty back, and turned the stallion's head toward the ranch. They traveled slowly. Many times the rider reeled recklessly, and came near tumbling off. At such times, the horse would stop and wait until Hank gave the word to go on again.

Fifteen cow-punchers were lolling away Sunday afternoon in the shade of the bunk house. Hank's absence was being discussed. Around a point two hundred yards away came the stallion. At the sight of the men he stopped quickly, and Hank narrowly saved himself from pitching headlong to the ground.

The stallion turned his head and looked at Hank. "It's all right, old fellow; I'll see you through. Go on!" And the horse went forward at an easy pace, with Hank clinging with his left hand tightly to the flowing mane.

Fifteen punchers held the attitude they were in when the horse appeared—they were frozen with astonishment. Not one of them broke the silence nor moved a hand.

At the gate the stallion stopped, and Hank crumpled into the arms of one of the punchers, and then to the ground. He lay quiet so long that the horse gently pawed at him and whinnied anxiously. "I'm all right, old pal." Hank said aloud, through clenched teeth. "You hit the trail; I'll see you again, when I'm able to travel."

With head and tail high, mane flowing in the breeze, the stallion galloped away, swinging his magnificent head from side to side as he went, and looking backward continually.

But not a man stirred.

PLANTATION STORIES

by Grace MacGowan Cooke

I.—MRS. PRAIRIE-DOG'S BOARDERS

Texas is a near-by land to the dwellers in the Southern States. Many of the poorer white people go there to mend their fortunes, and not a few of them come back from its plains, homesick for the mountains, and with these fortunes unmended. Daddy Laban, the half-breed, son of an Indian father and a Negro mother, who sometimes visited Broadlands plantation, had been a wanderer; and his travels had carried him as far afield as the plains of southwestern Texas. The Randolph children liked, almost better than any others, the stories he brought home from these extensive travels.

"De prairie-dog a mighty cur'ous somebody," he began one day, when they asked him for a tale. "Hit lives in de ground, more samer dan a ground-hog. But dey ain't come out for wood nor water; an' some folks thinks dey goes plumb down to de springs what feeds wells. I has knowed dem what say dey go fur enough down to find a place to warm dey hands— but dat ain't de tale I'm tellin'.

"A long time ago, dey was a prairie-dog what was left a widder, an' she had a big fambly to keep up. 'Oh, landy!' she say to dem dat come to visit her in her 'fliction, 'what I gwine do to feed my chillen?'

"De most o' de varmints tell Miz. Prairie-Dog dat de onliest way for her to git along was to keep boarders. 'You got a good home, an' you is a good manager,' dey say; 'you bound to do well wid a boardin'-house.'

"Well, Miz. Prairie-Dog done sent out de runners to run, de fliers to fly, de crawlers to crawl, an' tell each an' every dat she sot up a boardin'-house. She say she got room for one crawler, and one flier, an' dat she could take in a whole passel o' runners.

"Well, now you knows a flier's a bird— or hit mought be a bat. Ef you was lookin' for little folks, hit mought be a butterfly. Miz. Prairie-Dog ain't find no fliers what wants to live un'neath de ground. But crawlers—bugs an' worms an' sich-like— dey mostly does live un'neath de ground, anyhow, an' de fust pusson what come seekin' house-room with Miz. Prairie-Dog was Brother Rattlesnake.

"'I dest been flooded out o' my own house,' Mr. Rattlesnake say; 'an' I like to look at your rooms an' see ef dey suits me.'

"'I show you de rooms,' Miz. Prairie-Dog tell 'im. 'I bound you gwine like 'em. I got room for one crawler, an' you could be him; but—'

"Miz. Prairie-Dog look at her chillen. She ain't say no more—dest look at dem prairie-dog gals an' boys, an' say no more.

"Mr. Rattlesnake ain't like bein' called a crawler so very well; but he looks at dem rooms, an' low he'll take 'em. Miz. Prairie-Dog got somethin' on her mind, an' 'fore de snake git away dat somethin' come out.

367

'I's shore an' certain dat you an' me can git along,' she say, 'ef—ef—ef you vow an' promish not to bite my chillen. I'll have yo' meals reg'lar, so dat you won't be tempted.'

"Old Mr. Rattlesnake' powerful high-tempered—yas, law, he sho' a mighty quick somebody on de trigger. Zip! he go off, dest like dat—zip! Br-r-r! 'Tempted!' he hiss at de prairie-dog woman. He look at dem prairie-dog boys an' gals what been makin' mud cakes all mornin' (an' dest about as dirty as you-all is after you do de same). 'Tempted,' he say, 'I should hope not.'

"For, mind you, Brother Rattlesnake is a genterman, an' belongs to de quality. He feels hisself a heap too biggity to bite prairie-dogs. So *dat* turned out all right.

"De next what come to Miz. Prairie-Dog was a flier."

"A bird?" asked Patricia Randolph.

"Yes, little mistis," returned the old Indian. "One dese-hyer little, round, brown squinch-owls, what allers quakes an' quivers in dey speech an' walk. 'I gits so dizzy—izzy—wizzy! up in de top o' de trees,' de little brown owl say, as she swivel an' shake. 'An' I wanted to git me a home down on de ground, so dat I could be sure, an' double sure, dat I wouldn't fall. But dey is dem dat says ef I was down on de ground I might fall down a hole. Dat make me want to live in you' house. Hit's down in de ground, ain't hit? Ef I git down in you' house dey hain't no place for me to fall off of, an' fall down to, is dey?' she ax.

"Miz. Prairie-Dog been in de way o' fallin' down-stairs all her life; dat de onliest way she ever go inter her house—she fling up her hands an' laugh as you pass her by, and she drap back in de hole. But she tell de little brown owl dat dey ain't no place you could fall ef you go to de bottom eend o' her house. So, what wid a flier an' a crawler, an' de oldest prairie-dog boy workin' out, she manage to make tongue

and buckle meet. I is went by a many a prairie-dog hole an' seen de owl an' de rattlesnake what boards wid Miz. Prairie-Dog. Ef you was to go to Texas you'd see de same. But nobody in dat neck o' woods ever knowed how dese folks come to live in one house."

"Who told *you,* Daddy Laban?" asked Pate Randolph.

"My Injun gran'mammy," returned the old man. "She told me a many a tale, when I lived wid my daddy's people on de Cherokee Res'vation. Sometime I gwine tell you 'bout de little fawn what her daddy ketched for her when she's a little gal. But run home now, honey chillens, or yo' mammy done think Daddy Laban stole you an' carried you plumb away."

II.—SONNY BUNNY RABBIT'S GRANNY

OF all the animal stories which America, the nurse-girl, told to the children of Broadlands plantation, they liked best those about Sonny Bunny Rabbit.

"You listen now, Marse Pate an' Miss Patty an' my baby child, an' I gwine tell you de best tale yit, 'bout de rabbit," she said, one lazy summer afternoon when they were tired of playing marbles with china-berries.

"You see, de fox he mighty hongry all de time for rabbit meat; yit, at de same time, he 'fraid to buck up 'gainst a old rabbit, an' he always pesterin' after de young ones.

"Sonny Bunny Rabbit' granny was sick, an' Sonny Bunny Rabbit' mammy want to send her a mess o' sallet. She put it in a poke, an' hang de poke round de little rabbit boy's neck.

"'Now, my son,' she says, 'you tote dis sallet to yo' granny, an' don't stop to play wid none o' dey critters in de big Woods.'

"'Yassum, mammy,' say Sonny Bunny Rabbit.

"'Don't you pass de time o' day wid no foxes,' say Mammy Rabbit.

"'Yassum, mammy,' say Sonny Bunny Rabbit.

"Dest as he was passin' some thick chinkapin bushes, up hop a big red fox an' told him howdy.

nothin'—an' ain't know dat right good. 'Stead o' sayin', 'I'se gwine whar I's gwine —an' dat's whar I's gwine,' he answer right back: 'Dest 'cross de hill, suh. Won't you walk wid me, suh? Proud to have yo' company, suh.'

"'An' who-all is you gwine see on t'other side de hill?' ax Mr. Fox.

"'My granny,' answer Sonny Bunny Rabbit. 'I totin' dis sallet to her.'

"'Is yo' granny big?' ax de fox. 'Is yo' granny old?' he say. 'Is yo' granny mighty

" 'Come back Hyer, you rabbit trash, an' he'p me out o' dis trouble!' " he holler

"'Howdy,' say Sonny Bunny Rabbit. He ain't study 'bout what his mammy tell him now. He 'bleege to stop an' make a miration at bein' noticed by sech a fine pusson as Mr. Fox. 'Hit's a fine day—an' mighty growin' weather, Mr. Fox.'

"'Hit am dat,' say de fox. 'Yass, suh, hit sho'ly am dat. An' what you puttin' out for, ef I mought ax?' he say, mighty slick an' easy.

"Now, right dar," said America, impressively, "am whar dat little rabbit boy fergit his teachin'. He act like he ain't know

pore? Is yo' granny tough?' An' he ain't been nigh so slick an' sof' an' easy any mo' by dis time—he gittin' mighty hongry an' greedy.

"Right den an dere Sonny Bunny Rabbit wake up. Yaas, law! He come to he senses. He know mighty well an' good dat a pusson de size o' Mr. Fox ain't got no reason to ax ef he granny rough, less'n he want to git he teef in her. By dat he recomember what his mammy done told him. He look all 'bout. He ain't see no he'p nowhars. Den hit com in Sonny Bunny Rabbit' mind dat de boys on de farm done sot a trap down by de pastur' fence. Ef he kin git Mr. Fox to jump inter dat trap, his life done save.

" 'Oh, my granny mighty big,' he say; 'but dat's 'ca'se she so fat she cain't run. She hain't so mighty old, but she sleep all de time; an' I ain't know is she tough or not—you dest better come on an' find out,' he holler. Den he start off on er long, keen jump.

"Sonny Bunny Rabbit run as hard as he could. De fox run after, most nippin' his heels. Sonny Bunny Rabbit run by de place whar de fox-trap done sot, an' all kivered wid leaves an' trash, an' dar he le'p high in the air—an' over it. Mr. Fox ain't know dey ary trap in de grass; an', blam! he stuck he foot squar' in it!

" 'Oh-ow-ow! Hi-hi-hi! Hi-yi! Yi-yi-yi!' bark de fox. 'Come back hyer, you rabbit trash, an' he'p me out o' dis trouble!' he holler.

" 'Dat ain't no trouble,' say Sonny Bunny Rabbit, jumping high in de grass. 'Dat my granny, what I done told you 'bout. Ain't I say she so fat she cain't run? She dest love company so powerful well, dat I 'spect she holdin' on to you to hear you talk.'

"An' de fox talk," America giggled, as she looked about on her small audience.

THE TIME SHOP
by
John Kendrick Bangs

Of course it was an extraordinary thing for a clock to do, especially a parlor clock, which one would expect to be particularly dignified and well-behaved, but there was no denying the fact that the Clock did it. With his own eyes, Bobby saw it wink, and beckon to him with its hands. To be sure, he had never noticed before that the Clock had eyes, or that it had any fingers on its hands to beckon with, but the thing happened in spite of all that, and as a result Bobby became curious. He was stretched along the rug in front of the great open fireplace, where he had been drowsily gazing at the blazing log for a half hour or more, and looking curiously up at the Clock's now smiling face, he whispered to it.

"Are you beckoning to me?" he asked, rising up on his hands and knees.

"Of course I am," replied the Clock in a soft, silvery tone, just like a bell, in fact. "You didn't think I was beckoning to the piano, did you?"

"I didn't know," said Bobby.

"Not that I wouldn't like to have the piano come over and call upon me some day," the Clock went on, "which I most certainly would, considering him, as I do, the most polished four-footed creature I have ever seen, and all of his family have been either grand, square, or upright, and if properly handled, full of sweet music. Fact is, Bobby, I'd rather have a piano playing about me than a kitten or a puppy dog, as long as it didn't jump into my lap. It would be awkward to have a piano get frisky and jump into your lap, now, wouldn't it?"

Bobby had to confess that it would; "But what did you want with me?" he asked, now that the piano was disposed of.

"Well," replied the Clock, "I am beginning to feel a trifle run down, Bobby, and I thought I'd go over to the shop, and get in a little more time to keep me going. Christmas is coming along, and everybody is so impatient for its arrival that I don't want to slow down at this season of the year, and have all the children blame me because it is so long on the way."

"What shop are you going to?" asked Bobby, interested at once, for he was very fond of shops and shopping.

"Why, the Time Shop, of course," said the Clock. "It's a shop that my father keeps, and we clocks have to get our supply of time from him, you know, or we couldn't keep on going. If he didn't give it to us, why, we couldn't give it to you. It isn't right to give away what you haven't got."

"I don't think I understand," said Bobby, with a puzzled look on his face. "What is a Time Shop, and what do they sell there?"

"Oh, anything from a bunch of bananas

371

or a barrel of sawdust up to an automobile," returned the Clock. "Really, I couldn't tell you what they don't sell there if you were to ask me. I know of a fellow who went in there once to buy a great name for himself, and the floor-walker sent him up to the third floor, where they had fame, and prosperity, and greatness for sale, and ready to give anybody who was willing and able to pay for them, and he chose happiness instead, not because it was less expensive than the others, but because it was more worth having. What they've got in the Time Shop depends entirely upon what you want. If they haven't got it in stock, they will take your order for it, and will send it to you, but always C.O.D., which means you must pay when you receive the goods. Sometimes you can buy fame on the instalment plan, but that is only in special cases. As a rule, there is no charging things in the Time Shop. You've got to pay for what you get, and it is up to you to see that the quality is good. Did you ever hear of a man named George Washington?"

"Hoh!" cried Bobby, with a scornful grin. "Did I ever hear of George Washington! What a question! Was there anybody ever who hasn't heard of George Washington?"

"Well, yes," said the Clock. "There was Julius Cæsar. He was a pretty brainy sort of a chap, and he never heard of him. And old Father Adam never heard of him, and Mr. Methusaleh never heard of him, and I rather guess that Christopher Columbus, who was very much interested in American history, never heard of him."

"All right, Clocky," said Bobby, with a smile. "Go on. What about George Washington?"

"He got all that he ever won at the Time Shop; a regular customer, he was," said the Clock; "and he paid for what he got with the best years of his life, man or boy.

He rarely wasted a minute. Now I thought that having nothing to do for a little while but look at those flames trying to learn to dance, you might like to go over with me and visit the old shop. They'll all be glad to see you and maybe you can spend a little time there whilst I am laying in a fresh supply to keep me on the move."

"I'd love to go," said Bobby, starting up eagerly.

"Very well, then," returned the Clock. "Close your eyes, count seventeen backward, then open your eyes again, and you'll see what you will see."

Bobby's eyes shut; I was almost going to say with a snap. He counted from seventeen back to one with a rapidity that would have surprised even his school-teacher, opened his eyes again and looked around, and what he saw—well, that was more extraordinary than ever! Instead of standing on the parlor rug before the fireplace, he found himself in the broad aisle of the ground floor of a huge department store, infinitely larger than any store he had ever seen in his life before, and oh, dear me, how dreadfully crowded it was! The crowd of Christmas shoppers that Bobby remembered to have seen last year when he had gone out to buy a lead-pencil to put into his father's stocking was as nothing to that which thronged this wonderful place. Ah me, how dreadfully hurried some of the poor shoppers appeared to be, and how wistfully some of them gazed at the fine bargains to be seen on the counters and shelves, which either because they had not saved it, or had wasted it, they had not time to buy!

"Well, young gentleman," said a kindly floor-walker, pausing in his majestic march up and down the aisle, as the Clock, bidding Bobby to use his time well, made off to the supply shop, "what can we do for you to-day?"

"Nothing that I know of, thank you,

sir," said Bobby. "I have just come in to look around."

"Ah!" said the floor-walker with a look of disappointment on his face. "I'm afraid I shall have to take you to the Waste-Time Bureau, where they will find out what you want without undue loss of precious moments. I should think, however, that a nice-looking boy like you would be able to decide what he really wanted and go directly to the proper department and get it."

"Got any bicycles?" asked Bobby, seizing upon the first thing that entered his mind.

"Fine ones—best there are," smiled the pleasant floor-walker, very much relieved to find that Bobby did not need to be taken to the bureau. "Step this way, please. Mr. Promptness, will you be so good as to show this young gentleman our line of bicycles?"

Then turning to Bobby, he added: "You look like a rather nice young gentleman, my boy. Perhaps never having been here before, you do not know our ways, and have not provided yourself with anything to spend. To encourage business we see that new comers have a chance to avail themselves of the opportunities of the shop, so here are a few time-checks with which you can buy what you want."

The kindly floor-walker handed Bobby twenty round golden checks, twenty silver checks, and twenty copper ones. Each check was about the size of a five-cent piece, and all were as bright and fresh as if they had just been minted.

"What are these?" asked Bobby, as he jingled the coins in his hand.

"The golden checks, my boy, are days," said the floor-walker. "The silver ones are hours, and the coppers are minutes. I hope you will use them wisely, and find your visit to our shop so profitable that you will become a regular customer."

With this and with a pleasant bow the floor-walker moved along to direct a gray-haired old gentleman with a great store of years in his possession to the place where he could make his last payment on a stock of wisdom which he had been buying, and Bobby was left with Mr. Wiggins, the salesman, who immediately showed him all the bicycles they had in stock.

"This is a pretty good wheel for a boy of your age," said Mr. Promptness, pulling out a bright-looking little machine that was so splendidly under control that when he gave it a push it ran smoothly along the top of the mahogany counter, pirouetted a couple of times on its hind wheel, and then gracefully turning rolled back to Mr. Promptness again.

"How much is that?" asked Bobby, without much hope, however, of ever being able to buy it.

"Sixteen hours and forty-five minutes," said Mr. Promptness, looking at the price-tag, and reading off the figures. "It used to be a twenty-five-hour wheel, but we have marked everything down this season. Everybody is so rushed these days that very few people have any spare time to spend, and we want to get rid of our stock."

"What do you mean by sixteen hours and forty-five minutes?" asked Bobby. "How much is that in dollars?"

Mr. Promptness smiled more broadly than ever at the boy's question.

"We don't do business in dollars here, my lad," said he. "This is a Time Shop, and what you buy you buy with time: days, hours, minutes, and seconds."

"Got anything that costs as much as a year?" asked Bobby.

"We have things that cost a lifetime, my boy," said the salesman; "but those things, our rarest and richest treasures, we keep up-stairs."

"I should think that you would rather do business for money," said Bobby.

"Nay, nay, my son," said Mr. Promptness. "Time is a far better possession than money, and it often happens that it will buy things that money couldn't possibly purchase."

"Then I must be rich," said Bobby.

The salesman looked at the little fellow gravely.

"Rich?" he said.

"Yes," said Bobby, delightedly. "I've got no end of time. Seems to me sometimes that I've got all the time there is."

"Well," said Mr. Promptness, "you must remember that its value depends entirely upon how you use it. Time thrown away or wasted is of no value at all. Past time or future time are of little value compared to present time, so when you say that you are rich you may be misleading yourself. What do you do with yours?"

"Why—anything I happen to want to do," said Bobby.

"And where do you get your clothes, your bread and butter, your playthings?" asked the salesman.

"Oh, my father gets all those things for me," returned Bobby.

"Well, he has to pay for them," said Mr. Promptness, "and he has to pay for them in time, too, while you use yours for what?"

Bobby hung his head.

"Do you spend it well?" asked the salesman.

"Sometimes," said Bobby, "and sometimes I just waste it," he went on. "You see, Mr. Promptness, I didn't know there was a Time Shop where you could buy such beautiful things with it, but now that I do know you will find me here oftener spending what I have on things worth having."

"I hope so," said Mr. Promptness, patting Bobby affectionately on the shoulder. "How much have you got with you now?"

"Only these," said Bobby, jingling his time-checks in his pocket. "Of course next

week when my Christmas holiday begins I shall have a lot—three whole weeks— that's twenty-one days, you know."

"Well, you can only count on what you have in hand, but from the sounds in your pocket I fancy you can have the bicycle if you want it," said Mr. Promptness.

"At the price I think I can," said Bobby, "and several other things besides."

"How would you like this set of books about wild animals?" asked Mr. Promptness.

"How much?" said Bobby.

"Two days and a half, or sixty hours," said Mr. Promptness, inspecting the price-tag.

"Send them along with the rest," said Bobby. "How much is that electric railroad over there?"

"That's rather expensive," Mr. Promptness replied. "It will cost you two weeks, three days, ten minutes, and thirty seconds."

"Humph," said Bobby. "I guess that's a little too much for me. Got any marbles?"

"Yes," laughed Mr. Promptness. "We have china alleys, two for a minute, or plain miggles at ten for a second."

"Put me down for two hours' worth of china alleys, and about a half an hour's worth of miggles," said Bobby.

"Very good, sir," said Mr. Promptness, with a twinkling eye. "Now can you think of anything else?"

"Well, yes," said Bobby, a sudden idea flashing across his mind. "There is one thing I want very much, Mr. Promptness, and I guess maybe perhaps you can help me out. I'd like to buy a Christmas present for my mother, if I can get a nice one with the time I've got. I was afraid I couldn't get her much of anything with what little money I had saved. But if I can pay for it in time, Mr. Promptness—why, what couldn't I buy for her with those three whole weeks coming to me!"

"About how much would you like to spend on it?" asked Mr. Promptness, with a soft light in his eye.

"Oh, I'd *like* to spend four or five years on it," said Bobby, "but, of course—"

"That's very nice of you," said the salesman, putting his hand gently on Bobby's head, and stroking his hair. "But I wouldn't be extravagant, and once in a while we have special bargains here for kiddies like you. Why, I have known boys to give their mothers presents bought at this shop that were worth years, and years, and years, but which haven't cost them more than two or three hours because they have made up the difference in love. With love you can buy the best treasures of this shop with a very little expenditure in time. Now what do you think of this for your mother?"

Mr. Promptness reached up to a long shelf back of the counter and brought down a little card, framed in gold, and printed in beautiful colored letters, and illustrated with a lovely picture that seemed to Bobby to be the prettiest thing he had ever seen.

"This is a little thing that was written long ago," said Mr. Promptness, "by a man who spent much time in this shop buying things that were worth while, and in the end getting from our frame department a wonderful name which was not only a splendid possession for himself, but for the people among whom he lived. Thousands and thousands of people have been made happier, and wiser, by the way he spent his hours, and he is still mentioned among the great men of time. He was a fine, great-hearted fellow, and he put a tremendous lot of love into all that he did. His name was Thackeray. Can you read, Bobby?"

"A little," said Bobby.

"Then read this and tell me what you think of it," said Mr. Promptness.

He handed Bobby the beautiful card, and the little fellow, taking it in his hand, read the sentence: MOTHER IS THE NAME OF GOD IN THE LIPS AND HEARTS OF LITTLE CHILDREN.

"You see, my dear little boy," said the kindly salesman, "that is worth—oh, I don't know how many years, and your mother, I am sure, would rather know that that is what you think, and how you feel about her, than have you give her the finest jewels that we have to sell. And how much do you think we charge you for it?"

"Forty years!" gasped Bobby.

"No," replied Mr. Promptness. "Five minutes. Shall we put it aside for you?"

"Yes, indeed," cried Bobby, delighted to have so beautiful a Christmas gift for his mother.

So Mr. Promptness put the little card aside with the bicycle, and the wild animal books, and the marbles, putting down the price of each of the things Bobby had purchased on his sales slip.

They walked down the aisles of the great shop together, looking at the many things that time well expended would buy, and Bobby paused for a moment and spent two minutes on a glass of soda water, and purchased a quarter of an hour's worth of peanuts to give to Mr. Promptness. They came soon to a number of large rooms at one end of the shop, and in one of these Bobby saw quite a gathering of youngsters somewhat older than himself, who seemed to be very busy poring over huge books, and studying maps, and writing things down in little note-books, not one of them wasting even an instant.

"These boys are buying an education with their time," said Mr. Promptness, as they looked in at the door. "For the most part they haven't any fathers and mothers to help them, so they come here and spend what they have on the things that we have in our library. It is an interesting fact that what is bought in this room can never be stolen from you, and it happens more often than not that when they have spent hundreds of hours in here they win more time to spend on the other things that we have on sale. But there are others, I am sorry to say, who stop on their way here in the morning and fritter their loose change away in the Shop of Idleness across the way—a minute here, and a half hour there, sometimes perhaps a whole hour will be squandered over there, and when they arrive here they haven't got enough left to buy anything."

"What can you buy at the Shop of Idleness?" asked Bobby, going to the street door, and looking across the way at the shop in question, which seemed, indeed, to be doing a considerable business, if one could judge from the crowds within.

"Oh, a little fun," said Mr. Promptness. "But not the real, genuine kind, my boy. It is a sort of imitation fun that looks like the real thing, but it rings hollow when you test it, and on close inspection turns out to be nothing but frivolity."

"And what is that great gilded affair further up the street?" asked Bobby, pointing to a place with an arched entrance gilded all over and shining in the sunlight like a huge house of brass.

"That is a cake shop," said Mr. Promptness, "and it is run by an old witch named Folly. When you first look at her you think she is young and beautiful, but when you come to know her better you realize that she is old, and wrinkled, and selfish. She gives you things and tells you that you needn't pay until to-morrow and this goes on until some day to-morrow comes, and you find she has not only used up all the good time you had, but that you owe her even more, and when you can't pay she pursues you with all sorts of trouble. That's all anybody ever got at Folly's shop, Bobby —just trouble, trouble, trouble."

"There seem to be a good many people there now," said Bobby, looking up the highway at Folly's gorgeous place.

"Oh, yes," sighed Mr. Promptness. "A great many—poor things! They don't know any better, and what is worse they won't listen to those who do."

"Who is that pleasant-looking gentleman outside the Shop of Idleness?" asked Bobby, as a man appeared there and began distributing his card amongst the throng.

"He is the general manager of the Shop of Idleness," said the salesman. "As you say, he is a pleasant-looking fellow, but you must beware of him, Bobby. He is not a good person to have around. He is a very active business man, and actually follows people to their homes, and forces his way in, and describes his stock to them as being the best in the world. And all the time he is doing so he is peering around in their closets, in their chests, everywhere, with the intention of robbing them. The fact that he is so pleasant to look at makes him very popular, and I only tell you the truth when I say to you that he is the only rival we have in business that we are really afraid of. We can compete with Folly but—"

Mr. Promptness's words were interrupted by his rival across the way, who, observing Bobby standing in the doorway, cleverly tossed one of his cards across the street so that it fell at the little boy's feet. Bobby stooped down and picked it up and read it. It went this way:

THE SHOP OF IDLENESS

PROCRASTINATION,
General Manager.

Put Off Everything And Visit Our Shop.

"So he's Procrastination, is he?" said Bobby, looking at the man with much interest, for he had heard his father speak of him many a time, only his father called him "old Putoff."

"Yes, and he is truly what they say he is," said Mr. Promptness; "the thief of time."

"He doesn't look like a thief," said Bobby.

Now it is a peculiarity of Procrastination that he has a very sharp pair of ears, and he can hear a great many things that you wouldn't think could travel so far, and, as Bobby spoke, he turned suddenly and looked at him, waved his hand, and came running across the street, calling out to Bobby to wait. Mr. Promptness seized Bobby by the arm, and pulled him into the Time Shop, but not quickly enough, for he was unable to close the door before his rival was at their side.

"Glad to see you, my boy," said Procrastination, handing him another card. "Come on over to my place. It's much easier to find what you want there than it is here, and we've got a lot of comfortable chairs to sit down and think things over in. You needn't buy anything to-day, but just look over the stock."

"Don't mind him, Bobby," said Mr. Promptness, anxiously whispering in the boy's ear. "Come along with me and see the things we keep on the upper floors— I am sure they will please you."

"Wait just a minute, Mr. Promptness," replied Bobby. "I want to see what Mr. Procrastination looks like close to."

"But, my dear child, you don't seem to realize that he will pick your pocket if you let him come close—" pleaded Mr. Promptness.

But it was of no use, for the unwelcome visitor from across the way by this time had got his arm through Bobby's and was endeavoring to force the boy out through the door, although the elevator on which

Bobby and Mr. Promptness were to go up-stairs was awaiting them.

"When did you come over?" said Procrastination, with his pleasantest smile, which made Bobby feel that perhaps Mr. Promptness, and his father, too, for that matter, had been very unjust to him.

"Going up," cried the elevator boy.

"Come, Bobby," said Mr. Promptness, in a beseeching tone. "The car is just starting."

"Nonsense. What's your hurry?" said Procrastination. "You can take the next car just as well."

"All aboard!" cried the elevator boy.

"I'll be there in two seconds," returned Bobby.

"Can't wait," cried the elevator boy, and he banged the iron door to, and the car shot up to the upper regions where the keepers of the Time Shop kept their most beautiful things.

"Too bad!" said Mr. Promptness, shaking his head, sadly. "Too bad! Now, Mr. Procrastination," he added fiercely, "I must ask you to leave this shop, or I shall summon the police. You can't deceive us. Your record is known here, and—"

"Tutt-tutt-tutt, my dear Mr. Promptness!" retorted Procrastination, still looking dangerously pleasant, and smiling as if it must all be a joke. "This shop of yours is a public place, sir, and I have just as much right to spend my time here as anybody else."

"Very well, sir," said Mr. Promptness, shortly. "Have your own way if you prefer, but you will please remember that I warned you to go."

Mr. Promptness turned as he spoke and touched an electric button at the back of the counter, and immediately from all sides there came a terrific and deafening clanging of bells; and from up-stairs and down came rushing all the forces of time to the rescue of Bobby, and to put Procrastination out. They fell upon him like an army, and shouting, and struggling, but still smiling as if he thought it the greatest joke in the world, the unwelcome visitor was at last thrust into the street, and the doors were barred and bolted against his return.

"Mercy me!" cried Bobby's friend the Clock, rushing up just as the door was slammed to. "What's the meaning of all this uproar?"

"Nothing," said Mr. Promptness. "Only that wicked old Procrastination again. He caught sight of Bobby here—"

"He hasn't hurt him?" cried the Clock.

"Not much, if any," said Mr. Promptness.

"You didn't have anything to do with him, did you, Bobby?" asked the Clock, a trifle severely.

"Why, I only stopped a minute to say how do you do to him," began Bobby, sheepishly.

"Well, I'm sorry that you should have made his acquaintance," said the Clock; "but come along. It's getting late and we're due back home. Paid your bill?"

"No," said Mr. Promptness, sadly. "He hasn't had it yet, but there it is, Bobby. I think you will find it correct."

He handed the little visitor a memorandum of all the charges against him. Bobby ran over the items and saw that the total called for a payment of eight days, and fifteen hours, and twenty-three minutes, and nine seconds, well within the value of the time-checks the good floor-walker had given him, but alas! when he put his hand in his pocket to get them they were gone. Not even a minute was left!

Procrastination had succeeded only too well!

"Very sorry, Bobby," said Mr. Promptness, "but we cannot let the goods go out

of the shop until they are paid for. However," he added, "although I warned you against that fellow, I feel sorry enough for you to feel inclined to help you a little, particularly when I realize how much you have missed in not seeing our treasures on the higher floors. I'll give you five minutes, my boy, to pay for the little card for your mother's Christmas present."

He placed the card in the little boy's hand, and turned away with a tear in his eye, and Bobby started to express his sorrow at the way things had turned out, and his thanks for Mr. Promptness's generosity, but there was no chance for this. There was a whirr as of many wheels, and a flapping as of many wings. Bobby felt himself being whirled around, and around, and around, and then there came a bump. Somewhat terrified he closed his eyes for an instant, and when he opened them again he found himself back on the parlor rug, lying in front of the fire, while his daddy was rolling him over and over. The lad glanced up at the mantel-piece to see what had become of the Clock, but the grouchy old ticker stared solemnly ahead of him, with his hands pointed sternly at eight o'clock, which meant that Bobby had to go to bed at once.

"Oh, let me stay up ten minutes longer," pleaded Bobby.

"No, sir," replied his father. "No more Procrastination, my son—trot along."

And it seemed to Bobby as he walked out of the room, after kissing his father and mother good-night, that that saucy old Clock grinned.

INCIDENTALLY let me say that in the whirl of his return Bobby lost the card that the good Mr. Promptness had given him for his mother, but the little fellow remembered the words that were printed on it, and when Christmas morning came his mother found them painted in watercolors on a piece of cardboard by the boy's own hand; and when she read them a tear of happiness came into her eyes, and she hugged the little chap and thanked him, and said it was the most beautiful Christmas present she had received.

"I'm glad you like it," said Bobby. "It isn't so very valuable though, Mother. It only cost me two hours and a half, and I know where you can get better looking ones for five minutes."

Which extraordinary remark led Bobby's mother to ask him if he were not feeling well!

AN AZTEC FRAGMENT

—

It is not alone the dreadful morning bath
That fills this hieroglyphic Babe with wrath.
His complacent Brother's jeers
Start those two resentful tears,—
But behold! the Father cometh with a lath.

The King's Pie

by Abbie Farwell Brown

THERE was great excitement in Blessington, for the king was coming with his young bride, and the town was preparing to give them a famous welcome.

Hugh, the lord mayor, was at his wit's end with all that must be done. As he sat in the town hall holding his aching head, while a mob of decorators and artists and musicians, costumers, jewelers, and florists clamored about him, there came to him a messenger from Cedric, his son. Cedric was one of the king's own courtiers, and he knew his Majesty's taste well. So he had sent to the lord mayor a hint as to how the king might best be pleased. Being a man of few words, this is how his message ran:

"His Majesty is exceedingly fond of pie."

Long pondered the lord mayor over this mysterious message, reading it backward and forward, upside down and crisscross, and mixed up like an anagram. But he could make nothing of it except what it straightforwardly said: that the king was exceedingly fond of pie.

Now in those days pie meant but one thing—a pasty, that is, meat of some sort baked in a dish covered with dough. At that time there was no such thing known as a pie made of fruit or mincemeat. Pie was not even a dainty. Pie was vulgar, ordinary victuals, and the lord mayor was shocked at his son's even mentioning pie in connection with the king.

"Pie indeed!" he shuddered. "A pretty dish to set before a king on his wedding journey! How can pie be introduced into my grand pageant? The king can get pie anywhere, in any hut or hovel along his way. What has Blessington to do with pie?"

The lord mayor snorted scornfully, and was about to dismiss his son's hint from his mind, when he had an idea! A pie! A great, glorified, poetic, symbolic pie such as could be carried in procession decorated with flowers! That was a happy thought. The lord mayor dismissed every one else and sent for all the master cooks of the city.

It was decided to accept Cedric's hint for what it was worth, and make pie the feature of the day. There should be a grand pageant of soldiers and maskers and music. And, following the other guilds, last of all should come the cooks, with their ideas of pie presented as attractively as might be, for the edification of the king. Moreover, the lord mayor said, in dismissing the white-capped company:

"To whichever of you best pleases his Majesty with the pie, I will give this reward: a team of white oxen, a hundred sacks of white flour, and a hundred pieces of white silver."

"Hurrah!" shouted the cooks, waving their white caps. Then away they hurried to put on their *thinking*-caps instead and plan for the building of the king's pie.

Now, among the cooks of Blessington there were two brothers, Roger and Rafe. Roger, the elder, had one of the hugest kitchens and shops in Blessington. But Rafe, the younger, had only a little old house on an acre of land under a little red-apple tree, with a little red cow who gave a little rich cream every day. Rafe was very poor, and no richer for having a brother well-to-do like Roger. For the thrifty cook had little to do with Rafe, whose ways were not his ways.

Rafe cooked in his little kitchen for the poor folk of the town, charging small prices such as they could pay. Indeed, often as not he gave away what he had cooked for himself to some one who seemed hungrier. This is a poor way to make profit of gold, but an excellent way to make profit of affection. And Rafe was rich in the love of the whole town.

Roger was among the cooks whom the lord mayor summoned to consult about the king's pie. But Rafe knew nothing at all of it, until one afternoon he was surprised by a visit from his brother, who had not darkened his door for many a day.

"Well, Brother," said Roger, briefly, "I suppose you are not busy, as I am. Will you work for me for a day or two? In fact, I need you."

"Need me!" said Rafe, in surprise. "How can that be, Brother?"

"I have a great task at hand," said the master cook; "a task that needs extra help. You must come. Your own work can wait well enough, I judge."

Rafe hesitated. "I must cook for my poor people first," he said.

Roger sneered. "Your poor people, indeed! I am cooking for the king! Will you hesitate now?"

"Cooking for the king!" cried Rafe. "Ah, but he is not so hungry as my neighbors will be to-morrow without their rabbit-pies."

"Rabbit-pies! It is a pie for the king that I am making!" shouted Roger, in high dudgeon,—"such a pie as you and your louts never dreamed of. Now what say you? Will you come?"

"I must do my own small cooking first," said Rafe, firmly.

"Very well then," growled Roger. "Cook for your beggars first, but come to me to-morrow. Every cook in town but you is engaged. I must have your help."

"I will come," said Rafe, simply, and Roger bade him a surly good-by without thanks or promises.

The next morning, when his own simple tasks were done, Rafe hied him to his brother's kitchen, and there he found great doings. Roger was superintending the preparations for baking an enormous pie. A group of masons had just finished building the huge oven out of doors, and about a score of smiths were struggling with the pie-dish, which they had forged of iron. It was a circular dish ten feet across and four feet deep; and it looked more like a swimming-tank than anything else.

Rafe stared in amazement. "Is that to hold your pie, Brother?" he asked.

"Yes," growled Roger. "Now get to work with the other men, for the crust must be baked this morning."

Three assistant cooks in caps and aprons were busy sifting buckets of flour, measuring out handfuls of salt and butter. Others were practising with long rolling-pins made for the occasion, so big that a man had to be at each end. On the ground lay a great round piece of tin, ten feet across, pierced full of holes.

"What is that?" whispered Rafe to one of his fellow-cooks.

"That is to be the lid of the pie," answered the cook. "See, they are lifting it onto the dish now. It will have a strong hinge, and it will be covered with crust."

"And what is to fill this marvelous pie?" asked Rafe, wondering still more. "Tender capon? Rabbits? Venison? Peacocks? What is suitable for a king? I do not know."

"Ah, there you show your lack of imagination!" cried the cook. "Master is a great man. This is a poetic pie. It is to be filled with flowers, and on the flowers will be sitting ten beautiful little children, pink and sweet as cherubs, dressed all in wreaths of flowers. And when the pie reaches the king, the top will be opened, and they will all begin to sing a song in honor of their Majesties. Is it not a pretty thought?"

"Well, if the king be not too hungry," said the practical Rafe, doubtfully.

"Nonsense!" cried the cook, testily. "Would you make out our king to be a cannibal, indeed?"

"Nay," said Rafe; "that is why I doubt. However, I am here but to assist in this colossal plan. Hand me yon bag of salt."

All day long at Roger's kitchen the cooks worked over the king's pie. At noon came a band of ten mothers, each with a rosy, smiling baby. They placed the children in the great shell to see how they would look. Every one cried: "Charming! Superb! But ah! we must not tell any one, for Roger has paid us well, and the other cooks must not know how he is to win the prize tomorrow!"

Weary and unthanked, with his meager day's wage,—a little bag of flour and a pat of butter, sugar and a handful of salt,— Rafe went home, musing sadly. "A team of white oxen; a hundred sacks of white flour; a hundred pieces of white silver,— what a prize! If only I could earn these I should be rich indeed and able to help my poor neighbors. But Roger will win the prize," he thought.

He spread on the table his frugal supper. He had emptied his larder that morning for a sick woman. He had but a few apples and a bowl of cream. It was the first food that he had eaten that day, for his brother had forgotten to bid him to his table.

As he was taking a bite from one of the rosy-cheeked apples, there came a tap at the door.

"Enter!" cried Rafe, hospitably. The door creaked, and there tottered in a little, bent, old woman in a long black cloak, leaning on a staff.

"Good evening, Son," she said, in a cracked voice. "Are you a man of charity, or will you turn away a poor old soul who has had nothing to eat for many hours?"

Rafe rose and led her to the table. "Sit down, Mother," he said kindly. "Sit and share my poor supper: a few apples from my little tree, a sup of the cream which my good little red cow gives me,—that is all; but you are welcome."

"Thanks, Son," said the old woman, and without further words she began to eat. But when she had finished she sat for a few moments looking into the empty bowl. Then she said:

"Son, why do you not bake a pie for the king?"

"I!" cried Rafe, astonished. "How can I make a pie? You see all I have in my cupboard. There is nothing but a little bag of flour, a pat of butter, a handful of sugar and salt."

"It is enough," said the stranger. "Son, I will show you a secret. You have been kind to me. Now I will tell you that which until this day no man has known. You shall make the king a pie indeed!"

"But, Mother," interrupted Rafe, smiling, "you do not know what manner of pies are being made. I have seen but one— a giant pie, a glorious pie, all golden crust and flowers and pink little babies who sing!"

"Humph!" grunted the old woman. "A pie for a pasteboard king. Why not cook a pie to tempt a hungry man?"

"The king is indeed a man," mused Rafe.

have tasted them." She leaned forward, whispering earnestly: "Make your pie of them, my son!"

"Apples! A pie of apples!" cried Rafe. "Who ever heard of such a thing!" (And at this time, indeed, no one had.)

" 'Son, why do you not bake a pie for the king?' "

"But how shall I make a pie without viands of any sort?" (As I have said, to speak of a pie in those days meant always a dish of meat or game or poultry.)

"I will tell you," said the old woman. "Have you not a tree of red apples? Yes, luscious apples of a goodly flavor, for I

"Nay, you need not laugh so scornfully," said the old crone. "You shall see! I will help you."

At her command Rafe fetched out the bag of flour and the butter, salt and sugar. Then he went to gather a basket of apples, while the old woman mended the fire and mixed the dough. Wonderingly he watched her pare the apples, core and slice them, and cover all with a blanket of crust laid softly over, but not tucked in at the edges as for an ordinary pasty. Soon the pie was baked, all flaky and brown. When it came smoking hot from the oven, the old woman slipped a knife under the blanket of crust and lifted it aside.

"See," she said, "the apples are steamed and soft. Now I will mash them with a knife and mix the butter and sugar generously therein. This one must ever do, Son, last of all. This is the crown of my secret, the only recipe for a perfect pie."

Rafe watched her curiously, by no means convinced. Then, from a pouch somewhere concealed in her robe, she drew out a strange round nut, such as Rafe had never seen before.

"This is the final blessing," she said. "See, I will grate a little of this magic nut into the pie." Forthwith it was done, and a whiff of spicy fragrance reached Rafe's nose, and, more than anything, gave him confidence in this strange new pie.

"It smells worthy," said Rafe, hungrily.

Without a word the stranger drew from under a cover a little pie baked in a tiny tin, an exact copy of the other. "Eat," she said. "Eat and judge if my secret be worth keeping."

Rafe sunk his teeth into the warm, crisp crust and ate eagerly. His eyes sparkled, but he spoke no word till the last crumb was gone.

"Oh!" he said. "It is a magic pie! Never such have I met before! Never, in all my life!"

The old woman nodded. "A magic pie," she said. "And still better when you serve it with the yellow cream of your little red cow."

"It is a pie for a king," said Rafe. "But shall I be allowed in the procession, Mother?"

"All the cooks in Blessington who choose may march with that guild," said the old woman. "Bear your pie proudly in your own hands, wearing your cap and apron. I will send some one to walk beside you and carry the jug of cream. She shall be here to-morrow when you milk the little red cow. Treat her kindly for my sake."

"Mother, how can I ever thank you—" began Rafe. But, with a quickness which seemed impossible to her years, the old woman had slipped out of the door and was gone.

The next morning bright and early Rafe went out to milk his cow. And there in the stall stood a young maid, the fairest he had ever seen.

"Good morning, Rafe," said the maid, dropping a curtsy. "I am Meg, and I have come to help you carry the king's pie." She smiled so sweetly that Rafe's heart danced a jig. She was dressed in a neat little gown of blue, with a white apron and a dainty cook's cap on her flaxen curls. And she wore red stockings and shoes, with silver buckles. From under her apron she drew a little blue jug. "See, I have brought this to hold the cream," she said, "and it is full of red strawberries for your breakfast. Milk the little red cow, Rafe, and then we can eat and be gone as soon as the cream has risen."

In a happy daze Rafe did as she bade. Merrily they breakfasted together on milk and berries and a wheaten loaf which the maid had brought, as if she knew how hungry Rafe would be. Then Meg skimmed the cream for the blue jug, and they were ready to start. Rafe, in his white cap and apron, bore the precious pie, while Meg walked along at his side. A merry, handsome couple they were.

When they came to the market-place they found a great crowd assembled. "Ho, Rafe! Rafe!" people shouted to him, for every one knew and loved him. "Come here! Come with us!"

But Rafe answered: "Nay, I am going to walk in the procession with the other cooks. I have a pie for the king."

"A pie! A pie!" they cried good-naturedly. "Look at Rafe's pasty! Of what is it made, Rafe? Grasshoppers or mice?" For they knew how poor he was.

But Rafe only smiled and pushed his way to where the cooks were gathered. They, too, greeted him with jests. But he insisted that he must march with them. So they gave him place at the very end of the line, with the little maid at his side. But when he saw the wonderful pies all around him, he sighed and shook his head, looking ruefully at his own simple offering. The little maid, seeing him so look, said:

"Never mind, Rafe. You are giving your best to the king. No one can do more than that."

The people waited. The hands of the great clock in the market-place crept slowly around until they marked noon. Every one began to feel uneasy, for it was close upon the dinner-hour, and the long procession had not moved. The king and queen were late.

At last there sounded the blast of a trumpet, which told that the king and his bride had arrived, and that the lord mayor had led them to their seats on the balcony in front of the town hall. Every one gave a sigh of relief. But then there was another long wait, while the hands of the clock crept on—on, and the people watched and craned their necks eagerly. The lord mayor was making his speech, and it was very long. Finally arose more shouts and huzzas, not because the speech was good, but because it was ended. And presently another trumpet gave signal for the procession to start.

Off they went, through the streets full of cheering, hungry people. Soldiers and bands of music led the way; then came the maskers and the flower-maidens, the city guilds and all the arts and crafts. Finally passed along the yoke of snowy oxen, with ribbons in their ears, drawing a white wain in which were the bags of flour and silver, the prize for the best pie-maker of Blessington. When the company of white-capped cooks came within sight of the king, he laughed merrily and said:

"Cooks! Now we shall have something worth while, for I am growing hungry indeed!" And the young queen whispered: "So am I!"

Then came the pies. And such pies! Carried on the shoulders of sturdy boys, drawn by teams of ponies, wreathed in flowers and stuck over with mottos, the pies passed along before the hungry king. And not one of the pies was real! The king's smile gradually faded.

There was a wonderful big pie fashioned like a ship,—rigged with masts and sails and manned by sailor-dolls. There was a fine brown pasty like a bird's nest, and when it passed the king, off came the cover, and out flew four-and-twenty blackbirds croaking lustily.

"Good-by, dinner!" sighed the king, looking after them wistfully. The queen nudged him and said: "Sh! Behave, your Majesty!" But she also began to look hungrier and hungrier.

There passed a pie in a carriage drawn by six mules. It seemed piping hot, for steam came out of it. But when it reached the king it blew up with a *bang!* scattering showers of blossoms over the royal party.

"My faith!" cried the king, "methought this was the end of all things. But it seems not. Here come more and more empty pies!" The queen smelled of her salts and grew paler every moment.

One pie had a musical box inside and played a sweet tune as it passed the king.

In one was hidden a tiny dwarf, who popped out like a jack-in-the-box when the queen pulled a golden cord.

Still the procession moved on, and so did the hands of the clock, and the king's hands moved to his ample girdle, which he tightened sharply. But both he and the pale young queen were too polite to ask the lord mayor for buns or something to sustain them.

The pie which caused the greatest excitement as it passed along, drawn by four white horses, was that of Roger, the master cook, who walked proudly beside it. When he came opposite the king the carriage stopped, the cover was lifted, and ten beautiful babies on a bed of roses waved their little hands and began to sing. The queen leaned forward eagerly, forgetting to be hungry. "How sweet! The darlings!" she murmured. "Oh, this is the best of all!" Roger the cook heard her and flushed with triumph.

But the king grumbled: "Humph! They look good enough to eat, but—my faith, I hope that this is the end, for soon I must eat something, or I shall become a cannibal!"

"Your Majesty!" protested the queen, faintly. But the king interrupted her.

"What comes here?" he cried. "This looks sensible!" It was Rafe and the pretty maid bringing up the rear of the procession. Side by side they walked in cap and apron, he bearing the small, delicately browned pie, she with a jug of yellow cream. No one paid any attention to them, but closed in around them, following Roger's chariot.

When Rafe and Meg came opposite the king and queen, they turned and Rafe bowed low, holding up the pie as high as he could. The pretty maid curtsied gracefully, and offered the cream-jug with a winsome smile. The crowd was fain to hustle them on; but the king struck the floor with his staff and pointed eagerly at the pie.

"Hold!" he cried, "What have you there?"

Everyone stopped and began to stare. Rafe bowed again.

"'Tis a pie, your Majesty," said Rafe, simply, "an apple pie."

"With cream for the top," lisped the little maid, curtsying again.

"Apple pie!" cried the king. "Who ever heard of an apple pie! A pie should be of savory meat. But of *apples!*" Words failed to express his astonishment.

"Butter and sugar, Sire, go to the making of it, and the dust of a wondrous nut. Will you taste it, Sire?" Rafe held out the pie temptingly.

"With thick cream to pour on the top,— yellow, sweet, rich, thick cream!" said Meg, lingering over each word as if it melted on her lips.

"Give hither that pie!" almost shouted the hungry king. "I will look into this matter." And, drawing a dagger from his girdle, he seized and stabbed the pie to the heart. Sniffing at it eagerly, his eyes grew round, and he smacked his lips. "It is good, I wager my scepter!" he cried. "Hand me the cream, fair maid."

The little maid stepped up and daintily poured cream upon the shattered pie, and without more ado the king began to eat with his dagger. (This was not considered bad manners in those days.) After the first mouthful he stopped only to say: "Food of the fairies! Pie of the pixies! Cook, you are a magician!" He went on at a rate which threatened not to leave a mouthful. But the queen pulled at his sleeve. "A bite for me, your Majesty," she begged. And, with an apology, the king handed her what was left, watching her wistfully till she ate the last crumb.

"Delicious! I never tasted anything finer," she cried. "I must have the recipe."

"*I* must have the cook!" cried the king, turning to Rafe, with a broad grin on his merry, fat face. "You must come with me and cook such pies for every meal. Yes, I will have them for breakfast, too," he insisted, in response to a protest from the queen.

Then up stepped Hugh, the lord mayor.

"Sire," said he, bowing low, "will your Majesty deign to point out to me the pie which has best pleased you, that I may have it set in the place of honor, and give the prize to the maker?"

"That I cannot do," said the king, "for the pie no longer exists. It is *here,*" and he slapped his generous waistband. "But give whatever prize there may be to this worthy fellow, whom I now dub Baron Applepy. Baron, wear this ring in token of my pleasure in your pie." He drew a fine ruby from his finger and gave it to Rafe.

"And this is for the little maid," said the queen, taking a beautiful pearl necklace and tossing it over Meg's curls.

But Roger, the master cook, stood by and tore his hair when he saw what was happening.

Then up came the yoke of white oxen drawing the cart bearing the prize. And the lord mayor gave a goad into Rafe's hands, with words of congratulation.

"Now mount and come with me," said the king. But Rafe hesitated.

"Your Majesty," he replied, "I see no way to make another pie like this which has pleased you. For I have no more of the magic nuts wherewith to flavor a second."

The king frowned. "What! No more pie! Is this to be the first and the last? Sirrah, I am not pleased!"

Then little Meg stepped forth. "The magic nut is the nutmeg," said she. "My name is Meg, and Granny called the magic nuts after me. I know where is hidden a store of them. These are my dower." She emptied her pockets of the nuts which they held, and they were a precious handful.

"Ha!" cried the king, eagerly, "you must marry Baron Applepy, that he may use your dower in our behalf."

Rafe and the maid looked sidewise at one another.

"You are willing, my dear?" said the queen, smiling upon Meg.

"Yes," whispered she, with red-apple cheeks.

"Yes, indeed!" cried Rafe when the queen looked at him. But again he seemed troubled.

"Your Majesty," he said, "I cannot leave my poor neighbors. There will be no one to cook for them at my prices."

"You shall have your own price from me," said the king.

Rafe bowed low. "You do me great honor," he said humbly. "But I cannot leave my poor people, my house and my cow and my apple-tree; indeed I cannot."

The king looked very angry and raised his staff with a gesture of wrath. But the queen laid her hand upon his arm.

"Why may he not live where he will and yet cook the pies for us?" she said. "A messenger on a fleet horse can bring them to us every day. We shall then have pies like that first delicious one, made from apples from that very same red-apple tree of his. They would be best of all."

"True," said the king, reflecting for a moment.

"Please, your Majesty," said Meg, in her most winsome tones, "I do so long to help Rafe pick the red apples for your pies and skim the yellow cream of the little red cow. And please, I do so long to help him cook for his poor neighbors, who will miss him so. Now that we have the prize, we can do much for them. Please, your Majesty!"

"Please, your Majesty!" begged the queen. So the king hemmed and hawed and yielded. "But see, Baron Applepy," he said, "that you make me three fine pies every day, for which my swiftest messenger shall call. Now farewell to thee—and to all. We must be off."

"Heaven bless your Majesties," said Rafe and Meg, bowing and curtsying low. Then Rafe lifted the little maid into the white cart beside the hundred sacks of flour and the bag of silver, and amid shouts and cheers away they drove the white oxen toward the little house on the acre of land under the red-apple tree, where the little red cow was waiting for them. And there they lived happily ever after, making three pies a day for the king at an enormous price, and feeding the beloved poor people, his neighbors, for no price at all.

THE HIDDEN RILL
(*Translated from the Spanish*)

By WILLIAM CULLEN BRYANT

ACROSS a pleasant field, a rill unseen
   Steals from a fountain, nor does aught betray
Its presence, save a tint of livelier green,
   And flowers that scent the air along its way.
Thus secretly should charity attend
   Those who in want's dim chambers pine and grieve;
And nought should e'er reveal the aid we lend,
   Save the glad looks our kindly visits leave.

THE RIP VAN WINKLE MAN-O'-WAR

(AN "AS-IT-*MIGHT*-HAVE-HAPPENED" STORY)

by H. Irving Hancock

"SAIL two points off sta'bu'd bow, sir!" came up to the bridge from the bow watch of the second class battle-ship *Tecumseh,* of the United States Navy.

Lieutenant Rowland, officer of the watch, nodded slightly, spy-glass at his eyes, for he had made out the stranger at the same moment.

It was morning, just after daylight, on Monday, April 20, 1908. The *Tecumseh,* southbound, and going at slow cruising speed, was in latitude about 30° S. and longitude 35° W., that is to say, about six hundred and fifty miles southeast of Rio Janeiro.

Patches of light-brown, smoky, thick haze that is peculiar to the South Atlantic at this season of the year hung about the trim, bristling, white watercraft. Here and there were open streaks showing deep blue water and unclouded skies overhead.

Out of one of these patches of haze, less than a quarter of a mile away, poked a black bowsprit, topped by a spread of old yellow canvas. This was followed by the looming up of a rusty black hull, high out of water; and then a foremast came into view. But what caused officer and bow watch to start in intense astonishment was the muzzle of a long, old-style, 32-pounder bow-gun that, peering out of its canvas jacket, appeared at the stranger's starboard bow.

"The *Flying Dutchman?*" wondered the bow watch.

The men in the wheel-house and the few other members of the crew on duty forward rubbed their eyes. Whatever he felt within, the calm young officer on the bridge kept his outward composure admirably. The vessel that now came wholly out of the haze proved to be a wooden ship of nearly four thousand tons. Her three masts bore a full spread of much-patched, time-seared canvas, while from a single funnel wood smoke floated indolently. Steam was plainly only auxiliary on this craft. Despite the revolutions of the side paddle-wheels the stranger was making barely six knots an hour northward. A few deck-guns were visible, while white-painted, closed ports along the side perhaps concealed others.

It came as a shock to all beholders aboard the *Tecumseh* that this rather ghostly old craft displayed, aft, an old United States flag of many years ago.

"We'll soon know something about this marine ghost, or whatever it is!" said Lieutenant Rowland to himself, as, with a hand on the lever of the mechanical signaling apparatus, he gave the order for the stopping of the battle-ship's propeller-shafts. His verbal command to a marine brought Ensign Waite and Cadet Midshipman Ellis hastily forward.

"Give 'em a blank shot, Mr. Waite!" directed Rowland. "Mr. Ellis, my compliments to the captain and the executive officer, and tell 'em—"

As a puff of white smoke and a sharp report left one of the *Tecumseh's* lighter forward guns, the stranger's colors dipped, while a clump of signal-flags was hauled to the old craft's maintop and there broken out.

"I can't make out that bunting gibberish!" muttered Rowland, impatiently, as he studied the flags through his glass. "Any orders, sir?" he asked, from force of habit, as the executive officer reached the bridge just ahead of the captain.

"No," said both. "Wait."

As the old black craft, in slowly stopping headway, turned and came somewhat nearer, the *Tecumseh's* signal-flags shook out the challenge, "Who are you?" But the stranger replied only with a single deep-throated blast from her whistle.

"Mr. Thornton," said Captain Loring, turning to an ensign in the group of officers that had hastened close to the bridge, "you're our authority on everything ancient in the navy. Can you place the craft yonder?"

"She carries about an 1856 flag, sir, and looks like one of our old line-of-battle ships before the war. But there's no such craft in commission to-day, sir."

From the davits at the starboard waist of the stranger a cumbersome black rowing cutter was lowered in rather seamanlike manner, though the sailors going stiffly down a side gangway to the cutter appeared to be all old, white-haired men. A feeling somewhat of awe crept over the hundreds of watchers now on the white battle-ship's decks.

Though with a stiffness of movement suggestive of something between old age and rheumatism, the men in the cutter got away from their own vessel in good old naval style. Officers and blue-jackets on the *Tecumseh* watched the approaching cutter until Captain Loring roared through a megaphone: "What ship are you from?"

From a white-haired, venerable-faced man of at least seventy years, who sat in the stern-sheets of the cutter, and who wore a curious, dingy, old-style blue uniform, even to the ancient "cheese-box" cap of the old navy, came the response.

"We couldn't read your signals, sir, any better than you could make out ours. Our craft is the line-of-battle ship *Neponset*, United States Navy. Sailed from New York November 18, 1858, and frozen in below the Antarctic Circle almost ever since—now free, thank heaven, to return to the United States! Your flag, sir, and your strange, wonderful craft, show us that our country still lives! We—"

The ancient officer's speech ended in a huskiness that he could not choke down. Yet his words would not have been heard, for one blue-jacket on the *Tecumseh,* gazing hard, forgot discipline and roared hoarsely:

"Mates, we're gazing on wot's left of the Old Navy, that saved this country of our'n and kept it for the New Navy!"

What a mighty tempest of a cheer went up from six hundred throats as the meaning of that speech broke on these gallant sailors of to-day! Even their officers forgot their dignity and joined in the hearty salute. As the cutter came in closer, a side gangway was quickly lowered, while captain and executive officer hurried to receive the wonderful guests.

Only the aged officer who had answered the hail came up the narrow steps. He paused long enough to say to a white-haired brother officer in the cutter:

"Keep all hands in the boat, Midshipman."

"Aye, aye, sir!" came cheerily from that "boy" of past threescore. Then, as this ranking officer, looking as though he had stepped from an old-time print, started to ascend, Ensign Thornton, at a nod from his captain, ran down to give the old man a reverentially supporting arm.

"I am Captain Loring, and I welcome you most heartily, sir, on my own behalf and that of my brother officers," said the *Tecumseh's* commander in husky tones, as the pair reached the head of the gangway.

"I tender you my most respectful thanks, sir," came simply, in a now strong, clear voice from the old man. "I am Second Lieutenant Raymond, ranking surviving officer of the old *Neponset*. I have brought our crumbly old ship's papers, sir, for your inspection."

"Come down to my cabin," begged Captain Loring, and led the way.

While the two commanders were below, recovered discipline prevented any curious hails or conversation between the men on the battle-ship and those in the cutter that rode on the ground-swell at a little distance from the ship's side. It was not long ere the *Tecumseh's* executive officer, Mr. Stayton, was sent for. He soon returned to the deck, saying:

"Mr. Rowland, hail the cutter, and ask the men, with Captain Loring's compliments, to come aboard. Mr. Waite, clear away cutters number three and four, placing Mr. Ellis in charge of one. Go aboard the *Neponset* and hand this invitation to Lieutenant Clover. Gentlemen," to the other officers gathered about, "the captain presents his compliments and invites all not on duty to join our guest and guests-to-come in the ward-room."

As the officers filed below they found the mess-servants flying about in the greatest bustle.

"Gentlemen," began Captain Loring, "this strange tale of the *Neponset* seems proven by the papers that Mr. Raymond brought. You will not be surprised at learning that I have invited the other officers of the *Neponset*—only seven survive, I regret to say—to come aboard and breakfast with us. Until that meal has been met and vanquished I feel that we shall do well to postpone asking for the story that I know every one is waiting in the utmost suspense to hear."

In a few moments more Midshipman John Dalton, sixty-five years old, and the youngest survivor of the *Neponset,* came below, while his venerable-looking boat's crew were being received with tremendous cheers by the *Tecumseh's* enlisted men overhead. Nor were the two steam-launches long in reaching the old black craft and in returning with the remaining officers and some thirty members of the *Neponset's* crew. Undoubtedly the most disappointed man on the old-time fighting ship was Boatswain Peterson, who was obliged to remain in temporary command.

Only greetings and pleasantries of the day followed the introductions between the officers of the Old Navy and the New. They seated themselves at the ward-room tables, old Mr. Raymond at the post of honor.

For nearly an hour, on account of the tension of waiting for the story to come, the meal proceeded rather solemnly. Only once did Lieutenant Raymond touch upon the past, when, looking down at his plate, he sighed: "It seems good to eat such food again, after half a century."

His words were echoed by a murmur from the other aged officers of the *Neponset,* yet, being "youngsters" in point of service rank, they left the remarks mainly to their commanding officer.

When the meal was being cleared away the first surprise came to the nattier officers of the *Tecumseh*. The waiters brought the choicest cigars of the mess. Looking down into a box held before him, Lieutenant Raymond, with an odd, far-away expression in his eyes, said slowly:

"It is good to see the weed, thank you. We've been nearly fifty years away from tobacco, and so we've lost the habit. But we'd like to try these!"

Then Captain Loring asked:

"Will it be agreeable to you, now, sir, to begin some account of your fifty years in the navy but out of the world?"

"I fear you will be disappointed, there is so little to tell," smiled the old man. "We have about the same story to tell as Rip Van Winkle told when he came back from his long sleep. In fact, sir, of late years I've often thought of the good old *Neponset* as the Rip Van Winkle of the United States Navy.

"I have told you the date when we left New York. Our commanding officer, Captain Howard, was ordered by the Navy Department to go as far south of the Antarctic Circle as possible, for the double purpose of making magnetic observations and geographical discoveries. We were expected to be away for two years, and were provisioned for three. Our only stop was at Rio Janeiro, for more fuel.

"Then we plunged boldly southward. On that side of the equator, of course, the summer season is the reverse of that at the north. So we neared the extreme southern seas in what was the height of summer. It was an unusually warm year in the Antarctic, I remember. The sea was so open that we made for the South Orkney Islands without trouble. After stopping there for two days we went somewhat out of our direct course, passing several large tracts of land, but not stopping until we reached Graham Land, which, as you know, is just on the Antarctic Circle. At Graham Land we remained for a week. While some of our officers made volumes of magnetic observations and calculations, Captain Howard kept his eye on the sea conditions.

"Though icebergs dotted the sea in all directions, the water yet remained won-

derfully open for the South Polar region. Captain Howard, therefore, decided upon a swift dash southward, even though we ran the risk of becoming ice-bound until the following year.

"It seemed well worth the trying. I may add, sir and gentlemen, that we made the dash with bold and cheery hearts. Though we had to be content with slow progress past the increasing number of icebergs, yet for days we kept on to the southward. One daybreak found us close to a great wall of ice. That wall, sir, was at least two hundred feet high. Captain Howard decided to skirt that great barrier of ice. Going westward at only about four knots an hour, we followed that wall for over four hundred miles.

"Then, one morning, our eyes were amazed by the sight of great, snow-clad mountain peaks on the further side of the ice wall. Our mathematicians quickly figured that the three visible peaks were from eleven to twelve thousand feet high.

"Within two hours of that time, sir and gentlemen, we found an open passage through the ice wall. We followed that passage through, discovering the ice wall, at that point, to be some two thousand feet thick. But beyond, sir, at the bases of those great mountains, we found the bare black rocks jutting out. The water, too, near this land, was much warmer than any we had encountered in days. By noon we sighted a fourth mountain, a live volcano with smoke issuing from its top.

"As we neared the base of this fourth mountain Captain Howard determined to send several officers and two boats' crews ashore. Almost their first discovery was a rock-lined entrance to a cove beyond. Skirting the cove, hemmed in by the mountains, was a valley of warm, fertile land, comprising some three square miles. Throughout this tract of land geysers of warm water spouted and the creeks formed by their waters kept the land warm and genial in that Antarctic summer. Vegetation grew freely, and at least half of the valley was covered by trees that could not be called stunted in latitude 82° S."

"Eighty-two?" cried Captain Loring, astonished.

"Eighty-two, sir," replied Lieutenant Raymond, gravely.

"Pardon me, sir. I did not mean to interrupt you. But your expedition went further south than any before or since!"

"And *stayed there longer!*" sighed Mr. Raymond. "For we were fascinated, and reveled in explorations ashore until one morning, a fortnight later, we made the awful discovery that our gap in the ice wall had closed. It has remained closed, ever since, until about a fortnight ago."

A gasp of astonishment—almost of horror—went round the *Tecumseh's* officers.

"Well, sir," continued Lieutenant Raymond, "there is not much more to be told. We were unable to get out, but we kedged our stanch old *Neponset* into that cove, and later built an especial basin in which we kept her all these years, diverting enough of the flow of the geysers into that basin so that the water about our ship's hull never froze.

"The climate was, of course, cold in winter, but our little three-mile kingdom had as comfortable a climate, winter or summer, as New York can boast. We had plenty of timber for houses and fuel, while the great mountains kept off the iciest Antarctic blasts. Our apothecary had, in a chest, several kinds of vegetable seeds and wheat, from which we harvested a good crop the first summer. There were fish in the waters, a species of seal and several varieties of birds, so that we fared well enough. We were well stocked with cloth, and made much use also of sealskins and the skins of the larger birds.

"Through it all, sir and gentlemen, we tried never to forget that we belonged to the United States Navy, and that we had one of the nation's vessels and a proud old flag to be returned to the American people. As the years went on I will admit that we often despaired of ever seeing our beloved country again. Our officers fell from eighteen to seven, and our crew from two hundred and eighty-nine to seventy-one. Still we felt that we had enough stout hearts to take the old *Neponset* home. Never once did we grow slack in our duty of fitting in new ship's timbers wherever an old one showed signs of giving out. We actually hoarded our uniform cloths, sir, that we might return home with some of the dignity befitting our country's service.

"Even our paint supply we hoarded, that the good old ship herself might go home shipshape and clean. Our ammunition we could not keep, for, with our best care, it gradually became worthless.

"It was twenty-six years ago that Captain Howard, full of hope and the love of duty to the last, died. His last words were: 'Do not despair, gentlemen. We have all made a brave fight of it. You will yet get back home.'

"Sir and gentlemen, a fortnight ago we discovered an opening in the wall of ice; and we were ready, as we had been for fifty years. An hour we spent, in reverent homage, at the graves of our beloved comrades in that ice-bound little valley. Then, with the boldest hearts possible, we left the place of our ship's long sleep, came safely through the great ice barrier, and—well, the rest of our tale you see before you."

Lieutenant Raymond's fine old eyes gleamed wet as he slipped from his seat at the table for a look through one of the port-holes at the not far distant *Neponset*.

"Now," said Captain Loring, speaking very softly, though heard by all, "we younger men understand more of the spirit of the Old Navy. Your ship's company waited a full half-century for your one chance of escape, and then, with true American pluck, took it the first instant that the chance came. Mr. Raymond, may we again shake the hand of each of the *Neponset's* officers? It will make better American sailors of us."

Before the hand-shaking was finished it rounded off into hearty cheering by these younger men of the New Navy. During the tumult the *Neponset's* aged officers looked actually abashed.

"At the time we—left the world," said Lieutenant Raymond, "war with England was feared in our country. I would like to ask if that war ever came about?"

"No, sir; and England and the United States to-day, sir, are two of the firmest friends in the world. But," added Captain Loring, very gravely, "within three years after your enforced exile, the Northern and Southern States clashed in the most gigantic war of modern times. Ten years ago we fought Spain. To-day, a portion of the United States Navy has just completed a cruise around the world—the most formidable naval fleet that ever made so long a cruise."

"A cruise around the world by a whole fleet!" cried Lieutenant Raymond and some of his brother officers in concert. "And the North and South at war! Tell us about that, I beg you!" pleaded the *Neponset's* commander.

"Mr. Thornton, as our historian aboard, I think you are best qualified for that performance," suggested Captain Loring. "While you are getting ready I will pass the word for such of the *Neponset's* crew as are aboard to come and listen with their officers."

A score and a half of the visiting white-haired enlisted men, all scrupulously neat in their darned and mended, faded blue uniforms, came down, gathering at the far end of the ward-room. They would have

stood, but Captain Loring insisted that chairs be placed for these old heroes.

For nearly two hours Thornton described the deeds of the American navy in the Civil War. At first there was deep awe over the story of the great national quarrel. Later the speaker was often interrupted by hoarse cheers from his enthused listeners. Porter, Farragut, Van Brunt, Mercer, Tatnall, Rodgers, Parker, Morris —these and scores of other names were those of living comrades to the *Neponset's* officers and men, who cheered the valor of their old-time friends to the echo. There were few dry eyes.

Ensign Thornton passed at last to the few but bright glories of the war with Spain. Dewey was a youngster, known to Lieutenant Raymond and two of his brother officers, but Admirals Sampson, Schley, and Evans were names over which they shook their heads even while their eyes brightened.

"You will want books to read on the rest of your homeward cruise, that you may 'pick up' and get into the world again," wound up Mr. Thornton. "I will bring you all that I think will be of use to you."

As he went in search of the books, brother officers excused themselves on the same errand. In a few minutes the old-timers had been supplied with more reading matter than could be digested in a year.

"We shall be as poor in purse as in comprehension of to-day's world, I imagine," said Mr. Raymond, musingly. "Of course our pay will have been stopped long ago."

"Poor in purse!" Captain Loring exclaimed, bringing a hand down heavily on the table. "I wish I had your prospects of a rich old age. Why, sir, every officer and man of you will be entitled to fifty years of back pay, for you've never been mustered out. And the country will certainly compel Congress to add compound interest at at least four per cent."

"Can that be so?" murmured Mr. Raymond, looking rather uncomfortable.

"Why, it will mount up into millions, altogether!" cried old Midshipman Dalton, after doing some frantic figuring on paper.

"Can that be so?" repeated Mr. Raymond, glancing at his astonished-looking brother officers. "Can the United States stand such a drain?"

"Yes! yes! Of course it can! We are a very rich country, now!" laughed Captain Loring. "But, gentlemen of the *Tecumseh*, as our guests must all be mentally tired, I ask you to take them above for a turn in the deck air."

"We can't seem to pick up any craft between here and Rio that has a wireless installation, sir," reported Ensign Waite, approaching his commander. The guests stared so curiously at that that they had to listen, with heads that must have throbbed, to the wonderful story of the wireless telegraph.

Captain Loring arranged with Lieutenant Raymond to have both vessels now shape their course toward Rio Janeiro.

"From there we will cable the Navy Department at Washington," Captain Loring explained, and then remembered that even the submarine cable was new to these men of the Rip Van Winkle man-o'-war.

The guests were now taken to the turrets to inspect the great rifled guns, the wonderful aiming mechanisms, the range-finders, and electric firing apparatus. These men of the Old Navy gazed with awe even at the hoisting of massive ammunition from the depths of this steel monster. The torpedo-tubes and the great Whitehead messengers of destruction almost made them shudder. The twentieth-century engine-room fascinated them. They saw a thousand wonders and new inventions in quick succession, and tried to com-

prehend each new marvel, yet cried out that they could not.

"We shall suffer collapse if you show us more to-day," urged Lieutenant Raymond, with a wavering smile. "We have been asleep for fifty years! Now, by the great Paul Jones, it will take us another fifty to wake!"

"We will lunch, then," suggested Captain Loring, and led the way once more to the ward-room. Through the meal the seven guests sat in an almost stunned silence. They were doing their best to recollect what they had heard and seen of naval progress in fifty wonder-filled years.

"With your approval, sir, we shall return to our ship, to think over what has come to us to-day," proposed Lieutenant Raymond, when luncheon was over. "And to rest," he added truthfully. "You will understand, sir, when we say that our heads never seemed so near to bursting. But we shall be glad, sir, if as many of you as possible will board us, at dark, and dine with us on the simple fare of which we have an abundance."

That invitation was gladly accepted. Most of the officers and crew of the *Tecumseh* spent a good deal of the afternoon gazing across at the drowsy black hull of the *Neponset* lumbering along over the ground-swell.

Never had any officer of the big white battle-ship sat at a simpler meal than the guests of the evening partook of aboard the old Rip Van Winkle man-o'-war. The meats were unfamiliar flesh that had been hunted far below the Antarctic Circle, though most of the vegetables were ordinary. There was wheat bread, though of a peculiar flavor.

After dinner it needed but a bare hour for the guests to see the little that was to be seen aboard the old *Neponset*. To modern eyes it was a primitive wooden ship. The furnaces under the boilers would burn either wood or coal. Mr. Raymond explained that they were now burning the former but had coal in reserve. The cannon were of the old smooth-bore type; the few shells in the magazine were worthless from age.

Just as the *Tecumseh's* officers stepped out upon deck, accompanied by their hosts, the great electric search-light of the white battle-ship turned its glaring eye on them, flooding the old man-o'-war's decks with an intense glow. A cry of amazement and even fear went up from the white-haired old sailors forward. They turned their faces from this brilliant glare, strangest of all equipment wonders of a modern sea-fighter.

The leave-taking between visiting officers and their hosts was simple but affecting. Then, in a reverent silence, the younger, nattier men went over the side into the steam-launch.

For some time there was complete silence among the *Tecumseh* group. Finally Mr. Stayton, the executive officer, said: "It was the *men,* not the *machines,* that made the Old Navy great!"

THE course for the night had been arranged between the respective commanding officers. The vessels were to keep as close together as wisdom in ship-handling permitted. But, as it happened, by six bells, long before midnight, the sky had darkened so as to blot out of sight the stars. A half-hour later a gale suddenly arose that quickly gave the officers of both ships all they wanted to think about. It was like a veritable West Indian hurricane, with a roaring wind and blinding sheets of rain, so that in a jiffy, as it seemed, each vessel lost sight of the other's lights. At first, the old ship's whistle could be heard in answer to the *Tecumseh's* deep-throated notes. Then even the husky old whistle ceased as a sound of near-by presence. No officer

on the *Tecumseh* slept that night. The raging winds and waters gave even the modern cruiser a struggle for life, and every man had to be at his post. And the dawn brought no relief, for nothing could be seen even a few ship-lengths away through the solid wall of fiercely driven rain. But, about three hours after daylight, the storm abated, and then the *Tecumseh's* officers swept the sea in vain with their glasses. The *Neponset* had vanished.

Captain Loring searched unceasingly for three days. His officers, well-nigh sleepless, shared the stern vigil with him. The *Neponset* was not seen again, nor was a single piece of wreckage found.

"I cannot bear to think of those grand old fellows going to the bottom!" said Captain Loring, that night, when he dined in the ward-room.

"Do you know, sir," smiled Mr. Thornton, wistfully, "I've just a notion that neither the *Neponset* nor the crew went under the waves?"

'Why, what else can have befallen them, sir?" demanded the captain of his young subordinate.

"Well, sir," went on the ship's historian, slowly, "you remember how awed those fine old men felt over the way the world has gone ahead since their day. Then, too, they didn't have any comprehension of how our country has grown. Why, sir, officers and men alike seemed absolutely scared at thought of coming back into a world and life that were utterly strange to them!"

"So you think—"

"Think?" cried Mr. Thornton, while his brother officers gazed at him with varying emotions. "Why, sir, it looks to me like a nine-to-one chance that the *Neponset* did weather that gale. She was old, but had been admirably kept up. So, sir, what more likely than that the gale gave those splendid old fellows the impulse to put about and make off back to their cove at 82° South? They knew that their naval hulk and their report were almost worthless to the country; they felt awed, exiled, and behind the times; they were certain that none of their old comrades still lived nor the relatives they had once known. I overheard one of them say as much to a comrade."

As Thornton ceased, there was a very long pause.

Who *knew?* It seemed sacrilege merely to *guess.* The captain rose slowly.

"Any orders, sir?" asked the lieutenant.

"Keep to the course, Mr. Wildman. We will put in at Rio Janeiro and cable the Navy Department. I fear we are going to have a hard time finding people to believe us when the whole story is told. But—for ourselves—we shall always treasure loving thoughts of those fine men of the Old Navy!"

BETTY'S BEST CHRISTMAS

by Alice Hegan Rice

IT was a long, long time ago, in the early days of the Civil War, when two little cousins lay under the shade of a broad beech-tree in Kentucky, and asked each other, for all the world like little girls of the present day, "What can we do next?"

They had swung on the willow-boughs that hung above the creek where it ambled sleepily between its banks of fern and mint; they had climbed the hay-loft and jumped off until they were tired. Now, in the heat of the afternoon, they lay on the grass, eating large slices of bread and jam and trying to think of something to do next.

"I know what I'd say if you weren't a goody-goody!" said Betty, a fair-haired, blue-eyed person of nine, with red lips that pouted when they weren't smiling, and eyes that could dance while the tears still stood in them.

"I'm *not* a goody-goody!" said the older girl, indignantly, "only with Daddy sick in the hospital and Aunty and Grandmother both away, I think we ought to mind Mammy."

"There's always some reason!" said Betty, with a rebellious toss of her curls. "They've been telling us that the Yankees would get us if we did this or that, until I 'most wish they would!"

"They wouldn't hurt me," said Jane, proudly, "because my father is a Union man."

"Well, your grandfather ain't, or Mother, or me, or Mammy. We wouldn't be Yankees for anything!"

A troubled expression crossed Jane's delicate, serious face. She was only eleven, but the tragedy of the terrible war had already thrown its sinister shadows across her life. Her little home in the North had been broken up, her mother was off in a distant hospital nursing the dear father who had given his right arm for his country, and she was here at Hollycrest, her mother's old home in Kentucky, where she hardly dared mention her father's name. "Rebels" and "Yankees"! How she hated the words! It made her just as angry to hear her grandfather called the one, as it did to hear her father called the other.

"I know what I am going to do," announced Betty, whose thoughts had gone back to that forbidden something that started the argument. "I'm going over to the office."

The office was a one-room log-building across the road, where Grandfather kept his books and papers and fled for refuge when the big house became too noisy with the coming and going of kith and kin. It was the one place on the estate forbidden to the children, and, by a strange law of nature, also the most fascinating.

Betty was a person who always suited the action to the word, and before Jane could remonstrate she was leading the way across the yard. As they passed the milk-cellar they encountered an obstacle. In fact, they encountered two of them. Two woolly little colored girls, who had been sliding down the slanting door, disentangled themselves from the bunch in which they had landed, and demanded in one breath: "Whar you-all gwine at?"

"Not any place you can go," said Betty, with a superior air.

"Kin too! Can't I, Miss Jane?" asked the blackest of the little girls, whose name was Lily White. Then as she saw them about to slip off, she added: "I bet I knows whar you-all's gwine. You gwine slip in Marse Jim's office! Ef you don't take me 'long, I'm gwine tell Mammy on you!"

Mammy's voice could be heard from the depths of the milk-cellar singing "Swing Low, Sweet Chariot." A word from her would put an end to the expedition.

"Well, we can't take Rose," said Betty, impatiently; "what you going to do with her?"

They all looked at the fat little darkey, who stood stolidly awaiting the verdict. If it was favorable, all would be well; if unfavorable, she was prepared to make trouble.

Rose was only four, but she had found a way of getting everything she wanted in the world. When things did not go exactly to suit her, she drew in her breath in one long piercing shriek, and held it. Held it until her eyes rolled back in her head, and her short kinky hair stood on end, and Mammy had to be summoned to shake her and dash water in her face. Even Betty, who was in the habit of having her way about most things, had to give in to Rose.

"Oh, well," she said, "bring her along. But if we play Indian, she's got to be the white child that's scalped."

The little procession made its way round the big white house, with its pillared porticoes, down the oleander-bordered avenue, and across the road. The door of the office was always locked, but the windows were often left open, and it was easy for the nimble Betty to scramble over the low sill and lend a hand to the others. It took all three of the older girls to get the fat little Rose up and over, especially as she helped herself not at all, but hung like a bag of meal, half in and half out.

"Marse Jim'll be comin' back heah an' ketchin' us, fus' thing you know!" panted Lily.

"He won't either!" said Betty; "he's gone to town for the day, and he won't come back till he brings Grandmother and Mother from the quilting-bee. Come on; let's see what's in the secretary!"

Of all the forbidden things in the office the most alluring was the secretary. The top part was a bookcase, filled with queer, musty old volumes, and the lower part looked like a chest of drawers. But if two of you pulled very hard on the top knobs and pressed up as you pulled, a shelf opened out into a writing-desk and revealed all sorts of mysteries. There were dark little pigeonholes, and a secret drawer lined with velvet that none of the children could open except Betty, and she wouldn't do it unless you hid your eyes and crossed your heart and body. There was a queer, two-walled inkstand, and one side held red ink that wouldn't come off your fingers no matter how hard you rubbed.

"Let's paint Rosie's face with it," cried Betty, "and stick rooster-feathers in her hair, and play she's a Indian chief!"

The experiment was tried, but the red ink made no show on Rosie's chubby black cheeks, and the project was abandoned in favor of a more daring scheme.

"I wish we could reach those big books on the top shelf," said Betty, jumping up and down in the leather chair; "they're bound volumes of the old magazines, and they've pictures in them."

"Miss Jane, she could reach 'em ef we wuz to put de hassock on toppen de writin' desk," suggested Lily.

Jane did not want to do it, but she didn't want to be left out of the play, either; so she climbed up on the secretary while four black hands and two white ones steadied the hassock. By hooking one finger over the edge of one of the uniform volumes she was able to bring it crashing down in their midst.

They knelt on the floor around it while Betty turned the pages. The first five minutes proved disappointing; then suddenly the pictures took on a personal interest. There were fashion-plates of quaint ladies in frilled petticoats over wide hoop-skirts, with lace mantillas and small dress bonnets; there were adorable little girls in low-necked, short-sleeved frocks, with wide pantalettes and pointed black slippers with ankle-straps.

"Paper dolls!" cried Betty, and even Jane's pulse quickened at the thought.

"Grandfather will never miss them," went on Betty, "besides, he wouldn't want to read the fashions. Let's each choose a family and cut them out."

Excitement ran high, for each mother wanted a good old-fashioned family of not less than twelve children, and the volume had to be ransacked to supply the demand. Moreover, there was but one pair of scissors to be found, and argument over them waxed furious until Rose settled things by demanding, with a threatening wheeze, that her order be executed first.

At the end of an hour four large families of paper dolls had set up light housekeeping in the four corners of Squire Todd's private office, the floor was littered with cut paper, and a large mutilated volume lay face downward on the leather chair.

Suddenly two fair heads and two kinky black ones were raised with a jerk.

"Hush!" cried Jane. "What's that?"

The furious barking of dogs came up the avenue. "Somebody's comin'!" whispered Lily, the whites of her eyes gleaming in terror. "Let's climb outen de winder quick as we kin. I'll go fust, an' you-all han' me Rosie."

Betty dropped everything and did as she was bidden, following the fat Rosie over the window-sill as fast as her legs would carry her. But the conscientious Jane stopped to pick up some of the litter, and had just succeeded in getting her apron full when the key turned in the lock and the door was flung open.

Grandfather, bareheaded and panting, stood on the threshold. He didn't seem to see Jane at all, but strode to the desk and began dragging papers out of the pigeon-holes and drawers.

"Grandfather," began Jane timidly, "I am so sorry—"

But he cut her short. "Child," he said more sternly than he had ever spoken to her before, "stand there at the window and tell me the moment you hear horses' hoofs."

Jane took her position by the window, and her heart began to thump uncomfortably as she saw him tie up package after package of papers and fling them into an old valise.

"Grandfather," she asked fearfully, "is it —is it—the Yankees?"

But he did not seem to hear her; his whole mind was bent on the task before him. After a few moments he stopped, as if he suddenly remembered something.

"Jane," he said, "run up to the house as fast as you can and tell the servants to hide—"

A warning finger stopped him.

"I hear horses, Grandfather!" whispered Jane; "they are coming up the Smithfield pike!"

"Watch if they turn this way or go toward town!"

Jane could feel her heart thump, thumping against the window-sill as she leaned out. "They are coming this way," she said, "two—four—no, six of them!"

Grandfather flattened himself against the wall, and signaled for Jane to do likewise. The clatter of horses' hoofs was growing louder. They passed under the window, passed the open door, then turned into the avenue across the road that led up to the house.

"Jane," said Grandfather, and his words came quick and tense, "those men are after me! They mustn't know I have been here. Hide the rest of those papers and this money before they come back. Don't tell anybody where you put them. Don't tell that you have seen me!"

He seized the valise, and with three strides to the back window was over the sill and gone.

Meanwhile Betty, scrambling through the lilac-bushes with Lily and Rose, made the exciting discovery that it wasn't the family returning from town after all, but a troop of soldiers on horseback, who had reined up at the front porch.

"Whose place is this?" asked the officer.

"Grandfather's," said Betty.

"What is his name?"

"Squire Todd."

The officer nodded to the man behind him. "I thought so," he said. "We'll have a look around."

It was at this point that Mammy, attracted by the voices, opened the front door. At sight of the blue-coated soldiers she gathered the children close, like an old hen protecting her chicks.

"Naw, sir, dey ain't nobody at home," she said; "dey ain't nobody 't all at home." Then with growing alarm as she saw the soldiers dismounting she added: "I ain't gwine 'low you-all to come traipsin' through our house when ole Miss ain't here. She won't like it, I tell you! She—"

But the soldiers brushed right past Mammy and went marching through the wide front door without even stopping to wipe their muddy boots on the mat. When they came out, they carried Grandfather's old flint-lock musket and the two dueling-pistols that used to hang in the dining-room but of late had stood behind the hall door, where nobody was allowed to so much as peep at them.

"Any papers?" asked the officer.

"None of consequence," said a soldier.

Then the officer turned to Mammy. "When do you look for your master to return?"

"Not 'fore sunset, Boss. He gwine bring ole Miss an' Miss Sue home f'um de quiltin'-bee."

"You are sure he hasn't been here in the last hour?"

"Naw, sir, he ain't been here sence breakfus'. Is he, Betty?"

Betty shook a positive head.

The officer looked at them suspiciously. "Two of you men guard the house," he said; "the rest of us will search the premises."

They circled the grounds several times, looking in the milk-cellar and the smoke-house and the negro cabins and all about; then they came back and got on their horses and rode down the avenue.

"Is that a house over there in the bushes?" asked the officer, with a sharp glance at the small log-building across the road. "Better take a look inside."

One of the soldiers strode through the high grass and flung open the door.

Sitting on the floor was a sweet-faced, demure little girl, apparently absorbed in her paper dolls.

"Are you Squire Todd's daughter?" asked the soldier.

"No, sir," said the little girl, looking up. "I am Captain Mitchell's daughter, of the Fourteenth Massachusetts."

"A good little Yankee, eh?" said the soldier, smiling.

"Yes, sir," said Jane, "my father lost his arm at Chickamauga."

The soldier returned to his chief, and after a brief parley they rode away, two to the north and two to the south.

An hour later, Jane and Betty, hanging anxiously over the big gate at the end of the avenue waiting for Grandmother and Mother to come home, saw two of the horsemen returning, with somebody riding between them.

"Why, it's Grandfather!" cried Betty, joyfully, and she waved her hand.

But Grandfather looked neither to right nor left. His white hair blew back from his stern white face and his brows met in a heavy scowl.

"He's awful mad!" said Betty; "he's mad at us for cutting his book."

But Jane knew better. In a terrible flash of understanding she knew that he had been captured, that he was being marched away to prison. She wanted to scream out in fear and protest, but because she was the daughter of a soldier, and because she wanted very much to let him know that she had been true to her trust, she scrambled up on the gate-post and shouted out as loud as she could:

"Good-by, dear Grandfather! I'll take care of everything for you till you come back!"

"TILL he came back!" How little either of them dreamed that he was never to come back, and that even if he had, no little Jane would have met him at the gate. For at the end of the dreadful war Jane and her grandfather lay side by side in the old graveyard on the hill-top, and only Betty and her mother and poor crippled grandmother were left in the old homestead at the cross-roads.

And what a change had come to Holly-crest! The once beautiful garden, with its dancing daffodils and spicy old-fashioned pinks, was trampled under foot; fences were down, outhouses burned. In the house itself every window was broken, and quilts were tacked up to keep out the rain. Mammy no longer sang "Swing Low, Sweet Chariot" as she made fat butter-pats in the cool milk-cellar; Lily and Rose no longer tumbled in the sun. They were all gone, gone with the happy, care-free days that the war had banished forever.

For soon after that fatal day when Grandfather was captured and his old valise found to contain incriminating papers, General Banks's army had marched down from the north, sweeping everything before it. The big house at the cross-roads had been sacked and plundered; every paper of value, every piece of silver, every object of worth had been confiscated. At the end of the war all that Mother had left was the ruined homestead and a bag full of Confederate money that would purchase nothing.

The only bit of happiness left to the family was Betty, now a tall girl of fourteen. But even Betty's dancing blue eyes grew wistful, and the laugh died on her lips when she saw the shadow that never lifted from Grandmother's face and the worn look of her dear mother, who was fighting day by day to keep poverty from the door.

"If I could only help!" was Betty's constant cry.

"You do help, dear," said Mother, wearily. "You help in a hundred ways. If it weren't for you, Grandmother and I wouldn't have the courage to go on."

"But I want to be earning some money!" said Betty, "If I could only go to the art school and learn designing, then I could take care of us all!"

Mother sighed. The art school had been the goal of all their hopes, for Betty had inherited from her artist father a gift for drawing, and had taken all the prizes that her school had to offer. But ambitions and dreams had to give way to the immediate need for food and clothes. And now that winter had come, the problem of keeping warm was looming up biggest of all. All the front part of the house was closed, and only Grandmother's room and the kitchen were lived in.

Day after day Betty tried to think of some way she could make some money; but everybody in the neighborhood was poor like themselves, and there seemed nothing for a girl of fourteen to do. And then one day a happy thought came to her. She had seen at school a set of hand-painted paper dolls that had come from New York, and the idea occurred to her that perhaps, if she made some very pretty ones, she could sell them, too.

Without saying anything to anybody about her plan, she took her paint-box after lunch and went down to the little log-house across the road, the only spot about the place that had been left untouched since the old days. For an hour she worked, only at the end of it to tear up all that she had done. She could paint the little figures with real daintiness and skill, but it took a more experienced hand than hers to make the drawing sufficiently accurate. Very much discouraged, she was about to give up, when another happy thought popped into her head, this time a veritable inspiration!

Jumping up, she ran over to the old secretary, and, reaching up to the top shelf, took down one of the dusty volumes of the bound magazines that had never been disturbed since the day five years ago when Grandfather was marched away to prison.

There they were! The quaint old-fashioned ladies in frilled petticoats over wide hoop-skirts, with their lace mantillas and dress bonnets; and smiling little girls, low-necked and short-sleeved, with wide pantalettes showing below their knees.

All the afternoon Betty worked furiously, cutting the figures out and mounting them with great care on cardboard. Then came the fun of coloring them, and the result was even more charming than she had dreamed. When a set of six was finished, she sat looking at them for a long time, then she went over to the secretary and rummaged until she found a long envelope. This she addressed to the aunt in Massachusetts whose picture Grandmother kept on her bureau, but whose name was never mentioned. Betty wrote:

Dear Aunt Fan: Will you please see if you can sell these paper dolls for me, and get some orders for more? They are just like the ones Jane and I used to play with, and I thought maybe the little Boston girls might like them as much as we did. Mother wouldn't like it if she knew I was writing this, so please don't tell her.
Your loving niece,
BETTY TODD.

Every day after that for a week Betty watched for the mail-carrier, and got to the letter-box before he did; but he always shook his head and passed on. Just when she was giving up hope a letter came. It ran:

Dear Betty: Your letter was the first word I have had from Hollycrest for over two years, and it warmed my heart! It brought back the happy days before the war when my darling Jane was living and my family held me dear. Indeed I can sell your dolls for you. A friend wants twenty sets for her kindergarten, provided you can get that number finished in time for Christmas.
Your loving aunt,
FANNIE TODD MITCHELL.

Betty was so excited over the order that she scarcely thought of the rest of the letter. One hundred and twenty paper dolls to be made, and Christmas only a month off!

That afternoon, as soon as school was over, she rushed home to begin her task, but Mother met her at the door.

"Betty," she said, "I hate to ask you, dear, but you will have to help me with the ironing to-day."

A quick protest sprang to her lips, but one look at her mother's tired face made her get out the ironing-board and fall to work with what patience she could muster. Every afternoon it was the same way; sometimes the dishes had to be washed, sometimes an errand had to be run, and sometimes, hardest of all, she had to sit by the hour playing checkers with Grandmother, trying to help her forget the terrible sorrows that had come to her in her old age.

But whenever a spare moment came, she fled to the office and worked like mad, cutting and pasting and tinting until her fingers grew numb with the cold.

Now and then a crowd of boys and girls, with their skates hung over their shoulders, would pass on the road below, and Betty would lift her head long enough to send a wistful glance after them. But there was no time these days for play: all she asked was time for work. If she could only make some money to help Mother pay those terrible bills over which she cried until her pillow was wet every night!

When all the volumes but one had been ransacked, Betty met with a disappointment that brought her air-castle tumbling about her in ruins. On opening the musty book she found the fashion-plates already cut out! It was the very volume she and Jane had been playing with on the day the soldiers had taken Grandfather away.

Aunt Fan's condition had been that she should send the full number, and here at the last minute she found herself one set short.

Her head went down on the table and she sobbed as if her heart would break. How could she have forgotten to make allowance for that volume? There had been more than enough plates to start with, but she had destroyed all but the prettiest ones, thinking she had more than enough to choose from. And now all her hard work would go for nothing. Mother would find no gold-piece under her plate on Christmas morning, the bills would come in, and then—

She flung back her curls with resolution, and something of Grandfather Todd's rebel spirit flashed in her eyes. She wouldn't give up! She would search every book in that old secretary until she found something she could use! Snatching up the volume before her to put it back on the shelf, she saw something flutter out from its pages and fall on the floor at her feet. Betty had thought so much about money lately that she was almost afraid she was dreaming now; but when she stooped and put out her hand, her fingers actually touched a twenty-dollar bill very old and soft.

For a moment she stood looking at it in bewilderment, then her eyes flew back to the book in her hand. With a quick drawn breath she began feverishly turning its pages. Wherever the fashion-plates had been cut out lay row after row of neatly piled bills, and at the very back, as if it had been thrust there hurriedly, a sheaf of loose papers.

Betty tumbled the treasure, book and all, into her apron, and sped to the house as if she had wings on her feet.

"Mother! Mother!" she kept shouting every step of the way.

Mrs. Todd straightened her tired back above the ironing-board as the impetuous figure burst into the kitchen.

"Look what I've found, Mother!" cried Betty, breathlessly. "In one of Grandfather's old books. It's money! Heaps and heaps of money!"

Mrs. Todd touched the bills with trembling fingers. "In a book?" she kept repeating, like one dazed.

"Grandfather must have hid it there when he thought the soldiers were coming," said Betty. "Count it, Mother, quick! Will there be enough to pay what we owe?"

But Mrs. Todd was not thinking about the money; she was examining the papers with growing excitement.

"Why, these are bonds!" she cried, "for thousands and thousands of dollars! And they've been there all this time and we never knew! Oh, my little girl, my little girl!"

And Mother, who had been so brave during all the years of poverty, broke down completely, now that relief was in sight, and buried her head on Betty's shoulder. Then the story of the paper dolls came out, and Grandmother had to be told, and Aunt Fan's letter was produced and cried over and laughed over in the same breath.

And in the midst of the excitement, with Mother preparing to take the money and papers to the bank, and Grandmother actually writing to Aunt Fan for the first time since Lee's surrender, Betty suddenly remembered her unfinished task!

The sudden good fortune that had dropped from the skies would have made many a girl forget all about those six paper dolls. But Betty was not one to be easily turned aside from an undertaking. Rushing back to the office, she searched in the scrap-basket until she found enough pieces to get together one more little family. The last pink rose was painted on the last bonnet by the flickering light of a candle, and the twenty sets, neatly packed, were addressed and slipped into the mail-box before Betty, tired but happy, trudged up the snowy avenue in time for supper.

On Christmas morning, for the first time in years, a huge log crackled merrily on the stone hearth in the dining-room; Grandmother occupied her old place at the head of the table and poured the coffee; while Lily White, a tall girl now, flew back and forth from the kitchen, bearing plates of crisp brown batter-cakes and piles of hot beaten biscuit. And on the table in the corner were presents, beautiful presents that had come from Boston for everybody down to Mammy and fat little Rose, who had come back to live in the cabin under the hill.

"And the best of all is this!" cried Mother, with eyes as bright as Betty's own. And she held up a shining gold-piece and a card on which was written:

> *For dearest Mother. The first money I ever earned.*

THE ORIGIN OF A PROVERB

by Ralph Henry Barbour

WHAT I am going to tell you about happened many years ago, so many that you couldn't count them on your toes and fingers if you were twins. It happened in the Kingdom of Faraway, which, as you doubtless remember, lies between Hereabouts and Just-beyond. The capital of Faraway is the royal city of Tingalingo, a very wonderful city indeed, filled with beautiful houses and crowned by a golden palace, wherein, at the time of my story, good King Acorn the First lived and ruled. He was a very kind and just and wise monarch, and was greatly loved by all his subjects, as was also his lovely Queen Goldenheart.

And so when one day the bells in the palace towers rang merrily, and the royal heralds rode forth to announce the birth of an heir to the throne, all Tingalingo rejoiced. King Acorn was so pleased that he decreed a period of celebration to last seven days, during which all loyal subjects were to dance and sing and be merry. Moreover, declared the edict, any one found with a long face would be instantly banished. So every one took special pains to be happy and gay, and never before was there such dancing and singing and merry-making, since of course nobody wanted to be banished. At the end of the time you couldn't have heard a sound from one end of the kingdom to the other, for all the people were so tired from being happy that they fell right to sleep and didn't wake up for three days!

But up at the palace there was noise a-plenty. It seemed that the royal baby had just made up his royal mind to be bad right from the start. He cried and he cried and he *cried,* and the seven royal nurses and their seven assistants shook golden rattles in front of him, made all the funny faces they knew how to make,—and some of them were extremely funny indeed!—sang all the lullabies they had ever heard of, and did everything they could to make him stop crying; but all to no purpose. The louder the seven royal nurses and the seven assistant nurses shook the golden rattles, the louder Prince Nimblenod cried, and the lullabies and the funny faces had no effect at all.

I can assure you things got to a truly awful state at the palace! Nobody was able to sleep a wink, and everybody went about looking terribly worried.

At last the King issued a proclamation: any one who would make Prince Nimblenod stop crying was to receive thirty bags of gold, which, since the King, besides being a just king was also a wise one and knew the value of money, was considered very generous. So almost in a twinkling the palace courtyard was filled with persons who believed they could earn the reward. One by one they were conducted to the royal nursery where the prince lay in a beautiful gold cradle, surrounded by the seven royal nurses and their seven assistants, and kicked his royal heels in the air and cried just as hard as he knew how.

They tried all sorts of ways. Some sang, some danced, some stood on their heads, some walked on their hands, and some turned somersaults.

It was a very funny scene, and every one, including the King and the Queen, laughed until their sides shook. Every one, that is, except the royal baby. He just lay in his golden crib and howled and howled and *howled*. It seemed that nothing could stop him, and finally the King and the Queen and the Prime Minister and the Lord High Chamberlain and the First, Second, and Third Lords of the Treasury, and the Exalted Keeper of the King's Bees, and the thirty-three ladies in waiting, and —oh, the whole court of Faraway stopped laughing, and grew very much disturbed, and wrung their hands, and cried, "Oh dear! what shall we do?"

When, at last, all the persons who had come to seek the reward had each one sung or danced or turned somersaults without success, the King smote his hand with a royal thump on the arm of the throne (much to the distress of the Queen, who was very careful of the royal furniture), and said crossly:

"We never heard such nonsense! Do you mean to tell us that not one among you is able to stop a baby from crying? Eh? What? Why doesn't somebody say something? Why doesn't somebody *do* something? We are very much displeased— very much displeased indeed!"

Whereupon the Court Jester, whose name was Addlepate, arose from the step of the throne and bowed low before the King with "May it please Your Majesty!" He was a very sad-faced fellow, owing possibly to the fact that his parents, intending him for the position of court jester, had made him sleep each night in a bureau-drawer so that he would grow up a dwarf.

"Your Majesty," said the Jester, making a very comical face, "it may be that a pin is sticking into Prince Nimblenod."

"Ha!" said the King. "We feel certain that that is it! Why didn't some one think of it before? Examine the Prince at once!"

So the seven royal nurses, aided by their seven assistants, hurried to the cradle and made the examination; and sure enough, there was a pin sticking right into the royal baby's princely tumtum! Did you ever!

When they informed the King, he instantly shouted in a ter-r-rible voice, *"Behead it!"* So the pin was promptly beheaded by the royal executioner. And while the beheading was going on the Jester twitched the King's sleeve.

"Your Majesty," said Addlepate, making a perfectly ridiculous grimace which almost sent the thirty-three ladies in waiting into hysterics, "referring to the thirty bags of gold—"

"To be sure!" replied the King. And he summoned the First Lord of the Treasury and instructed him to deliver the reward forthwith to the Jester.

When he was surrounded by the thirty bags of gold and had signed a receipt for them, Addlepate was very much pleased, and everyone shook hands with him, and told him he was a fine fellow, and invited him to dinner or luncheon. Every one, that is, except the good King Acorn. Times were hard just then, and thirty bags of gold were not to be sneezed at. But, being a just king, he stood by his bargain. Subsequently, however, being also a wise king, he called the royal executioner to him.

"Tie those thirty bags of gold to this varlet and drop him into the moat," he said. "Afterward restore the gold to the royal treasury and advertise for a new jester."

"Your gracious Majesty," said Addlepate with rare presence of mind, "I have long been convinced that the possession of wealth does not make for happiness, and that poverty is the natural heritage of genius. Consequently, Your Majesty, I had determined to devote to charity the treasure which your bounty so generously bestowed upon me, and would request Your Majesty to take charge of it and dispose of it at your pleasure."

"H-m," said the good King Acorn,

"h-m! A very wise resolve. We will attend to the matter. Remove the gold."

Whereupon, Addlepate, watching the disappearance of his wealth, sighed with relief. Then he sighed again, this time with regret, and observed sadly, "A fool and his money are soon parted!"

A saying which has survived to this day.

THE MONEY-JUG
(*A Rhyme of the Doll-House*)

By Katharine Pyle

The earthen money-jug sat on the shelf,
   Fat with pennies, and round and red;
"You shall marry the little china doll
   When you are full," the old rag-mother
      said.
"Only a few more pennies," said he,
"Will fill me as full as I can be."

The poor little china doll below
   Sat in the doll-house, very sad,
For she did not want to marry the jug,

   In spite of the pennies and dimes he
      had;
And she would not look at the nursery
     shelf,
Where he sat in his pride and puffed him-
     self.

"Two more days and it's Christmas Day;
   I shall be quite full by then, I know,"
Said the money-jug; but sadder still
     Was the little doll in the house below.

A MATCH FOR HIS CAPTORS

by C. H. Claudy

CUTEY stood on her ear. Then she slithered sidewise down a mud-bank, waddled over its top, and stuck her nose down a ditch-side, into which, after pausing inquiringly, she dropped with a squashy, squelching sound of oozy mud and slime.

Cutey—*Little Cutey,* to give her full name—apparently liked her mud-bath and her acrobatics. But those who found refuge from mud, now, and would from shells and bullets, later, in the cavernous, clanking complication which was at once One-Sixty-Seven's interior department, engine-room, and fighting-top, had no appreciation of the beauties of *Little Cutey's* performance.

"The main—dif-ference," grunted Sandy McTodd, "between *Cutey* and—a bucking broncho—oh! is that—you can—get off a broncho—when you—want to—ugh!"

Punctuated with lurches, words shaken from him with vibration, interrupted with the inferno of noise which is inseparable from the operation of the best-brought-up tanks, Sandy voiced the feelings of all her crew. As Sergeant Dill said,—of course he was "Pickles" when off duty!—"It isn't as if we didn't know how to run the old girl! Here we've been training and trailing around in the mud for *years,* posilutely, and no action! Aren't they *ever* going to let us get in the scrap?"

They wanted to get "in the scrap," very badly. All the "tankers" did. But the military powers-that-be had a pale idea that those tanks which stayed longest in the mud-wallows and had the greatest amount of instruction from competent tank officers would probably do the most damage when, indeed, it did finally come their turn to go "over the top." And so the tanks—which had numbers officially, but were affectionately known to their crews as *Little Cutey,* and her sister *Mischievous Maud,* and their near relatives *Go Get 'em* and *Huncatcher* and *The Peacemaker* and *Skiddoo Bill*—wallowed around in the great mud-fields of the training-camp and learned to crawl uphill and down ditches, and tumble into deep trenches, and fall into shell-craters and claw their way up again, and to face about with the quickness of a scared cat (no automobile can turn around so quickly), and to retreat with the speed of chilly molasses flowing uphill. Meanwhile, the human occupants of these most curious of war's new weapons learned to use their cumbersome vehicle and shoot machine-guns, take care of the mechanism and keep their feet and not get seasick, no matter what didos the state of the terrain and the orders of the day caused their movable forts to perform, and not to fall into the machinery, and keep their faces away from gun-slits when duty didn't call them there, and understand signals which couldn't be heard, and not mind living all day in a noise like a boiler-factory.

Except for the impatience of waiting for

that day when their training should bear fruit in action, the tank corps as a whole and the crew of *Little Cutey* in particular were a happy lot. They believed in a great many things with a belief which simply couldn't be shaken. Starting with the Stars and Stripes, and Wilson and Pershing, and the Allies, and the undoubtedness of that sight-seeing trip to Berlin they had promised themselves, they kept right on believing that of all armies there was none as good as the U. S. Army, of all tank corps there was none like theirs, and of all tanks there was none quite so good and obedient and mudworthy and handleable and impregnable as *Little Cutey*. Even Sandy McTodd believed these things, although he was stubborn when it came to saying that a Scottish regiment wasn't just as good as any in the world. Sandy was a good American, but he had a weakness for the kilties of his ancestors. Not that he had very much trouble with his mates on that score—the war record of the kilted soldiers from Bonny Scotland needed no defense from any one!

What Sergeant Dill did want to quarrel with Sandy about rather often was Sandy's pipe. Not that Pickles had any objection to the pipe as a pipe, or to Sandy as a smoker thereof—something must be conceded to the best tank engineer in the outfit.

"But inside *Cutey* is no place for it, Sandy, and you know it. It wouldn't be so bad if she was filled from outside. But you know as well as I do that it's dangerous to have matches around gas-tanks. Suppose some one left the cap off? Now you mark my words—you keep on getting caught smoking in here, and I'll have you sent to the rear!"

And Sandy would smile gently and put out his pipe, only to light it again the next time Pickles was absent.

"What makes you so stubborn, Sandy?"

asked Reddy Baldwin, the youngest and most enthusiastic member of One-Sixty-Seven's enthusiastic crew, late one afternoon. "Pickles'll blow up some day, and then we'll go into action without you!"

"Well, wouldn't you like that?" countered Sandy. "You'd be chief engineer then!"

"Like fun I would! Me, with only three months tanking behind me? No, I'd rather have you boss the job until I learn more. Why wasn't *Cutey* built to fill outside, like *Maud?*"

"Ask the man who made her! Experimental, all these—"

"Hi—inside! Tumble out! Captain's inspecting!"

It was a voice through a slit, and *Little Cutey's* crew crawled out to stand at attention by the little iron door while Captain Hammond looked them over. Then he motioned and they made way for him to go inside. He went in alone, presumably looked the complicated interior arrangements over at his leisure, and then crawled out.

"Very clean and orderly. But I found this!" Captain Hammond held up a half-filled, somewhat dirty, box of ordinary safety-matches. "I don't know whom it belongs to. I don't want ever to find its mate. It's against orders in any tank—particularly in this one. If I find this again, One-Sixty-Seven will lack a member of her crew."

No one said anything. There was nothing to say. And Captain Hammond passed on to look into *The Peacemaker,* standing at attention a score of yards away, and left *Little Cutey's* crew to jump, as one man, on poor Sandy.

"You see?"

"Crazy Scot—want to bust up the crew?"

"If I catch you doing that again, I'll lick you myself—"

"Pickles'll whale you if I can't—"

"Here, lay off me, you fellows!" cried Sandy. "They must have fallen out of my pocket. I didn't—"

"You'd no business with them in your pocket, and you know it! Think they make the rule for fun?"

Sandy said no more. But there was no more smoking that day, nor for several days thereafter.

Reddy was glad of it. He liked Sandy, and he knew the man for a capable engineer, brave to the point of foolhardiness and cool-headed. Too young himself to have had much experience of the world, Reddy couldn't understand why "an old man like Sandy" (Sandy must have been all of thirty-five!) couldn't appreciate the danger of matches in a tank. Even he knew that! Gasolene will leak sometimes, and shells have been known to puncture tanks; and matches and gasolene together in the inside of an iron box out of which you cannot get without being shot to small pieces do not make a happy combination. Every man of the crew, of course, would infinitely prefer being killed with Hun bullets to roasting to death inside their own tank, but that wasn't the last of the argument. If the tank was to be abandoned it might easily be captured by the gray-clad host across No-Man's-Land, and used against the Allied line.

"And all so you can have a forbidden smoke inside, off duty!" stormed Pickles, when he had heard of Captain Hammond's leniency. "Well, he didn't want to know, and, though I do know, I won't ask. But if I catch any one with matches inside again, I'll report him as sure as my name's Dill! Now that's flat and final, and you all hear me. And if I don't, then some of you report me for neglect of duty!"

And Pickles stalked away in wrath.

"You won't any more, will you, Sandy?" asked Reddy, after mess. "I—I don't want to be chief. I'd rather fight under you!"

"Humph! Listen to the kid!" mocked Sandy, puffing, puffing (it was not forbidden outside). But his eyes were not mocking.

But two days later the whole matter was forgotten. For in place of morning practice in the mud, came a messenger for Sandy to report at headquarters, and when he returned, his face told the news long before his joyous shout.

They were going into action!

It is a strange thing, but a true one, that even when soldiers know that their branch of the service is unusually dangerous, and that the thing they are going to do is as likely as not to result in painful wounds, death, capture, suffering, they hail with delight the chance to do it. No lad gets in a tank corps without knowing that while a tank *may* go through a battle unscathed, she may be disabled in the field and her entire crew wiped out. But there was none of that knowledge evident in the grins which all *Cutey's* crew wrapped round their faces, and which lasted during the journey to the lines, slow, tedious, interminable. Not even the sound of the guns, hourly clearer and clearer, the filling of the ammunition racks, the last inspection, the filling of the fuel- and oil-tanks, the final grooming of the machinery, could make other than joyous impress on these hardy sons of the service, the motto of which is, "Treat 'em rough!"

The attack was to be at daylight. "We're *all* going!" Sergeant Dill told them at the last mess—a difficult mess, for it was a dark one, eaten in the shelter of a little patch of woods too thin to permit a fire. "Yes, *Maud'll* be on our left an' *Peacemaker* to the right. Now boys, for heaven's sake, remember what we've been taught and don't go making any bulls. You, Ben, if I see you so much as raise your head to look out, I'll brain you! Sandy, for the love o' Bonny Scotland, have your oil hot and keep the old bus going. Reddy, don't forget to repeat every order whether Sandy gets it or not. Ellis—" and so on and so on to the point of weariness.

But they listened and liked it and nudged one another and grinned in the darkness, nor thought at all of the possible horrors of the day to come.

At the moment of going into battle there may have been some blanched faces. If there were, it was from excitement, not fear. They were wild to go. But the last hour of waiting is trying, and the guns were very loud and—no one knew what the day might bring forth.

But when they were actually over and into No Man's Land, then there was no fear. The battle sounds were dimmed by the rattle of the machinery—even the guns are muffled by the boiler-plate noise of a tank. Then the shells began to come, and they knew they were sighted. Their own machine-guns began to talk; *Maud* and *Peacemaker* rolled snare-drums to right and left—some grenades jarred on top of *Cutey,* and the noise became homogeneous —a mere blare of sound filling ears and brain, completely swallowing any extraneous impression. Literally deafened with din, *Cutey's* crew kept cool and calm, read arm-signals, did their duty, tended guns and engines as if in training and wallowing around in no danger. Such is discipline.

Reddy wondered at his own coolness. He even smiled a wry smile and shook his head as his eye lit on a box of the forbidden matches reposing on a ledge near the exit. How very far away it all seemed now— Sandy's besetting sin, Captain Hammond's threat, and Pickles's proposal to report! And what did it matter? They were in action! There—something hit! He could feel the blow—how he wished to look! Were *Maud* and *Peacemaker* and the rest still near? Or were they going on alone? Some craters under tread—it was hard to

keep one's feet—Sandy and his matches! He'd steal those matches and throw them out when they got back—save old Sandy a wigging. When they got back—if they got back—

And meanwhile, oil in an oil-cup, hand to a bearing, watchful eye on mechanism and on Sandy, just as if at practice—

"Ah!" One-Sixty-Seven toppled head first into a hole, crawled up, staggered, stopped. A burst from the machine-gun, then a motion from Pickles, and the engines stopped. Instantly, as if plugs of cotton had been pulled from their ears, came the sound of bullets on the iron tank, of explosions in the distance, of the machine-guns somewhere near. And through it all, Dill's voice, a whisper, though he shouted:

"Stalled! They've trapped us—run us up an incline! Treads off ground—"

It was true—too true! Sandy was for going out and tackling the obstruction with a crowbar or a grenade. But Dill wouldn't let him. It was simply suicide. And there might be a chance, after dark—

It was a long, long day. Crowding the slits, careless of stray bullets, they watched the tide of battle recede, watched the enemy in the distance, saw him surround them, saw there was no chance. "Of course, we can kill a few when they come to us —but they'll blow us to bits if we do—hear that 'plane overhead? Better surrender while we can, and hope for a new attack and escape later—"

It was a despondent crew which marched out of One-Sixty-Seven, hands over heads. Gray-clad captors crowded about, curious rather than hostile. Of course, their clothes were taken from them, their shoes, their arms—even Pickles had to smile at the appearance of his crew when it was dressed in German nondescript and worn-out clothing. But it was a wry smile.

Taken to a dugout and herded in like cattle, unfed, thirsty, their lot was not a happy one. Then came an officer, demanding in precise English, "Which of you is engineer?"

Sandy and Reddy stepped forward. "Both of us—why?"

The officer looked them both up and down. Sandy was tall, athletic, strong. Reddy small, wiry, compact. "You," said the officer to Reddy, "Come."

A guard put forth a hand and Reddy, wondering, followed. They led him to the tank—and Reddy saw with interest that the sand-bags on which they had stuck had been removed.

"Inside!" commanded the officer, and Reddy crawled obediently in.

"Now," began the officer, "we want to know how this thing works. Explain, please."

Reddy looked around. There were two other men besides the officer—strong-looking young fellows, each with a rifle in his hand. The officer had an automatic at his hip.

"You want me to show you how the tank works? So you can use it against us?" asked Reddy, slowly, "I'll see you—further first."

The officer smiled. "Oh, I guess you will!" he answered. "Of course, we can puzzle it out for ourselves. But that means getting engineers here, and we want to use this now—to-night. There are two methods I can use to make you talk. This is one," and he tapped his automatic, "that is the other," he pointed to the door. "Show us the whole thing, work it for us, make us its masters, and—you can go."

"I'll—" Reddy stopped. His eye fell on that box of matches. A wild scheme flashed through his head.

"I'll—I'll do it!" he stammered. "You must close the door."

"Do it!" was the command.

Reddy closed it, fastened it elaborately, showing just how the operation was ac-complished. He picked up a handful of oily cotton-waste and wiped the handle, striving to do it casually. As casually, the oily-waste went into a pocket of the nondescript prisoner's clothing he wore. A sidelong look told him no one noted anything strange in the apparently natural action. Reddy sighed, internally. The first step in a hazardous plan was a success.

Then Reddy began. As if he liked the job, he told the story of *Cutey*. He took the officer from stem to stern, explaining the mechanism, told how it was run and started and steered. He showed one man where he stood to oil, the other how the machine-guns were operated, and answered their questions, asked in broken, but understandable, English, with perfect freedom. He smiled grimly to himself at the officer's look of contempt, and his resolution hardened. Finally, he started the engine and let it warm up.

"Better hold on when I start her," he yelled above the sound of the engine. "Tanking is right rough going—"

Would his scheme succeed? Could he do it? Would the men—ah! Reddy concealed his exultation. Both the guards laid down their rifles, the better to hold on. What had they to fear from an unarmed man—three to one?

Very slowly Reddy moved *Cutey* forward and demonstrated how she was steered.

The two guards, with their faces to slits, watched *Cutey's* slow progress over their own ground. And they didn't see, or, if they did, sensed no danger in, a careless hand which swept the box of matches from its resting-place to another pocket. The second step was taken.

Nor did the officer suspect when Reddy stopped One-Sixty-Seven and directed his attention to the gasoléne tanks. "They're filled *here*," said Reddy, pointing; "wait, I'll show you."

He unscrewed the filling top, and held it while the officer looked. The men were still gazing from the slit.

"Now, I'll show you where they are drained," said Reddy, easily. But his heart was in his mouth. Would he have an instant—just one instant—unobserved?

The officer turned away. Two hands flashed rapidly for an instant—Reddy had put the top to the gasolene inlet back. But he had not screwed it home.

The third step had been taken.

"They are drained here," Reddy pulled open a pet cock. Gasolene spurted out in a stream.

"Yes, I see. Shut it off! It smells."

Reddy shut it off.

"Now, we'll go back," announced the officer.

"When do I go free?" asked Reddy.

"Why, when the war is over, of course!" laughed the officer. "Did you think I meant *now?*"

"I know darn well you didn't!" said Reddy, to himself. But he let his face fall as if disappointed.

"I forgot to tell you one thing," he went on, "you know if a match should light this gasolene, you'd burn to death, or it would blow up and kill you that way. I let out too much gasolene. And the tank is open. And—" Reddy drew the match-box from his pocket and struck a match as he spoke —"Hands up, *quick,* or I drop it."

He held the lighted match with one hand and lifted the cap with the other. And he shook inside, but the flame burned steadily in fingers that never trembled.

"Here—you—what—"

"Hands up!" commanded Reddy, and his voice was exultant. "See it? The tank's open! This match—" he waved it as he spoke. It blazed, potent of a terrible death, in hands which were steady. "I drop it in the tank—see?" The match was close to the opening. "We'll all burn together! Back—*quick*—"

The officer's automatic was in his hand, but Reddy expected that. "Shoot, and the match drops in the gas on the floor!" he cried—"to kill me is to kill yourselves—"

The officer hesitated,—probably Reddy had never been closer to death,—but he might well hesitate; the prospect of being locked in an iron box full of burning and probably exploding gasolene is not a pleasant one. It was this that Reddy had calculated upon. Had all three been armed, he wouldn't have dared it. But the two guards had laid their rifles down the better to hold on. Had they possessed pistols, they would probably have shot. But the quicker intelligence of the officer saw that to shoot was to precipitate the result of Reddy's threat. As far as he was concerned, a lighted match dropping in gasolene from the hand of a dead prisoner was just as much to be feared as a live prisoner doing the same thing. Besides, it may have occurred to him that the flash of his pistol would be very likely to ignite the spilled gasolene.

"I'll give you five seconds—" Reddy calculated the length of the burning match. It all happened in half the time it needs to write it. "Three seconds, one, two—"

Horror shone on three pale faces. But, as if moved by a single spring, three pairs of hands rose in the air—one of them held an automatic; Reddy's courage flamed high, even as the match scorched his fingers.

But before he pinched it out he quickly lit another from it. "Now," he commanded. "*You*—drop that gun—"

It waved in the air.

"But—"

"I *mean* it!" Reddy cried. "One move, and we burn together. I give you another five seconds—one—two—three—four—" The gun fell with a sharp clang, at the same time the officer spat out a command in German.

"Stop it! You'll talk English! Kick that gun over here, you—"

"You'd—you'd never burn yourself—"

"Wouldn't I? Do you think your filthy German prison camps have such a reputation I want to go to one?" demanded Reddy. "If that gun isn't kicked over to me before I say 'five,' you can kiss yourself good night—one, two, three—"

But Reddy had won. In response to a shove of the foot, the gun slithered to Reddy's feet.

"Turn your backs!" was Reddy's next move. Again the match burned his fingers, again he lit another and pinched out the first.

Three gray-clad backs were presented to him.

Reddy stooped swiftly, picked up the gun, and heaved a sigh of relief. Then he picked up the rifles and felt better.

"Now we are more comfortable!" he remarked. "You with the shoulder-straps! Take off your belt and tie your friend's arms behind his back. See you tie him up tight! Don't make any mistake. I'll shoot a heap more readily than I'd have dropped the match!"

"But you can't escape! It will be very difficult for you. When they break in, you will be shot, you know!" The officer's protest lacked sincerity in Reddy's ears.

"There'll be four of us shot, then!" he grinned cheerfully. "And where do you get that 'can't escape' stuff? Get busy and tie him up!"

Well, it sounds absurd to think of one American lad bossing three German soldiers around that way, with their own guns, in their own lines. But believing, as most people do, that a match and gasolene *always* mean an explosion, what else could they do? Probably the danger was less

than the officer thought it, but a terrified man does not stop to reason.

And so the officer laced one guard's hands behind his back with a belt, and the other guard tied the officer's hands behind *his* back, and Reddy made the third lie down, after first taking off his belt, and attended to that job himself. After which he dragged them, with difficulty, to a little group in the center of the tank, just forward of the engine, set them back to back, and fastened them all together with wire from the pipe-cleaning coil!

Then Reddy started the engine again, *Little Cutey* moved off slowly, and ambled back over No-Man's-Land to her own lines! Not until she was half-way across did it occur to the Germans outside, apparently, that something was wrong. Then the rattle of rifle-bullets, the sound of a few grenades, but made Reddy smile. And by the time the distant artillery had been informed and had got into action, Reddy had climbed over his own front-line trench, waddled on and on and on until a fringe of wood hid him from possible visual gun-brackets—and the thing was done!

There was another attack that night. All the lost ground was recovered, and most of the prisoners the Germans had made were rescued. *Mischievous Maud* and *Peacemaker* played a heroic part in the rescue, and the latter was the better for an extra engineer, who was allowed to go, apparently, as a reward for bringing home his captured tank and three German prisoners. But the reward that pleased him most was not the special mention he received, but the look on the faces of the crew of *Little Cutey* when they were once more inside their own little inferno of steel plates, smelly oil and gasolene, and reverberatory noise.

"Reddy," asked Sandy McTodd, "if the

Germans had come at you when you threatened, would you have dropped the lighted match in the tank?"

"Don't ask me," laughed Reddy. "I *looked* as if I would, anyhow!"

"Reddy," asked Pickles, hearing the story in detail, while taking notes for the daily record, *"whose* were those matches?"

"Don't ask me, Sergeant," smiled Reddy. "If I tell, you'll have to can him. And suppose it was me?"

"Humph! Where is discipline going, I'd like to know? I think I'll have to have *Little Cutey* rechristened. How would *Matchless* do for a name?"

"Reddy," asked Captain Hammond, who heard him, "how did you dare hold a match so close to the open tank? Didn't you think you ran a hundred to one chance of an explosion from gasolene fumes?"

"No, sir!" answered Reddy, demurely. "You see, sir, that handful of oily waste— well, I *stuffed it down the filling neck when he wasn't looking*. He thought the match would drop into the tank. But—I didn't want to burn *Cutey* up if I could help it!"

"Certainly *not!*" agreed Captain Hammond, solemnly, and said never a word about the forbidden matches!

But under his breath he made the remark which did, indeed, rechristen *Little Cutey*. To the rest of the corps she is now known by the striking appellation of *"Some* Bluff!"

THE PATH OF THE SKY

by Samuel Scoville, Jr.

DEACON JIMMY WADSWORTH was probably the most upright man in Cornwall. It was he who drove five miles one bitter winter night and woke up Silas Smith, who kept the store at Cornwall Bridge, to give him back three cents over-change. Silas's language, as he went back to bed, almost brought on a thaw. The deacon lived on the tip top of the Cobble, one of the twenty-seven named hills of Cornwall, with Aunt Maria his wife, Hen Root his hired man, Nip Root, Hen's yellow dog, and—the Ducks. The deacon had rumpled white hair, a serene, clear-cut face, and, even when working, always wore a clean white shirt with a stiff bosom and no collar; while Aunt Maria was one of the salt of the earth. She was spry and short, with a little face all wrinkled with good-will and good works, and had twinkling eyes of horizon-blue. If any one was suddenly ill or had unexpected company or was getting married or buried, Aunt Maria was always on hand helping. As for Hen, he cared more for his dog than he did for any human. When a drive for the Liberty Loan was started in Cornwall, he bought a bond for himself and one for Nip, and had the latter wear a Liberty Loan button in his collar. Of course, the farm was cluttered up with horses, cows, chickens, and similar bric-à-brac, but the Ducks were part of the household. It came about in this way: Rashe Howe, who hunted everything except work, had given the deacon a tamed decoy-duck who

seemed to have passed her usefulness as a lure. It was evident, however, that she had been trifling with Rashe, for before she had been on the farm a month, somewhere in sky or stream she had found a mate. Later down by the ice-pond, she stole a nest, a beautiful basin made of leaves and edged with soft down from her black-and-buff breast. There she laid ten, blunt-ended, brown eggs which she brooded until she was carried off one night by a wandering fox. Her mate went back to the wilds, and Aunt Maria put the eggs under a big, clucking brahma hen, who hatched out four soft yellow ducklings. They had no more than come out of the shell when, with faint little quackings, they paddled out of the barnyard and started in single file for the pond. Although just hatched, each little duck knew its place in the line, and, from that day on, the order never changed. The old hen, clucking frantically, tried again and again to turn them back. Each time they scattered and, waddling past her, fell into line once more. When at last they reached the bank, their foster-mother scurried back and forth, squawking warnings at the top of her voice; but one after another, each disobedient duckling plunged in with a bob of its turned-up tail, and the procession swam around and around the pond as if it would never stop. This was too much for the old hen. She stood for a long minute watching the ungrateful brood, and then turned away and evidently disinherited them upon the spot. From that moment she gave up the duties of motherhood, stopped setting and clucking, and never again recognized her foster-children, as they found out to their sorrow after their swim. All the rest of that day they plopped sadly after her, only to be received with pecks whenever they came too near. She would neither feed nor brood them, and when night came, they had to huddle in their deserted coop in a soft little heap, shivering and quacking beseechingly until daylight. The next day Aunt Maria was moved by the sight of the four, weary, but still pursuing the indifferent hen, keeping up the while a chorus of soft, sorrowful little quackings which ought to have touched her heart—but didn't. By this time they were so weak that if Aunt Maria had not taken them into the kitchen and fed them and covered them up in a basket of flannel, they would never have lived through the second night. Thereafter, the old kitchen became a nursery. Four human babies could hardly have called for more attention or made more trouble or have been better loved than those four fuzzy, soft, yellow ducklings. In a few days the whole home-life on top of the Cobble centered around them. They needed so much nursing and petting and soothing that it almost seemed to Aunt Maria as if a half-century had rolled back and that she was once more looking after babies long, long lost to her. Even old Hen became attached to them enough to cuff Nip violently when that pampered animal growled at the newcomers and showed signs of abolishing them. From that moment, Nip joined the brahma hen in ignoring the ducklings completely. If any attention was shown them in his presence, he would stalk away majestically, as if overcome by astonishment that humans would spend their time over four yellow ducks instead of one yellow dog.

During the ducks' first days in the kitchen, some one had to be with them constantly. Otherwise, all four of them would go "Yip! yip! yip!" at the top of their voices. As soon as any one came to their cradle or even spoke to them, they would snuggle down contentedly under the flannel and sing like a lot of little tea-kettles, making the same kind of a sleepy hum that a flock of wild mallards gives when they are sleeping far out on the water. They liked the deacon and Hen, but they loved Aunt Maria. In a few days they followed her everywhere around the house and even out on the farm, paddling along just behind her in single file and quacking vigorously if she walked too fast. One day she tried to slip out and go down to the sewing circle at Mrs. Miner Rogers' at the foot of the hill, but they were on her trail before she had taken ten steps. They followed her all the way there and stood with their beaks pressed against the bay window, watching her as she sat in Mrs. Rogers' parlor. When they made up their minds that she had called long enough, they set up such a chorus of quackings and so embarrassed Aunt Maria that she had to come.

"Those pesky ducks will quack their heads off if I don't leave," she explained shamefacedly.

The road uphill was a long, long trail for the ducklings. Every now and then they would stop and cry, with their pathetic little yipping note, and lie down flat on their backs and hold their soft little paddles straight up in the air to show how sore they were. The last half of the journey they made in Aunt Maria's apron, singing away contentedly as she plodded up the hill. As they grew older they took an interest in every one who came, and, if they did not approve of the visitor, would quack deafeningly until he went. Once Aunt Maria happened to step suddenly around the corner of the house as a load of hay went past. Finding her gone, the ducks started solemnly down the road, following the hay-wagon, evidently convinced that she was hidden somewhere beneath the load. They were almost out of sight when Aunt Maria called to them. At the first sound of her voice they turned and hurried back, flapping their wings and paddling with all their might, quacking joyously as they came.

Aunt Maria and the flock had various little private games of their own. Whenever she sat down they would tug at the neatly tied bows of her shoe-laces until they had loosened them, whereupon she would jump up and rush at them, pretending great wrath, whereat they would scatter on all sides, quacking delightedly. When she turned back they would form a circle around her, snuggling their soft necks against her gown, until she scratched each uplifted head softly. If she wore button shoes, they would pry away at the loose buttons and pretend to swallow them. When she was working in her flower-garden they would bother her by swallowing some of the smallest bulbs and snatching up and running away with larger ones. At other times they would hide in dark corners and rush out at her with loud and terrifying quacks, at which Aunt Maria would pretend to be much frightened and scuttle away pursued by the whole flock.

All three of the family were forever grumbling about the flock. To hear them, one would suppose that their whole lives were embittered by the trouble and expense of caring for a lot of useless, greedy ducks. Yet when Hen suggested roast duck for Thanksgiving, Deacon Jimmy and Aunt Maria lectured him so severely for his cruelty that he was glad to explain that he was only joking. Once, when the ducks were sick, he dug angleworms for them all one winter afternoon in the corner of the pig-pen, where the ground still remained unfrozen, and Deacon Jimmy nearly bankrupted himself buying pickled oysters which he fed them as a tonic. It was not long before they outgrew their baby clothes and wore the mottled brown of the mallard duck, with a dark, steel-blue bar edged with white on either wing. Blackie, the leader, evidently had a strain of black duck in her blood. She was larger and lacked the trim bearing of the aristocratic mallard. On the other hand, she had all the wariness and sagacity of the black duck, than whom there is no wiser bird. As the winter came on a coop was fixed up for them not far from the kitchen, where they slept on warm straw in the coldest weather with their heads tucked under their soft, down-lined wings up to their round, bright eyes. The first November snow-storm covered their coop out of sight; but when Aunt Maria called, they quacked a cheery answer back from under the drift.

Then came the drake, a gorgeous mallard with a head of emerald-green and snow-white collar and with black-white-gray-and-violet wings, in all the pride and beauty of his prime. A few days and nights before he had been a part of the far North. Beyond the haunts of men, beyond the farthest forests where the sullen green of the pines gleamed against a silver sky, a great waste-land stretched clear to the tundras, beyond which is the ice of the arctic. In this wilderness, where long leagues of rushes hissed and whispered to the wind, the drake had dwelt. Here and there were pools of green-gray water, and beyond the rushes stretched the bleached brown reeds, deepening in the distance to a dark tan. In the summer, a heavy, sweet scent had hung over the marshland, like the breath of a herd of sleeping cattle. Here had lived uncounted multitudes of water-fowl.

As the summer passed, a bitter wind howled like a wolf from the north, with the hiss of snow in its wings. Sometimes by day, when little flurries of snow whirled over the waving rushes, sometimes by night, when a misty moon struggled through a gray rack of cloud, long lines and crowded masses of water-birds sprang into the air and started on the far journey southward. There were gaggles of wild geese flying in long wedges, with the strongest and the wisest gander leading the converging lines, wisps of snipe and badlings of duck of many kinds. The widgeons flew, with whistling wings, in long black streamers. The scaup came down the sky in dark masses, giving a rippling purr as they flew. Here and there, scattered couples of blue-winged teal shot past the groups of the slower ducks. Then down the sky, in a whizzing parallelogram, came a band of canvasbacks, with long red heads and necks and gray-white backs. Moving at the rate of a hundred and sixty feet a second, they passed pintails, black duck and mergansers as if they had been anchored, grunting as they flew. When the rest of his folk sprang into the air, the mallard drake had refused to leave the cold pools and the whispering rushes. Late that season he had lost his mate; and lonely without her and hoping still for her return, he lingered among the last to leave. As the nights went by, the marshes became more and more deserted. Then there dawned a cold, turquoise day. The winding streams showed sheets of sapphire and pools of molten silver. That afternoon the sun, a vast globe of molten red, sank through an old-rose sky which slowly changed to a faint golden-green. For a moment it hung on the knife-edge of the world and then dipped down and was gone. Through the violet twilight, five gleaming, misty-white birds of an unearthly beauty, glorious trumpeter swans, flew across the western sky in strong, swift,

majestic flight. As the shadows darkened like spilt ink, their clanging notes came down to the lonely drake. When the swans start south it is no time for lesser folk to linger. The night was aflame with its million candles as he sprang into the air, circled once and again, and followed southward the moon-path which lay like a long streamer of gold across the waste-lands. Night and day and day and night and night and day again, he flew, until, as he passed over the northwestern corner of Connecticut, that strange food sense which a migrating bird has brought him down from the upper sky into the one stretch of marshland that showed for miles around. It chanced to be close to the base of the Cobble.

All night long he fed full among the pools. Just as the first faint light showed in the eastern sky he climbed upon the top of an old muskrat house that showed above the reeds. At the first step, there was a sharp click, the fierce grip of steel, and he was fast in one of Hen's traps. There the old man found him at sunrise and brought him home wrapped up in his coat, quacking, flapping, and fighting every foot of the way. An examination showed his leg to be unbroken, and Hen held him while Aunt Maria, with a pair of long shears, clipped his beautiful wings. Then, all gleaming green and violet, he was set down among the four ducks, who had been watching him admiringly. The second he was loosed he gave his strong wings a flap that should have lifted him high above the hateful earth where tame folk set traps for wild folk. Instead of swooping toward the clouds, the clipped wings beat the air impotently and did not even raise his orange-webbed feet fom the ground. Again and again the drake tried in vain to fly, only to realize at last that he was clipped and shamed and earth-bound. Then for the first time he seemed to notice the four who stood by, watching him in silence. To them he fiercely quacked and quacked and quacked, and Aunt Maria had an uneasy feeling that she and her shears were the subject of his remarks. Suddenly he stopped, and all five started toward their winter quarters; and lo and behold, at the head of the procession marched the gleaming drake with the deposed Blackie trailing meekly in second place. From that day forth he was their leader, nor did he forget his wrongs. The sight of Aunt Maria was always a signal for a burst of impassioned quackings. Soon it became evident that the ducks were reluctantly convinced that the gentle little woman had been guilty of a great crime, and more and more they began to shun her. There were no more games and walks and caressings. Instead, the four followed the drake's lead in avoiding as far as possible humans who trapped and clipped the people of the air.

At first, the deacon put the whole flock in a great pen where the young calves were kept in spring, fearing lest the drake might wander away. This, of course, was no imprisonment to the ducks, who could fly over the highest fence. The first morning after they had been penned, they all sprang over the fence and started for the pond, quacking to the drake to follow. When he quacked back that he could not, the flock returned and showed him again and again how easy it was to fly over the fence. At last he evidently made them understand that for him flying was impossible. Several times they started for the pond, but each time at a quack from the drake they came back. It was Blackie who finally solved the difficulty. Flying back over the fence, she found a place where a box stood near one of the sides of the pen. Climbing up on top of this she fluttered to the top rail. The drake clambered up on the box and tried

to follow. As he was scrambling up the fence, with desperate flappings of his disabled wings, Blackie and the others, who had joined her on the top rail, reached down and pulled him upward with tremendous tugs from their flat bills until he finally scrambled to the top and was safely over. For several days this went on, and the flock would help him out and into the pen every day as they went to and from the pond. When at last Aunt Maria saw this experiment in prison-breaking she threw open the gate wide, and thereafter the drake had the freedom of the farm with the others. As the days went by, he seemed to become more reconciled to his fate and at times would even take food from Aunt Maria's hands, yet certain reserves and withdrawings on the part of the whole flock were always apparent to vex her.

At last and at last, just when it seemed as if winter would never go, spring came. There were flocks of wild geese beating, beating, beating up the sky, never soaring, never resting, thrusting their way north in a great black-and-white wedge, outflying spring, and often finding lakes and marshes still locked against them. Then came the strange wild call from the sky of the killdeer, who wore two black rings around his white breast, and the air was full of robin notes and bluebird calls and the shrill high notes of the hylas. On the sides of the Cobble the bloodroot bloomed, with its snowy petals and heart of gold and root dripping with burning, bitter blood, frail flowers which the wind kisses and kills. Then the beech-trees turned all lavender-brown and silver, and the fields of April wheat made patches of brilliant velvet-green. At last there came a day blurred with glory, when the grass was a green blaze and the woods dripped green and the new leaves of the apple-trees were like tiny jets of green flame among the pink-and-white blossoms. The sky was full of water-fowl going north. All that day the drake had been uneasy. One by one he had molted his clipped wing-feathers, and the long curved quills which had been his glory had come back again. Late in the afternoon, as he was leading his flock toward the kitchen, a great hub-bub of calls and cries floated down from the afternoon sky. The whole upper air was black with ducks. There were teal, wood-ducks, bald-pates, black-duck, pin-tails, little blue-bills, whistlers, and sud-denly a great mass of mallards, the green heads of the drakes gleaming against the sky. As they flew they quacked down to the little earth-bound group below. Sud-denly the great drake seemed to realize that his power was upon him once more. With a great sweep of his lustrous wings, he launched himself forth into the air in a long, arrowy curve and shot up through the sky toward the disappearing company —and not alone. Even as he left the ground before Aunt Maria's astonished eyes, faith-ful, clumsy, wary Blackie sprang into the air after him, and with the strong awk-ward flight of the black-duck, which plows its way through the air by main strength, she overtook her leader, and the two were lost in the distant sky.

Aunt Maria took what comfort she could out of the three which remained, but only now they had gone did she realize how dear to her had been Greentop, the beau-tiful, wild, resentful drake, and Blackie, awkward, wise, resourceful Blackie. The flock, too, was lost without them, and took chances and overlooked dangers which they never would have been allowed to do under the reign of their lost king and queen. At last fate overtook them one dark night when they were sleeping out. That vampire of the darkness, a wandering mink, came upon them. With their passing

went something of love and hope, which left the Cobble a very lonely place for the three old people.

As the nights grew longer, Aunt Maria would often dream that she heard the happy little flock singing like tea-kettles in their basket or that she heard them quack from their coop and would call out to comfort them. Yet always it was only a dream. Then the cold came, and one night a great storm of snow and sleet broke over the Cobble and the wind howled as it did the night before the drake was found. Suddenly Aunt Maria started out of her warm bed and listened. When she was sure she was not dreaming, she awakened the deacon and through the darkness they hurried down to the door, from the other side of which sounded tu-multuous and familiar quackings. With trembling hands she lighted the lamp, and, as they threw open the door, in marched a procession. It was headed by Greentop, resentful and reserved no more, but quacking joyously at the sight of light and shelter. Back of him, Blackie's soft, dark head rubbed lovingly against Aunt Maria's trembling knees with the little caressing, crooning note which Blackie al-ways made when she wanted to be petted. Back of her, quacking embarrassedly, wad-dled four more ducks, who showed their youth by their size and the newness of their feathering. Greentop and Blackie had come back, bringing their family with them. The tumult and the shoutings aroused old Hen, who hurried down in his night-clothes. These, by the way, were the same as his day-clothes, except for the shoes, for, as Hen said, he could not be bothered with dressing and undressing ex-cept during the bathing season, which was long past.

"Durned if it ain't them pesky ducks again!" he said, grinning happily.

"That's what it be," responded Deacon Jimmy. "I don't suppose now we'll have a moment's peace."

"Yes, it's them good-for-nothin'—" began Aunt Maria, but she gulped and something warm and wet trickled down her wrinkled cheeks as she stooped and pulled two dear-loved heads, one green and the other black, into her arms.

THISTLEDOWN

WHEN the nights are long and the dust is deep,
    The shepherd's at the door;
Hillo, the little white woolly sheep
    That he drives on before!

Never a sound does the shepherd make;
    His flock is as still as he;
Under the boughs their road they take,
    Whatever that road may be.

And one may catch on a shriveling brier,
    And one drop down at the door,
And some may lag, and some may tire,
    But the rest go on before.

The wind is that shepherd so still and sweet,
    And his sheep are the thistledown;
All August long, by alley and street,
    He drives them through the town.

Lizette Woodworth Reese

The Runaway Dory

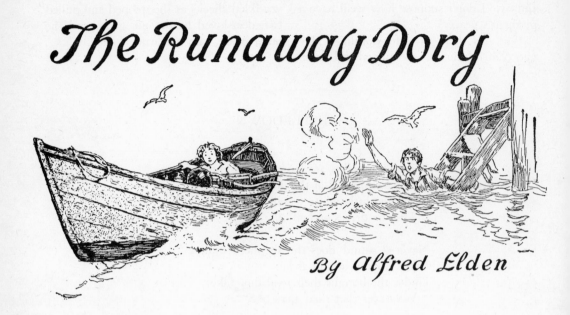

By Alfred Elden

"Now sit tight, kiddie, until I drop this bag of sand in," admonished Jack Maxon to his five-year-old sister Bess sitting in the little power-dory at the foot of the slimy steps.

"All right, Jackie," piped Bess, in her childish treble; "sister's waiting for you."

Jack Maxon was a strong youth for his age, having just turned his seventeenth birthday, but the big bag of white sea-sand he had obtained from the glistening beach at Crab Island was heavy, and he staggered under its weight as he picked his way down the rotting steps which led into the water from the old ramshackle wharf. The summer folks seldom came to this end of Crab Island, for the steamboat landing and the hotel were at the Western Point, and the crude wharf that had been built by the fishermen before the advent of the vacationists was now seldom used.

But Jack's mother knew that for scouring the kitchen floor nothing quite equaled the fine dry sand on the East Beach at Crab Island. And when the supply ran short, it was one of Jack's tasks, an agreeable one to be sure, to replenish it.

He took Bess with him everywhere in his power-dory, for she was an excellent sailor. She was never frightened, always sat where she was told to sit, and had the most implicit confidence in brother Jackie's ability to take her to and from any destination in the Big South Reach. Nor was it misplaced confidence, for the sons of Maine fishermen generally are as at home in a boat as the average farmer's boy is on a horse, and Jack Maxon was no exception to this rule.

During the school vacations he always went lobstering with his father, and Jacob Maxon soon taught his boy all the tricks of the trade. By the time he was twelve Jack could build a lobster-trap equal to any his father put together. He knew all about the proper kind of spruce saplings to cut for his end bows, and how to fashion his buoys and carve his name on them as the law required. He could even knit the heads and fasten them properly in place. So proficient did he become that Jacob bought him a dory when he was fourteen, and near Riggsport Jack had his own little gang of a dozen or so traps, which he baited and hauled as regularly as his father did the hundred or more he had set on a trawl farther off shore.

The motor was something new. Jack had saved every penny he could earn for it; but when the first of June came, he was still twenty-five dollars short of the required amount. Rather than have him lose the pleasure of another summer, Jacob Maxon had generously made up the deficiency, for he had learned, through the medium of his own big motor-Hampton, that the power-propelled craft is a business proposition,—a necessity, not a luxury, to the modern lobster-fisherman.

Jack left his motor running, with the clutch thrown into neutral, when he said good-bye to Bess and went after the sand. He would be absent only a few minutes, and he thought it hardly worth while to open the switch. He stopped on the third step from the water to rest a moment, and, looking off into the open Atlantic, noticed the white-winged coasters coming in, while the tang of the east wind was strong in his nostrils.

"Looks like a spell o' fog, kiddie," he grunted, as he lifted the bag preparatory to tossing it into the dory. "I'll just heave this old Crab Island sand in there and we'll send her over those three miles to Riggsport before any bad weather strikes us. Yo ho! Heave ho! Here she comes!" and he launched the bag at the stern of the dory.

As he gave the toss, there came a splintering sound, a splash, and Jack was struggling in the deep water under the wharf! The step had given way under his weight. Ordinarily a ducking would not have bothered him, for he could handle himself like a diving-loon in the water. But terrifying things were happening in the little power-dory. The breaking step had disconcerted Jack's aim, and the bag of sand, instead of falling in the stern, had landed squarely against the clutch, throwing it into the forward gear as truly as Jack's hand could have done it. As the water churned under her stern, the frail craft gave a plunge forward, snapped like a string the six-thread lobster-warp Jack had twisted around the old cleat, and chugged cheerily off— straight for the open ocean.

In a frenzy, Jack splashed around to the front of the steps, hauled himself out, and shouted at the top of his lungs: "Open the switch, Bess! Quick! Quick! Open the switch!"

But the wind was against Jack, and the smart little dory already was three or four hundred yards away. Moreover, the child did not know a switch from a carbureter. Beside himself with fear and excitement, Jack realized the gravity of the situation. The tank had been filled that morning, and, as the engine was lubricated by pouring the cylinder-oil directly into the gasoline rather than by feed cups, there was no possibility of the motor heating and refusing duty. For the first time in his life, he prayed that the engine might balk. But he knew its reliability only too well. Barring accidents, it would run for hours. Barring accidents! Jack turned pale at the thought. What perils might not be awaiting little Bess alone in the tiny dory with an open ocean and an increasing east wind confronting her?

Jack staggered up the shaky steps and quickly picked his way across the insecure planking. Wiping the blinding tears from his eyes, he looked once more at the rapidly receding dory. Already it was growing smaller, and he could just make out little Bess sitting bolt upright on the midship thwart, her flaxen hair showing plainly against the leaden background of the lowering sea and sky.

"She doesn't realize, she doesn't realize!" moaned the boy, and he started to run for help as fast as his water-soaked garments would permit.

It was full three miles to the western end of the island, where he would find the hotel, the cottages, and the boats which could give him assistance. And what might not happen to little Bess before he could cover the distance! Jack knew he must not keep up the mad pace he had struck, for already his breath was coming in short quick gasps, so he slowed down to a dog-trot, realizing that he would be better off in the end. Suddenly he stopped and looked down to the shore. There in little Gull Cove, bobbing easily at her moorings, was a handsome runabout. Jack gave an exultant shout and started like mad down over the bank for the only cottage in sight. It was owned by Mr. Derry, a Philadelphia merchant, who spent his vacations at Crab Island and had selected this out-of-the-way cove as an ideal place for rest. Jack had not thought of him. He seldom came until the latter part of July and it was now no more than mid-June. But there was the speedy runabout, and there was smoke curling from the cottage chimney.

Jack dashed up the cottage steps and pounded loudly on the door. As he did so, a white card fluttered to his feet. He picked it up and read: "Gone over to the city. Will be back on 5 o'clock boat." There could be no help from Mr. Derry then! Jack felt strangely weak as he hurried down the steps. The shock of falling overboard, the

excitement, and the strain of his unusual physical exertion were telling on him. But this would not do. He must continue his painful run.

Just then his eyes rested on the runabout again. Why could he not take it himself and go to Bess's rescue? He had never run the engine, but he had frequently been for a spin with Mr. Derry in summers past and felt sure he could manage it. It was a case of life and death. Surely there was no harm in it, there was nothing else for him to do, nothing else to be done. Mr. Derry would never call it stealing. So Jack argued with himself, but with Bess's life, perhaps, hanging in the balance, he already had his mind made up and with nervous fingers was untying the painter on the little landing-skiff. Dragging it to the water, he was soon alongside the runabout.

As Jack clambered aboard, his hand rested on one of the cylinders of the fourteen horse-power motor. It was noticeably warm. This was decidedly encouraging. It indicated that the craft was in running order and that Mr. Derry must have been trying out the motor that very morning. Seizing the starting lever, Jack pushed it into the ratchet as he had seen Mr. Derry do, closed the switch, and turned over the big fly-wheel. Nothing happened. Again and again the boy pulled and fumed at the lever, but the heavy fly-wheel ceased to move when he ceased his exertions. What could be the matter?

"I'm a fool!" exclaimed Jack, suddenly, as he scrambled forward. "Who could expect an engine to go without gas?" Opening the globe-valve under the forward deck he tried again, this time with better results. The motor picked up its cycles the first time Jack brought the wheel over the center. He soon had it adjusted and running smoothly. Then, giving the hard grease-cups a turn, he tossed off the mooring-painter, slowly threw in the clutch, and the runabout shot out of Gull Cove like a thing of life.

Rounding the Eastern Point, Jack headed for the open ocean and little Bess. Standing erect he peered ahead. There he made out a tiny dark object two or three miles distant which he knew to be the runaway dory and its precious human freight.

"A stern-chase ought not to be a long chase in this case," mused the lad. "I slowed the dory's motor down a little when I left it to go after the sand, so I don't believe it is making more than four or five miles an hour. This little flyer is doing twelve easily and I guess I could open her up to fourteen; but she's running so slick I won't take any chances of stopping her by monkeying around."

The runabout was fairly eating up the intervening gap between herself and the runaway and Jack began to breathe more easily. It was not going to be such a serious thing after all. He looked ahead again at the dark object which was rapidly assuming the outlines of his dory. Now he could make out a little upright figure on the seat and he knew it to be Bess. She was still all right, and he would soon have her safe in his arms.

But what was this? He strained his eyes ahead. The dory had vanished as if by magic! At the same time the hoarse drone of the fog siren on the Cape shore reached his ears. The fog was rolling in! Already it had enveloped the dory and Bess. So, too, was the wind increasing, and the slap of the waves against the bow of the runabout grew more vicious each moment, and frequent wisps of stinging spray struck him full in the face, half blinding him with the salty moisture.

Jack's heart sank within him. Then he thought of the compass. If he could keep the runabout headed about as she was he would probably come within sight of the dory again. It gave him a slight feeling of

encouragement as he remembered that he had left the steering-tiller in the center notch of the deck-comb. That meant the dory's rudder was straight fore-and-aft. And as the little craft carried but the very slightest port helm, she would not swerve much from a straight course. But it was getting nasty weather off shore, and the swells became higher and higher, longer and longer. The dory would ride them like a sheldrake, Jack reflected, but the runabout was built more for speed than for seaworthiness and was already beginning to act badly. He slid the cover back from the little brass-bound mahogany binnacle. There was no compass there! Jack then noticed for the first time that much of the regular equipment of the runabout was missing. Mr. Derry had not yet put it aboard. Jack bit his lips until the blood came.

"I must use my wits now. Darling Bess's life depends on me!" muttered the plucky boy, as he strove to keep back the tears. From all around there now came the usual Babel of noise that is synonymous with a foggy day. Hoarse blasts of ocean tugs, shriller alarms from harbor craft scurrying inshore, blatant squawkers and wheezy fish-horns from the coasters and trawlers hastening to reach port before the storm broke, now echoed across the water.

There was a possibility that some of these craft might sight the dory and rescue Bess. But Jack knew that in the thick atmosphere with no signal to make her whereabouts known the chances of this were indeed slight.

The runabout was equipped with an underwater exhaust, but the staccato clicking of the valves, as they seated and unseated, prevented Jack from hearing much of anything outside his own craft. He shut down the covers over the motor. That was better. He held his hand to his ears and listened. Faintly he could make out the rhythmic chug-chug-chug of the dory motor. He knew its tone as he knew a comrade's voice. It seemed to be off to the starboard a little. He shifted his wheel a trifle and opened the throttle another notch. The runabout leaped forward and nearly poked her nose through a big roller. Jack hastily slowed down.

"That won't do!" he ejaculated. "If she dives into one of those walls of water, she will keep right on to the bottom!"

But nearer and nearer sounded the exhaust and in another moment Jack made out the tiny craft no more than three or four hundred yards ahead. But where was Bess? There was no sign of her! In an agony of fear Jack clutched the spokes of the side steering wheel. Had she fallen overboard, or had she sunk exhausted to the wet floor-boards? He would soon know. Rapidly the runabout closed up the gap. In another minute it would shoot alongside the dory. Suddenly the motor began skipping and slowing! It would almost stop and then seem to pick up again for a moment, but its struggles became fainter and fainter, more frequent. Jack's heart sank. He was barely holding his own with the dory, and they were still a hundred yards apart.

Running forward he unscrewed the cap to the gasoline tank and peered in. It was too dark to see, but there was a piece of bamboo on the floor evidently used by Mr. Derry for just this purpose. Jack ran it to the bottom of the tank and quickly withdrew it. The end was barely wet half an inch. No gasoline! This settled it. There was nothing more he could do. Yes, there was—just one thing.

Like a madman Jack scrambled aft. Past his former seat, just forward of the motor, he crawled, and out on to the flat stern where his eye had fallen upon the brass steering quadrant to which the tiller ropes were fastened. He could steer by grasping

that, and his hundred and forty pounds weight might settle the stern enough to bring the bow a few inches higher. And this, in turn, might give the gasoline-piping from the tank sufficient pitch so that the last few cupfuls of precious fluid at the bottom would flow back to the carbureter and keep the rapidly dying motor alive until he came alongside the dory. It was a logical deduction, for instantly the motor picked up and ran again with its usual smoothness. But Jack knew it was only a temporary makeshift. However, he was now almost up to the dory. As he shot alongside, his heart gave a bound of joy, for he looked down on the form of little Bess. Tired out with fear and excitement of this strange kidnapping, unmindful of the buffetings of the sea, the child lay curled up on the dory's damp bottom, peacefully sleeping.

Just as Jack leaned out to open the dory's switch, the motor in the runabout stopped dead! Never could he tell just what emotions shot through him as the awful silence struck his ear. He gave one spring from the stern to the cock-pit, another tremendous one over the engine to the bow, and then, with a last, superhuman effort, jumped wildly into the air, both hands outstretched toward the dory. In that brief second it seemed to Jack the thoughts of a lifetime passed through his brain. If he missed, it probably would mean the end of them all, of everything; Bess, himself, and the two boats. And then his right hand closed over the very sternboard of the dory! He clawed his fingers into the unyielding wood as he was dragged along through the water like a huge fish at the end of a line, but in another second he relieved the awful strain by getting a reinforcing hold with his other hand.

He pulled himself forward until he got a good grasp on the starboard gunwale, and then it was a bit easier for him to hold on. But the dory careened frightfully as his weight drew it down. Once a pailful of water sloshed in, soaking little Bess, who awoke with a cry of fright at the strange apparition which, it seemed to her, emerged from the turbulent sea. With a word Jack reassured her, and by a supreme effort he drew himself through the water to the bow, where he reached the switch and opened it. The motor stopped for the first time since early that morning!

Jack allowed himself to slip back along the gunwale to the stern, over which, with a great deal of difficulty, he finally managed to climb. Soaked as he was, he clasped little Bess to his heart and sank exhausted on the dory's bottom. But this was no time for inaction. Quickly starting the motor again, Jack ran back to the runabout, which he could just make out through the fog, and after some difficulty succeeded in getting hold of her stout bow-painter. To this he bent his anchor-line and then paid off perhaps fifty feet, or a little better than eight fathoms. Again he sent his dory ahead and started off with his tow. But where should he steer? He had no compass in the dory, although he had planned to buy one as soon as he could afford it. The wind, he thought, was nearly due east, and he could run with the waves. This, at least, would be bringing him nearer the shore instead of carrying him out to sea. That is, unless the wind shifted!

Out of the mysterious shadows of the fog came a weird moaning. Louder and louder it sounded. It was the siren of some sort of steam craft which seemed to be approaching with terrifying swiftness. Frantically Jack blew back answering warnings with his little mouth chime-whistle. The thin tones were as impotent in carrying power against the rush of the waves and the roar of the wind as an infant's wail. Suddenly, cleaving through the wall of gray, came tearing a black monster. Scarce five hundred yards away it swept past, an ocean tramp bound up the coast to Portland, leaving in its wake a huge mountain of water that rolled on after the little dory and its tow, apparently bent upon engulfing them. But the dory has not been called "the broncho of the sea" for nothing, and gallantly it lifted itself to the very apex of the giant comber. Even more frightful was the dizzy slide down the sharply steep wall of water into the trough of the sea. But when the terror had passed, both tiny craft still floated.

"Whew!" muttered Jack, as he rubbed his hands across his eyes and peered after the monster, which was almost immediately swallowed in the fog, "that was a close shave! A few hundred yards this way, and it would have been all off with us. I don't believe those pilots even looked down at the water. Much they would care if they had crashed through us! I don't believe they would even stop her engines to see if they could help anybody. It is no wonder the poor fishermen on the banks in thick weather are frightened of their lives when they hear one of those ocean liners."

Soon Jack heard, off on his port bow, a low melodious whistle. One long and two short blasts it sounded. This was repeated every two or three minutes. "That's a towboat with some barges, Bess," he said. "Now, if I could get in that fellow's course, he would pick us up. He is moving slowly and there might be a chance." Nearer and nearer sounded the signal which indicated a steam craft with a tow was approaching. Then suddenly the black bow of the big railroad tug, *Antietam*, loomed through the mists. Frantically Jack blew four blasts.

He was now so near that, despite the roar of the elements, the tug captain heard him. He blew four more blasts. He was answered by a number of staccato toots. Down went a window in the pilot-house, and a man waved his hand reassuringly.

A big gong clanged in the engine room and the tug perceptibly slowed. The captain waved again at Jack, pointing ahead and beckoning as though for him to follow. "I know!" exclaimed the plucky boy; "he wants me to keep on until he loses headway, so his barges won't run over him. Keep a stiff upper lip, kiddie."

"I'm not 'fraid, now, Jackie. Brother's with me."

Soon the tow had slowed sufficiently for Jack to steer alongside. Willing hands caught the painter-rope he tossed them, and in a minute he and Bess were safe on board the staunch ocean-tug. The motorboats were allowed to drop astern and the tow proceeded. Up in the steam-heated pilot-house, for it was cold and raw outside this June day, the captain saw to it that Jack and Bess were dried, given hot coffee, and made comfortable. When he heard the story of the day's adventure, he patted Jack on the back and stroked the little girl's flaxen curls. He also caused the lad to turn an uncomfortable red when he slowly remarked, "This old world seems to go right on turning out heroes, my boy. Somehow, it runs in the Yankee blood, I guess. I know I'd be mighty proud if I had a son like you."

It was the luckiest sort of thing for Jack and Bess that the *Antietam* was going in to Riggsport to drop one barge before proceeding to Portland with the other two. It meant that late that afternoon the boy and girl were clasped in the loving arms of their parents, while the people of Riggsport came from far and near to hear the modestly told story of the miraculous escape and of Jack Maxon's courageous pursuit and rescue.

As for Mr. Derry, he received his runabout back again the next day safe and sound. Angry? Well, if he was, he showed it in a most peculiar manner, for on his next trip to the city he brought back the finest dory spirit-compass he could buy and presented it to Jack with his compliments.

IN A FOREST AFLAME

by H. S. Canfield

On a late summer morning, in the North woods of Wisconsin, Sam Kawagasaga, of the Chippewas, said to his hunting-mates:

"Those coals amount to little; the Brule is fifty miles away, and there are many deer; let us go."

So in Indian file, their moccasined feet scarce stirring a dead leaf, they moved northward, and the coals smoldered and smoked a little. Sam had broken the white man's standing law of the woods: "All camp-fires must be extinguished." But he cared little for white man's law. The only one of the pale-faced tribes whose word was weighty was the agent who tried to govern the Chippewa reservation, and his word was weighty only when he had supplies to give out.

One of the coals fell a little apart from its comrades and scorched the edge of a red maple-leaf. The edge curled back from the contact, charred, and burst into tiny flame. The flame, not larger than that of a burning match, touched two fallen leaves of a red birch, and they threw up answering signals. A slow breeze, wandering through the forest, turned over the birch-leaves as if to look at them, then picked them up, carried them a yard or so, and tossed them upon a pile of pine needles and twigs as large as a boy's hat, and for the first time a thin column of smoke arose. It was still a fire that a child could have put out with a pitcher of water; but the pine needles lay next to a thick carpet of leaves, and the carpet ran to the bottom of a dead hemlock, clothed only in tindery bark to its top. "The dry-salt crackling of this," as Thoreau would say, "was like mustard to the ear." The flames spiraled up the trunk gleefully, climbing almost as speedily as squirrels climb, and in a little while the hemlock was a flaring torch from bottom to top, signaling "Danger!"

This tree had grown alone in a space of thirty feet square; and if one man had been there to watch, it would have burned out harmlessly; but it roared unheeded, a slender tower of blaze, and its great limbs fell with crashes, one by one, sending their embers far. Finally it swooned to its fall. One flying fiery branch pitched at the foot of a rotting oak. A small cloud passing swiftly overhead, the only cloud in all the bending vault of blue, shed some drops upon it in its flight, but vainly. The flame caught the brown interior of the oak, and rushed up its hollow shaft, which acted like a chimney. The oak went down, and its upper end caught in the fork of a Norway pine, a noble tree forty inches through at the butt, and its first fork sixty feet from earth. It had stood majestic and columnar for centuries, baring its dark green head bravely to storm and sun, and, when the blasting hand of the fire fell on it, writhed and shivered in protest. With all of its upper part one red waving furnace, black strands of smoke rising from its resin, and

431

sparks pouring down from it in showers, a flashing cascade, it fought its last fight in despair; then, with a sound like the crack of a field-piece, split from fork to root, and fell widely. The conflagration was under headway then, and not any fire department of any city could have checked it for a moment. It was destined to spread havoc and death over a territory thirty miles wide by twenty deep. Looking back from afar, Kawagasaga saw the whirling pall of smoke against the blue of the sky, and hurried on.

It had been a dry summer. No rain had fallen for three months, and the woods were like tinder. So the great fire did not march. It leaped and ran, and old forest giants, green in their age, were withered before it touched them. The sound of it miles away was like the booming of distant thunder.

William Boyd, Jr., was eight years old. His mother called him "Willy," but he preferred to be known as plain "Bill." He always gave that name when asked. This was a North woods child, as different from a city boy as could be imagined—freckle-faced, snub-nosed, sturdy, with gnarled little hands, used to bruises and skin-scrapes in the timber, able to find his way through thickest forest, sound of wind, tireless of leg, and expert with a little ax which he valued above all things. One day, in shutting a new pocket-knife coaxed from his father, he cut a finger badly. Small June Lessard, a French orphan staying with the Boyds, turned pale and said:

"You had better go back to the kitchen, Willy, and wash your hand."

"No," he answered, gazing at the trickling crimson, and resenting both the "Willy" and the doubt of his stoicism; "the blood will wash it."

Through all of the densely shaded country lying along the north fork of the Flam-beau River, William Boyd, Jr., was known to loggers, chainers, skidders, and drivers as a "sliver of the old stump," which was their way of saying that Boyd the elder was only such another child grown taller and stronger.

Father and mother left the shack on the homestead, three miles from the Flam-beau, at daylight that morning, going to Pineville, fifteen miles away. They intended to return in the afternoon; but they had misgivings, not because the children would be left alone,—under ordinary conditions that would be safe enough,—but because the woods were dry.

Those people do not dread terrific winters, when the wolves come out of the timber. The horror of their lives is the forest fire: for they have seen its work. These two had to meet a lawyer, however, in the matter of the purchase of some wild land, and with them, as with all of their kind, a business engagement was paramount almost to life itself.

"Be good, Willy," said Mrs. Boyd, as she climbed into the wagon.

The boy, standing with his ax on his shoulder and a tuft of red hair sticking up through a hole in his hat, disdained to reply.

"Bill," said the father, genially, "take care of June, and split a lot of stove-wood by the time we're back."

That pleased him. "Look out for the bad log in the middle of the bridge over the slough," he advised. Then, as an afterthought: "Those horses will want water when you get to Pine Crick."

Boyd, Sr., laughed and drove off. Bill turned his attention to a large log in the rear of the house, using a wedge to rive stove-wood from it. June sat near him for company, drawing pictures with a charred stick on birch bark. Dinner had been cooked for them and left in the cupboard

—bread, venison, and a pan of milk. At ten o'clock Bill quit work, and said that it was dinner-time, or noon.

June dissented. There was a clock in the house, but it was a mystery to them both. Bill squinted critically at the sun, and declared with exactness.

"It wants ten minutes of dinner-time."

June, accustomed to obey, laid down the birch bark meekly. They dined, clearing up everything they could find. As befitted a man left in charge of the place, Bill strolled about, whistling shrilly and out of tune.

Everything seemed to be in order. The chickens, not realizing his importance, scratched busily and moved out of his way, clucking protests. The two cows and calves were in the four-acre pasture, browsing on brown grass, oblivious of his calls and orders. The black hound with a round tan spot above each eye refused wholly to notice him, lying half asleep on the porch floor, with his long ears spread upon the planking. Only June followed him about, patiently admiring, not daring to disturb his calm with questions.

Bill did not return to his ax and log, but sauntered jauntily, appraising the value of the timber which grew to the edge of the clearing, estimating the number of "feet" each tree would cut, and longing for the time when he could chop it all down and see it hauled to the mill. Desire to "fall" trees was in his blood.

Noon came, and the hound rose and threw up his muzzle and howled quaveringly. North and westward the sky was overspread by a dun cloud. The wind had freshened, and high up little glittering particles were floating past—ashes. There was a slight scent of burning wood in the air. Bill climbed a high stump, thinking he could see better from it, shaded his eyes with his hand, and said oracularly:

"There's a fire out yander."

"Yes," said June, indifferently.

"Fool Injuns, I guess," said Bill.

"Yes," said June.

"If I had my way with Injuns," said Bill, "I'd send 'em to Africa."

"Yes," said June.

Bill jumped eight feet down from the stump, and remarked, "Time f'r me to get at that log." He stopped half-way to it, however. The hound looked at him questioningly, then trotted into the woods, going east. Bill called and stormed, but the dog kept on. Across the back of the yard a rabbit scurried, its ears flat, its eyes bulging. It, too, was going east. A covey of ruffed grouse rose from the edge of the wood and whirred by, going east; then flocks of small birds twittered over, above them a gang of crows, above the crows a dozen hen-hawks, all going east. The river lay that way.

Bill went into the kitchen and locked the back door; though why he did so he could not have told. Passing through the house, he took a long drink of water, for the air was sultry. He saw June's sunbonnet lying on the floor, and picked it up. It was a characteristic of a North woods child that, before going out, he felt in his pocket and saw that knife and matches were safe. He kept the latter in a little glass bottle, tightly corked. He closed the front door behind him, locking that, too; then tied June's bonnet under her round chin. He was white under his freckles, but his brave gray eyes did not flicker as he looked at her.

"That fire's coming here, June," he said almost in a whisper; "we got ter hike."

Even then he ran swiftly back and snatched up his precious ax, patting the blade caressingly with his rough little hand and saying, "Come along, Betsy!"

The roar of the flames could be heard

plainly now—a steady, savage sound. Against the vast black background of smoke, deep crimson below, fading into rose above, sheets of burning bark and small limbs were whirled high. Its belly within a foot of the ground, its great antlers thrown back until the prongs touched its sides, a buck flashed past, distraught with terror. Grasping Jane's wrist firmly with his left hand, holding the ax in his right, Bill plunged into the woods, making for the river. He had no knowledge of the speed of forest fires, and believed that they were safe, but scurried on, determined to make the best time he could. The little girl went cheerfully, having utter confidence in him.

At first there was a trail nearly a yard wide, and along this they trotted comfortably, the boy slackening his pace to match hers, saying something now and then: wondering whether the house would be burned, whether the fire would reach Pineville, where the dog had gone, and so forth. Once, being struck strongly by the thought, he stopped long enough to pant, "It's a good thing we got that meat and milk," then started afresh. In the course of a half-mile, however, the trail narrowed to a foot in width. He placed June behind him and told her to take hold of the tail of his jacket. She did this, and, by leaning on him somewhat, found that she ran more lightly. She was almost as tireless as he, however. With them it was terribly a question of speed, not of endurance. The boy knew that the trail ran straight to the Flambeau,—he had been over it often,— and he headed for the stream because he hoped that its course would break the progress of the fire.

He could not help noticing, however, that, though they were doing their best, the roar of the flames grew louder and the heat more intense. Before they had gone a mile the perspiration was running into his eyes. He glanced back now and then, but the small orphan smiled at him cheerfully and seemed to be doing as well as he. They heard crashes and rustlings in the undergrowth on either hand, showing that many animals were fleeing for their lives. Most of these passed them easily. Some of them came into the path for a few steps, but when they saw the children behind them, turned again to the shelter of the woods.

They saw deer, does, bucks, and fawns half-grown, foxes and rabbits in numbers. The partridges thundered up around them, flying a quarter of a mile at a stretch, then dropping to the ground and running fiercely. Bill went silently over one deep indentation in the trail, and knew that a bear had gone by. They could beat the porcupines,—that was some satisfaction,—and they went past these lumbering creatures as if they had been standing still. It never occurred to them to feel fear of any of the animals. They seemed to know intuitively that at such a time there was universal truce. Once they stopped still for a second with beating hearts, for a great gray timber-wolf loped across the path not ten yards in front of them. Bill valiantly swung his ax high, with his throat thick; but the wolf only slung his head sidewise, glanced at them with a red eye, and went hurriedly on.

There was a half-mile yet to go, and the heat had become almost unbearable. June was sobbing in gasps that seemed to tear her little body. The wild voice of the conflagration was now so great that no other sound was audible. Great birds flapped along in sick fashion, or screamed in the smoke; but the children did not hear them. Looking up, they saw a mass of sparks rushing over them, darting along a hundred yards above the tallest trees, and above the sparks a solid curtain of pitch-black smoke. This smoke had descended to the ground and choked them. Often the wind seemed to bear down and drive the heat more strongly against them, and at such times their flesh smarted beneath their clothing; then it lifted and comparative coolness came.

The trail was barely visible now through the smoke, though all about them the trees still were green. They stumbled upon roots that crossed it, and its many holes; but the dogged fighting spirit of the boy— a spirit that came to him down a long line of woods-conquering folk—was awake, and he plowed on, not stopping to think whether or not he was beaten, possibly not caring, feeling only that his girl playmate was clinging to him, and the river was ahead, and he was going to get to it. He did not know it, but no finer, steadier courage burned in Richard Grenville when he strode the bloody deck of the "Revenge" and called to his sailors, "Fight on! Fight on!" while fifty Spanish sail ringed them around.

Then June fell—fell with a little sobbing cry, her arms helplessly spread out, her chubby face pressing the leaves, her red lips open, her shoulders heaving convulsively. Tired in her short legs was June, her fat knees bleeding from scratches, her cheeks tear-stained, her sunbonnet askew, her bright hair disordered. He turned instantly, and a terrified cry—his first and last—came from him as he saw, not three hundred yards behind them, that booming, sweeping, high-reaching wall of flame. Its breath, blown on him furiously, blistered one cheek even as he looked. The girl child's form was dim to him in the smoke, but he grasped her by both arms and dragged, calling frantically: "Come on, June! Come on!" dragged and tugged and strained, still facing the rushing furnace, then fell himself, down, down, and she with him. They had gone over the Flambeau's edge!

The rush of cold water revived him as he struggled to his feet, still holding to his comrade. The river came nearly to his shoulders, but like a muskrat he bored his way under the overhanging bank. The stream there had washed its way in deeply, and he had over him a roof of earth five feet thick and nearly as wide. Shivering, with the water eddying about his waist, both arms around June, he waited. The smoke swirled down to the surface of the river and far beyond; great brands fell in hissing and were extinguished; over all was the dominant roar of the fire itself. Upstream a great tree fell in and threw the drops high, lying across; fiery hazel-bushes seemed to be torn up by the roots and hurled blazing; the crashing was incessant. The Flambeau did not stop that fire. It was a hundred yards wide, but the flames leaped it as if it were a ditch, and went tearing on; they stopped only when the forest stopped, ten miles away.

The boy noted first the lessening of the noise; then a scorched porcupine, caught within six feet of the water, tumbled in and floated down, kicking feebly; then a wind blew down the river instead of across; fortunately it lifted the smoke a little, for he was almost choked.

There was a rocky ledge running two feet under the surface to a small island in the center of the river; he could mark its course by the water purling over it. They went along this, and clambered out. In the middle of the blackened bit of land a large log was burning, and they dried their clothing by this; the ground was not hot, as there had been little upon it to burn.

So they waited through the afternoon, not knowing what else to do. June snuggled to him, her young nerves still "twisted." Some men came down the river in a boat, looking for chance survivors. Luckily settlers were few, and they were about to turn back, after having hallooed lustily, when they were startled at hearing Bill's shrill "Whoopee!"

"Where's your dad and mam?" one of the men asked, as the children climbed in and squatted between the thwarts.

"Gone to town," said Bill. "He'll be back to-night. Seen our dorg?"

"No," said the man. "We'll put you off where the main tote-road crosses the river and your folks'll pick you up there. But you'll have to camp for a while, I guess. That fire ain't left any houses behind it. How you feeling?"

"Hungry," said Bill. "I think June's hungry, too; and—and I lost my ax."

JESSIE

By Bret Harte

Jessie is both young and fair,
Dewy eyes and sunny hair;
Sunny hair and dewy eyes
Are not where her beauty lies.

Jessie is both fond and true,
Heart of gold and will of yew;
Will of yew and heart of gold—
Still her charms are scarcely told.

If she yet remain unsung,
Pretty, constant, docile, young,
What remains not here compiled?
Jessie is a little child!

THE BLACK DUCK

by Virginia Woodward Cloud

YESTERDAY I found a delightful book, and of course it was in an attic. Our ancestors may not have stored things in attics expressly to have us discover them, but we continue to do so from time to time, and they are undoubtedly more interesting from being a bit cobwebby and mysterious. The attic in which I found the delicious book had in it hidden things which looked as if they might be the first patterns of everything we use now. Probably the most desirable trait about this attic was that it did not possess a place for anything or anything in its place.

For instance, I found a bonnet hanging on a pair of andirons.

But for the green silk strings no one would ever dream it was a bonnet. It looked much more like a coal-scuttle, and had as many enormous bones as a prehistoric skeleton. It must have belonged to a very-great-grandmother. No one without several greats before her name could have worn that bonnet! Behind the andirons was a cradle, and in the cradle was a long pole with a red silk arrangement which once meant a fire-screen. Beside it stood a clock with a moon face and long chains and weights. It looked so much like a Dutch doll, with just head and legs, that I laughed aloud. But an attic is not a place in which to laugh unless one has company. Everything was rebukingly still, and so was I immediately.

Near the clock was a table shaped like a long-legged spider. It looked as if just ready to walk off alone. I was quite sure it belonged to the bonnet and the fire-screen, and that somewhere there were blue cups and saucers, which one might break by talking too loud, and that they belonged to the table.

In a far corner stood a picture with its face to the wall.

I drew it out and rested it against the table. Of course it was dusty. I never heard of the right sort of an attic which was kept dusted. It was the picture of a lady. I knew that at once, just as we always know a lady when we see one. The picture was rather dim, but I could easily discern that she was very young and slim, with a white throat and bright, dark eyes. Her hair, done very high, was of a ruddy brown, and she had on a short-waisted white satin frock, and held a half-open fan primly in her hands.

It was easy to see that she was just where she belonged—beside the spider-legged table. I had no doubt that she could have told the whereabouts of the blue cups and saucers! Thinking about this lady, my eyes encountered another pair of eyes staring straight at mine. My heart jumped once and stood still, until I recognized the eyes as my own.

I was gazing into a mirror. It was a dim, queer mirror with a crack like an enormous smile across its face, and pale enough to hold only the ghost of light which once shone in it. Two rods supported it. They held a brass candlestick apiece, and rested on a little stand which had a drawer. I sat down on a hair-trunk before this little stand. The drawer had brass knobs and might have been locked once, but time or rust made it open easily, and then—such an assortment of odds and ends! Faded ribbons and flowers and beads, and a feather-fan which, when I opened it, filled the air with a musty dust that made me sneeze! Under these scraps was a box, and under the box was a book—*the* book.

The box first.

It held a silk bag, yellow with age—a bag which used to be called a reticule. In the reticule were a handkerchief, fine and lacy and also yellow; a tiny looking-glass set in shells; and a square of paper carefully pinned. The last contained only dry, yellow rose-leaves. Under the bag lay another fan. It had delicate sticks and a cord and tassel which once were rose-colored; and painted on one pale blue side was a young person in rose-colored panniers and enormous hoops, who was coyly accepting a bouquet from a young gentleman who wore crimson breeches and a white wig.

Where had I seen that fan? My eyes met those of the lady. Yes, the same fan was in her hand. I could just make out a glimpse of the rose-hued damsel and the bouquet. Inside the box-top was written one word, nearly faded out:

Lois

She was Lois, then, this young lady with the slim white throat and the dark eyes, and this was her fan; and Lois, I knew, had been my great-grandaunt. The book came next.

It had a square of paper pasted on its brown cover, and on it was written in unformed characters:

LOIS, HER BOOK

Underneath in the same childish letters:

"mother Says i shall Rite dayly in This book that Whitch doth impress Me most and Also that falt whitch needs Be coreckted."

She immediately adds:

"i need Care in My Riting and speling."

There begins from that date, on which she says she is eight years of age, a daily chronicle written with laborious care. It noted some occurrences which the child thought important, or some faults which she was trying to correct.

The second entry reads thus:

"the Ducks strayed to the Berynground [doubtless the churchyard] i Went to fetch them but Did not Want to."

The third entry:

"Father says i Can Hav Clovers Caf fore my Owne. i wud Hav it wen it Grows Bigger and Get More munny. Mother says Munny is A Root of Evle whitch I do not Understand We do Not plante munny."

These entries varied only according to the daily duties in the domestic régime, or the childish faults which were sometimes noted with a large black cross on certain days. On two occasions the pages were sadly smeared and blurred as if unwilling tears had been shed thereon. Once was when the Dominie made her turn her face to the wall for being late to school because she stopped to pick blackberries. Again was when her mother forced her to rip out a long seam twice and do it over. This last was evidently written in an outburst of childish rebellion, for the black cross was very heavy.

At a date two years later my Aunt Lois's handwriting and spelling had improved vastly. The steady, painstaking practice of writing daily in her book showed its results. In the time which followed she grew older rapidly, doubtless from hearing and experiencing the excitement shed around her by the expected War of the Revolution. The Day Book soon ceased to be a daily duty. When she wrote, it was with the grave fears and hopes which she heard uttered by her elders, yet, withal, a note here and there of her own vivacious spirit which she admits "doth cause my mother ofttimes to shake her head and rebuke me for having many words."

At the bursting of the war-cloud of American Revolution she goes on to tell of busy hours filled by herself and her mother in preparing food and supplies. Then comes the day when her father left home to enter the army, and again the page is blurred.

There is little of importance thereafter until the longest entry of all, which I will copy from my Aunt Lois's book, beginning under the date of January 10, 1777.

She writes:

When I awakened New Year's night and beheld my mother over me with a candle, I thought it was a dream, but she laid her hand on me and spake aloud:

"Lois! Lois! Awake quickly; I have need of thee!"

[The mother of my great-grandaunt being raised a Friend, both she and Aunt Lois had acquired their mode of speech. She continues:]

"It is not dawn," said I; for not having a man to help us, I must even go out to the barn at dawn and make ready for the day.

"No, God be thanked, it is not dawn," quoth my mother. "Thou must be up and away before break of dawn, my child; so hasten!"

I sprang up and quickly put on my clothing, knowing that my mother would explain it in her own time, for at best she hath few words. Coming nearer, she said, "Breathe it not, Lois, but thy father is here,—shot!"

"My father!—here—shot?" I began in

fear. But she urged me to hasten and pause not. My mother then made known to me how that my father had been given a most perilous errand,—namely, to gather some information, and bear it or send it by means of a paper to our Commander-in-chief, General Washington, he then being, as my father surmised, on his way from Trenton to Princeton, but nobody knew by what road. My father, in making a wide circuit around for better concealment, was shot; but not so "General," his horse, who rushed for the woods, and in so doing concealed my father the better. My mother went on to tell me that inasmuch as my father did lose several hours from unconsciousness and weakness, though still clinging to General's neck, he found himself when he roused all but home, whereto General had brought him straight.

"'T is wonderful he did not fall off!" spake my mother; "and, Lois, see to 't no one learns from thee of thy father's coming."

"Nay," quoth I; "there is no other gossip to prattle with saving thyself and Clover."

Then marked I my mother's face as she laid her hand upon her heart and let her eyes rest upon me, and some way I understood.

"Lois," quoth she, "thy father's errand must be finished for him. I dare not leave him to go."

"Nay," said I; "I will go, mother."

She spake not, but turned away, and I saw she was sorely troubled.

"Mother," spake I, hastening the more, "let it not fright thee. I know not what the errand be, but my father is wise and good, and I will but do as he saith. I have no fear!"

"Nay, hadst thou more I would fret less," spake my mother. "Thou art thy father again, Lois,—ever venturesome and knowing not of fear!"

While speaking she laid by me my heavy quilted petticoat and pelisse, for the snow which came after was already in the air. Then by the lantern's light, at my mother's bidding, I put my own saddle on General George, adding my father's saddle-pockets. For General, whom I have named after good General Washington, hath tremendous strength, and was already, having had a meal, fit to be off again. I then straightway ate a hasty bit which my mother had prepared, placing the remainder in the saddle-pockets. My mother then put on me her own quilted bonnet, and over it tied a heavy comforter: I still not knowing what it was I should undertake, but knowing I should hear in good time. I strove to push back the comforter, but my mother adjusted it, saying:

"Nay; let be! 'T were better to have thy face covered when a lass like thee goes about at such an hour."

Then in the dim light I sought my father's couch, where he had fallen an hour before.

"My daughter, are you there?" spake my father.

I answered, and drew nigh as he said:

"You are going an errand for me, daughter?"

"Yes, father," quoth I.

"Do you know its nature, Lois?" said he, weakly.

"No, father," said I.

"It is to bear that which is of value and intrusted to me. It must go to the first officer of the American army you can find this side of the town."

"The town!" quoth I, in wonderment; for that is full thirty miles away.

"And I would not have you go thinking it a safe or wise thing for a maid to do," quoth he. "There are dangers which I cannot even warn you against, not knowing them. Only this: you may be arrested and searched, Lois; hence you must bear

naught about your person. You must also feign some reason for going toward the town at this time; hence, your mother will put in the saddle-pockets two ducks she hath already killed. You are going to bear them to Mistress Van Tyne, who dwells this side of the town; they are a New Year's dinner from thy mother—" His voice failed from weakness, and my mother held a hot drink to his lips before he went on.

"One thing, my daughter: should you be halted on the way, and should they strive to take the ducks, give up the white one with a show of resistance, but hold to the black one with life and wit—"

"And why the black one, father?" I asked.

"The papers are in its craw."

I being too amazed at this to speak, he went on.

"Should you find no trouble, and should you meet with one of our own commanders, give him the paper or the duck, and tell him straightway what I have told you. Should no one meet or molest you, ride on to Mistress Van Tyne's, near by the town. Tell her all, and that 't is pressing needful that the black duck be sent on to General Washington. I know not where you may find any of our men six hours hence. Keep but your eye keen, your wit clear, and your trust in God. Go, now!" I kissed my father and went, as he bade me.

"The pass, which may be of use to thee, is stitched in the crown of thy hood, lest wind blow it away," said my mother, kissing me. She followed me with a lantern, as I went out and mounted General George.

It was very dark and cold; and my mother held my hand closely for an instant, and then went in and shut the door. There was no sound as General cantered down the lane, saving here and there the faint bark of a dog, and always the echo of the horse's hoofs on the frozen ground. I knew that he must not go too hard at the first; for both he and I would need the speed and exercise when it grew colder, as it soon did. I felt it but little for some time, so muffled was I by the comforter. Indeed, at cock's crow I marked two women going toward their barns with lanterns; but they would not have known me, and remembering I was about business of moment, I made no sign. Now and then I felt the saddle-pockets to be certain of the safety of the ducks, and of the bag of feed which mother had tied on for General.

Of the long, lonely ride in the darkness my Aunt Lois says but little. I think she must have been bent too seriously on her errand to feel actual fear, although once she speaks of being startled for an instant by a scarecrow in a field "which did come upon me suddenly." She continues:

The way was all alike save that as I rode I became more and more stiff and tired; but I feared to get down lest some one should come suddenly from ambush and steal the ducks. Mile after mile did General and I travel before the first summons to halt, which was about daybreak. The sudden stopping brought my heart into my mouth. I had turned a corner and come upon a clearing against a bit of woods. There was a small fire, and some men around it. Another did walk sentry-like to and fro. 'T was he who bade me halt. He scanned me most curiously, and then laid his hand on General's bridle.

"You are my prisoner, mother; so dismount!" quoth he, very superior-like.

"Nay, nay, good sir," said I, ducking a courtesy as well as one may on horseback. "I have often heard tell how that the brave British would fight only their equals or superiors in strength, whereas old women and children are by right left unmolested."

"Truly said, mother," quoth he, laughing. "You bear at least a ready tongue, but you may be bearing more than your tongue, for aught I know. Whither would you ride at this hour, and alone?"

"I go alone because I know each stick and stone of the way, good sir; and I go for that I bear a pair of ducks for Mistress Van Tyne as a New Year's gift from our own farm."

He shook his head, and the men near by began to gather around, while my heart did sink lower than the ground on which General was pawing. But at the instant two horsemen appeared out of the woods. One rode rapidly up and drew rein before me, and I marked that he was fair and well-built, with honest blue eyes and fearless of mien.

"Whom have we here?" he asked.

"A prisoner, sir," said the man at General's head.

"Nay," quoth the young officer, "'t is an old lady! What will you, mother? You had better turn about and go back home before you meet others."

"Nay, good sir," quoth I; "for I have a pass permitting my family to go to and from the town with supplies. But 't is stitched in the crown of my hood. So I would I might remove my hood, good sir, and prove it thee!"

At this the young officer laughed, and said he, "I am sorry, mother, to have you remove your hood in the cold; but it needs must be unless you become my prisoner before instead of afterward!"

"Nay, nay," quoth I; "I would fain remove my hood, then; for I have had that off before, but I have never yet been prisoner of war!" So dropping the reins on General's neck, I unwound the comforter. The air felt most grateful to my head, which was warm, and my face flushed; and as I pushed the hood back my hair did tumble all about my neck in troublesome confusion, and the soldier who had cried "Halt!" exclaimed aloud:

"By my sword, 't is a lass!"

The officer made a sign toward him, and as I looked up he bowed, his own face being quite flushed, and said:

I was fumbling at the saddle-pockets, meanwhile, with a show of courage which I did not feel, for my heart was thumping because of the black duck.

I drew it out,—for I saw he was waiting to see what I might carry,—and laid it

Lois delivers the black duck to General Mercer

"You will pardon me, fair Mistress, for mistaking your age!"

"Surely, sir, 't was the fault of the hood and comforter," quoth I, meeting his frank, blue eyes as I handed him the pass from out the hood.

"This allows no luggage, Mistress," he spake hesitatingly.

"Oh, I bear no luggage," said I, "save a New Year's dinner which I did raise myself."

across General's neck, meanwhile stroking its glossy plumage.

"And wilt thou help me lift the other one out, good sir," said I, "that thou mayest examine the saddle-pockets and the bag of feed for my horse?" So, holding the white duck in one hand, he examined the saddle-pockets with the other.

"Following my own will, Mistress," said he, "I would fain let you go on; but know you not that Lord Cornwallis hath already crossed the Assanpink, and hath his forces stationed in the town? Hence you will surely be arrested and searched this side of it. Therefore, Mistress, my duty is—" He paused, and in a second I saw that I had to do as my father had enjoined, and use my wit.

Taking up the black duck, I held it outward, saying, "Good sir, please hold this, too, for me an instant"; which he did; and I slipped from General's back, nearly falling from stiffness as I reached the ground. I shook out my petticoat, and showed the empty saddle; then I laid my hand upon his horse's neck, looking up in his face, and said I:

"Thou hast my word, sir, that thou dost hold in thy hands my sole reason for going up to town. I bear naught else about my person, and that I may prove the ducks quite good to eat, I pray thee keep one of them, and so share our New Year's dinner."

"Go to, little Mistress!" quoth he, looking down on me, with a laugh. "A skilful pleader for one so young! Thinkest to bribe the British army?"

"Nay," said I, meeting his honest blue eyes as I leaped back on General. "I think not, good sir, indeed; but I would fain thou shouldst keep one, for it is like as not thou art far from home." As I spoke, I took the black duck, and left the white one in his hand.

"Thank you kindly, sweet Mistress," said he; "but despite my will, I must do my duty, and I fear me thou must come with us."

Even as he spake there was a burst of musketry from the woods behind them, which made him wheel around, and every man spring to his feet. In a trice I had given General such a cut as he never had before, and darting ahead, dashed down the road to the left, whither I galloped like mad, pausing not to look behind until I knew there was a mile or more between us, and that I was not being overtaken. Then, halting, I fastened the duck again in the saddle-pocket, and let General take it slowly while I wondered what next to do.

My Aunt Lois then tells of her quandary on learning the town to be full of British.

"I did not fret to think of being a prisoner," she writes; "for at worst I knew they would not shoot a defenseless maid. But I feared me lest they should seize the black duck."

She then made up her mind to go straight ahead, and to hold until the last to the black duck—"which," she says, "they should not take from me unless by force of arms, and then I was determined to go likewise!"

She had no further stoppings until she found herself six miles from the town, riding by a piece of woods. She heard there the sounds of horses and of tramping.

"And then it was," she writes, "that I felt somewhat of fright, and straightway wheeled General into the woods, and waited. It was a body of men coming very rapidly and, methought, quietly, and my heart thumped loudly until—what was my joy to see the uniforms of our own American army! Knowing this, perhaps, to be my only chance, I rode out in the road straight before them, whereat they halted in much surprise."

Then Aunt Lois tells of her interview with their leader, General Mercer, who got his mortal wounds shortly after at Stony Bridge.

"He was in great haste," she writes, "and I said I did but bear a black duck of which I must tell him, whereupon he ordered his men to march on, and straightway said he, in some surprise:

"'Now, Mistress, what is it?'

"'It is my father's—John Bradley's—errand,' quoth I, 'to bear this black duck to one who would send it or its contents to General Washington this morn, immediately.'

"'So!' said he, drawing a long breath. 'And thy father?'

"'Was shot while making his way with the papers.'

"'And the papers?'

"'Are in the duck's craw, sir,' said I, drawing the bird from out my saddle-pocket.

"'And at what time didst start, little Mistress?'

"'At two o'clock this morn, sir.'

"'Well, well!' He took the duck and slung it across his saddle before him. 'I must hasten. I shall see General Washington within an hour, God willing, and he shall get the papers—if not by me, by some one else. Good day, Mistress Bradley.' He bowed. 'The American army has done well to count you in it!'

"'In truth, sir,' said I, 'if they count by hearts, and not by muskets, their biggest following is left behind!'

"Which, when I did tell my mother to-day, she shook her head at me from the buttery door, saying, 'Lois! Lois!' But my father, from his couch where he lieth weak, saith, 'Tut! Let the lass be, so that she doth but speak the truth!'—which from my heart I did."

My Aunt Lois's ride home was uneventful. As every step took her further from the approaching armies, she was unmolested, and feared naught save that General might give out. It was snowing hard for the greater part of her journey, and the horse stumbled homeward, stiff with cold and lame with fatigue. She writes:

"Twice after night-time I fell asleep on General's neck; and when I spied the candle-light from the kitchen window, from sheer joy I could have wept. But I called to mind what the officer had said about being in the American army, so bore up until my mother did open the door and fly outward. I could not stand alone, and fell forward when I slipped from General's back. They raised me and bore me into the house.

"But once in the light of the fire, I marked, for the first time in my life, the tears running down my mother's face as she held a hot posset to my lips.

"'Tell father it went safely,' said I,—'the black duck'; and then I must have fallen dead asleep at once, on the settle Whereunto my mother drew me."

My Aunt Lois must have slept for many hours after that ride, of the hardship of which she says so little, though she owns, the second day after, to "a sorely stiff and cramped feeling."

I think, though, that she was fully repaid even before her father showed her a letter, long afterward, signed "G. Washington," which among other things expressed the writer's thanks "for an important service rendered his country."

"I went a dangerous errand," said Aunt Lois's father; "but 't would have been naught save for thee, my daughter; so yours was the service!"

A year later my Aunt Lois writes lightheartedly of a short trip southward with her father, who was quite recovered "but for a slight lameness," when she attended a grand ball "with my hair done high, and wearing a new sleeveless white satin gown —the same which father hath had done in the portrait." On which occasion she had the honor of a presentation to General and Lady Washington; whereupon General Washington, who knew her father, said:

"And is this the Mistress Bradley who carried the duck?"

"Yes, your Excellency," said Aunt Lois, laughing,—"a *pair* of ducks; but I bethought me that thou wert sharing naught else with the British, hence I gave them one!"

"At which," she writes, "my mother doth shake her head, and say, 'Oh, Lois! Lois! Thou wilt ever have the last word!'"

Sweet, bright, brave Aunt Lois!

I closed the book, smiling at its blithe pages, and knowing that some time sad ones must follow. But, if they do, they belong solely to the dim, ghostly attic and the dead rose-leaves, whereas I know she would gladly have us read about the black duck!

MORNING

By Emily Dickinson

Will there really be a morning?
  Is there such a thing as day?
Could I see it from the mountains
  If I were as tall as they?

Has it feet like water-lilies?
  Has it feathers like a bird?
Is it brought from famous countries
  Of which I have never heard?

Oh, some scholar! Oh, some sailor!
  Oh, some wise man from the skies!
Please to tell a little pilgrim
  Where the place called morning lies!

ON A MOUNTAIN TRAIL

by Harry Perry Robinson

WE had no warning. It was as if they had deliberately lain in ambush for us at the turn in the trail. They seemed suddenly and silently to rise on all sides of the sleigh at once.

It is not often that the gray timberwolves, or "black wolves," as the mountaineers call them, are seen hunting in packs, though the animal is plentiful enough among the foot-hills of the Rockies. As a general rule they are met with singly or in pairs. At the end of a long and severe winter, however, they sometimes come together in bands of fifteen or twenty; and every old mountaineer has a tale to tell,—perhaps of his own narrow escape from one of their fierce packs, perhaps of some friend of his who started one day in winter to travel alone from camp to camp, and whose clean-picked bones were found beside the trail long afterward.

It was in February, and we, Gates and myself, were driving from Livingston, Montana, to Gulch City, fifty miles away, with a load of camp supplies—a barrel of flour and some bacon, coffee, and beans; a blanket or two, and some dynamite (or "giant powder," as the miners call it) for blasting; a few picks and shovels, and other odds and ends. We had started at daybreak. By five o'clock in the evening, with some ten miles more to travel, the worst of the trail was passed. There had been little snow that winter, so that even in the gulches and on the bottoms the exposed ground was barely covered; while, on the steep slopes, snow had almost entirely disappeared, leaving only ragged patches of white under overhanging boughs, and a thin coating of ice in the inequalities of the hard, frost-bound trail, making a treacherous footing for the horses' hoofs.

The first forty miles of the road had lain entirely over hills,—zigzagging up one side of a mountain only to zigzag down the other,—with the dense growth of pine and tamarack and cedar on both sides, wreathed here and there in mist. But at last we were clear of the foot-hills and reached the level. The tall forest trees gave place to a wilderness of thick underbrush, lying black in the evening air, and the horses swung contentedly from the steep grade into the level trail, where at last they could let their legs move freely in a trot.

Hardly had they settled into their stride, however, when both animals shied violently to the left side of the trail. A moment later they plunged back to the right side so suddenly as almost to throw me off into the brush.

Then, out of the earth and the shadow of the bushes, the grim, dark forms seemed to rise on all sides of us. There was not a sound,—not a snap nor a snarl; but in the gathering twilight of the February evening, we saw them moving noiselessly over the thin coat of snow which covered the ground. In the uncertain light, and moving as rapidly as we did, it was impossible to guess how many they were. An animal which was one moment in plain sight, running abreast of the horses, would, the next moment, be lost in the shadow of the bushes, while two more dark, silent forms would edge up to take its place. So, on both sides of us, they kept appearing and disappearing. In the rear, half a dozen jostled one another to push up nearer to the flying sleigh,—a black mass that filled the whole width of the trail. Behind those again, others, less clearly visible, crossed and recrossed the roadway from side to side. They might be twenty in all—or thirty—or forty. It was impossible to tell.

For a minute I did not think of danger. The individual wolf is the most skulking and cowardly of animals, and only by some such experience as we had that night does a hunter learn that wolves can be dangerous. But soon the stories of the old mountaineers came crowding into my mind, as the horses, terrified and snorting, plunged wildly along the narrow trail, while the ghost-like forms glided patiently alongside—appearing, disappearing, and reappearing. The silent pertinacity with which, apparently making no effort, they kept pace beside the flying horses was horrible. Even a howl or a yelp or a growl would have been a relief. But not so much as the sound of their footfalls on the snow was to be heard.

At the first sight of the wolves, I had drawn my revolver from the leather case in which it hung suspended from my belt. Gates, handling the reins, was entirely occupied with the horses; but I knew, without need of words, that he saw our pursuers and understood the peril as well as I. "Have you your gun?" I shouted in his ear.

A negative shake of the head was all the answer. So we must trust to the six cartridges in my revolver.

"How many wolves are there, do you suppose?" again I called.

Again he shook his head, as if to say that he could not guess.

So the minutes passed and we swept on, rising and falling and swaying with the inequalities in the trail. The dark forms, growing more indistinct each minute, were hanging doggedly to the sleigh.

Suddenly I became aware that a wolf was almost at my elbow; its head was on a level with my waist as I sat in the low sleigh. In the darkness I could plainly see the white teeth, and the dim circle of the eyes. I hardly had to lean over at all to place the muzzle of the revolver within a foot of the great round head before I fired. I saw the black form roll over and over in the snow as we went by. Simultaneously, two other shadowy shapes that had been running abreast of the horses, in advance of the animal that was shot, dropped back; and looking over my shoulder I could see them throw themselves upon their wounded fellow. As the sea-gulls, following in the wake of a vessel in mid-ocean, swoop from all directions upon some floating scrap that has been thrown overboard, so from both sides of the trail the dark figures rushed together into one struggling mass behind the sleigh; and for the first time we heard them snapping and snarling at one another, as they tore their comrade to pieces.

The horses appeared to know that in some way a gleam of hope had come. They ceased plunging and seemed to throw all their energies into putting as wide a space as possible between them and the yelping pack behind.

How long would the respite be? Seconds passed until half a minute had gone. Then a minute. Could it be that they had left us —that the horrible race was over?

But even as the hope was forming itself in my mind, I became aware of a dim, gray thing moving beside me. A moment later another appeared, close by the horses' heads, and behind us the trail was again full of the jostling pack.

It was terrible beyond expression, the utter noiselessness with which they resumed their places,—apparently tireless; keeping pace with the racing horses without a sign of effort; patient as fate itself. Have you ever been on a fast steamship— say a "P. and O." boat in Indian waters where the sea is transparent—and, leaning over the stern, watched a shark following the vessel? If so, you remember how, hour after hour and day after day, the dark, vaguely outlined body, not more distinct than the shadow of a cloud upon the waves, stayed, motionless to all appearance, just so many feet aft in the ship's wake, no matter how fast she moved. To me, and I think to every one who has seen it, that silent, persistent, haunting presence is the very embodiment of ruthlessness and untiring cruelty. There, in the twilight and shadow, was the same silence, the same indistinctness, the same awing impression of motionless speed, the same horror of the inevitable, in that pursuit by the wolves.

But soon their tactics changed. Either they had grown bolder, or the wolf they had eaten among them had put a keener edge upon their appetites. There were now four or five of the ghostlike forms moving abreast of the horses on my side of the sleigh alone. On the other side more were visible. They were now closing in upon us, with determination. Suddenly I saw one make a spring at the throat of the off horse, and, missing his aim, fall back. The horses had been terrified before; from that moment they lost all control of themselves. Neither the driver's voice nor his hands

upon the reins had any influence upon them as they tore wildly down the narrow path between the bushes, snorting, throwing their heads from side to side, and breaking now and again into short, shrill neighs of terror. The breath from their nostrils and the steam from their bodies made a white cloud in the wintry night air, almost enveloping them and us, and at times blotting out of sight the wolves beneath.

But the pack was again closing in. In front of all, I could see one running under the very noses of the horses, keeping just beyond the reach of their hoofs, and evidently waiting for the right moment to make a final leap at their throats. Leaning forward, and steadying my aim as well as I could in the rocking sleigh, I fired full at the whole dark mass in front. Apparently the ball passed harmlessly through them, but in an instant all had vanished—behind and into the bushes—as a swarm of flies vanish at the waving of a handkerchief. Only for a second, however, and one after another they were back again.

A second shot, fired again at random into the mass, was more successful; and once more we saw them drop back and crowd together in the trail behind us while the snapping and snarling grew fainter as the horses plunged on.

Half of the last ten miles had now been traveled, and five miles more would bring us to Gulch City and security. The excitement of that race was unspeakable: the narrow lane of the trail lying white ahead of us and behind us between the dark borders of the brush, seen fitfully through the steam from the maddened horses.

But the respite this time was shorter than before. Once more our relentless foes gathered round us, silently, one by one. The wolves seemed to know as well as we, that time was short and escape lay not far away; for hardly had the pack settled in their places round us before I saw one animal throw himself recklessly at the horses' throats. There was a sudden mad rearing up of both the horses, a wild, despairing neigh, a short yelp from the wolf's throat, and the dark form that had seemed to hang for a moment, leech-like, to the chest of one of our brave beasts was beaten down under the hoofs.

The others did not wait even for the sleigh to pass, but leaped upon the struggling form even as the runners were upon it. In my excitement I did a foolish thing. Leaning over, and thrusting my revolver almost against the skins of the fierce brutes, I fired two shots in quick succession. They had their effect, I know, for I saw one of the dark figures throw itself convulsively out of the mass into the brush, where others sprang upon it, and a death-cry went up in the night air. But we could ill spare the ammunition.

This idea evidently occurred to Gates. Leaning suddenly toward me, but with his eyes fixed on the horses and the road ahead, he called:

"How many shots have you left?"

"Only one."

"Not even one apiece for us?"

And I knew that he was in earnest. I knew also that he was right; that it would be better to die so, than to be torn to pieces by that snarling, hungry crew.

But it was too late now. Five shots out of the six were spent, and twenty minutes yet must pass before we could reach the camp. And even while these few words were being said the pack was close upon us again. Fiercer now, and more determined than ever to make an end of it, they crowded around. One even flung himself at the low side of the sleigh to snap at me, and his teeth caught for a moment in the sleeve of my coat as I struck him on the head with the clenched hand holding the pistol. On both sides, too, they jostled each other, to reach the flying horses, and I knew that in

a few seconds more I must sacrifice the last cartridge in my revolver.

As a forlorn hope I snatched the buffalo-robe which lay on Gates' knees, and threw it to them. But they hardly stopped to tear it to pieces. There was more satisfying food in the sleigh. And they closed around the horses again.

For the first time Gates turned to look at me.

"Jack!" he called excitedly, "the giant powder!"

For a moment I did not grasp his meaning. Seeing my indecision he shouted again:

"The giant powder, Jack!"

Then it came to me. Thrusting the pistol into its case, I scrambled over into the rear part of the sleigh, and as I did so the wolves that were following behind fell back a few feet. Hastily fumbling among the various supplies, I found the old sack in which the sticks of dynamite were wrapped, and with them the small package of caps and fuse. Taking three of the sticks, I tied them tightly together with my handkerchief and, quickly fitting the end of an inch of fuse— for, in this case, the shorter the piece the better—into a cap, I thrust the latter into the center of the three sticks. I was still at work, when a sudden swing of the sleigh and a cry from Gates warned me that something was the matter. The horses were plunging violently, and as the near horse reared I saw that a wolf had leaped upon its withers and was clinging, with its teeth apparently in the side of the horse's neck. In their terror, the horses had stopped, and were actually backing us into the brush. Something had to be done, and with some vague hope, I fired the last shot from the revolver into the dark circle which already surrounded the plunging horses. The shot had its effect, for one of the brutes leaped into the air with a yelp and fell backward into the bushes. The horse, too, sprang sud-

denly forward, and the wolf that was clinging to it fell to the ground and was trampled under the hoofs. In an instant, those of
the pack that had not already flung themselves upon the wounded animal in the
bushes, rushed upon this one that was lying
lifeless or stunned from the horses' feet;
and once more, for a few seconds, we had
breathing space, and the sleigh sped along
through the keen air, our enemies snarling
and quarreling behind us.

But the last shot was spent!

Turning my attention again to the giant
powder, I fixed the cap and fuse more
firmly in their place, and taking off my belt
wound that tightly round the whole.
Round that again I wrapped one of the old
sacks, and tearing off my coat made an
extra covering of that, knotting the sleeves
tightly on the outside, that the ravenous
teeth might be delayed in tearing the bundle apart. Crouching down in the sleigh, I
lighted a match, and, as I did so, I saw
that the wolves were upon us again, apparently as numerous and as tireless as
ever. The match went out; and a second.
Crouching lower still, I made a barricade
against the wind with anything I could lay
my hands on in the sleigh, and at last a
dull red spark caught the end of the fuse.

The pack was already crowding round
the terrified horses, which, it seemed to
me, were almost worn out, and moved
more heavily than heretofore. And how
slowly the fuse burned! Nursing it carefully with my hands, I blew upon the
spark and kept it glowing as it ate its way
slowly into the cotton. Why had I not
made it shorter? Every moment I expected
to feel the sudden jolt which told that the
wolves had pulled down one of the horses
and that the end had come!

At last the dull red glow had almost
reached the end of the cap. A few seconds
more and it would explode. Thrusting the
bundle hastily into another sack, forgetting
even the wolves in my terror lest it should
explode in my hands, I threw it with all
my force into the midst of the moving
forms abreast of the horses.

The beasts flung themselves upon it, and
as we swept by, the whole pack was again
collected into a struggling, snarling heap
beside the trail. We were sweeping round
a curve in the road, and before the horses
had taken a dozen strides, the brush shut
out the path behind us and the wolves.

A moment later and the air and the
earth shook around us. I was still half
standing, clutching the low side of the
sleigh, and the concussion threw me upon
my face. The report was not the crash of
a cannon nor the sharp noise of gunpowder, but a dull, heavy roar like an instantaneous clap of distant thunder. The stillness that followed was intense, but I
thought that I heard, from the direction
where the wolves had been, one broken,
muffled howl.

What had been the effect of it? Both
Gates and myself leaned forward and with
voice and hand urged the horses on. When
would those grim, gray, ruthless forms reappear? The seconds passed; minute followed minute, and the horses, breathing
painfully, labored on over the level trail.
With every yard traveled, hope grew
stronger, until leaning over again I said
to Gates:

"I don't believe they're coming, Char-
lie."

But his only reply was a shake of the
reins and another word to the horses.

Then suddenly there came a twinkle of
light in the distance. The brush fell away
from the trail and the white expanse of
the clearing of Gulch City was before us.

For a distance of fifty yards, at a point
about a mile and a half north of Gulch
City, the old Livingston trail had to be
abandoned. It would have been more labor

to repair it than to clear a new pathway through the brush. And when I left that part of the country two years afterward, the packers would still turn out of their way for a minute to look at "Giant Hole," and to kick up out of the weeds and brush that had grown around it the skull or part of the skeleton of a wolf.

SKATING

By Odell Shepard

We are off in a trice on the glittering ice
  Where the cold is as keen as a knife,
Where the winds at our back are a gallop-
    ing pack
  Of wolves on the warm scent of life,
And the frost-laden air is a blustering dare,
  A wager and challenge to strife.

Then, swifter than arrows, we speed
    through the narrows,
  We circle and quarter and reel,
We dodge and we race, play at prisoners'
    base,
  Snap-the-whip, figure-eight, and cart-
    wheel;
While the river-banks ring to the songs
    that we sing
  And the hiss of the glistening steel.

But the wind gathers might at the coming
    of night,
  And we ride on the wings of the gale
Down the river again o'er the glimmering
    plain
  Where the light is beginning to fail,
On the strength of the blast spinning diz-
    zily past
  The trees in the twilight pale.

Forgetful of care as the birds of the air,
  Or as boats on a breeze-bright sea,
We are wafted along with our laughter
    and song
  While the valleys reëcho our glee;
And our hearts are in tune with the cloud-
    driven moon
  And the boughs of the wind-blown tree.

Over the level ice, joining our revel,
  The snow, a dim flurry of white,
Drives drifting and rollicking by in a frolicking
  Dance through the halls of the night.
The stars are a-quiver with glee, and the river
  Rings with our shouts of delight
As we race on together before the keen weather,
  Borne by the wild wind's might.

HALF A MAN

by Walter Archer Frost

OFF outside the harbor the wind still lashed the smashing seas to a lather. The gale had blown the worst of itself out, but everything was loose yet and the sky looked dirty.

In the harbor, though, all was snug, and *The Charming Lass,* comfortable at her moorings, courtesied daintily, bow into the wind, her long, keen cut-water slitting the in-swaying seas.

She was a sixty-five-ton schooner, fitting out now for the cod-grounds, as everyone in Trinity Bay, Newfoundland, knew. But no one in all the bay knew it any better than Murdock Fraser.

The schooner had wintered at Trinity Bay. She'd shot her big anchor down in the lee of the island and slept soundly there, frozen in, comfortable as an eel in the mud. And all through the long cold weeks Murdock had looked at her with admiration and longing.

For he came of a long line of fishermen. The sea and the lure of the rigors of a fisherman's life—they were what he dreamed of; he hungered to be about the work which had summoned his father and his grandfather and those of his kin before them; he burned to be off on the banks, fishing for cod in one of the dories of a trim schooner that never took in a sail for anything.

That was why he watched *The Charming Lass* with such longing: he wanted to ship on her not as a cabin boy, but as a member of her crew. And word had gone about through Trinity Bay that the trig schooner was short-handed.

"It's my chance," Murdock said to his mother. "I'm only fourteen, but," he stretched himself, "I'm bigger'n one or two o' th' men on her. I'm goin' down an' try."

His mother smiled. He was good to her eyes: she knew that he was going to be big and brawny and powerful like his father. Murdock was her only son. She knew, too well, the dangers of a fisherman's life; and she winced at the thought of the boy's going. But she knew the call of the blue water. It was in her blood as in his. So she did not try to dissuade him.

"Try your luck, Murdock," she said, and touched his big-boned shoulder in veiled caress.

The boy laughed in his quiet way, and turned and walked down the path which led to the wharf. A dory was just putting out to the schooner, and Murdock jumped in, saying to the two men at the oars, "I want to see yer captain."

"Don't know's he'll want to see *you,*" said one of the men. But Murdock paid no attention.

A few moments later the dory made fast astern of the schooner, Murdock clambered over the rail, and stood on the deck. He was so dazed at finding himself here, where he'd dreamed of being, that he hardly felt, for the first second, the heavy hand which fell on his shoulder.

452

"I'm Cap'n Peter Johnson," a big voice rumbled above him. "You want to see me?"

"Yes," said the boy, "I hear you're short-handed," and he looked up confidently.

"Meanin'," the big voice rumbled with the laugh in it, "you want to help me out? I got a cabin-boy already."

"That's good," Murdock said, giving the captain a straight look from a pair of frank blue eyes. "It's fillin' out yer *crew* I'm thinking of."

Captain Peter Johnson smiled more than ever. "But you're only half a man. You could cut bait, mebby, but—"

"Yes, I kin cut bait as good as th' next," Murdock said, "but what I want is to do my trick at th' wheel, an' take my turn with th' oars in the dories, an' handle my lines *after* they've been baited. Then when I'm through, I want my *lay* like the other men."

Captain Johnson stopped smiling. "How old are you?" He liked the boy's confidence in himself, but half a man wasn't a whole one, and no captain that ever sailed blue water was more painstaking than Captain Johnson in picking men for his crew.

"I'm fourteen," said Murdock, honestly, "but my name's Murdock Fraser."

Captain Johnson nodded. He knew the Frasers of Trinity Bay. "You'll be a good man for me in four or five years, but now you couldn't even haul up the jumbo."

The "jumbo" was the big jib. Murdock knew this, and looked forward eagerly. "Lemme have a try at her! No," he corrected, like the sailor he said he was, "you don't want her set while you're fast to th' bottom."

Maybe Captain Johnson felt himself weakening; or it may be that he thought of the toll the sea already had taken of the Frasers. Be that as it may, he said sharply,

"Into th' dory, boy! I'll have two o' th' men take you back to shore!" Murdock said nothing. A lump had risen unexpectedly in his throat. He walked slowly astern, the captain following him.

Then, when the men started clambering over the side, the boy made one last appeal to Captain Johnson. "Mebby I am only half a man, like you say; but if you'd let me ship, you'd find I'd work like a whole one."

"Cast off that line!" was the captain's only answer. The boy leaped into the stern of the dory. Then, humiliated, and heavy with disappointment, Murdock was rowed ashore.

"But I'll ship on her yet!" he told his mother that evening at supper. "She'll take me 'long with 'er when she clears," he said, as the night came down. "I'll work like a man and get my lay like the rest, and the money'll help us here."

The *lay* meant the individual share of each member of the crew of the catch of cod. He was trying to reassure his mother and, understanding this, she nodded and said, "Yes, Murdock, it'd help." But, like him, she knew he was answering the irresistible summons of the sea.

So she was not surprised when he kissed her and his sisters good night, and, instead of going to his room, walked forth into the darkness which had held the harbor like a cloud of ink.

But through this seemingly impenetrable gloom the boy walked swiftly with sure tread; off, out there in the harbor, he could see the riding-lights of *The Charming Lass* as she swung: a red lantern to port and a green to starboard.

Half-way to the wharf he left the deeper path for one of his own making. A few moments later he was at the beach, where his own boat was moored. Easily she slid into the water, down the "slip" he'd made of spruce sticks. The oars found the locks apparently of their own instinct. Then he headed the boat for the stern of *The Charming Lass*.

In the rush of the waves he might have rowed without regard to the sound he made, for the click of his oarlocks was drowned by the breakers. But he rowed with his nicest pains. He pulled carefully, too, taking the larger seas bow on, and shipping not a cup of water.

On through the thick blackness he rowed, now sinking deep between towering black cliffs of water, now riding high on their snowy crests. Elated and confident, he rowed on. His spirits mounted even as he mounted the waves, but, unlike the waves, they suffered no depression.

He felt like shouting aloud in his ecstasy. Last night he would have so shouted. But he set his lips grimly now—as he thought a man would do—as he believed a sailor would do, a fisherman who was joining his mates aboard the schooner.

"Half a man?" Murdock said to himself. "I'll show 'em I'm a whole one!"

But there was that immediately ahead of him which was to tax severely this new manhood of his, and he knew it; once he reached the schooner's side, he could make her rail easily, but his own boat he must say good-by to.

Now was the ordeal, for he came suddenly on the schooner; checked the momentum of his rowboat by thrusting his hand against the schooner's side; in another moment was over her rail; for a long heart-beat tried to catch once more the clean lines of the boat he loved—then he let go her line and saw her drift astern into the blackness.

"I hope Rory McAuley remembers and watches out for her," Murdock said to himself. He had outlined his plans to Rory, his playmate.

Then the half a man, who was going to prove that he was a whole man on this cruise of *The Charming Lass*, stole noiselessly along the deck to the port stack of dories. The instant his hands found them, he undid the rope which made fast their canvas covering, crawled into the top dory, fastened the cover over the top again, and re-tied the rope as best he could.

Then he stretched himself comfortably on the dirty bottom of the dory. And when *The Charming Lass* got her hook up, just before dawn the next morning, and her sails sang up, and she sprang happily before the thrust of the fair wind, she carried forth on her over the blue water a half-a-man whose presence none of her crew was aware of, but whose heart was singing.

It was not until the schooner had raced over many miles of tumbling seas that Murdock slipped the rope and slid out to the deck from the dory. He had breakfasted on what his mother had put up for him. He had slept happily. He held his sturdy body well erect; the roll of the schooner was joy to him—but, for the moment, his heart was somewhere below his boot-tops.

Drawn by some power he could not explain, he turned, and met the keen eyes of the man at the wheel. A roll, as of thunder, seemed suddenly to envelop the boy. But it was only the roar of the helmsman. "Get below, an' tell th' old man we got a stow-'way!"

"Yes, sir," said Murdock. He obeyed, and he did it proudly: no matter what the result, he was being sent, as a member of the crew, with a message to the captain.

Knowing his way about a schooner as well as if he'd never been off her in his life, Murdock went swiftly to the captain's state-room, knocked, then, at the brusque command, opened the door and touched his thick hair:

"Man at th' wheel says we got a stow-

'way aboard, Cap'n," said Murdock Fraser. "W—w—what're we goin' to do with 'im, Cap'n?"

Captain Peter Johnson reflected, or seemed to. He was angry, and he was not one to forgive easily an infringement of his orders; he was on the high-seas now. On *The Charming Lass* Peter Johnson was a despot. That is to say, he was the captain of the schooner, and what he said *went*. On the other hand, this "stow'way's" obstinate perseverance appealed to him.

But Captain Johnson had selected his course and would not diverge from it, for he was obstinate himself. Fixing the boy with penetrating glance, the captain said. "Seen this stow'way, have you, Fraser?"

Murdock's heart leaped. "Yes, s-sir."

"Is he the Cape Bretoner that come aboard us in Trinity Bay, afternoon 'fore we cleared, Fraser?"

Murdock's brain reeled. "N-no, sir."

"What sort o' looking man *is* he, then?" asked Captain Johnson.

Murdock looked down, then up, straight into the captain's eyes. "He ain't very big, Cap'n, this man ain't, but he says he can do th' work—" Murdock gulped.

Peter Johnson leaned slightly toward Murdock. "Say, Fraser," he began, "you don't mean that kid I sent ashore in a dory's stowed away onto us?"

And poor Murdock could answer only, "Yes—sir."

The captain nailed the boy with a stern stare. "Then, Fraser, you tell this here stow'way to jump to the galley an' ask th' cook for a job peelin' potatoes. I remember that kid, he wasn't even half a man. Tell 'im if he touches a line or a dory or speaks to any man aboard but th' cook, I'll know what to do to 'im."

"He can do a man's work," Murdock cried desperately. "He'll *prove* it."

Captain Johnson was at the boy's side in one bound. "He'll learn obedience first!" roared the captain. "Get to the galley!"

"Yes, sir," Murdock cried once, then fled —as ordered.

"You'll peel potatoes, an' you'll wash dishes an' wipe 'em, an' you'll scrub decks, an' you'll clean bunks, an' you'll clean lamps, an' you'll sweep this galley, an' you'll sew on buttons, an' you'll mend clothes, an' you'll wait on th' table, an' you'll be cabin-boy's helper, an' you won't have time to be a fisherman," said the cook, grimly, having his orders from the captain.

And that, Murdock sorrowfully found, was what he'd won by stowing-away on *The Charming Lass*. On she flew, seeming to skim the blue water like a gull, on, on to the cod-grounds, the paradise of deep-sea fishermen.

Her decks were alive with the eager energy of the crew; the bait was of the best; the lines were sure; the hooks filed painstakingly; the dories tight; the oars and oar-locks ready for the water.

But Murdock, bending over his scrubbing, or spending himself on any one of his other monotonous duties, felt as far removed from the life of the flying schooner as if he'd been buried in the bottom of the Sydney mines.

More than that, the captain had forbidden him so much as to speak to any member of the crew. As a result, he was thrown for companionship on the cook and the cabin-boy. The former was taciturn. The latter, two years older than Murdock, was a blundering bully, who welcomed Murdock as one he could domineer over.

"Half-a-man," the cabin-boy would say, "get more elbow-grease into yer sweepin' this galley. Huh, you ain't even *half* a man; you're only a *quarter!*"

The cabin-boy's name was Herbert, and he threw his jeer at the boy who had been working since five in the morning like a Trojan. Then, as Murdock didn't so much as look up, Herbert began again: "You ain't even a quarter of a man. You're only a—"

"I'll show you what I am, if you want me to," Murdock said abruptly.

Herbert snatched the broom out of the other's hand, and stood over him. "Now show me!" Then, because he mistook Murdock's calmness for cowardice, Herbert sent his open hand to Murdock's face.

At the same instant, Herbert felt a solid fist crash against his side. He struck out with all his power, and Murdock slid across the narrow galley to the ladder. But Herbert's rush to pin the boy in the corner was met and broken before it was fairly started. All the larger boy knew was that something caught him with the clutch of a cable about his knees; he was lifted, swung clear off the floor, and slammed down with a force which dazed him. Then he was jerked to his feet and flung, big as he was, on the cook's bunk.

"You lie there!" a deep voice said quietly. And Herbert obeyed that quiet voice, for he'd found what was behind it. And when Herbert got up, some twenty minutes later, he'd lost all his bully and brag. He walked over to the other side of the little room and held out his hand.

"I was wrong: you're *more*'n half a man: you're blame near a whole man," said Herbert to Murdock Fraser.

After that, the two boys worked side by side and came to be good friends. But, though gratified, Murdock was not satisfied. He had convinced Herbert, but he wanted to convince the captain.

Murdock longed for some chance to show that, though he was only a boy in years, he could do a man's work on a fishing schooner. Hour after hour, while Herbert slept soundy in his bunk, Murdock wrestled with his problem. Every morning

he rose determined, that day, if any opportunity came, to prove the truth of his boast to the captain.

But it seemed that no chance would come. *The Charming Lass* made the fishing-grounds; the covers were snatched impatiently from the dories; the boats were shot to the water; in leaped the crew, two men to a dory, and off the boats raced to see which should make the first trip back laden down with cod.

There were nine men, counting the captain and crew, and Murdock hoped that he'd be allowed to make the tenth when the time came; but the fifth dory went out with only one man in her, and the boy watched her disconsolately. What wouldn't he have given to have pulled an oar and handled a line with the rest of them! What were tumbling mountains of water and floating ice to him? He yearned to be fighting them.

So it went, day after day. There was a wealth of cod running; the dories came back and back to the clean sides of *The Charming Lass,* emptied their loads, and went back to the fishing. Indeed, the cod were so keen in their biting that when the schooner was nearly full Captain Johnson ordered Herbert, the cabin-boy, to take a line with the ninth man in the fifth dory.

"Too bad, Murdock!" Herbert said honestly. "Wish t' you were comin', too."

But Murdock said nothing: by his promotion Herbert had been converted, for the time, to a member of the schooner's crew so Murdock could not speak to him.

The boy went back to his work in the galley, heavy-hearted. For he told himself that his last chance to prove himself in the big captain's eyes was gone now. In the morning would be begun the cruise home; on *The Charming Lass* he'd have showed his worth only in the galley.

There he seated himself listlessly on the cook's bunk. What was the use of hoping?

No use! He wasn't good for anything. If he had been, he'd have found a way of proving it. Over in the corner, between the foot of the bunk and the stove bolted to the floor, the cook dozed. All the work was done. Murdock set his teeth. How he hated this opportunity for idleness! How he sorrowed that no chance had come!

An hour passed, two, three.

Then something, instinct surely, roused him, sent him swiftly up the ladder, and turned his keen eyes over the schooner's rail. None too soon, either. For down from the Straits of Belle Isle had come a gigantic ice-floe. Now, silent as death, it was closing in grimly, inexorably, on *The Charming Lass;* once those two yawning jaws of ice closed up the blue water, nothing could save the schooner.

No time to cry out to the sleeping cook, Murdock knew. He sprang to the wheel, spun it over, and lashed it, having caught in a twinkling the narrow path of safe water that led to the open sea beyond. Like lightning, he had lashed the wheel, then he dashed forward to the "jumbo," the big jib, broke out the frozen rings, then flew to the sheet-line and began to haul.

"I got to get her up!" he cried aloud between his clenched teeth, as he hauled desperately. "I got to get her up, for we got to get steerageway!" Would the rope never start? He flung his weight on it again, but still it was not starting.

Then, as he'd seen men do, he made the rope fast on the cleat, and, catching the up-haul at shoulder-height, he hurled himself on it, then outward toward the rail, and the sheet sang free with a suddenness which almost sent him and the released line overboard. Then he hauled, hauled, hauled, felt *The Charming Lass* heel, hauled once more with all his strength, made fast and sure the line on the cleat, then dashed aft to the wheel, released its lashing with one hand, then spun the wheel until the schooner came in line with the safe lane of blue water and ploughed gaily ahead through it.

And that was the sight which gladdened the desperate eyes of Captain Peter Johnson, who, rowing hopelessly for the schooner on which he had seen, too late, the ice closing in, now sank back in his seat, his hand gripping on the thwart to steady himself.

"Who done *that?*" Captain Johnson demanded of the man in the bow seat. "Who knew enough to do th' only thing that could've saved her?"

"Not th' cook, he didn't," said the other man. "No, sir. He couldn't 've brung 'er out like that in a thousan' years. See 'er come! Look at 'er!"

The Charming Lass, though she had only the jumbo set, was dancing daintily along the blue lane as if she were laughing at the on-creeping ice each side of her. She had half a mile yet to go, but she didn't seem worried. Her jumbo filling until it stood rigid as sheet-iron, the schooner danced onward. Each instant the ice closed in more, but she continued on her way as if the whole thing were a joke, or as if she knew that, let the ice threaten as it would, she was safe in the capable hands of one who understood her and loved her.

"Bring 'er more to starb'rd," yelled Captain Johnson, though he knew his voice couldn't carry that far.

Simultaneously he saw the schooner's clean bow swing just the right degree to starboard; and while he watched, spellbound, *The Charming Lass* slid through the last fifty feet of the blue lane into the safe open water.

Then, as if that were not enough, she swung still farther around, though not enough to spill the wind out of the jumbo, and bore gracefully down to where the dories, now clustered, were watching her.

"I'm coming up into th' wind," called a voice from the wheel. "Then I'll stand by for you!"

And Captain Peter Johnson, good man that he was, sprang up in answer to that hail. He leaped up until he towered on the thwart, and he roared through his big hands, "Ay, ay, sir!"

The cook, white-faced, said: "He done it! I was below. Look here where the ice started piling over! It'd carried away the anchor, snapped th' chain, an' got a lot o' th' gear. Two minutes more, an' it'd got *us!*"

"Yes, of course," said Captain Peter Johnson. He looked about him. "Where's he gone to, that boy—I mean that *man?* Fraser," he said, when two of the crew dragged the boy up from where he had retreated to the galley, "where'd you have headed th' schooner for if we hadn't rowed for you?"

And Murdock said: "I'd 've took 'er to Lark Tickle Cove, sir," jerking his head over his right shoulder. "They's another schooner layin' there, an' I figured they might be able to spare us an anchor."

Captain Johnson looked down at the boy, then put a big hand on his shoulder. "Take the wheel again, Fraser," he said, "an' head where you was goin' to—Lark Tickle Cove. We need that anchor. In a little while I'll have *another* member of the crew relieve you at th' wheel. I want to see y'u."

And what Captain Peter Johnson said to Fraser, the new member of his crew, is best shown by the fact that when *The Charming Lass* danced back into Trinity Bay and shot her mud-hook down through the blue water, a sturdy boy went ashore with his mates in the dories. He'd signed articles for the next cruise; he had two hundred and fifty dollars in his pocket, representing his *lay* of *The Charming Lass's* record catch—nine hundred quintals of cod. His head was held well back, his chest swelled full, wide, and deep, he whistled a sea song as he faced off up the dock; and with a deep-sea roll, he strode up the path to his mother's cottage. For the half a man was a whole man, and he'd proved it!

THE "ARRIVAL" OF JIMPSON

BY RICHARD STILLMAN POWELL

I.—THE DEPARTURE

THE rain fell in a steady, remorseless drizzle upon the rain-coats and umbrellas of the throng that blocked the sidewalks and overflowed on to the car-tracks; but the fires of patriotism were unquenchable, and a thousand voices arose to the leaden sky in a fierce clamor of intense enthusiasm. It had rained all night. The streets ran water, and the spouts emptied their tides between the feet of the cheerers. The lumbering cars, their crimson sides glistening, clanged their way carefully through the crowds, and lent a dash of color to the scene. The back of Gray's loomed cheerless and bleak through the drizzle, and beyond, the college yard lay deserted. In store windows the plac-ards were hidden behind the blurred and misty panes, and farther up the avenue, the tattered red flag above Foster's hung limp and dripping.

Under the leafless elm, the barge, filled to overflowing with departing heroes, stood ready for its start to Boston. On the steps, bareheaded and umbrella-less, stood Benham, '95, who, with outstretched and waving arms, was tempting the throng into ever greater vocal excesses.

"Now, then, fellows! Three times three for Meredith."

"'Rah, 'rah, 'rah! 'rah, 'rah, 'rah! 'rah, 'rah, 'rah! Meredith!" A thousand throats raised the cry; umbrellas clashed wildly in mid-air; the crowd surged to and fro; horses curveted nervously; and the rain poured down impartially upon the reverend senior and the clamorous freshman.

459

"Fellows, you're not *half* cheering!" cried the relentless Benham. "Now, three times three, three long Harvards, and three times three for the eleven."

"'Rah, 'rah, 'rah! 'rah, 'rah, 'rah! 'rah, 'rah, 'rah! Har-vard; Har-vard, Har-vard! 'Rah, 'rah, 'rah! 'rah, 'rah, 'rah! 'rah, 'rah, 'rah! 'Leven!"

Inside the coach there was a babel of voices. Members of the eleven leaned out and conversed jerkily with friends on the sidewalk. Valises and suit-cases were piled high in the aisle and held in the owners' laps. The manager was checking off his list.

"Cowper?"

"Here."

"Turner?"

"All right."

"Truesdale?"

"Hey? Oh, yes; I'm here." The manager folded the list. Then a penciled line on the margin caught his eye.

"Who's Jameson? Jameson here?"

"Should be Jimpson," corrected the man next to him; and a low voice called from the far end of the barge:

"Here, sir." It sounded so much like the response of a school-boy to the teacher that the hearers laughed with the mirth begot of tight-stretched nerves. A youth wearing a faded brown ulster, who was between Gates, the big center, and the corner of the coach, grew painfully red in the face, and went into retirement behind the big man's shoulder.

"Who is this fellow Jimpson?" queried a man in a yellow mackintosh.

"Jimpson? He's a freshie. Trying for right half-back all fall. I suppose Brattle took him along, now that Ward's given up, to substitute Sills. They say he's an A 1 runner, and plucky. He's played some on the second eleven. Taunton told me, the other day, that he played great ball at Exeter, last year."

The strident strains of the "Washington Post" burst out on the air, urging the cheerers to even greater efforts. They were cheering indiscriminately now. The trainer, the rubbers, the coaches, even the bulldog "mascot," had received their shares of the ovation. But Benham, '95, with his coat soaked through, was still unsatisfied, and sought for further tests. Two professors, half hidden under umbrellas, had emerged from the yard, and were standing at a little distance, watching the scene.

"Three times three for Professor Dablee!" The cheers that followed were mixed with laughter, and the two professors moved off, but not until the identity of the second had been revealed, and the air had filled with the refrain of "Rah, 'rah, 'rah! Pollock!"

"They look as though they ought to win; don't you think so?" asked one of them.

The other professor frowned.

"Yes, they look like that; every eleven does. You'd think, to see them before a game, that nothing short of a pile-driver or dynamite could drive them an inch. And a few days later they return, heart-broken and defeated."

Across the square floated a husky bellow:

"Now, then, fellows! Once more! All together! Three times three for Harvard!"

The band played wildly, frenziedly, out of time and tune; the crowd strained its tired throats for one last farewell slogan; the men in the barge waved their hands; the horses jumped forward; a belated riser in Holyoke threw open a front window, and drowsily yelled, "Shut up"; and the Harvard eleven sped on its way up the avenue, and soon became a blur in the gray vista.

"Say, Bob, you forgot to cheer Jimpson."

The wearied youth faced his accuser, struck an attitude indicative of intense despair, and then joyfully seized the opportunity.

"Fellows! Fellows! Hold on! Three times three for Jim—Jim—who'd you say?"

"Jimpson," prompted the friend.

"Three times three for Jimpson! Now, then, all together!"

"Say—who *is* Jimpson?" shouted a dozen voices at once.

"Don't know. Don't care. Three times three for Jimpson!"

And so that youth, had he but known it, received a cheer, after all. But he didn't know it—at least, not until long afterward, when cheers meant so much less to him.

II.—A LETTER

New Haven, Conn., November 19.

Dear Mother: I can imagine your surprise upon receiving a letter from this place, when your dutiful son is supposed to be "grinding" in No. 30 College House, Cambridge. And the truth is that the dutiful son is surprised himself. Here am I, with some thirty-five other chaps, making ready for the big football game with Yale tomorrow. Here is how it happened:

Yesterday morning, Brattle—he's our captain—came to my room, routed me out of bed, and told me to report to the coaches for morning practise. You know, I've been trying for substitute right half-back. Ward, the regular, sprained his knee in the Dartmouth game, and a few days ago it went lame again. So now Sills has Ward's place, and I'm to substitute Sills. And if he gets laid out—and maybe I ought to hope he won't—I go in and play. What do you think of that? Of course Sills may last the entire game; but they say he has a weak back, only he won't own up to it, and may

have to give up after the first half. Gates told me this on the train. Gates is the big center, and weighs 196. He is very kind, and we chummed all the way from Boston. I didn't know any of the fellows, except a few by sight—just enough to nod to, you know.

We left Cambridge in a driving rain, and a big crowd stood out in it all, and cheered the eleven, and the captain, and the college, and everything they could think of. Every fellow on the first and second elevens, and every "sub" was cheered—all except Mr. Jimpson. They didn't know of his existence! But I didn't feel bad—not very, anyhow. I hope the rest of the fellows didn't notice the omission, however. But I made up my mind that if I get half a show, I'll make 'em cheer Jimpson, too. Just let me get on the field. I feel to-night as though I could go through the whole Yale team. Perhaps if I get out there, facing a big Yale man, I'll not feel so strong.

You know, you've always thought I was big. Well, to-day I overheard a fellow asking one of the men, "Who is that little chap with the red cheeks?" I'm a midget beside most of the other fellows. If I play tomorrow, I'll be the lightest man on the team, with the exception of Turner, our quarter-back, who weighs 158. I beat him by three pounds.

Such a hubbub as there is in this town to-night! Everybody seems crazy with excitement. Of course I haven't the slightest idea who is going to win, but to look at our fellows, you'd think they would have things their own way. I haven't seen any of the Yale players. We practised on their field for an hour or so this afternoon, but they didn't show up. There was a big crowd of Yale students looking on. Of course every fellow of us did his very worst; but the spectators didn't say anything—just looked wise.

Most of the fellows are terribly nervous to-night. They go around as though they were looking for something, and would cry if they didn't find it soon. And the trainer is the worst of all. Brattle, the captain, is fine, though. He isn't any more nervous than an alligator, and has been *sitting still all the evening,* talking with a lot of the old graduates about the game. Once he came in the writing-room, where I was sitting, and asked whom I was writing to. When I told him, he smiled, and said to tell you that if anything happened he'd look after my *remains* himself! Maybe he thought I was nervous. But if I am, I'm not the only one. Gates is writing to his mother, too, at the other table.

Give my love to Will and Bess. Tell Will to send my old skates to me. I shall want them. There is fine skating on Fresh Pond, which, by the way, is a lake.

We're ordered off to bed. I guess some of us won't sleep very well. I'm rather excited myself, but I guess I'm tired enough to sleep. I'll write again when I get back to college. With bushels of love to all,

Yours affectionately, Tom.

III.—THE "ARRIVAL"

JIMPSON sat on the ground and watched with breathless interest two charging, tattered, writhing lines of men. Jimpson felt a good deal like an outcast, and looked like a North American Indian. Only legs and face were visible; the rest of Jimpson was enveloped in a big gray blanket with barbaric red borders. Some two dozen counterparts of Jimpson sat or lay near by, stretching along the side-line in front of the Harvard section of the grand stand. Behind them a thousand en-

thusiastic mortals were shouting pæans to the goddess of victory, and, unless that lady was deaf, she must have heard the pæans, however little she approved of them. The most popular one was sung to a well-known air.

"As we're strolling through Fifth
     Avenue
With an independent air,
The ladies turn and stare,
The chappies shout, 'Ah, there!'
And the population cries aloud,
'Now, aren't they just the swell-
     est crowd,
The men that broke Old Eli at
     New Haven!'"

And a mighty response swept across the field from where a bank of blue rose from the green of the field to the lighter blue of the sky. It was a martial air, with a prophecy of victory:

"Shout aloud the battle-cry
     Of Yale, Yale, Yale!
Wave her standard far and high
     For Yale, Yale, Yale!
See the foe retreat before us,
Sons of Eli, shout the chorus,
     Yale, Yale, Yale, Yale, Yale!".

Harvard and Yale were doing battle once more, and thirty thousand people were looking on. The score-board announced: "Harvard, 4; Yale, 0, Yale's ball. 15 minutes to play."

The story of twenty minutes of the first half is soon told. It had been Yale's kick-off. Haag had sent the ball down the field to Harvard's 20-yard line, and Van Brandt had gathered it in his long arms, and, with Meredith ahead, had landed it back in the middle of the field. But the fourth down gave it to their opponents after a loss of two yards, and the pigskin went down again to Harvard's territory, coming to a stop at the white line that marked thirty-five yards. Here Harvard's new half-back kick had been tried, and the ball went high in air, and the field went after it; and when the Yale full-back got his hands on it, he was content with a bare five yards, and it was Yale's ball on her 40-yard line. Then happened a piece of ill luck for the wearers of the blue. On the second down, Kurtz fumbled the pass, the ball rolled toward Yale's goal, and Brattle broke through the opposing left-tackle and fell on it.

And while a thunderous roar of joy floated across the field from the followers of the Crimson, the teams lined up on Yale's thirty yards. Twice Meredith tried to go through between center and left guard, and a bare yard was the reward. Then Van Brandt had run back as for a kick; the ball was snapped, passed to Sills, Harvard's right half-back, and, with it safely under his arm, he had skirted the Yale left, and fallen and wriggled and squirmed across the goal-line for the first touch-down.

Then ensued five minutes of bedlam, and after the victorious seats had settled into excited complacency, Van Brandt had tried for goal. But success was too much to hope for, and the two teams trotted back to the middle of the field, with the score 4 to 0. Then had the sons of Eli shown of what they were made, and in the next ten minutes the ball had progressed with fatal steadiness from the center of the field to the region of the Crimson's twenty yards. And now it was Yale's ball on the second down, and the silence was so intense that the signal was heard as plainly by the watchers at the far end of the field as by the twenty-two stern-faced warriors who faced each other almost under the shadow of the goal-posts.

"Twelve, six, twelve, fifty—two!"

And the backs, led by the guards, hurled their weight against Harvard's right tackle; and when the ball was found, Baker held it within a few inches of the 10-yard line.

The cheers of Yale had now grown continuous; section after section passed the slogan along. The stand across the field looked to Jimpson like a field of waving blue gentians. On the Harvard seats the uproar was less intense, and seemed a trifle forced; and the men near by were breathing heavily, and restively creeping down the line.

Again the lines were formed. Jimpson could see the tall form of the gallant Gates settle down into a hunchback, toad-like position to receive the coming onslaught. Billings, the right tackle, was evidently expecting another experience like the last. He looked nervous, and Gates turned his head and spoke to him under cover of the first numbers of the signal.

The guards were back of the line again, and their elbows almost brushed as they stood between the half-backs. Silence reigned. The referee skipped nimbly out of the way.

"Seven, seventeen, eighty-one, thirty."

Again the weakening tackle was thrust aside, and although the Crimson line held better, the ball was three yards nearer home when the whistle blew, and Billings, somewhat dazed, had to call for a short delay.

"First down again," muttered a brawny sub, at Jimpson's elbow. "Why doesn't he take Billings out?"

Again the signal came. Again a jumbled mass of arms and legs for a moment hid the result. Then the men on the stand overlooking the goal-line arose *en masse,* and a mighty cheer traveled up the field, growing in volume until Jimpson could not hear his own groans nor the loud groans of a big sub. Back of the line, and almost equidistant from the posts, lay the

Yale full-back; and the ball was held tightly to earth between outstretched hands. The prostrate players were slowly gaining their feet; but Billings and Sills lay where they had fallen. Then Brattle stepped toward the side-line, holding up his hand. With a leap Jimpson was on his feet. But the big chap beside him had already pulled off his sweater, and now, tossing it into Jimpson's face, he sped gleefully toward the captain.

Jimpson sat down again in deep disappointment; and a moment later, Billings, supported on either side, limped from the gridiron, amidst the cheers of the Harvard supporters. Sills was on his feet again, and the trainer was talking to him. Jimpson could see the plucky fellow shaking his head. Then, after a moment of indecision, the trainer left him, the whistle sounded, the Crimson team lined up back of the line, and Kurtz was poising the ball for a try at a goal. The result was scarcely in doubt, and the ball sailed cleanly between the posts, a good two feet above the crossbar; and the scoreboard said, "Harvard, 4; Yale, 6"; and there were three minutes more of the half.

Back went the ball to the 55-yard line, and loud arose the cheers of the triumphant friends of Yale. Gates kicked off, and Warner sent the ball back again, with a gain of ten yards. Sills caught it and ran, but was downed well inside Harvard territory, and the half ended with the ball in Yale's hands. Jimpson seized his blanket, and trotted after the eleven to the quarters. He found Gates stripping for a rub-down.

"Well, my lad," panted the latter, "could you discern from where you were just what kind of a cyclone struck us?" But Jimpson was too much interested for such levity.

"Do you think I'll get in this half, Gates?"

"Can't say. Take a look at Sills, and judge for yourself."

That gentleman was having his lame back rubbed by a trainer, but he appeared to Jimpson good for at least another quarter of an hour.

It seemed but a moment after they had reached the rooms that the word of "Time's up, fellows," was passed, and renewed cheering from without indorsed the fact. But a moment or two still remained, and that moment belonged to Brattle. He stood on a bench and addressed the hearers very quietly:

"We're going to kick, this half, fellows. I want every man to get down the field on the instant, without stopping to hold. I don't think they can keep us from scoring at least once more; but every man has got to *work*. When the time comes to put the ball over the line, I expect it to go over with a rush. Let every man play the best game he knows, but *play together*. Remember that lack of team work has often defeated Harvard. And now, fellows, three times three for Harvard!"

And what a yell that was! Jimpson went purple in the face, and the head coach cheered his spectacles off. And then out they all went on a trot, big Gates doing a coltish hand-spring in mid-field, to the great delight of the Crimson's wearers. The college band played; thirty thousand people said something all together; and then the great quadrangle was silent, the whistle piped merrily, and the ball soared into air again.

Jimpson took up his position on the side-line once more, and watched with envious heart the lucky players. For the great, over-whelming desire of Jimpson's soul was to be out there on the torn turf, doing great deeds, and being trampled under foot. He watched the redoubtable Sills as a cat watches a mouse. Every falter of that player brought fresh hope to Jimpson. He would have liked to rise and make an impassioned speech in the interests of humanity, protesting against allowing a man in Sills' condition to remain in the game. Jimpson's heart revolted at the cruelty of it.

Some such idea as this he had expressed to Gates, that morning; and the big center had giggled in deep amusement; in fact he had refused to recognize the disinterested character of Jimpson's protest.

"Don't you think," Jimpson had pleaded, "that I might ask Brattle to give me a show in the second half?"

"No, I don't," Gates had answered bluntly. "You're an unknown quantity, my boy; as the Frenchies say, you haven't 'arrived.' For a player who hasn't 'arrived' to try to give the captain points would be shocking bad taste. That's how it is. Sills is a good player. As long as he can hold his head up, he'll be allowed to play. When he's laid out, Brattle will give you a show. He can't help himself; you're the only chap that he can trust in the position. And look here; when that time comes, just you remember the signals, and *keep your eye on the ball*. That's all you'll have to do. Don't take your eyes off the leather, even if the sky falls!"

Jimpson remembered the conversation, and thought ruefully that it was easy enough for a fellow who has everything that heart can desire to spout good advice to chaps on the side-lines. Perhaps if Gates were in his (Jimpson's) place he'd not be any too patient himself. The scoreboard said fifteen minutes to play. Sills still held up his stubborn head, and Jimpson's chances grew dimmer and dimmer as moments sped.

Harvard's kicking tactics had netted her long gains time and again, and twice had she reached Yale's 10-yard line, only to be grimly held and hurled back. Yale, on the other hand, had only once reached scoring-distance of their opponent's goal, and had been successfully held for downs. Veterans of the game declared enthusiastically, be-

tween bets, that it was "the snappiest game of the decade!" and supporters of Harvard said among themselves that it was beautifully conducive to heart-disease. Perhaps never had the two colleges turned out teams so evenly balanced in both offense and defense. The bets had become "one to two that Harvard doesn't score again."

Harvard's quarter had given place to a substitute, and her left guard had retired injured. Yale had fared no better, possibly worse, since her crack full-back had been forced to yield to a somewhat inferior sub. And now the hands on the score-board turned again, and only ten minutes remained.

The ball was down near Harvard's 40-yard line, and when it was snapped back Sills took it for a "round-the-end run." But Yale's big left half-back was waiting for him, and the two went to earth together near the side-line and almost at Jimpson's feet. And then it was that that youth's heart did queer feats inside him, and seemed trying to get out. For Sills lay awhile where he had fallen, and when he could walk the doctor had sent him from the field. Brattle beckoned to Jimpson. With trembling fingers Jimpson struggled with his sweater; but had not a neighbor come to his assistance, he would never have wriggled out of it before the game was called.

Brattle met him, and, laying an arm over his shoulder, walked him a few paces apart. Jimpson's heart, which had become more normal in action, threatened another invasion of his throat, and he wondered if everybody was looking on. Then he stopped speculating, and listened to what the captain was saying.

"We've only eight minutes to play. The ball has *got* to go over, Jimpson. I've seen you run, and I believe you can make it if you try. The ball is yours on the second down. Try the right end; don't be afraid of swinging out into the field. Whatever you do, don't let go of the ball. If Turner puts you through the line, keep your head down, but jump high. Now, go in, lad, and let's see what you can do." He gave Jimpson an encouraging slap on the back that almost precipitated that youth into the quarter, and Jimpson saw the broad backs before him settling down, and heard the labored breathing of the men.

"Ninety-one, twenty-eight, seventy-three, sixty-four—six!"

Jimpson suddenly found himself pushing the left half-back against a surging wall of tattered blue. Then some one seized him about the waist, and he picked himself up from the ground eight feet away from the scene of battle.

"That's what comes of being so small and light," he growled to himself, as he trotted back. But the thirst of battle was in Jimpson's soul, and he marked the Yale end who had treated him so contemptuously.

The try between right-tackle and end had netted a bare yard, and Jimpson tried to look self-possessed while his back was running with little chills and his throat was dry as dust. The next chance was his, and he waited the signal anxiously, to learn whether the pass was direct or double. The other half-back imperceptibly dropped back a foot. The quarter looked around. The lines swayed and heaved.

"Twenty-seven, sixty-three, forty-five, seventy-two—five!"

Jimpson leaped forward; the left half-back darted across him, the quarter passed neatly, and, with the Harvard left-end beside him, he was sweeping down to the right and into the field. The Yale end went down before the mighty Cowper; and Jimpson, sighting a clear space, sped through. He could feel the field trailing after him, and could hear the sounds of the falling men. Before him in the distance, a

little to the left, came the Yale full-back. Almost upon him was the Yale left-half, looking big and ugly. But, with a final spurt, Van Zandt ran even, and gave the shoulder to the enemy; and as they went down together, Jimpson leaped free, and, running on, knew that at last he was left to shift for himself. Of the foes behind he had no fear; of the full-back running cautiously down on him he feared everything. But he clutched the ball tighter, and raced on straight as an arrow toward the only player between him and the goal that loomed so far down the field.

He heard now the mighty sound of voices cheering him on, saw without looking the crowded stands to the right; and then something whispered of danger from behind, and, scarcely daring to do so, lest he trip and fall, glanced hurriedly over his shoulder into the staring eyes of a runner. And now he could hear the other's short, labored gasps. Before him but a scant ten yards was the full-back. Jimpson's mind was made up on the instant. Easing his pace the least bit, he swung abruptly to the left. He well knew the risk he ran, but he judged himself capable of making up the lost ground. As he had thought, the pursuer was little expecting such a deliberate divergence from the course, and, as a result, he overran, and then turned clumsily, striking for a point between Jimpson and the left goal-post. The full-back had noted the change of course on the instant, and was now running for about the same intersecting point as the other. The three runners formed a triangle. For the moment the pursuer was out of reckoning, and Jimpson could give all his skill to eluding the full-back, who faced him, ready for a tackle.

And here Jimpson's lighter weight stood him in good stead. Clutching the ball tightly, he made a feint to the left, and then flung himself quickly to the right. As he did so he spun around. The full-back's hand reached his canvas jacket, slipped, and found a slight hold upon his trousers; and Jimpson, scarcely recovered from his turn, fell on one knee, the full-back also falling in his effort to hold. At that moment the pursuer reached the spot, and sprang toward Jimpson.

The shouts had ceased, and thirty thousand persons were holding their breath. The next moment a shout of triumph went up, and Jimpson was speeding on toward the Yale goal. For as the last man had thrown himself forward, Jimpson had struggled to his feet, the full-back following, and the two Yale men had crashed together with a shock that left the full-back prostrate upon the turf. The other had regained himself quickly, and taken up the pursuit; but Jimpson was already almost ten yards to the good, and, although his breath was coming in short, painful gasps, and the white lines seemed rods apart, the goal became nearer and nearer. But the blue-stockinged runner was not done, and the cries of the Crimson well-wishers were stilled as the little space between the two runners grew perceptibly less.

Jimpson, with his eyes fixed in agony upon the last white line under the goal-posts, struggled on. One ankle had been wrenched in his rapid turn, and it pained frightfully as it took the ground. He could hear the steps of the pursuing foe almost at his heels, and, try as he might, he could not cover the ground any faster. His brain reeled, and he thought each moment that he must fall.

But the thought of what that touchdown meant, and the recollection of the captain's words, nerved him afresh. The goal-line was plain before him now; ten yards only remained. The air was filled with cheers; but to Jimpson everything save that little white line and the sound of the pounding steps behind him was obliterated.

Success seemed assured, when a touch on his shoulder made the landscape reel before his eyes. It was not a clutch—just fingers grasping at his smooth jacket, unable as yet to find a hold.

The last white line but one passed haltingly, slowly, under his feet. The fingers traveled upward, and suddenly a firm grasp settled upon his shoulder. He tried to swing free, faltered, stumbled, recovered himself with a last supreme effort, and, holding the ball at arm's length, threw himself forward, face down. And as the enemy crashed upon him, Jimpson tried hard to gasp "Down!" but found he couldn't, and then—didn't care at all.

When he came to he found a crowd of players about him. Faces almost strange to him were smiling, and the captain was holding his head. His right foot pained frantically, and the doctor and rubbers were busy over him.

"Was it—was it over?" he asked weakly.

"Easy, old chap—with an inch to spare," replied the lips above. "Listen!"

Jimpson tried to raise his head, but it felt so funny that he gave up the effort. But, despite the woolen sweater bunched up for a pillow, he heard a deep roar that sounded like the breakers on the beach at home. Then he smiled, and fainted once more.

But the score-board had changed its figures again: "Harvard, 8; Yale, 6. Touchdown. Harvard's ball. 3 minutes to play."

And the deep, exultant roar went on, resolving itself into "H-a-r-vard! H-a-r-vard!"

The band was playing "Washington Post." Harvard Square was bright under a lurid glow of red fire. Cheering humanity was packed tight from the street to the balustrade of Matthews, and from there up and across the yard. Cannon crackers punctuated the blare of noise with sharp detonations. The college was out in full force to welcome home the football heroes, and staid and prim old Cambridge lent her quota to the throng. From the back of Gray's the cheering grew louder, and the crowd surged toward the avenue. The band broke ranks and skeltered after. A four-horse barge drew up slowly at the curb, and, one after another, the men dropped out, tightly clutching their bags, and strove to slip away through the throng. But each was eventually captured, his luggage confiscated, and himself raised to the shoulders of riotous admirers. When all were out and up, the band started the strains of "Fair Harvard," and thousands of voices joined in. The procession moved. Jimpson, proud and happy and somewhat embarrassed, was well up in the line. When the corner was turned and the yard reached the roar increased in volume. Cheers for the eleven, for Harvard, for Brattle, were filling the air. And then suddenly Jimpson's heart leaped at sound

of his own name from thousands of throats.

"Now, fellows, three long Harvards, and three times three for Jimpson!" In the roar that followed Jimpson addressed his bearers.

"Won't you please let me go now? I—I'm not feeling very well, and—and I'm only a sub, you know."

The plea of illness moved his captors, and Jimpson was dropped to earth, and his valise restored. There was no notice taken of him as he slipped stealthily through the outskirts of the throng, and as he reached the corner of Holden Chapel he paused and listened.

To the dark heavens arose a prolonged, impatient demand from thousands of Harvard throats. The listener heard, and then fled toward the dark building across the street, and, reaching his room, locked the door behind him. But still he could hear the cries, loudly and impatiently repeated: "We—want—Jimpson! We—want—Jimpson! Jimp-son!"

THE BEARER OF GOOD TIDINGS

by Charles N. Lurie

I T was not by chance that Billy Briggs was loitering about the door of the church on Orange Street, in the town of Nantucket, on a warm, clear, sunny spring morning. His mother had sent him down to Marm Hopkins's for a spool of thread, and, returning to his home, diagonally opposite the church, he had seen Obed Macy enter the door of the church.

Only one thing could have brought Obed there on a week-day morning; he was going to climb into the gilded tower, and scan the water with his far-seeing eyes —trained by long gazing at ocean horizons —for a sign of a home-coming vessel. In all Nantucket there was no place like the tower of the Second Congregational Church for keeping watch for the return of the whaling ships from their long voyages in search of oil and bone. Sometimes four or even five years passed between the going forth of a whaler and her return.

While Obed mounted to his lookout, Billy waited, with the spool of thread in his pocket, and watched for the return of the one-armed sailorman. Of course, if his mother called him in, he would have had his trouble in vain. But Billy hoped that his mother would keep busy with her housework until Obed came down. When he did—well, it *might* mean a dollar or two in Billy's pocket. Dollars were mighty scarce in boys' pockets eighty years ago.

"I'm lucky," said Billy to himself. "None of the other boys are around to ask me why I'm waiting and watching the church."

It seemed to him a very long time before Obed reappeared at the door of the church, although it was only about ten minutes. The sailorman's eye fell on Billy, waiting impatiently. He did not need to ask why the boy waited; he was a Nantucket native himself, and he knew the customs of the island.

"All right, son," Obed said. "It's the *Minerva,* sure enough, back from her three years' trip to the Horn. I know her well; I was one of her crew last voyage when that 'bow-head' stove her boat and I lost my arm. Light out now for Captain Coffin's and see what you get."

"I'm going to Bicknells', too, to tell the mate's wife," shouted Billy, but Obed caught only the first part of the words, since Billy was running up the street as he spoke.

Captain Coffin and his wife lived on the road to Wannacomett, about half a mile from the outskirts of Nantucket town. It seemed to Billy that he did not run that half mile; he flew it.

There were only a few houses along that road then, and in one of them lived Bob Hussey, who was Billy's schoolmate, playfellow, and rival in all kinds of sports. He could run well, but not as fast as Billy; at the island "squantum" (picnic), the summer before, Billy had proved himself Bob's master, both in the sprints and longer races.

Bob was not at home when Billy, going like the winds that blow forever around Great Point, ran past the Husseys'. But Mrs. Hussey saw Billy flying down the road.

"The *Minerva's* in," she said to herself. "There's Billy Briggs going down to Mrs. Coffin's to tell her the news, and he'll get a dollar from her, sure. I wish Bob was home; I'd send him to Mrs. Bicknell's. Of all mornings to be away! I'm sorry I sent him to the cobbler's; his shoes could have waited another day; they weren't so bad; there's no reason why Billy Briggs should get *all* the money for bringing the good news."

In the meantime, Billy, out of breath, had reached Mrs. Coffin's. Without waiting to knock at the door, he lifted the latch, dashed through the hall, and to the kitchen.

"Oh, Mrs. Coffin!" he gasped. "The *Minerva's* coming in! Obed Macy saw her, rounding Sconset, from the church tower, and he sent me here to tell you!"

Mrs. Coffin was a true Nantucket woman. It took more than the news of her husband's safe return from a perilous three-year whaling voyage to upset her. She was a kinswoman—in spirit, at least— of the good wife of the island, who saw her husband coming up the street from a four years' voyage around the Horn, and, taking an empty water-pail from its place on her dresser, greeted him with, "Hullo, John, got back, have you? Here, go get me a bucket of water."

So the wife of Captain Coffin said quietly, to Billy:

"Well, I'll be glad to have Josiah back home. Thank you for coming to tell me. Wait a moment—here's a little gift for you." And she went to the old sea-chest that served her for a bureau, and handed Billy a silver dollar.

"Thank you, thank you, Mrs. Coffin," he said. "But excuse me—I'm off to Mrs. Bicknell's."

In a jiffy, Billy, his wind fully restored by his stop at the captain's house, was off again, at top speed, down the road along which he had come. "Perhaps I'll get to Mrs. Bicknell's before any one else brings the good news," he said to himself. In his mind, he had already spent the dollar which Mrs. Coffin had given him, and the one he hoped to get at the home of the mate.

But when he got almost to the Husseys' front gate, he saw Bob flinging it open, and starting to run in the same direction as himself. While Billy had been covering the short distance that lay between the Husseys' home and the Coffins', Bob had returned from the cobbler's, and had been told by his mother what was in the wind.

"He's gone to tell her of the *Minerva's* arrival," said she. "With a start, you can beat him to Mrs. Bicknell's, even if he can run faster than you."

It was a close race between the two boys, in the quarter of a mile that lay between the Husseys' and the Bicknells'. Despite Bob's start and Billy's weariness frim his run to the captain's house, the latter was right on the heels of Bob at the house of Mrs. Bicknell. When Bob rushed through the front door, Billy was close behind him, and they tumbled into the entry together, scaring Mrs. Bicknell half to death. No housewife can be expected to keep her composure when two boys of thirteen rush in on her like that, and fall through her doorway without even stopping to knock.

"Land's sake!" she said. "What's the matter?"

But when she understood what their

errand was, she laughed and cried all at once, and handed out a dollar, saying Billy and Bob might divide it. But Billy would no do that; by all the laws and rules of Nantucket's boys, and by the customs of the island, the money belonged rightfully to Bob, for he was the first one to cross Mrs. Bicknell's threshold with the good tidings of her husband's return.

"Anyway," said Billy, "I've got the dollar from Mrs. Coffin, and that makes it a pretty good morning's work for me. Besides, I think I'd better get that spool of thread home to Mother."

A NORSE LULLABY

By M. L. van Vorst

Over the crust of the hard white snow
The little feet of the reindeer go
(*Hush, hush, the winds are low*),
   And the fine little bells are ringing!
Nothing can reach thee of woe or harm—
Safe is the shelter of mother's arm
(*Hush, hush, the wind's a charm*),
   And mother's voice is singing.

Father is coming—he rides apace;
Fleet are the steeds with the winds that
   race
(*Hush, hush, for a little space*);
   The snow to his mantle's clinging.

His flying steed with the wind's abreast—
Here by the fire are warmth and rest
(*Hush, hush, in your little nest*),
   And mother's voice is singing.

Over the crust of the snow, hard by,
The little feet of the reindeer fly
(*Hush, hush, the wind is high*),
   And the fine little bells are ringing!
Nothing can reach us of woe or harm—
Safe is the shelter of father's arm
(*Hush, hush, the wind's a charm*),
   And mother's voice is singing.

"ONE MINUTE LONGER"

by Albert Payson Terhune

WOLF was a collie, red-gold and white of coat, with a shape more like his long-ago wolf ancestors' than like a domesticated dog's. It was from this ancestral throw-back that he was named Wolf.

He looked not at all like his great sire, Lad, nor like his dainty, thoroughbred mother, Lady. Nor was he like them in any other way, except that he inherited old Lad's stanchly gallant spirit and loyalty. No, in traits as well as in looks, he was more wolf than dog. He almost never barked, his snarl supplying all vocal needs.

The Mistress or the Master or the Boy —any of these three could romp with him, roll him over, tickle him, or subject him to all sorts of playful indignities. And Wolf entered gleefully into the fun of the romp. But let any human besides these three lay a hand on his slender body, and a snarling plunge for the offender's throat was Wolf's invariable reply to the caress.

It had been so since his puppyhood. He did not fly at accredited guests, nor, indeed, pay any heed to their presence, so long as they kept their hands off him. But to all of these the Boy was forced to say at the very outset of the visit:

"Pat Lad and Bruce all you want to, but leave Wolf alone. He doesn't care for people."

Then, to prove his own immunity, the Boy would proceed to tumble Wolf about, to the delight of them both.

In romping with humans whom they love, most dogs will bite more or less gently, —or pretend to bite,—as a part of the game. Wolf never did. In his wildest and roughest romps with the Boy or with the Boy's parents, Wolf did not so much as open his mighty jaws. Perhaps because he dared not trust himself to bite gently. Perhaps because he realized that a bite was not a joke, but an effort to kill.

There had been only one exception to Wolf's hatred for mauling at strangers' hands. A man came to The Place on a business call, bringing along a two-year-old daughter. The Master warned the baby that she must not go near Wolf, although she might pet any of the other collies. Then he became so much interested in the business talk that he and his guest forgot all about the child.

Ten minutes later, the Master chanced to shift his gaze to the far end of the room, and he broke off, with a gasp, in the very middle of a sentence.

The baby was seated astride Wolf's back, her tiny heels digging into the dog's sensitive ribs, and each of her chubby fists gripping one of his ears. Wolf was lying there, with an idiotically happy grin on his face and wagging his tail in ecstasy.

No one knew why he had submitted to the baby's tugging hands, except because she *was* a baby, and because the gallant heart of the dog had gone out to her helplessness.

Wolf was the official watch-dog of The Place, and his name carried dread to the loafers and tramps of the region. Also, he was the Boy's own special dog. He had been born on the Boy's tenth birthday, five years before this story of ours begins, and ever since then the two had been inseparable chums.

One sloppy afternoon in late winter, Wolf and the boy were sprawled, side by side, on the fur rug in front of the library fire. The Mistress and the Master had gone to town for the day. The house was lonely, and the two chums were left to entertain each other.

The boy was reading a magazine. The dog beside him was blinking in drowsy comfort at the fire. Presently, finishing the story he had been reading, the Boy looked across at the sleepy dog.

"Wolf," he said, "here's a story about a dog. I think he must have been something like you. Maybe he was your great-great-great-great-grandfather, because he lived an awfully long time ago—in Pompeii. Ever hear of Pompeii?"

Now, the Boy was fifteen years old, and he had too much sense to imagine that Wolf could possibly understand the story he was about to tell him; but long since he had fallen into a way of talking to his dog, sometimes, as if to another human. It was fun for him to note the almost pathetic eagerness wherewith Wolf listened and tried to grasp the meaning of what he was saying. Again and again, at sound of some familiar word or voice inflection, the collie would prick up his ears or wag his tail, as if in the joyous hope that he had at last found a clue to his owner's meaning.

"You see," went on the Boy, "this dog lived in Pompeii, as I told you. You've never been there, Wolf."

Wolf was looking up at the Boy in wistful excitement, seeking vainly to guess what was expected of him.

"And," continued the Boy, "the kid who owned him seems to have had a regular knack for getting into trouble all the time. And his dog was always on hand to get him out of it. It's a true story, the magazine says. The kid's father was so grateful to the dog that he bought him a solid silver collar. Solid silver! Get that, Wolfie?"

Wolf did not "get it." But he wagged his tail hopefully, his eyes alight with bewildered interest.

"And," said the Boy, "what do you suppose was engraved on the collar? Well, I'll tell you: *'This dog has thrice saved his little master from death. Once by fire, once by flood, and once at the hands of robbers!'* How's that for a record, Wolf? For one dog, too!"

At the words "Wolf" and "dog," the collie's tail smote the floor in glad comprehension. Then he edged closer to the Boy as the narrator's voice presently took on a sadder note.

"But at last," resumed the Boy, "there came a time when the dog couldn't save the kid. Mount Vesuvius erupted. All the sky was pitch-dark, as black as midnight, and Pompeii was buried under lava and ashes. The dog might have got away by himself—dogs can see in the dark, can't they, Wolf?—but he couldn't get the kid away. And he wouldn't go without him. You wouldn't have gone without me, either, would you, Wolf? Pretty nearly two thousand years later, some people dug through the lava that covered Pompeii. What do you suppose they found? Of course they found a whole lot of things. One of them was that dog—silver collar and inscription and all. He was lying at the feet of a child. It must have been the child he couldn't save. He was one grand dog—hey, Wolf?"

The continued strain of trying to understand began to get on the collie's high-strung nerves. He rose to his feet, quivering, and sought to lick the Boy's face, thrusting one upraised white fore paw at him in appeal for a handshake. The Boy slammed shut the magazine.

"It's slow in the house, here, with nothing to do," he said to his chum. "I'm going up the lake with my gun to see if any wild ducks have landed in the marshes yet. It's almost time for them. Want to come along?"

The last sentence Wolf understood perfectly. On the instant, he was dancing with excitement at the prospect of a walk. Being a collie, he was of no earthly help in a hunting-trip; but on such tramps, as everywhere else, he was the Boy's inseparable companion.

Out over the slushy snow the two started, the boy with his light single-barreled shotgun slung over one shoulder, the dog trotting close at his heels. The March thaw was changing to a sharp freeze. The deep and soggy snow was crusted over, just thick enough to make walking a genuine difficulty for both dog and boy.

The Place was a promontory that ran out into the lake, on the opposite bank from the mile-distant village. Behind, across the high-road, lay the winter-choked forest. At the lake's northerly end, two miles beyond The Place, were the reedy marshes where a month hence wild duck would congregate. Thither, with Wolf, the Boy plowed his way through the biting cold.

The going was heavy and heavier. A quarter-mile below the marshes the Boy struck out across the upper corner of the lake. Here the ice was rotten at the top, where the thaw had nibbled at it, but beneath it was still a full eight inches thick, easily strong enough to bear the Boy's weight.

Along the gray ice-field the two plodded. The skim of water, which the thaw had spread an inch thick over the ice, had frozen in the day's cold spell. It crackled like broken glass as the chums walked over it. The Boy had on big hunting-boots, so, apart from the extra effort, the glass-like ice did not bother him. To Wolf it gave acute pain. The sharp particles were forever getting between the callous black pads of his feet, pricking and cutting him acutely.

Little smears of blood began to mark the dog's course; but it never occurred to Wolf to turn back, or to betray by any sign that he was suffering. It was all a part of the day's work—a cheap price to pay for the joy of tramping with his adored young master.

Then, forty yards or so on the hither side of the marshes, Wolf beheld a right amazing phenomenon. The Boy had been walking directly in front of him, gun over shoulder. With no warning at all, the youthful hunter fell, feet foremost, out of sight through the ice.

The light shell of new-frozen water that covered the lake's thicker ice also masked an air-hole nearly three feet wide. Into this, as he strode carelessly along, the Boy had stepped. Straight down he had gone, with all the force of his hundred-and-ten pounds and with all the impetus of his forward stride.

Instinctively, he threw out his hands to restore his balance. The only effect of this was to send the gun flying ten feet away.

Down went the Boy through less than three feet of water (for the bottom of the lake at this point had started to slope upward toward the marshes) and through nearly two feet more of sticky marsh mud that underlay the lake-bed.

His outflung hands struck against the ice on the edges of the air-hole, and clung there. Sputtering and gurgling, the Boy brought his head above the surface and tried to raise himself, by his hands, high enough to wriggle out upon the surface of the ice. Ordinarily, this would have been simple enough for so strong a lad, but the glue-like mud had imprisoned his feet and the lower part of his legs and held them powerless.

Try as he would, the Boy could not wrench himself free of the slough. The water, as he stood upright, was on a level with his mouth. The air-hole was too wide for him, at such a depth, to get a good purchase on its edges and lift himself bodily to safety.

Gathering such a finger-hold as he could, he heaved with all his might, throwing every muscle of his body into the struggle. One leg was pulled almost free of the mud, but the other was driven deeper into it. And as the Boy's fingers slipped from the smoothly wet ice-edge, the attempt to restore his balance drove the free leg back, knee-deep into the mire.

Ten minutes of this hopeless fighting left the Boy panting and tired out. The icy water was numbing his nerves and chilling his blood into torpidity. His hands were without sense of feeling as far up as the wrists. Even if he could have shaken free his legs from the mud, now he had not strength enough left to crawl out of the hole.

He ceased his uselessly frantic battle and stood dazed. Then he came sharply to himself. For, as he stood, the water crept upward from his lips to his nostrils. He knew why the water seemed to be rising. It was not rising. It was he who was sinking. As soon as he stopped moving the mud began very slowly, but very steadily, to suck him downward.

This was not a quicksand, but it was a deep mud-bed, and only by constant motion could he avoid sinking farther and farther down into it. He had less than two inches to spare at best before the water should fill his nostrils; less than two inches of life, even if he could keep the water down to the level of his lips.

There was a moment of utter panic. Then the Boy's brain cleared. His only hope was to keep on fighting—to rest when he must for a moment or so, and then to renew his numbed grip on the ice-edge and try to pull his feet a few inches higher out of the mud. He must do this as long as his chilled body could be scourged into obeying his will.

He struggled again, but with virtually no result in raising himself. A second struggle, however, brought him chin-high above the water. He remembered confusedly that some of these earlier struggles had scarce budged him, while others had gained him two or three inches. Vaguely, he wondered why. Then turning his head, he realized.

Wolf, as he turned, was just loosing his hold on the wide collar of the Boy's mackinaw. His cut forepaws were still braced against a flaw of ragged ice on the air-hole's edge, and all his tawny body was tense.

His body was dripping wet, too. The Boy noted that; and he realized that the repeated effort to draw his master to safety must have resulted, at least once, in pulling the dog down into the water with the floundering Boy.

"Once more, Wolfie! Once more!" chattered the Boy through teeth that clicked together like castanets.

The dog darted forward, caught his grip afresh on the edge of the Boy's collar, and tugged with all his fierce strength, growling and whining ferociously the while.

The boy seconded the collie's tuggings by a supreme struggle that lifted him higher than before. He was able to get one arm and shoulder clear above the ice. His numb fingers closed about an upthrust tree-limb which had been washed down stream in the autumn freshets and had been frozen into the lake ice.

With this new purchase, and aided by the dog, the Boy tried to drag himself out of the hole. But the chill of the water had done its work. He had not the strength to move farther. The mud still sucked at his calves and ankles. The big hunting boots were full of water that seemed to weigh a ton.

He lay there, gasping and chattering. Then, through the gathering twilight, his eyes fell on the gun, lying ten feet away.

"Wolf!" he ordered, nodding toward the weapon, "Get it! *Get* it!"

Not in vain had the Boy talked to Wolf for years as if the dog were human. At the words and the nod, the collie trotted over to the gun, lifted it by the stock, and hauled it awkwardly along over the bumpy ice to his master, where he laid it down at the edge of the air-hole.

The dog's eyes were cloudy with trouble, and he shivered and whined as with ague. The water on his thick coat was freezing to a mass of ice. But it was from anxiety that he shivered, and not from cold.

Still keeping his numb grasp on the tree-branch, the boy balanced himself as best he could and thrust two fingers of his free hand into his mouth to warm them into sensation again.

When this was done, he reached out to where the gun lay, and pulled its trigger. The shot boomed deafeningly through the twilight winter silences. The recoil sent the weapon sliding sharply back along the ice, spraining the Boy's trigger finger and cutting it to the bone.

"That's all I can do," said the Boy to himself. "If any one hears it, well and good. I can't get at another cartridge. I couldn't put it into the breech if I had it. My hands are too numb."

For several endless minutes he clung there, listening. But this was a desolate part of the lake, far from any road, and the season was too early for other hunters to be abroad. The bitter cold, in any case, tended to make sane folk hug the fireside rather than to venture so far into the open. Nor was the single report of a gun uncommon enough to call for investigation in such weather.

All this the Boy told himself as the minutes dragged by. Then he looked again at Wolf. The dog, head on one side, still stood protectingly above him. The dog was cold and in pain, but, being only a dog, it did not occur to him to trot off home to the comfort of the library fire and leave his master to fend for himself.

Presently, with a little sigh, Wolf lay down on the ice, his nose across the Boy's arm. Even if he lacked strength to save his beloved master, he could stay and share the Boy's sufferings.

But the Boy himself thought otherwise. He was not at all minded to freeze to death, nor was he willing to let Wolf imitate the dog of Pompeii by dying helplessly at his master's side. Controlling for an instant the chattering of his teeth, he called:

"Wolf!"

The dog was on his feet again at the word, alert, eager.

"Wolf!" repeated the Boy. *"Go!* Hear me? *Go!"*

He pointed homeward.

Wolf stared at him, hesitant. Again the Boy called in vehement command, *"Go!"*

The collie lifted his head to the twilight sky in a wolf-howl, hideous in its grief and appeal—a howl as wild and discordant as that of any of his savage ancestors. Then, stooping first to lick the numb hand that clung to the branch, Wolf turned and fled.

Across the cruelly sharp film of ice he tore at top speed, head down, whirling through the deepening dusk like a flash of tawny light.

Wolf understood what was wanted of him. Wolf always understood. The pain in his feet was as nothing. The stiffness of his numbed body was forgotten in the urgency of speed.

The Boy looked drearily after the swift-vanishing figure which the dusk was swallowing. He knew the dog would try to bring help, as has many another and lesser dog in times of need. Whether or not that help could arrive in time, or at all, was a point on which the Boy would not let himself dwell. Into his benumbed brain crept the memory of an old Norse proverb he had read in school:

"Heroism consists in hanging on one minute longer."

Unconsciously he tightened his feeble hold on the tree-branch and braced himself.

FROM the marshes to The Place was a full two miles. Despite the deep and sticky snow, Wolf covered the distance in less than six minutes. He paused in front of the gate-lodge, at the highway entrance to the drive. But the gardener and his wife had gone to Paterson, shopping, that afternoon.

Down the drive to the house he dashed. The maids had taken advantage of their employers' day in New York to walk across the lake to the village to a motion-picture show.

Wise men claim that dogs have not the power to think or to reason things out in a logical way. So perhaps it was mere chance that next sent Wolf's flying feet across the lake to the village. Perhaps it was chance, and not the knowledge that where there is a village there are people.

Again and again, in the car, he had sat upon the front seat alongside the Mistress when she drove to the station to meet guests. There were always people at the station, and to the station Wolf now raced.

The usual group of platform idlers had been dispersed by the cold. A solitary baggageman was hauling a trunk and some boxes out of the express-coop on to the platform to be put aboard the five o'clock train from New York.

As the baggageman passed under the clump of station lights, he came to a sudden halt, for out of the darkness dashed a dog. Full tilt, the animal rushed up to him and seized him by the skirt of his overcoat.

The man cried out in scared surprise. He dropped the box he was carrying and struck at the dog to ward off the seemingly murderous attack. He recognized Wolf, and he knew the collie's repute.

But Wolf was not attacking. Holding tight to the coat-skirt, he backed away, trying to draw the man with him, and all the while whimpering aloud like a nervous puppy.

A kick from the man's heavy-shod boot broke the dog's hold on the coat-skirt, even as a second yell from the man brought four or five other people running out from the station waiting-room.

One of these, the telegraph operator, took in the scene at a single glance. With great presence of mind he bawled loudly: "MAD DOG!"

This, as Wolf, reeling from the kick, sought to gain another grip on the coat-skirt. A second kick sent him rolling over and over on the tracks, while other voices took up the panic cry of "Mad dog!"

Now, a mad dog is supposed to be a dog afflicted by rabies. Once in ten thousand times, at the very most, a mad-dog hue-and-cry is justified. Certainly not oftener. A harmless and friendly dog loses his Master on the street. He runs about, confused and frightened, looking for the owner he has lost. A boy throws a stone at him. Other boys chase him. His tongue hangs out, and his eyes glaze with terror. Then some fool bellows:

"Mad dog!"

And the cruel chase is on—a chase that ends in the pitiful victim's death. Yet in every crowd there is a voice ready to raise that asinine and murderously cruel shout.

So it was with the men who witnessed Wolf's frenzied effort to take aid to the imperiled Boy.

Voice after voice repeated the cry. Men groped along the platform edge for stones to throw. The village policeman ran puffing upon the scene, drawing his revolver.

Finding it useless to make a further attempt to drag the baggageman to the rescue, Wolf leaped back, facing the ever larger group. Back went his head again in that hideous wolf-howl. Then he galloped away a few yards, trotted back, howled once more, and again galloped lakeward.

All of which only confirmed the panicky crowd in the belief that they were threatened by a mad dog. A shower of stones hurtled about Wolf as he came back a third time to lure these dull humans into following him.

One pointed rock smote the collie's shoulder, glancing, cutting it to the bone. A shot from the policeman's revolver fanned the fur of his ruff as it whizzed past.

Knowing that he faced death, he nevertheless stood his ground, not troubling to dodge the fusillade of stones, but continuing to run lakeward and then trot back, whining with excitement.

A second pistol-shot flew wide. A third grazed the dog's hip. From all directions people were running toward the station. A man darted into a house next door, and emerged, carrying a shotgun. This he steadied on a veranda-rail not forty feet away from the leaping dog, and made ready to fire.

It was then the train from New York came in, and momentarily the sport of "mad-dog" killing was abandoned, while the crowd scattered to each side of the track.

From a front car of the train the Mistress and the Master emerged into a bedlam of noise and confusion.

"Best hide in the station, Ma'am!" shouted the telegraph operator, at sight of the Mistress. "There is a mad dog loose out here! He's chasing folks around, and—"

"Mad dog!" repeated the Mistress in high contempt. "If you knew anything about dogs, you'd know mad ones never 'chase folks around' any more than typhoid patients do. Then—"

A flash of tawny light beneath the station lamp, a scurrying of frightened idlers, a final wasted shot from the policeman's pistol, as Wolf dived headlong through the frightened crowd toward the voice he heard and recognized.

Up to the Mistress and the Master galloped Wolf. He was bleeding, his eyes were bloodshot, his fur was rumpled. He seized the astounded Master's gloved hand lightly between his teeth and sought to pull him across the tracks and toward the lake.

The Master knew dogs, especially he knew Wolf, and without a word he suffered himself to be led. The Mistress and one or two inquisitive men followed.

Presently, Wolf loosed his hold on the Master's hand and ran on ahead, darting back every few moments to make certain he was followed.

"Heroism — consists — in — hanging — on — one minute — longer," the Boy was whispering deliriously to himself for the hundredth time as Wolf pattered up to him in triumph across the ice, with the human rescuers a scant ten yards behind!

THE BUFFALO DANCE

by Cornelia Meigs

IN the cool silence and in the level light of the late afternoon, Chanuka's canoe seemed to be the only moving thing in the wide expanse of marshy lake country. There was so little breeze that the tall reeds stood motionless, knee-deep in the still water. The Indian boy was not hunting today, nor was he watching for any enemy, that he moved so silently. It was only his unwillingness to break that spell of utter quiet that made him guide his light craft so noiselessly across the narrow stretches of open water, over the shallows where the water grasses brushed softly along the birch bark bottom and between those tufts of green, where rocks, brush, and poplars or pines rose from the water here and there in a myriad of tiny green islands. Everywhere the tall rushes stood stiffly erect, so that he could not see, in any direction, more than a few yards beyond the high painted bow of his boat. Yet he moved forward steadily, threading his way without hesitation through that maze of concealing reeds and winding water lanes.

He liked to feel that he was the only human being within twenty, fifty or perhaps a hundred miles, that he and the fish and the water-fowl had all to themselves this stretch of lake and marsh and river which lay to the southward of the hunting grounds of his tribe. Somewhere beyond that watery domain lay the grassy open country where dwelt the Dacotahs, the unforgetting enemies of his tribe.

The older warriors still talked beside the camp-fire of the long wars which had raged intermittently and furiously between nation and nation for a hundred years. Neither tribe could ever call itself actually victorious; but fighting would cease at times from sheer exhaustion on both sides. For some years now there had been uneasy truce, with the smoldering hatred ready to break out into fierce flame again at any moment.

Once Chanuka had said to one of the old braves, "The Dacotahs live on the prairies and hunt the buffalo, and we dwell in the forest and get our meat from the deer and the moose. We do not need to quarrel over hunting grounds. Why should we be always at war with the prairie men?"

To which the scarred and wrinkled fighter had replied, "We hate them; so did our fathers, so will our sons. That is cause enough. And you will understand, when you grow older, that when spring comes, then the young warriors are ever restless and eager to be on the war-path. And for us the war-path must always lead southward."

Chanuka could understand the second explanation better than the first, for he knew that stirring of the spirit and the body in the spring, which might lead one anywhere.

Through those last years when there had been no fighting between Ojibway and Dacotah, both sides had avoided this special stretch of lake and swamp which lay between their two domains, so that it had long been left empty even of hunters. Now, moved by that same restlessness, which comes with the bursting loose of ice-imprisoned streams and the stir of life in the vast green wood, Chanuka had turned aside from his hunting to explore this unknown land and these unfamiliar waters. In spite of the knowledge that such journeying was forbidden by his chief, he could not forbear going farther and farther southward into the empty waste.

The last lake through which he had passed was wooded only on three sides, while the grassy prairie swept all the way up to its southern banks. This was proof indeed that he was coming close to the lands of the enemy. But the dense forest was still massed behind and immediately about him, and the sharp hoof-prints of deer and the big splay-footed tracks of moose had trampled the grass and mud of the shores where the wild creatures had come down to the water to drink or to feed on the lily-pads.

A blot of dense green, showing through the pale stems of the rushes, told him finally that he was approaching an island, solid ground in this empty wilderness of ripples and swaying reeds. He came near, dipping his blade easily and lightly, and then suddenly paused, with his paddle half lifted, frozen into an immovable statue of wary listening. He had heard a voice issuing from the dense undergrowth of the island, a voice which muttered, dropped into silence, then fell to muttering again or rose to a curious half-choked cry.

With a motion as soundless as that of a fish's quivering fin, Chanuka paddled nearer, yard by yard, until he was stealing under the drooping boughs of overhanging trees, until he was peering out at a bit of gravel beach and a narrow grassy clearing.

That which he saw first was a canoe, or rather had once been a canoe. It was not a trim birch-bark vessel such as was bearing Chanuka on his voyaging, but the clumsier dugout craft of the sort that the Indians dwelling on the southern rivers fashioned from tree trunks. It was battered and trampled now into hopeless ruin, stamped halfway into the soft ground, with the snapped blade of the paddle lying beside it along with a broken bow and a spilled quiver of arrows. After one long, silent survey, Chanuka stepped ashore and walked, without attempt at concealment, across the slope where the turf was plowed and torn by the stamping hoofs of some great animal.

The master of that broken vessel was extended at full length, half hidden below a thicket of brambles. One arm was crumpled under him; the other was flung before his face. Long, lean, and red-skinned, he lay inert and helpless, muttering and whispering to himself, taking no notice, even when Chanuka finally knelt down beside him on the grass. The arm under him was undoubtedly broken; his whole body was bruised and torn with a dozen jagged gashes, while the hot fever of untended wounds was evidently running like fire through his whole being. Chanuka laid his firm brown fingers against that burning skin and nodded.

"No one but a plains-dwelling Dacotah," he commented within himself, "would know so little as to stand against the charge of a wounded moose."

All up and down upon the grass was written the record of that encounter when the great ugly-tempered beast, wounded and furious, had turned upon the unwary hunter. Here were wounds of lashing, goring horns, here was the broken bow from which the arrow had sped too late.

"He thought he was hunting a creature like one of his stupid buffalo," the Ojibway boy reflected in scorn.

The Dacotah had evidently followed the animal through the marsh, not knowing that the moment it felt firm ground under its feet the moose would turn upon him in deadly attack. Canoe, weapons, the limp, helpless body under its feet—all alike were objects of the huge beast's blind onslaught. One final charge had carried it clean over the fallen quarry, and it had gone, plunging and splashing across the marsh, leaving the silent glade far behind. The keen eyes of the Indian boy could read plainly the whole tale.

Chanuka's eyes glinted with a sudden spark as he stooped over the wounded stranger. He had thought, more than once, as he paddled through the reeds and the rapids, of the black disfavor with which the chief of his village would greet him upon his return. The year before in the same foolhardy curiosity he had journeyed down into the prairie region and on his return had been met with severe reprimand and punishment as well.

"If a warrior seeks out the enemy's country, he must not come home empty-handed," the hard-faced old Indian had said and had set the boy to do squaw's work for the waxing and waning of the first snow-moon. The memory of that penalty had often burned hotly in Chanuka's heart; but it had not kept him back when the spring unrest set him once more to roving. And this time he would not come home empty-handed; he would bring a captive from the tribe of their foes, a Dacotah warrior, helpless in the bottom of his canoe.

He stooped and half lifted, half dragged the limp figure out from among the brambles to lie upon the open grass. As he did so the glittering light in his eyes died suddenly. For a long minute he stood frowning down upon that truth which a better view had revealed. Long of limb though the Dacotah might be, he was evidently not yet a grown warrior. His age must be much the same as Chanuka's own.

A boy, a boy taken with the same sudden impulse to wander into hostile country for no better reason than that it was forbidden! It would have been glorious triumph to carry home a captured brave. But would the triumph be quite the same, when the captive was a headlong, blundering lad, who had dared the same dangers as himself and had fallen into unexpected misfortune?

Hardly admitting, even in his own mind, just what was his final purpose, Chanuka stooped once more and began, as best he could, to tend the other's hurts. Every warrior knew a little of how bleeding wounds could be bound up with leaves and bark. Darkness fell while he was still at work; he kindled a fire, brought from his canoe a wild duck which he had shot earlier in the day and set it to broiling before the coals.

When the savory fowl was ready he attempted to feed the wounded Dacotah, but that burning throat would swallow nothing but water. After the first long cool draught from the bark cup which Chanuka set to his lips, the long lad's tossing and mumbling eased a little. He kept repeating a single word thereafter, which Chanuka began to understand stood for water—ever more water. In the end the Ojibway boy forgot to eat and bent all his absorbed effort upon bringing sufficient water, and moving the sufferer from time to time when one position became unbearable and he stirred and struggled feebly to shift to another.

The moon rose and stood high above the trees; the dark ripples lapped softly on the shore, and that muttering voice went on and on. There was never a groan, never a querulous note of complaint. Even with his mind and spirit wandering somewhere in that land of shadows which borders upon death, the young Dacotah's instinct held true. Not once did he cry out with the pain which was consuming him.

All night Chanuka toiled over him. It was only when the moon was dropping and the sky growing white to the eastward, that the fever seemed to abate and the Dacotah lay more quietly. When the morning broke over the silent marsh, the two Indian boys lay together upon the grass, side by side, both fast asleep.

There followed some days of strange comradeship. On the second morning the Dacotah tried to stand, but could not; on the third he made determined effort to walk, and by the fourth could move about, although but slowly and painfully. His wounds would give him pain for a long time still, and the scars would be with him throughout his life; but the iron strength of an Indian would not yield to weakness and fever for more than the briefest stretch of days.

The two could not talk together; nor did they make any real effort to communicate by that language of signs with which all red men are familiar. That they were enemies, brought together in surprising and accidental truce, was a thing which neither of them seemed able to forget. Yet they caught fish and cooked them together, snared rabbits and ate them in company, and, as on that first night, slept side by side upon the grass.

It was the Dacotah who made the only effort at further acquaintance. His name, it seemed, was Neosho. He offered this information and once or twice seemed to be trying, further, to give his rescuer some knowledge of the country in which he dwelt and the life of his people in their buffalo-skin lodges beside the big southward-flowing river. But Chanuka did not offer much attention to what the other was attempting to tell, and, after a little, the Dacotah ceased any efforts at a semblance

of talk. Had not Chanuka, on that foolhardy journey of seven moons ago, seen those same lodges of Neosho's people in the open country near that same river? He had stolen so close, under cover of the darkness, that he had actually lain hidden on one side of a small creek, while, upon the flat open ground of the opposite bank, the people of that Dacotah village had built their circle of fires and had danced the Buffalo Dance. He could see and hear them still, the red flames, the strangely moving dancers, the chanting voices and the thumping of the drums coming out of the darkness.

The Buffalo Dance celebrates the festival when the Dacotah braves have come home from their summer hunting, laden with the meat which is to be their provision against the winter. Only three dancers take part in it. First comes the warrior who represents the buffalo, wrapped in a brown, hairy robe and bearing the shaggy horned head pulled down over his own like a mask. He crouches and dances forward, tossing the head from side to side, imitating the lumbering gait of the buffalo. Next comes the horse, a man wrapped in a pony's hide and covering his face with the rude effigy of the animal's head. He moves it up and down, imitating the jogging motion of a horse loping along the buffalo trail. Last comes the hunter with his bow and arrows, rehearsing in pantomime all the adventures of the summer's chase.

Much as Chanuka would have liked to know more of the Dacotahs and their ways, he fought against paying heed to what Neosho was trying to tell him. He would sit beside the fire moody and brooding, or would go silently about his work of bringing food and caring for his comrade's wounds. There had been some idea in his mind, at first, of letting the Dacotah boy recover somewhat, and then of challenging him to mortal combat, as was fitting between enemies. But as he watched the other limping back and forth across the glade, slowly coming again to his former strength, the Ojibway's determination failed. The days passed, and no challenge came.

Even through their long silences, there was something growing up between them. Could it be called friendship between two mortal enemies? One had fallen into dire misfortune; the other had scorned to take advantage of his helplessness. Does such a thing make friends? Neither would betray by word or sign whether such were possible.

It was on the fifth day that they finally parted. The sun was rising red above the marsh when Chanuka signed to the other to take his place in the bow of the bark canoe. Neosho could not have known whether he was to be carried to freedom or back into the forest to fall into the hands of his deadly foes. He cast one glance at his broken bow still lying upon the ground and then with unchanging face stepped into the light craft which was already lifting to the ripples. Chanuka dipped his paddle and they slipped away through the rushes.

The unseen hand of a slight current bore them away southwestward, carried them at gathering speed through a narrow stream, then out upon the broad silver of a quiet lake. The forest was behind them; from the opposite shore the prairie lands, dotted with groves of trees, stretched away in green and rolling ridges. Chanuka brought the bow of the boat to land, and sat waiting without a word while his companion stepped out upon the grassy bank and strode away up the green rise. As he crossed the shoulder of the ridge, Neosho looked back and raised his hand. Chanuka lifted his paddle. That was the whole of their leave-taking before the Dacotah disappeared beyond the grassy summit. The Ojibway pushed off his vessel into deep water, swung the bow and set himself to paddling steadily northward.

If Chanuka wondered, on his homeward journey, what was to be the end of that forbidden adventure, he wondered still more when he arrived at his journey's end. He had been made to do sharp penance for that earlier expedition into the plains country; but this time, when he returned after an unexplained absence of eleven days and with nothing to show but a few wild ducks and a string of fish, no word was said. He was conscious that the eyes of the wrinkled old chief followed him as he went to and fro in the village. But if there was to be punishment for his disobeying, it was slow in coming.

The months of the summer passed with all the braves occupied by the season's hunting. Then the autumn began to draw on. The wild rice was ripening along the edges of the marshes, the swamp maples were turning red, and the dry rustle of the wind in the poplars foretold the coming of the winter tempests.

It was after a long day of hunting in the rice swamps that Chanuka was summoned at evening to the lodge of his chief. The great man sat alone before the smoldering fire and looked at the young brave with hard, narrow eyes. The moment of reckoning for that stolen expedition had come.

"You who have a heart so set upon voyages to the southward, are now to take a new journey," the chief said at last.

As a proper brave should, Chanuka waited in silence for the whole substance of his leader's commands.

"It may be that the time is coming close for us to do battle once more against our age-long enemies, the Dacotahs," the other went on. "The signs of sky and forest point to a hard winter; but our hunting has been good, so that our tribe will not have lost in strength before the spring. We must discover whether our foes are to fare as well through the season of the snows. That is to be your task."

He paused, seeming to search the boy's face for any sign of dismay. Yet Chanuka's countenance was as unmoving as his own, as the chief continued:

"You are to seek out that largest village of the Dacotahs which lies in a great grove of walnut-trees where one big river forks into three; and you are to go in haste so that you may see their braves come home from the buffalo hunt. If their store of dried meat for the winter is scanty, they will hunger and weaken when the snows begin and sickness will go from lodge to lodge. And then, when spring comes the Ojibway will fall upon them. It is of this matter that you are to bring news, whether the Dacotah hunters come home heavily or lightly laden. By the word which you carry we will determine whether there is to be war again, or longer peace."

A journey is apt to seem shorter each time that it is repeated. Chanuka, traveling over the now familiar waterways, seemed to approach his journey's end more swiftly than either time before. It almost seemed that his paddle lagged; but brisk autumn winds and streams brimming from autumn rains carried him relentlessly onward. It was not until he had passed over half the distance that a strange question began to form itself within his mind. Was it possible that he did not wish to go so quickly? Was he a reluctant messenger; had those days upon the island in the marsh so weakened the resolution of a proper warrior that he, the first one chosen for the war-path, was going forward unwillingly? The thought stung him as though it were one of the wild black bees who were gathering their final store of honey in the sheets of yellow flowers which bordered all the streams. He dipped his blade and sped southward with all the haste which his paddle could add to the breezes and currents behind him. Yet as he journeyed his face darkened; for ply his paddle as he would, he could not seem to leave that haunting question behind. He did not know that he was offering vain battle against a natural force far stronger than even the relentless will of an Indian warrior. Wars may last a hundred years, or a thousand; but the spirit of fellowship which can grow up between one growing youth and another is older and more powerful than tribal hatreds.

He came to that green shore where he had left Neosho; and from there hastened forward on foot until he came in sight of the forks of the big river and saw the Dacotah lodges scattered through the grove of walnut-trees. From daybreak until evening he lay in hiding on the opposite side of the stream, watching all those who went back and forth amongst the lodges or came down to the bank for water. At first it was plain that only squaws and children and old men inhabited the place, that all the young and able-bodied braves were still away hunting the buffalo. Chanuka's chief had timed well the sending of his messenger; for the boy had waited only a night and a day before he witnessed the return of the hunters.

They advanced across the plain in a cloud of dust, a long line of laden ponies and weary huntsmen. From the shouts and from the delight with which they were greeted by those who ran out to meet them and escort them to their own lodges, it seemed that the chase had been crowned with success. Of that, however, Chanuka could not be certain until he stole nearer. This it was his plan to do on the night when the Dacotahs lit their ceremonial fires on the flat bank just across from him and made ready to dance the Buffalo Dance.

Another warrior, so Chanuka reflected,

might be content to watch and spy and carry home his news gathered only by observing from a distance. But he was determined to steal through the whole village, to peer into every lodge, and to carry away, perhaps from the dwelling of the chief, some token of actual proof that he had walked among the very camp-fires of the enemy. A beaded pouch, a bow or a carved pipe, something he must surely have to bear away. Had not his chief said that he who seeks out the country of the enemy must not come home empty-handed? The darkness of the chosen night had fallen and the women were preparing the heaps of wood for the circle of fire, when he slipped into the river to swim silently across.

He came out dripping, and crouched under the low bank to listen. All the voices and movement were on the flat ground to the right of him, where the whole village seemed to be gathering. He found his way to a break in the slope of the shore and, under the scanty cover of wild blackberries and hickory brush, he crept unnoticed to the very edge of the camp. The lodges stood tenantless, with the embers of spent fires dying before every door. He peered into one empty dwelling, then another and another. It was even as he had guessed from afar, the stores were plenty; the hunt had been successful. The Dacotahs were rich indeed this season with dried meat and buffalo robes; there would be no starving when the winter came.

He had reached the very center of the camp and was looking about him to determine which was the chief's lodge, the most worthy dwelling to be plundered. It would be easy to bear away anything that he wished; for every living soul, it seemed, was on the open ground beside the river. A sudden tumult of voices almost at his elbow startled him into the knowledge that he was mistaken.

From the Medicine Lodge below the biggest walnut-tree there came forth a group of laughing, shouting warriors. The dull fire behind them and the light of the stars above showed him that here was the Medicine Man himself, with an escort of young braves, walking down through the lodges, to appear the last of all beside the river, and to give the signal for the dance to begin.

The young men spread their line out through the camp, perhaps to see whether every person had gone. There was nothing for Chanuka to do but to give way before them, slipping from one shadow to another, taking advantage of any possible cover, but still being driven steadily down toward that space of light and tumult where the whole village was gathered. In absolute desperation he took refuge at last under the edge of a great pile of firewood.

The shouting warriors passed close beside him. One of them even stopped, seemed to hesitate a moment, and then went on with the others. An old brave came hobbling up to the opposite side of the heap of fuel and gathered an armful to fling upon the fire just kindled not ten yards away. The flare of red light showed the crowding women and children, the warriors in their feathered head-dresses, and the fringed branches of the walnut-trees moving softly in the rush of hot air. It would be impossible now to slip from that hiding-place and reach the river unseen. From time to time more wood was thrown upon the fire, keeping the light ablaze and steadily lessening Chanuka's only cover. The drums thumped under the trees; the Medicine Man's voice rose in slow chant. The dance was about to begin.

Of a sudden, Chanuka, tense as a whipcord, felt a touch upon his arm. He started; in the pressure of his excitement he might have cried out. Some one was stooping over him, a queer misshapen figure quite unrecognizable in the firelight. But the voice which spoke Chanuka's name in a whisper was Neosho's.

At such highly wrought moments minds move quickly, and understanding comes without need of words. Neosho, it seemed, was to take the part of the horse, in the coming dance. Crouching low at the edge of the heap of wood, he wrapped about his former comrade the sheltering garments of horse-hide and thrust into his hands the wooden, skin-covered likeness of a horse's head. Already the brave who was to take the part of the buffalo was dancing and stamping his slow way around the circle inside the ring of fires. Every eye was upon that moving figure with its tossing horns and lashing tail. One round the buffalo was to make alone, then was to be followed by the horse, then by the hunter. So intent were all the spectators about the fires that no one noted the brief pause before the horse came out from the shadows and the second dancer joined the first.

As has been said, Chanuka had seen the dance before, watching from afar across the stream. It was well for him that an Indian's mind is trained to notice and to store up every detail which his eye has once seen. With his heart hammering against his ribs, and with his eyes peering desperately through the holes in the clumsy head, Chanuka set himself to imitate the stamping dance step of the man before him, while he moved the horse's head, up and down, up and down, just as he had seen the dancer, a year ago, imitate the jogging motion of a loping pony. In that breathless moment during which Dacotah and Ojibway had changed places, Neosho's quick eye had noted one detail which might have betrayed them both. He had kicked off his beaded moccasins, and had pointed to Chanuka's, cut and embroidered in a different fashion and proclaiming his tribe to any watchful eye. The long limbed

plainsman was larger than the lad of the forest, so that now Chanuka, dancing for his life, found the moccasins awkwardly big as he jerked and shuffled forward in the wake of the shuffling buffalo.

He had circled the ring of flickering red light, and now, from a shout behind him, knew that the hunter had joined the other two and that all interest and every glance was centered upon the final dancer alone. Once more they made the circuit, the three together. It seemed to the panting boy wrapped in the heavy horse-hide that the round of fire-lit grass had stretched to the compass of a mile. But at last he saw the buffalo stop, look backward over his shoulder and then step aside to mingle with the crowd. A few more steps he danced; then, where the spectators had dwindled to a broken line on the rough footing just above the river bank, the horse also slipped out of the circle and disappeared beyond the curtain of darkness that hung beyond the fire.

There was a soft splash in the water, as though a great fish had jumped. It attracted the attention of a single lean young warrior who alone turned to listen, and who, presently, edged his way to the brink of the river and there gathered up an abandoned horse-hide and the rudely fashioned model of a horse's head. Although he stood, silent and hearkening, for long minutes, there was no sound to be heard above the drums, no hint of a wet, supple figure clambering out of the stream on the opposite bank, and setting forth to bear a message northward.

It was three days later that Chanuka stood before his chief again and gave the news that the Dacotah tribe had had good hunting and that this was no time to prepare for renewing the war. The other heard him, frowning.

"And how do I know that you really traveled so far, that you speak the truth when you say that you actually peered into the Dacotah lodges beside the river?" he asked.

"By these," returned Chanuka briefly. He held up a pair of buffalo-hide moccasins, beaded and ornamented after a pattern never used by an Ojibway. And from the lodge pole of a certain dwelling of the Dacotahs, there swung at that same moment a pair of smaller moccasins, embroidered with bright porcupine quills, such as are worn by the forest hunters. For long years they hung there, the silent witness of a friendship of which no word had ever been spoken aloud.

THE BLACKBIRDS: A QUEER STORY

by Robert Emmet Ward

WHEN my Uncle Henry was about twelve years old, he had been "up to the Big Woods" one summer afternoon, and was coming home carrying a large watermelon. In that part of Kentucky, when forest land is cleared for growing tobacco, a portion is usually planted in melons the first summer, the ground being so rich that the yield is remarkably fine. The melon that Uncle Henry was "toting" home that afternoon, from the patch only that spring cut off the Big Woods, was so heavy and so ripe that when he happened to stub his bare toe against a projecting root and drop his burden, it burst wide open as it struck the ground.

Uncle Henry, even at that early stage of his history, had two marked characteristics —kindliness of disposition, and an impenetrable reticence. He stood looking at the ruin before him, nursing his stubbed toe, and saying nothing.

Presently the curious sense that one is being watched, which we all have experienced at times, caused him to glance around. On the rock-fence, not ten feet away, sat another boy, no older than himself, gazing at him in silence as unbroken as his own. He was, Uncle Henry thought, without exception, the thinnest, the most sunburnt, and most ragged boy he had ever seen.

"Howdy; want to help me to eat it?" Uncle Henry asked, hospitably, sitting down beside the melon's remains.

The boy nodded, joined him in the middle of the lane, and without further words, they both fell to.

There was little left, even of the fragments, except green rind and black seeds, when Uncle Henry's guest had finished. He drew the back of his thin hand across his mouth, and observed,

"That tas'e mighty good."

Uncle Henry looked at him, and reflected that he had never seen him before—he who knew everybody in several counties. Boys of twelve, however thin, do not blow along with the wind. It was no part of Uncle Henry's code to ask questions which might prove embarrassing, so he hesitated. But further reflection convinced him that here a question or two might prove justifiable.

"Going on a piece?" he ventured, politely.

"I reckon," answered the other boy, forlornly. "I dunno whereabouts I *am* goin'. Me and my father started out las' month from Buncombe County, No'th Caliny, after he done sold the farm; and he 'lowed we was goin' to Missoury. But I reckon he got tarred o' me taggin' along, fer he's done lef' me. I been lingerin' 'round lookin' fer 'im, but hit's three days now, and I ain't never seen 'im, so I reckon he's done lef' me fer good. So I'm jus' goin' along anywheres."

Uncle Henry made no display of the effect of this simple recital upon his warm, boyish heart. He only said cordially,

"Better come to my house for supper, and stay all night. My father'll be glad to see you. I live right near here. My name's Henry."

"Mine's Sam." No further acquiescence seemed, to either boy, necessary.

The two went along in amicable silence, occasionally exchanging ideas by means of a nod, a gesture, a half-articulated word, as some object of interest by the wayside attracted the attention of either. Once a flock of blackbirds flew up out of a field, and Sam, who had a crooked stick in his hand, threw it up to his shoulder, took careful aim at the birds, ejaculated *"Bing!"* with much fervor, and, after deliberately blowing down an imaginary barrel, let his weapon fall with evident satisfaction. Uncle Henry looked on with entire approval.

"Like shooting?" he asked, presently.

"I *kin*—but I ain't got no real sure-enough gun," returned Sam.

"You can shoot mine," responded Uncle Henry, promptly. "My father'll take us both out with him. That is, if you think you'd like to stay with us a while."

Sam made no reply. He may have been speechless; he may have thought reply superfluous. At any rate, welcomed with considerate courtesy by his new friend's father and mother, he stayed the night, and all the next day. His visit lengthened to a week, a month, and by the end of that month the whole family had forgotten that Sam was not by right of birth a member of the household.

The two boys grew up together, in much the same amity with which their acquaintance had begun over the watermelon. Both remained boys of few words. Sam's most marked peculiarity was one which seldom failed to strike the casual observer with surprise, although the family soon grew so accustomed to it that it excited no comment. In summer, the big old black locust-

trees on the lawn in front of the Hall are much frequented by blackbirds: and whenever a noisy flock would fly up into the boughs, Sam would dart into Uncle Henry's room, which was on the first floor, snatch his gun from the rack, dart out again on the porch, and fire. Whether he brought down several birds or none, the one shot seemed to content him; he would invariably blow down the barrel—thus ornamenting his countenance, around the mouth, with a black circle of powder, of which he never seemed aware—and then somewhat sheepishly replace the gun and go about his affairs without further concern. But that one shot he seemed obliged to have, just as surely as a flock of blackbirds came in sight; and he was never known to omit the ceremony of blowing down the barrel of the gun before he put it away.

He stayed on until Uncle Henry and he were a little over twenty-one years old: then he seemed to grow restless, and one day announced he wanted to "go West." Uncle Henry made no attempt to dissuade him. The whole family wished him God-speed, and, as suddenly as he had come, Sam went. Uncle Henry did not say that he missed him; but sometimes, when the blackbirds were especially noisy in the big locust-trees, he would glance up at them reminiscently, with what, from a less cheery, pleasant-hearted young fellow, would have been a sigh. Years passed, and it was as if there had never been a Sam.

Uncle Henry was a more than middle-aged man when, late one summer afternoon, as he was smoking on the porch, a stranger rode up the drive and stopped at the gate. A hearty hail brought him up to the house, where he and Uncle Henry fell into conversation that soon led to a cordial invitation to stay to supper. The stranger told Uncle Henry that he had heard a great deal of old Hurricane Hall—the first brick house to be built in that part of Kentucky—and had stopped to ask permission to see it. He was a well-dressed, prosperous-looking man, tall, spare, and gray-haired, and of much quiet dignity of manner; Uncle Henry fancied that they had met before, although he could not recall where. The guest, however, said nothing of himself or his affairs, and it still was no part of Uncle Henry's code to ask questions.

While they sat on the porch waiting to be summoned to supper, a flock of loud blackbirds swept across the lawn and up into the trees. Without a word Uncle Henry's visitor sprang from his seat, dashed into the house, and, returning with Uncle Henry's shot-gun, blazed away. Hardly noticing, it seemed, whether any birds fell, he carefully blew down the gunbarrel, and, oblivious of the powder mark around his mouth, walked back into the house to replace the gun on the rack in Uncle Henry's room, after which he returned composedly to his chair in the porch. The two men smoked in silence for several moments.

"Blackbirds," observed Uncle Henry then, "are unusually plentiful this year."

"I've noticed that," said the other.

No further remark was made, and an instant later, supper was announced. Open-hearted Southern hospitality gave the stranger welcome from all the family: it was enough that Uncle Henry brought him in. If any eye were arrested by the unusual decoration around the guest's grave mouth, none could detect the most fleeting glance of curiosity or surprise.

After supper the two men walked about the old place a little; but very soon the stranger, whose manner began to show a faint trace of constraint, declared he must be getting on, thanked his host briefly, shook hands with a hearty grip, and, mounting his horse, rode away into the gathering twilight.

Uncle Henry's eyes followed him for a little distance; then, turning back toward the house, he looked up into the trees where the blackbirds were now at rest for the night.

"Good old Sam!" he mused. "I doubt if we ever see him again."

And they never did.

THIS PLEASANT WORLD

by Rachel Field

CRANBERRY ROAD

I'D like to be walking the cranberry road,
  Where the sea shines blue through the
    bristling firs,
And the rocky pastures are overgrown
  With bayberry bushes and junipers;
Where orchards of bent old appletrees
  Go trooping down to the pebbly shore,
And the clapboard houses are seaward
    turned,
  With larkspur clumps at every door;
Where there's plenty of time to say good-
    day
  When friendly eyes from a window
    peer—
Oh, I'd like to be back on the cranberry
    road;
  I wish I were there instead of here!

IF ONCE YOU HAVE SLEPT ON AN ISLAND

IF once you have slept on an island,
  You'll never be quite the same;
You may look as you did the day before
  And go by the same old name;

You may bustle about in street and shop,
  You may sit at home and sew,
But you'll see blue water and wheeling
    gulls
  Wherever your feet may go.

You may chat with the neighbors of this
    and that,
  Or close to your fire keep,
But you'll hear ship-whistle and lighthouse
    bell
  And tides beat through your sleep.

Oh, you won't know why, and you can't
    say how
  Such change upon you came,
But—once you have slept on an island,
  You'll never be quite the same!

GENERAL STORE

SOME day I mean to keep a store,
With a tinkly bell hung over the door,
With real glass cases and counters wide
And drawers all spilly with things inside.

There'll be a little of everything—
Bolts of calico, balls of string,
Jars of peppermint, tins of tea,
Pots and kettles and crockery,
Seeds in packets, scissors bright,
Kegs of sugar brown and white,
Sarsaparilla for picnic lunches,
Bananas and rubber boots in bunches.
I'll fix the window and dust each shelf,
And take the money in all myself.
It will be my store and I will say:
"What can I do for *you* to-day?"

HOUSES

I LIKE old houses best, don't you?
They never go cluttering up a view
With roofs too red and paint too new,
With doors too green and blinds too blue.
The old ones look as if they *grew;*

Their bricks may be dingy, their clapboards
    askew
From sitting so many seasons through;
But they've learned, in a hundred years
    or two,
Not to go cluttering up a view!

TWO BIDDICUT BOYS

(AND THEIR ADVENTURES WITH A WONDERFUL TRICK DOG)

by J. T. Trowbridge

I

ON THE LAKE-SHORE

THE boys were putting on their clothes in the shadow of the ice-house, when a young man, walking along the edge of the railroad embankment, sauntered down to the shore, followed by a dog. The man had on a narrow-brimmed, speckled straw hat, and a loose sackcoat, and he carried a short stick jauntily in his hand.

He didn't seem to observe the boys, but the boys observed him.

"Looks like a lightning-rod man off on a vacation," said Cliff Chantry. "The one that rodded our new barn had just such a free and easy, I-own-the-earth sort of swagger."

"Bright-looking cur he's got," said Ike Ingalls, tugging at a stocking half-way on his wet foot.

"It's an Irish terrier," said Dick Swan, hopping on one foot to jar the water out of his ear.

"That's no terrier," said the tallest of the boys, as he stood buttoning his shirt-collar, with his elbows spread, his chin up, and a prominent nose high in the air. "It's some sort of a spaniel; don't you see the ears?"—lowering his chin and glancing in the direction of the dog and his master. "His legs are too long for any Irish terrier's."

"A spaniel it is, then; when Quint Whistler says a thing, that makes it so!"

Having uttered this sarcasm, Dick hopped on the other foot, to jounce the water out of his other ear.

Quint paid no attention to the taunt, but pulled down his wristbands under his coat-cuffs, and remarked dryly:

"What's that he has in his hand?—I mean the man, not the dog. It's too big for a toothpick, but not big enough for a walking-stick."

"I'll tell you," suggested Cliff Chantry. "He's the leader of a band, and that's his band-stick. Don't you know?"—and he stopped combing his wet hair with his fingers to make fantastic motions with an imaginary baton. "He's waving it now. See?"

"The dog's his band. He's waving it for him," said Quint. "There!"

The stick went splashing into the water a few rods from shore, and the dog went plunging and paddling after it.

"I knew he was a water-dog," said Quint.

"That's no sign," Cliff replied. "A terrier could do that. I'll ask him. I say, mister, what sort of a whelp is that?"

The young man waited until the dog brought him the stick, then turned to the boys coming down the slope and buttoning their last buttons.

"What sort of a whelp?" he repeated. "He's a sparkler. Didn't you ever see a sparkler?"

493

"Can't say I ever did," Cliff replied. "Never heard of one. What's a sparkler like?"

"As much like the animal you see here as your two thumbs are like each other. See him, and you see a sparkler. Hear him,"—at a motion of the stick the dog barked,—"and you hear a sparkler. Did you ever read Shakspere?"

"I know the dialogue between Brutus and Cassius, in the 'Advanced Speaker,' " Cliff replied. "I acted Cassius once, at a school exhibition, to this fellow's Brutus." He turned, and with a smile looked up at Quint Whistler, who was the last to come down to the shore, buttoning his vest by the way.

"Brutus — Marcus Brutus — this slab-sided chap with the gambrel-roof nose?" cried the dog's owner, with a laugh which infected the whole crowd of boys, except Quint himself.

He had, as has been suggested, an exceptionally bold nasal protuberance; and there was a break in the high slope of it, somewhat suggestive of the roof in question. Cliff's nose, on the contrary, was short, but shapely, belonging to a frank, freckled, mirthful face—the face of a farmer's boy about sixteen years old. He was of medium height, and rather stocky. Quint was perhaps a year older, fully a head taller, lank of face and bony of frame. His countenance was grave almost to sternness at this moment, as if he did not altogether relish the personal nature of the young man's remarks.

The young man confronted the two, looking from one to the other, with an air of lively satisfaction at having made their acquaintance. The boys' companions, half a dozen or more, gathered about them in a group, to listen to the conversation.

"Brutus has got the most nose, but Cassius knows the most," the stranger rattled on gaily. "Though it's easier to decide about the nose than about the knowledge. If I could see you two act Brutus and Cassius, that might help settle the question."

Quint kept his frowning countenance, but Cliff answered laughingly:

"He's great as Brutus! You should see him once! He used to step up on the teacher's platform to spout, 'When Marcus Brutus grows so covetous'; then when he got to,—'Be ready, gods, with all your thunderbolts! dash him to pieces!'—he would jump down on the floor with a jar that made the old school-house shake. Cassius was nowhere! But what have Shakspere, and Brutus and Cassius, to do with your pup?"

"That's what I was coming to," replied the pup's master, holding the stick again, ready to throw. "In one of the plays is a heroine, 'created,' as her lover says, 'of every creature's best.' That can't always be true. But it applies exactly to my dog. He is *multum in parvo, e pluribus unum, ne plus ultra.* He's a land-dog and a water-dog, a sheep-dog and a watch-dog; as honest a dog as ever you saw steal a sausage, and the cunningest trick-dog in the wide world; as sly as a fox, and as amusing as a monkey. Sparkler's his name, and Sparkler's his nature. Young gentlemen, that paragon is for sale, and I invite you to make an offer for him."

He threw the stick, and as the "paragon" went splashing after it, he added:

"What'll you give, Brutus? Name a figure, Cassius? Don't be bashful because I happen to be a stranger."

"I shouldn't think you would want to sell such a perfect creature as that," remarked Cliff Chantry.

"My young friend, you're right. Nothing but dire necessity could ever induce me to part with him. Necessity is a hard mistress; she'll part a good boy and his gran'ma, often a man and his money, sometimes a man and his dog. Have you a silver dollar, Brutus? You, Cassius, a quarter? I'd like to flip it into the lake, for you to see him paddle out and find it —dive to the bottom for it, and bring it ashore. Anybody got a piece of bright money?"

Brutus lifted his eyebrows at Cassius with a droll expression. Cassius drew down one side of his face with a sagacious wink. The other boys likewise winked and smiled, and two or three of them might have been observed to press their hands prudently on their pockets. Bright pieces with which to strew the bottom of the lake were not forthcoming.

"I am pained to perceive an air of incredulity among some of you," said the stranger. "But to convince you—" He put his hand into his own pocket, and asked, "How deep is it out where he is now?"

"About up to your neck," said Cliff.

"That's all right. This is the last quarter that remains to me out of a small fortune; but to show you the confidence I have in the sagacity of my four-footed friend— Here, Sparkler!"

Sparkler dropped the stick on the sand, put his nose to the coin, and yelped wishfully.

"Watch carefully!" his owner said to the boys. "Look alive, Sparkler!" And he tossed the coin boldly out into the lake, where it sank in a circle of ripples.

The dog swam swiftly after it, put down his head into the clear water two or three times as he neared the spot, and finally went down altogether. He seemed to be gone a long while; a few seconds seem a long while when you are watching a feat of that sort.

"I bet you he doesn't bring up any silver quarter," said Cliff Chantry.

"How much will you bet?" cried the dog's owner eagerly. "Any fellow here wants to make a bet? You, Brutus? Put up some money, some of you!"

"But you've no money to put up," said Quint Whistler.

"I've that quarter—"

"At the bottom of the lake!" Cliff laughed excitedly.

"I'll bet the dog! The dog against a dollar! That's a hundred to one! Quick!" cried the young man. "There he comes! Will you take the wager, on what he's got in his mouth?"

"I'm not in the habit of backing up my opinions with bets," remarked Quint Whistler. "All I can say is, I'm glad 't wasn't my quarter you flung."

"He's got his mouth shut," said Ike Ingalls. "It was open when he swam out."

"He's got a pebble in it! He's got his mouth full of sand! Ho, ho!" The boys clamored and jeered, at the same time watching with eager curiosity the dog paddling shoreward.

"Boys," said the young man, gaily, "you are a squad of young Solomons! You'll sprout wisdom when you get free from your mothers' apron-strings! Isn't that so, Sparkler?"—as the dog came dripping out of the lake, and dropped into his master's open palm, along with some gravel, before the eyes of the intensely interested spectators, the recovered piece of money!

II

A ROMANTIC STORY

"THAT's nothing to what he can do," said the young man, dipping the coin in the water and then wiping it with his handkerchief before returning it to his pocket. "Shake yourself, Sparkler!"

Sparkler shook himself, sending a

shower of spray into the faces of the recoiling and backward tumbling boys. Quint Whistler alone stood his ground, receiving the drops on his nose with an equanimity that amused the stranger.

"Now I see what that gambrel-roof is for—to shed water! My object, young gentlemen, was not to get the water on to you, as you may perhaps imagine, but to get it off from Sparkler, and reduce his weight by so much liquid; for now I am going to show you how he can jump. Sparkler!"

The young man held out the stick horizontally, about eighteen inches from the ground, and the dog leaped over it. He raised it six inches, and the dog went over it again. So he kept raising it, and the dog continued to jump over it, until it was finally placed across the top of Ike Ingall's head.

Ike shut his eyes, giggling nervously, and holding himself still, while the dog, just touching his shoulder lightly, went over the stick, and came down on the grass beyond.

"He's a regular trick-dog," said the stranger. "Now let me suggest a scheme. Brutus and Cassius will buy him for twenty-five dollars, and star the country with him. See? Play Shakspere and exhibit the dog! Can Mr. Whistler whistle?" He had heard the boys call Quint by his full name. "Can either of you sing a comic song? If you can, your fortune is made!"

"I can whistle," said Quint, "like an empty jug. And we can both sing like a couple of cats on a back shed at two o'clock in the morning. But I'm afraid that sort of whistling and singing wouldn't be popular, let alone our Shakspere!" Everybody laughed, except Quint himself, who looked up with an appearance of mild surprise, as if to see where the fun came in.

"The dog alone will be attraction enough," said the stranger. "See what else he can do." He took off his coat and laid it on the grass. "Watch it, Sparkler!"

The dog lay down beside it, with his paws on the collar.

"Now, would any of you young gentlemen like to earn a quarter? If so, bring away that coat, and the lucre is yours."

"I don't care for the quarter, but I can get that coat," said Dick Swan, stepping carefully toward it, undeterred by the growls of Sparkler.

All watched with excited interest till he made a sudden snatch at it. But before his hand grasped the garment, Sparkler's teeth were fast in his sleeve—so fast, indeed, that as he sprang back he left a piece of his cuff in the dog's mouth, amidst the loud laughter of his companions.

"He can do a hundred things," said the stranger. "Here's one."

Beside his coat on the grass he placed his handkerchief; beside that he laid his stick, and near that the silver quarter; then over the quarter he turned his hat.

"Now, boys," he said stepping back a few paces, "which of those articles shall he bring to me?"

"The handkerchief," said Cliff.

"You hear, Sparkler," said the master; "the handkerchief."

And without hesitation the dog picked it up and brought it to him.

"Now, Brutus, what will you have?"

"I say the thing that's under the hat," Quint replied.

"Very well, the money that's under the hat," said the master. Whereupon Sparkler tipped the hat over with his nose, nipped daintily at the coin, which, together with some grass, he took up and dropped into the young man's extended hand.

"That's judgmatical!" said Quint.

And Cliff exclaimed, "He's great! Why don't you exhibit him yourself?"

"That's what I am doing at this moment," said the dog's owner; "and that's what I've done to hundreds of delighted spectators. Sparkler never fails to sparkle. But to pass around the hat—that's another question. If I've a weak point, it's my modesty."

"Your modesty is as plain as a gambrel-roof nose," said Quint Whistler solemnly.

"Brutus," said the young man, laughing good-naturedly with the rest, "we're even. You owed me one, and you have paid it." He put on his coat, and proceeded: "I am the son of a distinguished lawyer, lately deceased; and I am now on my way to the bedside of a sick mother in Michigan, who has sent for me, without knowing that I have no money for the journey."

Cliff fondled the dog's wet head, and inquired: "How do you happen to be out of money so far from home?"

The young man pulled down his cuffs under his coat-sleeves, and smilingly answered:

"That's a long story; but it can be briefly told. I was employed as clerk in the big hotel in Bennington—the Stark Hotel, which was burnt two weeks ago. What? you didn't hear of that big fire? Well, you *would* have heard of it if you had been in town that night. 'Twas a clean sweep! The guests lost about everything —barely escaped with their lives. I was so busy getting out the hotel books, and helping the women and children, that I could not give any time to my own personal effects; so I lost all my clothing, except what I had on my back, and all my books and private papers. I had some money in my pocket, but I've spent that waiting to get my back salary from the proprietor. He owes me seven hundred dollars; but I couldn't get it, because he hadn't settled with the insurance companies. I was lucky in one thing—I saved my dog. I threw him from a three-story window."

"Seems to me that's a three-story kind of a story," observed Quint.

"Wait till I tell you," said the young man, not at all disconcerted. "That was twelve o'clock at night. Think of it! He saw I was in danger—would stick to my heels, you know, while I was rousing the guests; he really helped me, by barking up and down the corridors, till I tumbled a feather-bed out of a window, and dropped him on it."

"I don't see how you *can* part with him!" Cliff exclaimed, caressing the wonderful quadruped.

"Necessity—sheer necessity," answered the young man. "To be perfectly frank with you, I shall sell him conditionally, if at all,—with the privilege of buying him back, at double the price, any time within three months. Give me twenty-five dollars for him, and if I don't pay you fifty within ninety days, the dog is yours. I'm willing to put that in writing."

"I haven't got twenty-five dollars in the world," said Cliff, his eyes glistening with excitement as he looked appealingly at his companions. "And I know I couldn't raise so much."

"How much can you raise?"

"I don't know."

Cliff walked aside with Quint, two or three others following.

"You don't really think of buying him, do you?" said Ike Ingalls.

"I would, in a minute, if I could," said Cliff. "He's just wonderful! Say, Quint! what do you say to going in with me?"

"I'm afraid 't wouldn't work well for two boys to own one dog," replied Quint. "But I should like to see you own him; and I'll lend you a little money, if you like."

"Will you?" said Cliff eagerly.

"Yes, but let me give you something else first; that's advice. You are worked up now. You are more excitable than I am. You'd better wait till you've had time to think it over and ask your folks. You want to do a thing like this when your head is cool."

"My head is cool enough," said Cliff. "But, cool or not, I want that dog! As for my folks, I know they wouldn't consent if I should ask them. But if I take him home, show his tricks, and let out by degrees that I've bought him conditionally, to double my money when the owner comes for him,—if he ever does come: I shall hope he won't!—I don't think they'll say much."

"Well, you know best about it," said Quint. "I've got four or five dollars at home I can let you have."

"I can lend you three dollars," Ike Ingalls whispered, eager to see the sale go on.

Dick Swan, likewise interested in seeing so wonderful a dog brought into the neighborhood, offered to advance two more.

"Now, don't you appear too anxious!" Quint warned his enthusiastic friend.

"Oh, no!" said Cliff, with flushed cheeks and suffused eyes. "I'm as cool as a cucumber in an ice-house!"

III

THE STRANGER AND HIS DOG PART COMPANY

WHEN the friends went back to where the dog was, they found him sitting up in a comical attitude, with his fore paws pointing at the handkerchief thrown over the top of the stick, which was stuck in the turf.

"He feels a little chilly after his bath, and he is warming his hands," his master explained. "You may think it's rather a cold fire; but that's nothing to a dog that has a little imagination. Don't burn your fingers, Sparkler!"

The dog actually drew his paws back a little, showing his teeth and winking with his pleasant brown eyes, as if he enjoyed the humor of the situation.

"That will do. Now put out the fire."

The dog pulled the handkerchief from the stick, and put his paws upon it.

"You see what he is," cried the owner, turning to Cliff. "What do you say?"

Cliff was more than ever determined to possess so marvelous a creature. But keeping in mind his friend's caution, and remembering how he had seen shrewd jockeys swap horses, he assumed an indifferent air, and answered diplomatically:

"I can't raise the money; I told you before."

"How did you come by the dog?" Quint inquired.

"That's a part of the story I believe I didn't tell you," replied the young man. "He was a puppy one of the hostlers had in the hotel stables. I saw there was good stuff in him, bought him for a six-bladed jack-knife with a corkscrew and a gimlet, and gave my leisure time to training him."

Quint stooped to look at the dog's collar, and remarked that it bore no name or number.

"Has he ever been licensed?" he inquired.

"Licensed? yes," said the young man, with a smile of amusement at the simplicity of the question. "But in country places, where every dog is known, the law requiring names and license numbers on dogs' collars is apt to be a dead letter." He turned to Cliff. "How much can you raise?"

"I can raise five dollars; I'll give that for the dog," said Cliff, with a composed expression, such as he had noticed on the faces of horse-traders, but with a wildly throbbing heart.

The owner regarded him with a sad and pitying smile.

"I gave you credit for being a well-intentioned young man," he said; "and I supposed any one who had ever taken the great part of Cassius would have too high an appreciation of good acting to make such an offer for such a performer as my dog Sparkler. Why, sir, it would make him blush, it would make him hang his head for shame, to be sold for a paltry sum like that!"

It certainly made Cliff ashamed to have the pettiness of his offer held up to contempt in this way, and he would have blushed if his face had not been so very red before. He murmured something about having no more money.

"But your friends will lend you some; I see it in their eyes. Now, I'll tell you what I'll do. I believe you'll be a kind master; and I saw when you were stroking him that he had taken a liking to you. He knows a good dog-lover when he sees one, and he picked you out of the crowd. Give me twenty dollars, and the privilege of buying him back at forty, and he's yours."

"I'll give you ten," said Cliff quickly. "That's all I will give."

The other boys looked eagerly from his face to that of the young man, in which they saw signs of relenting. As Cliff couldn't be moved to raise his offer, the owner finally said:

"And I hold the right to buy him back?"

"Yes," replied Cliff, "at double the price."

The young man laughed, and shrugged. "On the whole," he said, "I think that will be as well for me. I shall save money when I come to reclaim him; and the ten dollars will take me as far as Buffalo, where I have friends who will help me over the rest of the journey. I wouldn't have sold him outright if you had offered a hundred."

He took a small cord from his pocket, which he made fast to the dog's collar.

"This is hardly necessary," he observed; "for if I tell him to go with you he will go. But it will be safer to place him under some restraint until I get well out of the way. I shall hurry down to the Junction, and take the first west-bound train." He stood ready to put the loose end of the cord into Cliff's hand. "Now where is your ten dollars, young man?"

"These boys are going to get it for me," said Cliff; "they live nearer here than I do. You'll give me a bill of sale?"

"Certainly, if you require it. Hurry up, and I'll wait here."

Some of the boys went off with Cliff and Quint, while the rest remained in the delightful company of the performing dog and his master. In a short time those who had departed came running back, Cliff at their head and Quint lagging in the rear; and Cliff, out of breath, paid with trembling hands his borrowed money. He received in return the end of the cord, and a leaf torn from the stranger's notebook. On this was penciled a memorandum of the transaction, signed "A. K. Winslow."

"My usual signature," said the dog's late owner. "Though I may as well tell you that the A. stands for Algernon, and the K. for Knight, and that my address will be Battle Creek, Michigan, till further notice. That is your receipted bill, with the redemption clause inserted. Now here is something for you to sign for my protection."

He held out his open note-book, in which Cliff read, on a penciled page:

"Purchased of A. K. Winslow, for ten dollars ($10), his trick-dog Sparkler, which I agree to re-deliver to him, or to his order, on the payment of twice that sum ($20), any time within three months."

This, like the bill of sale, was duly dated; and Cliff, after consulting with Quint, who thought it "judgmatical," attached his signature.

"I keep this, you keep that, and these friends of yours are our witnesses," said Algernon Knight Winslow, in the best of spirits, notwithstanding the present necessity of parting from his four-footed companion. "Sparkler! look alive!"

The dog sat up, with fore legs lifted and paws drooping, while his late master addressed him, with one forefinger pointed impressively:

"Sparkler, sharer of my fortunes, will you go with this young gentleman who holds you by the cord, stay with him faithfully, serve him obediently, and perform tricks for him as you would for me, till I send or come myself to claim you? Answer!"

Sparkler regarded him with half-closed, sleepy-looking eyes, and dropped one paw.

"That means 'yes,'" said Algernon K. Winslow. And now you have him."

"You don't mean to say he takes in all you've been saying?" Cliff queried wonderingly.

"He takes in the gist of it as well as any of you. Now, with regard to his tricks." And Mr. Winslow went on to give Cliff some useful hints on that all-important subject.

The dog was never to be whipped under any circumstances, but always to be treated kindly, and rewarded with nice bits from the table after each performance.

"And I advise you to feed him as soon as you get home; for he has been on rather short allowance lately. Now, good-by. Farewell! Adieu! Au revoir! Till we meet again!" cried A. K. Winslow gaily.

Cliff had still some questions to ask regarding the tricks, which being obligingly answered, he said, "Come, Sparkler!" and set off, cord in hand, accompanied by the dog, who went as readily as if he had been acting one of his well-understood parts. Cliff was overjoyed; and his friends, running beside him and the leashed animal, were almost as jubilant as he. Next to owning a trick-dog is the pleasure of having a friend own one.

"By-by!" Algernon K. Winslow called after them, waving his hand, as he turned and walked smilingly away.

IV

CLIFF BRINGS HOME HIS PURCHASE

"LAND'S sake alive! What's up?" exclaimed Mrs. Chantry, looking from the window of the old Chantry farm-house, and seeing a rabble of boys, headed by her son Clifford leading a strange dog, turn in at the gate.

On their way through the village the original party of six or seven had been joined by other boys eager to hear about the dog; and now two more, younger brothers of Cliff, ran out from the barn to meet the astonishing procession.

"What you got there? Where'd you get that dog?" cried the younger brothers, aged twelve and ten, almost with one voice.

"Bought him!" replied Cliff, walking proudly in, followed by his rabble.

"Where? What did you give? What's

he good for?" clamored the younger brothers, falling into the ranks.

"He's a trick-dog, and he's worth a hundred dollars!" replied Sparkler's new owner. "Say, just keep quiet, and let me get him tied up in the wood-house, before you scare him to death. I'll tell you all about it in a minute, ma!" he cried, passing on to the rear of the house, regardless of his mother's expostulations.

She intercepted him at the back door.

"Tell me now! Stop right where you are!" she commanded him. "Have you been buying a dog without permission from your father or me?"

"I didn't have time to get permission; 't wouldn't do to let such a chance slip. He's just the knowingest dog you ever saw or heard of! You and pa will both say it's all right when I tell you," said Cliff, leading his prize and his mob of boys into the wood-shed, a barn-like addition to the house, with one large door opening into the back yard, and a smaller one within, communicating with the kitchen.

"The boy's out of his head!" Mrs. Chantry exclaimed. "I should think they had all broken out of bedlam! Amos and Trafton have run wild with the rest. Where are *you* going, Susie?"

"I want to see the dog," said Susie, a fourteen-year-old sister of Cliff's.

"I declare, you're crazy too! Didn't anybody ever see a dog before?" cried the mother impatiently, but not ill-naturedly, for she was one of the indulgent sort. "Run and find your father, and tell him if he doesn't want his wood-house turned into a pandemonium, he'd better come quick!"

Having got Sparkler into the wood-shed and fastened him by his cord to the leg of a grindstone, Cliff told his brothers they might "just stroke his ears a little," but not to "fool with him," and charged Quint Whistler to look out for the other boys, who were crowding around; then he went bustling into the kitchen, calling out, "What can I feed him? Say, ma, what can I give my dog to eat?"

"That's a strange how-d'e-do!" Mrs. Chantry exclaimed; "before you've told me what dog it is, or how you came by him! As if I was your servant, to feed any stray creetur' you choose to bring into the house!"

"He isn't a stray creetur'!" cried Cliff, "and I don't ask you to feed him; I'll do that myself. The man I had him of said cold chicken was particularly nice for him."

He was already on his way to the cellar, where the cold victuals were kept.

Having relieved her feelings by scolding him for his folly, his mother helped him prepare a bountiful repast for Sparkler. She even showed her interest in his strange purchase so far as to go and stand in the doorway that opened from the kitchen into the wood-shed, and see the "stray creetur" fed.

There she was found by Susie, returning from the errand to her father.

"You are not going to be crazy too, are you, ma?" said the girl mischievously.

The good woman's countenance, which she endeavored to keep severe, beamed with kindness and curiosity.

"Law, no, child!" she said; "but I want to see that good victuals ain't wasted. I don't wonder you are surprised, father!"

"Father" was the father of the children, a sturdy, red-faced farmer, with a shaven chin hedged by long side-whiskers, who had just appeared at the outer door of the wood-shed. This door had been shut to prevent the possible escape of the dog; but he opened it to the width of his broad shoulders, and looked in with a scowl of humorous amazement.

"What's all this?" he demanded. "I

should think Barnum's 'Greatest Show on Earth' had settled itself on my premises!" Over the heads of the smaller boys he saw tall Quint Whistler standing by the grindstone, keeping back the crowd while the dog ate. "That your dog, Quint?"

"No; I don't own so much as a wag of his tail! Wish I did!" said Quint.

"He's got a mortgage on him; so have I," said Ike Ingalls. "He's a trick-dog, and a wonder!"

Just then Cliff got up from the floor.

"He's my dog," he said, turning only the side of his flushed face toward the outer door, without venturing to look at his father. "He's been trained to do almost anything. There's no end to the tricks that he can perform. And he's a good watch-dog, —look at Dick's coat-sleeve! He got that trying to pull a coat away from him after he had been told to guard it."

The mouth between the long sidewhiskers worked with grim humor, and said sarcastically:

"There seems to be another thing he can do pretty well—dispose of a plate of victuals! Did you pick him up in the street?"

"No, I didn't; you can't pick up such dogs as this in the street, nor anywhere else," Cliff replied with spirit.

"He bought him," spoke up his younger brother Amos, his face in a broad grin.

All eyes turned again to the father in the doorway, who gave a pull at the fleece of his left whisker, and exclaimed:

"You didn't pay money for a mangy cur like that, I hope!"

"He isn't a mangy cur!" Cliff declared indignantly. He didn't know just what "mangy" meant, but inferred that it must be something discreditable. "He's just as nice as he can be. Here, ma, take the plate. He has licked it clean of everything but the cold potato. Now stand a little further off, boys, and I'll show you his tricks."

V

THE ORIGIN OF THE WORD "DOGGED"

A SPACE was cleared for the first exhibition of Cliff's wonderful trick-dog. Some of the spectators climbed upon the piled wood; one stood on the frame of the grindstone, another on the choppingblock, two or three sat on a board placed across the tops of empty barrels, and the rest of the boys filled up the ring.

In the midst stood Quint Whistler and Ike Ingalls, in the distinguished capacity of Cliff's counselors and assistants: thus favored because they had advanced money for the purchase. Dick Swan's mother had refused to let him lend his money, greatly to his disappointment; but he had the next place, on account of the good-will he had shown.

In the kitchen-door stood smiling Mrs. Chantry, with Susie clinging excitedly to her elbow. Amos and Trafton were on the steps below. The father's broad shoulders and straight-brimmed straw hat were defined against the afternoon light in the partly opened wood-shed door, the sarcastic smile still playing about his mouth.

Cliff held in one hand the end of the cord, which he had detached from the leg of the grindstone, and in the other a thin stick of pine kindling. At his feet was the dog, couched on his paws, with his tongue out, looking complacent after his meal.

"Make him jump the first thing," said Ike Ingalls, proud of his part in the show. Then, turning to Mr. Chantry, Ike added: "He can jump over my head. He did it down on the shore."

"Get up, Sparkler!" Cliff commanded.

Sparkler lolled, without any apparent thought of stirring from his comfortable position.

"Say 'Look alive,'" Quint suggested, in a low voice.

"Look alive!" Cliff repeated, in a tone of authority.

As the trick-dog showed no disposition to obey, he gave the cord a jerk, which brought him to his feet.

"Now jump!" he said, holding his stick about eighteen inches from the floor, while Ike Ingalls made the nearest boys take a step or two backward, to give ample room for the leap.

But it was a useless trouble. Sparkler never moved.

"You hold it too high to begin with," said Quint.

So Cliff lowered the stick a few inches, and again commanded: "Jump now!" with no better result.

"Lower yet!" whispered Quint.

Cliff did so, and repeated his commands, at the same time jerking the cord, to rouse the wonderful trick-dog from his indifference. But Sparkler only lolled and looked stupid.

"Lay the stick on the floor," came from the whiskered face in the doorway. "Maybe he'll walk over it."

The spectators began to titter. Cliff, confused, covered with perspiration and blushes, pulled the cord and knocked the dog's paws with the stick, repeating sharply, "Jump, I say!" But Sparkler hung back.

The mother's face wore a look of disappointment and of pity for her son's humiliation; but the whiskered visage in the doorway was wreathed with ironic smiles.

"He *can* jump, but he won't," said Ike Ingalls. "He's balky."

"He's showing us the origin of the word *dogged*," said the amused father.

"He didn't like it because you yanked him by the cord," Quint Whistler argued. "Don't you remember his owner said you must never be rough with him?"

"I didn't think I was rough," Cliff replied.

He found a handkerchief somewhere in his pockets, and wiped his forehead, still looking down, with a face of perplexity and disgust, at the disobedient beast.

"Another thing he said, too, which I'd forgotten," Quint proceeded—"he said he must be fed after a performance, not before. You couldn't expect him to jump after a full meal."

"That's so!" Cliff assented, with a long breath.

"Try making him sit up," said Dick Swan.

Cliff was averse to the attempt, in the present state of the canine appetite; but as Dick's suggestion was clamorously backed up by the crowd of boys, and there was still a possibility of the dog's redeeming his reputation, he stroked and coaxed him; and finally, remembering the late owner's word and gesture, threw up the hand that held the stick, and cried out cheerily:

"Look alive now! look alive, Sparkler!"

Sparkler looked anything but alive; on the contrary, he looked quite asleep, as he stretched himself out, closing his languid eyes, by the leg of the grindstone.

"What a wonderful dog! Oh, Cliff!" jeered the boys who had previously been most envious of his purchase. "Why don't you brag some more about him?"

"There, there, boys! don't make fun," said Mrs. Chantry. "And don't feel bad, my son. The best of us are liable to be deceived in a bargain."

"Say, Cliff! How much did you give?" asked his brother Amos.

The father laughed pitilessly.

"If he gave ten cents, he got swindled," was his cruel comment. "Now quit your nonsense, and come and help me mend the pig-pen. When I said you could go in swimming, I didn't expect you to bring home a beggarly pup to fool with all the afternoon."

Cliff stood for some moments with bent brows, eying the "dogged" dog with extreme discontent. When he raised his head, his father's unwelcome face had disappeared, and his mother had drawn Susie back into the kitchen. The crowd was beginning to disperse, some laughing as they went, others lingering to hear what Cliff would have to say.

One lingered from a different motive: that was Ike Ingalls.

"If you'd just as lieves pay me the three dollars and a half I lent you,"—he began, in a low voice, at Cliff's ear.

Cliff turned upon him a scornful scowl.

"I'll pay you so quick it'll make your head swim!" he exclaimed, loud enough for all to hear. "You were glad enough to lend it, and help me buy the dog, and you felt easy enough about it till you began to think I'd been cheated. Ame, go up to my room and get my money-pouch out of the till of my chest; and say nothing to anybody."

"Don't mind about paying me," said Quint. "I wouldn't ask for my money even if I knew you'd bought a worthless dog; but I don't believe you have. You couldn't expect him to perform tricks in a crowd of strangers, before he'd got well acquainted with you."

"No, he hasn't got used to his new master," said Dick Swan, encouragingly. "I wouldn't come down on you for *my* money, would I? I'm sorrier'n I was before, ma wouldn't let me lend it to you."

"*You're* all right, Dick; so is Quint," Cliff replied, his brows clearing. "So am I! I don't give him up as a bad job—not yet! His dinner made him logy; that's what's the matter. Then again, father looking on the way he did, made me nervous. I knew he was just waiting to laugh at me. Ten

cents!" the boy repeated, with a dismal laugh.

"You never must be nervous when you are training an animal," Quint remarked. "That's so with horses, and it must be so with dogs. He'll come out all right, I know! If he don't, you needn't pay me back more than half my money; for it was partly my fault, your buying him."

"By jingo, Quint!" Cliff exclaimed, with a burst of grateful feeling, "you are a whole load of bricks! But I shall pay you every cent, all the same; some time, if not to-day. Give it here, Ame";—to the boy bringing the pouch of money.

Cliff untied the string, and began to count out silver half-dollars.

Ike, meanwhile, feeling that his eagerness to receive back his loan contrasted unfavorably with Quint's more generous conduct, and with what Dick would likewise have done in his place, looked furtively around for evidences of his own waning popularity on the faces of his companions.

"Here, Ike!" said Cliff, jingling seven half-dollars in his extended palm.

Ike was conscious of a chilly social atmosphere surrounding him; but he was nevertheless glad to see his money again.

"I didn't want you to think I was in any hurry for my pay," he said, as he reached out his hand for it. "I thought—"

"That's all right, Ike," said Cliff, without any show of resentment. "I can give you a part of yours, Quint,—"

"No, leave it now," replied Quint. "Or—just as you say." And Cliff insisting, he took the last of the silver which Cliff withdrew from the pouch. "And don't worry about the rest; let it go till—what's his name?—A. K. Winslow buys back his dog," he added, with a droll smile.

"Not a word, boys, about this money," Cliff cautioned his brothers. "I prefer to

tell father myself. Now, fellows, I've got
to shut up here; sorry to turn you out,
but—" tying the dog's cord again firmly
to the leg of the grindstone—"father wants
me, and I'm going to leave Master Sparkler to meditate upon his disgraceful conduct."

Having got the last of the boys out of the
wood-shed, and shut the large outer door,
he beckoned Quint to remain, and said to
him confidentially:

"Can't you come around this evening?
When everything is quiet, and he has
digested his dinner, I am going to try him
again, and see if he'll do his tricks any
better on an empty stomach."

Quint readily agreed to come.

VI

"DIDN'T I TELL YOU SO?"

WHILE the two were at work repairing the pig-pen, Mr. Chantry forbore to ask any questions
regarding the "beggarly pup" his son had
brought home.

"What he has to say about that will
keep," Cliff reflected ruefully, remembering that the paternal remarks never lost
any of their sharpness by being well
thought over. That they were in preparation he could see by an occasional quiet
smile in which his father indulged; but
he was glad to have them kept in for the
present.

"After I've had another chance to try
Sparkler," the boy said to himself, "then
he may ask questions and have his joke."

Mr. Chantry was particularly fond of a
joke at his children's expense. He never
struck them, but his stinging ridicule was
often worse than a whip.

"If Sparkler doesn't sparkle next time,
and I have to tell what I paid for him,
won't I get it!" thought Cliff, watching
the satirical quirk of the mouth in its
parenthesis of long, fine whiskers.

The afternoon waned, they finished their
work, and the subject uppermost in one
mind, if not in both, was not once mentioned. At the supper-table Susie and the
younger boys could talk of nothing but the
dog in the wood-shed; and the mother
scolded about it in her mild way, alternately blaming Cliff for bringing the
creetur' home, and blaming the creetur' for
ungratefully refusing to perform his tricks
after he had been fed so bountifully.

"He's been asleep almost ever since you
left him," said Amos. "I shouldn't think
he'd had any more sleep than victuals
lately. He wouldn't even open his eyes for
me."

"I told you not to go near him," said
Cliff, severely.

"I had to go there for an armful of
wood," was the younger brother's excuse. "You'll have to put him into a band-
box, if he's too precious to be looked at or
spoken to; or hang him in the well, as we
do butter in hot weather, when we are out
of ice."

The youngster's grin was a very good
reduced copy of the father's amused, ironic
smile. Father and son were much alike,
but for the paternal whiskers, and a difference of some thirty years in their ages.

After supper the cows were to be milked,
and other evening chores to be done; and
all the while the dog was left to his dreams
and reflections in the darkening wood-
shed. It was deep dusk when Quint Whistler strolled in at the front gate, and Cliff
went out to meet him.

"How's your ten-cent pup?" Quint inquired.

"He's humble, and I hope penitent,"

said Cliff. "Now, if we can have him by ourselves, we'll see whether he can perform tricks, or whether we've dreamed it."

He let Quint into the wood-shed, and went to the kitchen for a lamp. This he brought, followed by the younger boys, whom he cautioned to "keep quiet and hold their tongues," if they wanted to see the show.

"Now, Sparkler," he said, proceeding to remove the cord from the collar, "remember what you promised Mr. Winslow, and be a good dog. Treat me well, and I'll treat you well."

"I believe he understands," said Quint. "See how knowing he looks! I believe he's laughing!"

"We'll all laugh soon," Cliff exclaimed hopefully, looking for a suitable stick in the pile of kindling-wood. "Shut that door, Susie!"

"Father says bring the dog in," replied the girl, looking down from the kitchen doorway.

"Jehu! I can't do that," Cliff muttered. "It'll spoil everything. Tell him I don't want to—just yet."

Susie disappeared, but returned with a peremptory message.

"He says bring him in, whether you want to or not. If there's a show, he wants to see it."

"There won't be any show if I have him looking on and making fun," Cliff growled. "I suppose I shall have to, though. When he says a thing like that, he means it. You come too, Quint, and back me up. I know Sparkler won't do a thing!" And he threw down the stick in bitter discouragement.

To his surprise, Sparkler picked it up, and stood, with wagging tail, ready to follow him.

"See that! See that!" cried Amos and Trafton together. "He's going to perform!"

"It looks more like it—sure!" said Cliff, thrilled with joyous expectation. "Out of the way, boys!" Then to Susie: "Have all the doors shut in there, for it's a strange place, and there's no knowing what he may do."

Preceded by the boys, and followed by Sparkler bearing the stick, Cliff entered the large, old-fashioned, lamp-lighted kitchen, Quint lagging awkwardly behind.

Mrs. Chantry at the same time came in from a room beyond, with a half-knitted stocking in her hand. The bright needles shone in the lamp-light, and a dark thread of yarn meandered down across her white apron to a pocket, a bulge in which showed where the ball was lodged. The kindly face was crinkled with smiles of anticipation, as she saw Sparkler trotting along with the stick in his teeth.

Backed up toward a corner under the clock sat Mr. Chantry in a splint-bottomed rocker, parting his long, fleecy side-whiskers away from his shaven mouth and chin with the fingers of both hands, as his frequent habit was when preparing for a little pleasantry at the expense of the youngsters. Cliff, without looking at him, perceived the motion, and knew that his father's lips were twitching and his eyes twinkling in a manner that boded mischief. But he determined not to be disconcerted.

"Come along, Quint!" he cried, with an air of confidence. "Ame, give him a chair."

"I'm all right," said Quint, placing a flat stick across a corner of the wood-box, and sitting on it.

With his hat removed, exposing a high, robust forehead, he was a good-looking fellow, notwithstanding his disproportionate nose. He held his hat on his knee, and put an arm around Trafton, the youngest boy, who was standing at his side.

Cliff made his mother sit down, and

placed a chair for himself beside the table. There was a hush of suspense, in which the old clock was heard ticking loudly, and the farmer's chair squeaking, as he rocked gently.

Cliff sat down, with the dog at his feet, and looking up inquiringly into his face.

"Sparkler," said he, "what are you going to do with that stick?"

Immediately Sparkler got on his hind legs, holding up the stick before his new master. The youngsters shrieked with delight.

"I declare, that's complete!" said the mother, staying her hands, which had begun to ply the knitting-needles vigorously.

Mr. Chantry stopped rocking; he even stopped stroking his whiskers.

Trembling with joy, yet almost afraid to ask anything else of the dog, Cliff took the stick. Sparkler sat erect, with his fore paws at his breast, his bright, soft eyes wistfully studying his young master's face.

"Are you going to jump for me?" Cliff asked, in a tone of affectionate comradeship.

The dog's whole body gave an eager start, his tail wagged, and one paw dropped.

"That means 'yes,'" Quint interpreted, from his seat on the wood-box.

Cliff could hardly keep from hugging the animal, so intense was his delight.

"Jump, then!" he said, holding out the stick. Sparkler leaped over it. "Higher!" he cried, suiting the action to the word. "Higher yet! Higher!" At each command, with its accompanying upward movement of the stick, the dog leaped to and fro with extraordinary liveliness, describing at each rebound a loftier curve.

"Didn't I tell you so?" cried Cliff, triumphantly, with tears of pride and joy shining in his eyes. "He could jump over

Ame's head, but I won't have him try on this hard floor."

"Oh, yes, let him," said Amos. "I never had a dog jump over my head."

"Well, bring a rug for him to come down on," said Cliff.

But, seeing that Sparkler was panting, Quint suggested that he should be allowed to rest a minute.

"Winslow," he said, "always let him rest between his tricks. He's a beauty, isn't he, boys!"

Mrs. Chantry joined with the children in praising Sparkler's nimbleness and docility. Her husband forgot his whiskers, forgot his sarcasms, and leaned forward, with his arms on the arms of the chair, hardly less interested than the rest, although still wary of committing himself by any word of approval. The dog might yet make a failure, and give him an opportunity to get in some of his cutting remarks.

VII

CLIFF TRIUMPHANT

THE rug being put in place, and Sparkler having recovered his breath, he made the leap over Ame's head, in a manner that elicited applause from everybody but the non-committal farmer.

"Now roll over!" said Cliff; which Sparkler promptly did, choosing the rug for his performance. Then Cliff cried, "Look alive!" and Sparkler was erect before him in a moment. "Give me a handkerchief, somebody!"

Susie gave him hers, and he wrapped it around the end of the stick, which he set up between his feet.

"That's supposed to be a fire, and he's going to warm his hands. Warm your hands, Sparkler!"—which the dog did, sitting erect before the handkerchief, and holding up his paws before it, with amusing mimicry.

"How's that for a ten-cent pup?" Quint asked in his dry way, as soon as the tumult of admiring exclamations had subsided.

"Ten cents!" exclaimed Mrs. Chantry. "You don't mean to say that's what you paid?"

Cliff said nothing, but sat patting Sparkler's head, and breathing fast with excitement.

"That's the price father guessed, and he told Cliff he got cheated if he paid it," tittered Amos, while the father smiled, and watched the dog.

"Now I'll try his great trick, though I'm by no means sure it will succeed," said Cliff. "How is it, Sparkler?" Sparkler sat up. "Will you do your best?"

He dropped one of his fore paws affirmatively; and the children cried out in jubilant chorus: "He will! He says he will!"

Then Cliff laid in a row on the floor, before the kitchen sink, the handkerchief, the stick, and one of the boy's hats, calling each article by name as he placed it.

"Now, father," he said, when all was arranged, "which shall he fetch?"

Before Mr. Chantry could speak—the boys clamored for the hat; and Mrs. Chantry said: "Yes, Cliff, I'd like to see him fetch the hat."

Sparkler looked up inquiringly at Cliff.

"Fetch the hat," said Cliff; and the dog brought the hat and put it into his hands.

"It is past belief!" Mrs. Chantry exclaimed. "There's witchery in it!"

"The witchery is in his superior knowingness," said Cliff proudly. "You've no idea how bright he is. Fetch the stick, Sparkler!"

Sparkler brought the stick. Then Cliff replaced all the articles, and asked his father for a piece of money. Mr. Chantry hesitated, lifting his brows quizzically; but finally produced a half-dollar. Cliff took it and placed it under the hat.

"He'll go for that, of course," said Amos.

"You'll see," Cliff answered. "Ask for anything else."

So Amos named the handkerchief, which Sparkler brought, after waiting for his master to repeat the order. Then Cliff said, "Fetch the money"—which the dog did, after some trouble in getting the coin between his teeth.

The Mr. Chantry for the first time opened his lips; not, however, to utter sarcasms.

"How did you say you came by that dog?"

"A man named Winslow sold him to me, this afternoon, down by Gibson's ice-house."

"I can't conceive of the owner selling a dog like that for any such price as a boy like you is likely to give," said Mr. Chantry gravely. "There must be some hidden reason."

"Oh, he told us the reason," Cliff replied. "He was out of money; and he was on his way to his mother in Michigan. He was clerk in the big hotel in Bennington when it was burned, two weeks ago; he lost everything by the fire, and was obliged to part with the dog."

"Big hotel in Bennington?"

"Yes; the Stark Hotel, wasn't it, Quint?"

"Stark Hotel in Bennington?" pondered the farmer. "There may be a Stark Hotel there, for General Stark was in the battle of Bennington. Yet that's a small town, and I don't know what they should want of a big hotel there."

"Maybe for summer boarders," Mrs. Chantry suggested.

"Possibly. But if any such great hotel has

been burned lately, we should have seen something of it in the papers. And if he was on his way to Michigan, what brought him here?" Mr. Chantry argued. "This is out of his way."

"He didn't explain that," said Cliff. "Oh, I remember!—he was going to stop in Buffalo, where he has friends."

"That doesn't better the matter. I'm afraid there's some crookedness in the business. Ah!" Mr. Chantry had taken hold of the dog's collar, and was examining it. "No name, but here's a place for one."

The strap was of maroon-colored leather, ornamented with a row of nickel studs set about an inch and a half apart. There were, however, two vacancies in this row: one where the collar buckled at the throat, the other where, instead of the studs, there were two rivet-holes in the leather.

"I noticed those holes," said Quint; "and I supposed two of the studs had been lost out."

"It looks to me," said the farmer, "as if there had been a name-plate here, and as if it had been picked off. I'll wager something, the fellow stole the dog!"

"I can't think that," exclaimed Cliff. "He was very particular to put it into the bargain that he was to have the privilege of buying him back. He made me give that to him in writing."

"And did he give you any writing?"

"Yes; a regular bill of sale."

"Let me see it."

The paper was produced. Mr. Chantry read the writing carefully, and mused.

"So you gave ten dollars in cash?" he said, lifting his eyes, and looking straight at Cliff.

"Isn't he worth it?"

"I should say he was, and a good deal more. I don't at all approve of you buying him without my advice and consent; but 't was a temptation, and I shan't whale you for it." All the children laughed at what

appealed to them as a good joke,—Mr. Chantry not being in the habit of "whaling" his boys. "Did you have money enough to pay for him?"

"I still owe a little that I borrowed of Quint," Cliff answered.

"Pay it up," said his father, taking out his pocket-book.

But Cliff declined the proffered assistance.

"Quint is willing to wait," he said. "And I don't want anybody to have a claim on the dog except me—and Mr. Winslow. All I'm afraid of is that he'll come to get him back."

"I guess you'd better feed him a little now, hadn't you?" said his mother. "He can have some bread and milk as well as not."

"Let's have some more tricks first!" pleaded the youngsters.

"Well, just one or two, to please the children," she assented.

"Oh, ma!" Susie laughed, "you want to see the tricks just as much as we do!"

Cliff was glad to put Sparkler again through some of his performances. Then the dog was petted and fed, and taken back to the wood-shed. Cliff gave him the rug to lie on, and patted him, and talked to him, as he slipped the cord once more through his collar, and made him fast to the frame of the grindstone.

"I shan't have to do this many times more," he said to his friend Quint, standing by. "But for a while it's best to be on the safe side. Forgive me, Sparkler."

Taking affectionate leave of the dog, who licked his hand, he went out with Quint, and walked home with him, and they talked for half an hour longer, standing at Quint's gate.

"Well, good-night, Quint!" Cliff said at parting. "Hasn't it been a great day? I owe ever so much to you!"

Then he returned home. He took a last

peep at his prize curled up on the rug in the wood-shed; saw that everything was quiet, and all doors fast; said "Good-night" to his mother in a voice thrilling with happiness, received from her hand a candle she had lighted for him, and went up-stairs to bed. He was soon asleep, and dreaming of dogs that could swim in the air and balance poles on their noses.

VIII

ONE OF SPARKLER'S TRICKS

WHEN Cliff awoke in the morning, Sparkler was the first thing in his thoughts. He hurriedly put on his clothes, and hastened downstairs, eager to learn how his pet had passed the night; also to assure himself that the wonderful creature was a reality, and not a part of his vanished dreams.

He was astonished to meet Amos at the foot of the stairs. The boy was frightened, and hardly able to speak.

"What's the matter?" Cliff demanded.

"Gone!" Amos whimpered.

"Who's gone? What's gone?"

"The dog!"

"Not my trick-dog—not Sparkler?" Cliff exclaimed, in wild consternation.

"Yes! skedaddled!" said Amos. "I was hurrying to tell you."

"Who let him go?" Cliff asked fiercely, rushing past him.

"I didn't mean to," whined Amos. "I thought he was tied. I just opened the door to look at him, and he ran into the kitchen. That door was open, and he ran out."

"He *was* tied! Who untied him? Where is he?"

Cliff was already out of the house. At the corner of the wood-shed he met his mother, pale with excitement.

"Which way did he go?" he demanded, hardly pausing for her reply as he ran past her.

"Down the road—toward the village," she answered, catching her breath. "He had a piece of the cord tied to his collar."

"A piece of it?" cried Cliff, turning back.

"Yes; just a few inches. I was standing by the stove when he went by me like a flash; in at one door and out of the other, in an instant. I had just time to follow and get another glimpse of him before he was out of sight."

Cliff hurried to the wood-shed to examine the cord. He found one end tied to the grindstone, as he had left it; but Sparkler was off with the end fastened to his collar.

"He has gnawed it in two!" Cliff moaned.

Much the longer piece remained attached to the grindstone. With sudden resolution he untied it, twisted it into a loose ball, and thrust it into his pocket.

"What are you going to do?" his mother asked, as he was hurrying from the wood-shed.

"Follow him! Find him and bring him back!"

"Eat your breakfast first," she entreated.

"I haven't a minute's time!" he declared.

"You may be away longer than you think. I'll give you something to put in your pocket."

"Hurry up, then!"

He went with her into the kitchen, and came out presently with a piece of berry-pie in his hand, and his pockets bulging. He met his father approaching from the barn.

"What's the trouble?" cried the farmer. "What's the matter now?"

"My dog!" said Cliff. "He has gnawed off his cord and got away. Ame opened the door."

"Bah!" exclaimed his father. "That's one of his tricks his owner didn't tell you of. You never'll see him again."

"Yes, I will. He won't go farther than the Junction, where Winslow was to take the train. Or, if he does, I can trace him."

"Let me go too!" Amos entreated. "I can leg it as fast as Cliff can."

"No, no!" said Mr. Chantry. "It's bad enough to have one boy start off on such a wild-goose chase. You'd better not go far, Cliff." But Cliff was out of hearing, past the gate. "I wouldn't have had it happen for a good deal; I took quite a notion to that dog. Come, Amos. You must help about the chores."

"I let him out, and I ought to go and help find him," said Amos, making a merit of his share in the accident.

Just then the youngest son appeared, with hair uncombed, staring wildly, and highly incensed because he had been allowed to sleep at a time of such excitement.

"Any other morning I'd have been called six times!" he complained. "Why didn't you ketch him, ma, when he shot by you?"

"I might as well have tried to ketch a streak of lightning by the tail," replied his mother. "I just heard a pattering sound, and he was out in a jiffy. He's a mile away by this time, I warrant!"

IX

CLIFF IN PURSUIT

CLIFF ran fast until he came in sight of Quint Whistler's home, on the outskirts of the village, and saw Quint himself standing in the open barn door. Quint's father, a mason and contractor, had just driven away to look after some business in an adjoining town, leaving Quint to shut up the barn and take care of the premises.

"Quint! Quint!" called Cliff from the street. "My dog has got away!"

"Got away!" Quint called back, beginning to walk fast toward the gate. "Which way did he go?"

"Right past your place here; at least he started this way. He'll most likely go straight to the shore where he saw his master last, and then try to track him." Cliff stopped to gather breath, and added, "I'm so glad I've found you. Come along, won't you, and help me hunt him?"

"I don't know," said Quint doubtfully. "As I was off yesterday afternoon, I'm expected to do some hoeing in the garden this morning. That's the order, and it seems only reasonable."

"So was I expected to work to-day," said Cliff. "But I can make it up; and I'll help you for all the time you lose. We may overhaul him in an hour."

"And it may take all day. Besides, I haven't had my breakfast," was Quint's objection.

"Neither have I! Take a bite in your hand and something in your pocket, as I have," said Cliff.

As he spoke, Cliff seemed to remember the wedge of pie he carried, which he hadn't yet thought of eating. He took a deep mouthful, staining his lips with the juice of the berries with which it was filled; while Quint, as deliberate in thought and action as his friend was impetuous, balanced considerations.

"Of course I must help you out of this," he said at length. "I'll be with you in a minute."

He entered the house, and presently came out, stuffing the side pockets of his coat with doughnuts.

"Whether it's to be a long or a short chase," he said, "you can count me in. I helped you buy him, and I'll stick by you as long as there's a chance of running him down."

And the chase began.

X

THE BEGINNING OF THE CHASE

THE boys walked fast through the village, and broke into a run as they approached the lake-shore, where they hoped to find Sparkler looking for his master. But no dog was anywhere in sight.

Two men were loading ice into a wagon backed up against the ice-house. Cliff called out to them.

"Yes!" one called back, in reply to his inquiries. "We saw a dog come down to the pond just a little while ago. He snuffed around, and capered up and down for a while, then started off down the railroad track as fast as he could clip it."

"He seemed to have a little piece of rope, or something, dangling from his neck," said the other man.

"That's my dog! He's gone straight to the Junction!" Cliff said confidently to his companion, as they hurried on.

It was nearly a mile to the Junction; they kept the railroad track all the way, but saw nothing of the fugitive. On the platform they found the station-master checking a trunk; and Cliff accosted him breathlessly.

"No," he said; "I haven't noticed any such dog."

"That is strange," said Cliff. "Did you sell a ticket yesterday afternoon, at about four o'clock, to a young man—who had on a narrow-brimmed hat, kind of a checkered straw?"

The station-master remembered him very well; he had sold him a ticket, and noticed that he had no baggage, not even a gripsack, when he stepped aboard the train.

"That's all right," cried Cliff. "That man sold me a dog yesterday; he was a trick-dog, and he got away this morning."

The station-master called a switch-tender, who said:

"Yes, I saw that very dog, half or three quarters of an hour ago. He snuffed about the platform, then all of a sudden he seemed to remember a previous engagement, and put out toward Tressel, with a full head of steam on!"

Tressel was a station a mile or more beyond.

"Come on," cried Cliff eagerly. "He's going the wrong direction to find Winslow. He'll fetch up somewhere."

But Quint was deliberating. "Wait a minute! I want to be sure of a thing or two. You say that man bought a ticket. Was it to go West?"

"No; he bought a ticket for Kilbird." Kilbird was the first station beyond Tressel.

"He said he was going West!"

"No matter what he said, he boarded the east-bound accommodation train, here!"

It took Cliff a moment to recover from his bewilderment; then he turned to Quint and said:

"I'd like your company ever so much, and I don't know what I shall do without you; you think of more things than I do, and look further ahead. But I'm afraid this is going to be a long pull; and I know I ought not to drag you along."

"If you call it dragging, why, I'll turn back," said Quint. "I know I'm slow."

"I don't mean that!" cried Cliff. "But I've no right to ask so much of you; that's what I meant to say."

"Then don't say it again!" Quint replied, starting off resolutely on the road to Tressel and Kilbird. "Come along!"

The boys now settled down to a fast walk, discussing by the way Sparkler's chances of rejoining his late master. On reaching Tressel, they met three boys who gave them some interesting information. They had seen the dog with the dangling piece of cord pass through the village in the direction of Kilbird; and one of them reported having seen, the day before, a man offering to sell just such a dog to a teamster who had stopped to water his horses at the wayside trough.

Quint thought a moment, then observed:

"It's all plain to me. Winslow came from Kilbird, or some place around there, yesterday; he took the train to Kilbird after selling you the dog, and now the dog has gone back there to meet him. See?"

Cliff did see, greatly to his chagrin and vexation. Just then a locomotive whistled.

"Here comes the down-train," he exclaimed. "How would it do for one of us to board it for Kilbird, and try heading him off that way, while the other keeps the road?"

"That's judgmatical," said Quint. "We've just time to buy a ticket. Have you got any money?"

"Jehu! I forgot all about money," cried Cliff.

"Never mind," said Quint, consolingly. "The dog will be in Kilbird before the train will, if he isn't there already. It will be better for us to keep together."

The dangling cord was a fortunate circumstance; for it attracted attention to the runaway, and rendered the pursuit for a while comparatively easy.

They had been walking some time on a lonely country road, without meeting any one of whom they could make inquiries, when Cliff said: "There comes a team. We'll ask the driver."

Quint stopped suddenly, and stood star-ing straight before him down the turnpike. "By hokey, Cliff," he exclaimed, "I know that horse, for I harnessed him this morning! The wagon is our carryall, and the driver is my father."

Mr. Whistler was much surprised to meet his own boy and a neighbor's traveling that dusty road, so far from home. He listened with amused interest to Quint's story of the runaway dog.

"Did he bite you both, and give you the running-away distemper?" he asked. "Get into the wagon, and ride back with me, both of you. That's the wisest thing you can do."

"Quint can. I guess it's the wisest thing for him," said Cliff; "but I shall keep on till I find the dog, or drop down in my tracks."

"Get up here, Quint! No more nonsense!" the elder Whistler commanded. "Cliff can do as he likes."

"He would like to borrow a little money of you, anyway," said Quint. "We have both come away without any."

Mr. Whistler demurred. "I don't know what his father'll say to my lending him money for such a tom-fool expedition."

"My father knows what I am doing, and he'll be obliged to you for giving me a little help," Cliff put in.

"Well, about how much do you want?" said the mason and contractor, putting his hand in his pocket.

"Enough to take me home from Kilbird by the train, anyway," said Cliff, "and maybe a little over."

"Enough to take us both home," Quint added, "if I go with him."

"It's a foolish business," Mr. Whistler commented; "but if Cliff's father approves, I don't know why I should stand out." Leaning over the wagon side, he reached down a handful of small change. "Will this do?"

"Oh, yes; ever so much obliged!" cried

Cliff delightedly, pocketing the money. "If you see any of my folks, please tell 'em—"

"I'll tell 'em that I saw you going off in company with another lunatic," said the elder Whistler, driving on.

XI

ANOTHER DOG-HUNTER

THE boys resumed their tramp, keeping up their inquiries for Sparkler. Nobody on that part of the highway had seen a dog with a cord dangling from his collar, nor, indeed, any stray dog.

"He may have turned off on some other road, or taken to the fields," said Cliff at length. "What shall we do?"

"I believe our best way is to keep straight on to Kilbird," said Quint. "If we don't strike his trail there, we may at least hear from Winslow."

"There comes some one we can ask," said Cliff; for a man on horseback was approaching along a by-road. The horse was a heavy, hard-trotting animal, and the rider a stout little man, who at every jolt went up and down like a bouncing ball. The boys stopped to speak with him.

Before they could accost him he called out, with the jolts in his voice, as the animal's ponderous trot broke to a walk:

"Say — have — you — seen — a — stray — dog — along — here — anywheres?"

It seemed almost as if he must have known their business, and that he was a joker, who took this means of heading off their expected inquiries.

Quint gave Cliff a nudge, and said, with a droll twist of his mouth:

"It seems to be a pretty good day for stray dogs!"

"A rather small dog," said the man. "Kind of curly brown hair; a sort of spani'l. Had on a collar fastened with a buckle; sort of reddish-brown leather with bright studs in it."

The boys listened with astonishment, the description fitted Sparkler so exactly.

"What do you want of that dog?" Cliff demanded. "Does he belong to you?"

"He ought ter belong to me, for I bought him. Day before yes'day. A man brought him along and offered him for sale. I give a five-dollar bill for him! He wanted twenty-five, but I beat him down to five. My name is Miller; I live over in Wormwood."

Cliff's throat had become so dry that he couldn't utter another word. Quint took up the colloquy.

"How did he get away from you?"

Mr. Miller eased his position by leaning sidewise on his horse, and explained.

"The man advised me to keep him shet up for a day or two, and I put him in the barn. I fed him well, and he seemed as contented as if I'd always owned him. A couple of hours later I went to look at him. It was kind o' dusky in the barn,—I couldn't see him nowheres; so I spoke to him, and opened the door jest a crack wider—swish! he zipped past my legs, and out o' that door like a kicked foot-ball! That's the last I've seen of him. But half an hour ago a neighbor come over to say he'd seen that dog this morning, over by the Lippitt place, this side of Tressel. He tried to head him off, but he took to the woods, and he lost sight of him. So I jest throws a blanket on old Bob, and jogs off to hunt him up. You hain't seen no such animal around anywheres?" Mr. Miller continued, talking down to the boys.

"Not to-day," Quint replied; "but I saw that very dog yesterday afternoon. A man offered him for sale, over in Biddicut, and a neighbor of mine bought him for ten dollars. He got cheated more than you did."

"Yes, he did, for he bought my dog! Where is he?"

"The boy or the dog?" Quint inquired.

"Both," said Mr. Miller.

"The boy is right here before you," said Quint, laying his hand on Cliff's shoulder. "But where the dog is, we're as anxious to know as you are. He got away this morning, and we tracked him a good piece this side of Tressel village,—to about where your neighbor saw him, I should say."

Mr. Miller thereupon kicked his clumsy heels into the horse's ribs, slapped him with the looped end of the reins, clucked like a hen, threw up his arms like wings, and started off on his hard-trotting beast.

"Well, Cliff!" Quint said, with a strange smile.

Cliff was so astounded by the proof of Winslow's bad faith, that he made two or three attempts to speak before he finally replied:

"Quint, it's no use! We may as well turn around and go home."

"How do you work that out?" Quint inquired.

"Don't you see? I've no claim on that dog, anyway! If Winslow had a right to sell him, he belongs to Miller, who bought him before I did."

"I can't help laughing!" Quint suddenly broke forth. "Algernon K. Winslow is a man of genius. He has invented a new business—selling a dog! Who knows how many times he had sold him, before he sold him to Miller? Your title is probably as good as Miller's."

"It may be, and yet not be worth taking this tramp for."

"I beg to differ with you. If we get that dog," Quint continued, "we can hold him till somebody shows a better claim; and if the rightful owner turns up, I'm sure he'll be willing to pay your ten-dollar

mortgage on him, and other expenses. There's no discount on that dog, Cliff; the discount is all on Winslow."

Cliff's face brightened. "There's a good deal in what you say, Quint."

"It's judgmatical," said Quint.

He gave a last look at the disappearing horseman, and said smilingly:

"Mr. Miller is welcome to all the satisfaction he will get from his trip to the Lippitt place; we'll hunt for both man and dog at Kilbird. And it's my humble opinion that the man will be about as well worth catching as the dog. I'll squeeze your ten dollars out of him!" he concluded, clenching his fist, while his strong features settled into an expression of grim resolution.

XII

THE VILLAGE LANDLADY

AT Kilbird the boys traced their man to a hotel where he had been staying, and put their question to the landlady, who came out on the porch to speak with them.

"Why, yes," she said; "you mean Mr. Knight?—a very nice man! And the wonderfullest dog I ever did see! He spent the night here last night, and the night before. He hasn't been gone much more than half an hour."

"Gone?" Cliff gasped out, standing with one foot on the porch step. "And the dog—did he have the dog?"

"I'll tell you about that," replied the landlady. "He lost the dog some way, yesterday, and came back last evening without him. The dog didn't come till this morning; Mr. Knight seemed to be waiting for him. He said the dog had a bad trick of straying off, but that he always turned up again."

Cliff stepped up on the porch floor, and said earnestly:

"The man you call Mr. Knight told me his name was Algernon Knight Winslow; and he sold me that very same dog yesterday for ten dollars."

The landlady expressed a great deal of surprise and sympathy, and invited the boys to sit down and rest on a bench inside the cool porch.

"You look kind of beat out," she said, noticing that they were flushed and covered with dust.

But Cliff said they were not tired; they couldn't stop; they were bound to follow Winslow. And he asked:

"Did he take a train?"

"No; he hired my husband to drive him over to Corliss in his buggy."

Quint inquired, "Did he have any baggage?"

"Only a small linen bag, which he left here when he was off on excursions. But he took it with him this morning, saying he didn't expect to come back."

The landlady became exceedingly friendly and sympathetic, and insisted on opening a bottle of spruce beer for the wayfarers, while they rested on the shaded bench. It was a welcome refreshment, and Cliff offered to pay for it, but she laughingly told him to "put up his money." Then perceiving that they nibbled furtively at something they brought out from their pockets, between sips, she entered the house, and presently reappeared with two generous sandwiches, consisting of slices of excellent buttered bread, lined with cold sliced ham.

"You are taking too much trouble!" Cliff exclaimed, with hearty gratitude.

"You seem to be proper nice boys," she replied; "and I'm very glad to give you a little treat, after you have been so imposed upon. I shall want you to write your names in our book. I'll bring it right out here, with a pen, so you can be eating all the while."

"Cliff," said Quint, glancing over his shoulder, to see that she was out of hearing,—he held his glass in one hand and his bitten sandwich in the other,—"if I wasn't already fitted out with a tolerably good mother, I know where I'd go to adopt one!"

Cliff nodded and winked, and whispered, as he lifted his glass to his lips, "She's coming back."

She brought the hotel register, which was not a large one, and laying it open on Cliff's knee, offered him a freshly dipped pen.

"You write for both," said Quint.

Cliff wrote in a fair round hand, "J.Q.A. Whistler," saying as he raised the pen, "That small regiment of initials stands for John Quincy Adams; I was afraid there wouldn't be ink enough to write out the name in full, and I didn't want to keep you running to the inkstand."

Then Cliff wrote his own name, "Clifford P. Chantry," made a flourish against both names, and at the right of it put the address—"Biddicut."

"I declare!" exclaimed the landlady, looking down over the end of the bench. "I know your mother! She was Lucinda Clifford, and she married Jonathan Chantry. We were school-girls together, and I was at her wedding. Tell her you have made the acquaintance of Emmeline Small that was, now Mrs. Robert Grover; and that my husband keeps the Grover House, here in Kilbird."

"She'll be pleased enough," said Cliff. "And when I tell her how you treated two strange boys, it isn't going to make her sorry she ever knew you."

She offered to remove the hotel book, but Quint asked to look at it.

"Just a second," he said. "Here's our friend's name, Cliff; did you notice it? A little twisted,—'*A. W. Knight,*'—with a flourish as long as the cord he gave you to lead the dog by!"

"Burlington!" Cliff exclaimed, reading the address. "He told us Bennington; and here it is as plain as print,"—slapping the register,—"Burlington, Vermont!"

"The trouble with that man is, he forgets," said Quint. "He'll forget us, if we don't hurry along and overhaul him."

XIII

A NICE PET FOR AN OLD COUPLE

FROM Mrs. Grover's husband, whom they soon met, and from other persons of whom they made inquiries, they gained all needful information regarding the movements of Winslow and the dog. They followed fast, and in a little more than an hour, hot with haste, but high in hope, they entered a small village, to which they had traced the fugitives.

It was a village of scattered houses, in front of one of which they found a bareheaded man leaning over a gate. His back was toward them, and he seemed to be gazing very intently up the street. Farther on were other people in doorways or front yards, or standing in the street, all gazing in the same direction. By his leather apron and the sign over his door, the boys perceived that the man leaning on the gate was a shoemaker.

"What's the show?" Quint asked.

"Show!" said the man, turning upon them a look of disgust. "There's no show! And I've been fooled out of five dollars! Clean as a whistle!"

Cliff asked how that had come about, and the man told his story to an intensely interested audience of two.

"A man come along here about an hour ago, and stepped into my shop, to git me to rasp a nail out of his boot. He had a dog he bragged about, and made him do some tricks. We hain't got no children, and we'd been wishin' for some kind of a pet; and when my wife heard the man say he had got out of money, and would have to part with his dog, she looked at me, and I nodded, and then she says, 'How much do you ask for him?' she says. When he said, 'Twenty dollars,' I thought of course 't wa'n't no use for us to think of buyin' him; but as he wanted me to make him an offer, I looked at my wife, and she nodded to me, and I says, 'I'll give three,' I says, without the least idea he'd take me up. He didn't, exactly, but he come down to ten dollars, then to seven, then he said he'd split the difference; and I looked at my wife and she winked to me, and I says, 'All right,' I says, 'I'll give ye five, though I wish to gracious now I'd stuck to my first bid."

"Where's the dog now?" Cliff asked, although he knew well enough already.

The man pointed with his thumb over his shoulder, in the direction in which he and the other villagers had been gazing.

"Skipped!" he said. "Skipped like a hopper! We fed him in the shop, with the doors closed; and he was so nice and quiet, my wife wanted to have him a little while in the kitchen; and I said, 'Yes, but keep him shet in for the present,' I said; for the owner advised us to do that till he'd had time to get well out of the way. There was just a window open, over the kitchen sink; but we didn't think nothin' about that, and he didn't seem to, neither; till all to once—whish!—he was up on that sink and out o' that winder 'fore the scream was out of her mouth. I've got the rheumatiz, and can't run; but she rushed out. There she comes now!"

"Without the dog," said Cliff, gazing eagerly.

The shoemaker's wife had to run the gauntlet of questions from all her neigh-

XIV

AN UNPLEASANT SURPRISE

THE chase became exciting, and our Biddicut boys gave little heed to the circumstance that it was taking them farther and farther from home.

"Winslow will be waiting somewhere

bors, as she returned with excited looks and panting breath to her husband.

"I never see the beat on 't!" she said. "He went off like a sky-rocket, and it's my belief that we never shall see him again."

The boys asked for water, which she brought in a tin dipper, with a trembling hand. It was cold from the pump, and having drunk and condoled with the worthy couple for their loss, they resumed their tramp, without deeming it necessary to proclaim their own personal and peculiar interest in the many-times-sold dog.

for Sparkler to come up with him," Quint observed. "Then he'll be trying to sell him again; so we shall be gaining on him all the while."

Soon a team overtook them—a real "team" this time, consisting of a span of horses harnessed to an empty and clattering farm-wagon. The wayfarers turned up sweaty and appealing faces to the driver; and, pulling reins, he invited them to "hop in." It was a welcome change to the boys, enabling them not only to rest their limbs, but also to get over the road faster than they could have done on foot.

They told their story, while the driver, a farmer of the neighborhood, drove them on a mile or more farther to his own house. There a boy came out, and met them with the exciting news that a man with a thin linen bag had stopped at the door, a little while before, to ask for a glass of milk.

"Yes," he said, in answer to Cliff's eager questions; "the man hadn't been gone long when a dog came. We shouldn't have noticed him, only he ran into the yard and out again, and snuffed around, as if he was following the man."

"That's great news!" Quint exclaimed. "'T was a judgmatical idea of Winslow's, that glass of milk!" he said aside to Cliff. "I shouldn't object to sampling the pan myself."

"By the way," the farmer called to them as they were hurrying on, "wouldn't *you* like a glass of milk, or a bowl of milk, or a bowl of bread-and-milk? I'm just sitting down to my dinner, and I guess we can give you a plate of boiled victuals too, if you have time to eat it."

"We shouldn't have time for that," Quint replied. "But bread-and-milk and I are good friends. What do you say, Cliff?"

"We are in an awful hurry," said Cliff; "but—such an offer as that!"

They did, however, take time to give their hands and faces a much-needed washing, and to brush their dusty clothes on the back porch. Meanwhile, the farmer's daughters—two merry young girls, whose bright eyes made our Biddicut boys feel untidy and awkward—placed bread-and-milk on the table opposite the single plate set for their father's late dinner; his family having dined in his absence.

They were profuse in their thanks at parting. But the farmer said:

"You are quite welcome. If you come back this way, stop in. My name is Mills. You may want another bite by that time;

and I shall want to hear how you make out dog-hunting."

"Wasn't that bread-and-milk a godsend!" said Cliff, when they were once more on the road. "That meal may have to last us till we get home to supper."

"Home to supper!" Quint replied, with a laugh. "I gave that up hours ago. We shall be lucky if our folks see us at break-fast-time tomorrow—or dinner! We're in for it, Cliff!—did you know it?"

"The worst of it is," said Cliff, "we're beginning to look like a couple of tramps; anyhow, that's the way I feel."

"Was it the pretty girls back there that made you feel so?" Quint queried.

"I couldn't help looking at myself with their eyes, and wishing I had better clothes on," Cliff blushingly acknowledged. "And I wish we had more money. I'm afraid we shan't have enough to get home with."

"Winslow is our bank," replied Quint. "The farther we go, the more need there is of our catching him. We can't turn back."

They walked fast again, being sure of their trail, and soon got news of Winslow and the dog traveling together. It was easy to trace them; for as he went on through the well-settled but open country, Winslow offered the dog to almost everybody he met, stopping to talk often; so that our Biddicut boys felt at length that they had the trick-dog merchant almost within view.

They were unaccustomed to such journeys; their legs were beginning to ache. Cliff suffered from a pain in his side, Quint was unpleasantly reminded that his shoe hurt him, and both discovered that bread-and-milk, and the few berries they picked by the wayside, were a diet deficient in staying qualities. But now, inspired by the certain nearness of their game, they forgot soreness and fatigue; and Quint, whose breath held out better than Cliff's, proposed that they should try a trot.

"A *dog*-trot," he said, with a laugh. "Think you can stand it?"

"Yes, if my confounded side-ache doesn't take me again," replied Cliff.

They set their hands to their hips, each with his coat hooked on one arm, and jogged on in silence, Quint always a pace or two ahead.

"I'm getting my second wind," he said presently. "I feel more like running than I did two or three hours ago. Don't you?"

"Y-e-s!" said Cliff, admiring his companion's easy and steady lope. "We ought to get sight of 'em—from the top—of that knoll!" speaking with difficulty.

"Hello!" said Quint, "there's a crossing that's going to bother us."

Crossings and forks were their chief source of delay and vexation, but for which they must have overtaken the fugitives long before. This one, however, hindered them hardly long enough to enable Cliff to recover breath. Fresh dog-tracks were discovered, and a little further on they saw a man mowing briers by the roadside fence.

Yes, he had seen a man and a dog pass ten or fifteen minutes before.

"Did he want to sell his dog?"

"No; he just asked how far it was to the Snelling farm. That's a great stock-farm, where they have all sorts of live critters. You can see it from the top of the hill above here, a spread of buildings, with a tall windmill and a red-painted water-tank."

Wild roses in bloom, and raspberry bushes in full bearing, were the briers the man was cutting. The boys hurriedly picked and ate the berries while they talked.

"It seems too bad to cut them," said Quint.

"They spread into the fields," replied the man. "Wild roses don't do no good, and I never git none of the berries."

He slashed away at the briers, while the boys hastened on.

"Wild roses don't do no good!" Quint repeated disdainfully. "And he cuts the raspberries because he never gets none! A good man enough, I guess, but not exactly my style."

He had cut off a spray of the wild roses, which he stuck in his hat-band. Cliff carried a raspberry branch, plucking and eating the berries as they pushed on.

They were soon at the summit of the hill, gazing down upon a long stretch of open road; and near by, on the left, the orchards and buildings and windmill of the great Snelling farm.

"No such need of hurrying now," said Quint, wiping his forehead. "We must save our wind for emergencies. If he's there, he'll stay till we come. Then there's no knowing what will happen!" He laughed grimly.

They put on their coats, and talked in low tones, as they walked, still at a brisk pace, under the shelter of some orchard trees growing near the street.

"You look out for the dog; get hold of him the first thing, and leave me to deal with Winslow," said Quint. "Keep cool!" for he saw that Cliff was excited.

They came in sight of the great granite posts of the Snelling gateway, before entering which they stopped to wait for a carriage coming toward them along the road beyond. The driver answered their concise inquiries without drawing rein. He had met no man and dog.

"Then he's here!" Quint said to his companion, as with all their senses alert they turned in at the open gate.

One branch of a broad driveway curved in toward the front of the house; the other led to the rear, and to the farm-buildings beyond. This the boys followed, keeping close to a thick border of Norway spruces that thrust out heavy boughs above their heads. So they came to an open coach-house in the doorway of which an old coachman in overalls was polishing the brass mountings of a handsome harness.

"Have you seen a man and a dog come into the place lately?" Cliff asked, in a low voice, which he couldn't keep from trembling.

"I have, not many minutes ago," replied the old coachman. "He inquired for Mr. Snelling, and they have just gone into the yards together."

"The yards?—where are they?"

The old coachman dropped his polishing-brush on a chair, dusted his fingers on his overalls, and said, "Come along." The boys were careful to keep a little behind him, and partially concealed by his broad shoulders, as he passed the gate toward an open shed between two barns. There was a sound of voices in that direction, and presently the old man said:

"There's Mr. Snelling, patting the cow's neck, and there's your man with his dog."

The little group was in an angle of the shed, not twenty yards away. The boys peered over the shoulders of their guide, eager to command the situation, yet cautious of exposing themselves to view. He had stopped; they stopped too, in sudden amazement.

The man in the shed with Mr. Snelling was putting a rope on the cow's horns. He was an Irish laborer, and his dog was an ugly bull-terrier!

"Wasn't there another man?" Cliff gasped.

The old coachman had seen no other, and no other dog. Quint was utterly dismayed. But he soon recovered his equanimity, and questioned the Irish laborer.

The man had been sent for the cow from a farm about two miles away; and it appeared that he had come by the cross-road at the corner of which the boys had last stopped to look for tracks, and found them, although they were probably those of the wrong dog.

"Well, Quint, what now?" said Cliff, almost ready to cry with disappointment and vexation.

"What time is it?" Quint asked, turning to the coachman, who pulled out a big silver watch, and obligingly turned the full moon of its rimmed face toward the boys. "Thank you," said Quint. "Only half-past two. Earlier than I thought."

"We might get home to-night, if we start now," said Cliff. "We've lost the trail."

"But we may pick it up again," replied Quint. "If you are tuckered out and discouraged, you can rest here, while I start out alone to make discoveries."

"If you keep on, I shall," said Cliff. "It was partly on your account I felt we ought to take the shortest cut home."

Quint answered with a droll smile: "As for me, I'm just finding out what my gambrel-roof nose is for; it's to follow through thick and thin the man who named it. Come on!"

XV

"AN ENGLISH LORD WITH SIX TRUNKS"

THE cook of the Star Grove Hotel was old and lame and cross, and she was put into specially ill humor that afternoon by being called upon to broil a beefsteak for a late-arriving traveler.

"He's just as pleasant as he can be," said light-footed Jenny Ray, a college girl turned waitress for the summer, coming from the dining-room, after serving the traveler. "He told me to give this to the only cook he has found since he has been in the States who knows how to broil a beefsteak."

The old woman had seated herself in the broad-roofed, open passage connecting the dining-room and the summer kitchen, and was cooling her flushed face and heated temper in the breeze that blew freshly through.

"Huh!" she said, looking at the coin which Jenny dropped into her hand. "Since he has been in the States? He's an English gentleman, I'll be bound. Is there anything else he would like? There's a little of that sherbet left in the freezer."

The English gentleman *would* like the sherbet, and it was served accordingly.

"I hope he has come for the rest of the season," the old cook muttered to herself. "Well, what do *you* want?"

Two tired, dusty, forlorn-looking boys came around a corner of the hotel, and stood waiting to have a word with her.

"We don't find anybody in the office," said the younger of the two.

"The office generally runs itself from now till the five-o'clock coach arrives," she replied. "What might you be wanting in the office?"

"We are looking for an acquaintance," said the older boy, who was also the taller, and had a well-developed nose on a strong, honest face.

"We thought he might have come to this hotel."

"He had on a loose-fitting brown coat, and he had a dog with him, the last we heard," said the younger boy—Cliff Chantry, in short.

"There's been no such person here, with or without a dog," said the old woman sourly. "There's been no arrival this afternoon, but an English gentleman, about an hour ago."

Cliff's face wore a hopeless expression; it seemed useless to pursue the inquiry. But Quint queried:

"An English gentleman?"

"An English gentleman," she repeated haughtily. "He isn't the first one that's honored this house, and I hope he won't be the last. We had an English lord here once, and I'm thinking this is another."

That she was not to prove a treasury of obliging information was evident enough. But Quint said:

"Did he—your English lord—come afoot, and carry a linen grip-sack; was his shirt-collar just the least mite frayed about the edges?"

With her other excellent qualities the old cook possessed a bold imagination, to which she now gave free rein.

"He came in a carriage from the station, and he has six trunks coming this evening. He engaged the two best rooms in the house by letter, and ordered a beefsteak by telegraph. Not at all the sort of gentleman you claim as an acquaintance. Frayed shirt-collar, indeed!"

The glowering look with which she said this discouraged further questions. The boys stepped aside for a brief consultation.

It was now two hours since they had lost Winslow's trail; and they had worn out their strength and patience in the vain endeavor to pick it up again. Since the bread-and-milk they had had at the Mills farm-house, they had tasted nothing but cold water and wayside berries, and they were faint with hunger. At the close of their whispered consultation, Quint said:

"Beefsteaks are not exactly in our line; but if you can give us a couple of sandwiches, we'll be glad to pay you for your trouble."

The old cook answered tartly, "The Star Grove Hotel ain't a sandwich-shop, I'd have you know. There's a grocery in the village."

"I gave them a string of yarns as long as a kite-tail!" the old woman chuckled with malicious glee, as they disappeared around the corner of the hotel.

"But why did you?" said Jenny. "They seemed to be honest boys."

"Claiming any guest of this house as a friend of theirs, and asking for sandwiches!" scoffed the cook. "Of course they never expected to pay for 'em. An English lord—he, he! And six trunks!"

Meanwhile the possible British nobleman strolled into the reading-room, where he glanced at the newspapers for a few minutes; then he took a turn or two on the long hotel piazza, and finally came around to the roofed passage where the cook still sat at her ease cooling her round face in the refreshing breeze.

She was rather unpleasantly reminded of the two boys' description of their "friend," when she noticed the singular coincidence that this foreign tourist also had on a loosely fitting brown coat, and a standing shirt-collar frayed about the edges.

In suavity of manner, however, he was all that Jenny's words and her own fancy had painted him. With an ingratiating smile he inquired:

"Have you, madam, seen a stray dog about here anywhere, while I have been in the dining-room?"

This was another remarkable coincidence. Without waiting for a reply, he went on glibly:

"Mine chased a squirrel into some woods back here, and I left him barking up a tree. He'll turn up before long, and if he doesn't find me the first thing, he'll make for the kitchen door. That's a rule of his: a moral principle." He laughed and looked about him. "Your hotel is delightfully situated. That shady retreat is very inviting."

He walked back into the hotel, and presently reappearing with a light duster on, strolled out into the grove.

The old cook watched him with a curiously puzzled expression.

"An English lord with six trunks!" she repeated to herself with a derisive titter. "I suppose I ought to have told him his friends are looking for him; but that's none of my business. See the cheek of him now," she suddenly exclaimed; "stretching himself in Mrs. Mayhew's hammock, that she's so awful particular about. But that's not my affair either. I've something else to think of, from now till supper-time."

XVI

THE HOT BOX

ON their way to the grocery the boys noticed three or four wagons halted on a side street, and a group of men and boys standing near one of them. After they had provided themselves with a luncheon of crackers and cheese, Quint left Cliff sitting on the grocery steps, and went to speak with the teamsters.

An axle-box of a heavy draft-wagon loaded with wood had become heated by friction, and the wheel had ceased to revolve. It was a rear wheel, and three men were lifting that corner of the load by means of a plank used as a lever. Two others were swinging upon the wheel thus raised a few inches from the ground, while the one they were aiding gripped the spokes opposite the hub. One of the bystanders was holding a stick and a pot of grease, ready to give the axle the necessary oiling as soon as it was exposed.

Seeing the wheel loosening a little, Quint also laid hold of the spokes, and forgetting how weary he was from his all-day tramp, helped pull it off.

"You've a pretty good grip, young man!" the teamster said to him. "I'm much obliged to everybody."

Then, while the grease was being applied, Quint introduced his own business to a remarkably well-disposed audience. The driver of a light carryall remarked:

"Your man was a slim-waisted party, not above three or four and twenty?—and the dog looked like some kind of a spaniel? —had on a collar with nickel-headed studs on it?"

"The very same!" cried Quint.

"That party," said the driver of the light carryall, "begged a ride of me this afternoon, and took his dog with him into the wagon."

From the information he proceeded to give, Quint concluded that Winslow and Sparkler had been taken up not far from the crossing where he and Cliff lost track of them. The driver of the light carryall had come from that direction, and was now on his way back.

"How far did you carry them?" Quint inquired.

"May be a couple of miles in this direction, and then half a mile off on the Fulton road, where I had business with a man by the name of Ames. I left your chap there trying to sell his dog. I am driving right back in that direction. I can take you along and show you the house."

"I jump at that!" Quint exclaimed. "Only please wait till I can speak to my chum."

Cliff, as he confessed afterward, was feeling that he could never get up from those grocery steps, when Quint came hurrying toward him with the exciting news. He was off the steps in an instant, quite forgetting that he had ever known fatigue; and in three minutes they were riding away with their new friend. He was sociable and had a good deal to say about Winslow; among other things this:

"Before he got into my wagon, he took a long, glossy duster out of a bag, whipped the dust from his shoulders with it, and then put it on over his coat. There didn't seem to be much left in the bag; so he just made a roll of it, which he held in his lap, or under his arm. His dog lay in the bottom of the wagon, where he wouldn't be much noticed."

"That accounts for our losing trace of them so suddenly," said Cliff. "For we made inquiries all along that road."

They related their adventures, and Quint asked the driver if he knew the Mills farm-house, where they were treated to bread and milk, and were laughed at by two bright girls.

"I rather think I do!" the man replied, with a broadening smile. "My name is Putney. If you had mentioned it, those girls might have told you I won my wife in that house. She is their eldest sister."

The boys were delighted to hear this, and went on praising the hospitality of the Mills household in a way that caused their new friend to take to them more and more.

"It isn't over three quarters of a mile from my house to theirs, across country," he said. "Now, I'll tell you what I'll do. I'll drive you to Ames's; then if you find you've missed your man again, and don't see much chance of catching him or the dog, I'll put you on the way to my father-in-law's, where I advise you to pass the night; or I'll keep you over myself. Then you can start out fresh in the morning."

The boys were touched by the kindness of this proposal, and impressed by the wisdom of the advice. To Cliff particularly it seemed as if it would be the most blissful thing imaginable to settle down in some quiet farm-house for the night, talk over their adventures after a good supper, and then go to bed. He felt, as he told Quint afterward, as if he would like to sleep about forty hours out of the next twenty-four. He almost hoped that, if they didn't come upon Winslow or Sparkler, they might not get any encouraging news of them, so that they would not feel obliged to bestir themselves further in the thankless business.

The road was smooth, the country pleasant, the sun low, and the air cool; and the boys were enjoying greatly their restful mode of travel, when Quint suddenly threw up his hands, and uttered a startling cry.

"There! Look! Hold on!"—at the same time making an instinctive clutch at the reins.

Cliff looked, and saw before them, coming on the roadside, running fast, a dog—the dog they sought—there could be no doubt of it—the trick-dog Sparkler!

XVII

A MEETING AND A PARTING

"OH, jingo!" Cliff exclaimed. "Stop him! Stop him!" Whether he meant to "stop the horse," or "stop the dog," he himself could not have told. Before the wagon came to a halt, the boys tumbled themselves down over the wheel and foot-board, and rushed with outstretched hands to head off the fugitive. Sparkler was running directly toward them; and Cliff almost hoped for a moment that his pet was hastening to meet him, equally eager for their reunion.

But the dog's conduct quickly dispelled that fond fancy. There dangled from his collar just such a piece of cord as he started with in the morning, as if he had been running with it all day. He passed so near that Cliff actually reached down to clutch it, at the same time calling and coaxing, "Sparkler! Come, Sparkler!" when the animal turned suddenly aside, darted between the horse's legs, escaped under the wagon, and was rods away before the boys were fully aware what had happened.

"That's the dog," sair Mr. Putney.

"Of course it is!" cried Cliff, wildly excited. "He has been sold again!"

"And has gnawed his rope," said Quint.

"What will you do?" their new friend asked—"follow him, or drive on with me, and see if you can find his master?"

"His master has gone in the direction the dog took," said Quint. "Following one, we follow both."

"We can trace the dog more easily now, as we did in the morning, with the flying piece of cord to attract attention," cried Cliff, once more full of the ardor of pursuit.

"Sorry to bid you and your carryall good-by, Mr. Putney," said Quint; "but you see how it is." And the boys shouted back their thanks and good-bys as they ran.

The tide of human life, which had been at its lowest ebb when the Biddicut boys first touched at the Star Grove Hotel, was by this time rising again, in and about that favorite summer resort.

"Where's my maid?" cried a bustling and important woman, coming out upon the piazza. "Where's Betsy? Betsy!" as the maid appeared, trundling a baby-carriage. "Who is that man lounging in my new hammock? Go at once!—say you have orders to take the hammock in, as its owner thinks it will rain. Dear me, what dog is that? How strangely he acts! Don't dare to touch him, Philip! He may be mad."

The dog, just arrived, had a short piece of cord attached to his collar, and he was acting strangely indeed. There wasn't the slightest danger of Philip Mayhew or any other boy touching him, although two or three were soon trying to lay hold of the cord.

He ran in at the door and out again, darted between two of his pursuers, who bumped heads as he slipped through their fingers, capered around the corner of the hotel toward the kitchen, occasionally dropping his nose to the ground, and finally ran into the grove, where he jumped joyously upon the trousers of the stranger, who, at Betsy's request, was just then rolling out of the hammock.

"That your dog, mister?" cried Philip.

"He is mine—he is everybody's; at least, everybody seems to think so. What were you boys chasing him for?" said the stranger.

"I thought he had got away from somebody; I saw the rope on his neck," replied Philip.

"That cord is very useful in the performance of one of his favorite tricks," said the owner, with a peculiar laugh—stooping, however, and quickly removing the cord from the dog's collar. "He can do things that will astonish you. If enough of the boarders were interested, I could show you, right here in the grove, or on the hotel piazza, what a wonderful dog he is."

"Show us his tricks! Oh, mister, show us some of his tricks!" clamored the boys.

"Get some men—some ladies—somebody that can appreciate the most intelligent canine creature in the world," said the owner, looking around on his not very satisfactory audience of nurses and children. Just then the hotel gong sounded. "It's of no use now. Perhaps after supper—" He stooped again and caressed the dog. "Look alive now!"

The animal sat up immediately, raising his fore paws, to the delight of the boys and nurses.

"What do you want? Food?"

The dog made no motion, but watched his master with bright, intelligent eyes.

"No; he has been fed, and so have I. Walk? take a walk?" The dog dropped one of his lifted paws. "That means 'yes'; he would like to take a walk and see something of the beautiful country around here. I approve of his judgment. You see what sort of a prodigy he is, and you'll know what to expect if I am back in time to show you some of his tricks this evening."

About half an hour after this our two Biddicut boys came panting up the Star Grove driveway. They had had more trouble than they expected in following Sparkler, having lost track of him in consequence of an unexpected turn he had made; and had learned to their bewilderment, that such a dog had been seen going toward the very hotel they had so lately visited.

Eager to verify this report, they hastened up the piazza steps and met the office-clerk in the doorway. Yes, he said, a dog with a cord hanging from his collar had been dodging about there a little while ago, and he had last seen him running around the corner of the hotel pursued by some boys.

Where were the boys? At supper. Which corner of the hotel? He told them; and a minute later Quint and Cliff were standing on the spot where they had interviewed the crusty-tempered old cook.

The cook was no longer there, but presently Jenny Ray appeared, with some dishes on a tray, between the dining-room and the kitchen. She recognized them, and smiled at their question.

"The dog was here only a little while ago," she told them, "and I believe that the man himself was in the dining-room at the very time you were inquiring for him."

"The English lord!" exclaimed Cliff.

Jenny laughed. "The cook told me how she fooled you. It was too bad!"

"I'd like to fan her with her own gridiron!" said Quint indignantly. "Where is he now—the man who was in the dining-room?"

"I don't know; he was in the grove till his dog came and found him. But I can't stop longer!" And Jenny went on into the kitchen.

The boys hastened to the grove, where they found a nurse with two small children, and learned from her that Winslow had gone off with his dog shortly after the supper-gong sounded.

She showed the way he had taken through the grove, and they started in pursuit.

XVIII

THE WAYSIDE SHED

A DRIVEWAY skirting the grove in the rear of the hotel led to an open road not far beyond. This the boys soon reached, and they were fortunate in hearing of Winslow and the dog before much time was lost in looking for tracks along the road.

They found themselves in a beautiful upland, with the grove on their left, a rolling farm region on the other side, and before them a pleasant road stretching away to the westward, across a cool valley, toward distant wooded hills. The sun was not yet setting, but masses of black cloud with wondrously illuminated edges surging up in a wild sky cast a strange gloom over all the landscape.

"There's rain-water in that cloud," said Quint, "and thunder and lightning. I've felt a storm brewing all the afternoon."

"Do you believe it will come here?" Cliff asked.

"If it keeps on the way it is moving, we shall get it," Quint replied. "The lightning is having a circus!" as the black face of the cloud crinkled with sudden flashes.

At no time during the day had they felt more certain hope of coming up with their game. If Winslow did not turn back on his course, or lose time by offering Sparkler for sale, and so allow them to gain upon him, he must soon, they reasoned, seek shelter from the coming storm; and they determined not to pass a wayside house without stopping to make inquiries.

These stops caused some delay; but they succeeded in keeping his trail, and came at length to a gloomy hollow, where there was a solitary farm-house a little back from the street, and an open wagon-shed on the roadside. A short distance beyond this the road made a fork, arrived at which they were again puzzled, as they had been similarly so many times in the course of that day's adventure. Although it was not yet night, the shadow of the advancing storm was gathering so fast that they would hardly have been able to detect footprints, even if any had been impressed in the hard, gravelly road-bed.

"Well! what now, Quint?" said Cliff, his face showing pale and anxious in a gleam of lightning which just then lit up the landscape.

"I'll go ahead on this left-hand road, which shows most travel," Quint replied, "while you wait here, or perhaps go as far as the first farm-house on the other branch. Whether we find out anything or not, we'll both come back here; and the one who comes first will wait for the other under the shed. That will be as good a shelter as any when the storm breaks."

A feeling of dread came over Cliff at the

thought of parting from his friend, even for a brief interval, at such a crisis. The increasing darkness, the dazzling lightning, the far-off thunder rolling ever nearer, and the utter loneliness of their strange surroundings, filled him with vague forebodings. But without breathing a syllable of his shuddering fears, he agreed to Quint's plan. So they separated at the fork, and hurried on their separate ways, bushy and hilly fields soon hiding each from the other's view.

Cliff had not gone far before he came to a farm-house, where he was assured no such man as he inquired for had been seen. A little farther on he met a wagon, the driver of which pulled up his horses reluctantly, shook his head sullenly, and with an anxious look at the sky, whipped his horses on again.

Cliff did not stop long to consider what he should do. A dazzling zigzag rift running across the blackness of the heavens, followed by an appalling crash of thunder and splashes of rain, put an end to all irresolution.

"By jingo!" he exclaimed aloud, with thrills of fear crawling all over him, "I am going back!"

He hoped to find Quint in the shed before him; but it was empty. It was a most desolate place, but he was glad to have a roof between him and the lightning-riven sky and echoing thunder. He stood at the great opening and looked out, straining his eyes in the obscurity, or blinking at the glare, and listening for footsteps, caring little now for Winslow, but longing for Quint to come. He seemed to think that, whatever happened, it wouldn't be half so bad if his friend were present; such comfort is companionship in times of trouble.

He explored the shed. At one end was an old tip-cart, while nearer the center was a farm wagon, run in diagonally with the neap pushed into the vacant corner above a manger at the rear. He discovered, to his satisfaction, that the manger contained bundles of straw. This he gathered up, and made a bed of it on the ground against the end of the shed. Then again he stood in the opening, looking, listening, longing for his friend. A wind was rising, and the gusts blew whiffs of rain into his face, causing him to draw farther back beneath the roof.

"Wishing won't fetch him, and worrying won't do any good," he said; and yielding to a sense of overpowering weariness, he lay down upon his bed of straw.

He remembered how often, under the attic roof at home, he had been lulled to rest by the mild music of the wind and rain. Something like the same influence stole over him now, and he thought what comfort it would be to cuddle down there, forgetting Winslow and Sparkler and all anxiety and care, and sink into blissful slumber!

But where all the while was Quint?

It was darker again, but still light enough for him to perceive anybody who might be passing on the road. He still thought of Winslow, but his chief solicitude was to see the tall lank form of his friend appear at the opening. Had some accident happened to him? What could keep him so long? It had not rained hard at first, but now the torrents came down with a rushing sound.

He tried to console himself with the reflection that Quint had sought shelter in some farm-house; but that wouldn't be like Quint. All at once the tired boy stopped thinking altogether. A whole procession of dogs and Winslows might have passed; Quint's mysterious absence, his own pains and fatigues and disappointments, thunder and lightning and wind and rain—he was sweetly oblivious of all, fast asleep on his bed of straw.

XIV

"WHAT DO YOU WANT OF ME?"

QUINT proceeded some distance, making fruitless inquiries at farm-houses, and meeting no travelers. At length he came to a cross-road presenting the usual difficulties, and he saw the uselessness of keeping on.

"Cross-roads, I should say!" he muttered, as he stood and gazed off in the three directions, any one of which Winslow might have taken. "They make *me* cross enough. Well! that's rather sharp!"

It was a frightful flash of lightning, with its quickly following peal. Still he stood deliberating, holding out his hand to catch the raindrops.

It was a lonely situation, surrounded by barren and bushy fields, except on one side, where a clump of dark woods straggled down to the very corner of the cross-roads. He stood among the scattered trees,—stunted oaks and hard pines,—and strained his every nerve to watch and listen.

He was on the point of turning reluctantly back, when he heard quick footsteps, and presently perceived, a little way before him, the figure of a man walking fast in the middle of the road. Quint stepped out from the wayside to accost him.

"Good evening, stranger," he began, and stopped.

No need to put the inquiry that was on his lips. A lightning flash just then flooded heaven and earth, and poured its white instantaneous glare on the two human figures facing each other in that terrible solitude.

"Hullo!" said the dog-seller, skipping aside with an exceedingly alert movement, very much as if he had been stopped by a highwayman. "What do you want of me?"

Quint also took a step, so that he still confronted him. "You know pretty well what I want! I see you remember me."

"Remember you?" cried Winslow with a light laugh. "Brutus—or Cassius?—which is it? Brutus, I believe. Well, Marcus Brutus, what can I do for you? This is really like meeting an old friend!"

Quint had many times rehearsed to himself what he would do and say upon the chance of falling in with Winslow; but the present occasion was so different from any he had foreseen, that he hardly knew how he alone was to deal with the swindler. But his wits did not desert him. Cliff was too far away to be called to his assistance; he must then try to take Winslow to Cliff.

"If you don't object," he said, "I'll walk along with you."

"All right!" said Winslow. "But you seemed to be going in the opposite direction."

"You were going in that direction too, a short time ago," said Quint, falling in by his side.

"I was out for a little walk," said Winslow. "Now I am going back."

"Just my case," said Quint. "I was out for a walk, and now I am going back."

"And I've got to hurry, for I don't care to get wet," said Winslow, quickening his step.

"Just my case every time," said Quint, keeping at his side. "I don't fancy a wetting."

"I shall be drenched before I get back to the Star Grove Hotel, if I don't run for it!" And Winslow broke into a light trot.

"That's a nice house—worth running for," observed Quint, always within easy clutching distance of the dog-seller's right arm. And he calculated, with secret glee, that their present rate of speed would in five minutes bring them to the shed where Cliff would soon be, if he wasn't there already.

It seemed as if Winslow must have read his mind. He was certainly suspicious of Quint's too evident willingness to accompany him in that direction. All at once he stopped.

"It is too far," he said. "It will pour before I get half-way there. I am going back to a house I passed just before I saw you."

"There's a house only a little farther on," replied Quint; "and just beyond the forks of the road is a shed we can wait under till the shower is over."

Winslow turned and faced him with a sarcastic grin.

"The shed wouldn't be big enough for us both. I am going back."

"I'm afraid it will be lonesome there without you; guess I'll go back, too"; and turning as Winslow turned, Quint still kept close by his side.

"Now, look here, young man!" cried Winslow. "This is a great country—big as all outdoors! It almost seems as if there was room in it for me and you and your gambrel-roof nose without crowding."

"I'll try not to crowd you," Quint answered; "but the fact is, poor company is better than none on such a night as this."

"My amiable friend," cried Winslow, his tones growing hard and sharp and menacing, "doesn't it appeal to your common sense that a person has a right to choose his own company in this land of the free and home of the brave?"

"That's just what I think," said Quint; "and I choose yours."

For a moment Winslow made no response as he walked fast back toward the crossing, Quint's elbow constantly close to his own.

Quint would have yelled for Cliff, but he wasn't sure Cliff was within hearing; and he hoped Winslow would yet conclude

to return to the Star Grove Hotel. Upon one thing the boy from Biddicut was fully determined—to stick to him until, with or without Cliff's assistance, he had got back Cliff's money. The dog was not with his master; but Quint cared little for that often-sold animal.

Their hurried footsteps were the only sounds on that lonely road; but now and then the thunder tumbled down the cloudy crags of heaven, and the leaping lightning severed the gloom of the storm and night. On reaching the wooded corner, Winslow turned sharply on his unwelcome companion.

"I'm inclined to the opinion," he said, "that it's about time for you and me to come to some sort of an understanding."

"This seems to be a good place for it," Quint replied, sternly regarding him. "We needn't be afraid of an interruption."

"Then have the kindness to inform me just why you dog my footsteps in this way," said Winslow threateningly.

"Because I can't *dog* them in any other," Quint replied. "I'm not a Sparkler."

"I see the point," remarked Winslow. "State your case, and we'll settle it on the spot. If not in one way, then in another. A very good spot, as you say!"

"You know the case perfectly well," said Quint, without heeding the threat. "You go about the country selling that dog. You have sold him once too often. That's my case, Mr. Algernon Knight Winslow!"

"I never sold him to you!" Winslow retorted, insolent and defiant. "You are not Cassius."

"Cassius and I are solid in this business," said Quint. "You have got back your dog; now we want our money."

"How much?" Winslow asked, as coolly as if he had been prepared to fork out millions.

All the while the rain was slowly pattering, and the lightning was winking at them as they confronted each other on the edge of the lonely woods.

For a moment Quint had hope of bringing the dog-seller to an easy settlement.

"You remember the agreement you put your name to. We gave you ten dollars. I want the twenty you promised." And he held out his hand.

"Was that the bargain? Show me the paper you say I signed. Business is business," said Winslow.

"Come with me," Quint replied, "and I'll show you the paper in the presence of witnesses."

"Bring on your witnesses. I'll wait here," said Winslow, stepping under the trees on the dreary roadside, and placing his back against one of the largest trunks.

A DESPERATE ENCOUNTER

XX

QUINT also stepped aside under the trees and stood facing him.

The dark woodland beyond looked impenetrably dense until lighted up by a vivid flash that showed each silent trunk distinct in its space, and quiet saplings ranged on each side of a broken and ruined wayside wall. The utter solitude, the surrounding desolation, the fitful gleams and peals, the on-coming night and storm, might well have tried the nerves of one older and more experienced than Quint, but no one could have been more determined.

"I can wait here as long as you can," he said; coolly adding, "I don't think there's going to be much of a shower."

Winslow moved to a fallen tree-trunk and sat down upon it. Quint guessed there was room for two, and sat down beside him.

"How long have you been following me?" The dog-seller's tone was quite friendly now.

"All day," Quint replied. "Cassius and I have been on the war-path ever since the dog got away this morning."

"Seems to me you are giving yourselves a deal of trouble for a small matter," Winslow remarked sarcastically.

"It's no small matter to us, let me tell you," Quint replied. "Ten dollars is a big sum to a poor country boy. It's more than my chum had saved up in all his life; that's why he borrowed of me. Now we are bound to have it back, with something for our trouble."

"You are a precious pair of country bumpkins!" said Winslow laughing. "But I rather like your pluck. Come now, be reasonable. What will you settle for?"

"Twenty dollars," Quint responded in a direct and quiet tone.

"That's absurd! I haven't got so much money as that."

"You've got more than that, Mr. Winslow. Before you sold that dog to us you sold him to Mr. Miller in the town of Wormwood. To-day you sold him first to an old shoemaker, then again to somebody else, just before you went to the Star Grove Hotel, and you've sold him again this evening. How many more times you have sold him," Quint went on, "you know better than I do. You certainly have money, and the best thing in the world for you to do, Mr. Winslow, is to hand out mine." And he looked squarely at the dog-seller over four feet of pine log between them.

"And what if I decline to give up to you my hard-earned profits?" sneered Winslow.

"Then I'll see that you don't earn any more in that way; I'll see that you are put where even your dog can't find you! That's the size of it, Mr. Winslow."

The dog-seller laughed derisively.

"You imagine you can make people believe your absurd story? I deny every word of it. I never sold you and Cassius a dog. Never sold anybody a dog. My dog is not for sale; he is with my mother in Michigan. Besides, I never had a dog. If you have a paper signed with my name it's a forgery. I don't sign my name to papers. More than all that, my name is not Winslow."

He rattled this off with bewildering volubility, and taking a knife from his pocket, opened it with a peculiar motion, and began to stick the blade into the log they sat on—merely to display his weapon, Quint thought. It was not so dark but that Quint could see that the blade was long and bright. He also took out his knife and began to stab the log.

"It's funny, then," said he, "what we have hunted you all day for!"

"I know what for," cried Winslow. "You have trumped up false charges against me, and think you'll force me to buy you off. That's what I say and what I'll maintain."

"And the other people you've swindled, —I know just where to find some of them, —how will it be when they come to tell their stories?" Quint demanded.

"Brutus!" said the dog-seller, snapping his knife shut and putting it into his pocket, "I'll give you five dollars, and you shall go your way and I'll go mine."

Quint quietly closed and pocketed his own knife, and asked dryly:

"You will submit, then, to our 'false charges' as you call them?"

"I'll submit to anything for a dry skin. We're a couple of fools to sit here and palaver when our little affair can be compromised so easily."

"So I think. But five dollars won't compromise it," said Quint.

"Very well, then!" exclaimed Winslow, a blaze of lightning showing a sinister resolution on his keen face; "we'll sit it out. I've got on a waterproof; I think I can stand it, if you can!"

"I've got a better waterproof than that," said Quint, with ominously set lips. "I'm going to get mad by and by; that will keep me from caring about the weather. You'd better not put off settling too long."

The thunder was terrific. Then, between the peals, a rushing and roaring sound could be heard, distant and faint at first, then nearer and louder, and they knew that the storm, with tempest and down-pouring and fracas of tossing boughs, was sweeping toward them over the woods and fields. The lightning shot through fringes of the coming rain, and shone in the large, near, slant-streaking drops.

Winslow turned up the collar of his duster, or waterproof, and pulled the flaps over his exposed knees. Quint likewise turned up his coat-collar, and buttoned the top button, remarking coolly:

"When this tree gets wet through, we can move under another."

The pleasantry did not appeal to Winslow's sense of humor. He sprang to his feet with an outburst of unquotable adjectives, threw down his head against the gusts, and exclaiming," I'm going to get out of this!" started to run.

Quint started at the same time, catching him by the arm.

"Hands off!" Winslow yelled, in the turmoil of rain and wind and thrashing boughs. "Don't stop me! or I'll—. Take that—on your gambrel-roof nose!" with which half-stifled ejaculation, he whirled and aimed a furious blow at Quint's head.

Quint ducked in time to receive only a glancing stroke on his crown. Then throwing up an elbow to parry a second blow, he made a headlong dive at Winslow's waist; he closed with him, and in a minute the two were engaged in a desperate struggle.

They were about equally matched as to weight; but the lank Biddicut boy was the taller and longer-limbed of the two. He had had some school-boy practice at scuffling and wrestling; and his mates had usually found him what they termed a "tough customer" in their rough-and-tumble contests. If one attempted to lift him from the ground, his feet seemed to stick to it, as if they had glue on them, and his sinewy legs to stretch out like legs of india-rubber.

He gripped Winslow firmly about the waist, at first with the sole idea of holding him, and of shielding his own head and face from the blows. With his right arm he managed to secure his favorite under-hold, while his left fought, and finally grappled, Winslow's right.

Though slight of build, Winslow was lithe and athletic, and a more formidable adversary than he appeared. Forced to desist from his blows, he cried in a lull of the scuffle:

"Will you let go now and go your way, while I go mine?"

"Your way will be mine till you give me my money!" Quint replied.

"I'll give you a broken back over that log!" Winslow snarled. And the struggle recommenced, both settling down to business.

They tugged, and wrenched, and lifted, Winslow trying to throw Quint over the log; Quint avoiding it, and at the same time doing his utmost to get Winslow on his hip, fling him, and fall upon him.

Suddenly Winslow, freeing one hand, got it inside his waterproof, and into his trousers' pocket. But before he could fairly grasp the knife he was evidently reaching for, his arm was clutched again, he was forced violently backward; in another moment he was tripped over the log, and falling, both went down together.

XXI

CLIFF'S AMAZING DISCOVERIES

THROUGH all the tumult of the storm Cliff slumbered on his heap of straw, to be at last awakened by something like a blow grazing his cheek and striking him full upon the breast. He started from his dreams and put out his hand.

He thought he was in his bed at home, and that he had been hit by his brother Amos tumbling about in his sleep. Then it seemed as if something was moving in the room; he heard a rustling sound, and the hand he put out for his brother touched straw.

It was not so dark but that he could see the great open front of the shed, the overhanging roof, and the dim shape of the farm-wagon under it. Recollection returned with a shock, and he was terrified to find that he had fallen asleep while waiting for his friend; he couldn't imagine how long ago. It might have been hours.

"Hullo!" he cried out, in the wild hope that the movements he had heard were those of Quint, who might perhaps have returned.

No answer. But the movements continued. There was some live creature close behind him. The straw rustled at his very side. He started up, thrilled through and through with horrid fear.

Suddenly the blow on his breast was repeated, and a dark object came between him and the light. Something wet touched his hands; something warm and moist flashed, so to speak, across his face.

His companion in the shed was a dog. The wagging tail thumped his arm; the caressing tongue lapped his face. He uttered a sudden cry—something between a gasp of astonishment and a cry of joy.

"Sparkler! Oh, my gracious Jehu! Sparkler! Quint! Quint!" he called; "I've got him!"—as if Quint were near.

Securing a hold of the collar, he hugged the wet creature to his heart.

"You don't get away from me again, you rogue!" he said, in a tremor of excitement, as he pulled from his pocket the cord he had carried all day, slipped one end of it about the dog's collar, and fastened it with a firm knot. "Now this never goes out of my hand!"

Sparkler did not even try to get away; he seemed, on the contrary, to recognize Cliff with pleasure, to which his smiting tail gave vivacious expression.

"Why did you run away from me? Why did you come back? How did you find me here?" said the boy, talking as if his dumb companion could comprehend. "Oh, Sparkler, I wish you could speak! What a story you could tell!"

The exciting occurrence diverted his mind for a minute from its anxieties about Quint. But now he thought of him again with growing amazement and alarm at his mysterious absence. He stilled the dog's movements, and knelt upon the straw, listening and wondering; then advanced to the opening of the shed.

The storm was over; the few drops that fell upon his hand and shoulder came from the still dripping eaves. He went out upon the wet roadside, the dog capering at the end of his cord, and gazed up and down,

feeling sure that some dreadful thing had befallen his friend.

"Oh, Sparkler!" he exclaimed in his misery, "can't you tell me what to do?"

The dog had at first seemed averse to quitting the dark corner of the shed, even bounding back toward the manger when Cliff pulled him away. But now, on the open road, as if he had understood the boy's appeal, he began to tug at the cord in the direction in which Cliff was himself inclined to go.

"Go ahead!" cried Cliff, with sudden hope and confidence. "I'll trust you!"

He was still full of imaginary fears; but he was comforted by the companionship of the dog; and occasionally, through all his troubles, would break a gleam of pure joy at the thought of Sparkler once more in his possession.

At the same time the world was growing lighter and still lighter; and he perceived that the western sky was clearing. A bright star appeared beneath the edge of broken and low-hanging clouds, and shone with inexpressible beauty and purity in the opening rift. Then all at once a flood of white radiance filled the night. Cliff looked up, and there, almost overhead in the wild sky, was the moon. It peered over the edge of a great black rampart of cloud, as if to reassure the storm-buffeted sphere with its cold, placid smile.

Cliff kept on, often pausing, and taxing every sense to discern signs of his lost comrade, until suddenly Sparkler jumped up on the roadside, jerking at the cord. They were on the outskirts of a wood-lot, and a passing gust of wind shook down pattering drops from the branches overhead. The moonlight slanting through the boughs and silvering the undergrowth showed a dark log on the ground, toward which Sparkler led the way.

Near the log was a dark-gray object at

which Sparkler was presently sniffing. Cliff ran to it, stooped over it, caught it up and examined it with astonishment which quickly became consternation. It was a hat —a common felt hat, of a well-worn appearance, with a narrow rim and shapeless crown, crushed as if it had been trampled on, yet just such a hat as his friend had worn; and there, as if more certainly to identify it, was a spray of wild roses, such as Quint had stuck under the band that afternoon.

Cliff's fears were thus confirmed. Quint had certainly had an encounter with the desperate character they were pursuing; and that he had not had the best of it seemed proved by the fact that his hat, and not Winslow's, was left on the field.

But what had happened to him since? In continuing the struggle, he might have met with some terrible mishap, and Cliff's excited imagination pictured his friend lying on the ground, somewhere in the woods, disabled—possibly worse.

He stood in the edge of the moonlit woodland, and called with all his force of throat and lungs.

"Hello-o-o, Quint! Hello-o-o!"

His voice died away in the depths of the forest, and not even an echo came back. A curdling terror crept through his veins.

Sparkler meanwhile tugged at his leash, and sniffed along the ground. The drenching shower must have carried away, for the most part, such evidences of his master's presence as his delicate canine scent would otherwise have been quick to detect and follow; but he was strangely uneasy.

"Oh, Sparkler!" Cliff pleaded, "seek— seek him!"—in the fond belief that, by pursuing Winslow, the dog might help him find his friend.

Sparkler's nose stopped at something half-buried in a clump of moss. It was a bright object, with a shining edge turned up in the moonlight. Cliff darted to pick it up.

"Only a piece of knife-handle!" he exclaimed. "Have they been breaking knives?" he wondered. It appeared to have been trodden into the moss.

He would have thrown it away as something worthless, but for the possibility of its affording some clue to the harrowing mystery.

It was about the size and shape of the thing he took it for; but unlike any knife he had ever seen in Quint's hands. He was carefully scrutinizing it, holding it up in the moonlight with one hand,—the end of the cord in the other, along with Quint's hat,—wholly forgetting Sparkler in that moment of intense thought, when he was reminded of the dog in an unpleasantly surprising manner.

Sparkler, who had been sniffing again about his feet, gave a sudden bounce, the cord was jerked from Cliff's relaxed hold, and in an instant the dog darted away in the checkered moonshine, with the cord flying like a faint streak at his heels.

"He's gone!" said Cliff, in rage and despair. "Let him go! I don't care if I never see him again! I wish I had never seen him!"

XXII

CAPTOR OR CAPTIVE?

Quint's hat had been knocked off by the first glancing blow from Winslow's fist; and when, in the final struggle, he plunged after Winslow over the log, he struck his unprotected head against the root of a tree. Though partially stunnned, he was on his feet again almost immediately, but only in time to see a dim figure dart away in the rain, in the direction of the cross-road.

Without waiting to recover his hat or to search for the knife, which he thought flew from Winslow's pocket when he seized his arm, he started at once in pursuit, stumblingly at first, then with more certain steps as he rallied from the effect of his fall.

It was a strange race, in the midst of the mad storm, gusts of wind, rain that came down in veiling sheets, lightning gleams and crashes of thunder. A flash at a critical instant showed the fugitive taking the southern branch of the cross-road; and from that time Quint had little difficulty in following him.

At first the distance between them seemed to increase, then for a while to continue about the same. Each had started out with breath spent by the scuffle, and Quint was put to a still further disadvantage by his dive against the tree. Then gradually his forces returned; he drew deep breaths as he ran, and with the sense of restored power, the fury of his resolution came back.

So, though a fair match for him in a wrestling bout, the dog-seller soon found that he couldn't compete with the tall Biddicut boy in a foot-race. His breath was utterly gone, when, hearing Quint close at his heels, he turned and faced him.

"Aren't we a couple of fools!" he articulated pantingly.

"If you are speaking for yourself, I don't know of anybody that will dispute you," Quint replied, in much better breath and voice.

He didn't offer to lay hands on Winslow; but, bareheaded, his hair disordered, his features dripping in the rain, and showing a ghastly streak caused by the blow upon the left temple, he confronted the swindler.

"What do you intend to do now?" said the dog-seller.

"Stick by you," said Quint grimly.

"Hadn't you better go back and pick up your hat? You seem to have come off in a hurry," said Winslow, walking on.

His own duster, or waterproof, had been torn open in the scuffle, and he was holding it together over his breast.

"I've more important business just now," Quint answered, again keeping close to his side.

How extremely anxious he was to go back, he was careful not to betray. Not for his hat, indeed; but in following Winslow he was going farther and farther away from Cliff, of whose assistance he was in desperate need. But he would not go back without his captive, and he could not devise any means of taking his captive with him.

It was a singular dilemma—the captive leading away the captor! But there seemed to be no help for it, unless he abandoned his purpose; and this he had no thought of doing, although far more apprehensive than he appeared as to the outcome of the amazing adventure.

Winslow would no doubt have offered more liberal terms of settlement if he had known what sort of a boy was behind the "gambrel-roof nose." But a rogue may have pride as well as an honest man; and he was not one to give up his ill-gotten "profits" at the demand of a seventeen-year-old "country bumpkin." He knew no more than Quint did how the affair was to end; but he would trust to luck and his sharp wits to carry him through. While Quint was "sticking" to him, he was watching for an opportunity to get rid of Quint.

The thunder and lightning ceased, or became distant, but it rained steadily, and the darkness was increasing.

The road ran at right angles with the one to which Quint would gladly have returned. But he shrewdly guessed that it would soon strike one parallel to that, perhaps the main thoroughfare that traversed the village where he had bought crackers and cheese with Cliff, and had helped the teamsters with their hot box.

The two walked on without speaking, and before many minutes came to the very street of Quint's conjecture. The cross-road ended there, and a broader highway stretched away in the darkness to the right and left. To the right it led into an unknown region; to the left, it led back to the village Quint knew. There were no lights visible, except in the windows of a few scattered houses.

"Here's a lamp-post," said Winslow, stopping on a corner. "Why is there no light?"

"Because there is supposed to be a moon," replied Quint. "That's the way it is in Biddicut; no matter how dark and stormy the nights are, the street lamps are never lighted, if there happens to be a moon in the almanac."

"Do you know where we are?" Winslow inquired.

"We are about a mile and a half from the Star Grove Hotel, which lies in this direction," Quint answered, pointing.

"That's according to my calculation," Winslow remarked, as he turned the corner in the direction of the village, to the immense but secret satisfaction of his captor.

Another long silence. They were rapidly approaching the village.

"Are we going to keep this up all night?" the dog-seller inquired.

"That's for you to say," Quint replied.

"If you walk, I walk. After the shower is over, exercise will dry us."

Another silence. Then Winslow asked: "Where's Cassius all this time?"

"He's getting rested, so he'll be fresh for hooking on to you, if I find the thing growing monotonous."

"Well," said Winslow, decisively, "I'm going to the Star Grove Hotel!"—the lights of which were now visible, over the village roofs and trees. "I've engaged a room there."

"I'm with you," Quint remarked cheerfully. "The hotel will be a good place to call a convention of the people you've sold your dog to."

"That's what you're after, is it?" Winslow retorted.

"I'm not after anything. What I do will depend on you. I've only one plan—to get my money back, or to see you locked up. That's the kind of country bumpkin I am."

"You want to try that game?" cried Winslow defiantly. "Here's your chance!"

It was a chance Quint had been eagerly looking for, with but little hope, however, that he would be allowed to take advantage of it.

They had reached the center of the village, which he recognized, although its aspect was changed from what it had been when he and Cliff passed and repassed through its principal streets that afternoon. They were now plashy and deserted, and doors were closed against the storm. A little off from the corner, not far ahead, was the broadly lighted front window of the grocery, on the steps of which Cliff had rested and munched his crackers and cheese while Quint went to join the teamsters around the hot box.

On another corner, still nearer, was an establishment in which Quint was more intensely interested just now. This was the police station. Here he had stopped with

Cliff to make inquiries, while following Sparkler back through the village, and had told enough of their story to insure him a ready hearing, he believed, if he could now succeed in taking Winslow to the door.

He had hardly expected to bring him even within sight of it; for Winslow probably knew the town as well as he did, and that was one of the places which persons of his character are usually solicitous to avoid. Perhaps he had not been so quick as Quint, to recognize the situation; but he certainly recognized it now. For there, right across the way, on a broad transparency lighted from within, were the conspicuous letters—POLICE.

Winslow perceived the sign as soon as Quint did; but instead of retreating or hurrying by, he put on a bold front and repeated:

"Here's your chance! Think I'm afraid of that?"

Fearing some trick, but holding himself ready to fling himself upon Winslow the instant he should attempt any suspicious action, Quint answered promptly:

"All right! Cross over with me!"

"I'll do that," said Winslow, "and we'll soon see what your trumped-up charges will amount to."

So saying, he crossed over with Quint to the door of the station. It was closed, but the light from the window shone mistily upon them as they stood there a moment in the rain, alert, suspicious, each eager to fathom the other's intentions.

"Why don't you go ahead?" said Winslow, with an ironic smile.

"The elder first; age before beauty," Quint replied.

"Come along, then!" said the dog-seller, with an air of bravado, mounting the two steps that led to the door.

Quint was so intent upon getting him into the station and cutting off his retreat

in case he should turn back at the last moment, that he was wholly unprepared for what followed.

"Come along!" Winslow repeated, raising his voice as he threw open the door, at the same time clutching the astonished Biddicut boy by the collar and dragging him forward over the threshold. "Police!" he cried, "I've brought you a highway robber!"

Captor and captive had all at once changed places.

XXIII

"A PRODIGIOUS BLUNDER"

THERE was but one person in the room — a sturdy Americanized Irishman. Unfortunately he was not the officer of whom the boys had made inquiries that afternoon. He was writing at a desk, in a little railed-off space, with his broad back toward the door, when it was burst open in this extraordinary manner.

He stepped promptly outside the rail, and seized hold of Quint, who was struggling with Winslow.

"Be quiet, will you!" Then to the pretended captor: "What has he done?"

"Stopped me on the street!" Winslow exclaimed, showing his thin outer garment torn open at the breast. "Snatched my watch and ran! I caught him, and he flung it away—a few rods back here."

Quint meanwhile was holding fast to Winslow and trying to speak. His bare head, his drenched hair and garments, his rain-streaked features, showing the effects of his wearisome all-day tramp and of the present excitement, — rendered ghastly, moreover, by an ugly bruise on the temple, —all combined to give him the aspect of a desperate and disreputable character.

"Be quiet, or I'll quiet you!" said the officer roughly. "Take away your hand!"

Quint relaxed his hold upon Winslow.

"I'll be quiet," he said; "only allow me to tell my story."

"You'll have time for that," said the officer, quickly slipping a pair of handcuffs on the astounded prisoner.

"Wait till I pick up my watch; I know just where he dropped it," said Winslow.

"Keep him! keep him! Don't let him go!" Quint fairly howled.

But Winslow, without awaiting an answer, was already out of the station.

Even with the handcuffs on his wrists Quint would have rushed out in pursuit if the officer had not detained him.

"*He* is the robber! Let me go!" he cried, trying to get away.

"Will you quit?" demanded the officer, holding him firmly by one manacled wrist.

"I'll quit if I must," Quint replied fiercely. "But I never thought it was the business of the police to help the rogues instead of the honest men."

"We'll see who is the rogue in this case," said the officer, slightly disconcerted by Winslow's sudden disappearance, and by the prisoner's vehement protest; "when he comes back with the watch."

"There was no watch!" Quint declared. "He won't come back! If he does, you may believe I am the robber, and not that *he* has got *my* money."

It is not probable that the deliberate Biddicut boy had ever before spoken so volubly and vehemently. Fully roused, furiously indignant, he turned from gazing after the vanished figure, and glared upon the officer.

Only the pouring rain was heard outside the open door. The sound of fleeing footsteps had died away. No figure groping along the ground in search of a watch, nor any other moving object, was visible in the rainy street. After looking out and listening a moment, the officer addressed his prisoner:

"What were you resisting for?"

"I wasn't resisting. I was only trying to hold on to him, while you were letting him go. Couldn't you see what he was up to?" said Quint, his grim face wrathfully glowering. "*I* had brought *him* in, instead of his having brought me!"

"It didn't look so," said the officer, incredulous, but evidently disturbed. "He was dragging you after him."

"I'll tell you how that was," said Quint. "The minute I got him to the door, and was making him come in first, he grabbed me by the collar and snaked me over the top step so suddenly I stumbled; then you thought I was fighting to get away, when I was only keeping *him* from getting away."

The officer was all the while looking out for the returning watch-hunter, and frowning dubiously. Again he turned and looked Quint carefully over.

"It's an improbable story you tell," he declared. "You couldn't capture and bring in a man like him. Impossible!"

"Would it be any more possible for him to bring me in?" Quint retorted, standing at his full height, and looking sternly into the eyes of the officer, who, though a good-sized man, was hardly taller than he.

"You are bigger than I thought, when you came sprawling in."

"You thought then I was big enough to play the highway-robber. I own I couldn't have brought him here, if he hadn't been willing, any more than he could have brought me. I had been following him all day—I had just caught him—

and then to have the *police* help him get away!"

Quint crushed some angry word in his teeth, and his ghastly features worked with repressed emotion.

"How had he robbed you?" the officer demanded.

Quint told something of the dog-seller's operations, and went on:

"We followed him all the way from Biddicut through I don't know how many towns. I was alone when I fell in with him this evening. He tried to shake me off, and we had a squabble. But I stuck to him till we came in sight of your station. Then I should have called for help, if he hadn't himself proposed to come in. He must have had this rascally trick of his already planned."

"Did he give you that blow on the forehead?" the officer inquired.

Quint put up his hand. "I didn't know I had one! He struck me three or four times. But I must have got this when we fell over a log together, and my head tried to occupy the same place with the butt of a tree!" he explained solemnly.

The officer, evidently no longer expectant of Winslow, kept glancing up at the clock. He had told Quint he could sit down, but Quint remained standing.

"The chief will be here in a few minutes," the man said. "Then if we find you are telling a straight story, we'll see what we can do for you."

"You can't do anything now," Quint answered sullenly. "Unless you take off these bracelets. They aren't comfortable, and they aren't ornamental, and they happen to be on the wrong pair of wrists. The other pair is far enough out of your reach by this time. After all the trouble we'd had!" He choked a little. "Nobody is going to follow him again as we followed him!"

Footsteps were heard approaching along the wooden sidewalk. They had a heavier sound than would have been made by the tread of the light-heeled young dog-seller.

Another officer stepped up on the threshold. Quint recognized him as the one of whom he and Cliff had made inquiries that afternoon, but he at first said nothing.

The newcomer regarded the Biddicut boy with astonishment, recognizing him only after an effort of puzzled reflection.

"Hello!" he said, "what has happened to you?"

"Ask him!" Quint replied, with morose wrath.

"What is it, Terry?" the chief demanded, turning to the officer.

Terry told his story. Then Quint related all that was necessary of his. An expression of disgust settled upon the face of the chief —a much more refined and intelligent face than that of the subordinate.

"Terry," he said, "it's a prodigious blunder. This boy's story corresponds with what he and his chum told me this afternoon. That fellow won't find any watch; 'tisn't a good night for finding watches. Take off that pair of rings!"

Terry quickly removed the handcuffs.

"Now go out and see if you can find anything of the other party to this affair," said his superior. "I'll give you fifteen minutes to produce him, with or without the watch. If he doesn't put in an appearance by that time, we shall know he's a fraud."

With a sarcastic smile he watched Terry's departure on his ridiculous errand; then looked at Quint, silent, surly, his pale face rain-streaked and blood-stained, his wet clothes beginning to steam as they were dried in the warm air of the station.

"You may as well sit down, and take it easy," the chief said kindly, pushing a stool toward him.

"I'm too mad to sit down," said Quint. "Besides, my partner is waiting for me in that cart-shed, if he hasn't already started hunting for me. I must put out and find him, so soon as you make up your minds that I'm not a highwayman."

He seated himself on the stool, nevertheless, with a strangely haggard aspect.

"You've had a pretty hard time," observed the chief, regarding him curiously.

"I haven't had leisure to think of that," Quint replied. "If I had kept the fellow, that would have rested me for all my life! I shouldn't mind anything,—lost hat, empty stomach, broken head, wet skin! As it is—" he could say no more, for he choked up again with rage and grief.

"I'll dry you off," said the chief, stooping to open the door of an air-tight stove.

There were kindlings laid in it ready for lighting. He touched a match to them; and in a few seconds it was roaring and crackling close behind the boy's wet back.

"I wish—Cliff—was here!" Quint murmured, with a long-drawn sigh. Even he was breaking down at last.

Considerably within the allotted fifteen minutes, Terry returned, disconsolate, and obliged to confess that his watch-hunter was still missing.

"But he looked so respectable compared with—" he glanced at poor Quint as he spoke—"anybody might have made the mistake."

"Anyhow, it has been made," said the chief; "and now we must see what can be done to rectify it. We can't catch the scamp —not to-night, anyway; but we may do something for this boy. It's high time that we were thinking of that."

It was time indeed. His weariness and discouragement, the reaction from his late terrible excitement, his want of substantial food, and now the stifling heat of the stove and the odor of his own steaming garments, were producing an alarming effect upon the boy from Biddicut. He turned sick and dizzy, and the chief had but just time to spring to his support, when he reeled sidewise, tumbling limply from the stool into the officer's outstretched arms.

XXIV

WHAT WAS HIDDEN IN THE MANGER

THE last trick of the trick-dog had surprised Cliff at a moment when he was so full of trouble that in his despair he had exclaimed, "Let him go!" and cared little if he never beheld Sparkler again. What disappointments, what fatigues, that wily and treacherous animal had caused him!—and now had come this acme of the boy's woes, this horrible uncertainty as to what had befallen his faithful friend Quint. Nevertheless, even in his wretched state of mind, it was a matter of interest that Sparkler had gone back in the direction from which they had come —the way Cliff must now return.

He called again; he explored the ground all about, under the trees and on the corners of the intersecting roads; he looked in every direction in the vain hope of seeing a human figure start out from the shadows; then with a heavy heart he turned back toward the shed.

He had but a flickering hope of finding that Quint had reached there, and it died within him before he had fairly passed beneath the roof. He called Quint's name and kicked the heap of straw; for although Cliff's friend was foremost in his thoughts, he also remembered the bare possibility of Sparkler's having gone back again to that comfortable bed. But then neither the dog nor his friend made sound or sign in that solitary shelter.

He stood gazing up and down the road, when he perceived a light. It was evidently in motion; it was approaching in the middle of the highway. The moon's beams reduced its rays to a feeble glimmer and soon revealed a man carrying it; a stocky man, in a buttoned frock coat, and wearing a round-topped hat.

Cliff watched his approach and drew back into the shed to wait, filled with a fearful hope that the coming of the man with the lantern somehow concerned him and Quint.

Arrived at the shed, the man turned into it, and holding up the lantern where Cliff stood in the shadow, cast its light upon both their faces. His own was that of a ruddy, Americanized Irishman—our friend Terry, in short.

"Are you the boy from Biddicut?" he inquired, peering at Cliff curiously.

Cliff had already noticed that the stocky man wore the uniform of a police officer.

"The other Biddicut boy sent you?" he answered eagerly. "Where is he?"

"Down at the police station," the officer replied. "He has had a rough time. He was troubled about you, and so I offered to come and find out about you."

Cliff anxiously inquired of the officer what had happened to the other boy from Biddicut.

"Nothing very serious," Terry answered. "Only he caught your dog-seller, and had a set-to with him. But he stuck to him, and brought him to the station."

"Oh, Quint!—he's great!" cried Cliff, rejoicing too quickly.

" 'T was a fine piece of strategy," Terry admitted. "But at the last moment the rogue turned the tables on him by a cunning trick and got away."

"Oh!—how could he?" Cliff wailed.

"I'll tell you on the way back. We've made your friend pretty comfortable, and he wants you to join him. You have his hat? I was to look for that, as well as for you."

"To think," exclaimed Cliff, "that he should have caught Winslow and I should have caught the dog, and that both should have got away!"

He was explaining how Sparkler had found him on the straw there, when he paused in amazement at sight of an object revealed by the rays of Terry's lantern. It was a piece of most familiar-looking cord, hanging over the side of the manger. He sprang to seize it.

"The lantern! hold the lantern!" he cried, slipping his hand carefully along the cord toward some object to which it was attached.

Terry lifted the lantern, and exposed to view, curled up in the bottom of the manger and pretending to be fast asleep, but doubtless as wide-awake as any four-footed creature could be, the thrice-lost Sparkler! —Sparkler, wisest of dogs, yet not wise enough to know it was a short-sighted and ostrich-like policy, in hiding, to leave the piece of cord trailing at length behind him!

"I'll hold you this time, if I live!" Cliff exclaimed jubilantly. He fastened the cord about his wrist.

Sparkler seemed reluctant to leave the manger, but Cliff forced him to take the leap.

"What's this, do you believe? He was guarding something," said Terry, lowering his lantern so as to shed its light into the vacated manger.

Sparkler, seizing the officer's coat-tail, tugged at it with a menacing snarl.

"Sparkler!—behave!" Cliff commanded. "See what it is. I'll hold him."

Terry thereupon fished up a curiously-shaped roll, which fell open in his hand, and assumed the shape of a flat, empty bag; Sparkler growling, and springing to get at him.

"That's Winslow's!" cried Cliff, in high excitement. "It's his gray linen grip-sack! I understand the whole business now!"

As the officer was mystified, the boy briefly explained.

"He followed Winslow as long as he carried that. It might be a roll he could put into his pocket, or it might be a bag with his duster in it. But if he left it anywhere, then the dog knew he was to meet Winslow at that place, or wait for him there. He had come back to stay with the bag when he found me here."

"If that was the scheme," observed Terry, "then your man will return here. Leave the bag just as we found it."

"It must have been covered with straw; I got all of this litter out of the manger," said Cliff. "Now let's have it all back, and put out the light, and leave everything till my partner and I can come in the morning and waylay the crafty Mr. Winslow."

XXV

WHAT CLIFF CARRIED IN HIS POCKET

SPARKLER had become quiet after the bag was returned to its place; and he followed readily when Cliff led him from the shed and set off, guided by Terry, down the road.

"What time is it?" Cliff inquired.

The officer pulled out his watch and turned its white countenance up to the moon.

"Twenty minutes to nine."

"No later?" exclaimed Cliff. "Will any stores be open in the village?"

He explained his purpose, and on entering the village Terry took him to a store where small articles of hardware were retailed. He laid Quint's hat on the counter and inquired:

"Have you any copper wire?" Some samples being shown, he selected one that was sufficiently light and flexible, and said, "Cut me off three yards of this."

The piece obtained, he made one end fast to the dog's collar; then passed the rest in a long spiral around the entire cord, including the loop at his wrist. The two men watched him with interest, giving him such assistance as he required; but Sparkler looked sleepy and indifferent.

"He may gnaw the cord, but I defy him to bite off the wire! How much is to pay?"

As he said this he thrust his free hand into his pocket, and drew it out again with something that might have been silver or nickel, but wasn't money.

"What's this?" he muttered; and it was a moment before he recognized the shining object he had picked up near the spot where he found Quint's hat. He had not since given it a thought; indeed, he had hardly been conscious of slipping it into his pocket in the moment of surprise when Sparkler got away from him. Examined in the lamplight, it resembled less the part of a knife-handle, which he had at first taken it for. It was in shape a long oval, about three inches in length by nearly three quarters of an inch in width; thin and slightly curved; on the innermost surface were two short rivets. The outer surface was brightly polished, with rounded edges, and it bore an engraved inscription.

Cliff held it up to the light and read the lettering, with a face betraying the utmost astonishment, his eyes staring and his lips forming an inaudible exclamation. Then he flung himself upon Sparkler, as if with intent to throttle that unconcerned and impassive quadruped.

His immediate business, however, was not so much with the dog as with the dog's collar, a strap of maroon-colored leather, starred with nickel studs about an inch and a half apart, except in one place where two studs seemed to be missing.

With hands trembling in their eagerness, Cliff applied his metal plate to the space thus left, and found that it not only fitted, but that the rivets corresponded exactly with the two rivet holes in the collar.

He sprang to his feet, unwilling to tell any one of his discovery until he had imparted the tremendous secret to his friend. "What will Quint say," was the thought uppermost in his mind, as he accompanied Terry to the station.

The door was wide open, and within sat Quint with his back to the stove, and his coat and vest hanging near it on the office railing. On the stove were two bowls containing hot chocolate, and on a stool beside him was a tray containing a comfortable repast for two,—boiled eggs, as white as the saucer that held them, a loaf of bread, butter and salt, knives and spoons and plates. The air of the room was warm, despite the open door, and humid from the vapor of steaming garments.

This banquet set before him must have been tempting to the tired and hungry boy, now quite recovered from his faintness. But Quint was unwilling to taste food until his friend could partake of it with him.

The appearance of Cliff at the door, with Sparkler capering before him, very nearly proved disastrous to the contents of the tray, which Quint's knee knocked in his sudden attempt to rise. Fortunately he caught it, and steadied it on the stool.

"The dog?" he cried, his face lighting up joyfully. "Cliff, you've beaten me! I'm glad *one* of us has had some luck!"

"Don't say luck till I tell you," replied Cliff, in gleeful agitation. "Whether it's luck or not, I don't know. But it's great!" And he held out the metal plate.

No common adjective seemed strong enough to express Quint's astonishment as he read the inscription; but the famous words of Brutus, which he had so often spouted, broke from his lips with a force of feeling he had never put into them before:

"'Be ready, gods, with all your thunderbolts!' How did you come by that?"

"See how it fits," said Cliff, pulling Sparkler forward, parting his curls, and showing the place in the collar, which the plate and the rivets fitted. "I found it near your hat, up there in the woods. I feel certain Winslow must have lost it."

"And I know just how he lost it," exclaimed Quint.

"May I see?" asked the Chief.

"Yes, you can see it," said Cliff, passing the name-plate over to the chief, who read the inscription with delighted curiosity.

"'P. T. Barnum!'" he exclaimed. "'Bridgeport, Conn. License 373.' Thunderation, young fellows, that's Barnum's celebrated circus dog! He's worth a thousand dollars!"

Cliff stroked the spaniel's head affectionately.

"If he belongs to Barnum, Barnum must have him back again, I suppose. I only wish he was mine! Now tell about your tussle with Winslow, Quint."

"Begin your supper, boys," counseled the chief, "and tell your stories over your eggs and chocolate."

"That's judgmatical," observed Quint.

XXVI

HOW THE BOYS FOUND SUPPER AND LODGING

"SUPPER? our supper?" said Cliff, eyeing the contents of the bowl and tray with an interest which the more exciting question of the moment could not wholly eclipse. "How is that?"

"We sometimes have to feed a prisoner, and your friend here came so near to being one, that I thought we owed him a treat. He'll tell you about it; or perhaps Terry would prefer to. Eh, Terry? Well, lay to, boys, before the supper gets any colder."

He placed a second chair for Cliff opposite Quint's, with the tray on the stool between them, and handed them the chocolate. Hungry, happy, grateful, they cracked their eggs and told their stories, while Terry, kneeling before the open stove-door, toasted slices of bread for them on a fork.

Quint in his narrative cast no blame upon the officer, but called it a "very natural mistake," and took his slice of crisp toast from the friendly hands that prepared it, ate it with immense relish, declaring they "would have Winslow yet."

"He will certainly go back to the shed for the dog and his bag," he said; "and we must be there to nab him, very early in the morning, if we don't go to-night. I am getting dry, and rested. How is it with you, partner?"

"My little nap in the shed was almost as good as a night's sleep," Cliff replied. "Then there was a good deal of the right kind of medicine in catching the dog, finding you all right—and such a supper as this! I could start for home, if there was any hope of reaching it in three or four hours."

As that was out of the question, the chief offered to find lodgings for them in a house near by, where their supper had been ordered.

"You are kindness itself!" said Cliff. "But we can turn in for only a little while; and I mustn't be parted from this dog."

"Then allow me to make a suggestion," said the chief, between puffs of his cigar. "We've got a couple of cells downstairs, and they open into an airy room. Unoc-cupied—no bedding—straw mattresses—rather thin, but clean. You won't find 'em bad to sleep on; and you can keep the dog with you."

Cliff shrugged and lifted his eyebrows at Quint. Quint smiled his drollest smile and looked quizzically at Cliff over the devastated tray.

"It will be enough for me to brag that I've had on a pair of iron wristbands," he remarked. "If it should get to the boys in Biddicut that I'd slept in a police-station I wouldn't answer for the result. I'm afraid some of 'em would die of envy."

The chief laughed as he knocked the ashes off his cigar, while Terry stood by and grinned.

"If we could get into a barn somewhere and put in three or four hours' sleep on the hay," said Cliff, "that would be better than going back to the shed before day-light."

"That would suit me," said Quint. "I've more than once slept in a barn in summer, just for fun. I'm getting dry enough."

He put on his vest, but held his coat to the fire for a turn or two, while Cliff offered the fragments of their repast to Sparkler. At first the dog had declined food, and he now winked at it somewhat contemptuously as he lay curled up by the stove.

"If you had spoken about the barn a little earlier I might have managed it," said Terry. "Deacon Payson's barn," with a consulting glance at the chief. "Maybe I can now. The deacon is usually up later than this."

As the boys welcomed this suggestion, Terry, with the chief's approval, went out to see what arrangements could be made. In his absence the boys talked over their affairs with the chief and got his advice as to what they should do if they found Winslow, and what if they didn't, and as to their best course in regard to the dog that had in so strange a manner come into their possession.

Then Terry returned and said, "It's all right. Deacon Payson's haymow will accommodate you."

He relighted his lantern, Quint put on his coat and shoes, and Cliff, with a pull of the wire-wound cord, woke up Sparkler, who had been dozing by the stove. Then the boys shook hands with the chief, who wished them luck, and promised them further assistance, if they should require it; and they departed, preceded by Terry carrying his lantern, and followed by the dispirited spaniel.

A little way up the street, Terry knocked at a door, which was opened by an old gentleman in shirt sleeves.

"I've brought my young chaps, Mr. Payson," said the officer, stepping aside and holding his lantern so that his "young chaps" could be seen.

The old gentleman looked them over and fixed his eyes on Quint.

"I thought so," he remarked. "I've seen one of 'em before. Haven't I?"

"You were in the crowd around the hot box this afternoon when I was inquiring for a man and a dog," Quint replied, glad to recognize the kindly face.

"Terry tells me that you want to sleep in my barn," said the old gentleman. "I'll be with you in a second."

He stepped back into the room, and reappeared putting on his coat, then he led the way along a path lighted by the mingled rays of the moon and of Terry's lantern. Having unlocked a stable door, he took the lantern from Terry's hand and preceded the others, past a stall in which there was a horse lying down, into a well-filled barn beyond.

"Here's hay right here on the floor," he said, "and I can get you blankets."

"If it was my case," said Terry, "I should get up on this load of hay. Here's a ladder a-purpose. Then you'll be out of the way of rats."

Quint surveyed the premises with satisfaction, and said he wasn't afraid of rats.

"Particularly with the dog to watch us," Cliff added, laughing. "He's good for almost everything else; he ought to be death on rats; I believe he smells 'em now."

Sparkler was, in fact, sniffing about excitedly, putting his nose in the littered hay, whining, and finally setting his forefeet on a round of the ladder, with a wistful upward look, as if he understood and approved Terry's suggestion.

"The dog votes for the top of the load," said Quint; "and I'm not so sure but that will be the best place for us. It may be the safest for him, if he is going to try any more of his tricks."

"You mean, if he gets away from me!" said Cliff. "He isn't going to do that, I tell you! But if he should, he'd find his way down from that load quicker than you or I could!"

"I guess the best place is right here on the floor," Quint concluded. " 'Twon't do any harm to pull down a little more hay, will it?"

"None at all," Mr. Payson replied. "And here are some carriage cushions."

"Quint, this is luxury!" said Cliff.

"Cliff, this is judgmatical!" replied Quint. "We wouldn't ask anything more comfortable, if we had our choice of lodgings."

"I wish our folks could know!" said Cliff. "How are we to get out in the morning?"

"I shall have to lock you in," Mr. Payson answered; "but if you are stirring before my man comes round, you can open this big front door from the inside; I'll show you how the swivel-bar works. Or you can unbolt the door in the rear. Unless you start too early in the morning, my folks can give you some breakfast."

"If you want any help from us, you'll find the station open," said Terry. "I'll post the night officer, so there'll be no more mistakes at our end of the line."

The boys had made their bed between the side of the load and the front door, and were preparing to lie down in their clothes after kicking off their shoes.

"Come here now!" Cliff commanded, making Sparkler lie down by his side. "He heard us talk of rats, and can't forget it." He took the precaution to make a couple of turns with the leash about his arm in addition to the loop at his wrist. "Even if he should get loose, I don't suppose he can get out of the barn."

"Not before the doors are opened," Mr. Payson replied, regarding his guests with amused satisfaction. "I should say that you are pretty cozy."

With an exchange of good-nights, the men went out with the lantern; and the boys found themselves alone on the floor of the great, shadowy, moon-visited barn.

"I don't know how to thank folks," said Cliff. "Somehow, when anybody has been good to you, any words about it sound foolish."

"We have had more kindness shown to us than anything else on this trip," Quint replied, "even putting Winslow and the old cook into the opposite scale."

"I'm thinking," said Cliff, "we'd better let Winslow slide. Now that we have the dog, we can make enough out of him to pay for the trouble."

"I'm rather surprised at you, Cliff," Quint answered, after a moment's silence. "Just after we started on this expedition, and it was growing a little mite interesting, you'd have given it up two or three times, if it hadn't been for me."

"I've wished we had given it up more times than that," Cliff confessed. "Think of what you have gone through! Such a wetting as you got, and the trouble the rascal gave you, up there in the woods— let alone his turning you over to the police! It makes me laugh, though, to think of that!"

"We'll laugh at the whole thing when we're safe through it," said Quint. "Maybe we sha'n't get much satisfaction out of Algernon, in one way, even if we catch him. But as I owe him for the wetting, *and* the broken head, *and* the cold wristbands, not to mention other small items, I want to pay him in a lump, and get his receipt in full. In short, I mean to get even with Algernon K. if it takes another day to do it."

Cliff made no reply to this declaration, which suggested such possibilities of still further hardships and disappointments. Quint waited a minute, then went on in a tone which betrayed how deeply hurt he was by his friend's silence:

"You have the dog, and now you naturally want to hurry away with him. That's all right, Cliff; that's the important thing to you. The important thing to me is the bear-hug I am saving up for Winslow. This may be a weakness on my part; and I've no doubt the course you propose is the wisest. But if I don't get in that squeeze, I shall feel a want, as if I had missed something useful and agreeable, all the rest of my life."

"I feel just so too," Cliff replied. "Although we've secured the dog, I never shall feel quite happy about it unless we get Winslow. But I'm doubting whether the chance of catching him is worth what it will cost."

"We can find that out only by making the trial. Just give me a little help in the morning," said Quint; "then if we don't scoop him in, and if I should feel like sticking to his trail a little longer, I'll go ahead on my own account, and let you start for home without me."

Cliff reached over and gave Quint's arm an affectionate grip.

"See here, Quint," he said; "don't misunderstand me. Remember what Cassius says—'A friend should bear a friend's infirmities.' I've played that part to your Brutus too many times, to have a disagreement with you in earnest."

"Oh, it's no disagreement!" Quint protested.

"The fact is," said Cliff, "I was used up too soon on this tramp. I haven't anything of your tremendous 'stick-to-it-iveness'; and I—but no matter!" choking a little. "You've been such a friend to me—you've helped me to get the dog, which is your dog now just as much as he is mine; and now I'm going to help you overhaul Winslow again, no matter how long it takes; and you won't hear me say another word about turning back as long as you want to follow him."

"Cliff! you're the pluckiest fellow I ever saw!" Quint exclaimed; and the boys' two hands were clasped in a hearty pressure. "Pluckier than I am!"

"Don't be absurd!" Cliff remonstrated.

"I mean it!" said Quint. "You have stuck to this business when you've seen it would be wiser to give it up. I am a little more obstinate than you are, that's all. And now you offer to give up your wisdom to my obstinacy. Well, I think we've a good chance of trapping Winslow in the morning. We must stop talking now and get some sleep."

"I forgot you didn't have a nap, as I had," said Cliff. "I feel as if I could talk all night. Isn't it pleasant in here!—the moonlight slanting in at that window, and striking down over the stalls! Sparkler is sleeping, as quiet and contented as the most honest dog in the world."

Quint made no reply, and his heavy breathing soon showed that he was asleep. Nor was it long before Cliff succumbed to blissful drowsiness, and slept soundly on their bed of hay, between his friend and the dog.

The moonbeams mounted higher and higher over the stalls, and sent their radiance through the racks, as the great, slow, solemn, starry wheel of night rolled on. The last fading yesterday joined the countless yesterdays of the past, and another untried morrow was at hand.

Then a dark figure crept to the edge of the load of hay, put one foot after the other on the rounds of the ladder, and slowly and with the utmost caution began to descend.

The dog gave a whine and a start, tightening the cord about the arm at his side. Cliff roused instantly, put out his hand, felt the dog's head, and patting it, told him to lie still. His eyes opened enough to see that only a few feeble flecks of moonlight rested high up on the partition, and that all was quiet in the deepening gloom of the barn. Then he slept again.

During this slight disturbance, and for some minutes afterward, the figure on the ladder remained perfectly motionless against the side of the load. Then it put out a hand in the direction of the dog and waved it with an expressive downward gesture. From that time Sparkler made neither sound nor movement; the wary feet felt their way down the ladder, and Algernon K. Winslow stood upon the barn floor.

XXVII

"WHAT MAN-TRAP IS THAT?"

STANDING so close to the load of hay that he might have been taken for a part of it, the dog-seller contemplated the situation. He had slipped into the barn when the owner was bedding down his horses the evening before, found a lodging on top of the load, and had been, no doubt, highly edified by the conversation of the two boys on the floor below. Now the time had come for him to anticipate their well-laid plans by some shrewd action.

Quint's prominent features were distinctly visible in the dim, diffused light. His face was pale, and the shut eyelids with the discolored bruise on his temple gave it a sad and stern expression even in sleep. He lay on his back, with one relaxed arm on his breast, the other outstretched on the blanket, and with his shoes and hat beside him on the floor.

Nearer the silent standing figure lay Cliff, turned over on the arm to which the cord was attached, with his face toward Sparkler, curled up close by on the hay. Cliff's hat and shoes were under the corner of the load, at Winslow's very feet. All this the keen eye of the observer took in, even to the slender, serpent-like coil of gray cord about the dark sleeve.

He looked at the great door, then down at the legs in his way, and the eyes that would open, if they opened at all, upon any object moving in that direction. Thanks to overhearing Mr. Payson's explanations, he had knowledge of another door in the rear of the barn. He stooped to give Sparkler a quieting caress, and to look into his slyly blinking eyes, then glided away to make discoveries.

With movements so furtive that if they had been heard, nothing more than the presence of mice on the littered floor would have been suspected, he passed the load of hay, groped his way around the carriage beyond, and found the door he sought. He had no difficulty in slipping the bolt without noise, and in opening the door a little space, to see that his way of escape was clear. It was bright starlight without; the moon was near its setting, if not already set.

Leaving the door open a good arm's breadth, he stole back toward the front of the barn, observing every turn, and every obstacle to be avoided in any precipitate retreat. Within half a yard of Cliff's head, he got down upon his hands and knees, under the corner of the load of hay. It was darker now, and the faces of the sleepers were indistinct in shadow, but their steady breathing reassured him. He advanced his hand until he felt the cord.

He took out his knife intending to cut it, but something harder than hemp stayed his blade. Wire!—a long flexible piece encircling the cord, and extending from a small loop at the dog's collar to a larger one at the boy's wrist.

Upon making this discovery he was minded to cut the collar, but the boy was sleeping so heavily that he decided to unbuckle it. This he did without difficulty, and having freed it from both cord and wire he put it into his pocket.

He was now ready to depart and to take the dog with him; but he must first devise some means of delaying pursuit. He crept by the cushions that pillowed the boys' heads, and reached until his groping hand touched Quint's shoes. These he took, with the hat, and creeping back, placed them beside Cliff's hat and shoes. He was now ready for his last, most ingenious device, which he couldn't think of, even at that critical moment, without a chuckle of delight.

"Since he's determined to hold something, I'll oblige him," he whispered facetiously to himself, as he carried the released end of the cord toward one of the wagon-wheels, meaning to make it fast to the rim. "He sha'n't wake up and feel he has been wasting his time!"

But that very large substitute for the

dog's collar was too far away to permit a turn of the cord to be taken about it, without a coil or two from Cliff's arm; which could be had only at the risk of disturbing his slumber. Winslow thereupon produced from his pocket another piece of cord, which he had not found it necessary to part with, and was about to cut off enough for his purpose, when another happy thought struck him.

"No use being mean about a little string." His position, kneeling on the barn-floor, was becoming irksome; and having knotted his cord to the end of Cliff's, he rose to his feet. Then, instead of tying it to the wagon-wheel, he put it through the wheel, and made the end fast to the ladder, quite at his leisure. "To make things lively for 'em, if they start off in a hurry!" was his amiable intention.

So far all was well, from his own point of view; although our boys, if they had been awake to the situation, might have regarded it differently. He was prepared to resume his career in a gullible world, and only one other slight precaution remained to be taken.

He would have stolen their clothes if that had been possible. As it was, he could make free only with their hats and shoes.

The hats, one after another, he tossed up on the load of hay, where they lodged noiselessly. All this time the dog had lain as still as the sleeping boys; but now, at a signal from his master, he crouched on his paws, alert and intelligent, awaiting orders. Then in one hand Winslow gathered all the shoes except one; this he gave to Sparkler to carry, and with that too faithful accomplice, stole away, as silent as the shadows amid which they passed.

And still the tired Biddicut boys slept on.

At this juncture an astonishing thing occurred.

As Winslow approached the door, which he had left unlatched and slightly ajar, he was startled to see it swing all at once wide open, as if moved by an unseen hand. He stopped, half expecting a human form to appear in the square of star-lit space suddenly confronting him. But all was strangely quiet, and it seemed for a moment as if the door had opened magically, of its own accord, to let him pass.

The mystery was quickly solved; a wind was rising, and it had carried the outward-swinging door around on its hinges. He foresaw what might happen next, and hastened forward to prevent it. But he was too late. A counter-gust swung the door again, shutting it with a loud, rattling bang.

An indescribable hubbub ensued. The boys started up with cries of amazement, demanding of each other what had happened.

"It was a door that slammed!" exclaimed Quint.

"Somebody has been in the barn!" cried Cliff, feeling hurriedly for the dog.

"Where in thunder are my shoes?" Quint roared.

"The dog! the dog is gone!" said Cliff, in wild consternation. "He's here, though!"

He was on his feet, following up the cord, which was certainly attached to something, but which seemed to be miraculously lengthened, as if it had grown in the night.

"Jehu!—what's all this?"

His hand encountered the wired knot that had clasped Sparkler's collar; but instead of the collar he found more cord—more cord!

"The old Harry has been here!" he wailed, in mad bewilderment.

"It's the old Winslow!" said Quint. In springing up he had struck his head a stunning blow against the projecting frame of the hay-wagon. But without heeding the hurt, or waiting to find his shoes, he started for the door that had made the bang, and which was now slowly swinging open again.

In his headlong rush he passed between his friend and the load of hay.

"Look out!" Cliff implored. But Quint kept on, plunging over the cord, dragging Cliff after him, and bringing the ladder down upon both their shoulders. If Winslow had remained to witness the unqualified success of his scheme for "making things lively" in the deacon's barn, he would have had no cause to complain of the result.

"What man-trap is that?" murmured Quint, as he scrambled off, freeing his legs from the cord and his back from the encumbrance of the ladder, and made for the open door.

XXVIII

ANOTHER MYSTERIOUS MAN-TRAP

IT had taken the dazed Cliff some moments to assure himself that there was no dog at the other end of the cord. But he was thoroughly satisfied of the fact by this time. His shoulder had received a staggering blow from the tumbling ladder, and his wrist a tremendous wrench from the sharply drawn wire-wound loop; but he quickly disengaged himself from both, and forgot his hurts in the fury that possessed him to rush out in pursuit of the author of his woes.

Outside the barn he found night and silence, the dim earth outspread, and the starry firmament—nothing else. Not a footstep was heard, not a human figure was seen—not even Quint's.

"Quint! where are you?" Cliff called out in a thrilled voice, standing bareheaded amid the great mystery into which he had rushed. Then something which might have been a post detached itself from a fence near by and moved toward him. It was the shoeless Quint.

"Which way did he go?" Cliff demanded.

"That's more than I know," Quint replied. "He was out of sight and hearing before I pitched out of the door."

"I can't understand it!" said Cliff. "I'm sure somebody went out of the barn, not ten seconds before you did!"

"Ten seconds is a good while when you are racing with slippery Winslow!" Quint said.

"I believe he has dropped into a hiding-place somewhere," said Cliff. "Or he is half a mile away by this time. That dog! that dog!" he moaned in angry despair. "Just after we had found out about him, and I was so sure of holding fast to him this time!"

"The ground will be wet and soft, and we can track 'em by daylight," said Quint. "I don't see what else we can do. He must have been in the barn when Mr. Payson locked us in."

"That's what the dog's strange actions meant," replied Cliff. "You remember how he tried to bounce up the ladder? Winslow must have heard all our talk."

"Did he take your shoes too?" Quint inquired.

"I guess so; I didn't stop to hunt."

They were searching for some sign to guide them, when Cliff's unshod foot hit some dark object lying loose among the sparse weeds and stunted grass by the yard fence. It was so much like a shoe that he stooped and picked it up. And a shoe it was.

"Mine, I do believe!" he declared.

"Look for mine," said Quint. "We may track 'em by our own shoes!"

"Here's another!—and another!" said Cliff. "All right here by the fence!"

"This is the way he went; he dropped the shoes as he jumped over."

Beyond the fence was an open space lying between Mr. Payson's house and an apple orchard not far off. The boys concluded that Winslow had vanished among the trees. Cliff sprang upon the fence; Quint stood looking over it.

"What's that?" Cliff whispered, intently gazing and listening—"I hear something coming toward us."

"A dog?" Quint suggested.

"A dog, as sure as I am crazy!" said Cliff, in wild excitement; for what he saw appeared too marvelous to be true. He jumped down from the fence to meet the returning truant.

"Sparkler!—it's Sparkler!" he cried, darting forward to seize him.

But Sparkler had no intention of allowing himself to be so easily recaptured. As Cliff advanced, he retreated, turning and capering, as if to lead him on; and when Quint came up, he ran away toward some dark object lying on the ground. Just then, from that direction came a horrible groan.

"Jehu! What's that?" said Cliff, his imagination conjuring up appalling mysteries, in the strange night-scene they were exploring.

"I'll see what it is!" exclaimed Quint, striding eagerly forward over the wet turf.

The dark object became a man, and rose to a sitting posture. The dog leaped upon him, then ran back toward the boys, who were now within a few paces of the spot.

The ground was level, with no visible impediment anywhere; and yet here was a human being struggling up with pain and difficulty from the ground, upon which he had evidently fallen from no discernible cause—the human being they sought!

Even Quint was startled by the strangeness of the chance that had so suddenly and mysteriously interrupted Winslow's hasty flight. What could have happened to him? Why that dreadful groan? And why had he permitted his presence to be betrayed by the very dog he had been hurrying away?

The shadowy orchard was on the left. On the right were the kitchen porch and rear gable of the Payson house, only two or three rods distant. The boys slackened their speed, very fortunately, as it proved, and advanced cautiously, peeringly, along the open space, toward the man, who was by this time struggling to get upon his feet.

"No hurry! We've got him, sure!" said Quint.

Seeing the boys close upon him, Winslow sank down again, resting upon his knees.

"My young friends," he said, in a badly shaken tone of voice, "the luck is against me."

"What are you saying your prayers here for?" Quint demanded.

"That's what I'm trying to find out," Winslow answered, feeling his head and shoulders with both hands in a dazed sort of way. "I was running, just skipping along about as fast as I could go—it seemed to be a clear course—when all at once—"

He paused, turning his head tentatively, as if to make sure that the joints were still in working condition.

"What happened?" Quint inquired, bending over him.

"I've had my throat cut, and my neck broken. I was caught by a lasso, and jerked back and over and whirled in the air, and dropped on my back, which is another part of me that's badly damaged. I feel as if I had had a tussle with a cyclone."

Uttering these words disconnectedly, the dog-seller looked up and around, and felt his neck again, as if trying to realize the kind of calamity that had befallen him.

"Shall I tell you what did it?" said Quint.

"You'll oblige me," said Winslow, his eye following the motion of the boy's lifted hand.

"You tried to cut off your useless head with this galvanized-wire clothes-line. Do you see it running between these two posts?"

"The posts I see. I'll take your word for the wire clothes-line." It seemed painful for the injured man to look upward. "I've proof enough that it's there."

"It's a wonder it didn't kill you!" Quint exclaimed.

"Where's this dog's collar?" cried Cliff, who had succeeded in catching Sparkler.

"In my waterproof's pocket, I suppose; at least I put it there." It was produced, and Cliff replaced it on the dog's neck. "Did he bring you to me?" Winslow inquired.

"Sparkler? Yes," said Cliff. "He seemed to know you were in trouble, and needed help."

"I was in trouble, fast enough!" said Winslow. "But still, I could have dispensed with the help. Now what do you propose to do?"

"Bring a doctor, if you need one," replied Quint.

"No doctor for me!"

"Then a policeman."

"Worse yet! Of the two, I prefer the doctor every time," said Winslow. "But this isn't a case for either. Boys, can't we go back into the barn there, and talk this little business over, in an amicable sort of way? You needn't try to hold him"—to Cliff, who was attaching his handkerchief to the dog's collar. "You've got him; and with the help of a slamming door and a wire clothes-line, you've got me. That's the mournful truth, my young friends. I am yours to command. All I ask is, be reasonable. Oh, yes! I can walk; thanks!" as Quint handed him his hat, which he picked up from the ground.

"Perhaps you can tell us where *our* hats are," Quint said. "And the other half of my pair of shoes? I found only one of them."

"I'll square the shoe account, and the hat account, and all the other accounts, to your entire satisfaction," Winslow replied; "only give me a chance."

"And how about the tumble you gave me in the woods?" Quint inquired.

"I've had a worse tumble! Such a jar, and a wrench, and a shaking-up generally, as I never had before, in all the ups and downs of my varied career," said Winslow, who had risen to his feet, and was clasping the tightly drawn wire that had come so near to cutting the said career tragically short. "I believe that you're about even with me, boys!"

"We mean to be quite even," said Quint, "before we get through with you."

XXIX

IN DEACON PAYSON'S BARN

THEY were walking back toward the barn, Winslow assisted by an arm Quint had passed through one of his; Cliff leading Sparkler by his handkerchief tied to the dog's collar.

The way was clear before them, surrounding objects being more distinct. The darkness that precedes the dawn was dissolving by such delicate degrees that the change from minute to minute was not noticeable; the east was brightening behind the orchard trees. Then, in the orchard's edge, as they passed, a robin piped suddenly his familiar note among the boughs overhead. Another answered near by; then a song-sparrow trilled ecstatically; other tuneful throats joined in; and soon the whole choir of field and orchard birds burst into song.

The boys were not so absorbed in the sordid business of the moment as not to feel the beauty and freshness and melody that ushered in the daily miracle of the dawn. All the doubts of the night-time passed away; their sense of the morning was one with the hope and joy that filled their hearts. The object of their journey was accomplished, or nearly so; and soon they would be on their triumphant homeward way.

When they reached the fence, Winslow got over into the yard, still carefully guarded by Quint. As Sparkler couldn't leap back while confined by the handkerchief, Cliff handed him over to his friend, then got over himself.

"The missing shoe, the first thing," said Quint, finding the other three where he and Cliff had left them.

"If you'll give the dog a chance, he'll find it," said Winslow. "He had the handling of that one. You needn't be afraid to let him go; he'll come back, while you have me."

"I won't risk it," Cliff replied. "He and you are up to too many tricks."

"To convince you of my good will—here, Sparkler!" said Winslow, directing the dog's attention to the shoe in Quint's hand. "Find!"

As the dog began to pull the handkerchief in the direction of the barn, Cliff followed him to the plank-way that sloped up to the rear door. Under its edge Sparkler thrust his nose and brought out the missing shoe.

"You wouldn't have found it without

his help and mine," said Winslow, eager to gain credit with his captors.

"No; and I shouldn't have lost it without his help and yours!" Quint replied dryly.

The boys didn't stop to put on their shoes, but made Winslow carry back into the barn the three which he had carried out of it, while Sparkler likewise did penance by transporting the other in his teeth.

"Now, here's a kind of string puzzle which you can amuse yourself by undoing," said Quint, "if you are feeling well enough."

"Oh, that!" replied the dog-seller, with a feeble attempt at jocoseness. "When I took the cord from Sparkler's collar I wanted to put it where it would do the most good, so I pieced it out and tied it to the ladder. It seems to have got into a tangle."

"Untangle it!" commanded Quint.

Obeying with cheerful docility, Winslow began loosening the knots from the fallen ladder. As soon as he had freed the end of the cord, Quint made a noose in it, which he immediately slipped over the dog-seller's wrist and drew tight.

"You are not going to do such an ungentlemanly thing as that!" Winslow remonstrated, taken unawares.

"If that's what you call ungentlemanly, you set the example," Quint replied. "A while ago I had iron on my wrists, thanks to you; and you are going to have hemp on yours, thanks to me."

"Before going any further," said the dog-seller, "allow me to make a proposition."

"We'll hear that by and by," said Quint. "Just now, please, help my chum about those other knots."

The broadening daylight, coming in through the wide-open door, shone upon a strange group, there in Deacon Payson's barn. Quint held the cord, one end of which was fast to his captive's wrist, while his captor undid the knots of his own tying which united the two cords. Then Cliff, on his knees, turned Sparkler's head toward the door, and held him while Winslow unbuckled the collar, slipped it through the small wire-wound loop, and buckled it again; both boys looking on, to see that the thing was honestly done.

"You see, young gentlemen," said the dog-seller, never once losing his assurance, or betraying any sense of his humiliation, "I am doing everything I can to oblige you, trusting you will reciprocate. Now, I sha'n't even wait for you to ask me where your hats are. I'm still pretty stiff, but if my cracked joints are equal to the effort, please give me a little freedom of the cord, and I'll restore the missing articles."

He took the ladder from the floor, and replacing it against the load of hay, put one hand on his back and the other on his neck and begged that he might be allowed to breathe a moment.

"I was deucedly shaken up by that lasso business!" he remarked with a dreary grimace.

"You are getting over it faster than I thought you would," said Quint. "Take your time. You must have been in the barn when we came into it."

"That's a natural and just conclusion"; and the dog-seller frankly explained how he had got in. "I overheard all your talk, and I was pleased with the ingenuity of your plans. If it hadn't been for the dog, I should have left you undisturbed, to waylay me in the shed. As it was, I thought you would appreciate the means I took to let you know who had been your roommate. Now a little rope, Brutus!"

So saying, he mounted the ladder, drawing after him the cord still attached to his wrist, Quint paying it out through his fingers, as he looked up, with a humorous smile, to observe the dog-seller proceeding on his extraordinary errand. Cliff too stood

watching the movement; and Sparkler's soft, bright eyes were also upturned with an expression of intelligence almost human.

From the top of the ladder Winslow stepped upon the load of hay, Quint mounting a round or two at his request, to "give him more rope." Having picked up both hats, he descended the ladder, holding them by the rims.

"It has cost me a pang," he remarked; "for I feel as though every bone in my body had been run through a stone-crusher! But anything to oblige! The fact is, Brutus and Cassius, I am not the unconscionable scamp my conduct may have led you to suppose; and I am bound to do what I can to atone for the errors I have been betrayed into by the stress of circumstances. So allow me the pleasure—this is yours, I believe, Brutus. Cassius, with my compliments!" handing the hats with the airy politeness which not even the "lasso business" had jerked out of him.

As Quint put on his hat, he was reminded of the ugly bruise he had received in the tumble the man now in his power had given him. He gathered up the cord, and laid hold of his captor's unbound wrist. Winslow remonstrated.

"Have I done nothing to earn your confidence, but you still contemplate so—excuse me for saying it—so brutal a thing as that? I was just going to make my proposition."

"We'll hear your proposition," said Quint very coolly.

"Thanks, ever so much! And will you kindly allow me to recline against this ladder?" The dog-seller practically answered his own question by settling himself against the rungs. "My accident has left me as loose-jointed as a jumping-jack."

Quint suspected some crafty pretense in this. But he was willing his captive should play the jumping-jack as long as he himself held the string.

XXX

SETTLING WITH THE DOG-SELLER

"My proposition is to pay you the twenty dollars I agreed to pay, and to take back the dog," said the smiling Winslow.

"You had a fair chance to make that settlement," replied Quint. "Now it's too late. We are going to have our money, but you are not going to have the dog."

"We know whose dog it is," spoke up Cliff, sitting on a box and putting on his shoes.

The captive persisted in his smile, though it showed rather ghastly in the morning light, and asked with mock politeness:

"Will you have the kindness to inform me how you came by that interesting information?"

"You dropped it from your pocket when you reached for your knife to use on me," replied Quint.

"And I picked it up!" said Cliff, showing the engraved plate that had so evidently been removed from the dog's collar.

"You are giving it to me pretty straight, boys," the captive admitted, grinning at the piece of metal, while his free hand pressed his pocket.

"It's a good deal straighter than what you gave us about the burnt hotel and your sick mother in Michigan," Cliff said, returning the polished piece of nickel to his pocket.

"The burnt hotel was, I acknowledge, a myth," the captive answered. "But the sick mother, boys," he went on, with a change of tone; "she—well, I can't talk about her! Only—I'll tell you this. I've as good a mother as ever a bad son had!"

Quint, too, sat on the box preparing to put on his shoes.

"Then how happens it—?" he began.

"I know what you are about to ask," said Winslow, nursing with his free hand the cord-encircled wrist, and speaking in the deeper tone into which his feeling had surprised him. "How does any son of a good mother ever go wrong? I'll tell you what the trouble was in my case. I wanted to have the earth without paying for it. See?"

"No; I don't see," replied Cliff, with a growing interest which he was afraid might degenerate into pity. He was determined not to be guilty of that weakness.

"I'll explain. My mother was indulgent —too indulgent. But she was poor. It was all she could do to give me a fair education, but she did that. I think you'll allow that I have the language and breeding of a gentleman." And a smile of pride came back into the dog-seller's pale face.

"People's ideas of a gentleman differ," said Quint. "You've the 'gift of the gab' as folks hereabout call it; I won't dispute that."

"I suppose I deserve that sarcastic cut," said the captive, with a sad expression. "But it shuts off the gift, if I have it."

"Let him tell his story," Cliff interrupted, resolved beforehand not to believe half of it.

"Of course," Quint assented. "Though when he talks of the breeding of a gentleman after playing us such low-down tricks —but never mind!"

"Is your mother really sick?" Cliff inquired.

"Yes—sick with the bad-son affliction!" Winslow exclaimed. "And she'll have it worse than ever if she hears what I've been up to lately. The truth is just here, boys. I got into extravagant habits; I wanted more money than she could afford me; I wouldn't work for it, and the result was, I left home under what you may call a cloud. I have been a hotel clerk, and I have been many other things, but nothing very long at a time. I've been an actor—light comedy, and I've been in the show business—employed in Barnum's Circus, boys!" he added boastfully.

"I'll believe *that,*" said Cliff.

"That was my last situation, and I ought to have kept it," the captive continued; "but I was foolish. I got the idea that I was a bigger man than P. T. Barnum himself. Unfortunately, Barnum didn't see it in that light; and when I tried to run my end of the show in a way that didn't suit P. T., there was a little rumpus, and I found myself on the wrong side of the canvas. The trick-dog was one of my specialties, and it didn't require much of a trick to take him with me."

He looked down at Sparkler, who was looking up wistfully at him, wagging a sympathetic tail.

"Whatever you may think of *me,* boys, *he* is genuine all through! The best friend I ever had!" Winslow actually sniffed a little as he said this. "I had no thought of selling him when I started out. But necessity was the mother of that scheme. I had to raise money, and that was the way I raised it. I found it worked well, and I worked it for all it was worth. I could have made it more profitable but for one thing. Men who had money, and brains, too, and knew what such a dog was really worth, were—in short—suspicious. Then I couldn't sell him in the big towns without too much danger of losing him, so I played him off on the rustic population."

"My father knew he was stolen!" Cliff exclaimed.

"That's a mistake," the captive remonstrated. "I had the care of the dog, and when I left he left, too. I kept clear of the law in that."

"But not in selling him over and over again!" Quint averred sternly, seizing his unbound wrist.

"Now, see here!" said the captive. "If you march me to the police station and enter a complaint, what do you gain?"

"We're going to stop your little business of swindling the rustic population," Quint declared. "We'll gain so much!"

"Don't be too hard on me, boys," Winslow entreated. "I've made a clean breast of it." And he really seemed to think his confidences entitled him to their favorable consideration. "Put yourselves in my place. *You've* got good mothers, both of you, and one of *you* may be in a bad fix some time."

"He's trying the sentimental game," Quint said, with a frowning look at Cliff. "Are we going to be humbugged by him with our eyes open?"

"No," Cliff replied; "but I don't see the good of giving him over to the police. He can't sell the dog any more. And he'll give us back our money."

"Here it is waiting for you," Winslow exclaimed, producing his pocket-book with alacrity. "Here's your twenty dollars,"—putting a roll of bills into Cliff's hand. "And I promise to return the dog to Barnum's Circus just as soon as I can."

"We ought to have as much as this, after all our trouble," said Cliff, looking at the money. "But *you* are not going to return him to Barnum's Circus. I'm not going to give up Sparkler to you for one minute, am I, Quint?"

"That's judgmatical!" said Quint, with stern satisfaction. "If we want Barnum to have his property again, we should be fools to trust *him* to restore it."

XXXI

WINSLOW'S POCKET-KNIFE

WINSLOW besought them to stick to the bargain and give him the dog; then, finding they would not do this, he insisted upon Cliff's handing back to him ten dollars of the money.

"What do you think, Quint?" asked Cliff. "We are not robbers, though he tried to make you out one last evening. Our ten dollars we are bound to have, anyway; but we don't want any of the money he has swindled other people out of."

"No, sir!" exclaimed Quint; "but those other people want it, and we will see they have it, as far as the extra ten dollars will go. We'll begin with the old shoemaker and his wife. Won't they be glad? No, Cliff; don't give him back a dollar of it."

"You are right, as you are every time," said Cliff after a moment.

As Winslow strongly objected to this manner of settlement, Quint said: "What right have you to complain? You are getting off what you may call dog-cheap. I'm thinking we ought to hand you over to the police, after all, for the sake of those other people; and it's only the idea of our paying some of them that quiets my conscience in letting you off."

Winslow reflected a moment, then stooped from his seat on the ladder, and patted Sparkler affectionately.

"We part for good, Sparkler, this time! Boys," he said pathetically, "are you aware that I am not much more than a boy myself? I'm not twenty-two yet, and sha'n't be till next September."

"You look older than that," said Cliff.

"So will you at twenty-two, if you live the kind of life I've lived. 'Tisn't the right kind of life, boys, and I'm going to quit it. Live easy and pay to-morrow—the kind of to-morrow that never comes—that's been my style. That's what has brought me to this humiliation."

The captive didn't seem to take the humiliation very much to heart, however, for he added cheerfully:

"We part friends, I trust? And now I suppose I can dispense with this!" And he recommenced loosening the cord that was about his wrist.

"Not yet!" cried Quint. "I want to see the knife you tried to draw on me last night. Your knife!" he thundered, as Winslow answered evasively. "We have had enough of delay and palaver!"

The captive brought out reluctantly what seemed to be an ordinary but rather long pocket-knife, with a single blade. As it did not open in the ordinary way, Quint examined the handle and found in it a suspicious-looking rivet, which he pressed with a surprising result. A slender dirk-shaped blade flew out like a flash in the morning light, and he held in his hand a deadly weapon.

"Jehu! that's dangerous!" Cliff ejaculated, with a horrified backward start. "Think what he would have done to you last night!"

Quint gave a cruel laugh, as he turned upon the owner of the knife. "That's the sort of lady-bird you are!" he said with grim irony.

"I declare to you I never used it, and never meant to!" said Winslow earnestly.

"And I declare you never shall!"

So saying Quint drove the blade into the partition behind him, and snapped it short off. The stub that was left he pressed into a crack, where it stuck.

"None of that!"—as the captive was again at work loosening the cord. At the same time Quint seized his other wrist.

"It serves him right!" said Cliff, shuddering at the thought of what his friend had escaped the night before.

Quint drew the bound wrist behind the ladder, and drew its fellow around the other way to meet it.

"No nonsense!" he cried, as his captive resisted. "If you prefer the police-station, all right! But do you think I'm going to leave you to follow on our track, and keep the dog in sight till you can contrive some plot for getting him back again? Stop that!" he roared out; "if you don't stop working your wrists we'll march you to the station instanter! You tied my partner to the ladder; now it's your turn."

"I hoped," said the prisoner, yielding because he must—"I hoped I had gained your confidence, and I expected more honorable treatment."

"It will take something besides your cheap talk to gain much confidence with us; and it's droll to hear *you* preach about honorable treatment! How's this, Cliff?"

Quint showed the prisoner's hands bound behind him, and lashed to the ladder in knots above the utmost reach of his fingers, wriggle how they might. Then taking a turn with the remainder of the cord about the captive's wrist and back again, he made another knot in it, and tied the end to the ladder in a cluster of knots, which Cliff regarded with satisfaction.

"I've heard of jugglers getting out of such tangles," he said; "but they didn't have John Quincy Adams Whistler to tie the knots!"

"If I had known what you really meant to do with me, you never would have got me into this shape!" muttered the prisoner.

"Think so?" said Quint, good-humoredly. "One of us was enough for you last night; and you have had us both to deal with this morning. Besides, you had been monkeying with a galvanized-wire clothes-line."

"For my part, I feel as if we had been almost too easy with him," said Cliff; "though we might have been easier still if it hadn't been for the knife. I never can forgive that!"

"But we are doing this chiefly in self-defense," said Quint, giving a final tug at his hard knots. "Now if he follows us very soon, it will be with the ladder on his back."

The captive continued to protest and entreat, but Quint only said: "My partner was very near being taken in by your humble confessions and fine promises; but they won't hurt anybody now, and they won't do you any good. Talk away, if it will amuse you; try to console yourself for our absence. I know it will be a sad thing for you to see the last of my gambrel-roof nose!"

He was fastening the rear door; this done, the two Biddicut boys, accompanied by Sparkler, went out by the great front door, which they closed after them, leaving Winslow lashed to the ladder in the lonesome barn.

XXXII

HOMEWARD BOUND

As they were passing near Deacon Payson's kitchen porch, they were delighted to see the deacon himself coming out of the door.

"Starting so early?" said the good man. "I'd been hearing voices, and I thought I'd come out and see how you had got through the night."

Then if ever there was an amazed old gentleman at four o'clock on a fine summer morning, it was the worthy deacon, standing beside his kitchen porch and listening to the story of the strange happenings in his barn and orchard.

"My wife said she heard the voices outdoors first, but she didn't wake me. That wire clothes-line must have been a savage thing to run afoul of. No wonder it floored him! And he's in the barn there now? I never heard anything so surprising!"

"We think he had better stay there an hour or so until we get a good start," said Cliff; "then do what you please with the fellow."

"We make you a present of him," said Quint; "only hoping he won't give you much trouble."

"I'll leave him till my man comes; then I suppose we'd better cut him loose. Though I'm inclined to think," said the deacon, "that he ought to be put in pickle for all his misdemeanors. Come into the house," he went on; "you can't start off this way with nothing to eat."

He made the boys go in, which they did very willingly, and talked over with them their homeward trip, while his wife set before them butter and bread and cold sliced ham, and glasses of milk, and golden honey dripping from the comb; Sparkler also receiving a share. Then they took leave of these kind people; listened for sounds in the barn as they went out, but heard none; and set off in the cool morning air, on the clean-washed country roads, with the light of the new-risen sun on their glad faces.

Winslow did not follow them, with or without the ladder on his back, and they never saw him again.

The boys were minded to make directly for the nearest way-station, on the railroad connecting with the Biddicut branch. But it was early for trains; and remember-

ing their promise to Mr. Mills, they determined to take his house on their way, and report to him the success of their expedition. Perhaps they also wished to enjoy their triumph in the merry eyes of the two girls who had been so mischievously inclined to laugh at them.

They found a shorter course than the one by which they had hunted Winslow; and reached the farm-house just as the family were sitting down at table. They were heartily welcomed, treated to a second breakfast, which they accepted with frank good-will, and paid well for the hospitality in the entertainment the tale of their adventures afforded. There was open admiration as well as merriment in the bright eyes of the girls opposite them, as the boys took turns in the narrative, Cliff reciting the more dramatic portions in his impulsive way; and Quint setting off the whole with his droll commentary.

The meal over, Cliff would have had Sparkler perform some of his tricks. But the dog had also had a second breakfast; or his last parting with his late master had sobered him too much; or he resented the restraint of the cord, of which Cliff would on no account relieve him. Whatever the cause, he was in one of his sullen moods, and would do nothing.

Then Cliff took from his pocket five dollars of the money received from Winslow, and handed them to Mr. Mills for the old shoemaker, whom he knew, and whom he promised to see and reimburse for his loss within a few days.

"Now I have five dollars which I must manage to get to Mr. Miller of Wormwood," said Cliff. "Plenty more dog-purchasers may turn up, and there won't be money enough to go around; so first come, first served."

Having kept the boys as long as he could, the farmer offered to harness a horse and drive them over to a station on the connecting road. This offer they gratefully accepted, and the wagon was brought to the door.

Then adieus were said and smiles exchanged, the girls waved their handkerchiefs, and the boys their hats, the farmer touched up his nag, and our Biddicut adventurers felt that they were indeed on their way home.

They drove along the green-bordered country roads, where every wayside bush and tree glistened in the early sunshine.

"No stop now till we see Biddicut!" Cliff said exultantly; "only as we may have to wait for trains."

"I wouldn't stop now," observed Quint, "even to make a friendly call on Winslow working his passage in Deacon Payson's barn."

Yet it wasn't long before both boys called out simultaneously for a halt, as they were passing another barn, on their way through a small town.

It was a weather-worn structure, all of a dreary brown hue, except for one end, which was conspicuously and garishly red with enormous posters advertising the incomparable attractions of Barnum's combined circus and menagerie—"the Greatest Show on Earth." There were pictures of monkeys at their tricks; a big-muscled man grappling with a lion; a tiger pouncing upon a sleeping Arab; elephants playing at see-saw, or balancing themselves on rolling balls; and athletes in all sorts of startling and impossible positions, linked together, or leaping, or falling head-foremost through the air.

"They ought to have Sparkler here somewhere," said Cliff. But the boys searched in vain among the flaming marvels for a performing dog.

"Here's what we want to know!" exclaimed Quint, standing up in the wagon, in front of the red-gabled barn, and studying the dates and names of places advertised for appearances of "the Greatest Show on Earth."

XXXIII

BACK IN BIDDICUT

"He's coming! Cliff's coming! And he's got the dog! He's bringing the dog!"

Trafton Chantry, who had been watching at the gate for his absent brother, shrieked out this welcome news at about nine o'clock that morning.

Susie took up the cry: "Cliff is coming! Cliff is coming with the dog!" She flew through the kitchen, calling, "Amos! he's come! Tell pa, quick! He's come with the dog!"

The mother hastened to the door, to behold with her own amazed and happy eyes the return of the wanderer, of whom no word had been received since Quint's father brought news of the two boys the day before.

"I declare," she exclaimed, "wonders will never cease! My son!—and he has got the prize!" For to her, also, the appearance of the dog led captive was the crowning triumph of her boy's return.

Trafton had rushed out again to meet his brother, and they came into the yard together, walking fast and talking fast, with Sparkler trotting demurely between them. Amos came running and shouting, and Mr. Chantry appeared, his amused face quirking between his fleecy sidewhiskers; and soon a jubilant group was gathered, of which Cliff was the central figure and flushed hero.

He stood holding Sparkler by the cord, and with gleeful excitement answering, or attempting to answer, the volleys of questions of which he was the target.

"Pa said he'd bet a thousand dollars you wouldn't bring home any dog," cried Amos, glorying in his brother's glory.

"I wish I could have taken that bet!" Cliff retorted, while the father stood parting his whiskers with both hands, and smiling again with good-humored sarcasm.

"I didn't think you would get him," he said; "and I didn't see much use in it, even if you should. 'T would take a good many dogs to pay for the anxiety your mother suffered sitting up for you last night."

"I thought of that," Cliff replied, "and I would have helped it, if I could!"

"That's nothing now," said his mother. "Your father was just as anxious as I was. But we both had faith that you and Quint would be able to take care of yourselves. Do sit down, Cliff! You must be tired. And we'll all try to keep still and let you tell your story."

"I'm not a bit tired," Cliff protested, sitting down, nevertheless; "and I don't know what to tell first. Only this I'll say, first and last and all the time: I owe everything to Quint. He's great! You never saw such a fellow! And now—!"

He couldn't help telling the most surprising part of his story at the beginning.

"If you want to know who is the real owner of the dog, see here!" He held something clasped in his hand, which he opened under his father's peering gray eyes. "See how it fits the place on the collar! And the fellow himself owned up that he stole him from the circus. He's Barnum's famous performing spaniel!"

Any disappointment Cliff may have felt in consequence of his father's seeming lack of enthusiasm was amply compensated by the exclamations of wonder with which the others regarded the engraved plate and heard his account of how he came by it.

"P. T. Barnum" was a famous name in those days, known in every household in the land. In the minds of all, it added immensely to the importance of the dog lolling at their feet, and to the fact of Cliff's possession of him, to know that he belonged to the great traveling circus and menagerie they had read about.

Nor was Mr. Chantry's enthusiasm as unmoved as it appeared. There was a glistening brightness in his eyes as he held the plate in his hand and glanced at it occasionally while Cliff told his story; and finally, when he heard how the boys had followed Winslow through hardships and discouragements, and captured him at last, he no longer attempted to disguise his satisfaction.

"I always knew Quint Whistler had good stuff in him," he remarked; "and I don't see that the other Biddicut boy's conduct was anything to be very much ashamed of. Yes, Cliff; I think you did right to take the twenty dollars. But I'm glad you intend to keep only the ten you had been tricked out of. I've heard of your Mr. Miller in Wormwood, and I'm pretty sure Quint's father knows him; we'll get his five dollars to him in some way. And now"—Mr. Chantry glanced at the engraved name again—"now about the real owner of this dog with too many owners."

The younger boys were on their knees, patting and hugging the object of so much solicitude and excited discussion.

"Can't we buy him of Barnum?" was Trafton's pathetic appeal.

"That isn't likely," said the father. "Such a dog as that is worth too much money. Barnum must be notified the first thing."

"I wouldn't give him up!" said Susie.

"Nor I!" "Nor I!" chimed in the younger boys, while Cliff looked thoughtfully down at the pet crouched lazily between his feet.

"It isn't a question of what you would or you wouldn't do," said the father; "it's a question of what is right. Stolen property belongs to the owner, no matter what innocent hands it has fallen into. You said you looked up the names of the places where his show is to be the next few days?"

"It's in Lowell to-day," Cliff replied. "Next Monday it is to be in Worcester, and the day after in Springfield. I tell you, it was a temptation for Quint and me to go as straight to Lowell as we could, and have the business settled before there was a chance for any more accidents. But we concluded to come home and tell the news and consult our folks."

"A wise conclusion," said Mr. Chantry, who commonly put so much pepper in his praises of his children that any commendation of his that was free from such ironic condiment gave them all the greater satisfaction. "I don't see but you have acted, all through, about as discreetly as two boys could. Now we'll consult Quint's folks, and decide what's best to do."

"That's my idea," said Cliff; "for of course he has just as much interest in the dog now as I have. He stopped to see his folks, but he promised to come by and by, and talk the matter over."

"To-day is Saturday," Mr. Chantry mused aloud. "I believe Mr. Barnum generally travels with his show, but he may be going home to Bridgeport to spend Sunday. I'll write to Bridgeport. If he isn't there, the letter will be forwarded. A little delay may be unavoidable, but it won't do any harm."

"It seems to me," said Mrs. Chantry, "it would be a good idea for Cliff himself to write the letter; why not?"

"That's so! To be sure!" said her husband.

"Oh, I can't write a letter to Mr. Barnum!" Cliff exclaimed, looking up with frightened eyes.

"Do the best you can," said his father.

"Make it as brief and businesslike as possible, without trying to tell anything more than is necessary. You never wrote a letter to a great man, and very likely you never will have another chance."

And Mr. Chantry went out, laughing and stroking his whiskers, leaving the boy to face the formidable difficulty of the letter.

XXXIV

CLIFF WRITES A LETTER AND RECEIVES A TELEGRAM

HOWEVER, his father's hint had set the boy's mind to working, and while putting Sparkler into the shed, and afterward when he was refreshing himself with soap and water and clean clothing, he thought out the substance of what he would write.

"If I just say in plain words that I've found the dog, and would like to know what to do with him, won't that be enough?" Cliff asked his mother, as he seated himself at the sitting-room secretary.

"Why, that's just what you want to say," replied his mother. "Write just as you would talk. Now, boys, don't bother him; keep away till he has his letter written."

Cliff, nevertheless, chewed his penhandle a good deal, and started two or three letters, before he found just the "plain words" he wanted, and put them together in this way:

DEAR SIR: Two days ago a man calling himself Algernon K. Winslow came to this town and sold me a dog for ten dollars. The dog is a small spaniel of mixed breed, and he has been trained to perform tricks. The dog got away the next morning, and another boy and I followed him through five towns, and caught him last night, and brought him home to our house this forenoon. We found the dog had been sold to several different persons, and he had got away from everybody. There was no name on the dog's collar, but we think we have proof that he belongs to you. I like the dog, and would be glad to keep him; but if he is yours, and you want him, please let me know what you wish to have done with him.

This letter he signed in formal fashion and showed to his mother.

"Why, Clifford!" she said. "I think it is a very creditable letter, and I'm sure your father will say so, too!"

"I had no idea of writing so much, but it all came in," said Cliff, well pleased with his composition, now that she had commended it. "But I want to correct and copy it before father has a chance to make fun of it. I've got too many *dogs* in it, for one thing; I want to take out five or six."

He had the letter corrected and neatly copied (for Cliff wrote a very good hand), with the word *dog* occurring in only two places, by the time his father came in.

"Did you do all that without help from anybody?" said Mr. Chantry—the very question Cliff knew he would ask.

"Of course," said Cliff, carelessly. "I found there wasn't much to say. If it isn't all right, I can try again." The evidence of his previous trials had disappeared in the kitchen fire.

His father gave a nod of decided approval.

"Well, Clifford! I don't mind telling you I couldn't have done better myself."

"Isn't there too much of it?" said Cliff, trying to conceal his gratification.

"I don't see that there is. You tell how you came by the dog, and it's right to say something of the trouble you had in hunting him, and to let Mr. Barnum know that

you would like to keep him. No!" said Mr. Chantry, emphatically; "I don't find anything in it to alter; and now we'll see to posting it in time for the noon mail."

"I think I'd better not seal it till Quint sees it," pursued Cliff, "since it's his affair as much as mine."

"You are right, my boy—right in every particular!" said his father, quite forgetting that jeering habit of his by which, without ever seriously intending it, he had embittered for his children so many occasions when a single kindly word would have made them happy.

Quint came in soon after, and, being shown the letter, remarked:

"That's judgmatical! I don't see how it could be better—unless I had written it myself."

The two boys went together to mail it in the village; which done, Cliff drew a long breath, exclaiming:

"Now to wait for an answer! We are pretty sure none will come to-day or to-morrow, but after that Sparkler may be sent for at any time. It makes me feel blue to think of it."

"You ought to show off his tricks once more," Quint suggested. "I'd like to have my folks see him. And why not ask in a few friends?"

"I'll do it! I'll do it this very evening!" Cliff exclaimed. "Come over early, and bring along as many as you like. I'll try to have him in good condition—only a little hungry, so he sha'n't go back on us."

The entertainment took place in the Chantry sitting-room, with doors closed, and only screened windows open, and it proved delightfully successful. Quint's father and mother and sister were present, and there were, besides, a few boys of the neighborhood (Dick Swan and Ike Ingalls among them), who regarded the invitations as precious favors.

Sparkler performed his tricks, some of

them over and over again, with a charming alertness that won all hearts, and made the children more than ever unwilling to part with him. During the rests between, and afterward, Cliff and Quint, in response to many questions, gave a most diverting account of their adventures, with many details which Cliff had omitted from his previous narrative.

To Mr. Chantry, who sat quietly rocking and stroking his whiskers, what was most gratifying in this part of the entertainment was the generous forwardness each boy showed in attributing the chief credit of their exploit to his companion. For of what value, after all, are victories won and prizes gained, unless the character be at the same time enriched?

Sunday was a day of delicious rest to both our Biddicut boys; and Monday, fortunately, found them ready to renew their adventure.

No letter came from Mr. Barnum, but early in the forenoon a messenger-boy from the village brought a yellowish-brown envelope, which he displayed as, with pretended ignorance, he inquired for Clifford Chantry.

"What is it?" cried Cliff, running to receive it.

"It's a telegram," replied the boy, holding it behind him. "Who is Mr. Clifford Chantry, anyway, and where can I find the gentleman?"

"No fooling, Bob Elden!" said Cliff, pouncing upon the messenger, capturing the envelope, and tearing it open.

It contained a telegraphic blank, dated at Bridgeport, and filled out thus:

Deliver dog to Barnum's Circus, at Worcester to-day, or at Springfield to-morrow. Reward and expenses will be paid.
P. T. Barnum.

Cliff was reading this message in a highly excited state of mind when Quint arrived, having immediately followed the messenger-boy, who, as he passed the Whistler premises, had yelled out the startling news that he carried a despatch for Cliff.

All the Chantry household quickly gathered to hear and to discuss the momentous intelligence, and Mr. Chantry observed:

"The dog should go to-day, for you'll have so much farther to take him to-morrow. Now, which of you boys will go? Or shall I go in your place?" he asked quizzically.

"We'll both go!" said Cliff and Quint, speaking together.

"That's just the answer I expected," Mr. Chantry replied, laughing humorously. "And it's my opinion the sooner you start the better, for I don't know about the railroad connections."

Quint hastened home to put on suitable clothes, and to be rejoined by Cliff on his way with Sparkler to the station. Cliff also prepared himself for a possible interview with the great showman, and led Sparkler out from the shed by the cord, from which he had ventured to remove the wire. All the family followed him to the gate, the parents to give him good advice, and the children to pat and hug for the last time the wonderful quadruped.

"Let me go and see him off! Can't I?" pleaded Trafton.

"Me too!" cried Amos.

The granting of the request made Susie wish she was a boy, that she might claim the same privilege.

The three Chantry boys were joined by Quint as they passed the Whistler house; and as they went on, other village boys ran out to swell the procession, the surprising report having spread that Cliff had received a despatch from the great Barnum, and that he and Quint were on their way to return the dog to the circus at Worcester—an event that made the envious youngsters wish Winslow would come along with more trick-dogs, of which they might become the purchasers.

The two partners, with their captive, did not have long to wait for the train, which relieved them of their too noisy and officious host of friends, and soon set them down at the Junction. There they had to wait for another train; and they had still one more change of cars to make, and then a ride which seemed interminable to their impatience, before they alighted at the station in Worcester.

XXXV

HOW THE BOYS WENT TO THE CIRCUS

MANY people were getting out of the cars, evidently bound for the same destination as the two boys from Biddicut. Some climbed into omnibuses and wagons in waiting; others set off rapidly on foot.

"Shall we walk?" said Cliff. "We've only to follow the crowd."

"Since our expenses are to be paid, I rather think we can afford to ride," replied Quint, as they approached a wagon bearing a placard inscribed:

CIRCUS GROUNDS—10 CENTS.

They had already discussed the question, whether the word in the despatch meant that expenses would be paid for as many as might come with the dog, and had decided that it couldn't be strictly so construed. But they felt that their business was important, and that a little lavishness of expenditure would therefore be justifiable. Cliff took Sparkler in his arms, and, climbing to a seat in the wagon, made him lie down between his knees; Quint

took the only other vacant place; and they were soon passing the throngs of pedestrians in their rapid course to the circus grounds.

Cliff's bosom swelled mightily at sight of the great white tents, the swaying flags, and the converging crowds, with the blue dome of a perfect summer sky arching over all. He turned to see if Quint's face betrayed any unusual emotion, and Quint answered his look with a beaming smile.

They were out of the wagon almost as soon as it stopped, and found themselves in a stream of people before rows of small tents or booths containing side-shows, the venders of which were noisily advertised by hand-organs, drums, and shouting men.

Avoiding the stand of the ticket-sellers, the boys made directly to the main entrance of the circus tents. Two men were taking tickets from the throng passing between them. They hardly noticed anybody, and observed neither our Biddicut boys nor the dog until, as one held out his hand for Cliff's ticket, he received this extraordinary greeting:

"We've come to see Mr. Barnum—if he is here."

"He is here, or will be," replied the man. "You'll see him when he makes his speech. Your ticket!"

"We haven't any. I—"

"Don't come here without tickets!" exclaimed the ticket-taker sharply. "Stand aside and let the people pass!"

Cliff held his ground, with Quint close behind.

"I have this telegram from Mr. Barnum," he cried out, to the surprise of the entering spectators, and of the ticket-taker himself especially, "and we have brought the dog."

The man regarded Cliff more carefully, and cast his eye down at the poor little animal shrinking from the legs of the entering crowd.

"It's 'King Francis!'" he said to his fellow ticket-taker. "I never expected to see him again!"

He would have taken the telegram as if it had been a ticket; but Cliff kept tight hold of it, allowing him merely to glance at it.

"You should have gone to the private entrance. But all right! Dick," the man called to somebody within the tent, "here's King Francis back again! Go with that man," he said to Cliff, and went on with his ticket-taking, which had hardly been interrupted.

Cliff passed into the tent, but Quint was stopped in attempting to follow him.

"He's my partner!" Cliff called back, standing aside to let the crowd pass.

"He can't go in without a ticket," the man declared. "One of you is enough to go with the dog. Pass along! pass along!"

At the same time the attendant named Dick offered to take the cord from Cliff's hand; but Cliff exclaimed:

"The dog doesn't go without me, and I don't go without my partner! We are here on Mr. Barnum's business, and if we can't—"

"Go in! go in!" said the ticket-taker, nodding at Quint; and Quint, laughing at the effect of Cliff's defiant words, quickly rejoined him in the tent.

It was a sort of vestibule to the great wild-beast show and the greater amphitheater beyond. In it were a number of living curiosities, among which the boys noticed a very tame giant stalking about, and a human mite, placed, in effective contrast with him, on a low platform from which he shouted up at every spectator who passed: "How's the weather up where you are?"—his invariable salutation,—in a squeaking mite of a voice.

They passed in through a large circular tent redolent of wild beasts, with great iron-barred cages on either side, and a group of elephants chained, each by one foot, in the central space. There was the monarch of elephants, the mighty "Jumbo," rocking himself on his hips, and dusting himself with wisps of hay, which his huge, elastic, swinging trunk swept over his shoulders and back. Beyond were other trunks, like writhing and twisting anacondas, with open, upturned mouths, which they passed around like contribution-boxes, begging peanuts and bonbons of the spectators. In the cages were mischievous monkeys, restless hyenas walking to and fro, sleepy-looking lions, and beautiful pards and panthers, only glimpses of which could be had through the human groups pressing against the ropes, but which the boys promised themselves they would see more of before they left the show.

The attendant Dick looked down occasionally at the dog Cliff persisted in leading, and made a single remark as they passed the last of the cages:

"The old man will smile to see his pet back again!"—the "old man" being, as the boys understood, the great showman himself.

The next tent was vastly larger still; it was the "mammoth tent" of the circus performances, supported by tall masts, and hung, high overhead, with all the apparatus used by acrobats in their daring aërial feats. The benches, rising one above another from the ample ring, were rapidly filling with spectators; attendants were arranging spring-boards and laying mats for the tumblers; and the members of the band, wearing shining uniforms, and bearing shining instruments, some of prodigious size, were filing to their places. To the boys, who had never seen a great circus, there was in all this preparation an inspiring suggestiveness which filled them with wonder and joy.

Dick lifted the flap of a curtain, and

ushered them into a side-tent, where a troop of athletes in costume, and two or three fantastic clowns, were gossiping together, or walking about, as if waiting for their work to begin, now and then one stepping aside to turn a handspring or a backward somersault on the grass, in mere exuberance of spirits, hardly ceasing from his talk and laughter while whirling in the air.

Past this picturesque and interesting group Dick led the boys toward a part of the tent where a full-proportioned man in a black hat and a swallow-tailed coat, standing with his back toward them, was talking with two other men, one of whom had a ring-master's whip in his hand.

The large man was speaking earnestly, and did not look around until the ringmaster, seeing the boys approaching with the dog and their guide, broke out jovially:

"Ho, ho! There's his Majesty, Mr. Barnum! King Francis has arrived!"

Thereupon the man in the swallowtailed coat turned a full, genial face smilingly toward the boys, and snapped his thumb and finger at the dog. Sparkler had so far shown but little interest in anything he saw; but at this signal he darted forward the length of his leash, leaping up and manifesting the most joyous emotion under his real owner's caresses.

XXXVI

AN INTERVIEW WITH THE GREAT SHOWMAN

"Y ou have got along earlier than I expected," Mr. Barnum then said, looking pleasantly at Cliff.

Cliff stood with his hat off, flushed and panting; but the showman's genial manner quickly relieved him of the embarrassment the boy felt on finding himself in his presence.

"I started as soon as I got your message," he replied. "This is my partner, Quincy Whistler. I never could have got the dog back if it hadn't been for him; so I thought we'd better both come and fetch him."

Quint also stood with his hat off, gravely smiling—a youth without blemish, except for the bruised spot on his left temple. Cliff noticed that the showman's comprehensive glance rested for a moment on that discoloration, and hastened to explain:

"He got that in a tussle with Winslow —the man who sold me the dog. He might have got worse, for Winslow tried to draw a knife on him."

"Winslow?" queried the showman.

"That's one of the names he goes by," said Cliff, "though I don't suppose it is his real name. I've brought the bill of sale he signed when he sold me the dog"— producing the paper from his pocket.

The showman glanced his eye over it with a smile that struggled with a frown.

"I know the handwriting," he said, "and I know the man. A scapegrace, if ever there was one! You are quite right; his name is not Winslow."

"He told us—not when he sold me the dog, but after we had followed him up and caught him—he told us," said Cliff, "that he had been connected with your show."

"He told you the truth, for once," replied the showman. "I know his family— respectable Bridgeport people; for their sakes I set the fellow on his feet, when he was down, and gave him employment. He is smart enough,—he could make himself useful if he chose,—and I engaged him at a fair salary. But it wasn't safe to trust him with money; so I made him sign an agreement that all but a small part of his earnings should be reserved for the payment of his debts,—chiefly debts to his own father, who has ruined himself by helping him out of scrapes. Yes,"—in answer to a question from Cliff,—"he has a good mother, a refined, intelligent woman. From his boyhood, he has given them no end of trouble."

"He told us he was hardly more than a boy even now,—not yet twenty-two," said Cliff.

"He is twenty-four years old," said the showman. "I'd like to retain this,"—taking the bill of sale and putting it into his pocket. "He might have kept his place in my show, but he became dissatisfied with the arrangement, and demanded his wages, cash in hand. Knowing he would squander every dollar I gave him, I refused—for his own good and his family's, as he knew very well. He was intolerably conceited; he imagined 'the Greatest Show on Earth' couldn't be run without his assistance. I promptly dispelled that illusion; he became impertinent and disappeared with the dog."

"He gave us that part of the story pretty straight," observed Quint.

The showman regarded him with friendly interest, remarking:

"He's a reckless fellow; but I should hardly have supposed he would attempt to draw a knife on you."

"I was a little too quick for him; but his intentions were good," said Quint, with a smile.

"Instead of getting out his knife, my partner tripped him so suddenly he pulled out this, and dropped it," said Cliff, exhibiting the name-plate. "I picked it up afterward, and that's the way I came to know who was the real owner of the dog."

"That certainly resembles my name!" laughed the showman. After a little further talk with the boys, mainly about the frequent selling of the dog, he asked: "Have you seen any of his tricks?"

"Winslow showed us some of them," replied Cliff, "and I made him perform them afterward."

"Did he show you this? Take hold of that end of the cord."

It was the cord which another attendant (Dick had disappeared) took from Sparkler's collar. Cliff held an end of it, the showman swung it by the other end, and at a word the dog, running in, began to jump the rope with surprising ease and gracefulness.

"I wish I had known he could do that!" Cliff exclaimed admiringly. "Wouldn't it have pleased our folks!"—turning to Quint, who smiled amused assent.

"Here's another very pretty performance."

The showman tossed aside the cord, and reached for a drum brought by the attendant. He requested Cliff to hold one side of it, while he held the other, facing him, and raising the drum about three feet from the ground. At a word Sparkler made a swift dash and leaped straight through it, bursting both drumheads, with a double explosion, and landing on the turf beyond. The drumheads, as the boys perceived, were of paper.

Mr. Barnum then asked the boys a few questions about their adventure, and laughed heartily at the amusing parts of it.

"Have you seen a notice of the reward offered? I am having it posted now with the show-bills, and I've had it sent to a few country papers."

"I haven't seen it," Cliff replied; "I don't know anything about any reward, except what you said in your telegram."

Mr. Barnum was opening a long, well-filled pocket-book.

"I offered a moderate sum—forty dollars. Then, there are your expenses. Of course I meant your expenses bringing the dog from Biddicut; but I think, with all the trouble you've had, I ought to allow ten dollars on the expense account. Then, there's the money you paid for the dog— ten dollars more. Besides, there are two of you, and I am glad to get King Francis back at any price. How's this? Satisfactory?"

And he put into Cliff's hand six ten-dollar bank-notes.

"Oh, Mr. Barnum!" Cliff exclaimed, completely overcome by such unexpected munificence. "Forty dollars is enough— more than we expected! You needn't say anything about the expenses. And I forgot—I meant to tell you—Winslow gave me back *that* ten dollars."

"So much the better!" said the showman, smiling in hearty enjoyment of the surprise and pleasure he was able to afford two such honest-minded youths. "It is thirty dollars apiece. I think you have earned it; and if you are the sort of boys I take you for, a little nest-egg like that isn't going to do you any harm."

"It's a small fortune to us!" said Cliff, with glistening eyes. "Here, Quint! you must take charge of your share,"—dividing the money on the spot. "I am afraid to have so much money about me!"

"Well, thanks! and good fortune to you!" said the showman, holding out both hands to the boys.

"Oh! *we* thank *you,* Mr. Barnum!" replied Cliff. "I suppose I must say good-by to Sparkler, too; that's the only thing I am sorry for now. Sparkler isn't his name?" he said, looking up, as he gave the dog a parting caress.

"King Francis is the only name we know him by." Mr. Barnum then said: "Did you ever see my show?"

"Never; but we have always wanted to," said Cliff, with shining eyes.

The attendant who had carried away the drum now returned with two packages looking like books in wrappers. Mr. Barnum said, as he took them:

"Show these young men to the best reserved seats there are left." Then, presenting a package to each of the boys: "This is the story of my life. I hope you will find it instructive, and that your interest in it will not be lessened by the fact that you have seen and talked with the writer."

Cliff was stammering his thanks, when Quint in a low voice said something in his ear which the showman overheard.

"Write my autograph in the books? Certainly, if you wish it. Go to your places now, and I will send them around to you before the show is over."

The proud parade of the Roman hippodrome, with its horses and chariots and solemn elephants, glorious banners glittering and trumpets braying, was making its stately circuit of the triple-winged arena when the boys reëntered the great tent. Then, as they mounted to the places to which the attendant guided them, with opulence in their pockets and exultation in their hearts, the sonorous, brazen measures of the band burst forth, rivaling in sound the majestic movement and gorgeous colors of the pompous procession of the performers.

"Isn't this grand?" said Cliff, his face beaming as with the light of victory.

"It's judgmatical!" replied Quint, with a high and haughty smile.

WEEDS IN MY LANE

By Lucius A. Bigelow (age 8)

(GOLD BADGE)

I LIKE to live in nature's glory. I love the sunny silence of my lane, where everything grows with all its might. Why do people call weeds common? They are frequent, but very wonderful, and I have spent my happiest summer days among them. First, I find yellow dandelions peeping from the green grass. Because they are the first to appear, they seem dearest, for in winter only the faithful fir-trees bear us company. The dandelions have long, narrow petals, and French boys call them *dent de lion*. They soon pass into little balls of down, which scatter in the breeze. They sow early; therefore they are thrifty. Next arrive a multitude of buttercups. They also have a French name—*bouton d'or*. They are happy, and nod to each other in the wind. Soon I gather white and buff daisies. Sometimes I make a nosegay of several hundreds. I hunt for clover, not with my eyes, but with my nose and also my ears; for where I find fragrant clover, there hums the big bee, looking for a honey breakfast, and never disappointed. Butter-and-egg grows in my lane, but I do not approve the name. I have christened it "orange-and-lemon," after its cousin fruit. Have you ever noticed how gracefully this blossom sits in its calyx chair? The silver yarrow and the gold tansy grow abundantly. I love the strong smell of tansy, because it means midsummer, when everything splendid is in sight. Burdock has a cool, shady leaf, a pretty pink blossom, and little burs, which I use to make baskets for amusement. There are many other weeds in my lane. They are my intimate friends. I have noticed that yellow is the color often chosen by weeds—I suppose because yellow is so cheerful.

The nature studies in ST. NICHOLAS explain reasons. They interest me. I think about them a great deal. Last comes the tall goldenrod. It closes in my lane on each side, waving good-by; for with its arrival summer makes preparation to leave us.

THE LOST POCKET-BOOK

By Margaret E. Scott (age 13)

(HONOR MEMBER)

THE great ocean liner was just steaming out of the dock, and last farewells were being waved, when suddenly a wail of despair came from an elderly lady on the deck. "Oh, I've gone and lost my pocket-book! What shall I do! What shall I do?"

"Tell the captain," suggested a sympathetic passenger. "Maybe he can help you."

She rushed into the cabin and grasped the captain's hand. "Oh, captain!" she cried, "my pocket-book is gone! I must have dropped it on the pier. It was imitation black seal, with a strap across the back. Can't you stop the boat?"

"Madam," said the captain soothingly, "I can't do that, but I'll send a wireless back to port, asking if such a purse has been found. If it has, I'll have a tug sent after us with it."

"Oh, thank you, thank you!" said the old lady.

The captain hurried out and soon returned, beaming though breathless. "It's been found, Madam," he panted, "and the tug has started!"

Ten minutes later the tug came chugging to the side of the vessel. A man climbed over the rail and handed the pocket-book to the lady.

"Well, I *am* thankful," sighed she, "and so relieved."

"Was all your money in it?" asked the sympathetic passenger.

"No money was in it," said the old lady calmly, "I keep all that in my bag. But I value the purse so much! I bought it at a bargain-sale, when I was shopping with cousin Mehitabel. Now she's gone out west to live, and I may never see her again. The purse was so cheap, too. Only thirty-nine cents! I should have hated to lose it!"

The captain rubbed the perspiration off his forehead, and stood for some minutes gazing steadily out to sea.

"A Study from Life," by Frances Leone Robinson, age 12. (Gold badge)

TELL-TALE TONGUES

By Janet Denton (age 9)
(HONOR MEMBER. MERIT ENTRY)

ANIMALS cannot talk, yet their tongues can tell tales. If we will study the members of the animal kingdom, we will find that their tongues tell many tales—tales of how they live, and what they live on.

Our friend, Mr. Frog, has a long, slender tongue, with a little knob at the end, much like a pop-gun cork tied to a string. When a bug or fly alights near Mr. Frog's long, sticky tongue, it darts out like a streak of lightning, and the poor fly has been swallowed before he knows what has happened to him.

The humming-bird has an interesting tongue. It is long and slender, and it is hollow like a soda-water straw. The humming-bird poises over a flower, pushes his long tongue down the flower's throat, and sips the nectar that he finds there. The whole thing is as simple as drinking a chocolate soda through a straw.

The woodpecker has a cruel sort of tongue. It is long and needle-like, and it has pointed barbs on its tip, just as a fish-hook has. After boring into the tree and finding the worm he has been seeking, he darts his needle-like tongue into the hole and spears the worm on its barbs. Then he draws the worm out and eats it.

The ant-eater has an unusual tongue. It is slender and flexible, and is eight or nine inches long. The ant-eater plows up an ant hill with his nose, and then, as the startled ants dash about, he sweeps his long tongue back and forth over the ground, and gathers in the ants by the hundreds.

All the members of the cat family have tongues with a very rough surface. Let your cat lick your hand, and you will find that her tongue is as rough as sandpaper. This sort of tongue helps the cat in her method of drinking, lapping up the milk with her tongue. Her rough tongue also helps her in cleaning the meat of the bones that are given her.

Her larger cousins, the lion and the tiger, have tongues much rougher than hers. If a lion or a tiger should lick your hand, he would scrape the skin right off. Tame lions and tigers have sometimes turned savage by scraping the skin off their trainer's hands, and getting their first taste of human blood.

The prize tongue of all belongs to the whale, who has an enormous flabby tongue which weighs from one to two tons. Mr. Whale cannot stick out his tongue, because it is so securely attached that he cannot extend it.

When we study the way in which the whale feeds, we can understand why he needs such a tongue. The arctic waters in which he lives are swarming with millions of tiny sea animals. As the whale swims along, he scoops in a mouthful of water, and strains it out through the thick fringe of whalebone which hangs from the roof of his mouth, and this catches his food. It is his great tongue which enables him to force the water through this sieve.

"A Heading for May," by D. M. Shaw, age 14. (Gold badge)

WAVES

By Isadore Douglas (age 17)

(HONOR MEMBER)

From somewhere out of the woods by the
    lane
    An idle wind wanders and touches the
      wheat;
And where was but now a field of grain,
    A shimmering sea ripples out at my feet,
Whose waves go eddying up the hill,
    Stray over the field—now here, now
      there,
Then quicken, swayed by the mad wind's
    will,
    Race on to the fence where two fields
      meet,
To break in a swirling of daisy-heads
    And the tossing spray of bittersweet.

BE BRAVE, MY SOUL

By Robert Friend (age 17)

(HONOR MEMBER. CASH AWARD)

Be brave, my soul, though flesh be weak;
Be brave before the truths you seek.
    Though aching to the heart you find
    The truth compatible to mind,
Be faithful to the mind and speak.
I know the heart gives to the meek
The consolation that they seek
    When truth is hard to bear defined.
                Be brave, my soul.
But I have climbed the barren peak
Of truth and found the prospect bleak—
    And oh, how easy to be blind
    And to one's heart be false—but kind;
Yet say I like the stoic Greek:
                Be brave, my soul.

"A Heading for August," by Florence Mason, age 13. (Silver badge)

SPINACIA OLERACEA

By Sturges D. Dorrance, Jr. (age 14)

(HONOR MEMBER. CASH AWARD)

The family was in turmoil;
    Racked in civil strife.
The father stamped and tore his hair
    And shouted to his wife.

"See here, see here," he roared aloud,
    "Is there nothing which
Will make our little Benny eat
    His nice, fresh green spinach?"
His wife, she frowned a dreadful frown,
    And shed a salty tear.
Up little Benny piped at last,
    With voice so shrill and clear:
"Oh! Father, would you have me eat,

Assimilate, osmose
A plant, which like the spinach
    (As every wise man knows),
Is formed of protoplasm
    With chlorophyllous grains
In upper epidermis,
    And deliquescent veins
Which carbohydrates circulate
    And chromosome connects
With photosynthetic bast
    And plumuled green cortex?
The vasculary bundles
    With turgescence swell away
While hydrotropic elements
    Cross every small pith ray.
And Father, dear, remember,
    The lenticel's small slit,
And that the lowly spinach
    Has other things than grit."

The father's angry cries are stilled;
    Son's cruel words will harry
Till he doth find a solace
    In Cent'ry dictionary.

"What I Love Best." By William
H. Savin, age 15. (Honor member.)

SNOWY DAY

By Elizabeth Lehman (age 17)

(HONOR MEMBER)

Morning—

When snow first falls, the pines possess
    A new coquettish sort of grace—
Born of the trust of womankind
    In powder and bit of lace.

Afternoon—

Now they have lost the first delight.
    They seem a little sad and old;
Each clutching close a ragged shawl,
    Seeming to shiver with the cold.

Evening—

Like ladies at the opera
    How elegant and debonair!
Each tree in spotless ermine cloak,
    A star tiara in her hair.

A MIDSUMMER SONG

By Elizabeth H. Parsons (age 12)

The sun shines through the wind-swept,
    straggling clouds
That wander far across the summer sky;
O'er hills and valleys, over plains and seas,
The clouds will always wander, on and on.
Like ships that sail across an endless sea
To meet the golden sunsets of the West,
The clouds go onward, ever farther on,
As if in search of something that is lost.

SUMMER FAIRIES

By Lewis S. Combes
(age 8)

(GOLD BADGE)

Airy little fairies
  Dancing in the sun;
Playing all the daytime,
  Having lots of fun.

Hungry little fairies,
  Eating honey sweet
Hidden in the blossoms,
  Think it is a treat.

Thirsty little fairies,
  Sipping drops of dew
Sparkling on the roses
  And the grasses too.

Tired little fairies,
  Resting all the night;
Sleeping in the flowers,
  Cuddled up so tight.

A SONG OF THE WOODS

By Nellie Adams (age 13)

(SILVER BADGE)

Oh what so gay, on a summer day,
  When sultry and hot the hours,
As a forest scene, with its pine-trees green,
  And carpet of fairy flowers?
When the zephyrs sigh in the tree limbs high,
  And temper the sullen heat;
With the leaves aloft, and the mosses soft
  Spread smoothly for elfin feet?

Oh what so rare as the forest fair
  When autumn brings frosty cold;
The pine-trees green, with a bush between
  Aflame with crimson and gold?

But a winter night, when the snow is white,
  Is lovelier yet, by far;
When every flake the snow-clouds make
  Is a dazzling, diamond star.

But, oh! and it's spring when the glad hearts sing,
  And the shy white violets peep;
When the herald's mouth calls the birds from the South,
  And the wood-mice from their sleep.
And the wood folk sing, "From the fall 'til spring,
  And from spring again to fall,
You may seek and roam, but the pine-trees' home
  Is the loveliest spot of all."

IN VACATION

By Myra Bradwell Helmer
(age 11)

I'm tired of the world and its pleasures,
And gold coming in by the measures.
Give me something new, something else to do;
Give to me the sweet, still country town,
Where every one is met by a smile, not a frown;
Give to me the simple country church, with people dressed in modest style,
Not the city church, where oft they dress to show off in the aisle.
Let me be awakened by the crowing of the cock
Instead of the tones of a much-used silver clock;
Let me hear the little calves and the little lambs say "Baa!"
For this will do me much more good than a trip to Panama.

Oh, take the hothouse city flowers away
from my sight,
And give to me the country ones that have
God's rain and light;
Give to me the hearty farmer, with his
merry, laughing jokes,
And the rickety old wagon with hardly any
spokes;
I'd rather have that than the dude with the
automobile,
With perfumed handkerchief, stupid head,
and military heel.
My ears are full and ringing
Of the songs the birds are singing;

And my only sorrow is,
And a very sad one 'tis,
That the farmer will not let me pile up his
golden hay,
Like the lads and lassies round here, chant-
ing all a merry lay.
Oh, what fun to catch the russet apples as
they fall!
But one must haste away to the farmer's
wife's dinner-call.
Give to me the boiled dinner, with bread
and preserves.
If I stay here so very long I shall soon
regain my nerves.

"A Heading for November," by Anna Zucker, age 16. (Silver badge)

SPRING

By Elizabeth Connolly (age 9)

(SILVER BADGE)

Little snowdrop, lift your head
From the brown earth's wintry bed;
Blue-eyed violet, come up, too,
Blue-eyed violet, shy and true.
Spring has come to call you all.
Hark! I hear the bluebird's call!

THE DAY AFTER THANKSGIVING
By Aileen Hyland
(age 12)

"Our community's diminished," said the
turkey with a sigh.
"Indeed it is," the duck replied, tears stand-
ing in his eye.
"Alas, I am a widow!" cried poor young
Mrs. Hen,
"And so am I," sobbed Mrs. Goose, "My
husband's left the pen."

So they set up such a wailing that the
farmer was quite scared.
And his knees knocked on each other, for
he thought they had not cared.
But the day had been Thanksgiving and
the poultry had been caught,
And the farmer's wife had cooked them,
and to the table brought.

So within himself he whispered, "I will
take my things and go.
For one never kept an awful farm like this
I'm sure you know."
Then he got up, and he scuttled, and he's
not been heard of since.
And the feathered folk now rule there, and
the turkey cock is prince.

AN OFFERING

By Lucius A. Bigelow (age 8)

(A WINNER OF SILVER AND GOLD BADGES)

To St. Nicholas—this valentine:
A spray of spruce, with a branch of pine.

When the leaves fall, the doors into Tree-
land open wide. I can hear the cheerful
thud, thud of the dropping nuts and cones
as I enter in.

There is brightness everywhere, for summer has gathered up her garments of green
and glided away, leaving space for winter's
sun-gift. I like to look at the shapes of
trees; they make me think of strength. In
cold weather I can feel color more than in
summer days. The blue is brighter and
the evergreen seems darker, and there are
not so many other things to occupy my
mind.

The brown mat that arranges itself underneath the pines is composed of fine
needles.

Hemlock glistens in a breeze. Everything that nature uncovers has silver or
gold somewhere, if we carefully look. The
story of Socrates makes the name hemlock
solemn; but there is silver under that sad-
ness also.

I love the pine-tree. Its breath makes
everything around seem perfectly clean.
The spruce is not so loving in fragrance.
Often I shut my eyes; then I hear music.
It comes from the tree-tops as the wind
sweeps along.

Arbutus is the only flower that forces its
way up through the needles to the companionship of the pine. On cold winter
days, sitting by the open fire, I like to talk
of these happy things.

Pines persevere. They are our steadfast
friends. They do not go away to the south,
or hide in the earth, but remain brave and
glad the whole winter through; nor in
the summer do they leave us.

THE EBBING TIDE

(REFLECTIONS OF A SIX-YEAR-OLD)

By Betty Humphreys (age 14)

(HONOR MEMBER)

I love to stand upon the shore
When lower grows the tide,
And watch the many things it leaves
Upon the beach's side.

It always leaves a starfish
Half buried in the sand,
And pretty shells, and sea-weed,
Are thrown upon the land.

And once I found a funny thing—
An "urchin of the sea";
I thought it was a chestnut-bur—
It looked like that to me.

My mother thinks I'm careless
When I neglect my pets;
What would she say at all the things
The ebbing tide forgets?

GALATEA, AN ENGLISH SONNET

By Judith F. Mar (age 14)

(GOLD BADGE)

PYGMALION before his statue knelt.
He prayed high Aphrodite that his love,
By right of its own heat and aid divine,
    might melt
Cold marble. He sacrificed a dove
To please the goddess and propitiate
His cause. She heard and granted his desire
For Galatea as his living mate.
Through all her marble veins ran living
    fire.
Pygmalion cried out, "She lives!" but she
Stared straight ahead, was silent and stirred
    not.
In one brief flash she saw life's agony,
The pain that all too soon would be her lot.
For this her marble peace, that was so dear,
Was lost. In either eye there shone a tear.

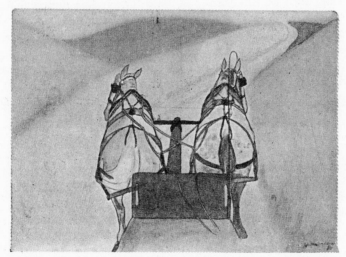

"The Object Before Me," by Laura Gardin, age 14. (Silver badge)

CHARADE

My *first,* an unknown quantity,
Yet represents my *second;*
If from it *third* should take my *fourth,* ·
But two could then be reckoned.

My *fourth* and *second* numbers are,
My *first* and *third* are letters;
To *whole* themselves before the law
Is often tried by debtors.

A. W. CLARK.

WORD-SQUARE

1. A violent gust of wind. 2. A weapon of war. 3. To join or attach. 4. Odor. 5. Passages of Scripture.

EDNA MASON CHAPMAN (League Member).

CONCEALED DIAGONAL

(*Silver Badge,*
St. Nicholas League Competition.)

ONE word is concealed in each sentence. When these have been rightly guessed and written one below another, the diagonal (beginning with the upper left-hand letter and ending with the lower right-hand letter) will spell something that comes in November.

1. The messenger she sent ran certainly very fast, but failed to reach here in time.
2. Should you slip, persons of all ranks would run to assist you.

3. Peleg, ancestor of Abraham, died at a very great age indeed.
4. Have you ever seen pitch in great quantities? I saw a barrel of it which had been buried by thieves.
5. The troops in action fought bravely, but were soon defeated.
6. In Paris I announced the coming of the great general to a large crowd.
7. She did not throw the bag over, nor did she push it through the fence.
8. That the recently captured fox is much tamer I can plainly see.

L. ARNOLD POST.

TWO ZIGZAGS

I. 1. A grain. 2. A gentle bird. 3. A large stone. 4. Soon. 5. A bag. 6. Solitary. 7. Part of a teapot. 8. A chill.
From 1 to 2, a harvest poem.
II. 1. A blemish. 2. A pain. 3. A Biblical name. 4. A small particle. 5. An outer garment. 6. A den. 7. A story. 8. To peel.
From 3 to 4, the author of the harvest poem.

KATHARINE H. WEAD (League Member).

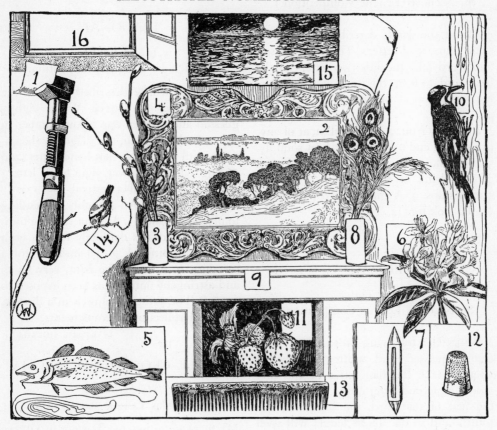

This differs from the ordinary numerical enigma in that the words forming it are pictured instead of described. When the sixteen objects have been rightly guessed, and the letters set down in the order given, the hundred and twenty-one letters will form a quotation appropriate to the season, from one of our best-loved poets.

Picture No. 1: 5-11-61-67-44-39-103-19-17-76-43-63.

No. 2: 91-83-57-96-33-10-66-24-9.

No. 3: 24-36-74-7-34-110-25-107-82-20-59-93.

No. 4: 88-119-75-31-6.

No. 5: 10-102-117-48-46-84-8.

No. 6: 26-45-50-73-30-87-54-95-92-115-120-76-21.

No. 7: 47-1-36-51-112-82-99.

No. 8: 18-2-94-40-98-86-41-23.

No. 9: 12-42-104-85-108-13-55-89-80-3-32.

No. 10: 121-60-35-69-55-116-3-67-80-101.

No. 11: 52-22-115-38-70-118-90-26-101-111-6-56.

No. 12: 97-79-89-5-100-82-68.

No. 13: 29-71-31-81.

No. 14: 15-49-12-78-27-62.

No. 15: 37-72-58-95-109-16-106-65-114.

No. 16: 53-113-119-64-14-105-4-91-77.

No. 28: is served at five o'clock.

A. R. W. and F. H. W.

ENDLESS CHAIN

(Gold Badge,
St. Nicholas League Competition.)

ALL of the words described contain the same number of letters. To form the second word take the last two letters of the first word, to form the third word take the last two letters of the second word, and so on.

1. A juicy fruit. 2. Mild. 3. Extent of anything from end to end. 4. To beat soundly. 5. To shake with cold. 6. A valuable fur. 7. The drink of the gods. 8. A fleet of armed ships. 9. A girl. 10. To pass away. 11. To look for. 12. To alter.

MARGARET ABBOTT.

ZIGZAG

(Silver Badge,
St. Nicholas League Competition.)

WHEN the following words have been rightly guessed, and written one below another, take the first letter of the first word, the second letter of the second word, the first of the third, the second of the fourth, and so on. These letters will spell a familiar word.

CROSS-WORDS: 1. An inn. 2. To flourish. 3. A season. 4. Yearly. 5. To light. 6. Mien. 7. The sound made by a turkey. 8. A ring. 9. A modest flower. 10. To separate. 11. Heed. 12. Terrified.

MARJORIE HOLMES.

MATHEMATICAL PUZZLE

(Gold Badge,
St. Nicholas League Competition.)

ADD together: one fourth of four, one, five hundred, five hundred, fifty, one third of ten, one seventh of billion, zero, and ten,

and you will find the sum in the ST. NICHOLAS Magazine.

SAMUEL WOHLGEMUTH.

DIAGONAL

(Gold Badge,
St. Nicholas League Competition.)

ALL the words described contain the same number of letters. When rightly guessed and written one below another in the order here given, the diagonal (beginning with the upper left-hand letter and ending with the lower right-hand letter) will spell a December festival.

CROSS-WORDS: 1. An assembly. 2. Tending to promote health. 3. A beautiful blue mineral. 4. Withdraws definitely from a high office. 5. Additional. 6. To find out for a certainty. 7. A plum-like fruit, very harsh and astringent until it has been exposed to frost. 8. The principal church in a diocese. 9. A full collection of implements.

MARJORIE HOLMES.

TRIPLE CROSS-WORD ENIGMA

(Gold Badge,
St. Nicholas League Competition.)

MY *firsts* are in butcher, but not in kill;
My *seconds,* in note, but not in bill;
My *thirds* are in gallon, but not in quart;
My *fourths* are in long, but not in short;
My *fifths* are in rain, and also in hail;
My *sixths* are in thunder, but not in gale;
My *sevenths,* in almond, but not in nut;
My *wholes,* three countries of Europe.

DAISY JAMES.

NUMERICAL ENIGMA

(Silver Badge,
St. Nicholas League Competition.)

I AM composed of eighty-one letters, and I form a quotation from one of Scott's poems.

My 76-61-54-73-47-19-21-58 is an old name for Christmas. My 59-42-30-69-77 are juicy fruits. My 72-66-67-15-80-10-31-60-57 is an ancient heathen emblem used at Christmas. My 24-44-9-12-81-71 are songs of joy. My 52-70-40-23-3-22-50 is a beverage formerly much used in England at Christmas. My 7-79-65-34-16 is merriment. My 5-14-35-20 is an ancient Norse deity. My 37-26-6-36-2-75 is the coldest season of the year. My 56-17-43-28 is part of a ship. My 25-13-4-33 is expectancy. My 64-49-32-68 is the handle of a sword. My 18-46-27-55 is to determine. My 11 is a point of the compass. My 29-8-41-1 mean a couple. My 63-74-53-45-78 is the summit. My 48-38-39-62-51 is to swing in a circle.   ETHEL PAINE.

CONNECTED DIAMONDS

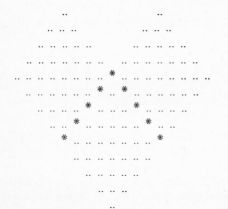

THESE diamonds are only to be read *across*. The long middle word, however, may be read either across or up and down.

I. UPPER LEFT-HAND DIAMOND: 1. In strong. 2. A cooking utensil. 3. A poet. 4. To associate with. 5. A flower named for a beautiful youth who became enamoured of his own image. 6. A vegetable. 7. A bowl. 8. The whole amount. 9. In strong.

II. UPPER RIGHT-HAND DIAMOND: 1. In strong. 2. A weapon of war. 3. A musical instrument. 4. A masculine name. 5. A large, showy flower. 6. A feminine name. 7. Birds of prey. 8. A large body of water. 9. In strong.

III. LOWER DIAMOND: 1. In strong. 2. To stuff. 3. The next after the eighth. 4. Pastures. 5. A small shore game-bird. 6. A fruit. 7. A scholar. 8. To perceive. 9. In strong.

DAISY JAMES (League Member).

CHARADE

MY first proclaims the peep of day;
  My *second*'s filled with sweetness;
My *second* smooths life's tangled snarls
  And aids the maiden's neatness.
My *whole* adorns my pompous *first;*
  My *whole* in pride is basking;
My *whole* believes that every maid
  Would wed him for the asking.

AUGUSTA L. HANCHETT.

CONCEALED PRIMAL ACROSTIC

One word is concealed in each sentence. When these have been rightly guessed and written one below another, the initials will spell the name of a famous cardinal.

1. If you fear a certain animal, avoid it.
2. He slid each time he passed the slippery path.
3. Tragic as the ending was, it made no great impression.
4. Hannah and I will join you soon.
5. Henry says the moon will disappear late to-night.
6. The animal ate all the food I offered.
7. I risked my life in climbing the steep cliff.
8. Grace picked a large bouquet this afternoon.
9. The house, repainted, looked as good as new.

MADGE OAKLEY (League Member).

SWORD PUZZLE

```
            .  .
          .  .  .
    1  * * * * * * * * * * * * * *  2
    .  .  .  .  .  .  .  .  .  .  .  .  .
    .  .  .  .
    .  .  .  .
    .  .  .  .  .
```

READING DOWNWARD: 1. A feminine name. 2. A book for autographs. 3. An organ of the body. 4. In addition. 5. A waterfall. 6. To endure. 7. A poem. 8. A swamp. 9. Skill. 10. An article. 11. Useful in a small boat. 12. A feminine name. 13. To lubricate. 14. Entire. 15. Consumed. 16. A measure of weight. 17. In cardinal.

From 1 to 2, a famous man who perished by the sword.   ANGUS M. BERRY.

ZIGZAG

(*Silver Badge,*
St. Nicholas League Competition.)

ALL the words described contain the same number of letters. When these have been rightly guessed and written one below another, the zigzag (beginning with the upper left-hand letter and ending with the lower left-hand letter) will spell the first and last names of a President of the United States.

CROSS-WORDS: 1. To tell over again. 2. Good sense. 3. Posture. 4. A cap worn in bed to protect the head. 5. A brief statement of facts concerning the health of some distinguished personage. 6. An absolute sovereign. 7. To establish the identity of. 8. One of the United States. 9. A severe snow-storm. 10. Faint-hearted. 11. Aloft. 12. The universe. 13. A pointed instrument of the dagger kind fitted on the muzzle of a rifle. 14. A formal method of performing acts of civility. 15. Approbation.

JEAN C. FREEMAN.

DIAGONAL

ALL of the words described contain the same number of letters. When rightly guessed and written one below another, the diagonal, beginning with the upper left-hand letter and ending with the lower right-hand letter, will spell the name of a famous musician.

CROSS-WORDS: 1. Method. 2. An engine of war. 3. A nose. 4. To conduct. 5. Showy clothes. 6. A sudden alarm.

RICHARD BLUCHER (age 9).

BEHEADINGS

1. DOUBLY behead to chide sharply, and leave aged. 2. Doubly behead high estimation, and leave a conjunction. 3. Doubly behead a kind of small type, and leave devoured. 4. Doubly behead the Mohammedan Bible, and leave raced. 5. Doubly behead passages out of a place, and leave a possessive pronoun. 6. Doubly behead a fish, and leave a place of refuge. 7. Doubly behead value, and leave a form of water. 8. Doubly behead the after-song, and leave a lyric poem. 9. Doubly behead to dress, and leave a line of light. 10. Doubly behead an inhabitant of Rome, and leave a human being. 11. Doubly behead a masculine name, and leave to conquer.

The initial letters of the words before beheading will spell the name of a very famous personage.

SAMUEL P. HALDENSTEIN
(League Member)

CONCEALED CENTRAL ACROSTIC

WE hold the merry Christmas cheer
And greetings of the glad new year.

CROSS-WORDS

(One word is concealed in each sentence.)

1. Minerva pinned, with perfect taste,
   A chestnut bur upon her waist.

2. A band of coral one inch wide
   Adorned her hat-brim's under-side.
3. And, as she walked, she swung with grace
   A parasol around her face.
4. Across the lawn she swiftly moved,
   But high-heeled boots her downfall proved.
5. For when the bordering walk she jumped,

She hurt her pride—her nose was bumped.
6. She tried to run because it rained,
   And found her foot was badly sprained.
7. She simply said: "I jumped too soon;
   One should not jump in May or June.
8. I've hurt my instep some—it feels
   As if I needed higher heels."

ANNA M. PRATT.

ANSWERS TO RIDDLE BOX PUZZLES

CHARADE. Extenuate (x-ten-u-8).

WORD-SQUARE. 1. Blast. 2. Lance. 3. Annex. 4. Scent. 5. Texas.

CONCEALED DIAGONAL. Election. CROSS-WORDS: 1. Entrance. 2. Slippers. 3. Elegance. 4. Pitching. 5. Inaction. 6. Parisian. 7. Governor. 8. American.

TWO ZIGZAGS. I. 1. Corn. 2. Dove. 3. Rock. 4. Anon. 5. Sack. 6. Lone. 7. Nose. 8. Ague. From 1 to 2, Corn-song. II. 1. Flaw. 2. Ache. 3. Levi. 4. Mite. 5. Coat. 6. Lair. 7. Tale. 8. Pare. From 3 to 4, Whittier.

ILLUSTRATED NUMERICAL ENIGMA.
He comes! He comes! The Frost Spirit comes!
You may trace his footsteps now
On the naked woods and the blasted fields
And the brown hill's withered brow.

J. G. WHITTIER.

ENDLESS CHAIN. 1. Orange. 2. Gentle. 3. Length. 4. Thrash. 5. Shiver. 6. Ermine. 7. Nectar. 8. Armada. 9. Damsel. 10. Elapse. 11. Search. 12. Change.

ZIGZAG. Thanksgiving. Cross-words: 1. Tavern. 2. Thrive. 3. Autumn. 4. Annual. 5. Kindle. 6. Aspect. 7. Gobble. 8. Circle. 9. Violet. 10. Divide. 11. Notice. 12. Aghast.

MATHEMATICAL PUZZLE. R-i-d-d-L-e B-o-x.

DIAGONAL. Christmas. Cross-words: 1. Concourse. 2. Wholesome. 3. Turquoise. 4. Abdicates. 5. Accessory. 6. Ascertain. 7. Persimmon. 8. Cathedral. 9. Apparatus.

TRIPLE CROSS-WORD ENIGMA. England, Holland, Belgium.

NUMERICAL ENIGMA.

Heap on more wood! The wind is chill,
But let it whistle as it will,
We'll keep our Christmas merry still.
  "Marmion," Introduction to Canto VI.

CONNECTED DIAMONDS. I. 1. N. 2. Pan. 3. Byron. 4. Consort. 5. Narcissus. 6. Parsnip. 7. Basin. 8. Sum. 9. S. II. 1. S. 2. Gun. 3. Banjo. 4. Wilfred. 5. Sunflower. 6. Dorothy. 7. Hawks. 8. Sea. 9. R. III. 1. S. 2. Pad. 3. Ninth. 4. Meadows. 5. Sandpiper. 6. Apricot. 7. Pupil. 8. See. 9. R.—CHARADE. Coxcomb.

CONCEALED PRIMAL ACROSTIC. Richelieu. 1. Race. 2. Idea. 3. Cast. 4. Hand. 5. Earl. 6. Late. 7. Iris. 8. Epic. 9. User.

SWORD PUZZLE. From 1 to 2, Alexander Hamilton. Downward: 1. Frances. 2. Album. 3. Heart. 4. Extra. 5. Cataract. 6.

Stand. 7. Ode. 8. Fen. 9. Art. 10. The. 11. Oar. 12. Amy. 13. Oil. 14. All. 15. Ate. 16. Ton. 17. N.

ZIGZAG. Rutherford Hayes. Cross-words: 1. Rehearse. 2. Judgment. 3. Attitude. 4. Nightcap. 5. Bulletin. 6. Autocrat. 7. Identify. 8. Colorado. 9. Blizzard. 10. Cowardly. 11. Overhead. 12. Creation. 13. Bayonets. 14. Ceremony. 15. Sanction.

DIAGONAL. Mozart. Cross-words: 1. Manner. 2. Mortar. 3. Nozzle. 4. Manage. 5. Finery. 6. Fright.

BEHEADINGS. Shakespeare. 1. Sc-old. 2. Ho-nor. 3. Ag-ate. 4. Ko-ran. 5. Ex-its. 6. Sh-ark. 7. Pr-ice. 8. Ep-ode. 9. Ar-ray. 10. Ro-man. 11. Ed-win.

CONCEALED CENTRAL ACROSTIC. Holidays. Cross-words: 1. Aches. 2. Alone. 3. Solar. 4. Thigh. 5. Order. 6. Train. 7. Mayor. 8. Epsom.